DC PUBLIC LIBRARY

3 1172 06012 9111

COMPLETE BOOK OF
GRADUATE PROGRAMS
IN THE ARTS AND SCIENCES

By
Christopher Maier and
The Staff of The Princeton Review

THE PRINCETON REVIEW

COMPLETE BOOK OF
GRADUATE PROGRAMS

IN THE ARTS AND SCIENCES

By
Christopher Maier and
The Staff of The Princeton Review

Random House, Inc., New York
2006 Edition
www.PrincetonReview.com

The Princeton Review, Inc.
2315 Broadway
New York, NY 10024
Email: bookeditor@review.com

© 2005 by The Princeton Review, Inc.
All rights reserved under International and Pan-American Copyright Conventions.
Published in the United States by Random House, Inc., New York, and simultaneously in Canada by Random
House of Canada Limited, Toronto.

ISBN 0-375-76501-8

Publisher: Robert Franek
Editors: Erik Olson and Spencer Foxworth
Production Editor: Christine LaRubio
Designer: Scott Harris
Production Coordinator: Greta Blau

Manufactured in the United States of America on partially recycled paper.
9 8 7 6 5 4 3 2 1

2006 Edition

CONTENTS

ACKNOWLEDGMENTS

This book could not have taken shape without the generous assistance of many graduate students and professionals. In particular, I'd like to thank the following people for sharing not only their expertise, but also their candid advice and valuable time:

Dianne Bryan, Graduate and Professional Studies Advisor, Dickinson College

Peter Diffley, Associate Dean of Graduate Studies, University of Notre Dame

Philip Graham, Director of Creative Writing, University of Illinois—Urbana-Champaign

Che Hutson, Doctoral Candidate and Student Representative for the Admissions Committee for the Neuroscience Graduate Program, University of California—Los Angeles

Thomas Kelley, Assistant Director for Campus Operations, National-Louis University—Tampa

Dale Kinney, Dean of the Graduate School of Arts and Sciences, Bryn Mawr College

Amy Lingafelter, Master of Fine Arts, Poetry, University of Iowa; Master of Library Science, University of Illinois—Urbana-Champaign

Mary Ann Mason, Dean of the Graduate Division, University of California—Berkeley

William J. Maxwell, Director of English Graduate Studies, University of Illinois—Urbana-Champaign

Barbara Pennypacker, Assistant Dean of the Graduate School, Pennsylvania State University

Bruce Rettig, Associate Dean of the Graduate School, Oregon State University

Joseph Russo, Director of Financial Aid, University of Notre Dame

Oday Salim, Doctoral Candidate, English, University of Illinois—Urbana-Champaign

Scott Samson, Chair of the Geology Department, Syracuse University

Carrie Scott, Doctoral Candidate, Art History, University of Washington

Robert Tignor, Chair of the History Department, Princeton University

INTRODUCTION

So you're thinking about graduate school. Maybe you're thinking about it quite seriously, or perhaps you simply want to thumb through some pages that'll help you decide whether or not grad school is really for you. Either way, you've come to the right place.

If you've read this far, that means that you must be at least *kind of* serious about graduate school. It's probably time that we hit you with the big questions that are at the center of this book: *Why are you considering grad school?* and *How do you determine which program is best for you?* Of course, each person's answers to these questions are going to have their own unique flavor—textured by an individual list of details and scenarios. Even if you've turned those details and scenarios over in your head dozens of times, it's worth some more thought. While the rewards of earning a graduate degree are numerous, they do not come without their costs.

In the pages that follow, we'll introduce you to the questions that prospective graduate students need to ask, the concerns that they need to address, and the rewards that they can expect. We'll rely on you to plug these considerations into your own equation and, ultimately, find the graduate program that suits you best.

So What Is a Graduate Degree, Anyway?

We've all heard it before: Alexis X pushed through her sociology major only to end up working as a chef. Or Ryan Y earned his undergraduate degree in philosophy and went on to pursue a career in computer security. Or Suzy Z majored in biology and wound up landing her first job out of college with a congressman on Capitol Hill. Uncertainty, to some degree, is par for the course with an undergraduate education these days. But the same cannot—and should not—be said for a graduate degree. The first thing you need to realize about a graduate degree—in any field—is this: You are embarking on a specific educational journey that will provide you with the thorough training necessary to succeed in a particular career or field. The pursuit of a graduate degree is a focused experience. With few exceptions, if you spend two years earning a master's degree in geology, you *are* training for a career in geology, *not* a *possible* career in geology.

But even if you're settled on a degree in geology, you still need to decide what sort of degree will serve you best. At Syracuse University, for instance, you can earn the following degrees in geology: a master of arts (MA), a master of science (MS), and a doctor of philosophy (PhD or doctorate). You'll find a similar situation in many other geology departments around the country, not to mention the various degrees offered through English departments, psychology departments, chemistry departments, and a whole mess of other departments that offer graduate degrees.

So what's the difference?

THE MASTER'S DEGREE

First, earning a master's degree is less time-intensive than going for a PhD. When we say this, we're talking about less time in years. (The daily schedule of a master's candidate is often as rigorous as that of a PhD candidate.) Generally, you can expect to put in two years of full-time study to earn your master's. This is not a hard-and-fast rule, though; plenty of institutions offer one-year degrees while a handful of others extend the degree to a third and, in lesser cases, a fourth year. But for now, if a master's degree is what you have in mind, you should expect to chisel out two years of your life to devote to it.

A master's degree involves a combination of comprehensive course work and, often, the production of a thesis (a lengthy research project)—or, in the cases of master of fine arts degrees, or MFAs, something along the lines of a creative manuscript, exhibit, or performance—that will be produced under the guidance of a faculty member and assessed by a committee of professors. (Students going straight from the master's degree to the PhD, however, are not always required to write a master's thesis.) Regardless, in the span of two years, you'll have the opportunity to work closely with accomplished academic professionals in your field at the same time that you'll be required to forge ahead with your own ideas. And this, of course, is exactly what you hope to do out in the "real world" when you have that degree in hand.

Although a master's degree will extend your knowledge of the field you choose, it is not the final rung, so to speak. In other words, a master's degree is not a *terminal degree*. (The exception to this is the MFA, as well as a wide number of professional degrees, such as the MBA.) By definition, a terminal degree is the highest degree possible in a field. It is, quite literally, "terminal"—the end of the educational line in that discipline. Because a master's is not a terminal degree, many people see it as a stepping stone to the PhD, which *is* terminal. And if you're uncertain about a PhD, that's okay. After all, if biology is your passion but after trying out the master's, you decide that the PhD isn't really what you want, you've still given yourself a stronger personal and professional base on which to stand. Although heading into any graduate degree on a whim is not a wise idea—for a number of reasons—it's not at all uncommon for people to show up at a university planning to earn a PhD and then, after a few years of study, deciding to take the master's and dive into the workforce.

Let us add one disclaimer here: No matter which graduate degree you're working toward, it *is* a graduate degree—a degree that will demand many things of you, including time, concentration, devotion, and money. It's not the kind of thing you want to jump into lightly.

While there are certainly a glut of master's programs across the country, it's *not* at the master's level that most top-grade research programs place their emphasis. Mary Ann Mason, dean of the graduate division at the University of California—Berkeley, confirms, "Major research universities like Berkeley don't have [many] functional master's degrees." And the numbers speak for themselves: Less than 15 percent of Berkeley's graduate degrees are stand-alone master's. The reason for this is that institutions dedicated to research want to produce the most well-prepared and highly qualified graduates possible, and, in most fields, a master's degree falls short of this goal.

As you've probably already noticed, underneath the master's umbrella you'll find a number of variations: MA, MS, MFA, MBA, MEd, MLS, and others. In the liberal arts and sciences, you're most likely to come across the MA and MS. As we've said, with few exceptions these are not terminal degrees. The primary difference between the types of master's degrees is one of focus. Looking at the MS and MA, you can assume that the MS will place a heavier emphasis on completing a hands-on research project. Case in point: As we mentioned earlier, the Syracuse University geology department offers both the MA and the MS. "The difference is that a student pursuing an MA does not write a research thesis, but takes courses only and then takes a final examination from a group of three faculty," says Scott Samson, chair of Syracuse's geology department. But, he adds, you won't find the department's MA option for much longer: "We are eliminating this degree … as it is of minimal use in earth sciences." Numerous other science departments, however, continue to offer both master of arts and master of science degrees. The value of every degree will vary depending on the particular department and the particular field in which you're interested. When examining a variety of degree options, be sure to ask yourself two questions. *What will each degree require of me in terms of time and money? Which degree will be most valued when I go into the workforce?*

As you begin to answer these questions, you'll want to look further than the general information that you find on graduate school websites and in promotional brochures. Contact professors. Get in touch with current students. Even pick up the phone and call potential employers; talking to people already ensconced in your projected profession can provide invaluable advice.

THE DOCTORATE

If you think of your education as a ladder, the doctorate, or PhD, is the final official rung. You can expect everything you find in the master's degree—after all, the course work of a master's degree is usually a prerequisite for a doctoral program—and more. Although you're likely to find variations among the programs you consider, you can generally expect that the doctorate will culminate in a project that will, at some point in the not-too-distant future, be ready for professional publication or presentation. And no, *you* won't be the judge of the project's quality. You'll have to present your project to a committee of faculty members (usually three to five professors) who will evaluate what you produce. Prior to this evaluation, you'll be working closely with your personal faculty advisor, and this advisor will look out for your best interests. In other words, if the advisor doesn't feel that your work is done, there's a slim chance that you'll be up for review by the other faculty members. Defending a dissertation is no easy process, but because doctoral students usually work so closely with their advisors, it's rare that a student fails to successfully defend his or her dissertation.

This point alone is reason enough to carefully investigate a graduate program's faculty prior to enrolling in it. Even though you might end up changing advisors once or twice during your graduate career, it's important to get a sense of faculty accessibility and participation with the students. Just as employees count on employers to let them know if they're performing their tasks to expectation, you want to immerse yourself in a community that will help guide the arc of your graduate career, letting you know when you're taking the right steps, as well as when you're messing up. In particular, you'll do yourself a favor by cozying up to a faculty member who seems particularly in sync with your interests and personality. After getting in touch with this person, ask yourself: Does this seem like a faculty member who will take an active role in my academic development after I show up on campus? To answer this question for yourself, try to get in touch with current advisees to see if your gut feeling can be confirmed.

In many cases, students matriculate directly from the master's to doctoral programs at the same institution. The process of climbing up to the doctoral rung can differ. Some programs will ask for a simple application. Others will expect students to write a master's thesis and defend it before moving up into position as a doctoral candidate. And yet others will fall somewhere in between these two possibilities, asking students to take an exam demonstrating their retention of knowledge they acquired in their studies for their master's distinction.

But the acquisition of a master's degree offers a grace period of sorts—a few moments to decide whether you really want to enroll in the university's PhD program or move on to something (or somewhere) else. And moving on to something else doesn't necessarily mean getting a job (this is, of course, one option). This is also a time to reflect on the academic and social bonds that you've formed during the years you've spent pursuing your master's degree. If something seems off kilter, you'll never have a better time to switch to a different university for your doctoral program. Hopping to a new department and a new locale will be no easy matter, but if you feel that you're not getting what you expected, explore the options. This opportunity may seem especially advantageous to students who settled for the program that accepted them rather than the program that they wanted (which rejected them). This often happens to grad school hopefuls going into fields that are different than their undergraduate majors. For instance, a psychology major wants to do a PhD in biology, but he hasn't completed the kind of course work that a top school is going to expect; earning his master's at a smaller, less reputable school just might allow him to build the base that'll launch him into upper-tier programs for his PhD.

Once in a PhD program, a student will need to fulfill a number of credit hours taking courses. Depending on the program in question, students may only be required to take courses the first two semesters, or the course work may carry over to year two and, even, year three. Regardless, most PhD candidates can expect to take three classes in each of their first two semesters. Then, most likely, the student will have to pass an intensive qualifying (or comprehensive) exam that proves he or she is an expert in the breadth and depth of available knowledge about that field. And from there on, the work becomes largely a matter of individual initiative—particularly in the social sciences and humanities, where latter-stage "group work" plays less of a role than it does in the laboratory sciences. While some programs have time limits, others allow PhD students to drag on for years and years, slowly chipping away at their dissertations. This is where personal discipline comes in. "A businesslike attitude is necessary," advises William J. Maxwell, University of Illinois's director of English graduate studies. What he means is this: One of the secrets to success in the late stages of graduate study is the ability to devise—and maintain—a steady work routine. "Set up a 9-to-5 schedule for yourself," Maxwell suggests. The students who make it from one end of the PhD to the other are not necessarily the prodigies; they're the people who have a sound work ethic and stick to it.

Stick-to-it-ness is a trait that's indispensable for those who hope to make it to the top of the educational ladder. In the final years of a PhD program, students do not take classes, so initiative, structure, and progress are largely determined by the students themselves. Ruts are easily dug and are difficult to leave. So a steady dose of stick-to-it-ness is as good as gold.

THE WEB OF DEGREES

Graduate degrees in the liberal arts and sciences are offered in the MA, MS, and PhD varieties. A variety of foci may be contained within a single department. For instance, the biology department at the University of North Dakota allows graduate students to specialize in the following areas: behavior, cell, and molecular biology; ecology; fisheries and wildlife biology; genetics; neurobiology; physiology; and systematics. And in the ever-expanding academic world of the twenty-first century, new possibilities for specialization are always turning up. Listed below is a sampling of specific graduate degree options in the liberal arts and sciences.

Life Sciences

Animal Sciences	Bacteriology
Behavioral Science	Biochemistry
Biophysics	Cell Biology
Developmental Biology	Ecology
Entomology	Environmental Sciences
Epidemiology	Forestry
Genetics	Immunology
Microbiology	Molecular Biology
Neuroscience	Physiology
Systematics	

Social Sciences

Agricultural Economics	Anthropology/Archaeology
Area/Regional Studies	Clinical Psychology
Cognitive Studies	Communications
Economics	Geography
History	International Relations
Linguistics	Political Science/Government
Psychology	Public Policy
Sociology	

Humanities

Art History	Classics
Comparative Literature	English Language and Literature
Music	Theater/Performance

Physical Science and Mathematics

Applied Mathematics	Astrophysics/Astronomy
Atmospheric Studies	Chemistry
Geoscience/Earth Science	Information Science
Mathematics	Oceanography
Physics	Statistics

Area, Ethnic, and Cultural Studies

American Studies	French
German	History and Philosophy of Science
Near Eastern Literature	Philosophy
Race, Ethnicity, and Postcolonial Studies	Religion/Theology
Slavic Literatures	Spanish and Portuguese

And even these categories, in some cases, can be broken down further. Take, for example, English Language and Literature. Among the possibilities for specialization are medieval British literature, early American literature, Native American literature, African American literature, critical theory, and too many others to possibly create a comprehensive catalogue. For this reason, it's important to understand the anatomy of the programs you're applying to. If African American literature is your interest, you probably won't be satisfied if you end up at a top-ranked school that doesn't happen to have a specialist in the field.

STATUS: TERMINAL

A terminal degree is not as ghastly as it sounds. In the realm of graduate degrees, the word "terminal" translates into the highest degree that a person can earn in a particular field of study. In many fields, a PhD is the terminal degree. In English literature, for instance, a student who earns a PhD is considered an expert in Shakespeare or James Joyce or the Harlem Renaissance, or whatever the specialty. There is no degree in English literature that he or she could earn to add girth to his or her qualifications (except, perhaps another PhD in a different subject). If, for some reason, the student would decide to earn some other degree in a parallel field, it's not likely that the credits would transfer; the credits have been used for all they're worth.

This said, "PhD" and "terminal degree" are not synonymous. A number of master's degrees lead students directly to, well, the end of the formal educational line. One such example is the MFA, which is earned by practicing artists in fields such as creative writing, visual arts, and theater. In the world of business administration degrees, an MBA is terminal. Although a little research might turn up a handful of PhD options in the creative arts or business, these are different monsters; they don't take away from the fact the person with the MFA or the MBA has a terminal degree.

We should remind you, however, that these days, the higher education system is evolving and progressing—like just about everything else in our society. New degrees are springing up all the time, including a growing number of hybrid degrees, and if you read the fine print, you just might discover some of these are terminal degrees. For instance, the new dual master's degree in Earth and Environmental Science Journalism at Columbia University is a program that mixes course work in earth sciences with professional training via the School of Journalism. This is a terminal degree, and it makes sense; after all, how many PhD opportunities in Earth and Environmental Science Journalism have you come across?

Yes, but so what? What does it matter if a degree's terminal or not? We'll tell you why it matters. Most institutes of higher learning only hire professors who've earned the terminal degree in their field. Remember when you were searching for a place to earn your bachelor's degree, and you came across stats at some school boasting that 97 percent of the faculty had earned the "highest degree possible"? What that school was implying is this: We're proud to say that the vast majority of our professors have a terminal degree. So if teaching at a university is your goal, a terminal degree will breathe some necessary life into your resume.

A FEW WORDS ABOUT THE MFA

The MFA is a terminal degree that, once earned, denotes substantial progress in any one of a number of creative arts. Artists-in-training can earn an MFA in a variety of specialties, including fiction writing, nonfiction writing, poetry, theater, dance, photography, painting, ceramics, and narrative media. Unlike traditional master's programs, the MFA offers students a chance to practice art, as opposed to responding to it. The culmination of an MFA is typically a demonstration of the artistic progress that was made during the years in residence. So, for instance, an MFA student concentrating on fiction can expect to produce a short-story collection or novel manuscript of publishable quality before getting that degree in hand; similarly, a dance student should prepare himself for a final assessment that'll involve either performing or choreographing a substantial piece.

As you're probably already realizing, the MFA is a unique sort of degree. It's unique because, in a sense, the MFA faculty tends to emphasize the creative process over the academic process. It's unique also because these degrees foster one of the most unmarketable aspirations around: the life of the artist. These days, it's rare for an artist to be self-supporting on art alone. Also, the jobs in the academy that many MFA students hope to fill are sparse and competitive. For these reasons, it's important to closely look at the financial assistance offered through each MFA program you're considering. Shop around. If you have to pay to attend an MFA program, you probably want to explore other options.

Another thing you'll want to keep your eyes on as you research MFA programs: each program's sense of "citizenship responsibilities," as Philip Graham, University of Illinois—Urbana-Champaign's director of creative writing, puts it. What Graham means is that you owe it to yourself to find out what sorts of opportunities the program will offer you to become marketable—aside from practicing your art, of course. For example, does the program give its students the chance to teach undergraduate writing courses? Are there publications affiliated with the program that students can participate in? Are there performance, exhibition, or curatorial opportunities in which you'll be able to participate?

Spend some time getting to know each program and its faculty before you apply. Programs have their own unique culture and often lean toward a particular aesthetic. Spending some time familiarizing yourself with the work of the faculty members can give you a better idea of what to expect once you're enrolled in the program. "You should be mature enough to find out who the teachers of a workshop are in a program and look up their work in the library," advises Graham. And by getting to know the people and culture of a program, you'll be able to give a clearer indication of *why* you want to be at that particular program when you write your personal statement.

And yes, the personal statement is very important when you apply to an MFA program—particularly a program in writing. The personal statement gives a clear indication of your ability to communicate as well as highlighting your personality. But what matters most when coming to a program is your work. Whether it's a novel excerpt or a portfolio of photographs, the quality of your efforts is what will catch an admissions committee's eye. Grades and GRE scores (if they're even required) matter less.

"An MFA is a place that you work your way toward," says Graham. And you work your way toward an MFA by practicing your art diligently, until you're convinced that devoting a few years to working on an MFA—even at the risk of walking away with a degree that doesn't earn you a job—is worth it.

Amy Lingafelter *earned an MFA in poetry from the Writer's Workshop at the University of Iowa in 2000 and a master's in library science from the University of Illinois—Urbana-Champaign in 2004.*

My MFA experience depended on two very unique ingredients: my classmates and my teachers. That said, it's worth noting that MFA programs (and the guidance they offer) vary vastly from year to year depending on the influx of students, teachers, and visiting writers.

Earning an MFA gave me two years to devote solely to writing poetry in a community of like-minded people. I would not have found that time, those people, or that relative financial freedom anywhere else in life. I often find it difficult to call myself a writer or talk about writing when I'm around my family, people I work with, and other nonwriters, and being at the University of Iowa completely normalized and demystified this very personal thing I do by giving me the freedom to write how I write with a bunch of other writers.

If you want nitty-gritty details, though my MFA contributed immensely to my evolution, it contributed little to my straight-up job marketability, and having an MFA does not change the fact that selling art is a strange and fickle thing to do. I went back to grad school, earned another master's degree to support myself, and I'm still learning ways to weave the writer side of me into the stable working side of me.

One last thought: I would not recommend attending an MFA program without funding from the university, and I would not rack up student loan debt getting an MFA. Earning an MFA guarantees that you'll have time to practice your art, but it definitely does not guarantee a job when it's all over.

WHY GET A GRADUATE DEGREE?

This is a question that we can trace all the way back to Plato. Well, maybe not this *exact* question. But in the seventh book of *Republic,* Plato did have something to say on the topic of education that isn't far from what many present-day graduate deans say: "In the first place, no student should be lame in his love of hard work." And "love" is the key word here. As you've probably already realized, "hard work" is the name of the game when you're earning a graduate degree, but a passion for the game is what keeps a student going.

And we're not just talking about fleeting passion here. We're talking about the passion to learn that drives the entire engine of academe. On this note, Barbara Pennypacker, assistant dean of the Graduate School at Pennsylvania State University, says, "To go to grad school is really making a commitment to study and the acquisition of knowledge." And as Dale Kinney, the dean of the Graduate School of Arts and Sciences at Bryn Mawr College says of graduate school applicants, "They have to be sure that they love the subject. Because loving the subject is the primary reward."

All three of these voices point us toward the most common—and most crucial—answer to that all-important question: *Why get a graduate degree?* The answer: Because the process of acquiring your advanced degree should be first and foremost a labor of love. Graduate school will require a lot of you, but if you have a true passion for the subject, the time and energy will seem like worthwhile sacrifices. If you're on the fence, however, you might want to consider holding off applying for a year or two or five or six. Wait until your passion for the subject is too hot to douse. The sad truth is that every year, many students walk away from their graduate studies because they realize that their head or heart, or both, are simply not in it.

High-minded academic principles are not the only reason people enroll in grad programs in the arts and sciences. There are, of course, perfectly valid professional motivations. But there are different brands of professional motivation that drive people back to the halls of the academy. For instance, a master's in biology—not a terminal degree—could give a boost to the credentials of a person making a living in pharmaceutical research. Similarly, an investment analyst could gain some additional professional respect by adding a master's in economics to her curriculum vitae. Or a master's in English could give an applicant an edge over the competition for a job in publishing. But it's worth noting that while graduate degrees in the arts and sciences can have professional benefits in a wide variety of industries, there are a few vocations for which most graduate programs in the arts and sciences are specifically geared, and those are research and teaching.

But even if you're dead set on getting that graduate degree in hand and marching off to the nearest university classroom, you have to face the reality of today's higher-ed job market. To put in nicely, the market is a competitive one. *Very* competitive. According to a 2003 article in *The Chronicle of Higher Education,* advertised jobs in the English field dropped from 983 to 792 in a one-year period—and of those, only about 50 percent were tenure-track positions. And as the article's author, the pseudonymous Thomas H. Benton points out, in 2000–2001, there were 977 English PhDs awarded, and these candidates were competing for jobs not only with their contemporaries, but also with those who earned doctorates in prior years and continued to hunt for a job.[1]

No, finding a job in academe is not impossible, but it's not exactly easy, either. As Benton explains, data from the Modern Language Association (MLA) notes that only one in five graduates entering an English program will actually land in a job with tenure—ever.[2] And while numbers surely vary among fields, it's fair to say that there's no guarantee that your years of hard work will lead you to your dream teaching job or even to a mildly satisfying one. So, as we said, if you're going to dive into a graduate program, make sure that your decision comes after calculating the risks and uncertainties. If you have a passion for the subject, the sacrifices of time, money, and stability might not seem so bad.

---

1 Thomas H. Benton, "So You Want to Go to Grad School?" *The Chronicle of Higher Education Career Network,* 6 June 2003, 3.

2 Ibid.

THE PART-TIME/FULL-TIME QUESTION

In our *Paying for Graduate School Without Going Broke* by Peter Diffley and Joseph Russo, both of the University of Notre Dame, you'll find four good reasons for attending graduate school full-time: *time, options, educational quality,* and *financing.*

In short, a full-time program tends to be exactly that: a full-time immersion into your field of study. And this means that you're more likely to focus—and less likely to succumb to other distractions, like the demands of a daytime job—thus making the most of your grad school efforts. In other words, full-time programs make better use of your *time.*

And full-time programs are, frankly, more prevalent. Because there are more full-time programs around, you'll have a wider pool of *options* when you apply. As we've already mentioned, graduate degrees in the arts and sciences are highly focused on producing top-quality researchers; and because top-quality researchers usually step away from graduate school with terminal degrees, part-time master's degrees are in less demand. And part-time doctoral programs, while not completely unavailable, are a relatively rare breed.

One of the reasons that full-time graduate programs are more common than part-time programs is that administrators know that students receive the highest *educational quality* when they do more than merely show up for class. Graduate school is largely about constructing professional networks. Those networks form best when students immerse themselves in a focused and lively academic environment. Often, this academic environment breeds cross-pollination, encouraging a student to associate with other disciplines and scholars beyond the seeming boundaries of her particular field.

And let's not forget money. Most universities reserve their assistantships, fellowships, and stipends for full-time students, not to mention the other perks, like health benefits and day care. It's true that you'll have to give up that 9-to-5 job if you want to go to school full-time, but you can also rest assured that, in almost all cases, you'll get more from the school financially than you would if you nickel and dime your academic progress.

We realize, though, that enrolling in school full-time might not be an option. Family and financial obligations, among others, can set limitations that require you to take the part-time route. In this case, you'll need to devote some hours to seeking out the part-time options available in the field that interests you. And you may need to narrow your scope even further because part-time students are often limited in terms of geography by the jobs that make full-time study impossible.

On this note, the benefits of a part-time degree are twofold. First, the corporate world is a world that often recognizes the achievement of a graduate degree with a nice pay hike. There is, of course, no guarantee that you'll be better paid once you get a graduate degree. So if you're thinking about devoting a few years' worth of evening hours to attain a degree solely for this reason, you'll do yourself a favor by talking with your employer *before* enrolling in a program. If he's able to assure you that your efforts will be rewarded with financial gain, then you have reason enough to march ahead. But be sure to find out exactly what types of degrees will shine the brightest in your employer's eyes. Part-time programs in academic subjects, like English literature or biology, are not as easy to find as professional programs, such as MBAs or master's degrees in marketing and nursing. And frankly, your efforts to earn a grad degree in English literature will most likely reap you less monetary rewards in the corporate world than your efforts to obtain a professional degree.

This brings us to the second benefit of the part-time degree. Like any other grad degree in the arts and sciences, a part-time degree gives you a chance to delve into a subject that you love. If your idea of a good time is coming home from work and kicking back with a steaming cup of tea and a few hundred pages of the *Illiad*, then a part-time master's in the classics might be right up your alley. If the thought of this—or the thought of doing any substantial brainwork after dinner—rubs you the wrong way, then you might want to step back and reconsider. Part-time does not mean *no*-time. You'll need to sacrifice many of your leisure hours to keep up with assignments, write essays, and, eventually, push through a dissertation.

There are also so-called "accelerated" programs that have components of both full-time and part-time approaches. These programs require students to take on full-time workloads with limited time in the classroom. Like part-time programs, accelerated programs cater to people with employment and family obligations, which limit the time they're able to spend on campus. At any of National-Louis University's many campuses, for instance, students working toward a graduate degree typically meet only one evening a week in a classroom. However, because these are full-time degrees, the students need to devote a healthy number of hours on the "off" nights to keeping up with their work. One of the notable differences between a traditional full-time degree and an accelerated full-time degree is one of self-discipline. As Thomas Kelley, assistant director for campus operations at National-Louis's Tampa campus, says, "It's up to you to make it happen." In other words, students in these sorts of programs need to set up a steady work schedule and stick to it; they can't count on daily (or even every other day) on-campus attendance requirements to keep them in the ball game.

CHOOSING A PROGRAM

When students are preparing for an undergraduate career, we encourage them to keep their options open until they feel satisfied that they've collected enough information from a variety of sources—including their own thoughts and feelings—to make a responsible decision about where they will spend the next few years of their life, as well as a lot of their own and their parents' money. At this point, however, as you contemplate plunging into graduate school, our advice is quite different. Perhaps you're nearing the end of your undergraduate days, or maybe you've graduated years ago. Either way, you've done some exploring and (hopefully) discovered some niche in that vast ocean of human knowledge. If you're considering a graduate degree, then you're toying with the idea of developing your knowledge within that niche. And it's proper to consider that word, *niche.* While this may sound like a generalization, it's fair to say that graduate school is much more about *depth* than breadth of knowledge.

But if *breadth is* something you're after, you should spend some time studying the requirements of the programs in which you are interested. You'll come across programs that largely dictate everything that students must take to complete the degree (you're most likely to find this in one- or two-year master's programs or in science programs). But you will find others that provide an overarching structure with plenty of room for electives.

Electives or no electives: even this is not a black-and-white issue. Some programs offer students elective credits, but those credits still need to be earned within the same department as the degree itself. Other programs, however, will allow—and sometimes encourage—students to put their feelers out in other departments and schools around campus. In these sorts of programs, for instance, a master's candidate in economics who's always had a hankering for Freud just might find herself spending a semester in a graduate seminar in the psychology building.

But certainly there are other things to think about when choosing a graduate program. Very likely, the issue of electives will be near the bottom of that list. Each person will bring his own set of circumstances and concerns to the table—and, as that individual, you owe it to yourself to do a lot of head-racking, soul-searching, and number-crunching. But don't worry—we're not going to leave you entirely on your own.

When Bruce Rettig, associate dean of the Graduate School at Oregon State University, talks about choosing a graduate school, he emphasizes "the extreme value of program match." In other words, doing thorough research to determine which program suits your particular needs and desires. But figuring out exactly how to determine what is—and is not—the right match for you can seem an elusive task. You have many things to consider: some of them academic, some of them social, some of them financial.

Here's a list of major things that you'll want to take into account—no matter who you are—as you proceed in your search for the graduate program that's the perfect match for you.

- Specialization
- Prestige/rankings
- Program availability
- Faculty accessibility
- Existing relationships with faculty
- Resources
- Cost and personal finances
- Alumni
- Location
- Family considerations

THE CALCULUS

As you're starting to realize, making the big decision is not as easy as one-two-three. But that doesn't mean that you can't use numbers to help you make your list of possible programs. Here we offer a simple but useful chart that can assist you as you try to come to terms with two aspects of the selection process that are beyond your control: Ranking and the Almighty Dollar. Of course, rankings can differ from source to source, and money is going to go a lot further in Athens, Georgia, than in San Francisco, California. But devising a schematic—whether duplicating this chart or coming up with something of your own—can give some rational shape to what might otherwise seem like a jumble of considerations.

School	Ranking	Stipend	Final
U of X	2	8 ($12,000)	10
U of Y	11	1 ($21,500)	12
U of Z	30	10 ($9,500)	40
Etc.	Etc.	Etc.	Etc

Such a chart can help you to visually assess your options. Assuming that lower is better, we can see that the Universities of X and Y offer preferable options to University of Z—at least in terms of these simple equations. Even though the numbers aren't far apart, each university brings a different sort of benefit to the table. The University of X offers a spike in prestige, while the University of Y provides nearly twice the stipend that X does. Because the University of Z offers neither the massive prestige nor the dough, it might drop into the background. (Note: Students planning to pursue a degree in the sciences or technologies may opt to create charts that include equations taking into account, say, the *difference* in funding; students in the humanities may decide to insert a column that asks, What Would Henry James Do? Ken Kesey?)

But the University of Z may not stay in the background. As we said, this is just one of many tools that you can devise to help you put your options into some sort of perspective. After all the calculus is done, you'll have personal factors to consider. If the University of X and the University of Y are both on the West Coast, and you're dying to live in the Big Apple—where the University of Z is—then you have some soul-searching to do. Or perhaps you're married, planning on starting a family while you're in graduate school—well, then, that extra $11,500 will come in handy. Big city or rural town? Large program or small one? East or West? Sardines or caviar?

Our point is this: Some sort of "calculus" can help you put your options into perspective, but you'll never solve the equation for yourself until you sit down with your own concerns and priorities and lay them all out on the scales. The University of X may have the top seat in some national ranking, but when all the factors are tallied the best option for you might be the University of Z.

SPECIALIZATION

One of the first things you'll want to think about as you begin the search for the program that's best for you is what exactly you want to specialize in. As you can see from "The Web of Degrees" on page 3, the possibilities for specialization within a given discipline are numerous. When we say "specialization," what we mean is the narrower focus (say, immunology) within an already narrow focus (biology). And this is the kind of thing you want to start thinking about now. On the one hand, the broader your sense of what you want to study, the more difficult it will be to predict the sort of academic experience you'll get out of a program; on the other hand, the more focused your sense of what you want to study, the more effective you'll be in pinpointing the program(s) that'll suit you best.

What if you're not exactly sure what you want to specialize in? Although you'll probably have some room to tweak your specialization once you're actually enrolled, it's a wise idea to begin doing some research now. After all, admissions committees are going to expect to get a sense of your specific focus when you apply. Go to the library of a nearby college or university and begin reading articles in academic journals related to the field of study in which you're interested. Try to get a sense of what sort of research is hot in the field these days. As you read through the articles, ask yourself, *Does this interest me?* If the answer you come up with is *No*, then you probably don't want to dedicate the next two or five or ten years of your life to studying that particular niche of knowledge.

As you research the various specializations in your broader field of study, you'll also be exposing yourself to the work of the major players in the discipline. Keep a notebook with you, and as you come across articles that interest you, jot down the names of the authors. At the beginning or end of an article, you'll find some biographical info on the author(s). If you're especially intrigued by particular authors, take note of where they teach and how their research is funded. In doing so, you're killing two birds with one stone: narrowing down the academic specializations that might become your pursuit in graduate school, as well as the programs to which you might apply.

PROGRAM AVAILABILITY

Among the very important questions that this book can help you answer is this: What are the programs in my intended field of study? This might seem like an obvious consideration, but it's an important one nonetheless. And it's the kind of thing you'll want to look into during the early stages of your grad school research.

As you're getting a firm grasp on *exactly* what it is that you'd like to study, you'll want to begin making a list of the places where you can do this. And when we say list, we mean *list*. Write it down. As you'll realize soon—if you haven't already—the more organized you are during this whole process, the more sanity you'll be able to maintain. Applying to graduate schools will require that you spend about a year poring over vast amounts of information, ranging from guides like this one to professional articles in your potential field to university websites and department-specific materials that you receive in the mail. And after a while, the information can start to blend together; you'll know you read something, but when it's time to take another look at that information, you may have some trouble remembering exactly where you saw it. So keeping careful notes can help you streamline the process.

As you do your research on program availability, you want to keep your eyes peeled for answers to several other specific questions.

- In my specialization, what degree (MA, PhD, etc.) options are offered at each school?

- How many students does each program accept per year? How many apply?

- How many faculty members are working in my specific area? What sort of research are they doing right now?

PRESTIGE AND RANKING

"Prestige" is a tricky word. Look it up in a dictionary—go ahead—and you'll find a definition like this: "Standing or estimation in the eyes of people." In other words, prestige is a general term that describes how a group of people decide to assign value to something—in our case, graduate programs. Well, as we've tried to hammer into your head, *you* are the most important person in this process. So even if it is presented to you by anyone else as highly prestigious, it doesn't mean that you should just sign up sight-unseen. What's best in somebody else's eyes will not necessarily be best in yours, and vice versa.

One primary way in which a program earns the designation "prestigious" is by its placement within educational rankings. We know a thing or two about rankings, and it is fair to assume that if a program continually rises to the top of several national rankings, for some reason or another, it probably deserves the reputation the rankings afford it. But you should not let rankings determine where you apply, or, especially, where you enroll.

When you do look at rankings, take some time to read the fine print. On what factors are the rankings based? Which of these factors matter to you? Which factors that matter to you aren't included in the rankings? How can you go about finding out that information on your own?

Che Hutson, a PhD candidate in neuroscience at the University of California—Los Angeles, points out that many national rankings fail to take into account some factors that should, in fact, be crucial to a person attempting to assess the value of a grad program. Among these factors are the following:

- The number of faculty members

- The number of publications published per faculty member

- The quality and quantity of student funding

- Student graduation rates

- The number of publications published among the student population

Some rankings, like those put out by the National Research Council (NRC), do take these sorts of factors into account, but because the NRC rankings are issued infrequently, it'll be largely up to you to acquire up-to-date answers to these types of questions.

You'll also want to consider the specificity of the rankings. In other words, if you're particularly interested in studying oceanography, simply assessing a school's ranking in the "geology" or "earth sciences" category might not be enough. A geology program that's superb in mineralogy might not even have a focused doctoral track in oceanography. And if it does, it might not match up in terms of financial aid offerings, post-degree job placement, research opportunities, resource availability, esteemed faculty, or any other of a number of factors that you'll want to take into account. This is your graduate career—and, probably, your lifelong career—that's at stake here, and you owe it to yourself to look very deep into each program you are considering.

We're not suggesting that rankings are worthless. Rankings are useful tools that you can use as you research your options. It's also quite true that the reputation of your grad school alma mater will probably affect the caliber and range of job opportunities that you find after graduation. But remember that just because a Nobel Prize winner whose pursuits you admire works in a top-ranked department doesn't mean that you'll have much chance to work with him or her. This is where a little bit of your own legwork—or fingerwork—can take you a long way. If at all possible, visit the campus of each program on your shortlist. Otherwise, make a few phone calls. Either way, try to get a general sense of the shape of a particular program's prestige. Is the competition ruthless? Are the star faculty available? Are graduate students treated more like peers or peons? On the one hand, a top-ranked program that makes students feel like fraternity pledges might not be what you're looking for. On the other hand, a top-ranked program in which Ms. Nobel Prize is accessible and student voices are welcomed might be a goal worth aiming for.

Either way, your ultimate success will depend on the quality of work you are able to produce. Doing mediocre or uninspired work in what's considered a highly prestigious program will not serve you as well as producing a top-quality dissertation at a program a few lines lower in the rankings.

FACULTY ACCESSIBILITY

If you enroll in a graduate program that's going to cost you sweat, time, and money, you want to be sure that the people you're going there to learn from will actually be available. As you're exploring this, keep in mind that accessibility and friendliness do not always go hand in hand. In other words, just because you speak to a well-respected, good-natured faculty member on the telephone during the courting process does not mean that you'll be able to spend much time with that faculty member once you begin your daily life on campus.

So how do you find out if faculty members are *really* going to be as accessible as you'd like them to be? You can, of course, ask each faculty member point-blank. But the most effective approach is to get in touch with students. After all, students who have to deal with faculty members on a day-to-day basis will be able to offer you the candid, insider's perspective on the experience that will most closely mirror your own if you were to enroll in the program. When you speak to students, be sure to have good, specific questions to ask and encourage them to expand on any answers they give you. You want to find out what they love and hate about a program; only then will you start to build a realistic picture of what daily life in the program is really like.

Don't simply ask if Professor T is accessible; ask if Professor T teaches classes frequently, if he plays favorites, whether he's looking for acolytes or innovators. Ask whatever comes to mind—whatever you'd like to know but might not want to ask Professor T himself.

And, of course, you can do some research on your own. Click your way into the university schedule of courses to see if Professor T is teaching classes this semester. Many universities will also list the previous and upcoming semesters' schedules; see Professor T on those? You should also be able to find a personal web page linked to the department's home page that will tell you what sort of office hours the good professor offers. Use these clues to help you get a sense of how much time and energy you can expect a professor to devote to you.

EXISTING RELATIONSHIPS WITH FACULTY

As you're applying to programs, you'll certainly want to keep your eyes open for faculty members in each program that you'd like to get to know—faculty members with highly-regarded reputations as teachers or academics. But it's also a good idea to be on the lookout for faculty members that you already know. There are two benefits to this. First, you probably have some sense of who they are, how they teach, and with what sort of rigor (and success) they approach their research. Second, if you decide you're truly interested in the program with which they are associated, you already have someone on the "inside" who can recognize your name among the dozens or hundreds of other names on the applicant list. If you know them well enough, they can even vouch for your candidacy. That said, you also want to be careful. You may be familiar with faculty members because they taught you as an undergrad. If this is the case, beware of limiting your options simply because you're enamored of a former professor.

Attending graduate school is a great chance to encounter new people and new opportunities. So don't simply decide that you'll return to your undergraduate institution for a program in philosophy because you enjoyed studying for your major in philosophy there. Instead, take advantage of your relationship with your mentors to ask for advice about programs elsewhere. You might end up deciding that your undergraduate alma mater is the place for you, but why limit yourself before you test the waters elsewhere?

RESOURCES

Without question, the quality and variety of resources at your fingertips greatly influences the overall success of your graduate studies. When we talk about resources, we're talking about money, yes, but we're also talking about the actual tools you need to accomplish every task necessary to earning your degree. In other words, the question of resources is twofold: First, will you receive the financial support that you need to carry out your studies to the best of your abilities? Second, will you have access to the cutting-edge equipment that you'll need to conduct your research?

Although we'll address the question of financial resources in further detail in the "Paying for a Graduate Degree" section, there are a few basic things that you should know right now. The financial resources that graduate students are most acquainted with are awarded by the host university. These come in the forms of **teaching assistantships** (TAships, in grad school vernacular), **research assistantships** (RAships), **graduate assistantships** (GAships), and **fellowships.** The first three options require something of the recipient, whether it's teaching undergraduate courses, grading essays or exams for a professor, assisting a professor with a research project, or filling another role, administrative or otherwise, within the department. In comparison, fellowships are freebies, requiring nothing more of the recipient than an honest day's academic work. As you might expect, fellowships are less common and harder to win than assistantships.

Every program you look at will offer its own perks and complications. For instance, some programs will offer different financial aid packages to different students. A perceived hotshot might receive a free ride, while the person who barely made the cut will have to pay half of his tuition and grade papers to make his monthly wage. In this sort of program, students are likely to encounter a more competitive atmosphere, in large part because classmates are vying for treasures out of the same pot of gold. On the other side of the coin is the sort of program that offers everyone who's accepted the same basic resources. Speaking about the graduate students in Princeton University's history department, department chair Robert Tignor says, "They all get the same package." Because of the equality, he says, the program participants enjoy a "very communal" atmosphere. As you assess the financial resources offered by a program, then, it's useful to think about how their distribution will affect the shape of the community.

The other sorts of financial resources to be aware of are the on-campus and off-campus opportunities for specific-project funding. For instance, if you're a psychology grad student who wants to attend the annual convention of the American Psychological Association (which, by the way, was held in Honolulu in 2004), does your department or university offer any sorts of subsidies to cover the costs? Or do you have to pay for the whole shebang out of your own pocket? And what about personal research expenses? After all, if you're a volcanologist and your research leads you to the volcanoes on the Russian peninsula of Kamchatka, will departmental administrators and faculty members point you toward accessible research funding, or will they roll their eyes? When you speak to departmental officers, it's important to find out what sorts of resources are available and how often they're used. It's also a good idea to check into the ways in which faculty members at the university are funded; this will give you a sense of what kind of campus and corporate funds tend to show up in the department.

And you'll also want to find out what sort of equipment you'll have available to you as you progress through the degree. The type of equipment that will benefit you will depend on the type of degree you're pursuing.

If you're planning to go into a degree in the arts or humanities, it's fair to say that your most important resource will be the library. So spend some time in the library, and if you can't visit the campus, at least spend some time on the campus library's website. How many volumes does it have? To what periodicals does it subscribe? How wide-ranging is its interlibrary loan program? What about the availability of online journals and databases?

Similarly, if you're studying in the sciences, you'll want to find out what sorts of equipment and programs are most advantageous in your field and then which schools provide the best equipment for graduate student use. A good way to learn what equipment you should expect to find is to talk with your undergraduate professors who are working in the field. When you're speaking with students and faculty in the prospective programs, use this knowledge to ask specific questions about the resources that are on hand.

SMALL SCHOOLS, LARGE SCHOOLS, AND THE QUESTION OF RESOURCES

You should expect to find a thinner allocation of resources at small, private schools than at large, state institutions. To make up for this dearth of resources, programs at small schools will often set up reciprocal arrangements with programs at larger schools. At Pennsylvania's Bryn Mawr College, for example, where only six graduate programs are offered, students take advantage of the reciprocal relationship with the nearby University of Pennsylvania. When schools say they have reciprocal relationships with other schools, they're referring to a partnership that's been set up to allow students to take advantage of the course offerings and resources at another institution.

Along these same lines, small schools often have what Bryn Mawr's graduate dean of arts and sciences, Dale Kinney, calls "lack of overlap." What she means is that small schools may only have one faculty member devoted to a particular specialization, whereas large schools might have four or five. "At small schools, you have to be enterprising," explains Kinney. "You need to network and reach out to faculty at other institutions." Such reaching out, of course, can have its benefits, like getting to know the academic movers and shakers (and maybe even members of the faculty hiring committees) at other schools. However, if there aren't a few other universities nearby that you can reach out to, the likelihood of finding the resources that you need might be slim and frustrating.

The preference for a small school or a large school is a personal one, but keep in mind that it's not simply a question of campus atmosphere. It's a question of research too. And you owe it to yourself to talk to the students and faculty at each program to clue yourself in to what exactly you can expect.

COST AND PERSONAL FINANCES

Here's a common complaint among graduate students: "I wish I'd put away some money before returning to grad school." And the reason this complaint is so common is that graduate schools—with very few exceptions—support their graduate students with pitifully low wages or small stipends. And that, of course, only pertains to students who actually receive *any* funding. In the liberal arts and sciences, you can expect to find the four primary modes of university-provided funding mentioned above: teaching assistantships, graduate assistantships, research assistantships, and fellowships. In many cases, these awards and appointments will be accompanied by tuition remission and health care. But this is not always the case. And sometimes the health care will cover no more than the bare-bones minimum. At some universities, tuition remission does not include university fees, which can soar toward the thousand-dollar mark.

Whether or not you receive university funding, you owe it to yourself to read the fine print in *all* of your financial contracts. (This is a good lesson to apply to all contracts in real life too.) We'll address this more specifically in the "Paying for a Graduate Degree" section, but for now, tuck these four important questions into the back of your mind:

- What is the sticker price of the education?

- How much of this cost do I actually have to pay?

- How much of my expenses are being covered?

- What am I obligated to do once I get in?

ALUMNI

So far we've given you a long list of people that you should talk to as you search for the program that's the best match for you: current students, faculty members, administrators, undergraduate professors, and corporate professionals. Well, it's time to add one more group to this list: alumni. And the reason that alumni can be such useful resources is that these are the people in a particular program who've gone from one end of the degree to the other—they've worn the shoes that you hope to soon fill—and they're now (hopefully) putting that degree to work. But what kind of work? Did they find it easy to get a job after graduation? Can they pinpoint strengths or weaknesses of the degree *now* that they weren't even aware of when they were studying in the program? Do they have regrets? Recommendations?

Of course, you won't be able to talk to every alumnus. So you'll want to ask department secretaries or students or faculty members to provide you with contacts for a handful of recent grads. Or perhaps your own research in the field has turned up the names of a few successful alums. It's important to make sure the majority of alums you try to contact are *recent* graduates, because the atmosphere of a department is likely to evolve; alums from 10 or 20 years ago probably have little to offer in terms of what the current day-to-day life of a student is like.

Aside from talking one-on-one with alums, stepping back and looking at a program's entire body of alumni can also provide you with a useful indication of the program's success ratio. A number of department websites will include a link to an "alumni" page that will give you a sense of what big names have passed through the program's doors, as well as what sorts of jobs alumni have gone on to hold and publications and projects they've been associated with. When you speak with a program director or a graduate dean, it's worth asking them for specific data on alumni. In particular, questions that you'll want to have answered include:

- How many graduates find work suited to their degrees within a year of graduation?

- Do graduates tend to work in academe, the private sector, or for governmental agencies? What's the breakdown for each category?

- If you're interested in teaching, find out what sorts of institutions graduates of the program tend to teach at.

- Are there any recent graduates who have established themselves as major players in the field? If so, what are they doing? Who did they work with when enrolled in the program? How do you get in touch with them?

LOCATION

Here's your situation: You're 39 years old; you're recently divorced; things at work are getting a little hairy; you've long considered returning to school for a PhD in English; you've never lived anywhere but the Pacific Northwest, and though you wouldn't mind picking up and going, it's not like you want to find yourself on another planet—like Ohio or something like that.

Or no, wait; *here's* your situation: You're living in Chicago; you're 28 years old; you've been married for three years; your mother's in a nursing home down in Joliet; you have a mortgage; you've realized that you can substantially increase your market value if you earn a master's in economics, which you'd like to do before you and your spouse start a family.

Oh, okay; *here's* your situation: You're 21 years old; you have one year left at a liberal arts college in Alabama; you'd like to earn an advanced degree in psychology, and you're willing to settle in Siberia if that's where you'll find the best psychology program for you.

Our point here is this: There's no one kind of person applying to graduate school, and because of this, there's no one easy rule that you can follow when choosing a school's location. As the hypothetical situations above show, depending on where you are in your life, you may have no geographic chains limiting you, or you may have many.

On the topic of location, Dianne Bryan, the graduate and professional studies advisor at Dickinson College, often offers students this food for thought: "A change of scenery and venue and opportunities is *very* important." Adapting to change is an important component of personal growth. So if you *do* have some room to maneuver, consider moving to an environment that will expose you to something new.

Whatever you decide, it's important to recognize that *location is very important*. If you're aiming to earn a PhD, you're going to be spending many years living and working in the city or town of your graduate school. If you're absolutely miserable—for whatever reason—in your surroundings, your studies won't benefit from your misery.

FAMILY CONSIDERATIONS

These come in all shapes and size, but whatever shape or size, they are never a small matter. If you have a partner or a child, if your family has car payments or house payments, or if you plan to send your child to a private school—if any of these situations sound vaguely pertinent, you'll want to keep in mind that the money you'll earn through a university stipend, even at best, is designed to provide a humble living wage for one person. In a 2001 article in *The Chronicle of Higher Education*, Scott Smallwood estimates that students in the social sciences and humanities can expect to bring in about $11,000–$12,000 annually, while students in the sciences average higher stipends, sometimes near $20,000.[3] Whether $11,000 or $20,000, this is not exactly a fortune. Savings, loans, fellowships, or spousal support will be necessary to carry a person with a family through the years you spend earning your PhD.

Above and beyond finances—which, let us emphasize, should be next to paramount in your mind—people with partners have their own brand of concerns. Children, too, raise specific issues. Sick relatives or other family responsibilities might limit the distance you're willing to go to study. While other individual family concerns might intervene, let's have a quick look at these three.

- **Partners.** If you have a partner, you can rest assured that it's not just *you* that's heading to graduate school; it's *both of you*. Unlike a 9-to-5 job, graduate school will likely dish out so many assignments and fodder for thought that you'll have trouble leaving the office (if you have an office, that is). When you're doing your course work or studying for your qualifying exams, you'll be back in homework mode, and this can intrude upon the time and energy that you'll have available to spend QT with your squeeze. And the leap to grad school will probably land you in the midst of an eclectic social circle—a social circle that will encourage you to swing out for departmental potlucks and academic lectures and, perhaps, a few hours at the pub. Of course, you can always decline the invitations. But it's important to remember that maintaining a social network will not only help keep you sane as you push through your degree, but can also evolve into a professional network that will serve you well after the degree's in hand.

  And let's not be selfish about it. You know exactly what *you'll* be doing during your time at the University of Anywhere, but what about your partner? Does he or she want to go back to school as well? If so, is there a program that suits his or her needs at the University of Anywhere? And what if he or she wants to continue working? How do the job prospects look in the town where the University of Anywhere is located? Is there a company that incorporates your partner's specialty? What about extracurricular activities? If you're both avid rock climbers, it's worth spending some time with a topographic map. And then, of course, there's always the bitter question of distance. If need be, are you willing to live apart while earning your degree? If not, is a healthy commute out of the question?

  All of these questions need to be addressed as you select schools and, particularly, as you prepare to sign on the dotted line.

- **Children.** As you might imagine, if you have children, you'll need to ask similar questions. What are the schools like? Looking into the schools before enrolling can help assure you that your child will get a decent education without being forced to commute 50 minutes each way. On this note, the good news is that colleges and universities are staffed by professors and administrators who, like you, demand a quality education for their children. In other words, you can usually find a school in a college town that will meet your expectations.

  A slew of other questions might come to mind. What are the neighborhoods in your budget range like? What's the deal with the town's crime rates? How about after-school programs, or little league, or the town's age demographic? Many universities will provide links from their main website to community web pages. This is a good place to start getting a feel for the city or town. But you should probably take it a step further; try to talk to other grad students with children and ask for their candid opinions. They might be able to give you more than the thumbs up or the thumbs down; they might also be able to point you to specific schools, quality neighborhoods, helpful realtors, hotspots for cool-but-affordable used furniture, and anything else you'll need to know as you prepare to settle into a new community.

- **"What is reality?"** writer Anne Sexton once asked. And it's the kind of question that you, too, should be asking yourself. More specifically, you should be asking yourself, *What is my reality?* As many soon-to-be students look ahead to a graduate career, they also have to consider their need to be close to relatives who might rely on them. For instance, an ailing parent might require constant care or frequent trips home. Our point here is not to offer you moral guidelines; rather, we're encouraging you to take into serious account the broader scope of your familial obligations and range of responsibilities. This may affect how far away you're willing to go. And if you don't think this over before moving a few thousand miles away, you might discover that the burden of distance is more than you can handle.

SHAMELESS SELF-PROMOTION 101

Any given application can have its own twists and turns, but generally speaking, you can expect to run into six major blocks as you construct your application: the application form itself, transcripts, test scores, the personal statement, sample work, and letters of recommendation. We'll say a little more about each of these, but before we do, let us offer you two words that will serve you well if you keep them at the front of your mind through the entire process: *neatness* and *punctuality*.

The presentation of your application says a lot about you—and admissions committees are well aware of this. If you turn in an application full of typos or an application three days past the deadline, you'll be sending a signal to the admissions committee, and not the kind of signal you want to send. Getting your application in six months early is not necessary—and will rarely win you preferential consideration—but sending your application in even one day late will unquestionably earn you an unwanted position in the "Questionable with regard to responsibility" pile of application. An application is your first opportunity to show an admissions committee what you're made of, and

---

3 Scott Smallwood, "Stipends are Key in Competition to Land Top Graduate Students," *Chronicle of Higher Education*, 28 September 2001, 24.

Complete Book of Graduate Programs in the Arts and Sciences

though it's a cliché, it's fair to say that you'll never have another chance to make a first impression on an admissions committee. So after you have your application packet assembled, look over it again. Look closely and scour it with a red pen and with an eye to all the specific requirements. Once you're done going over it, go over it again. Have a friend go over it. Use your spell check. Make sure your grammar is on the mark. Be certain that you haven't forgotten anything that's been specifically requested of you. Sending in a neat and punctual application might seem like one of the easiest parts of the process, but you'd be surprised how many people screw it up.

And presenting yourself in the best possible light is, of course, your goal. A recent study by the National Center for Education Statistics (NCES) shows that enrollment in graduate schools will increase by nearly 11 percent over the next eight years, which means that you'll want to do everything that you can to rise above the competition.[4]

THE FORM

When you apply to a program, you're actually applying to two separate entities: the graduate school and the department itself. In most cases, the application form you're required to complete will go to the graduate school. (You may be asked to send a photocopy of the completed form to the department office too.) This form will contain all the information that you'd expect, ranging from name and address to educational and employment history. Some people advise that you seek out a typewriter and fill out the forms the old-fashioned way; others will tell you that handwriting is fine. The best option is to complete the application online, if it's available (it's worth visiting our website, www.PrincetonReview.com, as it serves the online applications of hundreds of colleges and graduate schools). Whatever option you choose, the most important thing you can do is make sure the application is neat and easy to review—and this includes carefully following all instructions. After all, admissions committees are usually made up of busy professionals. You'll leave them with a sour taste in their mouths if they have to devote unnecessary time to deciphering anything about your application.

THE PAPERWORK

Transcripts are those records of your educational history that hide deep within the files of the computer network at each post-secondary institution (usually this means college) you've attended. And while they might not look too exciting, they're absolutely crucial to your moving on up through the ranks of the educational system.

Getting your hands on your transcripts isn't terribly hard, but that doesn't mean that you might not run into a few headaches along the way. The most important thing to think about is this: How long will it take your college(s) to process your request for a transcript? You can usually find this out by looking on the school's website or by phoning the registrar's office. If you're lucky, you might find an office that can turn around the document in a week or two, but as a rule you should *expect to wait eight to twelve weeks between the time that you order the transcript and the time that it is within your possession.* It is crucial that you factor this time into your total prep time for your grad school applications because when a school gives you a deadline for your application materials, it means that *everything*—including all supplementary materials like your transcript(s)—must be in by that date.

Some colleges will provide you with a small number of transcripts for free, but don't count on this generosity. To be on the safe side, when you're planning your application budget, expect to drop about 10 dollars per transcript. You may find that the transcripts cost only half of that. In that case, rent a movie to celebrate.

One final note on transcripts: Programs will ask for an "official transcript," which means that they want the transcript to come to them in a university envelope, with an official stamp or signature across the seal. So if you have an unofficial transcript sitting among your stacks of paperwork, don't think for a minute that a photocopy of this will suffice.

THE BIG TEST(S)

It's rare to find a graduate program that won't require you to submit your scores on one or more standardized tests. So get used to the idea now: you have at least one test standing between you and graduate school.

Practically every arts and sciences graduate program in the country will require that you take the **Graduate Record Examination (GRE)** General Test. The General Test (in its recently revised form) comprises three sections: verbal, quantitative, and analytic writing. In the United States, the General Test is administered by computer and can only be taken at specific GRE testing sites. In some foreign countries, written tests are an option. To take the test in the U.S. or a U.S. territory such as Puerto Rico, you'll need to shell out $115. The cost is $175 in China, Hong Kong, and Taiwan and $140 in all other countries. At the computer test centers in the United States, the test can be taken year-round, Monday through Saturday. Still, you need to register for the test in advance. The easiest way to do this is to go to the GRE website at www.gre.org.

As we said, the test itself comes in three parts. The verbal section tests your skills in reading comprehension. This will include understanding issues of syntax and diction, comprehending the concepts discussed in a passage, and analyzing the language of a text as you attempt to solve some problems presented in the reading.

The quantitative section tests your dexterity in mathematics, including your ability to work with the basic mathematical subjects that you wrestled with in high school: arithmetic, algebra, geometry, and data analysis. You'll obviously have an edge here if you're well-versed in math, but there's no need to take an emergency course in upper-level calculus. That said, you *should* spend some time brushing on up on your math skills if you're not currently using them on a daily basis.

In the analytic writing section—you guessed it—you'll be asked to write. In this section, which is broken into two parts, your ability to produce a clear, articulate argument will be tested. You'll be expected to think analytically and to incorporate complex ideas. Since 2003, responses to the analytic section have been made available to the schools to which you apply. Obviously, this adds extra weight to an already high-stakes test.

4 U.S. Department of Education, National Center for Education Statistics, Projections of Education Statistics to 2012, (NCES 2002-30), by Debra E. Gerald and William J. Hussar. Washington, DC: 2002.

One of the best ways to prepare for the general test is to take a GRE prep course. We are, of course, biased, but we are confident that Princeton Review courses are the best around. And these courses are available in classroom settings, as well as online. Whether you go with The Princeton Review or not, however, you should prep with someone. And you should complement this prep by spending some serious time with the preparation materials (paper and software versions available) that will be sent to you by the Education Testing Service (ETS), the company who writes the GRE. Practice tests, too, are available on the GRE website, at www.gre.org/pracmats.html. Take as many practice tests as your schedule allows, because the more familiar you are with the type of material you'll encounter and the format of the test itself, the more comfortable you'll be when you finally come face-to-face with the actual exam.

Aside from the general test, a GRE subject test will be required by a large number of programs. Subject tests are given in eight areas.

- Biochemistry, cell, and molecular biology

- Biology

- Chemistry

- Computer science

- Literature in English

- Mathematics

- Physics

- Psychology

As the name itself suggests, the subject test will assess your knowledge in a specific area of study. Depending on the subject test you take, you can expect to spend about three hours answering anywhere from 66 to 230 multiple-choice questions. If you want to nail a subject test, we'd recommend devoting time to the texts on the subject you studied as an undergraduate. Pull out your old notebooks. Make some study cards. Do whatever it takes. And pick up a study guide too. At practically every book superstore in the country, you'll find our test prep books for the biology, chemistry, literature, mathematics, and psychology subject tests.

It's true that high scores alone probably won't get you into the graduate school of your dreams, but doing well on the subject test will show an admissions committee that you're moving in the right direction. And doing poorly—well, this might show them something as well.

At the end of the subject test(s), which are administered with paper and pencil, and at the finale of the general test, you'll have the option to cancel your scores if you don't think you did well enough to have the results listed on your permanent record. (When schools receive your GRE scores, they receive the scores you received on *all* tests you have taken, not just the scores from your latest or best effort.) On the subject test, you simply fill in the appropriate bubbles at the end of the exam. On the general test, after you complete the exam's final question, a ticking clock will appear on the screen, giving you a few minutes to decide what to do. *Think carefully about this.* It's not so uncommon to walk away from a standardized test feeling that you fared worse than you actually did. And if you do choose to cancel, you won't receive a refund, nor will you ever find out how well you actually did. It's also worth noting that even if you cancel your scores, your test records will report the cancellation. For the computerized tests, if you choose not to cancel, you'll receive your unofficial scores immediately.

Whether you're taking the GRE general test, a subject test, or both, we strongly recommend that you review the testing schedules to find a time—with a several-month study cushion beforehand—that will work best for you, with one caveat: Choose a time that will allow you to get your scores to a graduate program before the application deadline. Registration information for the general test can be found at www.gre.org/generalreg.html. Also go to www.gre.org/pbstest.html#testreg to get the necessary info for the subject tests. Further details about test centers and test dates are also accessible through the GRE website. If you'd prefer to talk to someone in person, you can always call the GRE headquarters at (609) 771-7670.

If you're an undergraduate right now and you're looking ahead to the possibility of graduate school, we recommend that you take the GRE general and subject tests while you're still in school. The summer between your junior and senior years is an ideal time because you have a few months to study, and if after you get your results, you aren't satisfied, there's time to try again. Dianne Bryan, the graduate and professional studies advisor at Dickinson College, points out that taking the big test(s) while still in college is also a wise idea because at this point—as opposed to three years down the road—you're in an academic, test-taking frame of mind. And GRE scores are good for five years, so even if you don't plan on going back to grad school right away, it doesn't hurt to take it soon. Think about it: You'll have an easier time with the chemistry test if you take it when those chemistry courses are still fresh in your mind, as opposed to a few years later when the memories of those classes are fuzzier.

Foreign students have one additional exam to consider: the **Test of English as a Foreign Language,** known as the **TOEFL.** This test, which is required of international students by more than 4,300 higher-ed institutions in the United States, assesses a foreign speaker's ability to comprehend and effectively use written and spoken English. The four-hour test is broken into four parts: listening, structure, reading, and writing. In most cases, the test is administered on a computer. Whether you take the test on computer or paper depends on location. TOEFL test centers are stationed around the globe, but you should note that at least 80 test centers have been closed in recent years. A list of computer-based test centers is available at http://etsis4.ets.org/tcenter/cbt_fr.cfm. Five times a year, TOEFL/TSE services offers paper testing for people who aren't able to make it to a regional test center. The testing fee is US$130. If you will be paying the fee from an overseas account, only the following currencies are acceptable: Australian dollar, British pound, Canadian dollar, Danish krone, Euro, Hong Kong dollar, Japanese yen, New Zealand dollar, Norwegian krone, Singapore dollar, Swedish krona, and Swiss franc.

TEST TAKIN': QUICK FACTS

	GRE GENERAL TEST	GRE SUBJECT TESTS	TOEFL
Cost	$115 (U.S., territories, & Puerto Rico) $175 (China, Hong Kong, Taiwan, & Korea) $140 (all other countries)	$115 (U.S., territories, & Puerto Rico) $175 (China, Hong Kong, Taiwan, & Korea) $140 (all other countries)	$130
Dates	year-round*	November, December, & April**	year-round
Shelf-life	five years	five years	two years
Website	www.gre.org/gendir.html	www.gre.org/pbstest.html	www.toefl.org
Phone	800-473-2255 or 609-771-7670	800-473-2255 or 609-771-7670	800-468-6335 or 443-751-4862

* Students taking the test in countries other than the United States need to check with local testing centers for availability.

** Specific dates vary each year, though subject tests are generally administered twice in the fall semester and once in the spring. See www.gre.org/testdate.html#subdate for updated information.

THE STATEMENT

Remember how nerve-racking and frustrating it was to write that essay for your college application? Well, it's time to write another one. The personal statement you write for a graduate application, however, is a much different, more benevolent beast. The difficulty in writing a personal statement for a college application lies in how wide open the prompt often is, looking for insight into who you are as a person (Where to begin?) and less on you as the focused academic. But at this point, of course, you *are* a focused academic, and your academic ambitions are precisely what your personal statement should reflect.

Depending on your field of interest, your own experience, and the specific question posed to you, the personal statement you write might differ greatly from the personal statement written by someone else. But Robert Tignor, chair of the history department at Princeton University, has noticed three traits often found in successful statements:

1. Sophistication of thought (in other words, you don't want to come across as naive)

2. A demonstrated capacity to write coherently

3. An indication of why you want to study at *that* particular institution

You'll also want to focus on your specific progress in the field you want to enter, as well as any other personal experiences that pertain to your interest in it. (For instance, if you want to study the politics of Italy and you spent three years during your childhood living in Rome, mention it.) But while writing your statement, you should actively avoid repeating *anything* that you've laid out on your application form or, if required, in your resume. Focus is key here. You're making an argument for why *that* program and *that* field are perfect for you—and you'll need to do this in a page or two. If you go off on a tangent, you'll probably leave members of the admissions committee scratching their heads and flipping to the next application.

How much weight does an admissions committee place on the personal statement? There's no cut-and-dry answer to this question. The value of a personal statement differs between small schools and large schools, science programs and social science/humanities programs, department and department. Generally, you can assume that if you're applying for a spot in a social sciences or humanities program, your statement will be examined for not only its content, but also for its demonstration of writing ability. Also, smaller schools or programs with less applicants often have the time (and desire) to learn everything about an applicant that they can. However, large state schools with a pool of accomplished applicants often rely more on numbers and streamlined information than they do on written statements. But even if this is the case, a lousy personal statement can lead to a lousy letter in the mail.

THE SAMPLES

When a program requests that you send a sample piece of writing or research, what they're really saying is this: Send us a chunk of your work that will convince us that you have the skills that it takes to succeed in this field, that will prove to us that you know how to communicate according to the standards of the discipline, and that will show us that you're able to work in an innovative and organized fashion. "Make it look like the best such writing in your field," advises William J. Maxwell, director of graduate studies in the English department at the University of Illinois—Urbana-Champaign.

To make your sample stack up to the "best" writing in your discipline, you'll want to send a clean copy to the admissions committee. When we say clean copy, we mean a version of the essay that was revised specifically for the application, minus the glowing or critical red-ink comments that an undergrad professor scrawled in the margins. And even if you decide to send in an eight-page essay that earned an A during your junior year, you'll do yourself a favor by revisiting and revising the essay. Rework it according to your most recent understanding and knowledge of its subject, incorporating the writing standards of what makes an essay in your field successful. Pull out your own red pen and get to work. As many graduate deans have assured us, wooing an admissions committee with a strong writing sample can sometimes make up for slights in other areas, such as shaky GRE scores.

THE LETTERS

It's true that you can't write the letters of recommendation yourself, but this doesn't mean that you can't have an effect on what sorts of letters accompany your application. There are a number of things you can do to make sure you get the most out of your letters.

First, you are in charge of choosing who you ask to write your letters, and you should not take this decision lightly. You want to choose people who are both well-regarded in their field and well-versed in the art of writing recommendation letters. This means that no matter how well you did in a course taught by a teaching assistant, and no matter how terrific your rapport with that TA may be, asking a TA to be one of three official supporters is a bad decision. A teaching assistant just doesn't carry the same amount of distinction as a full-time professor, as most TAs will tell you themselves. Review your academic history (your transcript may come in helpful here) in search of *tenured* faculty members whose research or publications have gained enough attention in their respective fields that the admissions committee might recognize their names.

Also, make sure you *personally* know these professors. If you choose a professor who knows you only as one of 250 students in his or her bench chemistry lecture, there's little concrete evidence that he or she will be able to offer in terms of your personal performance and development.

You should also avoid asking employers (unless specifically related to the field) or other nonacademic acquaintances. You're vying for a coveted spot in a highly-focused academic program; the committee wants to hear about your performance in other academic environments.

Once you settle on which professors you'd like to recommend you, you must ask them to actually write the letters. Most professors will oblige you, provided you performed well in their class, which means you didn't earn anything lower than an A–. As a matter of fact, recommendation letter-writing for current or former students is often a part of their job description. But it's crucial that you make your request to the professors well in advance of when they are due—months before they're due is not a bad idea.

When a professor agrees to write a letter on your behalf, you can—again, politely—let them know what you'd like them to focus on. You don't want to be overbearing on this point because each professor will bring his or her own approach to the keyboard, but giving a little guidance can't hurt. Basically, you want professors to focus on the specific progress you've made in the field and the strong work ethic that you bring into your research. Remember: Survival in grad school is not simply about brains; it's also about discipline and determination. The more ways that you're able to prove to a committee that you're an organized, efficient, and effective worker, the better. Your professors' letters corroborating your own self-description as such a person will help in this regard.

NOW OR THEN? DECIDING WHEN TO APPLY

There's no single type of applicant to graduate school. However, we can break applicants down into two categories: 1) current undergraduate students and 2) people who've already earned their bachelor's degrees and taken some time to pursue other paths. As the NCES data in the previous section suggests, taking time off after college is the more common route. In fact, when considering master's candidates in general (not just those in the arts and sciences), about three-quarters take a break from academics before enrolling in graduate school. Approximately 50 percent of all students in master's programs spend between one and seven years working (or otherwise distracting themselves) before stepping back into the academic arena.

So what does all of this mean? It means that, as the numbers show, there's no need to rush into a graduate program if you're not sure that you're ready. After all, a 30-year-old PhD student is by no means a virtual senior citizen in the grad school society. In fact, a 30-year-old PhD student is a few years below the average.

And yes, timing is important. As Dianne Bryan says, she often meets with junior and senior undergraduates who are set to begin a frantic search for graduate school programs. If students show up at her office saying that they are interested in graduate school but they are not exactly sure in what field, she tells them, "You need to work a couple of years." She tells them this because, as many other folks involved with graduate schools have confirmed, students who arrive in a graduate program with a hazy sense of *why* they want to be there have a higher likelihood of cracking under the very specialized pressure that they're subjected to than students who have a clear, focused sense of what they want out of grad school. If you're on the fence, it's probably better to take a few years to work, to allow your passion to either develop or dissipate, and then reassess your options. Otherwise, you might wind up signing up for a graduate program, toiling through a year or two before realizing that it's not for you, and walking away with a handful of worthless course credits and a few new loans to repay.

Aside from giving yourself time to gain perspective, there's another benefit to putting a few years between the end of your undergraduate and the beginning of your graduate years: money. Even if you end up in a program that offers you a healthy fellowship or TAship, one that grants you free tuition, one that gives you a discounted rate at the nearest parking garage—even if you have all of these perks, the money that you bring in will still only allow you to lead a life bordering on pauperism. And this is why a few years earning paychecks makes sense: It gives you the chance to sock some money away, so if and when you find yourself in graduate school, you don't need to devote precious hours to deciding between food and rent.

We'll talk more about paying for graduate school in the following section. But for now, let's not forget about one more very important thing you get by spending some time in the "real world" after you graduate from college: life experience. If you've followed the traditional educational path, you've spent 13 years in K–12, followed immediately by four (or five or maybe six) years as an undergraduate. It might be time to step away from the classroom and see what else life has to offer. No doubt that graduate school will provide you with a rich intellectual experience, but the value of traveling, wandering, and working in the real world can add a different sort of perspective to your life that you might not otherwise be able to gain if you go straight into graduate school, then directly into the job pool, and end up landing a job as a professor, governmental researcher, or corporate administrator.

But if you've got fire in your belly for an advanced degree, don't let what we've said here discourage you. Just as there are a number of logical reasons to consider waiting a few years before going off to grad school, there's also a single, very solid reason for stepping in right after earning a bachelor's: *passion*. If the academic bug has bitten you and you're absolutely convinced that a PhD in psychology or biochemistry is exactly what you want, then it's probably time to take the plunge. Let us remind you what Dale Kinney of Bryn Mawr, says: Students "have to be sure they love the subject. Because loving the subject is the primary reward." And if you *are* sure—absolutely positive—then go for it and don't look back.

GRAD SCHOOL: LIFE CHANGING OR HARDLY A CHANGE?

Whether you're going straight from college to graduate school, or you're returning to school after a stint in the workplace, "You have to be prepared for a huge change in intensity and depth of concentration," says Dean Kinney of Bryn Mawr College. Graduate school is at once the quintessence of academic life and a clear step in a professional plan, and because of this duality, it's guaranteed to be an all-consuming experience, particularly for the majority of students who enroll in graduate school full-time. It's very likely that graduate school will require a brand of dedicated focus to which even the most scrupulous undergraduates are unaccustomed. And because many people in the professional world are in the habit of leaving their work at work, the endless hours will challenge them as well.

As if the hours of academic work aren't enough, students with assistantships will also have to find the time to prepare for the classes they teach, the essays they grade, and the conferences with undergraduates that they need to facilitate. It's a busy life, to be sure. As Kinney puts it, "You have to be 'on' all the time."

Aside from the hours, graduate students also have to get used to the dollars and sense of their new lives. As we've touched on in other sections of this book, grad-student living can hardly be described as luxurious. If Mom and Dad footed the undergraduate bills, there's little chance that they'll be doing this now. And if a professional paycheck—even a relatively small professional paycheck—has been the norm, there'll be a lesser norm to get used to now. It's a frugal life that graduate students live, and because incoming students might not be used to this, finances can provide one of the biggest hurdles in the process of adjustment.

But fortunately, many campuses are places of incredible intellectual activity—which is probably the most sought-after quality by prospective grad students. As students get to know their universities and disciplines better, they usually begin to realize that a wealth of affordable intellectual and cultural entertainment is at their fingertips—inside and outside of their field of study. Lectures, conferences, concerts, and organizations—all of these, for a few pennies or dollars or absolutely free—will allow you to enjoy yourself, expand your base of knowledge, and develop relationships with people of similar temperaments.

"Try some new things," urges Mary Ann Mason, the dean of the Graduate Division of the University of California—Berkeley. "Make these years *enjoyable*." This means not only taking advantage of the pulses of activity on campus or within your discipline, but also among the wider community in which the university exists. This advice is important, because students who fail to find enjoyable outlets away from solitary study lose the balance that saves them from burning out or flipping out.

GET OUT THE ASPIRIN: HEADACHES OF THE GRAD SCHOOL VARIETY

"Graduate students assume that the problem is going to be that they're going to come up against the wall of their own intelligence," says William J. Maxwell, director of graduate studies in English at the University of Illinois—Urbana-Champaign. In other words, students often turn up at graduate school afraid that they won't have the brains to keep up with the other people in the program. "That rarely happens," Maxwell says. And this is the reason: Admissions committees scour applications very carefully, admitting only those students who demonstrate an ability to at least tread water in the program. If you don't have the smarts and demonstrated drive to make it, chances are that you won't find an acceptance letter in your mailbox anyway.

But say that you *do* find that letter in your mailbox:

Dear You,

We're happy to inform you that you been accepted into the program of your choice at the university of your choice.

Sincerely,

Dean Killjoy

Does this mean that your worries are over? Not necessarily. Like anyone else who opts for a significant life change, you'll have to prepare yourself for an adaptation period. This means getting to know new classmates, new faculty, new administrators, a new town, a new school, a new gym, a new grocery store, a new bus schedule, a new landlord—well, you get the point. Many people are adaptable creatures by nature, and if you're this sort, these changes might even put a smile on your face. But if you're not the sort of person who takes well to change, you'll do yourself a favor by getting used to your new environs before you even show up. Talk to the secretary in your department's office and ask for the e-mail addresses of a few other incomers. (These may or may not be provided.) Use the telephone and Internet to develop a rapport with a few of your new professors. Spend some time looking at web pages related to the department, the university, the community, and the region. As you've probably already figured out, knowledge is comfort.

Upon arriving at the school, you may be pleased to find that there are offices and administrators dedicated to helping you find the answers that you need. There are offices dedicated to graduate students in a specific program. Some offices serve graduate students in a particular college and some offices are solely devoted to graduate funding. Other offices are devoted to helping international students assimilate into their new culture. But these offices are often swamped with students in need of *something*. And remember, if you choose to enroll in a large program, you may be one of several hundred people in that program alone who are searching for some sort of assistance. The result, as you might expect, is often red tape. Even the most well-meaning administrators find themselves bound up in a web of the nefarious red tape. For this reason, one of the best things you can come to graduate school with is a healthy stock of patience. It's as good as, and cheaper than, aspirin.

Here's a helpful hint that you should file away and never forget. (You'll thank us for telling you this later.) The secretaries and administrative assistants in an office are usually the people who get things done. They control all the access, and they have all the information. This is always true, even if it appears to you as though they could only be employable by miracle. Losing your patience with a secretary—even if you're absolutely convinced that you're right—will only lead to more snafus in the long run. On the flipside, if you treat the office staff with courtesy, they'll remember you, and when you need something from their office, you just might find yourself on the receiving end of a friendly wink and the expedited fulfillment of a request.

GRAD STUDENTS: A PROFILE

SELECTED PROFILES OF PERSONS WHO EARNED A PHD IN 2001

	Social Sciences	Humanities	Physical Science	Life Sciences
Age	33	35	31	32
Female	54%	51%	25%	47%
U.S. Citizen	74%	78%	52%	65%
Years enrolled in grad school	7.6	9.0	6.7	7.0
BA/BS in the same field as the PhD	58%	55%	64%	47%

* Data adapted from the Survey of Earned Doctorates, sponsored by the National Science Foundation, the National Institutes of Health, the U.S. Department of Education, the National Endowment for the Humanities, the U.S. Department of Agriculture, and the National Aeronautics and Space Administration. The full report is available at www.norc.uchicago.edu/issues/sed-2001.pdf. Updated and associated surveys can be found at www.norc.uchicago.edu/issues/docdata.htm.

There's no hard-and-fast rule that will tell you exactly what sort of person attends graduate school in the liberal arts and sciences. Grad schools have been known to play host to everyone from the 18-year-old prodigy to the 80-year-old retiree. But as the figures from the NSF above attest, the average person chipping away at a PhD is a 30-something who, when all is said and done, will have spent between seven and nine years working toward his or her degree.

This NSF data will give you a good idea of the general student-body shape you can expect to find in your specific program. Remember, though, that these are averages, which means that there are plenty of people who don't fit these generic molds. In other words, if you're a 23-year-old thinking about a degree in art history, you're probably not alone.

The data from the NCES study on the facing page shows that, in general, students in pursuit of a master's degree aren't too dissimilar from doctoral candidates. The largest discrepancy is in the "full-time student" row, in which 54 percent—or just over half—of master's students are going full-time as opposed to more than two-thirds of PhD students. One note about the NCES data: These include some professional and other nonresearch degrees, so while they give you a broad sense of who's going back to earn a graduate degree, they're not limited to merely research degrees in the liberal arts and sciences. In most top-notch programs in the arts and sciences—master's or PhD—you're more likely to find higher full-time numbers than what's reflected here.

Another point of interest is the number of international students. As the data show, nearly one-quarter of all PhD students in the United States are not U.S. citizens—a fact that brings a rich diversity of thought and experience into the graduate classrooms and laboratories. And other NCES studies show that the number of foreign students studying at American institutions of higher education is constantly increasing. For instance, in 1980–1981, there were 311,880 foreign students enrolled in grad and undergrad programs in the U.S. By 2000–2001, that number had nearly doubled, weighing in at 547,867.[5] Since the instituting of tighter controls on international student visas after September 11, 2001, however, many graduate programs have seen a decline in applications from foreign students. Many professors and graduate school administrators worry that in the long run such tight restrictions will have a negative impact on the quality of scholarship coming out of U.S. graduate schools as a whole.

5 U.S. Department of Education, National Center for Education Statistics, "Foreign students enrolled in institutions of higher education in the United States and outlying areas by continent, region, and selected countries of origin: 1980–1981 to 2000–2001."

	MA/MS/MFA	PhD
Age	33	34
Female	57%	50%
US Citizen	84%	76%
Married	56%	55%
With Dependents	27%	25%
African American	8%	6%
Asian American	15%	19%
Native American	1%	1%
Hispanic or Latino	7%	5%
Going to a Public University	55%	63%
Full-time Student	54%	69%
Started right after BA/BS	26%	25%
Waited less than 7 years after BA/BS	25%	35%

* Data adapted from an NCES study on student financing of graduate and first professional education.[6]

PAYING FOR A GRADUATE DEGREE

When we talked about graduate school headaches earlier, we left out one major headache: money. As we've already made clear, the financial obligations of a graduate student can range from minimal to suffocating. In this section, we'll introduce you to the basic types of financial aid that you'll need to be aware of as you prepare to pursue a degree. This is, however, merely an introduction. For a fuller consideration of the topic, we highly recommend checking out our *Paying for Graduate School Without Going Broke*, a reference guide put out by The Princeton Review that gives you the ins and outs of all aspects of financing a graduate school education, from finding fellowships to negotiating tax breaks and everything in between.

AID FROM THE UNIVERSITY

First thing's first: Earning a graduate degree in the liberal arts and sciences should be motivated by a desire for job satisfaction, not a desire to make millions. If lots of money is what you desire, that's fine, but there are other professional paths you can take, like law school and medical school, that will give you more return on your financial investment in dollar terms alone. With this in mind, you'll want to pay particular attention to the financial aid options available to you; the wiser you are with money now, the happier you'll be in years to come.

And what expenses will financial aid help you cover? The primary costs that graduate students confront are the following:

- Tuition & fees
- Room & board
- Books & supplies
- Personal expenses
- Transportation

6 U.S. Department of Education, National Center for Education Statistics, *Student Financing of Graduate and First-Professional Education, 1999–2000*, by S.P. Choy, S. Geis, and A.G. Malizio, U.S. Department of Education Document NCES 2002-166, 2002.

Many programs—particularly full-time doctoral programs—offer students tuition scholarships or waivers. Straight scholarships or waivers will require no work of the recipient; they are, basically, promises by the program to cover the cost the university charges for enrollment. As long as the student is not working to receive tuition remission, then the tuition remission will be considered nontaxable income.

In many cases, tuition waivers are paired with fellowships or assistantships. Most fellowships will offer a regular stipend—a monthly paycheck above and beyond the tuition remission that the student will need to take care of room and board, books and supplies, transportation, uncovered university fees, and other personal expenses. It also requires no additional work on the part of the recipient. Assistantships (for example, TAships, RAships, or GAships), however, will stipulate that students must perform certain duties if they hope to hold onto their waivers and stipends. Because this money is earned by the sweat of the student, it is considered taxable income.

The best programs provide some sort of funding for their students, especially at the doctoral level. So as you're doing your research, you'll probably find that either fellowships or assistantships will be coming your way after you enroll in a program. You shouldn't be simply satisfied, though, that you will be receiving some help. After you've narrowed your options (or, through a series of acceptances and rejections, your options have been narrowed for you), it's time to sit down for a session of comparing opportunities. When considering assistantships, there are two questions that you should ask.

- How many hours per week do I need to work to fulfill my obligations?

- How much money will I be paid?

Now don't be shocked when you see the answer to this second question; it'll probably be lower than you would like. Keep in mind, however, that the stipend coming your way will, at best, be designed to cover the living expenses of one person. If you have a family or other financial considerations that need to be taken into account, you'll do yourself a favor by speaking to program directors and current students with families. Finding out how others in a similar situation manage to make ends meet will help you figure out if you'll be able to do the same.

Before you sign on a dotted line—whichever one it ends up being—you'll want to have three other questions answered.

- For how many years is the stipend guaranteed?

- How many years does it usually take a student in a particular program to earn a particular degree?

- If there's a discrepancy between these two numbers, how do students survive in the years after the fellowship/assistantship ends but before they complete the degree?

AID FROM OUTSIDE OF THE UNIVERSITY

The two primary types of financial aid that come from outside of the university are *fellowships* and *loans*. Before we give you the skinny of these two sorts of funding, let us remind you that just because these monies come your way from beyond the university gates, it does not mean that there aren't folks at the university who can help you find them, apply for them, and accept them wisely. Financial aid and career and placement offices are tremendous sources of information and guidance—and you should certainly use them as you make your financial decisions.

EXTRAMURAL FELLOWSHIPS

So-called extramural fellowships come (in various sizes and shades of prestige) from two main wellsprings: the government and private foundations. Generally, these fellowships are set aside for PhD research students, and they provide funding for one to several years of study, research-related travel, or other academically pertinent endeavors.

The multiyear fellowships are almost exclusively for PhD candidates, and many are restricted to specific citizenship status (*definitely* check out any citizenship limitations for fellowships you'd like to win). Students can, however, often apply for these fellowships before they begin the degree. In the case of multiyear fellowships, applicants usually send in their paperwork in their senior year of college (if they are applying straight to graduate school straight from undergraduate) or first year of graduate work. Each fellowship will have its own requirements, but for the most part you shouldn't need to worry about having an intense focus laid out; the scope of focus presented in your fellowship application should be comparable to the amount of focus you were able to give in your graduate school application. There are many multiyear fellowships available through a wide variety of government and private bodies, and we list many of the most popular ones, along with descriptions and pertinent contact information for applying for them, in *Paying for Graduate School*.

As you sink deeper into your studies, you'll probably start eyeing the sort of fellowships that suit your specific circumstances—fellowships that'll cover the costs of things like travel, research materials, and free time to push ahead without the distractions of teaching or grading. These research fellowships usually go to students who've achieved considerable focus—typically not before the third year of PhD studies. As you scope out the research fellowship options available to you, pay particular attention to *what* exactly they're able to fund and *how long* they're willing to fund it for. While some fellowships grant the recipients stipends generous enough to carry them through a 12-month period, others are designed to fund specific, short-span research outings or needs.

Trying to dig up individual fellowships on the Internet can suck up a lot of unnecessary time. Instead, speak to the folks at the career and placement offices at your undergraduate (or potential graduate) institution to see where they'd recommend beginning. In *Paying for Graduate School*, Peter Diffley and Joseph Russo, over the span of nearly 30 pages, introduce you to about 120 of the most prominent fellowships opportunities in different disciplines. At the end of the listings, you'll find a concise guide to writing fellowship applications—a resource that could help you win thousands of dollars of support for your studies in the years to come.

"Free" money for your graduate education may also be available through other sources like your employer, the military, and the Peace Corps. Yes, we did put "free" in quotation marks for a reason, and the reason is this: An employer, like the military, will most likely require that you put that degree to work for the company after it's in hand. So as you assess your options, be sure to ask more than *What do I get?* Ask, too, *What do I have to sacrifice?* Then it's time to perform a cost-benefit analysis.

LOANS

"The best resources are free," says Joseph Russo. But as many people can surely testify, there's no guarantee that you'll actually stumble across the free resources that you're looking for. When the free money's gone—assistantships included—most students turn to loans.

These days, getting a loan is an easy process. In fact, it's often as easy as filling out some online forms and providing an electronic signature. When all the proper forms have been filed, the loan can be sent to your student or bank account electronically, often within a day or two. Easy!

Easy, yes, but "almost too easy," Russo says. Graduate life has historically been an exercise in austerity, and you'll do yourself a favor by keeping this mind—and keeping the loans light—while you're chipping away at your degree. This may seem like simple logic, but let us remind you that whatever you borrow, you have to pay back. Research degrees in the liberal arts and sciences lead graduates to a highly competitive job pool, and often the degree holders are vying for jobs with modest starting paychecks. So don't forget: A loan you take out today will stay with you for many years to come. If you can avoid it, do.

If you do have to take out loans—and yes, even the most frugal students sometimes find that a small loan is unavoidable—you'll likely come across one of two types of federally operated loans: the Federal Family Education Loan Program (FFELP) Stafford Loan and the William D. Ford Direct Loan. The type of loan you'll have available to you will depend on the institution you're attending. Today, about 70 percent of higher-ed institutions offer the Stafford, while the remaining 30 percent use the Direct Loan system. A small percentage of schools offer one or the other to different segments of the campus population. In either case, the borrower is not required to start paying back the loan until six months after he or she graduates. (This is the same for undergraduate loans.)

Regardless of which one you find at your chosen institution, you'll want to keep your eyes open for two important words when your financial awards letter arrives in the mail: *subsidized* and *unsubsidized*. While both subsidized and unsubsidized loans offer low interest rates, the critical distinction between the two is that, on the one hand, with a subsidized loan, the borrower does not have to pay interest on the loan until after she finishes (or leaves) school; with unsubsidized loans, on the other hand, the student is responsible for the interest on the loan as soon as the money is disbursed to her. With the unsubsidized loan, you don't have to actually pay the interest while you are in school, but the interest that you *don't* pay while you are in school will be capitalized (basically, this means it will be added to the total you will have to repay.) Even at low rates, this interest can add up to a big headache in the end. For this reason, it's not a bad idea to begin paying the interest, if you're able, while still in school.

To receive either a Stafford or a Direct Loan, a student must fill out the **Free Application for Federal Student Aid,** more commonly known as the **FAFSA.** You can find this form online at www.fafsa.ed.gov—and we recommend that you fill it out there, as the online form helps you weed out mistakes that can lead to the return of your unprocessed form. Be aware that you'll need to have a FAFSA form sent to each institution that you're applying to, and to do this, you'll need to include the name and federal identification code for each school. Codes are available online at the FAFSA website listed above or by phone at 800-4-FED-AID. A series of calculations will be used to determine your **expected family contribution (EFC)** to your graduate expenses and, by association, your ultimate loan eligibility. The institution that you're applying to will let you know the type and amount of your loan eligibility after you submit the FAFSA. To be eligible to receive federal financial aid, you must meet certain requirements. These requirements are listed on the Department of Education's website as well as in our book, *Paying for Graduate School Without Going Broke.*

ALTERNATIVE GRAD SCHOOL FINANCING

There are other financing possibilities that graduate students should consider. One such example is loans from a private lender. We won't spend much time on this because the details of these sorts of loans vary depending on the lender. We will say, though, that if you do consider private loans, you'll want to keep a few things in mind. Unlike government loans, most private loans cannot be consolidated with other government-based student loans, except in the case of government Stafford and private loans that have been negotiated through the same lender. (This is called "bundled billing.") Moreover, private loans usually include higher interest rates and lack interest caps. In other words, with each billing statement, a borrower from a private lender might find that her interest rate is creeping upward. Government loans, with either fixed interest rates or rates that are variable, but capped at a certain percentage, are far more attractive for this reason.

If you find yourself needing private loans to make up a financial shortfall, we urge you to read the fine print and proceed only if absolutely necessary. Debt might seem like an abstraction right now, but in a few years, it'll be a harsh reality that you'll have to contend with.

Other possibilities for financing a graduate education include borrowing on equity in property (like your house) or from life insurance policies or retirement programs. Granted, most grad students won't even have these options available to them. If they do, though, the benefit to this option is that, at least, the interest being paid is basically being paid to them.

Loan programs or arrangements through employers, parents' employers, or generous relatives are also potential sources for educational loans.

Aside from the Stafford and Direct Loan offers, the government provides other possibilities. These loan programs, however, are smaller in availability and resources. For instance, the Perkins Loan (which, like the other government loans, requires the student to file the FAFSA and demonstrate financial need) offers fixed interest rates and a 10-year repayment period. The yearly limit on Perkins Loans for graduate students is $6,000. The total you can borrow in Perkins Loans is $40,000 minus the total amount of Perkins Loans you borrowed as an undergraduate.

Off You Go

In this introduction, we hope we've given you a handle on the realities you'll have to face while you're considering, researching, and applying to graduate schools. As you can tell, there is no foolproof, step-by-step process that will get you from one end of the road to the other. It's a long road you're about to traverse. But as Lao Tse wisely said so long ago, "a journey of a thousand miles begins with a single step." Well, you've taken the first steps; you're on your way. Now, keep moving. If you move ahead with diligence and care, you'll find that every day, your grad school goals will get closer, even as the terrain shifts and moves—or, perhaps, stays exactly the same.

We'll close this chapter with the thoughts of some graduate students currently in the thick of things. Take their words to heart; maybe you can avoid some of the pitfalls they didn't and enjoy some of the big wins that they did.

If You Won't Take Our Word for It ...

STUDENT VOICES: THE BARGAINING TABLE

Oday Salim is a second-year PhD candidate in English literature at the University of Illinois—Urbana-Champaign.

Why did I choose one particular English graduate department over some other department, not to mention a med school or a law school? My undergraduate professors and fellow literature junkies hammered their own answers to this question into me as if their conclusions were holy mantras: They were doing it for the sensation of a lyric poem, they'd say, or for the irony of a postmodern novel. But not for the money—definitely not for the money. But when I found myself in the midst of the grad school decision-making process, I caught myself thinking: What was "it" that these academics were doing? The answer: hard work. Hard work that deserved compensation. And I don't just mean the pride that comes with practicing our profession, but money: money to eat, money to make car payments, money to see a movie. There was nothing special or spiritually uplifting about avoiding corpulence and high fashion in order to feel like an academic martyr. Even Marx admits that one must eat before one philosophizes. So I used leverage, turning the graduate director's desk into a bargaining table.

When I was visiting one university—the university that I ended up selecting—I made sure to tell the graduate director that I had offers from other schools, that these other schools were willing to value (literally *value*) my work for them, and that while I loved my visit and respected the faculty and cherished access to the many resources, I also wanted to be paid accordingly for my efforts. At the graduate level, almost every university has something extraordinary to offer. The trick is to convince them that you are extraordinary too. *Not for the money?* Maybe the people who explained that money was not their concern were sincere. Most likely, though, they didn't even know it was available. Well, it is.

I used my other offers as leverage, and I got what I wanted. Of course, there are ethics and procedures to keep in mind when you begin negotiating for the best financial package you can get.

As for concerns about *who, where,* and *when,* it's best to speak directly to the graduate director in his or her office. Negotiating over the phone takes away from the sincerity and forcefulness you can achieve with physical presence. (The phone is also not the typical communicative medium in most graduate departments. The same can be said about e-mail.) As for *when,* it's important that any negotiation be completed before official registration. Bargaining during a visit to the school is best because it signals to them that you're still shopping around, but you can also get away with doing it a couple weeks prior to matriculation.

As for ethics, common sense and preparation are your friends. Remember, we're graduate students; the term "six figures" is not something that applies to us. If they're offering $5,000, ask for $3,000 more, not $30,000 more. If they're stipulating a certain teaching load or insisting on an initial fellowship, don't demand changes in the first semester, but rather for future semesters, giving them time to adjust. And don't name-drop at least, not narrowly so. Mention that Yale is interested or that MIT is offering a lighter teaching load, but don't say that you're tight with Penn's dean of humanities. And do your research! Find out what fellowship amounts and teaching loads the department has traditionally offered. Look up—and be able to identify—the various grant-giving institutions on campus. This will prove to them your sincere interest in the program and will force them into details and specifics. Nothing is worse than angrily demanding $15,000 for your first year, only to find out that the $12,000 they're giving you is their maximum offer. Lastly, try to strike a balance between confidence and arrogance. I was nervous, and you will be too, but the pot of gold, or at least pot of bronze, awaits.

Now, instead of choosing between Whitman and a rib-eye steak (or tofu if you prefer), I can have both.

STUDENT VOICES: LIFE IN THE SCIENCES

Che Hutson is a second-year PhD candidate in neuroscience at the University of California—Los Angeles. He's also served as the student representative on the program's admissions committee.

The Princeton Review: *What were the biggest challenges you faced during the application process?*

Che Hutson: The biggest challenge for me was trying to determine to which schools I was going to apply. I think this problem comes from the horribly biased rankings of grad schools/programs by *U.S. News & World Report* and other books and magazines. These rankings are not based on the number of faculty, number of publications per faculty member, number of tenured faculty, number of grants per faculty member, student funding, number of fully funded graduate students, graduation rates, and publication rates of the students—all of these important things to know about when applying for a PhD in the sciences (and I imagine the arts as well). And the National Research Council, which uses some of these parameters, has not ranked graduate schools or programs in ten years, which makes it all the more difficult to find a school that would be a good fit.

After finding the programs, the next difficult task was keeping up with all the deadlines and making sure each school received all portions of my application. Every other school seemed to misplace a portion of the application or sometimes recommenders sent out the letters late. Just staying on top of everything when applying to a bunch of schools was a real pain.

The only other difficult part was writing the personal statement: what exactly you need to say, what you need to emphasize, and what you clearly need to leave out. It was not until being on the admissions committee this year that I actually realized exactly what one needs to emphasize about oneself when applying to graduate school.

TPR: So what does one need to emphasize about oneself when applying to graduate school in the sciences? In other words, what sorts of things give a candidate an edge?

CH: After being on the neuroscience admissions committee, I learned the following:

1. Letters from course instructors have little or no value because they say nothing about your scientific ability. Letters need to be from a laboratory that you volunteered or worked in. And make sure you get them from someone who can give you an outstanding letter of recommendation. If you are not sure, ask the professor.

   The letters need to describe the applicant's scientific potential and any scientific contributions made by the student. The letters should also rank the student. Applicants need to ask the writers of their recommendations to include these things.

2. Each personal statement should be tailor-made for each school to which you are applying. In the essay, mention the professors (and their research) with whom you have a desire to work. Do this for each school. In other words, match your interests with the professors at the school. Programs want students who have a big interest in their school. So, name drop in your essay, mention whom you have worked with, for how long, what you learned, how you contributed scientifically to the work, and how this makes you a perfect match with the faculty at the school to which you're applying.

3. Put in a CV or resume—even if they do not ask for one.

4. E-mail at least one or two professors at each school before applying. Building a rapport with professors can help ensure that you get an interview—and possibly admitted. It also shows you have a large interest in their program. Professors and schools are always going to push for students who are interested in their research because (among other reasons) students are cheap labor.

5. Apply for fellowships while applying to graduate school. On your CV/resume, include the fellowships for which you've applied. Getting the fellowship is not important; what *is* important is that you are showing that you are already thinking like a graduate student.

STUDENT VOICES: LIFE IN THE ARTS

Carrie Scott is a first-year PhD candidate in art history at the University of Washington in Seattle.

The Princeton Review: *What were the biggest challenges you faced during the application process?*

Carrie Scott: Oddly, I think the more administrative aspects of the application process were the biggest challenges. There is a lot to keep straight, details you have to know about and remember that can make the difference between getting into a program or not. You have to be sure you know which schools want what, when they want it, and whether you've sent it. You have to coordinate letters of recommendation with GRE scores and your personal statement. It all adds up to a lot of juggling.

But if you are asking about the biggest mental challenge, it was definitely the personal statement. Writing something that, in 400 words or less, exemplifies why you are not only interested in the program to which you are applying but are also qualified to contribute to the program is a difficult, not to mention daunting, task.

TPR: You obviously succeeded in landing a spot in one of your preferred grad programs. At this point—less than a year into the program—are there any things that you wish you'd considered before showing up at the University of Washington?

CS: Again, I've more of an administrative answer. Because, to be perfectly honest, I wish I'd been more prepared for the language requirements. Many graduate programs in the arts and humanities expect you to be fluent in two languages. They don't, however, work languages into your course load. Adding a hefty language course into your already hefty course load isn't ideal. You want to be focusing on your area, not meeting a requirement. In other words, I should have spent more time studying French and German—the languages I need to know—before I got here. Now, I just don't seem to find the time or the inclination; I'd rather be studying art.

TPR: Hefty course load, huh? How would you compare the work you're expected to do now to the work you were expected to do as an undergrad? More stress? And academics aside, what other sorts of headaches are you encountering?

CS: Grad school is definitely a different ball game. It's not really about more work, per se, but you have to take it that extra step. You have to really get into the material you were assigned to read before you get to class or seminar. You have to do your best to fully understand the texts before you get there and be prepared to discuss not the basic arguments, but the meaty topics that lie underneath the main points. You can't show up at class expecting to go over the basics. In grad school, it's almost like you get into the footnotes in your discussions. But that is the best part because class ends up being a really good learning environment that goes way beyond what you've simply read.
   But academics aside, the move out here was a pretty big shake-up. (I relocated to Seattle from Manhattan.) Moving to a new city where you don't know a soul and you don't have an apartment—well, that can be a confidence-shaking experience. More than that, you also really want to get outside and explore your new home. Problem is, however, you don't really have the time to do it. At least, I didn't. I showed up a week before the quarter began and that didn't really give me enough time to explore my new city. I'm getting there, slowly but surely.

HOW TO USE THIS BOOK

There are two main sections in this guide. The first one—the section preceding this one—is a primer on the major considerations that should go into your decision to attend graduate school, as well as the process you should follow to choose the right graduate program for you. The second section contains data listings of 1,516 graduate schools and programs. The data were collected from institutional administrators at the schools from Summer 2004 to Spring 2005 and represent the most recent year for which the school had complete data; in most schools' cases that is the previous academic year (2003–2004). Although not all data fields will appear for all graduate programs because they either were not reported by the school administrators or are not applicable, a complete data listing should be broken up into the following sections, with each section including various data fields. The sections are explained below.

THE HEADING

Here you will find the name of the parent institution, the name of the particular graduate school/program, and relevant contact information for the school/program, including the admissions office's mailing address, phone and fax numbers, e-mail address, and website. When the parent institution supports several graduate schools/programs, you will only see the parent institution's name once in the header, with all specific schools'/programs' individual listings below it.

INSTITUTIONAL INFORMATION

This section provides quick and thorough statistics on the graduate school/program and the parent institution. These include: whether the school is public or private (non-profit or proprietary); whether the school/program offers evening classes in addition to regular day classes; the total number of faculty members; the percent of the faculty that is female; the percent of the faculty that is part-time; the student/faculty ratio; and the total number of students in the parent institution.

PROGRAMS

Here you will find lists of the academic disciplines in which the program offers master's, doctorate, and first professional degrees.

STUDENT INFORMATION

Demographic breakdowns of the graduate student body, including the total number of students in the graduate school/program, the percent of total graduate students attending school full-time, the percent of total graduate students that is female, the percent of total graduate students from underrepresented minorities, and the percent of total graduate students from foreign countries.

RESEARCH FACILITIES

In this section, you will find descriptions written by school administrators of the special research resources (labs, computer databases, libraries, etc.) that are available for use by graduate students in the school/program. Prospective graduate students should not overlook research resources when considering in which graduate programs to enroll; graduate study is so much more focused on research than undergraduate study. It is worth following up directly with each graduate program about research resources if their descriptions here do not address all of your concerns.

EXPENSES/FINANCIAL AID

This is the bread and butter section. Here we list the graduate program's costs for a full academic year: tuition, room and board (on-campus cost/off-campus estimate), required fees, and books and supplies. Also included in this section are the range (minimum and maximum award amounts, per year) of the grants and/or scholarships graduate students receive and the range (minimum and maximum award amounts, per year) in loan packages for graduate students. Next, you will find the percentages of all graduate students in the school/program receiving *any* financial aid. The next few statistics break that number down further; of the number of students receiving any financial aid, we list the percentage that received 1) scholarships or grants, 2) loans, 3) assistantships, and 4) any other types of aid. Then, we list all types of aid available to graduate students in the school/program. Also reported here is the average student-loan debt of graduating students. The number of fellowships granted each year to graduate students, as well as the average amount of the fellowship award; and the number of teaching and research assistantships, as well as what assistantship compensation includes, all appear next. Finally, if the school reports an annual salary stipend awarded to graduate students, you will find that figure here.

ADMISSIONS INFORMATION

Here you will find listed any application fee(s) and deadlines, both priority and regular, as well as the regular notification date (when students are notified whether they have been accepted into the program) for the graduate school/program. If the program notifies applicants on a rolling basis, we'll tell you that here too. Information for transfer students (whether they are considered for admission into the program and any special policies that pertain to them regarding transfer credits, etc.) appears next. Statistics from the most recently completed admissions cycle also are listed here, including: the total number of applications received by the school/program, the percent of applicants accepted, the percent of admitted applicants who enrolled, the average undergraduate GPA of entering students, and the average GRE scores of entering students broken down by test section. Admission factors for the school/program are listed at the end of this section and broken out by whether they are required, recommended, specific to a certain program within the graduate division, or otherwise.

EMPLOYMENT INFORMATION

Listed in this section are a number of fields pertaining to careers, including one that reports whether the school/program has a placement office available to graduate students. The last four fields speak to outcomes for previous graduates of the school/program: the percent of students employed within six months of graduation, the percentages of master's, doctoral, and first professional degree graduates who were employed in their fields upon graduation, the rate of placement for all three student types, and the average starting salary of all graduating students.

THE GRADUATE PROGRAMS

ABILENE CHRISTIAN UNIVERSITY
College of Arts & Sciences

Address: 204 Hardin Administration Building
ACU Box 29140, Abilene, TX 79699-9140
Admissions Phone: 325-674-2656 · **Admissions Fax:** 325-674-6717
Admissions E-mail: gradinfo@acu.edu · **Web Address:** www.acu.edu/grad

INSTITUTIONAL INFORMATION
Public/Private: Private (nonprofit). **Total Faculty:** 41. **% Faculty Female:** 32. **Student/Faculty Ratio:** 7:1. **Students in Parent Institution:** 4,761.

STUDENT INFORMATION
Total Students in Program: 201. **% Full-time:** 49. **% Female:** 65. **% Minority:** 9. **% International:** 3.

RESEARCH FACILITIES
Research Facilities: Center for Speech and Language Disorders Voice Institute of West Texas, Pruett Gerontology Center, Center for Conflict Resolution, University Writing Center, Nonprofit Management Center.

EXPENSES/FINANCIAL AID
Annual Tuition: $10,200. **Room & Board:** $5,080. **Fees:** $540. **Books and Supplies:** $800. **Grants Range From:** $300-$5,084. **Loans Range From:** $526-$17,740. **% Receiving Financial Aid:** 81. **% Receiving Scholarships/Grants:** 70. **% Receiving Loans:** 74. **% Receiving Assistantships:** 34. **Types of Aid Available:** Graduate assistantships, grants, institutional work-study, loans, scholarships. **ber of teaching/research assistantships granted each year:** 38. **Assistantship compensation includes:** Partial tuition remission, salary/stipend. **Average Salary Stipend:** $5,800.

ADMISSIONS INFORMATION
Application Fee: $40. **Priority Application Deadline:** 3/1. **Regular Application Deadline:** 9/1. **Regular Notification:** Rolling. **Transfer Students Accepted?** Yes. **Transfer Policy:** Maximum one-quarter of total degree credits with a minimum grade of B may be transferred. **Number of Applications Received:** 155. **% of Applicants Accepted:** 81. **% Accepted Who Enrolled:** 71. **Average GRE Verbal:** 434. **Average GRE Quantitative:** 511. **Average GRE Analytical:** 513. **Average GRE Analytical Writing:** 4.
Required Admission Factors: Essays/personal statement, letters of recommendation, transcript.
Other Admission Factors: Undergrad GPA 3.0
Program-Specific Admission Factors: Writing sample required of English program applicants.

EMPLOYMENT INFORMATION
Placement Office Available? Yes.

ABILENE CHRISTIAN UNIVERSITY
University Studies

Address: 204 Hardin Administration Building
ACU Box 29140, Abilene, TX 79699-9105
Admissions Phone: 915-674-2354 · **Admissions Fax:** 915-674-6717
Admissions E-mail: thorntonl@acu.edu

INSTITUTIONAL INFORMATION
Public/Private: Private (nonprofit). **Evening Classes Available?** Yes. **Students in Parent Institution:** 4,739.

STUDENT INFORMATION
Total Students in Program: 447. **% Full-time:** 50. **% Female:** 47.

EXPENSES/FINANCIAL AID
Annual Tuition: In-state $8,904. **Room & Board:** $6,930. **Fees:** $520. **Books and Supplies:** $550. **Grants Range From:** $174-$15,328. **Loans Range**

From: $1,100-$18,500. **% Receiving Financial Aid:** 13. **% Receiving Scholarships/Grants:** 98. **% Receiving Loans:** 61. **% Receiving Assistantships:** 16. **Average student debt, upon graduation:** $21,086. **Number of teaching/research assistantships granted each year:** 30.

ADMISSIONS INFORMATION
Application Fee: $25. **Regular Notification:** Rolling. **Transfer Students Accepted?** No. **Number of Applications Received:** 17. **% of Applicants Accepted:** 47. **% Accepted Who Enrolled:** 88. **Average GRE Verbal:** 377. **Average GRE Quantitative:** 392. **Average GRE Analytical:** 332.
Required Admission Factors: Transcript.
Other Admission Factors: Minimum GRE score of 900 or minimum GMAT score of 40 and minimum 2.8 GPA required.

EMPLOYMENT INFORMATION
Placement Office Available? Yes.

ACADEMY OF ART UNIVERSITY
Graduate Admissions

Address: 79 New Montgomery, San Francisco, CA 94105
Admissions Phone: 800-544-ARTS, ext.2265 · **Admissions Fax:** 415-263-4130
Admissions E-mail: info@academyart.edu · **Web Address** www.academyart.edu

INSTITUTIONAL INFORMATION
Public/Private: Private (proprietary). **Evening Classes Available?** Yes. **Total Faculty:** 203. **% Faculty Female:** 43. **% Faculty Part-time:** 71. **Student/Faculty Ratio:** 15:1. **Students in Parent Institution:** 7,200.

PROGRAMS
Masters offered in: Acting; architecture (BArch, BA/BS, MArch, MA/MS, PhD); cinematography and film/video production; commercial and advertising art; commercial photography; computer graphics; design and visual communications; drawing; fashion/apparel design; fiber, textile, and weaving arts; film/cinema studies; film/video and photgraphic arts; fine/studio arts; graphic design; illustration; industrial design; interior architecture; interior design; metal and jewelry arts; painting; photography; playwriting and screenwriting; printmaking; sculpture; Web page, digital/multimedia, and information resources design; web/multimedia management and webmaster.

STUDENT INFORMATION
Total Students in Program: 1,359. **% Full-time:** 99.

RESEARCH FACILITIES
Research Facilities: All graduate candidates have access to specialized computer labs to develop advanced software expertise related to their area of discipline.

EXPENSES/FINANCIAL AID
Annual Tuition: $13,200. **Room & Board:** $12,000. **Fees:** $60. **Books and Supplies:** $810. **Grants Range From:** $100-$10,000. **Loans Range From:** $10,500-$18,500. **% Receiving Financial Aid:** 30. **% Receiving Scholarships/Grants:** 1. **% Receiving Loans:** 93. **Types of Aid Available:** Grants, loans, scholarships. **Average student debt, upon graduation:** $26,000.

ADMISSIONS INFORMATION
Application Fee: $100. **Regular Application Deadline:** 7/21. **Regular Notification:** Rolling. **Transfer Students Accepted?** Yes. **Number of Applications Received:** 657. **% of Applicants Accepted:** 96. **Average GPA:** 2.7.
Required Admission Factors: Essays/personal statement, transcript, portfolio.

EMPLOYMENT INFORMATION
Placement Office Available? Yes. **% Employed Within 6 Months:** 82. **% of master's grads employed in their field upon graduation:** 83. **Rate of placement:** 85%. **Average starting salary:** $65,000.

ACADIA UNIVERSITY
Division of Research and Graduate Studies

Address: 15 University Avenue, Wolfville, Nova Scotia, B4P 2R6 Canada
Admissions Phone: 902-585-1222 · Admissions Fax: 902-585-1081
Admissions E-mail: admissions@acadiau.ca
Web Address: www.acadiau.ca/reg/reg2.html

INSTITUTIONAL INFORMATION
Public/Private: Public. Students in Parent Institution: 4,045.

STUDENT INFORMATION
Total Students in Program: 254. % Full-time: 32. % Female: 65.

RESEARCH FACILITIES
Research Facilities: ACMA (Acadia Centre for Microstructural Analysis), EC Smith Herbarium.

EXPENSES/FINANCIAL AID
Annual Tuition: In-state $5,611. / Out-of-state $11,222. Room & Board: $6,110. Fees: $354. Books and Supplies: $850. Grants Range From: $500-$17,500. Loans Range From: $100-$18,500. Types of Aid Available: Fellowships, graduate assistantships, grants, loans, scholarships. Average amount of individual fellowships per year: Average Salary Stipend: $8,000.

ADMISSIONS INFORMATION
Application Fee: $50. Regular Application Deadline: 3/15. Regular Notification: Rolling. Transfer Students Accepted? Yes. Transfer Policy: Students may transfer up to 12 courses to a graduate program, provided they offer the minimum of 6 hours of graduate courses towards their Acadia degree. An evaluation of transfer credit is made by the academic unit in consultation with the registrar upon admission.
Required Admission Factors: GRE, letters of recommendation, transcript.
Other Admission Factors: Minimum 2.67 GPA required. TOEFL minimum acceptable score is 550 paper-based test (213 computer-based test).

ADELPHI UNIVERSITY
College of Arts & Sciences

Address: South Avenue, Garden City, NY 11530
Admissions Phone: 800-ADELPHI · Admissions Fax: 516-877-3039
Admissions E-mail: admissions@adelphi.edu
Web Address: http://academics.adelphi.edu/artsci/

INSTITUTIONAL INFORMATION
Public/Private: Private (nonprofit). Evening Classes Available? Yes. Student/Faculty Ratio: 11:1. Students in Parent Institution: 7,931.

PROGRAMS
Masters offered in: Environmental studies; fine/studio arts.

STUDENT INFORMATION
Total Students in Program: 77. % Full-time: 14. % Female: 70. % Minority: 19. % International: 4.

RESEARCH FACILITIES
Research Facilities: Derner Institute of Advanced Psychological Studies, Hy Weinberg Center for Communicative Disorders.

EXPENSES/FINANCIAL AID
Annual Tuition: $14,160. Room & Board: $8,600. Fees: $700. Books and Supplies: $950. Grants Range From: $500-$10,000. Loans Range From: $100-$18,500. % Receiving Financial Aid: 59. Types of Aid Available: Fellowships, graduate assistantships, institutional work-study, loans. Assistantship compensation includes: Full tuition remission, partial tuition remission, salary/stipend.

ADMISSIONS INFORMATION
Application Fee: $50. Regular Application Deadline: 9/1. Regular Notification: Rolling. Transfer Students Accepted? Yes. Number of Applications Received: 56. % of Applicants Accepted: 64. % Accepted Who Enrolled: 89. Average GPA: 3.2.
Required Admission Factors: Essays/personal statement, letters of recommendation, transcript.
Program-Specific Admission Factors: For environmental studies, courses required include basic microeconomics, political science, one year of introductory biology, one year of statistics and/or calculus, one year of chemistry and one year of physics for science majors. For art, a portfolio is required.

EMPLOYMENT INFORMATION
Placement Office Available? Yes. % Employed Within 6 Months: 70. % of master's grads employed in their field upon graduation: 40. Rate of placement: 70%. Average starting salary: $63,150.

ADELPHI UNIVERSITY
Gordon F. Derner Institute of Advanced Psychological Studies

Address: South Avenue, Garden City, NY 11530
Admissions Phone: 800-ADELPHI · Admissions Fax: 516-877-3039
Admissions E-mail: ross@adelphi.edu ·
Web Address: www.derner.adelphi.edu

INSTITUTIONAL INFORMATION
Public/Private: Private (nonprofit). Total Faculty: 27. % Faculty Female: 41. % Faculty Part-time: 11. Student/Faculty Ratio: 12:1. Students in Parent Institution: 7,931.

PROGRAMS
Masters offered in: Clinical psychology, counseling psychology, psychology, school psychology. Doctorate offered in: Clinical psychology.

STUDENT INFORMATION
Total Students in Program: 432. % Full-time: 70. % Female: 74. % Minority: 13. % International: 6.

RESEARCH FACILITIES
Research Facilities: Denver Institute of Advanced Psychological Studies, Hy Weinberg Center.

EXPENSES/FINANCIAL AID
Annual Tuition: $25,000. Fees: $500. Books and Supplies: $500. Grants Range From: $3,800-$20,000. Loans Range From: $5,000-$18,500. % Receiving Financial Aid: 90. % Receiving Scholarships/Grants: 5. % Receiving Loans: 80. % Receiving Assistantships: 60. Types of Aid Available: Graduate assistantships, loans, scholarships. Average student debt, upon graduation: $60,000. Number of teaching/research assistantships granted each year: 50. Assistantship compensation includes: Partial tuition remission. Average Salary Stipend: $6,000.

ADMISSIONS INFORMATION
Application Fee: $50. Regular Application Deadline: 1/15. Regular Notification: 4/1. Transfer Students Accepted? No. Number of Applications Received: 230. % of Applicants Accepted: 26. % Accepted Who Enrolled: 30. Average GPA: 3.5. Average GRE Verbal: 590. Average GRE Quantitative: 640.
Required Admission Factors: Essays/personal statement, GRE, interview, letters of recommendation, transcript. GRE subject exam(s) in psychology.
Other Admission Factors: We have no minimum for either GPA or GREs, and we try to evaluate applicants along a variety of relevent dimensions. However, most applicants whom we accept have verbal GREs of 600 or better.

EMPLOYMENT INFORMATION

Placement Office Available? Yes. % Employed Within 6 Months: 95. % of doctoral grads employed in their field upon graduation: 95. Rate of placement: 90%. Average starting salary: $51,500.

ADELPHI UNIVERSITY
School of Social Work

Address: 1 South Avenue, Garden City, NY 11530
Admissions Phone: 516-877-4360 · Admissions Fax: 516-877-4392
Admissions E-mail: admissions@adelphi.edu
Web Address: www.adelphi.edu/swk

INSTITUTIONAL INFORMATION

Public/Private: Private (nonprofit). Evening Classes Available? Yes. Student/Faculty Ratio: 15:1. Students in Parent Institution: 7,355.

STUDENT INFORMATION

Total Students in Program: 822. % Full-time: 60. % Female: 87. % Minority: 15. % International: 1.

RESEARCH FACILITIES

Research Facilities: Denver Institute of Advanced Psychological Studies, Hy Weinberg Center for Communicative Disorders, New York Statewide Breast Cancer Support Program, Program for Students with Learning Disabilities.

EXPENSES/FINANCIAL AID

Annual Tuition: $19,550. Room & Board: $7,700. Fees: $500. Books and Supplies: $950. Grants Range From: $590-$49,000. Loans Range From: $6,620-$17,800. % Receiving Financial Aid: 81. Types of Aid Available: Fellowships, graduate assistantships, loans, scholarships. agency tuition remission program. Number of teaching/research assistantships granted each year: 30. Assistantship compensation includes: Partial tuition remission.

ADMISSIONS INFORMATION

Application Fee: $50. Regular Application Deadline: 8/15. Regular Notification: Rolling. Transfer Students Accepted? Yes. Transfer Policy: Minimum grade point average of 3.0, transcript. course descriptions and syllabi. Number of Applications Received: 631. % of Applicants Accepted: 65. % Accepted Who Enrolled: 83. Average GPA: 3.3.
Required Admission Factors: Essays/personal statement, letters of recommendation, transcript.
Other Admission Factors: Minimum 3.0 GPA required.
Program-Specific Admission Factors: Three years professional experience, transcripts, three letters of recommendation, essay, and examples of professional writing. Doctor of Social Welfare program applicants require an MSW.

EMPLOYMENT INFORMATION

Placement Office Available? Yes. % Employed Within 6 Months: 85. % of master's/doctoral/first professional grads employed in their field upon graduation: 40/100/NR. Rate of placement: 95%. Average starting salary: $35,000.

AGNES SCOTT COLLEGE
Graduate Studies

Address: 141 East College Avenue, Atlanta/Decatur, GA 30030
Admissions Phone: 404-471-6440 · Admissions Fax: 404-471-5152
Admissions E-mail: graduatestudies@agnesscott.edu
Web Address: www.agnesscott.edu

INSTITUTIONAL INFORMATION

Public/Private: Private (nonprofit). Student/Faculty Ratio: 10:1. Students in Parent Institution: 901.

PROGRAMS

Masters offered in: Junior high/intermediate/middle school education and teaching, secondary education and teaching.

STUDENT INFORMATION

Total Students in Program: 24. % Full-time: 100. % Female: 33.

EXPENSES/FINANCIAL AID

Annual Tuition: $17,500. Fees: $170. Books and Supplies: $700. Loans Range From: $15,998-$18,500. % Receiving Financial Aid: 44. % Receiving Loans: 100. Types of Aid Available: Loans. Average student debt, upon graduation: $15,988.

ADMISSIONS INFORMATION

Application Fee: $35. Priority Application Deadline: 4/1. Regular Application Deadline: 4/30. Regular Notification: Rolling. Transfer Students Accepted? Yes. Number of Applications Received: 30. % of Applicants Accepted: 80. % Accepted Who Enrolled: 100. Average GPA: 3.0.
Required Admission Factors: Essays/personal statement, letters of recommendation, transcript. Praxis I or SAT.
Recommended Admission Factors: Interview. Other Admission Factors: Minimum 3.0 GPA and minimum combined GRE score of 1030 or minimum Praxis scores of 172 (reading), 173 (math), and 172 (writing) required.
Program-Specific Admission Factors: Recommended undergraduate degree in English, journalism, or communications.

EMPLOYMENT INFORMATION

Placement Office Available? Yes. % Employed Within 6 Months: 90. Rate of placement: 100%. Average starting salary: $35,000.

ALABAMA AGRICULTURAL AND MECHANICAL UNIVERSITY
School of Arts & Sciences

Address: PO Box 998, Normal, AL 35762
Admissions Phone: 256-858-5266
Web Address: www.aamu.edu/graduatestudies

INSTITUTIONAL INFORMATION

Public/Private: Public. Evening Classes Available? Yes. Student/Faculty Ratio: 5:1. Students in Parent Institution: 5,523.

STUDENT INFORMATION

Total Students in Program: 1,143. % Full-time: 41. % Female: 69.

RESEARCH FACILITIES

Research Facilities: Physics/materials science research laboratory.

EXPENSES/FINANCIAL AID

Annual Tuition: In-state $2,400. / Out-of-state $4,800. Fees: $400. Books and Supplies: $1,000. Grants Range From: $100-$1,500. Loans Range From: $100-$1,500. % Receiving Loans: 100.

ADMISSIONS INFORMATION

Application Fee: $15. Regular Notification: Rolling. Transfer Students Accepted? No. Number of Applications Received: 237. % of Applicants Accepted: 51. % Accepted Who Enrolled: 64. Average GPA: 3.5. Average GRE Verbal: 390. Average GRE Quantitative: 500. Average GRE Analytical: 380.
Required Admission Factors: GRE, transcript.
Other Admission Factors: Minimum GRE score of 1000 and minimum 2.5 GPA required.

EMPLOYMENT INFORMATION

Placement Office Available? Yes. Rate of placement: 55%.

ALABAMA STATE UNIVERSITY
College of Arts & Sciences

Address: 915 South Jackson Street, Montgomery, AL 36101-0271
Admissions Phone: 334-229-4275 · **Admissions Fax:** 334-229-4928
Admissions E-mail: aallen@asunet.alasu.edu

INSTITUTIONAL INFORMATION
Public/Private: Public. **Evening Classes Available?** Yes. **Student/Faculty Ratio:** 7:1. **Students in Parent Institution:** 5,589.

STUDENT INFORMATION
Total Students in Program: 879. **% Full-time:** 21. **% Female:** 76.

RESEARCH FACILITIES
Research Facilities: National Center for the Study of Civil Rights and African American Culture.

EXPENSES/FINANCIAL AID
Annual Tuition: In-state $2,484. / Out-of-state $4,968. **Room & Board:** $3,500. **Books and Supplies:** $800. **Grants Range From:** $828-$8,176. **Loans Range From:** $8,117-$14,213. **% Receiving Financial Aid:** 94. **% Receiving Scholarships/Grants:** 49. **% Receiving Loans:** 55. **Average student debt, upon graduation:** $31,437.

ADMISSIONS INFORMATION
Application Fee: $10. **Regular Notification:** Rolling. **Transfer Students Accepted?** Yes. **Transfer Policy:** Transfer applicants must complete transfer forms in graduate school and provide course descriptions. **Number of Applications Received:** 12. **% of Applicants Accepted:** 67. **% Accepted Who Enrolled:** 100. **Average GPA:** 2.5. **Average GRE Verbal:** 300. **Average GRE Quantitative:** 380. **Average GRE Analytical:** 400.
Required Admission Factors: Essays/personal statement, letters of recommendation, transcript.
Other Admission Factors: Minimum 2.5 GPA required.
Program-Specific Admission Factors: GRE or MAT required of history program applicants. Minimum 3.0 GPA required for biology program applicants; minimum 2.5 GPA for probationary acceptance.

EMPLOYMENT INFORMATION
Placement Office Available? Yes. **% Employed Within 6 Months:** 70. **% of master's grads employed in their field upon graduation:** 80. **Rate of placement:** 86%.

ALASKA PACIFIC UNIVERSITY
Graduate Programs

Address: 4101 University Drive, Anchorage, AK 99508
Admissions Phone: 800-252-7528 or 907-564-8248
Admissions Fax: 907-564-8317
Admissions E-mail: dmont@alaskapacific.edu

INSTITUTIONAL INFORMATION
Public/Private: Private (nonprofit). **Evening Classes Available?** Yes. **Student/Faculty Ratio:** 17:1. **Students in Parent Institution:** 563.

STUDENT INFORMATION
Total Students in Program: 202. **% Full-time:** 50. **% Female:** 65.

EXPENSES/FINANCIAL AID
Annual Tuition: $3,870. **Room & Board (On/Off Campus):** $3,025/$3,200. **Fees:** $80. **Books and Supplies:** $1,000. **Number of fellowships granted each year:** 3.0

ADMISSIONS INFORMATION
Application Fee: $25. **Transfer Students Accepted?** Yes. **Number of Applications Received:** 136. **% of Applicants Accepted:** 74. **% Accepted Who Enrolled:** 73.
Required Admission Factors: Letters of recommendation, transcript.
Other Admission Factors: Minimum 3.0 GPA and prerequisite courses required.

ALBANY STATE UNIVERSITY
School of Arts & Sciences

Address: 504 College Drive, Albany, GA 31705
Web Address: http://asuweb.asurams.edu/asu/

INSTITUTIONAL INFORMATION
Public/Private: Public. **Students in Parent Institution:** 3,151

STUDENT INFORMATION
Total Students in Program: 339. **% Female:** 73.

EXPENSES/FINANCIAL AID
Annual Tuition: In-state $1,680. / Out-of-state $6,141. **Fees:** $444. **Books and Supplies:** $750.

ADMISSIONS INFORMATION
Transfer Students Accepted? No.
Other Admission Factors: Minimum 2.5 GPA required.

ALCORN STATE UNIVERSITY
School of Graduate Studies

Address: 1000 ASU Drive, #689, Alcorn State, MS 39096
Admissions Phone: 601-877-6122 · **Admissions Fax:** 601-877-6995
Admissions E-mail: lulagr@alcorn.edu
Web Address: www.alcorn.edu/academic/academ/grads.htm

INSTITUTIONAL INFORMATION
Public/Private: Public. **Evening Classes Available?** Yes. **Students in Parent Institution:** 3,033.

EXPENSES/FINANCIAL AID
Annual Tuition: In-state $1,733. / Out-of-state $4,098. **Room & Board:** $20,016. **Fees:** $100. **Books and Supplies:** $500. **Types of Aid Available:** Graduate assistantships, institutional work-study, loans. **Assistantship compensation includes:** Full tuition remission, salary/stipend.

ADMISSIONS INFORMATION
Application Fee: $10. **Regular Application Deadline:** 7/30. **Regular Notification:** Rolling. **Transfer Students Accepted?** Yes. **Transfer Policy:** Maximum six credit hours may be transferred with a minimum grade of B.
Required Admission Factors: Letters of recommendation, transcript.
Other Admission Factors: Minimum 2.5 GPA required.

EMPLOYMENT INFORMATION
Placement Office Available? Yes.

ALDERSON-BROADDUS COLLEGE
Graduate Programs

Address: 500 College Hill Drive, Philippi, WV 26416
Admissions Phone: 304-457-6356 · **Admissions Fax:** 304-457-6308
Admissions E-mail: mercer@ab.edu

INSTITUTIONAL INFORMATION
Public/Private: Private (nonprofit). **Students in Parent Institution:** 737.

STUDENT INFORMATION
Total Students in Program: 57. **% Full-time:** 100. **% Female:** 44.

EXPENSES/FINANCIAL AID
Annual Tuition: $15,725. **Books and Supplies:** $500. **Grants Range From:** $6,000-$18,500. **Loans Range From:** $6,000-$18,500. **% Receiving Financial Aid:** 75. **% Receiving Loans:** 100. **Average student debt, upon graduation:** $15,000.

ADMISSIONS INFORMATION
Application Fee: $35. **Regular Notification:** Rolling. **Transfer Students Accepted?** No. **Number of Applications Received:** 50. **% of Applicants Accepted:** 80. **% Accepted Who Enrolled:** 80. **Average GPA:** 3.0
Required Admission Factors: Interview, letters of recommendation, transcript.
Other Admission Factors: Graduation of CAHEP approved PA Program required.

EMPLOYMENT INFORMATION
Placement Office Available? Yes. **% Employed Within 6 Months:** 100. **% of master's grads employed in their field upon graduation:** 100. **Rate of placement:** 100%.

ALFRED UNIVERSITY
The Graduate School— Non-Statutory Programs

Address: 1 Saxon Drive, Alfred, NY 14802-1205
Admissions Phone: 607-871-2141 · **Admissions Fax:** 607-871-2198
Admissions E-mail: gradinquiry@alfred.edu
Web Address: www.alfred.edu/gradschool

INSTITUTIONAL INFORMATION
Public/Private: Private (nonprofit). **Students in Parent Institution:** 2,355.

PROGRAMS
Masters offered in: Business administration/management; community organization and advocacy; counselor education/school counseling and guidance services; electrical, electronics, and communications engineering; mechanical engineering; reading teacher education; school psychology. **Doctorate offered in:** school psychology.

STUDENT INFORMATION
Total Students in Program: 207. **% Full-time:** 55. **% Female:** 70.

RESEARCH FACILITIES
Research Facilities: NYS Center for Advanced Ceramic Technology, NSF Industry-University Center for Glass Research, Whiteware Research Center, NSF Industry-University Center for Bioservices, Lab for Electronic Ceramics, PAC-MAN Center, Center for Environmental and Energy.

EXPENSES/FINANCIAL AID
Annual Tuition: $28,450. **Room & Board:** $9,416. **Fees:** $810. **Grants Range From:** $13,614-$27,228. **Loans Range From:** $1,000-$27,228. **% Receiving Financial Aid:** 100. **% Receiving Scholarships/Grants:** 5. **% Receiving Loans:** 75. **% Receiving Assistantships:** 100. **Types of Aid Available:** Graduate assistantships, loans, scholarships.

ADMISSIONS INFORMATION
Application Fee: $50. **Regular Application Deadline:** 8/1. **Regular Notification:** Rolling. **Transfer Students Accepted?** Yes. **Transfer Policy:** Maximum six credit hours may be transferred into any masters program; twenty to the PsyD program. MBA program will only accept transfer credit from other AASCB institutions. **Number of Applications Received:** 328. **% of Applicants Accepted:** 38. **% Accepted Who Enrolled:** 98.
Required Admission Factors: Essays/personal statement, letters of recommendation, transcript.
Other Admission Factors: Minimum 3.0/4.0 GPA recommended. All international students must submit official TOEFL scores; the TSE is recommended but not required.
Program-Specific Admission Factors: A statement of research interest is required of School Psychology PsyD applicants. Three letters of recommendation are required for all School Psychology degree programs. The general section of the GRE is required of School Psychology program applicants.

EMPLOYMENT INFORMATION
Placement Office Available? Yes.

ALFRED UNIVERSITY
The Graduate School— Statutory Programs

Address: Saxon Drive, Alfred, NY 14802-1205
Admissions Phone: 607-871-2141 · **Admissions Fax:** 607-871-2198
Admissions E-mail: johnsonc@alfred.edu
Web Address: http://alfred.edu/gradschool

INSTITUTIONAL INFORMATION
Public/Private: Public. **Students in Parent Institution:** 2,355.

PROGRAMS
Masters offered in: Biomedical/medical engineering; ceramic sciences and engineering, commercial and advertising art, materials engineering, sculpture. **Doctorate offered in:** Ceramic sciences and engineering, materials engineering.

STUDENT INFORMATION
Total Students in Program: 82. **% Full-time:** 95. **% Female:** 37.

RESEARCH FACILITIES
Research Facilities: NYS Center for Advanced Ceramic Technology, NSF Industry-University Center for Glass Research, Whiteware Research Center, NSF Industry-University Center for Bioservices, Lab for Electronic Ceramics, PAC-MAN Center, Center for Environmental and Energy

EXPENSES/FINANCIAL AID
Annual Tuition: $16,100. **Room & Board:** $9,416. **Fees:** $810. **Grants Range From:** $3,000-$33,100. **Loans Range From:** $1,000-$13,100. **% Receiving Financial Aid:** 100. **% Receiving Assistantships:** 100. **Types of Aid Available:** Fellowships, graduate assistantships, stipends.

ADMISSIONS INFORMATION
Application Fee: $50. **Regular Application Deadline:** 8/1. **Regular Notification:** Rolling. **Transfer Students Accepted?** Yes. **Transfer Policy:** 6 credit hours can be transferred for MS programs, 20 credit hours for PhD programs, none for MFA. **Number of Applications Received:** 387. **% of Applicants Accepted:** 17. **% Accepted Who Enrolled:** 67.
Required Admission Factors: Essays/personal statement, letters of recommendation, transcript.
Other Admission Factors: Minimum 3.0/4.0 GPA recommended. All international students must submit official TOEFL scores; the TSE is recommended but not required.

EMPLOYMENT INFORMATION
Placement Office Available? Yes. **% of master's/doctoral grads employed in their field upon graduation:** 100/90. **Rate of placement:** 96%.

ALFRED UNIVERSITY
New York State College of Ceramics

Address: Saxon Drive, Alfred, NY 14802-1205

INSTITUTIONAL INFORMATION
Public/Private: Private (nonprofit). **Students in Parent Institution:** 2,473.

STUDENT INFORMATION
Total Students in Program: 348. **% Full-time:** 54. **% Female:** 58.

RESEARCH FACILITIES
Research Facilities: NYS Center for Advanced Ceramic Technology, NSF Industry-University Center for Glass Research, Whiteware Research Center, NSF Industry-University Center for Bioservices, Lab for Electronic Ceramics, PAC-MAN Center, Center for Environmental and Energy.

EXPENSES/FINANCIAL AID
Annual Tuition: $23,554. **Room & Board:** $8,600. **Fees:** $698. **Grants Range From:** $11,500-$30,000. **Loans Range From:** $1,000-$22,444. **% Receiving Scholarships/Grants:** 5. **% Receiving Loans:** 75

ADMISSIONS INFORMATION
Transfer Students Accepted? No.

EMPLOYMENT INFORMATION
Placement Office Available? Yes. **Rate of placement:** 96%.

ALLEN COLLEGE
Graduate Programs

Address: 1825 Logan Avenue, Waterloo, IA 50703
Admissions Phone: 319-226-2000 · **Admissions Fax:** 319-226-2051
Admissions E-mail: allencollegeadmissions@ihs.org
Web Address: www.allencollege.edu

INSTITUTIONAL INFORMATION
Public/Private: Private (nonprofit). **Total Faculty:** 9. **% Faculty Female:** 100. **% Faculty Part-time:** 100. **Student/Faculty Ratio:** 4:1. **Students in Parent Institution:** 364.

STUDENT INFORMATION
Total Students in Program: 31. **% Full-time:** 32. **% Female:** 97.

EXPENSES/FINANCIAL AID
Annual Tuition: $9,800. **Room & Board (On/Off Campus):** $4,930/$4,930. **Fees:** $668. **Books and Supplies:** $804. **Grants Range From:** $100-$2,500. **Loans Range From:** $500-$19,498. **% Receiving Financial Aid:** 94. **% Receiving Scholarships/Grants:** 68. **% Receiving Loans:** 100. **% Receiving Other Aid (Tuition Reimbursement):** 6. **Types of Aid Available:** Grants, loans, scholarships. **Average student debt, upon graduation:** $28,146. **Number of fellowships granted each year:** 1. **Number of teaching/research assistantships granted each year:** 1.

ADMISSIONS INFORMATION
Application Fee: $50. **Priority Application Deadline:** 7/15. **Regular Application Deadline:** 7/15. **Regular Notification:** Rolling. **Transfer Students Accepted?** Yes. **Number of Applications Received:** 21. **% of Applicants Accepted:** 48. **% Accepted Who Enrolled:** 100.
Required Admission Factors: GRE, interview, letters of recommendation, transcript.
Other Admission Factors: Minimum 3.0 GPA, biographical sketch, and goal statement required.

EMPLOYMENT INFORMATION
Placement Office Available? Yes. **% Employed Within 6 Months:** 73. **% of master's grads employed in their field upon graduation:** 73. **Rate of placement:** 100%. **Average starting salary:** $60,000.

ALLIANT INTERNATIONAL UNIVERSITY
California School of Organizational Studies

Address: 10455 Pomerado Road, San Diego, CA 92131-1799
Admissions Phone: 866-825-5426 · **Admissions Fax:** 858-635-4355
Admissions E-mail: admissions@alliant.edu
Web Address: www.alliant.edu/csos

INSTITUTIONAL INFORMATION
Public/Private: Private (nonprofit). **Total Faculty:** 49. **% Faculty Female:** 41. **% Faculty Part-time:** 55. **Student/Faculty Ratio:** 11:1. **Students in Parent Institution:** 3,760.

PROGRAMS
Masters offered in: Industrial and organizational psychology; psychology. **Doctorate offered in:** Industrial and organizational psychology; psychology.

STUDENT INFORMATION
Total Students in Program: 318. **% Full-time:** 69. **% Female:** 66. **% Minority:** 33. **% International:** 6.

RESEARCH FACILITIES
Research Facilities: The Organizational Consulting Center (OCC) provides consulting services to individuals, groups and organizations.

EXPENSES/FINANCIAL AID
Annual Tuition: $20,000. **Room & Board (On/Off Campus):** $7,430/$11,440. **Fees:** $230. **Books and Supplies:** $1,500. **Grants Range From:** $350-$7,000. **Loans Range From:** $150-$26,140. **% Receiving Financial Aid:** 90. **% Receiving Scholarships/Grants:** 67. **% Receiving Loans:** 68. **% Receiving Assistantships:** 1. **% Receiving Other Aid (work aid):** 30. **Types of Aid Available:** Graduate assistantships, grants, institutional work-study, loans, scholarships. **Number of fellowships granted each year:** 1. **Number of teaching/research assistantships granted each year:** 25. **Assistantship compensation includes:** Salary/stipend. **Average Salary Stipend:** $1,600.

ADMISSIONS INFORMATION
Application Fee: $65. **Priority Application Deadline:** 2/1. **Regular Application Deadline:** 8/1. **Regular Notification:** Rolling. **Transfer Students Accepted?** Yes. **Transfer Policy:** same as other applicants. **Number of Applications Received:** 152. **% of Applicants Accepted:** 67. **% Accepted Who Enrolled:** 70. **Average GPA:** 3.2.
Required Admission Factors: Essays/personal statement, interview, letters of recommendation, transcript.
Other Admission Factors: 3.0 GPA or documentation relating to academic ability.

EMPLOYMENT INFORMATION
% Employed Within 6 Months: 80. **% of master's/doctoral grads employed in their field upon graduation:** 80/75. **Rate of placement:** 90%. **Average starting salary:** $75,000.

ALLIANT INTERNATIONAL UNIVERSITY
California School of Professional Psychology

Address: 10455 Pomerado Road, Admissions Processing Center, San Diego, CA 92131-1799
Admissions Phone: 866-825-5426 · **Admissions Fax:** 858-635-4355
Admissions E-mail: admissions@alliant.edu
Web Address: www.alliant.edu/cspp/

INSTITUTIONAL INFORMATION
Public/Private: Private (nonprofit). **Total Faculty:** 512. **% Faculty Female:**

21. **% Faculty Part-time:** 35. **Student/Faculty Ratio:** 12:1. **Students in Parent Institution:** 3,760.

PROGRAMS

Masters offered in: Clinical psychology, counseling psychology, psychology, psychopharmacology. **Doctorate offered in:** Clinical psychology, psychology.

STUDENT INFORMATION

Total Students in Program: 2,087. **% Full-time:** 74. **% Female:** 80. **% Minority:** 28. **% International:** 5.

RESEARCH FACILITIES

Research Facilities: Psychological services centers providing services to the communities and training opportunities for students exist on most campuses

EXPENSES/FINANCIAL AID

Annual Tuition: $18,900. **Room & Board (On/Off Campus):** $6,365/ $11,440. **Fees:** $230. **Books and Supplies:** $1,500. **Grants Range From:** $350-$10,000. **Loans Range From:** $150-$40,000. **% Receiving Financial Aid:** 84. **% Receiving Scholarships/Grants:** 51. **% Receiving Loans:** 65. **% Receiving Assistantships:** 4. **% Receiving Other Aid (work):** 24. **Types of Aid Available:** Graduate assistantships, grants, institutional work-study, loans, scholarships. work aid. **Average student debt, upon graduation:** $80,000. **Number of fellowships granted each year:** 1. **Number of teaching/research assistantships granted each year:** 75. **Assistantship compensation includes:** Salary/stipend. **Average Salary Stipend:** $1,600.

ADMISSIONS INFORMATION

Application Fee: $65. **Priority Application Deadline:** 1/15. **Regular Application Deadline:** 8/1. **Regular Notification:** Rolling. **Transfer Students Accepted?** Yes. **Transfer Policy:** Portfolio of previous graduate coursework required of transfer applicants. **Number of Applications Received:** 1,010. **% of Applicants Accepted:** 69. **% Accepted Who Enrolled:** 61. **Average GPA:** 3.3.
Required Admission Factors: Essays/personal statement, interview, letters of recommendation, transcript.
Other Admission Factors: Minimum 3.0 GPA required.
Program-Specific Admission Factors: See www.alliant.edu/admissions/gradapply.htm

EMPLOYMENT INFORMATION

% Employed Within 6 Months: 93. **% of master's/doctoral grads employed in their field upon graduation:** 85/90. **Rate of placement:** 80%. **Average starting salary:** $35,000.

ALLIANT INTERNATIONAL UNIVERSITY
College of Arts and Sciences

Address: 10455 Pomerado Road, San Diego, CA 92131-1799
Admissions Phone: 866-825-5426 · **Admissions Fax:** 858-635-4355
Admissions E-mail: admissions@alliant.edu
Web Address: www.alliant.edu/cas/

INSTITUTIONAL INFORMATION

Public/Private: Private (nonprofit). **Total Faculty:** 12. **% Faculty Female:** 58. **% Faculty Part-time:** 42. **Student/Faculty Ratio:** 13:1. **Students in Parent Institution:** 360.

PROGRAMS

Masters offered in: International relations and affairs. **Doctorate offered in:** Psychology.

STUDENT INFORMATION

Total Students in Program: 151. **% Full-time:** 85. **% Female:** 79. **% Minority:** 23. **% International:** 3.

EXPENSES/FINANCIAL AID

Annual Tuition: $18,900. **Room & Board (On/Off Campus):** $6,365/ $11,440. **Fees:** $230. **Books and Supplies:** $1,500. **Grants Range From:**

$370-$4,500. **Loans Range From:** $590-$22,374. **% Receiving Financial Aid:** 81. **% Receiving Scholarships/Grants:** 67. **% Receiving Loans:** 88. **% Receiving Assistantships:** 3. **Types of Aid Available:** Graduate assistantships, grants, institutional work-study, loans, scholarships. **Number of fellowships granted each year:** 1. **Number of teaching/research assistantships granted each year:** 7. **Assistantship compensation includes:** Salary/stipend. **Average Salary Stipend:** $5,634.

ADMISSIONS INFORMATION

Application Fee: $50. **Priority Application Deadline:** 1/2. **Regular Application Deadline:** 8/1. **Regular Notification:** Rolling. **Transfer Students Accepted?** Yes. **Transfer Policy:** Same as for other applicants. **Number of Applications Received:** 171. **% of Applicants Accepted:** 57. **% Accepted Who Enrolled:** 60. **Average GPA:** 3.2.
Required Admission Factors: Letters of recommendation, transcript.
Other Admission Factors: 3.0 GPA required for doctoral programs.
Program-Specific Admission Factors: Go to www.alliant.edu/admissions/gradapply.htm.

EMPLOYMENT INFORMATION

% Employed Within 6 Months: 97. **% of master's/doctoral grads employed in their field upon graduation:** 50/97. **Rate of placement:** 99%. **Average starting salary:** $55,000.

ALVERNO COLLEGE
Alverno College Graduate School

Address: 3400 South 43rd Street, PO Box 343922, Milwaukee, WI 53234-3922
Admissions Phone: 414-382-6100 or 800-933-3401 · **Admissions Fax:** 414-382-6332
Admissions E-mail: sarajane.kennedy@alverno.edu · **Web Address:** www.alverno.edu

INSTITUTIONAL INFORMATION

Public/Private: Private (nonprofit). **Total Faculty:** 197. **% Faculty Female:** 78. **% Faculty Part-time:** 49. **Student/Faculty Ratio:** 14:1. **Students in Parent Institution:** 2,241.

PROGRAMS

Masters offered in: Education.

STUDENT INFORMATION

Total Students in Program: 188. **% Full-time:** 3. **% Female:** 86. **% Minority:** 28. **% International:** 1.

RESEARCH FACILITIES

Research Facilities: Video conferencing center, multimedia production facility, computer center, assessment center, career development center.

EXPENSES/FINANCIAL AID

Annual Tuition: $6,976. **Room & Board:** $3,320. **Fees:** $200. **Loans Range From:** $2,600-$18,500. **% Receiving Financial Aid:** 54% **Receiving Loans:** 100. **Types of Aid Available:** Loans

ADMISSIONS INFORMATION

Application Fee: $20. **Regular Application Deadline:** 8/1. **Regular Notification:** Rolling. **Transfer Students Accepted?** Yes. **Transfer Policy:** Same as for new students, but must provide official transcript of graduate coursework to be considered for transfer. **Number of Applications Received:** 60. **% of Applicants Accepted:** 98. **% Accepted Who Enrolled:** 68.
Required Admission Factors: Essays/personal statement, letters of recommendation, transcript.
Other Admission Factors: Copy of teaching license, if applicable, and portfolio of communication samples from work setting required.

AMERICAN BAPTIST SEMINARY OF THE WEST
Graduate & Professional Programs

Address: 2606 Dwight Way, Berkeley, CA 94704-3029
Admissions Phone: 510-841-1905 · **Admissions Fax:** 510-841-2446
Admissions E-mail: admissions@absw.edu · **Web Address:** www.absw.edu

INSTITUTIONAL INFORMATION
Public/Private: Private (nonprofit). **Evening Classes Available?** Yes. **Total Faculty:** 10. **% Faculty Female:** 40. **% Faculty Part-time:** 60. **Student/Faculty Ratio:** 11:1. **Students in Parent Institution:** 65.

PROGRAMS
First Professional degree offered in: Divinity/ministry (BD, MDiv).

STUDENT INFORMATION
Total Students in Program: 5. **% Full-time:** 20. **% Female:** 80.

EXPENSES/FINANCIAL AID
Annual Tuition: $12,610. **Fees:** $550. **Books and Supplies:** $1,200. **Grants Range From:** $500-$10,000. **Loans Range From:** $1,000-$25,000. **% Receiving Financial Aid:** 70. **% Receiving Scholarships/Grants:** 90. **% Receiving Loans:** 41. **% Receiving Other Aid (work-study, depending upon seminary's needs.):** 16. **Types of Aid Available:** Grants, institutional work-study, loans, scholarships. **Assistantship compensation includes:** Partial tuition remission, salary/stipend.

ADMISSIONS INFORMATION
Application Fee: $25. **Priority Application Deadline:** 3/1. **Regular Application Deadline:** 8/1. **Regular Notification:** Rolling. **Transfer Students Accepted?** Yes. **Transfer Policy:** Syllabus required for each course to be considered for transfer credit. Academic dean reveiws all units transferable. **Number of Applications Received:** 23. **% of Applicants Accepted:** 91. **% Accepted Who Enrolled:** 90. **Average GPA:** 2.5.
Required Admission Factors: Essays/personal statement, letters of recommendation, transcript.
Other Admission Factors: Undergraduate degree with a minimum 2.5 GPA from an accredited institution, autobiographical statement, and three references (one pastor, two professors) required.

AMERICAN CONSERVATORY THEATER
Graduate Program in Acting

Address: 30 Grant Avenue, 6th Floor, San Francisco, CA 94108-5834
Admissions Phone: 415-439-2350 · **Admissions Fax:** 415-834-3300
Admissions E-mail: mfa@act-sf.org · **Web Address:** www.actactortraining.org

INSTITUTIONAL INFORMATION
Public/Private: Private (nonprofit). **Student/Faculty Ratio:** 4:1.

PROGRAMS
Masters offered in: Acting.

STUDENT INFORMATION
Total Students in Program: 50. **% Full-time:** 96. **% Female:** 42.

EXPENSES/FINANCIAL AID
Annual Tuition: $13,530. **Room & Board:** $9,000. **Books and Supplies:** $500. **Grants Range From:** $1,000-$21,000. **Loans Range From:** $8,500-$20,000. **% Receiving Financial Aid:** 80. **% Receiving Scholarships/Grants:** 48. **% Receiving Loans:** 98. **% Receiving Other Aid (work-study):** 55. **Types of Aid Available:** Grants, institutional work-study, loans, scholarships. federal work study. **Average student debt, upon graduation:** $52,000. **Number of teaching/research assistantships granted each year:** 3.

ADMISSIONS INFORMATION
Application Fee: $65. **Regular Application Deadline:** 1/15. **Regular Notification:** 4/1. **Transfer Students Accepted?** No. **Number of Applications**

Received: 362. **% of Applicants Accepted:** 5. **Average GPA:** 3.0.
Required Admission Factors: Essays/personal statement, interview, letters of recommendation, transcript.
Program-Specific Admission Factors: An audition of two selections that provide a contrast in mood and tone (one from a classical verse play and one from a contemporary play), not to exceed a total of 4 minutes for both pieces.

EMPLOYMENT INFORMATION
% Employed Within 6 Months: 50. **Rate of placement:** 75%. **Average starting salary:** $600.

AMERICAN FILM INSTITUTE
Conservatory

Address: 2021 North Western Avenue, Los Angeles, CA 90027
Admissions Phone: 323-856-7628 · **Admissions Fax:** 323-856-7720
Admissions E-mail: jjackman@AFI.com · **Web Address:** www.AFI.com

INSTITUTIONAL INFORMATION
Public/Private: Private (nonprofit). **Student/Faculty Ratio:** 8:1. **Students in Parent Institution:** 288.

STUDENT INFORMATION
Total Students in Program: 288. **% Full-time:** 100. **% Female:** 34.

RESEARCH FACILITIES
Research Facilities: National Center for Film & Video Preservation, Screen Actors' Guild Conservatory Office, National Moving Image Database, Catalog of Feature Films, Louis B. Mayer Library.

EXPENSES/FINANCIAL AID
Annual Tuition: In-state $22,000. / Out-of-state. **Fees:** $1,590. **Grants Range From:** $1,000-$25,000. **Loans Range From:** $6,625-$18,500. **% Receiving Financial Aid:** 57. **% Receiving Scholarships/Grants:** 17. **% Receiving Loans:** 57. **Number of teaching/research assistantships granted each year:** 7. **Average Salary Stipend:** $2,000.

ADMISSIONS INFORMATION
Application Fee: $75. **Regular Application Deadline:** 12/5. **Regular Notification:** 4/15. **Transfer Students Accepted?** No. **Number of Applications Received:** 535. **% of Applicants Accepted:** 25. **% Accepted Who Enrolled:** 92.
Required Admission Factors: Essays/personal statement, interview, letters of recommendation, transcript.
Other Admission Factors: Sample of work related to the filmmaking discipline being applied for, resume, narrative statement.

AMERICAN INTERCONTINENTAL UNIVERSITY— LOS ANGELES
Graduate School

Address: 12655 West Jefferson Boulevard, Los Angeles, CA 90066
Admissions Phone: 310-302-2000 · **Admissions Fax:** 310-302-2001
Admissions E-mail: atall@la.aiunic.edu · **Web Address:** www.aiula.com

INSTITUTIONAL INFORMATION
Public/Private: Private (proprietary). **Evening Classes Available?** Yes. **Students in Parent Institution:** 1,521.

PROGRAMS
Masters offered in: Business administration/management, educational/instructional media design, information technology.

STUDENT INFORMATION
Total Students in Program: 100. **% Full-time:** 100.

EXPENSES/FINANCIAL AID

Annual Tuition: $17,000. Fees: $100. Books and Supplies: $750. Grants Range From: $1,000-$2,000. Loans Range From: $1,000-$30,000. Types of Aid Available: Institutional work-study, loans.

ADMISSIONS INFORMATION

Application Fee: $50. Priority Application Deadline: 9/15. Regular Application Deadline: 10/4. Transfer Students Accepted? No. Number of Applications Received: 100. % of Applicants Accepted: 100. % Accepted Who Enrolled: 75. Average GPA: 2.8. Required Admission Factors: Interview, transcript.

EMPLOYMENT INFORMATION

Placement Office Available? Yes. % Employed Within 6 Months: 90. Rate of placement: 90%. Average starting salary: $35,000.

AMERICAN MILITARY UNIVERSITY
Graduate Programs

Address: 10648 Wakeman CT, Masassas, VA 20110-2026
Admissions Phone: 703-330-5398 · Admissions Fax: 703-330-5109
Admissions E-mail: ntilton@amunet.edu

INSTITUTIONAL INFORMATION

Public/Private: Private (proprietary). Evening Classes Available? Yes. Student/Faculty Ratio: 12:1. Students in Parent Institution: 1,750

STUDENT INFORMATION

Total Students in Program: 1,750. % Female: 9.

EXPENSES/FINANCIAL AID

Annual Tuition: $4,500. Books and Supplies: $900.

ADMISSIONS INFORMATION

Application Fee: $50. Regular Notification: Rolling. Transfer Students Accepted? Yes. Number of Applications Received: 150. % of Applicants Accepted: 100. % Accepted Who Enrolled: 93. Average GPA: 2.95. Required Admission Factors: Transcript.
Other Admission Factors: Minimum 2.6 GPA in last 60 credit hours required.

EMPLOYMENT INFORMATION

% Employed Within 6 Months: 100. % of first professional grads employed in their field upon graduation: 100. Average starting salary: $65,000.

AMERICAN UNIVERSITY
College of Arts & Sciences

Address: 4400 Massachusetts Avenue, NW, Washington, DC 20016-8107
Admissions Phone: 202-885-3620 · Admissions Fax: 202-885-1505
Admissions E-mail: casgrad@American.edu
Web Address: www.american.edu/cas/admissions

INSTITUTIONAL INFORMATION

Public/Private: Private (nonprofit). Evening Classes Available? Yes. Students in Parent Institution: 10,060.

STUDENT INFORMATION

Total Students in Program: 3,192. % Full-time: 45. % Female: 60.

RESEARCH FACILITIES

Research Facilities: On-campus laboratory facilities in biology, chemistry, and physics. Cooperative arrangements with laboratories in the Washington, DC area.

EXPENSES/FINANCIAL AID

Annual Tuition: In-state $14,274. Fees: $290. Books and Supplies: $800. Grants Range From: $500-$20,978. Loans Range From: $200-$18,500. %

Receiving Financial Aid: 41. % Receiving Scholarships/Grants: 12. % Receiving Loans: 82. % Receiving Assistantships: 12. Number of fellowships granted each year: 250. Average amount of individual fellowships per year: 10,856. Number of teaching/research assistantships granted each year: 184. Average Salary Stipend: $7,820.

ADMISSIONS INFORMATION

Application Fee: $50. Priority Application Deadline: 2/1. Regular Application Deadline: 8/20. Regular Notification: Rolling. Transfer Students Accepted? Yes. Transfer Policy: 6 transfer credit hours are accepted. Number of Applications Received: 1,403. % of Applicants Accepted: 78. % Accepted Who Enrolled: 31. Average GPA: 3.43. Average GRE Verbal: 543. Average GRE Quantitative: 637. Average GRE Analytical: 642.
Required Admission Factors: Essays/personal statement, letters of recommendation, transcript.
Other Admission Factors: Minimum 3.0 GPA in last 60 credit hours of undergraduate coursework or minimum 3.3 GPA in a completed master's program.
Program-Specific Admission Factors: For fellowships, January 15th deadline is required for: anthropoloty, art, arts management, history.

EMPLOYMENT INFORMATION

Placement Office Available? Yes. Rate of placement: 85%.

AMERICAN UNIVERSITY
School of Communication

Address: 4400 Massachusetts Avenue, NW, Mary Graydon Center Room 328, Washington, DC 20016-8017
Admissions Phone: 202-885-2040 · Admissions Fax: 202-885-2019
Admissions E-mail: gradcomm@American.edu
Web Address: http://soc.American.edu

INSTITUTIONAL INFORMATION

Public/Private: Private (nonprofit). Evening Classes Available? Yes. Total Faculty: 102. % Faculty Female: 45. % Faculty Part-time: 49. Student/Faculty Ratio: 9:1. Students in Parent Institution: 10,060.

STUDENT INFORMATION

Total Students in Program: 3,192. % Full-time: 45. % Female: 60.

RESEARCH FACILITIES

Research Facilities: On-campus laboratory facilities in biology, chemistry, and physics. Cooperative arrangements with laboratories in the Washington, DC area.

EXPENSES/FINANCIAL AID

Annual Tuition: $16,746. Fees: $290. Books and Supplies: $800. Grants Range From: $2,000-$25,740. Loans Range From: $200-$18,500. % Receiving Scholarships/Grants: 12. % Receiving Loans: 82. % Receiving Assistantships: 12. Types of Aid Available: Graduate assistantships, institutional work-study, loans, scholarships.

ADMISSIONS INFORMATION

Application Fee: $50. Priority Application Deadline: 2/1. Regular Application Deadline: 6/1. Regular Notification: Rolling. Transfer Students Accepted? Yes. Transfer Policy: Maximum of 6 credit hours may be transferred into master's programs. Number of Applications Received: 604. % of Applicants Accepted: 62. % Accepted Who Enrolled: 46. Average GPA: 3.4. Average GRE Verbal: 543. Average GRE Quantitative: 595. Average GRE Analytical: 567. Average GRE Analytical Writing: 5.3.
Required Admission Factors: Essays/personal statement, GRE, letters of recommendation, transcript.
Other Admission Factors: Minimum 3.0 GPA required.

EMPLOYMENT INFORMATION

Placement Office Available? Yes. Rate of placement: 85%.

AMERICAN UNIVERSITY
School of Public Affairs

Address: 4400 Massachusetts Avenue, NW, Washington, DC 20016-8022
Admissions Phone: 202-885-6230 · **Admissions Fax:** 202-885-1435
Admissions E-mail: spagrad@American.edu · **Web Address:** www.spa.american.edu

INSTITUTIONAL INFORMATION

Public/Private: Private (nonprofit). **Evening Classes Available?** Yes. **Students in Parent Institution:** 11,571.

STUDENT INFORMATION

Total Students in Program: 519. **% Full-time:** 100.

RESEARCH FACILITIES

Research Facilities: Center for Congressional and Presidential Studies, Campaign Management Institute, Public Affairs and Advocacy Institute, Institute for the Study of Public Policy Implementation, Women and Politics Institute, Justice Programs Office.

EXPENSES/FINANCIAL AID

Annual Tuition: $989. **Fees:** $300. **Books and Supplies:** $800. **Grants Range From:** $5,000-$25,740. **Loans Range From:** $200-$18,500. **% Receiving Financial Aid:** 22. **% Receiving Scholarships/Grants:** 12. **% Receiving Loans:** 82. **% Receiving Assistantships:** 12. **Types of Aid Available:** Fellowships, graduate assistantships, grants, institutional work-study, scholarships. **Number of fellowships granted each year:** 25. **Average amount of individual fellowships per year:** 23,135. **Number of teaching/research assistantships granted each year:** 20. **Assistantship compensation includes:** Full tuition remission, partial tuition remission, salary/stipend. **Average Salary Stipend:** $8,000.

ADMISSIONS INFORMATION

Application Fee: $55. **Priority Application Deadline:** 2/1. **Regular Application Deadline:** 6/1. **Regular Notification:** Rolling. **Transfer Students Accepted?** Yes. **Transfer Policy:** Maximum of 6 credit hours may be transferred into a traditional master's program. **Number of Applications Received:** 715. **% of Applicants Accepted:** 63. **% Accepted Who Enrolled:** 38. **Average GPA:** 3.5. **Average GRE Verbal:** 554. **Average GRE Quantitative:** 636. **Average GRE Analytical Writing:** 5.
Required Admission Factors: Essays/personal statement, letters of recommendation, transcript.
Other Admission Factors: Minimum 3.0 GPA in last 60 credit hours of undergraduate coursework required.
Program-Specific Admission Factors: Executive programs require substantial work experience prior to admission (contact program for details). Traditional programs require the GRE for admission (unless an applicant has 8 years of full-time experience or more).

EMPLOYMENT INFORMATION

Placement Office Available? Yes. **% Employed Within 6 Months:** 51. **Rate of placement:** 85%. **Average starting salary:** $40,000.

THE AMERICAN UNIVERSITY IN CAIRO
The Office of Graduate Studies and Research

Address: 113 Kasr El Aini Street, PO Box 2511, Cairo, 11511 60
Admissions Phone: 202-797-5612 · **Admissions Fax:** 202-795-7565
Admissions E-mail: emallawany@aucegypt.edu
Website: www.aucegypt.edu/academic/huss.html

INSTITUTIONAL INFORMATION

Public/private: Private (nonprofit). **Student/faculty Ratio:** 13:1. **Students in Parent Institution:** 5,294.

PROGRAMS

Masters offered in: Anthropology; business administration/management; communications, journalism, and related fields; comparative literature; computer and information sciences; construction engineering; development economics and international development; economics; engineering; environmental/environmental health engineering; foreign languages, literatures, and linguistics; industrial engineering; international relations and affairs; law, legal services, and legal studies; physics; political science and government; public administration; social sciences; sociology.

STUDENT INFORMATION

Total Students in Program: 928. **% Full-time:** 28. **% Female:** 59. **% International:** 16.

RESEARCH FACILITIES

Research Facilities: Social Research Center, Desert Development Center, Gender Studies Center.

EXPENSES/FINANCIAL AID

Annual Tuition: $13,000. **Room & Board:** $5,500. **Fees:** $300. **Books and Supplies:** $550. **Grants Range From:** $3,700-$11,500. **% Receiving Assistantships:** 50. **Types of Aid Available:** Fellowships, graduate assistantships, grants, institutional work-study, scholarships. financial aid.

ADMISSIONS INFORMATION

Application Fee: $50. **Priority Application Deadline:** 3/31. **Regular Application Deadline:** 6/1. **Regular Notification:** Rolling. **Transfer Students Accepted?** Yes. **Transfer Policy:** Maximum 6 credit hours may be transferred with minimum grade average of B. With recommendation of department, up to 9 credit hours can be transferred. **Number of Applications Received:** 728. **% of Applicants Accepted:** 55. **% Accepted Who Enrolled:** 65. **Average GPA:** 2.7. **Average GRE Verbal:** 300. **Average GRE Quantitative:** 350. **Average GRE Analytical:** 300.
Required Admission Factors: Essays/personal statement, letters of recommendation, transcript.
Other Admission Factors: Minimum 3.0 GPA required.
Program-Specific Admission Factors: GMAT for MBA, GRE for economics, higher TOEFL scores for teaching English as a foreign language and English and comparative literature.

EMPLOYMENT INFORMATION

Placement Office Available? Yes.

AMERICAN UNIVERSITY
School of International Service

Address: 4400 Massachusetts Avenue, NW, Washington, DC 20016-8071
Admissions Phone: 202-885-1646 · **Admissions Fax:** 202-885-2494
Admissions E-mail: sisgrad@American.edu
Web Address: www.American.edu/sis/

INSTITUTIONAL INFORMATION

Public/Private: Private (nonprofit). **Evening Classes Available?** Yes.

PROGRAMS

Masters offered in: International relations and affairs. **Doctorate offered in:** International relations and affairs.

STUDENT INFORMATION

Total Students in Program: 874.

EXPENSES/FINANCIAL AID

Annual Tuition: $16,740. **Room & Board:** $12,166. **Fees:** $1,800. **Books and Supplies:** $800. **Types of Aid Available:** Fellowships, graduate assistantships, scholarships.

ADMISSIONS INFORMATION

Application Fee: $50. **Priority Application Deadline:** 1/15. **Regular Application Deadline:** 5/1. **Regular Notification:** Rolling. **Transfer Students**

Accepted? Yes. **Number of Applications Received:** 2,586. **% of Applicants Accepted:** 30. **Average GPA:** 3.5. **Average GRE Verbal:** 608. **Average GRE Quantitative:** 614. **Average GRE Analytical:** 601. **Average GRE Analytical Writing:** 5.
Required Admission Factors: Essays/personal statement, GRE, letters of recommendation, transcript. resume.
Other Admission Factors: Average combined GRE score of 600 verbal and 640 quantitative and 5.1 analytical writing, average 3.5 undergraduate GPA, minimum 24 credit hours in social science/economics. Second language fluency recommended. Economics coursework recommended.
Program-Specific Admission Factors: Fall admission only for PhD program. PhD deadline of 1/1. Fluency in Japanese required of applicants to the dual master's program with Ritsumeikan U. Three letters of recommendation and GRE exam required of all doctoral program applicants.

EMPLOYMENT INFORMATION
Placement Office Available? Yes.

ANDERSON UNIVERSITY
Graduate Studies

Address: 1100 East Fifth Street, Anderson, IN 46012
Admissions Phone: 765-641-4360 · **Admissions Fax:** 765-641-4356
Admissions E-mail: ttruitt@anderson.edu

INSTITUTIONAL INFORMATION
Public/Private: Private (nonprofit). **Evening Classes Available?** Yes. **Students in Parent Institution:** 1,751.

STUDENT INFORMATION
Total Students in Program: 197. **% Full-time:** 2. **% Female:** 48.

EXPENSES/FINANCIAL AID
Annual Tuition: $10,915. **Books and Supplies:** $500. **% Receiving Financial Aid:** 47. **Average student debt, upon graduation:** $9,500.

ADMISSIONS INFORMATION
Application Fee: $20. **Regular Notification:** Rolling. **Transfer Students Accepted?** Yes.
Required Admission Factors: Interview, letters of recommendation, transcript.

ANDOVER NEWTON THEOLOGICAL SCHOOL
Graduate & Professional Programs

Address: 210 Herrick Road, Newton Centre, MA 02459
Admissions Phone: 800-964-1100 · **Admissions Fax:** 617-965-9756
Admissions E-mail: admissions@ants.edu · **Web Address:** www.ants.edu

INSTITUTIONAL INFORMATION
Public/Private: Private (nonprofit). **Students in Parent Institution:** 494.

PROGRAMS
Masters offered in: Theology/theological studies. **Doctorate offered in:** Pastoral studies/counseling; theology/theological studies. **First Professional degree offered in:** Divinity/ministry (BD/MDiv); religious education.

STUDENT INFORMATION
Total Students in Program: 399. **% Full-time:** 39. **% Female:** 67. **% Minority:** 18. **% International:** 4.

RESEARCH FACILITIES
Research Facilities: Boston Theological Institute.

EXPENSES/FINANCIAL AID
Annual Tuition: $5,634. **Fees:** $130. **% Receiving Financial Aid:** 65.

ADMISSIONS INFORMATION
Application Fee: $20. **Priority Application Deadline:** 4/15. **Regular Application Deadline:** 7/1. **Regular Notification:** Rolling. **Transfer Students Accepted?** Yes. **Transfer Policy:** One-half of all credit hours may be transferred into graduate programs. Letter from registrar indicating good standing is required of transfer applicants. **Number of Applications Received:** 172. **% of Applicants Accepted:** 97. **% Accepted Who Enrolled:** 71. **Average GPA:** 3.0.
Required Admission Factors: Essays/personal statement, transcript.
Recommended Admission Factors: Interview.

EMPLOYMENT INFORMATION
Placement Office Available? Yes.

ANDREWS UNIVERSITY
College of Arts & Sciences

Address: Graduate Admissions Office, Andrews University, Berrien Springs, MI 49104
Admissions Phone: 269-471-6321 or 800-253-2874
Admissions Fax: 269-471-6246 · **Admissions E-mail:** graduate@andrews.edu
Web Address: www.andrews.edu

INSTITUTIONAL INFORMATION
Public/Private: Private (nonprofit). **Students in Parent Institution:** 3,133.

PROGRAMS
Masters offered in: Biology teacher education; clinical/medical laboratory science and allied professions; communications, journalism, and related fields; community organization and advocacy; conducting; dietetics and clinical nutrition services; dietetics/dietician (RD); English language and literature; English/language arts teacher education; French language teacher education; history teacher education; multi/interdisciplinary studies; music pedagogy; music; music/music and performing arts studies; nursing; physical therapy/therapist; piano and organ; religious/sacred music; social work; Spanish language teacher education; teaching English as a second or foreign language/ESL language instructor.

STUDENT INFORMATION
Total Students in Program: 1,280. **% Full-time:** 62. **% Female:** 44.

RESEARCH FACILITIES
Research Facilities: Horn Museum of Archeology.

EXPENSES/FINANCIAL AID
Fees: $180. **Books and Supplies:** $1,155.

ADMISSIONS INFORMATION
Application Fee: $40. **Regular Notification:** Rolling. **Transfer Students Accepted?** Yes. **Transfer Policy:** Same as general admission.
Required Admission Factors: Essays/personal statement, GRE, letters of recommendation, transcript.
Other Admission Factors: 2.60 undergraduate GPA
Program-Specific Admission Factors: Contact professional programs directly for special requirements, especially physical therapy, social work, nursing.

EMPLOYMENT INFORMATION
Placement Office Available? Yes.

ANGELO STATE UNIVERSITY
Graduate School

Address: 2601 West Avenue N, San Angelo, TX 76904
Admissions Phone: 325-942-2169 · **Admissions Fax:** 325-942-2194
Admissions E-mail: graduate.school@angelo.edu ·
Web Address: www.angelo.edu/gradschool

INSTITUTIONAL INFORMATION

Public/Private: Public. **Evening Classes Available?** Yes. **Total Faculty:** 121. **% Faculty Female:** 40. **% Faculty Part-time:** 0. **Students in Parent Institution:** 6,137.

PROGRAMS

Masters offered in: Accounting, animal sciences, biology/biological sciences, business administration/management, communications studies/speech communication and rhetoric, counseling psychology, counselor education/school counseling and guidance services, creative writing, curriculum and instruction, education leadership and administration, educational/instructional media design, English language and literature, health and physical education, history, industrial and organizational psychology, multi/interdisciplinary studies, nursing clinical specialist, nursing, physical therapy/therapist, psychology, public administration, reading teacher education, special education. **First Professional degree offered in:** Physical therapy/therapist.

STUDENT INFORMATION

Total Students in Program: 425. **% Full-time:** 34. **% Female:** 65. **% Minority:** 20. **% International:** 1.

RESEARCH FACILITIES

Research Facilities: Management, Instruction, and Research Center.

EXPENSES/FINANCIAL AID

Annual Tuition: In-state $2,124 / Out-of-state $6,768. **Room & Board (On/off Campus):** $4,656/$5,428. **Fees:** $348. **Books and Supplies:** $1,000. **Grants Range From:** $350-$7,000. **Loans Range From:** $100-$8,500. **% Receiving Financial Aid:** 25. **% Receiving Scholarships/Grants:** 20. **% Receiving Loans:** 10. **% Receiving Assistantships:** 10. **Types of Aid Available:** Fellowships, graduate assistantships, grants, institutional work-study, loans, scholarships. **Number of teaching/research assistantships granted each year:** 59. **Assistantship compensation includes:** salary/stipend. **Average Salary Stipend:** $5,206.

ADMISSIONS INFORMATION

Application Fee: $25. **Priority Application Deadline:** 7/15. **Regular Application Deadline:** 8/30. **Regular Notification:** Rolling. **Transfer Students Accepted?** Yes. **Transfer Policy:** Same as new students. Number of credit hours allowed for transfer differs by program. Some allow 6; majority allow 9. Must be in good standing from previous institution. **Number of Applications Received:** 176. **% of Applicants Accepted:** 78. **% Accepted Who Enrolled:** 86. **Average GPA:** 3.2.
Required Admission Factors: Essays/personal statement, transcript.
Recommended Admission Factors:
Other Admission Factors: 2.5 overall GPA or 3.0 in the last 60 credits, recommended 24 hours of prerequisites in the field of interest test scores are looked at alongside the GPA and essay to help determine admission.
Program-Specific Admission Factors: Physical therapy applicants are required to also submit three letters of reference, proof of completion of 70 volunteer hours, and a self report transcript.

EMPLOYMENT INFORMATION

Placement Office Available? Yes.

ANTIOCH SOUTHERN CALIFORNIA— LOS ANGELES
Graduate School

Address: 13274 Fiji Way, Marina del Rey, CA 90292
Admissions Phone: 800-726-8462 · **Admissions Fax:** 310-822-4824

INSTITUTIONAL INFORMATION

Public/Private: Private (nonprofit). **Evening Classes Available?** Yes. **Student/Faculty Ratio:** 30:1. **Students in Parent Institution:** 614.

STUDENT INFORMATION

Total Students in Program: 431. **% Full-time:** 64. **% Female:** 75.

RESEARCH FACILITIES

Research Facilities: Tutoring.

EXPENSES/FINANCIAL AID

Annual Tuition: $15,845. **Fees:** $150. **Books and Supplies:** $1,000. **Grants Range From:** $1,000-$16,000. **Loans Range From:** $6,625-$18,500. **% Receiving Financial Aid:** 84. **% Receiving Scholarships/Grants:** 1. **% Receiving Loans:** 100. **Average student debt, upon graduation:** $24,500.

ADMISSIONS INFORMATION

Application Fee: $60. **Regular Notification:** Rolling. **Transfer Students Accepted?** Yes. **Number of Applications Received:** 216. **% of Applicants Accepted:** 71. **% Accepted Who Enrolled:** 71.
Required Admission Factors: Essays/personal statement, letters of recommendation, transcript.
Program-Specific Admission Factors: Interview required of psychology program applicants. Writing sample required of creative writing program applicants. Interview and resume required of organizational management program applicants.

ANTIOCH UNIVERSITY
Antioch New England Graduate School

Address: 40 Avon Street, Keene, NH 03431-3552
Admissions Phone: 603-357-6265 · **Admissions Fax:** 603-357-0718
Admissions E-mail: admissions@antiochne.edu · **Web Address:** www.antiochne.edu

INSTITUTIONAL INFORMATION

Public/Private: Private (nonprofit). **Total Faculty:** 124. **% Faculty Female:** 52. **% Faculty Part-time:** 65. **Student/Faculty Ratio:** 7:1. **Students in Parent Institution:** 862.

PROGRAMS

Masters offered in: Counseling psychology, educational administration and supervision, elementary and middle school administration/principalship, elementary education and teaching, environmental studies, human services, management science, psychology, science teacher education/general science teacher education, secondary school administration/principalship, teacher education (multiple levels); Waldorf/Steiner teacher education. **Doctorate offered in:** Clinical psychology, environmental studies. **First Professional degree offered in:** Health/health care administration/management.

STUDENT INFORMATION

Total Students in Program: 862. **% Full-time:** 83.

RESEARCH FACILITIES

Research Facilities: Harris Center for Conservation Education, Center for Place Based Education, Howes Center for Community Engagement, Craiglaw Center for Applied Research & Policy, Center for Research on Psychological Practice, Center for Tropical Ecology & Conservation.

EXPENSES/FINANCIAL AID

Annual Tuition: $18,000. **Fees:** $500. **Books and Supplies:** $500. **Grants Range From:** $300-$27,166. **Loans Range From:** $500-$35,167. **% Receiving Financial Aid:** 67.3. **% Receiving Scholarships/Grants:** 19.3. **% Receiving Loans:** 62.9. **% Receiving Assistantships:** 2. **Types of Aid Available:** institutional work-study, loans, scholarships. **Average student debt, upon graduation:** $28,238. **Number of teaching/research assistantships granted each year:** 20. **Assistantship compensation includes:** Salary/stipend.

ADMISSIONS INFORMATION

Application Fee: $40. **Regular Application Deadline:** 8/1. **Regular Notification:** Rolling. **Transfer Students Accepted?** Yes. **Transfer Policy:** A maximum of 25 percent of a degree program—10 credits for a 40-credit pro-

gram, 12 credits for a 50-credit program, or 15 credits for a 60-credit program—may be awarded for prior learning. Credits earned for prior graduate work must be from an accredited institution of higher education and have been earned within 5 years prior to matriculation. This coursework must be relevant in the applicant's area of concentration and degree plan and carry a grade of B or better. Earned graduate credits which have been applied toward another master's or doctoral degree may not be used toward an Antioch New England degree. **Number of Applications Received:** 632. **% of Applicants Accepted:** 79. **% Accepted Who Enrolled:** 47.
Required Admission Factors: Essays/personal statement, interview, letters of recommendation, transcript.
Other Admission Factors: Minimum 3.0 GPA strongly recommended.

EMPLOYMENT INFORMATION
% Employed Within 6 Months: 77. **Rate of placement:** 77%. **Average starting salary:** $40,000.

ANTIOCH UNIVERSITY (SEATTLE)
Graduate Programs

Address: 2326 Sixth Avenue, Seattle, WA 98121-1814
Admissions Phone: 206-268-4200 · **Admissions E-mail:** dlarsen@antiochsea.edu

INSTITUTIONAL INFORMATION
Public/Private: Private (nonprofit). **Evening Classes Available?** Yes. **Students in Parent Institution:** 1,000.

EXPENSES/FINANCIAL AID
Fees: $50. **Books and Supplies:** $600.

ADMISSIONS INFORMATION
Application Fee: $50. **Regular Notification:** Rolling. **Transfer Students Accepted?** Yes. **Number of Applications Received:** 300. **% of Applicants Accepted:** 83. **% Accepted Who Enrolled:** 85.
Required Admission Factors: Essays/personal statement, interview, transcript.
Program-Specific Admission Factors: Work in education (number of hours vary by program) required of education program applicants.

APPALACHIAN STATE UNIVERSITY
College of Arts & Sciences

Address: Dougherty Hall, Boone, NC 28608
Admissions Phone: 828-262-2130 · **Admissions Fax:** 828-262-2709
Admissions E-mail: huntleyed@appstate.edu
Web Address: www.graduate.appstate.edu

INSTITUTIONAL INFORMATION
Public/Private: Public. **Students in Parent Institution:** 14,653.

PROGRAMS
Masters offered in: Area studies; biology teacher education; biology/biological sciences; clinical psychology; computer and information sciences; English language and literature; English/language arts teacher education; experimental psychology; foreign language teacher education; French language and literature; French language teacher education; geography; history teacher education; history; industrial and organizational psychology; mathematics teacher education; mathematics; physics; political science and government; psychology; public administration; public/applied history and archival administration; romance languages, literatures, and linguistics; school psychology; social science teacher education; social sciences; Spanish language and literature; Spanish language teacher education.

STUDENT INFORMATION
Total Students in Program: 382. **% Full-time:** 63. **% Female:** 52.

RESEARCH FACILITIES
Research Facilities: Program for the Study of Environmental Change, Center for Appalachian Studies, National Center for Developmental Education, Center for Business Research.

EXPENSES/FINANCIAL AID
Annual Tuition: In-state $3,301. / Out-of-state $12,884. **Room & Board:** $4,758. **Books and Supplies:** $400. **Grants Range From:** $200-$5,000. **Loans Range From:** $500-$18,500. **Types of Aid Available:** Fellowships, graduate assistantships, grants, loans, scholarships. **Assistantship compensation includes:** Salary/stipend.

ADMISSIONS INFORMATION
Application Fee: $35. **Regular Application Deadline:** 7/1. **Regular Notification:** Rolling. **Transfer Students Accepted?** Yes. **Transfer Policy:** Maximum 9 semester hours may be transferred into a program requiring no thesis. **Number of Applications Received:** 381. **% of Applicants Accepted:** 55. **% Accepted Who Enrolled:** 68. **Average GPA:** 3.2. **Average GRE Verbal:** 496. **Average GRE Quantitative:** 565. **Average GRE Analytical:** 627. **Average GRE Analytical Writing:** 4.51.
Required Admission Factors: GRE, letters of recommendation, transcript.
Other Admission Factors: Admissions criteria vary by program.

EMPLOYMENT INFORMATION
Placement Office Available? Yes.

APPALACHIAN STATE UNIVERSITY
College of Fine & Applied Arts

Address: John E. Thomas Building—Rivers Street, Boone, NC 28608
Admissions Phone: 828-262-2130 · **Admissions Fax:** 828-262-2709
Admissions E-mail: huntleyed@appstate.edu · **Web Address:** www.faa.appstate.edu

INSTITUTIONAL INFORMATION
Public/Private: Public. **Students in Parent Institution:** 14,653.

PROGRAMS
Masters offered in: Dietetics and clinical nutrition services, dietetics/dietician (RD), family and consumer sciences/home economics teacher education, industrial technology/technician, kinesiology and exercise science, physical education teaching and coaching, technology teacher education/industrial arts teacher education.

STUDENT INFORMATION
Total Students in Program: 68. **% Full-time:** 69. **% Female:** 57.

RESEARCH FACILITIES
Research Facilities: Program for the Study of Environmental Change, Center for Appalachian Studies, National Center for Developmental Education, Center for Business Research.

EXPENSES/FINANCIAL AID
Annual Tuition: In-state $3,301. / Out-of-state $12,884. **Room & Board:** $4,758. **Books and Supplies:** $400. **Grants Range From:** $200-$5,000. **Loans Range From:** $500-$18,500. **Types of Aid Available:** Fellowships, graduate assistantships, grants, loans, scholarships. **Assistantship compensation includes:** Salary/stipend.

ADMISSIONS INFORMATION
Application Fee: $35. **Regular Application Deadline:** 2/1. **Transfer Students Accepted?** Yes. **Number of Applications Received:** 52. **% of Applicants Accepted:** 54. **% Accepted Who Enrolled:** 89. **Average GPA:** 3.3. **Average GRE Verbal:** 457. **Average GRE Quantitative:** 601. **Average GRE Analytical:** 660. **Average GRE Analytical Writing:** 4.33.
Required Admission Factors: GRE, letters of recommendation, transcript.

Other Admission Factors: Minimum entrance formula total of 2000 (GPA times 400 plus GRE verbal plus GRE quantative) required.

EMPLOYMENT INFORMATION
Placement Office Available? Yes.

APPALACHIAN STATE UNIVERSITY
Hayes School of Music

Address: John E. Thomas Building–Rivers Street, Boone, NC 28608
Admissions Phone: 828-262-2130 · **Admissions Fax:** 828-262-2709
Admissions E-mail: huntleyed@appstate.edu · **Web Address:** www.music.appstate.edu

INSTITUTIONAL INFORMATION
Public/Private: Public. **Students in Parent Institution:** 14,653.

PROGRAMS
Masters offered in: Conducting; music pedagogy; music performance; music teacher education; music theory and composition; music/music and performing arts studies; piano and organ; violin, viola, guitar, and other stringed instruments; voice and opera.

STUDENT INFORMATION
Total Students in Program: 970. **% Full-time:** 34. **% Female:** 78.

RESEARCH FACILITIES
Research Facilities: Program for the Study of Environmental Change, Center for Appalachian Studies, National Center for Developmental Education, Center for Business Research.

EXPENSES/FINANCIAL AID
Annual Tuition: In-state $3,301. / Out-of-state $12,884. **Room & Board:** $4,758. **Books and Supplies:** $400. **Grants Range From:** $200-$5,000. **Loans Range From:** $500-$18,500. **Types of Aid Available:** Fellowships, graduate assistantships, grants, loans, scholarships. **Assistantship compensation includes:** salary/stipend.

ADMISSIONS INFORMATION
Application Fee: $35. **Regular Application Deadline:** 7/1. **Regular Notification:** Rolling. **Transfer Students Accepted?** Yes. **Number of Applications Received:** 699. **% of Applicants Accepted:** 76. **% Accepted Who Enrolled:** 81. **Average GPA:** 3.2. **Average GRE Verbal:** 443. **Average GRE Quantitative:** 487. **Average GRE Analytical:** 496. **Average GRE Analytical Writing:** 4.05.
Required Admission Factors: GRE, letters of recommendation, transcript. **Other Admission Factors:** Minimum entrance formula total of 2000 (GPA times 400 plus GRE verbal plus GRE quantative) required.

EMPLOYMENT INFORMATION
Placement Office Available? Yes.

AQUINAS INSTITUTE OF THEOLOGY
Graduate and Professional Programs

Address: 3642 Lindell Boulevard, St. Louis, MO 63108-3396
Admissions Phone: 800-977-3869 · **Admissions Fax:** 314-977-7225
Admissions E-mail: aquinas@slu.edu · **Web Address:** www.ai.edu

INSTITUTIONAL INFORMATION
Public/Private: Private (nonprofit). **Evening Classes Available?** Yes. **Total Faculty:** 28. **% Faculty Female:** 43. **% Faculty Part-time:** 39. **Student/Faculty Ratio:** 10:1. **Students in Parent Institution:** 321.

PROGRAMS
Masters offered in: Bible/biblical studies; divinity/ministry (BD, MDiv); pastoral studies/counseling; theological and ministerial studies, theology/theologi-

cal studies; youth ministry. **First Professional degree offered in:** Divinity/ministry (BD, MDiv); theological and ministerial studies, theology/theological studies.

STUDENT INFORMATION
Total Students in Program: 321. **% Full-time:** 37.

RESEARCH FACILITIES
Research Facilities: Students have full access to Saint Louis University and all of its resources.

EXPENSES/FINANCIAL AID
Annual Tuition: $11,854. **Fees:** $200. **Books and Supplies:** $800. **Grants Range From:** $154-$11,854. **Loans Range From:** $900-$18,500. **% Receiving Financial Aid:** 18. **% Receiving Scholarships/Grants:** 97. **% Receiving Loans:** 32. **% Receiving Assistantships:** 3. **Types of Aid Available:** Graduate assistantships, grants, institutional work-study, loans, scholarships. **Average student debt, upon graduation:** $18,600. **Number of teaching/research assistantships granted each year:** 4. **Assistantship compensation includes:** Full tuition remission, salary/stipend. **Average Salary Stipend:** $1,600.

ADMISSIONS INFORMATION
Application Fee: $50. **Priority Application Deadline:** 3/15. **Regular Application Deadline:** 7/1. **Regular Notification:** Rolling. **Transfer Students Accepted?** Yes. **Transfer Policy:** Maximum one-third of total program credit hours may be transferred to MAPS and MDiv degrees. Maximum of six credits to MA degree. **Number of Applications Received:** 82. **% of Applicants Accepted:** 93. **% Accepted Who Enrolled:** 95. **Average GPA:** 3.3.
Required Admission Factors: Essays/personal statement, letters of recommendation, transcript.
Recommended Admission Factors: Interview.
Other Admission Factors: Minimum 3.0 GPA required.
Program-Specific Admission Factors: Video of homily required of doctor of ministry in preaching program applicants.

EMPLOYMENT INFORMATION
Placement Office Available? Yes.

ARCADIA UNIVERSITY
Graduate and Professional Studies

Address: 450 South Easton Road, Glenside, PA 19038-3295
Admissions Phone: 215-572-2910 · **Admissions Fax:** 215-572-4049
Admissions E-mail: admiss@arcadia.edu · **Web Address:** www.arcadia.edu

INSTITUTIONAL INFORMATION
Public/Private: Private (nonprofit). **Evening Classes Available?** Yes. **Total Faculty:** 332. **% Faculty Part-time:** 71. **Student/Faculty Ratio:** 12:1. **Students in Parent Institution:** 3,803.

PROGRAMS
Masters offered in: Art teacher education; biology teacher education; chemistry teacher education; computer teacher education; counselor education/school counseling and guidance services; education leadership and administration; education/teaching of individuals with mental retardation; education/teaching of individuals with multiple disabilities; education/teaching of individuals with orthopedic and other physical health impairments; educational administration and supervision; educational, instructional, and curriculum supervision; elementary and middle school administration/principalship; elementary education and teaching; English language and literature; English/language arts teacher education; genetic counseling/counselor; health teacher education; history teacher education; humanities/humanistic studies; international relations and affairs; mathematics teacher education; physical therapy/therapist; physician assistant; public health education and promotion; public health (MPH, DPH); reading teacher education; school librarian/school library media specialist; science teacher education/general science teacher education; sec-

ondary education and teaching; secondary school administration/principalship; social science teacher education; social studies teacher education; special education, superintendency and educational system administration. **Doctorate offered in:** Physical therapy/therapist; physician assistant; special education.

STUDENT INFORMATION

Total Students in Program: 1,382. **% Full-time:** 32. **% Female:** 77.

EXPENSES/FINANCIAL AID

Annual Tuition: $20,550. **Room & Board:** $14,000. **Fees:** $365. **Books and Supplies:** $1,200. **Grants Range From:** $1,000-$10,000. **Loans Range From:** $1,000-$32,000. **% Receiving Financial Aid:** 90. **% Receiving Scholarships/Grants:** 40. **% Receiving Loans:** 70. **% Receiving Assistantships:** 20. **Assistantship compensation includes:** Salary/stipend. **Average Salary Stipend:** $1,300.

ADMISSIONS INFORMATION

Application Fee: $35. **Regular Application Deadline:** 7/15. **Regular Notification:** Rolling. **Transfer Students Accepted?** No. **Number of Applications Received:** 763. **% of Applicants Accepted:** 56. **% Accepted Who Enrolled:** 43. **Average GPA:** 3.2.
Required Admission Factors: Essays/personal statement, letters of recommendation, transcript.
Other Admission Factors: A bachelor's degree with a B average (3.0 or higher) from an accredited four-year institution.

EMPLOYMENT INFORMATION

Placement Office Available? Yes.

ARGOSY UNIVERSITY/SARASOTA
College of Behavioral Sciences

Address: 5250 17th Street, Sarasota, FL 34235
Admissions Phone: 800-331-5995 · **Admissions Fax:** 941-379-5964
Web address: www.argosy.edu

INSTITUTIONAL INFORMATION

Public/Private: Private (nonprofit). **Evening Classes Available?** Yes. **Students in Parent Institution:** 1,853.

STUDENT INFORMATION

Total Students in Program: 1,853. **% Full-time:** 8. **% Female:** 57.

EXPENSES/FINANCIAL AID

Annual Tuition: In-state $6,678. **Fees:** $66. **Books and Supplies:** $600. **% Receiving Financial Aid:** 30. **% Receiving Loans:** 100.

ADMISSIONS INFORMATION

Application Fee: $50. **Regular Notification:** Rolling. **Transfer Students Accepted?** Yes. **Average GPA:** 3.4.
Required Admission Factors: Essays/personal statement, letters of recommendation, transcript.
Other Admission Factors: Minimum 3.0 GPA required.

ARIZONA STATE UNIVERSITY EAST
East College

Address: 7001 East Williams Field Road #140, Mesa, AZ 85212
Admissions Phone: 480-965-6113 · **Admissions Fax:** 480-965-5158
Admissions E-mail: girvin@asu.edu · **Web Address:** www.eastasu.edu/ecollege/

INSTITUTIONAL INFORMATION

Public/Private: Public. **Total Faculty:** 37. **% Faculty Female:** 38. **% Faculty Part-time:** 11. **Student/Faculty Ratio:** 3:1. **Students in Parent Institution:** 3,983.

PROGRAMS

Masters offered in: Curriculum and instruction; family and consumer sciences/human sciences; health and physical education/fitness; psychology.

STUDENT INFORMATION

Total Students in Program: 180. **% Full-time:** 42. **% Female:** 73. **% Minority:** 9. **% International:** 3.

RESEARCH FACILITIES

Research Facilities: Sustainable technologies, agribusiness, and resources center, microelectronics teaching factory, exercise/wellness/fitness lab.

EXPENSES/FINANCIAL AID

Annual Tuition: In-state $5,038. / Out-of-state $13,558. **Room & Board (on/off campus):** $5,155/$8,110. **Fees:** $41. **Books and Supplies:** $838. **Grants Range From:** $2,993-$18,225. **Loans Range From:** $4,152-$21,861. **% Receiving Financial Aid:** 100. **% Receiving Scholarships/Grants:** 87. **% Receiving Loans:** 100. **Types of Aid Available:** Fellowships, graduate assistantships, institutional work-study, loans, scholarships. **Number of teaching/research assistantships granted each year:** 25. **Assistantship compensation includes:** Partial tuition remission. **Average Salary Stipend:** $4,805.

ADMISSIONS INFORMATION

Application Fee: $50. **Regular Application Deadline:** 4/15. **Regular Notification:** Rolling. **Transfer Students Accepted?** Yes. **Transfer Policy:** Maximum 9 semester hours of related coursework and/or 20% of total program credits may be transferred. **Number of Applications Received:** 123. **% of Applicants Accepted:** 59. **% Accepted Who Enrolled:** 71. **Average GPA:** 3.5. **Average GRE Verbal:** 465. **Average GRE Quantitative:** 597.
Required Admission Factors: GRE, letters of recommendation, transcript.
Other Admission Factors: Minimum 3.0 GPA in last 2 years of undergraduate coursework, resume, and departmental application required.
Program-Specific Admission Factors: Anatomy/physiology with lab, biochemistry with lab chemistry with lab nutrition, introductory statistics, microbiology with lab, and organic chemistry with lab required of nutrition program applicants.

EMPLOYMENT INFORMATION

Placement Office Available? Yes.

ARIZONA STATE UNIVERSITY WEST
College of Arts & Sciences

Address: PO Box 37100, Phoenix, AZ 85069-7100
Admissions Phone: 602-543-6084 · **Admissions Fax:** 602-543-6004

INSTITUTIONAL INFORMATION

Public/Private: Public. **Student/Faculty Ratio:** 1:1. **Students in Parent Institution:** 5,325.

STUDENT INFORMATION

Total Students in Program: 1,540. **% Full-time:** 16. **% Female:** 65.

EXPENSES/FINANCIAL AID

Annual Tuition: In-state $2,412. / Out-of-state $10,278. **Books and Supplies:** $800. **Grants Range From:** $330-$6,952. **Loans Range From:** $350-$18,500. **% Receiving Scholarships/Grants:** 50. **% Receiving Loans:** 52.

ADMISSIONS INFORMATION

Application Fee: $45. **Regular Notification:** Rolling. **Transfer Students Accepted?** No. **Number of Applications Received:** 15.
Required Admission Factors: Essays/personal statement, GRE, letters of recommendation.

ARIZONA STATE UNIVERSITY WEST
College of Human Services

Address: PO Box 37100, Phoenix, AZ 85069-7100
Admissions Phone: 602-543-6600

INSTITUTIONAL INFORMATION
Public/Private: Public. **Evening Classes Available?** Yes. **Students in Parent Institution:** 5,325.

STUDENT INFORMATION
Total Students in Program: 1,540. **% Full-time:** 16. **% Female:** 65.

EXPENSES/FINANCIAL AID
Annual Tuition: In-state $2,412. / Out-of-state $10,278. **Books and Supplies:** $800. **Grants Range From:** $330-$6,952. **Loans Range From:** $350-$18,500. **% Receiving Scholarships/Grants:** 50. **% Receiving Loans:** 52.

ADMISSIONS INFORMATION
Application Fee: $45. **Regular Notification:** Rolling. **Transfer Students Accepted?** No. **Number of Applications Received:** 104. **% of Applicants Accepted:** 88. **% Accepted Who Enrolled:** 90.
Required Admission Factors: GRE, letters of recommendation.

ARKANSAS TECH UNIVERSITY
Graduate School

Address: 1507 North Boulder Avenue, Russellville, AR 72801-2222
Admissions Phone: 479-968-0398 · **Admissions Fax:** 479-968-0452
Admissions E-mail: graduate.school@mail.atu.edu
Web Address: www.graduate.atu.edu

INSTITUTIONAL INFORMATION
Public/Private: Public. **Evening Classes Available?** Yes. **Total Faculty:** 47. **% Faculty Female:** 43. **% Faculty Part-time:** 6. **Students in Parent Institution:** 6,483.

PROGRAMS
Masters offered in: College student counseling and personnel services, conservation biology, counselor education/school counseling and guidance services, education leadership and administration, education, education/teaching of the gifted and talented, educational/instructional media design, elementary education and teaching, English language and literature, English/language arts teacher education, history, information technology, liberal arts and sciences/liberal studies, mass communications/media studies, mathematics teacher education, physical education teaching and coaching, social studies teacher education, Spanish language and literature, teacher education and professional development, specific levels and methods, teaching English as a second or foreign language/ESL language instructor.

STUDENT INFORMATION
Total Students in Program: 392. **% Full-time:** 24. **% Female:** 68. **% Minority:** 6. **% International:** 10.

EXPENSES/FINANCIAL AID
Annual Tuition: In-state $1,467. / Out-of-state $2,934. **Room & Board:** $9,550. **Fees:** $212. **Books and Supplies:** $1,030. **Types of Aid Available:** Graduate assistantships, grants, institutional work-study, loans, scholarships.

ADMISSIONS INFORMATION
Application Fee:. **Priority Application Deadline:** 3/1. **Regular Application Deadline:** 7/1. **Regular Notification:** Rolling. **Transfer Students Accepted?** Yes. **Transfer Policy:** Approval from advisor, chair, and dean required of transfer applicants.
Required Admission Factors: Letters of recommendation, transcript. TOEFL.

Other Admission Factors: Minimum 2.5 GPA required. GRE or GMAT required before the completion of 12 credit hours.

ARMSTRONG ATLANTIC STATE UNIVERSITY
College of Arts & Sciences

Address: 11935 Abercorn Street, Savannah, GA 31419
Admissions Phone: 912-927-5377 · **Admissions Fax:** 912-921-5586
Admissions E-mail: simonemm@mail.armstrong.edu
Web Address: www.armstrong.edu

INSTITUTIONAL INFORMATION
Public/Private: Public. **Evening Classes Available?** Yes. **Total Faculty:** 64. **% Faculty Female:** 36. **% Faculty Part-time:** 8. **Student/Faculty Ratio:** 1:1. **Students in Parent Institution:** 6,653.

STUDENT INFORMATION
Total Students in Program: 56. **% Full-time:** 23. **% Female:** 57. **% Minority:** 20. **% International:** 2.

EXPENSES/FINANCIAL AID
Annual Tuition: In-state $1,998. / Out-of-state $7,974. **Room & Board:** $4,500. **Fees:** $390. **Books and Supplies:** $800. **Grants Range From:** $1.00-$4,000. **Loans Range From:** $500-$8,500. **Types of Aid Available:** Graduate assistantships, institutional work-study, loans, scholarships. **Average student debt, upon graduation:** $5,000. **Number of teaching/research assistantships granted each year:** 34. **Assistantship compensation includes:** Partial tuition remission, salary/stipend. **Average Salary Stipend:** $2,500.

ADMISSIONS INFORMATION
Application Fee: $20. **Regular Application Deadline:** 7/1. **Regular Notification:** Rolling. **Transfer Students Accepted?** Yes. **Average GRE Verbal:** 463. **Average GRE Quantitative:** 307. **Average GRE Analytical:** 700. **Required Admission Factors:** GRE, transcript.

EMPLOYMENT INFORMATION
Placement Office Available? Yes. **Rate of placement:** 90%.

ASHLAND UNIVERSITY
Graduate Programs

Address: 401 College Avenue, Ashland, OH 44805
Admissions Phone: 419-289-5967 · **Admissions Fax:** 419-289-5097

INSTITUTIONAL INFORMATION
Public/Private: Private (nonprofit). **Evening Classes Available?** Yes. **Student/Faculty Ratio:** 14:1. **Students in Parent Institution:** 5,779.

STUDENT INFORMATION
Total Students in Program: 2,964. **% Full-time:** 34. **% Female:** 65.

RESEARCH FACILITIES
Research Facilities: Ashbrook Center for Public Affaris.

EXPENSES/FINANCIAL AID
Annual Tuition: $230-$460 per credit. **Grants Range From:** $300-$1,000. **Loans Range From:** $500-$18,500. **% Receiving Scholarships/Grants:** 3.

ADMISSIONS INFORMATION
Application Fee: $25. **Regular Notification:** Rolling. **Transfer Students Accepted?** No. **Number of Applications Received:** 351. **% of Applicants Accepted:** 100. **% Accepted Who Enrolled:** 100. **Average GPA:** 3.0.
Required Admission Factors: Interview, letters of recommendation, transcript.
Other Admission Factors: Minimum 2.75 GPA required.

EMPLOYMENT INFORMATION
Placement Office Available? Yes.

ASPEN UNIVERSITY
Graduate Studies

Address: 501 South Cherry Street, Suite 350, Denver, CO 80246
Admissions Phone: 303-333-4224 · **Admissions Fax:** 303-336-1144
Admissions E-mail: admissions@aspen.edu · **Web Address:** www.aspen.edu

INSTITUTIONAL INFORMATION

Public/Private: Private (proprietary). **Student/Faculty Ratio:** 5:1. **Students in Parent Institution:** 525.

PROGRAMS

Masters offered in: Business administration and management; business administration/management; business/commerce, education leadership and administration; education; information resources management/cio training; management information systems and services; management information systems.

STUDENT INFORMATION

Total Students in Program: 350. **% Full-time:** 100. **% Female:** 11. **% International:** 4.

EXPENSES/FINANCIAL AID

Annual Tuition: $600 per credit. **Books and Supplies:** $500. **Grants Range From:** $600-$2,000. **% Receiving Financial Aid:** 5.

ADMISSIONS INFORMATION

Application Fee: $75. **Regular Notification:** Rolling. **Transfer Students Accepted?** Yes. **Transfer Policy:** Yes. **Number of Applications Received:** 153. **% of Applicants Accepted:** 40. **% Accepted Who Enrolled:** 100. **Average GPA:** 3.4.
Required Admission Factors: Letters of recommendation, transcript.

ASSEMBLIES OF GOD THEOLOGICAL SEMINARY
Assemblies of God Theological Seminary

Address: 1435 North Glenstone Avenue, Springfield, MO 65802
Admissions Phone: 417-268-1000 · **Admissions Fax:** 417-268-1001
Admissions E-mail: info@agts.edu · **Web Address:** www.agts.edu

INSTITUTIONAL INFORMATION

Public/Private: Private (nonprofit). **Evening Classes Available?** Yes. **Total Faculty:** 29. **% Faculty Female:** 24. **% Faculty Part-time:** 59. **Student/Faculty Ratio:** 12:1. **Students in Parent Institution:** 496.

PROGRAMS

Masters offered in: Divinity/ministry (BD, MDiv); missions/missionary studies and missiology; theological and ministerial studies, theology/theological studies. **Doctorate offered in:** Theological and ministerial studies.

STUDENT INFORMATION

Total Students in Program: 465. **% Full-time:** 49. **% Female:** 28.

EXPENSES/FINANCIAL AID

Annual Tuition: $8,040. **Room & Board:** $10,640. **Fees:** $375. **Books and Supplies:** $987. **Grants Range From:** $500-$4,000. **Loans Range From:** $7,819-$18,460. **% Receiving Scholarships/Grants:** 44. **% Receiving Loans:** 60. **Types of Aid Available:** Institutional work-study, loans, scholarships. **Average student debt, upon graduation:** $49,958.

ADMISSIONS INFORMATION

Application Fee: $35. **Priority Application Deadline:** 7/1. **Regular Application Deadline:** 8/1. **Transfer Students Accepted?** Yes. **Transfer Policy:** Application deadlines and admission requirements are the same as standard admission requirements. **Number of Applications Received:** 180. **% of Applicants Accepted:** 61. **% Accepted Who Enrolled:** 89.
Required Admission Factors: Essays/personal statement, letters of recommendation, transcript.

Other Admission Factors: Baccalaureate degree or it's equivalent from an acceptable 4-year college with a 2.5 minimum GPA.
Complete TJTA exam as part of the orientation/registration process.
Program-Specific Admission Factors: Master of divinity program requires first-year Greek as a prerequisite. Minimum acceptable grade for the Greek prerequisite is C. Doctor of ministry program requires a master of divinity degree with a minimum 3.0 GPA; three years of full-time ministry.

ASSOCIATED MENNONITE BIBLICAL SEMINARY
Graduate & Professional Programs

Address: 3003 Benham Avenue, Elkhart, IN 46517-1999
Admissions Phone: 574-296-6227 · **Admissions Fax:** 574-295-0092
Admissions E-mail: admissions@ambs.edu · **Web Address:** www.ambs.edu

INSTITUTIONAL INFORMATION

Public/Private: Private (nonprofit). **Evening Classes Available?** Yes. **Total Faculty:** 18. **% Faculty Female:** 33. **% Faculty Part-time:** 33. **Student/Faculty Ratio:** 11:1. **Students in Parent Institution:** 191.

PROGRAMS

Masters offered in: Bible/biblical studies, divinity/ministry (BD, MDiv); missions/missionary studies and missiology, pastoral studies/counseling, religious education, theology/theological studies, youth ministry. **First Professional degree offered in:** Divinity/ministry (BD, MDiv), missions/missionary studies and missiology, pastoral studies/counseling, religious education, youth ministry.

STUDENT INFORMATION

Total Students in Program: 191. **% Full-time:** 36. **% Female:** 59. **% Minority:** 3. **% International:** 7.

RESEARCH FACILITIES

Research Facilities: Institute of Mennonite Studies, Mission Study Center.

EXPENSES/FINANCIAL AID

Annual Tuition: $8,370. **Fees:** $40. **Books and Supplies:** $900. **Grants Range From:** $200-$8,370. **Loans Range From:** $3,000-$13,500. **% Receiving Financial Aid:** 75. **% Receiving Scholarships/Grants:** 75. **% Receiving Loans:** 15.

ADMISSIONS INFORMATION

Application Fee: $30. **Priority Application Deadline:** 5/1. **Regular Application Deadline:** 7/1. **Regular Notification:** Rolling. **Transfer Students Accepted?** Yes. **Transfer Policy:** Maximum two-thirds of an MDiv degree and one-half of an MA degree requirements may be transferred. **Number of Applications Received:** 70. **% of Applicants Accepted:** 89. **% Accepted Who Enrolled:** 74. **Average GPA:** 3.0.
Required Admission Factors: Essays/personal statement, letters of recommendation, transcript
Recommended Admission Factors: Interview.
Other Admission Factors: Minimum 2.5 GPA required for unconditional admission.

ASSUMPTION COLLEGE
Graduate School

Address: 500 Salisbury Street, Worcester, MA 01609-1296
Admissions Phone: 508-767-7387 · **Admissions Fax:** 508-767-7030
Admissions E-mail: adumas@assumption.edu
Web Address: www.assumption.edu/graduate

INSTITUTIONAL INFORMATION

Public/Private: Private (nonprofit). **Evening Classes Available?** Yes. **Total Faculty:** 43. **% Faculty Female:** 47. **% Faculty Part-time:** 70. **Student/Faculty Ratio:** 13:1. **Students in Parent Institution:** 2,808.

PROGRAMS

Masters offered in: Business administration/management; counseling psychology; rehabilitation counseling/counselor; special education. **First Professional degree offered in:** Rehabilitation counseling/counselor.

STUDENT INFORMATION

Total Students in Program: 290. **% Full-time:** 36. **% Female:** 78. **% Minority:** 6.

RESEARCH FACILITIES

Research Facilities: Aaron T. Beck Institute.

EXPENSES/FINANCIAL AID

Annual Tuition: $10,476. **Room & Board:** $14,900. **Fees:** $60. **Books and Supplies:** $800. **Grants Range From:** $4,696-$8,372. **Loans Range From:** $850-$18,500. **% Receiving Financial Aid:** 64. **% Receiving Scholarships/Grants:** 1. **% Receiving Loans:** 58. **% Receiving Assistantships:** 1. **% Receiving Other Aid (TBD):** 30. **Types of Aid Available:** Fellowships, graduate assistantships, loans, scholarships. **Average student debt, upon graduation:** $35,200. **Number of fellowships granted each year:** 11. **Number of teaching/research assistantships granted each year:** 4. **Assistantship compensation includes:** Partial tuition remission. **Average Salary Stipend:** $8,372.

ADMISSIONS INFORMATION

Application Fee: $30. **Priority Application Deadline:** 6/1. **Regular Application Deadline:** 7/1. **Regular Notification:** Rolling. **Transfer Students Accepted?** Yes. **Transfer Policy:** MBA–12 max number of transfer credit hours; Counseling Psychology; Rehabilitation Counseling, Special Education & School Counseling–6 max number of transfer credit hours. **Number of Applications Received:** 210. **% of Applicants Accepted:** 78. **% Accepted Who Enrolled:** 85. **Average GPA:** 3.3.
Required Admission Factors: Essays/personal statement, letters of recommendation, transcript.
Program-Specific Admission Factors: MBA—min 2.75 GPA, two letters of recommendation. GMAT, waiver possible. Counseling Psychology—min 3.0 GPA, six undergraduate courses in pyschology, 3 letters of recommendation. Rehabilitation Counseling—min 2.75 GPA, three letters of recommendation.

ATHABASCA UNIVERSITY
Centre for Integrated Studies / Master of Arts—Integrated Studies

Address: One University Drive, Athabasca, Alberta, T9S 3A3 Canada
Admissions Phone: 780-675-6792 · **Admissions Fax:** 780-675-6921
Admissions E-mail: mais@athabascau.ca
Web Address: www.athabascau.ca/mais/program.html

INSTITUTIONAL INFORMATION

Public/Private: Public. **Students in Parent Institution:** 24,257. **Total Students in Program:** 2,135. **% Female:** 49.

ADMISSIONS INFORMATION

Application Fee: $60. **Regular Application Deadline:** 3/1. **Transfer Students Accepted?** Yes. **Transfer Policy:** Application deadline for transfer applicants is the same as program application deadlines. Institution must be accredited and recognized by Athabasca University. **Number of Applications Received:** 25. **% of Applicants Accepted:** 100. **% Accepted Who Enrolled:** 100.
Required Admission Factors: Essays/personal statement, transcript. CV/ resume.
Program-Specific Admission Factors: Admissions essay is an "Intellectual Biography." Questionnaire to be completed as part of program application. MAIS 'Writing Diagnostic' is required as a condition of admission to the program.

ATHENAEUM OF OHIO
Graduate Programs

Address: 6616 Beechmont Avenue, Cincinnati, OH 45230-2091
Admissions Phone: 513-231-2223 · **Admissions Fax:** 513-231-3254
Admissions E-mail: msweeney@mtsm.org · **Web Address:** www.mtsm.org

INSTITUTIONAL INFORMATION

Public/Private: Private (nonprofit). **Evening Classes Available?** Yes. **Students in Parent Institution:** 225.

STUDENT INFORMATION

Total Students in Program: 93. **% Full-time:** 47. **% Female:** 62.

EXPENSES/FINANCIAL AID

Annual Tuition: $10,890. **Fees:** $30. **Grants Range From:** $720-$1,620. **Loans Range From:** $2,600-$6,400. **% Receiving Scholarships/Grants:** 80. **% Receiving Loans:** 20.

ADMISSIONS INFORMATION

Application Fee: $30. **Regular Notification:** Rolling. **Transfer Students Accepted?** Yes.
Required Admission Factors: Essays/personal statement, interview, letters of recommendation, transcript.

ATLANTIC SCHOOL OF THEOLOGY
Graduate & Professional Programs

Address: 660 Francklyn Street, Halifax, Nova Scotia, B3H 3B5 Canada
Admissions Phone: 902-423-6939 · **Admissions Fax:** 902-492-4048
Admissions E-mail: dmaclachlan@astheology.ns.ca
Web Address: www.astheology.ns.ca

INSTITUTIONAL INFORMATION

Public/Private: Public. **Evening Classes Available?** Yes. **Total Faculty:** 9. **% Faculty Female:** 33. **% Faculty Part-time:** 33. **Student/Faculty Ratio:** 16:1. **Students in Parent Institution:** 125.

STUDENT INFORMATION

Total Students in Program: 144. **% Full-time:** 24. **% Female:** 55. **% Minority:** 3.

RESEARCH FACILITIES

Research Facilities: Library.

EXPENSES/FINANCIAL AID

Annual Tuition: $4,840. **Fees:** $60. **Books and Supplies:** $1,250. **% Receiving Financial Aid:** 70. **Types of Aid Available:** Bursaries.

ADMISSIONS INFORMATION

Application Fee: $30. **Regular Application Deadline:** 2/1. **Regular Notification:** Rolling. **Transfer Students Accepted?** Yes. **Transfer Policy:** Full admission requirements need to be met. Transfer up to 50 % of degree program. **Number of Applications Received:** 33. **% of Applicants Accepted:** 85. **Average GPA:** 3.0.
Required Admission Factors: Essays/personal statement, interview, letters of recommendation, transcript.
Other Admission Factors: B average or above.

EMPLOYMENT INFORMATION

% Employed Within 6 Months: 50. **% of master's grads employed in their field upon graduation:** 50. **Rate of placement:** 100%. **Average starting salary:** $25,000.

AUBURN UNIVERSITY
College of Human Sciences

Address: 106 Hargis Hall, Auburn University, AL 36849
Admissions Phone: 334-844-4700 · **Admissions Fax:** 334-844-4348
Admissions E-mail: gradadm@auburn.edu · **Web Address:** www.grad.auburn.edu

INSTITUTIONAL INFORMATION

Public/Private: Public. **Total Faculty:** 40. **% Faculty Female:** 70. **Student/Faculty Ratio:** 5:1. **Students in Parent Institution:** 22,928.

PROGRAMS

Masters offered in: Apparel and textiles, human development and family studies, textile science. **Doctorate offered in:** Apparel and textiles, human development and family studies.

STUDENT INFORMATION

Total Students in Program: 85. **% Full-time:** 42. **% Female:** 81.

RESEARCH FACILITIES

Research Facilities: Space Power Institute, International Center for Aquaculture, Center for Arts & Humanities.

EXPENSES/FINANCIAL AID

Annual Tuition: In-state $4,610. / Out-of-state $13,830. **Room & Board:** $6,686. **Fees:** $218. **Books and Supplies:** $900. **Types of Aid Available:** Fellowships, graduate assistantships.

ADMISSIONS INFORMATION

Application Fee: $25. **Regular Application Deadline:** 5/1. **Transfer Students Accepted?** Yes. **Number of Applications Received:** 77. **% of Applicants Accepted:** 62. **% Accepted Who Enrolled:** 38. **Required Admission Factors:** GRE.

EMPLOYMENT INFORMATION

Placement Office Available? Yes. **% Employed Within 6 Months:** 83. **Rate of placement:** 70%. **Average starting salary:** $40,000.

AUBURN UNIVERSITY
College of Liberal Arts

Address: 106 Hargis Hall, Graduate School, Auburn University, AL 36849
Admissions Phone: 334-844-4700 · **Admissions Fax:** 334-844-4348
Admissions E-mail: gradadm@auburn.edu · **Web Address:** www.grad.auburn.edu

INSTITUTIONAL INFORMATION

Public/Private: Public. **Total Faculty:** 156. **% Faculty Female:** 99. **% Faculty Part-time:** 0. **Student/Faculty Ratio:** 5:1. **Students in Parent Institution:** 23,276

PROGRAMS

Masters offered in: Audiology/audiologist and speech-language pathology/pathologist, English language and literature, French language and literature, history, psychology, public administration, Spanish language and literature. **Doctorate offered in:** English language and literature, history, psychology, public administration. **First Professional degree offered in:** Audiology/audiologist and speech-language pathology/pathologist.

STUDENT INFORMATION

Total Students in Program: 414. **% Full-time:** 49. **% Female:** 66.

RESEARCH FACILITIES

Research Facilities: Space Power Institute, International Center for Aquaculture, Center for Arts & Humanities.

EXPENSES/FINANCIAL AID

Annual Tuition: In-state $4,610. / Out-of-state $13,830. **Room & Board:** $6,686. **Fees:** $218. **Books and Supplies:** $900. **Types of Aid Available:** Graduate assistantships.

ADMISSIONS INFORMATION

Application Fee: $25. **Regular Application Deadline:** 7/7. **Regular Notification:** Rolling. **Transfer Students Accepted?** Yes. **Number of Applications Received:** 557. **% of Applicants Accepted:** 42. **% Accepted Who Enrolled:** 59. **Average GPA:** 3.4.
Required Admission Factors: GRE.

EMPLOYMENT INFORMATION

Placement Office Available? Yes. **% Employed Within 6 Months:** 83. **Rate of placement:** 70%. **Average starting salary:** $38,000.

AUBURN UNIVERSITY
College of Sciences & Mathematics

Address: 106 Hargis Hall, Graduate School, Auburn University, AL 36849
Admissions Phone: 334-844-4700 · **Admissions Fax:** 334-844-4348
Admissions E-mail: gradadm@auburn.edu · **Web Address:** www.grad.auburn.edu

INSTITUTIONAL INFORMATION

Public/Private: Public. **Total Faculty:** 135. **% Faculty Female:** 9. **% Student/Faculty Ratio:** 5:1. **Students in Parent Institution:** 23,276.

PROGRAMS

Masters offered in: Applied mathematics, biology/biological sciences, botany/plant biology, chemistry, geology/earth science, physics. **Doctorate offered in:** Biology/biological sciences, botany/plant biology, chemistry, mathematics, physics.

STUDENT INFORMATION

Total Students in Program: 295. **% Full-time:** 56. **% Female:** 41.

RESEARCH FACILITIES

Research Facilities: Space Power Institute, International Center for Aquaculture, Center for Arts & Humanities.

EXPENSES/FINANCIAL AID

Annual Tuition: In-state $4,610. / Out-of-state $13,830. **Room & Board:** $6,686. **Fees:** $218. **Books and Supplies:** $900. **Types of Aid Available:** Fellowships, graduate assistantships, grants, institutional work-study, scholarships. internship.

ADMISSIONS INFORMATION

Application Fee: $25. **Regular Application Deadline:** 7/7. **Transfer Students Accepted?** Yes. **Number of Applications Received:** 200. **% of Applicants Accepted:** 56. **% Accepted Who Enrolled:** 56. **Average GPA:** 3.2.
Required Admission Factors: GRE.

EMPLOYMENT INFORMATION

Placement Office Available? Yes. **% Employed Within 6 Months:** 83. **Rate of placement:** 70%. **Average starting salary:** $40,000.

AUBURN UNIVERSITY
School of Forestry & Wildlife Sciences

Address: 106 Hargis Hall, Graduate School, Auburn University, AL 36849
Admissions Phone: 334-844-4700 · **Admissions Fax:** 334-844-4348
Admissions E-mail: gradadm@auburn.edu · **Web Address:** www.grad.auburn.edu

INSTITUTIONAL INFORMATION

Public/Private: Public. **Total Faculty:** 29. **% Faculty Female:** 10. **% Faculty Part-time:** 0. **Student/Faculty Ratio:** 5:1. **Students in Parent Institution:** 23,276.

PROGRAMS

Masters offered in: Forest sciences, forestry. **Doctorate offered in:** Forestry.

STUDENT INFORMATION
Total Students in Program: 59. % Full-time: 46. % Female: 36.

RESEARCH FACILITIES
Research Facilities: Space Power Institute, International Center for Aquaculture, Center for Arts & Humanities.

EXPENSES/FINANCIAL AID
Annual Tuition: In-state $4,610. / Out-of-state $13,830. Room & Board: $6,686. Fees: $218. Books and Supplies: $900. Types of Aid Available: Fellowships, graduate assistantships, grants, institutional work-study, loans, scholarships. internship.

ADMISSIONS INFORMATION
Application Fee: $25. Regular Application Deadline: 7/7. Regular Notification: Rolling. Transfer Students Accepted? Yes. Number of Applications Received: 38. % of Applicants Accepted: 58. % Accepted Who Enrolled: 68. Average GPA: 3.6.
Required Admission Factors: GRE.

EMPLOYMENT INFORMATION
Placement Office Available? Yes. % Employed Within 6 Months: 83. Rate of placement: 70%. Average starting salary: $40,000.

AUBURN UNIVERSITY AT MONTGOMERY
School of Sciences

Address: PO Box 244023, Montgomery, AL 36124-4023
Admissions Phone: 334-244-3690 · Admissions Fax: 334-244-3826
Admissions E-mail: Gray@mail.aum.edu · Web Address: www.aum.edu/sciences/

INSTITUTIONAL INFORMATION
Public/Private: Public. Evening Classes Available? Yes. Student/Faculty Ratio: 5:1. Students in Parent Institution: 4,982.

STUDENT INFORMATION
Total Students in Program: 816. % Full-time: 30. % Female: 67.

RESEARCH FACILITIES
Research Facilities: Centers for Business, Government, Demographics.

EXPENSES/FINANCIAL AID
Annual Tuition: In-state $3,072. / Out-of-state $9,216. Room & Board: $2,900. Books and Supplies: $600. Grants Range From: $100-$3,000. Loans Range From: $300-$12,000.

ADMISSIONS INFORMATION
Application Fee: $25. Priority Application Deadline: 8/9. Regular Application Deadline: 8/9. Regular Notification: Rolling. Transfer Students Accepted? Yes. Transfer Policy: Maximum of 6 semester hours may be transferred with a minimum 3.0 GPA (B or better). Good standing at previous institution. Average GRE Verbal: 500. Average GRE Quantitative: 463.
Required Admission Factors: Transcript.
Recommended Admission Factors: GRE, GMAT.
Other Admission Factors: No minimum test score—GPA and test scores are combined to derive a "decision score." Students can get "provisional status" while test scores are pending if undergraduate GPA less than 2.75
Program-Specific Admission Factors: Graduate programs will accept either GRE or GMAT.

EMPLOYMENT INFORMATION
Placement Office Available? Yes.

AUBURN UNIVERSITY MONTGOMERY
School of Liberal Arts

Address: PO Box 244023, Montgomery, AL 36124-4023
Admissions Phone: 334-244-3406 · Admissions Fax: 334-244-3740

INSTITUTIONAL INFORMATION
Public/Private: Public. Evening Classes Available? Yes. Student/Faculty Ratio: 2:1. Students in Parent Institution: 4,982.

STUDENT INFORMATION
Total Students in Program: 816. % Full-time: 30. % Female: 67.

RESEARCH FACILITIES
Research Facilities: Centers for Business, Government, Demographics.

EXPENSES/FINANCIAL AID
Annual Tuition: In-state $3,072. / Out-of-state $9,216. Room & Board: $2,900. Books and Supplies: $600. Grants Range From: $100-$3,000. Loans Range From: $300-$12,000.

ADMISSIONS INFORMATION
Application Fee: $25. Regular Notification: Rolling. Transfer Students Accepted? Yes. Transfer Policy: Maximum six semester hours may be transferred with a minimum 3.0 GPA. Good standing at previous institution. Average GRE Verbal: 465. Average GRE Quantitative: 415.
Required Admission Factors: Transcript.

EMPLOYMENT INFORMATION
Placement Office Available? Yes.

AUGSBURG COLLEGE
Master of Arts in Leadership

Address: 2211 Riverside Avenue, Minneapolis, MN 55454
Admissions Phone: 612-330-1101 · Admissions Fax: 612-330-1784
Admissions E-mail: malinfo@augsburg.edu · Web Address: www.augsburg.edu/mal

INSTITUTIONAL INFORMATION
Public/Private: Private (nonprofit). Students in Parent Institution: 3,375.

STUDENT INFORMATION
Total Students in Program: 92. % Full-time: 25.

EXPENSES/FINANCIAL AID
Annual Tuition: $6,918. Books and Supplies: $300. % Receiving Financial Aid: 100. Average student debt, upon graduation: $20,895.

ADMISSIONS INFORMATION
Application Fee: $35. Regular Application Deadline: 9/1. Regular Notification: Rolling. Transfer Students Accepted? Yes. Transfer Policy: Maximum two courses may be transferred. Number of Applications Received: 32. % of Applicants Accepted: 78. % Accepted Who Enrolled: 100. Average GPA: 3.
Required Admission Factors: Essays/personal statement, letters of recommendation, transcript.
Other Admission Factors: Minimum 3.0 GPA required.

AUGUSTA STATE UNIVERSITY
Psychology Department

Address: 2500 Walton Way, Augusta, GA 30904-2200
Admissions Phone: 706-737-1694 · Admissions Fax: 706-737-1538
Admissions E-mail: pboyd@aug.edu
Web Address: www.aug.edu/psychology

INSTITUTIONAL INFORMATION
Public/Private: Public. Total Faculty: 8. % Faculty Female: 62. % Faculty Part-time: 0. Student/Faculty Ratio: 4:1. Students in Parent Institution: 6,368.

STUDENT INFORMATION

Total Students in Program: 419. **% Full-time:** 32. **% Female:** 68. **% Minority:** 21. **% International:** 3.

RESEARCH FACILITIES

Research Facilities: The department has an animal laboratory.

EXPENSES/FINANCIAL AID

Annual Tuition: In-state $2,648. / Out-of-state $10,616. **Room & Board:** $3,633. **Fees:** $380. **Books and Supplies:** $450. **Loans Range From:** $200-$18,500. **Assistantship compensation includes:** Partial tuition remission.

ADMISSIONS INFORMATION

Application Fee: $20. **Regular Application Deadline:** 6/1. **Regular Notification:** Rolling. **Transfer Students Accepted?** Yes. **Transfer Policy:** Good academic standing at previous institution and requried courses of transfer applicants. **Number of Applications Received:** 33. **% of Applicants Accepted:** 70. **% Accepted Who Enrolled:** 74. **Average GPA:** 3.2. **Average GRE Verbal:** 487. **Average GRE Quantitative:** 526. **Average GRE Analytical Writing:** 4.
Required Admission Factors: GRE, letters of recommendation, transcript. **Other Admission Factors:** Have taken the GRE within the past 5 years with a minimum score of 400 on one of the subtests and at least 450 on the remaining two. If the GRE was taken after 10/01/02, the analytical score must be 3.5 or higher, one of the remaining scores must be 4.
Program-Specific Admission Factors: Prerequisite courses are abnormal psychology; quantitative, methods, and research methods.

EMPLOYMENT INFORMATION

Placement Office Available? Yes. **% Employed Within 6 Months:** 100. **% of master's grads employed in their field upon graduation:** 100. **Rate of placement:** 72%.

AUGUSTANA COLLEGE
Graduate Programs

Address: 2001 South Summit, Sioux Falls, SD 57197
Admissions Phone: 605-274-4043 · **Admissions Fax:** 605-274-4450
Admissions E-mail: graduate@augie.edu
Web Address: www.augie.edu/dept/graduate

INSTITUTIONAL INFORMATION

Public/Private: Private (nonprofit). **Evening Classes Available?** Yes. **Students in Parent Institution:** 1,783.

PROGRAMS

Masters offered in: Nursing; clinical specialist; public health/community; nurse/nursing; teacher education, multiple levels.

STUDENT INFORMATION

Total Students in Program: 56. **% Female:** 84. **% Minority:** 2.

RESEARCH FACILITIES

Research Facilities: Center for Western Studies.

EXPENSES/FINANCIAL AID

Annual Tuition: In-state $16,665. **Fees:** $162.

ADMISSIONS INFORMATION

Application Fee: $50. **Regular Application Deadline:** 8/15. **Regular Notification:** Rolling. **Transfer Students Accepted?** Yes. **Transfer Policy:** Same as for other students. Graduate catalog outlines requirements for credits to be accepted in transfer. **% Accepted Who Enrolled:** 100.
Required Admission Factors: Essays/personal statement, letters of recommendation, transcript.
Other Admission Factors: Minimum 3.0 GPA required.
Program-Specific Admission Factors: BACC degree in nursing, current licensure or eligiblity for licensure to practice nursing in state, and coursework in descriptive and inferential statistics required of nursing program applicants.

EMPLOYMENT INFORMATION

Placement Office Available? Yes.

AURORA UNIVERSITY
George Williams College
School of Social Work

Address: 347 South Gladstone Avenue, Aurora, IL 60506
Admissions Phone: 630-844-5533 · **Admissions Fax:** 630-844-5535
Admissions E-mail: admission@aurora.edu · **Web Address:** www.aurora.edu

INSTITUTIONAL INFORMATION

Public/Private: Private (nonprofit). **Evening Classes Available?** Yes. **Student/Faculty Ratio:** 12:1. **Students in Parent Institution:** 2,391.

STUDENT INFORMATION

Total Students in Program: 1,075. **% Full-time:** 33. **% Female:** 73.

EXPENSES/FINANCIAL AID

Annual Tuition: $13,368.

ADMISSIONS INFORMATION

Application Fee: $25. **Regular Application Deadline:** 6/1. **Regular Notification:** Rolling. **Transfer Students Accepted?** Yes. **Average GPA:** 3.08.
Required Admission Factors: Essays/personal statement, letters of recommendation, transcript.
Other Admission Factors: Minimum 2.75 GPA and statement of purpose required.

EMPLOYMENT INFORMATION

Placement Office Available? Yes. **% Employed Within 6 Months:** 96. **% of master's grads employed in their field upon graduation:** 100.

AURORA UNIVERSITY
School of Professional Studies

Address: 347 South Gladstone Avenue, Aurora, IL 60506
Admissions Phone: 630-844-5292 · **Admissions Fax:** 630-844-5535
Admissions E-mail: jzimmerm@aurora.edu

INSTITUTIONAL INFORMATION

Public/Private: Private (nonprofit). **Evening Classes Available?** Yes. **Students in Parent Institution:** 2,391.

STUDENT INFORMATION

Total Students in Program: 1,075. **% Full-time:** 33. **% Female:** 73.

EXPENSES/FINANCIAL AID

Annual Tuition: $13,368. **% Receiving Financial Aid:** 25. **Average student debt, upon graduation:** $20,000.

ADMISSIONS INFORMATION

Application Fee: $25. **Regular Notification:** Rolling. **Transfer Students Accepted?** Yes. **Number of Applications Received:** 276. **% of Applicants Accepted:** 74. **% Accepted Who Enrolled:** 83.
Required Admission Factors: Essays/personal statement, interview, letters of recommendation, transcript.
Other Admission Factors: Minimum 2.75 GPA required.

EMPLOYMENT INFORMATION

Placement Office Available? Yes.

AUSTIN PEAY STATE UNIVERSITY
College of Arts & Sciences

Address: 601 College Street, Clarksville, TN 37040
Admissions Phone: 931-221-7414 · **Admissions Fax:** 931-221-7641
Admissions E-mail: polstond@apsu.edu

INSTITUTIONAL INFORMATION
Public/Private: Public. **Evening Classes Available?** Yes. **Students in Parent Institution:** 7,440.

STUDENT INFORMATION
Total Students in Program: 455. **% Full-time:** 36. **% Female:** 77.

RESEARCH FACILITIES
Research Facilities: Center for Excellence in Field Biology.

EXPENSES/FINANCIAL AID
Annual Tuition: In-state $3,276. / Out-of-state $8,392. **Room & Board:** $4,280. **Books and Supplies:** $600. **% Receiving Financial Aid:** 37. **Average student debt, upon graduation:** $12,500. **Average Salary Stipend:** $6,450.

ADMISSIONS INFORMATION
Application Fee: $25. **Regular Notification:** Rolling. **Transfer Students Accepted?** Yes.
Required Admission Factors: GRE, letters of recommendation, transcript.
Other Admission Factors: Minimum GRE section scores of 350 (verbal and quantitative) and minimum 2.5 GPA required.
Program-Specific Admission Factors: Minimum GRE section scores of 400 (verbal and quantitative) required of psychology program applicants; interview possible.

EMPLOYMENT INFORMATION
Placement Office Available? Yes.

AUSTIN PRESBYTERIAN THEOLOGICAL SEMINARY
Graduate & Professional Programs

Address: 100 East 27th Street, Austin, TX 78705-5797
Admissions Phone: 512-472-6736 · **Admissions Fax:** 512-479-0738
Admissions E-mail: admissions@mail.austinseminary.edu
Web Address: www.austinseminary.edu

INSTITUTIONAL INFORMATION
Public/Private: Private (nonprofit). **Student/Faculty Ratio:** 14:1. **Students in Parent Institution:** 304.

PROGRAMS
Masters offered in: Bible/biblical studies, divinity/ministry (BD, MDiv), theological studies and religious vocations, theology/theological studies. **Doctorate offered in:** Divinity/ministry (BD, MDiv).

STUDENT INFORMATION
Total Students in Program: 153. **% Full-time:** 7. **% Female:** 36.

RESEARCH FACILITIES
Research Facilities: University of Texas at Austin.

EXPENSES/FINANCIAL AID
Annual Tuition: $6,750. **Room & Board:** $4,200. **Fees:** $85. **Books and Supplies:** $1,080. **Grants Range From:** $330-$13,000. **Loans Range From:** $1,000-$18,500. **% Receiving Financial Aid:** 72. **% Receiving Scholarships/Grants:** 72. **% Receiving Loans:** 25. **Types of Aid Available:** Institutional work-study, loans, scholarships. **Average student debt, upon graduation:** $20,495.

ADMISSIONS INFORMATION
Application Fee: $25. **Priority Application Deadline:** 2/15. **Regular Application Deadline:** 5/15. **Regular Notification:** Rolling. **Transfer Students Accepted?** Yes. **Transfer Policy:** Maximum 1/2 of credit hours required may be transferred. **Number of Applications Received:** 117. **% of Applicants Accepted:** 75.
Required Admission Factors: Essays/personal statement, interview, letters of recommendation, transcript.
Other Admission Factors: Minimum 2.75 GPA required.

EMPLOYMENT INFORMATION
Placement Office Available? Yes. **% Employed Within 6 Months:** 84. **% of master's grads employed in their field upon graduation:** 84. **Rate of placement:** 96%.

AVERETT UNIVERSITY (FORMERLY AVERETT COLLEGE)
Graduate Programs

Address: 420 West Main Street, Danville, VA 24541
Admissions Phone: 434-791-5650 · **Admissions Fax:** 434-799-0658
Admissions E-mail: pwright@averett.edu
Web Address: http://www.averett.edu/gps/mba.html

INSTITUTIONAL INFORMATION
Public/Private: Private (nonprofit). **Evening Classes Available?** Yes. **Total Faculty:** 145. **% Faculty Female:** 26. **% Faculty Part-time:** 95. **Students in Parent Institution:** 2,519.

STUDENT INFORMATION
Total Students in Program: 908. **% Female:** 44.

EXPENSES/FINANCIAL AID
Annual Tuition: $4,050. **% Receiving Financial Aid:** 22. **Average student debt, upon graduation:** $8,660.

ADMISSIONS INFORMATION
Application Fee: $20. **Regular Notification:** Rolling. **Transfer Students Accepted?** No.
Required Admission Factors: Transcript.
Other Admission Factors: Resume and three letters of reference required.

EMPLOYMENT INFORMATION
Placement Office Available? Yes.

AVILA UNIVERSITY (FORMERLY AVILA COLLEGE)
Graduate Programs

Address: 11901 Wornall Road, Kansas City, MO 64145-1698
Admissions Phone: 816-501-3601 · **Admissions Fax:** 816-501-2463
Admissions E-mail: millerdl@mail.avila.edu · **Web Address:** www.avila.edu

INSTITUTIONAL INFORMATION
Public/Private: Private (nonprofit). **Evening Classes Available?** Yes. **Student/Faculty Ratio:** 16:1. **Students in Parent Institution:** 1,800.

PROGRAMS
Masters offered in: Business administration/management; counseling psychology; education.

STUDENT INFORMATION
Total Students in Program: 164. **% Full-time:** 12. **% Female:** 71.

RESEARCH FACILITIES
Research Facilities: Repository of ERIC documents, Women Religious special collection, MOHELA college selection & career planning lab.

EXPENSES/FINANCIAL AID

Annual Tuition: $5,580. Fees: $54. Books and Supplies: $450. Loans Range From: $1,000-$18,500. % Receiving Loans: 100. Average student debt, upon graduation: $14,000.

ADMISSIONS INFORMATION

Application Fee: $20. Regular Application Deadline: 9/6. Regular Notification: Rolling. Transfer Students Accepted? Yes. Number of Applications Received: 60. % of Applicants Accepted: 82. % Accepted Who Enrolled: 86. Average GPA: 3.3.

Required Admission Factors: Interview, transcript.

Other Admission Factors: Program Specific.

EMPLOYMENT INFORMATION

Placement Office Available? Yes. Rate of placement: 96%.

AZUSA PACIFIC UNIVERSITY
College of Liberal Arts & Sciences

Address: 901 East Alosta, Azusa, CA 91702-7000
Admissions Phone: 626-815-5470 · Admissions Fax: 626-815-5447
Admissions E-mail: gradcenter@apu.edu · Web Address: www.apu.edu

INSTITUTIONAL INFORMATION

Public/Private: Private (nonprofit). Evening Classes Available? Yes. Students in Parent Institution: 8,218.

PROGRAMS

Masters offered in: Art/art studies; biochemistry; chemistry; communications and media studies; communications studies/speech communication and rhetoric; communications, journalism, and related fields; computer and information sciences and support services; computer and information sciences; computer and information sciences; engineering; English language and literature; English language and literature/letters; foreign languages/modern languages; graphic design; liberal arts and sciences studies and humanities; liberal arts and sciences/liberal studies; mathematics; physics.

STUDENT INFORMATION

Total Students in Program: 110. % Full-time: 17. % Female: 34.

EXPENSES/FINANCIAL AID

Annual Tuition: $395. Fees: $70. Books and Supplies: $400. Loans Range From: $10,500-$18,500. Types of Aid Available: Graduate assistantships, loans.

ADMISSIONS INFORMATION

Application Fee: $45. Regular Application Deadline: 7/1. Regular Notification: Rolling. Transfer Students Accepted? Yes.

Required Admission Factors: Transcript.

Other Admission Factors: Minimum 3.0 GPA required.

EMPLOYMENT INFORMATION

Placement Office Available? Yes.

AZUSA PACIFIC UNIVERSITY
School of Music

Address: 901 East Alosta, Azusa, CA 91702-7000
Admissions Phone: 626-815-5470 · Admissions Fax: 626-815-5447
Admissions E-mail: gradcenter@apu.edu · Web Address: www.apu.edu

INSTITUTIONAL INFORMATION

Public/Private: Private (nonprofit). Evening Classes Available? Yes. Students in Parent Institution: 8,218.

PROGRAMS

Masters offered in: Conducting, music performance, music, music and performing arts studies, voice and opera.

STUDENT INFORMATION

Total Students in Program: 31. % Full-time: 32. % Female: 71.

EXPENSES/FINANCIAL AID

Fees: $70. Books and Supplies: $400. Loans Range From: $10,500-$18,500.

ADMISSIONS INFORMATION

Application Fee: $45. Regular Application Deadline: 6/15. Regular Notification: Rolling. Transfer Students Accepted? Yes. Transfer Policy: 6 units.

Required Admission Factors: Essays/personal statement, interview, letters of recommendation, transcript.

Other Admission Factors: Minimum 3.0 GPA required.

Program-Specific Admission Factors: Audition requirement for masters in performance.

EMPLOYMENT INFORMATION

Placement Office Available? Yes.

BAKER COLLEGE CENTER FOR GRADUATE STUDIES
Graduate Programs

Address: Baker Online, 1116 West Bristol Road, Flint, MI 48507-5508
Admissions Phone: 800-469-3165 · Admissions Fax: 810-766-4399
Admissions E-mail: cgurde01@baker.edu · Web Address: www.baker.edu

INSTITUTIONAL INFORMATION

Public/Private: Private (nonprofit). Evening Classes Available? Yes. Total Faculty: 241. % Faculty Female: 53. % Faculty Part-time: 95. Student/Faculty Ratio: 8:1. Students in Parent Institution: 31,000.

STUDENT INFORMATION

Total Students in Program: 1,090. % Full-time: 62.

EXPENSES/FINANCIAL AID

Annual Tuition: $6,500. Books and Supplies: $900. Grants Range From: $2,625-$9,000. Loans Range From: $2,625-$9,000. % Receiving Financial Aid: 68. % Receiving Loans: 100. Types of Aid Available: Grants, loans. Average Salary Stipend: $0.

ADMISSIONS INFORMATION

Application Fee: $25. Priority Application Deadline: 7/1. Regular Application Deadline: 9/30. Regular Notification: Rolling. Transfer Students Accepted? Yes. Transfer Policy: Course must be from a regionally accredited school with a grade of 3.0 or better. Number of Applications Received: 890. % of Applicants Accepted: 74. % Accepted Who Enrolled: 94. Average GPA: 2.9.

Required Admission Factors: Essays/personal statement, letters of recommendation, transcript. Three years full-time work experience.

Recommended Admission Factors: GMAT, GRE.

Other Admission Factors: Minimum 2.5 GPA and at least three years of full-time work experience required.

EMPLOYMENT INFORMATION

Placement Office Available? Yes. Rate of placement: 98%.

BAKER UNIVERSITY
School of Professional & Graduate Studies

Address: 8001 College BoulevardSuite 100, Overland Park, KS 66210
Admissions Phone: 913-491-4432 · **Admissions Fax:** 913-491-0470
Admissions E-mail: jasnicar@bakeru.edu · **Web Address:** www.bakerspgs.edu

INSTITUTIONAL INFORMATION

Public/Private: Private (nonprofit). **Evening Classes Available?** Yes. **Total Faculty:** 304. **% Faculty Female:** 50. **% Faculty Part-time:** 99. **Student/Faculty Ratio:** 17:1. **Students in Parent Institution:** 3,192.

STUDENT INFORMATION

Total Students in Program: 918. **% Full-time:** 81. **% Female:** 48.

EXPENSES/FINANCIAL AID

Annual Tuition: In-state $3,510. **Books and Supplies:** $800. **% Receiving Financial Aid:** 37. **% Receiving Loans:** 100. **Average student debt, upon graduation:** $10,000.

ADMISSIONS INFORMATION

Application Fee: $20. **Regular Notification:** Rolling. **Transfer Students Accepted?** No. **Average GPA:** 3.0.
Required Admission Factors: Letters of recommendation, transcript.
Other Admission Factors: Minimum 2 full-time years of work experience required.

EMPLOYMENT INFORMATION

Placement Office Available? Yes.

BALL STATE UNIVERSITY
College of Communication, Information, & Media

Address: 2000 West University Avenue, Muncie, IN 47304
Admissions Phone: 765-285-6000 · **Admissions Fax:** 765-285-6002
Admissions E-mail: ccim@BSu.edu · **Web Address:** www.bsu.edu/cim/

INSTITUTIONAL INFORMATION

Public/Private: Public. **Evening Classes Available?** Yes. **Total Faculty:** 33. **Students in Parent Institution:** 18,043.

STUDENT INFORMATION

Total Students in Program: 200. **% Full-time:** 61. **% Female:** 56.

RESEARCH FACILITIES

Research Facilities: Center for Middletown Studies, Wellness Institute, Center for Gerontology, Center for Teaching and Learning Advancement, Center for Teaching Technology.

EXPENSES/FINANCIAL AID

Annual Tuition: In-state $4,068. / Out-of-state $8,284. **Room & Board:** $10,346. **Fees:** $204. **Books and Supplies:** $1,000. **Grants Range From:** $250-$10,000. **Loans Range From:** $250-$10,000. **% Receiving Assistantships:** 40. **Types of Aid Available:** Graduate assistantships, loans. **Number of teaching/research assistantships granted each year:** 80. **Assistantship compensation includes:** Full tuition remission, salary/stipend. **Average Salary Stipend:** $7,349.

ADMISSIONS INFORMATION

Application Fee: $35. **Priority Application Deadline:** 3/1. **Regular Application Deadline:** 3/1. **Regular Notification:** Rolling. **Transfer Students Accepted?** Yes. **Transfer Policy:** Same as for nontransfer students. **Number of Applications Received:** 137. **% Accepted Who Enrolled:** 65. **Average GPA:** 3.2.

Required Admission Factors: Transcript.
Other Admission Factors: 2.75 GPA

EMPLOYMENT INFORMATION

Placement Office Available? Yes. **% Employed Within 6 Months:** 80. **Rate of placement:** 90%. **Average starting salary:** $30,000.

BALL STATE UNIVERSITY
College of Fine Arts

Address: 200 West University Avenue, Muncie, IN 47304
Admissions Phone: 765-285-5502 · **Admissions Fax:** 765-285-5401
Admissions E-mail: kkoriat2@bsu.edu · **Web Address:** www.bsu.edu/cfal

INSTITUTIONAL INFORMATION

Public/Private: Public. **Evening Classes Available?** Yes. **Total Faculty:** 81. **Students in Parent Institution:** 18,043.

PROGRAMS

Masters offered in: Accounting and computer science; accounting; adult and continuing education administration; American literature (United States); anthropology; apparel and textiles; architecture (BArch, BA/BS, MArch, MA/MS, PhD); art/art studies; business administration/management; business teacher education; chemistry; city/urban, community, and regional planning; clinical psychology; cognitive psychology and psycholinguistics; communications studies/speech communication and rhetoric; computer and information sciences, counseling psychology; counselor education/school counseling and guidance services; creative writing; criminal justice/law enforcement administration; curriculum and instruction; dietetics/dietician (RD); digital communications and media/multimedia; education leadership and administration; educational psychology; elementary education and teaching; English composition; English language and literature; environmental science; family and consumer sciences/home economics teacher education; family and consumer sciences/human sciences; family practice nurse/nurse practitioner; foods, nutrition, and wellness studies, geography; geology/earth science, gerontology; health and physical education, historic preservation and conservation; history, information science/studies; journalism; landscape architecture (BS, BSLA, BLA, MSLA, MLA, PhD); linguistics; mathematics teacher education; mathematics; music performance, music theory and composition; music/music and performing arts studies, natural resources/conservation, nursing—registered nurse training (RN, ASN, BSN, MSN); nursing administration (MSN, MS, PhD); nursing clinical specialist; physical education teaching and coaching; physics teacher education; physics; physiology; political science and government; public administration; public relations/image management; school psychology; science teacher education/general science teacher education; secondary education and teaching; social psychology; social science teacher education; social sciences, sociology; special education; speech-language pathology/pathologist; statistics, teaching English as a second or foreign language/ESL language instructor; technology teacher education/industrial arts teacher education. **Doctorate offered in:** Adult and continuing education administration, American literature (united states), audiology/audiologist and hearing sciences, chemistry, computer and information sciences, counseling psychology.

STUDENT INFORMATION

Total Students in Program: 98. **% Full-time:** 53. **% Female:** 60. **% Minority:** 8. **% International:** 24.

RESEARCH FACILITIES

Research Facilities: Center for Middletown Studies, Wellness Institute, Center for Gerontology, Center for Teaching and Learning Advancement, Center for Teaching Technology.

EXPENSES/FINANCIAL AID

Annual Tuition: In-state $4,824. / Out-of-state $11,516. **Room & Board:** $10,346. **Fees:** $1,200. **Books and Supplies:** $1,000. **Grants Range From:** $4,000-$21,000. **Loans Range From:** $50-$5,000. **% Receiving Assistantships:** 40. **Types of Aid Available:** Fellowships, graduate assistantships, loans.

Number of teaching/research assistantships granted each year: 64. Average Salary Stipend: $7,167.

ADMISSIONS INFORMATION

Application Fee: $35. **Priority Application Deadline:** 3/1. **Regular Notification:** Rolling. **Transfer Students Accepted?** Yes. **Transfer Policy:** Same as for first-time graduate students. **Number of Applications Received:** 68. **% of Applicants Accepted:** 68. **% Accepted Who Enrolled:** 65. **Average GPA:** 3.3. **Average GRE Verbal:** 479. **Average GRE Quantitative:** 471. **Average GRE Analytical Writing:** 3.8.
Required Admission Factors: Transcript.
Program-Specific Admission Factors: Minimum 2.75 GPA or 3.0 in latter half required of master's programs applicants. Minimum 3.2 GPA in master's required of doctoral program applicants. Transcripts, interview, and essay required of doctoral program applicants; recommended for master's programs.

EMPLOYMENT INFORMATION

Placement Office Available? Yes. **% Employed Within 6 Months:** 70. **Rate of placement:** 90%. **Average starting salary:** $30,000.

BALL STATE UNIVERSITY
College of Sciences & Humanities

Address: 2000 West University Avenue, Muncie, IN 47304
Admissions Phone: 765-285-1042 · **Admissions Fax:** 765-285-8980
Admissions E-mail: ASKUS@bsu.edu · **Web Address:** www.bsu.edu/sh/

INSTITUTIONAL INFORMATION

Public/Private: Public. **Evening Classes Available?** Yes. **Total Faculty:** 304. **Students in Parent Institution:** 18,043.

STUDENT INFORMATION

Total Students in Program: 620. **% Full-time:** 59. **% Female:** 58.

RESEARCH FACILITIES

Research Facilities: Center for Middletown Studies, Wellness Institute, Center for Gerontology, Center for Teaching and Learning Advancement, Center for Teaching Technology.

EXPENSES/FINANCIAL AID

Annual Tuition: In-state $4,068. / Out-of-state $8,284. **Room & Board:** $10,346. **Fees:** $204. **Books and Supplies:** $1,000. **Grants Range From:** $250-$10,000. **Loans Range From:** $250-$10,000. **% Receiving Assistantships:** 40. **Types of Aid Available:** Graduate assistantships, loans. **Number of teaching/research assistantships granted each year:** 248. **Average Salary Stipend:** $14,460.

ADMISSIONS INFORMATION

Application Fee: $35. **Priority Application Deadline:** 3/1. **Regular Application Deadline:** 8/1. **Regular Notification:** Rolling. **Transfer Students Accepted?** Yes. **Transfer Policy:** Same as for nontransfers. **Number of Applications Received:** 517. **% of Applicants Accepted:** 68. **% Accepted Who Enrolled:** 56. **Average GPA:** 3.3.
Required Admission Factors: Transcript.
Other Admission Factors: 2.75 GPA.

EMPLOYMENT INFORMATION

Placement Office Available? Yes. **% Employed Within 6 Months:** 80. **Rate of placement:** 90%. **Average starting salary:** $30,000.

BALTIMORE HEBREW UNIVERSITY
Peggy Meyerhoff Pearlstone School of Graduate Studies

Address: 5800 Park Heights Avenue, Baltimore, MD 21215
Admissions Phone: 410-578-6967 · **Admissions Fax:** 410-578-6940
Admissions E-mail: keyser@bhu.edu · **Web Address:** www.bhu.edu

INSTITUTIONAL INFORMATION

Public/Private: Private (nonprofit). **Evening Classes Available?** Yes. **Student/Faculty Ratio:** 8:1. **Students in Parent Institution:** 192

STUDENT INFORMATION

Total Students in Program: 61. **% Full-time:** 15. **% Female:** 62.

EXPENSES/FINANCIAL AID

Annual Tuition: In-state $6,000. **Fees:** $30. **Books and Supplies:** $600. **Grants Range From:** $50-$5,000. **% Receiving Financial Aid:** 25. **% Receiving Scholarships/Grants:** 80. **% Receiving Loans:** 5. **Number of fellowships granted each year:** 2. **Average amount of individual fellowships per year:** $5,000.

ADMISSIONS INFORMATION

Application Fee: $35. **Regular Notification:** Rolling. **Transfer Students Accepted?** Yes. **Transfer Policy:** Maximum . credits may be transferred into master's programs. **Number of Applications Received:** 53. **% of Applicants Accepted:** 79. **% Accepted Who Enrolled:** 74.
Required Admission Factors: Interview, transcript.
Program-Specific Admission Factors: Five letters of recommendation required of doctoral program applicants.

EMPLOYMENT INFORMATION

% of master's grads employed in their field upon graduation: 80.

BANGOR THEOLOGICAL SEMINARY
Professional Program

Address: 300 Union Street, Bangor, ME 04401-4699
Admissions Phone: 800-287-6781, ext. 126
Admissions Fax: 207-990-1267
Admissions E-mail: enrollment@bts.edu · **Web Address:** www.bts.edu

INSTITUTIONAL INFORMATION

Public/Private: Private (nonprofit). **Evening Classes Available?** Yes. **Total Faculty:** 10. **% Faculty Female:** 30. **% Faculty Part-time:** 20. **Students in Parent Institution:** 180.

PROGRAMS

Masters offered in: Divinity/ministry (BD, MDiv), theological and ministerial studies, theological studies and religious vocations, theology/theological studies. **Doctorate offered in:** Divinity/ministry (BD, MDiv). **First Professional degree offered in:** Divinity/ministry (BD, MDiv).

STUDENT INFORMATION

Total Students in Program: 155. **% Full-time:** 23. **% Female:** 17.

EXPENSES/FINANCIAL AID

Annual Tuition: $9,090. **Room & Board:** $10,760. **Fees:** $50. **Books and Supplies:** $750. **Grants Range From:** $500-$2,500. **Loans Range From:** $1,000-$18,500. **% Receiving Financial Aid:** 98. **% Receiving Scholarships/Grants:** 100. **% Receiving Loans:** 80. **Types of Aid Available:** Graduate assistantships, grants, institutional work-study, loans, scholarships. **Average student debt, upon graduation:** $28,500.

ADMISSIONS INFORMATION

Application Fee: $40. **Priority Application Deadline:** 4/1. **Regular Application Deadline:** 7/15. **Regular Notification:** Rolling. **Transfer Students Accepted?** Yes. **Transfer Policy:** Minimum grade of C required of transfer applicants. **Number of Applications Received:** 98. **% of Applicants Accepted:** 65. **% Accepted Who Enrolled:** 94.
Required Admission Factors: Essays/personal statement, interview, letters of recommendation, transcript.

Program-Specific Admission Factors: Graduate programs require bachelor's degree except for the unique "Bangor Plan". This program is designed for those who feel a call to ministry but do not have a bachelor's degree.

EMPLOYMENT INFORMATION
% of doctoral grads employed in their field upon graduation: 100.

BAPTIST BIBLE COLLEGE
Graduate School

Address: 538 Venard Road, Clarks Summit, PA 18411
Admissions Phone: 570-585-9345 · **Admissions Fax:** 570-585-9359
Admissions E-mail: gradadmissions@bbc.edu
Web Address: www.bbc.edu

INSTITUTIONAL INFORMATION
Public/Private: Private (nonprofit). **Evening Classes Available?** Yes. **Total Faculty:** 29. **% Faculty Female:** 17. **% Faculty Part-time:** 90. **Student/Faculty Ratio:** 20:1. **Students in Parent Institution:** 735.

PROGRAMS
Masters offered in: Marriage and family therapy/counseling.

STUDENT INFORMATION
Total Students in Program: 166. **% Full-time:** 39. **% Female:** 70.

EXPENSES/FINANCIAL AID
Annual Tuition: $7,152. **Fees:** $250. **Books and Supplies:** $500. **Grants Range From:** $250-$2,500. **Loans Range From:** $1,000-$7,000. **% Receiving Financial Aid:** 20. **% Receiving Scholarships/Grants:** 100. **Types of Aid Available:** Grants, scholarships.

ADMISSIONS INFORMATION
Application Fee: $30. **Regular Application Deadline:** 7/1. **Regular Notification:** Rolling. **Transfer Students Accepted?** Yes. **Transfer Policy:** Send completed application, all references, and all transcripts. Registrar will determine number of credits that will transfer. **Number of Applications Received:** 43. **% of Applicants Accepted:** 100. **Average GPA:** 3.0.
Required Admission Factors: Letters of recommendation, transcript.
Other Admission Factors: Minimum GPA of 3.0 or must take GRE; theology prerequisites; TOEFL exam for international students is required.

EMPLOYMENT INFORMATION
Placement Office Available? Yes. **% Employed Within 6 Months:** 100. **% of master's grads employed in their field upon graduation:** 100. **Rate of placement:** 100%. **Average starting salary:** $25,000.

BARD COLLEGE
Bard Center for Environmental Policy

Address: PO Box 5000, Hegeman 001, Annandale-on-Hudson, NY 12504-5000
Admissions Phone: 845-758-7073 · **Admissions Fax:** 845-758-7636
Admissions E-mail: cep@bard.edu · **Web Address:** www.bard.edu/cep

INSTITUTIONAL INFORMATION
Public/Private: Private (nonprofit). **Student/Faculty Ratio:** 1:1. **Students in Parent Institution:** 1,423.

PROGRAMS
Masters offered in: Community organization and advocacy, cultural resources management and policy analysis, environmental studies, historic preservation and conservation, historic preservation and conservation, multi/interdisciplinary studies, natural resources management and policy, natural resources management and policy, public administration and services, public policy analysis, social sciences. **First Professional degree offered in:** Environmental stud-

ies, law (LLB, JD), natural resources management and policy, natural resources management and policy.

STUDENT INFORMATION
Total Students in Program: 117. **% Full-time:** 100. **% Female:** 50.

RESEARCH FACILITIES
Research Facilities: Ecology field station.
NYSERDA contract.

EXPENSES/FINANCIAL AID
Annual Tuition: $22,250. **Room & Board:** $14,000. **Fees:** $250. **Books and Supplies:** $300. **Grants Range From:** $1,000-$10,000. **Loans Range From:** $10,000-$20,000. **Types of Aid Available:** Fellowships, grants, loans, scholarships.

ADMISSIONS INFORMATION
Application Fee: $50. **Priority Application Deadline:** 11/15. **Regular Application Deadline:** 2/1. **Regular Notification:** 3/31. **Transfer Students Accepted?** No. **Number of Applications Received:** 100. **% of Applicants Accepted:** 50. **% Accepted Who Enrolled:** 40.
Required Admission Factors: Essays/personal statement, GRE, letters of recommendation, transcript.
Recommended Admission Factors: Interview.
Other Admission Factors: Samples of written work required.

BARD COLLEGE
Bard Graduate Center for Studies in the Decorative Arts, Design, & Culture

Address: 18 West 86th Street, New York, NY 10024
Admissions Phone: 212-501-3019 · **Admissions Fax:** 212-501-3079
Admissions E-mail: admissions@bgc.bard.edu · **Web Address:** www.bgc.bard.edu

INSTITUTIONAL INFORMATION
Public/Private: Private (nonprofit).

RESEARCH FACILITIES
Research Facilities: Ecology field station.

ADMISSIONS INFORMATION
Application Fee: $50. **Regular Application Deadline:** 2/5. **Transfer Students Accepted?** Yes. **Transfer Policy:** Transfer applicants accepted for fall term only. Maximum 12 credit hours may be transferred into master program.
Required Admission Factors: Essays/personal statement, GRE, interview, letters of recommendation, transcript.
Program-Specific Admission Factors: Reading knowledge of French, Italian, or German required of MA program applicants. Reading knowledge of any two of French, Italian, or German and MA in decorative arts or related field required of PhD program applicants.

BARD COLLEGE
Center for Curatorial Studies

Address: PO Box 5000, Annandale-on-Hudson, NY 12504-5000
Admissions Phone: 845-758-7598 · **Admissions Fax:** 845-758-2442
Admissions E-mail: CCS@bard.edu · **Web Address:** www.bard.edu/ccs/

INSTITUTIONAL INFORMATION
Public/Private: Private (nonprofit). **Students in Parent Institution:** 1,423.

PROGRAMS
Masters offered in: Art history, criticism, and conservation; visual and performing arts.

STUDENT INFORMATION
Total Students in Program: 117. % Full-time: 100. % Female: 50.

EXPENSES/FINANCIAL AID
Annual Tuition: $18,900. Room & Board: $15,115. Fees: $100. Books and Supplies: $1,320. % Receiving Financial Aid: 90. Types of Aid Available: Fellowships, graduate assistantships, scholarships.

ADMISSIONS INFORMATION
Application Fee: $50. Regular Application Deadline: 2/15. Regular Notification: 3/31. Transfer Students Accepted? No. Number of Applications Received: 60.
Required Admission Factors: Essays/personal statement, letters of recommendation, transcript.

EMPLOYMENT INFORMATION
% Employed Within 6 Months: 75. % of master's grads employed in their field upon graduation: 42. Rate of placement: 99.9%.

BARD COLLEGE
The Master of Arts in Teaching Program

Address: Bard College MAT Program, PO Box 5000, Annandale-on-Hudson, NY 12504-5000
Admissions Phone: 845-758-7145 · **Admissions Fax:** 845-758-7149
Admissions E-mail: mat@bard.edu · **Web Address:** www.bard.edu/mat

INSTITUTIONAL INFORMATION
Public/Private: Private (nonprofit). Total Faculty: 17. % Faculty Female: 53. % Faculty Part-time: 59. Student/Faculty Ratio: 3:1.

PROGRAMS
Masters offered in: English language and literature, mathematics, secondary education and teaching, social sciences. First Professional degree offered in: Secondary education and teaching.

STUDENT INFORMATION
Total Students in Program: 24. % Full-time: 100. % Female: 75. % Minority: 12. % International: 8.

EXPENSES/FINANCIAL AID
Annual Tuition: $24,500. Room & Board: $6,000. Fees: $400. Books and Supplies: $800. Grants Range From: $4,000-$18,000. Loans Range From: $4,000-$18,000. % Receiving Financial Aid: 90. Types of Aid Available: Fellowships, graduate assistantships, grants, loans, scholarships.

ADMISSIONS INFORMATION
Application Fee: $50. Regular Application Deadline: 1/21. Regular Notification: 2/18. Transfer Students Accepted? Yes. Transfer Policy: Students interested in transferring into the MAT program should contact the office to arrange a meeting and transcript review. Number of Applications Received: 49. % of Applicants Accepted: 82. % Accepted Who Enrolled: 60. Average GPA: 3.0. Required Admission Factors: Essays/personal statement, interview, letters of recommendation, transcript. Other Admission Factors: Program applicants must have received a bachelor's degree from an accredited institution in the liberal arts with a major in the discipline (or the equivalent) they intend to study at Bard.

BARD COLLEGE
Milton Avery Graduate School of the Arts

Address: PO Box 5000, Annandale-on-Hudson, NY 12504-5000
Admissions Phone: 845-758-7481 · **Admissions Fax:** 845-758-7507

INSTITUTIONAL INFORMATION
Public/Private: Private (nonprofit). Student/Faculty Ratio: 4:1. Students in Parent Institution: 1,423.

STUDENT INFORMATION
Total Students in Program: 117. % Full-time: 100. % Female: 50.

RESEARCH FACILITIES
Research Facilities: Ecology field station.

EXPENSES/FINANCIAL AID
% Receiving Financial Aid: 64. Average student debt, upon graduation: $17,000 Number of fellowships granted each year: 41.

ADMISSIONS INFORMATION
Application Fee: $50. Transfer Students Accepted? Yes.
Required Admission Factors: Essays/personal statement, letters of recommendation, transcript.

BARRY UNIVERSITY
School of Arts & Sciences

Address: 11300 N.E. Second Avenue, Miami Shores, FL 33161
Admissions Phone: 305-899-3100 · **Admissions Fax:** 305-899-2971
Admissions E-mail: admissions@mail.barry.edu

INSTITUTIONAL INFORMATION
Public/Private: Private (nonprofit). Evening Classes Available? Yes. Students in Parent Institution: 8,650.

STUDENT INFORMATION
Total Students in Program: 2,343. % Full-time: 34. % Female: 75.

RESEARCH FACILITIES
Research Facilities: Pediatric clinics.

EXPENSES/FINANCIAL AID
Annual Tuition: In-state $9,360. % Receiving Financial Aid: 28. Average student debt, upon graduation: $21,139. Number of teaching/research assistantships granted each year: 4.

ADMISSIONS INFORMATION
Application Fee: $30. Regular Notification: Rolling. Transfer Students Accepted? Yes. Transfer Policy: Maximum six credit hours relevant to area of study with a minimum 3.0 GPA may be transferred with ap. Number of Applications Received: 100. % of Applicants Accepted: 63. % Accepted Who Enrolled: 38. Average GPA: 3.26.
Required Admission Factors: Essays/personal statement, letters of recommendation, transcript.
Other Admission Factors: Minimum 3.0 GPA required; other requirements vary by program.
Program-Specific Admission Factors: Portfolio required of photography applicants.

BARRY UNIVERSITY
School of Human Performance

Address: 11300 N.E. Second Avenue, Miami Shores, FL 33161
Admissions Phone: 305-899-3490 · **Admissions Fax:** 305-899-3556
Admissions E-mail: dsherman@mail.barry.edu

INSTITUTIONAL INFORMATION
Public/Private: Private (nonprofit). Evening Classes Available? Yes. Students in Parent Institution: 8,650.

STUDENT INFORMATION
Total Students in Program: 2,343. % Full-time: 34. % Female: 75.

RESEARCH FACILITIES
Research Facilities: Pediatric clinics.

EXPENSES/FINANCIAL AID

Annual Tuition: In-state $9,360. **% Receiving Financial Aid:** 68. **Number of teaching/research assistantships granted each year:** 22.

ADMISSIONS INFORMATION

Application Fee: $30. **Regular Notification:** Rolling. **Transfer Students Accepted?** Yes. **Transfer Policy:** Maximum six credit hours with a minimum grade of B may be transferred. **Number of Applications Received:** 40. **% of Applicants Accepted:** 58. **% Accepted Who Enrolled:** 70. **Required Admission Factors:** GRE, letters of recommendation, transcript. **Other Admission Factors:** Minimum 3.0 GPA required.

BARRY UNIVERSITY
School of Social Work

Address: 11300 N.E. Second Avenue, Miami Shores, FL 33161
Admissions Phone: 305-899-3900 · **Admissions Fax:** 305-899-3934
Admissions E-mail: sswadm@mail.barry.edu

INSTITUTIONAL INFORMATION

Public/Private: Private (nonprofit). **Evening Classes Available?** Yes. **Students in Parent Institution:** 8,650.

STUDENT INFORMATION

Total Students in Program: 2,343. **% Full-time:** 34. **% Female:** 75.

RESEARCH FACILITIES

Research Facilities: Pediatric clinics.

EXPENSES/FINANCIAL AID

Annual Tuition: In-state $9,360. **% Receiving Financial Aid:** 69. **Average student debt, upon graduation:** $9,071.

ADMISSIONS INFORMATION

Application Fee: $30. **Transfer Students Accepted?** Yes. **Transfer Policy:** Maximum 28 credit hours may be transferred from an accredited social work program (maximum 6 credits). **Number of Applications Received:** 297. **% of Applicants Accepted:** 70. **% Accepted Who Enrolled:** 89. **Required Admission Factors:** Essays/personal statement, letters of recommendation, transcript. **Other Admission Factors:** Minimum 3.0 GPA required. **Program-Specific Admission Factors:** Additional criteria required of advanced standing program applicants.

BASTYR UNIVERSITY
Graduate Programs

Address: 14500 Juanita Drive, NE, Kenmore, WA 98028-4966
Admissions Phone: 425-602-3330 · **Admissions Fax:** 425.823.6222
Admissions E-mail: admiss@bastyr.edu · **Web Address:** www.bastyr.edu

INSTITUTIONAL INFORMATION

Public/Private: Private (nonprofit). **Evening Classes Available?** Yes. **Students in Parent Institution:** 996.

PROGRAMS

Masters offered in: Acupuncture and traditional Chinese/oriental medicine, clinical nutrition/nutritionist, dietetics/dietician (RD), nutrition sciences, psychology, systems science and theory. **Doctorate offered in:** Acupuncture and traditional Chinese/oriental medicine. **First Professional degree offered in:** Naturopathic medicine/naturopathy (ND).

STUDENT INFORMATION

Total Students in Program: 750. **% Full-time:** 89. **% Female:** 80.

RESEARCH FACILITIES

Research Facilities: Bastyr University Research Institute.

EXPENSES/FINANCIAL AID

Annual Tuition: $17,796. **Room & Board:** $4,500. **Books and Supplies:** $1,461. **Grants Range From:** $500-$5,000. **Loans Range From:** $8,500-$18,500. **Types of Aid Available:** Institutional work-study, loans, scholarships.

ADMISSIONS INFORMATION

Application Fee: $75. **Regular Application Deadline:** 3/15. **Transfer Students Accepted?** Yes. **Number of Applications Received:** 386. **% of Applicants Accepted:** 73. **% Accepted Who Enrolled:** 70. **Average GPA:** 3.3. **Required Admission Factors:** Essays/personal statement, letters of recommendation, transcript.

BAY PATH COLLEGE
The Graduate School at Bay Path College

Address: 588 Longmeadow Street, Longmeadow, MA 01106
Admissions Phone: 413-565-1332 · **Admissions Fax:** 413-565-1105
Admissions E-mail: graduate@baypath.edu
Web Address: www.baypath.edu/academics_gradschool.htm

INSTITUTIONAL INFORMATION

Public/Private: Private (nonprofit). **Evening Classes Available?** Yes. **Students in Parent Institution:** 1,417.

PROGRAMS

Masters offered in: Communications technologies and support services, occupational therapy/therapist.

STUDENT INFORMATION

Total Students in Program: 70. **% Full-time:** 83. **% Female:** 83.

EXPENSES/FINANCIAL AID

Annual Tuition: $7,704.

ADMISSIONS INFORMATION

Application Fee: $45. **Priority Application Deadline:** 5/1. **Regular Application Deadline:** 10/1. **Regular Notification:** Rolling. **Transfer Students Accepted?** Yes. **Required Admission Factors:** Essays/personal statement, GRE, interview, letters of recommendation, transcript.

BAYLOR COLLEGE OF DENTISTRY
Graduate Programs

Address: PO Box 660677, Dallas, TX 75266-0677
Admissions Phone: 214-828-8230 · **Admissions Fax:** 214-874-4567
Admissions E-mail: jward@bcd.tamhsc.edu · **Web Address:** www.bcd.tamhsc.edu

INSTITUTIONAL INFORMATION

Public/Private: Public. **Students in Parent Institution:** 538

STUDENT INFORMATION

Total Students in Program: 119. **% Full-time:** 68. **% Female:** 38.

EXPENSES/FINANCIAL AID

ADMISSIONS INFORMATION

Application Fee: $35. **Priority Application Deadline:** 10/1. **Regular Application Deadline:** 11/1. **Regular Notification:** Rolling. **Transfer Students Accepted?** No. **Number of Applications Received:** 910. **% of Applicants Accepted:** 10. **Average GPA:** 3.5. **Required Admission Factors:** Essays/personal statement, GRE, interview, letters of recommendation, transcript. TOEFL. **Other Admission Factors:** 3.0 is the minumum GPA.

BAYLOR UNIVERSITY
College of Arts & Sciences

Address: PO Box 97264, Waco, TX 76798-7264
Admissions Phone: 254-710-3584 · **Admissions Fax:** 254-710-3870
Admissions E-mail: debra_j_williams@baylor.edu
Web Address: www.baylor.edu

INSTITUTIONAL INFORMATION
Public/Private: Private (nonprofit). **Students in Parent Institution:** 13,719.

STUDENT INFORMATION
Total Students in Program: 1,287. **% Full-time:** 72. **% Female:** 51.

RESEARCH FACILITIES
Research Facilities: Centers for American and Jewish Studies, analytical spectroscopy, applied geographic and spatial research, astrophysics; space physics and engineering research, community research and development, family and community ministries, ministry effectiveness.

EXPENSES/FINANCIAL AID
Annual Tuition: In-state $9,096. **Fees:** $1,048. **% Receiving Financial Aid:** 66. **Number of fellowships granted each year:** 43. **Average amount of individual fellowships per year:** $8,632.

ADMISSIONS INFORMATION
Application Fee: $40. **Priority Application Deadline:** 2/15. **Regular Application Deadline:** 2/15. **Regular Notification:** Rolling. **Transfer Students Accepted?** Yes. **Transfer Policy:** Minimum grade of B on coursework completed within the last 5 years from an accredited university. **Number of Applications Received:** 260. **% of Applicants Accepted:** 75. **% Accepted Who Enrolled:** 95. **Average GPA:** 3.32. **Average GRE Verbal:** 522. **Average GRE Quantitative:** 602. **Average GRE Analytical:** 602.
Required Admission Factors: Letters of recommendation, transcript.
Other Admission Factors: Minimum 2.7 GPA (3.0 in major) required.

EMPLOYMENT INFORMATION
Placement Office Available? Yes. **% Employed Within 6 Months:** 80. **% of master's/doctoral grads employed in their field upon graduation:** 65/96.

BAYLOR UNIVERSITY
School of Music

Address: PO Box 97264, Waco, TX 76798-7264
Admissions Phone: 254-710-3584 · **Admissions Fax:** 254-710-3870
Admissions E-mail: debra_j_williams@baylor.edu

INSTITUTIONAL INFORMATION
Public/Private: Private (nonprofit). **Students in Parent Institution:** 13,719.

STUDENT INFORMATION
Total Students in Program: 1,287. **% Full-time:** 72. **% Female:** 51.

RESEARCH FACILITIES
Research Facilities: Centers for American and Jewish Studies, analytical spectroscopy, applied geographic and spatial research, astrophysics; space physics and engineering research, community research and development, family and community ministries, ministry effectiveness.

EXPENSES/FINANCIAL AID
Annual Tuition: In-state $9,096. **Fees:** $1,048. **% Receiving Financial Aid:** 85. **Number of teaching/research assistantships granted each year:** 10. **Average Salary Stipend:** $4,788.

ADMISSIONS INFORMATION
Application Fee: $25. **Regular Notification:** Rolling. **Transfer Students Accepted?** Yes. **Transfer Policy:** Maximum 15 semester hours with a mini-

mum grade of B taken within the last 5 years may be transferred. **Number of Applications Received:** 34. **% of Applicants Accepted:** 88. **% Accepted Who Enrolled:** 50. **Average GPA:** 3.45. **Average GRE Verbal:** 449. **Average GRE Quantitative:** 548. **Average GRE Analytical:** 528.
Required Admission Factors: Letters of recommendation, transcript.
Other Admission Factors: Minimum 2.7 GPA (3.0 GPA in major) required.
Program-Specific Admission Factors: Portfolio required of composition program applicants. Audition required of conducting and performance program applicants.

EMPLOYMENT INFORMATION
Placement Office Available? Yes.

BELLEVUE UNIVERSITY
Graduate Programs

Address: 1000 Galvin Road South, Bellevue, NE 68005
Admissions Phone: 402-293-3702 · **Admissions Fax:** 402-293-2020
Admissions E-mail: info@bellevue.edu · **Web Address:** www.bellevue.edu

INSTITUTIONAL INFORMATION
Public/Private: Private (nonprofit). **Evening Classes Available?** Yes. **Total Faculty:** 177. **% Faculty Female:** 45. **% Faculty Part-time:** 66. **Student/Faculty Ratio:** 16:1. **Students in Parent Institution:** 5,524.

PROGRAMS
Masters offered in: Business administration/management, communications and media studies, family and consumer sciences/human sciences, health services/allied health, information technology.

STUDENT INFORMATION
Total Students in Program: 1,231. **% Full-time:** 68. **% Female:** 50.

EXPENSES/FINANCIAL AID
Annual Tuition: $7,800. **Fees:** $95. **Books and Supplies:** $900. **Grants Range From:** $13-$6,847. **Loans Range From:** $128-$18,500. **% Receiving Financial Aid:** 51. **% Receiving Scholarships/Grants:** 4.5. **% Receiving Loans:** 95.5. **Types of Aid Available:** Graduate assistantships, grants, institutional work-study, loans, scholarships.

ADMISSIONS INFORMATION
Application Fee: $75. **Priority Application Deadline:** 8/29. **Regular Application Deadline:** 8/29. **Regular Notification:** Rolling. **Transfer Students Accepted?** Yes. **Transfer Policy:** Will only transfer courses with grade of B or higher.
Required Admission Factors: Essays/personal statement, letters of recommendation, transcript.
Other Admission Factors: Minimum GPA 2.5
Program-Specific Admission Factors: Minimum GPA for master of science in human services is 2.75

BELMONT UNIVERSITY
College of Arts & Sciences—English

Address: 1900 Belmont Boulevard, Nashville, TN 37212-3757
Admissions Phone: 615-460-6437 · **Admissions Fax:** 615-460-5084
Admissions E-mail: halll@mail.belmont.edu · **Web Address:** www.belmont.edu

INSTITUTIONAL INFORMATION
Public/Private: Private (nonprofit). **Evening Classes Available?** Yes. **Total Faculty:** 14. **% Faculty Female:** 71. **Student/Faculty Ratio:** 5:1. **Students in Parent Institution:** 3,941

PROGRAMS
Masters offered in: American literature (U.S.); creative writing; elementary education and teaching; junior high/intermediate/middle school education and

teaching; secondary education and teaching; teacher education, multiple levels.

STUDENT INFORMATION

Total Students in Program: 24. **% Full-time:** 17. **% Female:** 67. **% Minority:** 4. **% International:** 4.

EXPENSES/FINANCIAL AID

Annual Tuition: $7,840. **Books and Supplies:** $600. **Grants Range From:** $175-$3,800. **Loans Range From:** $1,850-$18,500. **% Receiving Financial Aid:** 55. **% Receiving Scholarships/Grants:** 33. **% Receiving Loans:** 86. **Types of Aid Available:** Fellowships. **Number of fellowships granted each year:** 15 **Average amount of individual fellowships per year:** $1,150.

ADMISSIONS INFORMATION

Application Fee: $50. **Regular Application Deadline:** 7/18. **Regular Notification:** Rolling. **Transfer Students Accepted?** Yes. **Transfer Policy:** GRE, transcripts, writing sample, letters of recommendation. **Number of Applications Received:** 66. **% of Applicants Accepted:** 80. **% Accepted Who Enrolled:** 51. **Average GPA:** 3.18. **Average GRE Verbal:** 502. **Average GRE Quantitative:** 517. **Average GRE Analytical:** 457.
Required Admission Factors: Essays/personal statement, GRE, interview, letters of recommendation, transcript.
Other Admission Factors: Minimum 2.75 GPA required.

EMPLOYMENT INFORMATION

Placement Office Available? Yes. **% Employed Within 6 Months:** 100. **% of master's grads employed in their field upon graduation:** 100. **Rate of placement:** 97%. **Average starting salary:** $30,000.

BELMONT UNIVERSITY
College of Visual & Performing Arts

Address: 1900 Belmont Boulevard, Nashville, TN 37212-3757
Admissions Phone: 615-460-8117 · **Admissions Fax:** 615-386-0239
Admissions E-mail: bridgesm@mail.belmont.edu
Web Address: www.belmont.edu/cvpa

INSTITUTIONAL INFORMATION

Public/Private: Private (nonprofit). **Total Faculty:** 40. **% Faculty Female:** 38. **% Faculty Part-time:** 40. **Student/Faculty Ratio:** 5:1. **Students in Parent Institution:** 3,941.

PROGRAMS

Masters offered in: Music pedagogy, music performance, music theory and composition, music.

STUDENT INFORMATION

Total Students in Program: 43. **% Full-time:** 30. **% Female:** 49. **% Minority:** 12.

EXPENSES/FINANCIAL AID

Annual Tuition: $7,440. **Room & Board (On/Off campus):** $8,138/$11,848. **Books and Supplies:** $600. **Grants Range From:** $175-$3,800. **Loans Range From:** $1,850-$18,500. **% Receiving Financial Aid:** 50. **% Receiving Scholarships/Grants:** 33. **% Receiving Loans:** 86. **Types of Aid Available:** Loans, scholarships. **Number of teaching/research assistantships granted each year:** 5. **Assistantship compensation includes:** Partial tuition remission. **Average Salary Stipend:** $1,000.

ADMISSIONS INFORMATION

Application Fee: $50. **Regular Application Deadline:** 4/1. **Regular Notification:** Rolling. **Transfer Students Accepted?** Yes. **Number of Applications Received:** 17. **% of Applicants Accepted:** 71. **% Accepted Who Enrolled:** 67. **Average GPA:** 3.6.
Required Admission Factors: Essays/personal statement, interview, letters of recommendation, transcript.
Other Admission Factors: Minimum 2.7 GPA required.
Program-Specific Admission Factors: Audition required of music program

applicants.

EMPLOYMENT INFORMATION

Placement Office Available? Yes. **% Employed Within 6 Months:** 55. **Rate of placement:** 97%. **Average starting salary:** $36,000.

BELMONT UNIVERSITY
School of Physical Therapy

Address: 1900 Belmont Boulevard, Nashville, TN 37212
Admissions Phone: 615-460-6727 · **Admissions Fax:** 615-460-6729
Admissions E-mail: budpt@mail.belmont.edu · **Web Address:** www.belmont.edu/pt

INSTITUTIONAL INFORMATION

Public/Private: Private (nonprofit). **Total Faculty:** 23. **% Faculty Female:** 57. **% Faculty Part-time:** 65. **Student/Faculty Ratio:** 12:1. **Students in Parent Institution:** 3,941.

PROGRAMS

Doctorate offered in: Physical therapy/therapist.

STUDENT INFORMATION

Total Students in Program: 95. **% Full-time:** 100. **% Female:** 79. **% Minority:** 5.

EXPENSES/FINANCIAL AID

Annual Tuition: $18,590.

ADMISSIONS INFORMATION

Application Fee: $50. **Regular Application Deadline:** 8/1. **Regular Notification:** Rolling. **Transfer Students Accepted?** No. **Number of Applications Received:** 157. **% of Applicants Accepted:** 45. **% Accepted Who Enrolled:** 46. **Average GPA:** 3.6. **Average GRE Verbal:** 470. **Average GRE Quantitative:** 620. **Average GRE Analytical Writing:** 4.5.
Required Admission Factors: GRE.
Other Admission Factors: Minimum GPA of 3.0.

EMPLOYMENT INFORMATION

Placement Office Available? Yes. **% Employed Within 6 Months:** 100. **% of first professional grads employed in their field upon graduation:** 100. **Rate of placement:** 100%. **Average starting salary:** $50,000.

BELMONT UNIVERSITY
School of Occupational Therapy

Address: 1900 Belmont Boulevard, Nashville, TN 37212
Admissions Phone: 615-460-6000 · **Admissions Fax:** 615-460-6475
Admissions E-mail: mcphees@mail.belmont.edu
Web Address: www.belmont.edu/ot/

INSTITUTIONAL INFORMATION

Public/Private: Private (nonprofit). **Total Faculty:** 18. **% Faculty Female:** 78. **% Faculty Part-time:** 67. **Students in Parent Institution:** 3,941.

STUDENT INFORMATION

Total Students in Program: 92. **% Full-time:** 96. **% Female:** 84. **% Minority:** 5.

EXPENSES/FINANCIAL AID

Annual Tuition: $18,990. **Room & Board:** $8,544. **Books and Supplies:** $950.

ADMISSIONS INFORMATION

Application Fee: $50. **Regular Application Deadline:** 8/31. **Regular Notification:** Rolling. **Transfer Students Accepted?** No. **Number of Applications Received:** 130. **% of Applicants Accepted:** 42. **% Accepted Who Enrolled:** 89. **Average GPA:** 3.2. **Required Admission Factors:** GRE,

GMAT. **Other Admission Factors:** 3.0 minimum GPA. **Program-Specific Admission Factors:** Minimum of 90 credit hours if student does not have a bachelors's degree.

EMPLOYMENT INFORMATION

Placement Office Available? Yes. **% Employed Within 6 Months:** 100. **% of master's/doctoral/first professional grads employed in their field upon graduation:** 100/100/95. **Rate of placement:** 98%. **Average starting salary:** $55,000.

BEMIDJI STATE UNIVERSITY
College of Arts & Letters

Address: 1500 Birchmont Drive NE #30, Bemidji, MN 56601-2699
Admissions Phone: 218-755-2027 · **Admissions Fax:** 218-755-3788
Admissions E-mail: mtadlock@bemidjistate.edu
Web Address: www.bemidjistate.edu/graduatestudies/

INSTITUTIONAL INFORMATION

Public/Private: Public. **Total Faculty:** 13. **% Faculty Female:** 62. **% Faculty Part-time:** 100. **Students in Parent Institution:** 4,833.

PROGRAMS

Masters offered in: Environmental studies, mathematics, science technologies/technicians.

STUDENT INFORMATION

Total Students in Program: 25. **% Full-time:** 60. **% Female:** 64.

RESEARCH FACILITIES

Research Facilities: Graduate Student Association, Center for Research & Innovation, American Indian Resource Center.

EXPENSES/FINANCIAL AID

Annual Tuition: In-state $3,906. / Out-of-state $6,192. **Room & Board:** $4,000. **Fees:** $355. **Books and Supplies:** $700. **Grants Range From:** $400-$1,000. **Loans Range From:** $1,000-$2,000. **Types of Aid Available:** Graduate assistantships, loans, scholarships.

ADMISSIONS INFORMATION

Application Fee: $20. **Priority Application Deadline:** 5/1. **Regular Application Deadline:** 5/1. **Regular Notification:** Rolling. **Transfer Students Accepted?** Yes. **Transfer Policy:** Credits must be from an accredited institution; credits must have been successfully completed within 7 years of the completion of the graduate program at BSU. **Number of Applications Received:** 7. **% of Applicants Accepted:** 100. **% Accepted Who Enrolled:** 100. **Average GPA:** 3.5.
Required Admission Factors: Letters of recommendation, transcript.
Other Admission Factors: Minimum 2.75 GPA required.

EMPLOYMENT INFORMATION

Placement Office Available? Yes. **Rate of placement:** 65%. **Average starting salary:** $45,000.

BEMIDJI STATE UNIVERSITY
College of Professional Studies

Address: 1500 Birchmont Drive NE #30, Bemidji, MN 56601-2699
Admissions Phone: 218-755-2027 · **Admissions Fax:** 218-755-3788
Admissions E-mail: mtadlock@bemidjistate.edu
Web Address: www.bemidjistate.edu/graduate studies/

INSTITUTIONAL INFORMATION

Public/Private: Public. **Total Faculty:** 47. **% Faculty Female:** 49. **Student/Faculty Ratio:** 19:1. **Students in Parent Institution:** 4,833.

PROGRAMS

Masters offered in: Education, mathematics teacher education, physical education teaching and coaching, reading teacher education, science teacher education/general science teacher education, social science teacher education, special education, technical teacher education, trade and industrial teacher education.

STUDENT INFORMATION

Total Students in Program: 101. **% Full-time:** 39. **% Female:** 39.

RESEARCH FACILITIES

Research Facilities: Graduate Student Association, Center for Research and Innovation, American Indian Resource Center.

EXPENSES/FINANCIAL AID

Annual Tuition: In-state $3,411. Out-of-state $5,400. **Room & Board:** $3,480. **Fees:** $605. **Books and Supplies:** $700. **Grants Range From:** $500-$8,500. **Loans Range From:** $500-$8,500. **Types of Aid Available:** Graduate assistantships, institutional work-study, loans, scholarships. **Number of teaching/research assistantships granted each year:** 58. **Assistantship compensation includes:** Partial tuition remission, salary/stipend. **Average Salary Stipend:** $8,000.

ADMISSIONS INFORMATION

Application Fee: $20. **Priority Application Deadline:** 5/1. **Regular Application Deadline:** 5/1. **Regular Notification:** Rolling. **Transfer Students Accepted?** Yes. **Transfer Policy:** Credits must be from an accredited university; credits must have been successfully completed within 7 years of graduation from a BSU graduate program. **Number of Applications Received:** 32. **% of Applicants Accepted:** 100. **% Accepted Who Enrolled:** 100. **Average GPA:** 3.3.
Required Admission Factors: Letters of recommendation, transcript.
Other Admission Factors: Minimum 2.75 GPA required; GRE may be required if undergraduate grade point average is below the 2.75.

EMPLOYMENT INFORMATION

Placement Office Available? Yes. **Rate of placement:** 65%. **Average starting salary:** $35,000.

BEMIDJI STATE UNIVERSITY
College of Social & Natural Sciences

Address: 1500 Birchmont Drive NE #30, Bemidji, MN 56601-2699
Admissions Phone: 218-755-2027 · **Admissions Fax:** 218-755-3788
Admissions E-mail: mtadlock@bemidjistate.edu
Web Address: www.bemidjistate.edu/graduatestudies/

INSTITUTIONAL INFORMATION

Public/Private: Public. **Total Faculty:** 67. **% Faculty Female:** 31. **% Faculty Part-time:** 100. **Students in Parent Institution:** 4,833

PROGRAMS

Masters offered in: Environmental studies, mathematics, science technologies/technicians.

STUDENT INFORMATION

Total Students in Program: 38. **% Full-time:** 68. **% Female:** 39.

RESEARCH FACILITIES

Research Facilities: Graduate Student Association, Center for Research and Innovation, American Indian Resource Center.

EXPENSES/FINANCIAL AID

Annual Tuition: In-state $3,906. / Out-of-state $6,192. **Room & Board:** $4,000. **Fees:** $355. **Books and Supplies:** $700. **Grants Range From:** $500-$8,500. **Loans Range From:** $500-$8,500. **Types of Aid Available:** Graduate assistantships, institutional work-study, loans, scholarships. **Number of teaching/research assistantships granted each year:** 52. **Assistantship com-**

pensation includes: Partial tuition remission, salary/stipend. **Average Salary Stipend:** $8,000.

ADMISSIONS INFORMATION

Application Fee: $20. **Regular Application Deadline:** 5/1. **Regular Notification:** Rolling. **Transfer Students Accepted?** Yes. **Transfer Policy:** Credits must come from an accredited university; must have been successfully completed within 7 years prior to graduation with the BSU graduate degree. **Number of Applications Received:** 14. **% of Applicants Accepted:** 100. **% Accepted Who Enrolled:** 100. **Average GPA:** 3.3.
Required Admission Factors: Essays/personal statement, GRE, transcript. **Other Admission Factors:** Minimum 2.75 GPA required; letter of intent required for biology; GRE required for biology and environmental studies. **Program-Specific Admission Factors:** Environmental studies required minimum GRE score for Verbal and Quantitative is 1050 and at least 4.0 on a scale of 0-6.0 for Analytical of environmental studies program applicants; letters of recommendation are not required.

EMPLOYMENT INFORMATION

Placement Office Available? Yes. **Rate of placement:** 65%. **Average starting salary:** $45,000.

BENEDICTINE UNIVERSITY
Graduate Programs

Address: 5700 College Road, Lisle, IL 60532-0900
Admissions Phone: 630-829-6300 · **Admissions Fax:** 630-630-6301
Admissions E-mail: admissions@ben.edu · **Web Address:** www.ben.edu

INSTITUTIONAL INFORMATION

Public/Private: Private (nonprofit). **Evening Classes Available?** Yes. **Students in Parent Institution:** 2,622.

PROGRAMS

Masters offered in: Clinical psychology, computer and information sciences, curriculum and instruction, education leadership and administration, elementary education and teaching, exercise physiology, kinesiology and exercise science, public health (MPH, DPH), secondary education and teaching, special education.

STUDENT INFORMATION

Total Students in Program: 827. **% Full-time:** 19. **% Female:** 65.

EXPENSES/FINANCIAL AID

Annual Tuition: $5,670.

ADMISSIONS INFORMATION

Application Fee: $30. **Regular Notification:** Rolling. **Transfer Students Accepted?** Yes. **Number of Applications Received:** 180. **% of Applicants Accepted:** 83. **% Accepted Who Enrolled:** 93.
Required Admission Factors: Essays/personal statement, GRE, interview, letters of recommendation, transcript.

EMPLOYMENT INFORMATION

Placement Office Available? Yes.

BENNINGTON COLLEGE
Graduate Programs

Address: One College Drive, Bennington, VT 05201
Admissions Phone: 802-440-4312 or 800-833-6845 · **Admissions Fax:** 802-440-4320
Admissions E-mail: admissions@bennington.edu · **Web Address:** www.bennington.edu

INSTITUTIONAL INFORMATION

Public/Private: Private (nonprofit). **Students in Parent Institution:** 793.

PROGRAMS

Masters offered in: Architecture (BArch, BA/BS, MArch, MA/MS, PhD); art teacher education; bilingual and multilingual education; creative writing; dance, drama, and dramatics/theater arts; East Asian languages, literatures, and linguistics; elementary education and teaching; English/language arts teacher education; fine/studio arts; foreign language teacher education; foreign languages/modern languages; French language and literature; German language and literature; liberal arts and sciences/liberal studies; mathematics teacher education; music performance; music teacher education; music theory and composition; painting; science teacher education/general science teacher education; secondary education and teaching; social science teacher education; social studies teacher education; Spanish language and literature; teacher education and professional development, specific subject areas; teaching English as a second or foreign language/ESL language instructor; visual and performing arts.

STUDENT INFORMATION

Total Students in Program: 153. **% Full-time:** 90. **% Female:** 70. **% International:** 4.

RESEARCH FACILITIES

Research Facilities: Computer Center, Visual and Performing Arts Complex (VAPA), Early Childhood Center, Isabelle Kaplan Center for Languages and Cultures.

EXPENSES/FINANCIAL AID

Annual Tuition: $17,500. **Room & Board:** $8,000. **Fees:** $725. **Books and Supplies:** $800. **Grants Range From:** $2,000-$11,500. **Loans Range From:** $1,000-$18,500. **% Receiving Scholarships/Grants:** 43. **% Receiving Loans:** 75. **% Receiving Assistantships:** 50. **Types of Aid Available:** Grants, institutional work-study, loans, scholarships. **Average student debt, upon graduation:** $28,363. **Assistantship compensation includes:** Full tuition remission, partial tuition remission.

ADMISSIONS INFORMATION

Application Fee: $50. **Regular Application Deadline:** 2/1. **Transfer Students Accepted?** No. **Number of Applications Received:** 247. **% of Applicants Accepted:** 25. **% Accepted Who Enrolled:** 31.
Required Admission Factors: Essays/personal statement, interview, letters of recommendation, transcript.

BETHANY THEOLOGICAL SEMINARY
Graduate & Professional Programs

Address: 615 National Road West, Richmond, IN 47374
Admissions Phone: 800-287-8822 · **Admissions Fax:** 765-983-1840
Admissions E-mail: shetlda@earlham.edu

INSTITUTIONAL INFORMATION

Public/Private: Private (nonprofit). **Total Faculty:** 14. **% Faculty Female:** 43. **% Faculty Part-time:** 43. **Students in Parent Institution:** 73.

STUDENT INFORMATION

Total Students in Program: 73. **% Full-time:** 56. **% Female:** 38.

EXPENSES/FINANCIAL AID

Annual Tuition: In-state $5,683. **Fees:** $150. **Books and Supplies:** $700. **% Receiving Financial Aid:** 100. **Average student debt, upon graduation:** $11,860.

ADMISSIONS INFORMATION

Application Fee: $25. **Regular Notification:** Rolling. **Transfer Students Accepted?** Yes. **Number of Applications Received:** 26. **% of Applicants Accepted:** 100. **% Accepted Who Enrolled:** 73.
Required Admission Factors: Essays/personal statement, interview, letters of recommendation, transcript.
Other Admission Factors: Minimum 2.5 GPA required.

EMPLOYMENT INFORMATION

Placement Office Available? Yes. Rate of placement: 95%.

BETHEL SEMINARY
Graduate & Professional Programs

Address: 3949 Bethel Drive, Street Paul, MN 55112
Admissions Phone: 651-638-6288 · **Admissions Fax:** 651-638-6002
Admissions E-mail: bsem-admit@bethel.edu · **Web Address:** www.bethel.edu

INSTITUTIONAL INFORMATION

Public/Private: Private (nonprofit). Evening Classes Available? Yes. Total Faculty: 96. % Faculty Female: 15. % Faculty Part-time: 74. Students in Parent Institution: 924.

STUDENT INFORMATION

Total Students in Program: 515. % Full-time: 52. % Female: 43.

EXPENSES/FINANCIAL AID

Annual Tuition: $9,420. Room & Board: $725. Fees: $195. Books and Supplies: $900. % Receiving Financial Aid: 75. % Receiving Scholarships/Grants: 70. % Receiving Loans: 30. Average student debt, upon graduation: $12,000.

ADMISSIONS INFORMATION

Application Fee: $20. Priority Application Deadline: 7/31. Regular Application Deadline: 8/31. Regular Notification: Rolling. Transfer Students Accepted? Yes. Number of Applications Received: 202. % of Applicants Accepted: 83. % Accepted Who Enrolled: 85.
Required Admission Factors: Essays/personal statement, letters of recommendation, transcript.

EMPLOYMENT INFORMATION

Placement Office Available? Yes. Rate of placement: 90%.

BETHEL UNIVERSITY
Graduate School

Address: 3900 Bethel Drive, Saint Paul, MN 55112-6999
Admissions Phone: 651-635-8000 · **Admissions Fax:** 651-635-8004
Admissions E-mail: gs@bethel.edu · **Web Address:** www.gs.bethel.edu

INSTITUTIONAL INFORMATION

Public/Private: Private (nonprofit). Evening Classes Available? Yes. Students in Parent Institution: 2,983.

PROGRAMS

Masters offered in: Art teacher education; biology teacher education; business administration/management; business, management, marketing, and related support services; chemistry teacher education; communications and media studies; counseling psychology; curriculum and instruction; education/teaching of individuals with emotional disturbances; education/teaching of individuals with specific learning disabilities; English/language arts teacher education; gerontology; health teacher education; history teacher education; junior high/intermediate/middle school education and teaching; mathematics teacher education; music teacher education; musicology and ethnomusicology; nursing; reading teacher education; science teacher education/general science teacher education; secondary education and teaching; social studies teacher education; special education; teacher education, multiple levels; teaching English as a second or foreign language/ESL language instructor. Doctorate offered in: Education leadership and administration; elementary and middle school administration/principalship; secondary school administration/principalship; superintendency and educational system administration.

STUDENT INFORMATION

Total Students in Program: 372. % Full-time: 34. % Female: 72. % Minority: 5. % International: 1.

EXPENSES/FINANCIAL AID

Annual Tuition: $7,000. Fees: $125. Books and Supplies: $600. Grants Range From: $500-$10,800. Loans Range From: $500-$18,500. % Receiving Scholarships/Grants: 17. % Receiving Loans: 83. Types of Aid Available: Loans.

ADMISSIONS INFORMATION

Application Fee: $25. Regular Application Deadline: 6/5. Regular Notification: Rolling. Transfer Students Accepted? Yes. Transfer Policy: Maximum number of credit hours which may be transferred varies by program. Number of Applications Received: 267. % of Applicants Accepted: 99. % Accepted Who Enrolled: 95. Average GPA: 3.3.
Required Admission Factors: Essays/personal statement, interview, letters of recommendation, transcript.
Other Admission Factors: Minimum 3.0 GPA.

BIOLA UNIVERSITY
Rosemead School of Psychology

Address: 13800 Biola Avenue, La Mirada, CA 90639
Admissions Phone: 562-903-4752 or 800-652-4652 · **Admissions Fax:** 562-903-4709
Admissions E-mail: herb.higueros@biola.edu · **Web Address:** www.rosemead.edu

INSTITUTIONAL INFORMATION

Public/Private: Private (nonprofit). Total Faculty: 24. % Faculty Female: 38. % Faculty Part-time: 50. Student/Faculty Ratio: 8:1. Students in Parent Institution: 3,872.

PROGRAMS

Doctorate offered in: Clinical psychology.

STUDENT INFORMATION

Total Students in Program: 1,186. % Full-time: 44. % Female: 41.

RESEARCH FACILITIES

Research Facilities: Institute for Research in Psychology and Spirituality, Counseling Center.

EXPENSES/FINANCIAL AID

Annual Tuition: $18,568. Room & Board (On/Off Campus): $6,400/$7,956. Fees: $1,000. Books and Supplies: $900. Grants Range From: $200-$18,000. Loans Range From: $200-$18,500. % Receiving Financial Aid: 77. % Receiving Scholarships/Grants: 96. % Receiving Loans: 51. % Receiving Assistantships: 50. % Receiving Other Aid (36% private scholarships. outside gifts): 36. Types of Aid Available: Fellowships, graduate assistantships, grants, institutional work-study, loans, scholarships. Average student debt, upon graduation: $56,698. Number of fellowships granted each year: 1. Average amount of individual fellowships per year: $22,000. Number of teaching/research assistantships granted each year: 40. Assistantship compensation includes: Salary/stipend. Average Salary Stipend: $3,000.

ADMISSIONS INFORMATION

Application Fee: $45. Regular Application Deadline: 1/15. Regular Notification: 4/1. Transfer Students Accepted? Yes. Transfer Policy: Maximum 30 psychology and 15 theology credit hours may be transferred into graduate programs. Credits must be obtained at a regionally accredited graduate program. Number of Applications Received: 116. % of Applicants Accepted: 30. % Accepted Who Enrolled: 71. Average GPA: 3.7.
Required Admission Factors: Essays/personal statement, GRE, interview, letters of recommendation, transcript. MMPI, GRE subject exam(s) in psychology.

Other Admission Factors: Minimum GRE score of 950 (Verbal and Quantitative) recommended, and minimum 3.0 GPA in psychology coursework required.

Program-Specific Admission Factors: Personal commitment to the Christian faith and interest in the interface between psychology and faith.

EMPLOYMENT INFORMATION

Placement Office Available? Yes. **% Employed Within 6 Months:** 80. **% of doctoral grads employed in their field upon graduation:** 90. **Rate of placement:** 90%. **Average starting salary:** $40,000.

BIOLA UNIVERSITY
School of Arts & Sciences

Address: 13800 Biola Avenue, La Mirada, CA 90639
Admissions Phone: 800-652-4652 · **Admissions Fax:** 562-903-4709
Admissions E-mail: tamara_wytsma@peter.biola.edu

INSTITUTIONAL INFORMATION

Public/Private: Private (nonprofit). **Evening Classes Available?** Yes. **Student/Faculty Ratio:** 8:1. **Students in Parent Institution:** 3,872.

STUDENT INFORMATION

Total Students in Program: 1,186. **% Full-time:** 44. **% Female:** 41.

EXPENSES/FINANCIAL AID

Annual Tuition: In-state $7,848. **Room & Board:** $5,640. **% Receiving Financial Aid:** 76. **% Receiving Scholarships/Grants:** 96. **% Receiving Loans:** 51. **Average student debt, upon graduation:** $24,112.

ADMISSIONS INFORMATION

Application Fee: $45. **Regular Notification:** Rolling. **Transfer Students Accepted?** Yes. **Number of Applications Received:** 103. **Average GPA:** 3.4.

Required Admission Factors: Letters of recommendation, transcript.

Program-Specific Admission Factors: Minimum 2.75 GPA required of teaching credential program applicants. Minimum 3.0 GPA required of MAEd program applicants.

EMPLOYMENT INFORMATION

Placement Office Available? Yes.

BIOLA UNIVERSITY
School of Intercultural Studies

Address: 13800 Biola Avenue, La Mirada, CA 90639
Admissions Phone: 562-903-4752 · **Admissions Fax:** 562-903-4709
Admissions E-mail: james.cho@biola.edu
Web Address: www.biola.edu/academics/sics/index.cfm

INSTITUTIONAL INFORMATION

Public/Private: Private (nonprofit). **Evening Classes Available?** Yes. **Total Faculty:** 18. **% Faculty Female:** 33. **% Faculty Part-time:** 17. **Student/Faculty Ratio:** 9:1. **Students in Parent Institution:** 5,370.

PROGRAMS

Masters offered in: Intercultural/multicultural and diversity studies, international/global studies, language interpretation and translation, linguistics, missions/missionary studies and missiology, teaching English as a second or foreign language/ESL language instructor. **Doctorate offered in:** Bilingual, multilingual, and multicultural education; missions/missionary studies and missiology; multicultural education. **First Professional degree offered in:** Teaching English as a second or foreign language/ESL language instructor, teaching English or French as a second or foreign language.

EXPENSES/FINANCIAL AID

Annual Tuition: $9,172. **Room & Board (On/Off Campus):** $5,640/$8,400. **Books and Supplies:** $500. **Grants Range From:** $200-$2,000. **Loans Range From:** $200-$18,000. **% Receiving Financial Aid:** 75. **% Receiving Scholarships/Grants:** 96. **% Receiving Loans:** 51. **Types of Aid Available:** Grants, loans. **Average student debt, upon graduation:** $21,396.

ADMISSIONS INFORMATION

Application Fee: $45. **Priority Application Deadline:** 4/15. **Regular Application Deadline:** 8/1. **Regular Notification:** Rolling. **Transfer Students Accepted?** Yes. **Number of Applications Received:** 106. **Average GPA:** 3.53.

Required Admission Factors: Essays/personal statement, letters of recommendation, transcript.

Program-Specific Admission Factors: Minimum 3.0 GPA required of MA program applicants. Minimum 3.3 GPA and at least 3 years cross-cultural experience required of doctoral program applicants.

EMPLOYMENT INFORMATION

Placement Office Available? Yes.

BIOLA UNIVERSITY
School of Professional Studies

Address: 13800 Biola Avenue, La Mirada, CA 90639
Admissions Phone: 800-652-4652 · **Admissions Fax:** 562-903-4709
Admissions E-mail: rebeca_delatorre@peter.biola.edu

INSTITUTIONAL INFORMATION

Public/Private: Private (nonprofit). **Evening Classes Available?** Yes. **Student/Faculty Ratio:** 9:1. **Students in Parent Institution:** 3,872.

STUDENT INFORMATION

Total Students in Program: 1,186. **% Full-time:** 44. **% Female:** 41.

EXPENSES/FINANCIAL AID

Annual Tuition: $7,848. **Room & Board:** $5,640. **% Receiving Financial Aid:** 39. **% Receiving Scholarships/Grants:** 96. **% Receiving Loans:** 51. **Average student debt, upon graduation:** $24,737.

ADMISSIONS INFORMATION

Application Fee: $45. **Regular Notification:** Rolling. **Transfer Students Accepted?** Yes. **Number of Applications Received:** 63.

Required Admission Factors: Letters of recommendation, transcript.
Other Admission Factors: Minimum 3.0 GPA required.

EMPLOYMENT INFORMATION

Placement Office Available? Yes.

BOB JONES UNIVERSITY
Graduate Programs

Address: 1700 Wade Hampton Boulevard, Greenville, SC 29614
Admissions Phone: 864-242-5100 · **Admissions Fax:** 800-232-9258
Admissions E-mail: admissions@bju.edu
Web Address: www.bju.edu/academics/gmajors.html

INSTITUTIONAL INFORMATION

Public/Private: Private (nonprofit). **Total Faculty:** 120. **% Faculty Female:** 26. **Student/Faculty Ratio:** 4:1. **Students in Parent Institution:** 4,280.

PROGRAMS

Masters offered in: Accounting; art teacher education; art/art studies; business administration/management; cinematography and film/video production; drama and dramatics/theater arts; education; education/teaching of individuals with emotional disturbances; education/teaching of individuals with multiple disabilities; elementary education and teaching; English/language arts teacher education; fine arts and art studies; fine/studio arts; graphic design; history teacher education; human resources management/personnel administration; illustration; mathematics teacher education; music pedagogy; music teacher education; piano and organ; radio and television; religious/sacred music; secondary education and teaching; special education; speech teacher education; violin, viola, guitar, and other stringed instruments; voice and opera. **Doctorate offered in:** Education, human resources management/personnel administration.

STUDENT INFORMATION

Total Students in Program: 487. **% Full-time:** 74. **% Female:** 39. **% International:** 8.

EXPENSES/FINANCIAL AID

Annual Tuition: $8,580. **Room & Board:** $4,860. **Fees:** $510. **Books and Supplies:** $1,940. **Types of Aid Available:** Graduate assistantships. **Number of teaching/research assistantships granted each year:** 100. **Assistantship compensation includes:** Partial tuition remission, salary/stipend.

ADMISSIONS INFORMATION

Application Fee: $45. **Regular Application Deadline:** 8/1. **Regular Notification:** Rolling. **Transfer Students Accepted?** Yes. **Transfer Policy:** College transcript, letters of recommendation, GPA 2.5 or greater. **Number of Applications Received:** 215. **% of Applicants Accepted:** 80. **% Accepted Who Enrolled:** 75.
Other Admission Factors: Minimum GPA 2.5.
Program-Specific Admission Factors: Students must have a 2.5 GPA. For specific program requirements, refer to the graduate catalog.

EMPLOYMENT INFORMATION

Placement Office Available? Yes.

BOISE STATE UNIVERSITY
College of Arts & Sciences

Address: 1910 University Drive, Math/Geosciences Building, Room #141, Boise, ID 83725
Admissions Phone: 208-426-3903 · **Admissions Fax:** 208-426-4061
Admissions E-mail: bnewkirk@boisestate.edu

INSTITUTIONAL INFORMATION

Public/Private: Public. **Evening Classes Available?** Yes. **Students in Parent Institution:** 17,853.

STUDENT INFORMATION

Total Students in Program: 3,318. **% Full-time:** 11. **% Female:** 72.

EXPENSES/FINANCIAL AID

Annual Tuition: $3,100. **Room & Board (On/Off Campus):** $4,394/$4,806. **Fees:** $3,695. **Books and Supplies:** $900. **Number of teaching/research assistantships granted each year:** 31.

ADMISSIONS INFORMATION

Application Fee: $20. **Regular Notification:** Rolling. **Transfer Students Accepted?** Yes. **Required Admission Factors:** Essays/personal statement, letters of recommendation, transcript. **Other Admission Factors:** Minimum 3.0 GPA in last 2 years required.
Program-Specific Admission Factors: GRE required of English, history, and public administration program applicants.

EMPLOYMENT INFORMATION

Placement Office Available? Yes.

BOISE STATE UNIVERSITY
College of Social Science & Public Affairs

Address: 1910 University Drive, Math/Geosciences Building, Room #141, Boise, ID 83725
Admissions Phone: 208-426-3903 · **Admissions Fax:** 208-426-4061
Admissions E-mail: bnewkirk@boisestate.edu

INSTITUTIONAL INFORMATION

Public/Private: Public. **Students in Parent Institution:** 17,853.

STUDENT INFORMATION

Total Students in Program: 3,318. **% Full-time:** 11. **% Female:** 72.

EXPENSES/FINANCIAL AID

Annual Tuition: $3,100. **Room & Board (On/Off Campus):** $4,394/$4,806. **Fees:** $3,695. **Books and Supplies:** $900. **Number of teaching/research assistantships granted each year:** 3.

ADMISSIONS INFORMATION

Application Fee: $20. **Transfer Students Accepted?** Yes. **Average GPA:** 3.16. **Average GRE Verbal:** 534. **Average GRE Quantitative:** 523. **Required Admission Factors:** Essays/personal statement, GRE, transcript. **Program-Specific Admission Factors:** Minimum 3.0 overall GPA or last 60 credit hours required of 2-year MS social work program applicants. Minimum 3.0 GPA in all social work courses required of advanced standing MS social work program applicants.

EMPLOYMENT INFORMATION

Placement Office Available? Yes.

BOSTON COLLEGE
Graduate School of Arts & Sciences

Address: 140 Commonwealth Avenue, Chestnut Hill, MA 02167
Admissions Phone: 617-552-3265 · **Admissions Fax:** 617-552-3700
Admissions E-mail: robert.howe@bc.edu · **Web Address:** www.bc.edu/gsas

INSTITUTIONAL INFORMATION

Public/Private: Private (nonprofit). **Total Faculty:** 391. **% Faculty Female:** 31. **Students in Parent Institution:** 14,379.

PROGRAMS

Masters offered in: Algebra and number theory; American government and politics (U.S.); American history (U.S.); American literature (U.S.); analysis and functional analysis; applied mathematics; applied mathematics; Asian history; Bible/Biblical studies; biochemistry, biophysics and molecular biology, biochemistry/biophysics, and molecular biology; biochemistry; bioinformatics; biology/biological sciences, biomathematics and bioinformatics; biomedical sciences; biophysics; biostatistics; Buddhist studies; Canadian government and politics; Canadian history; cell biology and anatomy; cell/cellular and molecular biology; cell/cellular biology and anatomical sciences, cell/cellular biology and histology; Christian studies; cognitive psychology and psycholinguistics; community psychology; computational mathematics; developmental and child psychology; developmental biology and embryology; English language and literature, English literature (British and commonwealth); ethics; European history; experimental psychology; genetics, genetics, geochemistry and petrology; geochemistry; geological and earth sciences/geosciences, geology/earth science, geometry/geometric analysis; geophysics and seismology; Hindu studies; history and philosophy of science and technology; history, humanities/humanistic studies; immunology; Islamic studies; Jewish/Judaic studies; logic; mathematical statistics and probability; mathematics and statistics, mathematics; microbiological sciences and immunology; microbiology, missions/missionary studies and missiology; molecular biochemistry; molecular biology; molecular biophysics; molecular genetics; neurobiology and neurophysiology; pastoral counseling and

---

specialized ministries, pastoral studies/counseling; personality psychology; philosophy and religion; philosophy; physiological psychology/psychobiology; political science and government; psychology; religion/religious studies; religious education; social psychology; sociology; statistics; structural biology; theological and ministerial studies, theology/theological studies; virology; work and family studies.

STUDENT INFORMATION
Total Students in Program: 1,037. **% Full-time:** 100. **% Female:** 49. **% Minority:** 11. **% International:** 20.

RESEARCH FACILITIES
Research Facilities: Institute for Scientific Research, Jesuit Institute, Center for Study of Testing Evaluation & Educational Policy, Social Welfare Research Institute, Weston Center for Family, Children, & Community Partnerships, Weston Observatory.

EXPENSES/FINANCIAL AID
Annual Tuition: $21,600. **Room & Board:** $9,585. **Fees:** $100. **Books and Supplies:** $800. **Loans Range From:** $1,500-$24,500. **% Receiving Financial Aid:** 60. **Types of Aid Available:** Fellowships, graduate assistantships, grants, loans, scholarships. **Assistantship compensation includes:** Full tuition remission, partial tuition remission, salary/stipend.

ADMISSIONS INFORMATION
Application Fee: $70. **Priority Application Deadline:** 1/2. **Regular Application Deadline:** 2/1. **Regular Notification:** Rolling. **Transfer Students Accepted?** Yes. **Number of Applications Received:** 2,500. **% of Applicants Accepted:** 14. **% Accepted Who Enrolled:** 71.
Required Admission Factors: Essays/personal statement, GRE, letters of recommendation, transcript.
Program-Specific Admission Factors: GRE general required by most programs, and GRE subject required by some. Three letters of recommendation required by most programs. Statement of purpose and abstract of coursework required by most programs.

EMPLOYMENT INFORMATION
Placement Office Available? Yes. **% Employed Within 6 Months:** 75. **Rate of placement:** 50%. **Average starting salary:** $50,000.

BOSTON COLLEGE
Graduate School of Social Work

Address: 140 Commonwealth Avenue, Chestnut Hill, MA 02167
Admissions Phone: 617-552-4024

INSTITUTIONAL INFORMATION
Students in Parent Institution: 14,696.

STUDENT INFORMATION
Total Students in Program: 4,840. **% Full-time:** 48. **% Female:** 58.

RESEARCH FACILITIES
Research Facilities: Institute for Scientific Research, Jesuit Institute, Center for Study of Testing Evaluation & Educational Policy, Social Welfare Research Institute, Weston Center for Family, Children, & Community Partnerships, Weston Observatory.

EXPENSES/FINANCIAL AID
Annual Tuition: $13,248. **Fees:** $100. **Books and Supplies:** $800.

ADMISSIONS INFORMATION
Application Fee: $40. **Regular Notification:** Rolling. **Transfer Students Accepted?** Yes. **Number of Applications Received:** 900. **% of Applicants Accepted:** 44. **% Accepted Who Enrolled:** 50. **Average GPA:** 3.4.
Required Admission Factors: Essays/personal statement, GRE, transcript.
Program-Specific Admission Factors: GRE or GRE subject exams required of doctoral program applicants.

EMPLOYMENT INFORMATION
Placement Office Available? Yes.

BOSTON UNIVERSITY
College of Communication

Address: 640 Commonwealth Avenue, Boston, MA 02215
Admissions Phone: 617-353-3481 or 800-992-6514 · **Admissions Fax:** 617-358-0399
Admissions E-mail: comgrad@bu.edu · **Web Address:** www.bu.edu/com/grad

INSTITUTIONAL INFORMATION
Public/Private: Private (nonprofit). **Evening Classes Available?** Yes. **Students in Parent Institution:** 25,137.

STUDENT INFORMATION
Total Students in Program: 7,716. **% Full-time:** 66. **% Female:** 54.

RESEARCH FACILITIES
Research Facilities: Communication research center.

EXPENSES/FINANCIAL AID
Annual Tuition: $25,872. **Fees:** $246. **Grants Range From:** $200-$41,276. **Loans Range From:** $725-$51,000. **% Receiving Financial Aid:** 62. **% Receiving Scholarships/Grants:** 78. **% Receiving Loans:** 53. **Average student debt, upon graduation:** $25,000.

ADMISSIONS INFORMATION
Application Fee: $60. **Regular Application Deadline:** 2/1. **Regular Notification:** 4/15. **Transfer Students Accepted?** No. **Number of Applications Received:** 617. **% of Applicants Accepted:** 72. **% Accepted Who Enrolled:** 45. **Average GPA:** 3.2.
Required Admission Factors: Essays/personal statement, letters of recommendation, transcript.
Other Admission Factors: TOEFL score must be 600 (250 computer based) or higher. No minimum required GPA or GRE scores. Average minimum GPA: 3.0. Average minimum GRE: 580 in each category.
Program-Specific Admission Factors: Portfolio required of photojournalism applicants. International student video required of all international applicants.

EMPLOYMENT INFORMATION
Placement Office Available? Yes.

BOSTON UNIVERSITY
College of Fine Arts

Address: CFA Graduate Admissions, 855 Commonwealth Avenue, Room 230, Boston, MA 02215
Admissions Phone: 617-353-3350 · **Admissions Fax:** 617-353-5331
Admissions E-mail: arts@bu.edu · **Web Address:** www.bu.edu/cfa

INSTITUTIONAL INFORMATION
Public/Private: Private (nonprofit). **Student/Faculty Ratio:** 6:1. **Students in Parent Institution:** 25,137.

STUDENT INFORMATION
Total Students in Program: 425. **% Full-time:** 100.

EXPENSES/FINANCIAL AID
Annual Tuition: $17,000. **Fees:** $246. **Books and Supplies:** $400. **Grants Range From:** $200-$17,000. **Loans Range From:** $725-$51,000. **% Receiving Financial Aid:** 60. **% Receiving Scholarships/Grants:** 78. **% Receiving Loans:** 53. **Types of Aid Available:** Graduate assistantships, institutional work-study, scholarships. **Average Salary Stipend:** $3,000.

ADMISSIONS INFORMATION

Application Fee: $60. **Regular Application Deadline:** 3/1. **Transfer Students Accepted?** Yes. **Number of Applications Received:** 1,126. **% of Applicants Accepted:** 37. **% Accepted Who Enrolled:** 42. **Required Admission Factors:** Letters of recommendation, transcript. **Program-Specific Admission Factors:** Minimum three letters of recommendation required of doctoral program applicants. GRE (General Exam) required for musicology only.

EMPLOYMENT INFORMATION

Placement Office Available? Yes.

BOSTON UNIVERSITY
Graduate School of Arts & Sciences

Address: 121 Bay State Road, Boston, MA 02215
Admissions Phone: 617-353-2696 · **Admissions Fax:** 617-358-0540

INSTITUTIONAL INFORMATION

Public/Private: Private (nonprofit). **Students in Parent Institution:** 25,137.

STUDENT INFORMATION

Total Students in Program: 7,716. **% Full-time:** 66. **% Female:** 54.

RESEARCH FACILITIES

Research Facilities: Communication research center.

EXPENSES/FINANCIAL AID

Annual Tuition: $25,872. **Fees:** $246. **Grants Range From:** $200-$41,276. **Loans Range From:** $725-$51,000. **% Receiving Financial Aid:** 55. **% Receiving Scholarships/Grants:** 78. **% Receiving Loans:** 53. **Types of Aid Available:** 1. **Number of fellowships granted each year:** 70. **Average amount of individual fellowships per year:** $14,000. **Number of teaching/research assistantships granted each year:** 670. **Average Salary Stipend:** $6,250.

ADMISSIONS INFORMATION

Application Fee: $60. **Transfer Students Accepted?** Yes. **Transfer Policy:** Maximum 8 credit hours may be transferred into master's programs; 16 may be transferred into post-master's programs. **Number of Applications Received:** 5,026. **% of Applicants Accepted:** 31. **% Accepted Who Enrolled:** 32. **Average GRE Verbal:** 562. **Average GRE Quantitative:** 673. **Average GRE Analytical:** 669. **Required Admission Factors:** Essays/personal statement, GRE, letters of recommendation, transcript. **Program-Specific Admission Factors:** Creative writing sample required of applicants to master's creative writing program. Three letters of recommendation required of some applicants.

EMPLOYMENT INFORMATION

Placement Office Available? Yes.

BOSTON UNIVERSITY
Metropolitan College

Address: 755 Commonwealth Avenue, Boston, MA 02215
Admissions Phone: 617-353-6000 · **Admissions Fax:** 617-353-2744
Admissions E-mail: MET@bu.edu · **Web Address:** www.bu.edu/met

INSTITUTIONAL INFORMATION

Public/Private: Private (nonprofit). **Evening Classes Available?** Yes. **Total Faculty:** 164. **% Faculty Female:** 37. **% Faculty Part-time:** 85. **Student/Faculty Ratio:** 15:1. **Students in Parent Institution:** 29,596.

PROGRAMS

Masters offered in: Actuarial science; advertising; arts management; business administration/management; city/urban, community, and regional planning; computer and information sciences; computer systems, networking, and telecommunications; corrections and criminal justice; criminal justice/law enforcement administration; information science/studies; liberal arts and sciences/liberal studies; multi/interdisciplinary studies; urban studies/affairs.

STUDENT INFORMATION

Total Students in Program: 1,492. **% Full-time:** 12. **% Female:** 39. **% Minority:** 3. **% International:** 16.

RESEARCH FACILITIES

Research Facilities: Communication research center.

EXPENSES/FINANCIAL AID

Annual Tuition: $29,988. **Room & Board (On/Off Campus):** $9,680/$10,454. **Fees:** $294. **Books and Supplies:** $852. **Grants Range From:** $260-$28,512. **Loans Range From:** $100-$43,625. **% Receiving Scholarships/Grants:** 57. **% Receiving Loans:** 7. **% Receiving Assistantships:** 49. **Types of Aid Available:** Graduate assistantships, loans, scholarships. **Average student debt, upon graduation:** $26,049.

ADMISSIONS INFORMATION

Application Fee: $70. **Regular Application Deadline:** N/A. **Regular Notification:** Rolling. **Transfer Students Accepted?** Yes. **Transfer Policy:** Varies by program Contact the graduate department via MET@bu.edu. **Number of Applications Received:** 845. **% of Applicants Accepted:** 98. **% Accepted Who Enrolled:** 57. **Average GPA:** 3.1. **Required Admission Factors:** Essays/personal statement, letters of recommendation, transcript. **Other Admission Factors:** Minimum 3.0 GPA recommended. **Program-Specific Admission Factors:** Three letters of recommendation required of applicants to some programs. Please see www.bu.edu/met for graduate admissions requirements by program.

EMPLOYMENT INFORMATION

Placement Office Available? Yes.

BOSTON UNIVERSITY
School of Social Work

Address: 264 Bay State Road, Boston, MA 02215
Admissions Phone: 617-353-3765 · **Admissions Fax:** 617-353-5612
Admissions E-mail: busswad@bu.edu · **Web Address:** www.bu.edu/ssw/

INSTITUTIONAL INFORMATION

Public/Private: Private (proprietary). **Evening Classes Available?** Yes. **Total Faculty:** 59. **% Faculty Female:** 71. **% Faculty Part-time:** 63. **Students in Parent Institution:** 391.

PROGRAMS

Masters offered in: Social work. **Doctorate offered in:** Sociology.

STUDENT INFORMATION

Total Students in Program: 507. **% Full-time:** 73.

RESEARCH FACILITIES

Research Facilities: Communication research center.

EXPENSES/FINANCIAL AID

Annual Tuition: $20,972. **Fees:** $284. **Books and Supplies:** $1,132. **Grants Range From:** $500-$20,972. **Loans Range From:** $600-$36,000. **% Receiving Financial Aid:** 90. **% Receiving Scholarships/Grants:** 30. **% Receiving Loans:** 90. **Types of Aid Available:** Grants, institutional work-study, loans, scholarships. **Average student debt, upon graduation:** $35,915. **Number of teaching/research assistantships granted each year:** 2. **Assistantship compensation includes:** Full tuition remission, salary/stipend. **Average Salary Stipend:** $1,000.

ADMISSIONS INFORMATION

Application Fee: $65. **Priority Application Deadline:** 2/3. **Regular Application Deadline:** 3/1. **Regular Notification:** Rolling. **Transfer Students Accepted?** Yes. **Transfer Policy:** Maximum 24 credit hours with a minimum 3.0 GPA may be transferred from a CSWE accredited social work program. The additional 41 credits required for graduation must be taken at Boston University School of Social Work. **Number of Applications Received:** 507. **% of Applicants Accepted:** 87. **% Accepted Who Enrolled:** 43. **Average GPA:** 3.4. **Required Admission Factors:** Essays/personal statement, letters of recommendation, transcript.
Recommended Admission Factors: Interview.
Other Admission Factors: GPA of 3.0 is recommended; no minimum test score needed; students will not be rejected for low test score alone.

EMPLOYMENT INFORMATION

% Employed Within 6 Months: 75. **Average starting salary:** $36,000.

BOSTON UNIVERSITY
University Professors Program

Address: 745 Commonwealth Avenue, Boston, MA 02215
Admissions Phone: 617-353-4022 · **Admissions Fax:** 617-353-5084
Admissions E-mail: enewmark@bu.edu · **Web Address:** www.bu.edu/uni/

INSTITUTIONAL INFORMATION

Public/Private: Private (nonprofit). **Total Faculty:** 36. **% Faculty Female:** 11. **Student/Faculty Ratio:** 1:1. **Students in Parent Institution:** 25,137.

STUDENT INFORMATION

Total Students in Program: 7,716. **% Full-time:** 66. **% Female:** 54.

RESEARCH FACILITIES

Research Facilities: Communication research center.

EXPENSES/FINANCIAL AID

Annual Tuition: $25,872. **Fees:** $246. **Books and Supplies:** $300. **Grants Range From:** $200-$41,276. **Loans Range From:** $725-$51,000. **% Receiving Financial Aid:** 55. **% Receiving Scholarships/Grants:** 78. **% Receiving Loans:** 53. **Types of Aid Available:** Grants, scholarships.

ADMISSIONS INFORMATION

Application Fee: $65. **Regular Application Deadline:** 1/15. **Regular Notification:** Rolling. **Transfer Students Accepted?** Yes. **Transfer Policy:** Same as for regular applicants. **Number of Applications Received:** 22. **% of Applicants Accepted:** 41. **% Accepted Who Enrolled:** 89.
Required Admission Factors: Essays/personal statement, GRE, letters of recommendation, transcript.
Other Admission Factors: Writing sample required.

EMPLOYMENT INFORMATION

Placement Office Available? Yes.

BOWIE STATE UNIVERSITY
Graduate Programs

Address: 14000 Jericho Park Drive, Bowie, MD 20715-9465
Admissions Phone: 301-860-3415 · **Admissions Fax:** 301-860-3438
Admissions E-mail: schanaiwa@bowiestate.edu · **Web Address:** www.bowiestate.edu

INSTITUTIONAL INFORMATION

Public/Private: Public. **Evening Classes Available?** Yes. **Total Faculty:** 80. **% Faculty Female:** 40. **% Faculty Part-time:** 40. **Student/Faculty Ratio:** 17:1. **Students in Parent Institution:** 5,415.

STUDENT INFORMATION

Total Students in Program: 1,388. **% Full-time:** 21. **% Female:** 74. **% Minority:** 79. **% International:** 1.

EXPENSES/FINANCIAL AID

Annual Tuition: In-state $3,103. / Out-of-state $9,519. **Room & Board (On/Off Campus):** $5,673/$7,668. **Fees:** $961. **Books and Supplies:** $1,172. **Grants Range From:** $100-$5,000. **Loans Range From:** $500-$18,500. **% Receiving Financial Aid:** 34. **% Receiving Scholarships/Grants:** 16. **% Receiving Loans:** 84. **% Receiving Assistantships:** 18. **Types of Aid Available:** Graduate assistantships, grants, loans, scholarships. **Average student debt, upon graduation:** $7,275. **Assistantship compensation includes:** Full tuition remission, salary/stipend. **Average Salary Stipend:** $2,880.

ADMISSIONS INFORMATION

Application Fee: $40. **Priority Application Deadline:** 4/1. **Regular Application Deadline:** N/A. **Regular Notification:** Rolling. **Transfer Students Accepted?** Yes. **Number of Applications Received:** 461. **% of Applicants Accepted:** 70. **Average GPA:** 3.5.
Required Admission Factors: Transcript.
Other Admission Factors: 2.5 or better

EMPLOYMENT INFORMATION

% Employed Within 6 Months: 6. **Average starting salary:** $42,000.

BOWLING GREEN STATE UNIVERSITY
College of Arts & Sciences

Address: Bowling Green, OH 43403
Admissions Phone: 419-372-2791 · **Admissions Fax:** 419-372-8569
Admissions E-mail: tlawren@bgnet.bgsu.edu

INSTITUTIONAL INFORMATION

Public/Private: Public. **Students in Parent Institution:** 18,739.

STUDENT INFORMATION

Total Students in Program: 2,871. **% Full-time:** 50. **% Female:** 61.

RESEARCH FACILITIES

Research Facilities: Center for Archival Collections, Mid-American Center for Contemporary Music, Philosophy Documentation Center, Center for Microscopy and Microanalysis, Center for Photochemical Sciences, Institute for GREat Lakes Research, Mid-America Drosophila Stock.

EXPENSES/FINANCIAL AID

Annual Tuition: In-state $6,750. / Out-of-state $12,648. **Books and Supplies:** $868.

ADMISSIONS INFORMATION

Application Fee: $30. **Regular Notification:** Rolling. **Transfer Students Accepted?** No. **Number of Applications Received:** 1,282. **% of Applicants Accepted:** 49. **% Accepted Who Enrolled:** 43. **Average GPA:** 3.42. **Average GRE Verbal:** 519. **Average GRE Quantitative:** 613. **Average GRE Analytical:** 610.
Required Admission Factors: GRE, transcript.
Program-Specific Admission Factors: Minimum 3.0 GPA required of master's program applicants. Minimum 3.2 GPA required of doctoral program applicants. GRE subject exam (psychology) recommended of psychology program applicants.

EMPLOYMENT INFORMATION

Placement Office Available? Yes.

BOWLING GREEN STATE UNIVERSITY
College of Musical Arts

Address: Bowling Green, OH 43403
Admissions Phone: 419-372-2791 · **Admissions Fax:** 419-372-8569
Admissions E-mail: tlawren@bgnet.bgsu.edu

INSTITUTIONAL INFORMATION
Public/Private: Public. **Students in Parent Institution:** 18,739.

STUDENT INFORMATION
Total Students in Program: 2,871. **% Full-time:** 50. **% Female:** 61.

RESEARCH FACILITIES
Research Facilities: Center for Archival Collections, Mid-American Center for Contemporary Music, Philosophy Documentation Center, Center for Microscopy and Microanalysis, Center for Photochemical Sciences, Institute for Great Lakes Research

EXPENSES/FINANCIAL AID
Annual Tuition: In-state $6,750. / Out-of-state $12,648. **Books and Supplies:** $868. **Number of teaching/research assistantships granted each year:** 80.

ADMISSIONS INFORMATION
Application Fee: $30. **Regular Notification:** Rolling. **Transfer Students Accepted?** No. **Number of Applications Received:** 101. **% of Applicants Accepted:** 65. **% Accepted Who Enrolled:** 56. **Average GPA:** 3.54. **Average GRE Verbal:** 474. **Average GRE Quantitative:** 549. **Average GRE Analytical:** 612.
Required Admission Factors: GRE, letters of recommendation, transcript.
Other Admission Factors: Minimum 3.0 GPA required.
Program-Specific Admission Factors: Audition required of perfomance and conducting program applicants. Examples of work required of music composition, music history, and music theory program applicants.

EMPLOYMENT INFORMATION
Placement Office Available? Yes.

BRADLEY UNIVERSITY
The Graduate School

Address: 1501 West Bradley Avenue, Peoria, IL 61625
Admissions Phone: 309-677-2375 · **Admissions Fax:** 309-677-3343
Admissions E-mail: bugrad2@bradley.edu · **Web Address:** www.bradley.edu/grad

INSTITUTIONAL INFORMATION
Public/Private: Private (nonprofit). **Evening Classes Available?** Yes. **Students in Parent Institution:** 6,069.

PROGRAMS
Masters offered in: Accounting; business administration/management; ceramic arts and ceramics; chemistry; civil engineering; commercial photography; community health services/liaison/counseling; computer and information sciences; counselor education/school counseling and guidance services; creative writing; curriculum and instruction; design and visual communications; drawing; education leadership and administration; education/teaching of individuals with specific learning disabilities; electrical, electronics, and communications engineering; English language and literature; fine/studio arts; human services; illustration; industrial engineering; information science/studies; liberal arts and sciences/liberal studies; manufacturing engineering; mechanical engineering; nurse anesthetist; nursing administration (MSN, MS, PhD); painting; photography; physical therapy/therapist; printmaking; sculpture; visual and performing arts.

STUDENT INFORMATION
Total Students in Program: 754. **% Full-time:** 29. **% Female:** 49. **% Minority:** 6. **% International:** 27.

EXPENSES/FINANCIAL AID
Annual Tuition: $10,170. **Room & Board:** $3,075. **Types of Aid Available:** Fellowships, graduate assistantships, grants, loans, scholarships.

ADMISSIONS INFORMATION
Application Fee: $40. **Regular Application Deadline:** 8/15. **Regular Notification:** Rolling. **Transfer Students Accepted?** Yes. **Number of Applications Received:** 787. **% of Applicants Accepted:** 69. **% Accepted Who Enrolled:** 44.
Required Admission Factors: Essays/personal statement, letters of recommendation, transcript.
Other Admission Factors: Minimum 2.5/4.0 overall GPA and 2.75/4.0 in major area of study for unconditional admission (some departments require higher GPA). Minimum TOEFL score of 550 or IELTS score of 6.5 for international applicants. Financial certification also required for international students.

EMPLOYMENT INFORMATION
Placement Office Available? Yes. **% Employed Within 6 Months:** 97. **Rate of placement:** 99%.

BRANDEIS UNIVERSITY
The Graduate School of Arts & Sciences

Address: 415 South Street, PO Box 9110 - MS 031, Waltham, MA 02254-9110
Admissions Phone: 781-736-3410 · **Admissions Fax:** 781-736-3412
Admissions E-mail: gradschool@brandeis.edu
Web Address: www.brandeis.edu/gsas/

INSTITUTIONAL INFORMATION
Public/Private: Private (nonprofit). **Students in Parent Institution:** 4,753.

PROGRAMS
Masters offered in: Algebra and number theory; American government and politics (U.S.); American history (U.S.); American literature (U.S.); analysis and functional analysis; anthropology; applied mathematics; applied mathematics; archeology; area, ethnic, cultural, and gender studies; Bible/Biblical studies; biochemistry; biophysics and molecular biology, biochemistry/biophysics and molecular biology; biochemistry; biophysics; cell/cellular and molecular biology; chemistry; Christian studies; cognitive science; computational mathematics; computer and information sciences; computer science; cultural resources management and policy analysis; education; elementary education and teaching; English language and literature, English literature (British and commonwealth); European history; genetics, geometry/geometric analysis; health/medical preparatory programs; inorganic chemistry; international relations and affairs; Islamic studies; Jewish/Judaic studies; mathematics; mathematics; molecular biology; near and middle eastern studies; neuroscience; organic chemistry; peace studies and conflict resolution; physical anthropology; political science and government, pre-dentistry studies; pre-medicine/premedical studies; pre-veterinary studies; psychology; religion/religious studies; social and philosophical foundations of education; sociology; structural biology; topology and foundations; women's studies.

STUDENT INFORMATION
Total Students in Program: 1,584. **% Full-time:** 72. **% Female:** 49.

RESEARCH FACILITIES
Research Facilities: Center for Human Resources, Center for Social Change, Center for Ethics, Justice, and Public Life, International Research Institute on Jewish Women, Volen National Center for Complex Systems, Rosenstiel Basic Medical Sciences Research Center.

EXPENSES/FINANCIAL AID

Annual Tuition: $31,366. Fees: $795. Books and Supplies: $700. Grants Range From: $2,500-$31,366. Loans Range From: $4,000-$18,500. % Receiving Financial Aid: 95. Types of Aid Available: Fellowships, graduate assistantships, grants, loans, scholarships. Number of fellowships granted each year: 360 Average amount of individual fellowships per year: $11,000. Assistantship compensation includes: Full tuition remission, salary/stipend.

ADMISSIONS INFORMATION

Application Fee: $55. Priority Application Deadline: 1/15. Regular Application Deadline: 5/15. Regular Notification: Rolling. Transfer Students Accepted? Yes. Transfer Policy: Maximum 1 year may be transferred. Number of Applications Received: 1,578. % of Applicants Accepted: 30. % Accepted Who Enrolled: 45. Average GRE Verbal: 584. Average GRE Quantitative: 582. Average GRE Analytical: 678. Required Admission Factors: Essays/personal statement, letters of recommendation, transcript.
Program-Specific Admission Factors: Acting: audition. Composition, design, studio art: portfolio.

BRANDEIS UNIVERSITY/THE HELLER SCHOOL FOR SOCIAL POLICY AND MANAGEMENT
PhD in Social Policy

Address: 415 South Street, MS 035, Waltham, MA 02454-9110
Admissions Phone: 800-279-4105 · Admissions Fax: 781-736-3881
Admissions E-mail: HellerAdmissions@brandeis.edu
Web Address: http://heller.brandeis.edu

INSTITUTIONAL INFORMATION

Public/Private: Private (nonprofit). Total Faculty: 75. Student/Faculty Ratio: 3:1. Students in Parent Institution: 4,852.

PROGRAMS

Doctorate offered in: Community organization and advocacy, demography/population studies, human services, international public health/international health, maternal and child health, political science and government, political science and government. First Professional degree offered in: Community organization and advocacy, demography/population studies, human services, international public health/international health, maternal and child health, political science and government, political science and government.

STUDENT INFORMATION

Total Students in Program: 1,795. % Full-time: 72.

RESEARCH FACILITIES

Research Facilities: Six social policy research centers contribute to the intellectual foundation and scholarship within The Heller School and strive to bridge the gap between theory and practice.

EXPENSES/FINANCIAL AID

Annual Tuition: $28,999. Room & Board: $14,070. Fees: $35. Books and Supplies: $1,075. Loans Range From: $500-$18,500. % Receiving Financial Aid: 100. % Receiving Scholarships/Grants: 100. % Receiving Loans: 25. Types of Aid Available: Fellowships, graduate assistantships, grants, loans, scholarships. Average student debt, upon graduation: $8,500 Number of fellowships granted each year: 15 Average amount of individual fellowships per year: $41,999. Assistantship compensation includes: Salary/stipend. Average Salary Stipend: $13,000.

ADMISSIONS INFORMATION

Application Fee: $50. Priority Application Deadline: 12/15. Regular Application Deadline: 12/15. Regular Notification: 2/28. Transfer Students Accepted? No. Number of Applications Received: 96. % of Applicants

Accepted: 36. % Accepted Who Enrolled: 60. Average GPA: 3.7. Average GRE Verbal: 592. Average GRE Quantitative: 645. Average GRE Analytical: 665. Average GRE Analytical Writing: 5.
Required Admission Factors: Essays/personal statement, GRE, letters of recommendation, transcript.
Recommended Admission Factors: Interview.
Other Admission Factors: Academic writing sample and resume or C.V.
Program-Specific Admission Factors: Master's degree or significant work experience preferred.

EMPLOYMENT INFORMATION

Placement Office Available? Yes. % Employed Within 6 Months: 95. Rate of placement: 100%.

BRANDON UNIVERSITY
Department of Rural Development

Address: 270 18th Street, Brandon, MB R7A 6A9 Canada
Admissions Phone: 204-727-9784 · Admissions Fax: 204-728-3221
Admissions E-mail: admissions@brandonu.ca
Web Address: www.brandonu.ca

INSTITUTIONAL INFORMATION

Public/Private: Public. Evening Classes Available? Yes. Student/Faculty Ratio: 6:1. Students in Parent Institution: 2,666.

STUDENT INFORMATION

Total Students in Program: 100. % Full-time: 7. % Female: 73.

RESEARCH FACILITIES

Research Facilities: Rural Development Institute.

EXPENSES/FINANCIAL AID

Annual Tuition: In-state $4,094. / Out-of-state $4,094. Room & Board: $5,216. Fees: $179. Books and Supplies: $1,000. Grants Range From: $300-$1,500.

ADMISSIONS INFORMATION

Application Fee: $35. Priority Application Deadline: 1/31. Regular Application Deadline: 1/31. Regular Notification: Rolling. Transfer Students Accepted? Yes. Number of Applications Received: 16. % of Applicants Accepted: 75. % Accepted Who Enrolled: 100. Average GPA: 3.2.
Required Admission Factors: Essays/personal statement, letters of recommendation, transcript.
Other Admission Factors: Minimum 3.0 GPA required.

EMPLOYMENT INFORMATION

Placement Office Available? Yes.

BRANDON UNIVERSITY
School of Music

Address: 270 18th Street, Brandon, Manitoba, R7A 6A9 Canada
Admissions Phone: 204-727-7388 · Admissions Fax: 204-728-6839

INSTITUTIONAL INFORMATION

Public/Private: Public. Students in Parent Institution: 2,666.

STUDENT INFORMATION

Total Students in Program: 100. % Full-time: 7. % Female: 73.

RESEARCH FACILITIES

Research Facilities: Rural Development Institute.

EXPENSES/FINANCIAL AID

Fees: $179. Books and Supplies: $1,000. Grants Range From: $300-$1,500. % Receiving Financial Aid: 80. Number of teaching/research assistantships granted each year: 3. Average Salary Stipend: $6,500.

ADMISSIONS INFORMATION

Application Fee: $35. Regular Notification: Rolling. Transfer Students Accepted? Yes. Number of Applications Received: 9. % of Applicants Accepted: 100. % Accepted Who Enrolled: 44.

Required Admission Factors: Essays/personal statement, letters of recommendation, transcript.

Other Admission Factors: Minimum 3.0 GPA required.

EMPLOYMENT INFORMATION

Placement Office Available? Yes.

BRESCIA UNIVERSITY
Brescia University Graduate Programs

Address: 717 Frederica Street, Owensboro, KY 42301-3023
Admissions Phone: 270-686-4316 · Admissions Fax: 270-686-4314
Admissions E-mail: bill_kuba@brescia.edu · Web Address: www.brescia.edu

INSTITUTIONAL INFORMATION

Public/Private: Private (nonprofit). Total Faculty: 8. % Faculty Female: 62. % Faculty Part-time: 12. Student/Faculty Ratio: 10:1. Students in Parent Institution: 751.

PROGRAMS

Masters offered in: Curriculum and instruction; management science.

STUDENT INFORMATION

Total Students in Program: 41. % Female: 59.

EXPENSES/FINANCIAL AID

Fees: $80. Books and Supplies: $400. Loans Range From: $1,000-$10,500. % Receiving Financial Aid: 15. % Receiving Loans: 100.

ADMISSIONS INFORMATION

Application Fee: $50. Regular Application Deadline: 6/1. Regular Notification: Rolling. Transfer Students Accepted? No. Number of Applications Received: 7. % of Applicants Accepted: 86. % Accepted Who Enrolled: 67. Average GPA: 3.4.

Required Admission Factors: Interview, transcript.

BRIGHAM YOUNG UNIVERSITY
College of Family, Home, & Social Sciences

Address: B-356 ASB, Provo, UT 84602-1339
Admissions Phone: 801-378-7308 · Admissions Fax: 801-378-5238
Admissions E-mail: claire_dewitt@byu.edu

INSTITUTIONAL INFORMATION

Public/Private: Private (nonprofit). Students in Parent Institution: 32,415.

STUDENT INFORMATION

Total Students in Program: 2,955. % Full-time: 55. % Female: 37.

RESEARCH FACILITIES

Research Facilities: Benson Science Building, combustion lab, Eyring Science Center, Center for Studies of the Family, Cancer Research Center.

EXPENSES/FINANCIAL AID

Books and Supplies: $750. Average student debt, upon graduation: $15,000.

ADMISSIONS INFORMATION

Application Fee: $30. Regular Notification: Rolling. Transfer Students Accepted? Yes. Transfer Policy: Maximum 10 credit hours may be transferred with departmental approval. Number of Applications Received: 371. Average GPA: 3.59. Average GRE Verbal: 530. Average GRE Quantitative: 566. Average GRE Analytical: 594.

Required Admission Factors: Essays/personal statement, GRE, letters of recommendation, transcript.

Other Admission Factors: Minimum 3.0 GPA required.

Program-Specific Admission Factors: Writing sample required of MA in history program applicants. MA thesis required of PhD in history program applicants. Proof of lanuage competency required of international and area studies program applicants.

EMPLOYMENT INFORMATION

Placement Office Available? Yes.

Other Admission Factors: Minimum 2.5 GPA required.

Program-Specific Admission Factors: For the master of science in curriculm and instruction, successful completion of the Praxis II specialty tests in candidate's subject area/s or successful completion of the NTE (National Teacher Exam).

BRIGHAM YOUNG UNIVERSITY
College of Fine Arts & Communications

Address: B-356 ASB, Provo, UT 84602-1339
Admissions Phone: 801-378-4541 · Admissions Fax: 801-378-5238
Admissions E-mail: claire_dewitt@byu.edu

INSTITUTIONAL INFORMATION

Public/Private: Private (nonprofit). Student/Faculty Ratio: 4:1. Students in Parent Institution: 32,415.

STUDENT INFORMATION

Total Students in Program: 2,955. % Full-time: 55. % Female: 37.

RESEARCH FACILITIES

Research Facilities: Benson Science Building, combustion lab, Eyring Science Center, Center for Studies of the Family, Cancer Research Center.

EXPENSES/FINANCIAL AID

Books and Supplies: $750.

ADMISSIONS INFORMATION

Application Fee: $30. Regular Notification: Rolling. Transfer Students Accepted? Yes. Transfer Policy: Maximum 10 credit hours may be transferred with departmental approval. Number of Applications Received: 83. % of Applicants Accepted: 59. Average GPA: 3.5. Average GRE Verbal: 507. Average GRE Quantitative: 545. Average GRE Analytical: 605.

Required Admission Factors: Essays/personal statement, letters of recommendation, transcript.

Program-Specific Admission Factors: Writing sample required of MA in music program applicants. Portfolio or audition tape required of MMus in music program applicants. Writing sample and portfolio required of theater program applicants. GRE subject exam of music required of music program.

EMPLOYMENT INFORMATION

Placement Office Available? Yes.

BRIGHAM YOUNG UNIVERSITY
College of Humanities

Address: B-356 ASB, Provo, UT 84602-1339
Admissions Phone: 801-378-7308 · Admissions Fax: 801-378-5238
Admissions E-mail: landes_holbrook@byu.edu

INSTITUTIONAL INFORMATION
Public/Private: Private (nonprofit). Students in Parent Institution: 32,415.

STUDENT INFORMATION
Total Students in Program: 2,955. % Full-time: 55. % Female: 37.

RESEARCH FACILITIES
Research Facilities: Benson Science Building, combustion lab, Eyring Science Center, Center for Studies of the Family, Cancer Research Center.

EXPENSES/FINANCIAL AID
Books and Supplies: $750. Average student debt, upon graduation: $15,000.

ADMISSIONS INFORMATION
Application Fee: $30. Regular Notification: Rolling. Transfer Students Accepted? Yes. Transfer Policy: Maximum 10 credit hours may be transferred with departmental approval. Number of Applications Received: 103. % of Applicants Accepted: 51. Average GPA: 3.49. Average GRE Verbal: 577. Average GRE Quantitative: 552. Average GRE Analytical: 616. Required Admission Factors: Essays/personal statement, GRE, letters of recommendation, transcript.
Other Admission Factors: Minimum 3.0 GPA required.
Program-Specific Admission Factors: Writing sample required by some programs. Competency in 1 or 2 foreign languages required by some programs.

EMPLOYMENT INFORMATION
Placement Office Available? Yes.

BRIGHAM YOUNG UNIVERSITY
College of Physical & Mathematical Sciences

Address: B-356 ASB, Provo, UT 84602-1339
Admissions Phone: 801-378-4091 · Admissions Fax: 801-378-5238
Admissions E-mail: landes_holbrook@byu.edu

INSTITUTIONAL INFORMATION
Public/Private: Private (nonprofit). Student/Faculty Ratio: 2:1. Students in Parent Institution: 32,415.

STUDENT INFORMATION
Total Students in Program: 2,955. % Full-time: 55. % Female: 37.

RESEARCH FACILITIES
Research Facilities: Benson Science Building, combustion lab, Eyring Science Center, Center for Studies of the Family, Cancer Research Center.

EXPENSES/FINANCIAL AID
Books and Supplies: $750. % Receiving Financial Aid: 100. Number of fellowships granted each year: 3. Number of teaching/research assistantships granted each year: 12. Average Salary Stipend: $14,600.

ADMISSIONS INFORMATION
Application Fee: $30. Regular Notification: Rolling. Transfer Students Accepted? Yes. Number of Applications Received: 238. % of Applicants Accepted: 30. Average GPA: 3.4. Average GRE Verbal: 500. Average GRE Quantitative: 570. Average GRE Analytical: 610.
Required Admission Factors: Essays/personal statement, GRE, letters of recommendation, transcript.
Other Admission Factors: Minimum 3.0 GPA required.

EMPLOYMENT INFORMATION
Placement Office Available? Yes. % Employed Within 6 Months: 100. % of doctoral grads employed in their field upon graduation: 100.

BROOKS INSTITUTE OF PHOTOGRAPHY
Graduate Program

Address: 801 Alston Road, Santa Barbara, CA 93108
Admissions Phone: 805-966-3888,ext. 217 · Admissions Fax: 805-565-1386
Admissions E-mail: admissions@brooks.edu

INSTITUTIONAL INFORMATION
Public/Private: Private (proprietary). Students in Parent Institution: 411.

STUDENT INFORMATION
Total Students in Program: 65. % Full-time: 100. % Female: 25.

EXPENSES/FINANCIAL AID
Annual Tuition: $15,840. Fees: $600.

ADMISSIONS INFORMATION
Application Fee: $35. Regular Notification: Rolling. Transfer Students Accepted? No. Number of Applications Received: 18. % of Applicants Accepted: 78. % Accepted Who Enrolled: 93. Average GPA: 3.0.
Required Admission Factors: Essays/personal statement, transcript.
Other Admission Factors: Minimum 3.0 GPA required.

EMPLOYMENT INFORMATION
Placement Office Available? Yes. Rate of placement: 84%.

BROWN UNIVERSITY
Graduate School

Address: 47 George Street, Box 1876, Brown University, Providence, RI 02912
Admissions Phone: 401-863-2600 · Admissions Fax: 401-863-3471
Admissions E-mail: Graduate_School@brown.edu · Web Address: www.brown.edu/gs

INSTITUTIONAL INFORMATION
Public/Private: Private (nonprofit). Students in Parent Institution: 7,700

PROGRAMS
Masters offered in: Acting; American history (U.S.); American literature (U.S.); American/U.S. studies/civilization; ancient studies/civilization; anthropology; applied mathematics; art history, criticism, and conservation; behavioral sciences; biochemistry/biophysics and molecular biology; biochemistry; biological and physical sciences; biostatistics; biotechnology; cell biology and anatomy; cell/cellular and molecular biology; cell/cellular biology and histology; chemistry; Christian studies; classics and classical languages, literatures, and linguistics; cognitive psychology and psycholinguistics; comparative literature; computer and information sciences; creative writing; dance; development economics and international development; drama and dramatics/theater arts; econometrics and quantitative economics; economics; English language and literature; English literature (British and commonwealth); environmental studies; experimental psychology; film/cinema studies; foreign languages/modern languages, French language and literature; general studies; geology/earth science; history; humanities/humanistic studies; Italian language and literature; Jewish/Judaic studies; liberal arts and sciences/liberal studies; linguistics; mathematics and computer science; mathematics; medieval and renaissance studies; molecular biochemistry; molecular biology; molecular pharmacology; museology/museum studies; music history, literature, and theory; music theory and composition; music; music/music and performing arts studies; musicology and ethnomusicology; natural sciences; neuroscience; pharmacology; philosophy; physical anthropology; physical sciences; physics; playwriting and screenwriting; political science and government; Portuguese language and literature; psychology; public administration; public health (MPH, DPH); public policy analysis; religion/religious studies; social sciences, sociology; Spanish language and literature; technical theater/theater design and technology; theater literature, history, and criticism; urban studies/affairs; visual and performing arts.

STUDENT INFORMATION
Total Students in Program: 1,650. % Full-time: 100.

EXPENSES/FINANCIAL AID
Annual Tuition: $30,672. Fees: $2,600. Books and Supplies: $1,000. Grants Range From: $500-$50,000. Loans Range From: $100-$18,500. Types of Aid Available: Fellowships, graduate assistantships, grants, loans. Number of fellowships granted each year: 463. Average amount of individual fellowships per year: $50,000. Number of teaching/research assistantships granted each year: 819. Assistantship compensation includes: Full tuition remission, salary/stipend. Average Salary Stipend: $17,000.

ADMISSIONS INFORMATION
Application Fee: $70. Regular Notification: Rolling. Transfer Students Accepted? Yes. Number of Applications Received: 5,592. % of Applicants Accepted: 17. % Accepted Who Enrolled: 46.
Other Admission Factors: Three letters of recommendation required.

EMPLOYMENT INFORMATION
Placement Office Available? Yes.

BRYN MAWR COLLEGE
Graduate School of Arts & Sciences

Address: 101 North Merion Avenue, Bryn Mawr, PA 19010-2899
Admissions Phone: 610-526-5072 · Admissions Fax: 610-526-5076
Admissions E-mail: gsas@brynmawr.edu · Web Address: www.brynmawr.edu/gsas/

INSTITUTIONAL INFORMATION
Public/Private: Private (nonprofit). Student/Faculty Ratio: 10:1. Students in Parent Institution: 1,503.

STUDENT INFORMATION
Total Students in Program: 187. % Full-time: 32. % Female: 78.

RESEARCH FACILITIES
Research Facilities: Archaeology/anthropology collections, print/drawing collection, mineral collections, Institat d'Etudes Francaises.

EXPENSES/FINANCIAL AID
% Receiving Financial Aid: 70. % Receiving Scholarships/Grants: 100. Average Salary Stipend: $9,300.

ADMISSIONS INFORMATION
Application Fee: $30. Priority Application Deadline: 1/15. Regular Application Deadline: 6/30. Regular Notification: Rolling. Transfer Students Accepted? No.
Required Admission Factors: Essays/personal statement, GRE, letters of recommendation, transcript.

EMPLOYMENT INFORMATION
Placement Office Available? Yes. Rate of placement: 85%.

BRYN MAWR COLLEGE
Graduate School of Social Work & Social Research

Address: 300 Airdale Road, Bryn Mawr, PA 19010
Admissions Phone: 610-520-2601 · Admissions Fax: 610-520-2655
Admissions E-mail: nkirby@brynmawr.edu · Web Address: www.brynmawr.edu

INSTITUTIONAL INFORMATION
Public/Private: Private (nonprofit). Evening Classes Available? Yes. Student/Faculty Ratio: 10:1. Students in Parent Institution: 1,503

STUDENT INFORMATION
Total Students in Program: 187. % Full-time: 32. % Female: 78.

RESEARCH FACILITIES
Research Facilities: Archaeology/anthropology collections, print/drawing collection, mineral collections, Institat d'Etudes Francaises.

EXPENSES/FINANCIAL AID
% Receiving Financial Aid: 68. % Receiving Scholarships/Grants: 100. Average student debt, upon graduation: $28,800. Number of teaching/research assistantships granted each year: 8. Average Salary Stipend: $9,300.

ADMISSIONS INFORMATION
Application Fee: $50. Regular Application Deadline: 3/15. Regular Notification: Rolling. Transfer Students Accepted? Yes. Transfer Policy: Must meet the same requirements for other applicants. Number of Applications Received: 248. % of Applicants Accepted: 81. % Accepted Who Enrolled: 49.
Required Admission Factors: Essays/personal statement, interview, letters of recommendation, transcript.

EMPLOYMENT INFORMATION
Placement Office Available? Yes. Rate of placement: 85%.

BUCKNELL UNIVERSITY
College of Arts & Sciences

Address: Graduate Studies, Lewisburg, PA 17837
Admissions Phone: 570-577-1304 · Admissions Fax: 570-577-3760
Admissions E-mail: gradstds@bucknell.edu
Web Address: www.bucknell.edu/Offices_Resources/Offices/Graduate_Studies

INSTITUTIONAL INFORMATION
Public/Private: Private (nonprofit). Students in Parent Institution: 3,723.

STUDENT INFORMATION
Total Students in Program: 158. % Full-time: 41. % Female: 55.

RESEARCH FACILITIES
Research Facilities: Greenhouse, poetry center, 63-acre nature site, herbarium, electron microscope, gas chromatograph/mass spectrometer.

EXPENSES/FINANCIAL AID
Grants Range From: $2,875-$11,500. % Receiving Financial Aid: 50. % Receiving Scholarships/Grants: 25. % Receiving Assistantships: 75. Number of teaching/research assistantships granted each year: 34. Average Salary Stipend: $7,500.

ADMISSIONS INFORMATION
Application Fee: $25. Regular Notification: Rolling. Transfer Students Accepted? Yes. Transfer Policy: Maximum eight credits or two courses may be transferred. Number of Applications Received: 183. % of Applicants Accepted: 46. % Accepted Who Enrolled: 76. Average GPA: 3.0. Average GRE Verbal: 500. Average GRE Quantitative: 500. Average GRE Analytical: 500.
Required Admission Factors: Essays/personal statement, GRE, letters of recommendation, transcript.
Other Admission Factors: Minimum 2.8 GPA required.
Program-Specific Admission Factors: Writing sample required for English program.

EMPLOYMENT INFORMATION
Placement Office Available? Yes. Rate of placement: 98%.

BUTLER UNIVERSITY
Jordan College of Fine Arts

Address: 4600 Sunset Avenue, Indianapolis, IN 46208
Admissions Phone: 888-940-8100 · **Admissions Fax:** 317-940-8150
Admissions E-mail: admission@butler.edu · **Web Address:** www.butler.edu

INSTITUTIONAL INFORMATION
Public/Private: Private (nonprofit). **Evening Classes Available?** Yes. **Total Faculty:** 52. **% Faculty Female:** 31. **Student/Faculty Ratio:** 7:1. **Students in Parent Institution:** 4,415.

PROGRAMS
Masters offered in: Conducting; music history, literature, and theory; music pedagogy; music performance; music theory and composition; piano and organ; violin, viola, guitar, and other stringed instruments; voice and opera.

STUDENT INFORMATION
Total Students in Program: 40. **% Full-time:** 40. **% Female:** 35. **% Minority:** 5. **% International:** 12.

EXPENSES/FINANCIAL AID
Annual Tuition: $5,400. **Room & Board:** $7,780. **Fees:** $160. **Books and Supplies:** $750. **Grants Range From:** $500-$2,000. **Loans Range From:** $1,000-$10,000. **% Receiving Loans:** 23. **% Receiving Assistantships:** 50. **Types of Aid Available:** Graduate assistantships, institutional work-study, loans. **Average student debt, upon graduation:** $2,000. **Number of teaching/research assistantships granted each year:** 20. **Assistantship compensation includes:** Full tuition remission. **Average Salary Stipend:** $2,000.

ADMISSIONS INFORMATION
Application Fee: $25. **Regular Application Deadline:** 8/15. **Regular Notification:** Rolling. **Transfer Students Accepted?** Yes. **Number of Applications Received:** 40. **% of Applicants Accepted:** 60. **% Accepted Who Enrolled:** 88. **Average GPA:** 3.3. **Average GRE Verbal:** 450. **Average GRE Quantitative:** 530. **Average GRE Analytical:** 580.
Required Admission Factors: GRE, interview, transcript.
Other Admission Factors: Minimum GRE score of 800, minimum 3.0 GPA, and undergraduate degree in music required.

EMPLOYMENT INFORMATION
% Employed Within 6 Months: 25. **% of master's grads employed in their field upon graduation:** 25. **Rate of placement:** 50%. **Average starting salary:** $30,000.

BUTLER UNIVERSITY
Liberal Arts & Sciences, English Program

Address: 4600 Sunset Avenue, Indianapolis, IN 46208
Admissions Phone: 888-940-8100 · **Admissions Fax:** 317-940-8150
Admissions E-mail: admission@butler.edu
Web Address: www.butler.edu/academics/ada_pharmacy.asp

INSTITUTIONAL INFORMATION
Public/Private: Private (nonprofit). **Evening Classes Available?** Yes. **Total Faculty:** 5. **% Faculty Female:** 40. **% Faculty Part-time:** 100. **Student/Faculty Ratio:** 1:1. **Students in Parent Institution:** 4,415.

PROGRAMS
Masters offered in: Creative writing; English language and literature.

RESEARCH FACILITIES
Research Facilities: Observatory, herbarium, performing arts hall.

EXPENSES/FINANCIAL AID
Annual Tuition: $5,400. **Room & Board:** $7,780. **Books and Supplies:** $350. **Loans Range From:** $15,000-$15,000. **% Receiving Financial Aid:** 100. **% Receiving Loans:** 100. **Types of Aid Available:** Loans. **Average student debt, upon graduation:** $15,000.

ADMISSIONS INFORMATION
Application Fee: $35. **Priority Application Deadline:** 5/15. **Regular Application Deadline:** 8/27. **Regular Notification:** Rolling. **Transfer Students Accepted?** Yes. **Number of Applications Received:** 3. **% of Applicants Accepted:** 33. **% Accepted Who Enrolled:** 100. **Average GPA:** 3.2. **Required Admission Factors:** Letters of recommendation, transcript. **Program-Specific Admission Factors:** Contact English department.

EMPLOYMENT INFORMATION
% Employed Within 6 Months: 50. **% of master's grads employed in their field upon graduation:** 50. **Rate of placement:** 50%. **Average starting salary:** $25,000.

BUTLER UNIVERSITY
Liberal Arts & Sciences, History Program

Address: 4600 Sunset Avenue, Indianapolis, IN 46208
Admissions Phone: 317-940-8100 or 888-940-8100
Admissions Fax: 317-940-8150 · **Admissions E-mail:** admission@butler.edu
Web Address: www.butler.edu/academics/aca_education.asp

INSTITUTIONAL INFORMATION
Public/Private: Private (nonprofit). **Evening Classes Available?** Yes. **Total Faculty:** 3. **% Faculty Female:** 33. **Student/Faculty Ratio:** 4:1. **Students in Parent Institution:** 4,415.

PROGRAMS
Masters offered in: History.

STUDENT INFORMATION
Total Students in Program: 4. **% Female:** 50. **% Minority:** 25.

RESEARCH FACILITIES
Research Facilities: Observatory. Performing Arts Hall

EXPENSES/FINANCIAL AID
Annual Tuition: $5,400. **Room & Board:** $7,780. **Books and Supplies:** $450. **Loans Range From:** $100-$5,000. **Types of Aid Available:** Loans.

ADMISSIONS INFORMATION
Application Fee: $35. **Regular Application Deadline:** 8/27. **Regular Notification:** Rolling. **Transfer Students Accepted?** Yes. **Number of Applications Received:** 1. **% of Applicants Accepted:** 100. **Average GPA:** 3.0. **Required Admission Factors:** Essays/personal statement, GRE, transcript. **Recommended Admission Factors:** Interview.

EMPLOYMENT INFORMATION
Placement Office Available? Yes. **% Employed Within 6 Months:** 100. **Rate of placement:** 95%. **Average starting salary:** $25,000.

CABRINI COLLEGE
Graduate Studies

Address: 610 King of Prussia Road, Radnor, PA 19087-3698
Admissions Phone: 610-902-8552 · **Admissions Fax:** 610-902-8508
Admissions E-mail: admit@cabrini.edu

INSTITUTIONAL INFORMATION
Public/Private: Private (nonprofit). **Evening Classes Available?** Yes. **Students in Parent Institution:** 2,043.

STUDENT INFORMATION
Total Students in Program: 312. **% Full-time** 3. **% Female:** 81.

EXPENSES/FINANCIAL AID
Annual Tuition: $6,750. **Loans Range From:** $2,000-$18,500. **% Receiving Loans:** 100.

ADMISSIONS INFORMATION

Application Fee: $35. **Regular Notification:** Rolling. **Transfer Students Accepted?** Yes. **Number of Applications Received:** 88. **% of Applicants Accepted:** 90. **% Accepted Who Enrolled:** 77.
Required Admission Factors: Essays/personal statement, letters of recommendation, transcript.
Other Admission Factors: Minimum 3.0 GPA required.
Program-Specific Admission Factors: Teacher certification required for special education program applicants. Minimum 5 years teaching experience recommended for educational leadership program applicants.

EMPLOYMENT INFORMATION

Placement Office Available? Yes.

CALDWELL COLLEGE
Graduate Studies

Address: 9 Ryerson Avenue, Caldwell, NJ 07006
Admissions Phone: 973-618-3408 · **Admissions Fax:** 973-618-3640
Admissions E-mail: graduate@caldwell.edu
Web Address: www.caldwell.edu/graduate

INSTITUTIONAL INFORMATION

Public/Private: Private (nonprofit). **Evening Classes Available?** Yes. **Total Faculty:** 43. **% Faculty Female:** 56. **% Faculty Part-time:** 51. **Student/Faculty Ratio:** 11:1. **Students in Parent Institution:** 2,175.

PROGRAMS

Masters offered in: Accounting and business/management; accounting; business administration and management; business administration/management; counseling psychology; counselor education/school counseling and guidance services; curriculum and instruction; education leadership and administration; education/teaching of individuals who are developmentally delayed; education/teaching of individuals with autism; educational, instructional, and curriculum supervision; educational/instructional media design; elementary and middle school administration/principalship; pastoral studies/counseling; psychology; special education; teacher education, multiple levels; theological studies and religious vocations.

STUDENT INFORMATION

Total Students in Program: 463. **% Full-time** 22. **% Female:** 79. **% Minority:** 19.

EXPENSES/FINANCIAL AID

Annual Tuition: $525. **Fees:** $50. **Books and Supplies:** $400. **Loans Range From:** $2,190-$10,500. **% Receiving Financial Aid:** 25. **% Receiving Loans:** 98. **Types of Aid Available:** Graduate assistantships, loans. **Assistantship Compensation Includes:** Full tuition remission, partial tuition remission, salary/stipend. **Average Salary Stipend:** $5,000.

ADMISSIONS INFORMATION

Application Fee: $40. **Regular Application Deadline:** 8/1. **Regular Notification:** Rolling. **Transfer Students Accepted?** Yes. **Transfer Policy:** Same as for first-time students; only courses with B or better may transfer. Amount of transfer credit based on individual program admitted to. **Number of Applications Received:** 242. **% of Applicants Accepted:** 62. **% Accepted Who Enrolled:** 85. **Average GPA:** 3.3. **Average GRE Verbal:** 455. **Average GRE Quantitative:** 462.
Required Admission Factors: Essays/personal statement, interview, letters of recommendation, transcript.
Other Admission Factors: Minimum 3.0 for psychology-related programs and pastoral ministry, 2.75 for MBA and education-related programs. Test scores considered in context of other credentials.
Program-Specific Admission Factors: Teaching experience or certification required for curriculum/instruction and educational administration programs. Portfolio required of at therapy applicants. Masters required for post-masters programs.

CALIFORNIA BAPTIST UNIVERSITY
Department of Kinesiology

Address: 8432 Magnolia Ave, Riverside, CA 92504
Admissions Phone: 951-343-4249 · **Admissions Fax:** 951-343-5095
Admissions E-mail: gradservice@calbaptist.edu
Web Address: www.calbaptiStreetedu

INSTITUTIONAL INFORMATION

Public/Private: Private (nonprofit). **Evening Classes Available?** Yes. **Total Faculty:** 4. **% Faculty Female:** 50. **% Faculty Part-time:** 25. **Student/Faculty Ratio:** 17:1. **Students in Parent Institution:** 2,905.

STUDENT INFORMATION

Total Students in Program: 662. **% Full-time** 32. **% Female:** 76. **% Minority:** 34. **% International:** 1.

RESEARCH FACILITIES

Research Facilities: Annie Gabriel Library, Metcalf Art Gallery.

EXPENSES/FINANCIAL AID

Annual Tuition: $7,632. **Room & Board (on/off campus):** $6,310/$7,408. **Fees:** $240. **Books and Supplies:** $1,330. **Grants Range From:** $1,074-$9,420. **Loans Range From:** $4,863-$18,500.

ADMISSIONS INFORMATION

Application Fee: $45. **Regular Application Deadline:** 9/1. **Regular Notification:** Rolling. **Transfer Students Accepted?** Yes. **Transfer Policy:** Syllabi and course description to be reviewed by chair of kinesiology dept and registrar. **Number of Applications Received:** 18. **% of Applicants Accepted:** 72. **Average GPA:** 3.0.
Required Admission Factors: Letters of recommendation, transcript.
Recommended Admission Factors: Essays/personal statement, interview,
Other Admission Factors: Minimum GPA of 2.75.
Program-Specific Admission Factors: Physical education emphasis: students need a minimum of 12 semester units of study in kinesiology including a basic movement anatomy or related course. Sports management emphasis also available.

CALIFORNIA BAPTIST UNIVERSITY
Department of Modern Languages & Literature

Address: 8432 Magnolia Avenue, Riverside, CA 92504
Admissions Phone: 951-343-4249 · **Admissions Fax:** 951-343-5095
Admissions E-mail: gradservice@calbaptist.edu
Web Address: www.calbaptist.edu

INSTITUTIONAL INFORMATION

Public/Private: Private (nonprofit). **Evening Classes Available?** Yes. **Total Faculty:** 5. **% Faculty Female:** 60. **% Faculty Part-time:** 40. **Student/Faculty Ratio:** 17:1. **Students in Parent Institution:** 2,905.

STUDENT INFORMATION

Total Students in Program: 662. **% Full-time** 32. **% Female:** 76. **% Minority:** 34. **% International:** 1.

RESEARCH FACILITIES

Research Facilities: Annie Gabriel Library, Metcalf Art Gallery.

EXPENSES/FINANCIAL AID

Annual Tuition: $7,632. **Room & Board (on/off campus):** $6,310/$7,408. **Fees:** $240. **Books and Supplies:** $1,300. **Loans Range From:** $4,863-$18,500. **% Receiving Financial Aid:** 12. **% Receiving Loans:** 100.

ADMISSIONS INFORMATION

Application Fee: $45. **Regular Application Deadline:** 9/1. **Regular Notification:** Rolling. **Transfer Students Accepted?** Yes. **Number of Applications Received:** 16. **% of Applicants Accepted:** 81. **Average GPA:** 3.3. **Required Admission Factors:** Essays/personal statement, letters of recommendation, transcript.
Recommended Admission Factors: Interview.
Other Admission Factors: Minimum GPA of 2.75 required, successful demonstration of writing competence required, a minimum of 18 semester units in English beyond freshman compostition with the grade of C or better required.

CALIFORNIA BAPTIST UNIVERSITY
MBA Program

Address: 8432 Magnolia Avenue, Riverside, CA 92504
Admissions Phone: 951-343-4249 · **Admissions Fax:** 951-343-5098
Admissions E-mail: gradservice@calbaptist.edu
Web Address: www.calbaptist.edu/business

INSTITUTIONAL INFORMATION

Public/Private: Private (nonprofit). **Evening Classes Available?** Yes. **Total Faculty:** 7. **% Faculty Female:** 43. **% Faculty Part-time:** 43. **Student/Faculty Ratio:** 17:1. **Students in Parent Institution:** 2,905.

PROGRAMS

Masters offered in: Business administration/management; business, management, marketing, and related support services

STUDENT INFORMATION

Total Students in Program: 662. **% Full-time** 32. **% Female:** 76. **% Minority:** 34. **% International:** 1.

EXPENSES/FINANCIAL AID

Annual Tuition: $8,280. **Room & Board (on/off campus):** $6,310/$7,408. **Fees:** $240. **Books and Supplies:** $1,300. **Grants Range From:** $1,074-$9,420. **Loans Range From:** $4,863-$18,500. **% Receiving Financial Aid:** 78. **% Receiving Scholarships/Grants:** 5. **% Receiving Loans:** 100. **Number of Fellowships Granted Each Year:** 1.

ADMISSIONS INFORMATION

Application Fee: $45. **Regular Application Deadline:** 9/1. **Regular Notification:** Rolling. **Transfer Students Accepted?** Yes. **Transfer Policy:** Catalog descriptions and syllabi of courses for transfer required of transfer applicants (reviewed by registrar and business school dean). **Number of Applications Received:** 33. **% of Applicants Accepted:** 79. **Average GPA:** 3.2. **Required Admission Factors:** Essays/personal statement, interview, letters of recommendation, transcript.
Other Admission Factors: Minimum GPA of 2.75.

EMPLOYMENT INFORMATION

Placement Office Available? Yes. **% Employed Within 6 Months:** 65. **Rate of placement:** 50%.

CALIFORNIA BAPTIST UNIVERSITY
School of Behavioral Sciences, Counseling Psychology Program

Address: 8432 Magnolia Avenue, Riverside, CA 92504
Admissions Phone: 951-343-4249 · **Admissions Fax:** 951-343-5095
Admissions E-mail: gradservice@calbaptist.edu ·
Web Address: www.calbaptist.edu/behavioral_sci/index.htm

INSTITUTIONAL INFORMATION

Public/Private: Private (nonprofit). **Evening Classes Available?** Yes. **Total**

Faculty: 9. **% Faculty Female:** 44. **% Faculty Part-time:** 22. **Student/Faculty Ratio:** 17:1. **Students in Parent Institution:** 2,905.

STUDENT INFORMATION

Total Students in Program: 662. **% Full-time** 32. **% Female:** 76. **% Minority:** 34. **% International:** 1.

RESEARCH FACILITIES

Research Facilities: Annie Gabriel Library, Metcalf Art Gallery.

EXPENSES/FINANCIAL AID

Annual Tuition: $9,180. **Room & Board (on/off campus):** $6,310/$7,408. **Fees:** $240. **Books and Supplies:** $1,300. **Grants Range From:** $1,074-$9,420. **Loans Range From:** $4,863-$18,500. **% Receiving Financial Aid:** 75. **% Receiving Scholarships/Grants:** 5. **% Receiving Loans:** 100.

ADMISSIONS INFORMATION

Application Fee: $45. **Regular Application Deadline:** 8/27. **Regular Notification:** Rolling. **Transfer Students Accepted?** Yes. **Transfer Policy:** Catalog descriptions and/or syllabi required of transfer applicants. **Number of Applications Received:** 83. **% of Applicants Accepted:** 73. **Average GPA:** 3.0.
Required Admission Factors: Essays/personal statement, interview, letters of recommendation, transcript.
Other Admission Factors: Minimum 3.0 GPA required; minimum 2.75 GPA required for conditional acceptance.
Program-Specific Admission Factors: Minnesota Multiphasic Personality Inventory (MMPI) and Myers Briggs Personality Inventory.

EMPLOYMENT INFORMATION

Placement Office Available? Yes. **% Employed Within 6 Months:** 90. **Rate of placement:** 90%.

CALIFORNIA COLLEGE OF PODIATRIC MEDICINE
Graduate Programs

Address: 1210 Scott Street, San Francisco, CA 94115
Admissions Phone: 800-443-2276 or 800-334-2276
Admissions Fax: 415-292-0439 · **Admissions E-mail:** pwhite@ccpm.edu

INSTITUTIONAL INFORMATION

Public/Private: Private (nonprofit). **Student/Faculty Ratio:** 11:1. **Students in Parent Institution:** 300.

STUDENT INFORMATION

Total Students in Program: 5. **% Female:** 20.

RESEARCH FACILITIES

Research Facilities: Educational affiliations with U. of California at San Francisco and U of Southern California.

EXPENSES/FINANCIAL AID

Annual Tuition: $19,980. **Fees:** $2,625. **Grants Range From:** $1,000-$10,000. **Loans Range From:** $8,500-$45,000. **% Receiving Financial Aid:** 98. **% Receiving Scholarships/Grants:** 1. **% Receiving Loans:** 99. **Average student debt, upon graduation:** $110,000.

ADMISSIONS INFORMATION

Application Fee: $95. **Regular Notification:** Rolling. **Transfer Students Accepted?** Yes. **Number of Applications Received:** 266. **% of Applicants Accepted:** 47. **% Accepted Who Enrolled:** 52. **Average GPA:** 3.19.
Required Admission Factors: Interview, letters of recommendation, transcript.

EMPLOYMENT INFORMATION

Placement Office Available? Yes. **Rate of placement:** 100%. **Average starting salary:** $50,000.

CALIFORNIA COLLEGE OF THE ARTS
Curatorial Practice

Address: 1111 Eighth Street, San Francisco, CA 94107
Admissions Phone: 415-703-9523 · **Admissions Fax:** 415-703-9539
Admissions E-mail: graduateprograms@cca.edu · **Web Address:** www.cca.edu

INSTITUTIONAL INFORMATION
Public/Private: Private (nonprofit). **Total Faculty:** 38. **% Faculty Female:** 50. **% Faculty Part-time:** 89. **Student/Faculty Ratio:** 2:1.

STUDENT INFORMATION
Total Students in Program: 10. **% Full-time** 100. **% Female:** 70. **% Minority:** 30. **% International:** 30.

EXPENSES/FINANCIAL AID
Annual Tuition: $27,100. **Room & Board (on/off campus):** $8,430. **Fees:** $290. **Books and Supplies:** $2,000.

ADMISSIONS INFORMATION
Application Fee: $50. **Regular Application Deadline:** 1/15. **Regular Notification:** 3/24. **Transfer Students Accepted?** No. **Number of Applications Received:** 27. **% of Applicants Accepted:** 56. **% Accepted Who Enrolled:** 100. **Average GPA:** 3.1.
Required Admission Factors: Essays/personal statement, interview, transcript. Portfolio of writing samples.
Other Admission Factors: Minimum TOEFL score of 600 (paper) or 250 (computer) for international applicants.

CALIFORNIA COLLEGE OF THE ARTS
Graduate Program in Design

Address: 1111 Eighth Street, San Francisco, CA 94107
Admissions Phone: 415-703-9523 · **Admissions Fax:** 415-703-9539
Admissions E-mail: graduateprograms@cca.edu · **Web Address:** www.cca.edu

INSTITUTIONAL INFORMATION
Public/Private: Private (nonprofit). **Total Faculty:** 38. **% Faculty Female:** 50. **% Faculty Part-time:** 89. **Student/Faculty Ratio:** 10:1. **Students in Parent Institution:** 1,213.

STUDENT INFORMATION
Total Students in Program: 97. **% Full-time** 85. **% Female:** 60.

RESEARCH FACILITIES
Research Facilities: Wattis Institute, Capp Street Project Residency Program, Design Book Review, Small Press Traffic, CCA Center for Art and Public Life.

EXPENSES/FINANCIAL AID
Annual Tuition: $26,100. **Room & Board (on/off campus):** $8,430. **Fees:** $290. **Books and Supplies:** $1,620. **Grants Range From:** $1,000-$17,500. **Loans Range From:** $4,250-$28,500. **% Receiving Financial Aid:** 77. **% Receiving Scholarships/Grants:** 97. **% Receiving Loans:** 94. **Average Salary Stipend:** $2,000.

ADMISSIONS INFORMATION
Application Fee: $50. **Regular Application Deadline:** 1/15. **Transfer Students Accepted?** No. **Number of Applications Received:** 49. **% of Applicants Accepted:** 39. **% Accepted Who Enrolled:** 47.
Required Admission Factors: Essays/personal statement, letters of recommendation, transcript.

EMPLOYMENT INFORMATION
Placement Office Available? Yes.

CALIFORNIA COLLEGE OF THE ARTS
Graduate Program in Fine Arts

Address: 1111 Eighth Street, San Francisco, CA 94107
Admissions Phone: 415-703-9523 · **Admissions Fax:** 415-703-9539
Admissions E-mail: graduateprograms@cca.edu · **Web Address:** www.cca.edu

INSTITUTIONAL INFORMATION
Public/Private: Private (nonprofit). **Total Faculty:** 28. **% Faculty Female:** 68. **% Faculty Part-time:** 121. **Student/Faculty Ratio:** 12:1. **Students in Parent Institution:** 1,213.

STUDENT INFORMATION
Total Students in Program: 97. **% Full-time** 85. **% Female:** 60.

RESEARCH FACILITIES
Research Facilities: Wattis Institute, Capp Street Project Residency Program, Design Book Review, Small Press Traffic, Center for Art and Public Life.

EXPENSES/FINANCIAL AID
Annual Tuition: $27,100. **Room & Board (on/off campus):** $8,430. **Fees:** $290. **Books and Supplies:** $1,620. **Grants Range From:** $1,000-$17,500. **Loans Range From:** $4,250-$28,500. **% Receiving Financial Aid:** 94. **% Receiving Scholarships/Grants:** 97. **% Receiving Loans:** 94. **Types of Aid Available:** Graduate assistantships, loans. **Average student debt, upon graduation:** $34,000. **Number of Teaching/Research Assistantships Granted Each Year:** 30. **Average Salary Stipend:** $500.

ADMISSIONS INFORMATION
Application Fee: $50. **Regular Application Deadline:** 1/15. **Transfer Students Accepted?** No. **Number of Applications Received:** 317. **% of Applicants Accepted:** 27. **% Accepted Who Enrolled:** 41. **Average GPA:** 3.0.
Required Admission Factors: Essays/personal statement, interview, letters of recommendation, transcript.
Other Admission Factors: Minimum 3.0 GPA required.

EMPLOYMENT INFORMATION
Placement Office Available? Yes.

CALIFORNIA COLLEGE OF THE ARTS
Graduate Program in Visual Criticism

Address: 1111 Eighth Street, San Francisco, CA 94107
Admissions Phone: 415-703-9523 · **Admissions Fax:** 415-703-9539
Admissions E-mail: graduateprograms@cca.edu · **Web Address:** www.cca.edu

INSTITUTIONAL INFORMATION
Public/Private: Private (nonprofit). **Total Faculty:** 38. **% Faculty Female:** 50. **% Faculty Part-time:** 89. **Student/Faculty Ratio:** 10:1. **Students in Parent Institution:** 1,213.

STUDENT INFORMATION
Total Students in Program: 97. **% Full-time** 85. **% Female:** 60.

RESEARCH FACILITIES
Research Facilities: Wattis Institute, Capp Street Project Residency Program, Design Book Review, Small Press Traffic, Center for Art and Public Life.

EXPENSES/FINANCIAL AID
Annual Tuition: $27,100. **Room & Board (on/off campus):** $8,430. **Fees:** $290. **Books and Supplies:** $1,620. **Grants Range From:** $1,000-$17,500. **Loans Range From:** $4,250-$28,500. **% Receiving Financial Aid:** 86. **% Receiving Scholarships/Grants:** 97. **% Receiving Loans:** 94. **Average Salary Stipend:** $2,000.

ADMISSIONS INFORMATION
Application Fee: $50. **Regular Application Deadline:** 1/15. **Transfer Students Accepted?** No. **Number of Applications Received:** 14. **% of Appli-**

cants Accepted: 86. % Accepted Who Enrolled: 58.
Required Admission Factors: Essays/personal statement, letters of recommendation, transcript.
Other Admission Factors: Two writing samples of no more than 5,000 words each required.

EMPLOYMENT INFORMATION
Placement Office Available? Yes.

CALIFORNIA COLLEGE OF THE ARTS
Graduate Program in Writing

Address: 1111 Eighth Street, San Francisco, CA 94107
Admissions Phone: 415-703-9523 · **Admissions Fax:** 415-703-9539
Admissions E-mail: graduateprograms@cca.edu · **Web Address:** www.cca.edu

INSTITUTIONAL INFORMATION
Public/Private: Private (nonprofit). **Total Faculty:** 38. **% Faculty Female:** 50. **% Faculty Part-time:** 89. **Student/Faculty Ratio:** 10:1. **Students in Parent Institution:** 1,319.

STUDENT INFORMATION
Total Students in Program: 268. **% Full-time** 91. **% Female:** 62.

RESEARCH FACILITIES
Research Facilities: Wattis Institute, Capp Street Project Residency Program, Design Book Review, Small Press Traffic, Center for Art and Public Life.

EXPENSES/FINANCIAL AID
Annual Tuition: $27,100. **Room & Board (on/off campus):** $8,430. **Fees:** $290. **Books and Supplies:** $1,620. **Grants Range From:** $1,000-$17,500. **Loans Range From:** $4,250-$28,500. **% Receiving Financial Aid:** 100. **% Receiving Scholarships/Grants:** 97. **% Receiving Loans:** 94. **Types of Aid Available:** Loans, scholarships. **Average Salary Stipend:** $2,000.

ADMISSIONS INFORMATION
Application Fee: $50. **Priority Application Deadline:** 1/15. **Regular Application Deadline:** 1/15. **Transfer Students Accepted?** No. **Number of Applications Received:** 20. **% of Applicants Accepted:** 90. **% Accepted Who Enrolled:** 44. **Average GPA:** 3.1.
Required Admission Factors: Essays/personal statement, letters of recommendation, transcript.
Other Admission Factors: Writing samples of no more than 20 pages required.

EMPLOYMENT INFORMATION
Placement Office Available? Yes.

CALIFORNIA INSTITUTE OF INTEGRAL STUDIES
Graduate Programs

Address: 1453 Mission Street, 4th Floor, San Francisco, CA 94103-2557
Admissions Phone: 415-575-6150 · **Admissions Fax:** 415-575-1268
Admissions E-mail: admissions@ciis.edu · **Web Address:** www.ciis.edu

INSTITUTIONAL INFORMATION
Public/Private: Private (nonprofit). **Total Faculty:** 94. **% Faculty Female:** 49. **% Faculty Part-time:** 44. **Student/Faculty Ratio:** 11:1. **Students in Parent Institution:** 1,000.

PROGRAMS
Masters offered in: Alternative and complimentary medicine and medical systems; alternative, complimentary, and somatic health and therapeutic services; anthropology; area, ethnic, cultural, and gender studies; Buddhist studies; Chinese language and literature; Chinese studies; community health services/liaison/counseling; counseling psychology; ethnic, cultural minority, and gender

studies; health/health care administration/management; Hindu studies; marriage and family therapy/counseling; mental health counseling/counselor; multi/interdisciplinary studies; philosophy and religion; philosophy; psychoanalysis and psychoptherapy; psychology; religion/religious studies, sanskrit and classical Indian languages, literatures, and linguistics; somatic bodywork; south asian studies; substance abuse/addiction counseling; Tibetan language and literature; women's studies. **Doctorate offered in:** Anthropology; area, ethnic, cultural, and gender studies; Buddhist studies; Chinese language and literature; Chinese studies; clinical psychology; ethnic, cultural minority, and gender studies; Hindu studies; humanities/humanistic studies.

STUDENT INFORMATION
Total Students in Program: 1,000. **% Full-time** 70. **% Female:** 75. **% Minority:** 11. **% International:** 10.

RESEARCH FACILITIES
Research Facilities: Consciousness & Physiology Research Laboratory; 4 Counseling Clinics; Cultural Integration Fellowship.

EXPENSES/FINANCIAL AID
Annual Tuition: $15,000. **Room & Board:** $10,300. **Fees:** $300. **Books and Supplies:** $950. **Grants Range From:** $2,000-$9,650. **Loans Range From:** $1,000-$18,500. **% Receiving Financial Aid:** 65. **% Receiving Scholarships/Grants:** 5. **% Receiving Loans:** 95. **Average student debt, upon graduation:** $23,000

ADMISSIONS INFORMATION
Application Fee: $65. **Priority Application Deadline:** 3/1. **Regular Application Deadline:** 6/15. **Regular Notification:** Rolling. **Transfer Students Accepted?** Yes. **Transfer Policy:** Maximum 1/6 of total credit hours required may be transferred. **Number of Applications Received:** 550. **% of Applicants Accepted:** 59. **% Accepted Who Enrolled:** 77. **Average GPA:** 3.25.
Required Admission Factors: Essays/personal statement, interview, letters of recommendation, transcript.
Other Admission Factors: Minimum 3.0 GPA required.
Program-Specific Admission Factors: Minimum 3.1 GPA required of PsyD program applicants.

EMPLOYMENT INFORMATION
Placement Office Available? Yes. **% Employed Within 6 Months:** 45. **% of master's/doctoral/first professional grads employed in their field upon graduation:** 57/38/42. **Rate of placement:** 98%. **Average starting salary:** $2,250.

CALIFORNIA INSTITUTE OF TECHNOLOGY
Graduate Studies

Address: 1200 East California Boulevard, Mail Code 230-87, Pasadena, CA 91125
Admissions Phone: 626-395-6346 · **Admissions Fax:** 626-577-9246
Admissions E-mail: gradofc@caltech.edu · **Web Address:** www.gradoffice.caltech.edu

INSTITUTIONAL INFORMATION
Public/Private: Private (nonprofit). **Student/Faculty Ratio:** 6:1. **Students in Parent Institution:** 1,924.

PROGRAMS
Masters offered in: Aerospace, aeronautical, and astronautical engineering; electrical, electronics and communications engineering; engineering; engineering mechanics; mechanical engineering. **Doctorate offered in:** Aerospace, aeronautical, and astronautical engineering; agricultural/biological engineering and bioengineering; algebra and number theory; analysis and functional analysis; analytical chemistry; applied mathematics.

STUDENT INFORMATION
Total Students in Program: 1,001. **% Full-time** 100. **% Female:** 23.

EXPENSES/FINANCIAL AID
Annual Tuition: In-state $20,904. **Fees:** $32. **Books and Supplies:** $1,097. **Grants Range From:** $16,000-$20,000. **% Receiving Financial Aid:** 8. **%**

Receiving Scholarships/Grants: 15. % Receiving Assistantships: 70. Number of Fellowships Granted Each Year: 125. Average amount of individual fellowships per year: $17,000. Number of Teaching/Research Assistantships Granted Each Year: 700 Average Salary Stipend: $16,000.

ADMISSIONS INFORMATION

Application Fee: $50. Regular Application Deadline: 1/15. Regular Notification: 4/1. Transfer Students Accepted? No. Number of Applications Received: 3,669. % of Applicants Accepted: 16. % Accepted Who Enrolled: 41. Average GPA: 3.8. Average GRE Verbal: 730. Average GRE Quantitative: 773. Average GRE Analytical: 783.
Required Admission Factors: Essays/personal statement, GRE, letters of recommendation, transcript.

EMPLOYMENT INFORMATION

Placement Office Available? Yes. Rate of placement: 40%.

CALIFORNIA INSTITUTE OF THE ARTS
School of Art

Address: 24700 McBean Parkway, Valencia, CA 91355
Admissions Phone: 661-255-1050 · Admissions Fax: 661-254-8352
Admissions E-mail: admiss@calarts.edu
Web Address: www.calarts.edu/schools/art/index.html

INSTITUTIONAL INFORMATION

Public/Private: Private (nonprofit). Total Faculty: 44. % Faculty Female: 48. % Faculty Part-time: 32. Student/Faculty Ratio: 7:1. Students in Parent Institution: 1,325.

PROGRAMS

Masters offered in: Art/art studies, commercial and advertising art; crafts/craft design, folk art and artisanry; design and applied arts; design and visual communications; drawing; fine arts and art studies; fine/studio arts; graphic design; intermedia/multimedia; painting; printmaking; sculpture; visual and performing arts.

STUDENT INFORMATION

Total Students in Program: 485. % Full-time 100. % Female: 51.

EXPENSES/FINANCIAL AID

Annual Tuition: $25,560. Room & Board: $3,900. Fees: $765. Books and Supplies: $400. Grants Range From: $100-$23,920. Loans Range From: $2,230-$39,000. % Receiving Financial Aid: 70. % Receiving Scholarships/Grants: 97. % Receiving Loans: 76. % Receiving Other Aid (4% work-study, tuition remission): 4. Types of Aid Available: Grants, institutional work-study, loans, scholarships.

ADMISSIONS INFORMATION

Application Fee: $60. Priority Application Deadline: 1/5. Regular Application Deadline: 1/5. Regular Notification: Rolling. Transfer Students Accepted? Yes. Number of Applications Received: 505. % of Applicants Accepted: 15. % Accepted Who Enrolled: 42. Average GPA: 3.0.
Required Admission Factors: Essays/personal statement, letters of recommendation, transcript. Portfolio required.

CALIFORNIA INSTITUTE OF THE ARTS
School of Dance

Address: 24700 McBean Parkway, Valencia, CA 91355
Admissions Phone: 661-255-1050 · Admissions Fax: 661-254-8352
Admissions E-mail: admiss@calarts.edu
Web Address: www.calarts.edu/schools/dance/index.html

INSTITUTIONAL INFORMATION

Public/Private: Private (nonprofit). Total Faculty: 17. % Faculty Female:

47. % Faculty Part-time: 65. Student/Faculty Ratio: 7:1. Students in Parent Institution: 1,325.

PROGRAMS

Masters offered in: Dance.

STUDENT INFORMATION

Total Students in Program: 485. % Full-time 100. % Female: 51.

EXPENSES/FINANCIAL AID

Annual Tuition: $25,560. Room & Board: $3,900. Fees: $765. Books and Supplies: $400. Grants Range From: $100-$20,930. Loans Range From: $2,230-$39,000. % Receiving Financial Aid: 70. % Receiving Scholarships/Grants: 97. % Receiving Loans: 76. % Receiving Other Aid (4% work-study, tuition remission): 4. Types of Aid Available: Grants, institutional work-study, loans, scholarships.

ADMISSIONS INFORMATION

Application Fee: $60. Priority Application Deadline: 1/5. Regular Application Deadline: 1/5. Regular Notification: Rolling. Transfer Students Accepted? Yes. Number of Applications Received: 16. % of Applicants Accepted: 44. % Accepted Who Enrolled: 29. Average GPA: 3.0.
Required Admission Factors: Essays/personal statement, letters of recommendation, transcript.
Program-Specific Admission Factors: Audition and video of choreography.

CALIFORNIA INSTITUTE OF THE ARTS
School of Film & Video

Address: 24700 McBean Parkway, Valencia, CA 91355
Admissions Phone: 661-255-1050 · Admissions Fax: 661-254-8352
Admissions E-mail: admiss@calarts.edu
Web Address: www.calarts.edu/schools/film/index.html

INSTITUTIONAL INFORMATION

Public/Private: Private (nonprofit). Total Faculty: 76. % Faculty Female: 29. % Faculty Part-time: 62. Student/Faculty Ratio: 8:1. Students in Parent Institution: 1,273.

PROGRAMS

Masters offered in: Cinematography and film/video production; film/cinema studies; film/video and photgraphic arts.

STUDENT INFORMATION

Total Students in Program: 474. % Full-time 99. % Female: 49.

EXPENSES/FINANCIAL AID

Annual Tuition: $23,920. Room & Board: $3,700. Fees: $765. Books and Supplies: $400. Grants Range From: $100-$23,920. Loans Range From: $2,230-$39,000. % Receiving Financial Aid: 70. % Receiving Scholarships/Grants: 97. % Receiving Loans: 76. % Receiving Other Aid: 4. Types of Aid Available: Grants, institutional work-study, loans, scholarships.

ADMISSIONS INFORMATION

Application Fee: $60. Priority Application Deadline: 1/5. Regular Application Deadline: 1/5. Regular Notification: Rolling. Transfer Students Accepted? No. Number of Applications Received: 340. % of Applicants Accepted: 30. % Accepted Who Enrolled: 43. Average GPA: 3.0.
Required Admission Factors: Essays/personal statement, letters of recommendation, transcript.
Program-Specific Admission Factors: Portfolio submission is required.

CALIFORNIA INSTITUTE OF THE ARTS
School of Music

Address: 24700 McBean Pkwy, Valencia, CA 91355
Admissions Phone: 661-255-1050 · **Admissions Fax:** 661-254-8352
Admissions E-mail: admiss@calarts.edu · **Web Address:** www.music.calarts.edu

INSTITUTIONAL INFORMATION
Public/Private: Private (nonprofit). **Total Faculty:** 57. **% Faculty Female:** 26. **% Faculty Part-time:** 40. **Student/Faculty Ratio:** 5:1. **Students in Parent Institution:** 1,325.

PROGRAMS
Masters offered in: Jazz/jazz studies; music pedagogy; music performance; music theory and composition; music; music/music and performing arts studies; musicology and ethnomusicology; piano and organ; violin, viola, guitar and other stringed instruments; visual and performing arts; visual and performing arts; voice and opera.

STUDENT INFORMATION
Total Students in Program: 483. **% Full-time** 100. **% Female:** 51.

EXPENSES/FINANCIAL AID
Annual Tuition: $23,920. **Room & Board:** $3,700. **Fees:** $765. **Books and Supplies:** $400. **Grants Range From:** $100-$23,920. **Loans Range From:** $2,230-$39,000. **% Receiving Financial Aid:** 75. **% Receiving Scholarships/Grants:** 97. **% Receiving Loans:** 76. **% Receiving Other Aid (4% work-study, tuition remission):** 4. **Types of Aid Available:** Grants, institutional work-study, loans, scholarships.

ADMISSIONS INFORMATION
Application Fee: $60. **Priority Application Deadline:** 1/5. **Regular Application Deadline:** 1/5. **Regular Notification:** Rolling. **Transfer Students Accepted?** Yes. **Number of Applications Received:** 144. **% of Applicants Accepted:** 40. **% Accepted Who Enrolled:** 86. **Average GPA:** 3.0.
Required Admission Factors: Essays/personal statement, letters of recommendation, transcript. Audition or portfolio.
Program-Specific Admission Factors: Audition or portfolio.

CALIFORNIA INSTITUTE OF THE ARTS
School of Theater

Address: 24700 McBean Parkway, Valencia, CA 91355
Admissions Phone: 661-255-1050 · **Admissions Fax:** 661-254-8352
Admissions E-mail: admiss@calarts.edu
Web Address: www.calarts.edu/schools/theater/index.html

INSTITUTIONAL INFORMATION
Public/Private: Private (nonprofit). **Total Faculty:** 45. **% Faculty Female:** 56. **% Faculty Part-time:** 33. **Student/Faculty Ratio:** 7:1. **Students in Parent Institution:** 1,325.

PROGRAMS
Masters offered in: Acting, directing and theatrical production, drama and dramatics/theater arts, dramatic/theater arts and stagecraft, playwriting and screenwriting, technical theater/theater design and technology.

STUDENT INFORMATION
Total Students in Program: 485. **% Full-time** 100. **% Female:** 51.

EXPENSES/FINANCIAL AID
Annual Tuition: $25,560. **Room & Board:** $3,700. **Fees:** $765. **Books and Supplies:** $400. **Grants Range From:** $100-$23,920. **Loans Range From:** $2,230-$39,000. **% Receiving Financial Aid:** 70. **% Receiving Scholarships/Grants:** 97. **% Receiving Loans:** 76. **% Receiving Other Aid (4% work-study, tuition remission):** 4. **Types of Aid Available:** Grants, institutional work-study, loans, scholarships.

ADMISSIONS INFORMATION
Application Fee: $60. **Priority Application Deadline:** 1/5. **Regular Application Deadline:** 1/5. **Regular Notification:** Rolling. **Transfer Students Accepted?** No. **Number of Applications Received:** 287. **% of Applicants Accepted:** 28. **% Accepted Who Enrolled:** 58. **Average GPA:** 3.0.
Required Admission Factors: Essays/personal statement, letters of recommendation, transcript. Audition or portfolio.
Program-Specific Admission Factors: Audition or portfolio.

CALIFORNIA LUTHERAN UNIVERSITY
Graduate Studies

Address: 60 West Olsen Road, Thousand Oaks, CA 91360-2787
Admissions Phone: 805-493-3127 · **Admissions Fax:** 805-493-3542

INSTITUTIONAL INFORMATION
Public/Private: Private (nonprofit). **Evening Classes Available?** Yes. **Students in Parent Institution:** 2,673.

STUDENT INFORMATION
Total Students in Program: 1,012. **% Full-time** 75. **% Female:** 60.

EXPENSES/FINANCIAL AID
Room & Board: $600. **Books and Supplies:** $700.

ADMISSIONS INFORMATION
Application Fee: $50. **Regular Notification:** Rolling. **Transfer Students Accepted?** Yes.
Required Admission Factors: Essays/personal statement, GRE, interview, letters of recommendation, transcript.
Other Admission Factors: Minimum 3.0 GPA required.

CALIFORNIA POLYTECHNIC STATE UNIVERSITY— SAN LUIS OBISPO
College of Liberal Arts

Address: San Luis Obispo, CA 93407-0005
Admissions Phone: 805-756-2311 · **Admissions E-mail:** jmaravia@calpoly.edu

INSTITUTIONAL INFORMATION
Public/Private: Public. **Students in Parent Institution:** 16,877.

STUDENT INFORMATION
Total Students in Program: 1,010. **% Full-time** 59. **% Female:** 56.

EXPENSES/FINANCIAL AID
Annual Tuition: $3,936. **Fees:** $2,213. **Books and Supplies:** $900. **Average Salary Stipend:** $576.

ADMISSIONS INFORMATION
Application Fee: $55. **Regular Notification:** Rolling. **Transfer Students Accepted?** No.
Required Admission Factors: Essays/personal statement, letters of recommendation, transcript.
Other Admission Factors: Minimum 3.0 GPA required.
Program-Specific Admission Factors: Four letters of recommendation may be required for some programs. Writing sample required of English program applicants.

EMPLOYMENT INFORMATION
Placement Office Available? Yes.

CALIFORNIA STATE POLYTECHNIC UNIVERSITY—POMONA
College of Environmental Design

Address: 3801 West Temple Avenue, Pomona, CA 91768-4019
Admissions Phone: 909-869-3210 · Admissions Fax: 909-869-4529
Admissions E-mail: admissions@csupomona.edu
Web Address: www.csupomona.edu/~env/

INSTITUTIONAL INFORMATION
Public/Private: Public. Evening Classes Available? Yes. Student/Faculty Ratio: 21:1. Students in Parent Institution: 19,002

PROGRAMS
Masters offered in: Agriculture; animal sciences; architecture (BArch, BA/BS, MArch, MA/MS, PhD); business administration/management; chemistry; city/urban, community, and regional planning; computer and information sciences; economics; education; electrical; electronics and communications engineering; engineering; English language and literature; health and physical education; history; industrial management; landscape architecture (BS, BSLA, BLA, MSLA, MLA, PhD); mathematics; mechanical engineering; natural resources management and policy; plant protection and integrated pest management; psychology; public administration; structural engineering.

STUDENT INFORMATION
Total Students in Program: 185. % Full-time 85. % Female: 48. % Minority: 34. % International: 4.

RESEARCH FACILITIES
Research Facilities: Center for Regenerative Studies.

EXPENSES/FINANCIAL AID
Annual Tuition: $7,232. Room & Board (on/off campus): $7,212/$7,968. Fees: $3,318. Books and Supplies: $1,260.

ADMISSIONS INFORMATION
Application Fee: $55. Regular Application Deadline: 6/15. Regular Notification: Rolling. Transfer Students Accepted? Yes. Transfer Policy: Maximum 13 quarter units may be transferred. Number of Applications Received: 292. % of Applicants Accepted: 40. % Accepted Who Enrolled: 44. Average GPA: 3.39.
Required Admission Factors: Essays/personal statement, transcript.
Other Admission Factors: Minimum 3.0 GPA recommended, GRE recommended for applicants whose GPA is below 3.0.
Program-Specific Admission Factors: Portfolio required of architecture and landscape architecture program applicants.

EMPLOYMENT INFORMATION
Placement Office Available? Yes.

CALIFORNIA STATE POLYTECHNIC UNIVERSITY—POMONA
College of Letters, Arts, & Social Sciences

Address: 3801 West Temple Avenue, Pomona, CA 91768-4019
Admissions Phone: 909-869-3210 · Admissions Fax: 909-869-4529
Admissions E-mail: admissions@csupomona.edu
Web Address: www.class.csupomona.edu/

INSTITUTIONAL INFORMATION
Public/Private: Public. Evening Classes Available? Yes. Student/Faculty Ratio: 21:1. Students in Parent Institution: 19,002

PROGRAMS
Masters offered in: Agriculture; animal sciences; architecture (BArch, BA/BS, MArch, MA/MS, PhD); business administration/management; chemistry, city/urban, community, and regional planning; computer and information sciences; economics; education; electrical, electronics, and communications engineering; engineering; English language and literature; health and physical education; history; industrial management; landscape architecture (BS, BSLA, BLA, MSLA, MLA, PhD); mathematics; mechanical engineering; natural resources management and policy; plant protection and integrated pest management; psychology; public administration; structural engineering.

STUDENT INFORMATION
Total Students in Program: 218. % Full-time 57. % Female: 59. % Minority: 50. % International: 6.

RESEARCH FACILITIES
Research Facilities: Center for Regenerative Studies.

EXPENSES/FINANCIAL AID
Annual Tuition: $7,232. Room & Board (on/off campus): $7,212/$7,968. Fees: $3,318. Books and Supplies: $1,260.

ADMISSIONS INFORMATION
Application Fee: $55. Regular Application Deadline: 6/15. Regular Notification: Rolling. Transfer Students Accepted? Yes. Number of Applications Received: 234. % of Applicants Accepted: 57. % Accepted Who Enrolled: 52. Average GPA: 3.3.
Required Admission Factors: Essays/personal statement, GRE, interview, letters of recommendation, transcript.
Other Admission Factors: Minimum 3.0 GPA required.
Program-Specific Admission Factors: Minimum 2.7 GPA (3.0 in upper-division economics courses) required of economics program applicants. Personal statement and minimum 24 semester hours (36 quarter hours) of upper-division psychology courses required of psychology program applicants.

EMPLOYMENT INFORMATION
Placement Office Available? Yes.

CALIFORNIA STATE POLYTECHNIC UNIVERSITY—POMONA
College of Science

Address: 3801 West Temple Avenue, Pomona, CA 91768-4019
Admissions Phone: 909-468-5020 · Admissions Fax: 909-869-4529
Admissions E-mail: admissions@csupomona.edu
Web Address: www.csupomona.edu/~sci/

INSTITUTIONAL INFORMATION
Public/Private: Public. Evening Classes Available? Yes. Student/Faculty Ratio: 21:1. Students in Parent Institution: 19,002.

PROGRAMS
Masters offered in: Agriculture; animal sciences; architecture (BArch, BA/BS, MArch, MA/MS, PhD); business administration/management; chemistry, city/urban, community, and regional planning; computer and information sciences; economics; electrical, electronics, and communications engineering; engineering; English language and literature; health and physical education; history; industrial management; landscape architecture (BS, BSLA, BLA, MSLA, MLA, PhD); mathematics; mechanical engineering; natural resources management and policy; plant protection and integrated pest management; psychology; public administration; structural engineering.

STUDENT INFORMATION
Total Students in Program: 203. % Full-time 42. % Female: 42. % Minority: 60. % International: 13.

RESEARCH FACILITIES

Research Facilities: Center for Regenerative Studies.

EXPENSES/FINANCIAL AID

Annual Tuition: Out-of-state $7,232. **Room & Board (on/off campus):** $7,212/$7,968. **Fees:** $3,318. **Books and Supplies:** $1,260. **% Receiving Financial Aid:** 15.

ADMISSIONS INFORMATION

Application Fee: $55. **Regular Application Deadline:** 6/1. **Regular Notification:** Rolling. **Transfer Students Accepted?** Yes. **Number of Applications Received:** 214. **% of Applicants Accepted:** 43. **% Accepted Who Enrolled:** 57. **Average GPA:** 3.2.
Required Admission Factors: Transcript.

EMPLOYMENT INFORMATION

Placement Office Available? Yes.

CALIFORNIA STATE UNIVERSITY—BAKERSFIELD
School of Humanities & Social Sciences

Address: 9001 Stockdale Highway, Bakersfield, CA 93311-1099
Admissions Phone: 661-664-3036 · **Admissions Fax:** 661-664-3389
Admissions E-mail: hmontalvo@csubak.edu

INSTITUTIONAL INFORMATION

Public/Private: Public. **Students in Parent Institution:** 6,397.

STUDENT INFORMATION

Total Students in Program: 1,588. **% Full-time** 48. **% Female:** 69.

RESEARCH FACILITIES

Research Facilities: Applied research center.

EXPENSES/FINANCIAL AID

Annual Tuition: $5,520. **Room & Board:** $4,400. **Fees:** $367. **Books and Supplies:** $450. **Grants Range From:** $400-$2,500. **Loans Range From:** $500-$8,500. **% Receiving Scholarships/Grants:** 20. **% Receiving Loans:** 80. **% Receiving Assistantships:** 20.

ADMISSIONS INFORMATION

Application Fee: $55. **Regular Notification:** Rolling. **Transfer Students Accepted?** Yes.
Required Admission Factors: Essays/personal statement, letters of recommendation, transcript.
Other Admission Factors: Minimum 3.0 GPA in last 90 quarter hours or minimum 3.0 GPA in major required.

EMPLOYMENT INFORMATION

Placement Office Available? Yes. **Rate of placement:** 78%.

CALIFORNIA STATE UNIVERSITY—CHICO
College of Natural Sciences

Address: Graduate & International Programs, California State University–Chico, Chico, CA 95929-0875
Admissions Phone: 530-898-6880 · **Admissions Fax:** 530-898-6889
Admissions E-mail: grin@csuchico.edu · **Web Address:** www.csuchico.edu/nsci/

INSTITUTIONAL INFORMATION

Public/Private: Public. **Students in Parent Institution:** 13,798.

STUDENT INFORMATION

Total Students in Program: 1,572. **% Female:** 60.

EXPENSES/FINANCIAL AID

Annual Tuition: $4,428. **Fees:** $2,108. **Books and Supplies:** $800.

ADMISSIONS INFORMATION

Application Fee: $55. **Regular Application Deadline:** 3/1. **Regular Notification:** Rolling. **Transfer Students Accepted?** No.
Required Admission Factors: Transcript.

CALIFORNIA STATE UNIVERSITY—CHICO
College of Behavioral and Social Sciences

Address: Graduate & International Programs, California State University, Chico, Chico, CA 95929-0875
Admissions Phone: 530-898-6880 · **Admissions Fax:** 530-898-6889
Admissions E-mail: grin@csuchico.edu
Web Address: www.csuchico.edu/bss/

INSTITUTIONAL INFORMATION

Public/Private: Public. **Students in Parent Institution:** 13,798.

STUDENT INFORMATION

Total Students in Program: 1,572. **% Female:** 60.

EXPENSES/FINANCIAL AID

Annual Tuition: $4,428. **Fees:** $2,108. **Books and Supplies:** $800.

ADMISSIONS INFORMATION

Application Fee: $55. **Regular Application Deadline:** 3/1. **Regular Notification:** Rolling. **Transfer Students Accepted?** No.
Required Admission Factors: Transcript.

CALIFORNIA STATE UNIVERSITY—CHICO
College of Humanities & Fine Arts

Address: Graduate & International Programs, California State University–Chico, Chico, CA 95929-0875
Admissions Phone: 530-898-6880 · **Admissions Fax:** 530-898-6889
Admissions E-mail: grin@csuchico.edu · **Web Address:** www.csuchico.edu/hfa/

INSTITUTIONAL INFORMATION

Public/Private: Public. **Students in Parent Institution:** 13,798.

STUDENT INFORMATION

Total Students in Program: 1,572. **% Female:** 60.

EXPENSES/FINANCIAL AID

Annual Tuition: $4,428. **Fees:** $2,108. **Books and Supplies:** $800.

ADMISSIONS INFORMATION

Application Fee: $55. **Regular Application Deadline:** 3/1. **Regular Notification:** Rolling. **Transfer Students Accepted?** No.
Required Admission Factors: Letters of recommendation, transcript.

CALIFORNIA STATE UNIVERSITY—DOMINGUEZ HILLS
College of Arts & Science

Address: 1000 East Victoria Street, Carson, CA 90747

INSTITUTIONAL INFORMATION

Public/Private: Public. **Evening Classes Available?** Yes. **Students in Parent Institution:** 12,848.

STUDENT INFORMATION

Total Students in Program: 5,115. **% Full-time** 29. **% Female:** 70.

EXPENSES/FINANCIAL AID
Annual Tuition: In-state $1,585. Fees: $350. Books and Supplies: $150.

ADMISSIONS INFORMATION
Transfer Students Accepted? Yes. Number of Applications Received: 326. % of Applicants Accepted: 82. % Accepted Who Enrolled: 55. Average GPA: 3.1.

CALIFORNIA STATE UNIVERSITY—EAST BAY
College of Arts, Letters, & Social Sciences

Address: 25800 Carlos Bee Boulevard, Hayward, CA 94542
Admissions Phone: 510-885-3286 · Admissions Fax: 510-885-4795
Admissions E-mail: gradprograms@csuhayward.edu
Web Address: isis.csuhayward.edu/DBSW/Home_Page.php

INSTITUTIONAL INFORMATION
Public/Private: Public. Evening Classes Available? Yes. Students in Parent Institution: 13,061.

STUDENT INFORMATION
Total Students in Program: 755. % Full-time 41. % Female: 76. % Minority: 57. % International: 8.

EXPENSES/FINANCIAL AID
Annual Tuition: In-state $3,194. / Out-of-state $8,616. Room & Board: $7,200. Fees: $1,815. Books and Supplies: $800. Grants Range From: $900-$10,000. Loans Range From: $1,000-$10,000. Types of Aid Available: Graduate assistantships, institutional work-study, scholarships.

ADMISSIONS INFORMATION
Application Fee: $55. Regular Application Deadline: 5/5. Regular Notification: Rolling. Transfer Students Accepted? Yes. Number of Applications Received: 268. % of Applicants Accepted: 59. % Accepted Who Enrolled: 100. Average GPA: 3.0.
Required Admission Factors: Essays/personal statement, letters of recommendation, transcript.
Other Admission Factors: Minimum 3.0 GPA in last 90 quarter units (60 semester units) required.

CALIFORNIA STATE UNIVERSITY—EAST BAY
College of Science

Address: 25800 Carlos Bee Boulevard, Hayward, CA 94542
Admissions Phone: 510-885-2784 · Admissions Fax: 510-885-4795
Admissions E-mail: adminfo@csuhayward.edu
Web Address: esweb.csuhayward.edu/becoming_student/

INSTITUTIONAL INFORMATION
Public/Private: Public. Evening Classes Available? Yes. Students in Parent Institution: 13,061.

STUDENT INFORMATION
Total Students in Program: 555. % Full-time 44. % Female: 59. % Minority: 49. % International: 31.

EXPENSES/FINANCIAL AID
Annual Tuition: In-state $3,194. / Out-of-state $8,616. Room & Board: $7,200. Fees: $1,815. Books and Supplies: $800. Grants Range From: $900-$10,000. Loans Range From: $1,000-$10,000.

ADMISSIONS INFORMATION
Application Fee: $55. Priority Application Deadline: 5/4. Regular Application Deadline: 5/5. Regular Notification: Rolling. Transfer Students Accepted? Yes. Number of Applications Received: 108. % of Applicants Accepted: 69. % Accepted Who Enrolled: 100. Average GPA: 3.0.

Required Admission Factors: Letters of recommendation, transcript.
Other Admission Factors: Minimum 2.75 GPA (3.0 in all biological science courses) required.

CALIFORNIA STATE UNIVERSITY—FRESNO
College of Arts & Humanities

Address: 5241 North Maple, MS TA51, Fresno, CA 93740-8027
Admissions Phone: 559-278-4073 · Admissions Fax: 559-278-8181
Admissions E-mail: vivian_franco@csufresno.edu

INSTITUTIONAL INFORMATION
Public/Private: Public. Evening Classes Available? Yes. Students in Parent Institution: 18,322.

STUDENT INFORMATION
Total Students in Program: 3,557. % Full-time 58. % Female: 65.

RESEARCH FACILITIES
Research Facilities: Instructional Technology Resource Center, Center for Irrigation Technology, Human Performance Labratory, Social Research Labrotory, Center for Agricultural Business.

EXPENSES/FINANCIAL AID
Annual Tuition: Out-of-state $7,710. Room & Board: $6,095. Fees: $1,806. Books and Supplies: $612.

ADMISSIONS INFORMATION
Application Fee: $55. Regular Notification: Rolling. Transfer Students Accepted? Yes. Number of Applications Received: 125. % of Applicants Accepted: 70. % Accepted Who Enrolled: 45.
Required Admission Factors: GRE, transcript.

EMPLOYMENT INFORMATION
Placement Office Available? Yes.

CALIFORNIA STATE UNIVERSITY—FRESNO
College of Science & Mathematics

Address: 5241 North Maple, MS TA51, Fresno, CA 93740-8027
Admissions Phone: 559-278-4073 · Admissions Fax: 559-278-8181
Admissions E-mail: vivian_franco@csufresno.edu

INSTITUTIONAL INFORMATION
Public/Private: Public. Evening Classes Available? Yes. Students in Parent Institution: 18,322.

STUDENT INFORMATION
Total Students in Program: 3,557. % Full-time 58. % Female: 65.

RESEARCH FACILITIES
Research Facilities: Instructional Technology Resource Center, Center for Irrigation Technology, Human Performance Labratory, Social Research Labrotory, Center for Agricultural Business.

EXPENSES/FINANCIAL AID
Annual Tuition: Out-of-state $7,710. Room & Board: $6,095. Fees: $1,806. Books and Supplies: $612.

ADMISSIONS INFORMATION
Application Fee: $55. Regular Notification: Rolling. Transfer Students Accepted? Yes. Number of Applications Received: 73. % of Applicants Accepted: 74. % Accepted Who Enrolled: 63.
Required Admission Factors: GRE, transcript.

EMPLOYMENT INFORMATION
Placement Office Available? Yes.

CALIFORNIA STATE UNIVERSITY—FRESNO
College of Social Sciences

Address: 5241 North Maple, MS TA51, Fresno, CA 93740-8027
Admissions Phone: 559-278-4073 · **Admissions Fax:** 559-278-8181
Admissions E-mail: vivian_franco@csufresno.edu

INSTITUTIONAL INFORMATION
Public/Private: Public. **Evening Classes Available?** Yes. **Students in Parent Institution:** 18,322.

STUDENT INFORMATION
Total Students in Program: 3,557. **% Full-time** 58. **% Female:** 65.

RESEARCH FACILITIES
Research Facilities: Instructional Technology Resource Center, Center for Irrigation Technology, Human Performance Labratory, Social Research Labrotory, Center for Agricultural Business.

EXPENSES/FINANCIAL AID
Annual Tuition: Out-of-state $7,710. **Room & Board:** $6,095. **Fees:** $1,806. **Books and Supplies:** $612.

ADMISSIONS INFORMATION
Application Fee: $55. **Regular Notification:** Rolling. **Transfer Students Accepted?** Yes. **Number of Applications Received:** 67. **% of Applicants Accepted:** 84. **% Accepted Who Enrolled:** 52.
Required Admission Factors: GRE, transcript.

EMPLOYMENT INFORMATION
Placement Office Available? Yes.

CALIFORNIA STATE UNIVERSITY—LONG BEACH
College of Liberal Arts

Address: 1250 Bellflower Boulevard, Long Beach, CA 90840
Admissions Phone: 562-985-5381 · **Admissions Fax:** 562-985-2463
Admissions E-mail: ffata@csulb.edu · **Web address:** www.csulb.edu

INSTITUTIONAL INFORMATION
Public/Private: Public. **Evening Classes Available?** Yes. **Students in Parent Institution:** 30,918.

STUDENT INFORMATION
Total Students in Program: 5,765. **% Full-time** 35. **% Female:** 64.

RESEARCH FACILITIES
Research Facilities: Center for Aerospace Sciences, Center for Behavioral Research and Services, Center for Criminal Justice Research and Training, Center for Health and Behavior Studies, Center for Language-Minority Education and Research, Science and Math Education Institute.

EXPENSES/FINANCIAL AID
Annual Tuition: Out-of-state $7,726. **Fees:** $1,846. **Books and Supplies:** $612. **Grants Range From:** $1,800-$2,000. **Loans Range From:** $5,000-$8,500. **% Receiving Scholarships/Grants:** 60. **% Receiving Loans:** 50. **Number of Teaching/Research Assistantships Granted Each Year:** 50. **Average Salary Stipend:** $700.

ADMISSIONS INFORMATION
Application Fee: $55. **Regular Notification:** Rolling. **Transfer Students Accepted?** Yes. **Number of Applications Received:** 385. **% of Applicants Accepted:** 73. **% Accepted Who Enrolled:** 67.
Required Admission Factors: Transcript.
Other Admission Factors: Minimum 2.5 GPA on last 60 credit hours required.
Program-Specific Admission Factors: Portfolio required of MFA program applicants.

EMPLOYMENT INFORMATION
Placement Office Available? Yes.

CALIFORNIA STATE UNIVERSITY—LONG BEACH
College of Natural Sciences
& Mathematics

Address: 1250 Bellflower Boulevard, Long Beach, CA 90840
Admissions Phone: 562-985-4931 · **Admissions Fax:** 562-985-2315
Admissions E-mail: bambos@csulb.edu · **Web address:** www.csulb.edu

INSTITUTIONAL INFORMATION
Public/Private: Public. **Evening Classes Available?** Yes. **Students in Parent Institution:** 30,918.

STUDENT INFORMATION
Total Students in Program: 5,765. **% Full-time** 35. **% Female:** 64.

RESEARCH FACILITIES
Research Facilities: Center for Aerospace Sciences, Center for Behavioral Research and Services, Center for Criminal Justice Research and Training, Center for Health and Behavior Studies, Center for Language-Minority Education and Research, Science and Math Education Institute.

EXPENSES/FINANCIAL AID
Annual Tuition: $7,726. **Fees:** $1,846. **Books and Supplies:** $612. **Grants Range From:** $1,800-$2,000. **Loans Range From:** $5,000-$8,500. **% Receiving Scholarships/Grants:** 60. **% Receiving Loans:** 50.

ADMISSIONS INFORMATION
Application Fee: $55. **Regular Notification:** Rolling. **Transfer Students Accepted?** Yes. **Number of Applications Received:** 116. **% of Applicants Accepted:** 45.
Required Admission Factors: GRE, transcript.
Other Admission Factors: Minimum 2.5 GPA on last 60 credit hours required.

EMPLOYMENT INFORMATION
Placement Office Available? Yes.

CALIFORNIA STATE UNIVERSITY—LONG BEACH
College of the Arts

Address: 1250 Bellflower Boulevard, Long Beach, CA 90840
Admissions Phone: 562-985-4364 · **Admissions Fax:** 562-985-7883
Admissions E-mail: harbinge@csulb.edu · **Web Address:** www.csulb.edu/~cota

INSTITUTIONAL INFORMATION
Public/Private: Public. **Total Faculty:** 273. **% Faculty Female:** 40. **% Faculty Part-time:** 61. **Students in Parent Institution:** 35,000

PROGRAMS
Masters offered in: Art history, criticism, and conservation; ceramic arts and ceramics; conducting; dance, directing, and theatrical production; drawing; fiber, textile, and weaving arts; intermedia/multimedia; jazz/jazz studies; metal and jewelry arts; music pedagogy; music theory and composition; musicology and ethnomusicology; painting; piano and organ; printmaking; sculpture; technical theater/theater design and technology; violin, viola, guitar, and other stringed instruments; voice and opera.

STUDENT INFORMATION
Total Students in Program: 230. **% Full-time** 80.

RESEARCH FACILITIES
Research Facilities: California Institute for the Preservation of Jazz

EXPENSES/FINANCIAL AID

Annual Tuition: $2,572. **Fees:** $158. **Books and Supplies:** $1,224. **Grants Range From:** $250-$2,500. **Loans Range From:** $100-$15,000. **Types of Aid Available:** Fellowships, graduate assistantships, grants, institutional work-study, loans, scholarships. **Number of Teaching/Research Assistantships Granted Each Year:** 35 **Assistantship Compensation Includes:** Salary/ stipend. **Average Salary Stipend:** $6,000.

ADMISSIONS INFORMATION

Application Fee: $55. **Regular Application Deadline:** 7/1. **Regular Notification:** Rolling. **Transfer Students Accepted?** Yes. **Number of Applications Received:** 676. **% of Applicants Accepted:** 48. **% Accepted Who Enrolled:** 71. **Average GPA:** 3.2.
Required Admission Factors: Transcript.
Other Admission Factors: Minimum 2.5 GPA on last 60 credit hours required.
Program-Specific Admission Factors: Art: portfolio; Dance: audition; Music: audition and/or portfolio; Theater: acting/audition; Theater (design): portfolio; Theater (management): interview.

EMPLOYMENT INFORMATION

Placement Office Available? Yes.

CALIFORNIA STATE UNIVERSITY—LOS ANGELES
College of Arts & Letters

Address: 5151 State University Drive, Los Angeles, CA 90032
Admissions Phone: 323-343-4001 · **Admissions Fax:** 323-343-6440
Admissions E-mail: Admission@CalStateLA.edu
Web Address: www.calstatela.edu/academic/al/

INSTITUTIONAL INFORMATION

Public/Private: Public. **Evening Classes Available?** Yes. **Students in Parent Institution:** 19,593.

STUDENT INFORMATION

Total Students in Program: 6,117. **% Full-time** 31. **% Female:** 65.

EXPENSES/FINANCIAL AID

Annual Tuition: $3,936. **Fees:** $1,878. **Books and Supplies:** $810. **Grants Range From:** $30-$30,000. **Loans Range From:** $100-$14,000. **% Receiving Scholarships/Grants:** 84. **% Receiving Loans:** 51.

ADMISSIONS INFORMATION

Application Fee: $55. **Regular Application Deadline:** 11/1. **Regular Notification:** Rolling. **Transfer Students Accepted?** Yes.
Other Admission Factors: Admission to art (MFA, MA), communication studies, English, modern languages (French), theater arts: 3.0 in last 90 units. Admission to modern languages (Spanish), philosophy: 2.75 in last 90 units. Admission to music: 2.5 in last 90 units.
Program-Specific Admission Factors: Departments may require portfolio review, writing sample, or auditions. Consult online university catalog for specific requirements.

EMPLOYMENT INFORMATION

Placement Office Available? Yes.

CALIFORNIA STATE UNIVERSITY—LOS ANGELES
College of Natural & Social Sciences

Address: 5151 State University Drive, Los Angeles, CA 90032
Admissions Phone: 323-343-2000 · **Admissions Fax:** 323-343-2011
Admissions E-mail: admission@calstatela.edu
Web Address: www.calstatela.edu/academic/nssd/

INSTITUTIONAL INFORMATION

Public/Private: Public. **Evening Classes Available?** Yes. **Students in Parent Institution:** 19,593.

PROGRAMS

Masters offered in: Biochemistry, molecular biology.

STUDENT INFORMATION

Total Students in Program: 6,117. **% Full-time** 31. **% Female:** 65.

EXPENSES/FINANCIAL AID

Annual Tuition: In-state $2,500. / Out-of-state $3,936. **Fees:** $1,878. **Books and Supplies:** $810. **Grants Range From:** $30-$30,000. **Loans Range From:** $100-$14,000. **% Receiving Scholarships/Grants:** 84. **% Receiving Loans:** 51.

ADMISSIONS INFORMATION

Application Fee: $55. **Regular Application Deadline:** 6/1. **Transfer Students Accepted?** Yes. **Transfer Policy:** Maximum 13 quarter units may be transferred. **Number of Applications Received:** 442. **% of Applicants Accepted:** 71. **% Accepted Who Enrolled:** 57. **Average GPA:** 3.11.
Required Admission Factors: Letters of recommendation, transcript.
Other Admission Factors: Minimum 2.5 GPA required; minimum 2.75-3.0 GPA required for some programs.
Program-Specific Admission Factors: Separate application required by some programs.

EMPLOYMENT INFORMATION

Placement Office Available? Yes.

CALIFORNIA STATE UNIVERSITY—NORTHRIDGE
College of Arts, Media, & Communication

Address: 18111 Nordhoff Street, Northridge, CA 91330
Admissions Phone: 818-677-2242 · **Admissions Fax:** 818-677-3046
Admissions E-mail: dave.y.moon@csun.edu

INSTITUTIONAL INFORMATION

Public/Private: Public. **Students in Parent Institution:** 29,066.

STUDENT INFORMATION

Total Students in Program: 6,513. **% Full-time** 38. **% Female:** 69.

EXPENSES/FINANCIAL AID

Annual Tuition: $4,428. **Fees:** $1,892.

ADMISSIONS INFORMATION

Transfer Students Accepted? No. **Number of Applications Received:** 254. **% of Applicants Accepted:** 73. **% Accepted Who Enrolled:** 57.
Required Admission Factors: Essays/personal statement, GRE, letters of recommendation, transcript.
Other Admission Factors: Minimum 3.0 GPA required.

CALIFORNIA STATE UNIVERSITY— SACRAMENTO

Address: 6000 J Street, Sacramento, CA 95819-6048
Admissions Phone: 916-278-3901 · **Admissions Fax:** 916-278-5603
Admissions E-mail: admissions@csus.edu · **Web Address:** www.csus.edu/

INSTITUTIONAL INFORMATION

Public/Private: Public. **Evening Classes Available?** Yes. **Total Faculty:** 522. **% Faculty Female:** 46. **% Faculty Part-time:** 32. **Student/Faculty Ratio:** 22:1. **Students in Parent Institution:** 27,972.

PROGRAMS

Masters offered in: Anthropology; art/art studies; audiology/audiologist and hearing sciences; audiology/audiologist and speech-language pathology/pathologist; behavioral sciences; bilingual and multilingual education; business administration/management; business, management, marketing, and related support services; cell/cellular and molecular biology; chemistry; city/urban, community and regional planning; civil engineering; communications studies/speech communication and rhetoric; community psychology; computer engineering; computer science; computer software engineering; conducting; conservation biology; corrections and criminal justice; counseling psychology; counselor education/school counseling and guidance services; creative writing; curriculum and instruction; drama and dramatics/theater arts; early childhood education and teaching; economics; education leadership and administration; education/teaching of individuals with hearing impairments, including deafness; education/teaching of individuals with speech or language impairments; electrical, electronics, and communications engineering; engineering; English language and literature, English language and literature/letters; family practice nurse; nurse practitioner; family psychology; finance; geology/earth science; health and physical education; health and physical education/fitness; higher education/higher education administration; history; human resources management/personnel administration; industrial and organizational psychology; international relations and affairs; international/global studies; kinesiology and exercise science; liberal arts and sciences/liberal studies; management information systems; marketing/marketing management; mathematics; mechanical engineering/mechanical technology/technician; mechanical engineering; multicultural education; music history, literature, and theory; music pedagogy; music performance; music theory and composition; music/music and performing arts studies; nursing-registered nurse training (RN, ASN, BSN, MSN); parks, recreation, and leisure facilities management; parks, recreation, leisure, and fitness studies; political science and government; psychology; public administration and services; public administration; public policy analysis; public/applied history and archival administration; school psychology; social work; sociology; Spanish language and literature; special education; speech-language pathology/pathologist; teacher education and professional development, specific subject areas; teaching English as a second or foreign language/ESL language instructor. **Doctorate offered in:** Public/applied history and archival administration.

STUDENT INFORMATION

Total Students in Program: 5,417. **% Full-time** 51. **% Female:** 68. **% Minority:** 17. **% International:** 4.

EXPENSES/FINANCIAL AID

Annual Tuition: In-state $3,310. / Out-of-state $13,480. **Room & Board:** $6,574. **Fees:** $490. **Books and Supplies:** $1,260. **Grants Range From:** $100-$20,769. **Loans Range From:** $15-$18,225. **% Receiving Financial Aid:** 31.2. **% Receiving Scholarships/Grants:** 60. **% Receiving Loans:** 86. **% Receiving Other Aid (Federal Work Study):** 4. **Types of Aid Available:** Fellowships, graduate assistantships, grants, institutional work-study, loans, scholarships. **Average student debt, upon graduation:** $21,081.

ADMISSIONS INFORMATION

Application Fee: $55. **Priority Application Deadline:** N/A. **Regular Application Deadline:** 5/1. **Regular Notification:** Rolling. **Transfer Students Accepted?** Yes. **Transfer Policy:** Must meet individual department requirements. **Number of Applications Received:** 12,515. **% of Applicants Accepted:** 51. **% Accepted Who Enrolled:** 37. **Average GPA:** 3.2. **Average GRE Verbal:** 420. **Average GRE Quantitative:** 525. **Average GRE Analytical:** 575.
Required Admission Factors: Transcript.
Program-Specific Admission Factors: Varies by department.

CALIFORNIA STATE UNIVERSITY— SAN BERNARDINO
College of Natural Sciences

Address: 5500 University Parkway, San Bernardino, CA 92407-2397
Admissions Phone: 909-880-5188 · **Admissions Fax:** 909-880-7034
Admissions E-mail: moreinfo@csusb.edu · **Web Address:** nsci.csusb.edu/

INSTITUTIONAL INFORMATION

Public/Private: Public. **Evening Classes Available?** Yes. **Total Faculty:** 207. **% Faculty Part-time:** 45. **Student/Faculty Ratio:** 21:1. **Students in Parent Institution:** 16,194

PROGRAMS

Masters offered in: Administration of special education; bilingual and multilingual education; business administration and management; clinical child psychology; clinical psychology; communications and media studies; communications studies/speech communication and rhetoric; communications, journalism, and related fields; computer and information sciences; counseling psychology; counselor education/school counseling and guidance services; curriculum and instruction; education; education/teaching of individuals with autism; education/teaching of individuals with emotional disturbances; education/teaching of individuals with hearing impairments, including deafness; education/teaching of individuals with multiple disabilities; education/teaching of individuals with specific learning disabilities; education/teaching of the gifted and talented; educational administration and supervision; educational, instructional, and curriculum supervision; elementary and middle school administration/principalship; environmental psychology; experimental psychology; mass communications/media studies; mathematics; multicultural education; psychology; public administration; secondary education and teaching; secondary school administration/principalship; social sciences; special education and teaching; teacher education, multiple levels.

STUDENT INFORMATION

Total Students in Program: 328. **% Full-time** 47. **% Female:** 53. **% Minority:** 40. **% International:** 14.

RESEARCH FACILITIES

Research Facilities: Behavioral Health Institute, Institute for Applied Supercomputing, Institute for Science Education, Institute for Applied Research and Policy Analysis, Water Institute.

EXPENSES/FINANCIAL AID

Annual Tuition: $8,136. **Room & Board:** $6,591. **Fees:** $3,398. **Books and Supplies:** $1,215. **Types of Aid Available:** Loans.

ADMISSIONS INFORMATION

Application Fee: $55. **Regular Application Deadline:** 11/1. **Regular Notification:** Rolling. **Transfer Students Accepted?** Yes. **Transfer Policy:** Varies by graduate program. **Number of Applications Received:** 268. **% of Applicants Accepted:** 52. **% Accepted Who Enrolled:** 25.
Required Admission Factors: GRE, letters of recommendation, transcript.
Other Admission Factors: Minimum 2.5 GPA required; minimum 3.0 GPA recommended.

EMPLOYMENT INFORMATION

Placement Office Available? Yes.

CALIFORNIA STATE UNIVERSITY— SAN BERNARDINO
College of Social & Behavioral Sciences

Address: 5500 University Parkway, San Bernardino, CA 92407-2397
Admissions Phone: 909-880-5188 · **Admissions Fax:** 909-880-7034
Admissions E-mail: moreinfo@csusb.edu · **Web Address:** csbs.csusb.edu/

INSTITUTIONAL INFORMATION
Public/Private: Public. **Evening Classes Available?** Yes. **Total Faculty:** 166. **% Faculty Part-time:** 36. **Student/Faculty Ratio:** 26:1. **Students in Parent Institution:** 16,194.

PROGRAMS
Masters offered in: Clinical psychology, criminal justice/law enforcement administration, developmental and child psychology, experimental psychology, industrial and organizational psychology, social sciences, social work.

STUDENT INFORMATION
Total Students in Program: 428. **% Full-time** 73. **% Female:** 70. **% Minority:** 45. **% International:** 4.

RESEARCH FACILITIES
Research Facilities: Behavioral Health Institute, Institute for Applied Supercomputing, Institute for Science Education, Institute for Applied Research and Policy Analysis, Water Institute.

EXPENSES/FINANCIAL AID
Annual Tuition: $8,136. **Room & Board:** $6,591. **Fees:** $3,398. **Books and Supplies:** $1,215. **Types of Aid Available:** Fellowships, graduate assistantships, grants, institutional work-study, loans, scholarships.

ADMISSIONS INFORMATION
Application Fee: $55. **Regular Application Deadline:** 11/1. **Regular Notification:** Rolling. **Transfer Students Accepted?** Yes. **Transfer Policy:** Separate applications to both university and program required of transfer applicants. **Number of Applications Received:** 488. **% of Applicants Accepted:** 42. **% Accepted Who Enrolled:** 73. **Average GPA:** 3.6.
Required Admission Factors: Essays/personal statement, GRE, letters of recommendation, transcript.
Other Admission Factors: Minimum 2.5 GPA required; minimum 3.0 GPA recommended.

EMPLOYMENT INFORMATION
Placement Office Available? Yes.

CALIFORNIA STATE UNIVERSITY— SAN MARCOS
College of Arts & Sciences

Address: 333 S. Twin Oaks Vallet Road, San Marcos, CA 92096-0001
Admissions Phone: 760-750-4848 · **Admissions Fax:** 760-750-3248
Admissions E-mail: apply@csusm.edu · **Web Address:** www.csusm.edu/A_S/

INSTITUTIONAL INFORMATION
Public/Private: Public. **Evening Classes Available?** Yes. **Total Faculty:** 226. **% Faculty Female:** 52. **% Faculty Part-time:** 44. **Students in Parent Institution:** 7,365

PROGRAMS
Masters offered in: Biology/biological sciences, computer and information sciences, English language and literature/letters, mathematics, psychology, sociology; Spanish language and literature.

STUDENT INFORMATION
Total Students in Program: 198. **% Full-time** 45. **% Female:** 63.

RESEARCH FACILITIES
Research Facilities: Center for the Study of Books in Spanish, Social and Behavioral Research Institute, Center for Border and Regional Affairs, National Latino Research Center.

EXPENSES/FINANCIAL AID
Annual Tuition: $10,170. **Room & Board (on/off campus):** $7,474/$8,061. **Fees:** $2,820. **Books and Supplies:** $1,195. **Grants Range From:** $438-$1,734. **Loans Range From:** $1,400-$18,500. **% Receiving Financial Aid:** 57. **% Receiving Scholarships/Grants:** 60. **% Receiving Loans:** 82. **Types of Aid Available:** Fellowships, graduate assistantships, grants, loans, scholarships.

ADMISSIONS INFORMATION
Application Fee: $55. **Priority Application Deadline:** 10/1. **Regular Application Deadline:** 11/30. **Regular Notification:** Rolling. **Transfer Students Accepted?** Yes. **Number of Applications Received:** 155. **% of Applicants Accepted:** 52. **% Accepted Who Enrolled:** 67. **Average GPA:** 3.0.
Required Admission Factors: Transcript.
Other Admission Factors: Most programs require a 3.0 GPA overall or for last 60 units completed.

EMPLOYMENT INFORMATION
Placement Office Available? Yes. **% Employed Within 6 Months:** 86. **Rate of placement:** 86%. **Average starting salary:** $40,000.

CALIFORNIA STATE UNIVERSITY—STANISLAUS
The Graduate School

Address: 801 West Monte Vista Avenue, Turlock, CA 95382
Admissions Phone: 209-667-3152 · **Admissions Fax:** 209-667-3788
Admissions E-mail: Outreach_Help_Desk@csustan.edu
Web Address: www.csustan.edu/Graduate_School/

INSTITUTIONAL INFORMATION
Public/Private: Public. **Students in Parent Institution:** 7,858.

PROGRAMS
Masters offered in: Biological and physical sciences, business administration/management, criminal justice/law enforcement administration, education, English language and literature, history; multi/interdisciplinary studies, psychology, public administration, social work.

STUDENT INFORMATION
Total Students in Program: 699. **% Full-time** 32. **% Female:** 67. **% Minority:** 25. **% International:** 2.

RESEARCH FACILITIES
Research Facilities: Center for Public Policy Studies.

EXPENSES/FINANCIAL AID
Annual Tuition: In-state $2,718. / Out-of-state $8,922. **Room & Board (on/off campus):** $7,596/$7,101. **Books and Supplies:** $1,224. **Grants Range From:** $300-$6,000. **Loans Range From:** $300-$14,000. **Types of Aid Available:** Graduate assistantships, grants, institutional work-study, loans, scholarships.

ADMISSIONS INFORMATION
Application Fee: $55. **Priority Application Deadline:** 11/30. **Regular Application Deadline:** 6/5. **Regular Notification:** Rolling. **Transfer Students Accepted?** Yes. **Transfer Policy:** College transcripts, good standing. **Number of Applications Received:** 532. **% of Applicants Accepted:** 83. **% Accepted Who Enrolled:** 33.
Required Admission Factors: Transcript.
Other Admission Factors: Students must be in good standing at the last college/university attended; minimum GPA of 2.5 in the last 60 semester units attempted; meet the professional, personal, scholastic, and other standards for graduate study, including qualifying examinations.

Program-Specific Admission Factors: 2.75 for MPA program/credential 3.0 for other MA programs.

CALIFORNIA UNIVERSITY OF PENNSYLVANIA
School of Graduate Studies & Research

Address: 250 University Drive, California, PA 15419
Admissions Phone: 724-938-4187 · **Admissions Fax:** 724-938-5712
Admissions E-mail: gradschool@cup.edu · **Web Address:** www.cup.edu/graduate

INSTITUTIONAL INFORMATION
Public/Private: Public. **Evening Classes Available?** Yes. **Students in Parent Institution:** 6,640.

PROGRAMS
Masters offered in: Animal behavior and ethology; audiology/audiologist and speech-language pathology/pathologist; biology teacher education; business administration/management; business, management, marketing, and related support services; business/commerce; communication disorders sciences and services; communication disorders; corrections and criminal justice; counseling psychology; counselor education/school counseling and guidance services; criminal justice/law enforcement administration; criminology; digital communications and media/multimedia; education; elementary and middle school administration/principalship; elementary education and teaching; environmental science; fishing and fisheries sciences and management; geography; geological and earth sciences/geosciences; geology/earth science; junior high/intermediate/middle school education and teaching; kinesiology and exercise science; law, legal services, and legal studies; physics teacher education; reading teacher education; school psychology; science teacher education/general science teacher education; secondary education and teaching; secondary school administration/principalship; social work; special education; speech-language pathology/pathologist; sports and fitness administration/management; superintendency and educational system administration; teacher education, multiple levels; technical teacher education; technology teacher education/industrial arts teacher education; Web page, digital/multimedia, and information resources design.

STUDENT INFORMATION
Total Students in Program: 1,185. **% Full-time** 51. **% Female:** 49.

EXPENSES/FINANCIAL AID
Annual Tuition: In-state $4,138. / Out-of-state $7,008. **% Receiving Assistantships:** 30.

ADMISSIONS INFORMATION
Application Fee: $25. **Priority Application Deadline:** 6/1. **Regular Application Deadline:** 8/15. **Regular Notification:** Rolling. **Transfer Students Accepted?** Yes. **Transfer Policy:** 3.0 GPA.
Required Admission Factors: Transcript.
Other Admission Factors: 3.0 GPA
Program-Specific Admission Factors: Please see website for additional department specific requirements.

EMPLOYMENT INFORMATION
Placement Office Available? Yes. **Rate of placement:** 95%.

CAMERON UNIVERSITY
School of Graduate Studies

Address: 2800 West Gore Boulevard, Lawton, OK 73505
Admissions Phone: 580-581-2987 · **Admissions Fax:** 580-581-5532
Admissions E-mail: graduate@cameron.edu · **Web Address:** www.cameron.edu

INSTITUTIONAL INFORMATION
Public/Private: Public. **Evening Classes Available?** Yes. **Total Faculty:** 132. **% Faculty Female:** 32. **% Faculty Part-time:** 59. **Student/Faculty Ratio:** 4:1. **Students in Parent Institution:** 5,626.

PROGRAMS
Masters offered in: Behavioral sciences; business administration/management; counseling psychology; education; teacher education and professional development, specific subject areas; teacher education, multiple levels.

STUDENT INFORMATION
Total Students in Program: 417. **% Full-time** 32. **% Female:** 71.

EXPENSES/FINANCIAL AID
Annual Tuition: In-state $2,027. / Out-of-state $4,817. **Room & Board:** $3,820. **Fees:** $15. **Books and Supplies:** $750. **Grants Range From:** $250-$500. **Loans Range From:** $100-$9,000. **% Receiving Financial Aid:** 75. **% Receiving Scholarships/Grants:** 5. **% Receiving Loans:** 35. **% Receiving Assistantships:** 5. **% Receiving Other Aid (VA and Military Tuition Assistance):** 55. **Number of Teaching/Research Assistantships Granted Each Year:** 10. **Assistantship Compensation Includes:** Salary/stipend.

ADMISSIONS INFORMATION
Application Fee: $15. **Regular Application Deadline:** 11/1. **Regular Notification:** Rolling. **Transfer Students Accepted?** Yes. **Number of Applications Received:** 220. **% of Applicants Accepted:** 97. **% Accepted Who Enrolled:** 58. **Average GPA:** 3.0.
Required Admission Factors: Transcript.
Recommended Admission Factors: GMAT, GRE.
Other Admission Factors: Minimum 3.0 GPA. If below 3.00, conditional admission can be granted.

CAMPBELLSVILLE UNIVERSITY
College of Arts & Sciences

Address: 1 University Drive, Campbellsville, KY 42718-2799
Admissions Phone: 270-789-5220 · **Admissions Fax:** 270-789-5050
Admissions E-mail: krdeaton@campbellsville.edu
Web Address: www.campbellsville.edu

INSTITUTIONAL INFORMATION
Public/Private: Private (nonprofit). **Evening Classes Available?** Yes. **Student/Faculty Ratio:** 7:1. **Students in Parent Institution:** 2,006.

PROGRAMS
Masters offered in: Social sciences.

STUDENT INFORMATION
Total Students in Program: 19. **% Full-time** 100. **% Female:** 400.

EXPENSES/FINANCIAL AID
Annual Tuition: $4,500. **Room & Board (on/off campus):** $4,976/$5,100. **Fees:** $200. **Books and Supplies:** $500. **Grants Range From:** $500-$2,700. **Loans Range From:** $500-$8,500. **% Receiving Financial Aid:** 30. **% Receiving Scholarships/Grants:** 30. **% Receiving Loans:** 70. **Types of Aid Available:** Graduate assistantships, loans, scholarships. **Assistantship Compensation Includes:** Partial tuition remission.

ADMISSIONS INFORMATION
Application Fee: $25. **Priority Application Deadline:** 6/1. **Regular Application Deadline:** 8/1. **Regular Notification:** Rolling. **Transfer Students Accepted?** Yes. **Number of Applications Received:** 6. **% of Applicants Accepted:** 100. **% Accepted Who Enrolled:** 83. **Average GPA:** 3.4.
Required Admission Factors: Letters of recommendation, transcript.
Other Admission Factors: Minimum 2.9 GPA required.

EMPLOYMENT INFORMATION

Placement Office Available? Yes. **% Employed Within 6 Months:** 60. **Rate of placement:** 75%. **Average starting salary:** $35,000.

CAMPBELLSVILLE UNIVERSITY
School of Music

Address: 1 University Drive, Campbellsville, KY 42718-2799
Admissions Phone: 270-789-5552 · **Admissions Fax:** 270-789-5071
Admissions E-mail: krdeaton@campbellsville.edu
Web Address: www.campbellsville.edu

INSTITUTIONAL INFORMATION

Public/Private: Private (nonprofit). **Evening Classes Available?** Yes. **Total Faculty:** 10. **Student/Faculty Ratio:** 8:1. **Students in Parent Institution:** 2,006.

PROGRAMS

Masters offered in: Music, music/music and performing arts studies.

STUDENT INFORMATION

Total Students in Program: 76. **% Full-time** 17.

RESEARCH FACILITIES

Research Facilities: Campus in Recife Brazil.

EXPENSES/FINANCIAL AID

Annual Tuition: $4,500. **Room & Board (on/off campus):** $4,976/$5,100. **Fees:** $200. **Books and Supplies:** $500. **Grants Range From:** $500-$4,000. **Loans Range From:** $500-$8,500. **% Receiving Financial Aid:** 18. **% Receiving Scholarships/Grants:** 80. **% Receiving Loans:** 50. **% Receiving Assistantships:** 20. **Types of Aid Available:** Graduate assistantships, grants, loans, scholarships. **Number of Teaching/Research Assistantships Granted Each Year:** 1 **Assistantship Compensation Includes:** Partial tuition remission. **Average Salary Stipend:** $2,700.

ADMISSIONS INFORMATION

Application Fee: $25. **Priority Application Deadline:** 6/1. **Regular Application Deadline:** 8/1. **Regular Notification:** Rolling. **Transfer Students Accepted?** Yes. **Number of Applications Received:** 19. **% of Applicants Accepted:** 100. **% Accepted Who Enrolled:** 100. **Average GPA:** 3.1.
Required Admission Factors: Essays/personal statement, letters of recommendation, transcript.
Recommended Admission Factors:
Other Admission Factors: Minimum 2.5 GPA (3.0 in major) required.
Program-Specific Admission Factors: Auditions for music program.

EMPLOYMENT INFORMATION

Placement Office Available? Yes. **% Employed Within 6 Months:** 100. **% of master's professional grads employed in their field upon graduation:** 75. **Rate of placement:** 75%. **Average starting salary:** $30,000.

CANADIAN THEOLOGICAL SEMINARY
Graduate Programs

Address: 630, 833-4th Avenue SW, Calgary, AB T2P 3T5 Canada
Admissions Phone: 403-410-2900 · **Admissions Fax:** 403-571-2556
Admissions E-mail: hmyers@auc-nuc.ca
Web Address: www.auc-nuc.ca/student_information/graduate/index.html

INSTITUTIONAL INFORMATION

Public/Private: Private (nonprofit). **Students in Parent Institution:** 144.

STUDENT INFORMATION

Total Students in Program: 144. **% Full-time** 49. **% Female:** 34.

RESEARCH FACILITIES

Research Facilities: Center for Church Ministries.

EXPENSES/FINANCIAL AID

Annual Tuition: In-state $5,400. **Fees:** $85. **Books and Supplies:** $600. **Grants Range From:** $500-$1,500. **Loans Range From:** $500-$8,000. **% Receiving Scholarships/Grants:** 86. **% Receiving Loans:** 14.

ADMISSIONS INFORMATION

Application Fee: $50. **Regular Application Deadline:** 8/1. **Regular Notification:** Rolling. **Transfer Students Accepted?** Yes. **Number of Applications Received:** 48. **% of Applicants Accepted:** 98. **% Accepted Who Enrolled:** 55.
Required Admission Factors: Essays/personal statement, letters of recommendation, transcript.
Other Admission Factors: Minimum 2.0 GPA and minimum 30 credits of arts/sciences undergraduate coursework required.
Program-Specific Admission Factors: Applicants for the master of arts (Biblical/theological studies) must have maintained a minimum cumulative undergraduate grade point average of 3.0.

EMPLOYMENT INFORMATION

Placement Office Available? Yes.

CAPELLA UNIVERSITY
Harold Abel School of Psychology

Address: 225 South Sixth Street, 9th Floor, Minneapolis, MN 55402
Admissions Phone: 888-227-3552 · **Admissions Fax:** 612-977-5060
Admissions E-mail: info@capella.edu · **Web Address:** www.capella.edu

INSTITUTIONAL INFORMATION

Public/Private: Private (proprietary). **Evening Classes Available?** Yes. **Student/Faculty Ratio:** 10:1.

EXPENSES/FINANCIAL AID

Books and Supplies: $100. **Loans Range From:** $5,000-$18,500. **% Receiving Financial Aid:** 40. **% Receiving Loans:** 100. **Average student debt, upon graduation:** $30,000.

ADMISSIONS INFORMATION

Application Fee: $50. **Regular Notification:** Rolling. **Transfer Students Accepted?** Yes. **Transfer Policy:** Maximum 9 semester hours or 15 quarter hours may be transferred into master's programs.
Required Admission Factors: Essays/personal statement, transcript.
Other Admission Factors: Minimum 2.7 GPA required.

CAPELLA UNIVERSITY
School of Human Services

Address: 225 South Sixth Street, 9th Floor, Minneapolis, MN 55402
Admissions Phone: 1-888-227-3552 · **Admissions Fax:** 612-977-5060
Admissions E-mail: info@capella.edu · **Web Address:** www.capella.edu

INSTITUTIONAL INFORMATION

Public/Private: Private (proprietary). **Evening Classes Available?** Yes.

EXPENSES/FINANCIAL AID

Books and Supplies: $100. **Loans Range From:** $5,000-$18,500. **% Receiving Financial Aid:** 40. **% Receiving Loans:** 100. **Average student debt, upon graduation:** $30,000.

ADMISSIONS INFORMATION

Application Fee: $50. **Regular Notification:** Rolling. **Transfer Students Accepted?** Yes. **Transfer Policy:** Maximum 12 credits may be transferred into

master's programs. Maximum 48 quarter credits may be transfered.
Required Admission Factors: Essays/personal statement, transcript.
Other Admission Factors: Minimum 2.7 GPA required.

CARDINAL STRITCH UNIVERSITY
College of Arts & Sciences

Address: 6801 North Yates Road, Milwaukee, WI 53217
Admissions Phone: 800-347-8822, ext. 4042

INSTITUTIONAL INFORMATION
Public/Private: Private (nonprofit). **Evening Classes Available?** Yes. **Students in Parent Institution:** 4,823.

STUDENT INFORMATION
Total Students in Program: 1,734. **% Full-time** 57. **% Female:** 63.

EXPENSES/FINANCIAL AID
Annual Tuition: In-state $6,660. **Fees:** $100. **Books and Supplies:** $500. **Number of Teaching/Research Assistantships Granted Each Year:** 2. **Average Salary Stipend:** $625.

ADMISSIONS INFORMATION
Application Fee: $25. **Regular Notification:** Rolling. **Transfer Students Accepted?** Yes. **Transfer Policy:** Maximum 9 credit hours taken within the last 7 years with a minimum grade of B may be transferred. **Number of Applications Received:** 21. **% of Applicants Accepted:** 95.
Required Admission Factors: Transcript.
Other Admission Factors: Minimum 2.75 GPA required.

EMPLOYMENT INFORMATION
Placement Office Available? Yes. **Rate of placement:** 95%.

CARIBBEAN CENTER FOR ADVANCED STUDIES
Graduate Programs

Address: Apartado 9023711
Old San Juan Station, San Juan, Puerto Rico 00923-3711
Admissions Phone: 787-725-6500, ext. 21 · **Admissions Fax:** 787-721-7187
Admissions E-mail: crodriguez@prip.ccas.edu

INSTITUTIONAL INFORMATION
Public/Private: Private (nonprofit). **Evening Classes Available?** Yes. **Student/Faculty Ratio:** 23:1. **Students in Parent Institution:** 703.

STUDENT INFORMATION
Total Students in Program: 567. **% Full-time** 70. **% Female:** 85.

EXPENSES/FINANCIAL AID
Books and Supplies: $1,521. **Grants Range From:** $500-$3,000. **Loans Range From:** $1,000-$8,500. **% Receiving Financial Aid:** 84. **% Receiving Scholarships/Grants:** 16. **% Receiving Loans:** 81. **% Receiving Other Aid:** 3. **Average student debt, upon graduation:** $51,000. **Average amount of individual fellowships per year:** $9,600.

ADMISSIONS INFORMATION
Application Fee: $75. **Regular Notification:** Rolling. **Transfer Students Accepted?** Yes. **Number of Applications Received:** 133. **% of Applicants Accepted:** 100. **% Accepted Who Enrolled:** 88. **Average GPA:** 3.35.
Required Admission Factors: Essays/personal statement, GRE, interview, letters of recommendation, transcript.
Other Admission Factors: Minimum 2.0 undergraduate GPA and minimum 3.0 graduate GPA required.

EMPLOYMENT INFORMATION
% Employed Within 6 Months: 100. **% of master's/doctoral grads employed in their field upon graduation:** 100/100.

CARLOW COLLEGE
Graduate Studies

Address: 3333 Fifth Avenue, Pittsburgh, PA 15213
Admissions Phone: 412-578-8764 · **Admissions Fax:** 412-578-8822
Admissions E-mail: kchrisman@carlow.edu

INSTITUTIONAL INFORMATION
Public/Private: Private (nonprofit). **Evening Classes Available?** Yes. **Total Faculty:** 22. **% Faculty Female:** 77. **% Faculty Part-time:** 73. **Student/Faculty Ratio:** 13:1. **Students in Parent Institution:** 1,925

STUDENT INFORMATION
Total Students in Program: 294. **% Full-time** 4. **% Female:** 89.

RESEARCH FACILITIES
Research Facilities: The A.J. Palumbo Hall of Science and Technology.

EXPENSES/FINANCIAL AID
Annual Tuition: In-state $13,468. **Fees:** $408. **Books and Supplies:** $700. **Loans Range From:** $115-$8,500. **% Receiving Financial Aid:** 41. **% Receiving Loans:** 100. **Average student debt, upon graduation:** $5,100.

ADMISSIONS INFORMATION
Application Fee: $35. **Regular Notification:** Rolling. **Transfer Students Accepted?** Yes. **Number of Applications Received:** 91. **% of Applicants Accepted:** 95. **% Accepted Who Enrolled:** 86. **Average GPA:** 2.85.
Required Admission Factors: Essays/personal statement, interview, letters of recommendation, transcript.
Other Admission Factors: Minimum 3.0 GPA required.
Program-Specific Admission Factors: Leadership dimension checklist required for educational leadership program applicants. Portfolio required of art education certificate and master's program applicants.

EMPLOYMENT INFORMATION
Placement Office Available? Yes. **% Employed Within 6 Months:** 71. **% of master's professional grads employed in their field upon graduation:** 71.

CARNEGIE MELLON UNIVERSITY
College of Fine Arts

Address: 5000 Forbes Avenue, Pittsburgh, PA 15213

INSTITUTIONAL INFORMATION
Public/Private: Private (nonprofit). **Students in Parent Institution:** 8,436.

STUDENT INFORMATION
Total Students in Program: 3,174. **% Full-time** 75. **% Female:** 30.

RESEARCH FACILITIES
Research Facilities: Software Engineering Institute, Carnegie Mellon Research Institute, NASA robotics consortium.

EXPENSES/FINANCIAL AID
Annual Tuition: In-state $24,760. **Fees:** $202.

ADMISSIONS INFORMATION
Regular Notification: Rolling. **Transfer Students Accepted?** Yes.
Required Admission Factors: Transcript.
Other Admission Factors: Requirements vary by department.
Program-Specific Admission Factors:

EMPLOYMENT INFORMATION
Placement Office Available? Yes.

CARNEGIE MELLON UNIVERSITY
College of Humanities & Social Sciences

Address: 5000 Forbes Avenue, Pittsburgh, PA 15213
Admissions E-mail: hssdean@andrew.cmu.edu · **Web Address:** www.hss.cmu.edu

INSTITUTIONAL INFORMATION
Public/Private: Private (nonprofit). **Student/Faculty Ratio:** 2:1. **Students in Parent Institution:** 8,436.

STUDENT INFORMATION
Total Students in Program: 3,174. **% Full-time** 75. **% Female:** 30.

RESEARCH FACILITIES
Research Facilities: Software Engineering Institute, Carnegie Mellon Research Institute, NASA robotics consortium.

EXPENSES/FINANCIAL AID
Annual Tuition: $24,760. **Fees:** $202. **% Receiving Financial Aid:** 100. **Average amount of individual fellowships per year:** $10,000. **Average Salary Stipend:** $10,000.

ADMISSIONS INFORMATION
Transfer Students Accepted? Yes. **Transfer Policy:** Maximum 1 year of coursework may be transferred into the doctoral English program. **Average GPA:** 3.5. **Average GRE Verbal:** 613. **Average GRE Quantitative:** 653. **Average GRE Analytical:** 652.
Required Admission Factors: Essays/personal statement, GRE, letters of recommendation, transcript.
Other Admission Factors: Minimum GRE score of 500 and minimum 3.0 GPA required; some departments have higher requirements.

EMPLOYMENT INFORMATION
Placement Office Available? Yes. **% Employed Within 6 Months:** 80. **% of master's/doctoral grads employed in their field upon graduation:** 75/95.

CARNEGIE MELLON UNIVERSITY
Mellon College of Science

Address: 5000 Forbes Avenue, Pittsburgh, PA 15213

INSTITUTIONAL INFORMATION
Public/Private: Private (nonprofit). **Students in Parent Institution:** 8,436.

STUDENT INFORMATION
Total Students in Program: 3,174. **% Full-time** 75. **% Female:** 30.

RESEARCH FACILITIES
Research Facilities: Software Engineering Institute, Carnegie Mellon Research Institute, NASA robotics consortium.

EXPENSES/FINANCIAL AID
Annual Tuition: $24,760. **Fees:** $202.

ADMISSIONS INFORMATION
Transfer Students Accepted? Yes.
Required Admission Factors: GRE, letters of recommendation, transcript.
Program-Specific Admission Factors: Minimum 3.0 GPA required of chemistry program applicants. Minimum GRE score in the 75th percentile and minimum 3.0 GPA required of biological sciences program applicants.

EMPLOYMENT INFORMATION
Placement Office Available? Yes.

CARNEGIE MELLON UNIVERSITY
School of Design

Address: 5000 Forbes Avenue, School of Design, Pittsburgh, PA 15213
Admissions Phone: 412-268-6843 · **Admissions Fax:** 412-268-3088
Admissions E-mail: grad-des@andrew.cmu.edu
Web Address: www.cmu.edu/cfa/design

INSTITUTIONAL INFORMATION
Public/Private: Private (nonprofit).

ADMISSIONS INFORMATION
Application Fee: $60. **Regular Application Deadline:** 2/1. **Regular Notification:** MArch. **Transfer Students Accepted?** No.
Required Admission Factors: Essays/personal statement, GRE, letters of recommendation, transcript.
Recommended Admission Factors: Interview.
Program-Specific Admission Factors: Portfolio recommendation for all; required for designers.

CARNEGIE MELLON UNIVERSITY
School of Drama

Address: Purnell Ceneter for the Arts, Pittsburgh, PA 15213
Admissions Phone: 412-268-7219 · **Admissions Fax:** 412-621-0281
Admissions E-mail: rblock@andrew.cmu.edu · **Web Address:** www.cmu.edu/cfa/drama

INSTITUTIONAL INFORMATION
Public/Private: Private (nonprofit). **Total Faculty:** 17. **% Faculty Female:** 35. **Student/Faculty Ratio:** 3:1.

PROGRAMS
First Professional degree offered in: Acting, playwriting and screenwriting, technical theater/theater design and technology, visual and performing arts.

EXPENSES/FINANCIAL AID
Annual Tuition: $29,000. **Room & Board:** $9,500. **Fees:** $150. **Books and Supplies:** $900. **% Receiving Financial Aid:** 100. **% Receiving Scholarships/Grants:** 100. **Types of Aid Available:** Institutional work-study, scholarships. **Assistantship Compensation Includes:** Partial tuition remission.

ADMISSIONS INFORMATION
Application Fee: $90. **Priority Application Deadline:** 12/1. **Regular Application Deadline:** 1/1. **Regular Notification:** 3/1. **Transfer Students Accepted?** Yes. **Transfer Policy:** Graduate transfer students are extremely rare but have been accepted on occasion. **Number of Applications Received:** 110. **% of Applicants Accepted:** 37. **% Accepted Who Enrolled:** 54. **Average GPA:** 3.3.
Required Admission Factors: Interview, letters of recommendation, transcript.
Recommended Admission Factors: GRE.
Program-Specific Admission Factors: Design/production: portfolio; dramatic writing: full-length and one-act play submission; directing: interview—a short list will direct a scene.

EMPLOYMENT INFORMATION
Placement Office Available? Yes. **% Employed Within 6 Months:** 90. **Rate of placement:** 90%.

CARNEGIE MELLON UNIVERSITY
School of Music

Address: 5000 Forbes Avenue, Pittsburgh, PA 15213
Admissions Phone: 412-268-4118 · **Admissions Fax:** 412-268-1431
Admissions E-mail: music-admissions@andrew.cmu.edu
Web Address: www.cmu.edu/cfa/music/

INSTITUTIONAL INFORMATION
Public/Private: Private (nonprofit). **Total Faculty:** 70. **% Faculty Female:** 29. **% Faculty Part-time:** 57. **Student/Faculty Ratio:** 4:1. **Students in Parent Institution:** 8,600.

PROGRAMS
Masters offered in: Conducting; music performance, music theory, and composition; music, piano and organ; violin, viola, guitar, and other stringed instruments; voice and opera.

STUDENT INFORMATION
Total Students in Program: 85. **% Full-time** 94.

EXPENSES/FINANCIAL AID
Annual Tuition: $28,200. **Room & Board:** $800. **Fees:** $386. **Books and Supplies:** $300. **% Receiving Financial Aid:** 95. **% Receiving Scholarships/Grants:** 10. **% Receiving Assistantships:** 75. **Types of Aid Available:** Fellowships, graduate assistantships, scholarships. **Number of Fellowships Granted Each Year:** 55 **Average amount of individual fellowships per year:** $18,200. **Number of Teaching/Research Assistantships Granted Each Year:** 45. **Assistantship Compensation Includes:** Partial tuition remission.

ADMISSIONS INFORMATION
Application Fee: $100. **Priority Application Deadline:** 12/1. **Regular Application Deadline:** 12/1. **Regular Notification:** Rolling. **Transfer Students Accepted?** Yes. **Transfer Policy:** Same as for regular applicants—in addition, submission of official transcript from previous graduate program. **Number of Applications Received:** 268. **% of Applicants Accepted:** 28. **% Accepted Who Enrolled:** 64. **Average GPA:** 3.4.
Required Admission Factors: Letters of recommendation, transcript. Audition or composition portfolio.
Recommended Admission Factors: Interview
Other Admission Factors: minimum GPA of 3.0.

EMPLOYMENT INFORMATION
Placement Office Available? Yes.

CARROLL COLLEGE
Graduate Programs

Address: 100 North East Avenue, Waukesha, WI 53186
Admissions Phone: 262-524-7216, 800-CARROLL

INSTITUTIONAL INFORMATION
Public/Private: Private (nonprofit). **Evening Classes Available?** Yes. **Student/Faculty Ratio:** 7:1. **Students in Parent Institution:** 2,902.

STUDENT INFORMATION
Total Students in Program: 221. **% Full-time** 23. **% Female:** 82.

EXPENSES/FINANCIAL AID
Fees: $235. **Books and Supplies:** $978. **Loans Range From:** $1,000-$29,000. **% Receiving Financial Aid:** 50. **% Receiving Loans:** 100. **Average student debt, upon graduation:** $40,000.

ADMISSIONS INFORMATION
Application Fee: $25. **Regular Notification:** Rolling. **Transfer Students Accepted?** Yes. **Number of Applications Received:** 121. **% of Applicants**

Accepted: 72. **% Accepted Who Enrolled:** 74.
Required Admission Factors: Interview, transcript.
Other Admission Factors: Minimum 2.5 GPA required.

EMPLOYMENT INFORMATION
% Employed Within 6 Months: 100.

CARSON-NEWMAN COLLEGE
Graduate Studies

Address: 1634 Russell Avenue, Jefferson City, TN 37760
Admissions Phone: 865-471-3463

INSTITUTIONAL INFORMATION
Public/Private: Private (nonprofit). **Students in Parent Institution:** 2,230.

STUDENT INFORMATION
Total Students in Program: 236. **% Full-time** 56. **% Female:** 81.

EXPENSES/FINANCIAL AID
Annual Tuition: In-state $3,600. **Books and Supplies:** $500. **Grants Range From:** $200-$4,800. **Loans Range From:** $500-$8,500. **% Receiving Financial Aid:** 50. **% Receiving Scholarships/Grants:** 17. **% Receiving Loans:** 85. **% Receiving Assistantships:** 11.

ADMISSIONS INFORMATION
Application Fee: $50. **Regular Notification:** Rolling. **Transfer Students Accepted?** No.
Required Admission Factors: Interview, transcript.

CARTHAGE COLLEGE
Graduate Program

Address: 2001 Alford Park Drive, Kenosha, WI 53140-1994
Admissions Phone: 262-551-5826 · **Admissions Fax:** 262-551-5704
Admissions E-mail: jschaumberg@carthage.edu · **Web Address:** www.carthage.edu

INSTITUTIONAL INFORMATION
Public/Private: Private (nonprofit). **Evening Classes Available?** Yes. **Student/Faculty Ratio:** 15:1. **Students in Parent Institution:** 2,500.

PROGRAMS
Masters offered in: Curriculum and instruction, education.

STUDENT INFORMATION
Total Students in Program: 132. **% Female:** 89.

EXPENSES/FINANCIAL AID
Books and Supplies: $200. **% Receiving Financial Aid:** 1.

ADMISSIONS INFORMATION
Application Fee: $25. **Regular Application Deadline:** 8/15. **Regular Notification:** Rolling. **Transfer Students Accepted?** Yes. **Transfer Policy:** Full-time enrollment is neither required nor recommended. Our graduate students are employed full-time and are part time students. **Number of Applications Received:** 15. **% of Applicants Accepted:** 100. **% Accepted Who Enrolled:** 100. **Average GPA:** 3.5.
Required Admission Factors: Essays/personal statement, interview, letters of recommendation, MAT, transcript.
Other Admission Factors: 3.0 minimum GPA on a 4.0 scale.

EMPLOYMENT INFORMATION
Placement Office Available? Yes. **% Employed Within 6 Months:** 100. **% of master's grads employed in their field upon graduation:** 100. **Rate of placement:** 100%. **Average starting salary:** $40,000.

CASE WESTERN RESERVE UNIVERSITY
College of Arts & Sciences

Address: 10900 Euclid Avenue, Cleveland, OH 44106

INSTITUTIONAL INFORMATION
Students in Parent Institution: 9,970

STUDENT INFORMATION
Total Students in Program: 6,291. % Full-time 56. % Female: 47.

RESEARCH FACILITIES
Research Facilities: Alzheimers Center, Cancer Research Center, Center for Automation & Intelligent Systems, Center for Managment of Science & Technology, Center for Human Genetics, Center on Aging & Health, Electronics Design Center, Center for Applied Polymer Research.

EXPENSES/FINANCIAL AID
Annual Tuition: In-state $17,800. Room & Board (on/off campus): $6,460/ $10,400. Books and Supplies: $800.

ADMISSIONS INFORMATION
Transfer Students Accepted? No.

EMPLOYMENT INFORMATION
Placement Office Available? Yes.

CASE WESTERN RESERVE UNIVERSITY
Mandel Center for Nonprofit Organizations

Address: 10900 Euclid Avenue, Cleveland, OH 44106
Admissions Phone: 216-368-8565 · **Admissions Fax:** 216-368-6624
Admissions E-mail: mjfio0po@cwru.edu

INSTITUTIONAL INFORMATION
Public/Private: NR. Evening Classes Available? Yes. Total Faculty: 35. Students in Parent Institution: 9,970.

STUDENT INFORMATION
Total Students in Program: 6,291. % Full-time 56. % Female: 47.

RESEARCH FACILITIES
Research Facilities: Alzheimers Center, Cancer Research Center, Center for Automation & Intelligent Systems, Center for Managment of Science & Technology, Center for Human Genetics, Center on Aging & Health, Electronics Design Center, Center for Applied Polymer Research.

EXPENSES/FINANCIAL AID
Annual Tuition: $17,800. Room & Board (on/off campus): $6,460/$10,400. Books and Supplies: $800.

ADMISSIONS INFORMATION
Application Fee: $25. Regular Notification: Rolling. Transfer Students Accepted? Yes. Number of Applications Received: 105.
Required Admission Factors: Essays/personal statement, transcript.
Other Admission Factors: Minimum 3.0 GPA required.

EMPLOYMENT INFORMATION
Placement Office Available? Yes.

CASE WESTERN RESERVE UNIVERSITY
Mandel School of Applied Social Sciences

Address: 10900 Euclid Avenue, Cleveland, OH 44106

INSTITUTIONAL INFORMATION
Students in Parent Institution: 9,970.

STUDENT INFORMATION
Total Students in Program: 6,291. % Full-time 56. % Female: 47.

RESEARCH FACILITIES
Research Facilities: Alzheimers Center, Cancer Research Center, Center for Automation & Intelligent Systems, Center for Managment of Science & Technology, Center for Human Genetics, Center on Aging & Health, Electronics Design Center, Center for Applied Polymer Research,

EXPENSES/FINANCIAL AID
Annual Tuition: In-state $17,800. Room & Board (on/off campus): $6,460/ $10,400. Books and Supplies: $800.

ADMISSIONS INFORMATION
Transfer Students Accepted? No.

EMPLOYMENT INFORMATION
Placement Office Available? Yes.

CASTLETON STATE COLLEGE
Graduate Programs

Address: Seminary Street South Street, Castleton, VT 05735
Admissions Phone: 802-468-1213 · **Admissions Fax:** 802-468-1476
Admissions E-mail: info@castleton.edu · **Web Address:** www.castleton.edu

INSTITUTIONAL INFORMATION
Public/Private: Public. Students in Parent Institution: 1,691.

PROGRAMS
Masters offered in: Education leadership and administration, education, psychology, special education and teaching.

STUDENT INFORMATION
Total Students in Program: 138. % Full-time 30. % Female: 68.

EXPENSES/FINANCIAL AID
Annual Tuition: In-state $4,624. / Out-of-state $10,836. Fees: $880. Books and Supplies: $300.

ADMISSIONS INFORMATION
Application Fee: $30. Transfer Students Accepted? No.
Required Admission Factors: Essays/personal statement, letters of recommendation, transcript.

THE CATHOLIC UNIVERSITY OF AMERICA
Benjamin T. Rome School of Music

Address: The Catholic University of America, Office of Graduate Admissions, Washington, DC 20064
Admissions Phone: 202-319-5057 · **Admissions Fax:** 202-319-6171
Admissions E-mail: cua-admissions@cua.edu
Website: http://admissions.cua.edu/graduate/

INSTITUTIONAL INFORMATION
Public/private: Private (nonprofit). Evening Classes Available? Yes. Total Faculty: 35. % Faculty Female: 40. % Faculty Part-time: 54. Student/ faculty Ratio: 7:1. Students in Parent Institution: 5,981.

PROGRAMS
Masters offered in: Conducting; music history, literature, and theory; music pedagogy; music performance; music theory and composition; music; piano and organ; violin, viola, guitar, and other stringed instruments; voice and opera.
Doctorate offered in: Music history, literature, and theory; music pedagogy;

music performance; music theory and composition; music; piano and organ; violin, viola, guitar, and other stringed instruments; voice and opera.

STUDENT INFORMATION
Total Students in Program: 131. **% Full-time:** 40. **% Female:** 70. **% Minority:** 12. **% International:** 21.

RESEARCH FACILITIES
Research Facilities: Center for Advanced Training in Cell & Molecular Biology, Center for Irish Studies, Center for Pastoral Studies, Center for Ward Method Studies, Institute for Biomolecular Studies, Institute for Christian Oriental Research.

EXPENSES/FINANCIAL AID
Annual Tuition: $22,200. **Room & Board (On/off Campus):** $9,002/$11,357. **Fees:** $940. **Books and Supplies:** $1,300. **Grants Range From:** $298-$22,200. **Loans Range From:** $250-$20,650. **% Receiving Financial Aid:** 53. **% Receiving Scholarships/Grants:** 61. **% Receiving Loans:** 42. **% Receiving Assistantships:** 19. **Types of Aid Available:** Fellowships, graduate assistantships, grants, institutional work-study, loans, scholarships. **Number of Teaching/Research Assistantships Granted Each Year:** 13. **Assistantship Compensation Includes:** Partial tuition remission, salary/stipend.

ADMISSIONS INFORMATION
Application Fee: $55. **Priority Application Deadline:** 2/1. **Regular Notification:** Rolling. **Transfer Students Accepted?** Yes. **Transfer Policy:** Students who wish to transfer into master's programs may transfer 6 credits from another program. Students who wish to transfer into doctoral programs may transfer 24 credits from another program. **Number of Applications Received:** 128. **% of Applicants Accepted:** 60. **% Accepted Who Enrolled:** 52. **Average GPA:** 3.0. **Average GRE Verbal:** 529. **Average GRE Quantitative:** 558. **Average GRE Analytical:** 598. **Average GRE Analytical Writing:** 4.7.
Required Admission Factors: Essays/personal statement, GRE, letters of recommendation, transcript.
Program-Specific Admission Factors: List of all repertoire publicly performed; audition is required for most programs. Please call 202-319-5414 for further information. Additional supporting documents, depending on specific program.

THE CATHOLIC UNIVERSITY OF AMERICA
National Catholic School of Social Service

Address: The Catholic University of America, Office of Graduate Admissions, Washington, DC 20064
Admissions Phone: 202-319-5057 · **Admissions Fax:** 202-319-6171
Admissions E-mail: cua-admissions@cua.edu
Website: http://admissions.cua.edu/graduate/

INSTITUTIONAL INFORMATION
Public/private: Private (nonprofit). **Evening Classes Available?** Yes. **Total Faculty:** 43. **% Faculty Female:** 88. **% Faculty Part-time:** 60. **Student/faculty Ratio:** 10:1. **Students in Parent Institution:** 5,981.

PROGRAMS
Masters offered in: Social work. **Doctorate offered in:** Social work.

STUDENT INFORMATION
Total Students in Program: 245. **% Full-time:** 49. **% Female:** 84. **% Minority:** 13. **% International:** 4.

RESEARCH FACILITIES
Research Facilities: Center for Advanced Training in Cell & Molecular Biology, Center for Irish Studies, Center for Pastoral Studies, Center for Ward Method Studies, Institute for Biomolecular Studies, Institute for Christian Oriental Research.

EXPENSES/FINANCIAL AID
Annual Tuition: $16,000. **Room & Board (On/off Campus):** $9,002/$11,357. **Fees:** $940. **Books and Supplies:** $1,300. **Grants Range From:** $557-$16,000. **Loans Range From:** $117-$18,500. **% Receiving Financial Aid:** 63. **% Receiving Scholarships/Grants:** 44. **% Receiving Loans:** 82. **% Receiving Assistantships:** 11. **% Receiving Other Aid (work-study):** 47. **Types of Aid Available:** Fellowships, graduate assistantships, grants, institutional work-study, loans, scholarships. **Number of Teaching/Research Assistantships Granted Each Year:** 15. **Assistantship Compensation Includes:** Partial tuition remission, salary/stipend.

ADMISSIONS INFORMATION
Application Fee: $55. **Priority Application Deadline:** 2/1. **Regular Notification:** Rolling. **Transfer Students Accepted?** Yes. **Transfer Policy:** Students who wish to transfer into master's programs may transfer 6 credits from another program. Students who wish to transfer into doctoral programs may transfer 24 credits from another program. **Number of Applications Received:** 222. **% of Applicants Accepted:** 80. **% Accepted Who Enrolled:** 66. **Average GPA:** 3. **Average GRE Verbal:** 498. **Average GRE Quantitative:** 547. **Average GRE Analytical:** 629. **Average GRE Analytical Writing:** 4.5.
Required Admission Factors: Essays/personal statement, GRE, letters of recommendation, transcript.
Other Admission Factors: Millers Analogies Test results can be submitted in place of GRE test results. GRE test results are required for scholarship consideration.

THE CATHOLIC UNIVERSITY OF AMERICA
School of Arts & Sciences

Address: The Catholic University of America, Office of Graduate Admissions, Washington, DC 20064
Admissions Phone: 202-319-5057 · **Admissions Fax:** 202-319-6171
Admissions E-mail: cua-admissions@cua.edu
Website: http://admissions.cua.edu/graduate/

INSTITUTIONAL INFORMATION
Public/private: Private (nonprofit). **Evening Classes Available?** Yes. **Total Faculty:** 256. **% Faculty Female:** 43. **% Faculty Part-time:** 41. **Student/faculty Ratio:** 9:1. **Students in Parent Institution:** 5,981.

PROGRAMS
Masters offered in: Acting; American government and politics (United States); American history (United States); anthropology; area studies; art teacher education; biology teacher education; cell, cellular biology, and histology; chemistry teacher education; classics and classical languages, literatures, and linguistics; comparative literature; counselor education/school counseling and guidance services; curriculum and instruction; drama and dance teacher education; drama, and dramatics, theater arts; economics; education leadership and administration; education; elementary education and teaching; English language and literature; English/language arts teacher education; European history; experimental psychology; fine/studio arts; foreign language teacher education; French language and literature; French language teacher education; Hebrew language and literature; history teacher education; history; international economics; international relations and affairs; Italian language and literature; Latin language and literature; medieval and Renaissance studies; Middle/Near Eastern and Semitic languages, literatures, and linguistics; multi/interdisciplinary studies; physics; playwriting and screenwriting; political science and government; psychology; romance languages, literatures, and linguistics; sociology; Spanish language and literature; Spanish language teacher education; special education; speech and rhetorical studies; teaching English as a second or foreign language/ESL language instructor; theater literature, history and criticism.
Doctorate offered in: Ancient/classical Greek language and literature; anthropology; cell, cellular biology, and histology; clinical psychology; comparative literature; economics; education leadership and administration; education; educational psychology.

STUDENT INFORMATION

Total Students in Program: 599. **% Full-time:** 28. **% Female:** 51. **% Minority:** 11. **% International:** 11.

RESEARCH FACILITIES

Research Facilities: Center for Advanced Training in Cell & Molecular Biology, Center for Irish Studies, Center for Pastoral Studies, Center for Ward Method Studies, Institute for Biomolecular Studies, Institute for Christian Oriental Research.

EXPENSES/FINANCIAL AID

Annual Tuition: $22,200. **Room & Board (On/off Campus):** $9,002/$11,357. **Fees:** $940. **Books and Supplies:** $1,300. **Grants Range From:** $245-$22,200. **Loans Range From:** $385-$20,650. **% Receiving Financial Aid:** 60. **% Receiving Scholarships/Grants:** 53. **% Receiving Loans:** 56. **% Receiving Assistantships:** 28. **% Receiving Other Aid (work-study):** 4. **Types of Aid Available:** Fellowships, graduate assistantships, grants, institutional work-study, loans, scholarships. **Number of Teaching/Research Assistantships Granted Each Year:** 87. **Assistantship Compensation Includes:** Partial tuition remission, salary/stipend.

ADMISSIONS INFORMATION

Application Fee: $55. **Priority Application Deadline:** 2/1. **Regular Notification:** Rolling. **Transfer Students Accepted?** Yes. **Transfer Policy:** Students who wish to transfer into master's programs may transfer 6 credits from another program. Students who wish to transfer into doctoral programs may transfer 24 credits from another program. **Number of Applications Received:** 666. **% of Applicants Accepted:** 55. **% Accepted Who Enrolled:** 43. **Average GPA:** 3.0. **Average GRE Verbal:** 580. **Average GRE Quantitative:** 614. **Average GRE Analytical:** 621. **Average GRE Analytical Writing:** 5.
Required Admission Factors: Essays/personal statement, GRE, letters of recommendation, transcript.
Other Admission Factors: Miller Analogies Test (MAT) results are accepted for education applicants.
Program-Specific Admission Factors: Students are required to submit a writing sample if they are applying to any of the following departments/programs: Comparative literature, English language and literature, Greek and Latin, Irish studies, medieval and Byzantine studies, rhetoric.

THE CATHOLIC UNIVERSITY OF AMERICA
School of Library & Information Science

Address: The Catholic University of America, Office of Graduate Admissions, Washington, DC 20064
Admissions Phone: 202-319-5057 · **Admissions Fax:** 202-319-6171
Admissions E-mail: cua-admissions@cua.edu
Website: http://admissions.cua.edu/graduate

INSTITUTIONAL INFORMATION

Public/private: Private (nonprofit). **Evening Classes Available?** Yes. **Total Faculty:** 23. **% Faculty Female:** 83. **% Faculty Part-time:** 70. **Student/faculty Ratio:** 8:1. **Students in Parent Institution:** 5,981.

PROGRAMS

Masters offered in: Library science/librarianship.

STUDENT INFORMATION

Total Students in Program: 251. **% Full-time:** 15. **% Female:** 84. **% Minority:** 10.

RESEARCH FACILITIES

Research Facilities: Center for Advanced Training in Cell & Molecular Biology, Center for Irish Studies, Center for Pastoral Studies, Center for Ward Method Studies, Institute for Biomolecular Studies, Institute for Christian Oriental Research.

EXPENSES/FINANCIAL AID

Annual Tuition: $22,200. **Room & Board (On/off Campus):** $9,002/$11,357. **Fees:** $940. **Books and Supplies:** $1,300. **Grants Range From:** $465-$11,100. **Loans Range From:** $750-$20,650. **% Receiving Financial Aid:** 58. **% Receiving Scholarships/Grants:** 60. **% Receiving Loans:** 59. **Types of Aid Available:** Fellowships, graduate assistantships, grants, institutional work-study, loans, scholarships. **Assistantship Compensation Includes:** Partial tuition remission, salary/stipend.

ADMISSIONS INFORMATION

Application Fee: $55. **Priority Application Deadline:** 2/1. **Regular Notification:** Rolling. **Transfer Students Accepted?** Yes. **Transfer Policy:** Students who wish to transfer into master's programs may transfer 6 credits from another program. **Number of Applications Received:** 191. **% of Applicants Accepted:** 77. **% Accepted Who Enrolled:** 70. **Average GPA:** 3.0.
Required Admission Factors: Essays/personal statement, GRE, letters of recommendation, transcript.
Other Admission Factors: The requirement for an official GRE score report is waived if a student achieved an undergraduate GPA of 3.0 or higher.

THE CATHOLIC UNIVERSITY OF AMERICA
School of Philosophy

Address: The Catholic University of America, Office of Graduate Admissions, Washington, DC 20064
Admissions Phone: 202-319-5057 · **Admissions Fax:** 202-319-6171
Admissions E-mail: cua-admissions@cua.edu
Website: http://admissions.cua.edu/graduate/

INSTITUTIONAL INFORMATION

Public/private: Private (nonprofit). **Evening Classes Available?** Yes. **Total Faculty:** 34. **% Faculty Female:** 26. **% Faculty Part-time:** 50. **Student/faculty Ratio:** 14:1. **Students in Parent Institution:** 5,981.

PROGRAMS

Masters offered in: Philosophy. **Doctorate offered in:** Philosophy.

STUDENT INFORMATION

Total Students in Program: 131. **% Full-time:** 40. **% Female:** 17. **% Minority:** 3. **% International:** 18.

RESEARCH FACILITIES

Research Facilities: Center for Advanced Training in Cell & Molecular Biology, Center for Irish Studies, Center for Pastoral Studies, Center for Ward Method Studies, Institute for Biomolecular Studies, Institute for Christian Oriental Research.

EXPENSES/FINANCIAL AID

Annual Tuition: $22,200. **Room & Board (On/off Campus):** $9,002/$11,357. **Fees:** $940. **Books and Supplies:** $1,300. **Grants Range From:** $425-$22,200. **Loans Range From:** $360-$18,500. **% Receiving Financial Aid:** 55. **% Receiving Scholarships/Grants:** 71. **% Receiving Loans:** 35. **% Receiving Assistantships:** 11. **Types of Aid Available:** Fellowships, graduate assistantships, grants, institutional work-study, loans, scholarships. **Number of Teaching/Research Assistantships Granted Each Year:** 7. **Assistantship Compensation Includes:** Partial tuition remission, salary/stipend.

ADMISSIONS INFORMATION

Application Fee: $55. **Priority Application Deadline:** 2/1. **Regular Notification:** Rolling. **Transfer Students Accepted?** Yes. **Transfer Policy:** Students who wish to transfer into master's programs may transfer 6 credits from another program. Students who wish to transfer into doctoral programs may transfer 24 credits from another program. **Number of Applications Received:** 106. **% of Applicants Accepted:** 66. **% Accepted Who Enrolled:** 46. **Average GPA:** 3. **Average GRE Verbal:** 659. **Average GRE Quantitative:** 691. **Average GRE Analytical:** 697. **Average GRE Analytical Writing:** 5.3.

Required Admission Factors: Essays/personal statement, GRE, interview, letters of recommendation, transcript.
Other Admission Factors: Undergraduate GPA of 3.0 and prior course work in symbolic logic.

CENTER FOR HUMANISTIC STUDIES
Graduate School

Address: 26811 Orchard Lake Road, Farmington Hills, MI 48334-4512
Admissions Phone: 248-476-1122, ext. 117
Admissions Fax: 248-476-1125 · **Admissions E-mail:** shawn@humanpsych.edu
Web Address: www.humanpsych.edu

INSTITUTIONAL INFORMATION
Public/Private: Private (nonprofit). **Students in Parent Institution:** 87.

STUDENT INFORMATION
Total Students in Program: 87. **% Full-time** 97. **% Female:** 71.

EXPENSES/FINANCIAL AID
Annual Tuition: $14,070. **Fees:** $175. **Books and Supplies:** $1,718. **Grants Range From:** $100-$2,750. **Loans Range From:** $100-$18,500. **% Receiving Financial Aid:** 71. **% Receiving Scholarships/Grants:** 39. **% Receiving Loans:** 71. **Average student debt, upon graduation:** $18,500.

ADMISSIONS INFORMATION
Application Fee: $75. **Regular Notification:** Rolling. **Transfer Students Accepted?** No. **Number of Applications Received:** 85. **% of Applicants Accepted:** 69. **% Accepted Who Enrolled:** 98. **Average GPA:** 3.07.
Required Admission Factors: Essays/personal statement, interview, letters of recommendation, transcript.
Other Admission Factors: Minimum 3.0 GPA, 1 to 3 years of work experience, and coursework in psychology, education, social work, guidance, and counseling required.

EMPLOYMENT INFORMATION
% Employed Within 6 Months: 100. **% of master's grads employed in their field upon graduation:** 90. **Average starting salary:** $30,000.

CENTRAL BAPTIST THEOLOGICAL SEMINARY
Graduate & Professional Programs

Address: 741 North 31st Street, Kansas City, KS 66102-3964
Admissions Phone: 800-677-2287 · **Admissions Fax:** 913-371-8110
Admissions E-mail: enrollment@cbts.edu · **Web Address:** www.cbts.edu

INSTITUTIONAL INFORMATION
Public/Private: Private (nonprofit). **Evening Classes Available?** Yes. **Total Faculty:** 17. **% Faculty Female:** 35. **% Faculty Part-time:** 47. **Student/Faculty Ratio:** 9:1. **Students in Parent Institution:** 120.

PROGRAMS
Masters offered in: Divinity/ministry (BD, MDiv); religious education.

STUDENT INFORMATION
Total Students in Program: 100. **% Full-time** 70.

RESEARCH FACILITIES
Research Facilities: Kansas Qumran Bibliographic Project (collection of Dead Sea Scrolls materials).

EXPENSES/FINANCIAL AID
Annual Tuition: $5,730. **Room & Board (on/off campus):** $4,500/$6,500. **Books and Supplies:** $500. **Grants Range From:** $250-$11,000. **Loans Range From:** $300-$18,500. **% Receiving Financial Aid:** 100. **Types of Aid Available:** Grants, loans, scholarships.

ADMISSIONS INFORMATION
Application Fee: $25. **Priority Application Deadline:** 5/31. **Regular Application Deadline:** 8/1. **Regular Notification:** Rolling. **Transfer Students Accepted?** Yes. **Transfer Policy:** Regular admission requirements. Transfer credits can only come from accredited schools. Transfer credits evaluated and approved after enrolling in classes and applied to academic record after completing 10 hours at Central. 30 hours of completed credit at Central is required. No more than 60 hours from previous degree program can be transferred. **Number of Applications Received:** 26. **% of Applicants Accepted:** 100. **% Accepted Who Enrolled:** 96.
Required Admission Factors: Essays/personal statement, letters of recommendation, transcript.
Other Admission Factors: Minimum 2.3 undergraduate GPA required.
Program-Specific Admission Factors: Masters programs require an endorsement form from church or denominational body. Copies of ministry license or ordination certificate, if applicable.

CENTRAL CONNECTICUT STATE UNIVERSITY
School of Arts & Sciences

Address: School of Graduate Studies, 1615 Stanley Street, New Britain, CT 06050
Admissions Phone: 860-832-2350 · **Admissions Fax:** 860-832-2362
Admissions E-mail: Abraham@ccsu.edu
Web Address: www.ccsu.edu/grad/admissions.htm

INSTITUTIONAL INFORMATION
Public/Private: Public. **Evening Classes Available?** Yes. **Students in Parent Institution:** 12,282.

STUDENT INFORMATION
Total Students in Program: 2,809. **% Full-time** 11. **% Female:** 67.

RESEARCH FACILITIES
Research Facilities: Center for Social Research, Center for International Education, Reading Clinic, Center for Innovation in Teaching and Technology, Center for Multicultural Research and Education.

EXPENSES/FINANCIAL AID
Annual Tuition: In-state $2,280. / Out-of-state $8,028. **Room & Board:** $3,480. **Grants Range From:** $500-$1,000. **Number of Teaching/Research Assistantships Granted Each Year:** 95.

ADMISSIONS INFORMATION
Application Fee: $50. **Priority Application Deadline:** 5/1. **Regular Application Deadline:** 7/1. **Regular Notification:** 7/1. **Transfer Students Accepted?** Yes. **Number of Applications Received:** 402. **% of Applicants Accepted:** 61. **Average GPA:** 2.7.
Required Admission Factors: Transcript.
Other Admission Factors: Minimum 2.7 GPA required; additional requirements vary by program.

EMPLOYMENT INFORMATION
Placement Office Available? Yes.

CENTRAL CONNECTICUT STATE UNIVERSITY
School of Graduate Studies

Address: School of Graduate Studies
1615 Stanley Street, New Britain, CT 06050
Admissions Phone: 860-832-2358 · **Admissions Fax:** 860-832-2362
Admissions E-mail: lemma@ccsu.edu

INSTITUTIONAL INFORMATION
Public/Private: Public. **Evening Classes Available?** Yes. **Students in Parent Institution:** 12,282.

STUDENT INFORMATION

Total Students in Program: 2,809. **% Full-time** 11. **% Female:** 67.

RESEARCH FACILITIES

Research Facilities: Center for Social Research, Center for International Education, Reading Clinic, Center for Innovation in Teaching and Technology, Center for Multicultural Research and Education.

EXPENSES/FINANCIAL AID

Annual Tuition: In-state $2,280. / Out-of-state $8,028. **Room & Board:** $3,480. **Grants Range From:** $500-$1,000. **Number of Teaching/Research Assistantships Granted Each Year:** 95.

ADMISSIONS INFORMATION

Application Fee: $40. **Regular Notification:** Rolling. **Transfer Students Accepted?** Yes. **Number of Applications Received:** 1,329. **% of Applicants Accepted:** 68. **% Accepted Who Enrolled:** 69. **Average GPA:** 2.7. **Required Admission Factors:** Transcript. **Other Admission Factors:** Minimum 2.70 GPA required; requirements may vary by program.

EMPLOYMENT INFORMATION

Placement Office Available? Yes.

CENTRAL METHODIST COLLEGE
Graduate Program

Address: 411 Central Methodist Square, Fayette, MO 65248
Admissions Phone: 660-248-6393 · **Admissions Fax:** 660-248-2622
Admissions E-mail: ghairsto@cmc.edu

INSTITUTIONAL INFORMATION

Public/Private: Private (nonprofit). **Evening Classes Available?** Yes. **Student/Faculty Ratio:** 12:1. **Students in Parent Institution:** 935

STUDENT INFORMATION

Total Students in Program: 38. **% Full-time** 3. **% Female:** 87.

EXPENSES/FINANCIAL AID

Annual Tuition: $3,330. **Books and Supplies:** $650. **Loans Range From:** $100-$18,500. **% Receiving Financial Aid:** 50. **% Receiving Loans:** 50.

ADMISSIONS INFORMATION

Application Fee: $25. **Transfer Students Accepted?** Yes. **Transfer Policy:** Minimum 2.75 GPA and two reference letters required of transfer applicants. **Number of Applications Received:** 20. **% of Applicants Accepted:** 100. **% Accepted Who Enrolled:** 100. **Required Admission Factors:** Letters of recommendation, transcript. **Other Admission Factors:** Minimum 2.75 GPA required.

EMPLOYMENT INFORMATION

Placement Office Available? Yes. **% of master's grads employed in their field upon graduation:** 100. **Rate of placement:** 97%. **Average starting salary:** $25,000.

CENTRAL MICHIGAN UNIVERSITY
College of Communication & Fine Arts

Address: Foust 100, Mount Pleasant, MI 48859
Admissions Phone: 517-774-GRAD · **Admissions Fax:** 517-774-1857
Admissions E-mail: grad@cmich.edu

INSTITUTIONAL INFORMATION

Public/Private: Public. **Evening Classes Available?** Yes. **Students in Parent Institution:** 24,012

STUDENT INFORMATION

Total Students in Program: 6,146. **% Full-time** 38. **% Female:** 79.

RESEARCH FACILITIES

Research Facilities: English Language Institute, biological station on Beaver Island.

EXPENSES/FINANCIAL AID

Annual Tuition: In-state $2,585. / Out-of-state $5,134. **Fees:** $480. **Average Salary Stipend:** $8,300.

ADMISSIONS INFORMATION

Application Fee: $30. **Transfer Students Accepted?** Yes. **Transfer Policy:** Minimum 15 credit hours may be transferred with a minimum 3.0 GPA. **Required Admission Factors:** Essays/personal statement, transcript. **Other Admission Factors:** Minimum 2.5 GPA required.

EMPLOYMENT INFORMATION

Placement Office Available? Yes.

CENTRAL MICHIGAN UNIVERSITY
College of Extended Learning

Address: Foust 100, Mount Pleasant, MI 48859
Admissions Phone: 517-774-GRAD · **Admissions Fax:** 517-774-1857
Admissions E-mail: grad@cmich.edu

INSTITUTIONAL INFORMATION

Public/Private: Public. **Evening Classes Available?** Yes. **Students in Parent Institution:** 24,012.

STUDENT INFORMATION

Total Students in Program: 6,146. **% Full-time** 38. **% Female:** 79.

RESEARCH FACILITIES

Research Facilities: English Language Institute, biological station on Beaver Island.

EXPENSES/FINANCIAL AID

Annual Tuition: In-state $2,585. / Out-of-state $5,134. **Fees:** $480. **% Receiving Financial Aid:** 66. **Average student debt, upon graduation:** $15,000.

ADMISSIONS INFORMATION

Application Fee: $50. **Regular Notification:** Rolling. **Transfer Students Accepted?** Yes. **Required Admission Factors:** Transcript. **Other Admission Factors:** Minimum 2.5 GPA required.

EMPLOYMENT INFORMATION

Placement Office Available? Yes.

CENTRAL MICHIGAN UNIVERSITY
College of Graduate Studies

Address: Foust 100, Mount Pleasant, MI 48859
Admissions Phone: 989-774-GRAD · **Admissions Fax:** 989-774-1857
Admissions E-mail: grad@cmich.edu · **Web Address:** www.grad.cmich.edu

INSTITUTIONAL INFORMATION

Public/Private: Public. **Evening Classes Available?** Yes. **Students in Parent Institution:** 24,012

STUDENT INFORMATION

Total Students in Program: 1,852. **% Full-time** 43. **% Female:** 6. **% International:** 100.

RESEARCH FACILITIES

Research Facilities: English Language Institute, Biological Station on Beaver Island, Central Michigan University Research Center.

EXPENSES/FINANCIAL AID

Annual Tuition: In-state $3,702. / Out-of-state $7,354. **Room & Board:** $500. **Fees:** $575. **Books and Supplies:** $2,000. **Grants Range From:** $500-$8,500. **Loans Range From:** $500-$20,000. **Types of Aid Available:** Fellowships, graduate assistantships, grants, institutional work-study, loans, scholarships. **Average Salary Stipend:** $8,550.

ADMISSIONS INFORMATION

Application Fee: $35. **Regular Application Deadline:** 8/1. **Regular Notification:** Rolling. **Transfer Students Accepted?** Yes. **Transfer Policy:** 3.0/4.0 graduate GPA, good academic standing at prior institution. **Number of Applications Received:** 1,642. **% of Applicants Accepted:** 60. **Average GPA:** 3.0.
Required Admission Factors: Essays/personal statement, transcript.
Other Admission Factors: Minimum 2.7 GPA required.
Program-Specific Admission Factors: MAT required of counseling program applicants. GMAT required of MBA program applicants.

EMPLOYMENT INFORMATION

Placement Office Available? Yes.

CENTRAL MICHIGAN UNIVERSITY
College of Humanities & Social & Behavioral Sciences

Address: Foust 100, Mount Pleasant, MI 48859
Admissions Phone: 517-774-GRAD · **Admissions Fax:** 517-774-1857
Admissions E-mail: grad@cmich.edu ·

INSTITUTIONAL INFORMATION

Public/Private: Public. **Evening Classes Available?** Yes. **Students in Parent Institution:** 24,012.

STUDENT INFORMATION

Total Students in Program: 6,146. **% Full-time** 38. **% Female:** 79.

RESEARCH FACILITIES

Research Facilities: English Language Institute, biological station on Beaver Island.

EXPENSES/FINANCIAL AID

Annual Tuition: In-state $2,585. / Out-of-state $5,134. **Fees:** $480. **Average Salary Stipend:** $8,300.

ADMISSIONS INFORMATION

Application Fee: $30. **Transfer Students Accepted?** Yes. **Transfer Policy:** Maximum 15 credit hours may be transferred with a minimum 3.0 GPA.
Required Admission Factors: Essays/personal statement, transcript.
Other Admission Factors: Minimum 2.5 GPA required.

EMPLOYMENT INFORMATION

Placement Office Available? Yes.

CENTRAL MISSOURI STATE UNIVERSITY
Department of Library Science & Information Services

Address: Warrensburg, MO 64093
Admissions Phone: 660-543-4621 or 800-SAY-CMSU
Admissions Fax: 660-543-8333 · **Admissions E-mail:** perrin@cmsu1.cmsu.edu

INSTITUTIONAL INFORMATION

Public/Private: Public. **Evening Classes Available?** Yes. **Students in Parent Institution:** 10,936.

STUDENT INFORMATION

Total Students in Program: 1,786. **% Full-time** 16. **% Female:** 64.

RESEARCH FACILITIES

Research Facilities: Centers for Business & Economic Research, Family Studies, Religious Studies, Technology & Small Business Development, English Language Center, Regional Professional Development Center, Radar Certification Center, Gerontology Institute.

EXPENSES/FINANCIAL AID

Annual Tuition: In-state $4,152. / Out-of-state $8,304. **Fees:** $48. **Books and Supplies:** $450. **Grants Range From:** $200-$7,200. **Loans Range From:** $1,000-$15,000. **% Receiving Scholarships/Grants:** 17. **% Receiving Loans:** 85. **% Receiving Assistantships:** 36. **% Receiving Other Aid:** 22. **Number of Teaching/Research Assistantships Granted Each Year:** 9. **Average Salary Stipend:** $3,500.

ADMISSIONS INFORMATION

Application Fee: $25. **Regular Notification:** Rolling. **Transfer Students Accepted?** Yes. **Transfer Policy:** Minimum 3.0 transfer GPA required of transfer applicants for regular admission.
Required Admission Factors: Transcript.
Other Admission Factors: Minimum 2.75 GPA required.
Program-Specific Admission Factors: Minimum 2.75 GPA required of MS degree program applicants. Minimum 3.25 GPA required of education specialist program applicants. 2 years of teaching experience required of applicants to school library media specialist K-12 certification program.

EMPLOYMENT INFORMATION

Placement Office Available? Yes. **% of master's grads employed in their field upon graduation:** 91. **Rate of placement:** 96%.

CENTRAL MISSOURI STATE UNIVERSITY
The Graduate School

Address: Warrensburg, MO 64093
Admissions Phone: 660-543-4621 or 800-729-2678 · **Admissions Fax:** 660-543-8333
Admissions E-mail: perrin@cmsu1.cmsu.edu

INSTITUTIONAL INFORMATION

Public/Private: Public. **Evening Classes Available?** Yes. **Students in Parent Institution:** 10,936.

STUDENT INFORMATION

Total Students in Program: 1,786. **% Full-time** 16. **% Female:** 64.

RESEARCH FACILITIES

Research Facilities: Centers for Business & Economic Research, Family Studies, Religious Studies, Technology & Small Business Development, English Language Center, Regional Professional Development Center, Radar Certification Center, Gerontology Institute.

EXPENSES/FINANCIAL AID

Annual Tuition: In-state $4,152. / Out-of-state $8,304. **Fees:** $48. **Books and Supplies:** $450. **Grants Range From:** $200-$7,200. **Loans Range From:** $1,000-$15,000. **% Receiving Scholarships/Grants:** 17. **% Receiving Loans:** 85. **% Receiving Assistantships:** 36. **% Receiving Other Aid:** 22. **Number of Teaching/Research Assistantships Granted Each Year:** 44. **Average Salary Stipend:** $3,500.

ADMISSIONS INFORMATION

Application Fee: $25. **Regular Notification:** Rolling. **Transfer Students Accepted?** Yes. **Transfer Policy:** Minimum 3.0 transfer GPA required of transfer applicants for regular admission.

Required Admission Factors: Transcript.
Program-Specific Admission Factors: Minimum 2.75 GPA required of English and history program applicants. Minimum 2.75 GPA with 3.0 GPA in upper level math classes required of math program applicants.

EMPLOYMENT INFORMATION
Placement Office Available? Yes. **% of master's grads employed in their field upon graduation:** 83. **Rate of placement:** 96%. **Average starting salary:** $29,500.

CENTRAL WASHINGTON UNIVERSITY
College of Arts & Humanities

Address: 400 East University Way, Ellensburg, WA 98926-7510
Admissions Phone: 509-963-3103 · **Admissions Fax:** 509-963-1799
Admissions E-mail: masters@cwu.edu · **Web Address:** www.cwu.edu

INSTITUTIONAL INFORMATION
Public/Private: Public. **Total Faculty:** 84. **% Faculty Female:** 35. **Students in Parent Institution:** 8,018

PROGRAMS
Masters offered in: Acting, ceramic arts and ceramics, conducting, drawing, English language and literature, fine/studio arts, history, metal and jewelry arts, music pedagogy, music performance, music theory and composition, painting, sculpture.

STUDENT INFORMATION
Total Students in Program: 74. **% Full-time** 80. **% Female:** 57. **% Minority:** 11. **% International:** 1.

EXPENSES/FINANCIAL AID
Annual Tuition: In-state $5,493. / Out-of-state $11,430. **Room & Board:** $5,442. **Fees:** $369. **Books and Supplies:** $720. **% Receiving Assistantships:** 24. **Types of Aid Available:** Graduate assistantships, loans. **Average Salary Stipend:** $7,120.

ADMISSIONS INFORMATION
Application Fee: $35. **Priority Application Deadline:** 4/1. **Regular Application Deadline:** 6/1. **Regular Notification:** Rolling. **Transfer Students Accepted?** No. **Number of Applications Received:** 51. **% of Applicants Accepted:** 47. **% Accepted Who Enrolled:** 83.
Required Admission Factors: Essays/personal statement, letters of recommendation, transcript.
Other Admission Factors: Minimum 3.0 GPA required.

CENTRAL WASHINGTON UNIVERSITY
College of the Sciences

Address: 400 East University Way, Ellensburg, WA 98926-7510
Admissions Phone: 509-963-3103 · **Admissions Fax:** 509-963-1799
Admissions E-mail: masters@cwu.edu · **Web Address:** www.cwu.edu

INSTITUTIONAL INFORMATION
Public/Private: Public. **Students in Parent Institution:** 8,451.

STUDENT INFORMATION
Total Students in Program: 424. **% Full-time** 51. **% Female:** 62.

EXPENSES/FINANCIAL AID
Annual Tuition: In-state $4,848. / Out-of-state $14,772. **Fees:** $324. **Books and Supplies:** $690. **% Receiving Assistantships:** 24. **Average Salary Stipend:** $7,120.

ADMISSIONS INFORMATION
Application Fee: $35. **Priority Application Deadline:** 2/1. **Regular Application Deadline:** 6/1. **Regular Notification:** Rolling. **Transfer Students Accepted?** No. **Number of Applications Received:** 102. **% of Applicants Accepted:** 74. **% Accepted Who Enrolled:** 68.
Required Admission Factors: Essays/personal statement, GRE, letters of recommendation, transcript.
Other Admission Factors: Minimum GPA 3.00
Program-Specific Admission Factors: GRE and GRE subject exam required of chemistry program applicants.

EMPLOYMENT INFORMATION
Placement Office Available? Yes.

CHAMINADE UNIVERSITY OF HONOLULU
Graduate Programs

Address: 3140 Waialae Avenue, Honolulu, HI 96816-1587

INSTITUTIONAL INFORMATION
Public/Private: Private (nonprofit). **Evening Classes Available?** Yes. **Student/Faculty Ratio:** 16:1. **Students in Parent Institution:** 2,740.

STUDENT INFORMATION
Total Students in Program: 711. **% Full-time** 58. **% Female:** 63.

EXPENSES/FINANCIAL AID
Annual Tuition: In-state $7,440. **Room & Board:** $500. **Fees:** $50. **Books and Supplies:** $700.

ADMISSIONS INFORMATION
Application Fee: $50. **Regular Notification:** Rolling. **Transfer Students Accepted?** Yes. **Transfer Policy:** Maximum 12 credit hours may be transferred with a minimum grade of B with approval of program. **Number of Applications Received:** 50. **% of Applicants Accepted:** 70. **% Accepted Who Enrolled:** 91. **Average GPA:** 3.21.
Required Admission Factors: Interview, letters of recommendation, transcript.
Other Admission Factors: Minimum 3.0 GPA required.

EMPLOYMENT INFORMATION
Placement Office Available? Yes.

CHAPMAN UNIVERSITY
Dodge College of Film & Media Arts

Address: One University Drive, Orange, CA 92866
Admissions Phone: 714-997-6765 · **Admissions Fax:** 714-997-6700
Admissions E-mail: ftvinfo@chapman.edu · **Web Address:** www.ftv.chapman.edu

INSTITUTIONAL INFORMATION
Public/Private: Private (nonprofit). **Total Faculty:** 50. **% Faculty Female:** 20. **% Faculty Part-time:** 46. **Students in Parent Institution:** 5,557.

PROGRAMS
Masters offered in: Cinematography and film/video production, film/cinema studies, playwriting and screenwriting

STUDENT INFORMATION
Total Students in Program: 1,400. **% Full-time** 28.

RESEARCH FACILITIES
Research Facilities: Center for Economic Research, Food Science Lab.

EXPENSES/FINANCIAL AID
% Receiving Financial Aid: 44.

ADMISSIONS INFORMATION

Application Fee: $40. **Priority Application Deadline:** 2/1. **Regular Application Deadline:** 5/1. **Regular Notification:** Rolling. **Transfer Students Accepted?** Yes. **Number of Applications Received:** 61. **% of Applicants Accepted:** 75.

Required Admission Factors: Essays/personal statement, letters of recommendation, transcript.

Other Admission Factors: Minimum cumulative GPA of 3.0 or better based on the last 60 units of graded undergraduate work.

Program-Specific Admission Factors: Statement of purpose, portfolio lsit and writing samples required of all students applying to the graduate school of film and television.

CHAPMAN UNIVERSITY
School of Communication Arts

Address: One University Drive, Orange, CA 92866
Admissions Phone: 714-997-6786 · **Admissions Fax:** 714-997-6713
Admissions E-mail: shoover@nexus.chapman.edu

INSTITUTIONAL INFORMATION

Public/Private: Private (nonprofit). **Evening Classes Available?** Yes. **Students in Parent Institution:** 3,896.

STUDENT INFORMATION

Total Students in Program: 1,115. **% Full-time** 35. **% Female:** 65.

RESEARCH FACILITIES

Research Facilities: Center for Economic Research, Food Science Lab.

EXPENSES/FINANCIAL AID

% Receiving Financial Aid: 44.

ADMISSIONS INFORMATION

Application Fee: $40. **Regular Notification:** Rolling. **Transfer Students Accepted?** Yes. **Transfer Policy:** Application, transcripts, statement of intent, and references required of transfer applicants. **Number of Applications Received:** 92. **% of Applicants Accepted:** 38. **% Accepted Who Enrolled:** 60.

Required Admission Factors: Letters of recommendation, transcript.

Other Admission Factors: Minimum 3.0 GPA recommended. If GPA is 2.5-2.99, applicant is required to take GRE or MAT.

Program-Specific Admission Factors: Portfolio required of creative writing applicants.

CHAPMAN UNIVERSITY
University College

Address: One University Drive, Orange, CA 92866

INSTITUTIONAL INFORMATION

Public/Private: Private (nonprofit). **Evening Classes Available?** Yes. **Students in Parent Institution:** 3,896.

STUDENT INFORMATION

Total Students in Program: 1,115. **% Full-time** 35. **% Female:** 65.

RESEARCH FACILITIES

Research Facilities: Center for Economic Research, Food Science Lab.

ADMISSIONS INFORMATION

Application Fee: $40. **Regular Notification:** Rolling. **Transfer Students Accepted?** Yes.

Required Admission Factors: Essays/personal statement, GRE, letters of recommendation, transcript.

Other Admission Factors: Minimum 3.0 GPA required. GRE or MAT required if GPA is below minimum.

CHAPMAN UNIVERSITY
Wilkinson College of Letters & Sciences

Address: One University Drive, Orange, CA 92866
Admissions Phone: 714-997-6711 · **Admissions Fax:** 714-997-6713
Admissions E-mail: gradadmit@chapman.edu · **Web Address:** www.chapman.edu/wcls

INSTITUTIONAL INFORMATION

Public/Private: Private (nonprofit). **Evening Classes Available?** Yes. **Students in Parent Institution:** 3,896.

STUDENT INFORMATION

Total Students in Program: 1,115. **% Full-time** 35. **% Female:** 65.

RESEARCH FACILITIES

Research Facilities: Center for Economic Research, Food Science Lab.

ADMISSIONS INFORMATION

Application Fee: $40. **Regular Notification:** Rolling. **Transfer Students Accepted?** Yes. **Transfer Policy:** Maximum 9 credit hours with a minimum grade of B may be transferred.

Required Admission Factors: Essays/personal statement, letters of recommendation, transcript.

Other Admission Factors: Minimum 2.5 GPA required.

CHARLESTON SOUTHERN UNIVERSITY
Graduate Programs

Address: PO Box 118087, 9200 University Boulevard, Charleston, SC 29423-8087
Admissions Phone: 800-947-7474 · **Admissions Fax:** 843-863-7070
Admissions E-mail: maustin@csuniv.edu · **Web Address:** www.charlestonsouthern.com

INSTITUTIONAL INFORMATION

Public/Private: Private (nonprofit). **Evening Classes Available?** Yes. **Total Faculty:** 33. **% Faculty Female:** 39. **Student/Faculty Ratio:** 15:1. **Students in Parent Institution:** 2,594.

PROGRAMS

Masters offered in: American/U.S. law/legal studies/jurisprudence (LLM, MCJ, JSD/SJD), business administration/management, education, elementary and middle school administration/principalship, secondary school administration/principalship.

STUDENT INFORMATION

Total Students in Program: 169.

EXPENSES/FINANCIAL AID

Annual Tuition: $7,646. **Books and Supplies:** $250. **Grants Range From:** $4,500-$8,500. **Loans Range From:** $4,500-$8,500. **% Receiving Loans:** 90. **% Receiving Assistantships:** 10. **Types of Aid Available:** Graduate assistantships, loans.

ADMISSIONS INFORMATION

Application Fee: $30. **Regular Application Deadline:** 8/5. **Regular Notification:** Rolling. **Transfer Students Accepted?** Yes. **Number of Applications Received:** 235. **% of Applicants Accepted:** 91. **% Accepted Who Enrolled:** 79. **Average GPA:** 3.0.

Required Admission Factors: Essays/personal statement, letters of recommendation, transcript.

Program-Specific Admission Factors: Minimum 2.75 GPA required of education program applicants. MBA applicants with a 2.5 GPA or higher are exempt from the GMAT. For all graduate examinations, CSU uses a formula based on the students GPA for acceptance.

EMPLOYMENT INFORMATION

Placement Office Available? Yes. **% Employed Within 6 Months:** 86. **% of master's grads employed in their field upon graduation:** 86. **Rate of placement:** 65%. **Average starting salary:** $50,000.

CHATHAM COLLEGE
Graduate Programs

Address: Woodland Road, Pittsburgh, PA 15232
Admissions Phone: 800-837-1290 · **Admissions Fax:** 412-365-1609
Admissions E-mail: admissions@chatham.edu · **Web Address:** www.chatham.edu

INSTITUTIONAL INFORMATION

Public/Private: Private (nonprofit). **Evening Classes Available?** Yes. **Total Faculty:** 106. **% Faculty Female:** 75. **% Faculty Part-time:** 53. **Student/Faculty Ratio:** 8:1. **Students in Parent Institution:** 1,249.

PROGRAMS

Masters offered in: Biology teacher education, biology/biological sciences, business administration/management, business/managerial operations, chemistry teacher education, community psychology, counseling psychology, counselor education/school counseling and guidance services, creative writing, early childhood education and teaching, education, elementary education and teaching, English/language arts teacher education, French language teacher education, interior architecture, landscape architecture (BS, BSLA, BLA, MSLA, MLA, PhD), landscaping and groundskeeping, mathematics teacher education, physician assistant, physics teacher education, psychology, secondary education and teaching, social studies teacher education, Spanish language teacher education, special education, technical and business writing. **Doctorate offered in:** Physical therapy/therapist.

STUDENT INFORMATION

Total Students in Program: 584. **% Full-time** 59. **% Female:** 85. **% Minority:** 14. **% International:** 1.

RESEARCH FACILITIES

Research Facilities: Rachel Carson Institute; Pennsylvania Center for Women, Politics, & Public Policy; Pittsburgh Teachers Institute; The Fourth River Journal and Website for writing and art.

EXPENSES/FINANCIAL AID

Annual Tuition: $13,500. **Fees:** $216. **Books and Supplies:** $1,500. **Loans Range From:** $5,300-$18,500. **Types of Aid Available:** Loans.

ADMISSIONS INFORMATION

Application Fee: $45. **Priority Application Deadline:** 1/15. **Regular Application Deadline:** 8/15. **Regular Notification:** Rolling. **Transfer Students Accepted?** Yes. **Transfer Policy:** Transfers accepted in some programs; transfer deadlines are rolling and can vary by program; call for details. **Number of Applications Received:** 623. **% of Applicants Accepted:** 59. **% Accepted Who Enrolled:** 63. **Average GPA:** 3.0
Required Admission Factors: Essays/personal statement, interview, letters of recommendation, transcript.
Other Admission Factors: Minimum 3.0 GPA required for all programs.
Program-Specific Admission Factors: Health care job shadowing, health care volunteer experience, & non-health care community service for physical therapy & physician assistant programs. Writing samples for MFA writing.

EMPLOYMENT INFORMATION

Placement Office Available? Yes. **% Employed Within 6 Months:** 85. **Rate of placement:** 99%. **Average starting salary:** $65,000.

CHESTNUT HILL COLLEGE
School of Graduate Studies

Address: 9601 Germantown Avenue, Philadelphia, PA 19118-2693
Admissions Phone: 215-248-7020 · **Admissions Fax:** 215-248-7161
Admissions E-mail: graddiv@chc.edu · **Web Address:** www.chc.edu

INSTITUTIONAL INFORMATION

Public/Private: Private (nonprofit). **Evening Classes Available?** Yes. **Total Faculty:** 77. **% Faculty Female:** 64. **% Faculty Part-time:** 88. **Student/**

Faculty Ratio: 8:1. **Students in Parent Institution:** 1,555.

PROGRAMS

Masters offered in: Clinical pastoral counseling/patient counseling; clinical psychology; computer/information technology services, administration, and management; counseling psychology; education leadership and administration; educational/instructional media design; elementary education and teaching; human services; pastoral counseling and specialized ministries. **Doctorate offered in:** Clinical psychology.

STUDENT INFORMATION

Total Students in Program: 649. **% Full-time** 14. **% Female:** 82. **% Minority:** 14. **% International:** 1.

EXPENSES/FINANCIAL AID

Annual Tuition: $10,440. **Room & Board:** $9,376. **Fees:** $75. **Books and Supplies:** $900. **Loans Range From:** $1,000-$18,500. **% Receiving Financial Aid:** 23. **% Receiving Loans:** 100. **Types of Aid Available:** loans, **Average student debt, upon graduation:** $27,545.

ADMISSIONS INFORMATION

Application Fee: $35. **Priority Application Deadline:** 7/15. **Regular Application Deadline:** 8/15. **Regular Notification:** Rolling. **Transfer Students Accepted?** Yes. **Transfer Policy:** Generally the same as first-time graduate students. **Number of Applications Received:** 332. **% of Applicants Accepted:** 92. **% Accepted Who Enrolled:** 41.
Required Admission Factors: Essays/personal statement, interview, letters of recommendation, transcript.
Other Admission Factors: Minimum GRE score of 1400, minimum MAT score of 30, and minimum 3.0 GPA required. Writing sample required.
Program-Specific Admission Factors: PsyD applicants must have master's degree in counseling and 300 hours of clinical experience. Holistic Spirituality applicants must have 18 credits in theology or philosophy.

THE CHICAGO SCHOOL OF
PROFESSIONAL PSYCHOLOGY
Graduate Program

Address: 325 North Wells, Chicago, IL 60610
Admissions Phone: 312-329-6666 · **Admissions Fax:** 312-644-3333
Admissions E-mail: admissions@csopp.edu · **Web Address:** www.csopp.edu

INSTITUTIONAL INFORMATION

Public/Private: Private (nonprofit). **Evening Classes Available?** Yes. **Total Faculty:** 44. **% Faculty Female:** 45. **% Faculty Part-time:** 32. **Student/Faculty Ratio:** 16:1. **Students in Parent Institution:** 846.

PROGRAMS

Masters offered in: Clinical psychology, counseling psychology, forensic psychology, industrial and organizational psychology, psychology. **Doctorate offered in:** Clinical psychology, industrial and organizational psychology.

STUDENT INFORMATION

Total Students in Program: 846 **% Female:** 81. **% Minority:** 22. **% International:** 4.

RESEARCH FACILITIES

Research Facilities: Doctoral students will complete 2 practicums at off-site locations, as well as a year-long full-time internship. Master of arts students will complete an internship or practicum.

EXPENSES/FINANCIAL AID

Grants Range From: $1,000-$10,000. **Loans Range From:** $500-$31,000. **% Receiving Financial Aid:** 87. **% Receiving Scholarships/Grants:** 12. **% Receiving Loans:** 98. **% Receiving Assistantships:** 11. **Types of Aid Available:** Fellowships, institutional work-study, loans, scholarships. faculty assistantships. **Average student debt, upon graduation:** $100,000. **Number of Fellowships Granted Each Year:** 1. **Average amount of individual fel-**

lowships per year: $8,500. **Number of Teaching/Research Assistantships Granted Each Year:** 35. **Assistantship Compensation Includes:** Partial tuition remission.

ADMISSIONS INFORMATION

Application Fee: $50. **Priority Application Deadline:** 1/15. **Regular Application Deadline:** 3/1. **Regular Notification:** Rolling. **Transfer Students Accepted?** Yes. **Transfer Policy:** Doctoral: maximum of 21 hours may be transferred. Masters: maximum of 12 hours may be transferred. **Number of Applications Received:** 838. **% of Applicants Accepted:** 80. **Average GPA:** 3.3.
Required Admission Factors: Essays/personal statement, letters of recommendation, transcript.
Recommended Admission Factors: GRE subject exam(s) in psychology.
Other Admission Factors: The GRE is required for our PsyD programs only. All doctoral programs recommend a GPA of 3.2. All masters programs recommend a GPA of a 3.0 on a 4.0 scale. Each program has specific courses required for enrollment.
Program-Specific Admission Factors: Clinical PsyD requires: 18 semester hours of psychology coursework, including 1 course in statistics, abnormal psychology and child/human development or life span. Business PsyD requires 12 semester hours of psychology coursework.

CHICAGO STATE UNIVERSITY
School of Graduate & Professional Studies

Address: Douglas Library, Room 338, 9501E South King Drive, Chicago, IL 60628
Admissions Phone: 773-995-2404 · **Admissions Fax:** 773-995-3671
Admissions E-mail: G-Studies1@csu.edu · **Web Address:** www.csu.edu/xgrad/

INSTITUTIONAL INFORMATION

Public/Private: Public. **Evening Classes Available?** Yes. **Students in Parent Institution:** 6,921.

PROGRAMS

Masters offered in: Bilingual and multilingual education, community health services/liaison/counseling, computer teacher education, counseling psychology, counselor education/school counseling and guidance services, creative writing, criminology, curriculum and instruction, education leadership and administration, education, elementary education and teaching, English language and literature, geography, health and physical education, higher education/higher education administration, history, library science/librarianship, mathematics teacher education, mathematics, occupational therapy/therapist, physical education teaching and coaching, reading teacher education, school librarian/school library media specialist, secondary education and teaching, social sciences, social work, special education, student counseling and personnel services, technology teacher education/industrial arts teacher education.

STUDENT INFORMATION

Total Students in Program: 1,854. **% Full-time** 17. **% Female:** 69.

EXPENSES/FINANCIAL AID

Annual Tuition: In-state $1,872 / Out-of-state $5,616. **Fees:** $314.

ADMISSIONS INFORMATION

Application Fee: $25. **Regular Application Deadline:** 3/15. **Regular Notification:** Rolling. **Transfer Students Accepted?** Yes.
Required Admission Factors: Transcript.
Other Admission Factors: Minimum 3.0 GPA required (2.75 for conditional admission) required.

EMPLOYMENT INFORMATION

Placement Office Available? Yes.

CHICAGO THEOLOGICAL SEMINARY
Graduate & Professional Programs

Address: 5757 South University Avenue, Chicago, IL 60637
Admissions Phone: 773-752-0213 · **Admissions Fax:** 773-752-1903
Admissions E-mail: admissions@ctschicago.edu
Web Address: www.ctschicago.edu

INSTITUTIONAL INFORMATION

Public/Private: Private (nonprofit). **Evening Classes Available?** Yes. **Student/Faculty Ratio:** 15:1. **Students in Parent Institution:** 209.

PROGRAMS

Masters offered in: Divinity/ministry (BD, MDiv); religion/religious studies
Doctorate offered in: Bible/biblical studies; divinity/ministry (BD, MDiv); theology/theological studies.

STUDENT INFORMATION

Total Students in Program: 209. **% Female:** 52. **% Minority:** 35. **% International:** 13.

RESEARCH FACILITIES

Research Facilities: Center for Community Transformation; Center for Jewish, Christian, and Islamic Studies.

EXPENSES/FINANCIAL AID

Annual Tuition: $8,496. **Room & Board (on/off campus):** $5,985/$6,900. **Fees:** $140. **Books and Supplies:** $1,200. **Grants Range From:** $896-$8,960. **Loans Range From:** $100-$18,500. **Types of Aid Available:** Grants, loans, scholarships.

ADMISSIONS INFORMATION

Application Fee: $50. **Priority Application Deadline:** 3/1. **Regular Application Deadline:** 3/1. **Transfer Students Accepted?** Yes. **Transfer Policy:** Same as other admissions procedures. **Number of Applications Received:** 75. **% of Applicants Accepted:** 87. **% Accepted Who Enrolled:** 66.
Required Admission Factors: Essays/personal statement, letters of recommendation, transcript.
Other Admission Factors: Minimum TOEFL (international students only): 550 for paper, 217 for computer
Program-Specific Admission Factors: DMin: project proposal STM: Focus paper. PhD: Sample research paper, GRE scores.

CHRIST THE KING SEMINARY
Graduate & Professional Programs

Address: 711 Knox Road
PO Box 607, East Aurora, NY 14052-0607
Admissions Phone: 716-652-8900 · **Admissions E-mail:** cksacad@cks.edu

INSTITUTIONAL INFORMATION

Public/Private: Private (nonprofit). **Evening Classes Available?** Yes. **Student/Faculty Ratio:** 5:1. **Students in Parent Institution:** 96.

STUDENT INFORMATION

Total Students in Program: 66. **% Full-time** 3. **% Female:** 56.

EXPENSES/FINANCIAL AID

Annual Tuition: In-state $6,825. **Fees:** $285. **Books and Supplies:** $325. **Grants Range From:** $200-$5,775. **Loans Range From:** $1,000-$5,000. **% Receiving Financial Aid:** 52. **% Receiving Scholarships/Grants:** 80. **% Receiving Loans:** 20. **Average student debt, upon graduation:** $8,500.

ADMISSIONS INFORMATION

Application Fee: $75. **Regular Notification:** Rolling. **Transfer Students Accepted?** Yes. **Transfer Policy:** Maximum of 6 credit hours may be trans-

ferred from an ATS-accredited program. **Number of Applications Received:** 26. **% of Applicants Accepted:** 92. **% Accepted Who Enrolled:** 88. **Average GPA:** 3.1.
Required Admission Factors: Essays/personal statement, interview, letters of recommendation, transcript.
Other Admission Factors: Minimum 2.5 GPA required.

CHRISTIAN THEOLOGICAL SEMINARY
Graduate Programs

Address: 1000 West 42nd Street, Indianapolis, IN 46208
Admissions Phone: 800-585-0117 · **Admissions Fax:** 317-923-1961
Admissions E-mail: admissions@cts.edu · **Web Address:** www.cts.edu

INSTITUTIONAL INFORMATION
Public/Private: Private (nonprofit). **Evening Classes Available?** Yes. **Student/Faculty Ratio:** 14:1. **Students in Parent Institution:** 360

STUDENT INFORMATION
Total Students in Program: 360. **% Full-time** 46. **% Female:** 56.

EXPENSES/FINANCIAL AID
Annual Tuition: In-state $4,590. **Fees:** $80. **% Receiving Financial Aid:** 41. **Average student debt, upon graduation:** $20,000.

ADMISSIONS INFORMATION
Application Fee: $30. **Regular Application Deadline:** 8/1. **Regular Notification:** Rolling. **Transfer Students Accepted?** Yes. **Transfer Policy:** Maximum of 1/3 of the total required credit hours may be transferred. **Number of Applications Received:** 107. **% of Applicants Accepted:** 93. **% Accepted Who Enrolled:** 79. **Average GPA:** 3.41.
Required Admission Factors: Essays/personal statement, interview, letters of recommendation, transcript.
Other Admission Factors: Minimum 2.5 GPA required.
Program-Specific Admission Factors: MAT required of counseling program applicants; GRE may be accepted. GRE required of church music program applicants.

CHRISTOPHER NEWPORT UNIVERSITY
College of Liberal Arts and Sciences

Address: 1 University Place, Administration Bldg Room 323,
Newport News, VA 23606-2998
Admissions Phone: 757-594-7544 or 800-333-4268
Admissions Fax: 757-594-7304
Admissions E-mail: gradstdy@cnu.edu · **Web Address:** www.cnu.edu/gradstudies

INSTITUTIONAL INFORMATION
Public/Private: Public. **Evening Classes Available?** Yes. **Students in Parent Institution:** 5,314.

PROGRAMS
Masters offered in: Art teacher education; artificial intelligence and robotics; biology teacher education; computer and information sciences; computer programming/programmer; computer science; computer systems networking and telecommunications; computer teacher education; early childhood education and teaching; English/language arts teacher education; environmental biology; foreign language teacher education; French language teacher education; history teacher education; mathematics teacher education; music teacher education; physics teacher education; Spanish language teacher education; teacher education, multiple levels.

STUDENT INFORMATION
Total Students in Program: 213.

RESEARCH FACILITIES
Research Facilities: MS in APCS has 5 major research labs & collaboration with NASA Langley Research Center & Thomas Jefferson National Accelerator Facility & The Applied Research Center. MS in environmental science has ecological study sites in Gloucester County, Hoffler Creek Nature Preserve.

EXPENSES/FINANCIAL AID
Annual Tuition: In-state $4,000. / Out-of-state $9,432. **Room & Board:** $6,800. **Fees:** $200. **Books and Supplies:** $650. **Grants Range From:** $2,000-$3,000. **Loans Range From:** $400-$10,700. **% Receiving Loans:** 100. **Types of Aid Available:** Graduate assistantships. **Assistantship Compensation Includes:** Partial tuition remission, salary/stipend. **Average Salary Stipend:** $2,000.

ADMISSIONS INFORMATION
Application Fee: $40. **Priority Application Deadline:** 5/1. **Regular Application Deadline:** 8/1. **Regular Notification:** Rolling. **Transfer Students Accepted?** Yes. **Transfer Policy:** Maximum of 6 semester hours of graduate level classes from a regionally accredited university may be transferred with a minimum grade point average of 3.0 on a 4.0 scale for each class.
Required Admission Factors: Letters of recommendation, transcript.
Other Admission Factors: Minimum 3.0 GPA on a 4.0 scale is required. Minimum combined score of 950 on the GRE General Test from the Verbal and Quantitative areas when applying for either master of science degree. PRAXIS I is a Teacher Education Program entrance requirement.
Program-Specific Admission Factors: Requirements for each program are listed on our website: www.cnu.edu/gradstudies

EMPLOYMENT INFORMATION
Placement Office Available? Yes.

CHURCH DIVINITY SCHOOL OF THE PACIFIC
Graduate & Professional Programs

Address: 2451 Ridge Road, Berkeley, CA 94709-1217
Admissions Phone: 510-204-0715 · **Admissions Fax:** 510-204-0749
Admissions E-mail: admissions@cdsp.edu · **Web Address:** www.cdsp.edu

INSTITUTIONAL INFORMATION
Public/Private: Private (nonprofit). **Total Faculty:** 22. **% Faculty Female:** 36. **% Faculty Part-time:** 55. **Student/Faculty Ratio:** 10:1. **Students in Parent Institution:** 136.

PROGRAMS
Masters offered in: Bible/biblical studies, divinity/ministry (BD, MDiv), religion/religious studies, religious education, theological studies and religious vocations, theology/theological studies.

STUDENT INFORMATION
Total Students in Program: 136. **% Full-time** 60. **% Female:** 51. **% Minority:** 10. **% International:** 9.

RESEARCH FACILITIES
Research Facilities: Graduate Theological Union, Graduate Theological Union Library, University of California—Berkeley, Mills College—Berkeley.

EXPENSES/FINANCIAL AID
Annual Tuition: In-state $9,568. **Books and Supplies:** $1,030.

ADMISSIONS INFORMATION
Application Fee: $30. **Priority Application Deadline:** 3/1. **Regular Application Deadline:** 5/1. **Regular Notification:** Rolling. **Transfer Students Accepted?** Yes. **Transfer Policy:** Transfer credit applicable if the work was not applied to a completed degree or certificate program. **Number of Applications Received:** 78. **% of Applicants Accepted:** 77. **% Accepted Who Enrolled:** 78. **Average GPA:** 3.4. **Average GRE Verbal:** 600. **Average GRE Quantitative:** 550. **Average GRE Analytical Writing:** 5.
Required Admission Factors: Essays/personal statement, letters of recommendation, transcript.

Other Admission Factors: GRE waived with a GPA of 3.0 or above and/or completed graduate degree(s). Minimum GRE score of 500 combined.
Program-Specific Admission Factors: Undergraduate degree required for all programs.

EMPLOYMENT INFORMATION
Placement Office Available? Yes. **% Employed Within 6 Months:** 80. **% of doctoral/first professional grads employed in their field upon graduation:** 70/60. **Rate of placement:** 60%. **Average starting salary:** $35,000.

CHURCH OF GOD THEOLOGICAL SEMINARY
Graduate & Professional Programs

Address: 900 Walker Street, NE, PO Box 3330, Cleveland, TN 37320-3330

INSTITUTIONAL INFORMATION
Public/Private: Private (nonprofit). **Students in Parent Institution:** 272

STUDENT INFORMATION
Total Students in Program: 272. **% Full-time** 62. **% Female:** 19.

RESEARCH FACILITIES
Research Facilities: Pentecostal Resource Center.

EXPENSES/FINANCIAL AID
Annual Tuition: In-state $3,150. **Fees:** $100. **Books and Supplies:** $500.

ADMISSIONS INFORMATION
Transfer Students Accepted? No.

EMPLOYMENT INFORMATION
Placement Office Available? Yes. **Rate of placement:** 95%.

THE CITADEL
College of Graduate & Professional Studies

Address: 171 Moultrie Street, Charleston, SC 29409
Admissions Phone: 843-953-5089 · **Admissions Fax:** 843-953-7630

INSTITUTIONAL INFORMATION
Public/private: Public. **Evening Classes Available?** Yes. **Students in Parent Institution:** 3,866.

STUDENT INFORMATION
Total Students in Program: 1,871. **% Full-time:** 8. **% Female:** 78.

EXPENSES/FINANCIAL AID
Annual Tuition: In-state $2,466/Out-of-state $4,806. **Fees:** $60. **Books and Supplies:** $1,000. **Loans Range From:** $250-$11,000. **% Receiving Loans:** 100. **Average Salary Stipend:** $7,000.

ADMISSIONS INFORMATION
Application Fee: $25. **Regular Notification:** Rolling. **Transfer Students Accepted?** Yes.
Required Admission Factors: GRE, letters of recommendation, transcript.

EMPLOYMENT INFORMATION
Placement Office Available? Yes.

CITY UNIVERSITY
Graduate Programs

Address: PO Box 90008, Bellevue, WA 98004

INSTITUTIONAL INFORMATION
Public/Private: Private (nonprofit). **Evening Classes Available?** Yes. **Students in Parent Institution:** 12,333.

STUDENT INFORMATION
Total Students in Program: 6,984. **% Full-time** 22. **% Female:** 48.

EXPENSES/FINANCIAL AID
Annual Tuition: In-state $5,292. **Books and Supplies:** $600. **Grants Range From:** $1,000-$5,000. **Loans Range From:** $4,000-$18,500. **% Receiving Scholarships/Grants:** 6. **% Receiving Loans:** 100.

ADMISSIONS INFORMATION
Application Fee: $75. **Regular Notification:** Rolling. **Transfer Students Accepted?** Yes.
Required Admission Factors: Essays/personal statement, letters of recommendation, transcript.
Program-Specific Admission Factors: Interview required of applicants to guidance & counseling, principalship, and teacher preparation programs.

CITY UNIVERSITY OF NEW YORK— BARUCH COLLEGE
Weissman School of Arts & Sciences

Address: 55 Lexington Avenue, Box B8-211, New York, NY 10010
Admissions Phone: 646-312-4490 · **Admissions Fax:** 646-312-4491
Admissions E-mail: wsas_graduate_studies@Baruch.cuny.edu
Web Address: www.baruch.cuny.edu/wsas/graduate_programs/

INSTITUTIONAL INFORMATION
Public/Private: Public. **Evening Classes Available?** Yes.

STUDENT INFORMATION
Total Students in Program: 2,500. **% Full-time** 50.

ADMISSIONS INFORMATION
Application Fee: $50. **Regular Application Deadline:** 4/1. **Transfer Students Accepted?** Yes. **Number of Applications Received:** 255. **% of Applicants Accepted:** 42. **% Accepted Who Enrolled:** 51. **Average GPA:** 3.3.
Required Admission Factors: Essays/personal statement, letters of recommendation, transcript.

CITY UNIVERSITY OF NEW YORK— BROOKLYN COLLEGE
Conservatory of Music

Address: 2900 Bedford Avenue, Brooklyn, NY 11210
Admissions Phone: 718-951-5001 · **Admissions Fax:** 718-951-4506
Admissions E-mail: mtynan@brooklyn.cuny.edu · **Web Address:** www.brooklyn.cuny.edu

INSTITUTIONAL INFORMATION
Public/Private: Public. **Evening Classes Available?** Yes. **Students in Parent Institution:** 15,513.

STUDENT INFORMATION
Total Students in Program: 4,553. **% Full-time** 9. **% Female:** 68. **% Minority:** 47. **% International:** 8.

EXPENSES/FINANCIAL AID
Annual Tuition: In-state $5,440. **Fees:** $280. **Books and Supplies:** $800. **Grants Range From:** $100-$6,800. **Loans Range From:** $500-$18,500. **% Receiving Loans:** 98.

ADMISSIONS INFORMATION
Application Fee: $50. **Priority Application Deadline:** 3/1. **Regular Notification:** Rolling. **Transfer Students Accepted?** Yes. **Number of Applica-**

tions Received: 63. **% of Applicants Accepted:** 65. **% Accepted Who Enrolled:** 71. **Average GPA:** 3.2.

Required Admission Factors: Letters of recommendation, transcript.

Program-Specific Admission Factors: Portfolio required of composition program applicants. Sample papers required of musicology program applicants. Audition and historical or analytical topic paper for performance practice applicants. Audition or tape submission for performance program.

EMPLOYMENT INFORMATION

Placement Office Available? Yes.

CITY UNIVERSITY OF NEW YORK— BROOKLYN COLLEGE
Graduate Studies and Research

Address: 2900 Bedford Avenue, James Hall Room 1602, Brooklyn, NY 11210
Admissions Phone: 718-951-5001 · **Admissions Fax:** 718-951-4506
Admissions E-mail: adminqry@brooklyn.cuny.edu
Web Address: www.brooklyn.cuny.edu

INSTITUTIONAL INFORMATION

Public/Private: Public. **Evening Classes Available?** Yes. **Student/Faculty Ratio:** 14:1. **Students in Parent Institution:** 15,384

PROGRAMS

Masters offered in: Accounting; acting; art history, criticism, and conservation; art teacher education; art/art studies; arts management; audiology/audiologist and hearing sciences; bilingual and multilingual education; biology teacher education; biology/biological sciences; chemistry teacher education; chemistry; communications studies/speech communication and rhetoric; computer and information sciences; computer science; counselor education/school counseling and guidance services; creative writing; directing and theatrical production; dramatic/theater arts and stagecraft; drawing; early childhood education and teaching; economics; education leadership and administration; education; education/teaching of individuals in early childhood special education programs; education/teaching of individuals with speech or language impairments; elementary education and teaching; English language and literature; English/language arts teacher education; experimental psychology; fine/studio arts; foods, nutrition, and wellness studies; foreign language teacher education; French language and literature; French language teacher education; geology/earth science; health and physical education; health services administration; health teacher education; health/health care administration/management; history teacher education; history; human nutrition; industrial and organizational psychology; information science/studies; intermedia/multimedia; Jewish/Judaic studies; junior high/intermediate/middle school education and teaching; kinesiology and exercise science; liberal arts and sciences/liberal studies; mathematics teacher education; mathematics; music history, literature, and theory; music pedagogy; music performance; music teacher education; music theory and composition; musicology and ethnomusicology; organizational behavior studies; painting; photography; physical education, teaching and coaching; physics teacher education; physics; playwriting and screenwriting; political science and government; political science and government; printmaking; psychology; public health (MPH, DPH); public health; radio and television; radio, television, and digital communications; reading teacher education; school psychology; science teacher education/general science teacher education; sculpture; secondary education and teaching; social science teacher education; social studies teacher education; sociology; Spanish language and literature; Spanish language teacher education; special education; speech-language pathology/pathologist; sports and fitness administration/management; teacher education, multiple levels; technical theater/theater design and technology; theater literature, history, and criticism; theater/theater arts management; urban studies/affairs; visual and performing arts; visual and performing arts. **First Professional degree offered in:** Dietetics and clinical nutrition services, multi/interdisciplinary studies.

STUDENT INFORMATION

Total Students in Program: 4,212. **% Full-time** 11. **% Female:** 69. **% Minority:** 46. **% International:** 7.

RESEARCH FACILITIES

Research Facilities: Walter W. Gerboth Music Library; Meier Bernstein Art Library; Costas Memorial Classics Library; Nathan Schmukler Investment Library; Boyd V. Sheets Memorial Library—speech; S. Eugene Scalia Memorial Library—Italian American studies.

EXPENSES/FINANCIAL AID

Annual Tuition: In-state $5,440. / Out-of-state $10,200. **Room & Board:** $6,971. **Fees:** $280. **Books and Supplies:** $800. **Grants Range From:** $100-$2,000. **Loans Range From:** $500-$18,500. **% Receiving Financial Aid:** 25. **% Receiving Scholarships/Grants:** 5. **% Receiving Loans:** 96. **Types of Aid Available:** Scholarships. **Average student debt, upon graduation:** $10,000.

ADMISSIONS INFORMATION

Application Fee: $125. **Priority Application Deadline:** 3/1. **Regular Application Deadline:** 3/1. **Regular Notification:** Rolling. **Transfer Students Accepted?** Yes. **Transfer Policy:** Matriculated students apply for advanced standing once enrolled. **Number of Applications Received:** 4,347. **% of Applicants Accepted:** 48. **% Accepted Who Enrolled:** 50.

Required Admission Factors: Letters of recommendation, transcript. **Other Admission Factors:** Minimum 3.0 GPA required.

Program-Specific Admission Factors: MFA art: portfolio and supplemental application; MA art teacher: portfolio; MFA creative writing: manuscript; Adv. certificate performance and interactive media arts: supplemental application; MA music teacher: performance/interview; MA musicology: writing.

EMPLOYMENT INFORMATION

Placement Office Available? Yes. **% Employed Within 6 Months:** 95. **Average starting salary:** $46,000.

CITY UNIVERSITY OF NEW YORK— CITY COLLEGE
College of Liberal Arts & Science

Address: Convent Avenue and 138th Street, New York, NY 10031
Admissions Phone: 212-650-6977 · **Admissions Fax:** 212-650-6417
Admissions E-mail: gradadm@ccny.cuny.edu · **Web Address:** www.ccny.cuny.edu

INSTITUTIONAL INFORMATION

Public/Private: Public. **Total Faculty:** 966. **% Faculty Female:** 60. **% Faculty Part-time:** 49. **Student/Faculty Ratio:** 11:1. **Students in Parent Institution:** 12,400.

PROGRAMS

Masters offered in: Anthropology; architecture (BArch, BA/BS, MArch, MA/MS, PhD); art history, criticism, and conservation; art teacher education; art/art studies; bilingual and multilingual education; biochemistry; biology teacher education; biomedical/medical engineering; chemical engineering; chemistry teacher education; chemistry; city/urban, community, and regional planning; civil engineering; computer and information sciences; creative writing; economics; education leadership and administration; education; educational administration and supervision; electrical, electronics, and communications engineering; elementary education and teaching; English composition; English language and literature; English/language arts teacher education; film/cinema studies; fine/studio arts; foreign language teacher education; geology/earth science; history; international relations and affairs; jazz/jazz studies; junior high/intermediate/middle school education and teaching; mathematics teacher education; mathematics; mechanical engineering; museology/museum studies; music performance; music teacher education; music theory and composition; music/music and performing arts studies; photographic and film/video technology/technician and assistant; physics teacher education; physics; psychology;

reading teacher education; science teacher education/general science teacher education; secondary education and teaching; social studies teacher education; sociology; Spanish language and literature; Spanish language teacher education; special education and teaching; structural engineering; teaching English as a second or foreign language/ESL language instructor; transportation and highway engineering; water resources engineering. **Doctorate offered in:** Mechanical engineering. **First Professional degree offered in:** Education leadership and administration, educational administration and supervision, reading teacher education.

STUDENT INFORMATION
Total Students in Program: 3,562. % Full-time 6. % Female: 58.

RESEARCH FACILITIES
Research Facilities: Levich Institute for Physiochemical Hydrodynmics, Center for Biomedical Engineering, Clean Fuels Institute, Center for Water Resources, Center for Water Resources and Environmental Research, Institute for Ultrfast Spectrocopy, Colin Powell Center for Policy Studies.

EXPENSES/FINANCIAL AID
Annual Tuition: In-state $4,350. / Out-of-state $7,600.

ADMISSIONS INFORMATION
Application Fee: $50. **Priority Application Deadline:** 4/15. **Regular Application Deadline:** 5/1. **Regular Notification:** Rolling. **Transfer Students Accepted?** Yes. **Transfer Policy:** Same admission requirements as regular applicants. **Number of Applications Received:** 5,359. **% of Applicants Accepted:** 50.
Required Admission Factors: Essays/personal statement, letters of recommendation, transcript.
Other Admission Factors: Minimum 3.0 GPA required.
Program-Specific Admission Factors: Portfolio required of media arts production, creative writing, and fine arts program applicants.

EMPLOYMENT INFORMATION
Placement Office Available? Yes.

CITY UNIVERSITY OF NEW YORK— THE COLLEGE OF STATEN ISLAND
Graduate Programs

Address: 2800 Victory Boulevard, Staten Island, NY 10314
Admissions Phone: 718-982-2010

INSTITUTIONAL INFORMATION
Public/Private: Public. **Evening Classes Available?** Yes. **Students in Parent Institution:** 11,980.

STUDENT INFORMATION
Total Students in Program: 1,373. % Full-time 8. % Female: 77.

RESEARCH FACILITIES
Research Facilities: Center for Developmental Neuroscience and Developmental Disabilities, and the Center for Environmental Science.

EXPENSES/FINANCIAL AID
Annual Tuition: In-state $4,350. / Out-of-state $7,600. **Fees:** $104.

ADMISSIONS INFORMATION
Application Fee: $40. **Regular Notification:** Rolling. **Transfer Students Accepted?** No.
Required Admission Factors: Essays/personal statement, interview, letters of recommendation, transcript.

EMPLOYMENT INFORMATION
Placement Office Available? Yes.

CITY UNIVERSITY OF NEW YORK— GRADUATE SCHOOL AND UNIVERSITY CENTER
Graduate Studies

Address: 365 Fifth Avenue, New York, NY 10016-4309
Admissions Phone: 212-817-7470 · **Admissions Fax:** 212-817-1624
Admissions E-mail: admiss@gc.cuny.edu · **Web Address:** www.gc.cuny.edu

INSTITUTIONAL INFORMATION
Public/Private: Public. **Evening Classes Available?** Yes. **Students in Parent Institution:** 4,313.

STUDENT INFORMATION
Total Students in Program: 3,886. % Full-time 91. % Female: 55.

RESEARCH FACILITIES
Research Facilities: 23 research centers and institutes.

EXPENSES/FINANCIAL AID
Annual Tuition: In-state $4,870. / Out-of-state $9,500. **Fees:** $219. **Books and Supplies:** $759. **Grants Range From:** $100-$28,870. **Loans Range From:** $200-$18,500. **Types of Aid Available:** Fellowships, graduate assistantships, institutional work-study, loans.

ADMISSIONS INFORMATION
Application Fee: $50. **Priority Application Deadline:** 2/1. **Regular Application Deadline:** 2/1. **Regular Notification:** Rolling. **Transfer Students Accepted?** Yes. **Number of Applications Received:** 3,796. **% of Applicants Accepted:** 42. **% Accepted Who Enrolled:** 48.
Required Admission Factors: Essays/personal statement, GRE, letters of recommendation, transcript.

CITY UNIVERSITY OF NEW YORK— HUNTER COLLEGE
School of Arts & Sciences

Address: 695 Park Avenue, New York, NY 10021
Admissions Phone: 212-772-4490 · **Admissions Fax:** 212-650-3472
Admissions E-mail: admissions@hunter.cuny.edu · **Web Address:** www.hunter.cuny.edu

INSTITUTIONAL INFORMATION
Public/Private: Public. **Evening Classes Available?** Yes. **Students in Parent Institution:** 20,243.

PROGRAMS
Masters offered in: Anthropology; applied mathematics; art history, criticism, and conservation; biochemistry; biology/biological sciences, communications studies/speech, communication, and rhetoric; comparative literature; creative writing; drama and dramatics/theater arts; ecology; economics; English language and literature; English literature (British and commonwealth); fine arts and art studies; geography; history; Italian language and literature; mathematics; music history, literature, and theory; music performance; physics; Portuguese language and literature; psychology, Russian studies; sociology; Spanish language and literature; urban studies/affairs

STUDENT INFORMATION
Total Students in Program: 914. % Full-time 15. % Female: 15.

RESEARCH FACILITIES
Research Facilities: Brookdale Center on Aging; Center on AIDS, Drugs & Community Health; Institute for Biomolecular Structure/Function; Center for Media/Learning; Center for Occupational/Environmental Health; Centro de Estudios Puertoriquenos.

EXPENSES/FINANCIAL AID

Annual Tuition: In-state $5,440. / Out-of-state $10,200. **Fees:** $176. **Books and Supplies:** $759. **Types of Aid Available:** Grants, institutional work-study, loans, scholarships.

ADMISSIONS INFORMATION

Application Fee: $50. **Regular Application Deadline:** 1/15. **Regular Notification:** Rolling. **Transfer Students Accepted?** Yes. **Number of Applications Received:** 1,423. **% of Applicants Accepted:** 34. **% Accepted Who Enrolled:** 69. **Average GPA:** 3.0.
Required Admission Factors: Essays/personal statement, letters of recommendation, transcript.
Other Admission Factors: Minimum 2.7 GPA (3.0 in major) required.

EMPLOYMENT INFORMATION

Placement Office Available? Yes.

CITY UNIVERSITY OF NEW YORK—
HUNTER COLLEGE
School of Social Work

Address: 129 East 79th Street, New York, NY 10021
Admissions Phone: 212-452-7005 · **Admissions Fax:** 212-452-7197
Admissions E-mail: admissions.hcssw@hunter.cuny.edu
Web Address: www.hunter.cuny.edu/socwork/index.html

INSTITUTIONAL INFORMATION

Public/Private: Public. **Evening Classes Available?** Yes. **Students in Parent Institution:** 20,243.

PROGRAMS

Masters offered in: Clinical/medical social work, health professions and related sciences.

STUDENT INFORMATION

Total Students in Program: 785. **% Full-time** 54. **% Female:** 79.

RESEARCH FACILITIES

Research Facilities: Brookdale Center on Aging; Center on AIDS, Drugs & Community Health; Institute for Biomolecular Structure/Function, Center for Media/Learning; Center for Occupational/Environmental Health; Centro de Estudios Puertoriquenos.

EXPENSES/FINANCIAL AID

Annual Tuition: In-state $5,940. / Out-of-state $10,560. **Fees:** $176. **Books and Supplies:** $759. **Types of Aid Available:** Grants, institutional work-study, loans, scholarships.

ADMISSIONS INFORMATION

Application Fee: $125. **Regular Application Deadline:** 1/1. **Regular Notification:** Rolling. **Transfer Students Accepted?** Yes. **Number of Applications Received:** 1,348. **% of Applicants Accepted:** 29. **% Accepted Who Enrolled:** 84. **Average GPA:** 3.2.
Required Admission Factors: Essays/personal statement, interview, letters of recommendation, transcript.
Other Admission Factors: Minimum 3.0 GPA required.

EMPLOYMENT INFORMATION

Placement Office Available? Yes.

CITY UNIVERSITY OF NEW YORK—
JOHN JAY COLLEGE OF
CRIMINAL JUSTICE
Graduate Studies

Address: 445 West 59th Street, Suite 4260, New York, NY 10019
Admissions Phone: 212-237-8863 or 212-237-2864 · **Admissions Fax:** 212-237-8777
Admissions E-mail: jbrosser@jjay.cuny.edu · **Web Address:** www.jjay.cuny.edu

INSTITUTIONAL INFORMATION

Public/Private: Public. **Evening Classes Available?** Yes. **Student/Faculty Ratio:** 14:1. **Students in Parent Institution:** 10,612

RESEARCH FACILITIES

Research Facilities: Center on Violence and Human Survival, Criminal Justice Center, Criminal Justice Research and Evaluation Center, Fire Science Institute, Institute for Criminal Justice Ethics, Institute on Alcohol and Substance Abuse, Toxicology Research and Training Center.

EXPENSES/FINANCIAL AID

Annual Tuition: In-state $4,350. / Out-of-state $7,600. **Loans Range From:** $1,000-$13,000. **% Receiving Scholarships/Grants:** 5. **% Receiving Loans:** 95.

ADMISSIONS INFORMATION

Application Fee: $125. **Regular Application Deadline:** 6/30. **Regular Notification:** Rolling. **Transfer Students Accepted?** Yes. **Number of Applications Received:** 564. **% of Applicants Accepted:** 85. **% Accepted Who Enrolled:** 65. **Average GPA:** 3.2.
Required Admission Factors: Essays/personal statement, letters of recommendation, transcript.
Program-Specific Admission Factors: Minimum 3.0 GPA required for most programs; minimum 2.7 GPA required for MPAdmin program.

EMPLOYMENT INFORMATION

Placement Office Available? Yes. **Rate of placement:** 80%.

CITY UNIVERSITY OF NEW YORK—
QUEENS COLLEGE
Aaron Copland School of Music

Address: 65-30 Kissena Boulevard, Flushing, NY 11367
Admissions Phone: 718-997-5200 · **Admissions Fax:** 718-997-5193
Admissions E-mail: mrc$admg@qcl.qc.edu ·

INSTITUTIONAL INFORMATION

Public/Private: Public. **Evening Classes Available?** Yes. **Students in Parent Institution:** 15,686

STUDENT INFORMATION

Total Students in Program: 4,120. **% Full-time** 9. **% Female:** 71.

RESEARCH FACILITIES

Research Facilities: American Museum of Natural History, CUNY Oceanography Program, Lamont-Doherty Geological Observatory, Smithsonian Institute.

EXPENSES/FINANCIAL AID

Annual Tuition: In-state $4,350. / Out-of-state $7,600. **Fees:** $104. **Books and Supplies:** $400. **Grants Range From:** $275-$5,000. **Loans Range From:** $2,000-$10,500. **% Receiving Financial Aid:** 25. **% Receiving Scholarships/Grants:** 12. **% Receiving Loans:** 29. **% Receiving Assistantships:** 2.

ADMISSIONS INFORMATION

Application Fee: $40. **Regular Notification:** Rolling. **Transfer Students Accepted?** Yes. **Number of Applications Received:** 103. **% of Applicants Accepted:** 44. **% Accepted Who Enrolled:** 53.
Required Admission Factors: Essays/personal statement, transcript.
Other Admission Factors: Minimum 3.0 GPA and 3 letters of reference required.
Program-Specific Admission Factors: Composition samples required of composition and theory program applicants, recent papers required of theory and history program applicants.

EMPLOYMENT INFORMATION

Placement Office Available? Yes.

CITY UNIVERSITY OF NEW YORK— QUEENS COLLEGE
Graduate School of Library & Information Studies

Address: 65-30 Kissena Boulevard, Flushing, NY 11367
Admissions Phone: 718-997-5200 · **Admissions Fax:** 718-997-5193
Admissions E-mail: mrc$admg@qc1.qc.edu ·

INSTITUTIONAL INFORMATION

Public/Private: Public. **Evening Classes Available?** Yes. **Students in Parent Institution:** 15,686.

STUDENT INFORMATION

Total Students in Program: 4,120. **% Full-time** 9. **% Female:** 71.

RESEARCH FACILITIES

Research Facilities: American Museum of Natural History, CUNY Oceanography Program, Lamont-Doherty Geological Observatory, Smithsonian Institute.

EXPENSES/FINANCIAL AID

Annual Tuition: In-state $4,350. / Out-of-state $7,600. **Fees:** $104. **Books and Supplies:** $400. **Grants Range From:** $275-$5,000. **Loans Range From:** $2,000-$10,500. **% Receiving Financial Aid:** 25. **% Receiving Scholarships/Grants:** 12. **% Receiving Loans:** 29. **% Receiving Assistantships:** 2.

ADMISSIONS INFORMATION

Application Fee: $40. **Regular Notification:** Rolling. **Transfer Students Accepted?** Yes. **Number of Applications Received:** 201. **% of Applicants Accepted:** 95. **% Accepted Who Enrolled:** 46. **Average GPA:** 3.0.
Required Admission Factors: Essays/personal statement, interview, transcript.
Other Admission Factors: Minimum 3.0 GPA, 3 letters of reference, and competency in word processing required.

EMPLOYMENT INFORMATION

Placement Office Available? Yes.

CLAREMONT GRADUATE UNIVERSITY
Botany Program

Address: 170 East 10th Street, McManus 131, Claremont, CA 91711-6163
Admissions Phone: 909-621-8069 · **Admissions Fax:** 909-607-7285
Admissions E-mail: botany@cgu.edu · **Web Address:** www.rsabg.org

INSTITUTIONAL INFORMATION

Public/Private: Private (nonprofit). **Students in Parent Institution:** 2,039.

STUDENT INFORMATION

Total Students in Program: 2,039. **% Full-time** 24. **% Female:** 53.

RESEARCH FACILITIES

Research Facilities: California Institute of Public Affairs, Institute for Antiquity and Christianity.

EXPENSES/FINANCIAL AID

Annual Tuition: In-state $21,580. **Fees:** $150. **% Receiving Financial Aid:** 100.

ADMISSIONS INFORMATION

Application Fee: $40. **Regular Notification:** Rolling. **Transfer Students Accepted?** No. **Number of Applications Received:** 7. **% of Applicants Accepted:** 57. **% Accepted Who Enrolled:** 75.
Required Admission Factors: Essays/personal statement, GRE, letters of recommendation, transcript.

EMPLOYMENT INFORMATION

Placement Office Available? Yes.

CLAREMONT GRADUATE UNIVERSITY
Centers for the Arts & Humanities

Address: 170 East 10th Street, McManus 131, Claremont, CA 91711-6163
Admissions Phone: 909-621-8069 · **Admissions Fax:** 909-607-7285

INSTITUTIONAL INFORMATION

Public/Private: Private (nonprofit). **Students in Parent Institution:** 2,039.

STUDENT INFORMATION

Total Students in Program: 2,039. **% Full-time** 24. **% Female:** 53.

RESEARCH FACILITIES

Research Facilities: California Institute of Public Affairs, Institute for Antiquity and Christianity.

EXPENSES/FINANCIAL AID

Annual Tuition: In-state $21,580. **Fees:** $150. **% Receiving Financial Aid:** 63.

ADMISSIONS INFORMATION

Application Fee: $40. **Regular Notification:** Rolling. **Transfer Students Accepted?** Yes. **Number of Applications Received:** 284. **% of Applicants Accepted:** 78. **% Accepted Who Enrolled:** 31.
Required Admission Factors: Essays/personal statement, GRE, letters of recommendation, transcript.
Program-Specific Admission Factors: Portfolio required of music program applicants.

EMPLOYMENT INFORMATION

Placement Office Available? Yes.

CLAREMONT GRADUATE UNIVERSITY
Department of Mathematics

Address: 170 East 10th Street, McManus 131, Claremont, CA 91711-6163
Admissions Phone: 909-621-8069 · **Admissions Fax:** 909-607-7285
Admissions E-mail: math@cgu.edu

INSTITUTIONAL INFORMATION

Public/Private: Private (nonprofit). **Students in Parent Institution:** 2,039.

STUDENT INFORMATION

Total Students in Program: 2,039. **% Full-time** 24. **% Female:** 53.

RESEARCH FACILITIES

Research Facilities: California Institute of Public Affairs, Institute for Antiquity and Christianity.

EXPENSES/FINANCIAL AID

Annual Tuition: In-state $21,580. **Fees:** $150.

ADMISSIONS INFORMATION

Application Fee: $40. **Regular Notification:** Rolling. **Transfer Students Accepted?** Yes. **Number of Applications Received:** 34. **% of Applicants Accepted:** 85. **% Accepted Who Enrolled:** 28.

Required Admission Factors: Essays/personal statement, GRE, letters of recommendation, transcript.

EMPLOYMENT INFORMATION

Placement Office Available? Yes.

CLAREMONT GRADUATE UNIVERSITY
School of Behavioral & Organizational Sciences

Address: 123 East Eighth Street, Claremont, CA 91711
Admissions Phone: 909-621-8069 · **Admissions Fax:** 909-607-7285
Admissions E-mail: psych@cgu.edu · **Web Address:** www.cgu.edu/pages/154.asp

INSTITUTIONAL INFORMATION

Public/Private: Private (nonprofit). **Evening Classes Available?** Yes. **Total Faculty:** 52. **% Faculty Female:** 54. **% Faculty Part-time:** 87. **Students in Parent Institution:** 2,039.

PROGRAMS

Masters offered in: Psychology. **Doctorate offered in:** Cognitive psychology and psycholinguistics, developmental and child psychology, industrial and organizational psychology, psychology, social psychology.

STUDENT INFORMATION

Total Students in Program: 2,039. **% Full-time** 24. **% Female:** 53.

RESEARCH FACILITIES

Research Facilities: California Institute of Public Affairs, Institute for Antiquity and Christianity, Institute of Organizatioal and Program Evaluation Research, Institute for Research on Social Issues.

EXPENSES/FINANCIAL AID

Annual Tuition: $25,250. **Fees:** $220. **Books and Supplies:** $300. **Grants Range From:** $3,410-$15,741. **Loans Range From:** $500-$25,250. **% Receiving Financial Aid:** 61.

ADMISSIONS INFORMATION

Application Fee: $50. **Priority Application Deadline:** 1/15. **Regular Application Deadline:** 1/15. **Regular Notification:** Rolling. **Transfer Students Accepted?** Yes. **Number of Applications Received:** 173. **% of Applicants Accepted:** 62. **% Accepted Who Enrolled:** 36. **Average GPA:** 3.4.

Required Admission Factors: Essays/personal statement, GRE, letters of recommendation, transcript.

EMPLOYMENT INFORMATION

% Employed Within 6 Months: 50. **Rate of placement:** 75%. **Average starting salary:** $40,000.

CLAREMONT GRADUATE UNIVERSITY
School of Information Science

Address: 170 East 10th Street, McManus 131, Claremont, CA 91711-6163
Admissions Phone: 909-621-8069 · **Admissions Fax:** 909-607-7285
Admissions E-mail: go.yoshida@cgu.edu · **Web Address:** www.cgu.edu

INSTITUTIONAL INFORMATION

Public/Private: Private (nonprofit). **Evening Classes Available?** Yes. **Students in Parent Institution:** 2,039

STUDENT INFORMATION

Total Students in Program: 2,039. **% Full-time** 24. **% Female:** 53.

RESEARCH FACILITIES

Research Facilities: California Institute of Public Affairs, Institute for Antiquity and Christianity.

EXPENSES/FINANCIAL AID

Annual Tuition: In-state $21,580. **Fees:** $150. **% Receiving Financial Aid:** 28.

ADMISSIONS INFORMATION

Application Fee: $55. **Priority Application Deadline:** 2/1. **Regular Application Deadline:** 6/30. **Regular Notification:** Rolling. **Transfer Students Accepted?** Yes. **Number of Applications Received:** 142. **% of Applicants Accepted:** 60. **% Accepted Who Enrolled:** 34.

Required Admission Factors: Essays/personal statement, GMAT, GRE, letters of recommendation, transcript.

Recommended Admission Factors: Interview.

Other Admission Factors: Minimum GPA 3.2; Average GRE: Analytical = 460, Quantitative = 726, Verbal = 517, Average GMAT: Total = 519; TOEFL Minimum = 550.

EMPLOYMENT INFORMATION

Placement Office Available? Yes.

CLAREMONT GRADUATE UNIVERSITY
School of Politics & Economics

Address: CGU Admissions, 160 East 10th Street, Claremont, CA 91711-6163
Admissions Phone: 909-621-8069 · **Admissions Fax:** 909-607-7285
Admissions E-mail: admiss@cgu.edu · **Web Address:** http://spe.cgu.edu

INSTITUTIONAL INFORMATION

Public/Private: Private (nonprofit). **Evening Classes Available?** Yes. **Student/Faculty Ratio:** 15:1. **Students in Parent Institution:** 2,039

PROGRAMS

Masters offered in: American government and politics (U.S.); applied economics; development economics and international development; econometrics and quantitative economics; economics, finance, and financial management services; finance; international business; international economics; international finance; international relations and affairs; international/global studies; multi/interdisciplinary studies; political science and government; political science and government; public finance; social sciences. **Doctorate offered in:** American government and politics (U.S.); applied economics; development economics and international development; econometrics and quantitative economics; economics; economics, finance, and financial management services.

STUDENT INFORMATION

Total Students in Program: 2,039. **% Full-time** 24. **% Female:** 53.

RESEARCH FACILITIES

Research Facilities: California Policy Institute at Claremont, Claremont Institute of Economic Policy Studies, Institute for Democratic Renewal, Institute for Antiquity and Christianity.

EXPENSES/FINANCIAL AID

Annual Tuition: $23,996. **Fees:** $200. **Books and Supplies:** $500. **Grants Range From:** $2,500-$25,000. **Loans Range From:** $2,500-$18,000. **% Receiving Financial Aid:** 58.

ADMISSIONS INFORMATION

Application Fee: $50. **Priority Application Deadline:** 2/15. **Regular Application Deadline:** 5/15. **Regular Notification:** Rolling. **Transfer Students Accepted?** Yes. **Transfer Policy:** Transfer applicants should fill out a complete application packet. **Number of Applications Received:** 298. **% of Applicants Accepted:** 58. **% Accepted Who Enrolled:** 40. **Average GPA:** 3.7.

Required Admission Factors: Essays/personal statement, GRE, letters of recommendation, transcript.

Recommended Admission Factors: GMAT, interview.

Other Admission Factors: Please see information regarding admission requirements on the following Web page: http://spe.cgu.edu/admissions/faqs.html

EMPLOYMENT INFORMATION
Placement Office Available? Yes.

CLAREMONT SCHOOL OF THEOLOGY
Graduate Programs

Address: 1325 North College Avenue, Claremont, CA 91711-3199
Admissions Phone: 800-626-7821, ext. 1220 · **Admissions Fax:** 909-626-7062
Admissions E-mail: admission@cstedu

INSTITUTIONAL INFORMATION
Public/Private: Private (nonprofit). **Evening Classes Available?** Yes. **Total Faculty:** 41. **% Faculty Female:** 44. **% Faculty Part-time:** 49. **Students in Parent Institution:** 520.

STUDENT INFORMATION
Total Students in Program: 335. **% Full-time** 57. **% Female:** 44.

RESEARCH FACILITIES
Research Facilities: Ancient Biblical Manuscript Center, Center for Pacific and Asian American Ministries, Center for Process Studies, Institute for Antiquity and Christianity, Mobilization for the Human Family, National United Methodist Native American Center.

EXPENSES/FINANCIAL AID
Annual Tuition: $9,750. **Room & Board:** $900. **Grants Range From:** $2,655-$12,500. **Loans Range From:** $8,500-$18,500. **% Receiving Financial Aid:** 75. **% Receiving Scholarships/Grants:** 70. **% Receiving Loans:** 80. **% Receiving Assistantships:** 5. **Average student debt, upon graduation:** $32,000. **Number of Teaching/Research Assistantships Granted Each Year:** 10. **Average Salary Stipend:** $2,000.

ADMISSIONS INFORMATION
Application Fee: $30. **Transfer Students Accepted?** Yes. **Number of Applications Received:** 201. **% of Applicants Accepted:** 76. **% Accepted Who Enrolled:** 71. **Average GPA:** 3.3.
Required Admission Factors: Essays/personal statement, letters of recommendation, transcript.
Program-Specific Admission Factors: Minimum GRE score of 1100 and minimum 3.25 GPA required of PhD program applicants. Minimum 3.25 GPA required of DMin program applicants. Minimum 2.75 GPA required of MDiv and MA program applicants.

EMPLOYMENT INFORMATION
Placement Office Available? Yes.

CLARION UNIVERSITY OF PENNSYLVANIA
College of Arts & Sciences

Address: Clarion, PA 16214
Admissions Phone: 814-393-2337 · **Admissions Fax:** 814-393-2722
Admissions E-mail: bdede@mail.clarion.edu

INSTITUTIONAL INFORMATION
Public/Private: Public. **Evening Classes Available?** Yes. **Students in Parent Institution:** 6,271.

STUDENT INFORMATION
Total Students in Program: 459. **% Full-time** 38. **% Female:** 75.

EXPENSES/FINANCIAL AID
Annual Tuition: In-state $4,600. / Out-of-state $7,554. **Fees:** $910. **Books and Supplies:** $400. **Grants Range From:** $948-$3,792. **Loans Range**

From: $100-$11,300. **% Receiving Loans:** 42. **% Receiving Assistantships:** 21. **Average Salary Stipend:** $4,002.

ADMISSIONS INFORMATION
Application Fee: $30. **Regular Notification:** Rolling. **Transfer Students Accepted?** Yes. **Transfer Policy:** Maximum 1/3 of total credit hours required with a minimum grade of B may be transferred. **Number of Applications Received:** 38. **% of Applicants Accepted:** 68. **% Accepted Who Enrolled:** 54.
Required Admission Factors: GRE, letters of recommendation, transcript.
Other Admission Factors: Minimum 2.75 GPA required.

EMPLOYMENT INFORMATION
Placement Office Available? Yes.

CLARK UNIVERSITY
Graduate School

Address: 950 Main Street, Worcester, MA 01610-1477
Admissions Phone: 508-793-7676 · **Admissions Fax:** 508-793-8834
Admissions E-mail: drobertson@clarku.edu · **Web Address:** www.clarku.edu/graduate

INSTITUTIONAL INFORMATION
Public/Private: Private (nonprofit). **Total Faculty:** 174. **% Faculty Female:** 41. **% Faculty Part-time:** 36. **Student/Faculty Ratio:** 6:1. **Students in Parent Institution:** 3,115.

STUDENT INFORMATION
Total Students in Program: 459. **% Full-time** 88. **% Female:** 61. **% Minority:** 5. **% International:** 39.

RESEARCH FACILITIES
Research Facilities: George Perkins Marsh Institute, Jacob Hiatt Center for Urban Education, Center for Holocaust Studies, Heinz Werner Institute, Higgens School of Humanities, IDRISI Project.

EXPENSES/FINANCIAL AID
Annual Tuition: $28,000. **Fees:** $30. **Books and Supplies:** $800. **Grants Range From:** $10,000-$28,000. **Loans Range From:** $500-$18,500. **Types of Aid Available:** Fellowships, graduate assistantships, scholarships. **Number of Fellowships Granted Each Year:** 5 **Average amount of individual fellowships per year:** $12,500. **Number of Teaching/Research Assistantships Granted Each Year:** 102. **Average Salary Stipend:** $12,500.

ADMISSIONS INFORMATION
Application Fee: $50. **Regular Application Deadline:** 1/15. **Regular Notification:** Rolling. **Transfer Students Accepted?** Yes. **Number of Applications Received:** 772. **% of Applicants Accepted:** 39. **% Accepted Who Enrolled:** 50. **Average GPA:** 3.8.
Required Admission Factors: Essays/personal statement, letters of recommendation, transcript.
Recommended Admission Factors: Interview.
Other Admission Factors: Minimum 2.7 GPA required; some programs may require a higher GPA.

EMPLOYMENT INFORMATION
Placement Office Available? Yes.

CLARKE COLLEGE
Graduate Programs

Address: 1550 Clarke Drive, Dubuque, IA 52001-3198
Admissions Phone: 563-588-3042 · **Admissions Fax:** 563-588-6789
Admissions E-mail: graduate@clarke.edu
Web Address: www.clarke.edu/graduate/index.htm

INSTITUTIONAL INFORMATION

Public/Private: Private (nonprofit). **Evening Classes Available?** Yes. Students in Parent Institution: 1,249

STUDENT INFORMATION

Total Students in Program: 142. **% Full-time** 30.

EXPENSES/FINANCIAL AID

Annual Tuition: In-state $6,480. **Fees:** $75. **Books and Supplies:** $300. **% Receiving Loans:** 90.

ADMISSIONS INFORMATION

Application Fee: $25. **Regular Application Deadline:** 8/15. **Regular Notification:** Rolling. **Transfer Students Accepted?** Yes.
Required Admission Factors: Letters of recommendation, transcript.

EMPLOYMENT INFORMATION

Placement Office Available? Yes.

CLARKSON UNIVERSITY
School of Science

Address: Box 5625, Potsdam, NY 13699
Admissions Phone: 315-268-3802 · **Admissions Fax:** 315-268-6670
Admissions E-mail: tony.collins@clarkson.edu

INSTITUTIONAL INFORMATION

Public/Private: Private (nonprofit). **Students in Parent Institution:** 2,877.

STUDENT INFORMATION

Total Students in Program: 338. **% Full-time** 93. **% Female:** 33.

RESEARCH FACILITIES

Research Facilities: Center for Advanced Materials Processing, Institute for Nonlinear Studies, Center for Canadian-U.S. Business Studies, Center for Environmental Management, Center for Global Competitiveness, Center for Excellence in Communication.

EXPENSES/FINANCIAL AID

Annual Tuition: In-state $21,420. **Fees:** $215. **Books and Supplies:** $1,000. **Loans Range From:** $500-$18,500. **% Receiving Financial Aid:** 100. **% Receiving Scholarships/Grants:** 14. **% Receiving Loans:** 28. **% Receiving Assistantships:** 81. **Number of Fellowships Granted Each Year:** 1. **Average amount of individual fellowships per year:** $16,100. **Number of Teaching/Research Assistantships Granted Each Year:** 37. **Average Salary Stipend:** $16,100.

ADMISSIONS INFORMATION

Regular Notification: Rolling. **Transfer Students Accepted?** No. **Transfer Policy:** Maximum 10 credit hours may be transferred into MS programs; maximum 30 credit hours may be transferred into doctorate programs. **Number of Applications Received:** 95. **% of Applicants Accepted:** 64. **% Accepted Who Enrolled:** 26. **Average GPA:** 3.6. **Average GRE Verbal:** 520. **Average GRE Quantitative:** 760. **Average GRE Analytical:** 630.
Required Admission Factors: GRE, letters of recommendation,

EMPLOYMENT INFORMATION

Placement Office Available? Yes.

CLEVELAND COLLEGE OF JEWISH STUDIES
Graduate Programs

Address: 26500 Shaker Boulevard, Beachwood, OH 44122
Admissions Phone: 216-464-4050 · **Admissions Fax:** 216-464-5827
Admissions E-mail: lrosen@ccjs.edu

INSTITUTIONAL INFORMATION

Public/Private: Private (nonprofit). **Evening Classes Available?** Yes. **Student/Faculty Ratio:** 10:1. **Students in Parent Institution:** 560

STUDENT INFORMATION

Total Students in Program: 90. **% Full-time** 12. **% Female:** 77.

RESEARCH FACILITIES

Research Facilities: Aaron Garber Library.

EXPENSES/FINANCIAL AID

Annual Tuition: In-state $5,400. **Fees:** $25. **Books and Supplies:** $250. **Grants Range From:** $100-$1,000. **% Number of Fellowships Granted Each Year:** 2. **Average amount of individual fellowships per year:** $6,300.

ADMISSIONS INFORMATION

Application Fee: $50. **Regular Notification:** Rolling. **Transfer Students Accepted?** Yes. **Number of Applications Received:** 23. **% of Applicants Accepted:** 78. **% Accepted Who Enrolled:** 100.
Required Admission Factors: Essays/personal statement, interview, letters of recommendation, transcript.

EMPLOYMENT INFORMATION

% Employed Within 6 Months: 95. **% of master's grads employed in their field upon graduation:** 95.

CLEVELAND INSTITUTE OF MUSIC
Graduate Programs

Address: 11021 East Boulevard, Cleveland, OH 44106-1776
Admissions Phone: 216-795-3107 · **Admissions Fax:** 216-791-3161
Admissions E-mail: ewf3@po.cwru.edu · **Web Address:** www.cim.edu

INSTITUTIONAL INFORMATION

Public/Private: Private (nonprofit). **Student/Faculty Ratio:** 7:1. **Students in Parent Institution:** 424.

STUDENT INFORMATION

Total Students in Program: 167. **% Full-time** 96. **% Female:** 63. **% International:** 28.

EXPENSES/FINANCIAL AID

Annual Tuition: $22,768. **Room & Board (on/off campus):** $7,260/$6,750. **Fees:** $451. **Books and Supplies:** $800. **Grants Range From:** $2,000-$15,000. **Loans Range From:** $2,000-$18,500. **% Receiving Financial Aid:** 95. **% Receiving Scholarships/Grants:** 98. **% Receiving Loans:** 72. **Average student debt, upon graduation:** $33,319 **Number of Fellowships Granted Each Year:** 10. **Average amount of individual fellowships per year:** $1,500.

ADMISSIONS INFORMATION

Application Fee: $100. **Regular Application Deadline:** 12/1. **Regular Notification:** 4/1. **Transfer Students Accepted?** Yes. **Transfer Policy:** High school transcript and SAT or ACT scores required of transfer applicants. **Number of Applications Received:** 474. **% of Applicants Accepted:** 35. **% Accepted Who Enrolled:** 52.
Required Admission Factors: Essays/personal statement, letters of recommendation, transcript.
Other Admission Factors: Audition and admission examinations required.

CLEVELAND STATE UNIVERSITY
College of Graduate Studies

Address: 1860 East 22nd Street, Rhodes Tower West, Suite 220, Cleveland, OH 44114
Admissions Phone: 216-687-5599 · **Admissions Fax:** 216-687-5400
Admissions E-mail: graduate.admissions@csuohio.edu
Web Address: www.csuohio.edu/gradcollege/admit/

INSTITUTIONAL INFORMATION
Public/Private: Public. **Evening Classes Available?** Yes. **Students in Parent Institution:** 15,746.

STUDENT INFORMATION
Total Students in Program: 4,480. **% Full-time** 12. **% Female:** 61.

RESEARCH FACILITIES
Research Facilities: DNA Analysis Facility, Animal Care Facility, Biomedical and Health Institute, Environmental Systems Institute, Bioethics Center, K'inal Winik Cultural Center.

EXPENSES/FINANCIAL AID
Annual Tuition: In-state $5,600. / Out-of-state $11,500.

ADMISSIONS INFORMATION
Application Fee: $30. **Priority Application Deadline:** 3/1. **Regular Application Deadline:** 8/1. **Regular Notification:** Rolling. **Transfer Students Accepted?** Yes.
Required Admission Factors: Transcript.
Recommended Admission Factors: GRE subject exam(s) in biology, chemistry.
Other Admission Factors: In general, minimum undergraduate GPA of 3.0 required.
Program-Specific Admission Factors: Each program has varying requirements. Applicants should consult the CSU online graduate catalogue at www.csuohio.edu/gradcollege/gradbulletin/.

EMPLOYMENT INFORMATION
Placement Office Available? Yes.

COASTAL CAROLINA UNIVERSITY
Graduate Studies

Address: 755 Highway 544, PO Box 261954, Conway, SC 29526
Admissions Phone: 843-349-2026 or 800-277-7000 · **Admissions Fax:** 843-349-2127
Admissions E-mail: dwiseman@coastal.edu
Web Address: www.coastal.edu/graduate/

INSTITUTIONAL INFORMATION
Public/Private: Public. **Total Faculty:** 46. **% Faculty Female:** 63. **% Faculty Part-time:** 93. **Student/Faculty Ratio:** 13:1. **Students in Parent Institution:** 7,021.

PROGRAMS
Masters offered in: Early childhood education and teaching; elementary education and teaching; marine biology and biological oceanography; secondary education and teaching; teacher education, multiple levels; technology teacher education/industrial arts teacher education.

STUDENT INFORMATION
Total Students in Program: 1,001. **% Full-time** 4. **% Female:** 87.

RESEARCH FACILITIES
Research Facilities: Off-campus marine research lab.

EXPENSES/FINANCIAL AID
Annual Tuition: In-state $6,200/ Out-of-state $14,480. **Books and Supplies:** $840. **Loans Range From:** $500-$18,500. **% Receiving Loans:** 100.

ADMISSIONS INFORMATION
Application Fee: $45. **Regular Application Deadline:** 8/15. **Regular Notification:** Rolling. **Transfer Students Accepted?** Yes. **Transfer Policy:** Maximum 12 credit hours with a minimum grade of B may be transferred from a regionally accredited institution. **Number of Applications Received:** 49. **% of Applicants Accepted:** 84. **% Accepted Who Enrolled:** 71. **Average GPA:** 3.0.
Required Admission Factors: Essays/personal statement, letters of recommendation, transcript.
Recommended Admission Factors:
Other Admission Factors: Minimum GRE score of 800 or minimum MAT score of 35 and evidence of teacher certification required.

EMPLOYMENT INFORMATION
Placement Office Available? Yes.

COLGATE ROCHESTER CROZER DIVINITY SCHOOL
Graduate & Professional Programs

Address: 1100 South Goodman Street, Rochester, NY 14620
Admissions Phone: 1-888-937-3732 · **Admissions Fax:** 1-585-271-8013
Admissions E-mail: admissions@crcds.edu · **Web Address:** www.crcds.edu

INSTITUTIONAL INFORMATION
Public/Private: Private (nonprofit). **Evening Classes Available?** Yes. **Total Faculty:** 19. **% Faculty Female:** 37. **% Faculty Part-time:** 53. **Student/Faculty Ratio:** 7:1. **Students in Parent Institution:** 134

PROGRAMS
Masters offered in: Divinity/ministry (BD, MDiv), theological studies and religious vocations. **Doctorate offered in:** Divinity/ministry (BD, MDiv). **First Professional degree offered in:** Divinity/ministry (BD, MDiv).

STUDENT INFORMATION
Total Students in Program: 134. **% Full-time** 100.

EXPENSES/FINANCIAL AID
Annual Tuition: $9,160. **Fees:** $205. **Books and Supplies:** $1,000. **Grants Range From:** $500-$9,160. **Loans Range From:** $2,000-$18,500. **% Receiving Financial Aid:** 70.6. **% Receiving Scholarships/Grants:** 53. **% Receiving Loans:** 41. **% Receiving Other Aid (Student Support from Denominations):** 23.5. **Types of Aid Available:** Grants, scholarships.

ADMISSIONS INFORMATION
Application Fee: $35. **Regular Application Deadline:** 8/31. **Regular Notification:** Rolling. **Transfer Students Accepted?** Yes. **Transfer Policy:** Letter of good standing from academic dean required of transfer applicants. **Number of Applications Received:** 60. **% of Applicants Accepted:** 77. **% Accepted Who Enrolled:** 50. **Average GPA:** 3.1.
Required Admission Factors: Essays/personal statement, letters of recommendation, transcript.
Program-Specific Admission Factors: Minimum 2.75 GPA required of M.Div. program applicants, minimum 3.0 GPA required of MA and DMin program applicants.

EMPLOYMENT INFORMATION
% Employed Within 6 Months: 80. **Rate of placement:** 90%. **Average starting salary:** $30,000.

COLLEGE FOR FINANCIAL PLANNING
Graduate Program

Address: 6161 South Syracuse Way, Greenwood Village, CO 80111-4707
Admissions Phone: 303-220-1200 · **Admissions Fax:** 303-220-4149
Admissions E-mail: Julianna.sanchez@apollogrp.edu · **Web Address:** www.fp.edu

INSTITUTIONAL INFORMATION

Public/Private: Private (proprietary). **Evening Classes Available?** Yes. **Total Faculty:** 15. **% Faculty Female:** 20. **% Faculty Part-time:** 53. **Students in Parent Institution:** 12,500.

PROGRAMS

Masters offered in: Accounting and finance; family resources management studies; finance, financial planning, and services; investments and securities.

STUDENT INFORMATION

Total Students in Program: 1,200 **% Female:** 20.

EXPENSES/FINANCIAL AID

Books and Supplies: $750.

ADMISSIONS INFORMATION

Application Fee: $75. **Regular Application Deadline:** 1/1. **Regular Notification:** Rolling. **Transfer Students Accepted?** Yes. **Transfer Policy:** The program is offered in the distance mode (no residency requirment or campus). Transfer of graduate level courses related to finance, financial planning, and financial analysis. **Number of Applications Received:** 250. **% of Applicants Accepted:** 90. **% Accepted Who Enrolled:** 93. **Average GPA:** 3.1. **Required Admission Factors:** Essays/personal statement, transcript. **Other Admission Factors:** Bachelor's degree from a regionally accredited institution of higher education is required. A minimum undergraduate GPA of 2.5 is recommended. **Program-Specific Admission Factors:** Consideration is given for work experience, prior education, licenses/designations in areas related to financial planning, financial analysis, and finance. Communication skills is also an important consideration.

EMPLOYMENT INFORMATION

% of master's grads employed in their field upon graduation: 100.

COLLEGE MISERICORDIA
Graduate Programs

Address: 301 Lake Street, Dallas, PA 18612
Admissions Phone: 570-674-6451 · **Admissions Fax:** 570-674-6232
Admissions E-mail: toneill@misericordia.edu · **Web Address:** www.misericordia.edu

INSTITUTIONAL INFORMATION

Public/Private: Private (nonprofit). **Evening Classes Available?** Yes. **Students in Parent Institution:** 2,150.

PROGRAMS

Masters offered in: Curriculum and instruction; education, educational, instructional, and curriculum supervision; educational/instructional media design.

STUDENT INFORMATION

Total Students in Program: 153. **% Minority:** 10.

EXPENSES/FINANCIAL AID

Annual Tuition: $13,780. **Fees:** $740.

ADMISSIONS INFORMATION

Application Fee: $25. **Priority Application Deadline:** 2/28. **Regular Application Deadline:** 6/1. **Regular Notification:** Rolling. **Transfer Students Accepted?** Yes. **Transfer Policy:** 3.0 GPA. **Number of Applications Received:** 50. **% of Applicants Accepted:** 50. **% Accepted Who Enrolled:** 80. **Average GPA:** 3.2. **Required Admission Factors:** Essays/personal statement, letters of recommendation, transcript. **Other Admission Factors:** Minimum 2.8 GPA and 50 of fieldwork required.

EMPLOYMENT INFORMATION

Placement Office Available? Yes.

COLLEGE OF MOUNT SAINT VINCENT
Graduate Programs

Address: 6301 Riverdale Avenue, Riverdale, NY 10471
Admissions Phone: 718-405-3267 · **Admissions Fax:** 718-549-7945
Admissions E-mail: admissns@cmsv.edu

INSTITUTIONAL INFORMATION

Public/Private: Private (nonprofit). **Evening Classes Available?** Yes. **Students in Parent Institution:** 1,615

STUDENT INFORMATION

Total Students in Program: 256. **% Full-time** 7. **% Female:** 85.

EXPENSES/FINANCIAL AID

Annual Tuition: In-state $17,030. **Fees:** $300. **Books and Supplies:** $800.

ADMISSIONS INFORMATION

Application Fee: $50. **Regular Notification:** Rolling. **Transfer Students Accepted?** Yes. **Required Admission Factors:** Interview, letters of recommendation, transcript.

EMPLOYMENT INFORMATION

Placement Office Available? Yes.

COLLEGE OF NEW ROCHELLE
Graduate School

Address: 29 Castle Place, 206 A Chidwick Hall, New Rochelle, NY 10805
Admissions Phone: 914-654-5334 · **Admissions Fax:** 914-654-5593
Admissions E-mail: info@cnr.edu · **Web Address:** www.cnr.edu

INSTITUTIONAL INFORMATION

Public/Private: Private (nonprofit). **Evening Classes Available?** Yes.

STUDENT INFORMATION

Total Students in Program: 1,089. **% Full-time** 100.

EXPENSES/FINANCIAL AID

Annual Tuition: $11,160. **Books and Supplies:** $500. **Grants Range From:** $500-$10,000. **Loans Range From:** $1,000-$11,000. **% Receiving Financial Aid:** 100. **% Receiving Scholarships/Grants:** 5. **% Receiving Loans:** 90. **% Receiving Assistantships:** 5. **Types of Aid Available:** Graduate assistantships, loans, scholarships. **Average amount of individual fellowships per year:** $10,000

ADMISSIONS INFORMATION

Application Fee: $35. **Priority Application Deadline:** 9/6. **Regular Application Deadline:** 9/6. **Regular Notification:** Rolling. **Transfer Students Accepted?** Yes. **Number of Applications Received:** 311. **% of Applicants Accepted:** 97. **% Accepted Who Enrolled:** 83. **Required Admission Factors:** Essays/personal statement, interview, letters of recommendation, transcript. **Recommended Admission Factors:** **Other Admission Factors:** Minimum 2.7 GPA (3.0 in major) required; GRE required of communication program applicants with GPA below minimum. Biography and writing sample required. **Program-Specific Admission Factors:** Minimum 36 credit hours in art recommended of art program applicants.

EMPLOYMENT INFORMATION

Placement Office Available? Yes.

COLLEGE OF NOTRE DAME
Graduate Programs

Address: 1500 Ralston Avenue, Belmont, CA 94002
Admissions Phone: 650-508-3527 · **Admissions Fax:** 650-508-3662
Admissions E-mail: grad.admit@cnd.edu

INSTITUTIONAL INFORMATION
Public/Private: Private (nonprofit). **Evening Classes Available?** Yes. **Total Faculty:** 121. **% Faculty Female:** 70. **% Faculty Part-time:** 84. **Student/Faculty Ratio:** 14:1. **Students in Parent Institution:** 1,671

STUDENT INFORMATION
Total Students in Program: 686. **% Full-time** 33. **% Female:** 75.

EXPENSES/FINANCIAL AID
Annual Tuition: In-state $9,306. **Fees:** $90. **Books and Supplies:** $700. **Grants Range From:** $700-$13,000. **Loans Range From:** $8,500-$18,500. **% Receiving Financial Aid:** 46. **% Receiving Scholarships/Grants:** 22. **% Receiving Loans:** 75.

ADMISSIONS INFORMATION
Application Fee: $50. **Regular Notification:** Rolling. **Transfer Students Accepted?** Yes. **Number of Applications Received:** 377. **% of Applicants Accepted:** 76. **% Accepted Who Enrolled:** 89. **Average GPA:** 3.1. **Required Admission Factors:** Transcript.
Other Admission Factors: Minimum 2.5 GPA required.

EMPLOYMENT INFORMATION
% Employed Within 6 Months: 98. **% of master's grads employed in their field upon graduation:** 98.

COLLEGE OF NOTRE DAME OF MARYLAND
Graduate Studies

Address: 4701 North Charles Street, Baltimore, MD 21210
Admissions Phone: 888-GRAD-CND · **Admissions E-mail:** knikolaidis@ndm.edu

INSTITUTIONAL INFORMATION
Public/Private: Private (nonprofit). **Evening Classes Available?** Yes. **Students in Parent Institution:** 1,224.

STUDENT INFORMATION
Total Students in Program: 1,224 **% Female:** 82.

EXPENSES/FINANCIAL AID
Annual Tuition: In-state $5,346. **Fees:** $120.

ADMISSIONS INFORMATION
Application Fee: $25. **Regular Notification:** Rolling. **Transfer Students Accepted?** Yes.
Required Admission Factors: Essays/personal statement, transcript.
Other Admission Factors: Minimum 3.0 GPA required.

EMPLOYMENT INFORMATION
% Employed Within 6 Months: 90. **% of master's grads employed in their field upon graduation:** 80.

COLLEGE OF OUR LADY OF THE ELMS
Graduate Programs

Address: 291 Springfield Street, Chicopee, MA 01013
Admissions Phone: 413-598-8520 · **Admissions Fax:** 413-592-4871
Admissions E-mail: admissions@elms.edu · **Web Address:** www.elms.edu

INSTITUTIONAL INFORMATION
Public/Private: Private (nonprofit). **Evening Classes Available?** Yes. **Total Faculty:** 28. **% Faculty Female:** 71. **% Faculty Part-time:** 39. **Student/Faculty Ratio:** 11:1. **Students in Parent Institution:** 998.

PROGRAMS
Masters offered in: Bilingual and multilingual education; biology teacher education; chemistry teacher education; education leadership and administration; education; elementary and middle school administration/principalship; elementary education and teaching; English/language arts teacher education; foreign language teacher education; history teacher education; junior high/intermediate/middle school education and teaching; liberal arts and sciences/liberal studies; mathematics teacher education; reading teacher education; secondary education and teaching; secondary school administration/principalship; Spanish language teacher education; special education; teacher education, multiple levels; teaching English as a second or foreign language/ESL language instructor; theology/theological studies.

STUDENT INFORMATION
Total Students in Program: 159. **% Full-time** 6. **% Female:** 92.

EXPENSES/FINANCIAL AID
Annual Tuition: $8,820. **Fees:** $40. **Books and Supplies:** $750. **Grants Range From:** $450-$800. **Loans Range From:** $200-$8,500. **% Receiving Financial Aid:** 20. **% Receiving Scholarships/Grants:** 4. **% Receiving Loans:** 97. **% Receiving Assistantships:** 2. **Types of Aid Available:** Loans. **Number of Teaching/Research Assistantships Granted Each Year:** 3. **Average Salary Stipend:** $1,170.

ADMISSIONS INFORMATION
Application Fee: $30. **Regular Application Deadline:** 7/1. **Regular Notification:** Rolling. **Transfer Students Accepted?** Yes. **Number of Applications Received:** 42. **% of Applicants Accepted:** 74. **% Accepted Who Enrolled:** 100. **Average GPA:** 3.14.
Required Admission Factors: Essays/personal statement, letters of recommendation, transcript.
Other Admission Factors: Minimum 3.0 GPA required.

EMPLOYMENT INFORMATION
% Employed Within 6 Months: 35. **Rate of placement:** 90%. **Average starting salary:** $25,000.

COLLEGE OF SAINT ELIZABETH
Graduate Programs

Address: 2 Convent Road, Morristown, NJ 07960-6989
Admissions Phone: 973-290-4600 · **Admissions Fax:** 973-290-4676
Admissions E-mail: mszarek@cse.edu · **Web Address:** www.cse.edu

INSTITUTIONAL INFORMATION
Public/Private: Private (nonprofit). **Evening Classes Available?** Yes.

STUDENT INFORMATION
Total Students in Program: 459. **% Female:** 90.

EXPENSES/FINANCIAL AID
Annual Tuition: In-state $6,930. **Books and Supplies:** $600. **Grants Range From:** $1,000-$4,000. **Loans Range From:** $1,074-$18,467. **% Receiving Loans:** 98. **% Receiving Assistantships:** 2. **Average student debt, upon graduation:** $11,364. **Number of Teaching/Research Assistantships Granted Each Year:** 1.

ADMISSIONS INFORMATION
Application Fee: $35. **Regular Application Deadline:** 8/15. **Regular Notification:** Rolling. **Transfer Students Accepted?** Yes. **Number of Applications Received:** 358. **% of Applicants Accepted:** 66. **% Accepted Who Enrolled:** 89.

Required Admission Factors: Essays/personal statement, letters of recommendation, transcript.

EMPLOYMENT INFORMATION

Placement Office Available? Yes. **% of master's grads employed in their field upon graduation:** 42.

THE COLLEGE OF SAINT ROSE
School of Arts & Humanities

Address: 432 Western Avenue, Albany, NY 12203
Admissions Phone: 518-454-5144 · **Admissions Fax:** 518-458-5479
Admissions E-mail: ace@strose.edu · **Website:** www.strose.edu/Future_Students/Graduate_Admission/graduate_programs.asp

INSTITUTIONAL INFORMATION

Public/private: Private (nonprofit). **Evening Classes Available?** Yes. **Student/faculty Ratio:** 2:1. **Students in Parent Institution:** 4,231.

PROGRAMS

Masters offered in: Art teacher education; communications and media studies; English language and literature; history; jazz/jazz studies; music pedagogy; music teacher education; music/music and performing arts studies; piano and organ; political science and government.

STUDENT INFORMATION

Total Students in Program: 1,505. **% Full-time:** 18. **% Female:** 74.

RESEARCH FACILITIES

Research Facilities: Winkler Speech-Language and Hearing Center.

EXPENSES/FINANCIAL AID

Annual Tuition: In-state $9,192. **Fees:** $150. **Books and Supplies:** $1,000. **Grants Range From:** $5,000. **Loans Range From:** $18,500. **% Receiving Financial Aid:** 84. **% Receiving Scholarships/Grants:** 9. **% Receiving Loans:** 80. **% Receiving Assistantships:** 10. **Types of Aid Available:** 1. **Number of Teaching/Research Assistantships Granted Each Year:** 10. **Average Salary Stipend:** $1,537.

ADMISSIONS INFORMATION

Application Fee: $35. **Priority Application Deadline:** 6/30. **Regular Application Deadline:** 6/30. **Regular Notification:** Rolling. **Transfer Students Accepted?** Yes. **Transfer Policy:** Maximum one-third of total credit hours required may be transferred. **Number of Applications Received:** 47. **Average GPA:** 3.0.

Required Admission Factors: Essays/personal statement, letters of recommendation, transcript.

Other Admission Factors: Minimum 3.0 GPA and writing sample required.

Program-Specific Admission Factors: Portfolio required for art education.

EMPLOYMENT INFORMATION

Placement Office Available? Yes. **Rate of placement:** 84%. **Average starting salary:** $28,000.

THE COLLEGE OF SAINT ROSE
School of Math & Science

Address: 432 Western Avenue, Albany, NY 12203
Admissions Phone: 518-454-5143 · **Admissions Fax:** 518-458-5479
Admissions E-mail: ace@mail.strose.edu

INSTITUTIONAL INFORMATION

Public/private: Private (nonprofit). **Evening Classes Available?** Yes. **Student/faculty Ratio:** 4:1. **Students in Parent Institution:** 4,231.

STUDENT INFORMATION

Total Students in Program: 1,505. **% Full-time:** 18. **% Female:** 74.

RESEARCH FACILITIES

Research Facilities: Winkler Speech-Language and Hearing Center.

EXPENSES/FINANCIAL AID

Annual Tuition: In-state $9,192. **Fees:** $150. **Books and Supplies:** $1,000. **Grants Range From:** $5,000. **Loans Range From:** $18,500. **% Receiving Financial Aid:** 84. **% Receiving Scholarships/Grants:** 9. **% Receiving Loans:** 80. **% Receiving Assistantships:** 10. **Types of Aid Available:** 1. **Average Salary Stipend:** $1,537.

ADMISSIONS INFORMATION

Application Fee: $30. **Regular Notification:** Rolling. **Transfer Students Accepted?** Yes. **Transfer Policy:** Maximum one-third of total credit hours may be transferred. **Number of Applications Received:** 22. **% of Applicants Accepted:** 100. **% Accepted Who Enrolled:** 91. **Average GPA:** 3.0. **Required Admission Factors:** Essays/personal statement, letters of recommendation, transcript.

Other Admission Factors: Minimum 3.0 GPA, 3 courses in undergraduate math, and courses in introduction to C++, data structure in C++, and database management systems required.

EMPLOYMENT INFORMATION

Placement Office Available? Yes. **Rate of placement:** 84%.

COLLEGE OF SANTA FE
Graduate Programs

Address: 1600 St. Michael's Drive, Santa Fe, NM 87505
Admissions Phone: 505-473-6211 · **Admissions Fax:** 505-473-6504

INSTITUTIONAL INFORMATION

Evening Classes Available? Yes. **Total Faculty:** 14. **Students in Parent Institution:** 1,667.

STUDENT INFORMATION

Total Students in Program: 264. **% Full-time** 17. **% Female:** 30.

EXPENSES/FINANCIAL AID

Annual Tuition: In-state $4,266. **Fees:** $10. **Books and Supplies:** $400. **Grants Range From:** $500-$1,000. **Loans Range From:** $8,500-$10,500. **% Receiving Scholarships/Grants:** 19. **% Receiving Loans:** 83.

ADMISSIONS INFORMATION

Application Fee: $25. **Regular Notification:** Rolling. **Transfer Students Accepted?** Yes. **Transfer Policy:** Coursework no more than 5 years old, minimum grade average of B, and requests for transfer. **Number of Applications Received:** 34. **% of Applicants Accepted:** 91. **Average GPA:** 3.4.

Required Admission Factors: Interview, letters of recommendation, transcript.

Recommended Admission Factors:

Other Admission Factors: Minimum 3.0 GPA recommended, two letters of recommendation required.

EMPLOYMENT INFORMATION

Placement Office Available? Yes.

THE COLLEGE OF ST. CATHERINE
Graduate Programs

Address: 2004 Randolph Avenue, St. Paul, MN 55105
Admissions Phone: 651-690-6933 · **Admissions Fax:** 651-690-6024
Admissions E-mail: stkate@stkate.edu

INSTITUTIONAL INFORMATION

Public/private: Private (nonprofit). **Evening Classes Available?** Yes. **Student/faculty Ratio:** 9:1. **Students in Parent Institution:** 3,443.

STUDENT INFORMATION
Total Students in Program: 898. **% Full-time:** 33. **% Female:** 90.

EXPENSES/FINANCIAL AID
Room & Board: $5,758. **Fees:** $60. **Books and Supplies:** $300. **Grants Range From:** $100-$10,300. **Loans Range From:** $505-$28,161. **% Receiving Financial Aid:** 63.

ADMISSIONS INFORMATION
Application Fee: $25. **Transfer Students Accepted?** No. **Number of Applications Received:** 524. **% of Applicants Accepted:** 79. **% Accepted Who Enrolled:** 71.
Required Admission Factors: GRE, letters of recommendation, transcript. **Other Admission Factors:** Minimum 3.0 GPA required for most programs. **Program-Specific Admission Factors:** GRE or MAT required of MA organizational leadership program applicants; GRE required of master of library/information sciences program applicants if GPA is less than 3.0. Three prerequisite courses (statistics, human biology, lifespan development psychology) and essay required of master of social work.

COLLEGE OF ST. JOSEPH
Graduate Programs

Address: 71 Clement Road, Rutland, VT 05701
Admissions Phone: 877-270-9998 · **Admissions Fax:** 802-773-5900
Admissions E-mail: pryan@csj.edu · **Web Address:** www.csj.edu

INSTITUTIONAL INFORMATION
Public/Private: Private (nonprofit). **Evening Classes Available?** Yes. **Total Faculty:** 30. **% Faculty Female:** 37. **% Faculty Part-time:** 100. **Student/Faculty Ratio:** 12:1. **Students in Parent Institution:** 486

PROGRAMS
Masters offered in: Business administration/management, clinical psychology, community psychology, counseling psychology, counselor education/school counseling and guidance services, education, elementary education and teaching, English/language arts teacher education, reading teacher education, secondary education and teaching, social studies teacher education, special education. **First Professional degree offered in:** Clinical psychology, counseling psychology, counselor education/school counseling and guidance services, elementary education and teaching, English/language arts teacher education, secondary education and teaching, social studies teacher education.

STUDENT INFORMATION
Total Students in Program: 219. **% Full-time** 24. **% Female:** 71.

EXPENSES/FINANCIAL AID
Annual Tuition: $9,750. **Fees:** $100. **Books and Supplies:** $700. **Grants:** $4,875. **Loans Range From:** $2,500-$18,500. **% Receiving Financial Aid:** 56. **% Receiving Loans:** 100. **Types of Aid Available:** Graduate assistantships, loans. **Assistantship Compensation Includes:** Partial tuition remission.

ADMISSIONS INFORMATION
Application Fee: $35. **Regular Application Deadline:** 9/5. **Regular Notification:** Rolling. **Transfer Students Accepted?** Yes. **Number of Applications Received:** 92. **% of Applicants Accepted:** 89. **% Accepted Who Enrolled:** 78. **Average GPA:** 3.1.
Required Admission Factors: Letters of recommendation, transcript.

EMPLOYMENT INFORMATION
% Employed Within 6 Months: 85. **Rate of placement:** 90%. **Average starting salary:** $28,000.

THE COLLEGE OF ST. SCHOLASTICA
Graduate Studies

Address: 1200 Kenwood Avenue, Duluth, MN 55811
Admissions Phone: 218-723-6285 · **Admissions Fax:** 218-733-2275
Admissions E-mail: gradstudies@css.edu · **Website:** http://grad.css.edu

INSTITUTIONAL INFORMATION
Public/private: Private (nonprofit). **Evening Classes Available?** Yes. **Total Faculty:** 121. **% Faculty Female:** 51. **% Faculty Part-time:** 58. **Students in Parent Institution:** 2,334.

PROGRAMS
Masters offered in: Adult health nurse, nursing; business administration and management; computer and information sciences; curriculum and instruction; educational/instructional media design; family practice nurse/nurse practitioner; health information/medical records administration/administrator; kinesiology and exercise science; nursing administration (MSN, MS, PhD); nursing clinical specialist; occupational therapy/therapist; psychiatric/mental health nurse/nursing. **First Professional degree offered in:** Physical therapy/therapist.

STUDENT INFORMATION
Total Students in Program: 571. **% Full-time:** 61. **% Female:** 76. **% Minority:** 6. **% International:** 1.

RESEARCH FACILITIES
Research Facilities: On-campus nursing home and preschool.

EXPENSES/FINANCIAL AID
Annual Tuition: $11,664. **Books and Supplies:** $800. **Grants Range From:** $200-$16,088. **Loans Range From:** $925-$37,981. **% Receiving Financial Aid:** 55. **% Receiving Scholarships/Grants:** 19. **% Receiving Loans:** 86. **% Receiving Assistantships:** 4. **Types of Aid Available:** Graduate assistantships, grants, institutional work-study, loans, scholarships, institutional discounts. **Number of Teaching/Research Assistantships Granted Each Year:** 12. **Assistantship Compensation Includes:** Salary/stipend. **Average Salary Stipend:** $1,742.

ADMISSIONS INFORMATION
Application Fee: $50. **Regular Application Deadline:** 8/1. **Regular Notification:** Rolling. **Transfer Students Accepted?** Yes. **Transfer Policy:** Need to have earned course grade that is 3.0 or above on 4.0 scale, submit course syllabus or other descriptive information. **Number of Applications Received:** 385. **% of Applicants Accepted:** 91. **% Accepted Who Enrolled:** 76. **Average GPA:** 3.3. **Average GRE Verbal:** 444. **Average GRE Quantitative:** 603. **Average GRE Analytical Writing:** 4.3.
Required Admission Factors: Essays/personal statement, letters of recommendation, transcript.
Other Admission Factors: Work experience required for some.

EMPLOYMENT INFORMATION
Placement Office Available? Yes.

THE COLLEGE OF WILLIAM & MARY IN VIRGINIA
School of Marine Science

Address: PO Box 8795, Williamsburg, VA 23187-8795
Admissions Phone: 804-684-7105 or 804-864-7106
Admissions E-mail: newman@vims.edu

INSTITUTIONAL INFORMATION
Public/private: Public. **Student/faculty Ratio:** 2:1. **Students in Parent Institution:** 7,530.

STUDENT INFORMATION
Total Students in Program: 1,424. **% Full-time:** 65. **% Female:** 53.

RESEARCH FACILITIES

Research Facilities: Applied Research Center, Virginia Institute of Marine Science, Omohundro Institute of Early American History and Culture.

EXPENSES/FINANCIAL AID

Annual Tuition: In-state $5,740/Out-of-state $17,276. **Books and Supplies:** $1,000. **Grants Range From:** $4,000-$15,000. **Loans Range From:** $200-$30,000. **% Receiving Scholarships/Grants:** 48. **% Receiving Loans:** 97. **Number of Fellowships Granted Each Year:** 5. **Average amount of individual fellowships per year:** $14,900. **Number of Teaching/Research Assistantships Granted Each Year:** 14. **Average Salary Stipend:** $14,900.

ADMISSIONS INFORMATION

Application Fee: $30. **Transfer Students Accepted?** No. **Number of Applications Received:** 141. **% of Applicants Accepted:** 34. **% Accepted Who Enrolled:** 54. **Average GPA:** 3.38. **Average GRE Verbal:** 570. **Average GRE Quantitative:** 678. **Average GRE Analytical:** 669.

Required Admission Factors: Essays/personal statement, GRE, letters of recommendation, transcript.

EMPLOYMENT INFORMATION

Placement Office Available? Yes. **% of master's/doctoral grads employed in their field upon graduation:** 85/92.

THE COLLEGE OF WILLIAM & MARY IN VIRGINIA
Faculty of Arts & Sciences

Address: PO Box 8795, Williamsburg, VA 23187-8795
Admissions Phone: 757-221-2467 · **Admissions Fax:** 757-221-4874
Admissions E-mail: apgrad@wm.edu · **Website:** www.wm.edu/graduate

INSTITUTIONAL INFORMATION

Public/private: Public. **Total Faculty:** 729. **% Faculty Female:** 36. **% Faculty Part-time:** 23. **Student/faculty Ratio:** 3:1. **Students in Parent Institution:** 7,749.

PROGRAMS

Masters offered in: Anthropology, chemistry, computer and information sciences, history, physical sciences, physics, psychology, social sciences. **Doctorate offered in:** Anthropology, clinical psychology, computer and information sciences, history, physical sciences, physics.

STUDENT INFORMATION

Total Students in Program: 2,001. **% Full-time:** 76. **% Female:** 49. **% Minority:** 11. **% International:** 10.

RESEARCH FACILITIES

Research Facilities: Applied Research Center, Virginia Institute of Marine Science, Omohundro Institute of Early American History and Culture, Center for Archaeological Research, The William and Mary Archaeological Conservation Center.

EXPENSES/FINANCIAL AID

Annual Tuition: In-state $6,138/Out-of-state $17,972. **Room & Board:** $1,991. **Books and Supplies:** $1,000. **Grants Range From:** $4,000-$15,000. **Loans Range From:** $200-$30,000. **% Receiving Scholarships/Grants:** 48. **% Receiving Loans:** 97. **Types of Aid Available:** Fellowships, graduate assistantships, grants, institutional work-study, loans, scholarships. **Average student debt, upon graduation:** $17,530. **Number of Fellowships Granted Each Year:** 9. **Average amount of individual fellowships per year:** 12,000. **Average Salary Stipend:** $8,500.

ADMISSIONS INFORMATION

Application Fee: $30. **Regular Application Deadline:** 4/15. **Regular Notification:** Rolling. **Transfer Students Accepted?** Yes. **Number of Applications Received:** 858. **% of Applicants Accepted:** 31. **% Accepted Who Enrolled:** 48. **Average GPA:** 3.47. **Average GRE Verbal:** 566. **Average GRE Quantitative:** 649. **Average GRE Analytical:** 657.

Required Admission Factors: GRE, letters of recommendation, transcript. **Other Admission Factors:** Minimum 2.5 GPA required.

EMPLOYMENT INFORMATION

Placement Office Available? Yes.

COLLEGE OF THE ATLANTIC
Graduate Program

Address: 105 Eden Street, Bar Harbor, ME 04609
Admissions Phone: 800-528-0025 · **Admissions Fax:** 207-288-4126
Admissions E-mail: jga@coa.edu · **Web Address:** www.coa.edu

INSTITUTIONAL INFORMATION

Public/Private: Private (nonprofit). **Student/Faculty Ratio:** 10:1. **Students in Parent Institution:** 285.

PROGRAMS

Masters offered in: Biology/biological sciences; conservation biology; ecology, evolution, and systematics; ecology; environmental science; evolutionary biology; humanities/humanistic studies; liberal arts and sciences studies and humanities; marine biology and biological oceanography; multi/interdisciplinary studies; natural resource economics; natural resources management and policy; natural resources/conservation; peace studies and conflict resolution; philosophy; psychology.

STUDENT INFORMATION

Total Students in Program: 10. **% Full-time** 110. **% Female:** 80.

RESEARCH FACILITIES

Research Facilities: Allied Whale, Center for Applied Human Ecology, Island Research Institute, GIS Lab.

EXPENSES/FINANCIAL AID

Annual Tuition: $16,950. **Fees:** $171. **Books and Supplies:** $450.

ADMISSIONS INFORMATION

Application Fee: $45. **Priority Application Deadline:** 5/15. **Regular Application Deadline:** 5/31. **Regular Notification:** Rolling. **Transfer Students Accepted?** Yes. **Number of Applications Received:** 13. **% of Applicants Accepted:** 69. **% Accepted Who Enrolled:** 56.

Required Admission Factors: Essays/personal statement, letters of recommendation, transcript.

Recommended Admission Factors: Interview.

Program-Specific Admission Factors: Strong emphasis placed on letters of reference. A good match between applicant and at least 2 faculty members is essential.

COLORADO CHRISTIAN UNIVERSITY
Graduate Programs

Address: 8787 West Alameda Avenue, Lakewood, CO 80226-7499
Admissions Phone: 303-963-3150 · **Admissions Fax:** 303-963-3141
Admissions E-mail: smountjoy@ccu.edu · **Web Address:** www.ccu.edu

INSTITUTIONAL INFORMATION

Public/Private: Private (nonprofit). **Total Faculty:** 16. **% Faculty Female:** 50. **% Faculty Part-time:** 100. **Student/Faculty Ratio:** 16:1. **Students in Parent Institution:** 2,082.

PROGRAMS

Masters offered in: Curriculum and instruction. **First Professional degree offered in:** Education.

EXPENSES/FINANCIAL AID

Annual Tuition: $365. **Fees:** $300. **Books and Supplies:** $900. **Grants Range From:** $200-$15,500. **Loans Range From:** $200-$15,500. **% Receiving Financial Aid: 70. % Receiving Loans: 100. Types of Aid Available: Loans.

ADMISSIONS INFORMATION

Application Fee: $50. Priority Application Deadline: 6/15. Regular Application Deadline: 8/15. Regular Notification: Rolling. Transfer Students Accepted? No. Transfer Policy: Maximum 3 credit hours with minimum grade of B in education courses, from an accredited university. Number of Applications Received: 35. % of Applicants Accepted: 80. % Accepted Who Enrolled: 100. Average GPA: 3.2.

Required Admission Factors: Essays/personal statement, interview, letters of recommendation, transcript.

Other Admission Factors: Minimum 2.75 GPA required.

EMPLOYMENT INFORMATION

% Employed Within 6 Months: 92. % of master's grads employed in their field upon graduation: 90. Rate of placement: 90%. Average starting salary: $35,000.

COLORADO SCHOOL OF MINES
Graduate School

Address: 1500 Illinois Street, Golden, CO 80401-9952
Admissions Phone: 303-273-3247 · Admissions Fax: 303-273-3244
Admissions E-mail: grad-school@mines.edu
Web Address: www.mines.edu/Admiss/grad

INSTITUTIONAL INFORMATION

Public/Private: Public. Total Faculty: 210. % Faculty Female: 16. Student/Faculty Ratio: 3:1. Students in Parent Institution: 3,581.

PROGRAMS

Masters offered in: Applied mathematics, chemical engineering, chemistry, computer and information sciences, environmental science, environmental health engineering, geochemistry, geological and earth sciences/geosciences, geological/geophysical engineering, geophysics and seismology, management sciences and quantitative methods, materials engineering, materials science, mathematics and computer science, metallurgical engineering, mining and mineral engineering, multi/interdisciplinary studies, natural resource economics, operations research, petroleum engineering, physics, systems engineering.

Doctorate offered in: Applied mathematics, chemical engineering, chemistry, computer and information sciences, environmental science, environmental/environmental health engineering, geochemistry, geological and earth sciences/geosciences, geophysics and seismology, management sciences and quantitative methods, materials engineering, materials science, mathematics and computer science, metallurgical engineering, mining and mineral engineering, multi/interdisciplinary studies, natural resource economics, operations research, petroleum engineering, physics, systems engineering.

STUDENT INFORMATION

Total Students in Program: 738. % Full-time 77. % Female: 28. % Minority: 8. % International: 28.

RESEARCH FACILITIES

Research Facilities: Over 25 research centers and institutes, including Colorado Energy Research Institute, ChevronTexaco Center of Research Excellence in Subsurface Geology, Center for Automation, Robotics, and Distributed Intelligence.

EXPENSES/FINANCIAL AID

Annual Tuition: In-state $6,336. / Out-of-state $19,240. Room & Board (on/off campus): $5,625/$6,750. Fees: $746. Books and Supplies: $1,200. Grants Range From: $500-$20,000. Loans Range From: $200-$18,500. % Receiving Financial Aid: 80. % Receiving Loans: 28.7. % Receiving Assistantships: 61. Types of Aid Available: Fellowships, graduate assistantships, loans, scholarships. Number of Fellowships Granted Each Year: 60. Number of Teaching/Research Assistantships Granted Each Year: 369 Assis-

tantship Compensation Includes: Full tuition remission, salary/stipend. Average Salary Stipend: $1,250.

ADMISSIONS INFORMATION

Application Fee: $50. Priority Application Deadline: 1/1. Regular Application Deadline: 7/1. Regular Notification: Rolling. Transfer Students Accepted? Yes. Transfer Policy: Same as for all other applicants. Number of Applications Received: 714. % of Applicants Accepted: 66. % Accepted Who Enrolled: 40. Average GPA: 3.3. Average GRE Verbal: 480. Average GRE Quantitative: 710. Average GRE Analytical: 660. Average GRE Analytical Writing: 4.5.

Required Admission Factors: Essays/personal statement, GRE, letters of recommendation, transcript.

Other Admission Factors: Minimum GPA of 3.0; minimum TOEFL of 550 PBT or 213 CBT; Resume and statement of goals required.

Program-Specific Admission Factors:

EMPLOYMENT INFORMATION

Placement Office Available? Yes. % Employed Within 6 Months: 94. % of master's/doctoral grads employed in their field upon graduation: 81/86. Rate of placement: 82%. Average starting salary: $56,500.

COLORADO STATE UNIVERSITY
College of Applied Human Sciences

Address: 204 Gibbons Building, Fort Collins, CO 80523
Admissions Phone: 970-491-5236 · Admissions Fax: 970-491-7859
Admissions E-mail: gschool@grad.colostate.edu
Web Address: www.cahs.colostate.edu

INSTITUTIONAL INFORMATION

Public/Private: Public. Total Faculty: 126. % Faculty Female: 49. % Faculty Part-time: 11. Students in Parent Institution: 25,042.

STUDENT INFORMATION

Total Students in Program: 856. % Full-time 59. % Female: 71. % Minority: 14. % International: 5.

EXPENSES/FINANCIAL AID

Annual Tuition: In-state $3,350 / Out-of-state $13,955. Room & Board: $6,045. Fees: $806. Books and Supplies: $205. Types of Aid Available: Fellowships, graduate assistantships, grants, institutional work-study, loans, scholarships. Number of Fellowships Granted Each Year: 39. Number of Teaching/Research Assistantships Granted Each Year: 131. Assistantship Compensation Includes: Full tuition remission, partial tuition remission, salary/stipend. Average Salary Stipend: $11,700.

ADMISSIONS INFORMATION

Application Fee: $50. Priority Application Deadline: 1/1. Regular Notification: Rolling. Transfer Students Accepted? Yes. Transfer Policy: Maximum 10 credit hours may be transferred for doctoral programs; maximum 6 credit hours may be transferred for masters programs. Number of Applications Received: 1,004. % of Applicants Accepted: 51. % Accepted Who Enrolled: 64.

Required Admission Factors: Letters of recommendation, transcript.

Other Admission Factors: Minimum 3.0 GPA required.

Program-Specific Admission Factors: Students should contact department for prerequisite requirements.

COLORADO STATE UNIVERSITY
College of Liberal Arts

Address: C138 Clark Building, Fort Collins, CO 80523
Admissions Phone: 970-491-5421 · **Admissions Fax:** 970-491-0528
Admissions E-mail: gschool@grad.colostate.edu
Web Address: www.colostate.edu/colleges/libarts

INSTITUTIONAL INFORMATION
Public/Private: Public. **Total Faculty:** 281. **% Faculty Female:** 36. **% Faculty Part-time:** 19. **Students in Parent Institution:** 25,042.

STUDENT INFORMATION
Total Students in Program: 566. **% Full-time** 58. **% Female:** 57. **% Minority:** 8. **% International:** 12.

EXPENSES/FINANCIAL AID
Annual Tuition: In-state $3,350 / Out-of-state $13,955. **Room & Board:** $6,045. **Fees:** $806. **Books and Supplies:** $900. **Types of Aid Available:** Fellowships, graduate assistantships, grants, institutional work-study, loans, scholarships. **Number of Fellowships Granted Each Year:** 28. **Number of Teaching/Research Assistantships Granted Each Year:** 173. **Assistantship Compensation Includes:** Full tuition remission, partial tuition remission, salary/stipend. **Average Salary Stipend:** $11,800.

ADMISSIONS INFORMATION
Application Fee: $50. **Regular Notification:** Rolling. **Transfer Students Accepted?** Yes. **Transfer Policy:** Maximum 10 credit hours may be transferred for doctoral programs; maximum 6 credit hours may be transferred for master's programs. **Number of Applications Received:** 766. **% of Applicants Accepted:** 49. **% Accepted Who Enrolled:** 48.
Required Admission Factors: Letters of recommendation, transcript.
Other Admission Factors: Minimum 3.0 GPA required of applicants to most programs.
Program-Specific Admission Factors: Requirements vary by department.

COLORADO STATE UNIVERSITY
College of Natural Resources

Address: 101 Natural Resources Building, Fort Collins, CO 80523
Admissions Phone: 970-491-6675 · **Admissions Fax:** 970-491-0279
Admissions E-mail: gschool@grad.colostate.edu · **Web Address:** www.cnr.colostate.edu

INSTITUTIONAL INFORMATION
Public/Private: Public. **Total Faculty:** 62. **% Faculty Female:** 19. **% Faculty Part-time:** 3. **Students in Parent Institution:** 25,042.

STUDENT INFORMATION
Total Students in Program: 154. **% Full-time** 70. **% Female:** 56. **% Minority:** 8. **% International:** 13.

EXPENSES/FINANCIAL AID
Annual Tuition: In-state $3,350. / Out-of-state $13,955. **Room & Board:** $6,045. **Fees:** $806. **Books and Supplies:** $900. **Types of Aid Available:** Fellowships, graduate assistantships, grants, institutional work-study, loans, scholarships. **Number of Fellowships Granted Each Year:** 11. **Number of Teaching/Research Assistantships Granted Each Year:** 95. **Assistantship Compensation Includes:** Full tuition remission, salary/stipend. **Average Salary Stipend:** $14,206.

ADMISSIONS INFORMATION
Application Fee: $50. **Regular Notification:** Rolling. **Transfer Students Accepted?** Yes. **Number of Applications Received:** 281. **% of Applicants Accepted:** 37. **% Accepted Who Enrolled:** 51.
Required Admission Factors: Essays/personal statement, letters of recommendation, transcript.

Recommended Admission Factors:
Other Admission Factors: Minimum 3.0 GPA required.
Program-Specific Admission Factors: Applicants to fishery/wildlife biology program must hold bachelor's in same or related discipline.

COLORADO STATE UNIVERSITY
College of Natural Sciences

Address: Fort Collins, CO 80523
Admissions Phone: 970-491-1300 · **Admissions Fax:** 970-491-6639
Admissions E-mail: gschool@grad.colostate.edu
Web Address: www.colostate.edu/Depts/NatSci/

INSTITUTIONAL INFORMATION
Public/Private: Public. **Total Faculty:** 197. **% Faculty Female:** 16. **% Faculty Part-time:** 7. **Students in Parent Institution:** 25,042.

STUDENT INFORMATION
Total Students in Program: 593. **% Full-time** 52. **% Female:** 39. **% Minority:** 10. **% International:** 32.

EXPENSES/FINANCIAL AID
Annual Tuition: In-state $3,350 / Out-of-state $13,955. **Room & Board:** $6,045. **Fees:** $806. **Books and Supplies:** $900. **Types of Aid Available:** Fellowships, graduate assistantships, grants, institutional work-study, loans, scholarships. **Number of Fellowships Granted Each Year:** 36. **Number of Teaching/Research Assistantships Granted Each Year:** 484.

ADMISSIONS INFORMATION
Application Fee: $50. **Priority Application Deadline:** 4/15. **Regular Notification:** Rolling. **Transfer Students Accepted?** Yes. **Number of Applications Received:** 1,711. **% of Applicants Accepted:** 23. **% Accepted Who Enrolled:** 39.
Required Admission Factors: Essays/personal statement, letters of recommendation, transcript.
Other Admission Factors: Minimum 3.0 GPA required for most programs.

COLORADO STATE UNIVERSITY—PUEBLO
College of Science & Mathematics

Address: 2200 Bonforte Boulevard, Pueblo, CO 81001
Admissions Phone: 719-549-2461 · **Admissions Fax:** 719-549-2419
Admissions E-mail: joe.marshall@colostate-pueblo.edu
Web Address: www.colostate-pueblo.edu

INSTITUTIONAL INFORMATION
Public/Private: Public. **Students in Parent Institution:** 5,811.

STUDENT INFORMATION
Total Students in Program: 689. **% Full-time** 11. **% Female:** 68.

RESEARCH FACILITIES
Research Facilities: Minority Biomedical Research Support Program; Nature Center; Center for Teaching, Learning, and Research.

EXPENSES/FINANCIAL AID
Annual Tuition: In-state $1,808 / Out-of-state $8,448. **Fees:** $462. **Books and Supplies:** $500. **Grants Range From:** $500-$2,500. **Loans Range From:** $500-$18,500. **% Receiving Scholarships/Grants:** 58. **% Receiving Loans:** 79. **% Receiving Assistantships:** 7.

ADMISSIONS INFORMATION
Application Fee: $35. **Priority Application Deadline:** 8/1. **Regular Application Deadline:** 8/29. **Regular Notification:** Rolling. **Transfer Students Accepted?** Yes. **Transfer Policy:** Maximum nine credit hours with a minimum grade average of B may be transferred with the approval of program

director. **Number of Applications Received:** 9. **% of Applicants Accepted:** 33. **% Accepted Who Enrolled:** 100.
Required Admission Factors: GRE, letters of recommendation, transcript.
Other Admission Factors: Minimum GPA of 2.5

EMPLOYMENT INFORMATION
Placement Office Available? Yes.

COLUMBIA COLLEGE (MO)
Graduate Programs

Address: 1001 Rogers, Columbia, MO 65216
Admissions Phone: 573-875-7356 or 800-231-2391, ext. 7356
Admissions Fax: 573-875-7506 · **Admissions E-mail:** admissions@email.ccis.edu

INSTITUTIONAL INFORMATION
Public/Private: Private (nonprofit). **Evening Classes Available?** Yes. **Student/Faculty Ratio:** 6:1. **Students in Parent Institution:** 996

STUDENT INFORMATION
Total Students in Program: 141. **% Full-time** 100. **% Female:** 67.

EXPENSES/FINANCIAL AID
Annual Tuition: $2,985. **Books and Supplies:** $400. **Grants Range From:** $448-$3,000. **Loans Range From:** $2,000-$27,598. **% Receiving Financial Aid:** 40. **% Receiving Scholarships/Grants:** 9. **% Receiving Loans:** 91.

ADMISSIONS INFORMATION
Application Fee: $25. **Regular Notification:** Rolling. **Transfer Students Accepted?** Yes. **Transfer Policy:** Maximum 9 credit hours with a minimum grade of B may be transferred. **Number of Applications Received:** 971. **% of Applicants Accepted:** 59. **% Accepted Who Enrolled:** 5. **Average GPA:** 3.29.
Required Admission Factors: Essays/personal statement, letters of recommendation, transcript.
Other Admission Factors: Minimum 3.0 GPA and related work experience required.

EMPLOYMENT INFORMATION
Placement Office Available? Yes.

COLUMBIA COLLEGE CHICAGO
(FORMERLY COLUMBIA COLLEGE)
Graduate School

Address: 600 South Michigan Avenue, Chicago, IL 60605-1996
Admissions Phone: 312-344-7260 · **Admissions Fax:** 312-344-8047
Admissions E-mail: dlapin@popmail.colum.edu

INSTITUTIONAL INFORMATION
Public/Private: Private (nonprofit). **Evening Classes Available?** Yes. **Total Faculty:** 70. **Students in Parent Institution:** 8,848.

STUDENT INFORMATION
Total Students in Program: 502. **% Full-time** 35. **% Female:** 67.

EXPENSES/FINANCIAL AID
Annual Tuition: $7,056.

ADMISSIONS INFORMATION
Application Fee: $50. **Regular Notification:** Rolling. **Transfer Students Accepted?** Yes. **Number of Applications Received:** 309. **% of Applicants Accepted:** 67. **% Accepted Who Enrolled:** 71.
Required Admission Factors: Essays/personal statement, letters of recommendation, transcript.
Other Admission Factors: Minimum 3.0 GPA required.

Program-Specific Admission Factors: Writing samples required of creative writing and journalism program applicants.

COLUMBIA INTERNATIONAL UNIVERSITY
Graduate School

Address: 7435 Monticello Road, Columbia, SC 29203
Admissions Phone: 800-777-2227,ext. 3335 · **Admissions Fax:** 803-333-0501
Admissions E-mail: pdye@ciu.edu

INSTITUTIONAL INFORMATION
Public/Private: Private (nonprofit). **Evening Classes Available?** Yes. **Students in Parent Institution:** 935.

STUDENT INFORMATION
Total Students in Program: 259. **% Full-time** 62. **% Female:** 39.

EXPENSES/FINANCIAL AID
Annual Tuition: $6,840. **Books and Supplies:** $800.

ADMISSIONS INFORMATION
Application Fee: $25. **Regular Notification:** Rolling. **Transfer Students Accepted?** Yes. **Number of Applications Received:** 27. **% of Applicants Accepted:** 37. **% Accepted Who Enrolled:** 70.
Required Admission Factors: Essays/personal statement, letters of recommendation, transcript.
Other Admission Factors: Minimum 2.7 GPA required.

EMPLOYMENT INFORMATION
Placement Office Available? Yes.

COLUMBIA THEOLOGICAL SEMINARY
Graduate Programs

Address: 701 Columbia Drive, PO Box 520, Decatur, GA 30031
Admissions Phone: 404-378-8821 · **Admissions Fax:** 404-377-9696
Admissions E-mail: adamsa@ctsnet.edu · **Web Address:** www.CTSnet.edu

INSTITUTIONAL INFORMATION
Public/Private: Private (nonprofit). **Total Faculty:** 28. **% Faculty Female:** 39. **Students in Parent Institution:** 552

PROGRAMS
Masters offered in: Divinity/ministry (BD, MDiv), theology/theological studies. **Doctorate offered in:** Divinity/ministry (BD, MDiv), theology/theological studies.

EXPENSES/FINANCIAL AID
Annual Tuition: $15,120. **Room & Board:** $6,127. **Books and Supplies:** $1,000. **Grants Range From:** $700-$18,500. **Loans Range From:** $1,000-$18,500. **% Receiving Financial Aid:** 90. **% Receiving Scholarships/Grants:** 91. **% Receiving Loans:** 24. **% Receiving Other Aid (68% institutional work-study):** 68. **Types of Aid Available:** Grants, institutional work-study, loans, scholarships. **Average student debt, upon graduation:** $11,300.

ADMISSIONS INFORMATION
Application Fee: $35. **Priority Application Deadline:** 3/15. **Regular Application Deadline:** 8/1. **Regular Notification:** Rolling. **Transfer Students Accepted?** Yes. **Number of Applications Received:** 124. **% of Applicants Accepted:** 92. **% Accepted Who Enrolled:** 78. **Average GPA:** 3.0.
Required Admission Factors: Essays/personal statement, interview, letters of recommendation, transcript.
Other Admission Factors: Minimum 2.7 GPA recommended.

Program-Specific Admission Factors: Local church endorsement for M.Div.

EMPLOYMENT INFORMATION

Placement Office Available? Yes. **% Employed Within 6 Months:** 97. **% of master's/doctoral grads employed in their field upon graduation:** 97/100. **Rate of placement:** 97%. **Average starting salary:** $25,000.

COLUMBIA UNIVERSITY
Graduate School of Journalism

Address: 109 Low Memorial Library, New York, NY 10027
Admissions Phone: 212-854-3828 · **Web Address:** www.jrn.columbia.edu

INSTITUTIONAL INFORMATION

Public/Private: Private (nonprofit). **Students in Parent Institution:** 3,200

PROGRAMS

Masters offered in: Journalism. **Doctorate offered in:** Journalism.

STUDENT INFORMATION

Total Students in Program: 3,200.

ADMISSIONS INFORMATION

Application Fee: $60. **Transfer Students Accepted?** No. **Number of Applications Received:** 1,100. **% of Applicants Accepted:** 25.
Required Admission Factors: Essays/personal statement, letters of recommendation, transcript.
Other Admission Factors: Resume, school-administerd writing test, and minimum typing speed of 35 words per minute required.

COLUMBIA UNIVERSITY
School of International & Public Affairs

Address: Admissions and Financial Aid, 420 West 118th Street, Room 408, New York, NY 10027
Admissions Phone: 212-854-6216 · **Admissions Fax:** 212-854-3010
Admissions E-mail: sipa_admission@columbia.edu
Web Address: www.sipa.columbia.edu/

INSTITUTIONAL INFORMATION

Public/Private: Private (nonprofit). **Student/Faculty Ratio:** 9:1.

PROGRAMS

Masters offered in: Public administration and services, public administration; public policy analysis.

STUDENT INFORMATION

Total Students in Program: 950. **% Full-time** 100.

EXPENSES/FINANCIAL AID

Annual Tuition: $31,066. **Fees:** $2,027. **Books and Supplies:** $1,000. **Grants Range From:** $5,000-$31,800. **Loans Range From:** $100-$50,000. **Types of Aid Available:** Fellowships, graduate assistantships, institutional work-study, loans, scholarships. **Average student debt, upon graduation:** $45,000. **Number of Fellowships Granted Each Year:** 310. **Average amount of individual fellowships per year:** $14,000. **Number of Teaching/Research Assistantships Granted Each Year:** 16 **Assistantship Compensation Includes:** Partial tuition remission, salary/stipend. **Average Salary Stipend:** $5,000.

ADMISSIONS INFORMATION

Application Fee: $75. **Priority Application Deadline:** 1/5. **Regular Application Deadline:** 2/15. **Regular Notification:** 1/4. **Transfer Students Accepted?** No. **Number of Applications Received:** 2,215. **% of Applicants Accepted:** 35. **% Accepted Who Enrolled:** 65. **Average GPA:** 3.6.

Required Admission Factors: Essays/personal statement, letters of recommendation, transcript.
Recommended Admission Factors: GRE.
Other Admission Factors: We highly recommend that applicants have taken basic microeconomics and macroeconomics classes before matriculation.

EMPLOYMENT INFORMATION

Placement Office Available? Yes. **% Employed Within 6 Months:** 98. **Rate of placement:** 98%. **Average starting salary:** $50,000.

COLUMBIA UNIVERSITY
School of Social Work

Address: 1255 Amsterdam Avenue, New York, NY 10027
Admissions Phone: 212-851-2400 · **Admissions Fax:** 212-851-2305
Admissions E-mail: cussw-admit@columbia.edu
Web Address: www.socialwork.columbia.edu

INSTITUTIONAL INFORMATION

Public/Private: Private (nonprofit).

PROGRAMS

Masters offered in: Social sciences. **Doctorate offered in:** Philosophy.

STUDENT INFORMATION

Total Students in Program: 950.

EXPENSES/FINANCIAL AID

Annual Tuition: $24,360. **Types of Aid Available:** Fellowships, graduate assistantships, grants, institutional work-study, loans, scholarships.

ADMISSIONS INFORMATION

Application Fee: $85. **Regular Application Deadline:** 3/1. **Regular Notification:** Rolling. **Transfer Students Accepted?** Yes. **Transfer Policy:** Transfer students from other U.S. accredited social work programs must have a 3.0 or better GPA in all social work coursework. 1 of 3 letters of recommendation must be a field work evaluation.
Required Admission Factors: Essays/personal statement, letters of recommendation, transcript.
Other Admission Factors: Applicants for admission into the Columbia MS degree program must have a BS or BA from accredited college or university, with a minimum GPA of 3.0, and 60 semester hours in the liberal arts (20 of which must be in the social or biological sciences).
Program-Specific Admission Factors: Letters of recommendation: 3 (required).

EMPLOYMENT INFORMATION

Placement Office Available? Yes.

COLUMBIA UNIVERSITY
School of the Arts

Address: 305 Dodge Hall, MC1808, 2960 Broadway, New York, NY 10027
Admissions Phone: 212-854-2134 · **Admissions Fax:** 212-854-1309
Admissions E-mail: admissions-arts@columbia.edu
Web Address: http://arts.columbia.edu

INSTITUTIONAL INFORMATION

Public/Private: Private (nonprofit). **Students in Parent Institution:** 764.

STUDENT INFORMATION

Total Students in Program: 764.

ADMISSIONS INFORMATION

Application Fee: $100. **Regular Notification:** Rolling. **Transfer Students Accepted?** No. **Number of Applications Received:** 2,400. **% of Applicants Accepted:** 14. **% Accepted Who Enrolled:** 64.

Required Admission Factors: Essays/personal statement, letters of recommendation, transcript.
Program-Specific Admission Factors: Portfolio in the field of application required of all applicants. Divisions have individual requirements.

COLUMBUS STATE UNIVERSITY
Graduate Programs

Address: 4225 University Avenue, Columbus, GA 31907-5645
Admissions Phone: 706-568-2035 · **Admissions Fax:** 706-568-5091
Admissions E-mail: thornton_katie@colstate.edu · **Web Address:** www.colstate.edu

INSTITUTIONAL INFORMATION
Public/Private: Public. **Evening Classes Available?** Yes. **Student/Faculty Ratio:** 19:1. **Students in Parent Institution:** 7,224.

PROGRAMS
Masters offered in: Art teacher education; biology teacher education; business administration and management; computer and information sciences; counselor education/school counseling and guidance services; criminal justice/law enforcement administration; early childhood education and teaching; education leadership and administration; educational/instructional media design; English/language arts teacher education; environmental science; French language teacher education; health and medical administrative services; history teacher education; human development, family studies, and related services; junior high/intermediate/middle school education and teaching; mathematics teacher education; music teacher education; physical education teaching and coaching; public administration; Spanish language teacher education; special education.

STUDENT INFORMATION
Total Students in Program: 924. **% Full-time** 27. **% Female:** 57.

RESEARCH FACILITIES
Research Facilities: River Center, Coca-Cola Space Center, Oxbow Environmental Research Center.

EXPENSES/FINANCIAL AID
Annual Tuition: In-state $2,106. / Out-of-state $10,230. **Room & Board:** $5,080. **Fees:** $486. **Books and Supplies:** $750.

ADMISSIONS INFORMATION
Application Fee: $25. **Priority Application Deadline:** 7/22. **Regular Application Deadline:** 7/22. **Regular Notification:** Rolling. **Transfer Students Accepted?** Yes. **Transfer Policy:** See website: www.colstate.edu.
Required Admission Factors: Transcript.
Other Admission Factors: Differs with program. See website: www.colstate.edu
Program-Specific Admission Factors: Differs with program. See website: www.colstate.edu

EMPLOYMENT INFORMATION
Placement Office Available? Yes.

CONCORDIA SEMINARY
Graduate Programs

Address: 801 Seminary Place, St. Louis, MO 63105
Admissions Phone: 314-505-7103 · **Admissions Fax:** 314-505-7003
Admissions E-mail: gradschool@csl.edu · **Web Address:** www.csl.edu/GradSchl.htm

INSTITUTIONAL INFORMATION
Public/Private: Private (nonprofit). **Evening Classes Available?** Yes. **Student/Faculty Ratio:** 15:1. **Students in Parent Institution:** 215

STUDENT INFORMATION
Total Students in Program: 215. **% Full-time** 34. **% Female:** 17.

RESEARCH FACILITIES
Research Facilities: Institute for Mission Studies, Center Reformation Research.

EXPENSES/FINANCIAL AID
Annual Tuition: In-state $9,840. **Room & Board (on/off campus):** $5,190/ $11,000. **Fees:** $155. **Books and Supplies:** $1,000. **% Receiving Financial Aid:** 100. **% Receiving Scholarships/Grants:** 100. **Number of Fellowships Granted Each Year:** 2. **Average amount of individual fellowships per year:** $10,500. **Number of Teaching/Research Assistantships Granted Each Year:** 6. **Average Salary Stipend:** $3,200.

ADMISSIONS INFORMATION
Application Fee: $50. **Regular Notification:** Rolling. **Transfer Students Accepted?** Yes. **Number of Applications Received:** 80. **% of Applicants Accepted:** 81. **% Accepted Who Enrolled:** 71.
Required Admission Factors: GRE, letters of recommendation, transcript.
Program-Specific Admission Factors: 3 letters of recommendation required for non graduates of Concordia Seminary. Minimum 3.0 GPA required of MA and STM program applicants. Minimum 3.5 GPA required of doctoral program applicants.

EMPLOYMENT INFORMATION
% of master's/doctoral grads employed in their field upon graduation: 100/100.

CONCORDIA UNIVERSITY
Faculty of Arts & Science

Address: 1455 de Maisonneuve Boulevard, W, Montreal, Quebec, H3G 1M8 Canada
Admissions Phone: 514-848-3800 · **Admissions Fax:** 514-848-2812

INSTITUTIONAL INFORMATION
Public/Private: Public. **Evening Classes Available?** Yes. **Students in Parent Institution:** 26,450.

STUDENT INFORMATION
Total Students in Program: 3,819. **% Full-time** 74. **% Female:** 49.

EXPENSES/FINANCIAL AID
Annual Tuition: In-state $1,001. / Out-of-state $4,475. **Fees:** $271. **Grants Range From:** $1,200-$19,100.

ADMISSIONS INFORMATION
Application Fee: $50. **Transfer Students Accepted?** No.
Required Admission Factors: Letters of recommendation, transcript.

EMPLOYMENT INFORMATION
Placement Office Available? Yes.

CONCORDIA UNIVERSITY
Faculty of Fine Arts

Address: 1455 de Maisonneuve Boulevard, W, Montreal, Quebec, H3G 1M8 Canada
Admissions Phone: 514-848-4612 · **Admissions Fax:** 514-848-7959

INSTITUTIONAL INFORMATION
Public/Private: Public. **Evening Classes Available?** Yes. **Students in Parent Institution:** 26,450.

STUDENT INFORMATION
Total Students in Program: 3,819. **% Full-time** 74. **% Female:** 49.

EXPENSES/FINANCIAL AID
Annual Tuition: In-state $1,001. / Out-of-state $4,475. **Fees:** $271. **Grants Range From:** $1,200-$19,100.

ADMISSIONS INFORMATION

Application Fee: $50. **Transfer Students Accepted?** No.
Required Admission Factors: Transcript.
Other Admission Factors: Portfolio required.

EMPLOYMENT INFORMATION

Placement Office Available? Yes.

CONCORDIA UNIVERSITY (ILLINOIS)
School of Graduate Studies

Address: 7400 Augusta Street, River Forest, IL 60305-1499
Admissions Phone: 408-209-4093 · **Admissions Fax:** 708-209-3454
Admissions E-mail: crfdngrad@curf.edu

INSTITUTIONAL INFORMATION

Public/Private: Private (nonprofit). **Evening Classes Available?** Yes. **Student/Faculty Ratio:** 5:1. **Students in Parent Institution:** 1,384.

STUDENT INFORMATION

Total Students in Program: 620. **% Full-time** 45. **% Female:** 83.

EXPENSES/FINANCIAL AID

Annual Tuition: In-state $8,280. **Books and Supplies:** $450.

ADMISSIONS INFORMATION

Regular Notification: Rolling. **Transfer Students Accepted?** Yes. **Transfer Policy:** Minimum B grade average in previous graduate work required of transfer applicants.
Required Admission Factors: Essays/personal statement, letters of recommendation, transcript.
Other Admission Factors: Minimum 2.25 GPA and four years of successful professional experience required.

EMPLOYMENT INFORMATION

Placement Office Available? Yes.

CONCORDIA UNIVERSITY (NEBRASKA)
Graduate Programs

Address: 800 North Columbia Avenue, Seward, NE 68434
Admissions Phone: 402-643-7377 or 800-535-5494 · **Admissions Fax:** 402-643-4073
Admissions E-mail: gradadmiss@seward.cune.edu · **Web Address:** www.cune.edu

INSTITUTIONAL INFORMATION

Public/Private: Private (nonprofit). **Evening Classes Available?** Yes. **Total Faculty:** 52. **% Faculty Female:** 31. **% Faculty Part-time:** 10. **Students in Parent Institution:** 1,355.

PROGRAMS

Masters offered in: Curriculum and instruction; educational, instructional, and curriculum supervision; elementary and middle school administration/principalship; human development and family studies; reading teacher education; secondary school administration/principalship.

STUDENT INFORMATION

Total Students in Program: 210. **% Full-time** 17.

EXPENSES/FINANCIAL AID

Annual Tuition: $3,870. **Fees:** $200. **Books and Supplies:** $500.

ADMISSIONS INFORMATION

Application Fee: $25. **Regular Application Deadline:** 12/31. **Regular Notification:** Rolling. **Transfer Students Accepted?** Yes. **Number of Applications Received:** 16. **% of Applicants Accepted:** 100. **% Accepted Who Enrolled:** 100. **Average GPA:** 3.0.
Required Admission Factors: GRE, letters of recommendation, GMAT,

---

transcript.
Other Admission Factors: Minimum 3.0 GPA required.

EMPLOYMENT INFORMATION

Placement Office Available? Yes.

CONNECTICUT COLLEGE
Graduate Programs

Address: 270 Mohegan Avenue, New London, CT 06320-4196
Admissions Phone: 860-439-2062 · **Admissions Fax:** 860-439-5416
Admissions E-mail: awwhi@conncoll.edu · **Web Address:** conncoll.edu

INSTITUTIONAL INFORMATION

Public/Private: Private (nonprofit). **Students in Parent Institution:** 2,002.

PROGRAMS

Masters offered in: Biology teacher education; botany/plant biology; chemistry teacher education; chemistry; English/language arts teacher education; foreign language teacher education; French language teacher education; German language teacher education; history teacher education; Latin teacher education; mathematics teacher education; music history, literature, and theory; music performance; music theory and composition; physics teacher education; psychology; science teacher education/general science teacher education; secondary education and teaching; social studies teacher education; Spanish language teacher education.

STUDENT INFORMATION

Total Students in Program: 12. **% Full-time** 67. **% Female:** 67.

RESEARCH FACILITIES

Research Facilities: Arboretum, GIS laboratory, observatory.

EXPENSES/FINANCIAL AID

Annual Tuition: $10,600. **Room & Board:** $9,000. **Books and Supplies:** $700. **Grants Range From:** $1,325-$2,650. **Loans Range From:** $500-$18,500. **% Receiving Loans:** 100. **Types of Aid Available:** Institutional work-study, loans, course remission.

ADMISSIONS INFORMATION

Application Fee: $55. **Regular Application Deadline:** 2/1. **Regular Notification:** Rolling. **Transfer Students Accepted?** No. **Number of Applications Received:** 25. **% of Applicants Accepted:** 72. **% Accepted Who Enrolled:** 39. **Average GPA:** 3.4. **Average GRE Verbal:** 478. **Average GRE Quantitative:** 572. **Average GRE Analytical:** 500. **Average GRE Analytical Writing:** 4.5.
Required Admission Factors: Essays/personal statement, GRE, letters of recommendation, transcript.
Recommended Admission Factors: Interview.
Program-Specific Admission Factors: Audition required of music program applicants.

EMPLOYMENT INFORMATION

Placement Office Available? Yes. **% Employed Within 6 Months:** 25. **Rate of placement:** 100%. **Average starting salary:** $25,000.

CONVERSE COLLEGE
Graduate Studies Programs

Address: 580 East Main Street, Spartanburg, SC 29302
Admissions Phone: 864-596-9082 · **Admissions Fax:** 864-596-9221
Admissions E-mail: Tom.McDaniel@Converse.edu · **Web Address:** www.converse.edu

INSTITUTIONAL INFORMATION

Public/Private: Private (nonprofit). **Evening Classes Available?** Yes. **Students in Parent Institution:** 1,628.

STUDENT INFORMATION
Total Students in Program: 858.

EXPENSES/FINANCIAL AID
Books and Supplies: $400.

ADMISSIONS INFORMATION
Application Fee: $35. Regular Notification: Rolling. Transfer Students Accepted? Yes. Number of Applications Received: 110. % of Applicants Accepted: 90. % Accepted Who Enrolled: 100. Average GPA: 3.0. Required Admission Factors: Essays/personal statement, GRE, interview, letters of recommendation, transcript.
Other Admission Factors: Minimum 3.0 GPA required.

EMPLOYMENT INFORMATION
Placement Office Available? Yes.

CONWAY SCHOOL OF LANDSCAPE DESIGN
Graduate Programs

Address: 332 South Deerfield Road, PO Box 179, Conway, MA 01341-0179
Admissions Phone: 413-369-4044 · Admissions E-mail: info@csld.edu
Web Address: www.csld.edu

INSTITUTIONAL INFORMATION
Public/Private: Private (nonprofit). Total Faculty: 4. % Faculty Female: 25. % Faculty Part-time: 25. Student/Faculty Ratio: 6:1. Students in Parent Institution: 18.

PROGRAMS
Masters offered in: Landscape architecture (BS, BSLA, BLA, MSLA, MLA, PhD).

STUDENT INFORMATION
Total Students in Program: 18. % Full-time 100. % Female: 44.

EXPENSES/FINANCIAL AID
Annual Tuition: $20,300. Room & Board: $20,000, Books and Supplies: $600. Grants: $500. Loans Range From: $100-$39,000. % Receiving Financial Aid: 80. % Receiving Scholarships/Grants: 10. % Receiving Loans: 80. Types of Aid Available: Loans, scholarships. Average student debt, upon graduation: $36,000.

ADMISSIONS INFORMATION
Application Fee: $50. Priority Application Deadline: 3/15. Regular Application Deadline: 3/15. Regular Notification: Rolling. Transfer Students Accepted? No. Number of Applications Received: 25. % of Applicants Accepted: 80. % Accepted Who Enrolled: 90.
Required Admission Factors: Essays/personal statement, interview, letters of recommendation, transcript.

EMPLOYMENT INFORMATION
% Employed Within 6 Months: 60. % of master's grads employed in their field upon graduation: 30.

CORNELL UNIVERSITY
The Graduate School

Address: 143 Caldwell Hall, Ithaca, NY 14853
Admissions Phone: 607-255-5816 · Admissions Fax: 607-255-1816
Admissions E-mail: bae2@cornell.edu · Web Address: www.gradschool.cornell.edu

INSTITUTIONAL INFORMATION
Public/Private: Private (nonprofit). Students in Parent Institution: 19,671.

STUDENT INFORMATION
Total Students in Program: 4,702. % Full-time 100. % Female: 41.

RESEARCH FACILITIES
Research Facilities: More than 20 institutional research centers.

EXPENSES/FINANCIAL AID
% Receiving Financial Aid: 76. % Receiving Assistantships: 65. Number of Fellowships Granted Each Year: 1,147. Number of Teaching/Research Assistantships Granted Each Year: 2,161. Average Salary Stipend: $13,185.

ADMISSIONS INFORMATION
Application Fee: $60. Regular Application Deadline: 8/1. Transfer Students Accepted? Yes. Transfer Policy: Maximum 2 registration units may be transferred into PhD program. Number of Applications Received: 15,322. % of Applicants Accepted: 24. % Accepted Who Enrolled: 42. Average GRE Verbal: 563. Average GRE Quantitative: 723. Average GRE Analytical: 687.
Required Admission Factors: Essays/personal statement, letters of recommendation, transcript.
Program-Specific Admission Factors: GRE required of applicants to most programs, minimum score required varies by program. GMAT required or may be substituted for GRE in some programs.

EMPLOYMENT INFORMATION
Placement Office Available? Yes.

COVENANT COLLEGE
Graduate Programs

Address: 14049 Scenic Highway, Lookout Mountain, GA 30750
Admissions Phone: 800-677-3626 · Admissions Fax: 706-820-0672

INSTITUTIONAL INFORMATION
Public/Private: Private (nonprofit). Student/Faculty Ratio: 7:1. Students in Parent Institution: 967.

STUDENT INFORMATION
Total Students in Program: 66. % Full-time 91. % Female: 64.

EXPENSES/FINANCIAL AID
Annual Tuition: $2,835. Fees: $96. Books and Supplies: $306. Grants Range From: $200-$3,600. Loans Range From: $2,160-$4,480. % Receiving Financial Aid: 67. % Receiving Scholarships/Grants: 97. % Receiving Loans: 26. Average student debt, upon graduation: $6,465.

ADMISSIONS INFORMATION
Application Fee: $35. Regular Notification: Rolling. Transfer Students Accepted? Yes. Number of Applications Received: 24. % of Applicants Accepted: 100. % Accepted Who Enrolled: 92. Average GRE Verbal: 522. Average GRE Quantitative: 604.
Required Admission Factors: Essays/personal statement, GRE, letters of recommendation, transcript.
Other Admission Factors: Minimum of 2 years work experience required.

COVENANT THEOLOGICAL SEMINARY
Graduate Programs

Address: 12330 Conway Road, St. Louis, MO 63141
Admissions Phone: 314-434-4044 or 800-264-8064 · Admissions Fax: 314-434-4819

INSTITUTIONAL INFORMATION
Public/Private: Private (nonprofit). Evening Classes Available? Yes. Student/Faculty Ratio: 18:1. Students in Parent Institution: 832.

STUDENT INFORMATION
Total Students in Program: 501. % Full-time 18. % Female: 37.

RESEARCH FACILITIES

Research Facilities: Francis Schaeffer Institute, Youth in Ministry Institute.

EXPENSES/FINANCIAL AID

Annual Tuition: In-state $7,800. **Fees:** $120. **Books and Supplies:** $450. **Grants Range From:** $500-$3,500. **Loans Range From:** $500-$8,500. **% Receiving Financial Aid:** 50. **% Receiving Scholarships/Grants:** 50. **% Receiving Loans:** 20. **Average student debt, upon graduation:** $14,000.

ADMISSIONS INFORMATION

Application Fee: $25. **Regular Notification:** Rolling. **Transfer Students Accepted?** Yes. **Number of Applications Received:** 292. **% of Applicants Accepted:** 82. **% Accepted Who Enrolled:** 83.
Required Admission Factors: Essays/personal statement, interview, letters of recommendation, transcript.

EMPLOYMENT INFORMATION

Placement Office Available? Yes. **% Employed Within 6 Months:** 97. **Rate of placement:** 98%.

CRANBROOK ACADEMY OF ART
Graduate Programs

Address: 39221 Woodward Avenue, PO Box 801, Bloomfield Hills, MI 48303-0801
Admissions Phone: 248-645-3300 · **Admissions Fax:** 248-646-0046
Admissions E-mail: kwillman@cranbrook.edu · **Web Address:** www.cranbrookart.edu

INSTITUTIONAL INFORMATION

Public/Private: Private (nonprofit). **Total Faculty:** 10. **% Faculty Female:** 30. **Student/Faculty Ratio:** 15:1. **Students in Parent Institution:** 152.

PROGRAMS

Masters offered in: Architecture (BArch, BA/BS, MArch, MA/MS, PhD); ceramic arts and ceramics; fiber, textile, and weaving arts; graphic design; industrial design; metal and jewelry arts; painting; photography; printmaking; sculpture.

STUDENT INFORMATION

Total Students in Program: 150. **% Full-time** 101. **% Female:** 49. **% Minority:** 9. **% International:** 9.

EXPENSES/FINANCIAL AID

Annual Tuition: $21,550. **Room & Board (on/off campus):** $1,900/$8,250. **Fees:** $600. **Books and Supplies:** $1,700. **Grants Range From:** $1,000-$6,500. **Loans Range From:** $5,000-$18,500. **% Receiving Financial Aid:** 92. **% Receiving Scholarships/Grants:** 86. **% Receiving Loans:** 90. **% Receiving Assistantships:** 30. **Types of Aid Available:** Institutional work-study, loans, scholarships. **Average student debt, upon graduation:** $32,800.

ADMISSIONS INFORMATION

Application Fee: $50. **Priority Application Deadline:** 2/1. **Regular Application Deadline:** 2/1. **Transfer Students Accepted?** No. **Number of Applications Received:** 460. **% of Applicants Accepted:** 27. **% Accepted Who Enrolled:** 67.
Required Admission Factors: Essays/personal statement, letters of recommendation, transcript.

CREIGHTON UNIVERSITY
Graduate School

Address: 2500 California Plaza, Omaha, NE 68178
Admissions Phone: 402-280-2870

INSTITUTIONAL INFORMATION

Public/Private: Private (nonprofit). **Evening Classes Available?** Yes. **Students in Parent Institution:** 6,297.

STUDENT INFORMATION

Total Students in Program: 474. **% Full-time** 38. **% Female:** 51.

EXPENSES/FINANCIAL AID

Annual Tuition: $8,046. **Fees:** $636. **Grants Range From:** $100-$20,000. **% Receiving Scholarships/Grants:** 25. **% Receiving Loans:** 75.

ADMISSIONS INFORMATION

Application Fee: $40. **Regular Notification:** Rolling. **Transfer Students Accepted?** Yes. **Number of Applications Received:** 503. **% of Applicants Accepted:** 48. **% Accepted Who Enrolled:** 65.
Required Admission Factors: GRE, letters of recommendation, transcript.

EMPLOYMENT INFORMATION

Placement Office Available? Yes.

CUMBERLAND COLLEGE
Graduate Programs

Address: 6178 College Station Drive, Williamsburg, KY 40769
Admissions Phone: 800-343-1609 · **Admissions Fax:** 606-539-4303
Admissions E-mail: admiss@cumberlandcollege.edu
Web Address: www.cumberlandcollege.edu

INSTITUTIONAL INFORMATION

Public/Private: Private (nonprofit). **Evening Classes Available?** Yes. **Total Faculty:** 10. **% Faculty Female:** 30. **% Faculty Part-time:** 20. **Student/Faculty Ratio:** 16:1. **Students in Parent Institution:** 1,747.

PROGRAMS

Masters offered in: Education; elementary and middle school administration/principalship; elementary education and teaching; junior high/intermediate/middle school education and teaching; secondary education and teaching; secondary school administration/principalship; teacher education, multiple levels.

STUDENT INFORMATION

Total Students in Program: 140. **% Full-time** 6. **% Female:** 82. **% Minority:** 1.

EXPENSES/FINANCIAL AID

Annual Tuition: $1,080. **Room & Board:** $4,926. **Fees:** $65. **Books and Supplies:** $150. **Grants Range From:** $225-$1,080. **Loans Range From:** $1,390-$18,500. **% Receiving Financial Aid:** 25. **% Receiving Loans:** 25. **% Receiving Assistantships:** 10. **Types of Aid Available:** Graduate assistantships, loans, scholarships. **Assistantship Compensation Includes:** Full tuition remission, partial tuition remission.

ADMISSIONS INFORMATION

Application Fee: $30. **Regular Application Deadline:** 9/1. **Regular Notification:** Rolling. **Transfer Students Accepted?** Yes. **Transfer Policy:** Application, fee, test scores, transcripts. **Number of Applications Received:** 39. **% of Applicants Accepted:** 100. **% Accepted Who Enrolled:** 95. **Average GPA:** 3.2.
Required Admission Factors: Transcript.

EMPLOYMENT INFORMATION

Placement Office Available? Yes. **% Employed Within 6 Months:** 98. **% of master's grads employed in their field upon graduation:** 98. **Rate of placement:** 100%. **Average starting salary:** $24,000.

CURRY COLLEGE
Graduate Programs

Address: 1071 Blue Hill Avenue, Milton, MA 02186
Admissions Phone: 617-333-2243 · **Admissions Fax:** 617-333-2045
Admissions E-mail: jbresnah0104@curry.edu · **Web Address:** www.curry.edu

INSTITUTIONAL INFORMATION

Public/Private: Private (nonprofit). **Evening Classes Available?** Yes. **Students in Parent Institution:** 2,599

PROGRAMS

Masters offered in: Criminology, education, elementary and middle school administration/principalship, elementary education and teaching, reading teacher education, special education.

STUDENT INFORMATION

Total Students in Program: 98.

RESEARCH FACILITIES

Research Facilities: Program for the Advancement of Learning (PAL), Educational Diagnostic Center.

EXPENSES/FINANCIAL AID

Annual Tuition: $365. **Books and Supplies:** $250. **Loans Range From:** $8,500-$18,500. **% Receiving Financial Aid:** 30. **% Receiving Loans:** 100. **Types of Aid Available:** Loans, **Average student debt, upon graduation:** $17,000.

ADMISSIONS INFORMATION

Application Fee: $50. **Priority Application Deadline:** 8/15. **Regular Application Deadline:** 9/1. **Regular Notification:** Rolling. **Transfer Students Accepted?** Yes. **Transfer Policy:** Same as for other applicants.
Required Admission Factors: Essays/personal statement, GRE, interview, letters of recommendation, MAT, transcript.
Program-Specific Admission Factors: Master of education also requires passing score on communication and literacy tests of the Massachusetts Test for Educator Licensure. Both programs require current resume.

DAEMEN COLLEGE
Graduate Programs

Address: 4380 Main Street, Amherst, NY 14226
Admissions Phone: 716-839-8225 · **Admissions Fax:** 716-839-8229
Admissions E-mail: tlee@daemen.edu · **Web Address:** www.daemen.edu

INSTITUTIONAL INFORMATION

Public/private: Private (nonprofit). **Evening Classes Available?** Yes. **Student/faculty Ratio:** 16:1. **Students in Parent Institution:** 2,186.

PROGRAMS

Masters offered in: Accounting; adult health nurse/nursing; biology teacher education; elementary education and teaching; English/language arts teacher education; French language teacher education; international business; mathematics teacher education; multi/interdisciplinary studies; nursing, physician assistant; social studies teacher education; Spanish language teacher education; special education. **First Professional degree offered in:** Physical therapy/therapist.

STUDENT INFORMATION

Total Students in Program: 592. **% Full-time:** 58. **% Female:** 71. **% International:** 47.

RESEARCH FACILITIES

Research Facilities: Natural & Health Sciences Research Center.

EXPENSES/FINANCIAL AID

Annual Tuition: $2,718. **Room & Board:** $7,000. **Fees:** $252. **Books and Supplies:** $400. **Grants Range From:** $500-$2,000. **Loans Range From:** $1,000-$8,500. **% Receiving Scholarships/Grants:** 62. **% Receiving Loans:** 52.

ADMISSIONS INFORMATION

Application Fee: $25. **Priority Application Deadline:** 5/1. **Regular Application Deadline:** 6/1. **Regular Notification:** Rolling. **Transfer Students Accepted?** No. **Number of Applications Received:** 479. **% of Applicants**

Accepted: 67. **% Accepted Who Enrolled:** 63.
Required Admission Factors: Essays/personal statement, letters of recommendation, transcript.

EMPLOYMENT INFORMATION

Placement Office Available? Yes.

DALHOUSIE UNIVERSITY
Faculty of Graduate Studies

Address: Room 314, Henry Hicks Academic Administration Building, 6299 South Street, Halifax, NS B3H 4H6 Canada
Admissions Phone: 902-494-2485 · **Admissions Fax:** 902-494-8797
Admissions E-mail: graduate.studies@dal.ca · **Web Address:** www.dalgrad.dal.ca

INSTITUTIONAL INFORMATION

Public/private: Public. **Students in Parent Institution:** 11,873.

STUDENT INFORMATION

Total Students in Program: 5,526.

ADMISSIONS INFORMATION

Application Fee: $70. **Regular Application Deadline:** 6/30. **Regular Notification:** Rolling. **Transfer Students Accepted?** No.
Required Admission Factors: Letters of recommendation, transcript.
Other Admission Factors: 3.0 GPA minimum.
Program-Specific Admission Factors: See website.

DALHOUSIE UNIVERSITY
Faculty of Science

Address: 1355 Oxford Street, Halifax, NS B3H 4J1 Canada
Admissions Phone: 902-494-2373 · **Admissions Fax:** 902-494-1123
Admissions E-mail: science@dal.ca · **Web Address:** www.dalgrad.dal.ca

INSTITUTIONAL INFORMATION

Public/private: Public. **Students in Parent Institution:** 11,873.

STUDENT INFORMATION

Total Students in Program: 5,526.

ADMISSIONS INFORMATION

Application Fee: $70. **Regular Application Deadline:** 6/1. **Transfer Students Accepted?** No.
Required Admission Factors: Letters of recommendation, transcript.

DALHOUSIE UNIVERSITY
School of Human
Communication Disorders

Address: 5599 Fenwick Street, Halifax, NS B3H 1R2 Canada
Admissions Phone: 902-494-7052 · **Admissions Fax:** 902-494-5151
Admissions E-mail: hcdwww@dal.ca · **Web Address:** www.dalgrad.dal.ca

INSTITUTIONAL INFORMATION

Public/private: Public. **Students in Parent Institution:** 11,873.
Total Students in Program: 5,526.

ADMISSIONS INFORMATION

Application Fee: $70. **Regular Application Deadline:** 1/15. **Transfer Students Accepted?** No.
Required Admission Factors: Letters of recommendation, transcript.

DALLAS BAPTIST UNIVERSITY
College of Humanities & Social Sciences

Address: 3000 Mountain Creek Parkway, Dallas, TX 75211-9299
Admissions Phone: 214-333-5242 · **Admissions Fax:** 214-333-5579
Admissions E-mail: graduate@dbu.edu · **Web Address:** www.dbu.edu

INSTITUTIONAL INFORMATION

Public/private: Private (nonprofit). **Evening Classes Available?** Yes. **Total Faculty:** 413. **% Faculty Female:** 44. **% Faculty Part-time:** 69. **Student/faculty Ratio:** 17:1. **Students in Parent Institution:** 4,714.

STUDENT INFORMATION

Total Students in Program: 1,173. **% Full-time:** 27. **% Female:** 66. **% Minority:** 28. **% International:** 8.

EXPENSES/FINANCIAL AID

Annual Tuition: $7,146. **Room & Board (On/off Campus):** $4,986/$7,290. **Fees:** $0. **Books and Supplies:** $738. **Types of Aid Available:** Institutional work-study, loans, scholarships.

ADMISSIONS INFORMATION

Application Fee: $25. **Regular Application Deadline:** 8/31. **Regular Notification:** Rolling. **Transfer Students Accepted?** Yes. **Transfer Policy:** Completed and approved transfer request form required of transfer applicants. **Number of Applications Received:** 90. **% of Applicants Accepted:** 56. **% Accepted Who Enrolled:** 78. **Average GPA:** 3.0.
Required Admission Factors: Essays/personal statement, GRE, letters of recommendation, transcript.
Other Admission Factors: Minimum 3.0 GPA required.

EMPLOYMENT INFORMATION

Placement Office Available? Yes.

DALLAS THEOLOGICAL SEMINARY
Graduate Programs

Address: 3909 Swiss Avenue, Dallas, TX 75204
Admissions Phone: 214-841-3661 or 800-992-0998, ext. 3661
Admissions Fax: 214-841-3664
Admissions E-mail: admissions@dts.edu · **Web Address:** www.dts.edu

INSTITUTIONAL INFORMATION

Public/private: Private (nonprofit). **Evening Classes Available?** Yes. **Total Faculty:** 98. **% Faculty Female:** 7. **% Faculty Part-time:** 36. **Student/faculty Ratio:** 18:1. **Students in Parent Institution:** 1,877.

PROGRAMS

Masters offered in: Bible/biblical studies, missions/missionary studies and missiology, pastoral counseling and specialized ministries, pastoral studies/counseling, religious education, theological and ministerial studies, theological studies and religious vocations, theology/theological studies, youth ministry. **Doctorate offered in:** Bible/biblical studies, theological and ministerial studies, theological studies and religious vocations, theology/theological studies.

STUDENT INFORMATION

Total Students in Program: 1,877. **% Full-time:** 41. **% Female:** 25.

RESEARCH FACILITIES

Research Facilities: Center for Christian Leadership.

EXPENSES/FINANCIAL AID

Annual Tuition: $8,400. **Room & Board:** $2,165. **Fees:** $310. **Books and Supplies:** $400. **Grants Range From:** $1,000-$3,000. **Loans Range From:** $1,000-$7,500. **% Receiving Financial Aid:** 60. **% Receiving Scholarships/Grants:** 60. **% Receiving Loans:** 12. **Types of Aid Available:** Loans, scholarships. **Average student debt, upon graduation:** $11,266.

ADMISSIONS INFORMATION

Application Fee: $50. **Priority Application Deadline:** 7/1. **Regular Application Deadline:** 7/1. **Regular Notification:** Rolling. **Transfer Students Accepted?** Yes. **Number of Applications Received:** 758. **% of Applicants Accepted:** 82. **% Accepted Who Enrolled:** 66. **Average GPA:** 3.2.
Required Admission Factors: Essays/personal statement, interview, letters of recommendation, transcript.
Recommended Admission Factors:
Other Admission Factors: Minimum 2.5 GPA recommended.
Program-Specific Admission Factors: Interview and testing required of biblical counseling program applicants.

EMPLOYMENT INFORMATION

Placement Office Available? Yes. **% Employed Within 6 Months:** 70. **% of master's grads employed in their field upon graduation:** 95. **Rate of placement:** 95%. **Average starting salary:** $40,000.

DARTMOUTH COLLEGE
School of Arts & Sciences

Address: Hanover, NH 03755
Admissions E-mail: g.hutchins@dartmouth.edu

INSTITUTIONAL INFORMATION

Public/private: Private (nonprofit). **Students in Parent Institution:** 5,386.

STUDENT INFORMATION

Total Students in Program: 1,058. **% Full-time:** 93. **% Female:** 35.

EXPENSES/FINANCIAL AID

Fees: $10. **% Receiving Financial Aid:** 100. **Average student debt, upon graduation:** $20,000. **Average Salary Stipend:** $15,876.

ADMISSIONS INFORMATION

Transfer Students Accepted? No. **Number of Applications Received:** 1,514. **% of Applicants Accepted:** 22. **% Accepted Who Enrolled:** 55. **Average GPA:** 3.51. **Average GRE Verbal:** 568. **Average GRE Quantitative:** 712. **Average GRE Analytical:** 684.
Required Admission Factors: Essays/personal statement, letters of recommendation, transcript.

EMPLOYMENT INFORMATION

Placement Office Available? Yes. **% of master's/doctoral grads employed in their field upon graduation:** 77/95.

DELTA STATE UNIVERSITY
College of Arts & Sciences

Address: Highway 8 West, Cleveland, MS 38733
Admissions Phone: 662-846-4100 · **Admissions Fax:** 662-846-4099
Admissions E-mail: srogers@deltastate.edu · **Web Address:** www.deltastate.edu

INSTITUTIONAL INFORMATION

Public/private: Public. **Evening Classes Available?** Yes. **Total Faculty:** 5. **% Faculty Female:** 40. **% Faculty Part-time:** 40. **Students in Parent Institution:** 3,853.

PROGRAMS

Masters offered in: Aviation/airway management and operations; biological and physical sciences; business administration/management; community organization and advocacy; counselor education/school counseling and guidance services; criminal justice/safety studies; education leadership and administration; elementary education and teaching; English/language arts teacher education; mathematics teacher education; music teacher education; nursing; physical education teaching and coaching; social science teacher education; social work; special education; teacher education and professional development, specific subject areas. **Doctorate offered in:** Education.

STUDENT INFORMATION
Total Students in Program: 31. **% Full-time:** 39. **% Female:** 68.

EXPENSES/FINANCIAL AID
Annual Tuition: In-state $3,348. / Out-of-state $7,965. **Room & Board:** $3,270. **Books and Supplies:** $1,000. **Grants Range From:** $400-$2,000. **Loans Range From:** $500-$18,500. **% Receiving Loans:** 57. **% Receiving Assistantships:** 14. **Types of Aid Available:** Graduate assistantships, grants, loans, scholarships.

ADMISSIONS INFORMATION
Application Fee: $35. **Priority Application Deadline:** 8/1. **Regular Application Deadline:** 8/30. **Regular Notification:** Rolling. **Transfer Students Accepted?** Yes. **Transfer Policy:** Maximum 6 credit hours may be transferred with minimum grade of B.
Required Admission Factors: GRE, transcript.
Other Admission Factors: Minimum 2.75 GPA overall (3.0 in major and relevant coursework) or 3 years of successful relevant professional experience supported by 3 letters of reference required.

EMPLOYMENT INFORMATION
Placement Office Available? Yes. **% Employed Within 6 Months:** 60. **% of master's/doctoral grads employed in their field upon graduation:** 80/70. **Rate of placement:** 70%. **Average starting salary:** $50,000.

DEPAUL UNIVERSITY
College of Liberal Arts & Sciences

Address: 2352 North Clifton, Suite 130, Chicago, IL 60614
Admissions Phone: 773-325-7315 · **Admissions Fax:** 773-325-7311
Admissions E-mail: graduate_la&s@depaul.edu
Web Address: www.depaul.edu

INSTITUTIONAL INFORMATION
Public/private: Private (nonprofit). **Evening Classes Available?** Yes. **Students in Parent Institution:** 19,549.

STUDENT INFORMATION
Total Students in Program: 6,603. **% Full-time:** 49. **% Female:** 49.

EXPENSES/FINANCIAL AID
Annual Tuition: $6,108. **Fees:** $30. **Books and Supplies:** $300.

ADMISSIONS INFORMATION
Application Fee: $25. **Regular Application Deadline:** 9/1. **Transfer Students Accepted?** Yes. **Number of Applications Received:** 1,012. **% of Applicants Accepted:** 49. **% Accepted Who Enrolled:** 60.
Required Admission Factors: Transcript.

EMPLOYMENT INFORMATION
Placement Office Available? Yes.

DEPAUL UNIVERSITY
School of Music

Address: 1 East Jackson Boulevard, Chicago, IL 60604-2287
Admissions Phone: 312-325-7444 · **Admissions Fax:** 773-325-7429
Admissions E-mail: rbeacraf@wppostdepaul.edu · **Web Address:** www.depaul.edu

INSTITUTIONAL INFORMATION
Public/private: Private (nonprofit). **Students in Parent Institution:** 19,549.

STUDENT INFORMATION
Total Students in Program: 6,603. **% Full-time:** 49. **% Female:** 49.

EXPENSES/FINANCIAL AID
Annual Tuition: $6,108. **Fees:** $30. **Books and Supplies:** $300.

ADMISSIONS INFORMATION
Application Fee: $25. **Regular Notification:** Rolling. **Transfer Students Accepted?** No. **Number of Applications Received:** 63. **% of Applicants Accepted:** 97. **% Accepted Who Enrolled:** 66.
Required Admission Factors: Transcript.
Other Admission Factors: Minimum grade average of B and bachleor's degree in music or related subject required.

EMPLOYMENT INFORMATION
Placement Office Available? Yes.

DEPAUL UNIVERSITY
Theater School

Address: 1 East Jackson Boulevard, Chicago, IL 60604-2287
Admissions Phone: 773-325-7999 · **Admissions Fax:** 773-325-7920
Admissions E-mail: mmeltzer@wppostdepaul.edu · **Web Address:** www.depaul.edu

INSTITUTIONAL INFORMATION
Public/private: Private (nonprofit). **Students in Parent Institution:** 19,549.

STUDENT INFORMATION
Total Students in Program: 6,603. **% Full-time:** 49. **% Female:** 49.

EXPENSES/FINANCIAL AID
Annual Tuition: $6,108. **Fees:** $30. **Books and Supplies:** $300.

ADMISSIONS INFORMATION
Application Fee: $35. **Regular Notification:** Rolling. **Transfer Students Accepted?** No. **Number of Applications Received:** 79. **% of Applicants Accepted:** 38. **% Accepted Who Enrolled:** 53.
Required Admission Factors: Interview, transcript.

EMPLOYMENT INFORMATION
Placement Office Available? Yes.

DESALES UNIVERSITY (FORMERLY ALLENTOWN COLLEGE OF SAINT FRANCIS DE SALES)
Graduate Programs

Address: 2755 Station Avenue, Center Valley, PA 18034-9568
Admissions Phone: 610-282-1100, ext. 1415 · **Admissions Fax:** 610-282-1893
Admissions E-mail: christine.bruce@desales.edu

INSTITUTIONAL INFORMATION
Public/private: Private (nonprofit). **Student/faculty Ratio:** 6:1. **Students in Parent Institution:** 2,549.

STUDENT INFORMATION
Total Students in Program: 680. **% Full-time:** 9. **% Female:** 60.

EXPENSES/FINANCIAL AID
Loans Range From: $500-$18,500. **% Receiving Financial Aid:** 95. **% Receiving Loans:** 100. **Average student debt, upon graduation:** $48,000.

ADMISSIONS INFORMATION
Application Fee: $35. **Transfer Students Accepted?** No. **Number of Applications Received:** 128. **% of Applicants Accepted:** 40. **% Accepted Who Enrolled:** 78. **Average GPA:** 3.3. **Average GRE Verbal:** 482. **Average GRE Quantitative:** 597. **Average GRE Analytical:** 603.
Required Admission Factors: Essays/personal statement, GRE, interview, letters of recommendation, transcript.

Other Admission Factors: Minimum GRE score of 500 in each section and minimum 3.0 GPA required.

EMPLOYMENT INFORMATION

Placement Office Available? Yes. % Employed Within 6 Months: 100. Average starting salary: $55,000.

DOANE COLLEGE
Graduate Studies

Address: 1014 Boswell, Crete, NE 68333
Admissions Phone: 402-464-1223 · Admissions Fax: 402-466-4228
Admissions E-mail: blinder@doane.edu

INSTITUTIONAL INFORMATION

Public/private: Private (nonprofit). Evening Classes Available? Yes. Students in Parent Institution: 2,165.

STUDENT INFORMATION

Total Students in Program: 626. % Full-time: 36. % Female: 75.

EXPENSES/FINANCIAL AID

% Receiving Financial Aid: 17. % Receiving Loans: 100. Average student debt, upon graduation: $7,552.

ADMISSIONS INFORMATION

Application Fee: $25. Transfer Students Accepted? Yes. Transfer Policy: Transfer hours not accepted until 9 credit hours are completed in the program. Number of Applications Received: 16. % of Applicants Accepted: 100. % Accepted Who Enrolled: 100.
Required Admission Factors: Essays/personal statement, letters of recommendation, transcript.
Other Admission Factors: Minimum 2.75 GPA and letter of intent required.

EMPLOYMENT INFORMATION

Placement Office Available? Yes.

DOMINICAN UNIVERSITY
Graduate School of Library & Information Science

Address: 7900 West Division Street, River Forest, IL 60305
Admissions Phone: 708-524-6845 · Admissions Fax: 708-524-6657
Admissions E-mail: gslis@dom.edu · Web Address: www.dom.edu/gslis

INSTITUTIONAL INFORMATION

Public/private: Private (nonprofit). Evening Classes Available? Yes. Students in Parent Institution: 2,200.

PROGRAMS

Masters offered in: Library science/librarianship.

STUDENT INFORMATION

Total Students in Program: 772. % Full-time: 100.

EXPENSES/FINANCIAL AID

Annual Tuition: $21,780. Room & Board: $5,580. Fees: $110. Books and Supplies: $100. Grants Range From: $1,815-$4,500. Loans Range From: $1,000-$14,500. % Receiving Financial Aid: 10. % Receiving Scholarships/Grants: 100. Types of Aid Available: Loans, scholarships.

ADMISSIONS INFORMATION

Application Fee: $25. Regular Application Deadline: 6/1. Regular Notification: Rolling. Transfer Students Accepted? Yes. Transfer Policy: Students may transfer up to 3 credit hours from another American Library Association accredited institution. Transfer of credits must be requested and reviewed at time of admission. Number of Applications Received: 219. % of Appli-

---

cants Accepted: 90. % Accepted Who Enrolled: 59. Average GPA: 3. Average GRE Verbal: 600. Average GRE Quantitative: 500. Average GRE Analytical Writing: 3.5.
Required Admission Factors: Essays/personal statement, letters of recommendation, transcript.

EMPLOYMENT INFORMATION

Placement Office Available? Yes. % Employed Within 6 Months: 80. Rate of placement: 90%. Average starting salary: $35,000.

DOMINICAN UNIVERSITY OF CALIFORNIA (FORMERLY DOMINICAN COLLEGE OF SAN RAFAEL)
School of Arts & Sciences

Address: 50 Acacia Avenue, San Rafael, CA 94901-2298
Admissions Phone: 415-485-3266 · Admissions Fax: 415-485-3205
Admissions E-mail: laudisio@dominican.edu

INSTITUTIONAL INFORMATION

Public/private: Private (nonprofit). Student/faculty Ratio: 15:1. Students in Parent Institution: 1,368.

STUDENT INFORMATION

Total Students in Program: 423. % Full-time: 56. % Female: 73.

EXPENSES/FINANCIAL AID

Annual Tuition: $14,760. Room & Board (On/off Campus): $9,400/$7,668. Fees: $350. Grants Range From: $319-$9,420. Loans Range From: $2,012-$18,500. % Receiving Financial Aid: 42. % Receiving Loans: 99. Number of Fellowships Granted Each Year: 35 Average amount of individual fellowships per year: 2543

ADMISSIONS INFORMATION

Application Fee: $40. Transfer Students Accepted? Yes. Number of Applications Received: 73. % of Applicants Accepted: 66. % Accepted Who Enrolled: 79.
Required Admission Factors: Essays/personal statement, interview, transcript.
Other Admission Factors: Minimum 3.0.

DORDT COLLEGE
Graduate Programs

Address: 498 Fourth Ave NE, Sioux Center, IA 51250
Admissions Phone: 712-722-6236 · Admissions Fax: 712-722-1185
Admissions E-mail: m_ed@dordt.edu · Web Address: www.dordt.edu/masters

INSTITUTIONAL INFORMATION

Public/private: Private (nonprofit). Total Faculty: 90. % Faculty Female: 44. % Faculty Part-time: 56. Student/faculty Ratio: 7:1. Students in Parent Institution: 1,430.

PROGRAMS

Masters offered in: Curriculum and instruction.

STUDENT INFORMATION

Total Students in Program: 52. % Full-time: 100. % Female: 63.

RESEARCH FACILITIES

Research Facilities: Center for Educational Studies.

EXPENSES/FINANCIAL AID

Annual Tuition: $690. Fees: $35. Books and Supplies: $150. % Receiving Financial Aid: 5. % Receiving Loans: 100. Types of Aid Available: Institutional work-study,

ADMISSIONS INFORMATION

Application Fee: $25. **Priority Application Deadline:** 1/1. **Regular Application Deadline:** 5/15. **Regular Notification:** Rolling. **Transfer Students Accepted?** Yes. **Transfer Policy:** Maximum of 6 credits can be transferred however up to 9 credits can be transferred if part of that work has been done at an ARIHE affiliated college. Transfer credit will not be given for any course for which a grade is lower than a B. **Number of Applications Received:** 7. **% of Applicants Accepted:** 100. **% Accepted Who Enrolled:** 100. **Average GPA:** 3.3.

Required Admission Factors: Essays/personal statement, GRE, letters of recommendation, MAT, transcript.

Other Admission Factors: Minimum 3.0 GPA required.

Program-Specific Admission Factors: One or more years of teaching experience. 15 hours of undergraduate work in education.

EMPLOYMENT INFORMATION

Placement Office Available? Yes. **% Employed Within 6 Months:** 100. **% of master's grads employed in their field upon graduation:** 100. **Rate of placement:** 90%. **Average starting salary:** $30,000.

DRAKE UNIVERSITY
Masters in Accounting

Address: 2507 University Avenue, Des Moines, IA 50311-4505
Admissions Phone: 515-271-2188 · **Admissions Fax:** 515-271-4518
Admissions E-mail: cbpa.gradprograms@drake.edu · **Web Address:** www.drake.edu

INSTITUTIONAL INFORMATION

Public/private: Private (nonprofit). **Total Faculty:** 58. **% Faculty Female:** 24. **% Faculty Part-time:** 14. **Student/faculty Ratio:** 20:1. **Students in Parent Institution:** 5,221.

STUDENT INFORMATION

Total Students in Program: 458. **% Full-time:** 5. **% Female:** 48. **% Minority:** 10. **% International:** 10.

RESEARCH FACILITIES

Research Facilities: Kelley Insurance Center; Pappajohn Institute; Center for Professional Studies; Career Center; Business Source Premier, Full-text of 2,260 business journals, Business Wire News, Lexis-Nexis Academic University, Full-text newspapers, periodicals and references.

EXPENSES/FINANCIAL AID

Annual Tuition: $6,600. **Room & Board:** $5,950. **Fees:** $300. **Books and Supplies:** $400. **% Receiving Other Aid (Employer tuition reimbursements):** 65. **Types of Aid Available:** Fellowships, graduate assistantships, grants, institutional work-study, loans, scholarships. employer tuition reimbursements.

ADMISSIONS INFORMATION

Application Fee: $25. **Priority Application Deadline:** 4/1. **Regular Application Deadline:** 8/15. **Regular Notification:** Rolling. **Transfer Students Accepted?** Yes. **Number of Applications Received:** 14. **% of Applicants Accepted:** 71. **Average GPA:** 3.2.

Required Admission Factors: GMAT, GRE.

EMPLOYMENT INFORMATION

Placement Office Available? Yes. **% Employed Within 6 Months:** 100. **% of master's/doctoral/first professional grads employed in their field upon graduation:** 100/100/100.

DRAKE UNIVERSITY
Master of Public Administration

Address: 2507 University Avenue, Des Moines, IA 50311-4505
Admissions Phone: 515-271-2188 · **Admissions Fax:** 515-271-4518
Admissions E-mail: cbpa.gradprograms@drake.edu · **Web Address:** www.drake.edu

INSTITUTIONAL INFORMATION

Public/private: Private (nonprofit). **Total Faculty:** 10. **% Faculty Female:** 10. **% Faculty Part-time:** 80. **Student/faculty Ratio:** 20:1. **Students in Parent Institution:** 5,221.

STUDENT INFORMATION

Total Students in Program: 458. **% Full-time:** 5. **% Female:** 48. **% Minority:** 10. **% International:** 10.

RESEARCH FACILITIES

Research Facilities: Cowles Library; Opperman Law Library; Kelley Insurance Center; Pappajohn Institute; Center for Professional Studies; Career Center; Business Source Premier/ Full-text of 2,260 business journals, Business Wire News, Lexis-Nexis Academic University.

EXPENSES/FINANCIAL AID

Annual Tuition: $6,600. **Room & Board:** $5,950. **Fees:** $300. **Books and Supplies:** $400. **Types of Aid Available:** Graduate assistantships, loans, employee tuition assistance.

ADMISSIONS INFORMATION

Application Fee: $25. **Priority Application Deadline:** 4/1. **Regular Application Deadline:** 8/15. **Regular Notification:** Rolling. **Transfer Students Accepted?** Yes. **Number of Applications Received:** 80. **% of Applicants Accepted:** 88. **Average GPA:** 3.2.

Required Admission Factors: Letters of recommendation, transcript.

EMPLOYMENT INFORMATION

Placement Office Available? Yes. **% Employed Within 6 Months:** 100. **% of master's/doctoral grads employed in their field upon graduation:** 100/100.

DREW UNIVERSITY
Caspersen School of Graduate Studies

Address: 36 Madison Avenue, Madison, NJ 07940
Admissions Phone: 973-408-3110 · **Admissions Fax:** 973-408-3242
Admissions E-mail: gradm@drew.edu · **Web Address:** www.drew.edu/grad

INSTITUTIONAL INFORMATION

Public/private: Private (nonprofit). **Evening Classes Available?** Yes. **Student/faculty Ratio:** 6:1. **Students in Parent Institution:** 2,521.

PROGRAMS

Masters offered in: American history (U.S.), American literature (U.S.), Bible/biblical studies, bioethics/medical ethics, bioethics/medical ethics, English language and literature, English language and literature/letters, English literature (British and commonwealth), European history, history, Holocaust and related studies, humanities/humanistic studies, liberal arts and sciences studies and humanities, multi/interdisciplinary studies, philosophy and religion, philosophy, religion/religious studies, religion/religious studies, religious/sacred music, theology/theological studies, women's studies. **Doctorate offered in:** American history (U.S.), American literature (U.S.), Bible/biblical studies, bioethics/medical ethics, bioethics/medical ethics, English language and literature, English language and literature/letters, English literature.

STUDENT INFORMATION

Total Students in Program: 552. **% Full-time:** 51. **% Female:** 51.

RESEARCH FACILITIES

Research Facilities: Center for Holocaust & Genocide Studies, Center for Study of the History of the Book, United Methodist Archives.

EXPENSES/FINANCIAL AID

Annual Tuition: $25,866. **Fees:** $800. **Books and Supplies:** $500. **Grants Range From:** $7,500-$28,000. **Loans Range From:** $100-$18,500. **% Receiving Financial Aid:** 80. **% Receiving Scholarships/Grants:** 85. **% Receiving Loans:** 75. **% Receiving Assistantships:** 10. **Types of Aid Available:** Fellowships, graduate assistantships, grants, institutional work-study, loans, scholarships. **Number of Teaching/Research Assistantships Granted Each Year:** 25 **Assistantship Compensation Includes:** Salary/stipend. **Average Salary Stipend:** $1,500.

ADMISSIONS INFORMATION

Application Fee: $45. **Regular Application Deadline:** 2/1. **Regular Notification:** 3/15. **Transfer Students Accepted?** Yes. **Number of Applications Received:** 290. **% of Applicants Accepted:** 52. **% Accepted Who Enrolled:** 65. **Average GPA:** 3.5. **Average GRE Verbal:** 573. **Average GRE Quantitative:** 563. **Average GRE Analytical:** 603. **Average GRE Analytical Writing:** 4.5.
Required Admission Factors: Essays/personal statement, GRE, letters of recommendation, transcript.
Other Admission Factors: 3.3 GPA recommended.

EMPLOYMENT INFORMATION

Placement Office Available? Yes. **Rate of placement:** 88%.

DREXEL UNIVERSITY
College of Arts & Sciences

Address: 3141 Chestnut Street, Philadelphia, PA 19104
Admissions Phone: 215-895-6700 · **Admissions Fax:** 215-895-5939
Admissions E-mail: mn23@drexel.edu · **Web Address:** www.drexel.edu/coas

INSTITUTIONAL INFORMATION

Public/private: Private (nonprofit). **Evening Classes Available?** Yes. **Total Faculty:** 266. **% Faculty Part-time:** 33. **Students in Parent Institution:** 12,015.

STUDENT INFORMATION

Total Students in Program: 2,483. **% Full-time:** 28. **% Female:** 40.

EXPENSES/FINANCIAL AID

Annual Tuition: $15,312. **Fees:** $225.

ADMISSIONS INFORMATION

Application Fee: $35. **Regular Notification:** Rolling. **Transfer Students Accepted?** No. **Number of Applications Received:** 760. **% of Applicants Accepted:** 41. **% Accepted Who Enrolled:** 23.
Required Admission Factors: Essays/personal statement, letters of recommendation, transcript.

EMPLOYMENT INFORMATION

Placement Office Available? Yes.

DREXEL UNIVERSITY
College of Media Arts & Design

Address: 3141 Chestnut Street, Philadelphia, PA 19104
Admissions Phone: 215-895-6700 · **Admissions Fax:** 215-895-5939
Admissions E-mail: mn23@drexel.edu · **Web Address:** www.drexel.edu/comad

INSTITUTIONAL INFORMATION

Public/private: Private (nonprofit). **Evening Classes Available?** Yes. **Total Faculty:** 136. **% Faculty Part-time:** 56. **Students in Parent Institution:** 12,015.

PROGRAMS

Masters offered in: Architecture (BArch, BA/BS, MArch, MA/MS, PhD), arts management, fashion/apparel design, interior design.

STUDENT INFORMATION

Total Students in Program: 2,483. **% Full-time:** 28. **% Female:** 40.

EXPENSES/FINANCIAL AID

Annual Tuition: $15,312. **Fees:** $225.

ADMISSIONS INFORMATION

Application Fee: $50. **Regular Application Deadline:** 8/24. **Regular Notification:** Rolling. **Transfer Students Accepted?** Yes. **Transfer Policy:** It is the same admissions procedure as a new student but all previous graduate level work must be submitted for consideration of transfer credits. **Number of Applications Received:** 89. **% of Applicants Accepted:** 81. **% Accepted Who Enrolled:** 47.
Required Admission Factors: Essays/personal statement, letters of recommendation, transcript.
Program-Specific Admission Factors: Portfolio required for fashion design program applicants.

EMPLOYMENT INFORMATION

Placement Office Available? Yes.

DUKE UNIVERSITY
Nicholas School of the Environment & Earth Sciences

Address: Enrollment Services, Box 90330, Duke University, A 142 LSRC, Research Drive, Durham, NC 27708
Admissions Phone: 919-613-8070 · **Admissions Fax:** 919-684-8741
Admissions E-mail: envadm@duke.edu · **Web Address:** www.nicholas.duke.edu

INSTITUTIONAL INFORMATION

Public/private: Private (nonprofit). **Total Faculty:** 116. **% Faculty Part-time:** 54. **Students in Parent Institution:** 11,794.

PROGRAMS

Doctorate offered in: Environmental science, forest management/forest resources management, forestry, natural resources and conservation, natural resources conservation and research, natural resources management and policy, natural resources/conservation. **First Professional degree offered in:** Environmental science, environmental studies, fishing and fisheries sciences and management, forest management/forest resources management, forestry, land use planning and management/development, natural resource economics, natural resources/conservation.

STUDENT INFORMATION

Total Students in Program: 4,162. **% Full-time:** 94. **% Female:** 45.

RESEARCH FACILITIES

Research Facilities: Levine Science Research Center, Supercomputing Center.

EXPENSES/FINANCIAL AID

Annual Tuition: $23,300. **Fees:** $644. **Books and Supplies:** $1,000. **Grants Range From:** $2,800-$12,000. **Loans Range From:** $1,000-$19,100. **Types of Aid Available:** Graduate assistantships, institutional work-study, loans, scholarships.

ADMISSIONS INFORMATION

Application Fee: $75. **Priority Application Deadline:** 2/1. **Regular Application Deadline:** 2/1. **Regular Notification:** 3/15. **Transfer Students Accepted?** No.
Required Admission Factors: Essays/personal statement, GRE, letters of recommendation, transcript. TOEFL for non-native English speakers.
Program-Specific Admission Factors: School wide prerequisites: college calculus course, college statistics course, background in social or natural sci-

ences relevant to area of natural resource interests, computer experience; additional prerequisites depending on program area.

EMPLOYMENT INFORMATION
Placement Office Available? Yes. **% Employed Within 6 Months:** 90. **Rate of placement:** 90%. **Average starting salary:** $39,500.

DUKE UNIVERSITY
The Graduate School

Address: Box 90065, 125 Allen Building, Durham, NC 27708-0065
Admissions Phone: 919-684-3913 · **Admissions Fax:** 919-684-2277
Admissions E-mail: grad-admissions@duke.edu
Web Address: www.gradschool.duke.edu

INSTITUTIONAL INFORMATION
Public/private: Private (nonprofit). **Total Faculty:** 940. **Students in Parent Institution:** 12,550.

PROGRAMS
Masters offered in: Biomedical/medical engineering; civil engineering; computer and information sciences; computer engineering; curriculum and instruction; East Asian languages, literatures, and linguistics; East Asian studies; economics; electrical; electronics and communications engineering; environmental science; environmental/environmental health; engineering; forest management/forest resources management; forest sciences; geology/earth science; history; humanities/humanistic studies; land use planning and management/development; liberal arts and sciences/liberal studies; materials science; mechanical engineering; music/music and performing arts studies; natural resource economics; philosophy; political science and government; public policy analysis; religion/religious studies; Slavic languages, literatures, and linguistics; Slavic studies; water, wetlands, and marine resources management. **Doctorate offered in:** Ancient studies/civilization, anthropology, art/art studies, biochemistry, bioinformatics, biology/biological sciences, biomedical/medical engineering, biophysics, business/commerce, cell biology and anatomy.

STUDENT INFORMATION
Total Students in Program: 2,694. **% Full-time:** 100. **% Female:** 48. **% Minority:** 12. **% International:** 33.

RESEARCH FACILITIES
Research Facilities: Levine Science Research Center, Supercomputing Center.

EXPENSES/FINANCIAL AID
Annual Tuition: $23,280. **Room & Board:** $7,353. **Fees:** $3,964. **Books and Supplies:** $1,000. **Grants Range From:** $1,000-$50,000. **Loans Range From:** $1,000-$50,000. **Types of Aid Available:** Fellowships, graduate assistantships, grants. **Average Salary Stipend:** $16,000.

ADMISSIONS INFORMATION
Application Fee: $65. **Priority Application Deadline:** 12/1. **Regular Application Deadline:** 12/31. **Regular Notification:** Rolling. **Transfer Students Accepted?** No. **Transfer Policy:** Up to 12 credit hours may be transferred by request after 1 full-time semester in residence. **Number of Applications Received:** 7,088. **% of Applicants Accepted:** 21. **% Accepted Who Enrolled:** 44. **Average GPA:** 3.5 **Average GRE Verbal:** 590. **Average GRE Quantitative:** 720.
Required Admission Factors: Essays/personal statement, GRE, letters of recommendation, transcript. TOEFL for international applicants,
Program-Specific Admission Factors: Some specific requirements vary by program.

EMPLOYMENT INFORMATION
Placement Office Available? Yes. **% Employed Within 6 Months:** 95. **Rate of placement:** 100%. **Average starting salary:** $75,000.

DUQUESNE UNIVERSITY
Bayer School of Natural & Environmental Sciences

Address: 600 Forbes Avenue, 100 Mellon Hall, Pittsburgh, PA 15282
Admissions Phone: 412-396-4900 · **Admissions Fax:** 412-396-4881
Admissions E-mail: gradinfo@duq.edu · **Web Address:** www.science.duq.edu

INSTITUTIONAL INFORMATION
Public/private: Private (nonprofit). **Evening Classes Available?** Yes. **Total Faculty:** 68. **% Faculty Female:** 32. **% Faculty Part-time:** 32. **Student/faculty Ratio:** 3:1.

PROGRAMS
Masters offered in: Biochemistry, cell biology and anatomy, cell/cellular and molecular biology, cell/cellular biology and histology, developmental biology and embryology, environmental science, microbiology, natural resources management and policy. **Doctorate offered in:** Analytical chemistry, biochemistry, cell biology and anatomy, cell/cellular and molecular biology, cell/cellular biology and histology, chemistry, developmental biology and embryology, inorganic chemistry, microbiology, organic chemistry.

STUDENT INFORMATION
Total Students in Program: 138. **% Full-time:** 61. **% Female:** 51. **% International:** 17.

RESEARCH FACILITIES
Research Facilities: Center for Biotechnology, Center for Computational Sciences, Center for Research & Education, Center for Microwave & Analytical Chemistry, Member Supercomputing Science Consortium

EXPENSES/FINANCIAL AID
Annual Tuition: $11,008. **Room & Board** $7,820. **Fees:** $1,040. **Books and Supplies:** $750. **Grants Range From:** $100-$12,048. **Loans Range From:** $100-$18,500. **Types of Aid Available:** Fellowships, graduate assistantships, institutional work-study, loans, scholarships, research assistantships. **Number of Fellowships Granted Each Year:** 3. **Average amount of individual fellowships per year:** $18,125. **Number of Teaching/Research Assistantships Granted Each Year:** 76. **Assistantship Compensation Includes:** Full tuition remission, salary/stipend. **Average Salary Stipend:** $16,000.

ADMISSIONS INFORMATION
Priority Application Deadline: 2/1. **Regular Application Deadline:** 5/1. **Regular Notification:** Rolling. **Transfer Students Accepted?** Yes. **Transfer Policy:** Minimum 3.0 GPA required of transfer applicants. **Number of Applications Received:** 69. **% of Applicants Accepted:** 65. **% Accepted Who Enrolled:** 58. **Average GPA:** 3.3. **Average GRE Verbal:** 464. **Average GRE Quantitative:** 632. **Average GRE Analytical:** 587.
Required Admission Factors: Essays/personal statement, GRE, letters of recommendation, transcript.
Recommended Admission Factors: GRE subject exam(s) in Biology.
Other Admission Factors: Minimum 3.0 GPA recommended.
Program-Specific Admission Factors: TOEFL required for international admission, TSE required for assistantship. GRE subject exams recommended (not required) of biological sciences.

EMPLOYMENT INFORMATION
Placement Office Available? Yes. **% Employed Within 6 Months:** 90. **% of master's/doctoral employed in their field upon graduation:** 80/100. **Rate of placement:** 80%. **Average starting salary:** $40,000.

DUQUESNE UNIVERSITY
Mary Pappert School of Music

Address: 600 Forbes Avenue, Pittsburgh, PA 15282
Admissions Phone: 412-396-5064 · **Admissions Fax:** 412-396-5719
Admissions E-mail: jordanof@duq.edu · **Web Address:** www.music.duq.edu

INSTITUTIONAL INFORMATION

Public/private: Private (nonprofit). **Evening Classes Available?** Yes. **Total Faculty:** 100. **% Faculty Female:** 22. **% Faculty Part-time:** 74. **Student/faculty Ratio:** 5:1. **Students in Parent Institution:** 9,667.

STUDENT INFORMATION

Total Students in Program: 2,974. **% Full-time:** 39. **% Female:** 60.

RESEARCH FACILITIES

Research Facilities: Biomedical Research/Bayer Learning Center, Multimedia Development Lab, City Music Center, Opera Workshop, Family Institute, research emphasizing human sciences and qualitative research including phenomenology hermeneutics, music career services office.

EXPENSES/FINANCIAL AID

Annual Tuition: $11,880. **Room & Board:** $5,000. **Fees:** $975. **Books and Supplies:** $350. **Grants Range From:** $100-$12,855. **Loans Range From:** $200-$29,440. **% Receiving Financial Aid:** 76. **% Receiving Scholarships/Grants:** 31. **% Receiving Loans:** 73. **% Receiving Assistantships:** 10. **Types of Aid Available:** Graduate assistantships, grants, loans. **Average Salary Stipend:** $1,350.

ADMISSIONS INFORMATION

Application Fee: $50. **Regular Application Deadline:** 8/1. **Regular Notification:** Rolling. **Transfer Students Accepted?** Yes. **Number of Applications Received:** 67. **% of Applicants Accepted:** 57. **Average GPA:** 3.0
Required Admission Factors: Letters of recommendation, transcript.
Other Admission Factors: Minimum 2.5 GPA (minimum 3.0 GPA in music courses) required.
Program-Specific Admission Factors: Portfolio required of theory/composition and music education program applicants. Audition required of sacred music and perfomance program applicants.

EMPLOYMENT INFORMATION

Placement Office Available? Yes. **Rate of placement:** 80%.

DUQUESNE UNIVERSITY
McAnulty College & Graduate School of Liberal Arts

Address: 600 Forbes Avenue, Pittsburgh, PA 15282
Admissions Phone: 412-396-6400 · **Admissions Fax:** 412-396-5265
Admissions E-mail: rendulic@duq.edu · **Web Address:** www.duq.edu

INSTITUTIONAL INFORMATION

Public/private: Private (nonprofit). **Evening Classes Available?** Yes. **Total Faculty:** 130. **Students in Parent Institution:** 9,667.

PROGRAMS

Masters offered in: Bioethics/medical ethics; communications, journalism, and related fields; computational mathematics; English language and literature; history; liberal arts and sciences/liberal studies; museology/museum studies; pastoral studies/counseling; peace studies and conflict resolution; philosophy; public policy analysis; religious education; theology/theological studies; Web page, digital/multimedia, and information resources design. **Doctorate offered in:** Bioethics/medical ethics; clinical psychology; English language and literature; philosophy; theology/theological studies.

STUDENT INFORMATION

Total Students in Program: 2,426. **% Full-time:** 49. **% Female:** 62. **% International:** 7.

RESEARCH FACILITIES

Research Facilities: Biomedical Research/Bayer Learning Center, Multimedia Development Lab, City Music Center, Opera Workshop, Family Institute, research emphasizing human sciences and qualitative research including phenomenology hermeneutics, music career services office.

EXPENSES/FINANCIAL AID

Annual Tuition: $11,808. **Room & Board (On/off Campus):** $7,820/$11,600. **Fees:** $1,170. **Books and Supplies:** $600. **Grants Range From:** $100-$17,131. **Loans Range From:** $200-$29,440. **% Receiving Financial Aid:** 94. **% Receiving Scholarships/Grants:** 31. **% Receiving Loans:** 73. **% Receiving Assistantships:** 10. **Types of Aid Available:** Graduate assistantships, institutional work-study, loans, scholarships. **Number of Teaching/Research Assistantships Granted Each Year:** 94. **Assistantship Compensation Includes:** Full tuition remission, partial tuition remission, salary/stipend. **Average Salary Stipend:** $9,000.

ADMISSIONS INFORMATION

Application Fee: $50. **Priority Application Deadline:** 2/1. **Regular Application Deadline:** 8/1. **Regular Notification:** Rolling. **Transfer Students Accepted?** No. **Number of Applications Received:** 350. **% of Applicants Accepted:** 72. **% Accepted Who Enrolled:** 63.
Required Admission Factors: Essays/personal statement, GRE, letters of recommendation, transcript.
Other Admission Factors: Minimum 3.0 GPA required. Minimum test score requirements vary by program.
Program-Specific Admission Factors: Portfolio required of multimedia program applicants.

EMPLOYMENT INFORMATION

Placement Office Available? Yes. **Rate of placement:** 80%. **Average starting salary:** $35,000.

D'YOUVILLE COLLEGE
Graduate Programs

Address: 320 Porter Avenue, Buffalo, NY 14201
Admissions Phone: 716-829-7676 · **Admissions Fax:** 716-829-7790
Admissions E-mail: graduateadmissions@dyc.edu · **Web Address:** www.dyc.edu

INSTITUTIONAL INFORMATION

Public/private: Private (nonprofit). **Evening Classes Available?** Yes. **Total Faculty:** 202. **% Faculty Female:** 57. **% Faculty Part-time:** 48. **Student/faculty Ratio:** 13:1. **Students in Parent Institution:** 2,729.

PROGRAMS

Masters offered in: Biology teacher education; business teacher education; dietetics/dietician (RD); elementary education and teaching; English/language arts teacher education; family practice/nurse/nurse practitioner; health services administration; health services/allied health; health/health care administration/management; history teacher education; international business; junior high/intermediate/middle school education and teaching; mathematics teacher education; nursing/registered nurse training (RN, ASN, BSN, MSN); nursing administration (MSN, MS, PhD); nursing, clinical specialist; nursing science (MS PhD); nursing, occupational therapy/therapist; physical therapy/therapist; science teacher education/general science teacher education; secondary education and teaching; special education. **First Professional degree offered in:** Chiropractic (DC), physical therapy/therapist.

STUDENT INFORMATION

Total Students in Program: 1,504. **% Full-time:** 100. **% Female:** 74. **% Minority:** 21. **% International:** 78.

RESEARCH FACILITIES

Research Facilities: Physical Therapy Gait Lab, Gross Anatomy Laboratory.

EXPENSES/FINANCIAL AID

Annual Tuition: $12,480. Room & Board: $7,340. Fees: $200. Books and Supplies: $850. Grants Range From: $200-$2,200. Loans Range From: $100-$18,500. % Receiving Financial Aid: 76. % Receiving Scholarships/Grants: 80. % Receiving Loans: 98. % Receiving Assistantships: 1. Types of Aid Available: Graduate assistantships, grants, institutional work-study, loans, scholarships. Number of Teaching/Research Assistantships Granted Each Year: 3. Average Salary Stipend: $3,000.

ADMISSIONS INFORMATION

Application Fee: $25. Regular Application Deadline: 8/15. Regular Notification: Rolling. Transfer Students Accepted? Yes. Transfer Policy: Submit application to graduate admissions, follow-up meeting with specific graduate department to determine transfer credit hours. Number of Applications Received: 1,205. % of Applicants Accepted: 67. % Accepted Who Enrolled: 55. Average GPA: 3.2.
Required Admission Factors: Interview, transcript.
Other Admission Factors: Minimum 3.0 GPA required.
Program-Specific Admission Factors: New York State RN licensure and 1 year of work experience required of nurse practitioner program applicants.

EMPLOYMENT INFORMATION

Placement Office Available? Yes. % Employed Within 6 Months: 96. % of master's employed in their field upon graduation: 96. Rate of placement: 96%. Average starting salary: $45,000.

EAST CAROLINA UNIVERSITY
School of Art

Address: The Graduate School, 131 Ragsdale, Greenville, NC 27858-4353
Admissions Phone: 282-328-6012 · Admissions Fax: 252-328-6071
Admissions E-mail: gradschool@mail.ecu.edu · Web Address: www.ecu.edu/art

INSTITUTIONAL INFORMATION

Public/private: Public. Evening Classes Available? Yes. Students in Parent Institution: 17,445.

PROGRAMS

Masters offered in: Art teacher education; fine/studio arts.

STUDENT INFORMATION

Total Students in Program: 3,103. % Full-time: 46. % Female: 62.

RESEARCH FACILITIES

Research Facilities: Numerous on-campus computer centers, state-of-the-art research labs.

EXPENSES/FINANCIAL AID

Annual Tuition: In-state $996. / Out-of-state $6,116. Fees: $610. Books and Supplies: $350. Types of Aid Available: Fellowships, graduate assistantships, grants, institutional work-study, loans, scholarships.

ADMISSIONS INFORMATION

Application Fee: $50. Regular Application Deadline: 10/15. Regular Notification: Rolling. Transfer Students Accepted? Yes. Transfer Policy: Can transfer 20% or required courses for program. Number of Applications Received: 48. % of Applicants Accepted: 100. % Accepted Who Enrolled: 100. Average GPA: 3.2.
Required Admission Factors: GRE, GMAT, transcript.
Program-Specific Admission Factors: MFA, MA: A portfolio of 20 slides of your work must be submitted with your application. These should be in a slide sheet with 2 copies of each slide. MAEd: Photocopy of current teaching license must be included.

EMPLOYMENT INFORMATION

Placement Office Available? Yes. % Employed Within 6 Months: 60. Rate of placement: 25%. Average starting salary: $40,000.

EAST CAROLINA UNIVERSITY
School of Human Environmental Sciences

Address: The Graduate School, Ragsdale Room 131, Greenville, NC 27858-4353

INSTITUTIONAL INFORMATION

Public/private: Public. Evening Classes Available? Yes. Students in Parent Institution: 17,445.

STUDENT INFORMATION

Total Students in Program: 3,103. % Full-time: 46. % Female: 62.

RESEARCH FACILITIES

Research Facilities: Numerous on-campus computer centers, state-of-the-art research labs.

EXPENSES/FINANCIAL AID

Annual Tuition: In-state $1,012. / Out-of-state $8,578. Number of Teaching/Research Assistantships Granted Each Year: 9.

ADMISSIONS INFORMATION

Application Fee: $40. Transfer Students Accepted? Yes.
Required Admission Factors: GRE, letters of recommendation, transcript.
Other Admission Factors: Minimum combined GRE score of 850 or MAT score of 35 required.

EMPLOYMENT INFORMATION

Placement Office Available? Yes.

EAST CAROLINA UNIVERSITY
School of Music

Address: The Graduate School, Ragsdale Room 131, Greenville, NC 27858-4353

INSTITUTIONAL INFORMATION

Public/private: Public. Students in Parent Institution: 17,445.

STUDENT INFORMATION

Total Students in Program: 3,103. % Full-time: 46. % Female: 62.

RESEARCH FACILITIES

Research Facilities: Numerous on-campus computer centers, state-of-the-art research labs.

EXPENSES/FINANCIAL AID

Annual Tuition: In-state $1,012. / Out-of-state $8,578.

ADMISSIONS INFORMATION

Transfer Students Accepted? No.

EMPLOYMENT INFORMATION

Placement Office Available? Yes.

EAST CAROLINA UNIVERSITY
Thomas Harriot College of Arts & Sciences

Address: The Graduate School, Ragsdale Hall Room 131, Greenville, NC 27858-4353
Admissions Phone: 252-328-6012 · **Admissions Fax:** 252-328-6071
Admissions E-mail: gradschool@mail.ecu.edu
Web Address: www.ecu.edu/gradschool

INSTITUTIONAL INFORMATION

Public/private: Public. **Evening Classes Available?** Yes. **Student/faculty Ratio:** 16:1. **Students in Parent Institution:** 17,445.

PROGRAMS

Masters offered in: Anthropology, applied mathematics, biochemistry, biotechnology, chemistry, clinical psychology, creative writing, economics, English composition, English language and literature, English/language arts teacher education, geography, history, mathematics, microbiology, molecular biology, physical sciences, physics, psychology, public administration, school psychology, sociology, speech and rhetorical studies, statistics, technical and business writing. **Doctorate offered in:** Physics.

STUDENT INFORMATION

Total Students in Program: 3,103. **% Full-time:** 46. **% Female:** 62.

RESEARCH FACILITIES

Research Facilities: Numerous on-campus computer centers, state-of-the-art research labs.

EXPENSES/FINANCIAL AID

Annual Tuition: In-state $1,012. / Out-of-state $8,578. **Number of Teaching/Research Assistantships Granted Each Year:** 63. **Average Salary Stipend:** $6,500.

ADMISSIONS INFORMATION

Application Fee: $50. **Priority Application Deadline:** 3/1. **Regular Application Deadline:** 6/1. **Regular Notification:** Rolling. **Transfer Students Accepted?** Yes. **Transfer Policy:** Submit same paperwork for new applicant. **Required Admission Factors:** Essays/personal statement, GRE, letters of recommendation, MAT, transcript.
Other Admission Factors: Minimum combined GRE score of 1000 (Verbal and Quantitative);

EMPLOYMENT INFORMATION

Placement Office Available? Yes.

EAST STROUDSBURG UNIVERSITY OF PENNSYLVANIA
Graduate School

Address: 200 Normal Street, East Stroudsburg, PA 18301
Admissions Phone: 570-422-3536 · **Admissions Fax:** 570-422-3506
Admissions E-mail: grad@po-box.esu.edu
Web Address: www.esu.edu/graduate/default.asp

INSTITUTIONAL INFORMATION

Public/private: Public. **Total Faculty:** 110. **% Faculty Female:** 40. **% Faculty Part-time:** 19. **Students in Parent Institution:** 6,162

PROGRAMS

Masters offered in: Audiology/audiologist and speech-language pathology/pathologist, biological and physical sciences, computer and information sciences, educational/instructional media design, elementary education and teaching, health and physical education/fitness, health teacher education, history, physical education teaching and coaching, political science and government,

public health (MPH, DPH), reading teacher education, rehabilitation and therapeutic professions, secondary education and teaching, special education.

STUDENT INFORMATION

Total Students in Program: 1,041. **% Full-time:** 30. **% Female:** 70. **% Minority:** 6. **% International:** 2.

EXPENSES/FINANCIAL AID

Annual Tuition: In-state $5,618. / Out-of-state $8,980. **Room & Board:** $4,464. **Fees:** $1,106. **Types of Aid Available:** Graduate assistantships, institutional work-study, loans, scholarships. **Average Salary Stipend:** $2,500.

ADMISSIONS INFORMATION

Application Fee: $50. **Regular Application Deadline:** 9/1. **Regular Notification:** Rolling. **Transfer Students Accepted?** Yes.
Required Admission Factors: GRE, transcript.
Other Admission Factors: Minimum 2.5 GPA overall (3.0 in major) required.

EMPLOYMENT INFORMATION

Placement Office Available? Yes.

EAST STROUDSBURG UNIVERSITY OF PENNSYLVANIA
School of Arts & Sciences

Address: East Stroudsburg, PA 18301
Admissions Phone: 570-422-3536 · **Admissions Fax:** 570-422-3506
Admissions E-mail: peter.hawkes@po-box.esu.edu

INSTITUTIONAL INFORMATION

Public/private: Public. **Students in Parent Institution:** 5,802.

STUDENT INFORMATION

Total Students in Program: 1,020. **% Full-time:** 29. **% Female:** 71.

EXPENSES/FINANCIAL AID

Annual Tuition: In-state $3,780. / Out-of-state $6,610. **Fees:** $724. **Books and Supplies:** $650. **Grants Range From:** $6,280-$11,610. **Loans Range From:** $1,000-$16,000. **% Receiving Financial Aid:** 12. **Number of Teaching/Research Assistantships Granted Each Year:** 111. **Average Salary Stipend:** $2,500.

ADMISSIONS INFORMATION

Application Fee: $15. **Regular Notification:** Rolling. **Transfer Students Accepted?** Yes.
Required Admission Factors: Transcript.
Other Admission Factors: Minimum 2.5 GPA (3.0 in major) required.

EMPLOYMENT INFORMATION

Placement Office Available? Yes.

EAST TENNESSEE STATE UNIVERSITY
College of Arts & Sciences

Address: 920 West Maple Streete, Box 70720, Johnson City, TN 37612-1710
Admissions Phone: 423-439-4221 · **Admissions Fax:** 423-439-5624
Admissions E-mail: gradsch@etsu.edu
Web Address: www.etsu.edu\gradstud

INSTITUTIONAL INFORMATION

Public/private: Public. **Evening Classes Available?** Yes. **Student/faculty Ratio:** 15:1. **Students in Parent Institution:** 12,111

PROGRAMS

Masters offered in: Anatomy, art/art studies, biochemistry, biology/biological sciences, biomedical sciences, ceramic arts and ceramics, chemistry, clinical psychology, counseling psychology, criminology, educational psychology, fine/studio arts, history, liberal arts and sciences/liberal studies, metal and jewelry arts, microbiology, psychology, school psychology, sociology, urban studies/affairs. **Doctorate offered in:** Anatomy, biochemistry, biomedical sciences, microbiology.

STUDENT INFORMATION
Total Students in Program: 338. **% Full-time:** 100. **% Female:** 386.

EXPENSES/FINANCIAL AID
Annual Tuition: In-state $1,845. / Out-of-state $3,479. **Fees:** $281. **Books and Supplies:** $300. **Grants Range From:** $6,000-$15,000. **Loans Range From:** $2,500-$4,500. **% Receiving Financial Aid:** 55. **Types of Aid Available:** Graduate assistantships, loans. **Number of Teaching/Research Assistantships Granted Each Year:** 55. **Average Salary Stipend:** $6,000.

ADMISSIONS INFORMATION
Application Fee: $25. **Priority Application Deadline:** 6/1. **Regular Application Deadline:** 8/1. **Transfer Students Accepted?** Yes. **Number of Applications Received:** 344. **% of Applicants Accepted:** 51. **Average GPA:** 3.2. **Average GRE Verbal:** 510. **Average GRE Quantitative:** 580. **Average GRE Analytical:** 620.
Required Admission Factors: Essays/personal statement, transcript.
Other Admission Factors: Each program in the College of Arts and Sciences has their specific requirements. Please refer to the graduate catalog for specifics.
Program-Specific Admission Factors: Each program in the College of Arts and Sciences has their specific requirements. Please refer to the graduate catalog for specifics.

EASTERN ILLINOIS UNIVERSITY
College of Arts & Humanities

Address: 600 Lincoln Avenue, Charleston, IL 61920

INSTITUTIONAL INFORMATION
Public/private: Public. **Total Faculty:** 124. **Students in Parent Institution:** 11,200.

STUDENT INFORMATION
Total Students in Program: 1,094. **% Full-time:** 50. **% Female:** 59.

EXPENSES/FINANCIAL AID
Annual Tuition: In-state $2,448. / Out-of-state $7,340. **Fees:** $591.

ADMISSIONS INFORMATION
Application Fee: $25. **Regular Notification:** Rolling. **Transfer Students Accepted?** Yes. **Transfer Policy:** Maximum 11 semester hours may be transferred.
Required Admission Factors: GRE, interview, transcript.
Other Admission Factors: Minimum 2.75 GPA required.

EMPLOYMENT INFORMATION
Placement Office Available? Yes. **Rate of placement:** 15%.

EASTERN KENTUCKY UNIVERSITY
College of Arts & Humanities

Address: Lancaster Avenue, Richmond, KY 40475-3102
Admissions Phone: 606-622-1405 · **Admissions Fax:** 859-622-1451
Admissions E-mail: andrew.schoolmaster@eku.edu · **Web Address:** www.cas.eku.edu

INSTITUTIONAL INFORMATION
Public/private: Public. **Evening Classes Available?** Yes. **Students in Parent Institution:** 16,183.

PROGRAMS
Masters offered in: Biology/biological sciences, chemistry, clinical psychology, computer science, English language and literature, geology/earth science, history, industrial and organizational psychology, mathematics, music, political science and government, public administration, school psychology.

STUDENT INFORMATION
Total Students in Program: 323. **% Full-time:** 57. **% Female:** 56. **% International:** 5.

EXPENSES/FINANCIAL AID
Annual Tuition: In-state $4,086. / Out-of-state $11,340. **Room & Board:** $4,658. **Fees:** $460. **Books and Supplies:** $800.

ADMISSIONS INFORMATION
Regular Application Deadline: 8/1. **Transfer Students Accepted?** Yes. **Transfer Policy:** Maximum of 9 credits may be transferred. Students with master's degree may transfer up to 12 credits. **Number of Applications Received:** 306. **% of Applicants Accepted:** 60. **% Accepted Who Enrolled:** 59.
Required Admission Factors: GRE, transcript.
Other Admission Factors: Minimum GRE score of 1000 and minimum 2.5 GPA required.

EMPLOYMENT INFORMATION
Placement Office Available? Yes.

EASTERN KENTUCKY UNIVERSITY
College of Justice & Safety

Address: Lancaster Avenue, Richmond, KY 40475-3102
Admissions Phone: 606-622-3565 · **Admissions Fax:** 859-622-6561
Admissions E-mail: allen.ault@eku.edu · **Web Address:** www.justice.eku.edu

INSTITUTIONAL INFORMATION
Public/private: Public. **Evening Classes Available?** Yes. **Total Faculty:** 31. **% Faculty Female:** 26. **% Faculty Part-time:** 3. **Students in Parent Institution:** 16,183.

PROGRAMS
Masters offered in: Corrections, criminal justice/police science, criminal justice/safety studies, juvenile corrections, protective services, securities services administration/management, technology teacher education/industrial arts teacher education.

STUDENT INFORMATION
Total Students in Program: 114. **% Full-time:** 47. **% Female:** 38. **% International:** 6.

EXPENSES/FINANCIAL AID
Annual Tuition: In-state $4,086. / Out-of-state $11,340. **Room & Board:** $4,658. **Fees:** $460. **Books and Supplies:** $800.

ADMISSIONS INFORMATION
Application Fee:. **Regular Application Deadline:** 8/1. **Transfer Students Accepted?** Yes. **Transfer Policy:** Maximum 9 credits may be transferred. Students with master's degree may transfer up to 12 credits. **Number of Applications Received:** 68. **% of Applicants Accepted:** 82. **% Accepted Who Enrolled:** 55.
Required Admission Factors: GRE, transcript.
Other Admission Factors: Minimum GRE score of 1250 and minimum 3.0 GPA required.

EMPLOYMENT INFORMATION
Placement Office Available? Yes.

EASTERN MENNONITE UNIVERSITY
Graduate Programs

Address: 1200 Park Road, Harrisonburg, VA 22802-2462
Admissions Phone: 540-432-4257 or 800-710-7871 · **Admissions Fax:** 540-432-4444
Admissions E-mail: yoderda@emu.edu

INSTITUTIONAL INFORMATION

Public/private: Private (nonprofit). **Student/faculty Ratio:** 12:1. **Students in Parent Institution:** 1,304.

STUDENT INFORMATION

Total Students in Program: 185. % Full-time: 31. % Female: 66.

RESEARCH FACILITIES

Research Facilities: Center for Evangelism and Church Planting, Institute for Peacebuilding.

EXPENSES/FINANCIAL AID

Room & Board: $6,235. **Fees:** $46. **Grants Range From:** $200-$20,000. **Loans Range From:** $700-$8,500. **% Receiving Financial Aid:** 22. **% Receiving Scholarships/Grants:** 88. **% Receiving Loans:** 51. **Average student debt, upon graduation:** $22,414. **Number of Teaching/Research Assistantships Granted Each Year:** 6. **Average Salary Stipend:** $1,200.

ADMISSIONS INFORMATION

Application Fee: $25. **Regular Notification:** Rolling. **Transfer Students Accepted?** Yes. **Number of Applications Received:** 94. **% of Applicants Accepted:** 94. **% Accepted Who Enrolled:** 66. **Average GPA:** 3.2. **Average GRE Verbal:** 451. **Average GRE Quantitative:** 507. **Average GRE Analytical:** 534.
Required Admission Factors: Essays/personal statement, letters of recommendation, transcript.
Other Admission Factors: Minimum 3.0 GPA required.
Program-Specific Admission Factors: Minimum 2 years of work experience required of conflict transformation program applicants.

EASTERN NEW MEXICO UNIVERSITY
College of Fine Arts

Address: Portales, NM 88130
Admissions Phone: 505-562-2147 · **Admissions Fax:** 505-562-2168
Admissions E-mail: phillip.shelley@enmu.edu

INSTITUTIONAL INFORMATION

Public/private: Public. **Students in Parent Institution:** 3,581.

STUDENT INFORMATION

Total Students in Program: 630. % Full-time: 17. % Female: 73.

RESEARCH FACILITIES

Research Facilities: Blackwater Draw Archeological Site.

EXPENSES/FINANCIAL AID

Annual Tuition: In-state $1,740. / Out-of-state $7,296. **Fees:** $588. **Grants Range From:** $510-$7,500. **Loans Range From:** $500-$14,400. **% Receiving Scholarships/Grants:** 19. **% Receiving Loans:** 75. **% Receiving Assistantships:** 34.

ADMISSIONS INFORMATION

Application Fee: $10. **Regular Notification:** Rolling. **Transfer Students Accepted?** Yes.
Required Admission Factors: GRE, transcript.
Other Admission Factors: Minimum 2.5 GPA required.

EMPLOYMENT INFORMATION

Placement Office Available? Yes.

EASTERN NEW MEXICO UNIVERSITY
College of Liberal Arts & Sciences

Address: 1500 South Avenue K, Portales, NM 88130
Admissions Phone: 505-562-2147 · **Admissions Fax:** 505-562-2168
Admissions E-mail: phillip.shelley@enmu.edu
Web Address: www.enmu.edu/academics/graduate/index.shtml

INSTITUTIONAL INFORMATION

Public/private: Public. **Evening Classes Available?** Yes. **Total Faculty:** 79. **% Faculty Female:** 41. **Student/faculty Ratio:** 5:1. **Students in Parent Institution:** 3,581.

PROGRAMS

Masters offered in: American literature (U.S.); analytical chemistry; anatomy; animal behavior and ethology; animal genetics; anthropology; anthropology; applied mathematics; archeology; bilingual and multilingual education; biochemistry/biophysics and molecular biology; biological and biomedical sciences; biology teacher education; botany/plant biology; broadcast journalism; business administration/management; cell/cellular biology and histology; chemistry teacher education; chemistry; communications and media studies; communications studies/speech communication and rhetoric; communications, journalism, and related fields; counselor education/school counseling and guidance services; creative writing; curriculum and instruction; education leadership and administration; education; educational, instructional, and curriculum supervision; elementary education and teaching; English composition; English language and literature; English literature (British and commonwealth); English/language arts teacher education; foreign language teacher education; genetics; health teacher education; higher education/higher education administration; human/medical genetics; inorganic chemistry; journalism; junior high/intermediate/middle school education and teaching; mass communications/media studies; mathematics; microbiology; molecular biology; molecular genetics; molecular physiology; multicultural education; organic chemistry; organizational communication; photojournalism; physical education teaching and coaching; physiology; plant genetics; plant molecular biology; public relations/image management; radio and television; reading teacher education; science teacher education/general science teacher education; secondary education and teaching; social science teacher education; social studies teacher education; special education; teacher education, multiple levels; teaching English as a second or foreign language/ESL language instructor; zoology/animal biology.

STUDENT INFORMATION

Total Students in Program: 630. % Full-time: 17. % Female: 73.

RESEARCH FACILITIES

Research Facilities: Blackwater Draw Archeological Site.

EXPENSES/FINANCIAL AID

Annual Tuition: In-state $2,064. / Out-of-state $7,632. **Room & Board:** $4,290. **Fees:** $696. **Books and Supplies:** $600. **Grants Range From:** $510-$7,500. **Loans Range From:** $500-$14,400. **% Receiving Financial Aid:** 50. **% Receiving Scholarships/Grants:** 19. **% Receiving Loans:** 75. **% Receiving Assistantships:** 34. **Types of Aid Available:** Fellowships, graduate assistantships, grants, institutional work-study, loans, scholarships.

ADMISSIONS INFORMATION

Application Fee: $10. **Priority Application Deadline:** 4/15. **Regular Application Deadline:** 8/10. **Regular Notification:** Rolling. **Transfer Students Accepted?** Yes. **Number of Applications Received:** 281. **% of Applicants Accepted:** 53. **% Accepted Who Enrolled:** 82. **Average GPA:** 3.0.
Required Admission Factors: GMAT, transcript.
Other Admission Factors: Cumulative 2.6 GPA for provisional admission; 3.0 GPA or greater for regular admissions.
Program-Specific Admission Factors: Minimum 3.0 GPA, undergraduate major in anthropology or related field, 2 letters of reference, writing sample, and vitae or letter of application required of anthropology program applicants.

EMPLOYMENT INFORMATION

Placement Office Available? Yes. % Employed Within 6 Months: 85. Rate of placement: 65%. Average starting salary: $30,000.

EASTERN NEW MEXICO UNIVERSITY
Graduate School

Address: 1500 South Avenue K, Station #24, Portales, NM 88130
Admissions Phone: 505-562-2147 · **Admissions Fax:** 505-562-2500
Admissions E-mail: phillip.shelley@enmu.edu
Web Address: www.enmu.edu/academics/graduate/index.shtml

INSTITUTIONAL INFORMATION

Public/private: Public. Evening Classes Available? Yes. Total Faculty: 101. % Faculty Female: 14. Students in Parent Institution: 3,725

PROGRAMS

Masters offered in: Anatomy; animal behavior and ethology; anthropology; archeology; bilingual and multilingual education; biochemistry; botany/plant biology; broadcast journalism; business administration/management; chemistry; communication disorders; communications studies/speech communication and rhetoric; counselor education/school counseling and guidance services; curriculum and instruction; education leadership and administration; education; elementary education and teaching; English language and literature; genetics, health and physical education; health, and physical education/fitness; health teacher education; journalism; mass communications/media studies; mathematics; microbiology; molecular biology; molecular genetics; neuroanatomy; public relations/image management; radio and television; secondary education and teaching; special education; speech-language pathology/pathologist; sports and fitness administration/management; teaching English as a second or foreign language/ESL language instructor; zoology/animal biology.

STUDENT INFORMATION

Total Students in Program: 701. % Full-time: 26. % Female: 73.

RESEARCH FACILITIES

Research Facilities: Blackwater Draw Archeological Site (the Clovis type site) and a natural history preserve.

EXPENSES/FINANCIAL AID

Annual Tuition: In-state $2,962. / Out-of-state $8,316. Room & Board: $5,100. Fees: $10. Books and Supplies: $570. Grants Range From: $962-$7,700. Loans Range From: $500-$14,400. % Receiving Financial Aid: 80. % Receiving Scholarships/Grants: 19. % Receiving Loans: 75. % Receiving Assistantships: 34. Types of Aid Available: Fellowships, graduate assistantships, grants, loans, scholarships. Number of Fellowships Granted Each Year: 4. Average amount of individual fellowships per year: $11,000. Number of Teaching/Research Assistantships Granted Each Year: 70. Assistantship Compensation Includes: Partial tuition remission, salary/stipend. Average Salary Stipend: $3,850.

ADMISSIONS INFORMATION

Application Fee: $10. Priority Application Deadline: 3/15. Regular Application Deadline: 8/1. Regular Notification: Rolling. Transfer Students Accepted? Yes. Number of Applications Received: 101. % of Applicants Accepted: 82. % Accepted Who Enrolled: 63. Average GPA: 3.1. Required Admission Factors: Transcript. Other Admission Factors: Minimum GRE score of 1000 (Verbal and Quantitative) and minimum 3.0 GPA or minimum GRE score of 900 (Verbal and Quantitative) and minimum 3.0 GPA required.

EMPLOYMENT INFORMATION

Placement Office Available? Yes. % Employed Within 6 Months: 5. Rate of placement: 88%. Average starting salary: $30,000.

EASTERN UNIVERSITY
Graduate Programs

Address: 1300 Eagle Road, St. Davids, PA 19087-3696
Admissions Phone: 610-341-5972 · **Admissions Fax:** 610-341-1466
Admissions E-mail: ljamison@eastern.edu · **Web Address:** www.eastern.edu

INSTITUTIONAL INFORMATION

Public/private: Private (nonprofit). Evening Classes Available? Yes. Students in Parent Institution: 2,757.

STUDENT INFORMATION

Total Students in Program: 855. % Full-time: 52. % Female: 61.

RESEARCH FACILITIES

Research Facilities: Institute for Urban Studies, Urban Ministry Center, Center for Global Applied Research.

EXPENSES/FINANCIAL AID

Annual Tuition: $7,110. Fees: $30. Books and Supplies: $750.

ADMISSIONS INFORMATION

Application Fee: $35. Regular Notification: Rolling. Transfer Students Accepted? Yes. Transfer Policy: Maximum 9 credit hours with minimum grade of B may be transferred. Number of Applications Received: 420. % of Applicants Accepted: 69. % Accepted Who Enrolled: 78. Required Admission Factors: Essays/personal statement, interview, letters of recommendation, transcript. Other Admission Factors: Minimum 2.5 GPA required.

EASTERN WASHINGTON UNIVERSITY
College of Arts & Letters

Address: 206 Showalter Hall, Cheney, WA 99004-2444
Admissions Phone: 509-359-6297 · **Admissions Fax:** 509-359-6044
Admissions E-mail: gradprograms@mail.ewu.edu

INSTITUTIONAL INFORMATION

Public/private: Public. Evening Classes Available? Yes. Students in Parent Institution: 8,597.

STUDENT INFORMATION

Total Students in Program: 1,101. % Full-time: 55. % Female: 67.

RESEARCH FACILITIES

Research Facilities: Turnbull Wildlife Refuge.

EXPENSES/FINANCIAL AID

Annual Tuition: In-state $4,470. / Out-of-state $13,161. Room & Board: $6,300. Fees: $139. Books and Supplies: $500. Grants Range From: $300-$3,000. Loans Range From: $8,500-$18,500. % Receiving Financial Aid: 65. Average Salary Stipend: $2,208.

ADMISSIONS INFORMATION

Application Fee: $35. Regular Notification: Rolling. Transfer Students Accepted? Yes. Required Admission Factors: Transcript. Other Admission Factors: Minimum 3.0 GPA in last 2 years of coursework required.

EMPLOYMENT INFORMATION

Placement Office Available? Yes.

EDEN THEOLOGICAL SEMINARY
Graduate Programs

Address: 475 East Lockwood Avenue, St. Louis, MO 63119-3192
Admissions Phone: 314-918-2504 · **Admissions Fax:** 314-918-2640
Admissions E-mail: dwindler@eden.edu · **Web Address:** www.eden.edu

INSTITUTIONAL INFORMATION

Public/private: Private (nonprofit). **Evening Classes Available?** Yes. **Total Faculty:** 26. **% Faculty Female:** 46. **% Faculty Part-time:** 38. **Student/faculty Ratio:** 13:1. **Students in Parent Institution:** 218.

STUDENT INFORMATION

Total Students in Program: 195. **% Full-time:** 79. **% Female:** 56. **% Minority:** 14. **% International:** 4.

RESEARCH FACILITIES

Research Facilities: Evangelical Synod Archives.

EXPENSES/FINANCIAL AID

Annual Tuition: $6,600. **Room & Board:** $3,339. **Fees:** $155. **Books and Supplies:** $600. **% Receiving Financial Aid:** 95. **Average student debt, upon graduation:** $1,500.

ADMISSIONS INFORMATION

Application Fee: $25. **Regular Application Deadline:** 7/15. **Regular Notification:** Rolling. **Transfer Students Accepted?** Yes. **Transfer Policy:** Minimum 3.0 GPA required of transfer applicants. Credit cannot be more than 7 years old. One year Eden residency (27 hours plus 2 units field education) required. **Number of Applications Received:** 75. **% of Applicants Accepted:** 77. **% Accepted Who Enrolled:** 100. **Average GPA:** 3.0.
Required Admission Factors: Essays/personal statement, interview, letters of recommendation, transcript.
Other Admission Factors: Minimum 2.7 GPA required.

EDGEWOOD COLLEGE
Graduate Studies

Address: 1000 Edgewood College Drive, Madison, WI 53711-1997
Admissions Phone: 608-663-2217 · **Admissions Fax:** 608-663-3291

INSTITUTIONAL INFORMATION

Public/private: Private (nonprofit). **Evening Classes Available?** Yes. **Student/faculty Ratio:** 13:1. **Students in Parent Institution:** 2,077.

STUDENT INFORMATION

Total Students in Program: 542. **% Full-time:** 10. **% Female:** 68.

EXPENSES/FINANCIAL AID

Annual Tuition: $3,438. **Books and Supplies:** $200. **Grants Range From:** $200-$6,650. **Loans Range From:** $200-$18,500. **% Receiving Loans:** 99.

ADMISSIONS INFORMATION

Application Fee: $25. **Regular Notification:** Rolling. **Transfer Students Accepted?** Yes.
Required Admission Factors: Essays/personal statement, letters of recommendation, transcript.
Other Admission Factors: Minimum 2.75 GPA required.

EMPLOYMENT INFORMATION

Placement Office Available? Yes. **% Employed Within 6 Months:** 80. **% of master's grads employed in their field upon graduation:** 82. **Rate of placement:** 90%. **Average starting salary:** $32,000.

EDINBORO UNIVERSITY OF PENNSYLVANIA
School of Liberal Arts

Address: Edinboro, PA 16444
Admissions Phone: 814-732-2856 or 888-845-2890
Admissions Fax: 814-732-2611
Admissions E-mail: mbevevino@edinboro.edu
Web Address: www.edinboro.edu/cwis/acaf/gradstudy/programs.htm

INSTITUTIONAL INFORMATION

Public/private: Public. **Evening Classes Available?** Yes. **Student/faculty Ratio:** 6:1. **Students in Parent Institution:** 7,498.

STUDENT INFORMATION

Total Students in Program: 814. **% Full-time:** 45. **% Female:** 70.

RESEARCH FACILITIES

Research Facilities: Miller Research Learning Center, Governor George Leader Speech and Hearing Center.

EXPENSES/FINANCIAL AID

Annual Tuition: In-state $4,600. / Out-of-state $7,554. **Room & Board:** $5,886/$5,500. **Fees:** $928. **Books and Supplies:** $650. **Grants Range From:** $350-$7,000. **Loans Range From:** $350-$14,100. **% Receiving Financial Aid:** 25. **% Receiving Scholarships/Grants:** 12. **% Receiving Loans:** 61. **% Receiving Assistantships:** 51. **Number of Teaching/Research Assistantships Granted Each Year:** 74. **Average Salary Stipend:** $1,575.

ADMISSIONS INFORMATION

Application Fee: $25. **Regular Notification:** Rolling. **Transfer Students Accepted?** Yes. **Transfer Policy:** Maximum 9 credit hours may be transferred into most programs. Maximum 12 credit hours may be transferred. **Average GRE Verbal:** 427. **Average GRE Quantitative:** 462. **Average GRE Analytical:** 548.
Required Admission Factors: Letters of recommendation, transcript.
Other Admission Factors: Minimum MAT score in the top 50% or minimum 2.5 GPA required for unconditional acceptance.
Program-Specific Admission Factors: Slides of recent work required of art program applicants. Minimum 2.8 GPA and essay describing professional goals required of social work applicants.

EMPLOYMENT INFORMATION

Placement Office Available? Yes.

ELMIRA COLLEGE
Graduate Programs

Address: One Park Place, Elmira, NY 14901
Admissions Phone: 607-735-1825 · **Admissions Fax:** 607-735-1150
Admissions E-mail: graduate@elmira.edu

INSTITUTIONAL INFORMATION

Public/private: Private (nonprofit). **Evening Classes Available?** Yes. **Student/faculty Ratio:** 15:1. **Students in Parent Institution:** 2,013.

STUDENT INFORMATION

Total Students in Program: 418. **% Full-time:** 11. **% Female:** 76.

EXPENSES/FINANCIAL AID

Annual Tuition: $13,248. **Fees:** $65. **Grants Range From:** $75-$550. **Loans Range From:** $2,000-$18,500. **% Receiving Financial Aid:** 45. **% Receiving Scholarships/Grants:** 6. **% Receiving Loans:** 100. **% Receiving Assistantships:** 12.

ADMISSIONS INFORMATION

Application Fee: $40. **Regular Notification:** Rolling. **Transfer Students Accepted?** Yes. **Transfer Policy:** Credits to be transferred must be graduate-level and have a minimum grade of B.

Required Admission Factors: Essays/personal statement, transcript.

EMPLOYMENT INFORMATION

Placement Office Available? Yes.

ELON UNIVERSITY
Office of Graduate Admissions

Address: 100 Campus Drive, 2750 Campus Box, Elon, NC 27244
Admissions Phone: 336-278-7600 · **Admissions Fax:** 336-278-7699
Admissions E-mail: gradadm@elon.edu · **Web Address:** www.elon.edu/graduate

INSTITUTIONAL INFORMATION

Public/private: Private (nonprofit). **Evening Classes Available?** Yes. **Total Faculty:** 59. **% Faculty Female:** 76. **% Faculty Part-time:** 17. **Student/faculty Ratio:** 20:1. **Students in Parent Institution:** 4,796.

PROGRAMS

Masters offered in: Business administration/management, education, elementary education and teaching, special education. **Doctorate offered in:** Physical therapy/therapist. **First Professional degree offered in:** Physical therapy/therapist.

STUDENT INFORMATION

Total Students in Program: 174. **% Full-time:** 51. **% Female:** 62.

RESEARCH FACILITIES

Research Facilities: The state-of-the-art Carol Grotnes Belk Library features the latest in information technology and is located at the center of campus, convenient to all graduate classrooms. Writing assistance and computer services also available.

EXPENSES/FINANCIAL AID

Annual Tuition: $21,412. **Books and Supplies:** $2,800. **Grants Range From:** $500-$14,817. **Loans Range From:** $1,700-$36,000. **% Receiving Financial Aid:** 49. **% Receiving Scholarships/Grants:** 13. **% Receiving Loans:** 95. **Types of Aid Available:** Loans, scholarships.

ADMISSIONS INFORMATION

Application Fee: $35. **Regular Application Deadline:** 9/1. **Regular Notification:** Rolling. **Transfer Students Accepted?** Yes. **Transfer Policy:** MEd: Maximum of 6 credit hours transferred; MBA: maximum of 9 credit hours transferred. **Number of Applications Received:** 259. **% of Applicants Accepted:** 59. **% Accepted Who Enrolled:** 78. **Average GPA:** 3.4. **Average GRE Verbal:** 470. **Average GRE Quantitative:** 610. **Average GRE Analytical:** 640. **Average GRE Analytical Writing:** 4.5.
Required Admission Factors: Essays/personal statement, letters of recommendation, transcript.
Recommended Admission Factors: Interview
Other Admission Factors: GPA of 3.0 or higher given admissions priority.
Program-Specific Admission Factors: Minimum GMAT score of 470 required of MBA program applicants. Minimum GRE score of 800 or minimum MAT score of 380-385 required of MEd program applicants. Recommended GRE score of 1000 requested of DPT program applicants.

EMPLOYMENT INFORMATION

% Employed Within 6 Months: 100. **Rate of placement:** 100%. **Average starting salary:** $47,000.

EMBRY-RIDDLE AERONAUTICAL UNIVERSITY
Graduate Programs

Address: 600 South Clyde Morris Boulevard, Daytona Beach, FL 32114-3900
Admissions Phone: 800-388-3728 · **Admissions Fax:** 386-226-7111
Admissions E-mail: graduate.admissions@erau.edu
Web Address: www.embryriddle.edu/graduate

INSTITUTIONAL INFORMATION

Public/private: Private (nonprofit). **Student/faculty Ratio:** 9:1. **Students in Parent Institution:** 4,900.

STUDENT INFORMATION

Total Students in Program: 300. **% Full-time:** 100. **% Female:** 21.

RESEARCH FACILITIES

Research Facilities: Affiliated research centers with Galaxy Scientific, McDonnell Douglas, Preston Group, Lockheed Martin, Harris Corportaion, Federal Aviation Administration, NASA/Global A/C, National Science Foundation.

EXPENSES/FINANCIAL AID

Annual Tuition: $13,140. **Fees:** $240. **Books and Supplies:** $800. **Grants Range From:** $1,000-$3,380. **Loans Range From:** $7,500-$18,500. **% Receiving Financial Aid:** 82. **% Receiving Loans:** 72. **Average student debt, upon graduation:** $28,585 **Number of Fellowships Granted Each Year:** 1. **Average amount of individual fellowships per year:** $18,580. **Number of Teaching/Research Assistantships Granted Each Year:** 93. **Average Salary Stipend:** $2,600.

ADMISSIONS INFORMATION

Application Fee: $50. **Regular Application Deadline:** 7/1. **Regular Notification:** Rolling. **Transfer Students Accepted?** Yes. **Transfer Policy:** Minimum grade average varies for each program. Minimum GPA varies depending on the program. Statement of objectives, official transcripts, resume, and 3 references are required. **Number of Applications Received:** 269. **% of Applicants Accepted:** 59. **% Accepted Who Enrolled:** 63.
Required Admission Factors: Essays/personal statement, letters of recommendation, transcript.
Other Admission Factors: Minimum GPA varies depending on the program. Statement of objectives, official transcripts, resume and 3 references are required.
Program-Specific Admission Factors: MBAA, Minimum GPA 3.0, GMAT required; MSA, Minimum GPA 2.5; MSAE, Minimum GPA 3.0, GRE preferred; MSE, Minimum GPA 3.0, GRE preferred; MSHFS, Minimum GPA 2.75, GRE required; MSSPS, Minimum GPA 3.0, GRE preferred.

EMPLOYMENT INFORMATION

Placement Office Available? Yes. **% of master's employed in their field upon graduation:** 90. **Rate of placement:** 96%. **Average starting salary:** $275,000.

EMERSON COLLEGE
School of the Arts and School of Communication

Address: Office of Graduate Admission, 120 Boylston Street, Boston, MA 02116-4624
Admissions Phone: 617-824-8610 · **Admissions Fax:** 617-824-8614
Admissions E-mail: gradapp@emerson.edu
Web Address: www.emerson.edu/graduate_admission

INSTITUTIONAL INFORMATION

Public/private: Private (nonprofit). **Evening Classes Available?** Yes. **Students in Parent Institution:** 4,398.

PROGRAMS

Masters offered in: Acting; advertising; broadcast journalism; business/corporate communications; cinematography and film/video production; communication disorders; communications, journalism, and related fields; creative writing; digital communications and media/multimedia; drama and dance teacher education; education/teaching of individuals with speech or language impairments; health communications; intermedia/multimedia; international business; international marketing; journalism; marketing; mass communications/media studies; organizational communication; organizational communications, public relations, and advertising; public health education and promotion; public relations/

image management; publishing; radio and television; radio, television, and digital communications; speech-language pathology/pathologist.

STUDENT INFORMATION

Total Students in Program: 980. **% Full-time:** 100.

RESEARCH FACILITIES

Research Facilities: Robbins Speech, Language, and Hearing Center; Thayer Lindsley Parent-Centered Preschool Nursery for the Hearing Impaired.

EXPENSES/FINANCIAL AID

Annual Tuition: $28,720. **Fees:** $2,600. **Books and Supplies:** $500. **% Receiving Scholarships/Grants:** 1. **% Receiving Loans:** 91. **% Receiving Assistantships:** 30.

ADMISSIONS INFORMATION

Application Fee: $60. **Regular Application Deadline:** 7/1. **Regular Notification:** Rolling. **Transfer Students Accepted?** Yes. **Number of Applications Received:** 1,458. **% of Applicants Accepted:** 58. **% Accepted Who Enrolled:** 48. **Average GPA:** 3.4. **Average GRE Verbal:** 522. **Average GRE Quantitative:** 572.

Required Admission Factors: Essays/personal statement, GRE, letters of recommendation, transcript.

EMPLOYMENT INFORMATION

Placement Office Available? Yes. **% Employed Within 6 Months:** 90.

EMMANUEL SCHOOL OF RELIGION
Graduate Programs

Address: One Walker Drive, Johnson City, TN 37601
Admissions Phone: 423-461-1535 or 800-933-3771 · **Admissions Fax:** 423-926-6198
Admissions E-mail: webmaster@esr.edu · **Web Address:** www.esr.edu

INSTITUTIONAL INFORMATION

Public/private: Private (nonprofit). **Students in Parent Institution:** 159.

PROGRAMS

Masters offered in: Divinity/ministry (BD, MDiv).

STUDENT INFORMATION

Total Students in Program: 64. **% Full-time:** 38. **% Female:** 23.

EXPENSES/FINANCIAL AID

Annual Tuition: $5,760. **Fees:** $320. **Books and Supplies:** $500. **Grants Range From:** $1,100-$5,000. **Loans Range From:** $1,000-$10,000. **% Receiving Scholarships/Grants:** 95. **% Receiving Loans:** 40. **% Receiving Assistantships:** 8.

ADMISSIONS INFORMATION

Application Fee: $25. **Regular Application Deadline:** 8/1. **Transfer Students Accepted?** Yes. **Number of Applications Received:** 56. **% of Applicants Accepted:** 98. **% Accepted Who Enrolled:** 84. **Average GPA:** 3.0. **Required Admission Factors:** Essays/personal statement, letters of recommendation, transcript.
Other Admission Factors: Minimum 2.75 GPA required.

EMPLOYMENT INFORMATION

Placement Office Available? Yes. **% Employed Within 6 Months:** 75. **Rate of placement:** 95%. **Average starting salary:** $50,000.

EMORY UNIVERSITY
Graduate School of Arts & Sciences

Address: 550 Asbury Circle, 200 Candler Library, Atlanta, GA 30322
Admissions Phone: 404-727-6028 · **Admissions Fax:** 404-727-4990
Admissions E-mail: gsoas@emory.edu · **Web Address:** www.emory.edu/GSOAS/

INSTITUTIONAL INFORMATION

Public/private: Private (nonprofit). **Students in Parent Institution:** 11,781.

PROGRAMS

Masters offered in: Computer science, film/cinema studies, Jewish/Judaic studies, junior high/intermediate/middle school education and teaching, music/music and performing arts studies, secondary education and teaching. **Doctorate offered in:** African studies; African-American/Black studies; American/U.S. studies/civilization; anthropology; biology/biological sciences; biomedical sciences; biomedical/medical engineering; biostatistics; chemistry, clinical psychology.

STUDENT INFORMATION

Total Students in Program: 1,626. **% Full-time:** 100. **% Female:** 60. **% Minority:** 31. **% International:** 6.

RESEARCH FACILITIES

Research Facilities: The university is linked to the Carter Center, an international leader in conflict resolution and democracy studies, the Yerkes Primate Center, and the U.S. Centers for Disease Control and Prevention. Additional resources are available for graduate students.

EXPENSES/FINANCIAL AID

Annual Tuition: $26,770. **Room & Board:** $9,474. **Fees:** $392. **Books and Supplies:** $1,000. **Grants Range From:** $13,000-$24,000. **% Receiving Financial Aid:** 95. **% Receiving Scholarships/Grants:** 100. **Types of Aid Available:** Fellowships, scholarships. **Assistantship Compensation Includes:** Full tuition remission, salary/stipend. **Average Salary Stipend:** $15,600.

ADMISSIONS INFORMATION

Application Fee: $50. **Regular Application Deadline:** 1/3. **Transfer Students Accepted?** Yes. **Transfer Policy:** Up to 12 semester hours of coursework; any amount over 12 hours must be approved by dean of graduate school with strong support from department. In no case will more than 24 hours be transferred. **Number of Applications Received:** 3,299. **% of Applicants Accepted:** 16. **% Accepted Who Enrolled:** 51. **Average GPA:** 3.4. **Average GRE Verbal:** 599. **Average GRE Quantitative:** 654. **Average GRE Analytical:** 657.

Required Admission Factors: Essays/personal statement, GRE, letters of recommendation, transcript.
Recommended Admission Factors: Interview.

EMPORIA STATE UNIVERSITY
Graduate Studies

Address: 1200 Commercial, Emporia, KS 66801
Admissions Phone: 620-341-5403 · **Admissions Fax:** 620-341-5909
Admissions E-mail: gradinfo@emporia.edu · **Web Address:** www.emporia.edu/grad

INSTITUTIONAL INFORMATION

Public/private: Public. **Evening Classes Available?** Yes. **Total Faculty:** 324. **% Faculty Female:** 50. **Students in Parent Institution:** 6,278.

PROGRAMS

Masters offered in: Advanced legal research/studies (LLM, MCL, MLI, MSL, JSD/SJD, art therapy/therapist, business administration/management, business teacher education, counselor education/school counseling and guidance services, curriculum and instruction, education leadership and administration, educational/instructional media design, elementary education and teaching, English language and literature, health and physical education, history, library science/librarianship, mathematics, physical sciences, psychology, rehabilitation counseling/counselor, school psychology, secondary education and teaching, social sciences, special education. **Doctorate offered in:** Library science/librarianship.

STUDENT INFORMATION

Total Students in Program: 1,343. **% Full-time:** 18. **% Female:** 71.

EXPENSES/FINANCIAL AID
Annual Tuition: In-state $2,556. / Out-of-state $6,572.

ADMISSIONS INFORMATION
Application Fee: $30. Regular Notification: Rolling. Transfer Students Accepted? Yes. Number of Applications Received: 412. % of Applicants Accepted: 55. % Accepted Who Enrolled: 85. Required Admission Factors: Transcript.

EMPLOYMENT INFORMATION
Placement Office Available? Yes.

ENDICOTT COLLEGE
Van Loan School of Graduate & Professional Studies

Address: 376 Hale Street, Beverly, MA 01915
Admissions Phone: 978-232-2084 · **Admissions Fax:** 978-232-3000
Admissions E-mail: psquarci@endicott.edu · **Web Address:** www.endicott.edu/gps

INSTITUTIONAL INFORMATION
Public/private: Private (nonprofit). Evening Classes Available? Yes. Total Faculty: 48. % Faculty Female: 54. % Faculty Part-time: 94. Student/faculty Ratio: 14:1. Students in Parent Institution: 2,023.

PROGRAMS
Masters offered in: Art teacher education, business administration/management, computer teacher education, education, elementary education and teaching, hospitality administration/management, international and comparative education, Montessori teacher education, nonprofit/public/organizational management, reading teacher education, special education and teaching, special education.

STUDENT INFORMATION
Total Students in Program: 264. % Full-time: 36. % Female: 70.

RESEARCH FACILITIES
Research Facilities: The Global Institute of Student Aspirations

EXPENSES/FINANCIAL AID
Loans Range From: $2,500-$18,500. % Receiving Financial Aid: 7. % Receiving Loans: 100.

ADMISSIONS INFORMATION
Application Fee: $50. Regular Application Deadline: 9/4. Regular Notification: Rolling. Transfer Students Accepted? Yes. Transfer Policy: Official gradaute transcript for the courses being requested to be transferred, course description/syllabus. Number of Applications Received: 120. % of Applicants Accepted: 100. % Accepted Who Enrolled: 83. Average GPA: 3.0
Required Admission Factors: Essays/personal statement, letters of recommendation, transcript.
Program-Specific Admission Factors: For Massachusetts Teacher Licensure programs, Massachusetts Tests for Educator Licensure and/or teaching licenses may be required.

EMPLOYMENT INFORMATION
Placement Office Available? Yes. % Employed Within 6 Months: 100. % of master's grads employed in their field upon graduation: 100. Rate of placement: 95%. Average starting salary: $45,000.

EPISCOPAL DIVINITY SCHOOL
Graduate Programs

Address: 99 Brattle Street, Cambridge, MA 02138
Admissions Phone: 617-868-3450, ext. 307 · **Admissions Fax:** 617-864-5385
Admissions E-mail: admissions@episdivschool.edu

INSTITUTIONAL INFORMATION
Public/private: Private (nonprofit). Student/faculty Ratio: 4:1. Students in Parent Institution: 99.

STUDENT INFORMATION
Total Students in Program: 99. % Full-time: 61. % Female: 69.

EXPENSES/FINANCIAL AID
Annual Tuition: $13,500. Room & Board: $3,945. Grants Range From: $2,000. Loans Range From: $1,000-$18,500. % Receiving Financial Aid: 63. % Receiving Scholarships/Grants: 93. % Receiving Loans: 100. Average student debt, upon graduation: $31,000.

ADMISSIONS INFORMATION
Application Fee: $50. Regular Notification: Rolling. Transfer Students Accepted? Yes.
Required Admission Factors: Essays/personal statement, GRE, interview, letters of recommendation, transcript.

EMPLOYMENT INFORMATION
Placement Office Available? Yes.

EPISCOPAL THEOLOGICAL SEMINARY OF THE SOUTHWEST
Graduate Programs

Address: PO Box 2247, 606 Rathervue Place, Austin, TX 78768-2247
Admissions Phone: 512-472-4133 · **Admissions Fax:** 512-472-3098
Admissions E-mail: jliro@etss.edu

INSTITUTIONAL INFORMATION
Public/private: Private (nonprofit). Evening Classes Available? Yes. Student/faculty Ratio: 7:1. Students in Parent Institution: 119.

STUDENT INFORMATION
Total Students in Program: 61. % Full-time: 7. % Female: 75.

RESEARCH FACILITIES
Research Facilities: Province VII Center for Hispanic Ministries, National Archives of the Episcopal Church.

EXPENSES/FINANCIAL AID
Annual Tuition: $9,826. Fees: $100. Books and Supplies: $500. Grants Range From: $1,224-$19,356. % Receiving Financial Aid: 45. % Receiving Scholarships/Grants: 45. Average student debt, upon graduation: $14,238.

ADMISSIONS INFORMATION
Application Fee: $30. Transfer Students Accepted? Yes. Transfer Policy: Maximum 1 year of credit hours may be transferred. Transcript, catalog, and syllabus required of transfer students. Number of Applications Received: 52. % of Applicants Accepted: 88. % Accepted Who Enrolled: 74. Average GRE Verbal: 576. Average GRE Quantitative: 542. Average GRE Analytical: 593.
Required Admission Factors: Essays/personal statement, interview, letters of recommendation, transcript.
Program-Specific Admission Factors: Support of the diocese recommended for MDiv program applicants.

ERSKINE THEOLOGICAL SEMINARY
Graduate Programs

Address: Drawer 668, Due West, SC 29639
Admissions Phone: 864-379-8885 · **Admissions Fax:** 864-379-2171
Admissions E-mail: jnelson@erskine.edu · **Web Address:** www.erskineseminary.org

INSTITUTIONAL INFORMATION

Public/private: Private (nonprofit). **Evening Classes Available?** Yes. **Students in Parent Institution:** 315

PROGRAMS

Masters offered in: Bible/biblical studies; pastoral studies/counseling; religious education; religious/sacred music. **Doctorate offered in:** Theology/theological studies. **First Professional degree offered in:** Divinity/ministry (BD, MDiv).

STUDENT INFORMATION

Total Students in Program: 315. **% Full-time:** 44. **% Female:** 32. **% International:** 5.

EXPENSES/FINANCIAL AID

Annual Tuition: $6,600. **Room & Board:** $5,315. **Fees:** $100. **Books and Supplies:** $550.

ADMISSIONS INFORMATION

Application Fee: $35. **Regular Application Deadline:** 8/1. **Regular Notification:** Rolling. **Transfer Students Accepted?** Yes.
Required Admission Factors: Essays/personal statement, letters of recommendation, transcript.
Recommended Admission Factors: Interview.

EVANGELICAL SCHOOL OF THEOLOGY
Graduate Programs

Address: 121 South College Street, Myerstown, PA 17067
Admissions Phone: 800-532-5775 · **Admissions Fax:** 717-866-4667
Admissions E-mail: admissions@evangelical.edu · **Web Address:** www.evangelical.edu

INSTITUTIONAL INFORMATION

Public/private: Private (nonprofit). **Evening Classes Available?** Yes. **Total Faculty:** 19. **% Faculty Female:** 21. **% Faculty Part-time:** 58. **Student/faculty Ratio:** 10:1. **Students in Parent Institution:** 200.

PROGRAMS

Masters offered in: Bible/biblical studies, marriage and family therapy/counseling, pastoral counseling and specialized ministries, pastoral studies/counseling, religious education, theological studies and religious vocations, theology/theological studies. **First Professional degree offered in:** Divinity/ministry (BD, MDiv).

STUDENT INFORMATION

Total Students in Program: 46. **% Full-time:** 4. **% Female:** 33.

RESEARCH FACILITIES

Research Facilities: Marriage and Family Center; Wenger Family Counseling Center.

EXPENSES/FINANCIAL AID

Annual Tuition: $9,120. **Room & Board:** $2,200. **Fees:** $50. **Books and Supplies:** $800. **Grants Range From:** $400-$9,120. **Loans Range From:** $2,500-$18,500. **% Receiving Financial Aid:** 75. **% Receiving Scholarships/Grants:** 78. **% Receiving Loans:** 58. **Types of Aid Available:** Grants, loans, scholarships.

ADMISSIONS INFORMATION

Application Fee: $30. **Priority Application Deadline:** 6/1. **Regular Notification:** Rolling. **Transfer Students Accepted?** Yes. **Transfer Policy:** Minimum 3.0 GPA required; 2.5-2.9 may be reviewed for transfer admission on probation and may be required to take either the GRE or GMAT. **Number of Applications Received:** 57. **% of Applicants Accepted:** 70. **% Accepted Who Enrolled:** 100.
Required Admission Factors: Essays/personal statement, letters of recommendation, transcript.
Other Admission Factors: Minimum 3.0 GPA required; 2.5-2.9 may be reviewed for admission on probation and may be required to take either the GRE or GMAT.

Program-Specific Admission Factors: Applicants for the MA, Marriage and Family Therapy should have familiarity with key terminology, concepts, and theories in the field of psychology. For those with little or no background in psychology or those who need a refresher, two prerequisite courses are required.

EMPLOYMENT INFORMATION

Placement Office Available? Yes.

EVANGELICAL SEMINARY OF PUERTO RICO
Graduate Programs

Address: 776 Ponce de Leon Avenue, San Juan, Puerto Rico 00925-2207
Admissions Phone: 787-763-6700, ext. 238 · **Admissions Fax:** 787-763-4773
Admissions E-mail: registro@mailhost.tld.net

INSTITUTIONAL INFORMATION

Public/private: Private (nonprofit). **Evening Classes Available?** Yes. **Student/faculty Ratio:** 15:1. **Students in Parent Institution:** 123.

STUDENT INFORMATION

Total Students in Program: 35.

RESEARCH FACILITIES

Research Facilities: Students have access to University of Puerto Rico and Inter-American University facilities.

EXPENSES/FINANCIAL AID

Annual Tuition: $1,800. **Fees:** $100. **Books and Supplies:** $500. **Grants Range From:** $250-$2,500. **% Receiving Financial Aid:** 86. **% Receiving Scholarships/Grants:** 8.

ADMISSIONS INFORMATION

Application Fee: $35. **Transfer Students Accepted?** Yes. **Transfer Policy:** Maximum 30 credit hours may be transferred into MA religion program. Maximum 60 credit hours may be transferred. **Number of Applications Received:** 29. **% of Applicants Accepted:** 100. **% Accepted Who Enrolled:** 97. **Average GPA:** 3.13.
Required Admission Factors: Essays/personal statement, interview, letters of recommendation, transcript.
Other Admission Factors: Minimum PAEG score of 486 and minimum 2.5 GPA recommended.
Program-Specific Admission Factors: Denominational endorsement required of MDiv. program applicants.

THE EVERGREEN STATE COLLEGE
Program in Environmental Studies

Address: 2700 Evergreen Parkway, NW, Olympia, WA 98505
Admissions Phone: 360-866-6000, ext. 6170

INSTITUTIONAL INFORMATION

Public/private: Public. **Evening Classes Available?** Yes. **Student/faculty Ratio:** 14:1. **Students in Parent Institution:** 4,125.

STUDENT INFORMATION

Total Students in Program: 224. **% Full-time:** 55. **% Female:** 56.

RESEARCH FACILITIES

Research Facilities: Washington Center for Improving the Quality of Undergraduate Education, Washington State Institute for Public Policy, Labor Education and Research Center, Evergreen Center for Educational Improvement (K-12), Northwest Indian Applied Research Institute.

EXPENSES/FINANCIAL AID

Annual Tuition: In-state $4,794/Out-of-state $15,249. **Books and Supplies:** $891. **Grants Range From:** $100-$22,738. **Loans Range From:** $100-

$21,342. % Receiving Financial Aid: 67. % Receiving Scholarships/Grants: 8. % Receiving Loans: 88. % Receiving Assistantships: 5. Average student debt, upon graduation: $30,436. Number of Fellowships Granted Each Year: 14. Average amount of individual fellowships per year: $2,500. Number of Teaching/Research Assistantships Granted Each Year: 5. Average Salary Stipend: $12.

ADMISSIONS INFORMATION

Application Fee: $35. Regular Notification: Rolling. Transfer Students Accepted? No. Transfer Policy: Maximum 12 credit hours of electives may be transferred. Number of Applications Received: 67. % of Applicants Accepted: 87. % Accepted Who Enrolled: 57. Average GPA: 3.42. Average GRE Verbal: 550. Average GRE Quantitative: 570. Average GRE Analytical: 600.
Required Admission Factors: Essays/personal statement, GRE, letters of recommendation, transcript.
Other Admission Factors: Minimum 3.0 GPA required of most applicants.

EMPLOYMENT INFORMATION

Placement Office Available? Yes. % Employed Within 6 Months: 70. Rate of placement: 86%.

THE EVERGREEN STATE COLLEGE
Program in Teaching

Address: 2700 Evergreen Parkway, NW, Olympia, WA 98505
Admissions Phone: 360-866-6000, ext. 6310
Admissions E-mail: welchj@evergreen.edu

INSTITUTIONAL INFORMATION

Public/private: Public. Student/faculty Ratio: 11:1. Students in Parent Institution: 4,125.

STUDENT INFORMATION

Total Students in Program: 224. % Full-time: 55. % Female: 56.

RESEARCH FACILITIES

Research Facilities: Washington Center for Improving the Quality of Undergraduate Education, Washington State Institute for Public Policy, Labor Education and Research Center, Evergreen Center for Educational Improvement (K-12), Northwest Indian Applied Research Institute.

EXPENSES/FINANCIAL AID

Annual Tuition: In-state $4,794/Out-of-state $15,249. Books and Supplies: $891. Grants Range From: $100-$22,738. Loans Range From: $100-$21,342. % Receiving Financial Aid: 67. % Receiving Scholarships/Grants: 8. % Receiving Loans: 88. % Receiving Assistantships: 5. Average student debt, upon graduation: $27,481. Number of Fellowships Granted Each Year: 6. Average amount of individual fellowships per year: $2,500. Number of Teaching/Research Assistantships Granted Each Year: 2. Average Salary Stipend: $12.

ADMISSIONS INFORMATION

Application Fee: $35. Regular Notification: Rolling. Transfer Students Accepted? No. Number of Applications Received: 71. % of Applicants Accepted: 66. % Accepted Who Enrolled: 85.
Required Admission Factors: Essays/personal statement, GRE, letters of recommendation, transcript.
Other Admission Factors: Minimum 3.0 GPA and teaching endorsments required.

EMPLOYMENT INFORMATION

Placement Office Available? Yes. Rate of placement: 86%.

EXCELSIOR COLLEGE (FORMERLY REGENTS COLLEGE)
Liberal Studies Program

Address: 7 Columbia Circle, Albany, NY 12203-5159
Admissions Phone: 888-647-2388 · Admissions Fax: 518-464-8777
Admissions E-mail: mls@excelsior.edu

INSTITUTIONAL INFORMATION

Public/private: Private (nonprofit). Evening Classes Available? Yes. Student/faculty Ratio: 6:1. Students in Parent Institution: 18,041.

STUDENT INFORMATION

Total Students in Program: 181 % Female: 23.

EXPENSES/FINANCIAL AID

Annual Tuition: $5,220. Books and Supplies: $150.

ADMISSIONS INFORMATION

Application Fee: $100. Regular Notification: Rolling. Transfer Students Accepted? Yes. Number of Applications Received: 23. % of Applicants Accepted: 87. % Accepted Who Enrolled: 85.
Required Admission Factors: Essays/personal statement, transcript.

FAIRFIELD UNIVERSITY
College of Arts & Sciences

Address: 1073 North Benson Road, Canisius Hall, Room 302, Fairfield, CT 06824-5195
Admissions Phone: 203-254-4184 · Admissions Fax: 203-254-4073
Admissions E-mail: gradadmis@mail.fairfield.edu
Web Address: www.fairfield.edu/academic/graduate.htm

INSTITUTIONAL INFORMATION

Public/private: Private (nonprofit). Evening Classes Available? Yes. Total Faculty: 128. % Faculty Female: 48. % Faculty Part-time: 88. Student/faculty Ratio: 10:1. Students in Parent Institution: 5,053.

PROGRAMS

Masters offered in: Area, ethnic, cultural, and gender studies; mathematics.

STUDENT INFORMATION

Total Students in Program: 56. % Full-time: 14. % Female: 46.

EXPENSES/FINANCIAL AID

Annual Tuition: $390. Fees: $25. Books and Supplies: $600. Grants Range From: $100-$1,000. Loans Range From: $200-$18,500. Types of Aid Available: Loans, assistantships available in student services.

ADMISSIONS INFORMATION

Application Fee: $55. Priority Application Deadline: 7/1. Regular Application Deadline: 7/1. Regular Notification: Rolling. Transfer Students Accepted? Yes. Transfer Policy: Maximum 6 credit hours (evaluated on an individual basis) may be transferred. Number of Applications Received: 18. % of Applicants Accepted: 89. % Accepted Who Enrolled: 100. Average GPA: 3.0.
Required Admission Factors: Essays/personal statement, letters of recommendation, transcript.
Recommended Admission Factors:
Other Admission Factors: Minimum 3.0 GPA required.

EMPLOYMENT INFORMATION

Placement Office Available? Yes. % Employed Within 6 Months: 100. % of master's grads employed in their field upon graduation: 100. Rate of placement: 90%. Average starting salary: $30,000.

FAIRLEIGH DICKINSON UNIVERSITY—
TEANECK-HACKENSACK CAMPUS
New College of General &
Continuing Studies

Address: 1000 River Road, Teaneck, NJ 07666
Admissions Phone: 201-692-2551

INSTITUTIONAL INFORMATION

Public/private: Private (nonprofit). **Evening Classes Available?** Yes. **Students in Parent Institution:** 9,079.

STUDENT INFORMATION

Total Students in Program: 2,682. **% Full-time:** 24.

EXPENSES/FINANCIAL AID

Annual Tuition: $10,746. **Grants Range From:** $1,000-$10,000. **Loans Range From:** $900-$18,500. **% Receiving Scholarships/Grants:** 20. **% Receiving Loans:** 100.

ADMISSIONS INFORMATION

Regular Notification: Rolling. **Transfer Students Accepted?** Yes. **Transfer Policy:** Minimum 3.0 GPA required of transfer applicants.
Required Admission Factors: Transcript.
Other Admission Factors: Minimum 2.7 GPA required.
Program-Specific Admission Factors: Work experience required of hospitality management studies program applicants.

EMPLOYMENT INFORMATION

Placement Office Available? Yes. **Rate of placement:** 76%.

FAIRLEIGH DICKINSON UNIVERSITY—
TEANECK-HACKENSACK CAMPUS
University College: Arts, Sciences, &
Professional Studies

Address: 1000 River Road, Teaneck, NJ 07666
Admissions Phone: 201-692-2551 · **Admissions Fax:** 201-692-2560
Admissions E-mail: anelson@mailbox.fdu.edu

INSTITUTIONAL INFORMATION

Public/private: Private (nonprofit). **Evening Classes Available?** Yes. **Students in Parent Institution:** 9,079

STUDENT INFORMATION

Total Students in Program: 2,682. **% Full-time:** 24.

EXPENSES/FINANCIAL AID

Annual Tuition: $10,746. **Grants Range From:** $1,000-$10,000. **Loans Range From:** $900-$18,500. **% Receiving Financial Aid:** 31. **% Receiving Scholarships/Grants:** 20. **% Receiving Loans:** 100. **Average student debt, upon graduation:** $24,985.

ADMISSIONS INFORMATION

Application Fee: $40. **Transfer Students Accepted?** Yes. **Transfer Policy:** Maximum 6 credit hours with a minimum grade of B may be transferred. **Number of Applications Received:** 1,596. **% of Applicants Accepted:** 74. **% Accepted Who Enrolled:** 58.
Required Admission Factors: Letters of recommendation, transcript.
Other Admission Factors: Minimum 2.75 GPA required of some programs.

EMPLOYMENT INFORMATION

Placement Office Available? Yes. **% of master's grads employed in their field upon graduation:** 62. **Rate of placement:** 76%.

FAULKNER UNIVERSITY
Graduate Programs

Address: 5345 Atlanta Highway, Montgomery, AL 36109
Admissions Phone: 334-386-7142 · **Admissions Fax:** 334-386-7143
Admissions E-mail: dnorris@faulkner.edu · **Web Address:** www.faulkner.edu

INSTITUTIONAL INFORMATION

Public/private: Private (nonprofit). **Students in Parent Institution:** 2,696.

PROGRAMS

Masters offered in: Bible/biblical studies; corrections and criminal justice; human resources management and services; law, legal services, and legal studies.

STUDENT INFORMATION

Total Students in Program: 50. **% Full-time:** 100.

EXPENSES/FINANCIAL AID

Annual Tuition: $12,000. **Room & Board:** $4,200. **Books and Supplies:** $1,000. **Grants Range From:** $500-$4,000. **Loans Range From:** $4,000-$12,000. **% Receiving Scholarships/Grants:** 2. **% Receiving Loans:** 98.

ADMISSIONS INFORMATION

Application Fee: $25. **Transfer Students Accepted?** No. **Number of Applications Received:** 78. **% of Applicants Accepted:** 77. **% Accepted Who Enrolled:** 83. **Average GPA:** 3.1.
Required Admission Factors: Transcript.
Other Admission Factors: Minimum GMAT score of 400, minimum 2.5 GPA, and resume required.

EMPLOYMENT INFORMATION

Placement Office Available? Yes.

FELICIAN COLLEGE
Graduate Studies

Address: 262 South Main Street, Lodi, NJ 07644
Admissions Phone: 201-559-6131 · **Admissions Fax:** 201-559-6188
Admissions E-mail: santaniellor@net.felician.edu

INSTITUTIONAL INFORMATION

Public/private: Private (nonprofit). **Evening Classes Available?** Yes. **Student/faculty Ratio:** 6:1. **Students in Parent Institution:** 1,559

STUDENT INFORMATION

Total Students in Program: 97. **% Full-time:** 4. **% Female:** 85.

EXPENSES/FINANCIAL AID

Annual Tuition: $7,470. **Room & Board:** $9,376. **Fees:** $475. **Grants Range From:** $750-$2,000. **Loans Range From:** $2,625-$10,500. **% Receiving Financial Aid:** 90. **% Receiving Scholarships/Grants:** 60. **% Receiving Loans:** 40. **Average student debt, upon graduation:** $15,000.

ADMISSIONS INFORMATION

Application Fee: $40. **Regular Notification:** Rolling. **Transfer Students Accepted?** Yes. **Number of Applications Received:** 105. **% of Applicants Accepted:** 74. **% Accepted Who Enrolled:** 77. **Average GPA:** 3.0.
Required Admission Factors: Essays/personal statement, letters of recommendation, transcript.
Other Admission Factors: Minimum 3.0 GPA required. 2 letters of recommendation required for MS Nursing program, three for education program, and 1 for religious education and English programs.

EMPLOYMENT INFORMATION

Placement Office Available? Yes. **% Employed Within 6 Months:** 100. **% of master's grads employed in their field upon graduation:** 100.

FIELDING GRADUATE UNIVERSITY
Graduate Programs

Address: 2112 Santa Barbara Street, Santa Barbara, CA 93105-3538
Admissions Phone: 800-340-1099 · **Admissions Fax:** 805-687-3296
Admissions E-mail: admissions@fielding.edu · **Web Address:** www.fielding.edu

INSTITUTIONAL INFORMATION
Public/private: Private (nonprofit). **Total Faculty:** 95. **% Faculty Female:** 53. **% Faculty Part-time:** 21. **Student/faculty Ratio:** 16:1. **Students in Parent Institution:** 1,546.

PROGRAMS
Masters offered in: Clinical psychology, education leadership and administration, human development and family studies, psychology, social sciences. **Doctorate offered in:** Clinical psychology, education leadership and administration, human development and family studies, psychology, social sciences.

STUDENT INFORMATION
Total Students in Program: 1,546. **% Full-time:** 94. **% Female:** 71. **% Minority:** 28. **% International:** 1.

RESEARCH FACILITIES
Research Facilities: Affiliated with the School of Human & Organization Development: Center for Innovation in the Nonprofit Sector. Affiliated with the school of Psychology: Alonso Center for Psychodynamic Studies.

EXPENSES/FINANCIAL AID
Annual Tuition: $16,980. **Room & Board:** $13,354. **Fees:** $1,161. **Books and Supplies:** $2,000. **Grants Range From:** $750-$2,500. **Loans Range From:** $500-$18,500. **% Receiving Financial Aid:** 78. **% Receiving Scholarships/Grants:** 7. **% Receiving Loans:** 93. **Types of Aid Available:** Loans, scholarships. **Average student debt, upon graduation:** $85,000.

ADMISSIONS INFORMATION
Application Fee: $75. **Regular Application Deadline:** 2/24. **Regular Notification:** 7/6. **Transfer Students Accepted?** Yes. **Number of Applications Received:** 552. **% of Applicants Accepted:** 55. **% Accepted Who Enrolled:** 68. **Average GPA:** 3.4.
Required Admission Factors: Essays/personal statement, interview, letters of recommendation, transcript.
Other Admission Factors: Minimum 3.0 GPA required.

FLORIDA AGRICULTURAL AND MECHANICAL UNIVERSITY
College of Arts & Sciences

Address: Tallahassee, FL 32307

INSTITUTIONAL INFORMATION
Public/private: Public. **Students in Parent Institution:** 13,070.

STUDENT INFORMATION
Total Students in Program: 543. **% Female:** 60.

EXPENSES/FINANCIAL AID
Room & Board: $2,982.

ADMISSIONS INFORMATION
Transfer Students Accepted? No.

FLORIDA ATLANTIC UNIVERSITY
Charles E. Schmidt College of Science

Address: 777 Glades Road, PO Box 3091, Boca Raton, FL 33431-0991
Admissions Phone: 561-297-2247 · **Admissions Fax:** 561-297-3792
Admissions E-mail: perryg@fau.edu · **Web Address:** www.science.fau.edu/

INSTITUTIONAL INFORMATION
Public/private: Public. **Evening Classes Available?** Yes. **Total Faculty:** 135. **% Faculty Female:** 21. **Students in Parent Institution:** 25,018.

PROGRAMS
Masters offered in: Applied mathematics, chemistry, environmental science, geography, geology/earth science, mathematics, physics, psychology. **Doctorate offered in:** Chemistry, experimental psychology, mathematics, physics, physiological psychology/psychobiology.

STUDENT INFORMATION
Total Students in Program: 363. **% Full-time:** 76. **% Female:** 54. **% Minority:** 18. **% International:** 22.

RESEARCH FACILITIES
Research Facilities: Center for Complex Systems & Brain Sciences, Center for Molecular Biology & Biotechnology, Center for Geo-Information Science.

EXPENSES/FINANCIAL AID
Annual Tuition: In-state $3,777. / Out-of-state $13,953. **Room & Board (On/off Campus):** $5,600/$7,415. **Books and Supplies:** $660. **Grants Range From:** $100-$12,500. **Loans Range From:** $100-$18,500. **% Receiving Scholarships/Grants:** 64. **% Receiving Loans:** 36. **Types of Aid Available:** Graduate assistantships, grants, loans, scholarships.

ADMISSIONS INFORMATION
Application Fee: $30. **Priority Application Deadline:** 7/1. **Regular Application Deadline:** 7/1. **Regular Notification:** Rolling. **Transfer Students Accepted?** Yes. **Number of Applications Received:** 277. **% of Applicants Accepted:** 55. **% Accepted Who Enrolled:** 72. **Average GPA:** 3.5. **Average GRE Verbal:** 527. **Average GRE Quantitative:** 644.
Required Admission Factors: GRE, transcript.
Other Admission Factors: 3.0 in last 60 hours of undergraduate work; GRE minimum 1000; GMAT minimum 500.

EMPLOYMENT INFORMATION
Placement Office Available? Yes.

FLORIDA ATLANTIC UNIVERSITY
Dorothy F. Schmidt College of Arts & Letters

Address: 777 Glades Road, PO Box 3091, Boca Raton, FL 33431-0991
Admissions Phone: 561-297-3040 · **Admissions Fax:** 561-297-2758
Admissions E-mail: keaton@fau.edu
Web Address: www.fau.edu/divdept/schmidt/index.htm

INSTITUTIONAL INFORMATION
Public/private: Public. **Evening Classes Available?** Yes. **Total Faculty:** 180. **% Faculty Female:** 47. **% Students in Parent Institution:** 25,018.

PROGRAMS
Masters offered in: Anthropology; drama and dramatics/theater arts; English language and literature; fine/studio arts; French language and literature; German language and literature; history; liberal arts and sciences/liberal studies; linguistics; music history, literature, and theory; political science and government; sociology; Spanish language and literature; speech and rhetorical studies; women's studies. **Doctorate offered in:** Multi/interdisciplinary studies.

STUDENT INFORMATION

Total Students in Program: 427. **% Full-time:** 56. **% Female:** 62. **% Minority:** 21. **% International:** 8.

RESEARCH FACILITIES

Research Facilities: Center for Complex Systems & Brain Sciences, Center for Molecular Biology & Biotechnology, Center for Geo-Information Science.

EXPENSES/FINANCIAL AID

Annual Tuition: In-state $3,777. / Out-of-state $13,953. **Room & Board (On/off Campus):** $5,600/$7,415. **Books and Supplies:** $660. **Grants Range From:** $100-$12,500. **Loans Range From:** $100-$18,500. **% Receiving Financial Aid:** 50. **% Receiving Scholarships/Grants:** 64. **% Receiving Loans:** 36. **Number of Fellowships Granted Each Year:** 5. **Average amount of individual fellowships per year:** $9,000. **Number of Teaching/Research Assistantships Granted Each Year:** 120. **Average Salary Stipend:** $3,500.

ADMISSIONS INFORMATION

Application Fee: $30. **Priority Application Deadline:** 7/1. **Regular Application Deadline:** 7/1. **Regular Notification:** Rolling. **Transfer Students Accepted?** Yes. **Number of Applications Received:** 257. **% of Applicants Accepted:** 68. **% Accepted Who Enrolled:** 77. **Average GPA:** 3.2. **Average GRE Verbal:** 483. **Average GRE Quantitative:** 503.
Required Admission Factors: GRE, transcript.
Other Admission Factors: Minimum GRE score of 1000 (verbal and quantitative or analytical) or minimum 3.0 GPA in final 60 credit hours required.

EMPLOYMENT INFORMATION

Placement Office Available? Yes.

FLORIDA ATLANTIC UNIVERSITY
Graduate Studies

Address: 777 Glades Road, PO Box 3091, Boca Raton, FL 33431-0991
Admissions Phone: 561-297-3040 · **Admissions Fax:** 561-297-2758
Admissions E-mail: admisweb@fau.edu · **Web Address:** www.fau.edu/

INSTITUTIONAL INFORMATION

Public/private: Public. **Evening Classes Available?** Yes. **Total Faculty:** 1688. **% Faculty Female:** 45. **% Faculty Part-time:** 40. **Student/faculty Ratio:** 18:1. **Students in Parent Institution:** 25,662.

PROGRAMS

Masters offered in: Accounting; applied mathematics; art teacher education; audiology/audiologist and speech-language pathology/pathologist; biology/biological sciences; biomedical sciences; business administration and management; chemistry; city/urban, community, and regional planning; civil engineering; computer and information sciences; computer engineering; counselor education/school counseling and guidance services; creative writing; curriculum and instruction; drama and dramatics/theater arts; early childhood education and teaching; economics; education leadership and administration; electrical; electronics and communications engineering; elementary education and teaching; English language and literature; environmental science; finance; fine/studio arts; French language and literature; geography; geology/earth science; German language and literature; health/health care administration/management; history; international business; kinesiology and exercise science; liberal arts and sciences/liberal studies; linguistics; mathematics; mechanical engineering; music; nonprofit/public/organizational management; nursing-registered nurse training (RN, ASN, BSN, MSN); ocean engineering; physics; political science and government; psychology; public administration; reading teacher education; social and philosophical foundations of education; social sciences; social work; sociology; Spanish language and literature; special education; speech and rhetorical studies; systems engineering; taxation; women's studies. **Doctorate offered in:** Biology/biological sciences, business administration and management, chemistry, computer and information sciences, computer engineering, counselor education/school counseling and guidance services, criminal justice.

STUDENT INFORMATION

Total Students in Program: 4,111. **% Full-time:** 34. **% Female:** 63. **% Minority:** 26. **% International:** 8.

RESEARCH FACILITIES

Research Facilities: Center for Complex Systems & Brain Sciences, Center for Molecular Biology & Biotechnology, Center for Geo-Information Science.

EXPENSES/FINANCIAL AID

Annual Tuition: In-state $3,777. / Out-of-state $13,953. **Room & Board (On/off Campus):** $5,600/$7,415. **Fees:** $30. **Books and Supplies:** $660. **Grants Range From:** $429-$2,700. **Loans Range From:** $100-$16,980. **% Receiving Financial Aid:** 37. **% Receiving Scholarships/Grants:** 29. **% Receiving Loans:** 71. **Types of Aid Available:** Fellowships, graduate assistantships, grants, institutional work-study, loans, scholarships. **Number of Teaching/Research Assistantships Granted Each Year:** 2. **Average Salary Stipend:** $7,000.

ADMISSIONS INFORMATION

Application Fee: $30. **Priority Application Deadline:** 7/1. **Regular Application Deadline:** 7/1. **Regular Notification:** Rolling. **Transfer Students Accepted?** Yes. **Number of Applications Received:** 2,173. **% of Applicants Accepted:** 60. **% Accepted Who Enrolled:** 38. **Average GPA:** 3.3. **Average GRE Verbal:** 486. **Average GRE Quantitative:** 553.
Required Admission Factors: Essays/personal statement, interview, letters of recommendation, transcript.
Program-Specific Admission Factors: Minimum GRE score of 1000 or minimum 3.0 GPA required of MFA in computer art and MA in library science program applicants.

EMPLOYMENT INFORMATION

Placement Office Available? Yes.

FLORIDA INSTITUTE OF TECHNOLOGY
School of Extended Graduate Studies

Address: 150 West University Boulevard, Melbourne, FL 32901-6975
Admissions Phone: 800-944-4348 · **Admissions Fax:** 321-723-9468
Admissions E-mail: cfarrior@fit.edu · **Web Address:** www.segs.fit.edu

INSTITUTIONAL INFORMATION

Public/private: Private (nonprofit). **Evening Classes Available?** Yes. **Total Faculty:** 154. **% Faculty Female:** 12. **% Faculty Part-time:** 86. **Student/faculty Ratio:** 10:1. **Students in Parent Institution:** 4,689.

PROGRAMS

Masters offered in: Business administration/management; business/managerial operations; e-commerce/electronic commerce; health/health care administration/management; human resources management/personnel administration; international business; logistics and materials management; management information systems; management science; nonprofit/public/organizational management; purchasing, procurement/acquisition, and contracts management.

STUDENT INFORMATION

Total Students in Program: 1,228. **% Full-time:** 8. **% Female:** 47. **% Minority:** 26. **% International:** 1.

EXPENSES/FINANCIAL AID

Annual Tuition: $6,750. **Fees:** $500. **Books and Supplies:** $500. **Grants Range From:** $1,000-$10,000. **Loans Range From:** $1,000-$10,000.

ADMISSIONS INFORMATION

Application Fee: $50. **Regular Application Deadline:** 3/15. **Regular Notification:** Rolling. **Transfer Students Accepted?** Yes. **Transfer Policy:** Review of transfer credit required of transfer applicants after acceptance and enrollment in program. **Number of Applications Received:** 299. **% of Applicants Accepted:** 46. **% Accepted Who Enrolled:** 54. **Average GPA:** 3.2. **Average GRE Verbal:** 537. **Average GRE Quantitative:** 638. **Average**

GRE Analytical: 570.
Required Admission Factors: Transcript.
Other Admission Factors: Minimum 3.0 GPA required for regular admission; provisional status possible with minimum 2.75 GPA.

EMPLOYMENT INFORMATION
% Employed Within 6 Months: 100. Rate of placement: 100%. Average starting salary: $50,000.

FLORIDA INSTITUTE OF TECHNOLOGY
College of Science

Address: 150 West University Boulevard, Melbourne, FL 32901-6975
Admissions Phone: 321-674-7118 · Admissions Fax: 321-723-9468
Admissions E-mail: cfarrior@fit.edu · Web Address: www.fit.edu/AcadRes/csla/

INSTITUTIONAL INFORMATION
Public/private: Private (nonprofit). Evening Classes Available? Yes. Total Faculty: 68. % Faculty Female: 13. % Faculty Part-time: 4. Student/faculty Ratio: 8:1. Students in Parent Institution: 4,689.

PROGRAMS
Masters offered in: Applied mathematics; astronomy and astrophysics; biotechnology; cell/cellular and molecular biology; chemistry; communications, journalism, and related fields; mathematics teacher education; oceanography; chemical and physical; operations research; organizational communication, physics; science teacher education/general science teacher education; secondary education and teaching. Doctorate offered in: Applied mathematics, astronomy and astrophysics, chemistry, mathematics teacher education, oceanography, chemical and physical, operations research, physics, science teacher education/general science teacher education.

STUDENT INFORMATION
Total Students in Program: 1,228. % Full-time: 8. % Female: 47. % Minority: 26. % International: 1.

RESEARCH FACILITIES
Research Facilities: Center for Airport Management and Development, Center for Computational Fluid Dynamics, Center for EDA Software Engingeering and Training, Center for Entrepreneurial Research, Center for Environmental Education.

EXPENSES/FINANCIAL AID
Annual Tuition: $13,410. Room & Board: $5,800. Fees: $1,000. Books and Supplies: $800. Grants Range From: $2,000-$10,000. Loans Range From: $1,000-$10,000. % Receiving Financial Aid: 60. % Receiving Loans: 15. % Receiving Assistantships: 50. Number of Teaching/Research Assistantships Granted Each Year: 78 Assistantship Compensation Includes: Partial tuition remission, salary/stipend. Average Salary Stipend: $18,000.

ADMISSIONS INFORMATION
Application Fee: $50. Regular Application Deadline: 3/15. Regular Notification: Rolling. Transfer Students Accepted? Yes. Transfer Policy: Minimum grade average of B and review of transfer credit required of transfer applicants after. Number of Applications Received: 299. % of Applicants Accepted: 82. % Accepted Who Enrolled: 30. Average GPA: 3.3. Average GRE Verbal: 537. Average GRE Quantitative: 638. Average GRE Analytical: 570.
Required Admission Factors: GRE, letters of recommendation, transcript.
Other Admission Factors: Minimum 3.0 GPA required of master's program applicants. Minimum 3.2 GPA required of doctoral program applicants.

EMPLOYMENT INFORMATION
% Employed Within 6 Months: 98. % of master's/doctoral grads employed in their field upon graduation: 100/100. Rate of placement: 99%. Average starting salary: $50,000.

FLORIDA INSTITUTE OF TECHNOLOGY
College of Psychology & Liberal Arts

Address: 150 West University Boulevard, Melbourne, FL 32901-6975
Admissions Phone: 800-944-4348 · Admissions Fax: 321-723-9468
Admissions E-mail: cfarrior@fit.edu · Web Address: www.fit.edu/AcadRes/psych/

INSTITUTIONAL INFORMATION
Public/private: Private (nonprofit). Evening Classes Available? Yes. Total Faculty: 27. % Faculty Female: 22. % Faculty Part-time: 41. Student/faculty Ratio: 8:1. Students in Parent Institution: 4,689.

PROGRAMS
Masters offered in: Industrial and organizational psychology, psychology. Doctorate offered in: Clinical psychology, industrial and organizational psychology.

STUDENT INFORMATION
Total Students in Program: 159. % Full-time: 95. % Female: 74. % Minority: 16. % International: 6.

RESEARCH FACILITIES
Research Facilities: Center for Airport Management and Development, Center for Computational Fluid Dynamics, Center for EDA Software Engingeering and Training, Center for Electronics Manufacturability, Center for Entrepreneurial Research, Center for Environmental Education.

EXPENSES/FINANCIAL AID
Annual Tuition: $12,000. Room & Board: $6,220. Fees: $100. Books and Supplies: $800. Grants Range From: $1,500-$3,500. Loans Range From: $1,000-$10,000. % Receiving Financial Aid: 55. % Receiving Loans: 14. % Receiving Assistantships: 41. Types of Aid Available: Graduate assistantships. Number of Teaching/Research Assistantships Granted Each Year: 20 Assistantship Compensation Includes: Partial tuition remission. Average Salary Stipend: $2,040.

ADMISSIONS INFORMATION
Application Fee: $50. Regular Application Deadline: 1/15. Regular Notification: Rolling. Transfer Students Accepted? Yes. Transfer Policy: Minimum grade average of B and review of transfer credit required of transfer applicants after. Number of Applications Received: 276. % of Applicants Accepted: 51. % Accepted Who Enrolled: 52. Average GPA: 3.4. Average GRE Verbal: 475.6. Average GRE Quantitative: 558.3. Average GRE Analytical: 588.5.
Required Admission Factors: Essays/personal statement, GRE, transcript.
Other Admission Factors: Minimum 3.0 GPA required of master's program applicants, minimum 3.2 GPA required of doctoral program applicants.

EMPLOYMENT INFORMATION
% Employed Within 6 Months: 100. % of master's/doctoral grads employed in their field upon graduation: 100/98. Rate of placement: 99%. Average starting salary: $45,000.

FLORIDA INTERNATIONAL UNIVERSITY
College of Arts & Sciences

Address: PO Box 659004, Miami, FL 33265
Admissions Phone: 305-348-7442 · Admissions Fax: 305-348-7441
Admissions E-mail: gradadm@fiu.edu · Web Address: www.fiu.edu/~casdean

INSTITUTIONAL INFORMATION
Public/private: Public. Evening Classes Available? Yes. Student/faculty Ratio: 14:1. Students in Parent Institution: 32,070.

PROGRAMS
Masters offered in: Creative writing, history, liberal arts and sciences/liberal studies, mathematics, music, psychology, sociology, visual and performing arts. Doctorate offered in: History, mathematics, psychology.

STUDENT INFORMATION

Total Students in Program: 6,416. % Full-time: 32. % Female: 60.

RESEARCH FACILITIES

Research Facilities: Center for Labor Research and Studies, Latin American and Caribbean Center, Drinking Water Research Center, Center on Nutrition and Aging.

EXPENSES/FINANCIAL AID

Annual Tuition: In-state $2,916. / Out-of-state $10,242. Room & Board: $6,242. Fees: $168. Books and Supplies: $1,058. Grants Range From: $200-$2,000. Loans Range From: $500-$18,500. % Receiving Financial Aid: 22. % Receiving Scholarships/Grants: 68. % Receiving Loans: 81. Average student debt, upon graduation: $8,500.

ADMISSIONS INFORMATION

Application Fee: $30. Regular Application Deadline: 6/1. Regular Notification: Rolling. Transfer Students Accepted? Yes. Number of Applications Received: 1,052. % of Applicants Accepted: 43. % Accepted Who Enrolled: 42. Average GPA: 3.51. Average GRE Verbal: 503. Average GRE Quantitative: 634.

Required Admission Factors: GRE, letters of recommendation, transcript. Other Admission Factors: Minimum GRE score of 1000 and minimum 3.0 GPA required.

Program-Specific Admission Factors: Minimum 9 undergraduate semester hours of creative writing and writing sample required of creative writing program applicants. Minimum GRE score of 1500 required of MA in economics program applicants.

EMPLOYMENT INFORMATION

Placement Office Available? Yes.

FLORIDA INTERNATIONAL UNIVERSITY
School of Journalism & Mass Communication

Address: PO Box 659004, Miami, FL 33265
Admissions Phone: 305-348-7442 · Admissions Fax: 305-348-7441
Admissions E-mail: gradadm@fiu.edu
Web Address: http://gradschool.fin.edu/colleges.html#50jmc

INSTITUTIONAL INFORMATION

Public/private: Public. Evening Classes Available? Yes. Student/faculty Ratio: 14:1. Students in Parent Institution: 32,070.

PROGRAMS

Masters offered in: Mass communications/media studies.

STUDENT INFORMATION

Total Students in Program: 6,416. % Full-time: 32. % Female: 60.

RESEARCH FACILITIES

Research Facilities: Center for Labor Research and Studies, Latin American and Caribbean Center, Drinking Water Research Center, Center on Nutrition and Aging.

EXPENSES/FINANCIAL AID

Annual Tuition: In-state $2,916. / Out-of-state $10,242. Room & Board: $6,242. Fees: $168. Books and Supplies: $1,058. Grants Range From: $200-$2,000. Loans Range From: $500-$18,500. % Receiving Financial Aid: 41. % Receiving Scholarships/Grants: 68. % Receiving Loans: 81. Average student debt, upon graduation: $8,500.

ADMISSIONS INFORMATION

Application Fee: $30. Regular Application Deadline: 6/1. Regular Notification: Rolling. Transfer Students Accepted? Yes. Number of Applications Received: 103. % of Applicants Accepted: 39. % Accepted Who Enrolled: 32. Average GPA: 3.42. Average GRE Verbal: 542. Average GRE Quantitative: 532.

Required Admission Factors: Essays/personal statement, GRE, transcript. Other Admission Factors: Minimum GRE score of 1000 (minimum 500 verbal), minimum GMAT score of 500, minimum PAEG score of 500, and minimum 3.0 GPA required.

EMPLOYMENT INFORMATION

Placement Office Available? Yes.

FLORIDA METROPOLITAN UNIVERSITY— BRANDON
Graduate Programs

Address: 3924 Coconut Palm Drive, Tampa, FL 33619
Admissions E-mail: dpearson@cci.edu

INSTITUTIONAL INFORMATION

Public/private: Private (proprietary). Evening Classes Available? Yes. Students in Parent Institution: 1,114.

EXPENSES/FINANCIAL AID

Annual Tuition: In-state $5,670. Fees: $200. Books and Supplies: $800. % Receiving Financial Aid: 100.

ADMISSIONS INFORMATION

Regular Notification: Rolling. Transfer Students Accepted? Yes. Transfer Policy: Minimum grade of C required of transfer applicants. Number of Applications Received: 7. % of Applicants Accepted: 100. % Accepted Who Enrolled: 100.

Required Admission Factors: Interview, transcript.
Other Admission Factors: Minimum 3.0 GPA required for regular admission.

EMPLOYMENT INFORMATION

Placement Office Available? Yes. % Employed Within 6 Months: 80. % of master's grads employed in their field upon graduation: 30. Average starting salary: $30,000.

FLORIDA METROPOLITAN UNIVERSITY— NORTH ORLANDO
Graduate Studies

Address: 5421 Diplomat Circle, Orlando, FL 32810
Admissions Phone: 407-628-5870

INSTITUTIONAL INFORMATION

Public/private: Private (proprietary). Evening Classes Available? Yes. Student/faculty Ratio: 6:1. Students in Parent Institution: 1,207

STUDENT INFORMATION

Total Students in Program: 43. % Full-time: 7. % Female: 58.

EXPENSES/FINANCIAL AID

Annual Tuition: $7,560. Fees: $150. Books and Supplies: $600. Loans Range From: $3,700-$18,500. % Receiving Financial Aid: 80. % Receiving Loans: 100. Average student debt, upon graduation: $17,000.

ADMISSIONS INFORMATION

Regular Notification: Rolling. Transfer Students Accepted? Yes.
Required Admission Factors: Interview, transcript.
Other Admission Factors: Minimum 3.0 GPA required for regular admission.

EMPLOYMENT INFORMATION

Placement Office Available? Yes. % of master's grads employed in their field upon graduation: 100. Rate of placement: 84%. Average starting salary: $36,700.

FLORIDA METROPOLITAN UNIVERSITY—
POMPANO BEACH
Graduate Programs

Address: 225 North Federal Highway, Pompano Beach, FL 33062-4319
Admissions Phone: 954-783-7339 · **Admissions Fax:** 954-943-2571
Admissions E-mail: wvasquez@cci.edu · **Web Address:** www.fmu.edu

INSTITUTIONAL INFORMATION
Public/private: Private (proprietary). **Evening Classes Available?** Yes. **Total Faculty:** 10. **% Faculty Female:** 30. **% Faculty Part-time:** 90. **Student/faculty Ratio:** 15:1.

EXPENSES/FINANCIAL AID
Annual Tuition: $7,560. **Fees:** $150. **Books and Supplies:** $600.

ADMISSIONS INFORMATION
Application Fee: $25. **Regular Application Deadline:** 10/10. **Regular Notification:** Rolling. **Transfer Students Accepted?** Yes. **Transfer Policy:** Students transferring from other institutions must provide evidence that the courses are comparable in content to the program of study at the university. Courses that show a grade below a B cannot be transferred.
Required Admission Factors: Interview, transcript.
Other Admission Factors: Degree seeking regular students seeking a graduate degree, must have achieved a cumulative GPA of not less than 3.0 for all undergraduate upper level division work, or must score not less than 470 on the GMAT.
Program-Specific Admission Factors: Certain prerequisite requirements prior to enrolling in managerial economics, international economic systems, quantitative methods, financial management, and certain graduate level accounting courses must be met.

FLORIDA METROPOLITAN UNIVERSITY—
SOUTH ORLANDO
Graduate Studies

Address: 2411 Sand Lake Road, Orlando, FL 32809
Admissions Phone: 407-851-2525

INSTITUTIONAL INFORMATION
Public/private: Private (proprietary). **Evening Classes Available?** Yes. **Student/faculty Ratio:** 20:1. **Students in Parent Institution:** 1,351.

STUDENT INFORMATION
Total Students in Program: 68. **% Full-time:** 100. **% Female:** 56.

EXPENSES/FINANCIAL AID
Annual Tuition: $7,560. **Fees:** $150. **Books and Supplies:** $750. **Loans Range From:** $7,128-$9,504. **% Receiving Loans:** 100.

ADMISSIONS INFORMATION
Transfer Students Accepted? Yes.

EMPLOYMENT INFORMATION
Placement Office Available? Yes. **% of master's grads employed in their field upon graduation:** 72. **Rate of placement:** 83%. **Average starting salary:** $30,000.

FLORIDA STATE UNIVERSITY
College of Arts & Sciences

Address: A2500 University Center, Tallahassee, FL 32306-2400
Admissions Phone: 850-644-3420 · **Admissions Fax:** 850-644-0197
Admissions E-mail: graduate@admin.fsu.edu · **Web Address:** www.fsu.edu/~fsuas/

INSTITUTIONAL INFORMATION
Public/private: Public. **Evening Classes Available?** Yes. **Total Faculty:** 538. **% Faculty Female:** 27. **Students in Parent Institution:** 38,886.

PROGRAMS
Masters offered in: Accounting and finance; accounting; acting; adult and continuing education administration; American government and politics (U.S.); American/U.S. studies/civilization; analytical chemistry; ancient/classical Greek language and literature; anthropology; apparel and textiles; applied mathematics; art history, criticism, and conservation; art teacher education; art/art studies; arts management; Asian studies/civilization; atmospheric sciences and meteorology; atomic/molecular physics; audiology/audiologist and speech-language pathology/pathologist; biochemistry; biological and physical sciences; biology/biological sciences; biomedical/medical engineering; business administration and management; central/middle and eastern European studies; chemical engineering; chemical physics; chemistry; child development; cinematography and film/video production; city/urban, community, and regional planning; civil engineering; classics and classical languages, literatures, and linguistics; clinical psychology; cognitive psychology and psycholinguistics; commercial and advertising art; communications studies/speech communication and rhetoric; communications technology/technician; community health services/liaison/counseling; computational mathematics; computer and information sciences; computer and information systems security; computer science; computer software engineering; conducting; consumer merchandising/retailing management; counselor education/school counseling and guidance services; creative writing; criminal justice/safety studies; criminology; dance; demography/population studies; dietetics/ dietitian (RD); directing and theatrical production; drama and dramatics/theater arts; early childhood education and teaching; economics, education leadership and administration; education; education/teaching of individuals with emotional disturbances; education/teaching of individuals with mental retardation; education/teaching of individuals with specific learning disabilities; education/teaching of individuals with vision impairments, including blindness; educational assessment, testing, and measurement; educational evaluation and research; educational psychology; educational statistics and research methods; educational/instructional media design; electrical, electronics, and communications engineering; elementary education and teaching; English language and literature; English/language arts teacher education; family and consumer sciences/home economics teacher education; family systems; fashion/apparel design; finance; fine/studio arts; foods, nutrition, and wellness studies; foreign language teacher education; French language and literature; geography; geology/earth science; German language and literature; health and physical education; health teacher education; health/health care administration/management; higher education/higher education administration; history; housing and human environments; human development and family studies; humanities/humanistic studies; industrial engineering; information science/studies; information technology; inorganic chemistry; interior design; international and comparative education; international relations and affairs; italian studies; jazz/jazz studies; kinesiology and exercise science; Latin language and literature; library science/librarianship; management information systems; management science; marine biology and biological oceanography; marketing/marketing management; mass communications/media studies; mathematics teacher education; mathematics; mechanical engineering; multicultural education; music performance; music teacher education; music theory and composition; music therapy/therapist; musicology and ethnomusicology; nursing-registered nurse training (RN, ASN, BSN, MSN); nutrition sciences; oceanography, chemical and physical; organic chemistry; parks, recreation, and leisure facilities management; philosophy; physical and theoretical chemistry; physical education teaching and coaching; physics; physiological psychology/psychobiology; piano and organ; political

communications; political science and government; psychology; public administration; reading teacher education; rehabilitation counseling/counselor; religion/religious studies; Russian studies; sales, distribution, and marketing operations; science teacher education; Slavic languages, literatures, and linguistics; social and philosophical foundations of education; social psychology; social science teacher education; social sciences, social work; sociology; Spanish language and literature; speech and rhetorical studies; sports and fitness administration/management; statistics; systems administration/administrator; theater/theater arts management; violin; viola, guitar and other stringed instruments; voice and opera. **Doctorate offered in:** See above.

STUDENT INFORMATION

Total Students in Program: 1,662. **% Full-time:** 77. **% Female:** 43. **% Minority:** 29. **% International:** 22.

EXPENSES/FINANCIAL AID

Annual Tuition: In-state $5,368. / Out-of-state $19,800. **Room & Board:** $6,076. **Grants Range From:** $50-$19,681. **Loans Range From:** $1,019-$29,894. **% Receiving Scholarships/Grants:** 33. **% Receiving Loans:** 82. **% Receiving Assistantships:** 1.

ADMISSIONS INFORMATION

Application Fee: $30. **Regular Application Deadline:** 7/1. **Regular Notification:** Rolling. **Transfer Students Accepted?** Yes. **Number of Applications Received:** 4,695. **% of Applicants Accepted:** 32. **% Accepted Who Enrolled:** 45. **Average GPA:** 3.5. **Average GRE Verbal:** 534. **Average GRE Quantitative:** 692. **Average GRE Analytical:** 676. **Average GRE Analytical Writing:** 4.

Required Admission Factors: GRE, transcript.
Other Admission Factors: State of Florida requires a minimum GRE score of 1000 or (a minimum junior/senior GPA of 3.0 or at least a 3.0 for an earned graduate degree). Most degree programs maintain higher minimum qualifications, therefore you should check departments websites for clarifications.
Program-Specific Admission Factors: Departmental websites can be located via the following link: www.fsu.edu/~fsuas/

FLORIDA STATE UNIVERSITY
College of Human Sciences

Address: A2500 University Center, Tallahassee, FL 32306-2400
Admissions Phone: 850-644-3420 · **Admissions Fax:** 850-644-0197
Admissions E-mail: graduate@admin.fsu.edu · **Web Address:** www.chs.fsu.edu

INSTITUTIONAL INFORMATION

Public/private: Public. **Evening Classes Available?** Yes. **Total Faculty:** 48. **% Faculty Female:** 71. **Students in Parent Institution:** 38,886.

PROGRAMS

Masters offered in: Anthropology; child development; city/urban, community, and regional planning; clinical psychology; cognitive psychology and psycholinguistics; counselor education/school counseling and guidance services; demography/population studies; research; educational psychology; family systems; health/health care administration/management; housing and human environments, human development and family studies; physiological psychology/psychobiology; psychology; rehabilitation counseling/counselor; social and philosophical foundations of education; social psychology; social work; sociology. **Doctorate offered in:** Anthropology; child development; city/urban, community, and regional planning; clinical psychology; cognitive psychology and psycholinguistics; counselor education/school counseling and guidance services; demography/population studies; research; educational psychology; family systems; health/health care administration/management; housing and human environments, human development and family studies; physiological psychology/psychobiology; psychology; rehabilitation counseling/counselor; social and philosophical foundations of education; social psychology; social work; sociology.

STUDENT INFORMATION

Total Students in Program: 173. **% Full-time:** 75. **% Female:** 81. **% Minority:** 38. **% International:** 10.

EXPENSES/FINANCIAL AID

Annual Tuition: In-state $3,332. / Out-of-state $11,577. **Grants Range From:** $50-$19,681. **Loans Range From:** $1,019-$29,894. **% Receiving Scholarships/Grants:** 33. **% Receiving Loans:** 82. **% Receiving Assistantships:** 1. **Number of Fellowships Granted Each Year:** 1. **Average amount of individual fellowships per year:** $6,300. **Number of Teaching/Research Assistantships Granted Each Year:** 55. **Average Salary Stipend:** $8,000.

ADMISSIONS INFORMATION

Application Fee: $20. **Regular Notification:** Rolling. **Transfer Students Accepted?** Yes. **Transfer Policy:** Maximum 6 credit hours may be transferred into master's programs; 9 into doctoral programs. **Number of Applications Received:** 339. **% of Applicants Accepted:** 59. **% Accepted Who Enrolled:** 30. **Average GPA:** 3.5. **Average GRE Verbal:** 485. **Average GRE Quantitative:** 621. **Average GRE Analytical:** 562. **Average GRE Analytical Writing:** 4.

Required Admission Factors: GRE, transcript.
Other Admission Factors: The State of Florida requires a minimum GRE score of 1000 or (a minimum junior/senior GPA of a 3.0 or at least a 3.0 for an earned graduate degree). Most degree programs maintain higher minimum qualifications therefore you should check departments websites for clarification.

FLORIDA STATE UNIVERSITY
College of Music

Address: A2500 University Center, Tallahassee, FL 32306-2400
Admissions Phone: 850-644-3420 · **Admissions Fax:** 850-644-0197
Admissions E-mail: graduate@admin.fsu.edu · **Web Address:** www.music.fsu.edu/

INSTITUTIONAL INFORMATION

Public/private: Public. **Evening Classes Available?** Yes. **Total Faculty:** 88. **% Faculty Female:** 34. **Students in Parent Institution:** 38,886.

PROGRAMS

Masters offered in: Conducting; jazz/jazz studies; music performance; music teacher education; music theory and composition; music therapy/therapist; musicology and ethnomusicology; piano and organ; violin, viola, guitar and other stringed instruments; voice and opera. **Doctorate offered in:** Conducting; jazz/jazz studies; music performance; music teacher education; music theory and composition; music therapy/therapist; musicology and ethnomusicology; piano and organ; violin, viola, guitar, and other stringed instruments; voice and opera.

STUDENT INFORMATION

Total Students in Program: 430. **% Full-time:** 74. **% Female:** 54. **% Minority:** 26. **% International:** 15.

EXPENSES/FINANCIAL AID

Annual Tuition: In-state $3,332. / Out-of-state $11,577. **Grants Range From:** $50-$19,681. **Loans Range From:** $1,019-$29,894. **% Receiving Scholarships/Grants:** 33. **% Receiving Loans:** 82. **% Receiving Assistantships:** 1.

ADMISSIONS INFORMATION

Application Fee: $30. **Regular Application Deadline:** 7/1. **Regular Notification:** Rolling. **Transfer Students Accepted?** Yes. **Number of Applications Received:** 1,149. **% of Applicants Accepted:** 47. **% Accepted Who Enrolled:** 43. **Average GPA:** 3.6. **Average GRE Verbal:** 509. **Average GRE Quantitative:** 607. **Average GRE Analytical:** 593. **Average GRE Analytical Writing:** 4.

Required Admission Factors: GRE, transcript.

Other Admission Factors: The State of Florida requires a minimum GRE score of 1000 or (a minimum junior/senior GPA of a 3.0 or at least a 3.0 for an earned gradute degree). Most degree programs maintain higher minimum qualifications, therefore you should check departments websites for clarification.

Program-Specific Admission Factors: Departmental websites can be located via the following link: www.coss.fsu.edu/

FLORIDA STATE UNIVERSITY
School of Criminology

Address: A2500 University Center, Tallahassee, FL 32306-2400
Admissions Phone: 850-644-3420 · **Admissions Fax:** 850-644-0197
Admissions E-mail: graduate@admin.fsu.edu · **Web Address:** www.criminology.fsu.edu/

INSTITUTIONAL INFORMATION
Public/private: Public. **Evening Classes Available?** Yes. **Total Faculty:** 28. **% Faculty Female:** 43. **Students in Parent Institution:** 38,886.

PROGRAMS
Masters offered in: Clinical psychology, cognitive psychology and psycholinguistics, criminal justice/safety studies, criminology, demography/population studies, housing and human environments, human development and family studies, physiological psychology/psychobiology, psychology, social psychology, sociology. **Doctorate offered in:** Clinical psychology, cognitive psychology and psycholinguistics, criminal justice/safety studies, criminology, demography/population studies, housing and human environments, human development and family studies, physiological psychology/psychobiology, psychology, social psychology, sociology.

STUDENT INFORMATION
Total Students in Program: 641. **% Full-time:** 28. **% Female:** 75. **% Minority:** 24. **% International:** 4.

EXPENSES/FINANCIAL AID
Annual Tuition: In-state $3,332. / Out-of-state $11,577. **Grants Range From:** $50-$19,681. **Loans Range From:** $1,019-$29,894. **% Receiving Financial Aid:** 15. **% Receiving Scholarships/Grants:** 33. **% Receiving Loans:** 82. **% Receiving Assistantships:** 1. **Number of Fellowships Granted Each Year:** 4. **Number of Teaching/Research Assistantships Granted Each Year:** 46.

ADMISSIONS INFORMATION
Application Fee: $30. **Regular Application Deadline:** 7/1. **Regular Notification:** Rolling. **Transfer Students Accepted?** Yes. **Number of Applications Received:** 1,152. **% of Applicants Accepted:** 84. **% Accepted Who Enrolled:** 71. **Average GPA:** 3.3. **Average GRE Verbal:** 524. **Average GRE Quantitative:** 543. **Average GRE Analytical:** 573. **Average GRE Analytical Writing:** 4.
Required Admission Factors: GRE, transcript.
Other Admission Factors: The State of Florida requires a minimumm GRE score of 1000 or (a minimum junior/senior GPA of 3.0 or at least a 3.0 for an earned gradute degree). Most degree programs maintain higher minimum qualifications, therefore you should check departments websites for clarification.
Program-Specific Admission Factors: Departmental websites can be located via the following link: http://www.lis.fsu.edu/

FLORIDA STATE UNIVERSITY
School of Motion Picture, Television, & Recording Arts

Address: A2500 University Center, Tallahassee, FL 32306-2400
Admissions Phone: 850-644-3420 · **Admissions Fax:** 850-644-0197
Admissions E-mail: graduate@admin.fsu.edu · **Web Address:** www.filmschool.fsu.edu

INSTITUTIONAL INFORMATION
Public/private: Public. **Evening Classes Available?** Yes. **Total Faculty:** 115. **% Faculty Female:** 23. **Students in Parent Institution:** 38,886.

PROGRAMS
Masters offered in: Acting, cinematography and film/video production, communications studies/speech communication and rhetoric, communications technology/technician, creative writing, directing and theatrical production, drama and dramatics/theater arts, theater/theater arts management. **Doctorate offered in:** Acting, cinematography and film/video production, communications studies/speech communication and rhetoric, communications technology/technician, creative writing, directing and theatrical production, drama and dramatics/theater arts, theater/theater arts management.

STUDENT INFORMATION
Total Students in Program: 592. **% Full-time:** 70. **% Female:** 48. **% Minority:** 31. **% International:** 13.

EXPENSES/FINANCIAL AID
Annual Tuition: In-state $3,332. / Out-of-state $11,577. **Grants Range From:** $50-$19,681. **Loans Range From:** $1,019-$29,894. **% Receiving Scholarships/grants:** 33. **% Receiving Loans:** 82. **% Receiving Assistantships:** 1.

ADMISSIONS INFORMATION
Application Fee: $20. **Regular Notification:** Rolling. **Transfer Students Accepted?** Yes. **Number of Applications Received:** 1,584. **% of Applicants Accepted:** 66. **% Accepted Who Enrolled:** 35. **Average GPA:** 3.4. **Average GRE Verbal:** 511. **Average GRE Quantitative:** 648. **Average GRE Analytical:** 660. **Average GRE Analytical Writing:** 4.
Required Admission Factors: GRE, transcript.
Other Admission Factors: The State of Florida requires a minimum GRE score of 1000 or (a minimum junior/senior GPA of a 3.0 or at least a 3.0 for an earned gradute degree). Most degree programs maintain higher minimum qualifications, therefore you should check departments websites for clarification.

FLORIDA STATE UNIVERSITY
School of Theater

Address: A2500 University Center, Tallahassee, FL 32306-2400
Admissions Phone: 850-644-3420 · **Admissions Fax:** 850-644-0197
Admissions E-mail: graduate@admin.fsu.edu · **Web Address:** www.theater.fsu.edu

INSTITUTIONAL INFORMATION
Public/private: Public. **Evening Classes Available?** Yes. **Total Faculty:** 26. **% Faculty Female:** 46. **Students in Parent Institution:** 38,886.

PROGRAMS
Masters offered in: Acting, directing and theatrical production, drama and dramatics/theater arts, theater/theater arts management. **Doctorate offered in:** Acting, directing and theatrical production, drama and dramatics/theater arts, theater/theater arts management.

STUDENT INFORMATION
Total Students in Program: 105. **% Full-time:** 90. **% Female:** 50. **% Minority:** 15. **% International:** 2.

EXPENSES/FINANCIAL AID

Annual Tuition: In-state $3,332. / Out-of-state $11,577. **Grants Range From:** $50-$19,681. **Loans Range From:** $1,019-$29,894. **% Receiving Financial Aid:** 85. **% Receiving Scholarships/Grants:** 33. **% Receiving Loans:** 82. **% Receiving Assistantships:** 1. **Number of Fellowships Granted Each Year:** 1 Average amount of individual fellowships per year: $6,300. **Number of Teaching/Research Assistantships Granted Each Year:** 62. **Average Salary Stipend:** $6,200.

ADMISSIONS INFORMATION

Application Fee: $30. **Regular Application Deadline:** 7/1. **Regular Notification:** Rolling. **Transfer Students Accepted?** Yes. **Number of Applications Received:** 184. **% of Applicants Accepted:** 47. **% Accepted Who Enrolled:** 63. **Average GPA:** 3.4. **Average GRE Verbal:** 537. **Average GRE Quantitative:** 599. **Average GRE Analytical:** 627. **Average GRE Analytical Writing:** 4.

Required Admission Factors: GRE, transcript.

Other Admission Factors: The State of Florida requires a minimum GRE score of 1000 or (a minimum junior/senior GPA of a 3.0 or at least a 3.0 for an earned graduate degree). Most degree programs have higher minimum qualifications, therefore you should check departments websites for clarification.

Program-Specific Admission Factors: Departmental websites can be located via the following link: www.theater.fsu.edu/

FLORIDA STATE UNIVERSITY
School of Visual Arts & Dance

Address: A2500 University Center, Tallahassee, FL 32306-2400
Admissions Phone: 850-644-3420 · **Admissions Fax:** 850-644-0197
Admissions E-mail: graduate@admin.fsu.edu · **Web Address:** www.fsu.edu/~svad

INSTITUTIONAL INFORMATION

Public/private: Public. **Evening Classes Available?** Yes. **Total Faculty:** 74. **% Faculty Female:** 50. **Students in Parent Institution:** 38,886.

PROGRAMS

Masters offered in: Apparel and textiles; art history, criticism, and conservation; art teacher education; art/art studies; arts management; commercial and advertising art; fashion/apparel design; fine/studio arts; interior design. **Doctorate offered in:** Apparel and textiles; art history, criticism, and conservation; art teacher education; art/art studies; arts management; dance; fashion/apparel design; fine/studio arts; interior design.

STUDENT INFORMATION

Total Students in Program: 232. **% Full-time:** 76. **% Female:** 77. **% Minority:** 23. **% International:** 8.

EXPENSES/FINANCIAL AID

Annual Tuition: In-state $3,332. / Out-of-state $11,577. **Grants Range From:** $50-$19,681. **Loans Range From:** $1,019-$29,894. **% Receiving Scholarships/Grants:** 33. **% Receiving Loans:** 82. **% Receiving Assistantships:** 1. **Number of Fellowships Granted Each Year:** 1. **Average Salary Stipend:** $2,900.

ADMISSIONS INFORMATION

Application Fee: $30. **Regular Application Deadline:** 7/1. **Regular Notification:** Rolling. **Transfer Students Accepted?** Yes. **Number of Applications Received:** 388. **% of Applicants Accepted:** 58. **% Accepted Who Enrolled:** 61. **Average GPA:** 3.4. **Average GRE Verbal:** 476. **Average GRE Quantitative:** 537. **Average GRE Analytical:** 546. **Average GRE Analytical Writing:** 4.

Required Admission Factors: GRE, letters of recommendation, transcript. **Other Admission Factors:** The State of Florida requires a minumum GRE of 1000 or (a minmum junior/senior GPA of a 3.0 or at least a 3.0 for an earned graduate degree). Most degree programs maintain higher minimum qualifications, therefore you should check departments websites for clarification. **Program-Specific Admission Factors:** Departmental websites can be located via the following link: www.fsu.edu/~svad/

FONTBONNE UNIVERSITY

Address: 6800 Wydown Boulevard, St. Louis, MO 63105
Admissions Phone: 314-889-1418 · **Admissions Fax:** 314-889-1451
Admissions E-mail: bfoster@fontbonne.edu/cdrury@fontbonne.edu
Web Address: www.fontbonne.edu

INSTITUTIONAL INFORMATION

Public/private: Private (nonprofit). **Evening Classes Available?** Yes. **Total Faculty:** 16. **% Faculty Female:** 6. **% Faculty Part-time:** 81. **Students in Parent Institution:** 2,827.

STUDENT INFORMATION

Total Students in Program: 811. **% Full-time:** 48. **% Female:** 74.

EXPENSES/FINANCIAL AID

Annual Tuition: $6,768.

ADMISSIONS INFORMATION

Application Fee: $25. **Regular Application Deadline:** 8/15. **Regular Notification:** Rolling. **Transfer Students Accepted?** Yes. **Transfer Policy:** Admission deadline is open. **Number of Applications Received:** 42. **% of Applicants Accepted:** 74. **% Accepted Who Enrolled:** 45.

Required Admission Factors: Letters of recommendation, transcript.

Other Admission Factors: Minimum 2.5 GPA and letters of reference required.

EMPLOYMENT INFORMATION

Placement Office Available? Yes. **% Employed Within 6 Months:** 87. **Rate of placement:** 98%.

FORDHAM UNIVERSITY
Graduate School of Arts & Sciences

Address: 441 East Fordham Road, Keating Hall, Room 216, New York, NY 10458
Admissions Phone: 718-817-4416 · **Admissions Fax:** 718-817-3566
Admissions E-mail: fuga@fordham.edu · **Web Address:** www.fordham.edu/gsas

INSTITUTIONAL INFORMATION

Public/private: Private (nonprofit). **Evening Classes Available?** Yes. **Students in Parent Institution:** 15,379.

PROGRAMS

Masters offered in: American government and politics (U.S.); American history (U.S.); American literature (U.S.); ancient/classical Greek language and literature; animal genetics; applied economics; artificial intelligence and robotics; bible/biblical studies; classics and classical languages, literatures, and linguistics; communications and media studies; computer and information sciences; computer science; computer systems networking and telecommunications; creative writing; criminology; demography/population studies; development economics and international development; ecology, evolution, and systematics; econometrics and quantitative economics; economics; English language and literature; English literature (British and commonwealth); ethics; European history; general studies; genetics; history; human/medical genetics; humanities/humanistic studies; immunology; information technology; international economics; international relations and affairs; international/global studies; Latin language and literature; liberal arts and sciences/liberal studies; logic; mass communications/media studies; medieval and renaissance studies; microbial and eukaryotic genetics; microbiological sciences and immunology; microbiology, molecular biology; molecular genetics; philosophy; plant genetics; political science and government; political science and government; sociology; system, networking, and lan/wan management/manager; systems administration/administrator; theology/theological studies. **Doctorate offered in:** See above. **First Professional degree offered in:** Hispanic-American, Puerto Rican, and Mexican-American/Chicano studies; Latin American studies.

STUDENT INFORMATION
Total Students in Program: 809. % Full-time: 100.

RESEARCH FACILITIES
Research Facilities: Archbishop Hughes Institute on Religion & Culture, Center for Advanced Management Studies, Center on European Community Law & International Antitrust, Center for Non-public Education, High School Principal's Center, Hispanic Research Center.

EXPENSES/FINANCIAL AID
Annual Tuition: $19,200. Fees: $316. Books and Supplies: $1,000. Grants Range From: $12,000-$17,000.

ADMISSIONS INFORMATION
Application Fee: $80. Priority Application Deadline: 1/15. Regular Application Deadline: 4/15. Regular Notification: Rolling. Transfer Students Accepted? Yes. Transfer Policy: Credits considered by petition upon matriculation. Number of Applications Received: 1,394. % of Applicants Accepted: 40. % Accepted Who Enrolled: 40.
Required Admission Factors: Essays/personal statement, GRE, letters of recommendation, transcript.
Other Admission Factors: Minimum 3.0 GPA required of master's program applicants. Minimum 3.5 GPA required of doctoral program applicants.

EMPLOYMENT INFORMATION
Placement Office Available? Yes.

FORDHAM UNIVERSITY
Graduate School of Social Service

Address: 113 West 60th Street, Suite 703, New York, NY 10023
Admissions Phone: 212-636-6600 · Admissions Fax: 212-636-6613
Admissions E-mail: gssadmission@fordham.edu · Web Address: www.fordham.edu/gss

INSTITUTIONAL INFORMATION
Public/private: Private (nonprofit). Evening Classes Available? Yes. Total Faculty: 138. % Faculty Female: 71. % Faculty Part-time: 70. Student/faculty Ratio: 11:1. Students in Parent Institution: 13,687.

PROGRAMS
Masters offered in: Social work. Doctorate offered in: Social work.

STUDENT INFORMATION
Total Students in Program: 5,176. % Full-time: 40. % Female: 65.

EXPENSES/FINANCIAL AID
Annual Tuition: $19,041. Room & Board: $12,400. Fees: $356. Books and Supplies: $800. Grants Range From: $1,000-$19,041. Loans Range From: $100-$18,500. % Receiving Financial Aid: 90. % Receiving Scholarships/Grants: 60. % Receiving Loans: 90. % Receiving Assistantships: 3. Types of Aid Available: Graduate assistantships, grants, institutional work-study, loans, scholarships. Average student debt, upon graduation: $37,000. Number of Teaching/Research Assistantships Granted Each Year: 28. Assistantship Compensation Includes: Partial tuition remission. Average Salary Stipend: $1,731.

ADMISSIONS INFORMATION
Application Fee: $40. Priority Application Deadline: 6/1. Regular Application Deadline: 6/1. Regular Notification: Rolling. Transfer Students Accepted? Yes. Transfer Policy: Letter from current program outlining progress is required of transfer applicants, as well as a copy of a field work evaluation if applicable. Number of Applications Received: 1,348. % of Applicants Accepted: 74. % Accepted Who Enrolled: 55. Average GPA: 3.2.
Required Admission Factors: Essays/personal statement, letters of recommendation, transcript.
Other Admission Factors: 3.00 GPA is the recommended minimum for acceptance. The school does not require any sort of testing.

Program-Specific Admission Factors: Applicants with a bachelors degree in social work may apply to the advanced standing (1 year) plan of study.

EMPLOYMENT INFORMATION
% Employed Within 6 Months: 90. % of master's/doctoral grads employed in their field upon graduation: 30/100. Average starting salary: $35,000.

FOREST INSTITUTE OF PROFESSIONAL PSYCHOLOGY
Graduate Studies

Address: 2885 West Battlefield Road, Springfield, MO 65807
Admissions Phone: 800-424-7793

INSTITUTIONAL INFORMATION
Public/private: Private (proprietary). Evening Classes Available? Yes. Students in Parent Institution: 103.

RESEARCH FACILITIES
Research Facilities: Mental health clinic.

EXPENSES/FINANCIAL AID
Annual Tuition: $8,640. Grants Range From: $1,080-$4,320. Loans Range From: $8,500-$31,500. % Receiving Scholarships/Grants: 2. % Receiving Loans: 90.

ADMISSIONS INFORMATION
Application Fee: $50. Regular Notification: Rolling. Transfer Students Accepted? Yes.
Required Admission Factors: Essays/personal statement, GRE, interview, letters of recommendation, transcript.
Program-Specific Admission Factors: Minimum 3.25 required of PsyD program applicants.

FORT HAYS STATE UNIVERSITY
College of Arts & Sciences

Address: 600 Park Street, Hays, KS 67601-4099
Admissions Phone: 785-628-4234

INSTITUTIONAL INFORMATION
Public/private: Public. Evening Classes Available? Yes. Students in Parent Institution: 5,335.

STUDENT INFORMATION
Total Students in Program: 1,121. % Full-time: 26. % Female: 73.

RESEARCH FACILITIES
Research Facilities: Herndon Speech/Language/Hearing Clinic, Gross Memorial Coliseum, geographic information systems lab, family healthcare clinic, Americorps program, small business development center.

EXPENSES/FINANCIAL AID
Annual Tuition: In-state $2,088. / Out-of-state $6,191. Room & Board: $4,749. Fees: $382. Books and Supplies: $700. Grants Range From: $200-$5,000. Loans Range From: $1,000-$13,500. % Receiving Scholarships/Grants: 8. % Receiving Loans: 98.

ADMISSIONS INFORMATION
Application Fee: $25. Transfer Students Accepted? Yes. Number of Applications Received: 47. % of Applicants Accepted: 94.
Required Admission Factors: Essays/personal statement, interview, letters of recommendation, transcript.
Other Admission Factors: Minimum 2.5 GPA required for some programs; minimum 3.0 GPA required for others.

EMPLOYMENT INFORMATION
Placement Office Available? Yes.

FRAMINGHAM STATE COLLEGE
Graduate Programs

Address: 100 State Street, Framingham, MA 01701
Admissions Phone: 508-626-4550 · **Admissions Fax:** 508-626-4030
Admissions E-mail: dgce@frc.mass.edu · **Web Address:** www.choosefsc.org

INSTITUTIONAL INFORMATION
Public/private: Public. Evening Classes Available? Yes. Students in Parent Institution: 5,310.

STUDENT INFORMATION
Total Students in Program: 1,035 % Female: 70.

EXPENSES/FINANCIAL AID
Annual Tuition: In-state $1,675. / Out-of-state $7,050.

ADMISSIONS INFORMATION
Application Fee: $50. Regular Notification: Rolling. Transfer Students Accepted? No.
Required Admission Factors: Essays/personal statement, GRE, letters of recommendation, transcript.

EMPLOYMENT INFORMATION
Placement Office Available? Yes.

FRANCIS MARION UNIVERSITY
Graduate Programs

Address: PO Box 100547, Florence, SC 29501-0547
Admissions Phone: 843-661-1284 · **Admissions Fax:** 843-661-4688
Admissions E-mail: graduate@fmarion.edu

INSTITUTIONAL INFORMATION
Public/private: Public. Evening Classes Available? Yes. Student/faculty Ratio: 22:1. Students in Parent Institution: 3,569.

STUDENT INFORMATION
Total Students in Program: 774. % Full-time: 5. % Female: 82.

EXPENSES/FINANCIAL AID
Annual Tuition: In-state $2,870. / Out-of-state $5,740. Room & Board (On/off Campus): $4,200/$6,000. Fees: $60. Books and Supplies: $400. Loans Range From: $500-$10,500. Number of Teaching/Research Assistantships Granted Each Year: 2. Average Salary Stipend: $3,000.

ADMISSIONS INFORMATION
Application Fee: $25. Transfer Students Accepted? No. Number of Applications Received: 40. % of Applicants Accepted: 52. % Accepted Who Enrolled: 67. Average GPA: 3.38. Average GRE Verbal: 474. Average GRE Quantitative: 515. Average GRE Analytical: 540.
Required Admission Factors: Essays/personal statement, GRE, interview, letters of recommendation, transcript.
Other Admission Factors: Minimum 3.0 GPA and minimum GRE scores of 400 each on verbal, quantitive and analytical required.

EMPLOYMENT INFORMATION
Placement Office Available? Yes. % Employed Within 6 Months: 100. % of master's grads employed in their field upon graduation: 100.

FRANCISCAN SCHOOL OF THEOLOGY
Graduate Programs

Address: 1712 Euclid Avenue, Berkeley, CA 94709
Admissions Phone: 510-848-5232 · **Admissions Fax:** 510-549-9466
Admissions E-mail: info@fstedu

INSTITUTIONAL INFORMATION
Public/private: Private (nonprofit). Student/faculty Ratio: 12:1. Students in Parent Institution: 98.

STUDENT INFORMATION
Total Students in Program: 59. % Full-time: 54. % Female: 54.

EXPENSES/FINANCIAL AID
Annual Tuition: $8,320. Room & Board (On/off Campus): $8,325/$14,400. Fees: $50. Books and Supplies: $400. Grants Range From: $500-$8,320. Loans Range From: $1,000-$6,000. % Receiving Financial Aid: 40. % Receiving Scholarships/Grants: 100. % Receiving Loans: 8.

ADMISSIONS INFORMATION
Application Fee: $25. Regular Notification: Rolling. Transfer Students Accepted? Yes. Number of Applications Received: 51. % of Applicants Accepted: 84. % Accepted Who Enrolled: 100. Average GPA: 3.8.
Required Admission Factors: Essays/personal statement, letters of recommendation, transcript.
Other Admission Factors: Minimum 3.0 GPA required.

EMPLOYMENT INFORMATION
% of master's grads employed in their field upon graduation: 20.

FRANCISCAN UNIVERSITY OF STEUBENVILLE
Graduate School

Address: 1235 University Boulevard, Steubenville, OH 43952-1763
Admissions Phone: 800-786-6220 · **Admissions Fax:** 740-284-5456
Admissions E-mail: admissions@franuniv.edu

INSTITUTIONAL INFORMATION
Public/private: Private (nonprofit). Evening Classes Available? Yes. Student/faculty Ratio: 13:1. Students in Parent Institution: 2,154.

STUDENT INFORMATION
Total Students in Program: 453. % Full-time: 36. % Female: 56.

EXPENSES/FINANCIAL AID
Room & Board: $5,500. Fees: $180. Books and Supplies: $800. Grants Range From: $600-$10,000. Loans Range From: $1,000-$18,500. % Receiving Financial Aid: 75. % Receiving Scholarships/Grants: 33. % Receiving Loans: 55. Average student debt, upon graduation: $35,076.

ADMISSIONS INFORMATION
Application Fee: $20. Regular Notification: Rolling. Transfer Students Accepted? Yes. Number of Applications Received: 135. % of Applicants Accepted: 98. % Accepted Who Enrolled: 67. Average GPA: 3.26. Average GRE Verbal: 465. Average GRE Quantitative: 482. Average GRE Analytical: 507.
Required Admission Factors: Letters of recommendation, transcript.
Other Admission Factors: Minimum 2.5 GPA required.

EMPLOYMENT INFORMATION
Placement Office Available? Yes. Rate of placement: 66%.

FRESNO PACIFIC UNIVERSITY
Graduate School

Address: 1717 South Chestnut Avenue, Fresno, CA 93702
Admissions Phone: 559-453-2256 · **Admissions Fax:** 559-453-2001
Admissions E-mail: edthiess@fresno.edu

INSTITUTIONAL INFORMATION
Public/private: Private (proprietary). **Evening Classes Available?** Yes. **Students in Parent Institution:** 1,887.

STUDENT INFORMATION
Total Students in Program: 947. **% Full-time:** 7. **% Female:** 71.

EXPENSES/FINANCIAL AID
Annual Tuition: In-state $5,760. **Books and Supplies:** $300. **Grants Range From:** $100-$2,000. **Loans Range From:** $100-$18,500. **% Receiving Financial Aid:** 70. **% Receiving Scholarships/Grants:** 20. **% Receiving Loans:** 80. **Average student debt, upon graduation:** $20,000.

ADMISSIONS INFORMATION
Application Fee: $75. **Regular Notification:** Rolling. **Transfer Students Accepted?** Yes. **Transfer Policy:** Official graduate transcripts from transfer institution (by 8/1) required of transfer applicant. **Number of Applications Received:** 152. **% of Applicants Accepted:** 90. **% Accepted Who Enrolled:** 100. **Average GPA:** 3.0
Required Admission Factors: Essays/personal statement, interview, letters of recommendation, transcript.
Other Admission Factors: Minimum 2.5 GPA, 2 professional writing samples, and personal statement required.

EMPLOYMENT INFORMATION
Placement Office Available? Yes. **Rate of placement:** 95%.

FROSTBURG STATE UNIVERSITY
College of Liberal Arts & Sciences

Address: 101 Braddock Road, Frostburg, MD 21532
Admissions Phone: 301-687-7053 · **Admissions Fax:** 301-687-4597
Admissions E-mail: rsmith@frostburg.edu

INSTITUTIONAL INFORMATION
Public/private: Public. **Students in Parent Institution:** 5,260.

STUDENT INFORMATION
Total Students in Program: 909. **% Full-time:** 19. **% Female:** 55.

RESEARCH FACILITIES
Research Facilities: Appalachian Environmental Lab.

EXPENSES/FINANCIAL AID
Annual Tuition: In-state $3,060. / Out-of-state $3,546. **Number of Teaching/Research Assistantships Granted Each Year:** 7. **Average Salary Stipend:** $5,000.

ADMISSIONS INFORMATION
Application Fee: $30. **Regular Notification:** Rolling. **Transfer Students Accepted?** Yes. **Number of Applications Received:** 50. **% of Applicants Accepted:** 36. **% Accepted Who Enrolled:** 39. **Average GPA:** 8.38. **Average GRE Verbal:** 483. **Average GRE Quantitative:** 523. **Average GRE Analytical:** 572.
Required Admission Factors: Essays/personal statement, GRE, interview, letters of recommendation, transcript.
Other Admission Factors: Minimum 3.0 GPA required.

EMPLOYMENT INFORMATION
Placement Office Available? Yes.

FULLER THEOLOGICAL SEMINARY
Graduate School of Intercultural Studies

Address: Office of Admissions, 135 North Oakland Avenue, Pasadena, CA 91182
Admissions Phone: 800-2-FULLER · **Admissions Fax:** 626-584-5449
Admissions E-mail: adm-email@dept.fuller.edu · **Web Address:** www.fuller.edu

INSTITUTIONAL INFORMATION
Public/private: Private (nonprofit). **Evening Classes Available?** Yes. **Students in Parent Institution:** 4,175.

PROGRAMS
Masters offered in: Anthropology, Christian studies, international/global studies, Islamic studies, Jewish/Judaic studies, missions/missionary studies and missiology, pastoral counseling and specialized ministries, theology/theological studies, urban studies/affairs. **Doctorate offered in:** Anthropology, Christian studies, international/global studies, Islamic studies, Jewish/Judaic studies, missions/missionary studies and missiology, pastoral counseling and specialized ministries, theology/theological studies, urban studies/affairs.

STUDENT INFORMATION
Total Students in Program: 572. **% Full-time:** 81. **% Female:** 37.

EXPENSES/FINANCIAL AID
Annual Tuition: $11,232. **Fees:** $103. **Books and Supplies:** $1,200. **Grants Range From:** $350-$10,000. **Loans Range From:** $100-$18,500. **% Receiving Financial Aid:** 62. **% Receiving Scholarships/Grants:** 85. **% Receiving Loans:** 56. **Types of Aid Available:** Grants, loans, scholarships, federal work-study. **Average student debt, upon graduation:** $18,100.

ADMISSIONS INFORMATION
Application Fee: $50. **Regular Application Deadline:** 8/28. **Regular Notification:** Rolling. **Transfer Students Accepted?** Yes. **Number of Applications Received:** 192. **% of Applicants Accepted:** 70.
Required Admission Factors: Essays/personal statement, letters of recommendation, transcript.
Other Admission Factors: Minimum 2.7 GPA required.

EMPLOYMENT INFORMATION
Placement Office Available? Yes.

FULLER THEOLOGICAL SEMINARY
Graduate School of Psychology

Address: Office of Admissions, 135 North Oakland Avenue, Pasadena, CA 91182
Admissions Phone: 800-2-FULLER · **Admissions Fax:** 626-584-5449
Admissions E-mail: adm-email@dept.fuller.edu · **Web Address:** www.fuller.edu

INSTITUTIONAL INFORMATION
Public/private: Private (nonprofit). **Students in Parent Institution:** 4,175.

PROGRAMS
Masters offered in: Clinical psychology, psychology. **Doctorate offered in:** Clinical psychology.

STUDENT INFORMATION
Total Students in Program: 354. **% Full-time:** 73. **% Female:** 65.

EXPENSES/FINANCIAL AID
Annual Tuition: $249-$482 per credit. **Fees:** $103. **Books and Supplies:** $1,200. **Grants Range From:** $350-$10,000. **Loans Range From:** $100-$18,500. **% Receiving Financial Aid:** 76. **% Receiving Scholarships/Grants:** 85. **% Receiving Loans:** 56. **Types of Aid Available:** Fellowships, grants, loans, scholarships. federal work-study. **Average student debt, upon graduation:** $86,340.

ADMISSIONS INFORMATION
Application Fee: $50. **Priority Application Deadline:** 11/30. **Regular Application Deadline:** 1/1. **Regular Notification:** 4/15. **Transfer Students**

Accepted? Yes. **Number of Applications Received:** 279. **% of Applicants Accepted:** 42. **Average GPA:** 3.71.
Required Admission Factors: Essays/personal statement, GRE, letters of recommendation, transcript.
Recommended Admission Factors: GRE subject exam(s) in psychology subject test.
Other Admission Factors: GRE score of 1100 and 3.5 GPA to be competitive (for clinical psychology degrees); GRE score of 1000 and 3.0 GPA to be competitive (for marriage & family therapy degrees)
Program-Specific Admission Factors: Admissions interview only required for clinical psychology applicants.

EMPLOYMENT INFORMATION
Placement Office Available? Yes.

FURMAN UNIVERSITY
Graduate Programs

Address: 3300 Poinsett Highway, Greenville, SC 29613
Admissions Phone: 864-294-2213 · **Admissions Fax:** 864-294-3579
Admissions E-mail: hazel.harris@furman.edu

INSTITUTIONAL INFORMATION
Public/private: Private (nonprofit). **Evening Classes Available?** Yes. **Total Faculty:** 55. **% Faculty Female:** 42. **% Faculty Part-time:** 95. **Student/faculty Ratio:** 10:1. **Students in Parent Institution:** 3,272.

STUDENT INFORMATION
Total Students in Program: 495. **% Full-time:** 12. **% Female:** 80.

EXPENSES/FINANCIAL AID
Annual Tuition: $5,280. **Books and Supplies:** $250. **Grants Range From:** $300-$7,000. **Loans Range From:** $1,380-$18,500. **% Receiving Financial Aid:** 16. **% Receiving Scholarships/Grants:** 34. **% Receiving Loans:** 51. **Types of Aid Available:** 1 **Average student debt, upon graduation:** $5,703.

ADMISSIONS INFORMATION
Application Fee: $30. **Regular Notification:** Rolling. **Transfer Students Accepted?** Yes.
Required Admission Factors: Transcript.
Program-Specific Admission Factors: Resume may be required of some applicants.

EMPLOYMENT INFORMATION
% Employed Within 6 Months: 98. **% of master's grads employed in their field upon graduation:** 98.

GALLAUDET UNIVERSITY
Graduate School &
Professional Programs

Address: 800 Florida Avenue, NE, HMB 4th floor, Washington, DC 20002
Admissions Phone: 202-651-5717 · **Admissions Fax:** 202-651-5295
Admissions E-mail: Graduate.School@Gallaudet.edu
Web Address: gradschool.gallaudet.edu/gradschool/index.html

INSTITUTIONAL INFORMATION
Public/private: Private (nonprofit). **Students in Parent Institution:** 1,834.

STUDENT INFORMATION
Total Students in Program: 627. **% Full-time:** 48. **% Female:** 79. **% Minority:** 20. **% International:** 4.

RESEARCH FACILITIES
Research Facilities: Graduate Research Center.

EXPENSES/FINANCIAL AID
Annual Tuition: $5,300. **Room & Board:** $8,420. **Fees:** $1,345. **Books and Supplies:** $600. **Grants Range From:** $1,000-$5,000. **Loans Range From:** $1,000-$16,000. **% Receiving Scholarships/Grants:** 85. **% Receiving Loans:** 71. **Types of Aid Available:** Fellowships, graduate assistantships, grants, institutional work-study, loans, scholarships. **Assistantship Compensation Includes:** Full tuition remission, partial tuition remission, salary/stipend.

ADMISSIONS INFORMATION
Application Fee: $50. **Priority Application Deadline:** 2/15. **Regular Application Deadline:** 2/15. **Regular Notification:** Rolling. **Transfer Students Accepted?** No. **Number of Applications Received:** 362. **% of Applicants Accepted:** 65. **% Accepted Who Enrolled:** 68. **Average GPA:** 3.0. **Average GRE Verbal:** 401. **Average GRE Quantitative:** 501.
Required Admission Factors: Essays/personal statement, letters of recommendation, transcript.
Other Admission Factors: Minimum 3.0 GPA required; other requirements vary by program.
Program-Specific Admission Factors: Special requirements to specific programs should be looked up in the graduate catalog: http://gradschool.gallaudet.edu/gradschool/catalog/gradcatalog.html

EMPLOYMENT INFORMATION
Placement Office Available? Yes. **% Employed Within 6 Months:** 90. **% of master's/doctoral/first professional grads employed in their field upon graduation:** 85/90/90. **Rate of placement:** 95%.

GANNON UNIVERSITY
College of Humanities

Address: University Square, Erie, PA 16541
Admissions Phone: 814-871-7474 · **Admissions Fax:** 814-871-5827

INSTITUTIONAL INFORMATION
Public/private: Private (nonprofit). **Evening Classes Available?** Yes. **Student/faculty Ratio:** 11:1. **Students in Parent Institution:** 3,292

STUDENT INFORMATION
Total Students in Program: 802. **% Full-time:** 23. **% Female:** 59.

RESEARCH FACILITIES
Research Facilities: Evironaut.

EXPENSES/FINANCIAL AID
Annual Tuition: $8,460. **Books and Supplies:** $650. **Grants Range From:** $200-$16,740. **Loans Range From:** $500-$18,500. **% Receiving Scholarships/Grants:** 15. **% Receiving Loans:** 80. **% Receiving Assistantships:** 2.

ADMISSIONS INFORMATION
Application Fee: $25. **Regular Notification:** Rolling. **Transfer Students Accepted?** Yes. **Transfer Policy:** Maximum 6 credit hours (9 for doctoral programs) may be transferred. **Number of Applications Received:** 75. **% of Applicants Accepted:** 75. **% Accepted Who Enrolled:** 75.
Required Admission Factors: GRE, interview, letters of recommendation, transcript.
Program-Specific Admission Factors: Minimum GRE score of 1400 and minimum 3.25 GPA required of counseling psychology program applicants.

EMPLOYMENT INFORMATION
Placement Office Available? Yes.

GARDNER-WEBB UNIVERSITY
Graduate School

Address: Main Street, Boiling Springs, NC 28017
Admissions Phone: 800-492-4723 · **Admissions Fax:** 704-406-4329
Admissions E-mail: gradschool@gardner-webb.edu

Complete Book of Graduate Programs in the Arts and Sciences

INSTITUTIONAL INFORMATION

Public/private: Private (nonprofit). **Evening Classes Available?** Yes. **Student/faculty Ratio:** 15:1. **Students in Parent Institution:** 3,193.

STUDENT INFORMATION

Total Students in Program: 718. **% Full-time:** 46. **% Female:** 54.

EXPENSES/FINANCIAL AID

Annual Tuition: $2,520. **Number of Fellowships Granted Each Year:** 22. **Average amount of individual fellowships per year:** $5,500.

ADMISSIONS INFORMATION

Application Fee: $25. **Regular Notification:** Rolling. **Transfer Students Accepted?** Yes. **Transfer Policy:** Maximum of 6 credit hours may be transferred into graduate programs. **Number of Applications Received:** 94. **% of Applicants Accepted:** 97. **% Accepted Who Enrolled:** 93. **Average GPA:** 3.2. **Average GRE Verbal:** 484. **Average GRE Quantitative:** 544. **Average GRE Analytical:** 480.
Required Admission Factors: Letters of recommendation, transcript.
Other Admission Factors: Minimum 2.5 GPA required.
Program-Specific Admission Factors: Minimum 2.7 GPA required for counseling and nursing program applicants.

EMPLOYMENT INFORMATION

Placement Office Available? Yes. **% of master's grads employed in their field upon graduation:** 98.

GARRETT-EVANGELICAL THEOLOGICAL SEMINARY
Graduate Programs

Address: 2121 Sheridan Road, Evanston, IL 60201
Admissions Phone: 847-866-3945 · **Admissions Fax:** 847-866-3957
Admissions E-mail: sean.recroft@garrett.edu ·

INSTITUTIONAL INFORMATION

Public/private: Private (nonprofit). **Student/faculty Ratio:** 8:1. **Students in Parent Institution:** 302.

STUDENT INFORMATION

Total Students in Program: 161. **% Full-time:** 40.

EXPENSES/FINANCIAL AID

Annual Tuition: $11,070. **Fees:** $30. **Books and Supplies:** $990. **Grants Range From:** $2,441-$14,445. **Loans Range From:** $200-$18,500. **% Receiving Financial Aid:** 54. **% Receiving Scholarships/Grants:** 94. **% Receiving Loans:** 72. **Average student debt, upon graduation:** $20,000 **Number of Fellowships Granted Each Year:** 36. **Average amount of individual fellowships per year:** $7,720.

ADMISSIONS INFORMATION

Regular Notification: Rolling. **Transfer Students Accepted?** Yes. **Transfer Policy:** Maximum 10 credit hours may be transferred into MA and MTS programs; maximum 15 credit. **Number of Applications Received:** 219. **% of Applicants Accepted:** 70. **% Accepted Who Enrolled:** 50. **Average GPA:** 3.3.
Required Admission Factors: Essays/personal statement, letters of recommendation, transcript.
Other Admission Factors: Minimum 2.5 GPA required.

GENEVA COLLEGE
Organizational Leadership Program

Address: 3200 College Avenue, Beaver Falls, PA 15010
Admissions Phone: 412-847-2715 · **Admissions Fax:** 412-847-4198
Admissions E-mail: kkuhlman@geneva.edu

INSTITUTIONAL INFORMATION

Public/private: Private (nonprofit). **Evening Classes Available?** Yes. **Student/faculty Ratio:** 10:1. **Students in Parent Institution:** 2,142.

STUDENT INFORMATION

Total Students in Program: 287. **% Full-time:** 71. **% Female:** 53.

RESEARCH FACILITIES

Research Facilities: The Geneva Professional Center for College and Community Services.

EXPENSES/FINANCIAL AID

Books and Supplies: $600. **Grants Range From:** $1,200-$2,400. **Loans Range From:** $500-$18,500.

ADMISSIONS INFORMATION

Application Fee: $15. **Regular Notification:** Rolling. **Transfer Students Accepted?** No. **Number of Applications Received:** 59. **% of Applicants Accepted:** 97. **% Accepted Who Enrolled:** 95. **Average GPA:** 2.9.
Required Admission Factors: Essays/personal statement, interview, letters of recommendation, transcript.
Other Admission Factors: Minimum 2.5 GPA, 3 to 5 years of full-time work experience, and writing sample required.

GEORGE FOX UNIVERSITY
Counseling Program

Address: 414 North Meridian Street, Newberg, OR 97132
Admissions Phone: 800-493-4937 · **Admissions Fax:** 503-554-6111
Admissions E-mail: dseipp@georgefox.edu

INSTITUTIONAL INFORMATION

Public/private: Private (nonprofit). **Students in Parent Institution:** 2,640.

STUDENT INFORMATION

Total Students in Program: 864. **% Full-time:** 31. **% Female:** 61.

RESEARCH FACILITIES

Research Facilities: Center for Peace Learning.

EXPENSES/FINANCIAL AID

Grants Range From: $150-$24,530. **Loans Range From:** $1,000-$30,000. **% Receiving Financial Aid:** 62. **% Receiving Scholarships/Grants:** 4. **% Receiving Loans:** 96.

ADMISSIONS INFORMATION

Application Fee: $40. **Regular Notification:** Rolling. **Transfer Students Accepted?** Yes. **Number of Applications Received:** 103. **% of Applicants Accepted:** 83. **% Accepted Who Enrolled:** 79.
Required Admission Factors: Essays/personal statement, interview, letters of recommendation, transcript.

GEORGE FOX UNIVERSITY
Graduate School of Clinical Psychology

Address: 414 North Meridian Street, Newberg, OR 97132
Admissions Phone: 800-631-0921 · **Admissions Fax:** 503-554-3856
Admissions E-mail: dseipp@georgefox.edu

INSTITUTIONAL INFORMATION

Public/private: Private (nonprofit). **Students in Parent Institution:** 2,640.

STUDENT INFORMATION

Total Students in Program: 864. **% Full-time:** 31. **% Female:** 61.

RESEARCH FACILITIES

Research Facilities: Center for Peace Learning.

EXPENSES/FINANCIAL AID

Grants Range From: $150-$24,530. Loans Range From: $1,000-$30,000. % Receiving Financial Aid: 80. % Receiving Scholarships/Grants: 4. % Receiving Loans: 96.

ADMISSIONS INFORMATION

Application Fee: $40. Transfer Students Accepted? Yes. Number of Applications Received: 35. % of Applicants Accepted: 66. % Accepted Who Enrolled: 65. Average GPA: 3.58. Average GRE Verbal: 520. Average GRE Quantitative: 527.

Required Admission Factors: Essays/personal statement, GRE, interview, letters of recommendation, transcript.

Other Admission Factors: Minimum 3.0 GPA and minimum 19 semester credits in psychology required.

GEORGE MASON UNIVERSITY
College of Arts & Sciences

Address: 4400 University Drive, Fairfax, VA 22030
Admissions Phone: 703-993-3699 · Admissions Fax: 703-993-8714
Admissions E-mail: gmugrad@gmu.edu

INSTITUTIONAL INFORMATION

Public/private: Public. Evening Classes Available? Yes.   Student/faculty Ratio: 15:1. Students in Parent Institution: 23,408.

STUDENT INFORMATION

Total Students in Program: 7,508. % Full-time: 16. % Female: 58.

RESEARCH FACILITIES

Research Facilities: Krasnow Institute.

EXPENSES/FINANCIAL AID

Annual Tuition: In-state $4,500. / Out-of-state $12,612. Books and Supplies: $700. % Receiving Financial Aid: 95. Number of Fellowships Granted Each Year: 15. Average amount of individual fellowships per year: $2,000. Number of Teaching/Research Assistantships Granted Each Year: 30. Average Salary Stipend: $4,000.

ADMISSIONS INFORMATION

Application Fee: $40. Transfer Students Accepted? Yes. Number of Applications Received: 1,316. % of Applicants Accepted: 51. % Accepted Who Enrolled: 53. Average GPA: 3.37. Average GRE Verbal: 534. Average GRE Quantitative: 599. Average GRE Analytical: 603.

Required Admission Factors: Essays/personal statement, letters of recommendation, transcript.

Other Admission Factors: Minimum 3.0 GPA in last 60 undergraduate credit hours required.

Program-Specific Admission Factors: Writing sample and 3 letters of recommendation may be required.

EMPLOYMENT INFORMATION

Placement Office Available? Yes.

GEORGE MASON UNIVERSITY
Institute of the Arts

Address: 4400 University Drive, Fairfax, VA 22030
Admissions Phone: 703-993-9989 or 703-993-1121· Admissions Fax: 703-993-8798
Admissions E-mail: gmugrad@gmu.edu

INSTITUTIONAL INFORMATION

Public/private: Public. Evening Classes Available? Yes. Students in Parent Institution: 23,408.

STUDENT INFORMATION

Total Students in Program: 7,508. % Full-time: 16. % Female: 58.

RESEARCH FACILITIES

Research Facilities: Krasnow Institute.

EXPENSES/FINANCIAL AID

Annual Tuition: In-state $4,500. / Out-of-state $12,612. Books and Supplies: $700. Number of Fellowships Granted Each Year: 2. Average amount of individual fellowships per year: $1,000. Number of Teaching/Research Assistantships Granted Each Year: 2. Average Salary Stipend: $7,500.

ADMISSIONS INFORMATION

Application Fee: $30. Regular Notification: Rolling. Transfer Students Accepted? Yes.

Required Admission Factors: Essays/personal statement, interview, letters of recommendation, transcript.

Other Admission Factors: Minimum 3.0 GPA required.

EMPLOYMENT INFORMATION

Placement Office Available? Yes. % of master's grads employed in their field upon graduation: 80.

GEORGE MASON UNIVERSITY
International Institute

Address: 4400 University Drive, Fairfax, VA 22030
Admissions Phone: 703-993-8200 · Admissions Fax: 703-993-8215
Admissions E-mail: gmugrad@gmu.edu

INSTITUTIONAL INFORMATION

Public/private: Public. Evening Classes Available? Yes. Total Faculty: 40. Students in Parent Institution: 23,408.

STUDENT INFORMATION

Total Students in Program: 7,508. % Full-time: 16. % Female: 58.

RESEARCH FACILITIES

Research Facilities: Krasnow Institute.

EXPENSES/FINANCIAL AID

Annual Tuition: In-state $4,500. / Out-of-state $12,612. Books and Supplies: $700. % Receiving Financial Aid: 41.

ADMISSIONS INFORMATION

Regular Notification: Rolling. Transfer Students Accepted? Yes. Transfer Policy: Maximum 6 transfer credits accepted from another university or 12 transfer credits from George Mason University. Number of Applications Received: 138. % of Applicants Accepted: 76. % Accepted Who Enrolled: 63. Average GPA: 2.9.

Required Admission Factors: Essays/personal statement, transcript.

Other Admission Factors: Minimum 3.0 GPA required.

EMPLOYMENT INFORMATION

Placement Office Available? Yes.

GEORGE MASON UNIVERSITY
School of Public Policy

Address: 3401 North Fairfax Drive, MS 3B1, Arlington, VA 22201
Admissions Phone: 703-993-8099 · Admissions Fax: 703-993-4876
Admissions E-mail: spp@gmu.edu · Web Address: http://policy.gmu.edu

INSTITUTIONAL INFORMATION

Public/private: Public. Evening Classes Available? Yes. Total Faculty: 74. % Faculty Female: 11. % Faculty Part-time: 41. Student/faculty Ratio: 10:1. Students in Parent Institution: 28,874.

STUDENT INFORMATION
Total Students in Program: 8,018. % Full-time: 20. % Female: 57. % Minority: 19. % International: 11.

RESEARCH FACILITIES
Research Facilities: Mason Enterprise Center, Center for Global Policy, Center for Regional Analysis, Policy Analysis Center, Office of International Medical Policy.

EXPENSES/FINANCIAL AID
Annual Tuition: In-state $6,498. / Out-of-state $11,862. Room & Board: $8,400. Fees: $60. Books and Supplies: $1,000. Grants Range From: $1,000-$1,500. Loans Range From: $1,000–$10,000.

ADMISSIONS INFORMATION
Application Fee: $60. Priority Application Deadline: 6/1. Regular Application Deadline: 6/1. Regular Notification: Rolling. Transfer Students Accepted? No. Number of Applications Received: 645. % of Applicants Accepted: 68. % Accepted Who Enrolled: 58. Average GPA: 3.5. Required Admission Factors: Essays/personal statement, letters of recommendation, transcript.
Other Admission Factors: Minimum 3.0 GPA, goals statement, resume, and 2 letters of recommendation required.
Program-Specific Admission Factors: Master's degree required of doctoral degree program applicants. Doctoral applicants must also submit GRE scores and a 10-25 page writing sample.

EMPLOYMENT INFORMATION
Placement Office Available? Yes. % Employed Within 6 Months: 80. Rate of placement: 70%. Average starting salary: $50,000.

THE GEORGE WASHINGTON UNIVERSITY
Columbian School of Arts & Sciences

Address: 2121 I Street, NW, Washington, DC 20052
Admissions Phone: 202-994-6211 · Admissions Fax: 202-994-6213

INSTITUTIONAL INFORMATION
Evening Classes Available? Yes. Students in Parent Institution: 16,741.

STUDENT INFORMATION
Total Students in Program: 9,435. % Full-time: 55. % Female: 49.

RESEARCH FACILITIES
Research Facilities: Biostatisics Center, Center for Washington Area Studies, Institute for the Environment, State Institute for Advancement of Flight Science, Institute for European, Russian and EurAsian Studies.

EXPENSES/FINANCIAL AID
Annual Tuition: In-state $13,365. Fees: $774.

ADMISSIONS INFORMATION
Application Fee: $55. Regular Notification: Rolling. Transfer Students Accepted? No. Number of Applications Received: 2,944. % of Applicants Accepted: 47. % Accepted Who Enrolled: 40.
Required Admission Factors: Essays/personal statement, GRE, interview, transcript.
Other Admission Factors: Minimum 3.0 GPA required.

EMPLOYMENT INFORMATION
Placement Office Available? Yes.

THE GEORGE WASHINGTON UNIVERSITY
Elliott School of International Affairs

Address: 1957 E Street, NW, Suite 301, Washington, DC 20052
Admissions Phone: 202-944-7050 · Admissions Fax: 202-994-9537
Admissions E-mail: esiagrad@gwu.edu · Website: www.gwu.edu/~elliott

INSTITUTIONAL INFORMATION
Public/private: Private (nonprofit). Evening Classes Available? Yes. Students in Parent Institution: 16,741.

PROGRAMS
Masters offered in: Area studies, international relations and affairs, international/global studies, peace studies and conflict resolution, regional studies (U.S., Canadian, foreign), science technologies/technicians.

STUDENT INFORMATION
Total Students in Program: 9,435. % Full-time: 55. % Female: 49.

RESEARCH FACILITIES
Research Facilities: Biostatisics Center, Center for Washington Area Studies, Institute for the Environment, State Institute for Advancement of Flight Science, Institute for European, Russian and EurAsian Studies, Sigur Center for Asian Studies, Center for International Science.

EXPENSES/FINANCIAL AID
Annual Tuition: In-state $13,365. Fees: $774.

ADMISSIONS INFORMATION
Application Fee: $60. Priority Application Deadline: 1/15. Regular Application Deadline: 2/1. Regular Notification: 4/1. Transfer Students Accepted? No. Number of Applications Received: 1,636. % of Applicants Accepted: 55. % Accepted Who Enrolled: 27. Average GPA: 3.4.
Required Admission Factors: Essays/personal statement, GRE, letters of recommendation, transcript.
Other Admission Factors: 2 years of a modern foreign language and 1 semester each of micro- and macroeconomics.

EMPLOYMENT INFORMATION
Placement Office Available? Yes.

GEORGETOWN UNIVERSITY
Graduate School of Arts & Sciences

Address: 37th and O Streets, NW, Washington, DC 20057
Admissions Phone: 202-687-5568 · Admissions Fax: 202-687-6802

INSTITUTIONAL INFORMATION
Students in Parent Institution: 12,618.

STUDENT INFORMATION
Total Students in Program: 6,244. % Full-time: 79. % Female: 46.

EXPENSES/FINANCIAL AID
Annual Tuition: $20,280.

ADMISSIONS INFORMATION
Application Fee: $50. Transfer Students Accepted? No.
Required Admission Factors: GRE, letters of recommendation, transcript.
Other Admission Factors: Minimum grade average of B required. Separate application form required for some programs.
Program-Specific Admission Factors: GRE subject exam (psychology) required of psychology program applicants.

GEORGIA COLLEGE AND STATE UNIVERSITY
College of Arts & Sciences

Address: Clark Street, Milledgeville, GA 31061
Admissions Phone: 912-445-4441 · Admissions Fax: 912-445-0873
Admissions E-mail: bpatters@mail.gcsu.edu ·

INSTITUTIONAL INFORMATION
Public/private: Public. Evening Classes Available? Yes. Students in Parent Institution: 5,076.

STUDENT INFORMATION

Total Students in Program: 1,096. % Full-time: 20. % Female: 69.

EXPENSES/FINANCIAL AID

Annual Tuition: In-state $2,286. / Out-of-state $9,108. Room & Board: $6,294. Fees: $500. Books and Supplies: $600. Loans Range From: $525-$12,300. Number of Teaching/Research Assistantships Granted Each Year: 26. Average Salary Stipend: $1,900.

ADMISSIONS INFORMATION

Application Fee: $25. Regular Notification: Rolling. Transfer Students Accepted? Yes.
Required Admission Factors: Transcript.

EMPLOYMENT INFORMATION

Placement Office Available? Yes.

GEORGIA INSTITUTE OF TECHNOLOGY
College of Sciences

Address: 225 North Avenue, NW, Atlanta, GA 30332

INSTITUTIONAL INFORMATION

Public/private: Public. Students in Parent Institution: 14,804.

STUDENT INFORMATION

Total Students in Program: 4,059. % Full-time: 80. % Female: 26.

RESEARCH FACILITIES

Research Facilities: Advanced Technology Development Center, Research Institute, Oceanography Institute, Nuclear Research Center.

EXPENSES/FINANCIAL AID

Annual Tuition: In-state $3,156. / Out-of-state $12,624. Room & Board: $5,534. Fees: $822. Grants Range From: $3,000-$24,000. Loans Range From: $8,500-$18,500. % Receiving Scholarships/Grants: 15. % Receiving Loans: 30. % Receiving Assistantships: 80.

ADMISSIONS INFORMATION

Transfer Students Accepted? No.

EMPLOYMENT INFORMATION

Placement Office Available? Yes.

GEORGIA INSTITUTE OF TECHNOLOGY
Ivan Allen College

Address: 225 North Avenue, NW, Atlanta, GA 30332
Admissions Phone: 404-894-1610 · Admissions Fax: 404-894-1609
Admissions E-mail: gradadmissions@gatech.edu · Web Address: www.iac.gatech.edu

INSTITUTIONAL INFORMATION

Public/private: Public. Students in Parent Institution: 14,804.

PROGRAMS

Masters offered in: American history (U.S.); European history; history and philosophy of science and technology; history; international relations and affairs; international/global studies; multi/interdisciplinary studies; public policy analysis; sociology. Doctorate offered in: American history (U.S.); European history; history and philosophy of science and technology; history, multi/interdisciplinary studies; public policy analysis; sociology.

STUDENT INFORMATION

Total Students in Program: 4,059. % Full-time: 80. % Female: 26.

RESEARCH FACILITIES

Research Facilities: Center for Women in Science and Technology; Center for International Strategy, Technology, and Policy; European Union Center; Technology Policy and Analysis Center.

EXPENSES/FINANCIAL AID

Annual Tuition: In-state $3,156. / Out-of-state $12,624. Room & Board: $5,534. Fees: $822. Books and Supplies: $350. Grants Range From: $3,000-$27,500. Loans Range From: $8,500-$18,500. % Receiving Scholarships/Grants: 15. % Receiving Loans: 30. % Receiving Assistantships: 80. Types of Aid Available: Fellowships, graduate assistantships, scholarships. tuition waivers. Assistantship Compensation Includes: Full tuition remission, salary/stipend. Average Salary Stipend: $12,500.

ADMISSIONS INFORMATION

Application Fee: $50. Priority Application Deadline: 2/1. Regular Notification: Rolling. Transfer Students Accepted? Yes.
Required Admission Factors: Essays/personal statement, GRE, letters of recommendation, transcript.
Other Admission Factors: TOEFL may be required for international students with less than 2 years' residency in U.S.
Program-Specific Admission Factors: Public policy PhD program recommends 1 semester of college calculus prior to enrollment.

EMPLOYMENT INFORMATION

Placement Office Available? Yes.

GEORGIA SOUTHERN UNIVERSITY
College of Liberal Arts & Social Sciences

Address: PO Box 8113, Statesboro, GA 30460-8113
Admissions Phone: 912-681-5384 · Admissions Fax: 912-681-0740
Admissions E-mail: gradschool@georgiasouthern.edu
Web Address: www.admissions.georgiasouthern.edu

INSTITUTIONAL INFORMATION

Public/private: Public. Evening Classes Available? Yes. Total Faculty: 152. % Faculty Female: 43. % Faculty Part-time: 2. Students in Parent Institution: 16,100.

PROGRAMS

Masters offered in: English language and literature, fine/studio arts, history, music, psychology, public administration, sociology.

STUDENT INFORMATION

Total Students in Program: 173. % Full-time: 59. % Female: 64. % Minority: 35. % International: 4.

RESEARCH FACILITIES

Research Facilities: Bureau of Public Affairs, Center for Africana Studies, Center for International Studies, Center for Irish Studies, Center for Social Gerontology.

EXPENSES/FINANCIAL AID

Annual Tuition: In-state $2,786. / Out-of-state $11,146. Room & Board: $6,000. Fees: $700. Books and Supplies: $700. Grants Range From: $250-$2,500. Loans Range From: $100-$18,500. % Receiving Financial Aid: 69. % Receiving Scholarships/Grants: 62. % Receiving Loans: 76. Types of Aid Available: Graduate assistantships, grants, institutional work-study, loans, scholarships. Average student debt, upon graduation: $24,902. Number of Teaching/Research Assistantships Granted Each Year: 44. Assistantship Compensation Includes: Partial tuition remission, salary/stipend. Average Salary Stipend: $5,500.

ADMISSIONS INFORMATION

Application Fee: $30. Priority Application Deadline: 3/1. Regular Application Deadline: 7/1. Regular Notification: Rolling. Transfer Students Accepted? Yes. Number of Applications Received: 84. % of Applicants Accepted: 86. % Accepted Who Enrolled: 78. Average GRE Verbal: 455. Average GRE Quantitative: 517. Average GRE Analytical: 453. Average GRE Analytical Writing: 4.3.
Required Admission Factors: Transcript.
Other Admission Factors: Varies by program.

Program-Specific Admission Factors: 3 letters of recommendation required of psychology and public administration program applicants. 2 letters of recommendation required for MA in English, history, music. Statement required for MA in sociology. Portfolio required for MFA.

GEORGIA SOUTHWESTERN STATE UNIVERSITY
Graduate School

Address: 800 Wheatley Street, Americus, GA 31709-4693
Admissions Phone: 229-931-2002 · **Admissions Fax:** 229-931-2021
Admissions E-mail: loliver@canes.gsw.edu · **Web Address:** www.gsw.edu

INSTITUTIONAL INFORMATION
Public/private: Public. **Students in Parent Institution:** 2,449.

PROGRAMS
Masters offered in: Business administration/management, computer and information sciences, education/teaching of individuals with emotional disturbances, education/teaching of individuals with mental retardation, education/teaching of individuals with specific learning disabilities, elementary education and teaching, English/language arts teacher education, junior high/intermediate/middle school education and teaching, mathematics teacher education, physical education teaching and coaching, reading teacher education, science teacher education/general science teacher education, secondary education and teaching, social science teacher education, social studies teacher education, special education.

STUDENT INFORMATION
Total Students in Program: 382. **% Full-time:** 40. **% Female:** 79.

EXPENSES/FINANCIAL AID
Annual Tuition: In-state $2,412. / Out-of-state $9,648. **Room & Board:** $3,926. **Fees:** $554. **Books and Supplies:** $850.

ADMISSIONS INFORMATION
Transfer Students Accepted? No.

EMPLOYMENT INFORMATION
Placement Office Available? Yes.

GEORGIA STATE UNIVERSITY
Andrew Young School of Policy Studies

Address: 14 Marietta Street NW, Suite G52, Atlanta, GA 30303
Admissions Phone: 404-651-3504 · **Admissions Fax:** 404-651-3536
Admissions E-mail: ayspsacademicassist@gsu.edu · **Web Address:** www.aysps.gsu.edu

INSTITUTIONAL INFORMATION
Public/private: Public. **Evening Classes Available?** Yes. **Students in Parent Institution:** 27,267.

PROGRAMS
Masters offered in: Business/managerial economics, economics, natural resources management and policy, nonprofit/public/organizational management, public administration, public policy analysis, urban studies/affairs. **Doctorate offered in:** Economics; natural resource economics, public policy analysis. **First Professional degree offered in:** Natural resources management and policy, nonprofit/public/organizational management.

STUDENT INFORMATION
Total Students in Program: 7,362. **% Full-time:** 100.

RESEARCH FACILITIES
Research Facilities: Domestic Studies Program, Environmental Policy Program, Fiscal Research Center, Georgia Health Policy Center, International Studies Program, Research Atlanta Inc., Program for Rehabilitation Leadership, Research Leadership Forum.

EXPENSES/FINANCIAL AID
Annual Tuition: In-state $4,044. / Out-of-state $16,170. **Room & Board:** $8,976. **Fees:** $786. **Books and Supplies:** $1,100. **Grants Range From:** $2,000-$15,000. **Loans Range From:** $300-$18,500. **% Receiving Scholarships/Grants:** 30. **% Receiving Loans:** 78. **% Receiving Assistantships:** 29. **Types of Aid Available:** Fellowships, graduate assistantships, loans. **Number of Teaching/Research Assistantships Granted Each Year:** 96. **Assistantship Compensation Includes:** Full tuition remission, salary/stipend. **Average Salary Stipend:** $2,400.

ADMISSIONS INFORMATION
Application Fee: $50. **Regular Application Deadline:** 4/1. **Regular Notification:** Rolling. **Transfer Students Accepted?** Yes. **Transfer Policy:** Admission requirements for transfer applicants are identical to other applicants. **Number of Applications Received:** 411. **% of Applicants Accepted:** 44. **% Accepted Who Enrolled:** 56. **Average GPA:** 3.3. **Required Admission Factors:** Essays/personal statement, GRE, transcript. **Other Admission Factors:** Minimum GRE score in the 50th percentile on all sections and minimum 3.0 GPA required.

EMPLOYMENT INFORMATION
Placement Office Available? Yes. **% of doctoral grads employed in their field upon graduation:** 100.

GEORGIA STATE UNIVERSITY
College of Arts & Sciences

Address: 33 Gilmer Street SE Unit 7, Atlanta, GA 30303-3087
Admissions Phone: 404-651-2297 · **Admissions Fax:** 404-651-0275
Admissions E-mail: gascas@langate.gsu.edu · **Web Address:** www.cas.gus.edu

INSTITUTIONAL INFORMATION
Public/private: Public. **Total Faculty:** 351. **Students in Parent Institution:** 23,618.

STUDENT INFORMATION
Total Students in Program: 6,581. **% Full-time:** 44. **% Female:** 60.

RESEARCH FACILITIES
Research Facilities: Asian Studies Center, NSF Center for Behavioral Neurosciences, Center for Biotechnology and Drug Design, Center for Brian and Health Sciences, Digital Arts and Entertainment, Center for Educational Partnerships in Music, Environmental Research Center.

EXPENSES/FINANCIAL AID
Annual Tuition: In-state $3,850. / Out-of-state $15,400. **Fees:** $356. **Books and Supplies:** $780. **Grants Range From:** $200-$24,000. **Loans Range From:** $300-$18,500. **% Receiving Scholarships/Grants:** 30. **% Receiving Loans:** 78. **% Receiving Assistantships:** 62. **Types of Aid Available:** Fellowships, graduate assistantships, loans, scholarships. **Assistantship Compensation Includes:** Full tuition remission, salary/stipend.

ADMISSIONS INFORMATION
Application Fee: $50. **Regular Application Deadline:** 4/15. **Regular Notification:** Rolling. **Transfer Students Accepted?** No. **Transfer Policy:** Maximum 6 semester hours may be transferred into master's programs; 30 semester hours may be transfered into doctoral programs. **Number of Applications Received:** 1,798. **% of Applicants Accepted:** 56. **Required Admission Factors:** GRE. **Recommended Admission Factors:** GMAT.

EMPLOYMENT INFORMATION
Placement Office Available? Yes.

GEORGIAN COURT UNIVERSITY
Graduate School

Address: 900 Lakewood Avenue, Lakewood, NJ 08701-2697
Admissions Phone: 732-364-2200 ext. 2760 · **Admissions Fax:** 732-364-4442
Admissions E-mail: admissions@georgian.edu · **Web Address:** www.georgian.edu

INSTITUTIONAL INFORMATION
Public/private: Private (nonprofit). **Evening Classes Available?** Yes. **Total Faculty:** 106. **% Faculty Female:** 46. **% Faculty Part-time:** 58. **Student/faculty Ratio:** 8:1. **Students in Parent Institution:** 2,976.

PROGRAMS
Masters offered in: Business administration/management; counseling psychology; education; educational instructional, and curriculum supervision; educational/instructional media design; health professions and related sciences; mathematics; special education; theology/theological studies.

STUDENT INFORMATION
Total Students in Program: 1,020. **% Full-time:** 10. **% Female:** 85. **% Minority:** 6.

EXPENSES/FINANCIAL AID
Annual Tuition: $9,540. **Fees:** $350. **Books and Supplies:** $1,000. **Grants Range From:** $200-$5,250. **Loans Range From:** $650-$12,187. **% Receiving Financial Aid:** 60. **% Receiving Scholarships/Grants:** 16. **% Receiving Loans:** 50. **Types of Aid Available:** Graduate assistantships, grants, loans, scholarships.

ADMISSIONS INFORMATION
Application Fee: $40. **Regular Application Deadline:** 00/00. **Regular Notification:** Rolling. **Transfer Students Accepted?** Yes. **Number of Applications Received:** 332. **% of Applicants Accepted:** 83. **% Accepted Who Enrolled:** 70. **Average GPA:** 3.3.
Required Admission Factors: Essays/personal statement, letters of recommendation, transcript. TOEFL for international students.
Other Admission Factors: Minimum 3.0 GPA and minimum 24 credit hours of coursework beyond the introductory level in biology and psychology required. Minimum 2.75 GPA required for theology program.

GODDARD COLLEGE
Graduate Programs

Address: 123 Pitkin Road, Plainfield, VT 05667
Admissions Phone: 800-468-4888 · **Admissions Fax:** 802-454-1029
Admissions E-mail: ellenc@earth.goddard.edu

INSTITUTIONAL INFORMATION
Public/private: Private (nonprofit). **Student/faculty Ratio:** 4:1. **Students in Parent Institution:** 577.

STUDENT INFORMATION
Total Students in Program: 221. **% Full-time:** 100. **% Female:** 73.

EXPENSES/FINANCIAL AID
Annual Tuition: $9,650. **Grants Range From:** $700. **% Receiving Scholarships/Grants:** 100.

ADMISSIONS INFORMATION
Regular Notification: Rolling. **Transfer Students Accepted?** Yes. **Number of Applications Received:** 73. **% of Applicants Accepted:** 86. **% Accepted Who Enrolled:** 51.
Required Admission Factors: Essays/personal statement, letters of recommendation, transcript.

GOLDEN GATE BAPTIST THEOLOGICAL SEMINARY
Graduate Programs

Address: 201 Seminary Drive, Box 278, Mill Valley, CA 94941
Admissions Phone: 888-442-8701 · **Admissions Fax:** 415-380-1602
Admissions E-mail: admissions@ggbts.edu · **Web Address:** www.ggbts.edu

INSTITUTIONAL INFORMATION
Public/private: Private (nonprofit). **Evening Classes Available?** Yes. **Total Faculty:** 139. **% Faculty Female:** 12. **% Faculty Part-time:** 76. **Student/faculty Ratio:** 15:1. **Students in Parent Institution:** 1,100.

PROGRAMS
Masters offered in: Divinity/ministry (BD, MDiv); religious education; theology/theological studies.

STUDENT INFORMATION
Total Students in Program: 1,100. **% Full-time:** 60.

EXPENSES/FINANCIAL AID
Annual Tuition: $140. **Fees:** $200. **Books and Supplies:** $700. **Grants Range From:** $200-$800. **Types of Aid Available:** Loans, scholarships.

ADMISSIONS INFORMATION
Application Fee: $35. **Priority Application Deadline:** 5/1. **Regular Application Deadline:** 7/15. **Regular Notification:** Rolling. **Transfer Students Accepted?** Yes. **Transfer Policy:** Must be from regionally accredited and/or ATS accredited schools; to graduate with a GGBTS degree, you must take at least 27 hours of a degree with GGBTS. **Number of Applications Received:** 246. **% of Applicants Accepted:** 98. **% Accepted Who Enrolled:** 81. **Average GPA:** 3.2.
Required Admission Factors: Essays/personal statement, letters of recommendation, transcript.
Other Admission Factors: 3.0 GPA for Global Studies Program; 2.7 MDiv GPA for Master of Theology.

EMPLOYMENT INFORMATION
Placement Office Available? Yes.

GOODING INSTITUTE OF NURSE ANESTHESIA
Graduate Programs

Address: Bay Medical Center
615 North Bonita Avenue, Panama City, FL 32401
Admissions Phone: 850-747-6918 · **Admissions Fax:** 850-747-6115

INSTITUTIONAL INFORMATION
Students in Parent Institution: 19.

STUDENT INFORMATION
Total Students in Program: 19. **% Full-time:** 100. **% Female:** 47.

EXPENSES/FINANCIAL AID
Annual Tuition: In-state $11,000. **Books and Supplies:** $250. **Grants Range From:** $500-$1,000. **% Receiving Financial Aid:** 85. **% Receiving Scholarships/Grants:** 65. **Average student debt, upon graduation:** $55,500.

ADMISSIONS INFORMATION
Application Fee: $40. **Transfer Students Accepted?** No. **Number of Applications Received:** 50. **% of Applicants Accepted:** 22. **% Accepted Who Enrolled:** 100. **Average GPA:** 3.25. **Average GRE Verbal:** 500. **Average GRE Quantitative:** 500. **Average GRE Analytical:** 500.
Required Admission Factors: GRE, interview, letters of recommendation, transcript.
Other Admission Factors: Minimum 3.0 GPA and RN license required.

EMPLOYMENT INFORMATION

% Employed Within 6 Months: 100. % of master's grads employed in their field upon graduation: 100. Rate of placement: 100%. Average starting salary: $85,000.

GORDON-CONWELL THEOLOGICAL SEMINARY
Graduate Programs

Address: 130 Essex Street, South Hamilton, MA 01982
Admissions Phone: 800-428-7329 · **Admissions Fax:** 978-646-4178
Admissions E-mail: adminfo@gcts.edu · **Web Address:** gordonconwell.edu

INSTITUTIONAL INFORMATION

Public/private: Private (nonprofit). **Total Faculty:** 46. **% Faculty Female:** 13. **Student/faculty Ratio:** 18:1. **Students in Parent Institution:** 2,064.

STUDENT INFORMATION

Total Students in Program: 2,064. **% Full-time:** 38. **% Female:** 37. **% Minority:** 26. **% International:** 4.

RESEARCH FACILITIES

Research Facilities: Library of the Advent Christian Church.

EXPENSES/FINANCIAL AID

Books and Supplies: $400.**% Receiving Financial Aid:** 50. **Average student debt, upon graduation:** $18,000.

ADMISSIONS INFORMATION

Application Fee: $35. **Regular Notification:** Rolling. **Transfer Students Accepted?** Yes. **Transfer Policy:** Letter of good standing required of transfer applicants. **Number of Applications Received:** 600. **% of Applicants Accepted:** 80. **% Accepted Who Enrolled:** 56. **Average GPA:** 3.4.
Required Admission Factors: Essays/personal statement, letters of recommendation, transcript.
Program-Specific Admission Factors: Psychological testing and interview required of MACouns program applicants. ThM program applicants must possess MDiv or equivalent. DMin program applicants must possess MDiv and minimum 3 years ministry experience.

EMPLOYMENT INFORMATION

Placement Office Available? Yes.

GOUCHER COLLEGE
Graduate Programs

Address: 1021 Dulaney Valley Road, Baltimore, MD 21204
Admissions Phone: 410-337-6047 · **Admissions Fax:** 410-337-6394
Admissions E-mail: sgray@goucher.edu

INSTITUTIONAL INFORMATION

Public/private: Private (nonprofit). **Evening Classes Available?** Yes. **Student/faculty Ratio:** 7:1. **Students in Parent Institution:** 1,973.

STUDENT INFORMATION

Total Students in Program: 778. **% Full-time:** 29. **% Female:** 79.

EXPENSES/FINANCIAL AID

Annual Tuition: $5,040. **Books and Supplies:** $400.

ADMISSIONS INFORMATION

Application Fee: $25. **Regular Notification:** Rolling. **Transfer Students Accepted?** Yes. **Average GPA:** 3.0.
Required Admission Factors: Letters of recommendation, transcript.

EMPLOYMENT INFORMATION

% Employed Within 6 Months: 100. % of master's grads employed in their field upon graduation: 75.

GOVERNORS STATE UNIVERSITY
College of Arts & Sciences

Address: University Parkway, 1 University Parkway, University Park, IL 60466
Admissions Phone: 708-534-4490 · **Admissions Fax:** 708-534-1640
Admissions E-mail: gsunow@govstedu · **Web Address:** www.govstedu/academics/cas/

INSTITUTIONAL INFORMATION

Public/private: Public. **Evening Classes Available?** Yes. **Students in Parent Institution:** 6,116.

STUDENT INFORMATION

Total Students in Program: 3,099. **% Full-time:** 7. **% Female:** 74.

RESEARCH FACILITIES

Research Facilities: Institute for public policy.

EXPENSES/FINANCIAL AID

Annual Tuition: In-state $2,520. / Out-of-state $7,560. **Fees:** $240. **Books and Supplies:** $550. **% Receiving Financial Aid:** 41. **% Receiving Scholarships/Grants:** 15. **% Receiving Loans:** 68. **% Receiving Assistantships:** 18.

ADMISSIONS INFORMATION

Application Fee: $25. **Regular Notification:** Rolling. **Transfer Students Accepted?** Yes. **Number of Applications Received:** 243. **% of Applicants Accepted:** 69. **% Accepted Who Enrolled:** 69. **Average GPA:** 3.2.
Required Admission Factors: Transcript.
Other Admission Factors: Minimum 2.5 GPA required.
Program-Specific Admission Factors: English requires GRE scores and letters of recommendation.

EMPLOYMENT INFORMATION

Placement Office Available? Yes.

GRACELAND UNIVERSITY
Graduate Studies

Address: 1 University Place, Lamoni, IA 50140
Admissions Phone: 866-GRACELAND · **Web Address:** www.graceland.edu

INSTITUTIONAL INFORMATION

Public/private: Private (nonprofit). **Student/faculty Ratio:** 20:1. **Students in Parent Institution:** 3,192.

STUDENT INFORMATION

Total Students in Program: 240. **% Full-time:** 10. **% Female:** 82.

EXPENSES/FINANCIAL AID

Annual Tuition: $7,884. **Fees:** $1,571. **Books and Supplies:** $800. **Grants Range From:** $570-$1,140. **Loans Range From:** $4,000-$4,347. **% Receiving Scholarships/Grants:** 8. **% Receiving Loans:** 8. **Average student debt, upon graduation:** $13,000.

ADMISSIONS INFORMATION

Application Fee: $80. **Regular Notification:** Rolling. **Transfer Students Accepted?** Yes. **Transfer Policy:** Maximum 10 semester hours with a minimum grade of B may be transferred. **Number of Applications Received:** 52. **% of Applicants Accepted:** 48. **% Accepted Who Enrolled:** 56. **Average GPA:** 3.5. **Average GRE Verbal:** 500. **Average GRE Quantitative:** 500.
Required Admission Factors: Essays/personal statement, letters of recommendation, transcript.
Other Admission Factors: Minimum 3.0 GPA and RN license required.

EMPLOYMENT INFORMATION

% Employed Within 6 Months: 80. % of master's grads employed in their field upon graduation: 80.

GRADUATE SCHOOL OF FIGURATIVE ART OF THE NEW YORK ACADEMY OF ART
Program in Figurative Art

Address: 111 Franklin Street, New York, NY 10013
Admissions Phone: 212-966-0300 · **Admissions Fax:** 212-966-3217
Admissions E-mail: info@nyaa.edu

INSTITUTIONAL INFORMATION
Public/private: Private (nonprofit). **Student/faculty Ratio:** 3:1. **Students in Parent Institution:** 123.

STUDENT INFORMATION
Total Students in Program: 123. **% Full-time:** 88. **% Female:** 50.

EXPENSES/FINANCIAL AID
Annual Tuition: $13,350. **Fees:** $400. **Books and Supplies:** $800. **Grants Range From:** $500-$5,000. **Loans Range From:** $1,000-$18,500. **% Receiving Financial Aid:** 78. **% Receiving Scholarships/Grants:** 70. **% Receiving Loans:** 76. **% Receiving Other Aid (teaching internships):** 50. **Average student debt, upon graduation:** $35,000 **Number of Fellowships Granted Each Year:** 8. **Average amount of individual fellowships per year:** $2,450. **Number of Teaching/Research Assistantships Granted Each Year:** 30.

ADMISSIONS INFORMATION
Application Fee: $40. **Regular Notification:** Rolling. **Transfer Students Accepted?** Yes. **Number of Applications Received:** 177. **% of Applicants Accepted:** 50. **% Accepted Who Enrolled:** 70.
Required Admission Factors: Essays/personal statement, letters of recommendation, transcript.

GRADUATE THEOLOGICAL UNION
Graduate Programs—PhD/ThD

Address: 2400 Ridge Road, Berkeley, CA 94709
Admissions Phone: 510-649-2460 · **Admissions Fax:** 510-649-1730
Admissions E-mail: gtuadm@gtu.edu · **Web Address:** www.gtu.edu

INSTITUTIONAL INFORMATION
Public/private: Private (nonprofit). **Total Faculty:** 132. **% Faculty Female:** 26. **Students in Parent Institution:** 366.

PROGRAMS
Masters offered in: African American/Black studies; American history (U.S.); American/U.S. studies/civilization; ancient Near Eastern and Biblical languages, literatures, and linguistics; ancient studies/civilization; ancient/classical Greek language and literature; anthropology; archeology; area, ethnic, cultural, and gender studies; art history, criticism, and conservation; art/art studies; Asian American studies; Bible/Biblical studies; Buddhist studies; Christian studies; classical, Mediterranean, and Near Eastern/Oriental studies and archaeology; classics and classical languages, literatures, and linguistics; community psychology; counseling psychology; dance; divinity/ministry (BD, MDiv); ethics; ethnic, cultural minority, and gender studies; European history; foreign languages, literatures, and linguistics; foreign languages/modern languages; gay/lesbian studies; Hebrew language and literature; history; industrial and organizational psychology; intercultural/multicultural and diversity studies; Jewish/Judaic studies; medieval and renaissance studies; Middle/Near Eastern and Semitic languages, literatures, and linguistics; multi/interdisciplinary studies; music; music/music and performing arts studies; musicology and ethnomusicology; pastoral counseling and specialized ministries; pastoral studies/counseling; peace studies and conflict resolution; philosophy and religion; philosophy; psychology; religion/religious studies; religious/sacred music; science, technology and society; semitic languages, literatures, and linguistics; social psychology; social sciences; sociology; theological and ministerial studies; theological studies and religious vocations; theology/theological studies; visual and performing arts; women's studies. **Doctorate offered in:** See Above.

STUDENT INFORMATION
Total Students in Program: 366. **% Full-time:** 94. **% Female:** 52. **% Minority:** 12. **% International:** 20.

RESEARCH FACILITIES
Research Facilities: Richard S. Dinner Center for Jewish Studies; Institute of Buddhist Studies; Patriarch Athenagoras Orthodox Institute; Center for the Arts, Religion and Education; Center for the Study of Religion and Culture; Center for Theology and the Natural Sciences.

EXPENSES/FINANCIAL AID
Annual Tuition: $18,160. **Room & Board:** $10,136. **Fees:** $0. **Books and Supplies:** $1,000. **Grants Range From:** $2,500-$25,000. **Loans Range From:** $1,000-$25,000. **Types of Aid Available:** Fellowships, grants, institutional work-study, loans, scholarships.

ADMISSIONS INFORMATION
Application Fee: $40. **Priority Application Deadline:** 12/15. **Regular Application Deadline:** 12/15. **Regular Notification:** Rolling. **Transfer Students Accepted?** Yes. **Number of Applications Received:** 142. **% of Applicants Accepted:** 46. **% Accepted Who Enrolled:** 60. **Average GPA:** 3.5. **Average GRE Verbal:** 600. **Average GRE Analytical Writing:** 5.
Required Admission Factors: Essays/personal statement, GRE, letters of recommendation, transcript, writing sample.
Other Admission Factors: Minimum score accepted for GRE verbal: 550. Minimum score accepted for TOEFL is 213(computer based).
Program-Specific Admission Factors: Applications to the PhD program are reviewed both by the GTU Admissions committee and the University of California at Berkeley.

EMPLOYMENT INFORMATION
% Employed Within 6 Months: 50. **Rate of placement:** 50%. **Average starting salary:** $40,000.

GRAND RAPIDS BAPTIST SEMINARY
Graduate Programs

Address: 1001 East Beltline Avenue, NE, Grand Rapids, MI 49525
Admissions Phone: 800-697-1133 · **Admissions Fax:** 616-222-1400
Admissions E-mail: grbs@cornerstone.edu

INSTITUTIONAL INFORMATION
Public/private: Private (nonprofit). **Evening Classes Available?** Yes. **Students in Parent Institution:** 256

STUDENT INFORMATION
Total Students in Program: 256. **% Full-time:** 35. **% Female:** 21.

EXPENSES/FINANCIAL AID
Annual Tuition: $7,080. **Fees:** $242. **Books and Supplies:** $450. **Grants Range From:** $250-$2,000.

ADMISSIONS INFORMATION
Application Fee: $25. **Regular Notification:** Rolling. **Transfer Students Accepted?** Yes. **Transfer Policy:** Maximum one half of total program credit hours may be transferred.
Required Admission Factors: Essays/personal statement, letters of recommendation, transcript.
Other Admission Factors: Minimum 2.5 GPA required.

EMPLOYMENT INFORMATION
Placement Office Available? Yes. **Rate of placement:** 85%.

GRAND VALLEY STATE UNIVERSITY
College of Science & Mathematics

Address: Allendale, MI 49401
Admissions Phone: 616-895-2025 · **Admissions Fax:** 616-895-2000

INSTITUTIONAL INFORMATION
Public/private: Public. **Students in Parent Institution:** 19,762.

STUDENT INFORMATION
Total Students in Program: 3,377. **% Full-time:** 18. **% Female:** 67.

RESEARCH FACILITIES
Research Facilities: Water resources institute.

EXPENSES/FINANCIAL AID
Annual Tuition: In-state $5,280. / Out-of-state $11,448. **Room & Board:** $5,830. **Grants Range From:** $1,000-$8,000. **Loans Range From:** $1,000-$16,500. **% Receiving Loans:** 96. **% Receiving Assistantships:** 7.

ADMISSIONS INFORMATION
Application Fee: $20. **Transfer Students Accepted?** Yes.
Required Admission Factors: Essays/personal statement, GRE, letters of recommendation, transcript.

EMPLOYMENT INFORMATION
Placement Office Available? Yes.

GRAND VALLEY STATE UNIVERSITY
Graduate Programs

Address: 1 Campus Drive, Allendale, MI 49401
Admissions Phone: 616-331-2025 · **Admissions Fax:** 616-331-2000
Admissions E-mail: go2gvsu@gvsu.edu · **Web Address:** www.gvsu.edu

INSTITUTIONAL INFORMATION
Public/private: Public. **Evening Classes Available?** Yes. **Student/faculty Ratio:** 18:1. **Students in Parent Institution:** 22,063

PROGRAMS
Masters offered in: Accounting; adult health nurse/nursing; biology teacher education; business administration/management; communications, journalism, and related fields; computer and information sciences; computer engineering; corrections and criminal justice; counselor education/school counseling and guidance services; education leadership and administration; education; education/teaching of individuals with emotional disturbances; education/teaching of individuals with specific learning disabilities; education/teaching of the gifted and talented; electrical, electronics, and communications engineering; elementary education and teaching; engineering, English language and literature; English/language arts teacher education; family practice nurse nurse practitioner; finance; higher education/higher education administration; history teacher education; junior high/intermediate/middle school education and teaching; manufacturing engineering; maternal/child health nurse/nursing; mathematics teacher education; mechanical engineering; music teacher education; nursing—registered nurse training (RN, ASN, BSN, MSN); nursing administration (MSN, MS, PhD); nursing; occupational therapy/therapist; physician assistant; physics teacher education; public administration and services; public administration; secondary education and teaching; social work; special education and teaching; special education; taxation; teacher education, multiple levels; teaching English as a second or foreign language/ESL language instructor. **Doctorate offered in:** Physical therapy/therapist.

STUDENT INFORMATION
Total Students in Program: 3,670. **% Full-time:** 22. **% Female:** 68.

RESEARCH FACILITIES
Research Facilities: Water Resources Institute.

EXPENSES/FINANCIAL AID
Annual Tuition: In-state $4,968. / Out-of-state $10,800. **Room & Board:** $6,160. **Grants Range From:** $1,000-$8,000. **Loans Range From:** $1,000-$18,500. **% Receiving Loans:** 96. **% Receiving Assistantships:** 7.

ADMISSIONS INFORMATION
Application Fee: $30. **Regular Notification:** Rolling. **Transfer Students Accepted?** Yes.
Required Admission Factors: Transcript.

EMPLOYMENT INFORMATION
Placement Office Available? Yes.

GRANTHAM UNIVERSITY
Graduate School

Address: 34641 Grnahtam College Road, Slidell, LA 70460
Admissions Phone: 985-649-4191 · **Admissions Fax:** 985-649-1812
Admissions E-mail: admissions@grantham.edu · **Web Address:** www.grantham.edu

INSTITUTIONAL INFORMATION
Public/private: Private (proprietary).

ADMISSIONS INFORMATION
Transfer Students Accepted? Yes.
Required Admission Factors: Transcript.
Other Admission Factors: 2.5 GPA

GRATZ COLLEGE
Graduate Programs

Address: 7605 Old York Road, Melrose Park, PA 19027
Admissions Phone: 215-635-7300, ext. 140 · **Admissions Fax:** 215-635-7320
Admissions E-mail: admissions@gratz.edu

INSTITUTIONAL INFORMATION
Public/private: Private (nonprofit). **Evening Classes Available?** Yes. **Student/faculty Ratio:** 12:1. **Students in Parent Institution:** 614.

STUDENT INFORMATION
Total Students in Program: 593. **% Full-time:** 2. **% Female:** 85.

EXPENSES/FINANCIAL AID
Annual Tuition: $9,950. **Books and Supplies:** $550.

ADMISSIONS INFORMATION
Application Fee: $50. **Regular Notification:** Rolling. **Transfer Students Accepted?** Yes. **Number of Applications Received:** 70. **% of Applicants Accepted:** 87. **% Accepted Who Enrolled:** 95.
Required Admission Factors: Essays/personal statement, letters of recommendation, transcript.
Other Admission Factors: Knowledge of Hebrew recommended.

EMPLOYMENT INFORMATION
Placement Office Available? Yes. **% Employed Within 6 Months:** 99. **Rate of placement:** 99%.

HAMLINE UNIVERSITY
Graduate Liberal Studies Program

Address: 1536 Hewitt Avenue, St. Paul, MN 55104
Admissions Phone: 651-523-2900 or 800-753-9753 · **Admissions Fax:** 651-523-2458
Admissions E-mail: gradprog@hamline.edu
Web Address: www.hamline.edu/gls/index.html

INSTITUTIONAL INFORMATION

Public/private: Private (nonprofit). **Evening Classes Available?** Yes. **Total Faculty:** 15. **% Faculty Female:** 60. **% Faculty Part-time:** 80. **Students in Parent Institution:** 4,490.

PROGRAMS

Masters offered in: Creative writing, liberal arts and sciences/liberal studies.

STUDENT INFORMATION

Total Students in Program: 190. **% Full-time:** 18.

EXPENSES/FINANCIAL AID

Annual Tuition: $344. **Fees:** $150. **Books and Supplies:** $150. **Types of Aid Available:** Loans.

ADMISSIONS INFORMATION

Application Fee: $30. **Regular Application Deadline:** 7/15. **Regular Notification:** Rolling. **Transfer Students Accepted?** Yes.
Required Admission Factors: Essays/personal statement, letters of recommendation, transcript.
Program-Specific Admission Factors: 20-page creative writing sample for the MFA program.

HAMPTON UNIVERSITY
Graduate College

Address: Graduate College, Hampton, VA 23368
Admissions Phone: 757-727-5454 · **Admissions Fax:** 757-727-5498
Admissions E-mail: hugrad@hamptonu.edu
Web Address: www.hamptonu.edu/academics/graduatecollege/index.htm

INSTITUTIONAL INFORMATION

Public/private: Private (nonprofit). **Evening Classes Available?** Yes. **Students in Parent Institution:** 5,135.

STUDENT INFORMATION

Total Students in Program: 396.

EXPENSES/FINANCIAL AID

Annual Tuition: $4,303. **Fees:** $50.

ADMISSIONS INFORMATION

Application Fee: $25. **Priority Application Deadline:** 4/1. **Regular Application Deadline:** 6/1. **Regular Notification:** Rolling. **Transfer Students Accepted?** Yes. **Transfer Policy:** All transfer work must be approved by the graduate program coordinator and the dean. A maximum of 9 credit hours transfer to a master's degree program, while up to 27 credit hours may transfer from a prior master's degree to a PhD program. Only graduate credits with a grade of B, or higher are eligible. **Number of Applications Received:** 348. **% of Applicants Accepted:** 68. **% Accepted Who Enrolled:** 36.
Required Admission Factors: Transcript.
Other Admission Factors: Minimum GPA for regular admission is 2.50 for master's degree programs and 3.00 for doctoral degree programs. The minimum acceptable GMAT Total Score is 400. The TOEFL is required for international students whose language of instruction was not English
Program-Specific Admission Factors: GMAT is required for admission to the MBA program, while the GRE can be used for all other master's degree programs and the physical therapy program. The MCAT or DAT can be used admission to the medical science program.

HARDIN-SIMMONS UNIVERSITY
Office of Graduate Studies

Address: PO Box 16210, Abilene, TX 79698
Admissions Phone: 915-670-1298 or 888-478-1222 · **Admissions Fax:** 915-670-1564
Admissions E-mail: gradoff@hsutx.edu

INSTITUTIONAL INFORMATION

Public/private: Private (nonprofit). **Evening Classes Available?** Yes. **Student/faculty Ratio:** 4:1. **Students in Parent Institution:** 2,276.

STUDENT INFORMATION

Total Students in Program: 276. **% Full-time:** 47. **% Female:** 61.

RESEARCH FACILITIES

Research Facilities: Rupert N. Richardson Research Center for the Southwest, instructional media center.

EXPENSES/FINANCIAL AID

Annual Tuition: $6,120. **Fees:** $650. **Books and Supplies:** $800. **Grants Range From:** $100-$6,120. **Loans Range From:** $50-$24,966. **% Receiving Financial Aid:** 94. **% Receiving Scholarships/Grants:** 87. **% Receiving Loans:** 57. **Average student debt, upon graduation:** $33,394. **Number of Fellowships Granted Each Year:** 68. **Average amount of individual fellowships per year:** $680.

ADMISSIONS INFORMATION

Application Fee: $25. **Regular Notification:** Rolling. **Transfer Students Accepted?** Yes. **Transfer Policy:** Work to be transferred must be from a regionally accredited institution of higher education. **Number of Applications Received:** 98. **% of Applicants Accepted:** 83. **% Accepted Who Enrolled:** 91. **Average GPA:** 3.0.
Required Admission Factors: Transcript.
Other Admission Factors: Minimum 2.7 GPA (3.0 in major) required.
Program-Specific Admission Factors: Minimum 2.8 GPA in last 60 credit hours required of physical therapy program applicants.

HARTFORD SEMINARY
Graduate Programs

Address: 77 Sherman Street, Hartford, CT 06105
Admissions Phone: 860-509-9512 · **Admissions Fax:** 860-509-9509
Admissions E-mail: kcobb@hartsem.edu

INSTITUTIONAL INFORMATION

Public/private: Private (nonprofit). **Evening Classes Available?** Yes. **Total Faculty:** 25. **% Faculty Part-time:** 44. **Students in Parent Institution:** 158.

STUDENT INFORMATION

Total Students in Program: 158. **% Full-time:** 5. **% Female:** 60.

RESEARCH FACILITIES

Research Facilities: Duncan Black Macdonald Center for the Study of Islam and Christian-Muslim Relations, Hartford Institute for Reliogion Research.

ADMISSIONS INFORMATION

Application Fee: $35. **Regular Notification:** Rolling. **Transfer Students Accepted?** Yes. **Transfer Policy:** Maximum 18 credit hours may be transferred into MA program; maximum 6 may be transferred into doctoral program. **Number of Applications Received:** 52. **% of Applicants Accepted:** 90. **% Accepted Who Enrolled:** 89.
Required Admission Factors: Essays/personal statement, interview, letters of recommendation, transcript.

HARVARD UNIVERSITY
Extension School

Address: 51 Brattle Street, Cambridge, MA 02138
Admissions Phone: 617-495-4024 · **Admissions Fax:** 617-496-2680
Admissions E-mail: extension@hudce.harvard.edu
Web Address: www.extension.harvard.edu

INSTITUTIONAL INFORMATION
Public/private: Private (nonprofit). **Students in Parent Institution:** 17,765.

STUDENT INFORMATION
Total Students in Program: 11,122. **% Female:** 44.

RESEARCH FACILITIES
Research Facilities: Woods Hole Oceanographic Institute, Arnold Arboretum, Dumbarton Oaks Library, Center for Hellenic Studies.

EXPENSES/FINANCIAL AID
Annual Tuition: $22,028. **Room & Board:** $6,500.

ADMISSIONS INFORMATION
Transfer Students Accepted? No.

HARVARD UNIVERSITY
Graduate School of Arts & Sciences

Address: Byerly Hall 2nd floor, 8 Garden Street, Cambridge, MA 02138
Admissions Phone: 617-495-5315 · **Admissions E-mail:** admiss@fas.harvard.edu
Web Address: www.gsas.harvard.edu

INSTITUTIONAL INFORMATION
Public/private: Private (nonprofit). **Students in Parent Institution:** 17,765.

STUDENT INFORMATION
Total Students in Program: 11,122. **% Female:** 44.

RESEARCH FACILITIES
Research Facilities: Woods Hole Oceanographic Institute, Arnold Arboretum, Dumbarton Oaks Library, Center for Hellenic Studies.

EXPENSES/FINANCIAL AID
Annual Tuition: $22,028. **Room & Board:** $6,500.

ADMISSIONS INFORMATION
Application Fee: $60. **Transfer Students Accepted?** No. **Number of Applications Received:** 3,049. **% of Applicants Accepted:** 12. **% Accepted Who Enrolled:** 57.
Required Admission Factors: Essays/personal statement, GRE, letters of recommendation, transcript.

HARVARD UNIVERSITY
Graduate School of Design

Address: Gund Hall 48 Quincy Street, Cambridge, MA 02138
Admissions Phone: 617-495-5453 · **Admissions Fax:** 617-495-8949
Admissions E-mail: admissions@gsd.harvard.edu · **Web Address:** www.gsd.harvard.edu

INSTITUTIONAL INFORMATION
Public/private: Private (nonprofit). **Students in Parent Institution:** 19,690.

PROGRAMS
Masters offered in: Architecture (BArch, BA/BS, MArch, MA/MS, PhD); city/urban, community and regional planning; landscape architecture (BS, BSLA, BLA, MSLA, MLA, PhD).

STUDENT INFORMATION
Total Students in Program: 12,690. **% Full-time:** 5. **% Female:** 48.

RESEARCH FACILITIES
Research Facilities: Woods Hole Oceanographic Institute, Arnold Arboretum, Dumbarton Oaks Library, Center for Hellenic Studies.

EXPENSES/FINANCIAL AID
Annual Tuition: $30,916. **Room & Board (On/off Campus):** $9,850. **Fees:** $2,908. **Books and Supplies:** $2,300. **Grants Range From:** $5,000-$12,000. **Loans Range From:** $18,500-$40,000. **% Receiving Financial Aid:** 80. **%**

Receiving Scholarships/Grants: 85. **% Receiving Loans:** 90. **Types of Aid Available:** Grants, institutional work-study, loans. **Average student debt, upon graduation:** $47,000.

ADMISSIONS INFORMATION
Application Fee: $75. **Regular Application Deadline:** 12/5. **Transfer Students Accepted?** No. **Number of Applications Received:** 1,511. **% of Applicants Accepted:** 24. **% Accepted Who Enrolled:** 71.
Required Admission Factors: Essays/personal statement, GRE, letters of recommendation, transcript.
Program-Specific Admission Factors: A portfolio is required of architecture, landscape architecture, and urban design applicants.

EMPLOYMENT INFORMATION
Placement Office Available? Yes. **% of doctoral/first professional grads employed in their field upon graduation:** 50/83.

HARVARD UNIVERSITY
John F. Kennedy School of Government

Address: 79 JFK Street, Belfer 110, Cambridge, MA 02138
Admissions Phone: 617-495-1155 · **Admissions Fax:** 617-496-1165
Admissions E-mail: ksg_admissions@harvard.edu
Web Address: www.ksg.harvard.edu

INSTITUTIONAL INFORMATION
Public/private: Private (nonprofit). **Total Faculty:** 154. **Student/faculty Ratio:** 6:1. **Students in Parent Institution:** 19,536.

PROGRAMS
Masters offered in: Development economics and international development, public administration, public policy analysis, urban studies/affairs. **Doctorate offered in:** Public policy analysis.

STUDENT INFORMATION
Total Students in Program: 970. **% Full-time:** 100. **% Female:** 42. **% Minority:** 24. **% International:** 37.

RESEARCH FACILITIES
Research Facilities: 13 research centers and dozens of policy programs. http://www.ksg.harvard.edu/

EXPENSES/FINANCIAL AID
Annual Tuition: $31,752. **Room & Board:** $18,160. **Fees:** $2,948. **Books and Supplies:** $1,735. **Grants Range From:** $1,000-$31,752. **Loans Range From:** $1,000-$68,439. **% Receiving Financial Aid:** 75. **% Receiving Scholarships/Grants:** 40. **% Receiving Loans:** 75. **Types of Aid Available:** Fellowships, graduate assistantships, grants, institutional work-study, loans, scholarships. http://www.ksg.harvard.edu/financialaid. **Average student debt, upon graduation:** $48,859. **Number of Fellowships Granted Each Year:** 36. **Average amount of individual fellowships per year:** $31,970.

ADMISSIONS INFORMATION
Application Fee: $80. **Regular Application Deadline:** 7/6. **Transfer Students Accepted?** No. **Number of Applications Received:** 2,300. **% of Applicants Accepted:** 35. **% Accepted Who Enrolled:** 74. **Average GPA:** 3.5. **Average GRE Verbal:** 585. **Average GRE Quantitative:** 681. **Average GRE Analytical:** 669. **Average GRE Analytical Writing:** 5.
Required Admission Factors: Essays/personal statement, GRE, letters of recommendation, transcript.

EMPLOYMENT INFORMATION
Placement Office Available? Yes. **% Employed Within 6 Months:** 99. **Rate of placement:** 99%. **Average starting salary:** $50,000.

HASTINGS COLLEGE
Graduate Programs

Address: 710 North Turner Avenue, Hastings, NE 68901-7621
Admissions Phone: 402-463-2402 · **Admissions Fax:** 402-461-7490
Admissions E-mail: fcondos@hastings.edu
Web Address: www.hastings.edu/academic/education/pageeight.html

INSTITUTIONAL INFORMATION

Public/private: Private (nonprofit). **Total Faculty:** 115. **% Faculty Female:** 37. **% Faculty Part-time:** 100. **Student/faculty Ratio:** 13:1. **Students in Parent Institution:** 1,153.

PROGRAMS

Masters offered in: Art teacher education; biology teacher education; business teacher education; chemistry teacher education; computer teacher education; drama and dance teacher education; education/teaching of individuals with specific learning disabilities; elementary education and teaching; English/language arts teacher education; foreign language teacher education; German language teacher education; history teacher education; mathematics teacher education; music teacher education; physical education teaching and coaching; physics teacher education; science teacher education/general science teacher education; secondary education and teaching; social science teacher education; social studies teacher education; Spanish language teacher education; speech teacher education; teacher education and professional development, specific subject areas; teacher education, multiple levels; teaching English as a second or foreign language/ESL language instructor.

STUDENT INFORMATION

Total Students in Program: 48. **% Full-time:** 62. **% Female:** 62.

EXPENSES/FINANCIAL AID

Annual Tuition: $3,780. **Room & Board (On/off Campus):** $4,000/$5,400. **Fees:** $650. **Books and Supplies:** $680. **Types of Aid Available:** Graduate assistantships, institutional work-study, loans.

ADMISSIONS INFORMATION

Application Fee: $20. **Regular Application Deadline:** 9/1. **Regular Notification:** Rolling. **Transfer Students Accepted?** Yes. **Number of Applications Received:** 15. **% of Applicants Accepted:** 100. **% Accepted Who Enrolled:** 100.
Required Admission Factors: GRE, interview, letters of recommendation, transcript.
Other Admission Factors: Minimum 2.5 GPA required.

EMPLOYMENT INFORMATION

Placement Office Available? Yes. **% Employed Within 6 Months:** 100. **Rate of placement:** 97%.

HAWAII PACIFIC UNIVERSITY
Graduate Programs

Address: 1164 Bishop Street, Suite 911, Honolulu, HI 96813
Admissions Phone: 808-544-1486 · **Admissions Fax:** 808-544-0280
Admissions E-mail: graduate@hpu.edu · **Web Address:** www.hpu.edu/grad

INSTITUTIONAL INFORMATION

Public/private: Private (nonprofit). **Evening Classes Available?** Yes. **Total Faculty:** 85. **% Faculty Female:** 44. **% Faculty Part-time:** 45. **Student/faculty Ratio:** 18:1. **Students in Parent Institution:** 8,340.

PROGRAMS

Masters offered in: Accounting; business administration/management; business, management, marketing, and related support services; business/corporate communications; communications and media studies; communications studies/speech communication and rhetoric; communications, journalism, and related

fields; computer and information sciences and support services; computer and information sciences; computer/information technology services, administration, and management; finance; human resources management/personnel administration; information science/studies; international business; international/global studies; marketing/marketing management; mass communications/media studies; military technologies; nursing—registered nurse training (RN, ASN, BSN, MSN); organizational behavior studies; organizational communications; organizational communications, public relations, and advertising; teaching English as a second or foreign language/ESL language instructor; tourism and travel services management.

STUDENT INFORMATION

Total Students in Program: 1,165. **% Full-time:** 53. **% Female:** 50. **% International:** 32.

RESEARCH FACILITIES

Research Facilities: The Oceanic Institute.

EXPENSES/FINANCIAL AID

Annual Tuition: $10,368. **Room & Board (On/off Campus):** $7,167/$9,900. **Fees:** $80. **Books and Supplies:** $1,865. **Grants Range From:** $250-$10,000. **Loans Range From:** $1,708-$18,500. **% Receiving Financial Aid:** 62. **% Receiving Scholarships/Grants:** 25. **% Receiving Loans:** 74. **% Receiving Assistantships:** 1. **Types of Aid Available:** Graduate assistantships, institutional work-study, scholarships. **Average student debt, upon graduation:** $17,000. **Average amount of individual fellowships per year:** $4,000. **Assistantship Compensation Includes:** Partial tuition remission.

ADMISSIONS INFORMATION

Application Fee: $50. **Regular Application Deadline:** 9/17. **Regular Notification:** Rolling. **Transfer Students Accepted?** Yes. **Number of Applications Received:** 1,066. **% of Applicants Accepted:** 71. **% Accepted Who Enrolled:** 41. **Average GPA:** 3.2. **Average GRE Verbal:** 527. **Average GRE Quantitative:** 595. **Average GRE Analytical:** 527.
Required Admission Factors: Essays/personal statement, letters of recommendation, transcript.
Other Admission Factors: Minimum 2.7 GPA required.
Program-Specific Admission Factors: Prerequisite coursework in accounting, computer science, economics, finance, mathematics, management, and marketing required of MBA program applicants. Prerequisite coursework in computer science and information science required of MS in information systems.

EMPLOYMENT INFORMATION

Placement Office Available? Yes. **% Employed Within 6 Months:** 85. **% of master's grads employed in their field upon graduation:** 33. **Rate of placement:** 65%. **Average starting salary:** $65,500.

HEBREW COLLEGE
Graduate School

Address: 160 Herrick Road, Newton Centre, MA 02459
Admissions Phone: 800-866-4814 · **Admissions Fax:** 618-559-8601
Admissions E-mail: admissions@hebrewcollege.edu
Web Address: www.hebrewcollege.edu

INSTITUTIONAL INFORMATION

Public/private: Private (nonprofit). **Evening Classes Available?** Yes. **Total Faculty:** 42. **% Faculty Female:** 33. **% Faculty Part-time:** 55.

STUDENT INFORMATION

Total Students in Program: 149. **% Full-time:** 38.

EXPENSES/FINANCIAL AID

Annual Tuition: $11,880. **Fees:** $200. **Books and Supplies:** $800. **Grants Range From:** $500-$2,000. **Loans Range From:** $4,000-$18,500. **% Receiving Financial Aid:** 60. **% Receiving Scholarships/Grants:** 80. **% Receiving Loans:** 20. **Types of Aid Available:** Fellowships, grants, loans, scholarships.

ADMISSIONS INFORMATION

Application Fee: $50. **Regular Application Deadline:** 5/30. **Regular Notification:** Rolling. **Transfer Students Accepted?** Yes. **Transfer Policy:** Maximum 6 credit hours with a minimum 3.0 GPA may be transferred. **Number of Applications Received:** 94. **% of Applicants Accepted:** 55. **% Accepted Who Enrolled:** 98. **Average GPA:** 3.0.
Required Admission Factors: Essays/personal statement, letters of recommendation, LSAT, transcript.
Recommended Admission Factors: GRE, interview.

EMPLOYMENT INFORMATION

% Employed Within 6 Months: 40. **Rate of placement:** 25%. **Average starting salary:** $25,000.

HEBREW UNION COLLEGE—JEWISH INSTITUTE OF RELIGION (NEW YORK)
School of Sacred Music

Address: One West Fourth Street, New York, NY 10012
Admissions Phone: 212-824-2225 · **Admissions Fax:** 212-388-1720
Admissions E-mail: igoldstein@huc.edu

INSTITUTIONAL INFORMATION

Public/private: Private (nonprofit). **Total Faculty:** 16. **% Faculty Part-time:** 75. **Students in Parent Institution:** 152.

STUDENT INFORMATION

Total Students in Program: 70. **% Full-time:** 61. **% Female:** 43.

EXPENSES/FINANCIAL AID

Fees: $100. **Grants Range From:** $500-$10,000. **Loans Range From:** $5,000-$18,500. **% Receiving Financial Aid:** 80. **% Receiving Scholarships/Grants:** 10. **% Receiving Loans:** 90.

ADMISSIONS INFORMATION

Application Fee: $75. **Regular Notification:** Rolling. **Transfer Students Accepted?** No. **Number of Applications Received:** 25. **% of Applicants Accepted:** 44. **% Accepted Who Enrolled:** 100.
Required Admission Factors: GRE.
Other Admission Factors: Hebrew and music theory sight reading required. Minimum GRE score of 1050 recommended.

EMPLOYMENT INFORMATION

Placement Office Available? Yes. **% Employed Within 6 Months:** 100. **% of master's grads employed in their field upon graduation:** 100. **Rate of placement:** 100%.

HENDERSON STATE UNIVERSITY
Graduate School

Address: 1100 Henderson Street, HSU Box 7802, Arkadelphia, AR 71999-0001
Admissions Phone: 870-230-5126 · **Admissions Fax:** 870-230-5479
Admissions E-mail: bellm@hsu.edu · **Web Address:** www.hsu.edu/dept/grad

INSTITUTIONAL INFORMATION

Public/private: Public. **Evening Classes Available?** Yes. **Total Faculty:** 25. **% Faculty Female:** 52. **% Faculty Part-time:** 12. **Student/faculty Ratio:** 17:1. **Students in Parent Institution:** 437.

PROGRAMS

Masters offered in: Business/commerce, counselor education/school counseling and guidance services, curriculum and instruction, education, special education, sports and fitness administration/management.

STUDENT INFORMATION

Total Students in Program: 437. **% Full-time:** 35. **% Female:** 25.

RESEARCH FACILITIES

Research Facilities: Huie Library.

EXPENSES/FINANCIAL AID

Annual Tuition: In-state $1,458. / Out-of-state $2,916. **Room & Board:** $4,096. **Fees:** $184. **Books and Supplies:** $600. **% Receiving Financial Aid:** 39. **Types of Aid Available:** Graduate assistantships, loans, scholarships. **Number of Teaching/Research Assistantships Granted Each Year:** 50. **Average Salary Stipend:** $2,000.

ADMISSIONS INFORMATION

Application Fee:. **Regular Application Deadline:** 8/16. **Regular Notification:** Rolling. **Transfer Students Accepted?** Yes. **Number of Applications Received:** 192. **% of Applicants Accepted:** 26. **% Accepted Who Enrolled:** 73.
Required Admission Factors: Transcript.
Other Admission Factors: Minimum 2.7 GPA required.

EMPLOYMENT INFORMATION

Placement Office Available? Yes.

HOFSTRA UNIVERSITY
College of Liberal Arts & Sciences

Address: Hofstra University, 105 Memorial Hall, Hempstead, NY 11549
Admissions Phone: 516-463-4723 or 866-GRAD-HOF
Admissions Fax: 516-463-4664 · **Admissions E-mail:** gradstudent@hofstra.edu
Web Address: www.hofstra.edu/Academics/HCLAS

INSTITUTIONAL INFORMATION

Public/private: Private (nonprofit). **Evening Classes Available?** Yes. **Total Faculty:** 116. **% Faculty Female:** 41. **% Faculty Part-time:** 29. **Student/faculty Ratio:** 4:1. **Students in Parent Institution:** 12,999.

PROGRAMS

Masters offered in: Applied mathematics; audiology/audiologist and hearing sciences; clinical psychology; community psychology; computer and information sciences; creative writing; education/teaching of individuals with speech or language impairments; English language and literature; English literature (British and commonwealth); foreign languages, literatures, and linguistics; human/medical genetics; humanities/humanistic studies; industrial and organizational psychology; industrial management; mathematics; psychology, school psychology; Spanish language and literature; speech-language pathology/pathologist.
Doctorate offered in: Clinical psychology, community psychology, industrial and organizational psychology, psychology, school psychology.

STUDENT INFORMATION

Total Students in Program: 494. **% Full-time:** 65. **% Female:** 71. **% Minority:** 13. **% International:** 3.

RESEARCH FACILITIES

Research Facilities: Marine lab in Jamaica, psychological evaluations research at counseling clinic, speech-language-hearing clinic.

EXPENSES/FINANCIAL AID

Annual Tuition: $11,700. **Room & Board (On/off Campus):** $8,590/$10,175. **Fees:** $920. **Books and Supplies:** $900. **Grants Range From:** $75-$17,050. **Loans Range From:** $3,637-$18,500. **% Receiving Financial Aid:** 56. **% Receiving Scholarships/Grants:** 23. **% Receiving Loans:** 50. **% Receiving Assistantships:** 5. **Types of Aid Available:** Fellowships, graduate assistantships, grants, institutional work-study, loans, scholarships. **Average student debt, upon graduation:** $31,805. **Number of Fellowships Granted Each Year:** 69 **Average amount of individual fellowships per year:** $4,850. **Number of Teaching/Research Assistantships Granted Each Year:** 53/ **Assistantship Compensation Includes:** Partial tuition remission, salary/stipend. **Average Salary Stipend:** $3,600.

ADMISSIONS INFORMATION

Application Fee: $60. **Regular Notification:** Rolling. **Transfer Students Accepted?** Yes. **Transfer Policy:** Same as new applicants. **Number of Applications Received:** 824. **% of Applicants Accepted:** 37. **% Accepted Who Enrolled:** 56. **Average GPA:** 3.4. **Average GRE Verbal:** 476. **Average GRE Quantitative:** 574. **Average GRE Analytical:** 501. **Average GRE Analytical Writing:** 4.44.
Required Admission Factors: Transcript. TOEFL for International students.

EMPLOYMENT INFORMATION

Placement Office Available? Yes. **% Employed Within 6 Months:** 78. **% of master's grads employed in their field upon graduation:** 56. **Rate of placement:** 94%. **Average starting salary:** $44,000.

HOLLINS UNIVERSITY
Graduate Programs

Address: PO Box 9603, Roanoke, VA 24020-1603
Admissions Phone: 540-362-6575 · **Admissions Fax:** 540-362-6288
Admissions E-mail: hugrad@hollins.edu · **Web Address:** www.hollins.edu

INSTITUTIONAL INFORMATION

Public/private: Private (nonprofit). **Evening Classes Available?** Yes. **Total Faculty:** 64. **% Faculty Female:** 50. **Student/faculty Ratio:** 10:1. **Students in Parent Institution:** 1,090.

PROGRAMS

Masters offered in: Art teacher education; biology teacher education; chemistry teacher education; cinematography and film/video production; creative writing; curriculum and instruction; dance; drama and dance teacher education; education; elementary education and teaching; English/language arts teacher education; film/cinema studies; foreign language teacher education; French language teacher education; general studies; history teacher education; humanities/humanistic studies; junior high/intermediate/middle school education and teaching; kindergarten/preschool education and teaching; liberal arts and sciences studies and humanities; liberal arts and sciences/liberal studies; mathematics teacher education; multi/interdisciplinary studies; music teacher education; playwriting and screenwriting; reading teacher education; science teacher education/general science teacher education; secondary education and teaching; social science teacher education; social sciences; social studies teacher education; Spanish language teacher education; teacher education, multiple levels; visual and performing arts.

STUDENT INFORMATION

Total Students in Program: 278. **% Full-time:** 24. **% Female:** 76.

RESEARCH FACILITIES

Research Facilities: Hollins Communications Research Institute.

EXPENSES/FINANCIAL AID

Annual Tuition: $18,500. **Books and Supplies:** $300. **Grants Range From:** $200-$18,500. **Loans Range From:** $850-$18,500. **% Receiving Financial Aid:** 53. **% Receiving Scholarships/Grants:** 59. **% Receiving Loans:** 89. **Types of Aid Available:** Loans, scholarships. **Average student debt, upon graduation:** $13,199. **Average amount of individual fellowships per year:** $16,960. **Number of Teaching/Research Assistantships Granted Each Year:** 4.

ADMISSIONS INFORMATION

Application Fee: $40. **Priority Application Deadline:** 2/2. **Regular Application Deadline:** 8/20. **Regular Notification:** Rolling. **Transfer Students Accepted?** Yes. **Transfer Policy:** Same admission requirements for transfers as for any applicant. A maximum of 8 credits may be considered for transfer. **Number of Applications Received:** 226. **% of Applicants Accepted:** 40. **% Accepted Who Enrolled:** 78.
Required Admission Factors: Essays/personal statement, letters of recommendation, transcript.

Other Admission Factors: No difference for in-state versus out-of-state applicants. Requirements vary by program. GRE may be submitted to support application, but is not required for any of our graduate programs.
Program-Specific Admission Factors: Creative writing, children's literature, and screenwriting all require portfolios/manuscripts demonstrating the applicant's best work. Our new MFA in dance requires a video with dance/choreography representative of the applicant's best work.

HOLY FAMILY UNIVERSITY
Graduate Programs

Address: 9701 Frankford Avenue, Philadelphia, PA 19114-2094
Admissions Phone: 215-637-7203 · **Admissions Fax:** 215-637-1478
Admissions E-mail: gradstudy@hfc.edu · **Web Address:** www.holyfamily.edu

INSTITUTIONAL INFORMATION

Public/private: Private (nonprofit). **Evening Classes Available?** Yes. **Student/faculty Ratio:** 18:1. **Students in Parent Institution:** 3,000.

PROGRAMS

Masters offered in: Business administration and management; business administration/management; community psychology; counseling psychology; counselor education/school counseling and guidance services; early childhood education and teaching; education leadership and administration; education; educational administration and supervision; educational, instructional, and curriculum supervision; elementary and middle school administration/principalship; elementary education and teaching; English/language arts teacher education; foreign language teacher education; French language teacher education; history teacher education; human resources management/personnel administration; junior high/intermediate/middle school education and teaching; management information systems; mathematics teacher education; nursing administration (MSN, MS, PhD); nursing; public health/community nurse/nursing; reading teacher education; science teacher education/general science teacher education; secondary education and teaching; secondary school administration/principalship; social science teacher education; social studies teacher education; special education and teaching; special education; teacher education, multiple levels; teaching English as a second or foreign language/ESL language instructor.

STUDENT INFORMATION

Total Students in Program: 1,145. **% Full-time:** 4. **% Female:** 51.

EXPENSES/FINANCIAL AID

Annual Tuition: $6,300. **Fees:** $170. **Books and Supplies:** $700.

ADMISSIONS INFORMATION

Application Fee: $25. **Priority Application Deadline:** 7/1. **Regular Application Deadline:** 8/30. **Regular Notification:** Rolling. **Transfer Students Accepted?** Yes. **Transfer Policy:** Credit to be transferred must have a minimum grade of B, and have been earned within the last 7 years. **Number of Applications Received:** 354. **% of Applicants Accepted:** 80. **% Accepted Who Enrolled:** 77. **Average GPA:** 3.45.
Required Admission Factors: Essays/personal statement, letters of recommendation, transcript.
Other Admission Factors: Minimum 3.0 GPA recommended; GRE or MAT required if GPA is lower than 3.0.
Program-Specific Admission Factors: Pennsylvania teaching certificate required of applicants to reading specialist program. Pennsylvania teaching certificate in elementary education required of applicants to special education and early childhood education programs.

EMPLOYMENT INFORMATION

Placement Office Available? Yes.

HOOD COLLEGE
Graduate School

Address: 401 Rosemont Avenue, Frederick, MD 21701-8575
Admissions Phone: 301-696-3600 · **Admissions Fax:** 301-696-3597
Admissions E-mail: hoodgrad@hood.edu · **Web Address:** www.hood.edu/graduate

INSTITUTIONAL INFORMATION
Public/private: Private (nonprofit). **Evening Classes Available?** Yes. **Students in Parent Institution:** 1,736.

STUDENT INFORMATION
Total Students in Program: 875. **% Full-time:** 6. **% Female:** 69.

EXPENSES/FINANCIAL AID
Annual Tuition: $5,580. **Grants Range From:** $750-$5,000. **Loans Range From:** $1,000-$18,500. **% Receiving Scholarships/Grants:** 5. **% Receiving Loans:** 100.

ADMISSIONS INFORMATION
Application Fee: $30. **Regular Application Deadline:** 8/17. **Regular Notification:** Rolling. **Transfer Students Accepted?** Yes. **Number of Applications Received:** 317. **% of Applicants Accepted:** 76. **% Accepted Who Enrolled:** 79.
Required Admission Factors: Transcript.
Other Admission Factors: Minimum 2.5 undergraduate GPA required.
Program-Specific Admission Factors: Minimum 2.75 GPA required of management of information technology program applicants.

EMPLOYMENT INFORMATION
Placement Office Available? Yes.

HOPE INTERNATIONAL UNIVERSITY
School of Graduate Studies

Address: 2500 East Nutwood Avenue, Fullerton, CA 92831
Admissions Phone: 714-879-3901 · **Admissions Fax:** 714-681-7450
Admissions E-mail: eyahumada@hiu.edu · **Web Address:** www.hiu.edu

INSTITUTIONAL INFORMATION
Public/private: Private (nonprofit). **Evening Classes Available?** Yes. **Student/faculty Ratio:** 7:1. **Students in Parent Institution:** 900.

STUDENT INFORMATION
Total Students in Program: 213. **% Full-time:** 45. **% Female:** 46.

EXPENSES/FINANCIAL AID
Fees: $40. **Books and Supplies:** $875. **Grants Range From:** $750-$4,260. **Loans Range From:** $2,000-$6,500. **% Receiving Financial Aid:** 44. **% Receiving Scholarships/Grants:** 40. **% Receiving Loans:** 85.

ADMISSIONS INFORMATION
Application Fee: $75. **Regular Application Deadline:** 10/4. **Regular Notification:** Rolling. **Transfer Students Accepted?** Yes. **Transfer Policy:** Graduate-level courses from accredited colleges only. **Number of Applications Received:** 79. **% of Applicants Accepted:** 89. **% Accepted Who Enrolled:** 50. **Average GPA:** 3.36.
Required Admission Factors: Essays/personal statement, GMAT, letters of recommendation, transcript.
Other Admission Factors: Minimum 3.0 GPA.

EMPLOYMENT INFORMATION
Rate of placement: 89%.

HOUSTON BAPTIST UNIVERSITY
College of Arts & Humanities

Address: 7502 Fondren Road, Houston, TX 77074
Admissions Phone: 281-649-3295 · **Admissions Fax:** 281-649-3011
Admissions E-mail: gradadm@hbu.edu · **Web Address:** www.hbu.edu

INSTITUTIONAL INFORMATION
Public/private: Private (nonprofit). **Evening Classes Available?** Yes. **Students in Parent Institution:** 2,227.

PROGRAMS
Masters offered in: Liberal arts and sciences/liberal studies, theological and ministerial studies.

STUDENT INFORMATION
Total Students in Program: 49. **% Full-time:** 71. **% Female:** 67. **% Minority:** 39. **% International:** 39.

EXPENSES/FINANCIAL AID
Annual Tuition: $8,100. **Room & Board (On/off Campus):** $4,566/$6,105. **Fees:** $855. **Books and Supplies:** $885. **Types of Aid Available:** Loans.

ADMISSIONS INFORMATION
Application Fee: $25. **Regular Application Deadline:** 9/1. **Regular Notification:** Rolling. **Transfer Students Accepted?** Yes. **Number of Applications Received:** 10. **% of Applicants Accepted:** 90. **% Accepted Who Enrolled:** 89.
Other Admission Factors: Minimum score of 900 on the GRE required of thelogy program applicants.
Program-Specific Admission Factors: Essay required of liberal arts program applicants.

EMPLOYMENT INFORMATION
Placement Office Available? Yes.

HOUSTON GRADUATE SCHOOL OF THEOLOGY
Graduate School

Address: 1311 Holman Street
#200, Houston, TX 77004-3833
Admissions Phone: 713-942-9505 · **Admissions Fax:** 713-942-9506

INSTITUTIONAL INFORMATION
Public/private: Private (nonprofit). **Total Faculty:** 23. **% Faculty Part-time:** 48. **Student/faculty Ratio:** 9:1. **Students in Parent Institution:** 210.

STUDENT INFORMATION
Total Students in Program: 210. **% Full-time:** 26. **% Female:** 36.

EXPENSES/FINANCIAL AID
Annual Tuition: $3,960. **Fees:** $200.

ADMISSIONS INFORMATION
Application Fee: $35. **Transfer Students Accepted?** No. **Transfer Policy:** Maximum 15 credit hours may be transferred for master's program. Maximum 30 credit hours may be transferred. **Number of Applications Received:** 48. **% of Applicants Accepted:** 85. **% Accepted Who Enrolled:** 93.
Required Admission Factors: Letters of recommendation, transcript.

EMPLOYMENT INFORMATION
Placement Office Available? Yes.

HOWARD UNIVERSITY
College of Fine Arts

Address: 2400 Sixth Street, NW, Washington, DC 20059

INSTITUTIONAL INFORMATION
Public/private: Private (nonprofit). **Students in Parent Institution:** 10,211.

STUDENT INFORMATION
Total Students in Program: 1,942. **% Full-time:** 65. **% Female:** 61.

RESEARCH FACILITIES
Research Facilities: Beltsville Biomedical Research Center.

EXPENSES/FINANCIAL AID
Annual Tuition: $10,500. **Room & Board:** $4,898. **Fees:** $405. **Books and Supplies:** $1,200.

ADMISSIONS INFORMATION
Transfer Students Accepted? No.

EMPLOYMENT INFORMATION
Placement Office Available? Yes.

HOWARD UNIVERSITY
School of Communications

Address: 2400 Sixth Street, NW, Washington, DC 20059

INSTITUTIONAL INFORMATION
Public/private: Private (nonprofit). **Students in Parent Institution:** 10,211.

STUDENT INFORMATION
Total Students in Program: 1,942. **% Full-time:** 65. **% Female:** 61.

RESEARCH FACILITIES
Research Facilities: Beltsville Biomedical Research Center.

EXPENSES/FINANCIAL AID
Annual Tuition: $10,500. **Room & Board:** $4,898. **Fees:** $405. **Books and Supplies:** $1,200.

ADMISSIONS INFORMATION
Transfer Students Accepted? No.

EMPLOYMENT INFORMATION
Placement Office Available? Yes.

HOWARD UNIVERSITY
Graduate School

Address: 4th & College Streets NW, Annex III Room 200, Washington, DC 20059
Admissions Phone: 202-806-7469 · **Admissions Fax:** 202-806-4664
Admissions E-mail: hugsadmission@howard.edu · **Web Address:** www.gs.howard.edu

INSTITUTIONAL INFORMATION
Public/private: Private (nonprofit). **Students in Parent Institution:** 10,211.

PROGRAMS
Masters offered in: African studies; artificial intelligence and robotics; biochemistry; chemical engineering; chemistry; civil engineering; clinical psychology; communications studies/speech communication and rhetoric; computer programming; computer science; computer systems analysis/analyst; counseling psychology; counselor education/school counseling and guidance services; curriculum and instruction; developmental and child psychology; economics; educational administration and supervision; educational psychology; electrical, electronics, and communications engineering; experimental psychology; genetics, history; mass communications/media studies; mathematics; mechanical engineering; molecular biology; organizational communication; pharmacology; philosophy; physics; political science and government; psychology; social psychology; sociology; special education. **Doctorate offered in:** See above.

STUDENT INFORMATION
Total Students in Program: 1,942. **% Full-time:** 65. **% Female:** 61.

RESEARCH FACILITIES
Research Facilities: Beltsville Biomedical Research Center.

EXPENSES/FINANCIAL AID
Annual Tuition: $10,500. **Room & Board:** $4,898. **Fees:** $405. **Books and Supplies:** $1,200.

ADMISSIONS INFORMATION
Application Fee: $45. **Regular Application Deadline:** 2/15. **Regular Notification:** Rolling. **Transfer Students Accepted?** No.
Required Admission Factors: Essays/personal statement, GRE, letters of recommendation, transcript.
Program-Specific Admission Factors: See graduate school website for specific program requirements.

EMPLOYMENT INFORMATION
Placement Office Available? Yes.

HUMBOLDT STATE UNIVERSITY
College of Arts, Humanities & Social Sciences

Address: 1 Harpst Street, Arcata, CA 95521-8299
Admissions Phone: 707-826-3949 · **Admissions Fax:** 707-826-3939
Admissions E-mail: schafer@humboldt.edu
Web Address: www.humboldt.edu/~gradst/gradinfo.shtml

INSTITUTIONAL INFORMATION
Public/private: Public. **Students in Parent Institution:** 7,725.

RESEARCH FACILITIES
Research Facilities: Schatz Energy Research Center, Institute for the Study of Altruistic Personality, Center for Applied Social Analysis and Education, Institute for the Study of Alternative Dispute Resolution.

EXPENSES/FINANCIAL AID
Annual Tuition: In-state $1,506. / Out-of-state $3,720. **Room & Board:** $3,500. **Books and Supplies:** $846. **Grants Range From:** $100-$1,500. **Loans Range From:** $100-$10,000. **% Receiving Scholarships/Grants:** 83. **% Receiving Loans:** 88.

ADMISSIONS INFORMATION
Application Fee: $55. **Regular Notification:** Rolling. **Transfer Students Accepted?** Yes. **Transfer Policy:** Maximum 9 credit hours may be transferred (16 for MFA program). **Number of Applications Received:** 206. **% of Applicants Accepted:** 33.
Required Admission Factors: Essays/personal statement, letters of recommendation, transcript.
Other Admission Factors: Minimum 3.0 GPA required. Other requirements vary by department.
Program-Specific Admission Factors: 3 letters of recommendation, a statement of purpose, and 2 official copies of transcripts from all schools attended. The GRE is required for English.

EMPLOYMENT INFORMATION
Placement Office Available? Yes.

HUMBOLDT STATE UNIVERSITY
College of Natural Resources & Sciences

Address: 1 Harpst Street, Arcata, CA 95521-8299
Admissions Phone: 707-826-3949 · **Admissions Fax:** 707-826-3939
Admissions E-mail: schafer@humboldt.edu
Web Address: www.humboldt.edu/~gradst/gradinfo.shtml

INSTITUTIONAL INFORMATION
Public/private: Public. **Students in Parent Institution:** 7,433.

PROGRAMS
Masters offered in: Fishing and fisheries sciences and management; forestry; land use planning and management/development; natural resources and conservation; water, wetlands, and marine resources management; wildlife and wildlands sciences and management.

STUDENT INFORMATION
Total Students in Program: 964. **% Full-time:** 66. **% Female:** 59.

RESEARCH FACILITIES
Research Facilities: Schatz Energy Research Center, Institute for the Study of Altruistic Personality, Center for Applied Social Analysis and Education, Institute for the Study of Alternative Dispute Resolution.

EXPENSES/FINANCIAL AID
Annual Tuition: $5,904. **Room & Board:** $2,093. **Fees:** $1,861. **Books and Supplies:** $846. **Grants Range From:** $100-$1,500. **Loans Range From:** $100-$10,000. **% Receiving Scholarships/Grants:** 83. **% Receiving Loans:** 88.

ADMISSIONS INFORMATION
Application Fee: $55. **Regular Application Deadline:** 2/1. **Regular Notification:** Rolling. **Transfer Students Accepted?** Yes. **Number of Applications Received:** 252. **% of Applicants Accepted:** 50. **% Accepted Who Enrolled:** 60.
Required Admission Factors: Essays/personal statement, letters of recommendation, transcript.
Program-Specific Admission Factors: 3 letters of recommendation, a statement of purpose, a resume, and 2 official copies of transcripts from all previous schools attended. The GRE is required for the fisheries option and recommended for all other options.

EMPLOYMENT INFORMATION
Placement Office Available? Yes.

HUMBOLDT STATE UNIVERSITY
College of Professional Studies

Address: 1 Harpst Street, Arcata, CA 95521-8299
Admissions Phone: 707-826-3949 · **Admissions Fax:** 707-826-3939
Admissions E-mail: schafer@humboldt.edu
Web Address: www.humboldt.edu/~gradst/gradinfo.shtml

INSTITUTIONAL INFORMATION
Public/private: Public. **Students in Parent Institution:** 7,725.

STUDENT INFORMATION
Total Students in Program: 964. **% Full-time:** 66. **% Female:** 59.

RESEARCH FACILITIES
Research Facilities: Schatz Energy Research Center, Institute for the Study of Altruistic Personality, Center for Applied Social Analysis and Education, Institute for the Study of Alternative Dispute Resolution.

EXPENSES/FINANCIAL AID
Annual Tuition: In-state $1,506. / Out-of-state $3,720. **Room & Board:** $3,500. **Fees:** $1,861. **Books and Supplies:** $846. **Grants Range From:**

$100-$1,500. **Loans Range From:** $100-$10,000. **% Receiving Scholarships/Grants:** 83. **% Receiving Loans:** 88. **Types of Aid Available:** Graduate assistantships, institutional work-study, loans, scholarships.

ADMISSIONS INFORMATION
Application Fee: $55. **Regular Application Deadline:** 00/00. **Regular Notification:** Rolling. **Transfer Students Accepted?** Yes. **Number of Applications Received:** 93. **% of Applicants Accepted:** 56. **% Accepted Who Enrolled:** 83.
Required Admission Factors: Letters of recommendation, transcript.
Other Admission Factors: GPA average of 2.5 for business, 3.0 for education, and 2.75 for kinesiology master's programs.
Program-Specific Admission Factors: 0 official transcripts from all schools previously attended. MBA program requires the GMAT. Education and kinesiology require 3 letters recommendation and a statement of purpose.

EMPLOYMENT INFORMATION
Placement Office Available? Yes.

IDAHO STATE UNIVERSITY
College of Arts & Sciences

Address: 741 South Seventh Avenue, Campus Box 8270, Pocatello, ID 83209-8270
Admissions Phone: 208-282-2475 · **Admissions Fax:** 208-282-4511
Admissions E-mail: info@isu.edu · **Web Address:** www.isu.edu

INSTITUTIONAL INFORMATION
Public/private: Public. **Evening Classes Available?** Yes. **Total Faculty:** 140. **% Faculty Female:** 25. **% Faculty Part-time:** 6. **Student/faculty Ratio:** 34:1. **Students in Parent Institution:** 13,802.

PROGRAMS
Master's offered in: Anthropology; art/art studies; biology/biological sciences; chemistry; clinical laboratory science/medical technology/technologist; communications studies/speech, communication, and rhetoric; drama and dramatics/theater arts; English language and literature; geological and earth sciences/geosciences; geology/earth science; geophysics and seismology; mathematics; microbiology; physics; political science and government; psychology; public administration; sociology. **Doctorate offered in:** Biology/biological sciences, clinical psychology, English language and literature, mathematics, political science and government.

STUDENT INFORMATION
Total Students in Program: 411. **% Full-time:** 61. **% Female:** 55. **% Minority:** 4. **% International:** 6.

RESEARCH FACILITIES
Research Facilities: Accelerator Center; Idaho National Laboratory, nearby; Business/Tech Center.

EXPENSES/FINANCIAL AID
Room & Board (On/off Campus): $6,090/$7,150. **Fees:** $660. **Books and Supplies:** $800. **Grants Range From:** $8,276-$10,807. **Loans Range From:** $100-$10,000. **% Receiving Financial Aid:** 80. **% Receiving Scholarships/Grants:** 6. **% Receiving Loans:** 14.5. **% Receiving Assistantships:** 8. **Types of Aid Available:** Fellowships, graduate assistantships, grants, institutional work-study, loans, scholarships. research assistantships, graduate studies, waiviers. **Number of Fellowships Granted Each Year:** 28 **Average amount of individual fellowships per year:** $15,847. **Number of Teaching/Research Assistantships Granted Each Year:** 82. **Assistantship Compensation Includes:** Full tuition remission, salary/stipend. **Average Salary Stipend:** $8,276.

ADMISSIONS INFORMATION
Application Fee: $35. **Priority Application Deadline:** 7/1. **Regular Application Deadline:** 7/1. **Regular Notification:** Rolling. **Transfer Students Accepted?** Yes. **Transfer Policy:** Master's level credits may be transferred from an accredited institution only if the courses were taken as resident credits

at the institution and are approved by the graduate school. Official transcripts are required before the credits will be transfered. Credits only will transfer, not the grades. **Number of Applications Received:** 791. **% of Applicants Accepted:** 42. **% Accepted Who Enrolled:** 28. **Average GPA:** 3.0. **Average GRE Verbal:** 505.5. **Average GRE Quantitative:** 577.8.
Required Admission Factors: GRE, transcript.
Other Admission Factors: Minimum 3.0 GPA in upper division courses. Total GRE scores must average at least the 50th percentile. Some programs require a higher average. International students are required to take the TOFEL exam and score 550 or higher on the paper exam.
Program-Specific Admission Factors: Foreign language is required for microbiology. Students with a verbal GRE below the 50th percentile are required to earn a B or higher in ENGL 607 during first semester.

EMPLOYMENT INFORMATION

Placement Office Available? Yes. **% Employed Within 6 Months:** 54. **Rate of placement:** 80%. **Average starting salary:** $35,000.

ILIFF SCHOOL OF THEOLOGY
Graduate Programs

Address: 2201 South University Boulevard, Denver, CO 80210
Admissions Phone: 303-765-3117 or 800-678-3360
Admissions Fax: 303-777-0164 · **Admissions E-mail:** admissions@iliff.edu
Web Address: www.iliff.edu

INSTITUTIONAL INFORMATION

Public/private: Private (nonprofit). **Evening Classes Available?** Yes. **Total Faculty:** 44. **% Faculty Female:** 41. **% Faculty Part-time:** 50. **Students in Parent Institution:** 346.

PROGRAMS

Master's offered in: Bible/biblical studies, pastoral counseling and specialized ministries, pastoral studies/counseling, religion/religious studies, theological and ministerial studies, theology/theological studies. **Doctorate offered in:** Bible/biblical studies, pastoral studies/counseling, religion/religious studies, theological and ministerial studies, theology/theological studies. **First Professional degree offered in:** Divinity/ministry (BD; MDiv), theological studies and religious vocations.

STUDENT INFORMATION

Total Students in Program: 346. **% Full-time:** 66. **% Female:** 59. **% Minority:** 11. **% International:** 6.

RESEARCH FACILITIES

Research Facilities: The Veteran's of Hope Project (focused on religion and social change).

EXPENSES/FINANCIAL AID

Annual Tuition: $11,445. **Room & Board (On/off Campus):** $12,000/$12,000. **Fees:** $10. **Books and Supplies:** $1,200. **Grants Range From:** $955-$14,445. **Loans Range From:** $500-$23,500. **% Receiving Financial Aid:** 80. **% Receiving Scholarships/Grants:** 82. **% Receiving Loans:** 61. **% Receiving Assistantships:** 3. **% Receiving Other Aid (church grants, private agencies):** 27. **Types of Aid Available:** Fellowships, grants, institutional work-study, loans, scholarships. **Average student debt, upon graduation:** $22,567.

ADMISSIONS INFORMATION

Application Fee: $40. **Priority Application Deadline:** 6/1. **Regular Application Deadline:** 9/1. **Regular Notification:** Rolling. **Transfer Students Accepted?** Yes. **Number of Applications Received:** 112. **% of Applicants Accepted:** 94. **% Accepted Who Enrolled:** 74. **Average GPA:** 3.0.
Required Admission Factors: Essays/personal statement, letters of recommendation, transcript.
Other Admission Factors: Minimum 2.5 GPA required of MDiv, MASM and MTS program applicants; minimum 3.0 GPA required of MA and PhD pro-

gram applicants. References, transcripts, and personal statement required of all applicants.
Program-Specific Admission Factors: GRE required for PhD applicants only.

ILLINOIS INSTITUTE OF TECHNOLOGY
Institute of Design

Address: 350 North LaSalle Street, 4th floor, Chicago, IL 60610
Admissions Phone: 312-595-4900 · **Admissions Fax:** 312-595-4901
Admissions E-mail: design@id.iit.edu · **Web Address:** www.id.iit.edu

INSTITUTIONAL INFORMATION

Public/private: Private (nonprofit). **Evening Classes Available?** Yes. **Total Faculty:** 20. **% Faculty Female:** 25. **% Faculty Part-time:** 50. **Student/faculty Ratio:** 7:1. **Students in Parent Institution:** 6,167.

PROGRAMS

Master's offered in: Aerospace, aeronautical, and astronautical engineering; analytical chemistry; applied mathematics; architectural engineering; biochemistry/biophysics and molecular biology; chemical engineering; chemistry; civil engineering; computer and information sciences; computer engineering; computer science; computer systems networking and telecommunications; computer teacher education; education; electrical, electronics, and communications engineering; engineering; environmental/environmental health engineering; food science; food technology and processing; geotechnical engineering; information science/studies; information technology; management information systems; manufacturing engineering; manufacturing technology/technician; mathematics teacher education; metallurgical engineering; physics; public administration; science teacher education/general science teacher education; specialized merchandising, sales, and related marketing operations; structural engineering; technical and business writing; transportation and highway engineering; water resources engineering **Doctorate offered in:** See above.

STUDENT INFORMATION

Total Students in Program: 122. **% Full-time:** 93.

EXPENSES/FINANCIAL AID

Annual Tuition: $28,584. **Room & Board:** $10,500. **Fees:** $391. **Books and Supplies:** $800. **Grants Range From:** $9,000-$28,584. **Loans Range From:** $10,000-$40,000. **% Receiving Financial Aid:** 15. **Types of Aid Available:** Fellowships, loans, competitive limited fellowships by merit. **Number of Fellowships Granted Each Year:** 10 **Average amount of individual fellowships per year:** $9,000.

ADMISSIONS INFORMATION

Application Fee: $50. **Priority Application Deadline:** 2/15. **Regular Application Deadline:** 4/1. **Transfer Students Accepted?** No. **Number of Applications Received:** 199. **% of Applicants Accepted:** 50. **% Accepted Who Enrolled:** 40. **Average GPA:** 3.5. **Average GRE Verbal:** 500. **Average GRE Quantitative:** 500. **Average GRE Analytical Writing:** 4.5.
Required Admission Factors: Essays/personal statement, letters of recommendation, transcript. TOEFL is required for international students.
Recommended Admission Factors: Interview.
Other Admission Factors: Minimum recommended GPA 3.0 on a 4.0 scale. TOEFL minimum 600 on paper based test; 250 on computer based test. Minimum GRE score for master's program is at least 1000 on the new scale and 1400 on the old scale.
Program-Specific Admission Factors: All PhD applicants are required to the GRE; the minimum score is 1600/2400 on the old scale and 1200/1600 on the new scale. All students without an undergraduate degree in industrial design or communication design are required to take the GRE.

EMPLOYMENT INFORMATION

Placement Office Available? Yes. **% Employed Within 6 Months:** 95. **% of master's/doctoral grads employed in their field upon graduation:** 95. **Rate of placement:** 50%. **Average starting salary:** $60,000.

ILLINOIS INSTITUTE OF TECHNOLOGY
Institute of Psychology

Address: 3101 South Dearborn Street, Room 252, Chicago, IL 60616
Admissions Phone: 312-567-3500 · **Admissions Fax:** 312-567-3493
Admissions E-mail: psychology@iit.edu · **Web Address:** www.iit.edu/colleges/psych

INSTITUTIONAL INFORMATION
Public/private: Private (nonprofit). **Total Faculty:** 18. **% Faculty Female:** 39. **Student/faculty Ratio:** 7:1. **Students in Parent Institution:** 6,167.

PROGRAMS
Master's offered in: Psychology, rehabilitation counseling/counselor. **Doctorate offered in:** Psychology.

STUDENT INFORMATION
Total Students in Program: 175. **% Full-time:** 61. **% Female:** 68. **% Minority:** 13. **% International:** 9.

EXPENSES/FINANCIAL AID
Annual Tuition: $11,304. **Room & Board (On/off Campus):** $6,282/$9,500. **Fees:** $534. **Books and Supplies:** $1,500. **Types of Aid Available:** Fellowships, graduate assistantships, loans, instititional work-study through the college. **Number of Fellowships Granted Each Year:** 15. **Average amount of individual fellowships per year:** $5,000. **Number of Teaching/Research Assistantships Granted Each Year:** 18. **Assistantship Compensation Includes:** Partial tuition remission, salary/stipend. **Average Salary Stipend:** $2,345.

ADMISSIONS INFORMATION
Application Fee: $40. **Priority Application Deadline:** 1/15. **Regular Application Deadline:** 3/15. **Transfer Students Accepted?** Yes. **Number of Applications Received:** 199. **% of Applicants Accepted:** 50. **% Accepted Who Enrolled:** 35.
Required Admission Factors: Essays/personal statement, letters of recommendation, transcript. TOEFL (for international students),
Other Admission Factors: Minimum GRE (Verbal and Quantitative) 1000. Minimum GPA 3.0.
Program-Specific Admission Factors: No GRE required for MAS in rehabilitation counseling.

EMPLOYMENT INFORMATION
Placement Office Available? Yes.

ILLINOIS STATE UNIVERSITY
College of Arts & Sciences

Address: Campus Box 2200, Normal, IL 61790
Admissions Phone: 800-366-2478 · **Admissions Fax:** 309-438-3932
Admissions E-mail: admissions@ilstu.edu · **Web Address:** www.admissions.ilstu.edu

INSTITUTIONAL INFORMATION
Public/private: Public. **Total Faculty:** 322. **% Faculty Female:** 35. **% Faculty Part-time:** 4. **Students in Parent Institution:** 20,860.

PROGRAMS
Master's offered in: Accounting; archeology; audiology/audiologist and speech-language pathology/pathologist; chemistry; counseling psychology; criminal justice/safety studies; drama and dramatics/theater arts; economics; English composition; English language and literature; family practice nurse nurse practitioner; fine/studio arts; foreign languages/modern languages; geological and earth sciences/geosciences; history, mathematics; music history, literature, and theory; music performance; political science and government; psychology; purchasing, procurement/acquisition and contracts management; school psychology; social work; sociology; visual and performing arts. **Doctorate offered in:** English language and literature, school psychology.

STUDENT INFORMATION
Total Students in Program: 994. **% Full-time:** 67. **% Female:** 66. **% Minority:** 9. **% International:** 17.

EXPENSES/FINANCIAL AID
Annual Tuition: In-state $2,205. Out-of-state $4,770. **Room & Board (On/off Campus):** $5,062/$7,058. **Fees:** $1,154. **Books and Supplies:** $686. **Grants Range From:** $108-$15,358. **Loans Range From:** $532-$18,500. **% Receiving Scholarships/Grants:** 95. **% Receiving Loans:** 29. **% Receiving Assistantships:** 51. **Number of Teaching/Research Assistantships Granted Each Year:** 288. **Average Salary Stipend:** $544.

ADMISSIONS INFORMATION
Application Fee: $30. **Regular Notification:** Rolling. **Transfer Students Accepted?** Yes. **Number of Applications Received:** 808. **% of Applicants Accepted:** 58. **% Accepted Who Enrolled:** 60. **Average GPA:** 3.4. **Average GRE Verbal:** 479. **Average GRE Quantitative:** 566. **Average GRE Analytical:** 545.
Required Admission Factors: GRE, transcript.
Other Admission Factors: Requirements vary by department.

EMPLOYMENT INFORMATION
Placement Office Available? Yes.

ILLINOIS STATE UNIVERSITY
College of Fine Arts

Address: Beaufort & School, Campus Box 5600, Normal, IL 61790
Admissions Phone: 800-366-2478 · **Admissions Fax:** 309-438-8318
Admissions E-mail: gradart@ilstu.edu · **Web Address:** www.arts.ilstu.edu

INSTITUTIONAL INFORMATION
Public/private: Public. **Total Faculty:** 83. **% Faculty Female:** 42. **% Faculty Part-time:** 2. **Students in Parent Institution:** 20,860

PROGRAMS
Master's offered in: Drama and dramatics/theater arts; fine/studio arts; music history, literature, and theory; music performance; music teacher education; music.

STUDENT INFORMATION
Total Students in Program: 137. **% Full-time:** 80. **% Female:** 56. **% Minority:** 2. **% International:** 16.

EXPENSES/FINANCIAL AID
Annual Tuition: In-state $2,205. / Out-of-state $4,770. **Room & Board (On/off Campus):** $5,062/$7,058. **Fees:** $1,154. **Books and Supplies:** $686. **Grants Range From:** $108-$15,358. **Loans Range From:** $532-$18,500. **% Receiving Scholarships/Grants:** 95. **% Receiving Loans:** 29. **% Receiving Assistantships:** 51. **Number of Teaching/Research Assistantships Granted Each Year:** 77 **Average Salary Stipend:** $384.

ADMISSIONS INFORMATION
Application Fee: $30. **Regular Notification:** Rolling. **Transfer Students Accepted?** Yes. **Number of Applications Received:** 158. **% of Applicants Accepted:** 48. **% Accepted Who Enrolled:** 63. **Average GPA:** 3.9. **Average GRE Verbal:** 532. **Average GRE Quantitative:** 568. **Average GRE Analytical:** 726.
Required Admission Factors: Transcript.
Other Admission Factors: Requirements vary by department.

EMPLOYMENT INFORMATION
Placement Office Available? Yes.

IMMACULATA UNIVERSITY
College of Graduate Studies

Address: 1145 King Road, Campus Box 500, Immaculata, PA 19345
Admissions Phone: 610-647-4400, ext. 3215 · **Admissions Fax:** 610-993-8550
Admissions E-mail: srollison@immaculata.edu · **Web Address:** www.immaculata.edu

INSTITUTIONAL INFORMATION
Public/private: Private (nonprofit). **Evening Classes Available?** Yes. **Students in Parent Institution:** 756.

STUDENT INFORMATION
Total Students in Program: 756. **% Full-time:** 10. **% Female:** 78.

EXPENSES/FINANCIAL AID
Annual Tuition: In-state $9,360. **Fees:** $80.

ADMISSIONS INFORMATION
Application Fee: $30. **Regular Notification:** Rolling. **Transfer Students Accepted?** Yes. **Number of Applications Received:** 274. **% of Applicants Accepted:** 74. **% Accepted Who Enrolled:** 74.
Required Admission Factors: Essays/personal statement, interview, letters of recommendation, transcript.
Other Admission Factors: Minimum GRE score of 1000 (or minimum MAT score of 45) and minimum 3.0 GPA required.

EMPLOYMENT INFORMATION
Placement Office Available? Yes.

INDIANA STATE UNIVERSITY
College of Graduate Studies

Address: Erickson Hall, Room 111, Terre Haute, IN 47809

INSTITUTIONAL INFORMATION
Public/private: Public. **Total Faculty:** 271. **Students in Parent Institution:** 12,565.

STUDENT INFORMATION
Total Students in Program: 1,514. **% Full-time:** 64. **% Female:** 55.

EXPENSES/FINANCIAL AID
Annual Tuition: In-state $3,696. / Out-of-state $8,424.

ADMISSIONS INFORMATION
Application Fee: $35. **Transfer Students Accepted?** Yes. **Number of Applications Received:** 359. **% of Applicants Accepted:** 53. **% Accepted Who Enrolled:** 68.
Required Admission Factors: Transcript.
Other Admission Factors: Minimum GRE section scores of 450 and minimum 2.5 GPA (minimum 3.0 GPA for doctoral programs) required.
Program-Specific Admission Factors: Minimum 3.0 GPA required of doctoral program applicants. Examinations may be required by some departments.

EMPLOYMENT INFORMATION
Placement Office Available? Yes.

INDIANA UNIVERSITY BLOOMINGTON
College of Arts & Sciences

Address: 300 North Jordan Avenue, Bloomington, IN 47405
Admissions Phone: 812-855-8931
Admissions E-mail: mbyler@indiana.edu

INSTITUTIONAL INFORMATION
Public/private: Public. **Students in Parent Institution:** 33,222.

STUDENT INFORMATION
Total Students in Program: 7,449. **% Female:** 53.

EXPENSES/FINANCIAL AID
Annual Tuition: In-state $4,046. / Out-of-state $11,787. **Fees:** $360.

ADMISSIONS INFORMATION
Application Fee: $40. **Transfer Students Accepted?** Yes. **% Accepted Who Enrolled:** 37. **Average GPA:** 3.48. **Average GRE Verbal:** 589. **Average GRE Quantitative:** 608. **Average GRE Analytical:** 625.
Required Admission Factors: Essays/personal statement, GRE, transcript.
Other Admission Factors: Minimum GRE score of 600 on at least one section and minimum 3.0 GPA required.

EMPLOYMENT INFORMATION
Placement Office Available? Yes.

INDIANA UNIVERSITY BLOOMINGTON
School of Informatics

Address: Informatics Graduate Studies Office, 901 East 10th Street, Bloomington, IN 47408
Admissions Phone: 812-856-6016 · **Admissions Fax:** 812-856-0999
Admissions E-mail: informat@indiana.edu
Web Address: http://informatics.indiana.edu

INSTITUTIONAL INFORMATION
Public/private: Public. **Total Faculty:** 25. **% Faculty Female:** 24. **Student/faculty Ratio:** 5:1. **Students in Parent Institution:** 6,876.

PROGRAMS

STUDENT INFORMATION
Total Students in Program: 62. **% Full-time:** 100. **% Female:** 35. **% Minority:** 8. **% International:** 48.

EXPENSES/FINANCIAL AID
Annual Tuition: In-state $4,700. / Out-of-state $13,750. **Room & Board:** $10,414. **Fees:** $400. **Books and Supplies:** $500. **% Receiving Financial Aid:** 40. **% Receiving Assistantships:** 38. **Types of Aid Available:** Fellowships, graduate assistantships, scholarships. **Number of Fellowships Granted Each Year:** 2. **Number of Teaching/Research Assistantships Granted Each Year:** 38. **Assistantship Compensation Includes:** Full tuition remission, salary/stipend. **Average Salary Stipend:** $13,000.

ADMISSIONS INFORMATION
Application Fee: $55. **Priority Application Deadline:** 1/15. **Regular Application Deadline:** 4/1. **Regular Notification:** 4/1. **Transfer Students Accepted?** No. **Number of Applications Received:** 108. **% of Applicants Accepted:** 76. **% Accepted Who Enrolled:** 37. **Average GPA:** 3.2. **Average GRE Verbal:** 523. **Average GRE Quantitative:** 710. **Average GRE Analytical:** 649. **Average GRE Analytical Writing:** 4.
Required Admission Factors: Essays/personal statement, GRE, letters of recommendation, transcript. TOEFL is required for non-native speakers of English.
Recommended Admission Factors: GRE subject exam(s) in chemistry, biology.
Other Admission Factors: Minimum overall GPA of 3.0 (on a 4.0 point scale). Minimum TOEFL score of 600.

INDIANA UNIVERSITY BLOOMINGTON
School of Journalism

Address: 300 North Jordan Avenue, Bloomington, IN 47405
Admissions Phone: 812-855-1699 · **Admissions Fax:** 812-855-0901
Admissions E-mail: ogan@indiana.edu

INSTITUTIONAL INFORMATION
Public/private: Public.   Students in Parent Institution: 33,222.

STUDENT INFORMATION
Total Students in Program: 7,449 % Female: 53.

EXPENSES/FINANCIAL AID
Annual Tuition: In-state $4,046. / Out-of-state $11,787. **Fees:** $360. **% Receiving Financial Aid:** 50.

ADMISSIONS INFORMATION
Application Fee: $40. Regular Notification: Rolling. Transfer Students Accepted? Yes. Number of Applications Received: 128. % of Applicants Accepted: 52. % Accepted Who Enrolled: 36.
Required Admission Factors: Essays/personal statement, GRE, transcript.
Other Admission Factors: Minimum GRE section score of 500 and minimum 3.0 GPA required.
Program-Specific Admission Factors: Clips of journalistic work may be submitted.

EMPLOYMENT INFORMATION
Placement Office Available? Yes.

INDIANA UNIVERSITY BLOOMINGTON
School of Library & Information Science

Address: 1320 East 10th Street, Main Library 011, Bloomington, IN 47405
Admissions Phone: 812-855-2018 · **Admissions Fax:** 812-855-6166
Admissions E-mail: slis@indiana.edu · **Web Address:** www.slis.indiana.edu

INSTITUTIONAL INFORMATION
Public/private: Public. Evening Classes Available? Yes. Students in Parent Institution: 37,000.

PROGRAMS
Master's offered in: Computer and information sciences, information science/studies, library science/librarianship. Doctorate offered in: Computer and information sciences, information science/studies, library science/librarianship.

STUDENT INFORMATION
Total Students in Program: 350. % Full-time: 94.

RESEARCH FACILITIES
Research Facilities: See the website: www.slis.indiana.edu/research.

EXPENSES/FINANCIAL AID
Annual Tuition: In-state $236. / Out-of-state $687. **Fees:** $1,000. **Books and Supplies:** $1,000. **Grants Range From:** $100-$22,000. **Loans Range From:** $1,000-$1,000. **% Receiving Financial Aid:** 10.

ADMISSIONS INFORMATION
Application Fee: $50. Priority Application Deadline: 1/15. Regular Application Deadline: 8/1. Regular Notification: Rolling. Transfer Students Accepted? Yes. Number of Applications Received: 300. % of Applicants Accepted: 83. % Accepted Who Enrolled: 48. Average GPA: 3.5.
Required Admission Factors: Essays/personal statement, letters of recommendation, transcript.
Other Admission Factors: Minimum 3.0 GPA for bachelor's degree; other requirements may apply (i.e., if first language is not English). Check our website for details.

EMPLOYMENT INFORMATION
Placement Office Available? Yes.

INDIANA UNIVERSITY OF PENNSYLVANIA
College of Fine Arts

Address: 101 Stright Hall, 210 South 10th Street, Indiana, PA 15705-1088
Admissions Phone: 724-357-2222 · **Admissions Fax:** 724-357-4862
Admissions E-mail: graduate_admissions@iup.edu · **Web Address:** www.arts.iup.edu/

INSTITUTIONAL INFORMATION
Public/private: Public. Evening Classes Available? Yes. Total Faculty: 29. % Faculty Female: 41. Students in Parent Institution: 13,998.

PROGRAMS
Master's offered in: Intermedia/multimedia, music.

STUDENT INFORMATION
Total Students in Program: 1,675. % Full-time: 39. % Female: 62.

RESEARCH FACILITIES
Research Facilities: Spatial Science Research Center, Applied Research Lab, Vandegraff accelerator.

EXPENSES/FINANCIAL AID
Annual Tuition: In-state $4,810 / Out-of-state $12,026. **Room & Board:** $4,898. **Fees:** $1,000. **Books and Supplies:** $900. **Types of Aid Available:** Fellowships, graduate assistantships, institutional work-study, loans. **Number of Teaching/Research Assistantships Granted Each Year:** 14 **Assistantship Compensation Includes:** Full tuition remission, partial tuition remission, salary/stipend. **Average Salary Stipend:** $4,740.

ADMISSIONS INFORMATION
Application Fee: $30. Regular Notification: Rolling. Transfer Students Accepted? Yes. Transfer Policy: Written request for transfer required of transfer applicants. Maximum 6 credit hours may be transferred. Average GPA: 3.28.
Required Admission Factors: Letters of recommendation, transcript.
Other Admission Factors: Minimum 2.6 GPA required; MAT required of applicants who do not meet GPA requirements.

EMPLOYMENT INFORMATION
Placement Office Available? Yes. % Employed Within 6 Months: 100. % of master's/doctoral grads employed in their field upon graduation: 100. Rate of placement: 92%.

INDIANA UNIVERSITY OF PENNSYLVANIA
College of Natural Science & Mathematics

Address: 101 Stright Hall, 210 South 10th Street, Indiana, PA 15705-1088
Admissions Phone: 724-357-2222 · **Admissions Fax:** 724-357-4862
Admissions E-mail: graduate_admissions@iup.edu
Web Address: www.iup.edu/natsciandmath/

INSTITUTIONAL INFORMATION
Public/private: Public. Evening Classes Available? Yes. Total Faculty: 78. % Faculty Female: 32. Students in Parent Institution: 13,998.

PROGRAMS
Master's offered in: Chemistry, mathematics, natural sciences, physics. Doctorate offered in: Clinical psychology.

STUDENT INFORMATION
Total Students in Program: 1,675. % Full-time: 39. % Female: 62.

RESEARCH FACILITIES

Research Facilities: Spatial Science Research Center, Applied Research Lab, Vandegraff accelerator.

EXPENSES/FINANCIAL AID

Annual Tuition: In-state $4,810. / Out-of-state $12,026. **Room & Board:** $4,898. **Fees:** $1,000. **Books and Supplies:** $900. **Types of Aid Available:** Fellowships, graduate assistantships, institutional work-study, loans. **Number of Fellowships Granted Each Year:** 2 **Average amount of individual fellowships per year:** $5,000. **Assistantship Compensation Includes:** Full tuition remission, salary/stipend. **Average Salary Stipend:** $5,800.

ADMISSIONS INFORMATION

Application Fee: $30. **Regular Notification:** Rolling. **Transfer Students Accepted?** Yes. **Transfer Policy:** Written request for transfer required of transfer applicants. Maximum 6 credit hours may be transferred. **Average GPA:** 3.16.
Required Admission Factors: Essays/personal statement, GRE, letters of recommendation, transcript.
Other Admission Factors: Minimum 2.6 GPA required. MAT required of applicants who do not meet GPA requirement.

EMPLOYMENT INFORMATION

Placement Office Available? Yes. **Rate of placement:** 92%.

INDIANA UNIVERSITY OF PENNSYLVANIA
College of Social Sciences & Humanities

Address: 101 Stright Hall, 210 South 10th Street, Indiana, PA 15705-1088
Admissions Phone: 724-357-2222 · **Admissions Fax:** 724-357-4862
Admissions E-mail: graduate_admissions@iup.edu · **Web Address:** www.chss.iup.edu/

INSTITUTIONAL INFORMATION

Public/private: Public. **Evening Classes Available?** Yes. **Total Faculty:** 97. **% Faculty Female:** 40. **Students in Parent Institution:** 13,998

PROGRAMS

Master's offered in: Criminology, English language and literature, geography, history, public administration, sociology. **Doctorate offered in:** Criminology, English language and literature, public administration and services.

STUDENT INFORMATION

Total Students in Program: 1,675. **% Full-time:** 39. **% Female:** 62.

RESEARCH FACILITIES

Research Facilities: Spatial Science Research Center, Applied Research Lab, Vandegraff accelerator.

EXPENSES/FINANCIAL AID

Annual Tuition: In-state $4,810. / Out-of-state $12,026. **Room & Board:** $4,898. **Fees:** $1,000. **Books and Supplies:** $900. **Types of Aid Available:** Fellowships, graduate assistantships, institutional work-study, loans. **Number of Fellowships Granted Each Year:** 8. **Average amount of individual fellowships per year:** $5,000. **Number of Teaching/Research Assistantships Granted Each Year:** 97. **Assistantship Compensation Includes:** Full tuition remission, partial tuition remission, salary/stipend. **Average Salary Stipend:** $5,000.

ADMISSIONS INFORMATION

Application Fee: $30. **Regular Notification:** Rolling. **Transfer Students Accepted?** Yes. **Transfer Policy:** Written request for transfer required of transfer applicants. Maximum 6 credit hours may be transferred. **Average GPA:** 3.24.
Required Admission Factors: Essays/personal statement, letters of recommendation, transcript.
Other Admission Factors: Minimum 2.6 GPA required; MAT requried of applicants who do not meet minimum GPA.

EMPLOYMENT INFORMATION

Placement Office Available? Yes. **% Employed Within 6 Months:** 70. **% of master's/doctoral grads employed in their field upon graduation:** 70/70. **Rate of placement:** 92%.

INDIANA UNIVERSITY SOUTH BEND
Graduate Programs

Address: 1700 Mishawaka Avenue
PO Box 7111, South Bend, IN 46634
Admissions Phone: 219-237-4839 · **Admissions Fax:** 219-237-4834

INSTITUTIONAL INFORMATION

Public/private: Public. **Evening Classes Available?** Yes. **Students in Parent Institution:** 7,417.

STUDENT INFORMATION

Total Students in Program: 1,347. **% Full-time:** 6. **% Female:** 65.

EXPENSES/FINANCIAL AID

Annual Tuition: In-state $3,393. / Out-of-state $8,268. **Fees:** $222. **Books and Supplies:** $592. **Loans Range From:** $200-$18,500.

ADMISSIONS INFORMATION

Application Fee: $40. **Transfer Students Accepted?** No. **Number of Applications Received:** 97. **Average GPA:** 2.91.
Required Admission Factors: Transcript.
Other Admission Factors: Minimum GMAT score of 450 and minimum 2.75 GPA required.

EMPLOYMENT INFORMATION

Placement Office Available? Yes.

INDIANA UNIVERSITY SOUTHEAST
Graduate Programs

Address: 4201 Grant Line Road, New Albany, IN 47150-6405
Admissions Phone: 812-941-2594 · **Admissions Fax:** 812-941-2668
Admissions E-mail: cabione@ius.edu

INSTITUTIONAL INFORMATION

Public/private: Public. **Evening Classes Available?** Yes. **Student/faculty Ratio:** 20:1. **Students in Parent Institution:** 5,813.

STUDENT INFORMATION

Total Students in Program: 575. **% Full-time:** 3.

EXPENSES/FINANCIAL AID

Annual Tuition: In-state $3,250. / Out-of-state $7,435. **Fees:** $224. **% Receiving Loans:** 100. **Average student debt, upon graduation:** $11,290.

ADMISSIONS INFORMATION

Regular Notification: Rolling. **Transfer Students Accepted?** Yes. **Transfer Policy:** Maximum 6 courses (15 from within Indiana University system) with a minimum grade of B may be transferred. **Number of Applications Received:** 65. **% of Applicants Accepted:** 100. **Average GPA:** 3.0.
Required Admission Factors: Letters of recommendation, transcript.
Other Admission Factors: Minimum 2.5 GPA required.
Program-Specific Admission Factors: Additional requirements for educational administration and counseling programs.

EMPLOYMENT INFORMATION

Placement Office Available? Yes. **% of master's/doctoral grads employed in their field upon graduation:** 90.

INDIANA UNIVERSITY—PURDUE UNIVERSITY INDIANAPOLIS
School of Public & Environmental Affairs

Address: 620 Union Drive, UN 518, Indianapolis, IN 46202
Admissions Phone: 317-274-4656 or 877-292-9321 · **Admissions Fax:** 317-274-5153
Admissions E-mail: mkeister@iupui.edu

INSTITUTIONAL INFORMATION
Public/private: Public. **Evening Classes Available?** Yes. **Students in Parent Institution:** 27,587.

RESEARCH FACILITIES
Research Facilities: Center on Philanthropy.

EXPENSES/FINANCIAL AID
Annual Tuition: In-state $3,933. / Out-of-state $11,348. **Fees:** $143. **Number of Fellowships Granted Each Year:** 2. **Average amount of individual fellowships per year:** $11,000 **Number of Teaching/Research Assistantships Granted Each Year:** 10. **Average Salary Stipend:** $700.

ADMISSIONS INFORMATION
Application Fee: $35. **Regular Notification:** Rolling. **Transfer Students Accepted?** Yes. **Number of Applications Received:** 56. **% Accepted Who Enrolled:** 66. **Average GPA:** 3.12. **Average GRE Verbal:** 464. **Average GRE Quantitative:** 630. **Average GRE Analytical:** 596.
Required Admission Factors: Essays/personal statement, GRE, letters of recommendation, transcript.
Other Admission Factors: Minimum GRE score of 1000 verbal and quantitative and minimum 3.0 GPA recommended.

EMPLOYMENT INFORMATION
Placement Office Available? Yes. **% Employed Within 6 Months:** 75.

INDIANA UNIVERSITY—PURDUE UNIVERSITY INDIANAPOLIS
School of Social Work

Address: 620 Union Drive
UN 518, Indianapolis, IN 46202
Admissions Phone: 317-274-6724 · **Admissions Fax:** 317-274-8630
Admissions E-mail: gpowers@iupui.edu

INSTITUTIONAL INFORMATION
Public/private: Public. **Students in Parent Institution:** 27,587.

RESEARCH FACILITIES
Research Facilities: Center on Philanthropy.

EXPENSES/FINANCIAL AID
Annual Tuition: In-state $3,933. / Out-of-state $11,348. **Fees:** $143. **% Receiving Financial Aid:** 85.

ADMISSIONS INFORMATION
Application Fee: $35. **Transfer Students Accepted?** Yes. **Number of Applications Received:** 13. **% of Applicants Accepted:** 38. **% Accepted Who Enrolled:** 100. **Average GPA:** 3.68. **Average GRE Verbal:** 620. **Average GRE Quantitative:** 610. **Average GRE Analytical:** 590.
Required Admission Factors: GRE, transcript.
Other Admission Factors: Minimum 3.0 GPA, resume, and sample of professional writing required.

EMPLOYMENT INFORMATION
Placement Office Available? Yes.

INSTITUTE FOR CLINICAL SOCIAL WORK
Graduate Programs

Address: 68 East Wacker Place
Suite 1400, Chicago, IL 60601-7202
Admissions Phone: 312-726-8480 · **Admissions Fax:** 312-726-7216

INSTITUTIONAL INFORMATION
Public/private: Private (nonprofit). **Student/faculty Ratio:** 2:1. **Students in Parent Institution:** 84.

STUDENT INFORMATION
Total Students in Program: 84. **% Full-time:** 77. **% Female:** 74.

EXPENSES/FINANCIAL AID
Annual Tuition: $21,100. **Books and Supplies:** $1,500. **Grants Range From:** $1,000-$2,000. **Loans Range From:** $1,000-$18,500. **% Receiving Financial Aid:** 30. **% Receiving Scholarships/Grants:** 2. **% Receiving Loans:** 100. **Average student debt, upon graduation:** $35,000.

ADMISSIONS INFORMATION
Application Fee: $50. **Regular Notification:** Rolling. **Transfer Students Accepted?** Yes. **Number of Applications Received:** 17. **% of Applicants Accepted:** 94. **% Accepted Who Enrolled:** 94.
Required Admission Factors: Essays/personal statement, interview, letters of recommendation, transcript.

EMPLOYMENT INFORMATION
% of doctoral grads employed in their field upon graduation: 100.

INTER-AMERICAN UNIVERSITY OF PUERTO RICO
Center for Graduate Studies

Address: PO Box 5100, San German, Puerto Rico 00683
Admissions Phone: 787-264-1912,ext. 7357, 7358
Admissions Fax: 787-892-7510

INSTITUTIONAL INFORMATION
Public/private: Private (nonprofit). **Evening Classes Available?** Yes. **Student/faculty Ratio:** 20:1. **Students in Parent Institution:** 5,425.

STUDENT INFORMATION
Total Students in Program: 806. **% Full-time:** 30. **% Female:** 64.

EXPENSES/FINANCIAL AID
Annual Tuition: $2,790. **Fees:** $183. **Books and Supplies:** $700. **Loans Range From:** $2,000-$8,500. **% Receiving Loans:** 86. **% Receiving Assistantships:** 14.

ADMISSIONS INFORMATION
Application Fee: $31. **Regular Notification:** Rolling. **Transfer Students Accepted?** Yes. **Transfer Policy:** PAEG or GMAT required of transfer applicants. **Number of Applications Received:** 307. **% of Applicants Accepted:** 88. **% Accepted Who Enrolled:** 69.
Required Admission Factors: Letters of recommendation, transcript.
Other Admission Factors: Coursework in economics (micro- and macro-), statistics, and accounting required.

EMPLOYMENT INFORMATION
Placement Office Available? Yes.

INTER-AMERICAN UNIVERSITY OF PUERTO RICO, METROPOLITAN CAMPUS
Graduate Programs

Address: PO Box 191293, San Juan, Puerto Rico 00919-1293
Admissions Phone: 787-765-1270 · **Admissions Fax:** 787-764-6963
Admissions E-mail: mfont@inter.edu

INSTITUTIONAL INFORMATION
Public/private: Private (nonprofit). **Evening Classes Available?** Yes. **Students in Parent Institution:** 10,586

STUDENT INFORMATION
Total Students in Program: 3,060. **% Full-time:** 27. **% Female:** 65.

EXPENSES/FINANCIAL AID
Annual Tuition: $2,970. **Books and Supplies:** $510.

ADMISSIONS INFORMATION
Application Fee: $31. **Regular Notification:** Rolling. **Transfer Students Accepted?** Yes. **Number of Applications Received:** 888. **% of Applicants Accepted:** 78. **% Accepted Who Enrolled:** 92. **Average GPA:** 2.5. **Required Admission Factors:** Letters of recommendation, transcript.

EMPLOYMENT INFORMATION
Placement Office Available? Yes.

INTERDENOMINATIONAL THEOLOGICAL CENTER
Graduate Programs

Address: 700 Martin Luther King, Jr. Drive, Atlanta, GA 30314
Admissions Phone: 404-527-7707 · **Admissions Fax:** 404-527-0901
Admissions E-mail: qrobertson@itc.edu

INSTITUTIONAL INFORMATION
Public/private: Private (nonprofit). **Evening Classes Available?** Yes. **Students in Parent Institution:** 460

STUDENT INFORMATION
Total Students in Program: 460. **% Full-time:** 65. **% Female:** 35.

EXPENSES/FINANCIAL AID
Annual Tuition: $6,378. **Room & Board:** $12,500. **% Receiving Financial Aid:** 95. **% Receiving Scholarships/Grants:** 60. **% Receiving Loans:** 80. **Average student debt, upon graduation:** $25,500.

ADMISSIONS INFORMATION
Application Fee: $25. **Regular Notification:** Rolling. **Transfer Students Accepted?** Yes. **Transfer Policy:** Letter of honorable withdrawal required of transfer applicants. **Number of Applications Received:** 223. **% of Applicants Accepted:** 71. **% Accepted Who Enrolled:** 81. **Average GPA:** 2.78. **Required Admission Factors:** Essays/personal statement, letters of recommendation, transcript. **Other Admission Factors:** Minimum 2.25 GPA and denominational endorsement required.

INTERNATIONAL SPACE UNIVERSITY
Central Campus

Address: 1 rue Jean-Dominique Cassini, Illkirch-Graffenstaden, 67400 France
Admissions Phone: +33-0-3-88-65-54-30 · **Admissions Fax:** +33-0-3-88-65-54-47
Admissions E-mail: admissions@isu.isunet.edu · **Web Address:** www.isunet.edu

INSTITUTIONAL INFORMATION
Public/private: Private (nonprofit).

PROGRAMS
Master's offered in: Aerospace, aeronautical, and astronautical engineering; astronomy; astrophysics; atmospheric sciences and meteorology; behavioral sciences; biological and biomedical sciences; business, management, marketing, and related support services; business/corporate communications; engineering; finance; health professions and related sciences; insurance; intercultural/multicultural and diversity studies; international business; international marketing; international/global studies; law, legal services, and legal studies; marketing; multi/interdisciplinary studies; peace studies and conflict resolution; physical sciences; physical sciences; science, technology, and society

EXPENSES/FINANCIAL AID
Annual Tuition: $11,500. **Grants Range From:** $12,500-$25,000. **% Receiving Financial Aid:** 60.

ADMISSIONS INFORMATION
Regular Application Deadline: 3/15. **Regular Notification:** Rolling. **Transfer Students Accepted?** Yes. **Required Admission Factors:** Essays/personal statement, letters of recommendation, transcript.

IONA COLLEGE
School of Arts & Science

Address: 715 North Avenue, New Rochelle, NY 10801
Admissions Phone: 914-633-2502 or 800-231-IONA · **Admissions Fax:** 914-633-2277
Admissions E-mail: nneville@iona.edu
Web Address: www.iona.edu/academic/arts_sci/arts_sci.htm

INSTITUTIONAL INFORMATION
Public/private: Private (nonprofit). **Evening Classes Available?** Yes. **Total Faculty:** 120. **% Faculty Female:** 33. **% Faculty Part-time:** 31. **Student/faculty Ratio:** 4:1. **Students in Parent Institution:** 4,329.

PROGRAMS
Master's offered in: Biology teacher education; computer and information sciences; computer systems, networking, and telecommunications; computer teacher education; counseling psychology; criminal justice/law enforcement administration; early childhood education and teaching; education leadership and administration; elementary education and teaching; English language and literature; English/language arts teacher education; experimental psychology; family and community services; health/health care administration/management; health/medical psychology; history; industrial and organizational psychology; journalism; mathematics teacher education; multicultural education; pastoral studies/counseling; psychology; public relations/image management; school psychology; secondary education and teaching; social studies teacher education; Spanish language and literature; Spanish language teacher education.

STUDENT INFORMATION
Total Students in Program: 532. **% Full-time:** 24. **% Female:** 70. **% Minority:** 19. **% International:** 2.

RESEARCH FACILITIES
Research Facilities: Ryan Library, Helen T. Arrirgoni Library/Technology Center: collections serving the departments of education, mass communication, computer science and the curriculum Library.

EXPENSES/FINANCIAL AID
Annual Tuition: $10,440. **Room & Board:** $12,000. **Fees:** $130. **Books and Supplies:** $700. **Grants Range From:** $50-$9,698. **Loans Range From:** $1,000-$18,500. **% Receiving Financial Aid:** 55. **% Receiving Scholarships/Grants:** 64. **% Receiving Loans:** 62. **Types of Aid Available:** Graduate assistantships, loans, scholarships. **Average student debt, upon graduation:** $21,539. **Number of Teaching/Research Assistantships Granted**

Each Year: 13. **Assistantship Compensation Includes:** Full tuition remission, salary/stipend.

ADMISSIONS INFORMATION

Application Fee: $50. **Regular Application Deadline:** 9/1. **Regular Notification:** Rolling. **Transfer Students Accepted?** Yes. **Transfer Policy:** Maximum 6 credit hours with a minimum grade of "B" may be transferred (with approval of department). **Number of Applications Received:** 478. **% of Applicants Accepted:** 72. **% Accepted Who Enrolled:** 67. **Average GPA:** 3.0.
Required Admission Factors: Letters of recommendation, transcript.
Other Admission Factors: Minimum 2.5 GPA required.
Program-Specific Admission Factors: If GPA is less than 3.0, GRE is required for the communication, journalism, marriage and therapy, and education programs.

EMPLOYMENT INFORMATION

Placement Office Available? Yes. **% Employed Within 6 Months:** 91. **% of master's/doctoral/first professional grads employed in their field upon graduation:** 85. **Rate of placement:** 81%.

ITHACA COLLEGE
Roy H. Park School of Communications

Address: 111 Towers Concourse, Ithaca, NY 14850-7142
Admissions Phone: 607-274-3527 · **Admissions Fax:** 607-274-1263
Admissions E-mail: rowland@ithaca.edu · **Web Address:** www.ithaca.edu/gradstudies

INSTITUTIONAL INFORMATION

Public/private: Private (nonprofit). **Evening Classes Available?** Yes. **Student/faculty Ratio:** 9:1. **Students in Parent Institution:** 6,170.

PROGRAMS

Master's offered in: Education; organizational communication.

STUDENT INFORMATION

Total Students in Program: 291. **% Full-time:** 100. **% Female:** 76. **% Minority:** 5. **% International:** 5.

RESEARCH FACILITIES

Research Facilities: Suzuki Institute, Kodaly Center of America/Musical Training Institute, Exercise Wellness Clinic, Sir Alexander Ewing Speech and Hearing Clinic, Gerontology Institute, Center for Trading and Analysis of Financial Instruments.

EXPENSES/FINANCIAL AID

Annual Tuition: $20,104. **Books and Supplies:** $838. **Grants Range From:** $68-$17,116. **Loans Range From:** $2,500-$18,500. **% Receiving Financial Aid:** 77. **% Receiving Scholarships/Grants:** 40. **% Receiving Loans:** 79. **% Receiving Assistantships:** 40. **Types of Aid Available:** Fellowships, graduate assistantships, institutional work-study, loans. **Number of Teaching/Research Assistantships Granted Each Year:** 19. **Assistantship Compensation Includes:** Full tuition remission, salary/stipend. **Average Salary Stipend:** $14,000.

ADMISSIONS INFORMATION

Application Fee: $40. **Priority Application Deadline:** 3/1. **Regular Application Deadline:** 7/30. **Regular Notification:** Rolling. **Transfer Students Accepted?** Yes. **Number of Applications Received:** 24. **% of Applicants Accepted:** 75. **% Accepted Who Enrolled:** 72. **Average GPA:** 3.4.
Required Admission Factors: Essays/personal statement, letters of recommendation, transcript.
Recommended Admission Factors: Interview.
Other Admission Factors: Minimum 3.0 GPA required. Two additional letters of recommendation required of applicants applying for assistantships. Current resume and statement of purpose.

EMPLOYMENT INFORMATION

Placement Office Available? Yes. **% Employed Within 6 Months:** 50. **Rate of placement:** 86%. **Average starting salary:** $45,000.

ITHACA COLLEGE
School of Music

Address: 111 Towers Concourse, Ithaca, NY 14850-7142
Admissions Phone: 607-274-3527 · **Admissions Fax:** 607-274-1263
Admissions E-mail: gradmusic@ithaca.edu
Web Address: www.ithaca.edu/gradstudies

INSTITUTIONAL INFORMATION

Public/private: Private (nonprofit). **Students in Parent Institution:** 6,170.

STUDENT INFORMATION

Total Students in Program: 264. **% Full-time:** 87. **% Female:** 78.

RESEARCH FACILITIES

Research Facilities: Suzuki Institute, Kodaly Center of America/Musical Training Institute, Exercise Wellness Clinic, Sir Alexander Ewing Speech and Hearing Clinic, Gerontology Institute.

EXPENSES/FINANCIAL AID

Annual Tuition: $20,104. **Books and Supplies:** $838. **Grants Range From:** $68-$17,116. **Loans Range From:** $2,500-$18,500. **% Receiving Financial Aid:** 97. **% Receiving Scholarships/Grants:** 40. **% Receiving Loans:** 79. **% Receiving Assistantships:** 40. **Number of Teaching/Research Assistantships Granted Each Year:** 29 **Average Salary Stipend:** $13,500.

ADMISSIONS INFORMATION

Application Fee: $40. **Regular Notification:** Rolling. **Transfer Students Accepted?** Yes. **Number of Applications Received:** 68. **% of Applicants Accepted:** 68. **% Accepted Who Enrolled:** 48.
Required Admission Factors: Interview, letters of recommendation, transcript.
Other Admission Factors: Minimum 3.0 GPA and undergraduate degree in music required. 2 additional letters of recommendation required of applicants applying for assistantship.
Program-Specific Admission Factors: Other requirements vary by program.

EMPLOYMENT INFORMATION

Placement Office Available? Yes.

JACKSONVILLE STATE UNIVERSITY
College of Arts & Sciences

Address: Jacksonville, AL 36265-9982
Admissions Phone: 256-782-5400

INSTITUTIONAL INFORMATION

Public/private: Public. **Evening Classes Available?** Yes. **Students in Parent Institution:** 8,749.

STUDENT INFORMATION

Total Students in Program: 1,329. **% Full-time:** 23. **% Female:** 67.

EXPENSES/FINANCIAL AID

Annual Tuition: In-state $2,640. / Out-of-state $5,280.

ADMISSIONS INFORMATION

Application Fee: $20. **Regular Notification:** Rolling. **Transfer Students Accepted?** Yes. **Number of Applications Received:** 513. **% of Applicants Accepted:** 95. **% Accepted Who Enrolled:** 73.
Required Admission Factors: Transcript.
Other Admission Factors: Undergraduate major in graduate field of study required.

EMPLOYMENT INFORMATION

Placement Office Available? Yes.

JACKSONVILLE UNIVERSITY
Graduate Programs

Address: 2800 University Boulevard North, Jacksonville, FL 32211
Admissions Phone: 904-256-8000 · **Admissions Fax:** 904-256-7463
Admissions E-mail: mba@ju.edu · **Web Address:** www.jacksonville.edu

INSTITUTIONAL INFORMATION

Public/private: Private (nonprofit). **Evening Classes Available?** Yes. **Students in Parent Institution:** 2,632.

PROGRAMS

Master's offered in: Art teacher education; business administration/management; education leadership and administration; education; elementary education and teaching; English/language arts teacher education; mathematics teacher education; music teacher education; nursing/registered nurse training (RN, ASN, BSN, MSN); nursing administration (MSN, MS, PhD); reading teacher education; teacher education and professional development, specific subject areas. **First Professional degree offered in:** Orthodontics/orthodontology (certificate, MS, PhD).

STUDENT INFORMATION

Total Students in Program: 418. **% Full-time:** 20. **% Female:** 55. **% Minority:** 22. **% International:** 2.

EXPENSES/FINANCIAL AID

Annual Tuition: $7,110. **Room & Board:** $2,500. **Books and Supplies:** $600. **Types of Aid Available:** Fellowships, loans.

ADMISSIONS INFORMATION

Application Fee: $50. **Regular Application Deadline:** 7/1. **Regular Notification:** Rolling. **Transfer Students Accepted?** Yes. **Transfer Policy:** Specific requirements apply to transfer credits; all other admissions requirements apply.
Required Admission Factors: Letters of recommendation, transcript.
Other Admission Factors: All international students are required to score a 550 on the TOEFL and a 220 on each of the TSE (Test of Spoken English) and TWE (Test of Written English). In some cases, international students will be asked to attend an interview. Requirements vary by program.

EMPLOYMENT INFORMATION

Placement Office Available? Yes.

JAMES MADISON UNIVERSITY
College of Arts & Letters

Address: Grace Street House MSC 6702, 17 West Grace Street, Harrisonburg, VA 22807
Admissions Phone: 540-568-6131 · **Admissions Fax:** 540-568-7860
Admissions E-mail: grad_school@jmu.edu · **Web Address:** caal.jmu.edu

INSTITUTIONAL INFORMATION

Public/private: Public. **Evening Classes Available?** Yes. **Total Faculty:** 61. **% Faculty Female:** 36. **% Faculty Part-time:** 2. **Students in Parent Institution:** 16,108.

PROGRAMS

Master's offered in: Art/art studies, English language and literature, history, music performance, public administration, technical and business writing.

STUDENT INFORMATION

Total Students in Program: 113. **% Full-time:** 65. **% Female:** 55. **% Minority:** 10. **% International:** 2.

EXPENSES/FINANCIAL AID

Annual Tuition: In-state $5,424. / Out-of-state $15,840. **Books and Supplies:** $750. **Grants Range From:** $150-$10,890. **Loans Range From:** $500-$18,500. **% Receiving Financial Aid:** 89. **% Receiving Scholarships/Grants:** 21. **% Receiving Loans:** 52. **% Receiving Assistantships:** 68. **% Receiving Other Aid (Tuition Waiver - Employee):** 10. **Types of Aid Available:** Graduate assistantships, grants, institutional work-study, loans, scholarships. **Average student debt, upon graduation:** $12,354. **Number of Teaching/Research Assistantships Granted Each Year:** 70 Assistantship Compensation Includes: Full tuition remission, partial tuition remission, salary/stipend. **Average Salary Stipend:** $2,837.

ADMISSIONS INFORMATION

Application Fee: $55. **Priority Application Deadline:** 7/1. **Regular Application Deadline:** 7/1. **Regular Notification:** Rolling. **Transfer Students Accepted?** Yes. **Transfer Policy:** Have a minimum grade of B.
Required Admission Factors: Essays/personal statement, GRE, letters of recommendation, MAT, transcript.
Other Admission Factors: GMAT or GRE required of public administration applicants.
Program-Specific Admission Factors: Art portfolio.

JAMES MADISON UNIVERSITY
College of Science & Mathematics

Address: Grace Street House MSC 6702, 17 West Grace Street, Harrisonburg, VA 22807
Admissions Phone: 540-568-6131 · **Admissions Fax:** 540-568-7860
Admissions E-mail: grad_school@jmu.edu · **Web Address:** csm.jmu.edu

INSTITUTIONAL INFORMATION

Public/private: Public. **Evening Classes Available?** Yes. **Total Faculty:** 19. **% Faculty Female:** 42. **% Faculty Part-time:** 11. **Students in Parent Institution:** 16,108.

PROGRAMS

Master's offered in: Biology/biological sciences, mathematics teacher education.

STUDENT INFORMATION

Total Students in Program: 14. **% Full-time:** 86. **% Female:** 50. **% Minority:** 14.

EXPENSES/FINANCIAL AID

Annual Tuition: In-state $5,424. / Out-of-state $15,840. **Books and Supplies:** $750. **Grants Range From:** $1,206-$10,285. **Loans Range From:** $500-$18,500. **% Receiving Financial Aid:** 78. **% Receiving Scholarships/Grants:** 9. **% Receiving Loans:** 28. **% Receiving Assistantships:** 81. **% Receiving Other Aid (JMU tuition waiver):** 9. **Types of Aid Available:** Graduate assistantships, grants, institutional work-study, loans, scholarships. **Average student debt, upon graduation:** $6,200. **Number of Teaching/Research Assistantships Granted Each Year:** 15. **Assistantship Compensation Includes:** Full tuition remission, partial tuition remission, salary/stipend. **Average Salary Stipend:** $3,100.

ADMISSIONS INFORMATION

Application Fee: $55. **Priority Application Deadline:** 2/15. **Regular Application Deadline:** 2/15. **Regular Notification:** Rolling. **Transfer Students Accepted?** Yes. **Transfer Policy:** Have a minimum grade of B.
Required Admission Factors: GRE, letters of recommendation, transcript. GRE subject exam(s) in biology.
Other Admission Factors: Undergraduate major with minimum 20 credit hours of biology and statement of professional goals and interests required.

JESUIT SCHOOL OF THEOLOGY AT BERKELEY
Graduate Programs

Address: 1735 LeRoy Avenue, Berkeley, CA 94709-1193
Admissions Phone: 800-824-0122 · **Admissions Fax:** 510-841-8536
Admissions E-mail: admissions@jstb.edu · **Web Address:** www.jstb.edu

INSTITUTIONAL INFORMATION
Public/private: Private (nonprofit). **Student/faculty Ratio:** 10:1. **Students in Parent Institution:** 170.

PROGRAMS
Master's offered in: Bible/biblical studies, theological and ministerial studies, theology/theological studies. **Doctorate offered in:** Bible/biblical studies, theological and ministerial studies, theology/theological studies. **First Professional degree offered in:** Divinity/ministry (BD, MDiv).

STUDENT INFORMATION
Total Students in Program: 114. **% Full-time:** 60. **% Female:** 33.

EXPENSES/FINANCIAL AID
Annual Tuition: $10,800. **Books and Supplies:** $1,081. **Grants Range From:** $1,200-$10,800. **Loans Range From:** $2,000-$10,000. **% Receiving Financial Aid:** 75. **% Receiving Scholarships/Grants:** 100. **% Receiving Loans:** 43. **Types of Aid Available:** Grants, institutional work-study, loans, scholarships.

ADMISSIONS INFORMATION
Application Fee: $40. **Regular Application Deadline:** 8/28. **Regular Notification:** Rolling. **Transfer Students Accepted?** Yes. **Transfer Policy:** Petition for advanced standing required of transfer applicants wishing to receive transfer credit. **Number of Applications Received:** 69. **% of Applicants Accepted:** 86. **% Accepted Who Enrolled:** 61.
Required Admission Factors: Essays/personal statement, GRE, letters of recommendation, transcript.
Other Admission Factors: Minimum GRE section scores of 550 and minimum 3.0 GPA required.

EMPLOYMENT INFORMATION
Placement Office Available? Yes. **% Employed Within 6 Months:** 100.

JOHN BROWN UNIVERSITY
Graduate Programs

Address: 2000 West University, Siloam Springs, AR 72761
Admissions Phone: 501-524-7287 · **Admissions Fax:** 501-524-4196
Admissions E-mail: smarkovi@jbu.edu · **Web Address:** www.jbu.edu/grad

INSTITUTIONAL INFORMATION
Public/private: Private (nonprofit). **Evening Classes Available?** Yes. **Student/faculty Ratio:** 10:1. **Students in Parent Institution:** 1,545

STUDENT INFORMATION
Total Students in Program: 132. **% Full-time:** 57. **% Female:** 62.

RESEARCH FACILITIES
Research Facilities: Center for Marriage/Family Studies, Center for Business Leadership/Ethics.

EXPENSES/FINANCIAL AID
Books and Supplies: $500. **Grants Range From:** $1,500-$8,100. **Loans Range From:** $790-$8,500. **% Receiving Financial Aid:** 28. **% Receiving Scholarships/Grants:** 36. **% Receiving Loans:** 46. **% Receiving Assistantships:** 18. **Average student debt, upon graduation:** $13,000. **Number of Fellowships Granted Each Year:** 24. **Average amount of individual fellowships per year:** $3,960. **Number of Teaching/Research Assistantships Granted Each Year:** 6. **Average Salary Stipend:** $8,100.

ADMISSIONS INFORMATION
Application Fee: $35. **Regular Application Deadline:** 8/3. **Regular Notification:** Rolling. **Transfer Students Accepted?** Yes. **Number of Applications Received:** 46. **% of Applicants Accepted:** 96. **% Accepted Who Enrolled:** 91. **Average GPA:** 3.1. **Average GRE Verbal:** 433. **Average GRE Quantitative:** 456. **Average GRE Analytical:** 496.
Required Admission Factors: Essays/personal statement, interview, letters of recommendation, transcript.
Other Admission Factors: Minimum 2.7 GPA required.
Program-Specific Admission Factors: Prerequisites required for MBA and ministry programs.

EMPLOYMENT INFORMATION
Placement Office Available? Yes. **% of master's/doctoral grads employed in their field upon graduation:** 40. **Rate of placement:** 90%.

JOHN CARROLL UNIVERSITY
Graduate School

Address: 20700 North Park Boulevard, Cleveland, OH 44118
Admissions Phone: 216-397-4284 · **Admissions Fax:** 216-397-3009
Admissions E-mail: gs_adm@jcu.edu · **Web Address:** www.jcu.edu/graduate

INSTITUTIONAL INFORMATION
Public/private: Private (nonprofit). **Evening Classes Available?** Yes. **Students in Parent Institution:** 4,384

STUDENT INFORMATION
Total Students in Program: 859. **% Full-time:** 24. **% Female:** 65.

EXPENSES/FINANCIAL AID
Annual Tuition: $9,594. **Fees:** $180. **Books and Supplies:** $600.

ADMISSIONS INFORMATION
Application Fee: $25. **Regular Application Deadline:** 7/15. **Regular Notification:** Rolling. **Transfer Students Accepted?** Yes.
Required Admission Factors: Letters of recommendation, transcript.
Other Admission Factors: Minimum G.P.A. is 2.5.
Program-Specific Admission Factors: School of psychology fall deadline is March 1 and spring deadline is October 15. Community counseling and school psychology require an additional questionnaire.

EMPLOYMENT INFORMATION
Placement Office Available? Yes. **Rate of placement:** 89%.

JOHN F. KENNEDY UNIVERSITY
Graduate School of
Professional Psychology

Address: 100 Ellinwood Way, Pleasant Hill, CA 94523
Admissions Phone: 800-696-5358 · **Admissions Fax:** 925-969-3136
Admissions E-mail: proginfo@jfku.edu · **Web Address:** www.jfku.edu

INSTITUTIONAL INFORMATION
Public/private: Private (nonprofit). **Evening Classes Available?** Yes. **Student/faculty Ratio:** 12:1. **Students in Parent Institution:** 1,567.

PROGRAMS
Master's offered in: Counseling psychology; industrial and organizational psychology; psychology. **Doctorate offered in:** Clinical psychology.

STUDENT INFORMATION
Total Students in Program: 522. **% Full-time:** 95.

RESEARCH FACILITIES
Research Facilities: JFKU has its own counseling center where students have supervision during their internships.

EXPENSES/FINANCIAL AID

Annual Tuition: $12,000. Fees: $24. Books and Supplies: $900. Grants Range From: $1,000-$5,000. Loans Range From: $10,000-$18,500. % Receiving Financial Aid: 68. % Receiving Scholarships/Grants: 5. % Receiving Loans: 95. Types of Aid Available: Loans.

ADMISSIONS INFORMATION

Application Fee: $50. Regular Application Deadline: 7/1. Regular Notification: Rolling. Transfer Students Accepted? Yes. Number of Applications Received: 206. % of Applicants Accepted: 71. % Accepted Who Enrolled: 66. Average GPA: 3.0.
Required Admission Factors: Essays/personal statement, interview,

EMPLOYMENT INFORMATION

% Employed Within 6 Months: 85. Average starting salary: $35,000.

JOHN F. KENNEDY UNIVERSITY
School of Education and Liberal Arts

Address: 100 Ellinwood Way, Pleasant Hill, CA 94523
Admissions Phone: 800-696-5358 · Admissions Fax: 925-969-3136
Admissions E-mail: proginfo@jfku.edu · Web Address: www.jfku.edu

INSTITUTIONAL INFORMATION

Public/private: Private (nonprofit). Evening Classes Available? Yes. Student/faculty Ratio: 12:1. Students in Parent Institution: 1,567

STUDENT INFORMATION

Total Students in Program: 1,055. % Full-time: 32. % Female: 80.

EXPENSES/FINANCIAL AID

Annual Tuition: $8,667. Fees: $27. Books and Supplies: $900. Grants Range From: $1,000-$5,000. Loans Range From: $10,000-$18,500. % Receiving Financial Aid: 68. % Receiving Scholarships/Grants: 5. % Receiving Loans: 95.

ADMISSIONS INFORMATION

Application Fee: $50. Regular Notification: Rolling. Transfer Students Accepted? Yes. Number of Applications Received: 47. % of Applicants Accepted: 66. % Accepted Who Enrolled: 61.
Required Admission Factors: Essays/personal statement, interview, transcript.

JOHN F. KENNEDY UNIVERSITY
School of Holistic Studies

Address: 100 Ellinwood Way, Pleasant Hill, CA 94523
Admissions Phone: 800-696-5358 · Admissions Fax: 925-969-3136
Admissions E-mail: proginfo@jfku.edu · Web Address: www.jfku.edu

INSTITUTIONAL INFORMATION

Public/private: Private (nonprofit). Evening Classes Available? Yes. Student/faculty Ratio: 12:1. Students in Parent Institution: 1,567

STUDENT INFORMATION

Total Students in Program: 1,055. % Full-time: 32. % Female: 80.

EXPENSES/FINANCIAL AID

Annual Tuition: $8,667. Fees: $27. Books and Supplies: $900. Grants Range From: $1,000-$5,000. Loans Range From: $10,000-$18,500. % Receiving Financial Aid: 68. % Receiving Scholarships/Grants: 5. % Receiving Loans: 95.

ADMISSIONS INFORMATION

Application Fee: $50. Regular Notification: Rolling. Transfer Students Accepted? Yes. Number of Applications Received: 155. % of Applicants Accepted: 94. % Accepted Who Enrolled: 81.

Required Admission Factors: Essays/personal statement, interview, transcript.

THE JOHNS HOPKINS UNIVERSITY
Peabody Conservatory of Music

Address: 3400 North Charles Street, Baltimore, MD 21218
Admissions Phone: 410-659-8110 · Admissions Fax: 410-659-8102
Admissions E-mail: dlane@peabody.jhu.edu · Website: www.peabody.jhu.edu

INSTITUTIONAL INFORMATION

Public/private: Private (nonprofit). Student/faculty Ratio: 3:1. Students in Parent Institution: 17,883.

STUDENT INFORMATION

Total Students in Program: 11,995. % Full-time: 34. % Female: 51.

RESEARCH FACILITIES

Research Facilities: Institute of Policy Studies, Mind/Brain Institute, Bioethics Institute, Space Telescope Science Institute, American Institute for Contemporary German Studies, Foreign Language Center.

EXPENSES/FINANCIAL AID

Annual Tuition: In-state $26,210. Books and Supplies: $800. Grants Range From: $1,000-$26,210. Loans Range From: $1,000-$18,500. % Receiving Financial Aid: 83. % Receiving Loans: 29. % Receiving Assistantships: 12. Average student debt, upon graduation: $20,000. Number of Teaching/Research Assistantships Granted Each Year: 62. Average Salary Stipend: $4,740.

ADMISSIONS INFORMATION

Application Fee: $55. Transfer Students Accepted? No. Number of Applications Received: 628. % of Applicants Accepted: 48. % Accepted Who Enrolled: 52. Average GPA: 3.54.
Required Admission Factors: Letters of recommendation, transcript.
Other Admission Factors: Minimum 3.0 GPA (exclusive of performance credits) required.

EMPLOYMENT INFORMATION

Placement Office Available? Yes. Rate of placement: 100%.

THE JOHNS HOPKINS UNIVERSITY
School of Advanced International Studies

Address: 1740 Massachusetts Avenue NW, N 200, Washington, DC 20036
Admissions Phone: 202-663-5700 · Admissions Fax: 202-663-7788
Admissions E-mail: admissions.sais@jhu.edu · Website: www.sais-jhu.edu/admissions

INSTITUTIONAL INFORMATION

Public/private: Private (nonprofit). Students in Parent Institution: 550.

PROGRAMS

Masters offered in: Development economics and international development; international economics; international relations and affairs; international/global studies; peace studies and conflict resolution; public policy analysis; science, technology, and society. Doctorate offered in: International relations and affairs, international/global studies.

STUDENT INFORMATION

Total Students in Program: 740. % Full-time: 100.

RESEARCH FACILITIES

Research Facilities: Institute of Policy Studies, Mind/Brain Institute, Bioethics Institute, Space Telescope Science Institute, American Institute for Contemporary German Studies, Foreign Language Center.

EXPENSES/FINANCIAL AID

Annual Tuition: $27,800. Room & Board: $11,000. Fees: $1,700. Books and Supplies: $1,000. Grants Range From: $1,000-$25,000. Loans Range From: $1,000-$18,500. % Receiving Financial Aid: 70. Types of Aid Available: Fellowships, institutional work-study, loans. Average student debt, upon graduation: $50,000. Average amount of individual fellowships per year: 5,600.

ADMISSIONS INFORMATION

Application Fee: $90. Priority Application Deadline: 1/15. Regular Application Deadline: 1/15. Regular Notification: 4/1. Transfer Students Accepted? No. Number of Applications Received: 1,861. % of Applicants Accepted: 35. % Accepted Who Enrolled: 47. Average GPA: 3.5. Average GRE Verbal: 625. Average GRE Quantitative: 670.
Required Admission Factors: Essays/personal statement, GRE, letters of recommendation, transcript.
Program-Specific Admission Factors: Foreign lanaguage background and prerequistes in introductory micro and macroeconomics required of MA program applicants; 9 years of professional work experience required for the MIPP program.

EMPLOYMENT INFORMATION

Placement Office Available? Yes. % Employed Within 6 Months: 80. % of master's grads employed in their field upon graduation: 60. Rate of placement: 100%. Average starting salary: $105,000.

THE JOHNS HOPKINS UNIVERSITY
Zanvyl Krieger School of Arts & Sciences

Address: 3400 North Charles Street, Wyman Park Bldg, Suite G1, Baltimore, MD 21218
Admissions Phone: 410-516-8174 · Admissions Fax: 410-516-6017
Admissions E-mail: grad_adm@jhu.edu · Website: www.jhu.edu

INSTITUTIONAL INFORMATION

Public/private: Private (nonprofit). Student/faculty Ratio: 10:1. Students in Parent Institution: 17,883.

STUDENT INFORMATION

Total Students in Program: 11,995. % Full-time: 34. % Female: 51.

RESEARCH FACILITIES

Research Facilities: Institute of Policy Studies, Mind/Brain Institute, Bioethics Institute, Space Telescope Science Institute, American Institute for Contemporary German Studies, Foreign Language Center.

EXPENSES/FINANCIAL AID

Annual Tuition: In-state $26,210. Books and Supplies: $800. Grants Range From: $1,000-$26,210. Loans Range From: $1,000-$18,500. % Receiving Financial Aid: 95. % Receiving Loans: 29. % Receiving Assistantships: 12. Average student debt, upon graduation: $18,000.

ADMISSIONS INFORMATION

Application Fee: $60. Regular Application Deadline: 1/15. Transfer Students Accepted? No. Number of Applications Received: 2,584. % of Applicants Accepted: 21. % Accepted Who Enrolled: 50. Average GPA: 3.5. Average GRE Verbal: 619. Average GRE Quantitative: 664. Average GRE Analytical: 658.
Required Admission Factors: Essays/personal statement, GRE, letters of recommendation, transcript.

EMPLOYMENT INFORMATION

Placement Office Available? Yes. % of master's/doctoral grads employed in their field upon graduation: 98/95. Rate of placement: 100%

JOHNSON & WALES UNIVERSITY
The Alan Shawn Feinstein Graduate School

Address: 8 Abbott Park Place, Providence, RI 02903
Admissions Phone: 401-598-1015 · Admissions Fax: 401-598-1286
Admissions E-mail: gradadm@jwu.edu · Web Address: www.jwu.edu/grad

INSTITUTIONAL INFORMATION

Public/private: Private (nonprofit). Evening Classes Available? Yes. Total Faculty: 28. % Faculty Female: 29. % Faculty Part-time: 57. Student/faculty Ratio: 27:1. Students in Parent Institution: 7,025.

PROGRAMS

Master's offered in: Accounting; business administration/management; business, management, marketing, and related support services; finance and financial management services; hospitality administration/management; hospitality administration/management; hospitality/travel services sales operations; hotel/motel administration/management; marketing/marketing management; office management and supervision; organizational behavior studies; resort management; tourism and travel services management; tourism promotion operations.

STUDENT INFORMATION

Total Students in Program: 740. % Full-time: 72.

EXPENSES/FINANCIAL AID

Annual Tuition: $4,860. Fees: $426. Books and Supplies: $750.

ADMISSIONS INFORMATION

Application Fee:. Priority Application Deadline: 7/15. Regular Application Deadline: 8/15. Regular Notification: Rolling. Transfer Students Accepted? Yes. Transfer Policy: Students can transfer comparable course content from accredited school; transfer must take at least 10 courses to earn a degree. Number of Applications Received: 610. % of Applicants Accepted: 59. % Accepted Who Enrolled: 72. Average GPA: 3.3.
Required Admission Factors: Transcript. TOEFL required for international students.
Recommended Admission Factors: Essays/personal statement, GMAT, GRE, letters of recommendation.
Other Admission Factors: 2.75 GPA.
Program-Specific Admission Factors: MA teaching ETS in Business.

EMPLOYMENT INFORMATION

Placement Office Available? Yes. Rate of placement: 98%.

THE JUILLIARD SCHOOL
Graduate Program in Music

Address: 60 Lincoln Center Plaza, New York, NY 10023-6588
Admissions Phone: 212-799-5000, ext. 223 · Admissions Fax: 212-724-0263

INSTITUTIONAL INFORMATION

Public/private: Private (nonprofit). Evening Classes Available? Yes. Student/faculty Ratio: 4:1. Students in Parent Institution: 784.

STUDENT INFORMATION

Total Students in Program: 290. % Full-time: 88. % Female: 48.

EXPENSES/FINANCIAL AID

Annual Tuition: In-state $17,400. Fees: $600. Books and Supplies: $3,100. Grants Range From: $100-$17,400. Loans Range From: $1,000-$18,500. % Receiving Financial Aid: 93. % Receiving Scholarships/Grants: 85. % Receiving Loans: 70. % Receiving Assistantships: 25. Average student debt, upon graduation: $27,100. Number of Teaching/Research Assistantships Granted Each Year: 50. Average Salary Stipend: $1,000.

ADMISSIONS INFORMATION

Application Fee: $100. **Transfer Students Accepted?** No. **Number of Applications Received:** 1,041. **% of Applicants Accepted:** 16. **% Accepted Who Enrolled:** 74.
Required Admission Factors: Essays/personal statement, transcript.

EMPLOYMENT INFORMATION

Placement Office Available? Yes.

KANSAS STATE UNIVERSITY
A.O. Miller School of Journalism & Mass Communications

Address: 103 Fairchild Hall, Manhattan, KS 66506-1103
Admissions Phone: 785-532-6890, 785-532-7066 · **Admissions Fax:** 785-532-5484
Admissions E-mail: journalism@k-state.edu · **Web Address:** jmc.ksu.edu/

INSTITUTIONAL INFORMATION

Public/private: Public. **Total Faculty:** 18. **% Faculty Female:** 44. **Students in Parent Institution:** 23,150.

PROGRAMS

Master's offered in: Mass communications/media studies.

STUDENT INFORMATION

Total Students in Program: 30. **% Full-time:** 60. **% Female:** 67. **% Minority:** 13. **% International:** 33.

RESEARCH FACILITIES

Research Facilities: For a complete list of our research facilities, visit: http://www.k-state.edu/Directories/research-facilities.html.

EXPENSES/FINANCIAL AID

Annual Tuition: In-state $3,978. / Out-of-state $10,530. **Fees:** $550. **Books and Supplies:** $250. **Grants Range From:** $200-$1,200. **Loans Range From:** $100-$17,000. **Types of Aid Available:** Graduate assistantships. **Number of Teaching/Research Assistantships Granted Each Year:** 13. **Assistantship Compensation Includes:** Salary/stipend. **Average Salary Stipend:** $7,500.

ADMISSIONS INFORMATION

Application Fee: $30. **Regular Application Deadline:** 2/1. **Regular Notification:** Rolling. **Transfer Students Accepted?** Yes. **Number of Applications Received:** 23. **% of Applicants Accepted:** 100. **% Accepted Who Enrolled:** 35. **Average GPA:** 3.2. **Average GRE Verbal:** 600. **Average GRE Quantitative:** 600. **Average GRE Analytical:** 600.
Required Admission Factors: Essays/personal statement, GRE, letters of recommendation, transcript.
Other Admission Factors: Minimum 3.0 GPA required.

EMPLOYMENT INFORMATION

Placement Office Available? Yes.

KANSAS STATE UNIVERSITY
College of Arts & Sciences

Address: 103 Fairchild Hall, Manhattan, KS 66506-1103
Admissions Phone: 785-532-6900 · **Admissions Fax:** 785-532-7004
Admissions E-mail: gradschool@k-state.edu · **Web Address:** www.k-state.edu/artsci/

INSTITUTIONAL INFORMATION

Public/private: Public. **Total Faculty:** 489. **% Faculty Female:** 35. **Students in Parent Institution:** 23,150.

PROGRAMS

Master's offered in: Biochemistry; biology/biological sciences; chemistry; cognitive psychology and psycholinguistics; creative writing; drama and dramat-

ics/theater arts; economics; English language and literature; English literature (British and commonwealth); fine/studio arts; foreign languages/modern languages; geography; geology/earth science; history; industrial and organizational psychology; mathematics; microbiology; music history, literature, and theory; music pedagogy; music performance; music theory and composition; personality psychology; physics; physiology, pathology, and related sciences; political science and government; psychology; public administration; sociology; speech and rhetorical studies; statistics. **Doctorate offered in:** See above.

STUDENT INFORMATION

Total Students in Program: 1,505. **% Full-time:** 36. **% Female:** 56. **% International:** 19.

RESEARCH FACILITIES

Research Facilities: For a complete list of our research facilities, visit: http://www.k-state.edu/Directories/research-facilities.html.

EXPENSES/FINANCIAL AID

Annual Tuition: In-state $3,978. / Out-of-state $10,530. **Books and Supplies:** $250. **Grants Range From:** $200-$1,200. **Loans Range From:** $100-$17,000. **Types of Aid Available:** Fellowships, graduate assistantships. **Number of Teaching/Research Assistantships Granted Each Year:** 566. **Assistantship Compensation Includes:** Salary/stipend. **Average Salary Stipend:** $11,500.

ADMISSIONS INFORMATION

Application Fee: $30. **Regular Application Deadline:** 2/1. **Regular Notification:** Rolling. **Transfer Students Accepted?** Yes. **Transfer Policy:** Maximum 10 credit hours may be transferred into the geography program. **Number of Applications Received:** 957. **% of Applicants Accepted:** 40. **% Accepted Who Enrolled:** 73.
Required Admission Factors: Essays/personal statement, transcript.
Other Admission Factors: Minimum 3.0 GPA required.

EMPLOYMENT INFORMATION

Placement Office Available? Yes.

KANSAS STATE UNIVERSITY
College of Human Ecology

Address: 103 Fairchild Hall, Manhattan, KS 66506-1103
Admissions Phone: 785-532-5500 · **Admissions Fax:** 785-532-5504
Admissions E-mail: humanecology@k-state.edu
Web Address: www.humec.k-state.edu/

INSTITUTIONAL INFORMATION

Public/private: Public. **Evening Classes Available?** Yes. **Total Faculty:** 71. **% Faculty Female:** 68. **Students in Parent Institution:** 23,150.

PROGRAMS

Master's offered in: Apparel and textile manufacture; apparel and textile marketing management; dietetics/ dietitian (RD); family and consumer sciences/human sciences; hospitality administration/management; human development and family studies; human development, family studies, and related services; human nutrition; public health (MPH, DPH); restaurant/food services management; textile science. **Doctorate offered in:** See above.

STUDENT INFORMATION

Total Students in Program: 302. **% Full-time:** 48. **% Female:** 72. **% International:** 13.

RESEARCH FACILITIES

Research Facilities: For a complete list of our research facilities, visit: http://www.k-state.edu/Directories/research-facilities.html.

EXPENSES/FINANCIAL AID

Annual Tuition: In-state $3,978. / Out-of-state $10,530. **Fees:** $550. **Books and Supplies:** $250. **Grants Range From:** $200-$1,200. **Loans Range From:** $100-$17,000. **Types of Aid Available:** Graduate assistantships. **Number of Teaching/Research Assistantships Granted Each Year:** 73. **Assis-**

tantship Compensation Includes: Salary/stipend. **Average Salary Stipend:** $11,000.

ADMISSIONS INFORMATION
Application Fee: $30. **Regular Application Deadline:** 2/1. **Transfer Students Accepted?** Yes. **Transfer Policy:** Maximum 10 credit hours may be transferred into hotel/restaurant management/dietetics program. **Number of Applications Received:** 150. **% of Applicants Accepted:** 60. **% Accepted Who Enrolled:** 78.
Required Admission Factors: Letters of recommendation, transcript.
Other Admission Factors: Minimum 3.0 GPA required.
Program-Specific Admission Factors: GRE requirement is waived for KSU students enrolled in the apparel and textiles degree program.

EMPLOYMENT INFORMATION
Placement Office Available? Yes.

KANSAS WESLEYAN UNIVERSITY
Graduate Programs

Address: 100 East Claflin, Salina, KS 67401
Admissions Phone: 785-827-5541, ext. 1283 · **Admissions Fax:** 785-827-0927
Admissions E-mail: kjeffm@acck.edu

INSTITUTIONAL INFORMATION
Public/private: Private (nonprofit). **Evening Classes Available?** Yes. **Student/faculty Ratio:** 8:1. **Students in Parent Institution:** 735

STUDENT INFORMATION
Total Students in Program: 51. **% Full-time:** 51. **% Female:** 63.

EXPENSES/FINANCIAL AID
Annual Tuition: $6,120. **Books and Supplies:** $200. **Loans Range From:** $1,000-$2,000. **% Receiving Financial Aid:** 60. **% Receiving Loans:** 100. **Average student debt, upon graduation:** $5,500.

ADMISSIONS INFORMATION
Application Fee: $30. **Regular Notification:** Rolling. **Transfer Students Accepted?** Yes. **Transfer Policy:** Syllabi review and transcript evaluation required of transfer applicants. **Number of Applications Received:** 36. **% of Applicants Accepted:** 86. **% Accepted Who Enrolled:** 68. **Average GPA:** 3.46.
Required Admission Factors: GRE, interview, transcript.
Other Admission Factors: Minimum 3.25 GPA, references, and writing sample required.

EMPLOYMENT INFORMATION
Placement Office Available? Yes.

KEAN UNIVERSITY
College of Arts, Humanities, & Social Services

Address: PO Box 411, Union, NJ 07083-0411
Admissions Phone: 908-527-2665 · **Admissions Fax:** 908-527-2286

INSTITUTIONAL INFORMATION
Public/private: Public. **Evening Classes Available?** Yes. **Student/faculty Ratio:** 15:1. **Students in Parent Institution:** 11,198

STUDENT INFORMATION
Total Students in Program: 1,971. **% Full-time:** 16. **% Female:** 79.

EXPENSES/FINANCIAL AID
Annual Tuition: In-state $3,373. / Out-of-state $5,070. **Fees:** $1,011. **% Receiving Assistantships:** 41.

ADMISSIONS INFORMATION
Application Fee: $35. **Regular Notification:** Rolling. **Transfer Students Accepted?** No.
Required Admission Factors: Essays/personal statement, GRE, interview, letters of recommendation, transcript.

EMPLOYMENT INFORMATION
Placement Office Available? Yes.

KEENE STATE COLLEGE
Graduate Studies

Address: 229 Main Street, Keene, NH 03435-2301
Admissions Phone: 603-358-2276 · **Admissions Fax:** 603-358-2767
Admissions E-mail: admissions@keene.edu · **Web Address:** www.keene.edu

INSTITUTIONAL INFORMATION
Public/private: Public. **Students in Parent Institution:** 4,573.

PROGRAMS
Master's offered in: Biology teacher education, chemistry teacher education, computer teacher education, counselor education/school counseling and guidance services, curriculum and instruction, education leadership and administration, English/language arts teacher education, foreign language teacher education, French language teacher education, geography teacher education, health teacher education, history teacher education, mathematics teacher education, music teacher education, physical education teaching and coaching, science teacher education/general science teacher education, social studies teacher education, Spanish language teacher education, special education, technology teacher education/industrial arts teacher education.

STUDENT INFORMATION
Total Students in Program: 276. **% Full-time:** 11. **% Female:** 63.

RESEARCH FACILITIES
Research Facilities: Child Development Center.

EXPENSES/FINANCIAL AID
Annual Tuition: In-state $5,060. / Out-of-state $11,500. **Room & Board:** $5,966. **Fees:** $1,840. **Books and Supplies:** $600. **Types of Aid Available:** Graduate assistantships, grants, loans.

ADMISSIONS INFORMATION
Application Fee: $35. **Priority Application Deadline:** 4/1. **Regular Application Deadline:** 4/1. **Regular Notification:** Rolling. **Transfer Students Accepted?** Yes. **Transfer Policy:** Up to 9 credits accepted as long as they are approved by an advisor and apply towards the degree program. Only grades of B or better will be accepted. Transfer credits do not apply toward GPA.
Required Admission Factors: Essays/personal statement, GRE, interview, letters of recommendation, transcript.
Other Admission Factors: Minimum 2.5 GPA required, GRE scores at or above the 50th percentile.
Program-Specific Admission Factors: Certifiability required of special education program applicants. Minimum 2 years of teaching experience required of educational administration applicants. PPST required for certification programs.

EMPLOYMENT INFORMATION
Placement Office Available? Yes.

KENNESAW STATE UNIVERSITY
College of Humanities & Social Sciences

Address: 1000 Chastain Road, Kennesaw, GA 30144-5591
Admissions Phone: 770-420-4377 · **Admissions Fax:** 770-423-6541
Admissions E-mail: ksugrad@kennesaw.com
Web Address: http://mapw.kennesaw.edu/

INSTITUTIONAL INFORMATION
Public/private: Public. **Evening Classes Available?** Yes.

PROGRAMS
Master's offered in: Creative writing, English language and literature/letters.

RESEARCH FACILITIES
Research Facilities: Educational technology center, instructional resource center, TRAC center.

EXPENSES/FINANCIAL AID
Annual Tuition: In-state $2,654. / Out-of-state $10,616. **Room & Board (On/off Campus):** $4,200/$6,500. **Fees:** $566. **Books and Supplies:** $750. **% Receiving Financial Aid:** 30. **Types of Aid Available:** Graduate assistantships, grants, loans, scholarships.

ADMISSIONS INFORMATION
Application Fee: $40. **Regular Application Deadline:** 7/9. **Regular Notification:** Rolling. **Transfer Students Accepted?** Yes.
Required Admission Factors: GMAT, GRE, letters of recommendation, transcript.
Other Admission Factors: Minimum 2.5 GPA and minimum GRE score of 1350 required.
Program-Specific Admission Factors: Writing sample and personal statement required of professional writing program applicants.

EMPLOYMENT INFORMATION
Placement Office Available? Yes. **Rate of placement:** 93%.

KENT STATE UNIVERSITY
College of Arts & Sciences

Address: PO Box 5190, Kent, OH 44242-0001

INSTITUTIONAL INFORMATION
Public/private: Public. **Students in Parent Institution:** 21,923.

STUDENT INFORMATION
Total Students in Program: 4,344. **% Full-time:** 46. **% Female:** 67.

RESEARCH FACILITIES
Research Facilities: Glenn H. Brown Liquid Crystal Institute.

EXPENSES/FINANCIAL AID
Annual Tuition: In-state $5,622. / Out-of-state $10,798. **Room & Board:** $4,410.

ADMISSIONS INFORMATION
Application Fee: $30. **Regular Notification:** Rolling. **Transfer Students Accepted?** No. **Transfer Policy:** Maximum 12 semester hours beyond master's may be transferred.
Required Admission Factors: Letters of recommendation, transcript.
Other Admission Factors: Minimum 2.75 GPA required.

EMPLOYMENT INFORMATION
Placement Office Available? Yes.

KENT STATE UNIVERSITY
College of Fine & Professional Arts

Address: PO Box 5190, Kent, OH 44242-0001
Admissions Phone: 330-672-2780

INSTITUTIONAL INFORMATION
Public/private: Public. **Students in Parent Institution:** 21,923.

STUDENT INFORMATION
Total Students in Program: 4,344. **% Full-time:** 46. **% Female:** 67.

RESEARCH FACILITIES
Research Facilities: Glenn H. Brown Liquid Crystal Institute.

EXPENSES/FINANCIAL AID
Annual Tuition: In-state $5,622. / Out-of-state $10,798. **Room & Board:** $4,410.

ADMISSIONS INFORMATION
Application Fee: $30. **Regular Notification:** Rolling. **Transfer Students Accepted?** No. **Transfer Policy:** Maximum 12 semester hours beyond master's may be transferred.
Required Admission Factors: Letters of recommendation, transcript.
Other Admission Factors: Minimum 2.75 GPA required.

EMPLOYMENT INFORMATION
Placement Office Available? Yes.

KENTUCKY STATE UNIVERSITY
College of Arts & Sciences

Address: East Main Street, Frankfort, KY 40601
Admissions Phone: 502-597-6664

INSTITUTIONAL INFORMATION
Public/private: Public. **Evening Classes Available?** Yes. **Students in Parent Institution:** 2,254.

STUDENT INFORMATION
Total Students in Program: 106. **% Full-time:** 43. **% Female:** 50.

RESEARCH FACILITIES
Research Facilities: Research farm.

EXPENSES/FINANCIAL AID
Annual Tuition: In-state $2,308. / Out-of-state $6,926. **Fees:** $340. **Loans Range From:** $7,500-$10,000. **% Receiving Scholarships/Grants:** 80. **% Receiving Loans:** 75. **% Receiving Assistantships:** 5.

ADMISSIONS INFORMATION
Application Fee: $15. **Transfer Students Accepted?** Yes.
Required Admission Factors: Essays/personal statement, GRE, letters of recommendation, transcript.
Other Admission Factors: Minimum GRE score of 1000 and minimum GPA of 3.0 required.

EMPLOYMENT INFORMATION
Placement Office Available? Yes. **Rate of placement:** 87%.

KETTERING UNIVERSITY
Graduate School

Address: 1700 West Third Avenue, Flint, MI 48504-4898
Admissions Phone: 810-762-9682 or 866-KU-GRADS
Admissions Fax: 810-762-9935 · **Admissions E-mail:** mkryska@kettering.edu
Web Address: http://graduate.kettering.edu

INSTITUTIONAL INFORMATION
Public/private: Private (nonprofit). **Evening Classes Available?** Yes. **Students in Parent Institution:** 3,331.

STUDENT INFORMATION
Total Students in Program: 699. **% Female:** 25.

RESEARCH FACILITIES
Research Facilities: Lubrizol Engine Test Cell, Mechatronics, Alternative Fuels, CIM, DFMA, Stress Analysis, and Polymer Processing Labs, Ford Design Simulation Studio.

EXPENSES/FINANCIAL AID

Annual Tuition: $8,370. **% Receiving Financial Aid:** 4. **% Receiving Assistantships:** 4. **Number of Fellowships Granted Each Year:** 4. **Average amount of individual fellowships per year:** $5,000 **Number of Teaching/Research Assistantships Granted Each Year:** 26. **Average Salary Stipend:** $1,190.

ADMISSIONS INFORMATION

Regular Application Deadline: 9/3. **Regular Notification:** Rolling. **Transfer Students Accepted?** Yes. **Number of Applications Received:** 553. **% of Applicants Accepted:** 88. **% Accepted Who Enrolled:** 71. **Average GRE Verbal:** 528. **Average GRE Quantitative:** 624. **Average GRE Analytical:** 699.
Required Admission Factors: Transcript.
Other Admission Factors: GPA for full admissions is 3.0 or higher GPA for provisional admissions is 2.5 or higher.
Program-Specific Admission Factors: All engineering and manufacturing Operations require letter of recommendation.

EMPLOYMENT INFORMATION

Placement Office Available? Yes. **% Employed Within 6 Months:** 100. **% of master's/doctoral grads employed in their field upon graduation:** 100. **Rate of placement:** 100%.

KING'S COLLEGE
College of Arts & Sciences

Address: 133 North River Street, Wilkes-Barre, PA 18711
Admissions Phone: 570-208-5991 · **Admissions Fax:** 570-825-9049
Admissions E-mail: eslott@kings.edu

INSTITUTIONAL INFORMATION

Public/private: Private (nonprofit). **Evening Classes Available?** Yes. **Student/faculty Ratio:** 10:1. **Students in Parent Institution:** 2,226.

STUDENT INFORMATION

Total Students in Program: 158. **% Full-time:** 35. **% Female:** 73.

EXPENSES/FINANCIAL AID

Annual Tuition: $9,216. **% Receiving Financial Aid:** 41.

ADMISSIONS INFORMATION

Application Fee: $35. **Regular Notification:** Rolling. **Transfer Students Accepted?** Yes. **Number of Applications Received:** 105. **% of Applicants Accepted:** 58. **% Accepted Who Enrolled:** 59.
Required Admission Factors: GRE, letters of recommendation, transcript.

EMPLOYMENT INFORMATION

Placement Office Available? Yes. **% of master's/doctoral grads employed in their field upon graduation:** 90.

KNOWLEDGE SYSTEMS INSTITUTE
Graduate Program

Address: 3420 Main Street, Skokie, IL 60076
Admissions Phone: 847-679-3135 · **Admissions Fax:** 847-679-3166
Admissions E-mail: office@ksi.edu

INSTITUTIONAL INFORMATION

Public/private: Private (nonprofit). **Evening Classes Available?** Yes. **Students in Parent Institution:** 87.

STUDENT INFORMATION

Total Students in Program: 87. **% Full-time:** 74. **% Female:** 26.

EXPENSES/FINANCIAL AID

Annual Tuition: In-state $7,560. **Room & Board:** $9,000. **Fees:** $140. **Books and Supplies:** $600. **% Receiving Financial Aid:** 10. **% Receiving Loans:** 100.

ADMISSIONS INFORMATION

Application Fee: $40. **Regular Notification:** Rolling. **Transfer Students Accepted?** Yes. **Transfer Policy:** Transfer requirements reviewed on an individual basis.
Required Admission Factors: Interview, letters of recommendation, transcript.

EMPLOYMENT INFORMATION

Placement Office Available? Yes. **Rate of placement:** 95%.

KUTZTOWN UNIVERSITY OF PENNSYLVANIA
College of Graduate Studies

Address: 15200 Kutztown Road, Kutztown, PA 19530-0730
Admissions Phone: 610-683-4200 · **Admissions Fax:** 610-683-1393
Admissions E-mail: hammann@kutztown.edu · **Web Address:** www.kutztown.edu

INSTITUTIONAL INFORMATION

Public/private: Public. **Evening Classes Available?** Yes. **Total Faculty:** 53. **% Faculty Female:** 47. **% Faculty Part-time:** 89. **Students in Parent Institution:** 9,008.

PROGRAMS

Master's offered in: Art teacher education, business administration/management, college student counseling and personnel services, counseling psychology, digital communications and media/multimedia, educational/instructional media design, elementary education and teaching, English language and literature, French language and literature, German language and literature, history, information technology, library science/librarianship, mathematics, political science and government, public administration, reading teacher education, Russian language and literature, secondary education and teaching, social sciences, social work, Spanish language and literature

STUDENT INFORMATION

Total Students in Program: 694. **% Full-time:** 23. **% Female:** 72. **% Minority:** 9.

EXPENSES/FINANCIAL AID

Annual Tuition: In-state $5,518. / Out-of-state $8,830. **Room & Board:** $5,510. **Fees:** $1,098. **Books and Supplies:** $750. **% Receiving Loans:** 88. **% Receiving Assistantships:** 41. **Types of Aid Available:** Graduate assistantships, institutional work-study, loans. **Number of Teaching/Research Assistantships Granted Each Year:** 30. **Average Salary Stipend:** $5,000.

ADMISSIONS INFORMATION

Application Fee: $35. **Regular Application Deadline:** 9/1. **Regular Notification:** Rolling. **Transfer Students Accepted?** Yes. **Number of Applications Received:** 442. **% of Applicants Accepted:** 92. **% Accepted Who Enrolled:** 36. **Average GPA:** 3.2. **Average GRE Verbal:** 451. **Average GRE Quantitative:** 503. **Average GRE Analytical:** 454.
Required Admission Factors: Letters of recommendation, transcript.
Other Admission Factors: Minimum GRE score of 1200 and minimum 3.0 GPA recommended.
Program-Specific Admission Factors: 3 letters of recommendation required of some programs.

EMPLOYMENT INFORMATION

Placement Office Available? Yes.

LaGRANGE COLLEGE
Graduate Programs

Address: 601 Broad Street, LaGrange, GA 30240
Admissions Phone: 706-880-8005 · **Admissions Fax:** 706-880-8010
Admissions E-mail: lgcadmis@lagrange.edu · **Web Address:** www.lagrange.edu

INSTITUTIONAL INFORMATION
Public/private: Private (nonprofit). **Evening Classes Available?** Yes. **Total Faculty:** 6. **% Faculty Female:** 67. **% Faculty Part-time:** 33. **Student/faculty Ratio:** 5:1. **Students in Parent Institution:** 1,020.

PROGRAMS
Master's offered in: Curriculum and instruction; education.

STUDENT INFORMATION
Total Students in Program: 48. **% Full-time:** 85. **% Female:** 69.

EXPENSES/FINANCIAL AID
Annual Tuition: $14,184. **Room & Board:** $6,018. **Books and Supplies:** $750. **% Receiving Financial Aid:** 67.

ADMISSIONS INFORMATION
Application Fee: $25. **Regular Application Deadline:** 8/15. **Regular Notification:** Rolling. **Transfer Students Accepted?** Yes. **Average GPA:** 3.0. **Average GRE Verbal:** 420. **Average GRE Quantitative:** 513.
Required Admission Factors: Essays/personal statement, interview, letters of recommendation, transcript.
Other Admission Factors: Minimum 2.5 GPA required.

LAKE ERIE COLLEGE
Graduate Programs

Address: 391 West Washington Street, Painesville, OH 44077
Admissions Phone: 440-375-7050 · **Admissions Fax:** 440-375-7005
Admissions E-mail: jcalhoun@lec.edu · **Web Address:** www.lec.edu

INSTITUTIONAL INFORMATION
Public/private: Private (nonprofit). **Evening Classes Available?** Yes. **Total Faculty:** 14. **% Faculty Female:** 36. **% Faculty Part-time:** 36. **Student/faculty Ratio:** 14:1. **Students in Parent Institution:** 720.

PROGRAMS
Master's offered in: Adult and continuing education and teaching; business administration/management; business/commerce; curriculum and instruction; education leadership and administration; education; educational, instructional, and curriculum supervision; teacher education and professional development, specific levels and methods.

STUDENT INFORMATION
Total Students in Program: 139. **% Female:** 71.

RESEARCH FACILITIES
Research Facilities: Indian Museum, International Center.

EXPENSES/FINANCIAL AID
Annual Tuition: $8,010. **Fees:** $450. **Books and Supplies:** $530. **Loans Range From:** $2,000-$18,500. **% Receiving Loans:** 100. **Types of Aid Available:** Graduate assistantships, loans.

ADMISSIONS INFORMATION
Application Fee: $25. **Regular Application Deadline:** 8/20. **Regular Notification:** Rolling. **Transfer Students Accepted?** Yes. **Number of Applications Received:** 47. **% of Applicants Accepted:** 91. **% Accepted Who Enrolled:** 74. **Average GPA:** 3.2.
Required Admission Factors: Interview, transcript.
Other Admission Factors: Managerial or administrative work experience recommended, prefer 3.0 or better.

LAKE FOREST COLLEGE
Graduate Program in Liberal Studies

Address: 555 North Sheridan Road, Box A8, Lake Forest, IL 60045
Admissions Phone: 847-735-5083 · **Admissions Fax:** 847-735-6291
Admissions E-mail: mls@lfc.edu · **Web Address:** www.lfc.edu/graduateprogram

INSTITUTIONAL INFORMATION
Public/private: Private (nonprofit). **Evening Classes Available?** Yes. **Total Faculty:** 15. **% Faculty Female:** 33. **Student/faculty Ratio:** 6:1. **Students in Parent Institution:** 1,350.

PROGRAMS
Master's offered in: African American/Black studies, American history (United States), American literature (United States), American/united states studies/civilization, Asian studies/civilization, English language and literature, English literature (British and commonwealth), European history, European studies/civilization, history and philosophy of science and technology, history, Latin American studies, liberal arts and sciences/liberal studies, mass communications/media studies, public/applied history and archival administration, religion/religious studies, social sciences, Western European studies.

STUDENT INFORMATION
Total Students in Program: 37. **% Female:** 54. **% Minority:** 3.

EXPENSES/FINANCIAL AID
Annual Tuition: $14,400. **Books and Supplies:** $250. **Grants:** $600. **Loans Range From:** $2,000-$2,500. **% Receiving Financial Aid:** 40. **% Receiving Scholarships/Grants:** 75. **% Receiving Loans:** 25. **Types of Aid Available:** Grants, loans. **Average student debt, upon graduation:** $1,000.

ADMISSIONS INFORMATION
Application Fee: $20. **Priority Application Deadline:** 6/1. **Regular Application Deadline:** 7/15. **Regular Notification:** Rolling. **Transfer Students Accepted?** Yes. **Number of Applications Received:** 23. **% of Applicants Accepted:** 39. **% Accepted Who Enrolled:** 100. **Average GPA:** 3.3.
Required Admission Factors: Essays/personal statement, interview, transcript.

EMPLOYMENT INFORMATION
% Employed Within 6 Months: 100. **% of master's/doctoral grads employed in their field upon graduation:** 100. **Rate of placement:** 90%. **Average starting salary:** $75,000.

LAMAR UNIVERSITY
College of Arts & Sciences

Address: 4400 MLK Parkway, Beaumont, TX 77710
Admissions Phone: 409-880-8356 · **Admissions Fax:** 409-880-8414
Admissions E-mail: dranes1@lub002.lamar.edu

INSTITUTIONAL INFORMATION
Public/private: Public. **Evening Classes Available?** Yes. **Students in Parent Institution:** 8,568.

STUDENT INFORMATION
Total Students in Program: 838. **% Full-time:** 47. **% Female:** 51.

RESEARCH FACILITIES
Research Facilities: Gulf Coast Hazardous Substance Research Center.

EXPENSES/FINANCIAL AID
Annual Tuition: In-state $1,634. / Out-of-state $5,522. **Fees:** $518. **Books and Supplies:** $500. **Grants Range From:** $1,000-$2,000. **% Receiving Financial Aid:** 7. **Average student debt, upon graduation:** $13,563.

ADMISSIONS INFORMATION

Application Fee: $25. **Regular Notification:** Rolling. **Transfer Students Accepted?** Yes. **Number of Applications Received:** 45. **% of Applicants Accepted:** 69. **% Accepted Who Enrolled:** 58. **Average GPA:** 2.5. **Required Admission Factors:** GRE, transcript. **Other Admission Factors:** Minimum GRE score of 950 (verbal and quantitative), and minimum 2.5 GPA overall (or minimum 2.75 GPA in last 60 credit hours) required.

EMPLOYMENT INFORMATION

Placement Office Available? Yes.   **Rate of placement:** 99%.

LAMAR UNIVERSITY
College of Fine Arts & Communication

Address: 4400 MLK Parkway, Beaumont, TX 77710
Admissions Phone: 409-880-8356 · **Admissions Fax:** 409-880-8414
Admissions E-mail: dranes1@lub002.lamar.edu

INSTITUTIONAL INFORMATION

Public/private: Public. **Evening Classes Available?** Yes. **Students in Parent Institution:** 8,568.

STUDENT INFORMATION

Total Students in Program: 838. **% Full-time:** 47. **% Female:** 51.

RESEARCH FACILITIES

Research Facilities: Gulf Coast Hazardous Substance Research Center.

EXPENSES/FINANCIAL AID

Annual Tuition: In-state $1,634. / Out-of-state $5,522. **Fees:** $518. **Books and Supplies:** $500. **Grants Range From:** $1,000-$2,000.   **% Receiving Financial Aid:** 7.   **Average student debt, upon graduation:** $13,563. **Average Salary Stipend:** $500.

ADMISSIONS INFORMATION

Application Fee: $25. **Regular Notification:** Rolling. **Transfer Students Accepted?** Yes. **Number of Applications Received:** 56. **% of Applicants Accepted:** 64. **% Accepted Who Enrolled:** 78. **Average GPA:** 2.6. **Average GRE Verbal:** 350. **Average GRE Quantitative:** 700. **Average GRE Analytical:** 350. **Required Admission Factors:** GRE, transcript. **Other Admission Factors:** Minimum entrance formula of 1350 ([GPA times 200] plus [GRE verbal and quantitative]) required.

EMPLOYMENT INFORMATION

Placement Office Available? Yes.   **Rate of placement:** 99%.

LASALLE UNIVERSITY
School of Arts & Sciences

Address: 1900 West Olney Avenue, Philadelphia, PA 19141-1199
Admissions Phone: 215-951-1100 · **Admissions E-mail:** reilly@lasalle.edu

INSTITUTIONAL INFORMATION

Public/private: Private (nonprofit). **Evening Classes Available?** Yes. **Students in Parent Institution:** 5,567

STUDENT INFORMATION

Total Students in Program: 1,606. **% Full-time:** 11. **% Female:** 59.

EXPENSES/FINANCIAL AID

Books and Supplies: $500. **Grants Range From:** $900-$1,500.

ADMISSIONS INFORMATION

Application Fee: $35. **Regular Notification:** Rolling. **Transfer Students Accepted?** Yes. **Number of Applications Received:** 283. **% of Applicants**

Accepted: 85. **% Accepted Who Enrolled:** 86.
Required Admission Factors: Letters of recommendation, transcript.

EMPLOYMENT INFORMATION

Placement Office Available? Yes.

LAURA AND ALVIN SIEGAL COLLEGE
Graduate School

Address: 26500 Shaker Boulevard, Cleveland, OH 44122
Admissions Phone: 216-464-4050 · **Admissions Fax:** 216-464-5827
Admissions E-mail: admissions@siegalcollege.edu
Web Address: www.siegalcollege.edu

INSTITUTIONAL INFORMATION

Public/private: Private (nonprofit). **Evening Classes Available?** Yes. **Total Faculty:** 40. **% Faculty Female:** 62. **% Faculty Part-time:** 70. **Student/faculty Ratio:** 10:1. **Students in Parent Institution:** 144.

PROGRAMS

Master's offered in: Curriculum and instruction; education leadership and administration; education; educational, instructional, and curriculum supervision; Hebrew language and literature; history; Jewish/Judaic studies; religion/religious studies.

STUDENT INFORMATION

Total Students in Program: 144. **% Full-time:** 9. **% Female:** 81.

EXPENSES/FINANCIAL AID

Annual Tuition: $5,850. **Fees:** $25. **Books and Supplies:** $300. **Grants Range From:** $500-$5,000. **% Receiving Financial Aid:** 40. **% Receiving Scholarships/Grants:** 35.   **Number of Fellowships Granted Each Year:** 15. **Average amount of individual fellowships per year:** $5,000.

ADMISSIONS INFORMATION

Application Fee: $50. **Priority Application Deadline:** 6/30. **Regular Application Deadline:** 9/30. **Regular Notification:** Rolling. **Transfer Students Accepted?** Yes. **Transfer Policy:** Application, fee, essay, transcripts, interview and 2 letters of recommendation. **Number of Applications Received:** 50. **% of Applicants Accepted:** 84. **% Accepted Who Enrolled:** 83. **Average GPA:** 3.3. **Required Admission Factors:** Essays/personal statement, interview, letters of recommendation, transcript.

EMPLOYMENT INFORMATION

% Employed Within 6 Months: 50. **Rate of placement:** 50%. **Average starting salary:** $35,000.

LEE UNIVERSITY
School of Music

Address: 1120 North Ocoee Street, Cleveland, TN 37311
Admissions Phone: 423-614-8245 · **Admissions Fax:** 423-614-8242

INSTITUTIONAL INFORMATION

Public/private: Private (nonprofit). **Student/faculty Ratio:** 3:1. **Students in Parent Institution:** 2,870.

STUDENT INFORMATION

Total Students in Program: 43. **% Full-time:** 28. **% Female:** 60.

EXPENSES/FINANCIAL AID

% Receiving Financial Aid: 100.

ADMISSIONS INFORMATION

Application Fee: $25. **Regular Notification:** Rolling. **Transfer Students Accepted?** Yes. **Number of Applications Received:** 7. **% of Applicants**

Accepted: 100. % Accepted Who Enrolled: 100. Average GPA: 3.0.
Required Admission Factors: Essays/personal statement, interview, letters of recommendation, transcript.
Other Admission Factors: Minimum 3.0 GPA or successfull tenure in profession required.

EMPLOYMENT INFORMATION
% Employed Within 6 Months: 100. % of master's/doctoral grads employed in their field upon graduation: 100.

LEHIGH UNIVERSITY
College of Arts & Sciences

Address: Maginnes Hall, 9 West Packer Avenue, Bethlehem, PA 18015-3035
Admissions Phone: 610-758-4280 · Admissions Fax: 610-758-6232
Admissions E-mail: ihp0@lehigh.edu
Web Address: www.lehigh.edu/gradarts-sciences

INSTITUTIONAL INFORMATION
Public/private: Private (nonprofit). Students in Parent Institution: 6,476.

PROGRAMS
Master's offered in: Chemistry, English language and literature, geological and earth sciences/geosciences, geology/earth science, history, optics/optical sciences, physics, political science and government, sociology. Doctorate offered in: Chemistry, English language and literature, geological and earth sciences/geosciences, geology/earth science, history, physics, psychology.

STUDENT INFORMATION
Total Students in Program: 1,791. % Full-time: 42. % Female: 44.

RESEARCH FACILITIES
Research Facilities: Biopharmaceutical Technology Institute, Building/Architectural Technology Institute, Center for Innovation Management Studies, International Center for Democracy and Social Change, Center for Manufacturing Systems Engineering.

EXPENSES/FINANCIAL AID
Annual Tuition: $8,550. Fees: $200. Books and Supplies: $400. Grants Range From: $12,500-$16,500. Loans Range From: $120-$17,000. % Receiving Financial Aid: 60. % Receiving Scholarships/Grants: 10. % Receiving Assistantships: 50. Types of Aid Available: Fellowships, graduate assistantships, scholarships.

ADMISSIONS INFORMATION
Application Fee: $50. Priority Application Deadline: 1/15. Regular Application Deadline: 7/1. Regular Notification: Rolling. Transfer Students Accepted? Yes. Transfer Policy: Maximum 6 credit hours may be transferred into master's programs. Number of Applications Received: 424. % of Applicants Accepted: 38. % Accepted Who Enrolled: 61. Average GPA: 3.2.
Required Admission Factors: Letters of recommendation, transcript.
Other Admission Factors: Minimum 2.75 GPA required.

EMPLOYMENT INFORMATION
Placement Office Available? Yes. Rate of placement: 97%.

LEMOYNE COLLEGE
Graduate Programs

Address: 1419 Salt Springs Road, Syracuse, NY 13214-1399
Admissions Phone: 315-445-4786 (MBA program), 315-445-4376 (education program) · Admissions Fax: 315-445-4787 (MBA program), 315-445-4744 (education program)

INSTITUTIONAL INFORMATION
Public/private: Private (nonprofit). Evening Classes Available? Yes. Total Faculty: 62. % Faculty Female: 47. % Faculty Part-time: 47. Student/faculty Ratio: 22:1. Students in Parent Institution: 3,130.

STUDENT INFORMATION
Total Students in Program: 731. % Full-time: 6. % Female: 59.

EXPENSES/FINANCIAL AID
Books and Supplies: $450. Loans Range From: $1,000-$18,500. % Receiving Financial Aid: 28. % Receiving Loans: 100. Average student debt, upon graduation: $16,000.

ADMISSIONS INFORMATION
Application Fee: $25. Regular Notification: Rolling. Transfer Students Accepted? Yes. Transfer Policy: Maximum 9 credit hours may be transferred into education programs; maximum 21 credit hours may be transferred into MBA programs. Number of Applications Received: 175. % of Applicants Accepted: 90. % Accepted Who Enrolled: 87. Average GPA: 3. Average GRE Verbal: 460. Average GRE Quantitative: 480. Average GRE Analytical: 530.
Required Admission Factors: Letters of recommendation, transcript.
Program-Specific Admission Factors: Minimum GMAT score of 450 and minimum 3.0 GPA (or minimum entrance formula of 1050 [200 times GPA plus GMAT score]) and admissions interview required of MBA program applicants. Minimum 3.0 GPA, GRE, and admissions essay required of education program.

EMPLOYMENT INFORMATION
Placement Office Available? Yes. % Employed Within 6 Months: 100. % of master's/doctoral grads employed in their field upon graduation: 100.

LENOIR-RHYNE COLLEGE
Graduate School

Address: PO Box 7420, Hickory, NC 28603
Admissions Phone: 828-328-7275 · Admissions Fax: 828-328-7368

INSTITUTIONAL INFORMATION
Public/private: Private (nonprofit). Evening Classes Available? Yes. Student/faculty Ratio: 10:1. Students in Parent Institution: 1,456.

STUDENT INFORMATION
Total Students in Program: 140. % Full-time: 14. % Female: 67.

RESEARCH FACILITIES
Research Facilities: Area Health Education Center (AHEC).

EXPENSES/FINANCIAL AID
Fees: $175. Books and Supplies: $500. Loans Range From: $1,000-$11,799. % Receiving Loans: 100.

ADMISSIONS INFORMATION
Application Fee: $25. Regular Notification: Rolling. Transfer Students Accepted? Yes. Transfer Policy: Minimum grade average of B required of transfer applicants. Number of Applications Received: 28. % of Applicants Accepted: 89. % Accepted Who Enrolled: 100. Average GPA: 2.94.
Required Admission Factors: Essays/personal statement, letters of recommendation, transcript.
Program-Specific Admission Factors: Minimum GMAT score of 450, minimum 2.7 GPA, business experience, and undergraduate business core required of business program applicants. Minimum combined GRE score of 1350, minimum GRE verbal score of 450, and minimum 2.7 undergraduate GPA (minimum 3.0 GPA in major).

LESLEY UNIVERSITY
Graduate School of Arts & Social Sciences

Address: 29 Everett Street, Cambridge, MA 02138-2790
Admissions Phone: 617-349-8300 · **Admissions Fax:** 617-349-8313
Admissions E-mail: jconley@mail.lesley.edu · **Web Address:** www.lesley.edu

INSTITUTIONAL INFORMATION
Public/private: Private (nonprofit). **Evening Classes Available?** Yes. **Student/faculty Ratio:** 14:1. **Students in Parent Institution:** 8,521.

PROGRAMS
Master's offered in: Administration of special education, art teacher education, computer teacher education, counseling psychology, counselor education/school counseling and guidance services, creative writing, cultural resources management and policy analysis, curriculum and instruction, early childhood education and teaching, education leadership and administration, education, education/teaching of individuals in early childhood special education programs, education/teaching of individuals who are developmentally delayed, education/teaching of individuals with autism, education/teaching of individuals with mental retardation, education/teaching of individuals with multiple disabilities, education/teaching of individuals with specific learning disabilities, elementary and middle school administration/principalship, elementary education and teaching, English/language arts teacher education, history teacher education, intercultural/multicultural and diversity studies, international and comparative education, international/global studies, junior high/intermediate/middle school education and teaching, kindergarten/preschool education and teaching, mathematics teacher education, multi/interdisciplinary studies, peace studies and conflict resolution, reading teacher education, science teacher education/general science teacher education, secondary school administration/principalship, social science teacher education, social studies teacher education, special education, superintendency and educational system administration, technology teacher education/industrial arts teacher education. **Doctorate offered in:** Computer teacher education, curriculum and instruction, early childhood education and teaching, education, elementary education and teaching, history teacher education, junior high/intermediate/middle school education and teaching. **First Professional degree offered in:** Art teacher education, computer teacher education, curriculum and instruction, early childhood education and teaching, education leadership and administration, education, education/teaching of individuals with traumatic brain injuries.

STUDENT INFORMATION
Total Students in Program: 2,412. **% Full-time:** 30. **% Female:** 89. **% Minority:** 6. **% International:** 7.

RESEARCH FACILITIES
Research Facilities: Kresge Center for Teaching Resources, Center for Mathematics, Science, & Technology in Education.

EXPENSES/FINANCIAL AID
Annual Tuition: $12,600. **Room & Board:** $11,250. **Fees:** $30. **Books and Supplies:** $585. **Grants Range From:** $1,000-$5,000. **Loans Range From:** $1,000-$7,500. **% Receiving Scholarships/Grants:** 2. **% Receiving Loans:** 45. **Types of Aid Available:** Graduate assistantships, grants, institutional work-study, loans. **Assistantship Compensation Includes:** Salary/stipend. **Average Salary Stipend:** $3,000.

ADMISSIONS INFORMATION
Application Fee: $50. **Regular Notification:** Rolling. **Transfer Students Accepted?** Yes. **Number of Applications Received:** 999. **% of Applicants Accepted:** 88. **% Accepted Who Enrolled:** 72. **Average GPA:** 3.5.
Required Admission Factors: Essays/personal statement, interview, letters of recommendation, transcript.
Program-Specific Admission Factors: MAT required of counseling psychology program applicants.

EMPLOYMENT INFORMATION
Placement Office Available? Yes. **% Employed Within 6 Months:** 94. **Rate of placement:** 90%. **Average starting salary:** $39,000.

LEWIS UNIVERSITY
College of Arts & Sciences

Address: One University Parkway, Office of Graduate and Adult Recruitment, Romeoville, IL 60446
Admissions Phone: 815-836-5570 · **Admissions Fax:** 815-838-8990
Admissions E-mail: grad@lewisu.edu
Web Address: www.lewisu.edu/academics/grad.htm

INSTITUTIONAL INFORMATION
Public/private: Private (nonprofit). **Evening Classes Available?** Yes. **Students in Parent Institution:** 4,826.

PROGRAMS
Master's offered in: Computer and information systems security, criminal justice/police science, mental health counseling/counselor, non-profit/public/organizational management, protective services.

STUDENT INFORMATION
Total Students in Program: 530. **% Full-time:** 19. **% Female:** 65. **% Minority:** 23. **% International:** 1.

EXPENSES/FINANCIAL AID
Annual Tuition: $10,584. **Room & Board:** $7,200. **Books and Supplies:** $500. **Grants Range From:** $500-$9,180. **Loans Range From:** $150-$18,500. **% Receiving Financial Aid:** 22. **% Receiving Scholarships/Grants:** 28. **% Receiving Loans:** 57. **% Receiving Assistantships:** 18. **Types of Aid Available:** Graduate assistantships, institutional work-study, loans, scholarships. **Assistantship Compensation Includes:** Full tuition remission, partial tuition remission, salary/stipend. **Average Salary Stipend:** $5,000.

ADMISSIONS INFORMATION
Application Fee: $40. **Regular Application Deadline:** 8/15. **Regular Notification:** Rolling. **Transfer Students Accepted?** Yes. **Number of Applications Received:** 110. **% of Applicants Accepted:** 85. **% Accepted Who Enrolled:** 77.
Required Admission Factors: Transcript.
Recommended Admission Factors: GRE.

LEXINGTON THEOLOGICAL SEMINARY
Graduate Programs

Address: 631 South Limestone Street, Lexington, KY 40508
Admissions Phone: 859-252-0361, ext. 235 · **Admissions Fax:** 859-281-6042
Admissions E-mail: zfuqua@lextheo.edu · **Web Address:** www.lextheo.edu

INSTITUTIONAL INFORMATION
Public/private: Private (nonprofit). **Evening Classes Available?** Yes. **Total Faculty:** 26. **% Faculty Female:** 23. **% Faculty Part-time:** 54. **Student/faculty Ratio:** 7:1.

PROGRAMS
Master's offered in: Bible/biblical studies, divinity/ministry (BD, MDiv), religious education, religious/sacred music, theology/theological studies, youth ministry. **Doctorate offered in:** Divinity/ministry (BD, MDiv).

RESEARCH FACILITIES
Research Facilities: Children's Worship and Wonder Training Center.

EXPENSES/FINANCIAL AID

Annual Tuition: $4,680. **Room & Board:** $355. **Fees:** $184. **Books and Supplies:** $500. **Grants:** $4,680. **Loans:** $8,500. **% Receiving Financial Aid:** 100. **% Receiving Scholarships/Grants:** 100. **% Receiving Loans:** 10.

ADMISSIONS INFORMATION

Application Fee: $25. **Regular Application Deadline:** 7/1. **Regular Notification:** Rolling. **Transfer Students Accepted?** Yes. **Transfer Policy:** Maximum of 30 credit hours for MDiv; 15 credit hours for MA both with minimum grade average of 2.5.
Required Admission Factors: Essays/personal statement, interview, letters of recommendation, transcript.
Other Admission Factors: Minimum 2.5 GPA required.

LIBERTY UNIVERSITY
College of Arts & Sciences

Address: 1971 University Boulevard, Lynchburg, VA 24502-2269
Admissions Phone: 434-582-2021 · **Admissions Fax:** 434-582-2617
Admissions E-mail: wewegert@liberty.edu

INSTITUTIONAL INFORMATION

Public/private: Private (nonprofit). **Students in Parent Institution:** 6,192.

STUDENT INFORMATION

Total Students in Program: 704. **% Full-time:** 25. **% Female:** 44.

EXPENSES/FINANCIAL AID

Annual Tuition: $5,130. **Fees:** $500. **Books and Supplies:** $700.

ADMISSIONS INFORMATION

Application Fee: $35. **Regular Notification:** Rolling. **Transfer Students Accepted?** Yes. **Number of Applications Received:** 150. **% of Applicants Accepted:** 87. **% Accepted Who Enrolled:** 77.
Required Admission Factors: GRE, transcript.
Other Admission Factors: Minimum 3.0 GPA and at least 6 semester hours in psychology or a closely related field required.

EMPLOYMENT INFORMATION

Placement Office Available? Yes.

LINCOLN CHRISTIAN SEMINARY
Graduate Programs

Address: 100 Campus View Drive, Lincoln, IL 62656-2111
Admissions Phone: 217-732-3168, ext. 2275 · **Admissions Fax:** 217-732-1821
Admissions E-mail: lswanson@lccs.edu

INSTITUTIONAL INFORMATION

Public/private: Private (nonprofit). **Evening Classes Available?** Yes. **Student/faculty Ratio:** 8:1. **Students in Parent Institution:** 240.

STUDENT INFORMATION

Total Students in Program: 158. **% Full-time:** 36. **% Female:** 35.

EXPENSES/FINANCIAL AID

Annual Tuition: $4,302. **Fees:** $630. **Books and Supplies:** $600. **% Receiving Financial Aid:** 38. **Average student debt, upon graduation:** $16,489 **Number of Teaching/Research Assistantships Granted Each Year:** 33. **Average Salary Stipend:** $1,000.

ADMISSIONS INFORMATION

Application Fee: $20. **Regular Notification:** Rolling. **Transfer Students Accepted?** Yes. **Number of Applications Received:** 89. **% of Applicants Accepted:** 98. **% Accepted Who Enrolled:** 79. **Average GPA:** 3.33.
Required Admission Factors: Essays/personal statement, letters of recommendation, transcript.

Other Admission Factors: Minimum 2.5 GPA required.

EMPLOYMENT INFORMATION

% Employed Within 6 Months: 90. **% of master's grads employed in their field upon graduation:** 90. **Average starting salary:** $25,000.

LINCOLN MEMORIAL UNIVERSITY
School of Graduate Studies

Address: Cumberland Gap Parkway, Harrogate, TN 37752
Admissions Phone: 423-869-6374 · **Admissions Fax:** 423-869-6261
Admissions E-mail: graduate@inetlmu.lmunet.edu

INSTITUTIONAL INFORMATION

Public/private: Private (nonprofit). **Evening Classes Available?** Yes. **Student/faculty Ratio:** 22:1. **Students in Parent Institution:** 1,701.

STUDENT INFORMATION

Total Students in Program: 826. **% Full-time:** 69. **% Female:** 70.

EXPENSES/FINANCIAL AID

Annual Tuition: $4,050. **Fees:** $50. **Books and Supplies:** $300. **Grants Range From:** $2,700-$12,000. **Loans Range From:** $2,700-$12,000. **% Receiving Financial Aid:** 60. **% Receiving Scholarships/Grants:** 1. **% Receiving Loans:** 96. **% Receiving Assistantships:** 3. **Number of Teaching/Research Assistantships Granted Each Year:** 25.

ADMISSIONS INFORMATION

Application Fee: $25. **Regular Notification:** Rolling. **Transfer Students Accepted?** Yes. **Transfer Policy:** Maximum 9 semester hours with a minimum grade of B may be transferred. **Number of Applications Received:** 879. **% of Applicants Accepted:** 84. **% Accepted Who Enrolled:** 85.
Required Admission Factors: GRE, letters of recommendation, transcript.
Other Admission Factors: Minimum 3.0 GPA required.

EMPLOYMENT INFORMATION

Placement Office Available? Yes.

LINCOLN UNIVERSITY
Graduate Program

Address: PO Box 179, Lincoln University, PA 19352
Admissions Phone: 610-932-8300, ext. 3252 · **Admissions Fax:** 610-932-5511

INSTITUTIONAL INFORMATION

Public/private: Public. **Evening Classes Available?** Yes. **Student/faculty Ratio:** 9:1. **Students in Parent Institution:** 2,084.

STUDENT INFORMATION

Total Students in Program: 508. **% Full-time:** 73. **% Female:** 67.

EXPENSES/FINANCIAL AID

Annual Tuition: In-state $3,748. / Out-of-state $6,256. **Fees:** $2,318. **Loans Range From:** $3,638-$13,805. **% Receiving Loans:** 100.

ADMISSIONS INFORMATION

Application Fee: $50. **Regular Notification:** Rolling. **Transfer Students Accepted?** No. **Number of Applications Received:** 236. **% of Applicants Accepted:** 89. **% Accepted Who Enrolled:** 100.
Required Admission Factors: Essays/personal statement, letters of recommendation, transcript.
Other Admission Factors: Minimum 5 years experience in human service field and current employment in field required.

EMPLOYMENT INFORMATION

Placement Office Available? Yes. **% Employed Within 6 Months:** 100. **% of master's/doctoral grads employed in their field upon graduation:** 100. **Average starting salary:** $35,000.

LINDSEY WILSON COLLEGE
Graduate Programs

Address: 210 Lindsey Wilson Street, Columbia, KY 42728

INSTITUTIONAL INFORMATION
Public/private: Private (nonprofit). **Evening Classes Available?** Yes. **Student/faculty Ratio:** 10:1. **Students in Parent Institution:** 1,274.

EXPENSES/FINANCIAL AID
Annual Tuition: $9,648. **Books and Supplies:** $600. **Grants Range From:** $1,000-$5,000. **Loans Range From:** $1,000-$18,000. **% Receiving Assistantships:** 8.

ADMISSIONS INFORMATION
Application Fee: $30. **Transfer Students Accepted?** Yes. **Number of Applications Received:** 16. **% of Applicants Accepted:** 100. **% Accepted Who Enrolled:** 100.
Required Admission Factors: Essays/personal statement, letters of recommendation, transcript.
Other Admission Factors: Minimum 3.0 GPA required.

EMPLOYMENT INFORMATION
% Employed Within 6 Months: 100. **% of master's/doctoral/first professional grads employed in their field upon graduation:** 100. **Average starting salary:** $32,000.

LOCK HAVEN UNIVERSITY OF PENNSYLVANIA
Master's in Liberal Arts Program

Address: Lock Haven, PA 17745
Admissions Phone: 570-893-2124 · **Admissions Fax:** 570-893-2734
Admissions E-mail: jsmalley@eagle.lhup.edu

INSTITUTIONAL INFORMATION
Public/private: Public. **Students in Parent Institution:** 3,945.

STUDENT INFORMATION
Total Students in Program: 109. **% Full-time:** 70. **% Female:** 61.

EXPENSES/FINANCIAL AID
Annual Tuition: In-state $4,140. / Out-of-state $7,002. **Fees:** $996. **Books and Supplies:** $600. **% Receiving Scholarships/Grants:** 10. **% Receiving Loans:** 80. **% Receiving Assistantships:** 10. **Number of Teaching/Research Assistantships Granted Each Year:** 8. **Average Salary Stipend:** $4,500.

ADMISSIONS INFORMATION
Application Fee: $25. **Regular Notification:** Rolling. **Transfer Students Accepted?** No. **Number of Applications Received:** 18. **% of Applicants Accepted:** 89. **% Accepted Who Enrolled:** 81. **Average GPA:** 3.0.
Required Admission Factors: Interview, transcript.
Other Admission Factors: Minimum 3.0 GPA required.

EMPLOYMENT INFORMATION
Placement Office Available? Yes. **Rate of placement:** 96%.

LONDON SCHOOL OF ECONOMICS
AND POLITICAL SCIENCE
Graduate School

Address: Houghton Street, London, WC2A 2AE United Kingdom
Admissions Phone: 44-0-20-7955-7160 · **Admissions Fax:** 44-0-20-7955-6137
Admissions E-mail: s.beattie@lse.ac.uk
Web Address: www.lse.ac.uk/collections/graduateAdmissions/

INSTITUTIONAL INFORMATION
Public/private: Public. **Total Faculty:** 489. **% Faculty Female:** 31. **% Faculty Part-time:** 9. **Student/faculty Ratio:** 16:1. **Students in Parent Institution:** 8,574.

STUDENT INFORMATION
Total Students in Program: 4,170. **% Full-time:** 93. **% Female:** 53. **% International:** 86.

RESEARCH FACILITIES
Research Facilities: Language Centre. www.lse.sc.uk/depts/language

EXPENSES/FINANCIAL AID
Annual Tuition: $11,958. **Room & Board:** $5,700. **Books and Supplies:** $500. **Grants Range From:** $500-$21,500. **% Receiving Financial Aid:** 36. **% Receiving Scholarships/Grants:** 100. **% Receiving Loans:** 2.

ADMISSIONS INFORMATION
Application Fee: $48. **Regular Notification:** Rolling. **Transfer Students Accepted?** No. **Number of Applications Received:** 23,539. **% of Applicants Accepted:** 25. **% Accepted Who Enrolled:** 55. **Average GPA:** 3.6. **Average GRE Quantitative:** 800.
Required Admission Factors: Essays/personal statement, letters of recommendation, transcript.
Other Admission Factors: Minimum UK Honours degree second class or equivalent (minimum 3.5 GPA) required.
Program-Specific Admission Factors: Minimum GRE quantitative and analytical section scores in the 90th percentile required of some applicants. Minimum GMAT score of 650 required of some applicants.

EMPLOYMENT INFORMATION
% Employed Within 6 Months: 71.

LONG ISLAND UNIVERSITY—
BROOKLYN CAMPUS
Richard L. Conolly College of Liberal Arts & Sciences

Address: One University Plaza, Brooklyn, NY 11201
Admissions Phone: 718-488-1011

INSTITUTIONAL INFORMATION
Public/private: Private (nonprofit). **Evening Classes Available?** Yes. **Students in Parent Institution:** 7,971.

STUDENT INFORMATION
Total Students in Program: 1,992. **% Full-time:** 37. **% Female:** 68.

EXPENSES/FINANCIAL AID
Annual Tuition: $8,226.

ADMISSIONS INFORMATION
Application Fee: $30. **Regular Notification:** Rolling. **Transfer Students Accepted?** Yes. **Number of Applications Received:** 335. **% of Applicants Accepted:** 44. **% Accepted Who Enrolled:** 72.
Required Admission Factors: Essays/personal statement, letters of recommendation, transcript.

EMPLOYMENT INFORMATION
Placement Office Available? Yes.

LONG ISLAND UNIVERSITY—
C.W. POST CAMPUS
College of Liberal Arts & Sciences

Address: 720 Northern Boulevard, Brookville, NY 11548-1300
Admissions Phone: 519-299-2900 · **Admissions Fax:** 516-299-2137
Admissions E-mail: enroll@cwpost.liu.edu · **Web Address:** www.liu.edu/postlas

INSTITUTIONAL INFORMATION

Public/private: Private (nonprofit). **Evening Classes Available?** Yes. **Student/faculty Ratio:** 25:1. **Students in Parent Institution:** 8,421.

PROGRAMS

Master's offered in: Applied mathematics, English language and literature, environmental studies, experimental psychology, history, multi/interdisciplinary studies, political science and government, Spanish language and literature. **Doctorate offered in:** Clinical psychology.

STUDENT INFORMATION

Total Students in Program: 254. **% Full-time:** 41. **% Female:** 65. **% International:** 6.

RESEARCH FACILITIES

Research Facilities: Center for Business Research, Library and Information Science Computer Lab, media studies lab, music lab.

EXPENSES/FINANCIAL AID

Annual Tuition: $12,690. **Room & Board:** $8,240. **Fees:** $580. **Books and Supplies:** $500. **Grants Range From:** $300-$28,800. **Loans Range From:** $500-$18,500. **% Receiving Scholarships/Grants:** 7. **% Receiving Loans:** 85. **Types of Aid Available:** Fellowships, graduate assistantships, grants, loans, scholarships.

ADMISSIONS INFORMATION

Application Fee: $30. **Regular Application Deadline:** 9/1. **Regular Notification:** Rolling. **Transfer Students Accepted?** Yes. **Number of Applications Received:** 366. **% of Applicants Accepted:** 40. **% Accepted Who Enrolled:** 56. **Average GPA:** 3.3.
Required Admission Factors: Essays/personal statement, letters of recommendation, transcript.

EMPLOYMENT INFORMATION

Placement Office Available? Yes.

LONG ISLAND UNIVERSITY—
C.W. POST CAMPUS
School of Public Service

Address: 720 Northern Boulevard, Brookville, NY 11548-1300
Admissions Phone: 516-299-2900 · **Admissions Fax:** 516-299-2137
Admissions E-mail: enroll@cwpost.liu.edu
Web Address: www.cwpost.liu.edu/cwis/cwp/colofman/public/graduate.html

INSTITUTIONAL INFORMATION

Public/private: Private (nonprofit). **Evening Classes Available?** Yes. **Total Faculty:** 14. **% Faculty Female:** 29. **Students in Parent Institution:** 8,421.

PROGRAMS

Master's offered in: Criminal justice/law enforcement administration, health/health care administration/management, public administration and services, public administration, social work.

RESEARCH FACILITIES

Research Facilities: Center for Business Research, Library and Information Science Computer Lab, Media Studies Lab, Music Lab.

EXPENSES/FINANCIAL AID

Annual Tuition: $12,690. **Room & Board:** $8,240. **Fees:** $580. **Books and Supplies:** $400. **Grants Range From:** $300-$28,800. **Loans Range From:** $500-$18,500. **% Receiving Scholarships/Grants:** 7. **% Receiving Loans:** 85. **Types of Aid Available:** Fellowships, graduate assistantships, grants, institutional work-study, loans, scholarships.

ADMISSIONS INFORMATION

Application Fee: $30. **Regular Application Deadline:** 8/15. **Transfer Students Accepted?** Yes. **Number of Applications Received:** 134. **% of Applicants Accepted:** 80. **% Accepted Who Enrolled:** 51. **Average GPA:** 3.1. **Required Admission Factors:** Essays/personal statement, letters of recommendation, transcript.

EMPLOYMENT INFORMATION

Placement Office Available? Yes.

LONG ISLAND UNIVERSITY—
C.W. POST CAMPUS
School of Visual & Performing Arts

Address: 720 Northern Boulevard, Brookville, NY 11548-1300
Admissions Phone: 516-299-2900 · **Admissions Fax:** 516-299-2137
Admissions E-mail: enroll@cwpost.liu.edu · **Web Address:** www.liu.edu/svpa

INSTITUTIONAL INFORMATION

Public/private: Private (nonprofit). **Evening Classes Available?** Yes. **Student/faculty Ratio:** 10:1. **Students in Parent Institution:** 8,421

PROGRAMS

Master's offered in: Art/art studies; art/art studies; commercial and advertising art; drama and dramatics/theater arts; fine/studio arts; intermedia/multimedia; music history, literature, and theory; music theory and composition; music; music/music and performing arts studies.

STUDENT INFORMATION

Total Students in Program: 175. **% Full-time:** 58. **% Female:** 75. **% International:** 14.

RESEARCH FACILITIES

Research Facilities: Center for Business Research, Library and Information Science Computer Lab, Media Studies Lab, Music Lab.

EXPENSES/FINANCIAL AID

Annual Tuition: $12,690. **Room & Board:** $8,240. **Fees:** $580. **Books and Supplies:** $400. **Grants Range From:** $300-$28,800. **Loans Range From:** $500-$18,500. **% Receiving Scholarships/Grants:** 7. **% Receiving Loans:** 85. **Types of Aid Available:** Fellowships, graduate assistantships, grants, institutional work-study, loans, scholarships.

ADMISSIONS INFORMATION

Application Fee: $30. **Regular Application Deadline:** 8/15. **Regular Notification:** Rolling. **Transfer Students Accepted?** Yes. **Number of Applications Received:** 139. **% of Applicants Accepted:** 71. **% Accepted Who Enrolled:** 64. **Average GPA:** 3.3.
Required Admission Factors: Essays/personal statement, letters of recommendation, transcript.
Program-Specific Admission Factors: Portfolio required for all art programs. Audition/interview required for art therapy, music, music education, theater.

EMPLOYMENT INFORMATION

Placement Office Available? Yes.

LONG ISLAND UNIVERSITY— SOUTHAMPTON COLLEGE
MFA Program in English and Writing

Address: 239 Montauk Highway, Southampton, NY 11968
Admissions Phone: 631-287-8010 · **Admissions Fax:** 631-287-8130
Admissions E-mail: admissions@southampton.liu.edu
Web Address: www.southampton.liu.edu

INSTITUTIONAL INFORMATION
Public/private: Private (nonprofit). **Total Faculty:** 21. **% Faculty Female:** 38. **% Faculty Part-time:** 57. **Student/faculty Ratio:** 9:1. **Students in Parent Institution:** 1,453.

PROGRAMS
Master's offered in: Accounting, creative writing, elementary education and teaching, reading teacher education, special education.

STUDENT INFORMATION
Total Students in Program: 50. **% Full-time:** 50. **% Female:** 54.

RESEARCH FACILITIES
Research Facilities: English Language Institute, The Center for Creative Retirement, Children's School, Institute for Sustainable Development.

EXPENSES/FINANCIAL AID
Annual Tuition: $15,792. **Room & Board (On/Off Campus):** $10,010/ $10,200. **Fees:** $1,050. **Books and Supplies:** $600. **Grants Range From:** $210-$2,420. **Loans Range From:** $8,500-$18,500. **% Receiving Financial Aid:** 88. **% Receiving Scholarships/Grants:** 72. **% Receiving Loans:** 70. **% Receiving Assistantships:** 12. **Types of Aid Available:** Graduate assistantships, loans, scholarships. teaching assistantships; alternative loans. **Average student debt, upon graduation:** $22,000. **Number of Fellowships Granted Each Year:** 15. **Average amount of individual fellowships per year:** $2,000. **Number of Teaching/Research Assistantships Granted Each Year:** 20. **Assistantship Compensation Includes:** Full tuition remission, partial tuition remission, salary/stipend.

ADMISSIONS INFORMATION
Application Fee: $30. **Regular Application Deadline:** 8/15. **Regular Notification:** Rolling. **Transfer Students Accepted?** Yes. **Transfer Policy:** Submit an official transcript with your application material. **Number of Applications Received:** 68. **% of Applicants Accepted:** 56. **% Accepted Who Enrolled:** 47. **Average GPA:** 3.1.
Required Admission Factors: Essays/personal statement, letters of recommendation, transcript.
Program-Specific Admission Factors: Portfolio (use 8 1/2 X 11 paper and do not bind) and 1-page personal statement required of writing program applicants.

EMPLOYMENT INFORMATION
Placement Office Available? Yes.

LONGWOOD UNIVERSITY
Graduate Studies

Address: 201 High Street, Farmville, VA 23909-1899
Admissions Phone: 434-395-2707 · **Admissions Fax:** 434-395-2750
Admissions E-mail: graduate@longwood.edu
Web Address: www.longwood.edu/graduatestudies

INSTITUTIONAL INFORMATION
Public/private: Public. **Evening Classes Available?** Yes. **Student/faculty Ratio:** 10:1. **Students in Parent Institution:** 4,115.

PROGRAMS
Master's offered in: Counselor education/school counseling and guidance services, creative writing, curriculum and instruction, education leadership and administration, education, education/teaching of individuals with multiple disabilities, elementary education and teaching, English language and literature, French language teacher education, German language teacher education, music teacher education, reading teacher education, school librarian/school library media specialist, sociology, Spanish language teacher education, teaching English as a second or foreign language/ESL language instructor.

STUDENT INFORMATION
Total Students in Program: 377. **% Full-time:** 3.

EXPENSES/FINANCIAL AID
Annual Tuition: In-state $308. / Out-of-state $552. **Books and Supplies:** $275. **Grants Range From:** $1,000-$5,000. **Loans Range From:** $1,000-$5,000. **% Receiving Financial Aid:** 38. **% Receiving Scholarships/Grants:** 13. **% Receiving Loans:** 100. **Types of Aid Available:** Loans. **Average student debt, upon graduation:** $14,569.

ADMISSIONS INFORMATION
Application Fee: $40. **Regular Application Deadline:** 6/30. **Regular Notification:** Rolling. **Transfer Students Accepted?** Yes. **Transfer Policy:** Same for other applicants plus submission of course descriptions and/or syllabi of course work to be considered for transfer. **Number of Applications Received:** 85. **% of Applicants Accepted:** 88. **% Accepted Who Enrolled:** 87. **Average GPA:** 3.0.
Required Admission Factors: Essays/personal statement, letters of recommendation, transcript.
Other Admission Factors: Minimum 2.75 GPA required.
Program-Specific Admission Factors: Valid teaching license required of most education program applicants. Passing Praxis I scores (or equivalent SAT/ACT scores) required for initial licensure programs.

EMPLOYMENT INFORMATION
Placement Office Available? Yes. **% Employed Within 6 Months:** 85. **Average starting salary:** $30,000.

LOUISIANA STATE UNIVERSITY (FORMERLY LOUISIANA STATE UNIVERSITY AND AGRICULTURAL AND MECHANICAL COLLEGE)
College of Art & Design

Address: Baton Rouge, LA 70803-2750
Admissions Phone: 225-578-5400 · **Admissions Fax:** 225-578-5040
Web Address: http://www.design.lsu.edu

INSTITUTIONAL INFORMATION
Public/private: Public. **Students in Parent Institution:** 29,881.

STUDENT INFORMATION
Total Students in Program: 4,792. **% Full-time:** 61. **% Female:** 50.

RESEARCH FACILITIES
Research Facilities: Frey Computing Services Center, Center for Faculty Development, System Network Computer Center, Center for Instructional Technology, Measurement and Evaluation Center, Harry T. Williams Center for Oral History, Center for French and Francophone Studies.

EXPENSES/FINANCIAL AID
Annual Tuition: In-state $3,368. / Out-of-state $8,668. **Books and Supplies:** $1,000. **Grants Range From:** $100-$31,550. **Loans Range From:** $100-$17,500. **% Receiving Financial Aid:** 70. **% Receiving Scholarships/Grants:** 30. **% Receiving Loans:** 22. **% Receiving Assistantships:** 42.

Number of Fellowships Granted Each Year: 3. **Average amount of individual fellowships per year:** $11,800. **Number of Teaching/Research Assistantships Granted Each Year:** 81. **Average Salary Stipend:** $4,700.

ADMISSIONS INFORMATION

Application Fee: $25. **Regular Notification:** Rolling. **Transfer Students Accepted?** No. **Number of Applications Received:** 130. **% of Applicants Accepted:** 48. **% Accepted Who Enrolled:** 65. **Average GPA:** 3.15. **Average GRE Verbal:** 528. **Average GRE Quantitative:** 557.
Required Admission Factors: GRE, letters of recommendation, transcript. **Program-Specific Admission Factors:** Statement of interest required.

EMPLOYMENT INFORMATION

Placement Office Available? Yes.

LOUISIANA STATE UNIVERSITY (FORMERLY LOUISIANA STATE UNIVERSITY AND AGRICULTURAL AND MECHANICAL COLLEGE)
College of Arts & Sciences

Address: Baton Rouge, LA 70803-2750
Admissions Phone: 225-578-2311 · **Admissions Fax:** 225-578-2112
Web Address: http://www.artsci.lsu.edu

INSTITUTIONAL INFORMATION

Public/private: Public. **Students in Parent Institution:** 29,881.

STUDENT INFORMATION

Total Students in Program: 4,792. % Full-time: 61. % Female: 50.

RESEARCH FACILITIES

Research Facilities: Frey Computing Services Center, Center for Faculty Development, System Network Computer Center, Center for Instructional Technology, Measurement and Evaluation Center, Harry T. Williams Center for Oral History, Center for French and Francophone Studies.

EXPENSES/FINANCIAL AID

Annual Tuition: In-state $3,368. / Out-of-state $8,668. **Books and Supplies:** $1,000. **Grants Range From:** $100-$31,550. **Loans Range From:** $100-$17,500. **% Receiving Financial Aid:** 75. **% Receiving Scholarships/Grants:** 30. **% Receiving Loans:** 22. **% Receiving Assistantships:** 42. **Number of Fellowships Granted Each Year:** 108. **Average amount of individual fellowships per year:** $8,700. **Number of Teaching/Research Assistantships Granted Each Year:** 420. **Average Salary Stipend:** $7,700.

ADMISSIONS INFORMATION

Application Fee: $25. **Regular Notification:** Rolling. **Transfer Students Accepted?** No. **Number of Applications Received:** 679. **% of Applicants Accepted:** 35. **% Accepted Who Enrolled:** 51. **Average GPA:** 2.99. **Average GRE Verbal:** 550. **Average GRE Quantitative:** 566.

EMPLOYMENT INFORMATION

Placement Office Available? Yes.

LOUISIANA STATE UNIVERSITY (FORMERLY LOUISIANA STATE UNIVERSITY AND AGRICULTURAL AND MECHANICAL COLLEGE)
College of Basic Sciences

Address: Baton Rouge, LA 70803-2750
Admissions Phone: 225-578-2311 · **Admissions Fax:** 225-578-2112
Web Address: http://science.lsu.edu

INSTITUTIONAL INFORMATION

Public/private: Public. **Students in Parent Institution:** 29,881.

STUDENT INFORMATION

Total Students in Program: 4,792. % Full-time: 61. % Female: 50.

RESEARCH FACILITIES

Research Facilities: Frey Computing Services Center, Center for Faculty Development, System Network Computer Center, Center for Instructional Technology, Measurement and Evaluation Center, Harry T. Williams Center for Oral History, Center for French and Francophone Studies.

EXPENSES/FINANCIAL AID

Annual Tuition: In-state $3,368. / Out-of-state $8,668. **Books and Supplies:** $1,000. **Grants Range From:** $100-$31,550. **Loans Range From:** $100-$17,500. **% Receiving Financial Aid:** 85. **% Receiving Scholarships/Grants:** 30. **% Receiving Loans:** 22. **% Receiving Assistantships:** 42. **Number of Fellowships Granted Each Year:** 56. **Average amount of individual fellowships per year:** $6,300. **Number of Teaching/Research Assistantships Granted Each Year:** 370. **Average Salary Stipend:** $10,400.

ADMISSIONS INFORMATION

Application Fee: $25. **Regular Notification:** Rolling. **Transfer Students Accepted?** No. **Number of Applications Received:** 93. **% of Applicants Accepted:** 26. **% Accepted Who Enrolled:** 62. **Average GPA:** 2.99. **Average GRE Verbal:** 579. **Average GRE Quantitative:** 665.

EMPLOYMENT INFORMATION

Placement Office Available? Yes.

LOUISIANA STATE UNIVERSITY (FORMERLY LOUISIANA STATE UNIVERSITY AND AGRICULTURAL AND MECHANICAL COLLEGE)
College of Music & Dramatic Arts

Address: Baton Rouge, LA 70803-2750
Admissions Phone: 225-578-3261 · **Admissions Fax:** 225-578-2562
Admissions E-mail: bgrimes@lsu.edu · **Web Address:** http://www.cmda.lsu.edu

INSTITUTIONAL INFORMATION

Public/private: Public. **Students in Parent Institution:** 29,881.

STUDENT INFORMATION

Total Students in Program: 4,792. % Full-time: 61. % Female: 50.

RESEARCH FACILITIES

Research Facilities: Frey Computing Services Center, Center for Faculty Development, System Network Computer Center, Center for Instructional Technology, Measurement and Evaluation Center, Harry T. Williams Center for Oral History, Center for French and Francophone Studies.

EXPENSES/FINANCIAL AID

Annual Tuition: In-state $3,368. / Out-of-state $8,668. **Books and Supplies:** $1,000. **Grants Range From:** $100-$31,550. **Loans Range From:** $100-$17,500. **% Receiving Financial Aid:** 76. **% Receiving Scholarships/Grants:** 30. **% Receiving Loans:** 22. **% Receiving Assistantships:** 42. **Number of Fellowships Granted Each Year:** 10. **Average amount of individual fellowships per year:** $12,100. **Number of Teaching/Research Assistantships Granted Each Year:** 88. **Average Salary Stipend:** $4,800.

ADMISSIONS INFORMATION

Application Fee: $25. **Regular Notification:** Rolling. **Transfer Students Accepted?** No. **Number of Applications Received:** 107. **% of Applicants Accepted:** 54. **% Accepted Who Enrolled:** 52. **Average GPA:** 2.85. **Average GRE Verbal:** 493. **Average GRE Quantitative:** 550.
Required Admission Factors: GRE, transcript.
Other Admission Factors: Minimum combined GRE score of 1000 required

of applicants to musicology programs. Examples of research reports required of applicants to music theory, musicology, and music education programs.

EMPLOYMENT INFORMATION
Placement Office Available? Yes.

LOUISIANA STATE UNIVERSITY (FORMERLY LOUISIANA STATE UNIVERSITY AND AGRICULTURAL AND MECHANICAL COLLEGE)
Manship School of Mass Communication

Address: Baton Rouge, LA 70803-2750
Admissions Phone: 225-578-2336 · **Admissions Fax:** 225-578-2125
Admissions E-mail: htaylor@lsu.edu · **Web Address:** www.manship.lsu.edu

INSTITUTIONAL INFORMATION
Public/private: Public. **Students in Parent Institution:** 29,881.

STUDENT INFORMATION
Total Students in Program: 4,792. **% Full-time:** 61. **% Female:** 50.

RESEARCH FACILITIES
Research Facilities: Frey Computing Services Center, Center for Faculty Development, System Network Computer Center, Center for Instructional Technology, Measurement and Evaluation Center, Harry T. Williams Center for Oral History, Center for French and Francophone Studies.

EXPENSES/FINANCIAL AID
Annual Tuition: In-state $3,368. / Out-of-state $8,668. **Books and Supplies:** $1,000. **Grants Range From:** $100-$31,550. **Loans Range From:** $100-$17,500. **% Receiving Financial Aid:** 66. **% Receiving Scholarships/Grants:** 30. **% Receiving Loans:** 22. **% Receiving Assistantships:** 42. **Number of Teaching/Research Assistantships Granted Each Year:** 25. **Average Salary Stipend:** $4,000.

ADMISSIONS INFORMATION
Application Fee: $25. **Regular Notification:** Rolling. **Transfer Students Accepted?** No. **Number of Applications Received:** 35. **% of Applicants Accepted:** 71. **% Accepted Who Enrolled:** 68. **Average GPA:** 3.17. **Average GRE Verbal:** 501. **Average GRE Quantitative:** 649.
Required Admission Factors: GRE, transcript.
Other Admission Factors: Minimum 3.0 GPA and minimum combined GRE score of 100 recommended.

EMPLOYMENT INFORMATION
Placement Office Available? Yes.

LOUISIANA STATE UNIVERSITY (FORMERLY LOUISIANA STATE UNIVERSITY AND AGRICULTURAL AND MECHANICAL COLLEGE)
School of Library & Information Science

Address: Baton Rouge, LA 70803-2750
Admissions Phone: 225-578-3158 · **Admissions Fax:** 225-578-4581
Admissions E-mail: bpaskoff@lsu.edu · **Web Address:** http://slis.lsu.edu

INSTITUTIONAL INFORMATION
Public/private: Public. **Students in Parent Institution:** 29,881.

STUDENT INFORMATION
Total Students in Program: 4,792. **% Full-time:** 61. **% Female:** 50.

RESEARCH FACILITIES
Research Facilities: Frey Computing Services Center, Center for Faculty

---

Development, System Network Computer Center, Center for Instructional Technology, Measurement and Evaluation Center, Harry T. Williams Center for Oral History, Center for French and Francophone Studies.

EXPENSES/FINANCIAL AID
Annual Tuition: In-state $3,368. / Out-of-state $8,668. **Books and Supplies:** $1,000. **Grants Range From:** $100-$31,550. **Loans Range From:** $100-$17,500. **% Receiving Financial Aid:** 59. **% Receiving Scholarships/Grants:** 30. **% Receiving Loans:** 22. **% Receiving Assistantships:** 42. **Number of Fellowships Granted Each Year:** 1. **Average amount of individual fellowships per year:** $17,600. **Number of Teaching/Research Assistantships Granted Each Year:** 69. **Average Salary Stipend:** $4,000.

ADMISSIONS INFORMATION
Application Fee: $25. **Regular Notification:** Rolling. **Transfer Students Accepted?** No. **Number of Applications Received:** 66. **% of Applicants Accepted:** 95. **% Accepted Who Enrolled:** 68. **Average GPA:** 2.78. **Average GRE Verbal:** 526. **Average GRE Quantitative:** 504.
Required Admission Factors: GRE, letters of recommendation, transcript.
Other Admission Factors: Essay required of applicants to some programs.

EMPLOYMENT INFORMATION
Placement Office Available? Yes.

LOUISIANA STATE UNIVERSITY (FORMERLY LOUISIANA STATE UNIVERSITY AND AGRICULTURAL AND MECHANICAL COLLEGE)
School of Social Work

Address: Baton Rouge, LA 70803-2750
Admissions Phone: 225-578-1351 · **Admissions Fax:** 225-578-1357
Admissions E-mail: swrose@lsu.edu · **Web Address:** www.socialwork.lsu.edu

INSTITUTIONAL INFORMATION
Public/private: Public. **Students in Parent Institution:** 29,881.

STUDENT INFORMATION
Total Students in Program: 4,792. **% Full-time:** 61. **% Female:** 50.

RESEARCH FACILITIES
Research Facilities: Frey Computing Services Center, Center for Faculty Development, System Network Computer Center, Center for Instructional Technology, Measurement and Evaluation Center, Harry T. Williams Center for Oral History, Center for French and Francophone Studies.

EXPENSES/FINANCIAL AID
Annual Tuition: In-state $3,368. / Out-of-state $8,668. **Books and Supplies:** $1,000. **Grants Range From:** $100-$31,550. **Loans Range From:** $100-$17,500. **% Receiving Financial Aid:** 64. **% Receiving Scholarships/Grants:** 30. **% Receiving Loans:** 22. **% Receiving Assistantships:** 42. **Number of Fellowships Granted Each Year:** 1. **Average amount of individual fellowships per year:** $5,800. **Number of Teaching/Research Assistantships Granted Each Year:** 22. **Average Salary Stipend:** $6,100.

ADMISSIONS INFORMATION
Application Fee: $25. **Regular Notification:** Rolling. **Transfer Students Accepted?** No. **Number of Applications Received:** 191. **% of Applicants Accepted:** 51. **% Accepted Who Enrolled:** 62. **Average GPA:** 3.2. **Average GRE Verbal:** 455. **Average GRE Quantitative:** 495.
Required Admission Factors: Letters of recommendation, transcript.
Other Admission Factors: Minimum 3.0 GPA, minimum combined (Verbal+Quanitative) GRE score of 1000, and letter of intent required.

EMPLOYMENT INFORMATION
Placement Office Available? Yes.

LOUISIANA STATE UNIVERSITY (FORMERLY LOUISIANA STATE UNIVERSITY AND AGRICULTURAL AND MECHANICAL COLLEGE)
School of the Coast & Environment

Address: Baton Rouge, LA 70803-2750
Admissions Phone: 225-578-6768 · **Admissions Fax:** 225-578-5328
Admissions E-mail: rallen2@lsu.edu

INSTITUTIONAL INFORMATION
Public/private: Public. **Students in Parent Institution:** 29,881.

STUDENT INFORMATION
Total Students in Program: 4,792. **% Full-time:** 61. **% Female:** 50.

RESEARCH FACILITIES
Research Facilities: Frey Computing Services Center, Center for Faculty Development, System Network Computer Center, Center for Instructional Technology, Measurement and Evaluation Center, Harry T. Williams Center for Oral History, Center for French and Francophone Studies.

EXPENSES/FINANCIAL AID
Annual Tuition: In-state $3,368. / Out-of-state $8,668. **Books and Supplies:** $1,000. **Grants Range From:** $100-$31,550. **Loans Range From:** $100-$17,500. **% Receiving Financial Aid:** 60. **% Receiving Scholarships/Grants:** 30. **% Receiving Loans:** 22. **% Receiving Assistantships:** 42. **Number of Fellowships Granted Each Year:** 2. **Average amount of individual fellowships per year:** $10,900. **Number of Teaching/Research Assistantships Granted Each Year:** 19. **Average Salary Stipend:** $6,100.

ADMISSIONS INFORMATION
Transfer Students Accepted? No. **Number of Applications Received:** 50. **% of Applicants Accepted:** 64. **% Accepted Who Enrolled:** 72. **Average GPA:** 2.97. **Average GRE Verbal:** 476. **Average GRE Quantitative:** 592. **Required Admission Factors:** GRE, letters of recommendation, transcript.

EMPLOYMENT INFORMATION
Placement Office Available? Yes.

LOUISIANA STATE UNIVERSITY IN SHREVEPORT
College of Liberal Arts

Address: One University Place, Shreveport, LA 71115
Admissions Phone: 318-797-5061 · **Admissions Fax:** 318-797-5286
Admissions E-mail: admissions@pilot.lsus.edu · **Web Address:** www.lsus.edu

INSTITUTIONAL INFORMATION
Public/private: Public. **Evening Classes Available?** Yes. **Total Faculty:** 34. **% Faculty Female:** 47. **% Faculty Part-time:** 26. **Students in Parent Institution:** 4,401.

PROGRAMS
Master's offered in: Humanities/humanistic studies, liberal arts and sciences/liberal studies.

STUDENT INFORMATION
Total Students in Program: 39. **% Full-time:** 23. **% Female:** 72. **% Minority:** 28.

EXPENSES/FINANCIAL AID
Annual Tuition: In-state $2,780. / Out-of-state $7,740. **Books and Supplies:** $1,000. **% Receiving Financial Aid:** 8. **Number of Teaching/Research Assistantships Granted Each Year:** 4. **Average Salary Stipend:** $900.

ADMISSIONS INFORMATION
Application Fee: $10. **Regular Application Deadline:** 6/30. **Regular Notification:** Rolling. **Transfer Students Accepted?** Yes. **Number of Applications Received:** 16. **% of Applicants Accepted:** 100. **% Accepted Who Enrolled:** 19. **Average GPA:** 3.0.
Required Admission Factors: Essays/personal statement, interview, transcript.
Other Admission Factors: Minimum 2.5 GPA required on undergraduate degree. Minimum 3.0 on graduate work.
Program-Specific Admission Factors: Varies from program to program.

EMPLOYMENT INFORMATION
Placement Office Available? Yes. **% Employed Within 6 Months:** 50.

LOUISIANA STATE UNIVERSITY IN SHREVEPORT
College of Sciences

Address: One University Place, Shreveport, LA 71115
Admissions Phone: 318-797-5061 · **Admissions Fax:** 318-797-5286
Admissions E-mail: admissions@pilot.lsus.edu · **Web Address:** www.lsus.edu

INSTITUTIONAL INFORMATION
Public/private: Public. **Evening Classes Available?** Yes. **Total Faculty:** 33. **% Faculty Female:** 33. **Student/faculty Ratio:** 14:1. **Students in Parent Institution:** 4,401.

PROGRAMS
Master's offered in: Computer/information technology services administration and management.

STUDENT INFORMATION
Total Students in Program: 24. **% Full-time:** 42. **% Female:** 46. **% Minority:** 50.

EXPENSES/FINANCIAL AID
Annual Tuition: In-state $2,780. / Out-of-state $7,740. **Books and Supplies:** $1,000. **Number of Teaching/Research Assistantships Granted Each Year:** 2. **Average Salary Stipend:** $800.

ADMISSIONS INFORMATION
Application Fee: $10. **Regular Application Deadline:** 6/30. **Regular Notification:** Rolling. **Transfer Students Accepted?** Yes. **Number of Applications Received:** 17. **% of Applicants Accepted:** 100. **Average GPA:** 3.
Required Admission Factors: Interview, transcript.
Other Admission Factors: Minimum 2.5 GPA on undergraduate degree. Minimum 3.0 on graduate work.
Program-Specific Admission Factors: Courses in calculus, statistics, and programming. Minimum 900 on sum of Verbal and Quantitative portions of GRE.

EMPLOYMENT INFORMATION
Placement Office Available? Yes. **% Employed Within 6 Months:** 95. **% of master's/doctoral grads employed in their field upon graduation:** 90.

LOUISIANA TECH UNIVERSITY
College of Applied & Natural Sciences

Address: PO Box 10197, 913 Prescott Library, Ruston, LA 71272
Admissions Phone: 318-257-4287 · **Admissions Fax:** 318-257-5060
Admissions E-mail: campbell@latech.edu · **Web Address:** www.ans.latech.edu

INSTITUTIONAL INFORMATION
Public/private: Public. **Student/faculty Ratio:** 1:1. **Students in Parent Institution:** 10,393.

STUDENT INFORMATION
Total Students in Program: 1,627. **% Full-time:** 62. **% Female:** 55.

EXPENSES/FINANCIAL AID

Annual Tuition: In-state $3,504. / Out-of-state $11,504. Books and Supplies: $600. Grants Range From: $100-$15,000. Loans Range From: $135-$16,854. % Receiving Scholarships/Grants: 28. % Receiving Loans: 97. Average student debt, upon graduation: $10,000. Number of Fellowships Granted Each Year: 3. Average amount of individual fellowships per year: $600. Number of Teaching/Research Assistantships Granted Each Year: 7. Average Salary Stipend: $5,000.

ADMISSIONS INFORMATION

Application Fee: $20. Regular Application Deadline: 8/1. Regular Notification: Rolling. Transfer Students Accepted? Yes. Transfer Policy: Maximum 1/3 of total credit hours required may be transferred with a minimum grade of B. Number of Applications Received: 10. % of Applicants Accepted: 100. % Accepted Who Enrolled: 80. Average GPA: 3.44. Average GRE Verbal: 425. Average GRE Quantitative: 538. Average GRE Analytical: 541.

Required Admission Factors: GRE, transcript.

Other Admission Factors: Minimum 3.0 GPA required for regular admission; conditional admission possible with minimum 2.5 GPA. Minimum 30 semester hours in the areas of biology, chemistry (through organic and with laBS), and college algebra required.

EMPLOYMENT INFORMATION

Placement Office Available? Yes.

LOUISIANA TECH UNIVERSITY
College of Liberal Arts

Address: PO Box 7923, Ruston, LA 71272
Admissions Phone: 318-257-2660 · Admissions Fax: 318-257-3935
Admissions E-mail: dminor@gans.latech.edu

INSTITUTIONAL INFORMATION

Public/private: Public. Students in Parent Institution: 10,393.

STUDENT INFORMATION

Total Students in Program: 1,627. % Full-time: 62. % Female: 55.

EXPENSES/FINANCIAL AID

Annual Tuition: In-state $3,504. / Out-of-state $11,504. Books and Supplies: $600. Grants Range From: $100-$15,000. Loans Range From: $135-$16,854. % Receiving Financial Aid: 40. % Receiving Scholarships/Grants: 28. % Receiving Loans: 97.

ADMISSIONS INFORMATION

Application Fee: $20. Regular Notification: Rolling. Transfer Students Accepted? Yes. Number of Applications Received: 138. % of Applicants Accepted: 29. % Accepted Who Enrolled: 100. Average GPA: 3. Average GRE Verbal: 498. Average GRE Quantitative: 451. Average GRE Analytical: 477.

Required Admission Factors: GRE, letters of recommendation, transcript.
Other Admission Factors: Minimum 3.0 GPA requried.

EMPLOYMENT INFORMATION

Placement Office Available? Yes.

LOUISIANA TECH UNIVERSITY
School of Human Ecology

Address: PO Box 7923, Ruston, LA 71272
Admissions Phone: 318-257-4287 · Admissions Fax: 318-257-5060
Admissions E-mail: campbell@latech.edu

INSTITUTIONAL INFORMATION

Public/private: Public. Evening Classes Available? Yes.   Student/faculty Ratio: 7:1. Students in Parent Institution: 10,393

PROGRAMS

STUDENT INFORMATION

Total Students in Program: 1,627. % Full-time: 62. % Female: 55.

EXPENSES/FINANCIAL AID

Annual Tuition: In-state $3,504. / Out-of-state $11,504. Books and Supplies: $600. Grants Range From: $100-$15,000. Loans Range From: $135-$16,854. % Receiving Scholarships/Grants: 28. % Receiving Loans: 97. Average student debt, upon graduation: $10,000. Number of Fellowships Granted Each Year: 3. Number of Teaching/Research Assistantships Granted Each Year: 5. Average Salary Stipend: $4,000.

ADMISSIONS INFORMATION

Application Fee: $20. Regular Notification: Rolling. Transfer Students Accepted? Yes. Transfer Policy: Maximum one-third of total credit hours required may be transferred with a minimum grade average of B. Number of Applications Received: 10. % of Applicants Accepted: 90. % Accepted Who Enrolled: 67. Average GPA: 3.09. Average GRE Verbal: 402. Average GRE Quantitative: 471. Average GRE Analytical: 496.

Required Admission Factors: GRE, letters of recommendation, transcript.
Other Admission Factors: Minimum 2.75 GPA required for regular admission; minimum 2.5 GPA required for conditional admission.
Program-Specific Admission Factors: Eligibility to be a registered dietitian required of nutrition program applicants.

EMPLOYMENT INFORMATION

Placement Office Available? Yes.

LOUISVILLE PRESBYTERIAN THEOLOGICAL SEMINARY
Graduate Programs

Address: 1044 Alta Vista Road, Louisville, KY 40205-1798
Admissions Phone: 502-895-3411 or 800-264-1839
Admissions Fax: 502-992-9399 · Admissions E-mail: admissions@lpts.edu
Web Address: www.lpts.edu

INSTITUTIONAL INFORMATION

Public/private: Private (nonprofit). Total Faculty: 48. % Faculty Female: 44. % Faculty Part-time: 60. Student/faculty Ratio: 11:1. Students in Parent Institution: 193.

PROGRAMS

Master's offered in: Bible/biblical studies, religious education, theology/theological studies. First Professional degree offered in: Divinity/ministry (BD, MDiv), pastoral studies/counseling.

STUDENT INFORMATION

Total Students in Program: 193. % Full-time: 58. % Female: 58. % Minority: 13. % International: 2.

RESEARCH FACILITIES

Research Facilities: Louisville Institute, Center for Congregations & Family Ministries, Continuing Education Programs, Louisville Counseling Ministry.

EXPENSES/FINANCIAL AID

Annual Tuition: $8,250. Room & Board: $3,200. Fees: $71. Books and Supplies: $950. Grants Range From: $900-$15,000. Loans Range From: $1,000-$8,500. % Receiving Financial Aid: 81. % Receiving Scholarships/Grants: 75. % Receiving Loans: 36. Types of Aid Available: Grants, institutional work-study, loans, scholarships. Average student debt, upon graduation: $19,818. Number of Fellowships Granted Each Year: 9. Average amount of individual fellowships per year: $14,000.

ADMISSIONS INFORMATION

Application Fee: $30. Priority Application Deadline: 2/1. Regular Application Deadline: 8/1. Regular Notification: Rolling. Transfer Students Accepted? Yes. Transfer Policy: Minimum grade of B- received within the last 5 years from an ATS accredited seminary. Number of Applications Received: 122. % of Applicants Accepted: 74. % Accepted Who Enrolled: 58. Average GPA: 3.2.
Required Admission Factors: Essays/personal statement, letters of recommendation, transcript.
Other Admission Factors: Minimum 2.5 GPA required.

EMPLOYMENT INFORMATION

Placement Office Available? Yes. % Employed Within 6 Months: 75. % of master's/doctoral grads employed in their field upon graduation: 50/100. Rate of placement: 90%. Average starting salary: $35,000.

LOYOLA COLLEGE IN MARYLAND

Address: 4501 North Charles Street, Baltimore, MD 21210-2699
Admissions Phone: 410-617-5020 · Admissions Fax: 410-617-2002
Admissions E-mail: graduate@loyola.edu · Web Address: www.loyola.edu

INSTITUTIONAL INFORMATION

Public/private: Private (nonprofit). Evening Classes Available? Yes. Students in Parent Institution: 6,073.

PROGRAMS

Master's offered in: Accounting; business administration/management; business/commerce; clinical psychology; computer and information sciences; computer engineering; counseling psychology; counselor education/school counseling and guidance services; curriculum and instruction; education leadership and administration; educational, instructional, and curriculum supervision; electrical, electronics, and communications engineering; finance; international business; liberal arts and sciences/liberal studies; management information systems and services; marketing/marketing management; Montessori teacher education; pastoral studies/counseling; reading teacher education; special education; speech-language pathology/pathologist; technology teacher education/industrial arts teacher education. Doctorate offered in: Clinical psychology; pastoral studies/counseling.

STUDENT INFORMATION

Total Students in Program: 2,597. % Full-time: 24. % Female: 60.

EXPENSES/FINANCIAL AID

Annual Tuition: $400. Books and Supplies: $540. Grants Range From: $250-$7,500. Loans Range From: $500-$18,500. % Receiving Financial Aid: 19. % Receiving Scholarships/Grants: 10. % Receiving Loans: 74. % Receiving Assistantships: 16. Average student debt, upon graduation: $12,750. Number of Teaching/Research Assistantships Granted Each Year: 80.

ADMISSIONS INFORMATION

Application Fee: $50. Transfer Students Accepted? Yes. Number of Applications Received: 1,136. % of Applicants Accepted: 72. % Accepted Who Enrolled: 68. Average GPA: 3.26.
Required Admission Factors: Essays/personal statement, letters of recommendation, transcript.
Program-Specific Admission Factors: All programs require resume. Montessori Education (PRAXIS I and PRAXIS II).

EMPLOYMENT INFORMATION

Placement Office Available? Yes.

LOYOLA MARYMOUNT UNIVERSITY
College of Liberal Arts

Address: One LMU Drive, 2500, Los Angeles, CA 90045-2659
Admissions Phone: 310-338-2721 · Admissions Fax: 310-338-6086
Admissions E-mail: ckouyoum@lmu.edu · Web Address: www.lmu.edu

INSTITUTIONAL INFORMATION

Public/private: Private (nonprofit). Evening Classes Available? Yes. Students in Parent Institution: 7,157.

PROGRAMS

Master's offered in: Creative writing, English language and literature, pastoral studies/counseling, philosophy, psychology, speech and rhetorical studies, theology/theological studies.

EXPENSES/FINANCIAL AID

Annual Tuition: $695. Room & Board: $6,640. Fees: $50. Books and Supplies: $400. Grants Range From: $500-$5,000. Loans Range From: $10,000-$18,500. % Receiving Financial Aid: 70. Average student debt, upon graduation: $50,000. Number of Fellowships Granted Each Year: 20. Average amount of individual fellowships per year: $7,000. Number of Teaching/Research Assistantships Granted Each Year: 20. Assistantship Compensation Includes: Salary/stipend. Average Salary Stipend: $15,000.

ADMISSIONS INFORMATION

Application Fee: $50. Regular Application Deadline: 6/1. Regular Notification: Rolling. Transfer Students Accepted? Yes. Transfer Policy: Minimum 3.0 GPA required of transfer applicants. Number of Applications Received: 159. % of Applicants Accepted: 67. % Accepted Who Enrolled: 71.
Required Admission Factors: Essays/personal statement, GRE, letters of recommendation, transcript.
Recommended Admission Factors: Interview.
Other Admission Factors: 3.0 GPA, GRE score varies.

EMPLOYMENT INFORMATION

Placement Office Available? Yes. Rate of placement: 90%.

LOYOLA UNIVERSITY, CHICAGO
The Graduate School

Address: 820 North Michigan Avenue, Chicago, IL 60611
Admissions Phone: 773-508-3396 · Admissions Fax: 773-508-2460
Admissions E-mail: mgramza@luc.edu

INSTITUTIONAL INFORMATION

Public/private: Private (nonprofit). Total Faculty: 570. Students in Parent Institution: 12,605.

STUDENT INFORMATION

Total Students in Program: 4,212. % Full-time: 44. % Female: 66.

RESEARCH FACILITIES

Research Facilities: Parmly Institute for Hearing Science, Center for Urban Research and Learning, Center for Ethics.

EXPENSES/FINANCIAL AID

Annual Tuition: $18,016. Fees: $120. Books and Supplies: $800. % Receiving Financial Aid: 100. Average student debt, upon graduation: $27,000. Number of Fellowships Granted Each Year: 50. Average amount of individual fellowships per year: $10,000. Number of Teaching/Research Assistantships Granted Each Year: 300. Average Salary Stipend: $10,000.

ADMISSIONS INFORMATION

Application Fee: $40. **Regular Notification:** Rolling. **Transfer Students Accepted?** Yes. **Transfer Policy:** Maximum 6 credit hours may be transferred into master's programs. **Number of Applications Received:** 2,249. **% of Applicants Accepted:** 33. **% Accepted Who Enrolled:** 43.
Required Admission Factors: Essays/personal statement, GRE, letters of recommendation, transcript.
Other Admission Factors: Minimum 3.0 GPA required.
Program-Specific Admission Factors: GRE subject exam required of some applicants; essay required of some applicants.

EMPLOYMENT INFORMATION

Placement Office Available? Yes.

LOYOLA UNIVERSITY, CHICAGO
School of Social Work

Address: 820 North Michigan Avenue, Chicago, IL 60611
Admissions Phone: 312-915-7005
Admissions E-mail: jgonza@luc.edu

INSTITUTIONAL INFORMATION

Public/private: Private (nonprofit). **Evening Classes Available?** Yes. **Student/faculty Ratio:** 16:1. **Students in Parent Institution:** 12,605.

STUDENT INFORMATION

Total Students in Program: 4,212. **% Full-time:** 44. **% Female:** 66.

RESEARCH FACILITIES

Research Facilities: Parmly Institute for Hearing Science, Center for Urban Research and Learning, Center for Ethics.

EXPENSES/FINANCIAL AID

Annual Tuition: $18,016. **Fees:** $120. **Books and Supplies:** $800. **% Receiving Financial Aid:** 10. **Number of Fellowships Granted Each Year:** 2. **Average amount of individual fellowships per year:** $5,000. **Average Salary Stipend:** $200.

ADMISSIONS INFORMATION

Application Fee: $50. **Regular Notification:** Rolling. **Transfer Students Accepted?** Yes. **Number of Applications Received:** 370. **% of Applicants Accepted:** 81. **% Accepted Who Enrolled:** 43. **Average GPA:** 3.4.
Required Admission Factors: Essays/personal statement, letters of recommendation, transcript.
Other Admission Factors: Minimum 3.0 GPA required.

EMPLOYMENT INFORMATION

Placement Office Available? Yes. **% Employed Within 6 Months:** 90. **% of master's/doctoral grads employed in their field upon graduation:** 90/100. **Average starting salary:** $45,000.

LOYOLA UNIVERSITY NEW ORLEANS
College of Arts & Sciences

Address: 6363 St. Charles Avenue, New Orleans, LA 70118-6195
Admissions Phone: 504-865-3240 or 800-4-LOYOLA · **Admissions Fax:** 504-865-3383
Admissions E-mail: stieffel@loyno.edu

INSTITUTIONAL INFORMATION

Public/private: Private (nonprofit). **Student/faculty Ratio:** 12:1. **Students in Parent Institution:** 5,279.

STUDENT INFORMATION

Total Students in Program: 880. **% Full-time:** 11. **% Female:** 67.

RESEARCH FACILITIES

Research Facilities: Archives of New Orleans province of the Society of Jesus, RATHE College of Business Lab.

EXPENSES/FINANCIAL AID

Fees: $512. **Books and Supplies:** $650. **Grants Range From:** $1,000-$19,000. **Loans Range From:** $1-$18,500. **% Receiving Financial Aid:** 37. **% Receiving Scholarships/Grants:** 19. **% Receiving Loans:** 88. **% Receiving Assistantships:** 1. **Average student debt, upon graduation:** $26,690. **Number of Teaching/Research Assistantships Granted Each Year:** 6.

ADMISSIONS INFORMATION

Application Fee: $20. **Transfer Students Accepted?** Yes. **Number of Applications Received:** 78. **% of Applicants Accepted:** 96. **% Accepted Who Enrolled:** 96. **Average GPA:** 3.12. **Average GRE Verbal:** 519. **Average GRE Quantitative:** 502. **Average GRE Analytical:** 540.
Required Admission Factors: GRE, letters of recommendation, transcript.
Program-Specific Admission Factors: At least 15 credit hours in communications, resume, and personal statement required of communications program applicants. Minimum 2.5 GPA required of religous studies program applicants. Three letters of recommendation and MAT required of education programs.

EMPLOYMENT INFORMATION

Placement Office Available? Yes.

LOYOLA UNIVERSITY NEW ORLEANS
City College Graduate Programs

Address: 6363 St. Charles Avenue, New Orleans, LA 70118-6195
Admissions Phone: 504-865-3142 · **Admissions Fax:** 504-865-3254
Admissions E-mail: ccgay@loyno.edu

INSTITUTIONAL INFORMATION

Public/private: Private (nonprofit). **Student/faculty Ratio:** 16:1. **Students in Parent Institution:** 5,279.

STUDENT INFORMATION

Total Students in Program: 880. **% Full-time:** 11. **% Female:** 67.

RESEARCH FACILITIES

Research Facilities: Archives of New Orleans province of the Society of Jesus, RATHE College of Business Lab.

EXPENSES/FINANCIAL AID

Fees: $512. **Books and Supplies:** $650. **Grants Range From:** $1,000-$19,000. **% Receiving Financial Aid:** 83. **% Receiving Scholarships/Grants:** 19. **% Receiving Loans:** 88. **% Receiving Assistantships:** 1. **Average student debt, upon graduation:** $13,393.

ADMISSIONS INFORMATION

Application Fee: $20. **Regular Notification:** Rolling. **Transfer Students Accepted?** Yes. **Number of Applications Received:** 14. **% of Applicants Accepted:** 100. **% Accepted Who Enrolled:** 100.
Required Admission Factors: GRE, interview, letters of recommendation, transcript.
Other Admission Factors: Minimum 2.8 GPA, B.S. Nursing from a NLN accredited institute, license to practice in state, goal statement, and at least one year of recent work experience required.

EMPLOYMENT INFORMATION

Placement Office Available? Yes.

LOYOLA UNIVERSITY NEW ORLEANS
College of Music

Address: 6363 St. Charles Avenue, New Orleans, LA 70118-6195
Admissions Phone: 504-865-3240,-800-4-LOYOLA · **Admissions Fax:** 504-865-3383
Admissions E-mail: stieffel@loyno.edu

INSTITUTIONAL INFORMATION

Public/private: Private (nonprofit). Student/faculty Ratio: 2:1. Students in Parent Institution: 5,279.

STUDENT INFORMATION

Total Students in Program: 880. % Full-time: 11. % Female: 67.

RESEARCH FACILITIES

Research Facilities: Archives of New Orleans province of the Society of Jesus, RATHE College of Business Lab.

EXPENSES/FINANCIAL AID

Fees: $512. Books and Supplies: $650. Grants Range From: $1,000-$19,000. Loans Range From: $1-$18,500. % Receiving Financial Aid: 71. % Receiving Scholarships/Grants: 19. % Receiving Loans: 88. % Receiving Assistantships: 1. Average student debt, upon graduation: $27,355. Number of Teaching/Research Assistantships Granted Each Year: 8.

ADMISSIONS INFORMATION

Application Fee: $20. Regular Notification: Rolling. Transfer Students Accepted? Yes. Number of Applications Received: 13. % of Applicants Accepted: 85. % Accepted Who Enrolled: 64. Average GPA: 3.27.
Required Admission Factors: Essays/personal statement, letters of recommendation, transcript.
Other Admission Factors: Minimum 3.0 GPA and resume required. Conditional admission available to those whose undergraduate major was not music or have a GPA below 3.0.
Program-Specific Admission Factors: Placement exams required of MM and MMed program applicants.

EMPLOYMENT INFORMATION

Placement Office Available? Yes.

LUBBOCK CHRISTIAN UNIVERSITY
Graduate Studies

Address: 5601 19th Street, Lubbock, TX 79407
Admissions Phone: 806-720-7662 · Admissions Fax: 806-720-7661
Admissions E-mail: donna.taylor@lcu.edu · Web Address: www.lcu.edu/graduate

INSTITUTIONAL INFORMATION

Public/private: Private (nonprofit). Total Faculty: 16. % Faculty Female: 6. % Faculty Part-time: 31. Student/faculty Ratio: 10:1. Students in Parent Institution: 1,972

PROGRAMS

Master's offered in: Christian studies, philosophy and religion, religion/religious studies

STUDENT INFORMATION

Total Students in Program: 67. % Full-time: 37. % Female: 15. % Minority: 13. % International: 4.

EXPENSES/FINANCIAL AID

Annual Tuition: $3,000. Fees: $120. Books and Supplies: $400. Grants Range From: $300-$2,000. Loans Range From: $500-$2,000. % Receiving Financial Aid: 100. % Receiving Scholarships/Grants: 100. % Receiving Loans: 50. Types of Aid Available: Loans, Average student debt, upon graduation: $5,000.

ADMISSIONS INFORMATION

Application Fee: $35. Regular Application Deadline: 8/23. Regular Notification: Rolling. Transfer Students Accepted? Yes. Transfer Policy: Transfer as follows: 12 for MS, 9 for MA, 48 for MDiv. Number of Applications Received: 45. % of Applicants Accepted: 56. % Accepted Who Enrolled: 100. Average GPA: 3.6. Average GRE Verbal: 600.
Required Admission Factors: Letters of recommendation, transcript.
Other Admission Factors: Minimum 2.5 GPA required of MS and MDiv program applicants; minimum 3.0 GPA required of MA program applicants.

EMPLOYMENT INFORMATION

Placement Office Available? Yes. % Employed Within 6 Months: 100. % of master's grads employed in their field upon graduation: 100. Rate of placement: 90%. Average starting salary: $40,000.

LUTHER SEMINARY
Graduate Programs

Address: 2481 Como Avenue, St. Paul, MN 55108
Admissions Phone: 651-641-3203 · Admissions Fax: 651-641-3425
Admissions E-mail: gte@luthersem.edu
Web Address: www.luthersem.edu/gradstudies

INSTITUTIONAL INFORMATION

Public/private: Private (nonprofit).

STUDENT INFORMATION

Total Students in Program: 46. % Full-time: 20.

EXPENSES/FINANCIAL AID

Annual Tuition: $11,700. Fees: $1,400. Books and Supplies: $800. Grants Range From: $500-$10,000. Loans Range From: $500-$10,000. % Receiving Financial Aid: 50.

ADMISSIONS INFORMATION

Application Fee: $50. Regular Application Deadline: 1/1. Transfer Students Accepted? Yes. Transfer Policy: Maximum three courses may be transferred. Number of Applications Received: 65. % of Applicants Accepted: 71. % Accepted Who Enrolled: 100. Average GPA: 3.1.
Required Admission Factors: Essays/personal statement, GRE, letters of recommendation, transcript.
Other Admission Factors: GRE taken within 5 years; and minimum 3.25 GPA required. First master's degree in theology required.

EMPLOYMENT INFORMATION

% Employed Within 6 Months: 60. Rate of placement: 100%.

LUTHERAN SCHOOL OF THEOLOGY AT CHICAGO
ThM/ PhD Program

Address: 1100 East 55th Street, Room 343, Chicago, IL 60615-5199
Admissions Phone: 773-256-0762 · Admissions Fax: 773-256-0782
Admissions E-mail: jrodrigu@lstc.edu

INSTITUTIONAL INFORMATION

Public/private: Public. Students in Parent Institution: 64.

EXPENSES/FINANCIAL AID

% Receiving Financial Aid: 80. Number of Fellowships Granted Each Year: 11. Average amount of individual fellowships per year: $3,000. Number of Teaching/Research Assistantships Granted Each Year: 4. Average Salary Stipend: $500.

ADMISSIONS INFORMATION

Application Fee: $25. Regular Notification: Rolling. Transfer Students Accepted? Yes. Number of Applications Received: 26. % of Applicants Accepted: 58. % Accepted Who Enrolled: 93. Average GRE Verbal: 660. Average GRE Quantitative: 550. Average GRE Analytical: 600.
Required Admission Factors: GRE, transcript.
Program-Specific Admission Factors: 2 letters of recommendation required of ThM program applicants; 4 letters of recommendation required of doctoral program applicants.

EMPLOYMENT INFORMATION

% Employed Within 6 Months: 50.

LUTHERAN THEOLOGICAL SEMINARY AT GETTYSBURG
Graduate Programs

Address: 61 Seminary Ridge, Gettysburg, PA 17325-1795
Admissions E-mail: admissions@hgs.edu

INSTITUTIONAL INFORMATION
Public/private: Private (nonprofit). **Evening Classes Available?** Yes. **Students in Parent Institution:** 189.

STUDENT INFORMATION
Total Students in Program: 11. **% Full-time:** 82. **% Female:** 55.

RESEARCH FACILITIES
Research Facilities: Washington, DC Theological Consortium.

EXPENSES/FINANCIAL AID
Annual Tuition: $7,000. **Fees:** $1,835. **Books and Supplies:** $825. **Grants Range From:** $1,000-$7,800. **% Receiving Financial Aid:** 95. **% Receiving Scholarships/Grants:** 95. **% Receiving Loans:** 55.

ADMISSIONS INFORMATION
Application Fee: $35. **Regular Notification:** Rolling. **Transfer Students Accepted?** Yes. **Transfer Policy:** Maximum 59 credit hours may be transferred. Good academic standing required of transfer applicants. **Number of Applications Received:** 83. **% of Applicants Accepted:** 93. **% Accepted Who Enrolled:** 83. **Average GPA:** 2.7.
Required Admission Factors: Essays/personal statement, letters of recommendation, transcript.

LUTHERAN THEOLOGICAL SEMINARY AT PHILADELPHIA
Graduate School

Address: 7301 Germantown Avenue, Philadelphia, PA 19119
Admissions Phone: 215-248-6304 · **Admissions Fax:** 215-248-4577

INSTITUTIONAL INFORMATION
Public/private: Private (nonprofit). **Evening Classes Available?** Yes. **Students in Parent Institution:** 249.

STUDENT INFORMATION
Total Students in Program: 51. **% Full-time:** 8. **% Female:** 25.

EXPENSES/FINANCIAL AID
Annual Tuition: $7,800. **Books and Supplies:** $800. **Grants Range From:** $500-$5,600. **Loans Range From:** $500-$18,500. **% Receiving Financial Aid:** 40. **% Receiving Scholarships/Grants:** 100. **% Receiving Loans:** 80. **Average student debt, upon graduation:** $18,000.

ADMISSIONS INFORMATION
Application Fee: $25. **Regular Notification:** Rolling. **Transfer Students Accepted?** Yes. **Number of Applications Received:** 75. **% of Applicants Accepted:** 93. **% Accepted Who Enrolled:** 86. **Average GPA:** 3.0.
Required Admission Factors: Essays/personal statement, letters of recommendation, transcript.
Other Admission Factors: Minimum 3.0 GPA recommended.

LUTHERAN THEOLOGICAL SOUTHERN SEMINARY
Graduate Programs

Address: 4201 North Main Street, Columbia, SC 29203-5898
Admissions Phone: 800-804-5233
Admissions E-mail: thenderson@ltss.edu

INSTITUTIONAL INFORMATION
Public/private: Private (nonprofit). **Student/faculty Ratio:** 11:1. **Students in Parent Institution:** 172.

STUDENT INFORMATION
Total Students in Program: 172. **% Full-time:** 77. **% Female:** 46.

EXPENSES/FINANCIAL AID
Annual Tuition: $7,867. **Room & Board:** $4,500. **Books and Supplies:** $600. **% Receiving Financial Aid:** 90. **Average student debt, upon graduation:** $39,000. **Number of Teaching/Research Assistantships Granted Each Year:** 18.

ADMISSIONS INFORMATION
Application Fee: $35. **Regular Notification:** Rolling. **Transfer Students Accepted?** Yes. **Number of Applications Received:** 63. **% of Applicants Accepted:** 97. **% Accepted Who Enrolled:** 84.
Required Admission Factors: Essays/personal statement, letters of recommendation, transcript.
Other Admission Factors: Minimum 2.75 GPA required.

LYNN UNIVERSITY
The Graduate School

Address: 3601 North Military Trail, Boca Raton, FL 33431-5598
Admissions Phone: 561-237-7841 · **Admissions Fax:** 561-237-7100
Admissions E-mail: psieredzki@lynn.edu

INSTITUTIONAL INFORMATION
Public/private: Private (nonprofit). **Evening Classes Available?** Yes. **Students in Parent Institution:** 1,806.

STUDENT INFORMATION
Total Students in Program: 120. **% Full-time:** 28. **% Female:** 58.

EXPENSES/FINANCIAL AID
Annual Tuition: $10,560. **Room & Board:** $10,000. **Fees:** $120. **Books and Supplies:** $1,000.

ADMISSIONS INFORMATION
Application Fee: $50. **Regular Notification:** Rolling. **Transfer Students Accepted?** Yes. **Transfer Policy:** Course material may be required of transfer applicants for credit transfer. **Number of Applications Received:** 52. **% of Applicants Accepted:** 85. **% Accepted Who Enrolled:** 86. **Average GPA:** 3.1.
Required Admission Factors: Essays/personal statement, letters of recommendation, transcript.
Other Admission Factors: Minimum GMAT score of 400 and minimum 3.0 GPA required.

EMPLOYMENT INFORMATION
Placement Office Available? Yes.

MALONE COLLEGE
Graduate School

Address: 515 25th Street, NW, Canton, OH 44709
Admissions Phone: 330-471-8500 · **Admissions Fax:** 330-471-8343
Admissions E-mail: jbartolet@malone.edu · **Web Address:** gradschool@malone.edu

INSTITUTIONAL INFORMATION

Public/private: Private (nonprofit). **Evening Classes Available?** Yes. **Total Faculty:** 73. **% Faculty Female:** 49. **% Faculty Part-time:** 58. **Student/faculty Ratio:** 12:1. **Students in Parent Institution:** 2,134.

PROGRAMS

Master's offered in: Business administration/management; counselor education/school counseling and guidance services; curriculum and instruction; educational, instructional, and curriculum supervision; family practice nurse nurse practitioner; mental health counseling/counselor; nursing clinical specialist; pre-theology/pre-ministerial studies; reading teacher education; special education.

STUDENT INFORMATION

Total Students in Program: 269. **% Female:** 53.

EXPENSES/FINANCIAL AID

Annual Tuition: $6,120. **Books and Supplies:** $226. **Loans Range From:** $700-$12,000. **% Receiving Financial Aid:** 41. **% Receiving Scholarships/Grants:** 1. **% Receiving Loans:** 96. **Types of Aid Available:** Loans. **Average student debt, upon graduation:** $14,873.

ADMISSIONS INFORMATION

Application Fee: $25. **Regular Application Deadline:** 8/1. **Regular Notification:** Rolling. **Transfer Students Accepted?** Yes. **Number of Applications Received:** 152. **% of Applicants Accepted:** 95. **% Accepted Who Enrolled:** 60.
Required Admission Factors: Interview, letters of recommendation, transcript.
Other Admission Factors: Minimum 3.0 GPA required for regular admission; probationary admission possible.

EMPLOYMENT INFORMATION

Placement Office Available? Yes.

MANHATTAN SCHOOL OF MUSIC
Graduate Programs in Music

Address: 120 Claremont Avenue, New York, NY 10027
Admissions Phone: 212-749-2802, ext. 2 · **Admissions Fax:** 212-749-3025
Admissions E-mail: admission@msmnyc.edu

INSTITUTIONAL INFORMATION

Public/private: Private (nonprofit). **Student/faculty Ratio:** 8:1. **Students in Parent Institution:** 831.

STUDENT INFORMATION

Total Students in Program: 436. **% Full-time:** 97. **% Female:** 60.

EXPENSES/FINANCIAL AID

Annual Tuition: $21,100. **Fees:** $400. **Books and Supplies:** $800. **Grants Range From:** $1,000-$21,100. **Loans Range From:** $1,000-$18,500. **% Receiving Financial Aid:** 72. **% Receiving Scholarships/Grants:** 40. **% Receiving Loans:** 95. **Average student debt, upon graduation:** $40,000. **Number of Fellowships Granted Each Year:** 15. **Average amount of individual fellowships per year:** $3,000. **Number of Teaching/Research Assistantships Granted Each Year:** 4. **Average Salary Stipend:** $3,500.

ADMISSIONS INFORMATION

Application Fee: $100. **Transfer Students Accepted?** Yes. **Number of Applications Received:** 1,280. **% of Applicants Accepted:** 41. **% Accepted Who Enrolled:** 45.
Required Admission Factors: Essays/personal statement, transcript.
Other Admission Factors: Minimum 2.9 GPA required.

EMPLOYMENT INFORMATION

Placement Office Available? Yes.

MANHATTANVILLE COLLEGE
School of Graduate & Professional Studies

Address: 2900 Purchase Street, Purchase, NY 10577
Admissions Phone: 914-694-3425 · **Admissions Fax:** 914-694-3488
Admissions E-mail: rdowd@mville.edu

INSTITUTIONAL INFORMATION

Public/private: Private (nonprofit). **Students in Parent Institution:** 1,848.

STUDENT INFORMATION

Total Students in Program: 866. **% Female:** 89.

RESEARCH FACILITIES

Research Facilities: Holocaust and Human Rights Center.

EXPENSES/FINANCIAL AID

Annual Tuition: $9,000. **Fees:** $60.

ADMISSIONS INFORMATION

Application Fee: $40. **Regular Notification:** Rolling. **Transfer Students Accepted?** Yes. **Transfer Policy:** Maximum six credit hours may be transferred. **Number of Applications Received:** 20. **% of Applicants Accepted:** 90. **% Accepted Who Enrolled:** 100. **Average GPA:** 3.1.
Required Admission Factors: Essays/personal statement, interview, transcript.
Other Admission Factors: Minimum 2.5 GPA required.
Program-Specific Admission Factors: Students must have 3 to 5 years of work experience (some exceptions made for younger students).

EMPLOYMENT INFORMATION

Placement Office Available? Yes.

MANNES COLLEGE OF MUSIC
Graduate Program

Address: 150 West 85th Street, New York, NY 10024
Admissions Phone: 212-580-0210, ext. 247 · **Admissions Fax:** 212-580-1738
Admissions E-mail: mannesadmissions@newschool.edu

INSTITUTIONAL INFORMATION

Public/private: Private (nonprofit). **Student/faculty Ratio:** 2:1. **Students in Parent Institution:** 285.

STUDENT INFORMATION

Total Students in Program: 151. **% Full-time:** 100. **% Female:** 55.

EXPENSES/FINANCIAL AID

Fees: $230. **Books and Supplies:** $1,950. **Grants Range From:** $3,000-$16,600. **Loans Range From:** $8,500-$18,500. **% Receiving Financial Aid:** 85. **% Receiving Scholarships/Grants:** 85. **% Receiving Loans:** 96. **Average student debt, upon graduation:** $18,000.

ADMISSIONS INFORMATION

Application Fee: $100. **Transfer Students Accepted?** Yes. **Number of Applications Received:** 712.
Required Admission Factors: Interview, letters of recommendation, transcript.
Program-Specific Admission Factors: Placement exams in music theory, ear training, and dictation required.

MANSFIELD UNIVERSITY OF PENNSYLVANIA
Graduate Studies

Address: Academy Street, Alumni Hall G-11, Mansfield, PA 16933
Admissions Phone: 717-662-4806 · **Admissions Fax:** 717-662-4121
Admissions E-mail: jbrayer@mansfield.edu · **Web Address:** www.mansfield.edu

INSTITUTIONAL INFORMATION

Public/private: Public. **Student/faculty Ratio:** 20:1. **Students in Parent Institution:** 3,556.

PROGRAMS

Master's offered in: Nursing—registered nurse training (RN, ASN, BSN, MSN). **First Professional degree offered in:** Accounting, broadcast journalism, business administration/management, history, human resources management/personnel administration, international business, journalism, marketing/marketing management, nursing—registered nurse training (RN, ASN, BSN, MSN).

STUDENT INFORMATION

Total Students in Program: 429. **% Full-time:** 24. **% Female:** 79. **% Minority:** 4.

EXPENSES/FINANCIAL AID

Annual Tuition: In-state $5,772. / Out-of-state $9,236. **Room & Board:** $5,456. **Types of Aid Available:** Graduate assistantships, institutional work-study, loans. **Number of Teaching/Research Assistantships Granted Each Year:** 25. **Assistantship Compensation Includes:** Salary/stipend. **Average Salary Stipend:** $4,212.

ADMISSIONS INFORMATION

Application Fee: $25. **Regular Notification:** Rolling. **Transfer Students Accepted?** Yes. **Number of Applications Received:** 372. **% of Applicants Accepted:** 75. **% Accepted Who Enrolled:** 73. **Average GPA:** 3.03.
Required Admission Factors: Letters of recommendation, transcript. **Other Admission Factors:** Minimum 3.0 GPA required.

EMPLOYMENT INFORMATION

Placement Office Available? Yes. **% Employed Within 6 Months:** 100. **% of master's/doctoral grads employed in their field upon graduation:** 100.

MARIAN COLLEGE OF FOND DU LAC
Graduate Studies

Address: 45 South National Avenue, Fond du Lac, WI 54935
Admissions Phone: 800-262-7426, ext.7651 · **Admissions Fax:** 920-923-7167

INSTITUTIONAL INFORMATION

Public/private: Private (nonprofit). **Evening Classes Available?** Yes. **Students in Parent Institution:** 2,559.

STUDENT INFORMATION

Total Students in Program: 930. **% Full-time:** 5. **% Female:** 65.

EXPENSES/FINANCIAL AID

Annual Tuition: $4,482. **Books and Supplies:** $360. **Grants Range From:** $900-$6,900. **Loans Range From:** $1,000-$13,735. **% Receiving Scholarships/Grants:** 7. **% Receiving Loans:** 95.

ADMISSIONS INFORMATION

Application Fee: $25. **Regular Notification:** Rolling. **Transfer Students Accepted?** Yes. **Transfer Policy:** 3 years of work experience required of transfer applicants.
Required Admission Factors: Essays/personal statement, letters of recommendation, transcript.

MARLBORO COLLEGE
Graduate Center

Address: 28 Vernon Street, Brattleboro, VT 05363
Admissions Phone: 802-258-9209 or 888-258-5665 · **Admissions Fax:** 802-258-9201
Admissions E-mail: mdonahue@gradcenter.marlboro.edu
Web Address: www.gradcenter.marlboro.edu

INSTITUTIONAL INFORMATION

Public/private: Private (nonprofit). **Evening Classes Available?** Yes. **Students in Parent Institution:** 360

STUDENT INFORMATION

Total Students in Program: 70. **% Full-time:** 73. **% Female:** 59.

EXPENSES/FINANCIAL AID

Annual Tuition: $18,000. **Books and Supplies:** $500. **Grants Range From:** $1,000-$32,585. **Loans Range From:** $960-$32,585. **% Receiving Scholarships/Grants:** 5. **% Receiving Loans:** 100. **Types of Aid Available:** Loans.

ADMISSIONS INFORMATION

Regular Application Deadline: 8/15. **Regular Notification:** Rolling. **Transfer Students Accepted?** Yes. **Number of Applications Received:** 90. **% of Applicants Accepted:** 82. **% Accepted Who Enrolled:** 78. **Average GPA:** 3.0.
Required Admission Factors: Essays/personal statement, interview, letters of recommendation, transcript.
Program-Specific Admission Factors: Programming experience and knowledge of programming language required of Internet engineering program applicants.

MARQUETTE UNIVERSITY
College of Arts & Sciences

Address: PO Box 1881, Milwaukee, WI 53201-1881
Admissions Phone: 414-288-7137 · **Admissions Fax:** 414-288-1902
Admissions E-mail: debra.mccormick@mu.edu
Web Address: www.grad.marquette.edu

INSTITUTIONAL INFORMATION

Public/private: Private (nonprofit). **Students in Parent Institution:** 11,355.

PROGRAMS

Master's offered in: American government and politics (United States), American history (United States), analytical chemistry, applied economics, Bible/biblical studies, biochemistry/biophysics and molecular biology, biochemistry, bioinformatics, biological and physical sciences, biomathematics and bioinformatics, cell biology and anatomy, cell/cellular and molecular biology, cell/cellular biology and anatomical sciences, cell/cellular biology and histology, chemical physics, chemistry, clinical psychology, community psychology, developmental biology and embryology, economics, educational psychology, European history, exercise physiology, genetics, history, inorganic chemistry, international economics, international relations and affairs, mathematics, microbiology, molecular biochemistry, molecular biology, molecular biophysics, multi/interdisciplinary studies, neurobiology and neurophysiology, organic chemistry, philosophy and religion, philosophy, physical and theoretical chemistry, political science and government, religion/religious studies, reproductive biology, school psychology, theology/theological studies. **Doctorate offered in:** See above.

STUDENT INFORMATION

Total Students in Program: 202. **% Full-time:** 74. **% Female:** 44.

RESEARCH FACILITIES

Research Facilities: More than 40 research centers and labs.

EXPENSES/FINANCIAL AID

Annual Tuition: $10,800. **Room & Board:** $8,000. **Books and Supplies:** $400. **Grants Range From:** $600-$24,650. **Types of Aid Available:** Fellowships, graduate assistantships, loans, scholarships. **Number of Teaching/Research Assistantships Granted Each Year:** 21. **Assistantship Compensation Includes:** Full tuition remission, salary/stipend. **Average Salary Stipend:** $10,800.

ADMISSIONS INFORMATION

Application Fee: $40. **Regular Application Deadline:** 8/1. **Regular Notification:** Rolling. **Transfer Students Accepted?** Yes. **Transfer Policy:** Contact individual program for specific information. A list of program Webpages can be found at http://www.grad.mu.edu/programs.html. **Average GRE Verbal:** 536.5. **Average GRE Quantitative:** 611.2. **Average GRE Analytical:** 646.1. **Average GRE Analytical Writing:** 4.8.
Required Admission Factors: Essays/personal statement, letters of recommendation, transcript.
Other Admission Factors: Contact individual program for specific information. A list of program Web pages can be found at http://www.grad.mu.edu/programs.html.
Program-Specific Admission Factors: Contact individual program for specific information. A list of program webpages can be found at http://www.grad.mu.edu/programs.html.

EMPLOYMENT INFORMATION

Placement Office Available? Yes. **% Employed Within 6 Months:** 100. **% of master's grads employed in their field upon graduation:** 100. **Rate of placement:** 100%. **Average starting salary:** $35,000.

MARQUETTE UNIVERSITY
College of Communication

Address: PO Box 1881, Milwaukee, WI 53201-1881
Admissions Phone: 414-288-7137 · **Admissions Fax:** 414-288-1902
Admissions E-mail: debra.mccormick@mu.edu

INSTITUTIONAL INFORMATION

Public/private: Private (nonprofit). **Evening Classes Available?** Yes. **Students in Parent Institution:** 10,780.

STUDENT INFORMATION

Total Students in Program: 2,272. **% Full-time:** 38. **% Female:** 47.

RESEARCH FACILITIES

Research Facilities: More than 40 research centers and labs.

EXPENSES/FINANCIAL AID

Annual Tuition: $9,630. **Books and Supplies:** $400. **Grants Range From:** $335-$23,010. . **Number of Teaching/Research Assistantships Granted Each Year:** 18. **Average Salary Stipend:** $9,540.

ADMISSIONS INFORMATION

Application Fee: $40. **Regular Notification:** Rolling. **Transfer Students Accepted?** Yes. **Number of Applications Received:** 52. **% of Applicants Accepted:** 67. **% Accepted Who Enrolled:** 46. **Average GPA:** 3.56. **Average GRE Verbal:** 520. **Average GRE Quantitative:** 590. **Average GRE Analytical:** 580.

Required Admission Factors: Essays/personal statement, GRE, letters of recommendation, transcript.
Other Admission Factors: Minimum grade average of B and a 300-word statement of academic and professional goals required.

EMPLOYMENT INFORMATION

Placement Office Available? Yes.

MARSHALL UNIVERSITY GRADUATE COLLEGE
College of Fine Arts

Address: 1 John Marshall Drive, Huntington, WV 25755

INSTITUTIONAL INFORMATION

Public/private: Public. **Students in Parent Institution:** 13,643.

STUDENT INFORMATION

Total Students in Program: 3,820. **% Full-time:** 27. **% Female:** 68.

RESEARCH FACILITIES

Research Facilities: Center for Environmental, Geotechnical, & Applied Sciences, Office of Research & Economic Development. Marshall University merged with West Virginia Graduate College in July 1997 to form the Marshall University Graduate College.

EXPENSES/FINANCIAL AID

Annual Tuition: In-state $3,996. / Out-of-state $7,670. **Fees:** $488. **Grants Range From:** $500-$20,000. **Loans Range From:** $200-$18,500. **% Receiving Scholarships/Grants:** 48. **% Receiving Loans:** 90.

ADMISSIONS INFORMATION

Transfer Students Accepted? No.

EMPLOYMENT INFORMATION

Placement Office Available? Yes. **Rate of placement:** 85%.

MARSHALL UNIVERSITY GRADUATE COLLEGE
College of Liberal Arts

Address: 1 John Marshall Drive, Huntington, WV 25755

INSTITUTIONAL INFORMATION

Public/private: Public. **Students in Parent Institution:** 13,643

STUDENT INFORMATION

Total Students in Program: 3,820. **% Full-time:** 27. **% Female:** 68.

RESEARCH FACILITIES

Research Facilities: Center for Environmental, Geotechnical, & Applied Sciences, Office of Research & Economic Development. Marshall University merged with West Virginia Graduate College in July 1997 to form the Marshall University Graduate College.

EXPENSES/FINANCIAL AID

Annual Tuition: In-state $3,996. / Out-of-state $7,670. **Fees:** $488. **Grants Range From:** $500-$20,000. **Loans Range From:** $200-$18,500. **% Receiving Scholarships/Grants:** 48. **% Receiving Loans:** 90.

ADMISSIONS INFORMATION

Transfer Students Accepted? No.

EMPLOYMENT INFORMATION

Placement Office Available? Yes. **Rate of placement:** 85%.

MARSHALL UNIVERSITY GRADUATE COLLEGE
College of Science

Address: 1 John Marshall Drive, Huntington, WV 25755

INSTITUTIONAL INFORMATION
Public/private: Public. **Students in Parent Institution:** 13,643.

STUDENT INFORMATION
Total Students in Program: 3,820. **% Full-time:** 27. **% Female:** 68.

RESEARCH FACILITIES
Research Facilities: Center for Environmental, Geotechnical, & Applied Sciences, Office of Research & Economic Development. Marshall University merged with West Virginia Graduate College in July 1997 to form the Marshall University Graduate College.

EXPENSES/FINANCIAL AID
Annual Tuition: In-state $3,996. / Out-of-state $7,670. **Fees:** $488. **Grants Range From:** $500-$20,000. **Loans Range From:** $200-$18,500. **% Receiving Scholarships/Grants:** 48. **% Receiving Loans:** 90.

ADMISSIONS INFORMATION
Transfer Students Accepted? No.

EMPLOYMENT INFORMATION
Placement Office Available? Yes. **Rate of placement:** 85%.

MARSHALL UNIVERSITY GRADUATE COLLEGE
W. Page Pitt School of Journalism & Mass Communications

Address: 1 John Marshall Drive, Huntington, WV 25755

INSTITUTIONAL INFORMATION
Public/private: Public. **Evening Classes Available?** Yes. **Students in Parent Institution:** 13,643.

STUDENT INFORMATION
Total Students in Program: 3,820. **% Full-time:** 27. **% Female:** 68.

RESEARCH FACILITIES
Research Facilities: Center for Environmental, Geotechnical, & Applied Sciences, Office of Research & Economic Development. Marshall University merged with West Virginia Graduate College in July 1997 to form the Marshall University Graduate College.

EXPENSES/FINANCIAL AID
Annual Tuition: In-state $3,996. / Out-of-state $7,670. **Fees:** $488. **Grants Range From:** $500-$20,000. **Loans Range From:** $200-$18,500. **% Receiving Scholarships/Grants:** 48. **% Receiving Loans:** 90.

ADMISSIONS INFORMATION
Application Fee: $15. **Regular Notification:** Rolling. **Transfer Students Accepted?** Yes.
Required Admission Factors: GRE, transcript.
Other Admission Factors: Minimum 2.0 GPA required.

EMPLOYMENT INFORMATION
Placement Office Available? Yes. **Rate of placement:** 85%.

MARY BALDWIN COLLEGE
Graduate Program

Address: Staunton, VA 24401
Admissions Phone: 540-887-7211 · **Admissions Fax:** 540-887-7187
Admissions E-mail: jurquhart@mbc.edu

INSTITUTIONAL INFORMATION
Public/private: Private (nonprofit). **Evening Classes Available?** Yes. **Student/faculty Ratio:** 10:1. **Students in Parent Institution:** 1,564.

STUDENT INFORMATION
Total Students in Program: 75. **% Full-time:** 49. **% Female:** 81.

RESEARCH FACILITIES
Research Facilities: Access to Black Friars Theater.

EXPENSES/FINANCIAL AID
Annual Tuition: $6,210. **Books and Supplies:** $600. **Grants Range From:** $1,500-$3,000. **Loans Range From:** $3,100-$16,120. **% Receiving Loans:** 100.

ADMISSIONS INFORMATION
Application Fee: $35. **Regular Notification:** Rolling. **Transfer Students Accepted?** Yes. **Transfer Policy:** Maximum 6 courses (must be comparable) may be transferred. **Number of Applications Received:** 33. **% of Applicants Accepted:** 91. **% Accepted Who Enrolled:** 83. **Average GPA:** 3.0.
Required Admission Factors: Essays/personal statement, letters of recommendation, transcript.
Other Admission Factors: Minimum 3.0 GPA required.
Program-Specific Admission Factors: Audition required of theater program applicants.

EMPLOYMENT INFORMATION
Placement Office Available? Yes.

MARYGROVE COLLEGE
Graduate Admissions

Address: 8425 West McNichols Road, Detroit, MI 48221-2599
Admissions Phone: 1-800-627-9476, ext. 8200 · **Admissions Fax:** 313-927-1505
Admissions E-mail: ployd@marygrove.edu
Web Address: www.marygrove.edu/graduate/programs/index.asp

INSTITUTIONAL INFORMATION
Public/private: Private (nonprofit). **Evening Classes Available?** Yes. **Total Faculty:** 61. **% Faculty Female:** 69. **% Faculty Part-time:** 77. **Students in Parent Institution:** 6,097.

PROGRAMS
Master's offered in: Adult and continuing education administration; adult and continuing education and teaching; education leadership and administration; education; elementary education and teaching; English language and literature; human resources management/personnel administration; intercultural/multicultural and diversity studies; multi/interdisciplinary studies; reading teacher education; religion/religious studies; secondary education and teaching; teacher education and professional development, specific levels and methods.

STUDENT INFORMATION
Total Students in Program: 5,218. **% Full-time:** 97. **% Female:** 80.

EXPENSES/FINANCIAL AID
Annual Tuition: $9,000. **Fees:** $450. **Books and Supplies:** $600. **Grants Range From:** $1,375-$2,750. **Loans Range From:** $8,500-$18,500. **% Receiving Financial Aid:** 95. **% Receiving Scholarships/Grants:** 85. **% Receiving Loans:** 100. **Types of Aid Available:** Loans.

ADMISSIONS INFORMATION
Application Fee: $25. **Priority Application Deadline:** 3/1. **Regular Application Deadline:** 9/1. **Regular Notification:** Rolling. **Transfer Students Accepted?** Yes. **Number of Applications Received:** 1,875. **% of Applicants Accepted:** 80. **% Accepted Who Enrolled:** 96. **Average GPA:** 3.2.
Required Admission Factors: Essays/personal statement, transcript.
Recommended Admission Factors: MTTC (for Initial Teacher Certification Programs).

Other Admission Factors: Minimum 3.0 GPA and career plan required.

EMPLOYMENT INFORMATION
Placement Office Available? Yes.

MARYLAND INSTITUTE COLLEGE OF ART
Graduate Studies

Address: 1300 Mount Royal Avenue, Baltimore, MD 21217-4134
Admissions Phone: 410-225-2256 · **Admissions Fax:** 410-225-2408
Admissions E-mail: skelly@mica.edu
Web Address: www.mica.edu/academic/grad.cfm

INSTITUTIONAL INFORMATION
Public/private: Private (nonprofit). **Total Faculty:** 45. **% Faculty Female:** 60. **% Faculty Part-time:** 27. **Student/faculty Ratio:** 5:1. **Students in Parent Institution:** 1,608.

PROGRAMS
Master's offered in: Art teacher education, fine arts and art studies, graphic design, painting, photography, sculpture.

STUDENT INFORMATION
Total Students in Program: 206. **% Full-time:** 96. **% Female:** 65. **% Minority:** 16. **% International:** 4.

EXPENSES/FINANCIAL AID
Annual Tuition: $24,474. **Room & Board:** $6,980. **Fees:** $730. **Books and Supplies:** $3,500. **Grants Range From:** $1,500-$15,000. **% Receiving Financial Aid:** 85. **Types of Aid Available:** Fellowships, loans, scholarships, teaching internships.

ADMISSIONS INFORMATION
Application Fee: $50. **Regular Application Deadline:** 2/15. **Regular Notification:** 4/1. **Transfer Students Accepted?** No.
Required Admission Factors: Essays/personal statement, letters of recommendation, transcript.
Other Admission Factors: A curriculum vitae/resume is required as well as a portfolio of art work consisting of 18-20 images.

MARYLHURST UNIVERSITY
Graduate College

Address: 17600 Pacific Highway
PO Box 261, Marylhurst, OR 97036-0261
Admissions Phone: 503-699-6268 · **Admissions Fax:** 503-636-9526
Admissions E-mail: mking@marylhurst.edu

INSTITUTIONAL INFORMATION
Public/private: Private (nonprofit). **Evening Classes Available?** Yes. **Student/faculty Ratio:** 6:1. **Students in Parent Institution:** 988.

STUDENT INFORMATION
Total Students in Program: 231. **% Full-time:** 27. **% Female:** 63.

EXPENSES/FINANCIAL AID
Annual Tuition: $5,706. **Fees:** $195. **Books and Supplies:** $900. **Grants Range From:** $500-$2,000. **Loans Range From:** $2,000-$14,000. **% Receiving Financial Aid:** 47. **% Receiving Scholarships/Grants:** 15. **% Receiving Loans:** 75. **Average student debt, upon graduation:** $24,000.

ADMISSIONS INFORMATION
Application Fee: $80. **Regular Notification:** Rolling. **Transfer Students Accepted?** Yes. **Transfer Policy:** Maximum 9 credit hours with a minimum

grade average of B may be transferred. **Number of Applications Received:** 96. **% of Applicants Accepted:** 95. **% Accepted Who Enrolled:** 85. **Average GPA:** 3.2.
Required Admission Factors: Essays/personal statement, interview, letters of recommendation, transcript.
Other Admission Factors: Minimum 3.0 GPA and writing sample required.

MARYMOUNT UNIVERSITY
School of Arts & Sciences

Address: 2807 North Glebe Road, Arlington, VA 22207-4299
Admissions Phone: 703-284-5901 · **Admissions Fax:** 703-527-3815
Admissions E-mail: francesca.reed@marymount.edu
Web Address: www.marymount.edu/admissions/grad/sas.html

INSTITUTIONAL INFORMATION
Public/private: Private (nonprofit). **Evening Classes Available?** Yes. **Student/faculty Ratio:** 4:1. **Students in Parent Institution:** 3,590.

PROGRAMS
Master's offered in: Computer and information sciences; English language and literature; humanities/humanistic studies; interior architecture.

STUDENT INFORMATION
Total Students in Program: 1,478. **% Full-time:** 26. **% Female:** 71.

RESEARCH FACILITIES
Research Facilities: Center for Ethical Concerns.

EXPENSES/FINANCIAL AID
Annual Tuition: $9,216. **Fees:** $90. **Books and Supplies:** $500. **Grants Range From:** $930-$10,000. **Loans Range From:** $3,000-$18,500. **% Receiving Scholarships/Grants:** 10. **% Receiving Loans:** 86. **% Receiving Assistantships:** 2.

ADMISSIONS INFORMATION
Application Fee: $35. **Regular Notification:** Rolling. **Transfer Students Accepted?** Yes. **Number of Applications Received:** 50. **% of Applicants Accepted:** 98. **% Accepted Who Enrolled:** 65. **Average GPA:** 3.3. **Average GRE Verbal:** 411. **Average GRE Quantitative:** 586. **Average GRE Analytical:** 530.
Required Admission Factors: Interview, letters of recommendation, transcript.
Other Admission Factors: Minimum 3.0 GPA required.
Program-Specific Admission Factors: For computer science, applicants must have an undergraduate degree in computer science or engineering. Otherwise, applicants can enter the certificate program to meet prerequistes.

MARYWOOD UNIVERSITY
College of Liberal Arts and Sciences

Address: 2300 Adams Avenue, Scranton, PA 18509-1598
Admissions Phone: 570-340-6002 or 866-279-9663
Admissions Fax: 570-961-4744 · **Admissions E-mail:** grad_adm@marywood.edu
Web Address: www.marywood.edu

INSTITUTIONAL INFORMATION
Public/private: Private (nonprofit). **Evening Classes Available?** Yes. **Student/faculty Ratio:** 12:1. **Students in Parent Institution:** 2,925.

STUDENT INFORMATION
Total Students in Program: 1,257. **% Full-time:** 31. **% Female:** 77.

RESEARCH FACILITIES
Research Facilities: Psychological services clinic.

EXPENSES/FINANCIAL AID

Annual Tuition: $9,972. **Fees:** $650. **Books and Supplies:** $500. **Grants Range From:** $1,000-$15,500. **Loans Range From:** $1,500-$18,500. **% Receiving Financial Aid:** 50. **% Receiving Scholarships/Grants:** 35. **% Receiving Loans:** 90. **% Receiving Assistantships:** 5. **Types of Aid Available:** 1. **Average student debt, upon graduation:** $17,125. **Number of Teaching/Research Assistantships Granted Each Year:** 15 **Average Salary Stipend:** $350.

ADMISSIONS INFORMATION

Application Fee: $25. **Regular Notification:** Rolling. **Transfer Students Accepted?** Yes. **Transfer Policy:** Maximum number of credits that may be transferred varies by program. **Number of Applications Received:** 606. **% of Applicants Accepted:** 83. **% Accepted Who Enrolled:** 62. **Required Admission Factors:** Letters of recommendation. **Other Admission Factors:** Minimum 3.0 GPA required.

EMPLOYMENT INFORMATION

Placement Office Available? Yes. **Rate of placement:** 95%.

MASSACHUSETTS COLLEGE OF ART
Graduate Programs

Address: 621 Huntington Avenue, Boston, MA 02115-5882
Admissions Phone: 617-879-7200

INSTITUTIONAL INFORMATION

Public/private: Public. **Evening Classes Available?** Yes. **Student/faculty Ratio:** 4:1. **Students in Parent Institution:** 2,315.

STUDENT INFORMATION

Total Students in Program: 101. **% Full-time:** 72. **% Female:** 67.

EXPENSES/FINANCIAL AID

Annual Tuition: $9,200. **Fees:** $950. **Books and Supplies:** $100. **Loans :** $18,500. **% Receiving Financial Aid:** 79. **% Receiving Scholarships/Grants:** 2. **% Receiving Loans:** 96. **% Receiving Assistantships:** 90. **Number of Teaching/Research Assistantships Granted Each Year:** 50. **Average Salary Stipend:** $1,500.

ADMISSIONS INFORMATION

Application Fee: $75. **Transfer Students Accepted?** Yes. **Number of Applications Received:** 333. **% of Applicants Accepted:** 24. **% Accepted Who Enrolled:** 52.
Required Admission Factors: Essays/personal statement, letters of recommendation, transcript.

MASSACHUSETTS COLLEGE OF LIBERAL ARTS
Graduate Programs

Address: 375 Church Street, North Adams, MA 01247
Admissions Phone: 413-662-5381 · **Admissions Fax:** 413-662-5174

INSTITUTIONAL INFORMATION

Public/private: Public. **Evening Classes Available?** Yes. **Students in Parent Institution:** 1,520.

STUDENT INFORMATION

Total Students in Program: 128 **% Female:** 63.

EXPENSES/FINANCIAL AID

Annual Tuition: $2,610. **% Receiving Loans:** 100.

ADMISSIONS INFORMATION

Regular Notification: Rolling. **Transfer Students Accepted?** Yes.
Required Admission Factors: Essays/personal statement, interview, letters of recommendation, transcript.
Other Admission Factors: Minimum 2.75 GPA and writing sample required.

EMPLOYMENT INFORMATION

Placement Office Available? Yes.

MASSACHUSETTS INSTITUTE OF TECHNOLOGY
School of Humanities, Arts, & Social Sciences

Address: 77 Massachusetts Avenue, Room 3-103, Cambridge, MA 02139-4307
Admissions Phone: 617-253-2917 · **Admissions Fax:** 617-258-8304
Admissions E-mail: mitgrad@mit.edu
Web Address: web.mit.edu/admissions/www/graduate/

INSTITUTIONAL INFORMATION

Public/private: Private (nonprofit). **Total Faculty:** 145. **% Faculty Female:** 29. **% Faculty Part-time:** 1. **Student/faculty Ratio:** 2:1. **Students in Parent Institution:** 10,340.

PROGRAMS

Master's offered in: Economics; journalism; mass communications/media studies; political science and government; science, technology, and society. **Doctorate offered in:** Economics; linguistics; philosophy; political science and government; science, technology, and society.

STUDENT INFORMATION

Total Students in Program: 331. **% Full-time:** 98. **% Female:** 38. **% Minority:** 2. **% International:** 39.

RESEARCH FACILITIES

Research Facilities: There are a number of school-supported or affiliated research labs and centers. Please visit http://web.mit.edu/research/ for more information.

EXPENSES/FINANCIAL AID

Annual Tuition: $29,400. **Room & Board:** $8,710. **Fees:** $200. **Books and Supplies:** $1,050. **Grants Range From:** $2,450-$91,005. **Loans Range From:** $2,054-$48,000. **% Receiving Loans:** 9. **Types of Aid Available:** Graduate assistantships, loans, scholarships. **Number of Fellowships Granted Each Year:** 115. **Number of Teaching/Research Assistantships Granted Each Year:** 135. **Assistantship Compensation Includes:** Full tuition remission, salary/stipend.

ADMISSIONS INFORMATION

Application Fee: $70. **Regular Application Deadline:** 12/31. **Regular Notification:** 4/1. **Transfer Students Accepted?** No. **Number of Applications Received:** 1,633. **% of Applicants Accepted:** 8. **% Accepted Who Enrolled:** 51. **Average GRE Verbal:** 649. **Average GRE Quantitative:** 740. **Average GRE Analytical:** 732.
Required Admission Factors: Essays/personal statement, GRE, letters of recommendation, transcript.
Other Admission Factors: Minimum TOEFL is 600 (paper) and 250 (computer) except linguistics and philosophy requires 577 (paper) and 233 (computer).
Program-Specific Admission Factors: The School of Humanities, Arts & Social Sciences includes the departments of comparable media studies, economics, linguistics and philosophy, political science, science, technology and sociology, and writing and humanity studies. Please check with departments for specific admission policies.

% Employed Within 6 Months: 52.4. % of master's/doctoral grads employed in their field upon graduation: 39.6/12.7. Rate of placement: 63.5%.

MASSACHUSETTS INSTITUTE OF TECHNOLOGY
School of Science

Address: 77 Massachusetts Avenue, Room 3-103, Cambridge, MA 02139-4307
Admissions Phone: 617-253-2917 · **Admissions Fax:** 617-258-8304
Admissions E-mail: mitgrad@mit.edu
Web Address: web.mit.edu/admissions/www/graduate/

INSTITUTIONAL INFORMATION
Public/private: Private (nonprofit). **Total Faculty:** 270. **% Faculty Female:** 13. **Student/faculty Ratio:** 4:1. **Students in Parent Institution:** 10,340.

PROGRAMS
Master's offered in: Atmospheric sciences and meteorology; chemistry; geology/earth science; geophysics and seismology; meteorology; oceanography, chemical and physical; physics; planetary astronomy and science. **Doctorate offered in:** Atmospheric sciences and meteorology; chemistry; geology/earth science; geophysics and seismology; mathematics; meteorology; multi/interdisciplinary studies; neuroscience; oceanography, chemical and physical; physics; planetary astronomy and science.

STUDENT INFORMATION
Total Students in Program: 1,107. **% Full-time:** 98. **% Female:** 34. **% Minority:** 4. **% International:** 33.

RESEARCH FACILITIES
Research Facilities: There are a number of school-supported or affiliated research labs and centers. Please visit http://web.mit.edu/research/ for more information.

EXPENSES/FINANCIAL AID
Annual Tuition: $29,400. **Room & Board:** $8,710. **Fees:** $200. **Books and Supplies:** $1,050. **Grants Range From:** $2,145-$88,010. **Loans Range From:** $3,105-$27,545. **% Receiving Loans:** 3. **Types of Aid Available:** Fellowships, graduate assistantships, loans, scholarships. **Number of Fellowships Granted Each Year:** 328. **Number of Teaching/Research Assistantships Granted Each Year:** 766. **Assistantship Compensation Includes:** Full tuition remission, salary/stipend.

ADMISSIONS INFORMATION
Application Fee: $70. **Regular Application Deadline:** 12/15. **Regular Notification:** 4/1. **Transfer Students Accepted?** No. **Number of Applications Received:** 2,812. **% of Applicants Accepted:** 19. **% Accepted Who Enrolled:** 37. **Average GRE Verbal:** 606. **Average GRE Quantitative:** 766. **Average GRE Analytical:** 720.
Required Admission Factors: Essays/personal statement, GRE, letters of recommendation, transcript.
Other Admission Factors: TOEFL minimum is 600 (paper) and 250 (computer).
Program-Specific Admission Factors: The School of Science includes the departments of biology; brain and cognitive science; chemistry; Earth, atmospheric and planetary science; mathematics; and physics. Please check with departments for specific admission policies. See http://web.mit.edu/education/

EMPLOYMENT INFORMATION
% Employed Within 6 Months: 40.4. % of master's/doctoral grads employed in their field upon graduation: 31.6/8.9. Rate of placement: 63.5%. Average starting salary: $58,431.

MASSACHUSETTS SCHOOL OF PROFESSIONAL PSYCHOLOGY
Graduate Program

Address: 221 Rivermoor Street, Boston, MA 02132
Admissions Phone: 617-327-6777 or 888-664-MSPP
Admissions Fax: 617-327-4447 · **Admissions E-mail:** mmurga@mspp.edu
Web Address: www.mspp.edu

INSTITUTIONAL INFORMATION
Public/private: Private (nonprofit). **Student/faculty Ratio:** 13:1. **Students in Parent Institution:** 177.

PROGRAMS
Doctorate offered in: Clinical psychology; psychology.

STUDENT INFORMATION
Total Students in Program: 177. **% Full-time:** 81. **% International:** 15.

EXPENSES/FINANCIAL AID
Room & Board: $18,131. **Fees:** $0. **Books and Supplies:** $742. **Grants Range From:** $500-$3,000. **Loans Range From:** $500-$18,500. **% Receiving Financial Aid:** 57. **% Receiving Scholarships/Grants:** 90. **% Receiving Loans:** 100. **Average student debt, upon graduation:** $42,022. **Number of Teaching/Research Assistantships Granted Each Year:** 28. **Assistantship Compensation Includes:** Salary/stipend. **Average Salary Stipend:** $1,240.

ADMISSIONS INFORMATION
Application Fee: $50. **Regular Application Deadline:** 1/9. **Regular Notification:** March. **Transfer Students Accepted?** No. **Number of Applications Received:** 250. **% of Applicants Accepted:** 32. **% Accepted Who Enrolled:** 71. **Average GPA:** 3.34. **Average GRE Verbal:** 547. **Average GRE Quantitative:** 584.
Required Admission Factors: Essays/personal statement, GRE, interview, letters of recommendation, transcript.
Other Admission Factors: Minimum 3.0 GPA recommended.

EMPLOYMENT INFORMATION
% Employed Within 6 Months: 90. Average starting salary: $40,000.

MCGILL UNIVERSITY
Graduate and Postdoctoral Studies

Address: 845 Sherbrooke Street West, Room 400, Montreal, Quebec, QC H3A 2T5 Canada
Admissions Phone: 514-398-3990 · **Admissions Fax:** 514-398-1626
Admissions E-mail: graduate.admissions@mcgill.ca · **Web Address:** www.mcgill.ca/gps

INSTITUTIONAL INFORMATION
Public/private: Public. **Students in Parent Institution:** 32,532

PROGRAMS
Master's offered in: Accounting; agricultural economics; agricultural/biological engineering and bioengineering; animal sciences; anthropology; architectural engineering; architectural history and criticism; architecture (BArch, BA/BS, MArch, MA/MS, PhD); architecture and related programs; art history, criticism, and conservation; atmospheric sciences and meteorology; biochemistry; biomedical/medical engineering; biotechnology; business/managerial economics; business/managerial operations; cell biology and anatomy; chemical engineering; city/urban, community, and regional planning; civil engineering; communications studies/speech communication and rhetoric; counseling psychol-

ogy; counselor education/school counseling and guidance services; dental clinical sciences (ms, PhD); East Asian studies; economics; education leadership and administration; education; educational psychology; electrical, electronics, and communications engineering; entomology; entrepreneurship/entrepreneurial studies; environmental design/architecture; finance; food science; French studies; genetic counseling/counselor; geography; German studies; Hispanic American, Puerto Rican, and Mexican American/Chicano studies; history; human/medical genetics; immunology; international business; international finance; Islamic studies; Italian studies; Jewish/Judaic studies; law (LLB, JD); library science/librarianship; linguistics; marketing/marketing management; mathematics; mechanical engineering; microbiological sciences and immunology; microbiology; mining and mineral engineering; music history, literature, and theory; music performance; music teacher education; music theory and composition; music; musicology and ethnomusicology; Near and Middle Eastern studies; nursing—registered nurse training (RN, ASN, BSN, MSN); operations management and supervision; oral/maxillofacial surgery (certification MS, PhD); parasitology; pathology/experimental pathology; philosophy; physics; physiology; plant sciences; psychology; Russian studies; Slavic studies; sociology; Spanish and Iberian studies; teaching English as a second or foreign language/ESL language instructor; teaching English or French as a second or foreign language; teaching French as a second or foreign language; theology/theological studies; urban studies/affairs. **Doctorate offered in:** Architecture (BArch, BA/BS, MArch, MA/MS, PhD), East Asian studies, French studies, German studies, Near and Middle Eastern studies, Russian studies, Slavic studies, Spanish and Iberian studies.

STUDENT INFORMATION

Total Students in Program: 7,812. **% Full-time:** 73. **% Female:** 52. **% International:** 20.

RESEARCH FACILITIES

Research Facilities: As one of North America's leading research institutions, McGill University works in close cooperation with researchers at other institutions in Quebec, in Canada and throughout the world.

EXPENSES/FINANCIAL AID

Annual Tuition: Native Canadians $1,668. / Non-Canadians $4,173. **Room & Board (On/off Campus):** $8,082/$9,600. **Fees:** $1,300. **Books and Supplies:** $1,000. **Types of Aid Available:** Fellowships, graduate assistantships, grants, institutional work-study, loans, scholarships. **Assistantship Compensation Includes:** Partial tuition remission, salary/stipend.

ADMISSIONS INFORMATION

Application Fee: $60. **Regular Application Deadline:** 6/1. **Regular Notification:** Rolling. **Transfer Students Accepted?** Yes. **Transfer Policy:** Please consult the individual departments for application procedures and deadlines. The listing is at http://www.mcgill.ca/applying/graduate/. **Number of Applications Received:** 9,843. **% of Applicants Accepted:** 34. **% Accepted Who Enrolled:** 59.
Required Admission Factors: Letters of recommendation, transcript.
Other Admission Factors: Minimum 3.0 on 4.0 Cumulative GPA required (N.B. some departments have higher minimum CGPA requirements). TOEFL or IELTS required for non-Canadian applicants whose mother tongue is not English.
Program-Specific Admission Factors: Follow links from www.mcgill.ca/applying/graduate to individual department sites for specific requirements for each department, including application deadlines.

EMPLOYMENT INFORMATION

Placement Office Available? Yes.

MEDICAL COLLEGE OF OHIO
Graduate School

Address: 3000 Arlington
PO Box 10008, Toledo, OH 43699-0008
Admissions Phone: 419-383-4112 · **Admissions Fax:** 419-383-6140

INSTITUTIONAL INFORMATION

Public/private: Public. **Student/faculty Ratio:** 2:1. **Students in Parent Institution:** 933.

STUDENT INFORMATION

Total Students in Program: 341. **% Full-time:** 50. **% Female:** 64.

EXPENSES/FINANCIAL AID

Room & Board: $600. **Fees:** $420. **Books and Supplies:** $1,300. **Loans Range From:** $1,000-$18,500. **% Receiving Scholarships/Grants:** 6. **% Receiving Loans:** 85. **% Receiving Assistantships:** 4.

ADMISSIONS INFORMATION

Application Fee: $30. **Regular Notification:** Rolling. **Transfer Students Accepted?** Yes. **Transfer Policy:** Maximum 1/3 of total credit hours required may be transferred for some programs. **Number of Applications Received:** 103. **% of Applicants Accepted:** 58. **% Accepted Who Enrolled:** 57. **Average GPA:** 3.64. **Average GRE Verbal:** 475. **Average GRE Quantitative:** 632. **Average GRE Analytical:** 610.
Required Admission Factors: GRE, letters of recommendation, transcript.
Other Admission Factors: Minimum 3.0 GPA required.

EMPLOYMENT INFORMATION

% Employed Within 6 Months: 98. **% of master's/doctoral grads employed in their field upon graduation:** 96/98.

MEDICAL UNIVERSITY OF SOUTH CAROLINA
College of Graduate Studies

Address: 171 Ashley Avenue, Charleston, SC 29425-2970
Admissions Phone: 843-792-9620 · **Admissions Fax:** 843-792-6590
Admissions E-mail: youngh@musc.edu

INSTITUTIONAL INFORMATION

Public/private: Public. **Students in Parent Institution:** 2,357.

STUDENT INFORMATION

Total Students in Program: 946. **% Full-time:** 56. **% Female:** 71.

RESEARCH FACILITIES

Research Facilities: The MUSC Medical Center, The Medical University Hospital, The Albert Florens Storm Memorial Eye Institute, The Children's Hospital, The Hollings Cancer Center, The Institute of Psychiatry, and the Walton Research Building.

EXPENSES/FINANCIAL AID

% Receiving Scholarships/Grants: 39. **% Receiving Loans:** 90.

ADMISSIONS INFORMATION

Application Fee: $55. **Regular Notification:** Rolling. **Transfer Students Accepted?** Yes. **Number of Applications Received:** 145. **% of Applicants Accepted:** 60. **Average GRE Verbal:** 519. **Average GRE Quantitative:** 656. **Average GRE Analytical:** 655.
Required Admission Factors: GRE, letters of recommendation, transcript.
Other Admission Factors: Minimum GRE score of 1650 and minimum 3.0 GPA required.

MEMORIAL UNIVERSITY OF NEWFOUNDLAND
Faculty of Arts

Address: St. John's, Newfoundland, A1B 3X5 Canada

INSTITUTIONAL INFORMATION

Public/private: Public. **Students in Parent Institution:** 16,000.

RESEARCH FACILITIES

Research Facilities: Canadian Centre for International Fisheries Training and Development, Centre for Earth Resources Research, Centre for International Business Studies, Centre for Management Development, Centre for Material Culture Studies, Institute for Folklore Studies.

EXPENSES/FINANCIAL AID
Fees: $60. Books and Supplies: $1,500. Grants Range From: $3,000-$17,000.

ADMISSIONS INFORMATION
Application Fee: $40. Transfer Students Accepted? No.
Required Admission Factors: Letters of recommendation, transcript.

MEMORIAL UNIVERSITY OF NEWFOUNDLAND
Marine Institute

Address: St. John's, Newfoundland, A1B 3X5 Canada
Admissions Phone: 800-563-5799

INSTITUTIONAL INFORMATION
Public/private: Public. Students in Parent Institution: 16,000.

RESEARCH FACILITIES
Research Facilities: Canadian Centre for International Fisheries Training and Development, Centre for Earth Resources Research, Centre for International Business Studies, Centre for Management Development, Centre for Material Culture Studies, Institute for Folklore Studies.

EXPENSES/FINANCIAL AID
Fees: $60. Books and Supplies: $1,500. Grants Range From: $3,000-$17,000.

ADMISSIONS INFORMATION
Application Fee: $40. Regular Notification: Rolling. Transfer Students Accepted? No. Number of Applications Received: 17. % of Applicants Accepted: 47. % Accepted Who Enrolled: 62.
Required Admission Factors: Letters of recommendation, transcript.

MEMORIAL UNIVERSITY OF NEWFOUNDLAND
School of Human Kinetics & Recreation

Address: St. John's, Newfoundland, A1B 3X5 Canada
Admissions Phone: 709-737-8130 · Admissions Fax: 709-737-3979
Admissions E-mail: mdwhite@mun.ca

INSTITUTIONAL INFORMATION
Public/private: Public. Students in Parent Institution: 16,000.

RESEARCH FACILITIES
Research Facilities: Canadian Centre for International Fisheries Training and Development, Centre for Earth Resources Research, Centre for International Business Studies, Centre for Management Development, Centre for Material Culture Studies, Institute for Folklore Studies.

EXPENSES/FINANCIAL AID
Fees: $60. Books and Supplies: $1,500. Grants Range From: $3,000-$17,000. % Receiving Financial Aid: 80. Number of Fellowships Granted Each Year: 2. Number of Teaching/Research Assistantships Granted Each Year: 3.

ADMISSIONS INFORMATION
Application Fee: $40. Regular Notification: Rolling. Transfer Students Accepted? Yes.
Required Admission Factors: Letters of recommendation, transcript.
Other Admission Factors: Minimum grade average of 65% required.

MEMORIAL UNIVERSITY OF NEWFOUNDLAND
School of Social Work

Address: St. John's, Newfoundland, A1B 3X5 Canada
Admissions Phone: 709-737-4859 · Admissions Fax: 709-737-2408
Admissions E-mail: mhutchen@mun.ca

INSTITUTIONAL INFORMATION
Public/private: Public. Student/faculty Ratio: 2:1. Students in Parent Institution: 16,000.

RESEARCH FACILITIES
Research Facilities: Canadian Centre for International Fisheries Training and Development, Centre for Earth Resources Research, Centre for International Business Studies, Centre for Management Development, Centre for Material Culture Studies, Institute for Folklore Studies.

EXPENSES/FINANCIAL AID
Fees: $60. Books and Supplies: $1,500. Grants Range From: $3,000-$17,000. % Receiving Financial Aid: 20. Number of Fellowships Granted Each Year: 12. Average amount of individual fellowships per year: $1,000.

ADMISSIONS INFORMATION
Application Fee: $40. Transfer Students Accepted? Yes.
Required Admission Factors: Essays/personal statement, letters of recommendation, transcript.
Program-Specific Admission Factors: Minimum 2 years of social work experience and BSW with a minimum grade average of B required of master's program applicants. Minimum 3 years of social work experience and MSW required of doctoral program applicants.

EMPLOYMENT INFORMATION
% Employed Within 6 Months: 100. % of master's grads employed in their field upon graduation: 100.

MEMPHIS COLLEGE OF ART
Graduate Programs

Address: Overton Park
1930 Poplar Avenue, Memphis, TN 38104
Admissions Phone: 901-272-5151 · Admissions Fax: 901-272-5158
Admissions E-mail: amoore@mca.edu

INSTITUTIONAL INFORMATION
Public/private: Private (nonprofit). Student/faculty Ratio: 4:1. Students in Parent Institution: 284.

STUDENT INFORMATION
Total Students in Program: 34. % Full-time: 88. % Female: 47.

EXPENSES/FINANCIAL AID
Annual Tuition: $12,940. Fees: $250. Books and Supplies: $1,200. Grants Range From: $1,000-$4,000. Loans Range From: $5,000-$18,500. % Receiving Financial Aid: 90. % Receiving Scholarships/Grants: 97. % Receiving Loans: 69. Number of Teaching/Research Assistantships Granted Each Year: 4. Average Salary Stipend: $2,200.

ADMISSIONS INFORMATION
Application Fee: $25. Regular Notification: Rolling. Transfer Students Accepted? Yes. Number of Applications Received: 70. % of Applicants Accepted: 60. % Accepted Who Enrolled: 38. Average GPA: 3.0.
Required Admission Factors: Essays/personal statement, letters of recommendation, transcript.

Other Admission Factors: 15-piece portfolio required. Minimum 3.0 GPA recommended.

EMPLOYMENT INFORMATION
Placement Office Available? Yes.

MEMPHIS THEOLOGICAL SEMINARY
Graduate Programs

Address: 168 East Parkway South, Memphis, TN 38104-4395
Admissions Phone: 800-822-0687 or 901-458-8232 · Admissions Fax: 901-452-4051

INSTITUTIONAL INFORMATION
Public/private: Private (nonprofit). Evening Classes Available? Yes. Student/faculty Ratio: 27:1. Students in Parent Institution: 278.

STUDENT INFORMATION
Total Students in Program: 26. % Full-time: 100. % Female: 35.

EXPENSES/FINANCIAL AID
Annual Tuition: $4,680. Books and Supplies: $500.

ADMISSIONS INFORMATION
Application Fee: $25. Regular Notification: Rolling. Transfer Students Accepted? Yes. Transfer Policy: Minimum 2.0 GPA required of transfer applicants. Number of Applications Received: 87. % of Applicants Accepted: 97. % Accepted Who Enrolled: 90. Average GPA: 2.89.
Required Admission Factors: Essays/personal statement, letters of recommendation, transcript.
Other Admission Factors: Minimum 2.5 GPA required.

EMPLOYMENT INFORMATION
Placement Office Available? Yes. Rate of placement: 90%.

MERCY COLLEGE
Graduate Programs

Address: 555 Broadway, Dobbs Ferry, NY 10522
Admissions Phone: 800-MERCY-NY
Admissions E-mail: benoma@mercynet.edu

INSTITUTIONAL INFORMATION
Public/private: Private (nonprofit). Evening Classes Available? Yes. Students in Parent Institution: 9,254.

STUDENT INFORMATION
Total Students in Program: 1,922. % Full-time: 32. % Female: 70.

EXPENSES/FINANCIAL AID
Annual Tuition: $9,960.

ADMISSIONS INFORMATION
Application Fee: $35. Regular Notification: Rolling. Transfer Students Accepted? Yes.
Required Admission Factors: Interview, transcript.
Other Admission Factors: Minimum 3.0 GPA required.

EMPLOYMENT INFORMATION
Placement Office Available? Yes.

MERCYHURST COLLEGE
Graduate Program

Address: Glenwood Hills, Erie, PA 16546
Admissions Phone: 814-824-2297 · Admissions Fax: 814-824-2055

INSTITUTIONAL INFORMATION
Public/private: Private (nonprofit). Evening Classes Available? Yes. Students in Parent Institution: 2,708.

STUDENT INFORMATION
Total Students in Program: 150. % Full-time: 51. % Female: 60.

EXPENSES/FINANCIAL AID
Annual Tuition: $6,096. Fees: $125. Grants Range From: $4,000-$5,000. % Receiving Assistantships: 25.

ADMISSIONS INFORMATION
Application Fee: $35. Regular Notification: Rolling. Transfer Students Accepted? Yes. Transfer Policy: Maximum 9 credit hours with a minimum grade of B may be transferred. Average GPA: 3.0.
Required Admission Factors: Essays/personal statement, transcript.
Other Admission Factors: Minimum MAT score in the 50th percentile and minimum 3.0 GPA required.

EMPLOYMENT INFORMATION
Placement Office Available? Yes.

MEREDITH COLLEGE
The John E. Weems Graduate School— Master of Music Performance & Pedagogy

Address: 3800 Hillsborough Street, Raleigh, NC 27607-5298
Admissions Phone: 919-760-8423 · Admissions Fax: 919-760-2898
Admissions E-mail: graduate@meredith.edu
Web Address: www.meredith.edu/graduate/academics/mm.htm

INSTITUTIONAL INFORMATION
Public/private: Private (nonprofit). Evening Classes Available? Yes. Students in Parent Institution: 2,543.

PROGRAMS
Master's offered in: Music pedagogy, music performance.

STUDENT INFORMATION
Total Students in Program: 142. % Full-time: 54. % Female: 100.

EXPENSES/FINANCIAL AID
Annual Tuition: $6,030. Books and Supplies: $300.

ADMISSIONS INFORMATION
Application Fee: $50. Priority Application Deadline: 7/1. Regular Application Deadline: 7/1. Regular Notification: Rolling. Transfer Students Accepted? Yes. Number of Applications Received: 2. % of Applicants Accepted: 100. % Accepted Who Enrolled: 100.
Required Admission Factors: Essays/personal statement, interview, letters of recommendation, transcript.

METHODIST THEOLOGICAL SCHOOL IN OHIO
Graduate Programs

Address: 3081 Columbus Pike
PO Box 8004, Delaware, OH 43015-8004
Admissions Phone: 800-333-6876 or 740-362-3371 · Admissions Fax: 740-362-3135
Admissions E-mail: admit@mtso.edu

INSTITUTIONAL INFORMATION

Public/private: Private (nonprofit). **Evening Classes Available?** Yes. **Student/faculty Ratio:** 17:1. **Students in Parent Institution:** 277..

STUDENT INFORMATION

Total Students in Program: 87. **% Full-time:** 100.

EXPENSES/FINANCIAL AID

Annual Tuition: $10,640. **Fees:** $25. **Books and Supplies:** $1,176. **Grants Range From:** $300-$11,900. **Loans Range From:** $300-$18,500. **% Receiving Financial Aid:** 80. **% Receiving Scholarships/Grants:** 96. **% Receiving Loans:** 57. **Average student debt, upon graduation:** $15,770.

ADMISSIONS INFORMATION

Application Fee: $35. **Transfer Students Accepted?** Yes. **Transfer Policy:** One-half of degree requirements may be transferred. Letter of honorable dismissal from academic dean. **Number of Applications Received:** 125. **Average GPA:** 3.12.
Required Admission Factors: Essays/personal statement, letters of recommendation, transcript.
Other Admission Factors: Minimum 2.5 GPA, autobiographical statement, and three letters of recommendation required.
Program-Specific Admission Factors: Interview required of counseling ministries program applicants.

MIAMI UNIVERSITY
Graduate School

Address: 102 Roudebush Hall, Oxford, OH 45056
Admissions Phone: 513-529-3734 · **Admissions Fax:** 513-529-3762
Admissions E-mail: gradschool@muohio.edu
Web Address: www.miami.muohio.edu/graduate/

INSTITUTIONAL INFORMATION

Public/private: Public. **Students in Parent Institution:** 19,351.

STUDENT INFORMATION

Total Students in Program: 1,308. **% Full-time:** 78. **% Female:** 59. **% Minority:** 24. **% International:** 14.

EXPENSES/FINANCIAL AID

Annual Tuition: In-state $5,954. / Out-of-state $13,628. **Room & Board:** $6,500. **Fees:** $1,185. **Books and Supplies:** $1,500.

ADMISSIONS INFORMATION

Application Fee: $35. **Regular Application Deadline:** 3/1. **Regular Notification:** Rolling. **Transfer Students Accepted?** Yes. **Transfer Policy:** Each program determines what credits/courses they will accept from another accreditated university. We have several application deadlines from 11/1 to 3/1 for fall enrollment. Otherwise admission and applications are on a rolling basis. **Number of Applications Received:** 1,290. **% of Applicants Accepted:** 48. **% Accepted Who Enrolled:** 51. **Average GRE Verbal:** 491. **Average GRE Quantitative:** 593. **Average GRE Analytical:** 599. **Average GRE Analytical Writing:** 5.
Required Admission Factors: Transcript.
Other Admission Factors: 2.75 (4.0 scale), a minimum 3.0 for all graduate level work attempted.

EMPLOYMENT INFORMATION

Placement Office Available? Yes.

MICHIGAN TECHNOLOGICAL UNIVERSITY
College of Sciences & Arts

Address: 1400 Townsend Drive, Houghton, MI 49931-1295
Admissions Phone: 906-487-2327 · **Admissions Fax:** 906-487-2245

Admissions E-mail: jeoliver@mtu.edu

INSTITUTIONAL INFORMATION

Public/private: Public. **Student/faculty Ratio:** 1:1. **Students in Parent Institution:** 6,336.

STUDENT INFORMATION

Total Students in Program: 670. **% Full-time:** 81. **% Female:** 31.

RESEARCH FACILITIES

Research Facilities: Center for Experimental Computation, Center for Advanced Manufacturing Research, Environmental Engineering Center, Lake States Forest Resource and Environmental Management Coorperative, Lake Superior Ecosystem Research Center.

EXPENSES/FINANCIAL AID

Annual Tuition: In-state $4,872. / Out-of-state $10,008. **Fees:** $136. **Books and Supplies:** $600. **Loans Range From:** $300-$15,000. **% Receiving Financial Aid:** 95. **% Receiving Loans:** 3. **% Receiving Assistantships:** 82. **Average student debt, upon graduation:** $12,580. **Number of Fellowships Granted Each Year:** 11. **Average amount of individual fellowships per year:** $14,700. **Number of Teaching/Research Assistantships Granted Each Year:** 172. **Average Salary Stipend:** $4,475.

ADMISSIONS INFORMATION

Application Fee: $30. **Regular Notification:** Rolling. **Transfer Students Accepted?** No. **Transfer Policy:** Maximum 1/3 of total non-research credit hours required may be transferred. **Number of Applications Received:** 336. **% of Applicants Accepted:** 51. **% Accepted Who Enrolled:** 43. **Average GRE Verbal:** 532. **Average GRE Quantitative:** 724. **Average GRE Analytical:** 671.
Required Admission Factors: Essays/personal statement, GRE, transcript. **Other Admission Factors:** Minimum 2.7 GPA recommended for most programs.

EMPLOYMENT INFORMATION

Placement Office Available? Yes. **% Employed Within 6 Months:** 90. **% of master's/doctoral grads employed in their field upon graduation:** 95/95. **Rate of placement:** 95%. **Average starting salary:** $55,000.

MICHIGAN TECHNOLOGICAL UNIVERSITY
School of Forestry & Wood Products

Address: 1400 Townsend Drive, Houghton, MI 49931-1295
Admissions Phone: 906-487-2352 · **Admissions Fax:** 906-487-2915
Admissions E-mail: mrgale@mtu.edu

INSTITUTIONAL INFORMATION

Public/private: Public. **Student/faculty Ratio:** 4:1. **Students in Parent Institution:** 6,336.

STUDENT INFORMATION

Total Students in Program: 670. **% Full-time:** 81. **% Female:** 31.

RESEARCH FACILITIES

Research Facilities: Center for Experimental Computation, Center for Advanced Manufacturing Research, Environmental Engineering Center, Lake States Forest Resource and Environmental Management Coorperative, Lake Superior Ecosystem Research Center.

EXPENSES/FINANCIAL AID

Annual Tuition: In-state $4,872. / Out-of-state $10,008. **Fees:** $136. **Books and Supplies:** $600. **Loans Range From:** $300-$15,000. **% Receiving Financial Aid:** 95. **% Receiving Loans:** 3. **% Receiving Assistantships:** 82. **Average student debt, upon graduation:** $19,112. **Number of Fellowships Granted Each Year:** 6. **Average amount of individual fellowships per year:** $14,700. **Number of Teaching/Research Assistantships Granted Each Year:** 32. **Average Salary Stipend:** $4,475.

ADMISSIONS INFORMATION

Application Fee: $30. **Regular Notification:** Rolling. **Transfer Students Accepted?** No. **Transfer Policy:** Maximum 1/3 of total non-research credit hours required may be transferred. **Number of Applications Received:** 35. **% of Applicants Accepted:** 71. **% Accepted Who Enrolled:** 48. **Average GRE Verbal:** 531. **Average GRE Quantitative:** 616. **Average GRE Analytical:** 583.

Required Admission Factors: Essays/personal statement, GRE, letters of recommendation, transcript.

Other Admission Factors: Minimum 3.0 GPA and minimum GRE score of 1500 recommended.

EMPLOYMENT INFORMATION

Placement Office Available? Yes. **% Employed Within 6 Months:** 97. **% of master's/doctoral grads employed in their field upon graduation:** 97/100. **Rate of placement:** 95%. **Average starting salary:** $60,000.

MICHIGAN THEOLOGICAL SEMINARY
Graduate Programs

Address: 41550 Ann Arbor Trail, Plymouth, MI 48170
Admissions Phone: 734-207-9581 · **Admissions Fax:** 734-207-9582
Admissions E-mail: registrar@mts.edu

INSTITUTIONAL INFORMATION

Public/private: Private (nonprofit). **Evening Classes Available?** Yes. **Students in Parent Institution:** 165.

EXPENSES/FINANCIAL AID

Annual Tuition: $7,500. **Fees:** $330.

ADMISSIONS INFORMATION

Application Fee: $25. **Regular Notification:** Rolling. **Transfer Students Accepted?** Yes. **Number of Applications Received:** 25. **% of Applicants Accepted:** 100. **% Accepted Who Enrolled:** 72.

Required Admission Factors: Essays/personal statement, letters of recommendation, transcript.

Other Admission Factors: Minimum 2.5 GPA required.

MID-AMERICA BAPTIST THEOLOGICAL SEMINARY
Graduate Programs

Address: 2216 Germantown Road South, Germantown, TN 38138
Admissions Phone: 901-751-8453 · **Admissions Fax:** 901-754-8454

INSTITUTIONAL INFORMATION

Public/private: Private (nonprofit). **Students in Parent Institution:** 331.

STUDENT INFORMATION

Total Students in Program: 166. **% Full-time:** 88. **% Female:** 13.

EXPENSES/FINANCIAL AID

Annual Tuition: $1,600. **Books and Supplies:** $600.

ADMISSIONS INFORMATION

Application Fee: $25. **Regular Notification:** Rolling. **Transfer Students Accepted?** Yes.

Required Admission Factors: Essays/personal statement, interview, letters of recommendation, transcript.

Program-Specific Admission Factors: Minimum MAT and minimum 2.0 GPA required of doctoral program applicants.

EMPLOYMENT INFORMATION

Placement Office Available? Yes. **Rate of placement:** 68%.

MIDAMERICA NAZARENE UNIVERSITY
Graduate Studies in Counseling

Address: 2030 East College Way, Olathe, KS 66062-1899
Admissions Phone: 913-791-3449 · **Admissions Fax:** 913-791-3402

INSTITUTIONAL INFORMATION

Public/private: Private (nonprofit). **Evening Classes Available?** Yes. **Student/faculty Ratio:** 10:1. **Students in Parent Institution:** 1,695.

STUDENT INFORMATION

Total Students in Program: 393. **% Full-time:** 38. **% Female:** 74.

EXPENSES/FINANCIAL AID

Annual Tuition: $7,860. **% Receiving Scholarships/Grants:** 6. **% Receiving Loans:** 89.

ADMISSIONS INFORMATION

Application Fee: $75. **Transfer Students Accepted?** Yes. **Number of Applications Received:** 30. **% of Applicants Accepted:** 100. **% Accepted Who Enrolled:** 67. **Average GPA:** 3.0.

Required Admission Factors: Essays/personal statement, GRE, interview, letters of recommendation, transcript.

Other Admission Factors: Minimum 3.0 GPA required.

MIDDLE TENNESSEE STATE UNIVERSITY
College of Basic & Applied Sciences

Address: 114 Cope Administration Building, Murfreesboro, TN 37132
Admissions Phone: 615-898-2840 · **Admissions Fax:** 615-904-8020
Admissions E-mail: dcurry@mtsu.edu

INSTITUTIONAL INFORMATION

Public/private: Public. **Students in Parent Institution:** 20,073.

STUDENT INFORMATION

Total Students in Program: 1,943. **% Full-time:** 9. **% Female:** 61.

RESEARCH FACILITIES

Research Facilities: Center for Study & Treatment of Dyslexia, Center for Historic Preservation, Business & Economic Research Center, Weatherford Chair of Finance, Adams Chair of Excellence in Health Care Services, Center for Environmental Education.

EXPENSES/FINANCIAL AID

Annual Tuition: In-state $3,432. / Out-of-state $8,298. **Fees:** $638. **Books and Supplies:** $800. **Grants Range From:** $3,938-$7,875. **Loans Range From:** $250-$18,172. **% Receiving Financial Aid:** 55. **% Receiving Scholarships/Grants:** 1. **% Receiving Loans:** 87. **% Receiving Assistantships:** 59. **Average student debt, upon graduation:** $15,000. **Number of Teaching/Research Assistantships Granted Each Year:** 75. **Average Salary Stipend:** $5,900.

ADMISSIONS INFORMATION

Application Fee: $25. **Transfer Students Accepted?** Yes. **Number of Applications Received:** 137.

Required Admission Factors: Transcript.

EMPLOYMENT INFORMATION

Placement Office Available? Yes. **% of master's grads employed in their field upon graduation:** 100.

MIDDLE TENNESSEE STATE UNIVERSITY
College of Graduate Studies

Address: 114 Cope Administration Building, 717 Brushy Ridge,
Murfreesboro, TN 37132
Admissions Phone: 615-898-2840 · **Admissions Fax:** 615-904-8020
Admissions E-mail: graduate@mtsu.edu · **Web Address:** www.mtsu.edu/~graduate

INSTITUTIONAL INFORMATION

Public/private: Public. **Evening Classes Available?** Yes. **Total Faculty:**
360. **Students in Parent Institution:** 22,422.

PROGRAMS

Master's offered in: Accounting and computer science; accounting; air transportation services; aviation/airway management and operations; bioinformatics; biology teacher education; biology/biological sciences; biostatistics; biotechnology; business administration and management; business administration/management; business teacher education; business, management, marketing, and related support services; business/managerial economics; chemistry; child care and support services management; child development; clinical psychology; cognitive psychology and psycholinguistics; communications and media studies; computer and information sciences; computer science; conducting; counseling psychology; counselor education/school counseling and guidance services; criminal justice/law enforcement administration; curriculum and instruction; drafting and design technology/technician; driver and safety teacher education; early childhood education and teaching; economics; education leadership and administration; education; education/teaching of individuals with mental retardation; education/teaching of individuals with multiple disabilities; education/teaching of individuals with specific learning disabilities; education/teaching of individuals with vision impairments, including blindness; education/teaching of the gifted and talented; educational administration and supervision; elementary and middle school administration/principalship; elementary education and teaching; engineering technology; English language and literature; English language and literature/letters; English/language arts teacher education; experimental psychology; family and consumer sciences/home economics teacher education; food science; foods, nutrition, and related services; foreign language teacher education; French language teacher education; German language teacher education; health and physical education; health and physical education/fitness; health professions and related sciences; health teacher education; higher education/higher education administration; historic preservation and conservation; history teacher education; history; human development and family studies; human nutrition; industrial and organizational psychology; jazz/jazz studies; junior high/intermediate/middle school education and teaching; kinesiology and exercise science; library science; management information systems; mass communications/media studies; mathematics and statistics; mathematics teacher education; mathematics; multi/interdisciplinary studies; music performance; music teacher education; music theory and composition; music; music; musicology and ethnomusicology; nursing—registered nurse training (RN, ASN, BSN, MSN); nursing administration (MSN, MS, PhD); nursing; nutrition sciences; occupational safety and health technology/technician; parks, recreation and leisure studies; physical education teaching and coaching; psychology; psychometrics and quantitative psychology; public/applied history and archival administration; quality control technology/technician; reading teacher education; school librarian/school library media specialist; school psychology; science teacher education/general science teacher education; secondary education and teaching; secondary school administration/principalship; social science teacher education; sociology; Spanish language teacher education; special education and teaching; special education; sports and fitness administration/management; teacher education and professional development, specific subject areas; teacher education, multiple levels; teaching English as a second or foreign language/ESL language instructor; teaching French as a second or foreign language. **Doctorate offered in:** Chemistry, economics, English language and literature, English language and literature/letters, public/applied history and archival administration.

STUDENT INFORMATION

Total Students in Program: 2,134. **% Full-time:** 52.

RESEARCH FACILITIES

Research Facilities: Center for Study & Treatment of Dyslexia, Center for Historic Preservation, Business & Economic Research Center, Weatherford Chair of Finance, Adams Chair of Excellence in Health Care Services, Center for Environmental Education, Martin Chair of Insurance.

EXPENSES/FINANCIAL AID

Annual Tuition: In-state $4,500. / Out-of-state $12,988. **Room & Board:** $2,324. **Fees:** $638. **Books and Supplies:** $800. **Grants Range From:** $3,938-$7,875. **Loans Range From:** $250-$18,172. **% Receiving Scholarships/Grants:** 1. **% Receiving Loans:** 87. **% Receiving Assistantships:** 59. **Types of Aid Available:** Fellowships, graduate assistantships, loans, scholarships. **Number of Teaching/Research Assistantships Granted Each Year:** 340. **Assistantship Compensation Includes:** Full tuition remission, salary/stipend. **Average Salary Stipend:** $6,750.

ADMISSIONS INFORMATION

Application Fee: $25. **Regular Application Deadline:** 8/15. **Regular Notification:** Rolling. **Transfer Students Accepted?** Yes. **Number of Applications Received:** 975. **% of Applicants Accepted:** 38. **Average GPA:** 3.0. **Required Admission Factors:** Transcript.
Other Admission Factors: All applicants to the College of Graduate Studies must have an overall undergraduate grade point average (GPA) of 2.75 (on a 4.00 scale) to be considered for unconditional admission.
Program-Specific Admission Factors: The Jennings A. Jones College of Business does not have a minimum GPA requirement, but rather uses the following formula: GPA x 200 + GMAT = 950 or Upper Division GPA x 200 + GMAT = 1000. The GMAT test is required.

EMPLOYMENT INFORMATION

Placement Office Available? Yes. **% Employed Within 6 Months:** 70. **Rate of placement:** 75%. **Average starting salary:** $41,641.

MIDDLE TENNESSEE STATE UNIVERSITY
College of Liberal Arts

Address: 114 Cope Administration Building, Murfreesboro, TN 37132
Admissions Phone: 615-898-2840 · **Admissions Fax:** 615-904-8020
Admissions E-mail: dcurry@mtsu.edu

INSTITUTIONAL INFORMATION

Public/private: Public. **Students in Parent Institution:** 20,073.

STUDENT INFORMATION

Total Students in Program: 1,943. **% Full-time:** 9. **% Female:** 61.

RESEARCH FACILITIES

Research Facilities: Center for Study & Treatment of Dyslexia, Center for Historic Preservation, Business & Economic Research Center, Weatherford Chair of Finance, Adams Chair of Excellence in Health Care Services, Center for Environmental Education.

EXPENSES/FINANCIAL AID

Annual Tuition: In-state $3,432. / Out-of-state $8,298. **Fees:** $638. **Books and Supplies:** $800. **Grants Range From:** $3,938-$7,875. **Loans Range From:** $250-$18,172. **% Receiving Financial Aid:** 55. **% Receiving Scholarships/Grants:** 1. **% Receiving Loans:** 87. **% Receiving Assistantships:** 59. **Average student debt, upon graduation:** $15,000. **Number of Teaching/Research Assistantships Granted Each Year:** 61. **Average Salary Stipend:** $4,550.

ADMISSIONS INFORMATION

Application Fee: $25. **Transfer Students Accepted?** Yes. **Number of Applications Received:** 90.

Required Admission Factors: Transcript.

EMPLOYMENT INFORMATION
Placement Office Available? Yes.

MIDDLE TENNESSEE STATE UNIVERSITY
College of Mass Communications

Address: 114 Cope Administration Building, Murfreesboro, TN 37132
Admissions Phone: 615-898-2840 · **Admissions Fax:** 615-904-8020

INSTITUTIONAL INFORMATION
Public/private: Public. Evening Classes Available? Yes. Students in Parent Institution: 20,073.

STUDENT INFORMATION
Total Students in Program: 1,943. % Full-time: 9. % Female: 61.

RESEARCH FACILITIES
Research Facilities: Center for Study & Treatment of Dyslexia, Center for Historic Preservation, Business & Economic Research Center, Weatherford Chair of Finance, Adams Chair of Excellence in Health Care Services, Center for Environmental Education.

EXPENSES/FINANCIAL AID
Annual Tuition: In-state $3,432. / Out-of-state $8,298. Fees: $638. Books and Supplies: $800. Grants Range From: $3,938-$7,875. Loans Range From: $250-$18,172. % Receiving Scholarships/Grants: 1. % Receiving Loans: 87. % Receiving Assistantships: 59.

ADMISSIONS INFORMATION
Application Fee: $25. Regular Notification: Rolling. Transfer Students Accepted? Yes. Number of Applications Received: 32.
Required Admission Factors: GRE, letters of recommendation.

EMPLOYMENT INFORMATION
Placement Office Available? Yes.

MIDDLEBURY COLLEGE
Bread Loaf School of English

Address: Freeman International Center, Middlebury College, Middlebury, VT 05753
Admissions Phone: 802-443-5418 · **Admissions Fax:** 802-443-2060
Admissions E-mail: sandy_legault@breadnet.middlebury.edu
Web Address: www.middlebury.edu/academics/blse/

INSTITUTIONAL INFORMATION
Public/private: Private (nonprofit). Student/faculty Ratio: 9:1.

RESEARCH FACILITIES
Research Facilities: Interactive Multimedia Center for Languages.

EXPENSES/FINANCIAL AID
Books and Supplies: $150. Grants Range From: $130-$5,915. Loans Range From: $25-$7,515. % Receiving Financial Aid: 35.

ADMISSIONS INFORMATION
Application Fee: $50. Priority Application Deadline: 2/1. Regular Application Deadline: 5/15. Regular Notification: Rolling. Transfer Students Accepted? Yes. Transfer Policy: Maximum 2 courses may be transferred from other programs after the completion of 1 summer term.
Required Admission Factors: Essays/personal statement, letters of recommendation, transcript.
Program-Specific Admission Factors: The only exception to the BA requirement for our program is that a small number of undergraduates between their junior and senior years may apply to the undergraduate Honors Program.

EMPLOYMENT INFORMATION
Placement Office Available? Yes.

MIDDLEBURY COLLEGE
Language Schools

Address: Sunderland Language Center, Middlebury, VT 05753
Admissions Phone: 802-443-5510 · **Admissions Fax:** 802-443-2075
Admissions E-mail: languages@middlebury.edu
Web Address: www.middlebury.edu/ls

INSTITUTIONAL INFORMATION
Public/private: Private (nonprofit). Students in Parent Institution: 2,298

PROGRAMS
Master's offered in: Foreign languages/modern languages, French language and literature, German language and literature, Italian language and literature, Russian language and literature, Spanish language and literature. Doctorate offered in: Foreign languages and literatures; foreign languages, literatures, and linguistics; foreign languages/modern languages; French language and literature; German language and literature; Italian language and literature; Russian language and literature.

STUDENT INFORMATION
Total Students in Program: 6. % Full-time: 6,667. % Female: 83.

RESEARCH FACILITIES
Research Facilities: Interactive Multimedia Center for Languages.

EXPENSES/FINANCIAL AID
Annual Tuition: $3,600. Room & Board: $1,989. Books and Supplies: $50. Grants Range From: $100-$6,620. Loans Range From: $100-$7,410. % Receiving Financial Aid: 36. Types of Aid Available: Grants, loans, scholarships. Number of Teaching/Research Assistantships Granted Each Year: 5. Average Salary Stipend: $500.

ADMISSIONS INFORMATION
Application Fee: $50. Priority Application Deadline: 1/1. Regular Application Deadline: 5/15. Regular Notification: Rolling. Transfer Students Accepted? No. Transfer Policy: Up to 3 courses taken after successful completion of initial summer at Middlebury may be transferred, with permission of the director. Number of Applications Received: 1,000. % of Applicants Accepted: 20. % Accepted Who Enrolled: 88. Average GPA: 3.8.
Required Admission Factors: Essays/personal statement, letters of recommendation, transcript.
Other Admission Factors: Candidates must have majored in the language in which the MA is sought, or must have completed the course work equivalent to a major in the language.

EMPLOYMENT INFORMATION
Placement Office Available? Yes.

MIDWESTERN BAPTIST THEOLOGICAL SEMINARY
Graduate Programs

Address: 5001 North Oak Street Trafficway, Kansas City, MO 64118
Admissions Phone: 800-944-3287 or 816-414-3733 · **Admissions Fax:** 816-414-3797

INSTITUTIONAL INFORMATION
Evening Classes Available? Yes. Student/faculty Ratio: 15:1. Students in Parent Institution: 466.

STUDENT INFORMATION
Total Students in Program: 215. % Full-time: 81. % Female: 15.

RESEARCH FACILITIES
Research Facilities: Center for Biblical Revival, Morton Museum of Biblical Archeology, MBTS Missions Resource Center.

EXPENSES/FINANCIAL AID
Annual Tuition: $1,170.

ADMISSIONS INFORMATION
Application Fee: $25. Regular Notification: Rolling. Transfer Students Accepted? Yes. Number of Applications Received: 160. % of Applicants Accepted: 93. % Accepted Who Enrolled: 86.
Required Admission Factors: Letters of recommendation, transcript.
Other Admission Factors: Church endorsment, 3 references, and physical exam required.
Program-Specific Admission Factors: GRE required of DMin.

EMPLOYMENT INFORMATION
Placement Office Available? Yes. % Employed Within 6 Months: 65. % of master's/doctoral grads employed in their field upon graduation: 50/100. Rate of placement: 80%.

MIDWESTERN STATE UNIVERSITY
Graduate Studies

Address: 3410 Taft Boulevard, Wichita Falls, TX 76308
Admissions Phone: 940-397-4334 · Admissions Fax: 940-397-4672
Admissions E-mail: admissions@mwsu.edu · Web Address: www.mwsu.edu

INSTITUTIONAL INFORMATION
Public/private: Public. Evening Classes Available? Yes. Total Faculty: 16. % Faculty Female: 50. % Faculty Part-time: 50. Student/faculty Ratio: 21:1. Students in Parent Institution: 6,348.

STUDENT INFORMATION
Total Students in Program: 742. % Full-time: 23. % Female: 65. % Minority: 13. % International: 8.

RESEARCH FACILITIES
Research Facilities: Bureau of Business/Government Research, Small Business Development Center.

EXPENSES/FINANCIAL AID
Annual Tuition: In-state $1,440. / Out-of-state $6,048. Room & Board: $4,844. Fees: $2,852. Books and Supplies: $1,200. Grants Range From: $100-$3,560. Loans Range From: $300-$8,955. % Receiving Scholarships/Grants: 20. % Receiving Loans: 25. Types of Aid Available: Graduate assistantships, grants, institutional work-study, loans, scholarships. Number of Teaching/Research Assistantships Granted Each Year: 114. Assistantship Compensation Includes: Salary/stipend. Average Salary Stipend: $7,500.

ADMISSIONS INFORMATION
Application Fee: $35. Priority Application Deadline: 7/1. Regular Application Deadline: 8/7. Regular Notification: Rolling. Transfer Students Accepted? Yes. Transfer Policy: All official must be received. Number of Applications Received: 324. % of Applicants Accepted: 68. % Accepted Who Enrolled: 52. Average GPA: 3.2. Average GRE Verbal: 451. Average GRE Quantitative: 492. Average GRE Analytical Writing: 4.
Other Admission Factors: Minimum GMAT score of 400 required. Admission into the graduate program is based on the admission index which = 200 X GPA on last 60 hours of college work plus GRE score.
Program-Specific Admission Factors: Biology—GRE analytical writing

score 3.5 or higher. Computer Science—TOEFL score 573 paper based exam and 230 computer based exam.

MILLERSVILLE UNIVERSITY OF PENNSYLVANIA
School of Humanities & Social Sciences

Address: PO Box 1002, Millersville, PA 17551-0302
Admissions Phone: 717-872-3030 · Admissions Fax: 717-872-2022
Admissions E-mail: duncan.perry@millersville.edu

INSTITUTIONAL INFORMATION
Public/private: Public. Evening Classes Available? Yes. Student/faculty Ratio: 17:1. Students in Parent Institution: 7,378.

STUDENT INFORMATION
Total Students in Program: 881. % Full-time: 17. % Female: 70.

RESEARCH FACILITIES
Research Facilities: Center for the Study of Politics, Center for Opinion Research.

EXPENSES/FINANCIAL AID
Annual Tuition: In-state $4,600. / Out-of-state $7,554. Fees: $519. Books and Supplies: $600. Average Salary Stipend: $4,000.

ADMISSIONS INFORMATION
Application Fee: $30. Regular Notification: Rolling. Transfer Students Accepted? Yes. Transfer Policy: Maximum 1/3 of total required credit hours may be transferred from an accredited institution. Number of Applications Received: 12. % of Applicants Accepted: 67. % Accepted Who Enrolled: 62.
Required Admission Factors: Essays/personal statement, letters of recommendation, transcript.
Other Admission Factors: Minimum 2.75 GPA required for most programs.

EMPLOYMENT INFORMATION
Placement Office Available? Yes.

MILLERSVILLE UNIVERSITY OF PENNSYLVANIA
School of Science & Mathematics

Address: PO Box 1002, Millersville, PA 17551-0302
Admissions Phone: 717-872-3030 · Admissions Fax: 717-872-2022
Admissions E-mail: duncan.perry@millersville.edu

INSTITUTIONAL INFORMATION
Public/private: Public. Evening Classes Available? Yes. Student/faculty Ratio: 17:1. Students in Parent Institution: 7,378.

STUDENT INFORMATION
Total Students in Program: 881. % Full-time: 17. % Female: 70.

RESEARCH FACILITIES
Research Facilities: Center for the Study of Politics, Center for Opinion Research.

EXPENSES/FINANCIAL AID
Annual Tuition: In-state $4,600. / Out-of-state $7,554. Fees: $519. Books and Supplies: $600. Number of Teaching/Research Assistantships Granted Each Year: 1 Average Salary Stipend: $4,000.

ADMISSIONS INFORMATION
Application Fee: $30. Regular Notification: Rolling. Transfer Students Accepted? Yes. Transfer Policy: Maximum 1/3 of total required credit hours

may be transferred from an accredited institution. **Number of Applications Received:** 9. **% of Applicants Accepted:** 67.

Required Admission Factors: Essays/personal statement, GRE, letters of recommendation, transcript.

Other Admission Factors: Minimum 2.75 GPA required for most departments.

EMPLOYMENT INFORMATION

Placement Office Available? Yes.

MILLIGAN COLLEGE
Graduate Programs

Address: PO Box 210, Milligan College, TN 37682
Admissions Phone: 423-461-8782 · **Admissions Fax:** 423-461-8789

INSTITUTIONAL INFORMATION

Public/private: Private (nonprofit). **Student/faculty Ratio:** 13:1. **Students in Parent Institution:** 906.

STUDENT INFORMATION

Total Students in Program: 116. **% Full-time:** 69. **% Female:** 74.

EXPENSES/FINANCIAL AID

Fees: $200. **Books and Supplies:** $400.

ADMISSIONS INFORMATION

Application Fee: $30. **Regular Notification:** Rolling. **Transfer Students Accepted?** No.

Required Admission Factors: Essays/personal statement, GRE, interview, letters of recommendation, transcript.

Other Admission Factors: Minimum GRE score of 1000 (verbal and quantitative) and minimum 3.0 GPA required.

Program-Specific Admission Factors: At least 40 hours of documneted volunteer experience in an occupational therapy setting required of occupational therapy program applicants.

MILLS COLLEGE
Graduate Studies

Address: 5000 MacArthur Boulevard, Oakland, CA 94613
Admissions Phone: 510-430-3309 · **Admissions Fax:** 510-430-2159
Admissions E-mail: grad-studies@mills.edu · **Web Address:** www.mills.edu

INSTITUTIONAL INFORMATION

Public/private: Private (nonprofit). **Total Faculty:** 114. **% Faculty Female:** 75. **% Faculty Part-time:** 50. **Student/faculty Ratio:** 12:1. **Students in Parent Institution:** 1,256.

PROGRAMS

Master's offered in: Business administration/management; computer and information sciences; creative writing; curriculum and instruction; dance; early childhood education and teaching; education; elementary education and teaching; English language and literature; fine/studio arts; junior high/intermediate/middle school education and teaching; music performance; music theory and composition; music; science teacher education/general science teacher education; secondary education and teaching; teacher education, multiple levels. **Doctorate offered in:** Education leadership and administration. **First Professional degree offered in:** Premedicine/premedical studies.

STUDENT INFORMATION

Total Students in Program: 494. **% Full-time:** 89. **% Female:** 79. **% Minority:** 31. **% International:** 6.

RESEARCH FACILITIES

Research Facilities: Center for Contemporary Music, Children's School, Women's Leadership Institute.

EXPENSES/FINANCIAL AID

Annual Tuition: $15,300. **Room & Board:** $9,955. **Fees:** $1,405. **Books and Supplies:** $846. **Grants Range From:** $500-$11,700. **Loans Range From:** $500-$18,500. **% Receiving Scholarships/Grants:** 65. **% Receiving Loans:** 75. **% Receiving Assistantships:** 50. **Types of Aid Available:** Fellowships, graduate assistantships, grants, institutional work-study, loans, scholarships.

ADMISSIONS INFORMATION

Application Fee: $50. **Regular Application Deadline:** 2/1. **Regular Notification:** Rolling. **Transfer Students Accepted?** No. **Number of Applications Received:** 709. **% of Applicants Accepted:** 61. **% Accepted Who Enrolled:** 59.

Required Admission Factors: Essays/personal statement, letters of recommendation, transcript.

EMPLOYMENT INFORMATION

Placement Office Available? Yes.

MILWAUKEE SCHOOL OF ENGINEERING
Lifelong Learning Institute

Address: 1025 North Broadway, Milwaukee, WI 53202-3109
Admissions Phone: 414-277-6763 · **Admissions Fax:** 414-277-7475
Admissions E-mail: boomsma@msoe.edu

INSTITUTIONAL INFORMATION

Public/private: Private (nonprofit). **Evening Classes Available?** Yes. **Student/faculty Ratio:** 9:1. **Students in Parent Institution:** 2,620.

STUDENT INFORMATION

Total Students in Program: 341. **% Full-time:** 21. **% Female:** 20.

RESEARCH FACILITIES

Research Facilities: St. Luke's Perfusion Lab, Rapid Prototyping Center, Fluid Power Institute, Applied Research Center, Photonics and Applied Optics Center, High Impact Materials and Structures, Construction Science and Engineering Center, Medical College of Wisconsin.

EXPENSES/FINANCIAL AID

Annual Tuition: $7,920. **Books and Supplies:** $2,340. **Loans Range From:** $1,000-$18,500. **% Receiving Loans:** 80.

ADMISSIONS INFORMATION

Application Fee: $30. **Regular Notification:** Rolling. **Transfer Students Accepted?** Yes. **Number of Applications Received:** 168. **% of Applicants Accepted:** 52. **% Accepted Who Enrolled:** 71. **Average GPA:** 3.2. **Average GRE Verbal:** 464. **Average GRE Quantitative:** 656. **Average GRE Analytical:** 574.

Required Admission Factors: Letters of recommendation, transcript.

Other Admission Factors: Minimum 2.8 GPA required.

Program-Specific Admission Factors: Three letters of recommendation required for some programs.

EMPLOYMENT INFORMATION

Placement Office Available? Yes. **% Employed Within 6 Months:** 99. **% of master's/doctoral grads employed in their field upon graduation:** 99. **Rate of placement:** 99%.

MINNESOTA STATE UNIVERSITY, MOORHEAD
Graduate Studies

Address: 1104 Seventh Avenue South, Moorhead, MN 56563
Admissions Phone: 218-477-2344 · **Admissions Fax:** 218-477-2482
Admissions E-mail: wengerk@mnstate.edu · **Web Address:** www.mnstate.edu/graduate

INSTITUTIONAL INFORMATION

Public/private: Public. **Evening Classes Available?** Yes. **Total Faculty:** 138. **% Faculty Female:** 46. **Students in Parent Institution:** 7,642.

PROGRAMS

Master's offered in: Adult health nurse/nursing; counselor education/school counseling and guidance services; creative writing; curriculum and instruction; education leadership and administration; family practice nurse/nurse practitioner; liberal arts and sciences/liberal studies; music history, literature, and theory; music performance; music theory and composition; nursing—registered nurse training (RN, ASN, BSN, MSN); nursing science (MS PhD); public administration and services; reading teacher education; school psychology; special education; speech-language pathology/pathologist.

STUDENT INFORMATION

Total Students in Program: 277. **% Full-time:** 45. **% Female:** 77. **% Minority:** 3. **% International:** 2.

EXPENSES/FINANCIAL AID

Annual Tuition: In-state $5,504. / Out-of-state $10,644. **Room & Board:** $4,360. **Types of Aid Available:** Graduate assistantships, institutional work-study, loans.

ADMISSIONS INFORMATION

Application Fee: $20. **Regular Application Deadline:** 4/15. **Regular Notification:** Rolling. **Transfer Students Accepted?** Yes. **Transfer Policy:** Students may transfer up to 1/2 of the total requirements for the specific program. **Number of Applications Received:** 213. **% of Applicants Accepted:** 69. **Required Admission Factors:** Transcript.

EMPLOYMENT INFORMATION

Placement Office Available? Yes.

MINNESOTA STATE UNIVERSITY—MANKATO
College of Arts & Humanities

Address: 125 Wigley Administration Center, Mankato, MN 56001
Admissions Phone: 507-389-2697 · **Admissions Fax:** 507-389-5974
Admissions E-mail: joni.roberts@mankato.edu

INSTITUTIONAL INFORMATION

Public/private: Public. **Evening Classes Available?** Yes. **Students in Parent Institution:** 12,085.

STUDENT INFORMATION

Total Students in Program: 1,643. **% Full-time:** 28. **% Female:** 64.

EXPENSES/FINANCIAL AID

Annual Tuition: In-state $3,785. / Out-of-state $5,687. **Average student debt, upon graduation:** $9,500.

ADMISSIONS INFORMATION

Application Fee: $20. **Regular Notification:** Rolling. **Transfer Students Accepted?** Yes. **Number of Applications Received:** 283. **% of Applicants Accepted:** 58. **% Accepted Who Enrolled:** 96. **Average GPA:** 3.28. **Required Admission Factors:** GRE, letters of recommendation, transcript. **Other Admission Factors:** Minimum 3.0 GPA (2.75 for some programs), minimum GRE score of 1350, and minimum MAT score of 45 required.

EMPLOYMENT INFORMATION

Placement Office Available? Yes.

MINNESOTA STATE UNIVERSITY—MANKATO
College of Social & Behavioral Sciences

Address: 125 Wigley Administration Center, Mankato, MN 56001
Admissions Phone: 507-389-2697 · **Admissions Fax:** 507-389-5974
Admissions E-mail: joni.roberts@mankato.msus.edu

INSTITUTIONAL INFORMATION

Public/private: Public. **Evening Classes Available?** Yes. **Total Faculty:** 107. **% Faculty Female:** 32. **Students in Parent Institution:** 12,085.

STUDENT INFORMATION

Total Students in Program: 1,643. **% Full-time:** 28. **% Female:** 64.

EXPENSES/FINANCIAL AID

Annual Tuition: In-state $3,785. / Out-of-state $5,687. **Average student debt, upon graduation:** $9,500.

ADMISSIONS INFORMATION

Application Fee: $20. **Regular Notification:** Rolling. **Transfer Students Accepted?** Yes. **Number of Applications Received:** 197. **% of Applicants Accepted:** 74. **% Accepted Who Enrolled:** 38. **Average GPA:** 3.28. **Required Admission Factors:** Letters of recommendation, transcript. **Other Admission Factors:** Minimum 3.0 GPA (2.75 for some programs), minimum GRE score of 1350, and minimum MAT score of 45 required. **Program-Specific Admission Factors:** GRE and GRE subject exam required of psychology program applicants.

EMPLOYMENT INFORMATION

Placement Office Available? Yes.

MINOT STATE UNIVERSITY
Graduate School

Address: Graduate School
500 University Avenue West, Minot, ND 58707
Admissions Phone: 800-777-0750 or 701-858-3250 · **Admissions Fax:** 701-839-6933

INSTITUTIONAL INFORMATION

Public/private: Public. **Evening Classes Available?** Yes. **Students in Parent Institution:** 3,294.

STUDENT INFORMATION

Total Students in Program: 174. **% Full-time:** 28. **% Female:** 81.

RESEARCH FACILITIES

Research Facilities: North Dakota Center for Persons with Disabilities, Federal Law Enforcer Training Center.

EXPENSES/FINANCIAL AID

Annual Tuition: In-state $3,095. / Out-of-state $7,794. **Room & Board:** $3,706. **Grants Range From:** $500-$4,500. **Average Salary Stipend:** $4,000.

ADMISSIONS INFORMATION

Application Fee: $30. **Regular Notification:** Rolling. **Transfer Students Accepted?** Yes. **Average GPA:** 3.0. **Required Admission Factors:** Essays/personal statement, letters of recommendation, transcript. **Other Admission Factors:** Minimum GRE score of 1200 and minimum 3.0 GPA required. **Program-Specific Admission Factors:** Minimum GRE score of 1600 required of school psychology program applicants.

EMPLOYMENT INFORMATION

Placement Office Available? Yes. **Rate of placement:** 92%.

MISSISSIPPI COLLEGE
College of Arts & Sciences

Address: 200 West College Street, Clinton, MS 39058
Admissions Phone: 601-925-3225 · **Admissions Fax:** 601-925-3889
Admissions E-mail: mcmilla@mc.edu

INSTITUTIONAL INFORMATION

Public/private: Private (nonprofit). **Evening Classes Available?** Yes. **Student/faculty Ratio:** 15:1. **Students in Parent Institution:** 3,560.

STUDENT INFORMATION

Total Students in Program: 667. **% Full-time:** 13. **% Female:** 65.

EXPENSES/FINANCIAL AID

Annual Tuition: $7,392. **Fees:** $230. **Books and Supplies:** $600. **Grants Range From:** $300-$7,000. **Loans Range From:** $1,000-$14,350. **% Receiving Scholarships/Grants:** 56. **% Receiving Loans:** 40. **% Receiving Assistantships:** 6.

ADMISSIONS INFORMATION

Application Fee: $25. **Regular Notification:** Rolling. **Transfer Students Accepted?** Yes. **Transfer Policy:** Maximum 6 credit hours may be transferred with a minimum grade average of B. **Number of Applications Received:** 73. **% of Applicants Accepted:** 96. **% Accepted Who Enrolled:** 60. **Required Admission Factors:** GRE, transcript. **Other Admission Factors:** Minimum GRE score of 850 and minimum 2.5 GPA required.

EMPLOYMENT INFORMATION

Placement Office Available? Yes.

MISSISSIPPI STATE UNIVERSITY
College of Arts & Sciences

Address: PO Box G, Mississippi State, MS 39762
Admissions Phone: 662-325-2224 · **Admissions Fax:** 662-325-7360
Admissions E-mail: admit@admissions.msstate.edu

INSTITUTIONAL INFORMATION

Public/private: Public. **Evening Classes Available?** Yes. **Student/faculty Ratio:** 4:1. **Students in Parent Institution:** 16,561.

STUDENT INFORMATION

Total Students in Program: 3,064. **% Full-time:** 51. **% Female:** 51.

EXPENSES/FINANCIAL AID

Annual Tuition: In-state $3,586. / Out-of-state $8,128. **Books and Supplies:** $750. **Grants Range From:** $200-$15,625. **Loans Range From:** $130-$31,670. **% Receiving Financial Aid:** 43. **% Receiving Scholarships/Grants:** 10. **% Receiving Loans:** 47. **% Receiving Assistantships:** 62. **Number of Teaching/Research Assistantships Granted Each Year:** 200.

ADMISSIONS INFORMATION

Application Fee: $25. **Regular Notification:** Rolling. **Transfer Students Accepted?** No. **Number of Applications Received:** 361. **% of Applicants Accepted:** 98. **% Accepted Who Enrolled:** 40. **Average GPA:** 3.34. **Average GRE Verbal:** 485. **Average GRE Quantitative:** 614. **Average GRE Analytical:** 592. **Required Admission Factors:** Essays/personal statement, letters of recommendation, transcript. **Other Admission Factors:** Minimum GRE score of 1000 required for some programs. Minimum 2.75 GPA required; minimum 3.0 GPA recommended. **Program-Specific Admission Factors:** Writing sample required of doctoral history program applicants.

EMPLOYMENT INFORMATION

Placement Office Available? Yes.

MISSISSIPPI STATE UNIVERSITY
College of Forest Resources

Address: PO Box G, Mississippi State, MS 39762
Admissions Phone: 662-325-2224 · **Admissions Fax:** 662-325-7360
Admissions E-mail: admit@admissions.msstate.edu

INSTITUTIONAL INFORMATION

Public/private: Public. **Students in Parent Institution:** 16,561.

STUDENT INFORMATION

Total Students in Program: 3,064. **% Full-time:** 51. **% Female:** 51.

EXPENSES/FINANCIAL AID

Annual Tuition: In-state $3,586. / Out-of-state $8,128. **Books and Supplies:** $750. **Grants Range From:** $200-$15,625. **Loans Range From:** $130-$31,670. **% Receiving Financial Aid:** 82. **% Receiving Scholarships/Grants:** 10. **% Receiving Loans:** 47. **% Receiving Assistantships:** 62. **Number of Teaching/Research Assistantships Granted Each Year:** 8. **Average Salary Stipend:** $12,000.

ADMISSIONS INFORMATION

Application Fee: $25. **Regular Notification:** Rolling. **Transfer Students Accepted?** Yes. **Transfer Policy:** Maximum 2 years of graduate work may be transferred. **Number of Applications Received:** 51. **% of Applicants Accepted:** 49. **% Accepted Who Enrolled:** 100. **Average GPA:** 3.17. **Average GRE Verbal:** 477. **Average GRE Quantitative:** 550. **Average GRE Analytical:** 600. **Required Admission Factors:** Essays/personal statement, letters of recommendation, transcript. **Other Admission Factors:** Minimum 2.75 GPA required. Minimum 3.0 GPA required for some programs.

EMPLOYMENT INFORMATION

Placement Office Available? Yes. **% Employed Within 6 Months:** 89. **% of master's/doctoral grads employed in their field upon graduation:** 100/100. **Average starting salary:** $41,500.

MISSISSIPPI UNIVERSITY FOR WOMEN
Graduate Studies

Address: W-Box 1613, Columbus, MS 39701
Admissions Phone: 662-329-7110 · **Admissions Fax:** 662-329-8515
Admissions E-mail: bmoore@muw.edu

INSTITUTIONAL INFORMATION

Public/private: Public. **Evening Classes Available?** Yes. **Student/faculty Ratio:** 13:1. **Students in Parent Institution:** 2,328

STUDENT INFORMATION

Total Students in Program: 162. **% Full-time:** 43. **% Female:** 93.

EXPENSES/FINANCIAL AID

Annual Tuition: In-state $3,054. / Out-of-state $7,375. **Grants Range From:** $250-$2,556. **Loans Range From:** $500-$17,500. **% Receiving Scholarships/Grants:** 35. **% Receiving Loans:** 65. **Number of Teaching/Research Assistantships Granted Each Year:** 2. **Average Salary Stipend:** $8.

ADMISSIONS INFORMATION

Regular Notification: Rolling. **Transfer Students Accepted?** Yes. **Transfer Policy:** Maximum 6 semester hours may be transferred with a minimum grade of B. **Average GPA:** 3.0. **Required Admission Factors:** GRE, letters of recommendation, transcript.

MISSISSIPPI VALLEY STATE UNIVERSITY
Departments of Criminal Justice & Social Work

Address: 14000 Highway 82 West, Itta Bena, MS 38941-1400
Admissions Phone: 662-254-3347 · **Admissions Fax:** 662-254-3655
Admissions E-mail: admsn@mvsu.edu

INSTITUTIONAL INFORMATION
Public/private: Public. Student/faculty Ratio: 23:1. Students in Parent Institution: 2,509.

STUDENT INFORMATION
Total Students in Program: 297. % Full-time: 6. % Female: 81.

EXPENSES/FINANCIAL AID
Annual Tuition: In-state $2,719. / Out-of-state $2,900. Books and Supplies: $450.

ADMISSIONS INFORMATION
Regular Notification: Rolling. Transfer Students Accepted? Yes. Transfer Policy: Maximum 6 credit hours from an accredited institution may be transferred. Number of Applications Received: 108. % of Applicants Accepted: 81. % Accepted Who Enrolled: 36.
Required Admission Factors: Letters of recommendation, transcript.
Other Admission Factors: Minimum 2.5 GPA required.

EMPLOYMENT INFORMATION
Placement Office Available? Yes.

MOLLOY COLLEGE
Graduate Programs

Address: 1000 Hempstead Avenue, PO Box 5002, Rockville Centre, NY 11571-5002
Admissions Phone: 516-678-5000, ext. 6230 · Admissions Fax: 516-256-2247
Admissions E-mail: admissions@molloy.edu · Web Address: www.molloy.edu

INSTITUTIONAL INFORMATION
Public/private: Private (nonprofit). Evening Classes Available? Yes. Students in Parent Institution: 3,007.

PROGRAMS
Master's offered in: Accounting; adult health nurse/nursing; biology teacher education; business administration/management; elementary education and teaching; English/language arts teacher education; family practice nurse, nurse practitioner; foreign language teacher education; history teacher education; junior high/intermediate/middle school education and teaching; maternal/child health nurse/nursing; mathematics teacher education; nursing—registered nurse training (RN, ASN, BSN, MSN); nursing administration (MSN, MS, PhD); nursing clinical specialist; nursing; pediatric nurse/nursing; psychiatric/mental health nurse/nursing; reading teacher education; science teacher education/general science teacher education; secondary education and teaching; social science teacher education; social studies teacher education; Spanish language teacher education; special education; teacher education, multiple levels; teaching English as a second or foreign language/ESL language instructor.

STUDENT INFORMATION
Total Students in Program: 696. % Full-time: 14. % Female: 86.

EXPENSES/FINANCIAL AID
Annual Tuition: $13,320. Fees: $360. Books and Supplies: $1,200. Grants Range From: $500-$13,320. Loans Range From: $1,500-$13,320. Types of Aid Available: Graduate assistantships, loans. Assistantship Compensation Includes: Partial tuition remission, salary/stipend.

ADMISSIONS INFORMATION
Application Fee: $60. Regular Application Deadline: 9/8. Regular Notification: Rolling. Transfer Students Accepted? Yes. Number of Applications Received: 270. % of Applicants Accepted: 77. % Accepted Who Enrolled: 94. Average GPA: 3.2.
Required Admission Factors: Essays/personal statement, interview, letters of recommendation, transcript.

EMPLOYMENT INFORMATION
Placement Office Available? Yes. % Employed Within 6 Months: 96. Rate of placement: 90%. Average starting salary: $56,000.

MONMOUTH UNIVERSITY
School of Humanities & Social Sciences

Address: 400 Cedar Avenue, West Long Branch, NJ 07764-1898
Admissions Phone: 732-571-3452, 800-320-7754 · Admissions Fax: 732-263-5123
Admissions E-mail: gradadm@monmouth.edu · Web Address: www.monmouth.edu/academics/humanities.asp

INSTITUTIONAL INFORMATION
Public/private: Private (nonprofit). Evening Classes Available? Yes. Total Faculty: 53. % Faculty Female: 45. % Faculty Part-time: 19. Students in Parent Institution: 6,212.

PROGRAMS
Master's offered in: Communications, journalism, and related fields; counseling psychology; criminal justice/safety studies; liberal arts and sciences/liberal studies; social sciences; social work.

STUDENT INFORMATION
Total Students in Program: 495. % Full-time: 35. % Female: 73. % Minority: 11. % International: 1.

EXPENSES/FINANCIAL AID
Annual Tuition: $10,386. Room & Board: $13,600. Fees: $568. Books and Supplies: $800. Grants Range From: $1,000-$10,450. Loans Range From: $549-$19,509. % Receiving Financial Aid: 74.8. % Receiving Scholarships/Grants: 1.6. % Receiving Loans: 64.2. % Receiving Assistantships: 6.5. Types of Aid Available: Fellowships, graduate assistantships, grants, loans, scholarships. Number of Teaching/Research Assistantships Granted Each Year: 22. Assistantship Compensation Includes: Partial tuition remission.

ADMISSIONS INFORMATION
Application Fee: $35. Regular Application Deadline: 8/1. Regular Notification: Rolling. Transfer Students Accepted? Yes. Number of Applications Received: 335. % of Applicants Accepted: 91. % Accepted Who Enrolled: 61. Average GPA: 3.1.
Required Admission Factors: Letters of recommendation, transcript.
Other Admission Factors: Minimum 3.0 GPA in major (2.5 overall) required.
Program-Specific Admission Factors: Candidates for advanced standing MSW must have a BSW from an accredited program within 6 years of the date of application.

EMPLOYMENT INFORMATION
Placement Office Available? Yes. % Employed Within 6 Months: 95. Rate of placement: 95%.

MONTANA STATE UNIVERSITY—BILLINGS
College of Professional Studies & Lifelong Learning

Address: 1500 North 30th Street, Billings, MT 59101-0298
Admissions Phone: 406-657-2238 · Admissions Fax: 406-657-2299

INSTITUTIONAL INFORMATION
Public/private: Public. Students in Parent Institution: 4,279.

STUDENT INFORMATION
Total Students in Program: 402. % Full-time: 38. % Female: 68.

EXPENSES/FINANCIAL AID

Annual Tuition: In-state $3,495. / Out-of-state $8,670. **Books and Supplies:** $800. **Grants Range From:** $100-$500. **Loans Range From:** $200-$11,000. **% Receiving Scholarships/Grants:** 40. **% Receiving Loans:** 72. **% Receiving Assistantships:** 35.

ADMISSIONS INFORMATION

Application Fee: $40. **Transfer Students Accepted?** No. **Required Admission Factors:** Essays/personal statement, GRE, letters of recommendation, transcript. **Other Admission Factors:** Minimum GRE score of 1350 and minimum 3.0 GPA required.

EMPLOYMENT INFORMATION

Placement Office Available? Yes. **Rate of placement:** 88%.

MONTANA STATE UNIVERSITY—BILLINGS
College of Arts & Sciences

Address: 1500 University Drive, Billings, MT 59101-0298
Admissions Phone: 406-657-2238 · **Admissions Fax:** 406-657-2299
Admissions E-mail: admissions@msubillings.edu · **Web Address:** www.msubillings.edu

INSTITUTIONAL INFORMATION

Public/private: Public. **Evening Classes Available?** Yes. **Students in Parent Institution:** 4,423.

PROGRAMS

Master's offered in: Clinical psychology; organizational communications, public relations, and advertising; psychology; public administration and services; public administration; public relations/image management.

STUDENT INFORMATION

Total Students in Program: 402. **% Full-time:** 40. **% Female:** 86.

EXPENSES/FINANCIAL AID

Annual Tuition: In-state $4,546. / Out-of-state $10,322. **Room & Board:** $5,370. **Books and Supplies:** $900. **Grants Range From:** $1,000-$4,500. **Loans Range From:** $200-$11,000. **% Receiving Scholarships/Grants:** 40. **% Receiving Loans:** 72. **% Receiving Assistantships:** 30. **Types of Aid Available:** Graduate assistantships, institutional work-study, loans, scholarships. **Assistantship Compensation Includes:** Partial tuition remission, salary/stipend.

ADMISSIONS INFORMATION

Application Fee: $40. **Regular Application Deadline:** 4/1. **Transfer Students Accepted?** Yes. **Required Admission Factors:** GRE, letters of recommendation, transcript. **Recommended Admission Factors:** GMAT.

EMPLOYMENT INFORMATION

Placement Office Available? Yes.

MONTANA TECH OF THE UNIVERSITY OF MONTANA
Graduate School

Address: 1300 West Park Street, Butte, MT 59701-8997
Admissions Phone: 406-496-4304 · **Admissions Fax:** 406-496-4334
Admissions E-mail: cdunstan@mtech.edu · **Web Address:** www.mtech.edu/gradschl

INSTITUTIONAL INFORMATION

Public/private: Public. **Evening Classes Available?** Yes. **Total Faculty:** 81. **% Faculty Female:** 20. **Student/faculty Ratio:** 2:1. **Students in Parent Institution:** 1,869.

PROGRAMS

Master's offered in: Civil engineering, communications and media studies, engineering, environmental/environmental health engineering, geological/geophysical engineering, mechanical engineering, metallurgical engineering, mining and mineral engineering, occupational health and industrial hygiene, petroleum engineering.

STUDENT INFORMATION

Total Students in Program: 102. **% Full-time:** 78. **% Female:** 41. **% International:** 6.

RESEARCH FACILITIES

Research Facilities: Center for Advanced Mineral & Metallurgical Processing.

EXPENSES/FINANCIAL AID

Annual Tuition: In-state $5,217. / Out-of-state $16,320. **Room & Board:** $4,790. **Books and Supplies:** $650. **Grants Range From:** $500-$8,000. **Loans Range From:** $1,000-$10,000. **% Receiving Financial Aid:** 85. **% Receiving Loans:** 60. **% Receiving Assistantships:** 47. **Types of Aid Available:** Graduate assistantships, loans. **Average student debt, upon graduation:** $10,000. **Number of Teaching/Research Assistantships Granted Each Year:** 30. **Assistantship Compensation Includes:** Salary/stipend. **Average Salary Stipend:** $8,000.

ADMISSIONS INFORMATION

Application Fee: $30. **Priority Application Deadline:** 4/1. **Regular Application Deadline:** 8/1. **Regular Notification:** Rolling. **Transfer Students Accepted?** Yes. **Transfer Policy:** Admission requirements are the same as for regular applicants. **Number of Applications Received:** 103. **% of Applicants Accepted:** 69. **% Accepted Who Enrolled:** 58. **Average GPA:** 3.2. **Average GRE Verbal:** 459. **Average GRE Quantitative:** 601. **Average GRE Analytical:** 568. **Average GRE Analytical Writing:** 4. **Required Admission Factors:** Essays/personal statement, GRE, letters of recommendation, transcript. **Other Admission Factors:** Minimum 2.7 GPA required. 3.0 GPA preferred. **Program-Specific Admission Factors:** Two-year work requirement for online industrial hygiene master degree program.

EMPLOYMENT INFORMATION

Placement Office Available? Yes. **% Employed Within 6 Months:** 98. **% of master's/doctoral grads employed in their field upon graduation:** 98. **Rate of placement:** 98%. **Average starting salary:** $54,000.

MONTCLAIR STATE UNIVERSITY
School of the Arts

Address: One Normal Avenue, Upper Montclair, NJ 07043-1624
Admissions Phone: 973-655-5147 or 800-331-9207
Admissions Fax: 973-655-7869 · **Admissions E-mail:** narrettc@mail.montclair.edu

INSTITUTIONAL INFORMATION

Public/private: Public. **Evening Classes Available?** Yes. **Total Faculty:** 52. **Students in Parent Institution:** 13,502.

STUDENT INFORMATION

Total Students in Program: 3,314. **% Full-time:** 18. **% Female:** 70.

RESEARCH FACILITIES

Research Facilities: Curriculum Resource Center.

EXPENSES/FINANCIAL AID

Annual Tuition: In-state $4,680. / Out-of-state $6,552. **Room & Board:** $4,113. **Fees:** $564. **Books and Supplies:** $805.

ADMISSIONS INFORMATION

Application Fee: $40. **Regular Notification:** Rolling. **Transfer Students Accepted?** Yes. **Number of Applications Received:** 60. **% of Applicants Accepted:** 75. **% Accepted Who Enrolled:** 84. **Average GPA:** 3.11. **Average GRE Verbal:** 443. **Average GRE Quantitative:** 453.

Required Admission Factors: Essays/personal statement, transcript.

EMPLOYMENT INFORMATION
Placement Office Available? Yes.

MONTCLAIR STATE UNIVERSITY
College of Science & Mathematics

Address: One Normal Avenue, Montclair, NJ 07043-1624
Admissions Phone: 973-655-5147 or 800-331-9207 · **Admissions Fax:** 973-655-7869
Admissions E-mail: aielloa@mail.montclair.edu
Web Address: www.montclair.edu/graduate

INSTITUTIONAL INFORMATION
Public/private: Public. **Evening Classes Available?** Yes. **Total Faculty:** 83. **Students in Parent Institution:** 15,204.

STUDENT INFORMATION
Total Students in Program: 3,829. **% Full-time:** 21. **% Female:** 71.

RESEARCH FACILITIES
Research Facilities: Curriculum Resource Center.

EXPENSES/FINANCIAL AID
Annual Tuition: In-state $4,680. / Out-of-state $6,552. **Room & Board:** $4,113. **Fees:** $564. **Books and Supplies:** $805.

ADMISSIONS INFORMATION
Application Fee: $60. **Regular Application Deadline:** 7/1. **Regular Notification:** Rolling. **Transfer Students Accepted?** Yes. **Number of Applications Received:** 153. **% of Applicants Accepted:** 76. **% Accepted Who Enrolled:** 71. **Average GPA:** 3.3. **Average GRE Verbal:** 439. **Average GRE Quantitative:** 622.
Required Admission Factors: Essays/personal statement, GRE, letters of recommendation, transcript.
Other Admission Factors: Minimum 24 semester hours in biology and coursework in chemistry, math, and physics required.

EMPLOYMENT INFORMATION
Placement Office Available? Yes.

MONTCLAIR STATE UNIVERSITY
The Graduate School

Address: One Normal Avenue, Montclair, NJ 07043
Admissions Phone: 973-655-5147 or 800-955-GRAD
Admissions Fax: 973-655-7869 · **Admissions E-mail:** aielloa@mail.montclair.edu
Web Address: www.montclair.edu/graduate

INSTITUTIONAL INFORMATION
Public/private: Public. **Evening Classes Available?** Yes. **Students in Parent Institution:** 15,637.

PROGRAMS
Master's offered in: Anthropology; biology/biological sciences; communication disorders; communications and media studies; communications studies/speech, communication, and rhetoric; computer science; education leadership and administration; education; educational psychology; English language and literature; French language and literature; health and physical education; linguistics; mathematics; organizational communication; pre-law studies; psychology; public relations/image management; social sciences; sociology; Spanish language and literature; statistics. **Doctorate offered in:** Education. **First Professional degree offered in:** Molecular biology.

STUDENT INFORMATION
Total Students in Program: 3,818. **% Full-time:** 22. **% Female:** 71. **% Minority:** 20. **% International:** 4.

RESEARCH FACILITIES
Research Facilities: Curriculum Resource Center.

EXPENSES/FINANCIAL AID
Annual Tuition: In-state $4,680. / Out-of-state $6,552. **Room & Board:** $4,113. **Fees:** $564. **Books and Supplies:** $805.

ADMISSIONS INFORMATION
Application Fee: $60. **Regular Application Deadline:** 8/1. **Regular Notification:** Rolling. **Transfer Students Accepted?** Yes. **Number of Applications Received:** 2,805. **% of Applicants Accepted:** 84. **% Accepted Who Enrolled:** 84. **Average GPA:** 3.2. **Average GRE Verbal:** 452. **Average GRE Quantitative:** 521.
Required Admission Factors: Essays/personal statement, GRE, letters of recommendation, transcript.

EMPLOYMENT INFORMATION
Placement Office Available? Yes.

MONTEREY INSTITUTE OF INTERNATIONAL STUDIES
Graduate School of International Policy Studies

Address: 460 Pierce Street, Monterey, CA 93940
Admissions Phone: 831-647-4123 · **Admissions Fax:** 831-647-6405
Admissions E-mail: admit@miis.edu · **Web Address:** www.miis.edu

INSTITUTIONAL INFORMATION
Public/private: Private (nonprofit). **Total Faculty:** 45. **% Faculty Female:** 24. **% Faculty Part-time:** 69. **Student/faculty Ratio:** 12:1. **Students in Parent Institution:** 780.

STUDENT INFORMATION
Total Students in Program: 364. **% Full-time:** 96. **% Female:** 62. **% Minority:** 1. **% International:** 22.

RESEARCH FACILITIES
Research Facilities: Center for Nonproliferation Studies, Program for Arms Control, Disarmament and Conversion, Business and Economic Development Center, Project OCEANS, Center for Russian and Eurasian Studies, and the Center for East Asian studies.

EXPENSES/FINANCIAL AID
Annual Tuition: $25,500. **Room & Board:** $7,400. **Fees:** $200. **Books and Supplies:** $900. **Grants Range From:** $2,000-$12,000. **Loans Range From:** $1,000-$37,000. **% Receiving Financial Aid:** 80. **% Receiving Scholarships/Grants:** 72. **% Receiving Loans:** 80. **Types of Aid Available:** Grants, institutional work-study, loans, scholarships. **Average student debt, upon graduation:** $45,000.

ADMISSIONS INFORMATION
Application Fee: $50. **Priority Application Deadline:** 12/1. **Regular Application Deadline:** 8/1. **Regular Notification:** Rolling. **Transfer Students Accepted?** Yes. **Transfer Policy:** Course descriptions are required to petition for transfer credits. Must have achieved grades of B or better on transfer courses. **Number of Applications Received:** 356. **% of Applicants Accepted:** 97. **% Accepted Who Enrolled:** 40. **Average GPA:** 3.3.
Required Admission Factors: Essays/personal statement, letters of recommendation, transcript.
Recommended Admission Factors: GRE.
Other Admission Factors: Minimum 3.0 GPA on a 4.0 scale. Student must be able to demonstrate that they can work at a 3rd-year college level in a second language.

EMPLOYMENT INFORMATION

Placement Office Available? Yes. % Employed Within 6 Months: 65. % of master's/doctoral grads employed in their field upon graduation: 40. Rate of placement: 85%. Average starting salary: $43,000.

MONTEREY INSTITUTE OF INTERNATIONAL STUDIES
Graduate School of Translation & Interpretation

Address: 460 Pierce Street, Monterey, CA 93940
Admissions Phone: 831-647-4123 · **Admissions Fax:** 831-647-6405
Admissions E-mail: admit@miis.edu
Web Address: www.miis.edu/gsti-about-overview.html

INSTITUTIONAL INFORMATION

Public/private: Private (nonprofit). Total Faculty: 39. % Faculty Female: 62. % Faculty Part-time: 56. Student/faculty Ratio: 7:1. Students in Parent Institution: 780.

STUDENT INFORMATION

Total Students in Program: 165. % Full-time: 98. % Female: 80. % Minority: 11. % International: 59.

RESEARCH FACILITIES

Research Facilities: Center for Nonproliferation Studies, Program for Arms Control, Disarmament and Conversion, Business and Economic Development Center, Project OCEANS, Center for Russian and Eurasian Studies, and the Center for East Asian studies.

EXPENSES/FINANCIAL AID

Annual Tuition: $25,500. Room & Board: $7,400. Fees: $200. Books and Supplies: $900. Grants Range From: $2,000-$12,000. Loans Range From: $1,000-$37,000. % Receiving Financial Aid: 80. % Receiving Scholarships/Grants: 72. % Receiving Loans: 80. Types of Aid Available: Grants, institutional work-study, loans, scholarships. Average student debt, upon graduation: $37,000.

ADMISSIONS INFORMATION

Application Fee: $50. Priority Application Deadline: 12/1. Regular Application Deadline: 8/1. Regular Notification: Rolling. Transfer Students Accepted? Yes. Transfer Policy: Course descriptions required to petititon for transfer credit. Number of Applications Received: 192. % of Applicants Accepted: 71. % Accepted Who Enrolled: 67. Average GPA: 3.3.
Required Admission Factors: Essays/personal statement, letters of recommendation, transcript.
Recommended Admission Factors: GRE, interview.
Other Admission Factors: Minimum 3.0 GPA required.
Program-Specific Admission Factors: Must be native-level speaker of Chinese, English, French, German, Japanese, Korean, Russian, or Spanaish and near-native-level in English or another foreign language above.

EMPLOYMENT INFORMATION

Placement Office Available? Yes. % Employed Within 6 Months: 80. % of master's/doctoral grads employed in their field upon graduation: 85. Rate of placement: 80%. Average starting salary: $40,000.

MOODY BIBLE INSTITUTE
Moody Graduate School

Address: 820 North LaSalle Boulevard, Chicago, IL 60610
Admissions Phone: 312-329-4265 · **Admissions Fax:** 312-329-8987

INSTITUTIONAL INFORMATION

Public/private: Private (nonprofit). Evening Classes Available? Yes. Students in Parent Institution: 1,471.

STUDENT INFORMATION

Total Students in Program: 177. % Full-time: 82. % Female: 34.

EXPENSES/FINANCIAL AID

Annual Tuition: In-state $2,070. / Fees: $1,323. Books and Supplies: $240. Grants Range From: $500-$1,500. % Receiving Financial Aid: 20. % Receiving Scholarships/Grants: 100.

ADMISSIONS INFORMATION

Application Fee: $35. Regular Notification: Rolling. Transfer Students Accepted? No. Number of Applications Received: 48. % of Applicants Accepted: 88. % Accepted Who Enrolled: 50. Average GPA: 3.2.
Required Admission Factors: Essays/personal statement, letters of recommendation, transcript.
Other Admission Factors: Minimum 2.75 GPA required.

EMPLOYMENT INFORMATION

Placement Office Available? Yes.

MOREHEAD STATE UNIVERSITY
Caudill College of Humanities

Address: 701 Ginger Hall, Morehead, KY 40351
Admissions Phone: 606-783-2039 · **Admissions Fax:** 606-783-5061
Admissions E-mail: graduate@moreheadstate.edu
Web Address: www.moreheadstate.edu

INSTITUTIONAL INFORMATION

Public/private: Public. Evening Classes Available? Yes. Students in Parent Institution: 7,583.

STUDENT INFORMATION

Total Students in Program: 768. % Full-time: 24. % Female: 65.

EXPENSES/FINANCIAL AID

Annual Tuition: In-state $2,470. / Out-of-state $6,710. Room & Board: $1,610. % Receiving Assistantships: 84.

ADMISSIONS INFORMATION

Application Fee:. Priority Application Deadline: 6/1. Regular Application Deadline: 7/1. Regular Notification: Rolling. Transfer Students Accepted? Yes. Number of Applications Received: 98. Average GPA: 3.0.
Required Admission Factors: Transcript.
Other Admission Factors: Minimum graduate school GPA is 2.5.

EMPLOYMENT INFORMATION

Placement Office Available? Yes.

MORGAN STATE UNIVERSITY
School of Graduate Studies

Address: 1700 East Cold Spring Lane, Suite 206 Holmes Hall, Baltimore, MD 21251
Admissions Phone: 443-885-3185 · **Admissions Fax:** 443-885-8226
Admissions E-mail: jwaller@moac.morgan.edu
Web Address: www.morgan.edu/academic/Grad-Studies/

INSTITUTIONAL INFORMATION

Public/private: Public. Evening Classes Available? Yes. Total Faculty: 202. % Faculty Part-time: 10. Student/faculty Ratio: 4:1. Students in Parent Institution: 6,640

PROGRAMS

Master's offered in: African American/Black studies; architecture (BArch, BA/BS, MArch, MA/MS, PhD); bioinformatics; business administration/management; chemistry; city/urban, community, and regional planning; civil engineering; communications and media studies; economics; electrical, electronics and communications engineering; elementary education and teaching; English language and literature; history; industrial engineering; international/global studies; junior high/intermediate/middle school education and teaching; landscape architecture (BS, BSLA, BLA, MSLA, MLA, PhD); mathematics; music performance; physics; public health (MPH, DPH); science teacher education/general science teacher education; social work; sociology; transportation and materials moving services. **Doctorate offered in:** See above.

STUDENT INFORMATION

Total Students in Program: 690. **% Full-time:** 48. **% Female:** 40.

RESEARCH FACILITIES

Research Facilities: Morris A. Sopher Library & Information Technology Center, McKeldin University Center, office of international student affairs, Institute of Urban Research, career development

EXPENSES/FINANCIAL AID

Annual Tuition: In-state $297 per credit. / Out-of-state $490 per credit. **Fees:** $52. **Books and Supplies:** $500. **Grants Range From:** $400-$5,000. **Loans Range From:** $4,500-$18,000. **% Receiving Financial Aid:** 45. **% Receiving Scholarships/Grants:** 41. **% Receiving Loans:** 35. **Types of Aid Available:** Fellowships, graduate assistantships, grants, scholarships. Title III funding. **Assistantship Compensation Includes:** Partial tuition remission, salary/stipend. **Average Salary Stipend:** $10,500.

ADMISSIONS INFORMATION

Priority Application Deadline: 2/1. **Regular Application Deadline:** 2/1. **Regular Notification:** Rolling. **Transfer Students Accepted?** Yes. **Number of Applications Received:** 746. **% of Applicants Accepted:** 40. **% Accepted Who Enrolled:** 71. **Average GPA:** 3.2.
Required Admission Factors: Essays/personal statement, letters of recommendation, transcript.
Other Admission Factors: Minimum 2.5 GPA required for conditional admission to most programs.
Minimum 3.0 GPA required for unconditional admission.

EMPLOYMENT INFORMATION

Placement Office Available? Yes. **Average starting salary:** $40,000.

MOUNT ALLISON UNIVERSITY
Graduate Studies

Address: Sackville, New Brunswick, E4L 1E4 Canada
Admissions Phone: 506-364-2500 · **Admissions Fax:** 506-364-2505
Admissions E-mail: iehrman@mta.ca

INSTITUTIONAL INFORMATION

Public/private: Public. **Students in Parent Institution:** 2,484

STUDENT INFORMATION

Total Students in Program: 2. **% Full-time:** 100. **% Female:** 100.

RESEARCH FACILITIES

Research Facilities: Digital Microscopy Facility, Wetlands Institute.

EXPENSES/FINANCIAL AID

Annual Tuition: $500 per credit. **Room & Board:** $6,750. **Books and Supplies:** $300. **Grants Range From:** $12,000-$15,000.

ADMISSIONS INFORMATION

Application Fee: $40. **Regular Notification:** Rolling. **Transfer Students Accepted?** No. **Number of Applications Received:** 7.
Required Admission Factors: Letters of recommendation, transcript.
Other Admission Factors: Minimum 3.0 GPA required.

EMPLOYMENT INFORMATION

% Employed Within 6 Months: 100. **% of master's/doctoral grads employed in their field upon graduation:** 100.

MOUNT ANGEL SEMINARY
Graduate Program

Address: St. Benedict, OR 97373
Admissions Phone: 503-845-3951 · **Admissions Fax:** 503-845-3126
Admissions E-mail: registrar@mtangel.edu

INSTITUTIONAL INFORMATION

Students in Parent Institution: 193.

STUDENT INFORMATION

Total Students in Program: 105. **% Full-time:** 79. **% Female:** 17.

EXPENSES/FINANCIAL AID

Books and Supplies: $300.

ADMISSIONS INFORMATION

Transfer Students Accepted? Yes.
Required Admission Factors: Letters of recommendation, transcript.
Other Admission Factors: Minimum 2.5 GPA required.

MOUNT MARY COLLEGE
Graduate Programs

Address: 2900 North Menomonee River Parkway, Milwaukee, WI 53222
Admissions Phone: 414-256-1252

INSTITUTIONAL INFORMATION

Public/private: Private (nonprofit). **Evening Classes Available?** Yes. **Total Faculty:** 31. **Student/faculty Ratio:** 7:1. **Students in Parent Institution:** 1,309

STUDENT INFORMATION

Total Students in Program: 135. **% Full-time:** 23. **% Female:** 96.

EXPENSES/FINANCIAL AID

Annual Tuition: $6,660. **Room & Board:** $4,650. **Fees:** $600. **Books and Supplies:** $1,560.

ADMISSIONS INFORMATION

Application Fee: $35. **Transfer Students Accepted?** Yes.
Required Admission Factors: Transcript.
Program-Specific Admission Factors: Slide portfolio required of some applicants.

EMPLOYMENT INFORMATION

Placement Office Available? Yes.

MOUNT SAINT MARY COLLEGE
Graduate Programs

Address: 330 Powell Avenue, Newburgh, NY 12550-3598
Admissions Phone: 914-569-3582 · **Admissions Fax:** 914-569-3885
Admissions E-mail: atsunyo@msmc.edu

INSTITUTIONAL INFORMATION

Public/private: Private (nonprofit). **Evening Classes Available?** Yes. **Student/faculty Ratio:** 12:1. **Students in Parent Institution:** 2,085.

STUDENT INFORMATION
Total Students in Program: 438. % Full-time: 4. % Female: 78.

EXPENSES/FINANCIAL AID
Annual Tuition: $8,838. Fees: $45. Books and Supplies: $300.

ADMISSIONS INFORMATION
Application Fee: $20. Regular Notification: Rolling. **Transfer Students Accepted?** Yes. **Transfer Policy:** Maximum 21 credit hours taken within the past five years may be transferred after evaluation. **Number of Applications Received:** 26. % of Applicants Accepted: 92. % Accepted Who Enrolled: 96. Average GPA: 3.21.
Required Admission Factors: Essays/personal statement, interview, letters of recommendation, transcript.
Other Admission Factors: Minimum 2.5 GPA required.

EMPLOYMENT INFORMATION
% Employed Within 6 Months: 94.

MOUNT SAINT MARY'S COLLEGE
Graduate Studies

Address: 16300 Old Emmitsburg Road, Emmitsburg, MD 21727-7796
Admissions Phone: 301-447-5326 · **Admissions Fax:** 301-447-5755
Admissions E-mail: drega@msmary.edu

INSTITUTIONAL INFORMATION
Public/private: Private (nonprofit). **Evening Classes Available?** Yes. **Total Faculty:** 15. % Faculty Part-time: 27. **Student/faculty Ratio:** 16:1. **Students in Parent Institution:** 1,859.

STUDENT INFORMATION
Total Students in Program: 244. % Full-time: 32. % Female: 50.

EXPENSES/FINANCIAL AID
Annual Tuition: $4,680. Room & Board: $6,860. Fees: $200. Books and Supplies: $600. % Receiving Assistantships: 3. Number of Teaching/Research Assistantships Granted Each Year: 12. Average Salary Stipend: $6,000.

ADMISSIONS INFORMATION
Application Fee: $35. Regular Notification: Rolling. **Transfer Students Accepted?** Yes. **Number of Applications Received:** 67. % of Applicants Accepted: 93. % Accepted Who Enrolled: 98. Average GPA: 3.0.
Required Admission Factors: Transcript.
Other Admission Factors: Minimum GMAT score of 500 required if undergraduate GPA is less than 2.75.

EMPLOYMENT INFORMATION
Placement Office Available? Yes. % Employed Within 6 Months: 98. % of master's/doctoral grads employed in their field upon graduation: 98.

MOUNT SAINT VINCENT UNIVERSITY
Graduate Programs

Address: Halifax, Nova Scotia, B3M 2J6 Canada
Admissions Phone: 902-457-6128

INSTITUTIONAL INFORMATION
Public/private: Public. **Evening Classes Available?** Yes.

EXPENSES/FINANCIAL AID
Annual Tuition: Canadians $5,375. / Non-Canadians $8,075. Fees: $400. Books and Supplies: $1,200. Grants Range From: $100-$3,000.

ADMISSIONS INFORMATION
Transfer Students Accepted? No.

Required Admission Factors: Essays/personal statement, letters of recommendation, transcript.

EMPLOYMENT INFORMATION
Placement Office Available? Yes.

MOUNT SINAI SCHOOL OF MEDICINE
Graduate School of Biological Sciences

Address: One Gustave L. Levy Place, Campus Box 1022, New York, NY 10029
Admissions Phone: 212-241-6546 · **Admissions Fax:** 212-241-0651
Admissions E-mail: grads@mssm.edu · **Web Address:** www.mssm.edu/gradschool

INSTITUTIONAL INFORMATION
Public/private: Private (nonprofit). **Students in Parent Institution:** 650

PROGRAMS
Doctorate offered in: Biochemistry, biophysics, and molecular biology; biological and biomedical sciences; biomathematics and bioinformatics; biotechnology; cell/cellular and molecular biology; genetics; human/medical genetics; microbiological sciences.

STUDENT INFORMATION
Total Students in Program: 105. % Full-time: 133.

RESEARCH FACILITIES
Research Facilities: Flow Cytometry; Hybridoma; Microarray; Microscopy; Microvascular Surgery; Mouse Genetics.

EXPENSES/FINANCIAL AID
Annual Tuition: $18,540. Books and Supplies: $250. **Grants Range From:** $25,500-$25,500. % Receiving Financial Aid: 100. **Types of Aid Available:** fellowships. **Average amount of individual fellowships per year:** $25,500. **Number of Teaching/Research Assistantships Granted Each Year:** 26. **Assistantship Compensation Includes:** Full tuition remission, salary/stipend. **Average Salary Stipend:** $25,500.

ADMISSIONS INFORMATION
Application Fee: $60. Regular Application Deadline: 1/15. Regular Notification: Rolling. **Transfer Students Accepted?** Yes. **Transfer Policy:** Must apply in regular application cycle for admission in fall. Applicants must provide recommendation from current program director or research mentor. **Number of Applications Received:** 402. % of Applicants Accepted: 15. % Accepted Who Enrolled: 39. Average GPA: 3.5.
Required Admission Factors: Essays/personal statement, GRE, interview, letters of recommendation, transcript.
Other Admission Factors: Research experience and undergraduate major in the sciences, mathematics or engineering required. Demonstrated commitment to a research career.

EMPLOYMENT INFORMATION
% of master's/doctoral grads employed in their field upon graduation: 100.

MURRAY STATE UNIVERSITY
College of Humanities & Fine Arts

Address: PO Box 9, Murray, KY 42071
Admissions Phone: 270-762-3756 · **Admissions Fax:** 270-762-3780
Admissions E-mail: barbara.thompson@murraystate.edu

INSTITUTIONAL INFORMATION
Public/private: Public. **Evening Classes Available?** Yes. **Students in Parent Institution:** 9,141.

STUDENT INFORMATION

Total Students in Program: 1,649. % Full-time: 27. % Female: 69.

EXPENSES/FINANCIAL AID

Annual Tuition: In-state $2,879. / Out-of-state $8,007. Loans Range From: $400-$18,500. % Receiving Financial Aid: 65. % Receiving Scholarships/Grants: 1. % Receiving Loans: 99.

ADMISSIONS INFORMATION

Application Fee: $20. Regular Notification: Rolling. Transfer Students Accepted? Yes. Number of Applications Received: 60. % of Applicants Accepted: 78. % Accepted Who Enrolled: 72.
Required Admission Factors: GRE, transcript.

EMPLOYMENT INFORMATION

Placement Office Available? Yes. Rate of placement: 68%

NAROPA UNIVERSITY
Graduate Programs

Address: 2130 Arapahoe Avenue, Boulder, CO 80302
Admissions Phone: 303-546-3572

INSTITUTIONAL INFORMATION

Public/private: Private (nonprofit). Student/faculty Ratio: 11:1. Students in Parent Institution: 1,127.

STUDENT INFORMATION

Total Students in Program: 664. % Full-time: 65. % Female: 70.

EXPENSES/FINANCIAL AID

Annual Tuition: In-state $10,766. Fees: $560. Books and Supplies: $600. Grants Range From: $250-$10,000. Loans Range From: $1-$18,500. % Receiving Financial Aid: 58. % Receiving Scholarships/Grants: 20. % Receiving Loans: 94. Average student debt, upon graduation: $43,489.

ADMISSIONS INFORMATION

Application Fee: $50. Regular Notification: Rolling. Transfer Students Accepted? No. Number of Applications Received: 487. % of Applicants Accepted: 82. % Accepted Who Enrolled: 61.
Required Admission Factors: Essays/personal statement, interview, letters of recommendation, transcript.
Program-Specific Admission Factors: Portfolio required of art therapy program applicants. Audition required of music therapy and dance therapy program applicants. Writing sample required of writing program applicants.

NATIONAL THEATER CONSERVATORY
Graduate Programs

Address: 1050 13th Street, Denver, CO 80204
Admissions Phone: 303-446-4855

INSTITUTIONAL INFORMATION

Public/private: Private (nonprofit). Total Faculty: 30. % Faculty Female: 17. % Faculty Part-time: 83. Student/faculty Ratio: 1:1. Students in Parent Institution: 22.

STUDENT INFORMATION

Total Students in Program: 22. % Full-time: 100. % Female: 45.

RESEARCH FACILITIES

Research Facilities: Voice Research Center.

EXPENSES/FINANCIAL AID

Room & Board: $600. Books and Supplies: $200. Grants Range From: $26,800-$28,750. % Receiving Scholarships/Grants: 100.

ADMISSIONS INFORMATION

Application Fee: $50. Transfer Students Accepted? No. Number of Applications Received: 385. % of Applicants Accepted: 2. % Accepted Who Enrolled: 100. Average GPA: 3.0.
Required Admission Factors: Interview, letters of recommendation, transcript.

EMPLOYMENT INFORMATION

% Employed Within 6 Months: 100.

NATIONAL-LOUIS UNIVERSITY
College of Arts & Sciences

Address: 122 South Michigan Avenue, Chicago, IL 60603
Admissions Phone: 888-NLU-TODAY

INSTITUTIONAL INFORMATION

Public/private: Private (nonprofit). Evening Classes Available? Yes. Student/faculty Ratio: 13:1. Students in Parent Institution: 6,558.

STUDENT INFORMATION

Total Students in Program: 3,217. % Full-time: 25. % Female: 81.

RESEARCH FACILITIES

Research Facilities: Baker Demonstration School (pre-kindergarten through grade 8 lab school).

EXPENSES/FINANCIAL AID

Books and Supplies: $750. % Receiving Financial Aid: 32.

ADMISSIONS INFORMATION

Application Fee: $25. Regular Notification: Rolling. Transfer Students Accepted? Yes. Number of Applications Received: 131. % of Applicants Accepted: 96. % Accepted Who Enrolled: 63.
Required Admission Factors: GRE, letters of recommendation, transcript.
Other Admission Factors: Minimum 3.0 GPA in final 2 years of course work and written statement required.

EMPLOYMENT INFORMATION

Placement Office Available? Yes.

NAVAL POSTGRADUATE SCHOOL
Graduate Programs

Address: 589 Dyer Road, Room 100, Monterey, CA 93943-5100
Admissions Phone: 831-656-3093 · Admissions Fax: 831-656-2891
Admissions E-mail: tcalhoon@nps.navy.mil

INSTITUTIONAL INFORMATION

Public/private: Public. Total Faculty: 349. % Faculty Part-time: 3. Students in Parent Institution: 1,504.

ADMISSIONS INFORMATION

Regular Notification: Rolling. Transfer Students Accepted? No.
Required Admission Factors: GRE, transcript.
Program-Specific Admission Factors: GRE required of doctoral program applicants only.

NAZARETH COLLEGE OF ROCHESTER
Graduate Programs

Address: 4245 East Avenue, Rochester, NY 14618
Admissions Phone: 716-389-2815 · Admissions Fax: 716-586-2452
Admissions E-mail: gfzappia@naz.edu

INSTITUTIONAL INFORMATION

Public/private: Private (nonprofit). **Evening Classes Available?** Yes. **Total Faculty:** 12. **% Faculty Female:** 8. **% Faculty Part-time:** 67. **Students in Parent Institution:** 3,075.

STUDENT INFORMATION

Total Students in Program: 1,165. **% Full-time:** 21. **% Female:** 81.

RESEARCH FACILITIES

Research Facilities: The Marie Callahan Reading Clinic, Speech and Hearing Clinic, The Graduate Learning Clinic.

EXPENSES/FINANCIAL AID

Annual Tuition: In-state $8,028. **Fees:** $40. **Grants Range From:** $75-$13,680. **Loans Range From:** $500-$18,500. **% Receiving Scholarships/Grants:** 27. **% Receiving Loans:** 85.

ADMISSIONS INFORMATION

Application Fee: $40. **Regular Notification:** Rolling. **Transfer Students Accepted?** Yes. **Transfer Policy:** Maximum 6 credit hours may be transferred with a minimum grade of B. **Number of Applications Received:** 22. **% of Applicants Accepted:** 86. **% Accepted Who Enrolled:** 79.
Required Admission Factors: Essays/personal statement, interview, letters of recommendation, transcript.
Other Admission Factors: Minimum 2.7 cumulative GPA, minimum 3.0 GPA in major, and course work in introductory management, marketing, accounting, business law, computer use, and statistics required.

EMPLOYMENT INFORMATION

Placement Office Available? Yes.

NEUMANN COLLEGE
Graduate Programs

Address: One Neumann Drive, Aston, PA 19014-1298
Admissions E-mail: sbogard@neumann.edu

INSTITUTIONAL INFORMATION

Public/private: Private (nonprofit). **Evening Classes Available?** Yes. **Student/faculty Ratio:** 6:1. **Students in Parent Institution:** 1,625.

STUDENT INFORMATION

Total Students in Program: 180. **% Full-time:** 38. **% Female:** 72.

RESEARCH FACILITIES

Research Facilities: Franciscan Center.

EXPENSES/FINANCIAL AID

Annual Tuition: $7,380.

ADMISSIONS INFORMATION

Transfer Students Accepted? No.
Required Admission Factors: Interview, letters of recommendation, transcript.
Other Admission Factors: At least 1 year in clinical nursing practice required of nursing program applicants.

EMPLOYMENT INFORMATION

Placement Office Available? Yes. **% Employed Within 6 Months:** 100. **% of master's grads employed in their field upon graduation:** 100. **Rate of placement:** 89%.

NEW JERSEY INSTITUTE OF TECHNOLOGY
College of Computing Sciences

Address: Office of University Admissions, University Heights, Newark, NJ 07102
Admissions Phone: 973-596-3300 · **Admissions Fax:** 973-596-3461
Admissions E-mail: admissions@njit.edu
Website: www.njit.edu/admissions/index.php

INSTITUTIONAL INFORMATION

Public/private: Public. **Evening Classes Available?** Yes. **Total Faculty:** 90. **% Faculty Female:** 16. **% Faculty Part-time:** 27. **Student/faculty Ratio:** 13:1. **Students in Parent Institution:** 8,249.

PROGRAMS

Masters offered in: Applied mathematics; architecture (BArch, BA/BS, MArch, MA/MS, PhD); biology/biological sciences; biomathematics and bioinformatics; biomedical/medical engineering; business administration/management; business/managerial operations; chemical engineering; chemistry; civil engineering; computer and information sciences; computer engineering; electrical, electronics, and communications engineering; engineering science; engineering; engineering-related technologies/technicians; environmental science; environmental/environmental health engineering; history; industrial engineering; industrial management; information science/studies; manufacturing engineering; materials engineering; mechanical engineering; multi/interdisciplinary studies; nursing science (MS, PhD); physical sciences; physics; public health (MPh, DPh); public policy analysis; statistics; technical and business writing; transportation and highway engineering. **Doctorate offered in:** Biology/biological sciences; biomedical/medical engineering; chemical engineering; chemistry; civil engineering; computer and information sciences; computer engineering; computer science; electrical, electronics, and communications engineering; nursing science (MS, PhD); physical sciences; physics; public health (MPh, DPh).

STUDENT INFORMATION

Total Students in Program: 787. **% Full-time:** 46. **% Female:** 30. **% Minority:** 7. **% International:** 48.

RESEARCH FACILITIES

Research Facilities: Architecture and Building Science Group, Center for Manufacturing Systems, Hazardous Substance Management Research Center, Air Emissions Research Center, Center for Microwave and Lightwave Engineering, Center for Communication and Signal Processing.

EXPENSES/FINANCIAL AID

Annual Tuition: In-state $9,620. / Out-of-state $13,542. **Room & Board (On/off Campus):** $7,896/$10,000. **Fees:** $1,148. **Books and Supplies:** $1,200. **Grants Range From:** $1,000-$26,000. **Loans Range From:** $1,000-$20,000. **% Receiving Scholarships/Grants:** 30. **% Receiving Loans:** 30. **% Receiving Assistantships:** 25. **Types of Aid Available:** Fellowships, graduate assistantships, grants, institutional work-study, loans, scholarships. **Assistantship Compensation Includes:** Full tuition remission, partial tuition remission, salary/stipend. **Average Salary Stipend:** $1,350.

ADMISSIONS INFORMATION

Application Fee: $60. **Priority Application Deadline:** 1/15. **Regular Application Deadline:** 6/1. **Regular Notification:** Rolling. **Transfer Students Accepted?** Yes. **Number of Applications Received:** 1,579. **% of Applicants Accepted:** 76. **% Accepted Who Enrolled:** 70. **Average GPA:** 2.8. **Average GRE Verbal:** 435. **Average GRE Quantitative:** 723. **Average GRE Analytical:** 668. **Average GRE Analytical Writing:** 3.7.
Required Admission Factors: Letters of recommendation, transcript.
Other Admission Factors: Cumulative GPA no lower than 2.8 on a 4.0 scale.

EMPLOYMENT INFORMATION

Placement Office Available? Yes. **% Employed Within 6 Months:** 75. **Rate of placement:** 85%. **Average starting salary:** $50,000.

NEW JERSEY INSTITUTE OF TECHNOLOGY
College of Science and Liberal Arts

Address: University Heights, Newark, NJ 07102-1982
Admissions Phone: 973-596-3300 · **Admissions Fax:** 973-596-3461
Admissions E-mail: admissions@njit.edu · **Website:** http://csla.njit.edu

INSTITUTIONAL INFORMATION

Public/private: Public. **Evening Classes Available?** Yes. **Total Faculty:** 228. **% Faculty Female:** 20. **% Faculty Part-time:** 32. **Student/faculty Ratio:** 13:1. **Students in Parent Institution:** 8,249.

PROGRAMS

Masters offered in: Applied mathematics; biomathematics and bioinformatics; biomedical/medical engineering; business administration/management; business/managerial operations; chemical engineering; chemistry; civil engineering; computer engineering; electrical, electronics, and communications engineering; engineering; environmental/environmental health engineering; history; industrial engineering; industrial management; manufacturing engineering; materials engineering; mechanical engineering; natural resources/conservation; nursing science (MS, PhD); physics; public health (MPh, DPh); public policy analysis; statistics; technical and business writing; transportation and highway engineering. **Doctorate offered in:** Biomedical/medical engineering; chemical engineering; chemistry; civil engineering; computer engineering; electrical, electronics, and communications engineering; environmental/environmental health engineering; industrial engineering.

STUDENT INFORMATION

Total Students in Program: 271. **% Full-time:** 42. **% Female:** 42. **% Minority:** 10. **% International:** 43.

RESEARCH FACILITIES

Research Facilities: Architecture and Building Science Group, Center for Manufacturing Systems, Hazardous Substance Management Research Center, Air Emissions Research Center, Center for Microwave and Lightwave Engineering, Center for Communication and Signal Processing.

EXPENSES/FINANCIAL AID

Annual Tuition: In-state $9,620. / Out-of-state $13,542. **Room & Board (On/off Campus):** $7,896/$10,000. **Fees:** $1,148. **Books and Supplies:** $1,200. **Grants Range From:** $1,000-$26,000. **Loans Range From:** $1,000-$20,000. **% Receiving Scholarships/Grants:** 30. **% Receiving Loans:** 30. **% Receiving Assistantships:** 25. **Types of Aid Available:** Fellowships, graduate assistantships, grants, institutional work-study, loans, scholarships. **Assistantship Compensation Includes:** Full tuition remission, partial tuition remission, salary/stipend. **Average Salary Stipend:** $1,350.

ADMISSIONS INFORMATION

Application Fee: $60. **Priority Application Deadline:** 1/15. **Regular Application Deadline:** 6/1. **Regular Notification:** Rolling. **Transfer Students Accepted?** Yes. **Transfer Policy:** Minimum 2.8 GPA required of transfer applicants. **Number of Applications Received:** 310. **% of Applicants Accepted:** 71. **% Accepted Who Enrolled:** 38. **Average GPA:** 2.8. **Average GRE Verbal:** 480. **Average GRE Quantitative:** 723. **Average GRE Analytical:** 636. **Average GRE Analytical Writing:** 3.9.
Required Admission Factors: Letters of recommendation, transcript.
Other Admission Factors: For MS admission: 2.8 minimum GPA; 1 letter of recommendation. For PhD admission: 3.5 minimum GPA; GRE; 3 letters of recommendation; statement of purpose.
Program-Specific Admission Factors: MS in biology, applied math, applied physics require GRE.

EMPLOYMENT INFORMATION

Placement Office Available? Yes. **% Employed Within 6 Months:** 75. **Rate of placement:** 85%. **Average starting salary:** $50,000.

NEW MEXICO INSTITUTE OF MINING & TECHNOLOGY
Graduate Studies

Address: 801 Leroy Place, Socorro, NM 87801
Admissions Phone: 505-835-5513 · **Admissions Fax:** 505-835-5476
Admissions E-mail: djohnson@prism.nmt.edu

INSTITUTIONAL INFORMATION

Public/private: Public. **Student/faculty Ratio:** 12:1. **Students in Parent Institution:** 1,547.

STUDENT INFORMATION

Total Students in Program: 312. **% Full-time:** 74. **% Female:** 37.

RESEARCH FACILITIES

Research Facilities: 10 institutional research centers, National Seismic Instrumentation Center.

EXPENSES/FINANCIAL AID

Annual Tuition: In-state $1,989. / Out-of-state $8,012. **Fees:** $684. **Books and Supplies:** $800. **Grants Range From:** $175-$16,300. **Loans Range From:** $600-$8,500. **% Receiving Financial Aid:** 67. **% Receiving Scholarships/Grants:** 8. **% Receiving Loans:** 25. **% Receiving Assistantships:** 93.

ADMISSIONS INFORMATION

Application Fee: $16. **Regular Notification:** Rolling. **Transfer Students Accepted?** Yes. **Transfer Policy:** Maximum 12 credit hours with a minimum B average may be transferred with approval by committee. **Number of Applications Received:** 604. **% of Applicants Accepted:** 61. **% Accepted Who Enrolled:** 19. **Average GPA:** 3.1. **Average GRE Verbal:** 410. **Average GRE Quantitative:** 685. **Average GRE Analytical:** 520.
Required Admission Factors: GRE, letters of recommendation, transcript. **Other Admission Factors:** Minimum 3.0 GPA required.

EMPLOYMENT INFORMATION

Placement Office Available? Yes. **% of master's/doctoral grads employed in their field upon graduation:** 28/100. **Rate of placement:** 40%. **Average starting salary:** $52,700.

NEW MEXICO STATE UNIVERSITY
College of Arts & Sciences

Address: Box 30001, MSC 3A, Las Cruces, NM 88003-8001

INSTITUTIONAL INFORMATION

Public/private: Public. **Student/faculty Ratio:** 21:1. **Students in Parent Institution:** 14,958.

STUDENT INFORMATION

Total Students in Program: 2,505. **% Full-time:** 51. **% Female:** 53.

EXPENSES/FINANCIAL AID

Annual Tuition: In-state $3,234. / Out-of-state $10,278. **Room & Board:** $5,414. **Books and Supplies:** $664.

ADMISSIONS INFORMATION

Regular Notification: Rolling. **Transfer Students Accepted?** No. **Number of Applications Received:** 634. **% of Applicants Accepted:** 62. **% Accepted Who Enrolled:** 37. **Average GPA:** 3.3. **Average GRE Verbal:** 513. **Average GRE Quantitative:** 630. **Average GRE Analytical:** 644. **Required Admission Factors:** Transcript.

EMPLOYMENT INFORMATION

Placement Office Available? Yes.

NEW MEXICO STATE UNIVERSITY
Graduate School

Address: Box 30001, MSC 3A, Las Cruces, NM 88003-8001
Admissions Phone: 505-646-3918 · **Admissions Fax:** 505-646-6846
Admissions E-mail: plammers@nmsu.edu

INSTITUTIONAL INFORMATION
Public/private: Public. **Students in Parent Institution:** 14,958.

STUDENT INFORMATION
Total Students in Program: 2,505. **% Full-time:** 51. **% Female:** 53.

EXPENSES/FINANCIAL AID
Annual Tuition: In-state $3,234. / Out-of-state $10,278. **Room & Board:** $5,414. **Books and Supplies:** $664. **% Receiving Financial Aid:** 95.

ADMISSIONS INFORMATION
Regular Notification: Rolling. **Transfer Students Accepted?** Yes. **Transfer Policy:** Concurrence of current major advisor and appropriate paperwork required of transfer applicants. **Number of Applications Received:** 54. **% of Applicants Accepted:** 87. **Average GPA:** 3.1. **Average GRE Verbal:** 516. **Average GRE Quantitative:** 580. **Average GRE Analytical:** 656.
Required Admission Factors: Essays/personal statement, letters of recommendation, transcript.
Other Admission Factors: Minimum GRE score of 1000 (Verbal and Quantitative), minimum 3.0 GPA, and personal letter of interest required; minimum GRE score of 1200 (verbal and quantitative) and minimum 3.3 GPA recommended.

EMPLOYMENT INFORMATION
Placement Office Available? Yes.

NEW SCHOOL UNIVERSITY
Actors Studio Drama School

Address: New School University Admissions, 55 West 13th Street, New York, NY 10011
Admissions Phone: 212-229-5150 or 877-528-3321
Admissions Fax: 212-229-5199 · **Admissions E-mail:** keltym@newschool.edu
Website: www.newschool.edu/academic/drama

INSTITUTIONAL INFORMATION
Public/private: Private (nonprofit). **Students in Parent Institution:** 7,867.

PROGRAMS
Masters offered in: Acting, playwriting, and screenwriting.

STUDENT INFORMATION
Total Students in Program: 208. **% Full-time:** 100.

RESEARCH FACILITIES
Research Facilities: Center for Economic Policy Analysis, World Policy Institute, Center for Studies of Social Change, Community Development Research Center, European Union Center of New York, Health Policy Research Center.

EXPENSES/FINANCIAL AID
Annual Tuition: $24,420. **Fees:** $200. **Books and Supplies:** $2,000. **Grants Range From:** $1,000-$20,000. **Loans Range From:** $100-$45,000. **% Receiving Financial Aid:** 85. **% Receiving Scholarships/Grants:** 60. **% Receiving Loans:** 85. **% Receiving Assistantships:** 15. **Average student debt, upon graduation:** $57,000. **Number of Fellowships Granted Each Year:** 5. **Average amount of individual fellowships per year:** $ 20,000.

ADMISSIONS INFORMATION
Application Fee: $50. **Priority Application Deadline:** 1/10. **Regular Application Deadline:** 1/10. **Regular Notification:** 4/2. **Transfer Students Accepted?** No. **Number of Applications Received:** 252. **% of Applicants Accepted:** 46. **% Accepted Who Enrolled:** 72. **Average GPA:** 3.0.

Required Admission Factors: Essays/personal statement, interview, letters of recommendation, transcript.
Other Admission Factors: For actors: headshot and artistic resume; for playwrights: writing sample; for directors: directing portfolio.
Program-Specific Admission Factors: Audition (with scene) required of acting applicants; directing audition required of directing applicants; interview required of playwriting applicants.

NEW SCHOOL UNIVERSITY
Graduate Faculty of Political & Social Science

Address: 66 West 12th Street, New York, NY 10011
Admissions Phone: 212-259-6710 · **Admissions Fax:** 212-989-7102
Admissions E-mail: inquiry@newschool.edu

INSTITUTIONAL INFORMATION
Public/private: Private (nonprofit). **Evening Classes Available?** Yes. **Students in Parent Institution:** 7,867.

STUDENT INFORMATION
Total Students in Program: 3,121. **% Full-time:** 63. **% Female:** 63.

RESEARCH FACILITIES
Research Facilities: Center for Economic Policy Analysis; World Policy Institute; Center for Studies of Social Change; Community Development Research Center; European Union Center of New York; Health Policy Research Center.

EXPENSES/FINANCIAL AID
Fees: $200. **Grants Range From:** $1,000-$22,000. **Loans Range From:** $100-$20,500. **% Receiving Financial Aid:** 60. **% Receiving Scholarships/Grants:** 60. **% Receiving Loans:** 85. **% Receiving Assistantships:** 15. **Average student debt, upon graduation:** $45,039. **Number of Fellowships Granted Each Year:** 110. **Average amount of individual fellowships per year:** 5,800. **Number of Teaching/Research Assistantships Granted Each Year:** 110. **Average Salary Stipend:** $1,888.

ADMISSIONS INFORMATION
Application Fee: $30. **Regular Notification:** Rolling. **Transfer Students Accepted?** No. **Transfer Policy:** Review of transfer credits by department required of transfer applicants. **Number of Applications Received:** 744. **% of Applicants Accepted:** 91. **% Accepted Who Enrolled:** 28.
Required Admission Factors: Essays/personal statement, letters of recommendation, transcript.
Other Admission Factors: Minimum general GRE score of 580 and minimum 3.2 GPA recommended.

NEW YORK INSTITUTE OF TECHNOLOGY
School of Arts, Sciences, & Communication

Address: PO Box 8000, Old Westbury, NY 11568-8000
Admissions Phone: 516-686-7519 · **Admissions Fax:** 516-626-0419
Admissions E-mail: admissions@nyit.edu

INSTITUTIONAL INFORMATION
Public/private: Private (nonprofit). **Evening Classes Available?** Yes. **Student/faculty Ratio:** 11:1. **Students in Parent Institution:** 8,965

STUDENT INFORMATION
Total Students in Program: 2,588. **% Full-time:** 29. **% Female:** 48.

RESEARCH FACILITIES
Research Facilities: Center for Urban/Suburban Studies, Center for Neighborhood Revitalization, *Long Island News*, Carleton Group, Parkinson's Dis-

ease Treatment Center, Center for Energy Policy and Research, Center for Labor and Industrial Relations.

EXPENSES/FINANCIAL AID

Annual Tuition: In-state $9,810. **Room & Board (On/off Campus):** $7,800/$9,600. **Books and Supplies:** $530. **Grants Range From:** $75-$25,126. **Loans Range From:** $100-$29,025. **% Receiving Financial Aid:** 56. **% Receiving Scholarships/Grants:** 39. **% Receiving Loans:** 41. **% Receiving Assistantships:** 4. **Number of Teaching/Research Assistantships Granted Each Year:** 30.

ADMISSIONS INFORMATION

Application Fee: $50. **Regular Notification:** Rolling. **Transfer Students Accepted?** Yes. **Transfer Policy:** Maximum 8 credit hours may be transferred with minimum grade of B. **Number of Applications Received:** 156. **% of Applicants Accepted:** 76. **% Accepted Who Enrolled:** 56. **Average GPA:** 3.1. **Average GRE Verbal:** 323. **Average GRE Quantitative:** 503. **Required Admission Factors:** Essays/personal statement, transcript. **Other Admission Factors:** Minimum 2.9 GPA required.

EMPLOYMENT INFORMATION

Placement Office Available? Yes. **% Employed Within 6 Months:** 53. **Average starting salary:** $40,000.

NEW YORK THEOLOGICAL SEMINARY
Graduate Programs

Address: 5 West 29th Street, New York, NY 10001-4599
Admissions Phone: 212-532-4012, ext. 253 · **Admissions Fax:** 212-684-0757
Admissions E-mail: ruiz@nyts.edu

INSTITUTIONAL INFORMATION

Public/private: Private (nonprofit). **Student/faculty Ratio:** 8:1. **Students in Parent Institution:** 293.

STUDENT INFORMATION

Total Students in Program: 57. **% Full-time:** 25. **% Female:** 23.

EXPENSES/FINANCIAL AID

Annual Tuition: In-state $4,750. **Fees:** $325. **Books and Supplies:** $500. **Grants Range From:** $500-$3,500. **% Receiving Financial Aid:** 24. **% Receiving Scholarships/Grants:** 100.

ADMISSIONS INFORMATION

Application Fee: $50. **Regular Notification:** Rolling. **Transfer Students Accepted?** No. **Number of Applications Received:** 178. **% of Applicants Accepted:** 61. **% Accepted Who Enrolled:** 82. **Average GPA:** 3.4. **Required Admission Factors:** Essays/personal statement, interview, letters of recommendation, transcript. **Other Admission Factors:** Minimum 3.0 GPA required.

EMPLOYMENT INFORMATION

% Employed Within 6 Months: 30. **% of doctoral grads employed in their field upon graduation:** 95.

NEW YORK UNIVERSITY
Gallatin School of Individualized Study

Address: 715 Broadway, 6th Floor, New York, NY 10003
Admissions Phone: 212-998-7370 · **Admissions Fax:** 212-995-4150
Admissions E-mail: gallatin.gradadmissions@nyu.edu · **Website:** www.nyu.edu/gallatin

INSTITUTIONAL INFORMATION

Public/private: Private (nonprofit). **Evening Classes Available?** Yes. **Total Faculty:** 37. **% Faculty Female:** 51. **% Faculty Part-time:** 24. **Students in Parent Institution:** 38,188.

PROGRAMS

Masters offered in: Multi/interdisciplinary studies.

STUDENT INFORMATION

Total Students in Program: 200. **% Full-time:** 28. **% Female:** 76. **% Minority:** 32. **% International:** 5.

RESEARCH FACILITIES

Research Facilities: Inter-University Doctoral Consortium with the City University of New York Graduate Center, Columbia University, Fordham University, New School University, Princeton University, Rutgers University, SUNY Stony Brook, Teacher College at Columbia University.

EXPENSES/FINANCIAL AID

Annual Tuition: $21,480. **Room & Board:** $15,200. **Fees:** $1,650. **Books and Supplies:** $720. **Grants Range From:** $202-$30,461. **Loans Range From:** $2,800-$43,125. **% Receiving Financial Aid:** 58. **% Receiving Scholarships/Grants:** 58. **% Receiving Loans:** 93. **% Receiving Other Aid (Work-Study):** 14. **Types of Aid Available:** Fellowships, graduate assistantships, grants, institutional work-study, loans, scholarships. **Average student debt, upon graduation:** $54,863. **Number of Fellowships Granted Each Year:** 1. **Average amount of individual fellowships per year:** $10,000. **Number of Teaching/Research Assistantships Granted Each Year:** 2. **Average Salary Stipend:** $6,375.

ADMISSIONS INFORMATION

Application Fee: $45. **Priority Application Deadline:** 2/1. **Regular Application Deadline:** 3/1. **Regular Notification:** Rolling. **Transfer Students Accepted?** Yes. **Transfer Policy:** Transfer credit is evaluated after student has enrolled. Priority housing/financial aid deadline 2/1. **Number of Applications Received:** 224. **% of Applicants Accepted:** 48. **% Accepted Who Enrolled:** 45. **Average GPA:** 3.3. **Required Admission Factors:** Essays/personal statement, letters of recommendation, transcript.

EMPLOYMENT INFORMATION

Placement Office Available? Yes. **% Employed Within 6 Months:** 85. **% of master's grads employed in their field upon graduation:** 50. **Rate of placement:** 95%. **Average starting salary:** $40,000.

NEW YORK UNIVERSITY
Graduate School of Arts & Science

Address: One-half Fifth Avenue, New York, NY 10003
Admissions Phone: 212-998-8050 · **Admissions Fax:** 212-995-4557
Admissions E-mail: gsas.admissions@nyu.edu · **Website:** www.nyu.edu/gsas

INSTITUTIONAL INFORMATION

Public/private: Private (nonprofit). **Total Faculty:** 1,023. **% Faculty Part-time:** 32. **Students in Parent Institution:** 39,408.

PROGRAMS

Masters offered in: African studies; American government and politics (United States); American literature (United States); American/United States studies/civilization; art history, criticism, and conservation; biochemistry; biological and biomedical sciences; biological and physical sciences; botany/plant biology; Caribbean studies; cell/cellular and molecular biology; computer and information sciences; creative writing; developmental biology and embryology; East Asian studies; economics; English literature (British and commonwealth); European studies/civilization; film/cinema studies; French language and literature; French studies; genetics; German language and literature; history; humanities/humanistic studies; immunology; industrial and organizational psychology; information science/studies; international relations and affairs; Italian studies; Jewish/Judaic studies; journalism; Latin American studies; mathematics and computer science; mathematics and statistics; mathematics; microbiology; molecular biology; molecular genetics; multi/interdisciplinary studies; museology/museum studies; music history, literature, and theory; musicology

Complete Book of Graduate Programs in the Arts and Sciences

and ethnomusicology; Near and Middle Eastern studies; philosophy; physiology; political science and government; Portuguese language and literature; psychology; public/applied history and archival administration; religion/religious studies; romance languages, literatures, and linguistics; Russian studies; Slavic studies; Spanish language and literature; virology; visual and performing arts. **Doctorate offered in:** American government and politics (United States); American literature (United States); American/United States studies/civilization; anthropology; applied mathematics; archaeology; art history, criticism, and conservation; biochemistry.

STUDENT INFORMATION

Total Students in Program: 3,961. **% Full-time:** 68. **% Female:** 55. **% Minority:** 10. **% International:** 27.

RESEARCH FACILITIES

Research Facilities: Inter-University Doctoral Consortium with the City University of New York Graduate Center, Columbia University, Fordham University, New School University, Princeton University, Rutgers University, SUNY Stony Brook, Teacher College at Columbia University.

EXPENSES/FINANCIAL AID

Annual Tuition: $22,056. **Room & Board:** $15,200. **Fees:** $1,664. **Books and Supplies:** $720. **Grants Range From:** $1,000-$18,000. **Loans Range From:** $1,000-$76,000. **Types of Aid Available:** Fellowships, graduate assistantships, loans. **Average amount of individual fellowships per year:** 40,000. **Assistantship Compensation Includes:** Full tuition remission, salary/stipend. **Average Salary Stipend:** $18,000.

ADMISSIONS INFORMATION

Application Fee: $75. **Regular Application Deadline:** 1/4. **Regular Notification:** Rolling. **Transfer Students Accepted?** Yes. **Transfer Policy:** Maximum 8 credit hours may be transferred into master's programs, maximum 40 credit hours into PhD. **Number of Applications Received:** 10,322. **% of Applicants Accepted:** 30. **% Accepted Who Enrolled:** 37. **Average GPA:** 3.5. **Average GRE Verbal:** 575. **Average GRE Quantitative:** 662. **Average GRE Analytical:** 656. **Average GRE Analytical Writing:** 4.9. **Required Admission Factors:** Essays/personal statement, GRE, letters of recommendation, transcript. **Program-Specific Admission Factors:** We also require a resume or CV, and most programs require a writing sample.

EMPLOYMENT INFORMATION

Placement Office Available? Yes.

NEW YORK UNIVERSITY
Robert F. Wagner Graduate School of Public Service

Address: 295 Lafayette Street, 2nd Floor, New York, NY 10012-9604
Admissions Phone: 212-998-7414 · **Admissions Fax:** 212-995-4164
Admissions E-mail: bethany.godsoe@nyu.edu · **Website:** www.nyu.edu/wagner/

INSTITUTIONAL INFORMATION

Public/private: Private (nonprofit). **Evening Classes Available?** Yes. **Total Faculty:** 88. **% Faculty Female:** 59. **% Faculty Part-time:** 68. **Student/faculty Ratio:** 10:1. **Students in Parent Institution:** 39,408.

PROGRAMS

Masters offered in: Public administration. **Doctorate offered in:** Public administration.

STUDENT INFORMATION

Total Students in Program: 854. **% Full-time:** 54. **% Female:** 72. **% Minority:** 27. **% International:** 11.

RESEARCH FACILITIES

Research Facilities: Inter-University Doctoral Consortium with the City University of New York Graduate Center, Columbia University, Fordham Uni-

---

versity, New School University, Princeton University, Rutgers University, SUNY Stony Brook, Teacher College at Columbia University.

EXPENSES/FINANCIAL AID

Annual Tuition: $16,200. **Room & Board:** $15,200. **Fees:** $1,554. **Books and Supplies:** $720. **Grants Range From:** $1,000-$25,000. **Loans Range From:** $1,000-$47,000. **% Receiving Financial Aid:** 75. **% Receiving Scholarships/Grants:** 30. **% Receiving Loans:** 70. **% Receiving Assistantships:** 4. **Types of Aid Available:** Graduate assistantships, scholarships. **Average student debt, upon graduation:** $30,000. **Number of Fellowships Granted Each Year:** 280. **Average amount of individual fellowships per year:** 6,500. **Number of Teaching/Research Assistantships Granted Each Year:** 16. **Assistantship Compensation Includes:** Full tuition remission, salary/stipend. **Average Salary Stipend:** $1,300.

ADMISSIONS INFORMATION

Application Fee: $65. **Priority Application Deadline:** 1/15. **Regular Application Deadline:** 6/1. **Regular Notification:** Rolling. **Transfer Students Accepted?** Yes. **Number of Applications Received:** 1,387. **% of Applicants Accepted:** 59. **% Accepted Who Enrolled:** 36. **Average GPA:** 3.5. **Required Admission Factors:** Essays/personal statement, letters of recommendation, transcript. **Other Admission Factors:** Minimum 3.0 GPA required. **Program-Specific Admission Factors:** 3 letters of recommendation required for doctoral studies.

EMPLOYMENT INFORMATION

% Employed Within 6 Months: 90. **% of master's/doctoral grads employed in their field upon graduation:** 83/75. **Average starting salary:** $50,050.

NEW YORK UNIVERSITY
School of Continuing & Professional Studies

Address: 145 Fourth Avenue, Room 219, New York, NY 10003
Admissions Phone: 212-998-7100 · **Admissions Fax:** 212-995-4674
Admissions E-mail: scps.gradadmissions@nyu.edu · **Website:** www.scps.nyu.edu

INSTITUTIONAL INFORMATION

Public/private: Private (nonprofit). **Evening Classes Available?** Yes. **Total Faculty:** 176. **% Faculty Female:** 24. **% Faculty Part-time:** 89. **Student/faculty Ratio:** 9:1. **Students in Parent Institution:** 39,408.

PROGRAMS

Masters offered in: Design and visual communications, educational/instructional media design, hospitality administration/management, international/global studies, management information systems, marketing, publishing, real estate, systems administration/administrator, tourism and travel services management. **First Professional degree offered in:** Hospitality administration/management, management information systems, marketing, real estate, tourism and travel services management.

STUDENT INFORMATION

Total Students in Program: 1,047. **% Full-time:** 29. **% Female:** 41. **% International:** 22.

RESEARCH FACILITIES

Research Facilities: Inter-University Doctoral Consortium with the City University of New York Graduate Center, Columbia University, Fordham University, New School University, Princeton University, Rutgers University, SUNY Stony Brook, Teacher College at Columbia University.

EXPENSES/FINANCIAL AID

Annual Tuition: $22,020. **Room & Board:** $15,200. **Fees:** $1,470. **Books and Supplies:** $750. **Grants Range From:** $162-$27,506. **Loans Range From:** $3,000-$49,090. **% Receiving Financial Aid:** 82. **% Receiving Schol-**

arships/Grants: 95. % Receiving Loans: 54. Types of Aid Available: Institutional work-study, loans. **Average student debt, upon graduation:** $45,241.

ADMISSIONS INFORMATION

Application Fee: $50. **Priority Application Deadline:** 6/1. **Regular Application Deadline:** 8/15. **Regular Notification:** Rolling. **Transfer Students Accepted?** Yes. **Transfer Policy:** Minimum standardized test scores in the 50th percentile, minimum 3.0 GPA, and at least 2 years of work experience preferred. **Number of Applications Received:** 1,071. **% of Applicants Accepted:** 84. **% Accepted Who Enrolled:** 67. **Average GPA:** 3.2. **Average GRE Verbal:** 479. **Average GRE Quantitative:** 613. **Average GRE Analytical:** 588.
Required Admission Factors: Essays/personal statement, GMAT, GRE, letters of recommendation, transcript.
Other Admission Factors: Minimum standardized test scores in the 50th percentile, minimum 3.0 GPA, and at least 2 years of work experience preferred. **Program-Specific Admission Factors:** MS in digital imaging requires a portfolio.

EMPLOYMENT INFORMATION

Placement Office Available? Yes.

NEW YORK UNIVERSITY
School of Social Work

Address: One Washington Square North, New York, NY 10003
Admissions Phone: 212-998-5910 · **Admissions Fax:** 212-995-4171
Admissions E-mail: essw.admissions@nyu.edu · **Website:** www.nyu.edu/socialwork/

INSTITUTIONAL INFORMATION

Public/private: Private (nonprofit). **Evening Classes Available?** Yes. **Total Faculty:** 174. **% Faculty Female:** 75. **% Faculty Part-time:** 78. **Student/faculty Ratio:** 13:1. **Students in Parent Institution:** 39,408.

PROGRAMS

Masters offered in: Social work. **Doctorate offered in:** Social work.

STUDENT INFORMATION

Total Students in Program: 1,085. **% Full-time:** 65. **% Female:** 86. **% Minority:** 31.

RESEARCH FACILITIES

Research Facilities: Inter-University Doctoral Consortium with the City University of New York Graduate Center, Columbia University, Fordham University, New School University, Princeton University, Rutgers University, SUNY Stony Brook, Teacher College at Columbia University.

EXPENSES/FINANCIAL AID

Annual Tuition: $24,800. **Room & Board (On/off Campus):** $15,614/$15,700. **Fees:** $1,084. **Books and Supplies:** $743. **Grants Range From:** $2,000-$12,000. **Loans Range From:** $1,000-$18,500. **% Receiving Financial Aid:** 85. **% Receiving Scholarships/Grants:** 85. **% Receiving Loans:** 90. **% Receiving Assistantships:** 1. **Types of Aid Available:** Fellowships, graduate assistantships, grants, institutional work-study, loans, scholarships, stipends. **Average student debt, upon graduation:** $48,000. **Number of Teaching/Research Assistantships Granted Each Year:** 5. **Assistantship Compensation Includes:** Full tuition remission, salary/stipend. **Average Salary Stipend:** $12,500.

ADMISSIONS INFORMATION

Application Fee: $50. **Regular Application Deadline:** 3/15. **Regular Notification:** Rolling. **Transfer Students Accepted?** Yes. **Transfer Policy:** For MSW program, completion of a comparable first-year program in an accredited school of social work. **Number of Applications Received:** 1,513. **% of Applicants Accepted:** 79. **% Accepted Who Enrolled:** 46. **Average GPA:** 3.3. **Required Admission Factors:** Essays/personal statement, letters of recommendation, transcript.

EMPLOYMENT INFORMATION

% Employed Within 6 Months: 93. **% of master's/doctoral grads employed in their field upon graduation:** 91/100. **Rate of placement:** 93%. **Average starting salary:** $40,000.

NEW YORK UNIVERSITY
Tisch School of the Arts

Address: 721 Broadway, 8th Floor, New York, NY 10003-6807
Admissions Phone: 212-998-1918 · **Admissions Fax:** 212-995-4060
Admissions E-mail: tisch.gradadmissions@nyu.edu · **Website:** www.tisch.nyu.edu

INSTITUTIONAL INFORMATION

Public/private: Private (nonprofit). **Total Faculty:** 216. **% Faculty Female:** 35. **% Faculty Part-time:** 100. **Students in Parent Institution:** 39,408.

PROGRAMS

Masters offered in: Acting; animation, interactive technology, video graphics, and special effects; cinematography and film/video production; dance; film/cinema studies; playwriting and screenwriting; technical theater/theater design and technology; visual and performing arts. **Doctorate offered in:** Film/cinema studies.

STUDENT INFORMATION

Total Students in Program: 961. **% Full-time:** 69. **% Female:** 51.

RESEARCH FACILITIES

Research Facilities: Inter-University Doctoral Consortium with the City University of New York Graduate Center, Columbia University, Fordham University, New School University, Princeton University, Rutgers University, SUNY Stony Brook, Teacher College at Columbia University.

EXPENSES/FINANCIAL AID

Annual Tuition: $31,264. **Room & Board:** $15,200. **Fees:** $1,766. **Books and Supplies:** $721. **Grants Range From:** $41-$31,264. **Loans Range From:** $192-$55,340. **% Receiving Financial Aid:** 72. **% Receiving Scholarships/Grants:** 37. **% Receiving Loans:** 53. **Types of Aid Available:** Fellowships, graduate assistantships, grants, institutional work-study, loans, scholarships. **Number of Fellowships Granted Each Year:** 125. **Average amount of individual fellowships per year:** 23,612. **Number of Teaching/Research Assistantships Granted Each Year:** 111. **Average Salary Stipend:** $9,700.

ADMISSIONS INFORMATION

Application Fee: $75. **Transfer Students Accepted?** No. **Number of Applications Received:** 2,770. **% of Applicants Accepted:** 22. **% Accepted Who Enrolled:** 56.
Required Admission Factors: Essays/personal statement, letters of recommendation, transcript.
Program-Specific Admission Factors: Portfolio required of film production, design, dramatic writing, and musical theater writing applicants. Audition required of acting and dance applicants. Resume and writing sample required of cinema studies and performance studies applicants.

EMPLOYMENT INFORMATION

Placement Office Available? Yes.

NICHOLLS STATE UNIVERSITY
College of Arts & Sciences

Address: PO Box 2015, Thibodaux, LA 70310
Admissions Phone: 504-448-4380 · **Admissions Fax:** 504-448-4927
Admissions E-mail: math-dmb@nicholls.edu

INSTITUTIONAL INFORMATION
Public/private: Public. Student/faculty Ratio: 1:1. Students in Parent Institution: 7,345.

STUDENT INFORMATION
Total Students in Program: 780. % Full-time: 12. % Female: 76.

EXPENSES/FINANCIAL AID
Annual Tuition: In-state $2,340. / Out-of-state $7,790. Room & Board: $3,902. % Receiving Financial Aid: 50. % Receiving Assistantships: 19. Number of Fellowships Granted Each Year: 2. Average amount of individual fellowships per year: 5,000. Number of Teaching/Research Assistantships Granted Each Year: 9. Average Salary Stipend: $3,000.

ADMISSIONS INFORMATION
Application Fee: $20. Regular Notification: Rolling. Transfer Students Accepted? Yes. Number of Applications Received: 7. % of Applicants Accepted: 86. % Accepted Who Enrolled: 100.
Required Admission Factors: GRE, transcript.
Other Admission Factors: Minimum GPA of 2.5 and minimum entrance score of 1100 on last 60 credit hours required.

EMPLOYMENT INFORMATION
Placement Office Available? Yes. % Employed Within 6 Months: 100. % of master's grads employed in their field upon graduation: 75.

NORTH CAROLINA A&T STATE UNIVERSITY
College of Arts & Sciences

Address: 1601 East Market Street, Greensboro, NC 27411
Admissions Phone: 336-334-7920 · Admissions Fax: 336-334-7282
Admissions E-mail: gradsch@ncat.edu · Website: www.ncat.edu/~gradsch/

INSTITUTIONAL INFORMATION
Public/private: Public. Evening Classes Available? Yes. Students in Parent Institution: 7,354.

STUDENT INFORMATION
Total Students in Program: 987. % Full-time: 43. % Female: 59.

EXPENSES/FINANCIAL AID
Annual Tuition: In-state $1,022. / Out-of-state $8,292. Fees: $503.

ADMISSIONS INFORMATION
Application Fee: $35. Regular Application Deadline: 7/1. Regular Notification: Rolling. Transfer Students Accepted? Yes. Number of Applications Received: 2,146. % of Applicants Accepted: 68. % Accepted Who Enrolled: 44.
Required Admission Factors: Essays/personal statement, letters of recommendation, transcript.
Other Admission Factors: Minimum 3.0 GPA required for unconditional admission.

EMPLOYMENT INFORMATION
Placement Office Available? Yes.

NORTH CAROLINA SCHOOL OF THE ARTS
School of Design & Production

Address: 1533 South Main Street, Winston-Salem, NC 27117-2189
Admissions Phone: 336-770-3215
Admissions E-mail: admissions@ncarts.edu

INSTITUTIONAL INFORMATION
Public/private: Public. Students in Parent Institution: 768.

STUDENT INFORMATION
Total Students in Program: 76. % Full-time: 96. % Female: 55.

EXPENSES/FINANCIAL AID
Annual Tuition: In-state $12,000. / Out-of-state $21,000. Books and Supplies: $800. Grants Range From: $1,000-$16,000. Loans Range From: $200-$18,500. % Receiving Financial Aid: 84. % Receiving Scholarships/Grants: 88. % Receiving Loans: 59. % Receiving Assistantships: 63. Average student debt, upon graduation: $41,973. Number of Teaching/Research Assistantships Granted Each Year: 24. Average Salary Stipend: $3,000.

ADMISSIONS INFORMATION
Application Fee: $45. Regular Notification: Rolling. Transfer Students Accepted? No. Number of Applications Received: 19. % of Applicants Accepted: 74. % Accepted Who Enrolled: 64.
Required Admission Factors: Interview, letters of recommendation, transcript.

NORTH CAROLINA SCHOOL OF THE ARTS
School of Music

Address: 1533 South Main Street, Winston-Salem, NC 27117-2189
Admissions Phone: 336-770-3255 · Admissions Fax: 336-770-3248
Admissions E-mail: admissions@ncarts.edu

INSTITUTIONAL INFORMATION
Public/private: Public. Students in Parent Institution: 768.

STUDENT INFORMATION
Total Students in Program: 76. % Full-time: 96. % Female: 55.

EXPENSES/FINANCIAL AID
Annual Tuition: In-state $12,000. / Out-of-state $21,000. Books and Supplies: $800. Grants Range From: $1,000-$16,000. Loans Range From: $200-$18,500. % Receiving Financial Aid: 66. % Receiving Scholarships/Grants: 88. % Receiving Loans: 59. % Receiving Assistantships: 63. Average student debt, upon graduation: $21,544. Number of Fellowships Granted Each Year: 10. Average amount of individual fellowships per year: $5,000. Number of Teaching/Research Assistantships Granted Each Year: 8. Average Salary Stipend: $2,000.

ADMISSIONS INFORMATION
Application Fee: $45. Regular Notification: Rolling. Transfer Students Accepted? No. Number of Applications Received: 40. % of Applicants Accepted: 78. % Accepted Who Enrolled: 77.
Required Admission Factors: Interview, letters of recommendation, transcript.

NORTH CAROLINA STATE UNIVERSITY
College of Design

Address: Box 7102, Raleigh, NC 27695-7102

INSTITUTIONAL INFORMATION
Public/private: Public. Students in Parent Institution: 25,472.

STUDENT INFORMATION
Total Students in Program: 5,621. % Full-time: 63. % Female: 42.

RESEARCH FACILITIES
Research Facilities: Triangle Universities Nuclear Laboratory, Research Triangle Institute, Highlands Biological Station, National Humanities Center, North Carolina Microelectronics Center, North Carolina Japan Center.

EXPENSES/FINANCIAL AID

Annual Tuition: In-state $3,496. / Out-of-state $13,807. **Fees:** $1,050. **Books and Supplies:** $600. **Number of Fellowships Granted Each Year:** 11. **Average amount of individual fellowships per year:** $ 6,022. **Number of Teaching/Research Assistantships Granted Each Year:** 37. **Average Salary Stipend:** $2,279.

ADMISSIONS INFORMATION

Application Fee: $55. **Transfer Students Accepted?** No. **Transfer Policy:** Maximum 9 credits may be transferred into master's programs. **Number of Applications Received:** 276. **% of Applicants Accepted:** 49. **% Accepted Who Enrolled:** 59. **Average GPA:** 3.3. **Average GRE Verbal:** 510. **Average GRE Quantitative:** 631. **Average GRE Analytical:** 608. **Required Admission Factors:** Letters of recommendation. **Other Admission Factors:** Minimum 3.0 GPA required; other requirements vary by program.

NORTH CAROLINA STATE UNIVERSITY
College of Humanities & Social Sciences

Address: Box 7102, Raleigh, NC 27695-7102

INSTITUTIONAL INFORMATION

Public/private: Public. **Students in Parent Institution:** 25,472.

STUDENT INFORMATION

Total Students in Program: 5,621. **% Full-time:** 63. **% Female:** 42.

RESEARCH FACILITIES

Research Facilities: Triangle Universities Nuclear Laboratory, Research Triangle Institute, Highlands Biological Station, National Humanities Center, North Carolina Microelectronics Center, North Carolina Japan Center.

EXPENSES/FINANCIAL AID

Annual Tuition: In-state $3,496. / Out-of-state $13,807. **Fees:** $1,050. **Books and Supplies:** $600. **Number of Fellowships Granted Each Year:** 16. **Average amount of individual fellowships per year:** $4,402. **Number of Teaching/Research Assistantships Granted Each Year:** 147. **Average Salary Stipend:** $4,463.

ADMISSIONS INFORMATION

Application Fee: $55. **Transfer Students Accepted?** No. **Transfer Policy:** Maximum 9 credits may be transferred into master's programs. **Number of Applications Received:** 468. **% of Applicants Accepted:** 49. **% Accepted Who Enrolled:** 68. **Average GPA:** 3.33. **Average GRE Verbal:** 509. **Average GRE Quantitative:** 556. **Average GRE Analytical:** 593. **Required Admission Factors:** Letters of recommendation. **Other Admission Factors:** Minimum 3.0 GPA required; other requirements vary by program.

NORTH CAROLINA STATE UNIVERSITY
College of Natural Resources

Address: Box 7102, Raleigh, NC 27695-7102

INSTITUTIONAL INFORMATION

Public/private: Public. **Students in Parent Institution:** 25,472.

STUDENT INFORMATION

Total Students in Program: 5,621. **% Full-time:** 63. **% Female:** 42.

RESEARCH FACILITIES

Research Facilities: Triangle Universities Nuclear Laboratory, Research Triangle Institute, Highlands Biological Station, National Humanities Center, North Carolina Microelectronics Center, North Carolina Japan Center.

EXPENSES/FINANCIAL AID

Annual Tuition: In-state $3,496. / Out-of-state $13,807. **Fees:** $1,050. **Books and Supplies:** $600. **Number of Fellowships Granted Each Year:** 3. **Average amount of individual fellowships per year:** 4,270. **Number of Teaching/Research Assistantships Granted Each Year:** 96. **Average Salary Stipend:** $4,404.

ADMISSIONS INFORMATION

Application Fee: $55. **Transfer Students Accepted?** No. **Transfer Policy:** Maximum 9 credits may be transferred into master's programs. **Number of Applications Received:** 126. **% of Applicants Accepted:** 52. **% Accepted Who Enrolled:** 73. **Average GPA:** 3.2. **Average GRE Verbal:** 485. **Average GRE Quantitative:** 632. **Average GRE Analytical:** 586. **Required Admission Factors:** Letters of recommendation. **Other Admission Factors:** Minimum 3.0 GPA required; other requirements vary by program.

NORTH CAROLINA STATE UNIVERSITY
College of Physical & Mathematical Sciences

Address: Box 7102, Raleigh, NC 27695-7102

INSTITUTIONAL INFORMATION

Public/private: Public. **Students in Parent Institution:** 25,472.

STUDENT INFORMATION

Total Students in Program: 5,621. **% Full-time:** 63. **% Female:** 42.

RESEARCH FACILITIES

Research Facilities: Triangle Universities Nuclear Laboratory, Research Triangle Institute, Highlands Biological Station, National Humanities Center, North Carolina Microelectronics Center, North Carolina Japan Center.

EXPENSES/FINANCIAL AID

Annual Tuition: In-state $3,496. / Out-of-state $13,807. **Fees:** $1,050. **Books and Supplies:** $600. **Number of Fellowships Granted Each Year:** 42. **Average amount of individual fellowships per year:** $7,177. **Number of Teaching/Research Assistantships Granted Each Year:** 436. **Average Salary Stipend:** $6,536.

ADMISSIONS INFORMATION

Application Fee: $55. **Transfer Students Accepted?** No. **Transfer Policy:** Maximum 9 credits may be transferred into master's programs. **Number of Applications Received:** 701. **% of Applicants Accepted:** 43. **% Accepted Who Enrolled:** 57. **Average GPA:** 3.4. **Average GRE Verbal:** 528. **Average GRE Quantitative:** 739. **Average GRE Analytical:** 676. **Required Admission Factors:** Letters of recommendation. **Other Admission Factors:** Minimum 3.0 GPA required; other requirements vary by program.

NORTH CAROLINA STATE UNIVERSITY
College of Textiles

Address: Box 7102, Raleigh, NC 27695-7102

INSTITUTIONAL INFORMATION

Public/private: Public. **Students in Parent Institution:** 25,472.

STUDENT INFORMATION

Total Students in Program: 5,621. **% Full-time:** 63. **% Female:** 42.

RESEARCH FACILITIES

Research Facilities: Triangle Universities Nuclear Laboratory, Research Triangle Institute, Highlands Biological Station, National Humanities Center, North Carolina Microelectronics Center, North Carolina Japan Center.

EXPENSES/FINANCIAL AID

Annual Tuition: In-state $3,496. / Out-of-state $13,807. **Fees:** $1,050. **Books and Supplies:** $600. **Number of Fellowships Granted Each Year:** 1. **Average amount of individual fellowships per year:** $6,773. **Number of Teaching/Research Assistantships Granted Each Year:** 71. **Average Salary Stipend:** $5,523.

ADMISSIONS INFORMATION

Application Fee: $55. **Transfer Students Accepted?** No. **Transfer Policy:** Maximum 9 credits may be transferred into master's programs. **Number of Applications Received:** 93. **% of Applicants Accepted:** 44. **% Accepted Who Enrolled:** 78. **Average GPA:** 3.4. **Average GRE Verbal:** 481. **Average GRE Quantitative:** 704. **Average GRE Analytical:** 623.
Required Admission Factors: Letters of recommendation.
Other Admission Factors: Minimum 3.0 GPA required; other requirements vary by program.

NORTH CENTRAL COLLEGE
Graduate Programs

Address: 30 North Brainard Street, Naperville, IL 60566-7063
Admissions Phone: 630-637-5840 · **Admissions Fax:** 630-637-5819
Admissions E-mail: grad@noctrl.edu · **Website:** www.northcentralcollege.edu

INSTITUTIONAL INFORMATION

Public/private: Private (nonprofit). **Evening Classes Available?** Yes. **Students in Parent Institution:** 2,458.

PROGRAMS

Masters offered in: Business administration/management, computer and information sciences, curriculum and instruction, education leadership and administration, information science/studies, liberal arts and sciences/liberal studies, multi/interdisciplinary studies.

STUDENT INFORMATION

Total Students in Program: 372. **% Full-time:** 17. **% Female:** 51.

EXPENSES/FINANCIAL AID

Annual Tuition: $7,290. **Room & Board:** $9,600. **Fees:** $60. **Books and Supplies:** $200. **Loans Range From:** $100-$8,500. **% Receiving Loans:** 100. **Types of Aid Available:** Loans.

ADMISSIONS INFORMATION

Application Fee: $25. **Priority Application Deadline:** 6/1. **Regular Application Deadline:** 8/15. **Regular Notification:** Rolling. **Transfer Students Accepted?** Yes. **Transfer Policy:** Transfer applicants must be in good academic standing. Courses are evaluated on an individual basis. **Number of Applications Received:** 148. **% of Applicants Accepted:** 88. **% Accepted Who Enrolled:** 82. **Average GPA:** 3.2.
Required Admission Factors: Essays/personal statement, interview, transcript.
Recommended Admission Factors: Letters of recommendation.
Program-Specific Admission Factors: MAEd and Type 75 only students should have full-time teaching experience; 2 years of experience is recommended.

EMPLOYMENT INFORMATION

Placement Office Available? Yes. **% Employed Within 6 Months:** 90. **Rate of placement:** 91%. **Average starting salary:** $50,000.

NORTH DAKOTA STATE UNIVERSITY
College of Arts, Humanities, & Social Sciences

Address: PO Box 5790, Fargo, ND 58105

INSTITUTIONAL INFORMATION

Public/private: Public. **Students in Parent Institution:** 9,745.

STUDENT INFORMATION

Total Students in Program: 1,010. **% Full-time:** 58. **% Female:** 41.

EXPENSES/FINANCIAL AID

Annual Tuition: In-state $2,690. / Out-of-state $7,182. **Fees:** $406.

ADMISSIONS INFORMATION

Transfer Students Accepted? No.
Required Admission Factors: GRE.

EMPLOYMENT INFORMATION

Placement Office Available? Yes.

NORTH GEORGIA COLLEGE & STATE UNIVERSITY
Graduate Programs

Address: Dahlonega, GA 30597
Admissions Phone: 706-864-1543 · **Admissions Fax:** 706-867-2795

INSTITUTIONAL INFORMATION

Public/private: Public. **Evening Classes Available?** Yes. **Total Faculty:** 90. **% Faculty Female:** 47. **Student/faculty Ratio:** 17:1. **Students in Parent Institution:** 3,990.

STUDENT INFORMATION

Total Students in Program: 380. **% Full-time:** 91. **% Female:** 66.

EXPENSES/FINANCIAL AID

Annual Tuition: In-state $2,292. / Out-of-state $7,530. **Room & Board (On/off Campus):** $3,800/$5,800. **% Receiving Financial Aid:** 15. **Average student debt, upon graduation:** $500.

ADMISSIONS INFORMATION

Application Fee: $25. **Transfer Students Accepted?** Yes. **Transfer Policy:** Good academic standing from previous school required of transfer applicants. **Number of Applications Received:** 150. **% of Applicants Accepted:** 80. **Average GPA:** 3. **Average GRE Verbal:** 500. **Average GRE Quantitative:** 400.
Required Admission Factors: GRE, letters of recommendation, transcript.
Other Admission Factors: Minimum 2.5 GPA required.

EMPLOYMENT INFORMATION

Placement Office Available? Yes. **% Employed Within 6 Months:** 90. **% of master's grads employed in their field upon graduation:** 90. **Average starting salary:** $45,000.

NORTH PARK THEOLOGICAL SEMINARY
Graduate Programs

Address: 3225 West Foster Avenue, Chicago, IL 60625-4895
Admissions Phone: 800-964-0101 · **Admissions Fax:** 773-244-6244
Admissions E-mail: semadmissions@northpark.edu

INSTITUTIONAL INFORMATION

Public/private: Private (nonprofit). **Student/faculty Ratio:** 8:1. **Students in Parent Institution:** 142.

STUDENT INFORMATION

Total Students in Program: 142. **% Full-time:** 100. **% Female:** 34.

EXPENSES/FINANCIAL AID

Annual Tuition: In-state $7,970. **Room & Board:** $800. **Fees:** $410. **Books and Supplies:** $300. **% Receiving Scholarships/Grants:** 60. **% Receiving Loans:** 45.

ADMISSIONS INFORMATION

Application Fee: $25. **Regular Notification:** Rolling. **Transfer Students Accepted?** Yes. **Number of Applications Received:** 86. **% of Applicants Accepted:** 66. **% Accepted Who Enrolled:** 82.

Required Admission Factors: Essays/personal statement, interview, letters of recommendation, transcript.

Other Admission Factors: Minimum 2.5 GPA required.

EMPLOYMENT INFORMATION

Rate of placement: 95%.

NORTHEASTERN ILLINOIS UNIVERSITY
College of Arts & Sciences

Address: 5500 North St. Louis Avenue, Chicago, IL 60625
Admissions Phone: 773-442-6008 · **Admissions Fax:** 773-442-6020
Admissions E-mail: a-umeh@neiu.edu

INSTITUTIONAL INFORMATION

Public/private: Public. **Evening Classes Available?** Yes. **Students in Parent Institution:** 10,937.

STUDENT INFORMATION

Total Students in Program: 2,732. **% Full-time:** 12. **% Female:** 68.

RESEARCH FACILITIES

Research Facilities: Center for Inner City Studies, Advocate Health Care Network, Advocate Medical Group.

EXPENSES/FINANCIAL AID

Annual Tuition: In-state $3,168. / Out-of-state $9,504. **Fees:** $463. **Books and Supplies:** $1,250. **% Receiving Financial Aid:** 89. **Types of Aid Available:** 1. **Average student debt, upon graduation:** $20,000. **Number of Teaching/Research Assistantships Granted Each Year:** 53. **Average Salary Stipend:** $550.

ADMISSIONS INFORMATION

Regular Notification: Rolling. **Transfer Students Accepted?** Yes. **Number of Applications Received:** 164. **% of Applicants Accepted:** 82. **Average GPA:** 3.1.

Required Admission Factors: Essays/personal statement, letters of recommendation, transcript.

Other Admission Factors: Minimum 2.75 GPA required.

EMPLOYMENT INFORMATION

Placement Office Available? Yes. **% of master's grads employed in their field upon graduation:** 15. **Rate of placement:** 80%.

NORTHEASTERN STATE UNIVERSITY
College of Social & Behavioral Sciences

Address: Tahlequah, OK 74464
Admissions Phone: 918-456-5511, ext. 3690 · **Admissions Fax:** 918-458-2061
Admissions E-mail: underwoo@cherokee.nsuok.edu

INSTITUTIONAL INFORMATION

Public/private: Public. **Evening Classes Available?** Yes. **Total Faculty:** 22. **Students in Parent Institution:** 9,250.

STUDENT INFORMATION

Total Students in Program: 1,536. **% Full-time:** 52.

EXPENSES/FINANCIAL AID

Annual Tuition: In-state $1,259. / Out-of-state $2,964. **Fees:** $25.

ADMISSIONS INFORMATION

Transfer Students Accepted? Yes. **Transfer Policy:** Maximum 8 credit

hours may be transferred into American studies program. **Number of Applications Received:** 46. **% of Applicants Accepted:** 61. **% Accepted Who Enrolled:** 93.

Required Admission Factors: GRE, transcript.

Program-Specific Admission Factors: Minimum GRE score of 900 (Verbal and Quantitative), minimum 2.75 GPA, interview, essay, 3 references, autobiography, and statement of career goals required of counseling psychology program applicants.

EMPLOYMENT INFORMATION

Placement Office Available? Yes.

NORTHEASTERN UNIVERSITY
Graduate School of Arts & Sciences

Address: 360 Huntington Avenue, 124 Meserve Hall, Boston, MA 02115
Admissions Phone: 617-373-5990 · **Admissions Fax:** 617-373-7281
Admissions E-mail: gsas@neu.edu · **Website:** www.cas.neu.edu/graduate

INSTITUTIONAL INFORMATION

Public/private: Private (nonprofit). **Evening Classes Available?** Yes. **Total Faculty:** 238. **Students in Parent Institution:** 16,628.

STUDENT INFORMATION

Total Students in Program: 3,749. **% Full-time:** 55. **% Female:** 48.

RESEARCH FACILITIES

Research Facilities: More than 30 institutional research centers.

EXPENSES/FINANCIAL AID

Number of Teaching/Research Assistantships Granted Each Year: 265. **Average Salary Stipend:** $10,100.

ADMISSIONS INFORMATION

Application Fee: $50. **Regular Application Deadline:** 7/5. **Regular Notification:** Rolling. **Transfer Students Accepted?** Yes. **Transfer Policy:** Please refer to www.cas.neu.edu/graduate for admission requirements and deadlines. **Number of Applications Received:** 1,008. **% of Applicants Accepted:** 60.

Required Admission Factors: Letters of recommendation, transcript.

Other Admission Factors: Requirements vary by program.

EMPLOYMENT INFORMATION

Placement Office Available? Yes. **Rate of placement:** 94%.

NORTHEASTERN UNIVERSITY
Graduate School of Criminal Justice

Address: 360 Huntington Avenue, Boston, MA 02115
Admissions Phone: 617-373-3327 · **Admissions Fax:** 617-373-8723

INSTITUTIONAL INFORMATION

Public/private: Private (nonprofit). **Evening Classes Available?** Yes. **Students in Parent Institution:** 16,628.

STUDENT INFORMATION

Total Students in Program: 3,749. **% Full-time:** 55. **% Female:** 48.

RESEARCH FACILITIES

Research Facilities: More than 30 institutional research centers.

ADMISSIONS INFORMATION

Application Fee: $50. **Regular Notification:** Rolling. **Transfer Students Accepted?** No. **Number of Applications Received:** 133. **% of Applicants Accepted:** 70. **Average GPA:** 3.6.

Required Admission Factors: Essays/personal statement, GRE, letters of recommendation, transcript.

EMPLOYMENT INFORMATION
Placement Office Available? Yes. **Rate of placement:** 94%.

NORTHERN ARIZONA UNIVERSITY
College of Arts & Sciences

Address: PO Box 4125, Flagstaff, AZ 86011-4125
Admissions Phone: 520-523-4348 · **Admissions Fax:** 520-523-8950

INSTITUTIONAL INFORMATION
Public/private: Public. **Students in Parent Institution:** 19,728.

STUDENT INFORMATION
Total Students in Program: 5,988. **% Full-time:** 29. **% Female:** 70.

RESEARCH FACILITIES
Research Facilities: Museum of Northern Arizona, U.S. Geological Survey's Flagstaff Field Center, Rocky Mountain Forest & Range Experiment Station, Lowell Observatory, Naval Observatory.

EXPENSES/FINANCIAL AID
Annual Tuition: In-state $2,488. / Out-of-state $10,354. **Books and Supplies:** $1,500.

ADMISSIONS INFORMATION
Application Fee: $45. **Transfer Students Accepted?** No. **Number of Applications Received:** 380. **% of Applicants Accepted:** 54. **% Accepted Who Enrolled:** 65.
Required Admission Factors: Transcript.
Program-Specific Admission Factors: GRE required of PhD program applicants; GRE subject exam required of PhD in linguistics program applicants.

EMPLOYMENT INFORMATION
Placement Office Available? Yes. **Rate of placement:** 94%.

NORTHERN ARIZONA UNIVERSITY
College of Social & Behavioral Sciences

Address: PO Box 4125, Flagstaff, AZ 86011-4125
Admissions Phone: 520-523-4348 · **Admissions Fax:** 520-523-8950

INSTITUTIONAL INFORMATION
Public/private: Public. **Students in Parent Institution:** 19,728.

STUDENT INFORMATION
Total Students in Program: 5,988. **% Full-time:** 29. **% Female:** 70.

RESEARCH FACILITIES
Research Facilities: Museum of Northern Arizona, U.S. Geological Survey's Flagstaff Field Center, Rocky Mountain Forest & Range Experiment Station, Lowell Observatory, Naval Observatory.

EXPENSES/FINANCIAL AID
Annual Tuition: In-state $2,488. / Out-of-state $10,354. **Books and Supplies:** $1,500.

ADMISSIONS INFORMATION
Application Fee: $45. **Transfer Students Accepted?** Yes. **Transfer Policy:** Petition to apply transfer credit toward degree required of transfer applicants. **Number of Applications Received:** 264. **% of Applicants Accepted:** 35. **% Accepted Who Enrolled:** 60.
Required Admission Factors: Transcript.

EMPLOYMENT INFORMATION
Placement Office Available? Yes. **Rate of placement:** 94%.

NORTHERN ARIZONA UNIVERSITY
School of Performing Arts

Address: PO Box 4125, Flagstaff, AZ 86011-4125
Admissions Phone: 520-523-4348 · **Admissions Fax:** 520-523-8950

INSTITUTIONAL INFORMATION
Public/private: Public. **Students in Parent Institution:** 19,728.

STUDENT INFORMATION
Total Students in Program: 5,988. **% Full-time:** 29. **% Female:** 70.

RESEARCH FACILITIES
Research Facilities: Museum of Northern Arizona, U.S. Geological Survey's Flagstaff Field Center, Rocky Mountain Forest & Range Experiment Station, Lowell Observatory, Naval Observatory.

EXPENSES/FINANCIAL AID
Annual Tuition: In-state $2,488. / Out-of-state $10,354. **Books and Supplies:** $1,500.

ADMISSIONS INFORMATION
Application Fee: $45. **Regular Notification:** Rolling. **Transfer Students Accepted?** No. **Number of Applications Received:** 19. **% of Applicants Accepted:** 79. **% Accepted Who Enrolled:** 93.
Required Admission Factors: Transcript.
Other Admission Factors: Performance auditions may be required of some applicants.
Program-Specific Admission Factors: Music audition may be required of some applicants.

EMPLOYMENT INFORMATION
Placement Office Available? Yes. **Rate of placement:** 94%.

NORTHERN BAPTIST THEOLOGICAL SEMINARY
Graduate Programs

Address: 660 East Butterfield Road, Lombard, IL 60148
Admissions Phone: 630-620-2128 or 800-YES-NBTS
Admissions Fax: 630-620-2194

INSTITUTIONAL INFORMATION
Public/private: Private (nonprofit). **Evening Classes Available?** Yes. **Students in Parent Institution:** 209.

STUDENT INFORMATION
Total Students in Program: 209. **% Full-time:** 43. **% Female:** 36.

RESEARCH FACILITIES
Research Facilities: Member of Chicago Association of Theological Seminaries; resource-sharing possible.

EXPENSES/FINANCIAL AID
Annual Tuition: $9,500. **Fees:** $210. **Books and Supplies:** $500. **Grants Range From:** $1,000-$7,600. **% Receiving Financial Aid:** 89. **% Receiving Scholarships/Grants:** 100.

ADMISSIONS INFORMATION
Application Fee: $35. **Regular Notification:** Rolling. **Transfer Students Accepted?** Yes. **Transfer Policy:** Church letter, 3 references, and autobiographical statement required of transfer applicants. **Number of Applications Received:** 121. **% of Applicants Accepted:** 79. **% Accepted Who Enrolled:** 68.
Required Admission Factors: Essays/personal statement, transcript.
Other Admission Factors: Minimum 2.5 GPA required.

EMPLOYMENT INFORMATION
Placement Office Available? Yes. **Rate of placement:** 90%.

NORTHERN ILLINOIS UNIVERSITY
College of Liberal Arts & Sciences

Address: DeKalb, IL 60115
Admissions Phone: 815-753-0395 · **Admissions Fax:** 815-753-6366

INSTITUTIONAL INFORMATION
Public/private: Public. **Students in Parent Institution:** 23,248.

STUDENT INFORMATION
Total Students in Program: 5,791. **% Full-time:** 10. **% Female:** 61.

RESEARCH FACILITIES
Research Facilities: Plant Molecular Biology Center, Center for Southeast Asian Studies, Center for Governmental Studies, Center for Black Studies, Center for Latino/Latin American Studies, Women's Studies Center, Center for Biochemical/Biophysical Studies.

EXPENSES/FINANCIAL AID
Annual Tuition: In-state $2,443. / Out-of-state $4,887. **Room & Board:** $11,940. **Fees:** $49.

ADMISSIONS INFORMATION
Application Fee: $30. **Regular Notification:** Rolling. **Transfer Students Accepted?** Yes. **Transfer Policy:** Maximum 15 credit hours may be transferred into master's programs. **Number of Applications Received:** 860. **% of Applicants Accepted:** 62. **% Accepted Who Enrolled:** 54.
Required Admission Factors: Essays/personal statement, GRE, letters of recommendation, transcript.
Program-Specific Admission Factors: Minimum 2.75 GPA required of master's program applicants. Minimum 3.2 graduate GPA and 3 letters of recommendation required of PhD program applicants.

EMPLOYMENT INFORMATION
Placement Office Available? Yes.

NORTHERN ILLINOIS UNIVERSITY
College of Visual & Performing Arts

Address: DeKalb, IL 60115
Admissions Phone: 815-753-0395 · **Admissions Fax:** 815-753-6366

INSTITUTIONAL INFORMATION
Public/private: Public. **Students in Parent Institution:** 23,248.

STUDENT INFORMATION
Total Students in Program: 5,791. **% Full-time:** 10. **% Female:** 61.

RESEARCH FACILITIES
Research Facilities: Plant Molecular Biology Center, Center for Southeast Asian Studies, Center for Governmental Studies, Center for Black Studies; Center for Latino/Latin American Studies, Women's Studies Center, Center for Biochemical/Biophysical Studies.

EXPENSES/FINANCIAL AID
Annual Tuition: In-state $2,443. / Out-of-state $4,887. **Room & Board:** $11,940. **Fees:** $49.

ADMISSIONS INFORMATION
Application Fee: $30. **Regular Notification:** Rolling. **Transfer Students Accepted?** Yes. **Transfer Policy:** Maximum 15 credit hours may be transferred into most programs; maximum 9 credit hours may be transferred. **Number of Applications Received:** 124. **% of Applicants Accepted:** 73. **% Accepted Who Enrolled:** 69.
Required Admission Factors: Essays/personal statement, letters of recommendation, transcript.
Other Admission Factors: Minimum 2.75 GPA required.
Program-Specific Admission Factors: Portfolio required of some theater

---

applicants. Audition required of performance music program applicants. Portfolio required of studio art program applicants.

EMPLOYMENT INFORMATION
Placement Office Available? Yes.

NORTHERN KENTUCKY UNIVERSITY
Office of Graduate Programs

Address: LAC 400, Nunn Drive, Highland Heights, KY 41099-7010
Admissions Phone: 859-572-6659 or 859-572-5220
Admissions Fax: 859-572-6665

INSTITUTIONAL INFORMATION
Public/private: Public. **Evening Classes Available?** Yes. **Student/faculty Ratio:** 17:1. **Students in Parent Institution:** 12,101.

STUDENT INFORMATION
Total Students in Program: 871. **% Full-time:** 7. **% Female:** 67.

EXPENSES/FINANCIAL AID
Annual Tuition: In-state $2,682. / Out-of-state $7,596. **Fees:** $270. **% Receiving Financial Aid:** 5. **Average student debt, upon graduation:** $8,500.

ADMISSIONS INFORMATION
Application Fee: $25. **Regular Notification:** Rolling. **Transfer Students Accepted?** Yes. **Number of Applications Received:** 272. **% of Applicants Accepted:** 82. **% Accepted Who Enrolled:** 57.
Required Admission Factors: Essays/personal statement, GRE, transcript.

EMPLOYMENT INFORMATION
Placement Office Available? Yes.

NORTHERN STATE UNIVERSITY
Graduate Studies

Address: 1200 South Jay Street, Aberdeen, SD 57401
Admissions Phone: 605-626-2558 · **Admissions Fax:** 605-626-3022
Admissions E-mail: griffith@northern.edu · **Website:** www.northern.edu

INSTITUTIONAL INFORMATION
Public/private: Public. **Evening Classes Available?** Yes. **Total Faculty:** 83. **% Faculty Female:** 27. **Student/faculty Ratio:** 8:1. **Students in Parent Institution:** 2,284.

PROGRAMS
Masters offered in: Counselor education/school counseling and guidance services, elementary and middle school administration/principalship, elementary education and teaching, health occupations teacher education, secondary education and teaching, secondary school administration/principalship, special education and teaching, teaching assistants/aides, technical teacher education.

STUDENT INFORMATION
Total Students in Program: 113. **% Full-time:** 19. **% Female:** 62.

EXPENSES/FINANCIAL AID
Annual Tuition: In-state $4,479. / Out-of-state $9,736. **Fees:** $1,200. **Books and Supplies:** $700. **Grants Range From:** $425-$500. **Loans Range From:** $200-$14,900. **Types of Aid Available:** Graduate assistantships, institutional work-study, loans, scholarships.

ADMISSIONS INFORMATION
Application Fee: $35. **Regular Application Deadline:** 9/1. **Regular Notification:** Rolling. **Transfer Students Accepted?** Yes. **Number of Applications Received:** 60. **% of Applicants Accepted:** 53. **Average GPA:** 3.0 **Average GRE Verbal:** 400. **Average GRE Quantitative:** 400. **Average GRE Analytical Writing:** 2.5.

Required Admission Factors: Letters of recommendation, transcript.
Other Admission Factors: Minimum 2.75 overall GPA or minimum 3.0 GPA in last 64 credit hours or minimum 3.25 GPA in major required.

EMPLOYMENT INFORMATION

Placement Office Available? Yes. **% Employed Within 6 Months:** 45.
Rate of placement: 50%. **Average starting salary:** $32,000.

NORTHWEST CHRISTIAN COLLEGE
Graduate Programs

Address: 828 East 11th Avenue, Eugene, OR 97401-3727
Admissions Phone: 541-684-7214

INSTITUTIONAL INFORMATION

Public/private: Private (nonprofit). **Evening Classes Available?** Yes. **Student/faculty Ratio:** 13:1. **Students in Parent Institution:** 490.

STUDENT INFORMATION

Total Students in Program: 49. **% Full-time:** 88. **% Female:** 59.

EXPENSES/FINANCIAL AID

Annual Tuition: In-state $10,000. **Books and Supplies:** $750. **% Receiving Financial Aid:** 57. **% Receiving Scholarships/Grants:** 10. **% Receiving Loans:** 90. **Average student debt, upon graduation:** $11,000.

ADMISSIONS INFORMATION

Application Fee: $25. **Regular Notification:** Rolling. **Transfer Students Accepted?** Yes. **Number of Applications Received:** 60. **% of Applicants Accepted:** 93. **% Accepted Who Enrolled:** 66. **Average GPA:** 3.4. **Average GRE Verbal:** 520. **Average GRE Quantitative:** 500. **Average GRE Analytical:** 500.
Required Admission Factors: Essays/personal statement, interview, letters of recommendation, transcript.
Other Admission Factors: Minimum GRE score of 1000 (on 2 of 3 sections) or minimum GMAT score of 500, and minimum 3.0 GPA required.

EMPLOYMENT INFORMATION

Rate of placement: 90%.

NORTHWEST MISSOURI STATE UNIVERSITY
College of Arts & Sciences

Address: 800 University Drive, Maryville, MO 64468
Admissions Phone: 660-562-1145
Admissions E-mail: gradsch@nwmissouri.edu

INSTITUTIONAL INFORMATION

Public/private: Public. **Evening Classes Available?** Yes. **Student/faculty Ratio:** 3:1. **Students in Parent Institution:** 6,625.

STUDENT INFORMATION

Total Students in Program: 1,023. **% Full-time:** 17. **% Female:** 72.

EXPENSES/FINANCIAL AID

Annual Tuition: In-state $2,776. / Out-of-state $4,626. **Fees:** $90. **Books and Supplies:** $300. **Grants Range From:** $250-$7,524. **Loans Range From:** $1,000-$17,838. **% Receiving Scholarships/Grants:** 9. **% Receiving Loans:** 64. **% Receiving Assistantships:** 69. **Number of Teaching/Research Assistantships Granted Each Year:** 21 **Average Salary Stipend:** $5,250.

ADMISSIONS INFORMATION

Regular Notification: Rolling. **Transfer Students Accepted?** Yes. **Number of Applications Received:** 10. **% of Applicants Accepted:** 90. **% Accepted Who Enrolled:** 44. **Average GPA:** 2.78. **Average GRE Verbal:** 480. **Average GRE Quantitative:** 460. **Average GRE Analytical:** 550.
Required Admission Factors: GRE, transcript.

Other Admission Factors: Minimum GRE score of 800 on Verbal and Analytical sections, minimum 2.5 GPA, and writing sample required.
Program-Specific Admission Factors: Minimum GRE score of 700 on Verbal and Quantitative sections required of math teaching, music teaching, and science education program applicants. Minimum GRE score of 1200 required of biology program applicants.

EMPLOYMENT INFORMATION

Placement Office Available? Yes. **Rate of placement:** 79%.

NORTHWEST NAZARENE UNIVERSITY
(FORMERLY NORTHWEST NAZARENE COLLEGE)
School of Applied Studies

Address: 623 Holly Street, Nampa, ID 83686
Admissions Phone: 208-467-8345 · **Admissions Fax:** 208-467-8339
Admissions E-mail: ddcartwright@nnu.edu

INSTITUTIONAL INFORMATION

Public/private: Private (nonprofit). **Total Faculty:** 69. **Student/faculty Ratio:** 10:1. **Students in Parent Institution:** 1,368.

STUDENT INFORMATION

Total Students in Program: 274. **% Full-time:** 68. **% Female:** 66.

EXPENSES/FINANCIAL AID

Fees: $15. **Books and Supplies:** $1,000. **% Receiving Financial Aid:** 70. **% Receiving Loans:** 100.

ADMISSIONS INFORMATION

Application Fee: $25. **Regular Notification:** Rolling. **Transfer Students Accepted?** No. **Transfer Policy:** Maximum 9 to 19 credit hours may be transferred.
Required Admission Factors: Letters of recommendation, transcript.
Other Admission Factors: Minimum 2.8 GPA (minimum 3.0 GPA in final 30 semester hours) required.
Program-Specific Admission Factors: Interview and on-site writing exercise required of counseling program applicants. Minimum GMAT score of 425 required of master of business administration program applicants.

NORTHWESTERN OKLAHOMA
STATE UNIVERSITY
Graduate School

Address: 709 Oklahoma Boulevard, Alva, OK 73717
Admissions Phone: 580-327-8410

INSTITUTIONAL INFORMATION

Public/private: Public. **Students in Parent Institution:** 7,470.

STUDENT INFORMATION

Total Students in Program: 323. **% Full-time:** 15. **% Female:** 69.

EXPENSES/FINANCIAL AID

Annual Tuition: In-state $1,406. / Out-of-state $3,368. **Grants Range From:** $200-$1,000. **Loans Range From:** $200-$6,200. **% Receiving Scholarships/Grants:** 5. **% Receiving Loans:** 95.

ADMISSIONS INFORMATION

Transfer Students Accepted? Yes.
Required Admission Factors: Transcript.
Other Admission Factors: Minimum 2.75 GPA required.

NORTHWESTERN STATE UNIVERSITY OF LOUISIANA
Graduate Studies & Research

Address: College Avenue, Natchitoches, LA 71497
Admissions Phone: 318-357-5851 · **Admissions Fax:** 318-357-5091
Admissions E-mail: henderson@nsula.edu
Website: www.nsula.edu/graduate_studies

INSTITUTIONAL INFORMATION

Public/private: Public. **Evening Classes Available?** Yes. **Total Faculty:** 79. **% Faculty Female:** 58. **% Faculty Part-time:** 16. **Students in Parent Institution:** 9,415.

PROGRAMS

Masters offered in: Adult and continuing education administration; adult and continuing education and teaching; adult health nurse/nursing; biology teacher education; business teacher education; chemistry teacher education; clinical psychology; computer teacher education; counselor education/school counseling and guidance services; curriculum and instruction; education leadership and administration; education; education/teaching of the gifted and talented; educational administration and supervision; educational, instructional, and curriculum supervision; educational/instructional media design; elementary and middle school administration/principalship; elementary education and teaching; English language and literature; English/language arts teacher education; family and consumer sciences/home economics teacher education; family practice nurse/nurse practitioner; health and physical education; health and physical education/fitness; health teacher education; mathematics teacher education; Montessori teacher education; music teacher education; nursing/registered nurse training (RN, ASN, BSN, MSN); nursing clinical specialist; pediatric nurse/nursing; physical education teaching and coaching; psychology; public health/community nurse/nursing; reading teacher education; science teacher education/general science teacher education; secondary education and teaching; secondary school administration/principalship; social studies teacher education; special education and teaching; special education; sports and fitness administration/management; student counseling and personnel services; teacher education, multiple levels. **First Professional degree offered in:** Education, school librarian/school library media specialist.

STUDENT INFORMATION

Total Students in Program: 863. **% Full-time:** 29.

EXPENSES/FINANCIAL AID

Annual Tuition: In-state $2,600. / Out-of-state $7,000. **Fees:** $267. **Books and Supplies:** $1,000. **Grants Range From:** $3,000-$12,000. **Loans Range From:** $3,000-$12,000. **% Receiving Financial Aid:** 13.

ADMISSIONS INFORMATION

Application Fee: $20. **Regular Application Deadline:** 8/15. **Regular Notification:** Rolling. **Transfer Students Accepted?** Yes. **Transfer Policy:** Eligibility to return to previous university required of tranfer applicants. **Number of Applications Received:** 469. **% of Applicants Accepted:** 98. **% Accepted Who Enrolled:** 68. **Average GPA:** 2.9. **Average GRE Verbal:** 472. **Average GRE Quantitative:** 491.
Required Admission Factors: GRE, letters of recommendation, transcript. **Other Admission Factors:** Minimum GRE score of 800 (900 for psychology program) and minimum 2.5 GPA (3.0 for psychology and nursing programs) required.

EMPLOYMENT INFORMATION

Placement Office Available? Yes. **% Employed Within 6 Months:** 92. **Rate of placement:** 66%. **Average starting salary:** $22,000.

NORTHWESTERN UNIVERSITY
Graduate School

Address: Rebecca Crown Center, 633 Clark Street, Evanston, IL 60208-1113
Admissions Phone: 847-491-7264 · **Admissions Fax:** 847-491-5070
Admissions E-mail: gradapp@northwestern.edu
Website: www.northwestern.edu/graduate/

INSTITUTIONAL INFORMATION

Public/private: Private (nonprofit). **Evening Classes Available?** Yes. **Students in Parent Institution:** 17,113.

STUDENT INFORMATION

Total Students in Program: 6,449. **% Full-time:** 72. **% Female:** 41.

RESEARCH FACILITIES

Research Facilities: The Searle Center for Teaching Excellence, Center for Biotechnology, Center for Catalysis and Surface Science, Center for Circadian Biology and Medicine, Center for Mathematical Studies in Economics and Management Science, Center for Reproductive Science.

EXPENSES/FINANCIAL AID

Annual Tuition: In-state $24,840. **Fees:** $1,184. **Books and Supplies:** $1,695. **Loans Range From:** $1,000-$39,375. **% Receiving Scholarships/Grants:** 4. **% Receiving Loans:** 8. **% Receiving Assistantships:** 46.

ADMISSIONS INFORMATION

Application Fee: $60. **Regular Application Deadline:** 12/31. **Regular Notification:** Rolling. **Transfer Students Accepted?** Yes. **Transfer Policy:** Admission requirements are the same for transfer students as they are for new graduate students. Fall admission deadline is 12/31, except for School of Engineering, which has a 1/15 deadline. Admission deadline for any quarter other than fall; for U.S. citizens and permanent residents deadline is 4 weeks before the first day of class for that quarter. International students are encouraged to submit their materials 3 months before domestic applicants. Many programs admit only in fall quarter. **Number of Applications Received:** 6,922. **% of Applicants Accepted:** 20. **Average GRE Verbal:** 579. **Average GRE Quantitative:** 714. **Average GRE Analytical:** 711.
Required Admission Factors: Essays/personal statement, letters of recommendation, transcript.
Other Admission Factors: Varies by discipline; contact academic program directly.

EMPLOYMENT INFORMATION

Placement Office Available? Yes.

NORWICH UNIVERSITY
Online Graduate Programs

Address: 158 Harmon Drive , Northfield, VT 05663
Admissions Phone: 800-686.6546 · **Admissions Fax:** 802-485-2533
Admissions E-mail: mba@grad.norwich.edu · **Website:** www.mba.norwich.edu

INSTITUTIONAL INFORMATION

Public/private: Private (nonprofit). **Total Faculty:** 23. **% Faculty Female:** 30. **% Faculty Part-time:** 52. **Student/faculty Ratio:** 13:1. **Students in Parent Institution:** 1,008.

PROGRAMS

Masters offered in: Business administration/management, civil engineering, computer and information systems security, criminology, international relations and affairs, structural engineering, water resources engineering.

STUDENT INFORMATION

Total Students in Program: 350. **% Full-time:** 100. **% Female:** 43.

RESEARCH FACILITIES

Research Facilities: Regional Center for the Study of Computer Crime and Counter Terrorism.

EXPENSES/FINANCIAL AID

Annual Tuition: $11,976. **Fees:** $600. **Books and Supplies:** $600. **Grants Range From:** $12,000-$15,000. **Loans Range From:** $400-$19,500. **% Receiving Scholarships/Grants:** 5. **% Receiving Loans:** 95.

ADMISSIONS INFORMATION

Application Fee: $50. **Priority Application Deadline:** 6/1. **Regular Application Deadline:** 7/1. **Regular Notification:** Rolling. **Transfer Students Accepted?** Yes. **Transfer Policy:** Maximum number of credits that may by transferred varies by program. **Number of Applications Received:** 300. **% of Applicants Accepted:** 67. **% Accepted Who Enrolled:** 75. **Average GPA:** 3.2.

Required Admission Factors: Essays/personal statement, interview, letters of recommendation, transcript. **Other Admission Factors:** 2.5 GPA. **Program-Specific Admission Factors:** Permission of employer to use IT system for a case study for MSIA students.

EMPLOYMENT INFORMATION

Placement Office Available? Yes. **% Employed Within 6 Months:** 90. **Rate of placement:** 85%. **Average starting salary:** $39,000.

NOVA SCOTIA AGRICULTURAL COLLEGE
Research & Graduate Studies Office

Address: PO Box 550, 62 Cumming Drive, Truro, Nova Scotia, B2N 5E3, Canada
Admissions Phone: 902-893-6502 · **Admissions Fax:** 902-893-3430
Admissions E-mail: jrogers@nsac.ns.ca · **Website:** www.nsac.ns.ca

INSTITUTIONAL INFORMATION

Public/private: Public. **Total Faculty:** 52. **% Faculty Female:** 12. **% Faculty Part-time:** 23. **Student/faculty Ratio:** 1:1. **Students in Parent Institution:** 753.

PROGRAMS

Masters offered in: Animal physiology, plant molecular biology, plant physiology.

STUDENT INFORMATION

Total Students in Program: 67. **% Full-time:** 64. **% Female:** 54. **% International:** 18.

RESEARCH FACILITIES

Research Facilities: Atlantic Poultry Research Institute, Atlantic Poultry Research Centre, Bio-Environmental Engineering Centre, Atlantic Pasture Research Centre, Canadian Centre for Fur Animal Research, Organic Agriculture Centre of Canada.

EXPENSES/FINANCIAL AID

Annual Tuition: In-state $6,723. / Out-of-state $11,553. **Room & Board:** $550. **Fees:** $420. **Books and Supplies:** $150. **Grants Range From:** $500-$7,000. **Loans Range From:** $100-$10,000. **% Receiving Financial Aid:** 77. **% Receiving Scholarships/Grants:** 38. **% Receiving Assistantships:** 77. **Types of Aid Available:** Graduate assistantships, scholarships. **Number of Fellowships Granted Each Year:** 5. **Average amount of individual fellowships per year:** $5,000. **Number of Teaching/Research Assistantships Granted Each Year:** 20. **Assistantship Compensation Includes:** Salary/stipend. **Average Salary Stipend:** $15,000.

ADMISSIONS INFORMATION

Application Fee: $70. **Regular Application Deadline:** 6/1. **Regular Notification:** Rolling. **Transfer Students Accepted?** Yes. **Transfer Policy:** 3 credit hours (1 full graduate course) may be transferred. **Number of Applications Received:** 28. **% of Applicants Accepted:** 79. **% Accepted Who Enrolled:** 59. **Average GPA:** 3.2.

Required Admission Factors: Essays/personal statement, letters of recommendation, transcript.
Other Admission Factors: Minimum 3.0 GPA required.
Program-Specific Admission Factors: BS degree with honors or the equivalent of honors standing. A 4-year degree may be considered as equivalent to honors if there is evidence of independent research capacity such as a research project as part of a course.

EMPLOYMENT INFORMATION

Placement Office Available? Yes. **% Employed Within 6 Months:** 42. **% of master's grads employed in their field upon graduation:** 42. **Rate of placement:** 90%. **Average starting salary:** $45,000.

NOVA SCOTIA COLLEGE OF ART AND DESIGN
Graduate Programs

Address: 5163 Duke Street, Halifax, Nova Scotia, NS B3J 3J6, Canada
Admissions Phone: 902-494-8129 · **Admissions Fax:** 902-425-2987
Admissions E-mail: tbailey@nscad.ns.ca · **Website:** www.nscad.ns.ca

INSTITUTIONAL INFORMATION

Public/private: Public. **Students in Parent Institution:** 954.

STUDENT INFORMATION

Total Students in Program: 15. **% Full-time:** 100. **% Female:** 40.

EXPENSES/FINANCIAL AID

Books and Supplies: $1,900. **Grants Range From:** $1,500. **% Receiving Financial Aid:** 100. **% Receiving Assistantships:** 100. **Number of Teaching/Research Assistantships Granted Each Year:** 16. **Average Salary Stipend:** $2,500.

ADMISSIONS INFORMATION

Application Fee: $35. **Transfer Students Accepted?** No. **Number of Applications Received:** 121. **% of Applicants Accepted:** 7. **% Accepted Who Enrolled:** 100.
Required Admission Factors: Essays/personal statement, letters of recommendation, transcript.

NOVA SOUTHEASTERN UNIVERSITY
Center for Psychological Studies

Address: 3301 College Avenue, Fort Lauderdale, FL 33314
Admissions Phone: 954-262-5760 · **Admissions Fax:** 954-262-3893
Admissions E-mail: cpsinfo@cps.nova.edu

INSTITUTIONAL INFORMATION

Public/private: Private (nonprofit). **Evening Classes Available?** Yes. **Students in Parent Institution:** 18,587.

STUDENT INFORMATION

Total Students in Program: 11,450. **% Full-time:** 29. **% Female:** 68.

RESEARCH FACILITIES

Research Facilities: Oceanographic Center, Family Center, University School (K-12).

EXPENSES/FINANCIAL AID

Annual Tuition: In-state $13,320. **Room & Board:** $8,490. **Fees:** $250. **% Receiving Financial Aid:** 90.

ADMISSIONS INFORMATION

Application Fee: $50. **Transfer Students Accepted?** Yes. **Transfer Policy:** Maximum 15 credit hours may be transferred into doctoral programs; maximum 6 credit hours may be transferred. **Number of Applications Received:** 412. **% of Applicants Accepted:** 39. **% Accepted Who Enrolled:** 66. **Average GPA:** 3.33. **Average GRE Verbal:** 528. **Average GRE Quantitative:** 583. **Average GRE Analytical:** 602.

Required Admission Factors: Essays/personal statement, GRE, letters of recommendation, transcript.
Other Admission Factors: Minimum 3.0 GPA required.
Program-Specific Admission Factors: Minimum GRE score of 1000, minimum 3.5 GPA, interview, and minimum 18 credit hours of course work in psychology including 3 hours of experimental psychology and 3 hours of statistics required of doctoral program applicants.

NOVA SOUTHEASTERN UNIVERSITY
Graduate School of Humanities & Social Sciences

Address: 3301 College Avenue, Fort Lauderdale, FL 33314
Admissions Phone: 954-262-3000 · **Admissions Fax:** 954-262-3968
Admissions E-mail: mamanda@nova.edu · **Website:** http://shss.nova.edu

INSTITUTIONAL INFORMATION
Public/private: Private (nonprofit). **Evening Classes Available?** Yes. **Student/faculty Ratio:** 18:1. **Students in Parent Institution:** 18,587.

PROGRAMS
Masters offered in: Behavioral sciences, community health services/liaison/counseling, criminology, marriage and family therapy/counseling, peace studies and conflict resolution. **Doctorate offered in:** Community health services/liaison/counseling, marriage and family therapy/counseling, peace studies and conflict resolution. **First Professional degree offered in:** Community health services/liaison/counseling, marriage and family therapy/counseling, multi/interdisciplinary studies, peace studies and conflict resolution, work and family studies.

STUDENT INFORMATION
Total Students in Program: 11,450. **% Full-time:** 29. **% Female:** 68.

RESEARCH FACILITIES
Research Facilities: Oceanographic Center, Family Center, University School (K-12).

EXPENSES/FINANCIAL AID
Annual Tuition: $13,320. **Room & Board:** $8,490. **Fees:** $250. **Books and Supplies:** $300. **% Receiving Financial Aid:** 74. **Types of Aid Available:** 1. **Number of Teaching/Research Assistantships Granted Each Year:** 6. **Average Salary Stipend:** $1,000.

ADMISSIONS INFORMATION
Application Fee: $50. **Regular Application Deadline:** 11/1. **Regular Notification:** Rolling. **Transfer Students Accepted?** Yes. **Transfer Policy:** Transfer of credit form required of transfer applicants. **Number of Applications Received:** 145. **Average GPA:** 3.0.
Required Admission Factors: Essays/personal statement, interview, letters of recommendation, transcript.
Other Admission Factors: Minimum 3.0 GPA recommended.

NOVA SOUTHEASTERN UNIVERSITY
Oceanographic Center

Address: 8000 North Ocean Drive, Dania Beach, FL 33004
Admissions Phone: 954-262-3600 · **Admissions Fax:** 954-262-4020
Admissions E-mail: imcs@nova.edu · **Website:** www.nova.edu/ocean

INSTITUTIONAL INFORMATION
Public/private: Private (nonprofit). **Evening Classes Available?** Yes. **Total Faculty:** 24. **% Faculty Female:** 12. **Student/faculty Ratio:** 10:1. **Students in Parent Institution:** 18,587.

PROGRAMS
Masters offered in: Environmental science; natural resources conservation and research; water, wetlands, and marine resources management. **Doctorate offered in:** Oceanography, chemical and physical.

STUDENT INFORMATION
Total Students in Program: 11,450. **% Full-time:** 29. **% Female:** 68.

RESEARCH FACILITIES
Research Facilities: Oceanographic Center on the Atlantic Ocean, 8 research vessels.

EXPENSES/FINANCIAL AID
Annual Tuition: $13,000. **Room & Board (On/off Campus):** $8,490/$10,800. **Fees:** $250. **Books and Supplies:** $200. **Grants Range From:** $1-$23,999. **Loans Range From:** $1-$23,000. **% Receiving Financial Aid:** 90. **% Receiving Scholarships/Grants:** 10. **% Receiving Loans:** 70. **% Receiving Assistantships:** 5. **% Receiving Other Aid (employee tuition waivers):** 10. **Types of Aid Available:** Graduate assistantships, institutional work-study, loans. **Average student debt, upon graduation:** $17,500. **Number of Teaching/Research Assistantships Granted Each Year:** 15. **Assistantship Compensation Includes:** Salary/stipend. **Average Salary Stipend:** $11,000.

ADMISSIONS INFORMATION
Application Fee: $50. **Regular Application Deadline:** 7/31. **Regular Notification:** Rolling. **Transfer Students Accepted?** Yes. **Number of Applications Received:** 72. **% of Applicants Accepted:** 69. **% Accepted Who Enrolled:** 62. **Average GPA:** 3.04. **Average GRE Verbal:** 501. **Average GRE Quantitative:** 560. **Average GRE Analytical:** 590. **Average GRE Analytical Writing:** 4.
Required Admission Factors: Essays/personal statement, GRE, letters of recommendation, transcript.
Other Admission Factors: GRE score in 50th percentile and minimum 3.0 GPA in major (2.75 overall) required for regular admission; GRE score in 40th percentile and minimum 2.9 GPA in major (2.5 overall) required for provisional acceptance. Statement of interest required.
Program-Specific Admission Factors: Undergraduate major in a natural science is required of marine biology program applicants. Natural science major or concentration required of coastal zone management and marine environmental sciences program applicants.

EMPLOYMENT INFORMATION
% Employed Within 6 Months: 80. **% of master's/doctoral grads employed in their field upon graduation:** 90/100. **Rate of placement:** 50%. **Average starting salary:** $34,000.

OAKLAND CITY UNIVERSITY
School of Adult Programs & Professional Studies

Address: 143 Lucretia Street, Oakland City, IN 47660
Admissions Phone: 800-737-5126 · **Admissions Fax:** 812-749-1294

INSTITUTIONAL INFORMATION
Public/private: Private (nonprofit). **Evening Classes Available?** Yes. **Students in Parent Institution:** 1,268.

STUDENT INFORMATION
Total Students in Program: 81 **% Female:** 37.

EXPENSES/FINANCIAL AID
Books and Supplies: $800. **% Receiving Scholarships/Grants:** 75.

ADMISSIONS INFORMATION
Application Fee: $25. **Regular Notification:** Rolling. **Transfer Students Accepted?** Yes. **Number of Applications Received:** 83. **% of Applicants Accepted:** 100. **% Accepted Who Enrolled:** 100. **Average GPA:** 3.0.
Required Admission Factors: Essays/personal statement, GRE, interview, letters of recommendation, transcript.

Other Admission Factors: Minimum 3.0 GPA required.

EMPLOYMENT INFORMATION

Placement Office Available? Yes. % of master's grads employed in their field upon graduation: 95.

OBERLIN COLLEGE
Conservatory of Music

Address: 39 West College Street, Oberlin, OH 44074
Admissions Phone: 440-775-8413 · Admissions Fax: 440-775-6972
Admissions E-mail: conservatory.admissions@oberlin.edu
Website: www.oberlin.edu/con

INSTITUTIONAL INFORMATION

Public/private: Private (nonprofit). Total Faculty: 76. % Faculty Part-time: 16. Students in Parent Institution: 2,984.

STUDENT INFORMATION

Total Students in Program: 23.

EXPENSES/FINANCIAL AID

Annual Tuition: In-state $26,410. Fees: $170. Books and Supplies: $700. % Receiving Financial Aid: 100. Average student debt, upon graduation: $12,000.

ADMISSIONS INFORMATION

Application Fee: $75. Regular Application Deadline: 1/15. Regular Notification: 4/1. Transfer Students Accepted? No. Number of Applications Received: 48. % of Applicants Accepted: 27. % Accepted Who Enrolled: 69.
Required Admission Factors: Letters of recommendation, transcript.
Program-Specific Admission Factors: Audition required of music program applicants.

EMPLOYMENT INFORMATION

Placement Office Available? Yes.

OBLATE SCHOOL OF THEOLOGY
Graduate Programs

Address: 285 Oblate Drive, San Antonio, TX 78216-6693
Admissions Phone: 210-341-1366, ext. 212 · Admissions Fax: 210-341-4519
Admissions E-mail: oblate@connecti.com

INSTITUTIONAL INFORMATION

Public/private: Private (nonprofit). Student/faculty Ratio: 5:1. Students in Parent Institution: 175.

STUDENT INFORMATION

Total Students in Program: 101. % Full-time: 33. % Female: 23.

EXPENSES/FINANCIAL AID

Annual Tuition: $7,944. Fees: $265.

ADMISSIONS INFORMATION

Application Fee: $30. Regular Notification: Rolling. Transfer Students Accepted? Yes. Number of Applications Received: 29. % of Applicants Accepted: 24.
Required Admission Factors: Essays/personal statement, interview, letters of recommendation, transcript.

EMPLOYMENT INFORMATION

% Employed Within 6 Months: 95. % of master's grads employed in their field upon graduation: 95.

OGI SCHOOL OF SCIENCE AND ENGINEERING AT OHSU
Graduate Studies

Address: 20000 NW Walker Road, Portland, OR 97006-8921
Admissions Phone: 503-748-1382 · Admissions Fax: 503-748-1285
Admissions E-mail: pickertl@ohsu.edu · Website: www.ogi.edu

INSTITUTIONAL INFORMATION

Public/private: Private (nonprofit). Students in Parent Institution: 594.

PROGRAMS

Masters offered in: Biomedical/medical engineering; computer engineering; computer hardware engineering; computer software engineering; electrical, electronics, and communications engineering; environmental/environmental health engineering. Doctorate offered in: Biomedical/medical engineering, computer engineering, computer hardware engineering, computer software engineering, environmental/environmental health engineering.

STUDENT INFORMATION

Total Students in Program: 594. % Full-time: 27. % Female: 23.

RESEARCH FACILITIES

Research Facilities: Center for Human-Computer Communication, Center for Groundwater Research, Center for Spoken Language Understanding, Center for Software Systems Research, Center for Coastal/Land-Margin Research.

EXPENSES/FINANCIAL AID

Annual Tuition: $21,420. Books and Supplies: $850. Grants Range From: $800-$21,420. % Receiving Scholarships/Grants: 70. % Receiving Loans: 8. % Receiving Assistantships: 12. Types of Aid Available: Graduate assistantships, loans, scholarships.

ADMISSIONS INFORMATION

Application Fee: $65. Regular Application Deadline: 7/1. Regular Notification: Rolling. Transfer Students Accepted? Yes. Number of Applications Received: 597. % of Applicants Accepted: 50. % Accepted Who Enrolled: 38. Average GPA: 3.5.
Required Admission Factors: Essays/personal statement, letters of recommendation, transcript.
Other Admission Factors: Minimum 3.0 GPA required.

EMPLOYMENT INFORMATION

% Employed Within 6 Months: 50. Average starting salary: $50,000.

OGLETHORPE UNIVERSITY
Graduate Program

Address: 4484 Peachtree Road, NE, Atlanta, GA 30319
Admissions Phone: 404-364-8314 · Admissions Fax: 404-364-8500
Admissions E-mail: jwaller@oglethorpe.edu

INSTITUTIONAL INFORMATION

Public/private: Private (nonprofit). Evening Classes Available? Yes. Students in Parent Institution: 1,288.

STUDENT INFORMATION

Total Students in Program: 110. % Full-time: 15. % Female: 71.

EXPENSES/FINANCIAL AID

Annual Tuition: $5,700.

ADMISSIONS INFORMATION

Application Fee: $30. Regular Notification: Rolling. Transfer Students Accepted? Yes. Average GPA: 3.4.
Required Admission Factors: Essays/personal statement, GRE, letters of recommendation, transcript.

Other Admission Factors: Minimum 3.0 GPA and demonstrated leadership and strong character required.

THE OHIO STATE UNIVERSITY—COLUMBUS
College of Biological Sciences

Address: 3rd Floor Lincoln Tower, 1800 Cannon Drive, Columbus, OH 43210-1200
Admissions Phone: 614-292-9444 · **Admissions Fax:** 614-292-3895
Website: www.biosci.ohio-state.edu

INSTITUTIONAL INFORMATION
Public/private: Public. **Students in Parent Institution:** 48,352.

STUDENT INFORMATION
Total Students in Program: 12,866. **% Full-time:** 68. **% Female:** 52.

EXPENSES/FINANCIAL AID
Annual Tuition: In-state $5,472. / Out-of-state $14,172. **Room & Board:** $9,500. **Books and Supplies:** $1,200.

ADMISSIONS INFORMATION
Transfer Students Accepted? No.

THE OHIO STATE UNIVERSITY—COLUMBUS
College of Human Ecology

Address: 3rd Floor Lincoln Tower, 1800 Cannon Drive, Columbus, OH 43210-1200
Admissions Phone: 614-292-3980 · **Admissions Fax:** 614-292-4818
Website: www.hec.ohio-state.edu

INSTITUTIONAL INFORMATION
Public/private: Public. **Students in Parent Institution:** 48,352.

STUDENT INFORMATION
Total Students in Program: 12,866. **% Full-time:** 68. **% Female:** 52.

EXPENSES/FINANCIAL AID
Annual Tuition: In-state $5,472. / Out-of-state $14,172. **Room & Board:** $9,500. **Books and Supplies:** $1,200.

ADMISSIONS INFORMATION
Application Fee: $30. **Regular Notification:** Rolling. **Transfer Students Accepted?** No. **Number of Applications Received:** 188. **% of Applicants Accepted:** 45. **% Accepted Who Enrolled:** 58.
Required Admission Factors: Essays/personal statement, transcript.
Other Admission Factors: Minimum 2.7 GPA required; GRE or GMAT required of applicants whose GPA is below minimum.

THE OHIO STATE UNIVERSITY—COLUMBUS
College of Humanities

Address: 3rd Floor Lincoln Tower, 1800 Cannon Drive, Columbus, OH 43210-1200
Admissions Phone: 614-292-9444 · **Admissions Fax:** 614-292-3895
Website: www.cohums.ohio-state.edu

INSTITUTIONAL INFORMATION
Public/private: Public. **Students in Parent Institution:** 48,352.

STUDENT INFORMATION
Total Students in Program: 12,866. **% Full-time:** 68. **% Female:** 52.

EXPENSES/FINANCIAL AID
Annual Tuition: In-state $5,472. / Out-of-state $14,172. **Room & Board:** $9,500. **Books and Supplies:** $1,200.

ADMISSIONS INFORMATION
Application Fee: $30. **Regular Notification:** Rolling. **Transfer Students Accepted?** No. **Number of Applications Received:** 1,321. **% of Applicants Accepted:** 27. **% Accepted Who Enrolled:** 51.
Required Admission Factors: Essays/personal statement, transcript.
Other Admission Factors: Minimum 2.7 GPA required; GRE or GMAT required of applicants whose GPA is below minimum.

THE OHIO STATE UNIVERSITY—COLUMBUS
College of Social & Behavioral Sciences

Address: 3rd Floor Lincoln Tower, 1800 Cannon Drive, Columbus, OH 43210-1200
Admissions Phone: 614-292-9444 · **Admissions Fax:** 614-292-3895
Website: www.sbs.ohio-state.edu

INSTITUTIONAL INFORMATION
Public/private: Public. **Students in Parent Institution:** 48,352.

STUDENT INFORMATION
Total Students in Program: 12,866. **% Full-time:** 68. **% Female:** 52.

EXPENSES/FINANCIAL AID
Annual Tuition: In-state $5,472. / Out-of-state $14,172. **Room & Board:** $9,500. **Books and Supplies:** $1,200.

ADMISSIONS INFORMATION
Application Fee: $30. **Regular Notification:** Rolling. **Transfer Students Accepted?** No. **Number of Applications Received:** 2,436. **% of Applicants Accepted:** 20. **% Accepted Who Enrolled:** 43.
Required Admission Factors: Essays/personal statement, transcript.
Other Admission Factors: Minimum 2.7 GPA required; GRE or GMAT required of applicants whose GPA is below minimum.

THE OHIO STATE UNIVERSITY—COLUMBUS
College of Social Work

Address: 3rd Floor Lincoln Tower, 1800 Cannon Drive, Columbus, OH 43210-1200
Admissions Phone: 614-292-2972 · **Admissions Fax:** 614-292-6940
Website: www.csw.ohio-state.edu

INSTITUTIONAL INFORMATION
Public/private: Public. **Evening Classes Available?** Yes. **Students in Parent Institution:** 48,352.

STUDENT INFORMATION
Total Students in Program: 12,866. **% Full-time:** 68. **% Female:** 52.

EXPENSES/FINANCIAL AID
Annual Tuition: In-state $5,472. / Out-of-state $14,172. **Room & Board:** $9,500. **Books and Supplies:** $1,200.

ADMISSIONS INFORMATION
Application Fee: $30. **Regular Notification:** Rolling. **Transfer Students Accepted?** Yes. **Number of Applications Received:** 487. **% of Applicants Accepted:** 44. **% Accepted Who Enrolled:** 64.
Required Admission Factors: Essays/personal statement, transcript.
Other Admission Factors: Minimum 2.7 GPA required; GRE required of applicants whose GPA is below minimum.

THE OHIO STATE UNIVERSITY—COLUMBUS
College of the Arts

Address: 3rd Floor Lincoln Tower, 1800 Cannon Drive, Columbus, OH 43210-1200
Admissions Phone: 614-292-9444 · **Admissions Fax:** 614-292-3895
Website: www.arts.ohio-state.edu

INSTITUTIONAL INFORMATION
Public/private: Public. **Students in Parent Institution:** 48,352.

STUDENT INFORMATION
Total Students in Program: 12,866. **% Full-time:** 68. **% Female:** 52.

EXPENSES/FINANCIAL AID
Annual Tuition: In-state $5,472. / Out-of-state $14,172. **Room & Board:** $9,500. **Books and Supplies:** $1,200.

ADMISSIONS INFORMATION
Application Fee: $30. **Regular Notification:** Rolling. **Transfer Students Accepted?** No. **Number of Applications Received:** 717. **% of Applicants Accepted:** 32. **% Accepted Who Enrolled:** 59.
Required Admission Factors: Essays/personal statement, transcript.
Other Admission Factors: Minimum 2.7 GPA or GRE/GMAT scores required.

OHIO UNIVERSITY
Center for International Studies

Address: Athens, OH 45701-2979
Admissions Phone: 740-593-2800 · **Admissions Fax:** 740-593-4625
Admissions E-mail: gradstu@www.ohiou.edu

INSTITUTIONAL INFORMATION
Public/private: Public. **Students in Parent Institution:** 19,920.

STUDENT INFORMATION
Total Students in Program: 2,792. **% Full-time:** 72. **% Female:** 49.

EXPENSES/FINANCIAL AID
Annual Tuition: In-state $2,195. / Out-of-state $4,218. **Room & Board:** $3,916.

ADMISSIONS INFORMATION
Application Fee: $30. **Transfer Students Accepted?** No. **Number of Applications Received:** 258. **% of Applicants Accepted:** 81. **% Accepted Who Enrolled:** 26.
Required Admission Factors: Letters of recommendation, transcript.
Other Admission Factors: Minimum 3.0 GPA required.

EMPLOYMENT INFORMATION
% Employed Within 6 Months: 70. **% of master's grads employed in their field upon graduation:** 40.

OHIO UNIVERSITY
College of Communication

Address: Athens, OH 45701-2979
Admissions Phone: 740-593-2800 · **Admissions Fax:** 740-593-4625
Admissions E-mail: gradstu@www.ohiou.edu

INSTITUTIONAL INFORMATION
Public/private: Public. **Students in Parent Institution:** 19,920.

STUDENT INFORMATION
Total Students in Program: 2,792. **% Full-time:** 72. **% Female:** 49.

EXPENSES/FINANCIAL AID
Annual Tuition: In-state $2,195. / Out-of-state $4,218. **Room & Board:** $3,916.

ADMISSIONS INFORMATION
Application Fee: $30. **Transfer Students Accepted?** No. **Number of Applications Received:** 313. **% of Applicants Accepted:** 56. **% Accepted Who Enrolled:** 46.
Required Admission Factors: GRE, letters of recommendation, transcript.
Other Admission Factors: Minimum 3.0 GPA required.

EMPLOYMENT INFORMATION
% Employed Within 6 Months: 94. **% of master's/doctoral grads employed in their field upon graduation:** 55/78.

OHIO UNIVERSITY
College of Fine Arts

Address: Athens, OH 45701-2979
Admissions Phone: 740-593-2800 · **Admissions Fax:** 740-593-4625
Admissions E-mail: gradstu@www.ohiou.edu

INSTITUTIONAL INFORMATION
Public/private: Public. **Students in Parent Institution:** 19,920.

STUDENT INFORMATION
Total Students in Program: 2,792. **% Full-time:** 72. **% Female:** 49.

EXPENSES/FINANCIAL AID
Annual Tuition: In-state $2,195. / Out-of-state $4,218. **Room & Board:** $3,916.

ADMISSIONS INFORMATION
Application Fee: $30. **Transfer Students Accepted?** No. **Number of Applications Received:** 402. **% of Applicants Accepted:** 43. **% Accepted Who Enrolled:** 58.
Required Admission Factors: GRE, letters of recommendation, transcript.
Other Admission Factors: Minimum 3.0 GPA required.

EMPLOYMENT INFORMATION
% Employed Within 6 Months: 70. **% of master's/doctoral grads employed in their field upon graduation:** 38/100.

OKLAHOMA BAPTIST UNIVERSITY
Graduate Programs

Address: 500 West University, Shawnee, OK 74801
Admissions Phone: 405-878-2225 or 800-654-3285
Admissions Fax: 405-878-2225

INSTITUTIONAL INFORMATION
Public/private: Private (nonprofit). **Evening Classes Available?** Yes. **Students in Parent Institution:** 2,017.

EXPENSES/FINANCIAL AID
Annual Tuition: $7,200. **Fees:** $200. **Loans Range From:** $5,500-$8,500. **% Receiving Loans:** 100. **Average student debt, upon graduation:** $6,800.

ADMISSIONS INFORMATION
Application Fee: $50. **Transfer Students Accepted?** Yes. **Number of Applications Received:** 17. **% of Applicants Accepted:** 88. **% Accepted Who Enrolled:** 80. **Average GPA:** 3.3. **Average GRE Verbal:** 510. **Average GRE Analytical:** 512.
Required Admission Factors: Essays/personal statement, GRE, letters of recommendation, transcript.
Other Admission Factors: Minimum admission index of 1600 required.

OKLAHOMA CITY UNIVERSITY
Petree College of Arts & Sciences

Address: 2501 North Blackwelder, Oklahoma City, OK 73106
Admissions Phone: 405-521-5351 · **Admissions Fax:** 405-521-5356
Admissions E-mail: gadmissions@okcu.edu · **Website:** www.tgimatocu.com

INSTITUTIONAL INFORMATION
Public/private: Private (nonprofit). **Evening Classes Available?** Yes. **Students in Parent Institution:** 3,695.

PROGRAMS
Masters offered in: Accounting and business/management; accounting; acting; art/art studies; business administration/management; business/managerial economics; commercial photography; computer and information sciences; computer science; conducting; creative writing; criminal justice/law enforcement administration; criminology; curriculum and instruction; drama and dramatics/theater arts; dramatic/theater arts and stagecraft; education; elementary education and teaching; finance; general studies; history; human resources management/personnel administration; information technology; international business; law (LLB, JD); liberal arts and sciences studies and humanities; liberal arts and sciences/liberal studies; management science; marketing/marketing management; Montessori teacher education; music performance; music theory and composition; music; music/music and performing arts studies; nursing/registered nurse training (RN, ASN, BSN, MSN); nursing administration (MSN, MS, PhD); painting; philosophy; photography; religion/religious studies; religious education; sculpture; secondary education and teaching; technical theater, theater design, and technology; visual and performing arts; voice and opera; women's studies.

STUDENT INFORMATION
Total Students in Program: 554. **% Full-time:** 84.

RESEARCH FACILITIES
Research Facilities: B.D. Eddie Business Research and Consulting Center.

EXPENSES/FINANCIAL AID
Annual Tuition: $9,540. **Fees:** $150. **Books and Supplies:** $500. **Grants Range From:** $1,500-$9,540. **Loans Range From:** $1,500-$18,000. **% Receiving Financial Aid:** 85.

ADMISSIONS INFORMATION
Application Fee: $35. **Regular Notification:** Rolling. **Transfer Students Accepted?** Yes. **Number of Applications Received:** 132. **% of Applicants Accepted:** 100. **% Accepted Who Enrolled:** 72. **Average GPA:** 3.25.
Required Admission Factors: Letters of recommendation, transcript.
Other Admission Factors: Minimum 3.0 GPA required.

EMPLOYMENT INFORMATION
Placement Office Available? Yes.

OKLAHOMA CITY UNIVERSITY
Wanda L. Bass School of Music

Address: 2501 North Blackwelder, Oklahoma City, OK 73106
Admissions Phone: 405-521-5351 · **Admissions Fax:** 405-521-5356
Admissions E-mail: gadmissions@okcu.edu · **Website:** www.tgimatocu.com

INSTITUTIONAL INFORMATION
Public/private: Private (nonprofit). **Student/faculty Ratio:** 4:1. **Students in Parent Institution:** 3,695.

PROGRAMS
Masters offered in: Conducting, music performance, music theory and composition, music, music/music and performing arts studies, piano and organ, visual and performing arts, voice and opera.

STUDENT INFORMATION
Total Students in Program: 47. **% Full-time:** 100. **% International:** 23.

RESEARCH FACILITIES
Research Facilities: B.D. Eddie Business Research and Consulting Center.

EXPENSES/FINANCIAL AID
Annual Tuition: $9,540. **Fees:** $150. **Books and Supplies:** $150. **Grants Range From:** $1,000-$9,540. **Loans Range From:** $1,000-$9,540. **% Receiving Financial Aid:** 85. **Types of Aid Available:** Graduate assistantships, institutional work-study, loans, scholarships.

ADMISSIONS INFORMATION
Application Fee: $35. **Regular Notification:** Rolling. **Transfer Students Accepted?** Yes. **Transfer Policy:** Minimum 3.0 GPA required of transfer applicants. **Number of Applications Received:** 29. **% of Applicants Accepted:** 86. **% Accepted Who Enrolled:** 68. **Average GPA:** 3.6.
Required Admission Factors: Essays/personal statement, letters of recommendation, transcript.
Other Admission Factors: Minimum 3.0 GPA required.
Program-Specific Admission Factors: All students must complete a successful audition and satisfy all admission criteria before being admitted to the School of Music.

EMPLOYMENT INFORMATION
Placement Office Available? Yes.

OKLAHOMA STATE UNIVERSITY
College of Arts & Sciences

Address: Stillwater, OK 74078
Admissions Phone: 405-744-6368 · **Admissions Fax:** 405-744-0355
Website: www.cas.okstate.edu

INSTITUTIONAL INFORMATION
Public/private: Public. **Evening Classes Available?** Yes. **Students in Parent Institution:** 21,087.

STUDENT INFORMATION
Total Students in Program: 4,590. **% Full-time:** 36. **% Female:** 44.

EXPENSES/FINANCIAL AID
Annual Tuition: In-state $1,843. / Out-of-state $5,236. **Room & Board:** $6,510. **Fees:** $100. **Books and Supplies:** $435.

ADMISSIONS INFORMATION
Application Fee: $25. **Regular Notification:** Rolling. **Transfer Students Accepted?** Yes. **Transfer Policy:** Maximum of 9 master's level credit hours may be transferred.
Required Admission Factors: Letters of recommendation, transcript.
Other Admission Factors: Minimum 3.0 GPA required for most programs.

EMPLOYMENT INFORMATION
Placement Office Available? Yes.

OKLAHOMA STATE UNIVERSITY
College of Human Environmental Sciences

Address: Stillwater, OK 74078
Admissions Phone: 405-744-6368 · **Admissions Fax:** 405-744-0355
Website: www.ches.okstate.edu

INSTITUTIONAL INFORMATION
Public/private: Public. **Evening Classes Available?** Yes. **Students in Parent Institution:** 21,087.

STUDENT INFORMATION
Total Students in Program: 4,590. **% Full-time:** 36. **% Female:** 44.

EXPENSES/FINANCIAL AID
Annual Tuition: In-state $1,843. / Out-of-state $5,236. **Room & Board:** $6,510. **Fees:** $100. **Books and Supplies:** $435.

ADMISSIONS INFORMATION
Application Fee: $25. **Transfer Students Accepted?** Yes. **Transfer Policy:** Maximum of 9 master's-level credit hours may be transferred. **Required Admission Factors:** Transcript.

EMPLOYMENT INFORMATION
Placement Office Available? Yes.

OLD DOMINION UNIVERSITY
College of Arts & Letters

Address: 5215 Hampton Boulevard, Norfolk, VA 23529-0050

INSTITUTIONAL INFORMATION
Public/private: Public. **Evening Classes Available?** Yes. **Student/faculty Ratio:** 5:1. **Students in Parent Institution:** 19,627.

STUDENT INFORMATION
Total Students in Program: 6,529. **% Full-time:** 22. **% Female:** 58.

RESEARCH FACILITIES
Research Facilities: Institute for the Study of Race and Ethnicity; Institute of Asian Studies; International Maritime, Ports, and Logistics Management Institute; Center for Global Business and Executive Education; Insurance and Financial Services Center.

EXPENSES/FINANCIAL AID
Annual Tuition: In-state $4,848. / Out-of-state $12,816. **Fees:** $152. **Books and Supplies:** $700. **Grants Range From:** $1,000-$19,360. **Loans Range From:** $1,000-$18,500. **% Receiving Scholarships/Grants:** 32. **% Receiving Loans:** 56. **% Receiving Assistantships:** 28. **Number of Teaching/Research Assistantships Granted Each Year:** 80. **Average Salary Stipend:** $8,000.

ADMISSIONS INFORMATION
Application Fee: $30. **Regular Notification:** Rolling. **Transfer Students Accepted?** Yes. **Number of Applications Received:** 159. **% of Applicants Accepted:** 82. **% Accepted Who Enrolled:** 71. **Average GPA:** 3.3. **Average GRE Verbal:** 510. **Average GRE Quantitative:** 474. **Average GRE Analytical:** 531.
Required Admission Factors: Essays/personal statement, GRE, letters of recommendation, transcript.
Other Admission Factors: Minimum 2.5 GPA required for some programs.

EMPLOYMENT INFORMATION
Placement Office Available? Yes.

OLD DOMINION UNIVERSITY
College of Sciences

Address: 5215 Hampton Boulevard, Norfolk, VA 23529-0050

INSTITUTIONAL INFORMATION
Public/private: Public. **Evening Classes Available?** Yes. **Student/faculty Ratio:** 6:1. **Students in Parent Institution:** 19,627

STUDENT INFORMATION.
Total Students in Program: 6,529. **% Full-time:** 22. **% Female:** 58.

RESEARCH FACILITIES
Research Facilities: Institute for the Study of Race and Ethnicity; Institute of Asian Studies; International Maritime, Ports, and Logistics Management Insti-

tute; Center for Global Business and Executive Education; Insurance and Financial Services Center.

EXPENSES/FINANCIAL AID
Annual Tuition: In-state $4,848. / Out-of-state $12,816. **Fees:** $152. **Books and Supplies:** $700. **% Receiving Scholarships/Grants:** 32. **% Receiving Loans:** 56. **% Receiving Assistantships:** 28. **Number of Fellowships Granted Each Year:** 1. **Average amount of individual fellowships per year:** $10,000. **Number of Teaching/Research Assistantships Granted Each Year:** 54.

ADMISSIONS INFORMATION
Application Fee: $30. **Regular Notification:** Rolling. **Transfer Students Accepted?** Yes. **Number of Applications Received:** 601. **% of Applicants Accepted:** 63. **% Accepted Who Enrolled:** 55. **Average GPA:** 3.5. **Required Admission Factors:** Essays/personal statement, GRE, letters of recommendation, transcript.
Other Admission Factors: Minimum 2.5 GPA required for some programs.

EMPLOYMENT INFORMATION
Placement Office Available? Yes.

OTIS COLLEGE OF ART AND DESIGN
Graduate Writing Program

Address: 9045 Lincoln Boulevard, Los Angeles, CA 90045
Admissions Phone: 310-665-6891 or 310-665-6818
Admissions E-mail: grads@otis.edu · **Website:** www.otis.edu

INSTITUTIONAL INFORMATION
Public/private: Private (nonprofit). **Evening Classes Available?** Yes. **Student/faculty Ratio:** 4:1. **Students in Parent Institution:** 925.

STUDENT INFORMATION
Total Students in Program: 31. **% Full-time:** 97. **% Female:** 58.

EXPENSES/FINANCIAL AID
Annual Tuition: In-state $19,894. **Fees:** $450. **Grants Range From:** $1,000-$6,000. **Loans Range From:** $8,500-$18,500. **% Receiving Financial Aid:** 100. **% Receiving Scholarships/Grants:** 60. **% Receiving Loans:** 100. **Average student debt, upon graduation:** $31,000 **Number of Fellowships Granted Each Year:** 5. **Number of Teaching/Research Assistantships Granted Each Year:** 6.

ADMISSIONS INFORMATION
Application Fee: $40. **Transfer Students Accepted?** Yes. **Transfer Policy:** Interview required of transfer applicants. **Number of Applications Received:** 62. **% of Applicants Accepted:** 19. **% Accepted Who Enrolled:** 92. **Required Admission Factors:** Essays/personal statement, letters of recommendation, transcript.
Other Admission Factors: Resume, portfolio (35-millimeter slides), statement of intent, and bachelor's or equivalent in art with minimum of 45 semester hours in studio art, and minimum 15 semester hours in art history required. **Program-Specific Admission Factors:** Portfolio required of writing program applicants.

EMPLOYMENT INFORMATION
Placement Office Available? Yes.

OTTAWA UNIVERSITY—ARIZONA
Office of Graduate Studies

Address: 10020 North 25th Avenue, Phoenix, AZ 85021
Admissions Phone: 800-235-9586 · **Admissions Fax:** 602-371-0035
Admissions E-mail: admiss.az@ottawa.edu · **Website:** www.ottawa.edu

INSTITUTIONAL INFORMATION

Public/private: Private (nonprofit). **Evening Classes Available?** Yes. **Total Faculty:** 48. **% Faculty Female:** 44. **% Faculty Part-time:** 92. **Student/faculty Ratio:** 12:1. **Students in Parent Institution:** 4,302.

PROGRAMS

Masters offered in: Bilingual and multilingual education, business administration and management, college student counseling and personnel services, counseling psychology, counselor education/school counseling and guidance services, curriculum and instruction, education leadership and administration, educational administration and supervision, human resources development, human resources management and services, human resources management/personnel administration, marriage and family therapy/counseling, Montessori teacher education, organizational behavior studies, school psychology, substance abuse/addiction counseling, teacher education and professional development, specific levels and methods, teaching English as a second or foreign language/ESL language instructor.

STUDENT INFORMATION

Total Students in Program: 598. **% Full-time:** 44. **% Female:** 74. **% Minority:** 15. **% International:** 1.

EXPENSES/FINANCIAL AID

Annual Tuition: $375. **Books and Supplies:** $800. **Loans Range From:** $1,000-$18,500. **% Receiving Financial Aid:** 62. **% Receiving Loans:** 100. **Types of Aid Available:** Loans.

ADMISSIONS INFORMATION

Application Fee: $50. **Priority Application Deadline:** 7/1. **Regular Application Deadline:** 8/1. **Regular Notification:** Rolling. **Transfer Students Accepted?** Yes. **Transfer Policy:** Transfer course work must be from a regionally accredited institution. **Number of Applications Received:** 156. **% of Applicants Accepted:** 91. **% Accepted Who Enrolled:** 70. **Average GPA:** 3.0.
Required Admission Factors: Essays/personal statement, interview, letters of recommendation, transcript.
Other Admission Factors: Minimum 3.0 GPA, preparatory course work, professional experience, and career development essay.
Program-Specific Admission Factors: Undergraduate course work in statistics required for human resources program. Undergraduate course work in accounting and economics required for MBA program. MAEd: some concentrations require teaching certification.

OTTAWA UNIVERSITY—KANSAS CITY
Office of Graduate Studies

Address: 20 Corporate Woods, 10865 Grandview Drive, Overland Park, KS 66210
Admissions Phone: 888-404-6852 · **Admissions Fax:** 913-451-0806
Admissions E-mail: admiss.kc@ottawa.edu · **Website:** www.ottawa.edu

INSTITUTIONAL INFORMATION

Public/private: Private (nonprofit). **Evening Classes Available?** Yes. **Total Faculty:** 12. **% Faculty Female:** 42. **% Faculty Part-time:** 67. **Student/faculty Ratio:** 6:1. **Students in Parent Institution:** 850.

PROGRAMS

Masters offered in: Business administration/management, human resources management and services.

STUDENT INFORMATION

Total Students in Program: 67. **% Full-time:** 55. **% Female:** 70. **% Minority:** 15.

EXPENSES/FINANCIAL AID

Annual Tuition: $375. **Books and Supplies:** $800. **Loans Range From:** $1,000-$18,500. **% Receiving Financial Aid:** 52. **% Receiving Loans:** 100. **Types of Aid Available:** Loans.

ADMISSIONS INFORMATION

Application Fee: $50. **Regular Application Deadline:** 8/31. **Regular Notification:** Rolling. **Transfer Students Accepted?** Yes. **Transfer Policy:** Transfer course work must be from a regionally accredited institution. **Number of Applications Received:** 47. **% of Applicants Accepted:** 89. **% Accepted Who Enrolled:** 48. **Average GPA:** 3.0.
Required Admission Factors: Essays/personal statement, interview, letters of recommendation, transcript.
Other Admission Factors: Minimum 3.0 GPA, preparatory course work, professional experience, and career development essay.
Program-Specific Admission Factors: Undergraduate course work in statistics required for human resources program. Undergraduate course work in accounting and economics required for MBA program.

OTTERBEIN COLLEGE
Office of Graduate Programs

Address: One Otterbein College, Westerville, OH 43081
Admissions Phone: 614-823-3210 · **Admissions Fax:** 614-823-3208
Admissions E-mail: grad@otterbein.edu · **Website:** www.otterbein.edu

INSTITUTIONAL INFORMATION

Public/private: Private (nonprofit). **Evening Classes Available?** Yes. **Students in Parent Institution:** 2,917.

PROGRAMS

Masters offered in: Adult health nurse/nursing, business administration/management, curriculum and instruction, family practice nurse/nurse practitioner, nursing administration (MSN, MS, PhD), nursing, reading teacher education.

STUDENT INFORMATION

Total Students in Program: 392. **% Full-time:** 1. **% Female:** 67.

EXPENSES/FINANCIAL AID

Annual Tuition: $8,128. **Room & Board:** $5,952. **Books and Supplies:** $400. **Loans Range From:** $500-$15,000. **% Receiving Loans:** 25. **Types of Aid Available:** Loans.

ADMISSIONS INFORMATION

Application Fee: $35. **Regular Application Deadline:** 9/15. **Regular Notification:** Rolling. **Transfer Students Accepted?** Yes. **Transfer Policy:** Transfer hours vary by program.
Required Admission Factors: Letters of recommendation, transcript.
Program-Specific Admission Factors: MAE: Must be a practicing teacher and be certified/licensed. MSN: Must be currently licensed as an RN in Ohio.

EMPLOYMENT INFORMATION

Placement Office Available? Yes.

OUR LADY OF HOLY CROSS COLLEGE
Graduate Studies

Address: 4123 Woodland Drive, New Orleans, LA 70131-7399
Admissions Phone: 504-398-2214 · **Admissions Fax:** 504-391-2421
Admissions E-mail: jmiranti@olhcc.edu · **Website:** www.olhcc.edu

INSTITUTIONAL INFORMATION

Public/private: Private (nonprofit). **Evening Classes Available?** Yes. **Students in Parent Institution:** 1,434.

STUDENT INFORMATION

Total Students in Program: 82. **% Full-time:** 49. **% Female:** 67.

EXPENSES/FINANCIAL AID

Grants Range From: $5,000. **Loans Range From:** $1,000-$1,800. **% Receiving Financial Aid:** 70. **% Receiving Loans:** 100. **% Receiving Assis-**

tantships: 50. **Number of Fellowships Granted Each Year:** 10. **Average amount of individual fellowships per year:** $2,500.

ADMISSIONS INFORMATION

Application Fee: $15. **Regular Application Deadline:** 7/31. **Regular Notification:** Rolling. **Transfer Students Accepted?** Yes. **Number of Applications Received:** 65. **% of Applicants Accepted:** 80. **% Accepted Who Enrolled:** 100. **Average GPA:** 3.0. **Average GRE Verbal:** 400. **Average GRE Quantitative:** 400. **Average GRE Analytical Writing:** 4.
Required Admission Factors: Essays/personal statement, interview, letters of recommendation, transcript.
Other Admission Factors: Minimum 3.0 GPA required.
Program-Specific Admission Factors: Writing sample.

EMPLOYMENT INFORMATION

Placement Office Available? Yes.

OUR LADY OF THE LAKE UNIVERSITY
College of Arts & Sciences

Address: 411 Southwest 24th Street, San Antonio, TX 78207-4689

INSTITUTIONAL INFORMATION

Public/private: Private (nonprofit). **Evening Classes Available?** Yes. **Total Faculty:** 9. **% Faculty Female:** 56. **Students in Parent Institution:** 3,324.

STUDENT INFORMATION

Total Students in Program: 1,128. **% Full-time:** 22. **% Female:** 70.

EXPENSES/FINANCIAL AID

Annual Tuition: $10,536. **Fees:** $258. **Books and Supplies:** $720. **Grants Range From:** $100-$2,000. **Loans Range From:** $500-$18,500. **% Receiving Scholarships/Grants:** 60. **% Receiving Loans:** 82. **% Receiving Assistantships:** 5.

ADMISSIONS INFORMATION

Application Fee: $25. **Regular Notification:** Rolling. **Transfer Students Accepted?** Yes.
Required Admission Factors: Transcript.
Other Admission Factors: Minimum 2.5 GPA (3.0 in major) and 2 letters of recommendation required.

EMPLOYMENT INFORMATION

Placement Office Available? Yes.

OUR LADY OF THE LAKE UNIVERSITY
Worden School of Social Service

Address: 411 Southwest 24th Street, San Antonio, TX 78207-4689
Admissions Phone: 210-434-6711, ext. 372 or 800-436-6558
Admissions Fax: 210-436-2314 · **Admissions E-mail:** millr@lake.ollusa.edu

INSTITUTIONAL INFORMATION

Public/private: Private (nonprofit). **Evening Classes Available?** Yes. **Students in Parent Institution:** 3,324.

STUDENT INFORMATION

Total Students in Program: 1,128. **% Full-time:** 22. **% Female:** 70.

EXPENSES/FINANCIAL AID

Annual Tuition: $10,536. **Fees:** $258. **Books and Supplies:** $720. **Grants Range From:** $100-$2,000. **Loans Range From:** $500-$18,500. **% Receiving Scholarships/Grants:** 60. **% Receiving Loans:** 82. **% Receiving Assistantships:** 5. **Number of Teaching/Research Assistantships Granted Each Year:** 6.

ADMISSIONS INFORMATION

Application Fee: $25. **Regular Notification:** Rolling. **Transfer Students Accepted?** Yes. **Transfer Policy:** Letter of endorsement from advisor required of transfer applicants. **Number of Applications Received:** 148. **% of Applicants Accepted:** 78. **% Accepted Who Enrolled:** 73.
Required Admission Factors: Essays/personal statement, transcript.
Other Admission Factors: Minimum 2.5 GPA and undergraduate concentration in liberal arts or social science recommended.

EMPLOYMENT INFORMATION

Placement Office Available? Yes.

PACE UNIVERSITY
Dyson College of Arts & Sciences

Address: Pace Plaza, New York, NY 10038
Admissions Phone: 212-346-1531 (NYC) or 914-422-4283 (White Plains)
Admissions Fax: 212-346-1585 (NYC) or 914-422-4287 (White Plains)
Admissions E-mail: gradnyc@pace.edu, gradwp@pace.edu · **Website:** www.pace.edu

INSTITUTIONAL INFORMATION

Public/private: Private (nonprofit). **Evening Classes Available?** Yes. **Total Faculty:** 73. **% Faculty Part-time:** 66. **Students in Parent Institution:** 13,962.

PROGRAMS

Masters offered in: Business, management, marketing, and related support services; hospital and health care facilities administration/management; multi/interdisciplinary studies; nonprofit/public/organizational management; political science and government; psychology; school psychology; substance abuse/addiction counseling. **Doctorate offered in:** Psychology.

STUDENT INFORMATION

Total Students in Program: 4,325. **% Full-time:** 19. **% Female:** 55. **% Minority:** 17. **% International:** 13.

EXPENSES/FINANCIAL AID

Annual Tuition: $700. **Room & Board (On/off Campus):** $8,120/$16,340. **Fees:** $412. **Books and Supplies:** $720. **Grants Range From:** $370-$28,922. **Loans Range From:** $646-$77,800. **% Receiving Financial Aid:** 62. **% Receiving Scholarships/Grants:** 39. **% Receiving Loans:** 81. **% Receiving Assistantships:** 10. **% Receiving Other Aid (jobs):** 5. **Types of Aid Available:** Graduate assistantships, grants, institutional work-study, loans, scholarships. **Average student debt, upon graduation:** $25,119. **Number of Teaching/Research Assistantships Granted Each Year:** 15. **Assistantship Compensation Includes:** Full tuition remission, salary/stipend. **Average Salary Stipend:** $5,100.

ADMISSIONS INFORMATION

Application Fee: $65. **Priority Application Deadline:** 8/1. **Regular Notification:** Rolling. **Transfer Students Accepted?** Yes. **Number of Applications Received:** 634. **% of Applicants Accepted:** 54. **% Accepted Who Enrolled:** 45. **Average GPA:** 3.2. **Average GRE Verbal:** 493. **Average GRE Quantitative:** 537.
Required Admission Factors: Essays/personal statement, letters of recommendation, transcript.
Program-Specific Admission Factors: 3 letters of recommendation required of MSEd and PsyD program applicants.

EMPLOYMENT INFORMATION

Placement Office Available? Yes.

PACIFIC GRADUATE SCHOOL OF PSYCHOLOGY
Graduate Programs

Address: 935 East Meadow Drive, Palo Alto, CA 94303-4232
Admissions Phone: 650-843-3419 or 800-818-6136
Admissions Fax: 650-493-6147 · **Admissions E-mail:** admissions@pgsp.edu
Website: www.pgsp.edu

INSTITUTIONAL INFORMATION
Public/private: Private (nonprofit). **Total Faculty:** 45. **% Faculty Female:** 42. **Students in Parent Institution:** 299.

STUDENT INFORMATION
Total Students in Program: 299. **% Full-time:** 94. **% Female:** 72.

RESEARCH FACILITIES
Research Facilities: Research library, computer lab.

EXPENSES/FINANCIAL AID
Annual Tuition: $21,181. **Fees:** $305. **Grants Range From:** $1,000-$5,000. **Average student debt, upon graduation:** $100,000. **Number of Fellowships Granted Each Year:** 10. **Average amount of individual fellowships per year:** $5,000. **Number of Teaching/Research Assistantships Granted Each Year:** 39. **Average Salary Stipend:** $900.

ADMISSIONS INFORMATION
Application Fee: $50. **Priority Application Deadline:** 1/15. **Regular Application Deadline:** 7/15. **Regular Notification:** Rolling. **Transfer Students Accepted?** Yes. **Transfer Policy:** Prospective student must submit completed application and course syllabi for those courses they wish to transfer. **Number of Applications Received:** 113. **% of Applicants Accepted:** 84. **% Accepted Who Enrolled:** 67. **Average GPA:** 3.4. **Average GRE Verbal:** 581. **Average GRE Quantitative:** 634. **Average GRE Analytical:** 606. **Required Admission Factors:** Essays/personal statement, GRE, letters of recommendation, transcript.
Other Admission Factors: References and autobiographical & professional statements required; mean GRE 1050, 3.3 mean undergraduate GPA.
Program-Specific Admission Factors: Joint JD/PhD program requires admission to Golden Gate University. Joint MBA/PhD program requires admission to University of San Francisco.

PACIFIC LUTHERAN THEOLOGICAL SEMINARY
Graduate Programs

Address: 2770 Marin Avenue, Berkeley, CA 94708-5264
Admissions Phone: 510-524-5264 · **Admissions Fax:** 510-524-2408
Admissions E-mail: admissions@plts.edu

INSTITUTIONAL INFORMATION
Public/private: Private (nonprofit). **Student/faculty Ratio:** 9:1. **Students in Parent Institution:** 186.

EXPENSES/FINANCIAL AID
Annual Tuition: In-state $6,800. **Books and Supplies:** $500. **% Receiving Financial Aid:** 100. **Average student debt, upon graduation:** $20,000. **Number of Fellowships Granted Each Year:** 5. **Number of Teaching/Research Assistantships Granted Each Year:** 5. **Average Salary Stipend:** $1,500.

ADMISSIONS INFORMATION
Application Fee: $35. **Regular Notification:** Rolling. **Transfer Students Accepted?** Yes. **Transfer Policy:** Applicant must submit transcript, recommendation, and autobiographical statement. **Number of Applications Received:** 65. **% of Applicants Accepted:** 85. **% Accepted Who Enrolled:** 55. **Average GPA:** 2.9.
Required Admission Factors: Essays/personal statement, letters of recommendation, transcript.

Other Admission Factors: Minimum 3.0 GPA required.
EMPLOYMENT INFORMATION
% Employed Within 6 Months: 75.

PACIFIC LUTHERAN UNIVERSITY
Marriage and Family Therapy

Address: 1010 122nd Street, Tacoma, WA 98447
Admissions Phone: 253-535-7151 · **Admissions Fax:** 253-536-5136
Admissions E-mail: admissions@plu.edu · **Website:** www.plu.edu

INSTITUTIONAL INFORMATION
Public/private: Private (nonprofit). **Evening Classes Available?** Yes. **Total Faculty:** 6. **% Faculty Female:** 50. **Students in Parent Institution:** 3,462.

PROGRAMS
Masters offered in: Marriage and family therapy/counseling.

STUDENT INFORMATION
Total Students in Program: 45. **% Full-time:** 84. **% Female:** 76. **% Minority:** 22. **% International:** 7.

EXPENSES/FINANCIAL AID
Annual Tuition: $14,688. **Room & Board:** $6,105. **Books and Supplies:** $700. **Grants Range From:** $500-$4,087. **Loans Range From:** $3,000-$28,200. **% Receiving Financial Aid:** 70. **% Receiving Scholarships/Grants:** 7. **% Receiving Loans:** 80. **% Receiving Assistantships:** 22.

ADMISSIONS INFORMATION
Application Fee: $35. **Regular Application Deadline:** 1/31. **Transfer Students Accepted?** No. **Number of Applications Received:** 26. **% of Applicants Accepted:** 85. **% Accepted Who Enrolled:** 100. **Average GPA:** 3.2. **Required Admission Factors:** Essays/personal statement, interview, letters of recommendation, transcript.
Other Admission Factors: Minimum 3.0 GPA and 5-page autobiographical statement required.

PACIFIC OAKS COLLEGE
Graduate School

Address: 5 Westmoreland Place, Pasadena, CA 91103
Admissions Phone: 626-397-1349 or 800-684-0900
Admissions Fax: 626-577-3502 · **Admissions E-mail:** admissions@pacificoaks.edu
Website: www.pacificoaks.edu

INSTITUTIONAL INFORMATION
Public/private: Private (nonprofit). **Evening Classes Available?** Yes. **Total Faculty:** 29. **% Faculty Female:** 79. **% Faculty Part-time:** 159. **Student/faculty Ratio:** 11:1. **Students in Parent Institution:** 909.

PROGRAMS
Masters offered in: Human development and family studies, marriage and family therapy/counseling.

STUDENT INFORMATION
Total Students in Program: 699. **% Full-time:** 22. **% Female:** 93.

RESEARCH FACILITIES
Research Facilities: Center for Democracy and Social Change.

EXPENSES/FINANCIAL AID
Annual Tuition: $8,800. **Fees:** $60. **Books and Supplies:** $500. **Grants Range From:** $500-$2,000. **Loans Range From:** $5,000-$18,500. **% Receiving Financial Aid:** 90. **% Receiving Scholarships/Grants:** 15. **% Receiving Loans:** 80. **Average student debt, upon graduation:** $25,000.

ADMISSIONS INFORMATION

Application Fee: $55. Priority Application Deadline: 4/15. Regular Application Deadline: 6/1. Regular Notification: Rolling. Transfer Students Accepted? No. Number of Applications Received: 150. % of Applicants Accepted: 84. % Accepted Who Enrolled: 75.
Required Admission Factors: Essays/personal statement, letters of recommendation, transcript.
Other Admission Factors: Work experience in human services recommended.
Program-Specific Admission Factors: Questionnaires required of the life experience admission option, teacher education, and marriage/family/child counseling programs.

PACIFIC SCHOOL OF RELIGION
Graduate Programs

Address: 1798 Scenic Avenue, Berkeley, CA 94709
Admissions Phone: 510-849-8253 · Admissions Fax: 510-845-8948
Admissions E-mail: admissions@psr.edu · Website: www.psr.edu

INSTITUTIONAL INFORMATION
Public/private: Private (nonprofit). Students in Parent Institution: 221

PROGRAMS
Masters offered in: Bible/biblical studies, divinity/ministry (BD, MDiv), theology/theological studies.

RESEARCH FACILITIES
Research Facilities: Member school of the Graduate Theological Union.

EXPENSES/FINANCIAL AID
Annual Tuition: In-state $9,000. Room & Board: $4,156. Fees: $50. % Receiving Financial Aid: 55. Average student debt, upon graduation: $14,000.

ADMISSIONS INFORMATION
Application Fee: $50. Priority Application Deadline: 2/1. Regular Application Deadline: 8/1. Regular Notification: Rolling. Transfer Students Accepted? Yes. Number of Applications Received: 147. % of Applicants Accepted: 90. % Accepted Who Enrolled: 55.
Required Admission Factors: Essays/personal statement, letters of recommendation, transcript.
Other Admission Factors: Minimum 3.5 GPA required for GTU common MA. Minimum 3.0 GPA required for all other programs.

PACIFIC UNIVERSITY
School of Occupational Therapy

Address: 2043 College Way, Forest Grove, OR 97116
Admissions Phone: 503-352-2900 or 800-933-9308
Admissions Fax: 503-352-2975 · Admissions E-mail: larsenj@pacificu.edu
Website: www.pacificu.edu

INSTITUTIONAL INFORMATION
Public/private: Private (nonprofit). Student/faculty Ratio: 3:1. Students in Parent Institution: 2,064.

PROGRAMS
Masters offered in: Occupational therapy/therapist.

STUDENT INFORMATION
Total Students in Program: 651. % Full-time: 78. % Female: 71.

EXPENSES/FINANCIAL AID
Annual Tuition: $18,500. Fees: $500. Books and Supplies: $1,000. Grants Range From: $100-$40,114. Loans Range From: $542-$40,380. % Receiv-

ing Financial Aid: 94. % Receiving Scholarships/Grants: 31. % Receiving Loans: 96. % Receiving Assistantships: 2. Types of Aid Available: Graduate assistantships, institutional work-study, loans, scholarships. Average student debt, upon graduation: $50,000.

ADMISSIONS INFORMATION
Application Fee: $55. Priority Application Deadline: 12/5. Regular Application Deadline: 1/15. Regular Notification: Rolling. Transfer Students Accepted? No. Number of Applications Received: 55. % of Applicants Accepted: 45. % Accepted Who Enrolled: 80. Average GPA: 3.3.
Required Admission Factors: Essays/personal statement, interview, letters of recommendation, transcript.

EMPLOYMENT INFORMATION
% Employed Within 6 Months: 100. % of master's grads employed in their field upon graduation: 20. Rate of placement: 100%. Average starting salary: $42,000.

PACIFIC UNIVERSITY
School of Physical Therapy

Address: 2043 College Way, Forest Grove, OR 97116
Admissions Phone: 503-359-2900 or 800-933-9308
Admissions Fax: 503-359-2975 · Admissions E-mail: larsenj@pacificu.edu
Website: www.pacificu.edu

INSTITUTIONAL INFORMATION
Public/private: Private (nonprofit). Student/faculty Ratio: 4:1. Students in Parent Institution: 2,064.

PROGRAMS
Doctorate offered in: Physical therapy/therapist.

STUDENT INFORMATION
Total Students in Program: 651. % Full-time: 78. % Female: 71.

EXPENSES/FINANCIAL AID
Annual Tuition: $19,000. Room & Board: $2,700. Fees: $500. Books and Supplies: $1,000. Grants Range From: $100-$40,114. Loans Range From: $542-$40,380. % Receiving Financial Aid: 86. % Receiving Scholarships/Grants: 31. % Receiving Loans: 96. % Receiving Assistantships: 2. Average student debt, upon graduation: $42,424.

ADMISSIONS INFORMATION
Application Fee: $55. Regular Application Deadline: 12/5. Regular Notification: 3/3. Transfer Students Accepted? No. Number of Applications Received: 230. % of Applicants Accepted: 20. % Accepted Who Enrolled: 78. Average GPA: 3.5.
Required Admission Factors: Essays/personal statement, interview, letters of recommendation, transcript.
Other Admission Factors: Minimum 3.0 GPA required.

EMPLOYMENT INFORMATION
% Employed Within 6 Months: 100. Rate of placement: 100%. Average starting salary: $45,000.

PACIFIC UNIVERSITY
School of Professional Psychology

Address: 2043 College Way, Forest Grove, OR 97116
Admissions Phone: 503-359-2900 or 800-933-9308
Admissions Fax: 503-359-2975 · Admissions E-mail: landstra@pacifcu.edu

INSTITUTIONAL INFORMATION
Public/private: Private (nonprofit). Student/faculty Ratio: 5:1. Students in Parent Institution: 2,064.

STUDENT INFORMATION

Total Students in Program: 651. % Full-time: 78. % Female: 71.

EXPENSES/FINANCIAL AID

Grants Range From: $100-$40,114. Loans Range From: $542-$40,380. % Receiving Financial Aid: 65. % Receiving Scholarships/Grants: 31. % Receiving Loans: 96. % Receiving Assistantships: 2. Average student debt, upon graduation: $38,829. Number of Teaching/Research Assistantships Granted Each Year: 24. Average Salary Stipend: $3,000.

ADMISSIONS INFORMATION

Application Fee: $40. Transfer Students Accepted? No. Number of Applications Received: 169. % of Applicants Accepted: 57. % Accepted Who Enrolled: 55. Average GPA: 3.2. Average GRE Verbal: 537. Average GRE Quantitative: 553. Average GRE Analytical: 622.

Required Admission Factors: Essays/personal statement, GRE, interview, letters of recommendation, transcript.

Other Admission Factors: Minimum GRE score of 1100 (Verbal and Quantitative or Analytical), minimum GRE subject exam score of 600, and minimum 3.0 GPA in the last 2 years of undergraduate study required.

PACIFICA GRADUATE INSTITUTE
Graduate School

Address: 249 Lambert Road, Carpinteria, CA 93013
Admissions Phone: 805-969-3626, ext. 128 or 189 · Admissions Fax: 805-565-1932
Admissions E-mail: admissions@pacifica.edu · Website: www.pacifica.edu

INSTITUTIONAL INFORMATION

Public/private: Private (proprietary).

PROGRAMS

Masters offered in: Counseling psychology. Doctorate offered in: Clinical psychology.

EXPENSES/FINANCIAL AID

Annual Tuition: $19,170.

ADMISSIONS INFORMATION

Application Fee: $60. Transfer Students Accepted? No.

Required Admission Factors: Essays/personal statement, interview, letters of recommendation, transcript.

PARDEE RAND GRADUATE SCHOOL OF POLICY STUDIES
Graduate Programs

Address: 1700 Main Street, PO Box 2138, Santa Monica, CA 90407-2138
Admissions Phone: 310-393-0411, ext. 7690 · Admissions Fax: 310-451-6978
Admissions E-mail: alex_duke@rgs.edu · Website: www.rgs.edu

INSTITUTIONAL INFORMATION

Public/private: Private (nonprofit). Student/faculty Ratio: 1:1. Students in Parent Institution: 70.

STUDENT INFORMATION

Total Students in Program: 70. % Full-time: 100. % Female: 31.

EXPENSES/FINANCIAL AID

Annual Tuition: In-state $18,000. Books and Supplies: $600. % Receiving Financial Aid: 100.

ADMISSIONS INFORMATION

Application Fee: $50. Regular Application Deadline: 2/1. Transfer Students Accepted? No. Number of Applications Received: 92. % of Applicants Accepted: 38. % Accepted Who Enrolled: 57. Average GRE Verbal: 650. Average GRE Quantitative: 750.

Required Admission Factors: Essays/personal statement, GRE, letters of recommendation, transcript.

EMPLOYMENT INFORMATION

Placement Office Available? Yes. Rate of placement: 100%.

PARK UNIVERSITY (FORMERLY PARK COLLEGE)
Graduate and Professional Studies

Address: 8700 River Park Drive, Parkville, MO 64152
Admissions Phone: 816-584-6384 · Admissions Fax: 816-505-5454
Admissions E-mail: rachelle.freese@park.edu · Website: www.park.edu

INSTITUTIONAL INFORMATION

Public/private: Private (nonprofit). Evening Classes Available? Yes. Student/faculty Ratio: 10:1. Students in Parent Institution: 1,349.

PROGRAMS

Masters offered in: Business administration/management, education, elementary and middle school administration/principalship, public administration and services, secondary school administration/principalship, special education.

STUDENT INFORMATION

Total Students in Program: 531.

EXPENSES/FINANCIAL AID

Annual Tuition: $4,500. Books and Supplies: $500. Grants Range From: $500. % Receiving Financial Aid: 33. Types of Aid Available: Graduate assistantships, loans, scholarships. Average student debt, upon graduation: $6,000.

ADMISSIONS INFORMATION

Application Fee: $50. Regular Notification: Rolling. Transfer Students Accepted? Yes. Transfer Policy: Maximum 9 graduate level credit hours from an accredited college or university may be transferred. Number of Applications Received: 103. % of Applicants Accepted: 89. % Accepted Who Enrolled: 35. Average GPA: 3.0. Average GRE Verbal: 500. Average GRE Quantitative: 450. Average GRE Analytical: 400.

Required Admission Factors: Transcript.

Other Admission Factors: Minimum 2.75 GPA in last 60 hours of undergraduate work required.

EMPLOYMENT INFORMATION

Placement Office Available? Yes. % of master's grads employed in their field upon graduation: 95.

PARSONS SCHOOL OF DESIGN
Graduate Programs

Address: 66 Fifth Avenue, New York, NY 10011
Admissions Phone: 212-229-8910 · Admissions Fax: 212-229-8975
Admissions E-mail: inquiry@newschool.edu

INSTITUTIONAL INFORMATION

Public/private: Private (nonprofit). Students in Parent Institution: 2,815.

STUDENT INFORMATION

Total Students in Program: 382. % Full-time: 75. % Female: 69.

RESEARCH FACILITIES

Research Facilities: Gimbel Library, Bobst Library, and Cooper Union Library.

EXPENSES/FINANCIAL AID

Annual Tuition: In-state $22,090. Fees: $200. Books and Supplies: $1,850. Grants Range From: $2,000-$22,000. Loans Range From: $18,500-

$20,500. **% Receiving Financial Aid:** 48. **% Receiving Scholarships/Grants:** 79. **Average student debt, upon graduation:** $36,844.

ADMISSIONS INFORMATION
Application Fee: $40. **Regular Notification:** Rolling. **Transfer Students Accepted?** Yes. **Number of Applications Received:** 654. **% of Applicants Accepted:** 67. **% Accepted Who Enrolled:** 42.
Required Admission Factors: GRE, letters of recommendation, transcript.
Program-Specific Admission Factors: GRE required of architecture program aplicants and recommended of history of decorative arts program applicants.

EMPLOYMENT INFORMATION
Placement Office Available? Yes.

PENNSYLVANIA STATE UNIVERSITY —UNIVERSITY PARK
College of Earth & Mineral Sciences

Address: 114 Kern Graduate Building, University Park, PA 16802
Admissions Phone: 814-865-1795 · **Admissions Fax:** 814-863-4627
Admissions E-mail: gradm@psu.edu

INSTITUTIONAL INFORMATION
Public/private: Public. **Students in Parent Institution:** 41,289.

STUDENT INFORMATION
Total Students in Program: 6,465. **% Full-time:** 81. **% Female:** 47. **% Minority:** 6. **% International:** 36.

EXPENSES/FINANCIAL AID
Annual Tuition: In-state $6,886. / Out-of-state $14,118.

ADMISSIONS INFORMATION
Application Fee: $45. **Regular Notification:** Rolling. **Transfer Students Accepted?** Yes. **Number of Applications Received:** 810. **% of Applicants Accepted:** 23. **% Accepted Who Enrolled:** 49. **Average GPA:** 3.5. **Average GRE Verbal:** 534. **Average GRE Quantitative:** 722. **Average GRE Analytical:** 679. **Average GRE Analytical Writing:** 4.4.
Required Admission Factors: Essays/personal statement, GRE, letters of recommendation, transcript, TOEFL (international).
Other Admission Factors: GPA 3.0; TOEFL 550 paper, 213 computer.

PENNSYLVANIA STATE UNIVERSITY AT HARRISBURG
School of Humanities

Address: 777 West Harrisburg Pike, Middletown, PA 17057
Admissions Phone: 717-948-6250 · **Admissions Fax:** 717-948-6325
Admissions E-mail: hbgadmit@psu.edu · **Website:** www.hbg.psu.edu

INSTITUTIONAL INFORMATION
Public/private: Public. **Evening Classes Available?** Yes. **Students in Parent Institution:** 3,564.

PROGRAMS
Masters offered in: American history (United States), humanities/humanistic studies.

STUDENT INFORMATION
Total Students in Program: 1,366. **% Female:** 44.

EXPENSES/FINANCIAL AID
Annual Tuition: In-state $6,000. / Out-of-state $12,000. **Room & Board (On/off Campus):** $5,960/$5,976. **Fees:** $500. **Books and Supplies:** $928.

Grants Range From: $1,000-$2,500. **Loans Range From:** $9,250-$18,500. **% Receiving Financial Aid:** 32. **% Receiving Scholarships/Grants:** 2. **% Receiving Loans:** 30. **Types of Aid Available:** Graduate assistantships, institutional work-study, loans. **Average student debt, upon graduation:** $38,000. **Assistantship Compensation Includes:** Full tuition remission.

ADMISSIONS INFORMATION
Application Fee: $45. **Priority Application Deadline:** 2/15. **Regular Application Deadline:** 2/15. **Regular Notification:** Rolling. **Transfer Students Accepted?** Yes.
Required Admission Factors: Essays/personal statement, interview, letters of recommendation, transcript.
Other Admission Factors: 3.0 minimum GPA.

PENNSYLVANIA STATE UNIVERSITY— GREAT VALLEY GRADUATE CENTER
School of Graduate Professional Studies

Address: 30 East Swedesford Road, Malvern, PA 19355
Admissions Phone: 610-648-3200 · **Admissions Fax:** 610-725-5296
Admissions E-mail: gradmiss@psu.edu

INSTITUTIONAL INFORMATION
Public/private: Public. **Evening Classes Available?** Yes. **Student/faculty Ratio:** 18:1. **Students in Parent Institution:** 1,687.

STUDENT INFORMATION
Total Students in Program: 1,687. **% Full-time:** 8. **% Female:** 42.

EXPENSES/FINANCIAL AID
Annual Tuition: In-state $7,752. / Out-of-state $13,476. **Grants Range From:** $500-$1,500. **Loans Range From:** $1,000-$18,500. **% Receiving Financial Aid:** 70. **% Receiving Scholarships/Grants:** 5. **% Receiving Loans:** 98. **% Receiving Assistantships:** 2. **Average student debt, upon graduation:** $8,000. **Number of Fellowships Granted Each Year:** 1. **Average amount of individual fellowships per year:** $25,000. **Number of Teaching/Research Assistantships Granted Each Year:** 4. **Average Salary Stipend:** $11,000.

ADMISSIONS INFORMATION
Application Fee: $60. **Regular Notification:** Rolling. **Transfer Students Accepted?** Yes. **Number of Applications Received:** 646. **% of Applicants Accepted:** 81. **% Accepted Who Enrolled:** 86. **Average GPA:** 3.2. **Average GRE Verbal:** 476. **Average GRE Quantitative:** 540. **Average GRE Analytical:** 547.
Required Admission Factors: GRE, letters of recommendation, transcript.

PEPPERDINE UNIVERSITY
School of Public Policy

Address: 24255 Pacific Coast Highway, Malibu, CA 90263-4375
Admissions Phone: 310-506-7493 · **Admissions Fax:** 310-506-7494

INSTITUTIONAL INFORMATION
Public/private: Private (nonprofit). **Student/faculty Ratio:** 9:1. **Students in Parent Institution:** 7,708.

RESEARCH FACILITIES
Research Facilities: Psychology clinic.

EXPENSES/FINANCIAL AID
Annual Tuition: $15,800. **Fees:** $70. **Books and Supplies:** $500. **Number of Teaching/Research Assistantships Granted Each Year:** 10. **Average Salary Stipend:** $1,500.

ADMISSIONS INFORMATION

Application Fee: $50. **Regular Notification:** Rolling. **Transfer Students Accepted?** Yes. **Number of Applications Received:** 78. **% of Applicants Accepted:** 85. **% Accepted Who Enrolled:** 47. **Average GPA:** 3.1. **Required Admission Factors:** Essays/personal statement, GRE, letters of recommendation, transcript.
Other Admission Factors: Current resume or curriculum vitae required.

EMPLOYMENT INFORMATION

Placement Office Available? Yes.

PEPPERDINE UNIVERSITY
Seaver College

Address: 24255 Pacific Coast Highway, Malibu, CA 90263-4375
Admissions Phone: 310-506-4392 · **Admissions Fax:** 310-506-4861

INSTITUTIONAL INFORMATION

Public/private: Private (nonprofit). **Evening Classes Available?** Yes. **Student/faculty Ratio:** 12:1. **Students in Parent Institution:** 7,708.

RESEARCH FACILITIES

Research Facilities: Psychology clinic.

EXPENSES/FINANCIAL AID

Annual Tuition: In-state $15,800. **Fees:** $70. **Books and Supplies:** $500.

ADMISSIONS INFORMATION

Application Fee: $55. **Regular Notification:** Rolling. **Transfer Students Accepted?** Yes. **Number of Applications Received:** 97. **% of Applicants Accepted:** 66. **Average GPA:** 3.2. **Average GRE Verbal:** 477. **Average GRE Quantitative:** 490. **Average GRE Analytical:** 581.
Required Admission Factors: Essays/personal statement, GRE, letters of recommendation, transcript.

EMPLOYMENT INFORMATION

Placement Office Available? Yes.

PHILADELPHIA BIBLICAL UNIVERSITY
Graduate School

Address: 200 Manor Avenue, Langhorne, PA 19047-2990
Admissions Phone: 215-702-4365 · **Admissions Fax:** 215-702-4248
Admissions E-mail: graduate@pbu.edu · **Website:** www.pbu.edu

INSTITUTIONAL INFORMATION

Public/private: Private (nonprofit). **Evening Classes Available?** Yes. **Total Faculty:** 31. **% Faculty Female:** 32. **% Faculty Part-time:** 61. **Student/faculty Ratio:** 10:1. **Students in Parent Institution:** 1,397.

STUDENT INFORMATION

Total Students in Program: 350. **% Full-time:** 10. **% Female:** 57. **% Minority:** 31. **% International:** 3.

EXPENSES/FINANCIAL AID

Annual Tuition: $7,470. **Room & Board:** $7,650. **Fees:** $10. **Books and Supplies:** $800. **Grants Range From:** $60-$2,000. **Loans Range From:** $1,200-$13,500. **% Receiving Financial Aid:** 26. **% Receiving Scholarships/Grants:** 81. **% Receiving Loans:** 71. **Average student debt, upon graduation:** $12,100.

ADMISSIONS INFORMATION

Application Fee: $25. **Regular Notification:** Rolling. **Transfer Students Accepted?** Yes. **Number of Applications Received:** 217. **% of Applicants Accepted:** 69. **% Accepted Who Enrolled:** 83.
Required Admission Factors: Essays/personal statement, letters of recom-

mendation, transcript.
Other Admission Factors: Minimum 2.5 GPA required; writing exam required if GPA is less than 2.5.

EMPLOYMENT INFORMATION

% of master's grads employed in their field upon graduation: 65.

PHILADELPHIA UNIVERSITY
Graduate Programs

Address: School House Lane and Henry Avenue, Philadelphia, PA 19144
Admissions Phone: 215-951-2943 · **Admissions Fax:** 215-951-2907

INSTITUTIONAL INFORMATION

Public/private: Private (nonprofit). **Students in Parent Institution:** 3,316.

STUDENT INFORMATION

Total Students in Program: 507. **% Full-time:** 26. **% Female:** 70.

EXPENSES/FINANCIAL AID

Annual Tuition: In-state $8,946. **Books and Supplies:** $750.

ADMISSIONS INFORMATION

Transfer Students Accepted? No. **Number of Applications Received:** 79. **% of Applicants Accepted:** 73. **% Accepted Who Enrolled:** 64.

EMPLOYMENT INFORMATION

Placement Office Available? Yes.

PHILLIPS GRADUATE INSTITUTE
Graduate Programs

Address: 5445 Balboa Boulevard, Encino, CA 91316-1509
Admissions Phone: 818-386-5634 · **Admissions Fax:** 818-386-5699
Admissions E-mail: admit@pgi.edu

INSTITUTIONAL INFORMATION

Public/private: Private (nonprofit). **Evening Classes Available?** Yes. **Student/faculty Ratio:** 6:1. **Students in Parent Institution:** 200.

STUDENT INFORMATION

Total Students in Program: 200. **% Full-time:** 100. **% Female:** 89.

RESEARCH FACILITIES

Research Facilities: Adjoining counseling center.

EXPENSES/FINANCIAL AID

Fees: $2,600. **Books and Supplies:** $1,200. **Grants Range From:** $500-$7,000. **Loans Range From:** $8,500-$18,500. **% Receiving Financial Aid:** 76. **% Receiving Scholarships/Grants:** 1. **% Receiving Loans:** 76. **Average student debt, upon graduation:** $21,000.

ADMISSIONS INFORMATION

Application Fee: $50. **Regular Notification:** Rolling. **Transfer Students Accepted?** Yes. **Number of Applications Received:** 80. **% of Applicants Accepted:** 89. **% Accepted Who Enrolled:** 85. **Average GPA:** 3.0.
Required Admission Factors: Essays/personal statement, letters of recommendation, transcript.
Other Admission Factors: Minimum 3.0 GPA required for regular admission.

EMPLOYMENT INFORMATION

Placement Office Available? Yes. **Rate of placement:** 100%.

PIEDMONT COLLEGE
School of Business

Address: 165 Central Avenue, Demorest, GA 30535-0010
Admissions Phone: 800-277-7020 or 706-778-8500, ext. 1181
Admissions Fax: 706-776-6635 · **Admissions E-mail:** ckokesh@piedmont.edu
Website: www.piedmont.edu

INSTITUTIONAL INFORMATION
Public/private: Private (nonprofit). **Evening Classes Available?** Yes. **Student/faculty Ratio:** 12:1. **Students in Parent Institution:** 1,728.

STUDENT INFORMATION
Total Students in Program: 702. **% Full-time:** 27. **% Female:** 84.

EXPENSES/FINANCIAL AID
Annual Tuition: $11,160. **Books and Supplies:** $850. **Grants Range From:** $1,000-$7,500. **Loans Range From:** $1,260-$14,200. **% Receiving Financial Aid:** 90. **% Receiving Scholarships/Grants:** 10. **% Receiving Loans:** 86. **% Receiving Assistantships:** 4. **Types of Aid Available:** Graduate assistantships, loans.

ADMISSIONS INFORMATION
Application Fee: $30. **Regular Application Deadline:** 7/15. **Regular Notification:** Rolling. **Transfer Students Accepted?** Yes. **Transfer Policy:** Transfer courses must be evaluated by director of MBA and the registrar and may not substitute for specialty courses.
Required Admission Factors: GRE, letters of recommendation, transcript.
Other Admission Factors: Minimum 2.8 GPA, minimum GRE score of 800 required, job description, and resume.
Program-Specific Admission Factors: Non-business majors may have to take prerequisite courses specifically designed to prepare for the MBA.

EMPLOYMENT INFORMATION
Placement Office Available? Yes.

PITTSBURGH THEOLOGICAL SEMINARY
Graduate Programs

Address: 616 North Highland Avenue, Pittsburgh, PA 15206
Admissions Phone: 800-451-4194

INSTITUTIONAL INFORMATION
Public/private: Private (nonprofit). **Evening Classes Available?** Yes. **Total Faculty:** 24. **% Faculty Female:** 21. **Students in Parent Institution:** 324.

STUDENT INFORMATION
Total Students in Program: 158. **% Full-time:** 88. **% Female:** 24.

EXPENSES/FINANCIAL AID
Annual Tuition: $7,992. **Fees:** $48. **Books and Supplies:** $750.

ADMISSIONS INFORMATION
Application Fee: $25. **Regular Notification:** Rolling. **Transfer Students Accepted?** Yes. **Number of Applications Received:** 70. **% of Applicants Accepted:** 97. **% Accepted Who Enrolled:** 87. **Average GPA:** 2.95.
Required Admission Factors: Essays/personal statement, interview, letters of recommendation, transcript.
Other Admission Factors: Minimum 2.7 GPA required.
Program-Specific Admission Factors: Church endorsement required of MDiv program applicants. MDiv and 3 years of active ministry required of doctorate in ministry program applicants.

EMPLOYMENT INFORMATION
Placement Office Available? Yes. **Rate of placement:** 98%.

POINT LOMA NAZARENE UNIVERSITY
Graduate Programs

Address: 3900 Lomaland Drive, San Diego, CA 92106-2899

INSTITUTIONAL INFORMATION
Public/private: Private (nonprofit). **Student/faculty Ratio:** 10:1. **Students in Parent Institution:** 2,733.

STUDENT INFORMATION
Total Students in Program: 429. **% Full-time:** 65. **% Female:** 67.

EXPENSES/FINANCIAL AID
Annual Tuition: In-state $14,800. **Fees:** $500. **Books and Supplies:** $900.

ADMISSIONS INFORMATION
Application Fee: $25. **Transfer Students Accepted?** Yes.
Required Admission Factors: Essays/personal statement, letters of recommendation, transcript.
Program-Specific Admission Factors: Minimum GRE score of 400 Verbal and 400 Quantitative (minimum MAT score of 35) and minimum 3.0 GPA required of MA program applicants. At least 1 year of full-time Christian ministry and interview required of master in ministry program applicants.

EMPLOYMENT INFORMATION
Placement Office Available? Yes.

POINT PARK UNIVERSITY
Conservatory of Performing Arts

Address: 201 Wood Street, Pittsburgh, PA 15222
Admissions Phone: 412-392-3808 · **Admissions Fax:** 412-392-6164
Admissions E-mail: saps@pointpark.edu · **Website:** www.pointpark.edu

INSTITUTIONAL INFORMATION
Public/private: Private (nonprofit).

STUDENT INFORMATION
Total Students in Program: 5. **% Full-time:** 100. **% Female:** 60.

EXPENSES/FINANCIAL AID
Annual Tuition: $8,748. **Room & Board:** $7,000. **Fees:** $270. **Books and Supplies:** $1,000. **Grants Range From:** $900-$1,800. **Loans Range From:** $18,333-$27,750. **% Receiving Financial Aid:** 100. **% Receiving Loans:** 60. **% Receiving Assistantships:** 5. **Types of Aid Available:** Graduate assistantships, grants, loans. **Average student debt, upon graduation:** $16,499. **Number of Teaching/Research Assistantships Granted Each Year:** 5. **Average Salary Stipend:** $560.

ADMISSIONS INFORMATION
Application Fee: $30. **Regular Notification:** Rolling. **Transfer Students Accepted?** Yes. **Number of Applications Received:** 6.
Required Admission Factors: Interview, letters of recommendation, transcript.
Recommended Admission Factors: Essays/personal statement.
Program-Specific Admission Factors: Audition, experience, selection from COPA experience.

POINT PARK UNIVERSITY
Curriculum & Instruction Department

Address: 201 Wood Street, Pittsburgh, PA 15222
Admissions Phone: 412-392-3808 · **Admissions Fax:** 412-392-6164
Admissions E-mail: kballas@ppc.edu

INSTITUTIONAL INFORMATION

Public/private: Private (nonprofit). **Students in Parent Institution:** 2,842.

STUDENT INFORMATION

Total Students in Program: 305. **% Full-time:** 60. **% Female:** 51.

EXPENSES/FINANCIAL AID

Annual Tuition: In-state $10,080. **Grants Range From:** $300-$7,700. **Loans Range From:** $100-$17,908. **% Receiving Scholarships/Grants:** 85. **% Receiving Loans:** 94. **Types of Aid Available:** 1. **Number of Teaching/Research Assistantships Granted Each Year:** 1. **Average Salary Stipend:** $4,500.

ADMISSIONS INFORMATION

Application Fee: $30. **Regular Notification:** Rolling. **Transfer Students Accepted?** Yes. **Number of Applications Received:** 47. **% of Applicants Accepted:** 89. **% Accepted Who Enrolled:** 79. **Average GPA:** 3.25. **Required Admission Factors:** Letters of recommendation, transcript. **Other Admission Factors:** Minimum 2.75 GPA, ACT 34 criminal check, and ACT 51 child abuse clearance required.

EMPLOYMENT INFORMATION

Placement Office Available? Yes. **Rate of placement:** 90%.

POINT PARK UNIVERSITY
Department of Journalism & Mass Communication

Address: 201 Wood Street, Pittsburgh, PA 15222
Admissions Phone: 412-392-3808 · **Admissions Fax:** 412-392-6164
Admissions E-mail: saps@ppc.edu · **Website:** www.ppc.edu

INSTITUTIONAL INFORMATION

Public/private: Private (nonprofit). **Evening Classes Available?** Yes. **Total Faculty:** 9. **% Faculty Part-time:** 44. **Student/faculty Ratio:** 5:1. **Students in Parent Institution:** 2,842.

PROGRAMS

Masters offered in: Communications, journalism, and related fields.

STUDENT INFORMATION

Total Students in Program: 305. **% Full-time:** 60. **% Female:** 51.

EXPENSES/FINANCIAL AID

Annual Tuition: $10,080. **Grants Range From:** $300-$7,700. **Loans Range From:** $100-$17,908. **% Receiving Financial Aid:** 17. **% Receiving Scholarships/Grants:** 85. **% Receiving Loans:** 94. **Types of Aid Available:** 1. **Number of Fellowships Granted Each Year:** 2. **Average amount of individual fellowships per year:** 4,500. **Average Salary Stipend:** $4,500.

ADMISSIONS INFORMATION

Application Fee: $30. **Regular Application Deadline:** 9/10. **Regular Notification:** Rolling. **Transfer Students Accepted?** Yes. **Number of Applications Received:** 40. **% of Applicants Accepted:** 68. **% Accepted Who Enrolled:** 93. **Average GPA:** 3.09. **Required Admission Factors:** Essays/personal statement, letters of recommendation, transcript. **Other Admission Factors:** 2.75 overall GPA required, 3.0 GPA in major. **Program-Specific Admission Factors:** 500-word essay required; GRE scores may be required for some applicants.

EMPLOYMENT INFORMATION

Placement Office Available? Yes. **Rate of placement:** 90%.

POINT PARK UNIVERSITY
School of Arts and Sciences

Address: 201 Wood Street, Pittsburgh, PA 15222
Admissions Phone: 412-392-3808 · **Admissions Fax:** 412-392-6164
Admissions E-mail: saps@pointpark.edu · **Website:** www.pointpark.edu

INSTITUTIONAL INFORMATION

Public/private: Private (nonprofit). **Evening Classes Available?** Yes. **Total Faculty:** 23. **% Faculty Female:** 61. **% Faculty Part-time:** 70. **Students in Parent Institution:** 3,292.

STUDENT INFORMATION

Total Students in Program: 125. **% Full-time:** 38. **% Female:** 60. **% Minority:** 16. **% International:** 5.

EXPENSES/FINANCIAL AID

Annual Tuition: $8,748. **Room & Board:** $7,000. **Fees:** $270. **Books and Supplies:** $1,000. **Grants Range From:** $900-$1,800. **Loans Range From:** $18,333-$27,750. **% Receiving Financial Aid:** 63. **% Receiving Scholarships/Grants:** 43. **% Receiving Loans:** 55. **Types of Aid Available:** Graduate assistantships, grants, loans. **Average student debt, upon graduation:** $31,173. **Number of Fellowships Granted Each Year:** 1. **Average amount of individual fellowships per year:** $1,000. **Number of Teaching/Research Assistantships Granted Each Year:** 2. **Average Salary Stipend:** $560.

ADMISSIONS INFORMATION

Application Fee: $30. **Regular Notification:** Rolling. **Transfer Students Accepted?** Yes. **Number of Applications Received:** 140. **% of Applicants Accepted:** 59. **% Accepted Who Enrolled:** 61. **Required Admission Factors:** Essays/personal statement, letters of recommendation, transcript. **Other Admission Factors:** 2.75 GPA.

POINT PARK UNIVERSITY
School of Adult and Professional Studies

Address: 201 Wood Street, Pittsburgh, PA 15222
Admissions Phone: 412-392-3808 · **Admissions Fax:** 412-392-6164
Admissions E-mail: saps@pointpark.edu · **Website:** www.pointpark.edu

INSTITUTIONAL INFORMATION

Public/private: Private (nonprofit). **Total Faculty:** 15. **% Faculty Female:** 20. **% Faculty Part-time:** 80. **Students in Parent Institution:** 3,292.

PROGRAMS

Masters offered in: Criminal justice/safety studies.

STUDENT INFORMATION

Total Students in Program: 38. **% Full-time:** 87. **% Female:** 71. **% Minority:** 68.

EXPENSES/FINANCIAL AID

Annual Tuition: $8,748. **Room & Board:** $7,000. **Fees:** $270. **Books and Supplies:** $1,000. **Grants Range From:** $900-$1,800. **Loans Range From:** $18,333-$27,750. **% Receiving Financial Aid:** 96. **% Receiving Scholarships/Grants:** 75. **% Receiving Loans:** 95. **Types of Aid Available:** Grants, loans. **Average student debt, upon graduation:** $36,007.

ADMISSIONS INFORMATION

Application Fee: $30. **Priority Application Deadline:** 8/20. **Regular Notification:** Rolling. **Transfer Students Accepted?** Yes. **Number of Applications Received:** 34. **% of Applicants Accepted:** 76. **% Accepted Who Enrolled:** 85. **Required Admission Factors:** Essays/personal statement, letters of recommendation, transcript.

Other Admission Factors: 2.75 GPA, resume required.

EMPLOYMENT INFORMATION
Placement Office Available? Yes.

POLYTECHNIC UNIVERSITY
Graduate Programs

Address: 6 MetroTech Center, Brooklyn, NY 11201
Admissions Phone: 718-260-3182 · **Admissions Fax:** 718-260-3624
Admissions E-mail: gradinfo@poly.edu · **Website:** www.poly.edu/admissions/graduate

INSTITUTIONAL INFORMATION
Public/private: Private (nonprofit). **Evening Classes Available?** Yes. Student/faculty Ratio: 5:1. Students in Parent Institution: 2,429.

PROGRAMS
Masters offered in: Aerospace, aeronautical, and astronautical engineering; chemical engineering; chemistry; civil engineering; computer and information sciences; computer engineering; electrical, electronics, and communications engineering; environmental/environmental health engineering; industrial engineering; journalism; manufacturing engineering; materials science; mathematics; mechanical engineering; physics; polymer/plastics engineering; systems engineering; technical and business writing; transportation and highway engineering. **Doctorate offered in:** Chemical engineering; civil engineering; computer and information sciences; computer engineering; electrical, electronics, and communications engineering; mathematics; mechanical engineering.

STUDENT INFORMATION
Total Students in Program: 937. % Full-time: 44. % Female: 23.

RESEARCH FACILITIES
Research Facilities: Center for Large-scale Computing, Center for Technology and Financial Services, and Institute for Imaging Sciences.

EXPENSES/FINANCIAL AID
Annual Tuition: $13,050. Fees: $600. Books and Supplies: $700. Grants Range From: $140-$10,000. Loans Range From: $500-$18,500. % Receiving Financial Aid: 21. % Receiving Scholarships/Grants: 40. % Receiving Loans: 88. Average student debt, upon graduation: $23,000.

ADMISSIONS INFORMATION
Application Fee: $45. Regular Application Deadline: 8/31. Regular Notification: Rolling. Transfer Students Accepted? Yes. Number of Applications Received: 1,287. % of Applicants Accepted: 60. % Accepted Who Enrolled: 43.
Required Admission Factors: Letters of recommendation, transcript.
Recommended Admission Factors: Essays/personal statement.
Other Admission Factors: Minimum 2.7 GPA required for some programs, minimum 3.0 GPA required for other programs.

EMPLOYMENT INFORMATION
Placement Office Available? Yes. % Employed Within 6 Months: 94. % of master's/doctoral grads employed in their field upon graduation: 85/82. Rate of placement: 94%. Average starting salary: $95,000.

POLYTECHNIC UNIVERSITY, LONG ISLAND CENTER CAMPUS
Graduate Programs

Address: Route 110, Farmingdale, NY 11735
Admissions Phone: 516-755-4200 · **Admissions Fax:** 516-755-4229
Admissions E-mail: jkerge@poly.edu

INSTITUTIONAL INFORMATION
Public/private: Private (nonprofit). **Evening Classes Available?** Yes. Students in Parent Institution: 454.

STUDENT INFORMATION
Total Students in Program: 171. % Full-time: 5. % Female: 14.

EXPENSES/FINANCIAL AID
Annual Tuition: $13,050. Fees: $600. Books and Supplies: $700. Grants Range From: $140-$10,000. Loans Range From: $500-$18,800. % Receiving Financial Aid: 4. % Receiving Scholarships/Grants: 25. % Receiving Loans: 75. Average student debt, upon graduation: $22,000.

ADMISSIONS INFORMATION
Application Fee: $45. Regular Notification: Rolling. Transfer Students Accepted? Yes. Transfer Policy: Maximum 27 credit hours with a minimum 2.7 GPA may be transferred. Number of Applications Received: 110. % of Applicants Accepted: 78. % Accepted Who Enrolled: 71.
Required Admission Factors: Letters of recommendation, transcript.
Other Admission Factors: Minimum grade average of B required.

EMPLOYMENT INFORMATION
Placement Office Available? Yes. % Employed Within 6 Months: 94. % of master's/doctoral grads employed in their field upon graduation: 85/82. Rate of placement: 94%. Average starting salary: $95,000.

POLYTECHNIC UNIVERSITY, WESTCHESTER GRADUATE CENTER
Westchester Graduate Center

Address: 40 Saw Mill River Road, Hawthorne, NY 10532
Admissions Phone: 718-260-3200 · **Admissions Fax:** 718-260-3446
Admissions E-mail: jkerge@poly.edu

INSTITUTIONAL INFORMATION
Public/private: Private (nonprofit). **Evening Classes Available?** Yes. Students in Parent Institution: 176.

STUDENT INFORMATION
Total Students in Program: 176. % Full-time: 41. % Female: 26.

EXPENSES/FINANCIAL AID
Annual Tuition: $13,050. Fees: $135. Books and Supplies: $700. Grants Range From: $137-$10,000. Loans Range From: $500-$18,500. % Receiving Financial Aid: 10. % Receiving Scholarships/Grants: 25. % Receiving Loans: 85. Average student debt, upon graduation: $23,000.

ADMISSIONS INFORMATION
Application Fee: $45. Regular Notification: Rolling. Transfer Students Accepted? Yes. Transfer Policy: Maximum 9 credit hours with a minimum 2.7 GPA may be transferred. Number of Applications Received: 97. % of Applicants Accepted: 75. % Accepted Who Enrolled: 85.
Required Admission Factors: Letters of recommendation, transcript.
Other Admission Factors: GRE and other admission requirements vary by department.
Program-Specific Admission Factors: Executive format programs require interview and essay.

EMPLOYMENT INFORMATION
Placement Office Available? Yes. % Employed Within 6 Months: 94. % of master's grads employed in their field upon graduation: 85. Rate of placement: 94%. Average starting salary: $95,000.

PORTLAND STATE UNIVERSITY
College of Liberal Arts & Sciences

Address: PO Box 751, Portland, OR 97207-0751
Admissions Phone: 503-725-3511 or 800-547-8887
Admissions Fax: 503-725-5525 · **Admissions E-mail:** admissions@pdx.edu
Website: www.clas.pdx.edu

INSTITUTIONAL INFORMATION

Public/private: Public. **Evening Classes Available?** Yes. **Total Faculty:** 446. **% Faculty Female:** 48. **% Faculty Part-time:** 34. **Students in Parent Institution:** 21,030.

PROGRAMS

Masters offered in: Anthropology, biology teacher education, chemistry teacher education, chemistry, Chinese language and literature, communications studies/speech communication and rhetoric, developmental and child psychology, economics, English composition, English language and literature, English/language arts teacher education, environmental science, experimental psychology, foreign language teacher education, French language and literature, French language teacher education, geography, geology/earth science, German language and literature, German language teacher education, history, industrial and organizational psychology, Japanese language and literature, mathematics teacher education, mathematics, natural resources management and policy, peace studies and conflict resolution, philosophy, physical sciences, physics, psychology, Russian language and literature, science teacher education/general science teacher education, social psychology, social science teacher education, sociology, Spanish language and literature, Spanish language teacher education, speech-language pathology/pathologist, statistics, systems science and theory, teaching English as a second or foreign language/ESL language instructor. **Doctorate offered in:** Chemistry, economics, environmental science, geography, geology/earth science, mathematics teacher education, mathematics, physics, psychology, sociology, systems science and theory.

STUDENT INFORMATION

Total Students in Program: 991. **% Full-time:** 61. **% Female:** 60. **% Minority:** 10. **% International:** 9.

RESEARCH FACILITIES

Research Facilities: Center for Black Studies, Center for Science Education.

EXPENSES/FINANCIAL AID

Annual Tuition: In-state $6,210. / Out-of-state $11,226. **Room & Board:** $8,175. **Fees:** $1,002. **Books and Supplies:** $1,200. **Grants Range From:** $250-$15,046. **Loans Range From:** $1,547-$21,500. **% Receiving Financial Aid:** 55. **% Receiving Scholarships/Grants:** 8. **% Receiving Loans:** 69. **% Receiving Assistantships:** 46. **% Receiving Other Aid:** 12. **Types of Aid Available:** Fellowships, graduate assistantships, grants, institutional work-study, loans, scholarships. **Number of Fellowships Granted Each Year:** 6. **Number of Teaching/Research Assistantships Granted Each Year:** 248. **Assistantship Compensation Includes:** Full tuition remission, salary/stipend. **Average Salary Stipend:** $7,698.

ADMISSIONS INFORMATION

Application Fee: $50. **Priority Application Deadline:** 4/1. **Regular Application Deadline:** 4/1. **Regular Notification:** Rolling. **Transfer Students Accepted?** Yes. **Transfer Policy:** Varies by program. **Number of Applications Received:** 705. **% of Applicants Accepted:** 59. **% Accepted Who Enrolled:** 89. **Average GPA:** 3.5.
Program-Specific Admission Factors: Some programs require written work samples. Some programs have minimum GPA requirement in program subject.

PORTLAND STATE UNIVERSITY
College of Urban & Public Affairs

Address: PO Box 751, Portland, OR 97207-0751
Admissions Phone: 503-725-3511 or 800-547-8887
Admissions Fax: 503-725-5525 · **Admissions E-mail:** admissions@pdx.edu
Website: www.upa.pdx.edu

INSTITUTIONAL INFORMATION

Public/private: Public. **Evening Classes Available?** Yes. **Total Faculty:** 128. **% Faculty Female:** 38. **% Faculty Part-time:** 57. **Students in Parent Institution:** 21,030.

PROGRAMS

Masters offered in: City/urban, community, and regional planning; criminal justice/law enforcement administration; health services administration; political science and government; public administration; public health (MPh, DPh); social science teacher education. **Doctorate offered in:** City/urban, community, and regional planning; public administration.

STUDENT INFORMATION

Total Students in Program: 523. **% Full-time:** 52. **% Female:** 58. **% Minority:** 12. **% International:** 7.

RESEARCH FACILITIES

Research Facilities: Population Research Center, Center for Urban Studies, Center for Public Health Studies, Institute of Portland Metropolitan Studies, Institute on Aging, Criminal Justice Policy Research Institue, Executive Leadership Institute.

EXPENSES/FINANCIAL AID

Annual Tuition: In-state $6,210. / Out-of-state $11,226. **Room & Board:** $8,175. **Fees:** $1,002. **Books and Supplies:** $1,200. **Grants Range From:** $500-$18,068. **Loans Range From:** $1,645-$25,889. **% Receiving Financial Aid:** 49. **% Receiving Scholarships/Grants:** 8. **% Receiving Loans:** 83. **% Receiving Assistantships:** 23. **% Receiving Other Aid:** 16. **Types of Aid Available:** Graduate assistantships, grants, institutional work-study, loans, scholarships. **Number of Teaching/Research Assistantships Granted Each Year:** 60. **Assistantship Compensation Includes:** Full tuition remission, salary/stipend. **Average Salary Stipend:** $5,089.

ADMISSIONS INFORMATION

Application Fee: $50. **Priority Application Deadline:** 1/15. **Regular Application Deadline:** 1/15. **Regular Notification:** Rolling. **Transfer Students Accepted?** Yes. **Number of Applications Received:** 330. **% of Applicants Accepted:** 69. **% Accepted Who Enrolled:** 75. **Average GPA:** 3.4. **Required Admission Factors:** Essays/personal statement, GRE, letters of recommendation, transcript.
Other Admission Factors: Minimum 3.0 GPA required.

EMPLOYMENT INFORMATION

Placement Office Available? Yes.

PORTLAND STATE UNIVERSITY
Graduate School of Social Work

Address: PO Box 751, Portland, OR 97207-0751
Admissions Phone: 503-725-3511 or 800-547-8887
Admissions Fax: 503-725-5525 · **Admissions E-mail:** putnamj@pdx.edu
Website: www.ssw.pdx.edu

INSTITUTIONAL INFORMATION

Public/private: Public. **Total Faculty:** 31. **% Faculty Female:** 61. **% Faculty Part-time:** 23. **Student/faculty Ratio:** 13:1. **Students in Parent Institution:** 21,030.

PROGRAMS

Masters offered in: Social work. **Doctorate offered in:** Social work.

STUDENT INFORMATION

Total Students in Program: 373. **% Full-time:** 84. **% Female:** 83. **% Minority:** 16. **% International:** 3.

RESEARCH FACILITIES

Research Facilities: Regional Research Institute, Child Welfare Partnership & Center for the Study of Mental Health Policy and Services.

EXPENSES/FINANCIAL AID

Annual Tuition: In-state $6,210. / Out-of-state $11,226. **Room & Board:** $8,175. **Fees:** $1,002. **Books and Supplies:** $1,200. **Grants Range From:** $811-$14,718. **Loans Range From:** $2,100-$33,500. **% Receiving Financial Aid:** 76. **% Receiving Scholarships/Grants:** 13. **% Receiving Loans:** 95. **% Receiving Assistantships:** 2. **% Receiving Other Aid:** 19. **Types of Aid Available:** Graduate assistantships, grants, institutional work-study, loans, scholarships. **Number of Teaching/Research Assistantships Granted Each Year:** 7. **Assistantship Compensation Includes:** Full tuition remission, salary/stipend. **Average Salary Stipend:** $7,367.

ADMISSIONS INFORMATION

Application Fee: $50. **Regular Application Deadline:** 2/1. **Regular Notification:** Rolling. **Transfer Students Accepted?** Yes. **Number of Applications Received:** 1,026. **% of Applicants Accepted:** 57. **% Accepted Who Enrolled:** 28. **Average GPA:** 3.4.
Required Admission Factors: Essays/personal statement, letters of recommendation, transcript.
Other Admission Factors: Minimum 2.75 GPA required.
Program-Specific Admission Factors: 4 references, personal statement, research outline, and writing sample required of PhD program applicants.

EMPLOYMENT INFORMATION

Placement Office Available? Yes.

PORTLAND STATE UNIVERSITY
School of Fine & Performing Arts

Address: PO Box 751, Portland, OR 97207-0751
Admissions Phone: 503-725-3511 or 800-547-8887
Admissions Fax: 503-725-5525 · **Admissions E-mail:** admissions@pdx.edu
Website: www.fpa.pdx.edu

INSTITUTIONAL INFORMATION

Public/private: Public. **Total Faculty:** 140. **% Faculty Female:** 44. **% Faculty Part-time:** 60. **Students in Parent Institution:** 21,030.

PROGRAMS

Masters offered in: Conducting, fine/studio arts, music performance.

STUDENT INFORMATION

Total Students in Program: 63. **% Full-time:** 59. **% Female:** 60. **% Minority:** 8. **% International:** 8.

EXPENSES/FINANCIAL AID

Annual Tuition: In-state $6,210. / Out-of-state $11,226. **Room & Board:** $8,175. **Fees:** $1,002. **Books and Supplies:** $1,200. **Grants Range From:** $75-$3,000. **Loans Range From:** $2,834-$21,500. **% Receiving Financial Aid:** 79. **% Receiving Scholarships/Grants:** 24. **% Receiving Loans:** 68. **% Receiving Assistantships:** 50. **% Receiving Other Aid:** 34. **Types of Aid Available:** Graduate assistantships, grants, institutional work-study, loans, scholarships. **Number of Teaching/Research Assistantships Granted Each Year:** 25. **Assistantship Compensation Includes:** Full tuition remission, salary/stipend. **Average Salary Stipend:** $2,660.

ADMISSIONS INFORMATION

Application Fee: $50. **Regular Application Deadline:** 3/1. **Regular Notification:** Rolling. **Transfer Students Accepted?** Yes. **Transfer Policy:** Maximum 15 credit hours may be transferred into MFA program with approval.
Number of Applications Received: 97. **% of Applicants Accepted:** 45. **% Accepted Who Enrolled:** 52. **Average GPA:** 3.6.
Required Admission Factors: Transcript.
Other Admission Factors: Minimum 2.75 GPA required.
Program-Specific Admission Factors: MFA applicants must submit a portfolio; music applicants must take a music entrance examination, includes performance.

EMPLOYMENT INFORMATION

Placement Office Available? Yes.

PRATT INSTITUTE
School of Art & Design

Address: 200 Willoughby Avenue, Brooklyn, NY 11205
Admissions Phone: 718-636-3669 or 800-331-0834
Admissions Fax: 718-636-3670 · **Admissions E-mail:** yhah@pratt.edu
Website: www.pratt.edu/ad/index.html

INSTITUTIONAL INFORMATION

Public/private: Private (nonprofit). **Evening Classes Available?** Yes. **Student/faculty Ratio:** 14:1. **Students in Parent Institution:** 4,119.

STUDENT INFORMATION

Total Students in Program: 1,277. **% Full-time:** 56. **% Female:** 69.

RESEARCH FACILITIES

Research Facilities: Pratt Institute Center for Community and Environmental Development.

EXPENSES/FINANCIAL AID

Annual Tuition: $18,000. **Fees:** $530. **Books and Supplies:** $500. **Grants Range From:** $200-$5,000. **Loans Range From:** $8,500-$18,500. **% Receiving Financial Aid:** 51. **% Receiving Scholarships/Grants:** 30. **% Receiving Loans:** 67. **% Receiving Assistantships:** 37. **Average student debt, upon graduation:** $60,000. **Number of Fellowships Granted Each Year:** 2. **Average amount of individual fellowships per year:** 1,740. **Number of Teaching/Research Assistantships Granted Each Year:** 221.

ADMISSIONS INFORMATION

Application Fee: $40. **Priority Application Deadline:** 2/1. **Regular Application Deadline:** 2/1. **Regular Notification:** Rolling. **Transfer Students Accepted?** Yes. **Number of Applications Received:** 1,087. **% of Applicants Accepted:** 46. **% Accepted Who Enrolled:** 53. **Average GPA:** 3.3.
Required Admission Factors: Essays/personal statement, letters of recommendation, transcript.
Other Admission Factors: Minimum 3.0 GPA required.
Program-Specific Admission Factors: Three years professional experience for arts and cultural management and design management.

EMPLOYMENT INFORMATION

Placement Office Available? Yes. **% Employed Within 6 Months:** 86. **% of master's grads employed in their field upon graduation:** 94. **Rate of placement:** 97%. **Average starting salary:** $36,000.

PRATT INSTITUTE
School of Information & Library Science

Address: 200 Willoughby Avenue, Brooklyn, NY 11205
Admissions Phone: 718-636-3683 or 718-636-6514
Admissions Fax: 718-636-3670 · **Admissions E-mail:** gladmdir@pratt.edu

INSTITUTIONAL INFORMATION

Public/private: Private (nonprofit). **Evening Classes Available?** Yes. **Student/faculty Ratio:** 14:1. **Students in Parent Institution:** 4,119.

STUDENT INFORMATION

Total Students in Program: 1,277. % Full-time: 56. % Female: 69.

RESEARCH FACILITIES

Research Facilities: Pratt Institute Center for Community and Environmental Development.

EXPENSES/FINANCIAL AID

Annual Tuition: In-state $18,000. Fees: $530. Books and Supplies: $500. Grants Range From: $200-$5,000. Loans Range From: $8,500-$18,500. % Receiving Financial Aid: 67. % Receiving Scholarships/Grants: 30. % Receiving Loans: 67. % Receiving Assistantships: 37. Average student debt, upon graduation: $60,000. Number of Fellowships Granted Each Year: 10. Average amount of individual fellowships per year: 500. Number of Teaching/Research Assistantships Granted Each Year: 29.

ADMISSIONS INFORMATION

Application Fee: $40. Regular Notification: Rolling. Transfer Students Accepted? Yes. Transfer Policy: Credits awarded on provisional basis by departmental chair. Number of Applications Received: 78. % of Applicants Accepted: 49. Average GPA: 3.3.

Required Admission Factors: Essays/personal statement, letters of recommendation, transcript.

Other Admission Factors: Statement of purpose required; minimum 3.0 GPA recommended.

EMPLOYMENT INFORMATION

Placement Office Available? Yes. % Employed Within 6 Months: 98. % of master's grads employed in their field upon graduation: 99. Rate of placement: 97%. Average starting salary: $45,000.

PRESCOTT COLLEGE
Master of Arts Program

Address: 220 Grove Avenue, Prescott, AZ 86301
Admissions Phone: 928-776-5180 · Admissions Fax: 928-776-5242
Admissions E-mail: mapmail@prescott.edu
Website: http://prescott.edu/academics/map/index.html

INSTITUTIONAL INFORMATION

Public/private: Private (nonprofit). Student/faculty Ratio: 1:1. Students in Parent Institution: 1,000.

STUDENT INFORMATION

Total Students in Program: 221. % Full-time: 61. % Female: 53.

RESEARCH FACILITIES

Research Facilities: Kino Bay Marine Biology Center, Wolfberry Farm.

EXPENSES/FINANCIAL AID

Annual Tuition: In-state $10,200. Books and Supplies: $683. Grants Range From: $300-$9,000. Loans Range From: $800-$18,500. % Receiving Financial Aid: 69. % Receiving Scholarships/Grants: 8. % Receiving Loans: 92. Average student debt, upon graduation: $22,900.

ADMISSIONS INFORMATION

Application Fee: $40. Priority Application Deadline: 2/15. Regular Notification: Rolling. Transfer Students Accepted? No. Number of Applications Received: 78.

Required Admission Factors: Essays/personal statement, letters of recommendation, transcript.

PRINCETON THEOLOGICAL SEMINARY
Graduate Programs

Address: 64 Mercer Street, PO Box 821, Princeton, NJ 08542-0803
Admissions Phone: 609-497-7805 or 800-622-6767, ext. 7805
Admissions Fax: 609-497-7870 · Admissions E-mail: admissions@ptsem.edu
Website: www.ptsem.edu

INSTITUTIONAL INFORMATION

Public/private: Private (nonprofit). Students in Parent Institution: 785

STUDENT INFORMATION

Total Students in Program: 785. % Full-time: 100. % Female: 39.

EXPENSES/FINANCIAL AID

Annual Tuition: $8,250. Fees: $620. Books and Supplies: $1,200. Grants Range From: $1,000-$8,250. Loans Range From: $1-$23,500. % Receiving Financial Aid: 89. % Receiving Scholarships/Grants: 87. % Receiving Loans: 50.

ADMISSIONS INFORMATION

Application Fee: $40. Regular Application Deadline: 3/1. Regular Notification: Rolling. Transfer Students Accepted? Yes. Number of Applications Received: 675. % of Applicants Accepted: 58. % Accepted Who Enrolled: 62.

Required Admission Factors: Essays/personal statement, letters of recommendation, transcript.

EMPLOYMENT INFORMATION

Placement Office Available? Yes. % Employed Within 6 Months: 63. Rate of placement: 70%. Average starting salary: $59,723.

PRINCETON UNIVERSITY
Graduate School

Address: 307 Nassau Hall, Princeton, NJ 08544
Admissions Phone: 609-258-3034 · Admissions Fax: 609-258-6180
Admissions E-mail: gsadmit@princeton.edu · Website: www.princeton.edu

INSTITUTIONAL INFORMATION

Public/private: Private (nonprofit). Total Faculty: 1,052. % Faculty Female: 28. % Faculty Part-time: 24. Student/faculty Ratio: 5:1.

PROGRAMS

Masters offered in: Aerospace, aeronautical, and astronautical engineering; architecture (BArch, BA/BS, MArch, MA/MS, PhD); chemical engineering; chemistry; computer science; electrical, electronics, and communications engineering; finance; mechanical engineering; operations research; public policy analysis; Semitic languages, literatures, and linguistics; structural engineering; water resources engineering. Doctorate offered in: Algebra and number theory, American history (United States), American literature (United States), ancient/classical Greek language and literature, anthropology, applied mathematics, Arabic language and literature, architectural history and criticism.

RESEARCH FACILITIES

Research Facilities: Center for Teaching and Learning.

EXPENSES/FINANCIAL AID

Annual Tuition: $31,450. Room & Board (On/off Campus): $21,040/$22,607. Fees: $1,000. % Receiving Assistantships: 23. Types of Aid Available: Fellowships, graduate assistantships, institutional work-study. Number of Fellowships Granted Each Year: 1,800. Average amount of individual fellowships per year: $33,960. Number of Teaching/Research Assistantships Granted Each Year: 1,040. Assistantship Compensation Includes: Full tuition remission, partial tuition remission, salary/stipend.

Complete Book of Graduate Programs in the Arts and Sciences

ADMISSIONS INFORMATION

Application Fee: $55. Regular Application Deadline: 12/1. Regular Notification: 3/15. Transfer Students Accepted? No. Number of Applications Received: 7,738. % of Applicants Accepted: 14. % Accepted Who Enrolled: 51.
Required Admission Factors: Essays/personal statement, GRE, letters of recommendation, transcript.

EMPLOYMENT INFORMATION

Placement Office Available? Yes.

PROVIDENCE COLLEGE
Graduate School

Address: 549 River Avenue, Providence, RI 02918-0001
Admissions Phone: 401-865-2247 · **Admissions Fax:** 401-865-1147

INSTITUTIONAL INFORMATION

Public/private: Private (nonprofit). Evening Classes Available? Yes. Student/faculty Ratio: 12:1. Students in Parent Institution: 5,336.

STUDENT INFORMATION

Total Students in Program: 931. % Full-time: 8. % Female: 67.

EXPENSES/FINANCIAL AID

Annual Tuition: $4,248. Books and Supplies: $650. Loans Range From: $2,000-$8,500. % Receiving Financial Aid: 4. % Receiving Loans: 60. % Receiving Assistantships: 40. Average student debt, upon graduation: $10,400. Number of Teaching/Research Assistantships Granted Each Year: 39. Average Salary Stipend: $700.

ADMISSIONS INFORMATION

Application Fee: $50. Regular Notification: Rolling. Transfer Students Accepted? Yes. Number of Applications Received: 169. % of Applicants Accepted: 96. % Accepted Who Enrolled: 92. Average GPA: 3.2. Average GRE Verbal: 439. Average GRE Quantitative: 451. Average GRE Analytical: 500.
Required Admission Factors: Essays/personal statement, GRE, letters of recommendation, transcript.
Other Admission Factors: Minimum MAT score of 45 and minimum 2.75 GPA required.

EMPLOYMENT INFORMATION

Placement Office Available? Yes. Rate of placement: 95%.

PURDUE UNIVERSITY
School of Consumer & Family Sciences

Address: 170 Young Graduate House, West Lafayette, IN 47906-6208
Admissions Phone: 765-494-8213

INSTITUTIONAL INFORMATION

Public/private: Public. Students in Parent Institution: 37,871.

RESEARCH FACILITIES

Research Facilities: AIDS research center, cancer research center, engineering experiment station, and 400 research labs.

EXPENSES/FINANCIAL AID

Annual Tuition: In-state $4,536. / Out-of-state $13,568. Books and Supplies: $750.

ADMISSIONS INFORMATION

Application Fee: $30. Regular Notification: Rolling. Transfer Students Accepted? No. Number of Applications Received: 234. % of Applicants Accepted: 47. % Accepted Who Enrolled: 50. Average GPA: 3.46. Aver-

age GRE Verbal: 560. Average GRE Quantitative: 625. Average GRE Analytical: 630.
Required Admission Factors: Transcript.

EMPLOYMENT INFORMATION

Placement Office Available? Yes.

QUINNIPIAC UNIVERSITY
Division of Education

Address: 275 Mount Carmel Avenue, Hamden, CT 06518
Admissions Phone: 203-582-8672 · **Admissions Fax:** 203-582-3443
Admissions E-mail: graduate@quinnipiac.edu · **Website:** www.quinnipiac.edu

INSTITUTIONAL INFORMATION

Public/private: Private (nonprofit). Total Faculty: 31. % Faculty Female: 71. % Faculty Part-time: 77. Student/faculty Ratio: 10:1. Students in Parent Institution: 7,121.

PROGRAMS

Masters offered in: Elementary education and teaching, junior high/intermediate/middle school education and teaching, secondary education and teaching.

STUDENT INFORMATION

Total Students in Program: 146. % Full-time: 92. % Female: 75. % Minority: 12.

EXPENSES/FINANCIAL AID

Annual Tuition: $8,100. Fees: $450. Books and Supplies: $1,000. Loans Range From: $760-$18,500. % Receiving Financial Aid: 80. % Receiving Loans: 93. % Receiving Assistantships: 7. Types of Aid Available: Graduate assistantships, loans, mat internship with partial tuition waiver. Assistantship Compensation Includes: Partial tuition remission.

ADMISSIONS INFORMATION

Application Fee: $45. Priority Application Deadline: 3/15. Regular Application Deadline: 7/30. Regular Notification: Rolling. Transfer Students Accepted? Yes. Number of Applications Received: 135. % of Applicants Accepted: 86. % Accepted Who Enrolled: 86. Average GPA: 2.9.
Required Admission Factors: Essays/personal statement, interview, letters of recommendation, transcript.
Other Admission Factors: Minimum 2.67 GPA, Praxis I test (or waiver), and U.S. history survey course required.

QUINNIPIAC UNIVERSITY
School of Communications

Address: 275 Mount Carmel Avenue, Hamden, CT 06518
Admissions Phone: 800-462-1944 · **Admissions Fax:** 203-582-3443
Admissions E-mail: graduate@quinnipiac.edu · **Website:** www.quinnipiac.edu

INSTITUTIONAL INFORMATION

Public/private: Private (nonprofit). Evening Classes Available? Yes. Total Faculty: 8. % Faculty Part-time: 38. Student/faculty Ratio: 6:1. Students in Parent Institution: 7,121.

PROGRAMS

Masters offered in: Communications, journalism, and related fields; journalism.

STUDENT INFORMATION

Total Students in Program: 58. % Full-time: 36. % Female: 69. % Minority: 17.

EXPENSES/FINANCIAL AID

Annual Tuition: $15,000. Fees: $450. Books and Supplies: $1,000. Loans Range From: $760-$35,000. % Receiving Loans: 92. % Receiving Assistantships: 7. **Types of Aid Available:** Fellowships, graduate assistantships, loans. **Number of Fellowships Granted Each Year:** 1. **Average amount of individual fellowships per year:** $8,000.

ADMISSIONS INFORMATION

Application Fee: $45. **Regular Application Deadline:** 7/30. **Regular Notification:** Rolling. **Transfer Students Accepted?** Yes. **Number of Applications Received:** 53. **% of Applicants Accepted:** 91. **% Accepted Who Enrolled:** 58. **Average GPA:** 3.0.
Required Admission Factors: Essays/personal statement, interview, letters of recommendation, transcript.
Other Admission Factors: 2.8 GPA.
Program-Specific Admission Factors: Minimum 2.8 GPA and portfolio sample required.

RADFORD UNIVERSITY
College of Arts & Sciences

Address: PO Box 6890, Radford, VA 24142
Admissions Phone: 540-831-5431 · **Admissions Fax:** 540-831-6061
Admissions E-mail: sgunter@radford.edu

INSTITUTIONAL INFORMATION

Public/private: Public. **Student/faculty Ratio:** 3:1. **Students in Parent Institution:** 8,837.

STUDENT INFORMATION

Total Students in Program: 1,215. **% Full-time:** 38. **% Female:** 73.

RESEARCH FACILITIES

Research Facilities: Center for Brain Research, Center for Gender Studies, Institute for Engineering Geosciences, Center for Music Technology, multimedia center.

EXPENSES/FINANCIAL AID

Annual Tuition: In-state $2,564. / Out-of-state $6,314. **Fees:** $1,440. **Books and Supplies:** $650. **Grants Range From:** $200-$6,000. **Loans Range From:** $200-$14,525. **% Receiving Financial Aid:** 30. **% Receiving Scholarships/Grants:** 25. **% Receiving Loans:** 38. **% Receiving Assistantships:** 30. **Average student debt, upon graduation:** $21,295. **Number of Fellowships Granted Each Year:** 14. **Average amount of individual fellowships per year:** 9,712. **Number of Teaching/Research Assistantships Granted Each Year:** 109. **Average Salary Stipend:** $5,535.

ADMISSIONS INFORMATION

Application Fee: $25. **Regular Notification:** Rolling. **Transfer Students Accepted?** Yes. **Transfer Policy:** Maximum 6 credit hours may be transferred with a minimum grade of B with approval. **Number of Applications Received:** 303. **% of Applicants Accepted:** 64. **% Accepted Who Enrolled:** 53. **Average GPA:** 3.2. **Average GRE Verbal:** 447. **Average GRE Quantitative:** 484. **Average GRE Analytical:** 513.
Required Admission Factors: GRE, letters of recommendation, transcript.
Other Admission Factors: Minimum GRE score of 1000 and minimum 2.7 GPA required.

EMPLOYMENT INFORMATION

Placement Office Available? Yes. **% Employed Within 6 Months:** 85. **Rate of placement:** 97%.

RADFORD UNIVERSITY
College of Visual & Performing Arts

Address: PO Box 6890, Radford, VA 24142
Admissions Phone: 540-831-5431 · **Admissions Fax:** 540-831-6061
Admissions E-mail: sgunter@radford.edu

INSTITUTIONAL INFORMATION

Public/private: Public. **Student/faculty Ratio:** 1:1. **Students in Parent Institution:** 8,837.

STUDENT INFORMATION

Total Students in Program: 1,215. **% Full-time:** 38. **% Female:** 73.

RESEARCH FACILITIES

Research Facilities: Center for Brain Research, Center for Gender Studies, Institute for Engineering Geosciences, Center for Music Technology, multimedia center.

EXPENSES/FINANCIAL AID

Annual Tuition: In-state $2,564. / Out-of-state $6,314. **Fees:** $1,440. **Books and Supplies:** $650. **Grants Range From:** $200-$6,000. **Loans Range From:** $200-$14,525. **% Receiving Financial Aid:** 4. **% Receiving Scholarships/Grants:** 25. **% Receiving Loans:** 38. **% Receiving Assistantships:** 30. **Average student debt, upon graduation:** $21,295. **Number of Fellowships Granted Each Year:** 12. **Average amount of individual fellowships per year:** 6,810. **Number of Teaching/Research Assistantships Granted Each Year:** 4. **Average Salary Stipend:** $4,650.

ADMISSIONS INFORMATION

Application Fee: $25. **Regular Notification:** Rolling. **Transfer Students Accepted?** Yes. **Transfer Policy:** Maximum 6 credit hours with a minimum grade of B may be transferred with approval. **Number of Applications Received:** 44. **% of Applicants Accepted:** 52. **% Accepted Who Enrolled:** 43. **Average GPA:** 3.25. **Average GRE Verbal:** 470. **Average GRE Quantitative:** 510. **Average GRE Analytical:** 540.
Required Admission Factors: Essays/personal statement, letters of recommendation.
Other Admission Factors: Minimum 2.7 GPA (2.7 in major) required.
Program-Specific Admission Factors: Portfolio of 20 slides of recent artwork required for art program applicants. 3 letters of recommendation and audition required of music program applicants.

EMPLOYMENT INFORMATION

Placement Office Available? Yes. **Rate of placement:** 97%.

REED COLLEGE
Master of Arts in Liberal Studies

Address: 3203 Southeast Woodstock Boulevard, Portland, OR 97202-8199
Admissions Phone: 503-777-7259 · **Admissions Fax:** 503-777-7581
Admissions E-mail: mals@reed.edu
Website: http://web.reed.edu/academic/MALS/index.html

INSTITUTIONAL INFORMATION

Public/private: Private (nonprofit). **Evening Classes Available?** Yes. **Total Faculty:** 15. **% Faculty Female:** 27. **% Faculty Part-time:** 100. **Student/faculty Ratio:** 10:1. **Students in Parent Institution:** 1,341.

PROGRAMS

Masters offered in: Liberal arts and sciences/liberal studies.

STUDENT INFORMATION

Total Students in Program: 29 **% Female:** 69. **% Minority:** 3.

EXPENSES/FINANCIAL AID

Annual Tuition: $695. **Books and Supplies:** $100. **Grants Range From:** $500-$2,000. **Loans Range From:** $3,500-$18,000. **% Receiving Financial Aid:** 40. **% Receiving Loans:** 100. **Types of Aid Available:** Loans. **Average student debt, upon graduation:** $10,000.

ADMISSIONS INFORMATION

Application Fee: $50. **Priority Application Deadline:** 5/1. **Regular Application Deadline:** 7/15. **Regular Notification:** Rolling. **Transfer Students Accepted?** Yes. **Transfer Policy:** Students may transfer up to a maximum of 2 units (8 semester credits). All work submitted for transfer must be approved

Complete Book of Graduate Programs in the Arts and Sciences

by the registrar and by the committee on graduate studies. The course work must be from a regionally accredited college or university, may not be applied toward another degree, and should represent B or better work. **Number of Applications Received:** 14. **% of Applicants Accepted:** 43. **% Accepted Who Enrolled:** 83. **Average GPA:** 3.5.
Required Admission Factors: Essays/personal statement, interview, letters of recommendation, transcript.
Other Admission Factors: Minimum 3.0 GPA and writing sample are recommended.

REGENT UNIVERSITY
Robertson School of Government

Address: 1000 Regent University Drive, Virginia Beach, VA 23464
Admissions Phone: 888-8001-7735 · **Admissions Fax:** 757-226-4735
Admissions E-mail: govschool@regent.edu · **Website:** www.regent.edu/acad/schgov/

INSTITUTIONAL INFORMATION
Public/private: Private (nonprofit). **Evening Classes Available?** Yes. **Total Faculty:** 10. **% Faculty Female:** 20. **Student/faculty Ratio:** 8:1. **Students in Parent Institution:** 3,000

PROGRAMS
Masters offered in: Political science and government, public administration, public policy analysis. **First Professional degree offered in:** Public policy analysis.

STUDENT INFORMATION
Total Students in Program: 2,836. **% Full-time:** 38.

RESEARCH FACILITIES
Research Facilities: American Center for Law & Justice (ACLJ), Center for Faith & Culture, Center for Leadership Studies, World Reach.

EXPENSES/FINANCIAL AID
Annual Tuition: $575. **Fees:** $500. **Books and Supplies:** $500. **Grants Range From:** $100-$10,725. **Loans Range From:** $1,650-$34,988. **% Receiving Financial Aid:** 88. **% Receiving Scholarships/Grants:** 85. **% Receiving Loans:** 59. **% Receiving Assistantships:** 1. **Types of Aid Available:** Fellowships, graduate assistantships, loans, scholarships.

ADMISSIONS INFORMATION
Application Fee: $40. **Regular Application Deadline:** 7/15. **Regular Notification:** Rolling. **Transfer Students Accepted?** Yes. **Transfer Policy:** Good standing at an accredited institution required of transfer applicants. **Number of Applications Received:** 65. **% of Applicants Accepted:** 72. **% Accepted Who Enrolled:** 87. **Average GPA:** 3.1. **Average GRE Verbal:** 482. **Average GRE Quantitative:** 493.
Required Admission Factors: Essays/personal statement, interview, letters of recommendation, transcript.
Other Admission Factors: Minimum GRE score in 50th percentile and minimum 3.0 GPA.

EMPLOYMENT INFORMATION
Placement Office Available? Yes. **% Employed Within 6 Months:** 25. **Rate of placement:** 70%. **Average starting salary:** $40,000.

REGENT UNIVERSITY
School of Communication & the Arts

Address: 1000 Regent University Drive, COM 200, Virginia Beach, VA 23464
Admissions Phone: 757-226-4243 · **Admissions Fax:** 757-226-4394
Admissions E-mail: comcollege@regent.edu
Website: www.regent.edu/communication

INSTITUTIONAL INFORMATION
Public/private: Private (nonprofit). **Student/faculty Ratio:** 8:1. **Students in Parent Institution:** 2,166.

STUDENT INFORMATION
Total Students in Program: 1,547. **% Full-time:** 50. **% Female:** 48.

RESEARCH FACILITIES
Research Facilities: Center for Leadership Studies, Center for Latin American Leadership, SLS Research Center, Center for Faith & Culture, World Reach, American Center for Law & Justice (ACLJ).

EXPENSES/FINANCIAL AID
Fees: $500. **Books and Supplies:** $500. **Grants Range From:** $100. **Loans Range From:** $1,650-$34,988. **% Receiving Scholarships/Grants:** 85. **% Receiving Loans:** 59. **% Receiving Assistantships:** 1. **Number of Teaching/Research Assistantships Granted Each Year:** 10.

ADMISSIONS INFORMATION
Application Fee: $40. **Priority Application Deadline:** 3/1. **Regular Application Deadline:** 7/31. **Regular Notification:** Rolling. **Transfer Students Accepted?** Yes. **Transfer Policy:** Transferred courses must be comparable to courses required in the program in which admission is sought. Course syllabi must accompany transfer credit evaluation request. **Number of Applications Received:** 220. **% of Applicants Accepted:** 65. **% Accepted Who Enrolled:** 68. **Average GPA:** 3.0.
Required Admission Factors: Essays/personal statement, interview, letters of recommendation, transcript.
Other Admission Factors: Minimum 2.75 GPA required. A GPA of 3.0 is preferred.
Program-Specific Admission Factors: Certain programs may require specific writing samples. An audition is required for the MFA acting and MFA acting/directing programs.

EMPLOYMENT INFORMATION
Placement Office Available? Yes. **% Employed Within 6 Months:** 70. **Rate of placement:** 80%. **Average starting salary:** $35,000.

REGENT UNIVERSITY
School of Leadership Studies

Address: 1000 Regent University Drive, Virginia Beach, VA 23464
Admissions Phone: 757-226-4550 · **Admissions Fax:** 757-226-4634
Admissions E-mail: leadership@regent.edu · **Website:** www.regent.edu/leadership

INSTITUTIONAL INFORMATION
Public/private: Private (nonprofit). **Total Faculty:** 28. **% Faculty Part-time:** 68. **Student/faculty Ratio:** 20:1. **Students in Parent Institution:** 2,938.

PROGRAMS
Masters offered in: Multi/interdisciplinary studies, nonprofit/public/organizational management, organizational behavior studies. **Doctorate offered in:** Multi/interdisciplinary studies, nonprofit/public/organizational management, organizational behavior studies.

RESEARCH FACILITIES
Research Facilities: Center for Leadership Studies, Center for Latin American Leadership, SLS Research Center, Center for Faith & Culture, World Reach, American Center for Law & Justice (ACLJ).

EXPENSES/FINANCIAL AID
Annual Tuition: $445. **Fees:** $60. **Books and Supplies:** $1,500. **Grants Range From:** $330-$14,400. **Types of Aid Available:** Fellowships, grants, loans, scholarships. **Number of Fellowships Granted Each Year:** 7. **Number of Teaching/Research Assistantships Granted Each Year:** 1.

ADMISSIONS INFORMATION
Application Fee: $100. **Regular Application Deadline:** 5/1. **Regular Notification:** Rolling. **Transfer Students Accepted?** Yes. **Transfer Policy:** Maxi-

mum 8 credit hours may be transferred into master's program; maximum 9 credit hours may be applied toward the elective course work in the PhD program. **Number of Applications Received:** 264. **% of Applicants Accepted:** 78. **% Accepted Who Enrolled:** 57. **Average GPA:** 3.6.
Required Admission Factors: Essays/personal statement, letters of recommendation, transcript.
Other Admission Factors: Minimum 3.0 GPA required.
Program-Specific Admission Factors: Academic writing sample required of doctoral program applicants. Goal statement required of all program applicants. Computer literacy evaluation for all programs applicants.

EMPLOYMENT INFORMATION
% of master's/doctoral grads employed in their field upon graduation: 90/90.

REGENT UNIVERSITY
School of Psychology & Counseling

Address: 1000 Regent University Drive, Virginia Beach, VA 23464
Admissions Phone: 757-226-4498 · **Admissions Fax:** 757-226-4282
Admissions E-mail: rennhit@regent.edu · **Website:** www.regent.edu/counseling

INSTITUTIONAL INFORMATION
Public/private: Private (nonprofit). **Evening Classes Available?** Yes. **Student/faculty Ratio:** 21:1. **Students in Parent Institution:** 2,166

STUDENT INFORMATION
Total Students in Program: 1,547. **% Full-time:** 50. **% Female:** 48.

RESEARCH FACILITIES
Research Facilities: American Center for Law & Justice (ACLJ), Center for Faith & Culture, Center for Leadership Studies, World Reach.

EXPENSES/FINANCIAL AID
Fees: $500. **Books and Supplies:** $500. **Grants Range From:** $100. **Loans Range From:** $1,650-$34,988. **% Receiving Financial Aid:** 80. **% Receiving Scholarships/Grants:** 85. **% Receiving Loans:** 59. **% Receiving Assistantships:** 1. **Average student debt, upon graduation:** $20,000. **Number of Fellowships Granted Each Year:** 5. **Average amount of individual fellowships per year:** $10,000. **Number of Teaching/Research Assistantships Granted Each Year:** 5. **Average Salary Stipend:** $10,000.

ADMISSIONS INFORMATION
Application Fee: $40. **Regular Application Deadline:** 3/1. **Regular Notification:** Rolling. **Transfer Students Accepted?** Yes. **Transfer Policy:** Maximum 25% of total credit hours required may be transferred. **Average GPA:** 3.4. **Average GRE Verbal:** 449. **Average GRE Quantitative:** 481. **Average GRE Analytical:** 506.
Required Admission Factors: Essays/personal statement, GRE, interview, letters of recommendation, transcript. GRE Writing Assessment (now part of GRE).
Other Admission Factors: Minimum 2.75 GPA required.
Program-Specific Admission Factors: Minimum 3.0 GPA required of doctoral program applicants.

EMPLOYMENT INFORMATION
Placement Office Available? Yes. **% Employed Within 6 Months:** 50. **% of master's grads employed in their field upon graduation:** 50. **Rate of placement:** 80%. **Average starting salary:** $32,000.

REGIS UNIVERSITY
School for Professional Studies

Address: 3333 Regis Boulevard, Denver, CO 80221-1099
Admissions Phone: 800-677-9270 or 303-458-4080 · **Admissions Fax:** 303-964-5538
Admissions E-mail: masters@regis.edu

INSTITUTIONAL INFORMATION
Public/private: Private (nonprofit). **Evening Classes Available?** Yes. **Total Faculty:** 500. **Student/faculty Ratio:** 15:1. **Students in Parent Institution:** 9,233.

RESEARCH FACILITIES
Research Facilities: New Ventures for International Education, corporate partnerships, community service.

EXPENSES/FINANCIAL AID
Books and Supplies: $300. **Number of Fellowships Granted Each Year:** 12.

ADMISSIONS INFORMATION
Application Fee: $75. **Regular Notification:** Rolling. **Transfer Students Accepted?** Yes. **Number of Applications Received:** 957. **% of Applicants Accepted:** 86. **% Accepted Who Enrolled:** 95.
Required Admission Factors: Essays/personal statement, transcript.
Program-Specific Admission Factors: 2 years of full-time business experience required of master of business administration program applicants. 3 years full-time administrative or supervisory experience required of MS in management program applicants. Nonprofit experience required of MS in nonprofit management program applicants.

EMPLOYMENT INFORMATION
Placement Office Available? Yes.

RENSSELAER POLYTECHNIC INSTITUTE
School of Humanities & Social Sciences

Address: 110 Eighth Street, Troy, NY 12180-3590
Admissions Phone: 518-276-6216 · **Admissions Fax:** 518-276-4072
Admissions E-mail: admissions@rpi.edu

INSTITUTIONAL INFORMATION
Public/private: Private (nonprofit). **Evening Classes Available?** Yes. **Students in Parent Institution:** 8,022.

STUDENT INFORMATION
Total Students in Program: 2,855. **% Full-time:** 53. **% Female:** 27.

RESEARCH FACILITIES
Research Facilities: Center for Image Processing Research, NYS Center for Polymer Synthesis, Center for Integrated Electronics & Electronics Manufacturing, Center for Composite Materials & Structures, Lighting Research Center, Darrin Fresh Water Institute.

EXPENSES/FINANCIAL AID
Annual Tuition: $12,600. **Fees:** $1,317. **Books and Supplies:** $1,800. **Loans Range From:** $100-$8,500.

ADMISSIONS INFORMATION
Application Fee: $45. **Regular Notification:** Rolling. **Transfer Students Accepted?** Yes. **Transfer Policy:** Maximum 6 credit hours may be transferred into master's programs; maximum 45 credit horus may be transferred. **Number of Applications Received:** 203. **% of Applicants Accepted:** 70. **% Accepted Who Enrolled:** 41. **Average GPA:** 3.4. **Average GRE Verbal:** 576. **Average GRE Quantitative:** 649. **Average GRE Analytical:** 641.
Required Admission Factors: Essays/personal statement, GRE, letters of recommendation, transcript.
Program-Specific Admission Factors: Portfolio required of MFA program applicants.

EMPLOYMENT INFORMATION
Placement Office Available? Yes. **Average starting salary:** $65,194.

RENSSELAER POLYTECHNIC INSTITUTE
School of Science

Address: 110 Eighth Street, Troy, NY 12180-3590
Admissions Phone: 518-276-6216 · **Admissions Fax:** 518-276-4072
Admissions E-mail: admissions@rpi.edu

INSTITUTIONAL INFORMATION
Public/private: Private (nonprofit). **Evening Classes Available?** Yes. Students in Parent Institution: 8,022.

STUDENT INFORMATION
Total Students in Program: 2,855. **% Full-time:** 53. **% Female:** 27.

RESEARCH FACILITIES
Research Facilities: Center for Image Processing Research, NYS Center for Polymer Synthesis, Center for Integrated Electronics & Electronics Manufacturing, Center for Composite Materials & Structures, Lighting Research Center, Darrin Fresh Water Institute.

EXPENSES/FINANCIAL AID
Annual Tuition: In-state $12,600. **Fees:** $1,317. **Books and Supplies:** $1,800. **Loans Range From:** $100-$8,500.

ADMISSIONS INFORMATION
Application Fee: $45. **Regular Notification:** Rolling. **Transfer Students Accepted?** Yes. **Transfer Policy:** Maximum 6 credit hours may be transferred into master's programs; maximum 45 credit hours may be transferred into PhD programs. **Number of Applications Received:** 878. **% of Applicants Accepted:** 43. **% Accepted Who Enrolled:** 49. **Average GPA:** 3.4. **Average GRE Verbal:** 538. **Average GRE Quantitative:** 749. **Average GRE Analytical:** 691.
Required Admission Factors: Essays/personal statement, GRE, letters of recommendation, transcript.

EMPLOYMENT INFORMATION
Placement Office Available? Yes. **Average starting salary:** $65,194.

RHODE ISLAND COLLEGE
School of Social Work

Address: Providence, RI 02908
Admissions Phone: 401-456-8042 · **Admissions Fax:** 401-456-8620
Admissions E-mail: gmetrey@grog.ric.edu

INSTITUTIONAL INFORMATION
Public/private: Public. **Total Faculty:** 13. **% Faculty Female:** 69. **Students in Parent Institution:** 8,513.

STUDENT INFORMATION
Total Students in Program: 1,596. **% Full-time:** 19. **% Female:** 80.

EXPENSES/FINANCIAL AID
Annual Tuition: In-state $3,060. / Out-of-state $6,390. **Fees:** $338. **Books and Supplies:** $600.

ADMISSIONS INFORMATION
Application Fee: $25. **Transfer Students Accepted?** Yes. **Number of Applications Received:** 222. **% of Applicants Accepted:** 45. **% Accepted Who Enrolled:** 80. **Average GPA:** 3.35.
Required Admission Factors: Essays/personal statement, transcript.
Other Admission Factors: Minimum 3.0 GPA and minimum 15 credit hours of course work in social & behavioral science and course content in human biology required.

EMPLOYMENT INFORMATION
Placement Office Available? Yes. **Rate of placement:** 75%.

RHODE ISLAND SCHOOL OF DESIGN
Graduate Studies

Address: 2 College Street, Providence, RI 02903
Admissions Phone: 401-454-6300 · **Admissions Fax:** 401-454-6309
Admissions E-mail: admissions@risd.edu · **Website:** www.risd.edu

INSTITUTIONAL INFORMATION
Public/private: Private (nonprofit). **Students in Parent Institution:** 2,282.

PROGRAMS
Masters offered in: Architecture (BArch, BA/BS, MArch, MA/MS, PhD); art teacher education; ceramic arts and ceramics; cinematography and film/video production; fiber, textile, and weaving arts; graphic design; industrial design; interior architecture; intermedia/multimedia; landscape architecture (BS, BSla, Bla, MSLA, MLA, PhD); metal and jewelry arts; painting; photography; printmaking; sculpture; visual and performing arts.

STUDENT INFORMATION
Total Students in Program: 400. **% Full-time:** 100. **% Female:** 62. **% Minority:** 19. **% International:** 14.

RESEARCH FACILITIES
Research Facilities: Edna Lawrence Nature Lab, The Center for Design and Business, The Sheridan Center for Teaching and Learning at Brown University.

EXPENSES/FINANCIAL AID
Annual Tuition: $27,510. **Room & Board:** $7,720. **Fees:** $445. **Books and Supplies:** $2,000. **Grants Range From:** $500-$11,750. **Loans Range From:** $18,500-$33,000. **% Receiving Financial Aid:** 90. **% Receiving Scholarships/Grants:** 3. **% Receiving Loans:** 50. **% Receiving Assistantships:** 60. **% Receiving Other Aid (college work-study program):** 46. **Types of Aid Available:** Fellowships, graduate assistantships, institutional work-study, scholarships, presidential scholarships, awards of excellence. **Number of Teaching/Research Assistantships Granted Each Year:** 240. **Assistantship Compensation Includes:** Salary/stipend.

ADMISSIONS INFORMATION
Application Fee: $50. **Regular Application Deadline:** 1/21. **Regular Notification:** 3/24. **Transfer Students Accepted?** No. **Number of Applications Received:** 1,874. **% of Applicants Accepted:** 21. **% Accepted Who Enrolled:** 48. **Average GPA:** 3.3.
Required Admission Factors: Essays/personal statement, letters of recommendation, transcript.
Other Admission Factors: Portfolio of artwork reflecting interest in the applicant's intended major.

EMPLOYMENT INFORMATION
Placement Office Available? Yes.

RICE UNIVERSITY
School of Humanities

Address: 6100 Main Street MS13, Houston, TX 77005
Admissions Phone: 713-527-4002

INSTITUTIONAL INFORMATION
Students in Parent Institution: 4,400.

STUDENT INFORMATION
Total Students in Program: 1,724. **% Full-time:** 97. **% Female:** 37.

RESEARCH FACILITIES
Research Facilities: Center for Research on Parallel Computation, Computer and Information Technology Institute, Energy and Environmental Systems Institute, Institute of Biosciences and Bioengineering, Rice Quantum Institute.

EXPENSES/FINANCIAL AID
Annual Tuition: $17,800. Fees: $250.

ADMISSIONS INFORMATION
Application Fee: $25. Transfer Students Accepted? No. Number of Applications Received: 266. % of Applicants Accepted: 28. % Accepted Who Enrolled: 75.

Required Admission Factors: GRE, transcript.

Other Admission Factors: GRE subject exam and essay may be required for some programs. Interview recommended by some departments. GPA requirements vary by program/department.

Program-Specific Admission Factors: Writing sample required of applicants to history, French studies, linguistics, and literature programs. Applicants to Spanish program must have near-native command of Spanish language.

EMPLOYMENT INFORMATION
Placement Office Available? Yes.

RICE UNIVERSITY
School of Social Sciences

Address: 6100 Main Street MS13, Houston, TX 77005
Admissions E-mail: stein-a@rice.ecu

INSTITUTIONAL INFORMATION
Students in Parent Institution: 4,400.

STUDENT INFORMATION
Total Students in Program: 1,724. % Full-time: 97. % Female: 37.

RESEARCH FACILITIES
Research Facilities: Center for Research on Parallel Computation, Computer and Information Technology Institute, Energy and Environmental Systems Institute, Institute of Biosciences and Bioengineering, Rice Quantum Institute.

EXPENSES/FINANCIAL AID
Annual Tuition: $17,800. Fees: $250. % Receiving Financial Aid: 71.

ADMISSIONS INFORMATION
Application Fee: $25. Transfer Students Accepted? Yes. Number of Applications Received: 270. % of Applicants Accepted: 19. % Accepted Who Enrolled: 62. Average GPA: 3.49. Average GRE Verbal: 625. Average GRE Quantitative: 753.

Required Admission Factors: Essays/personal statement, GRE, transcript.

Other Admission Factors: Minimum GRE score in 75th percentile required. Other exams may be required; specific tests vary by department.

EMPLOYMENT INFORMATION
Placement Office Available? Yes.

RICE UNIVERSITY
Shepherd School of Music

Address: 6100 Main Street MS532, Houston, TX 77005
Admissions Phone: 713-348-4854 · Admissions Fax: 713-348-5317
Admissions E-mail: gasmith@ruf.rice.edu · Website: www.rice.edu/music

INSTITUTIONAL INFORMATION
Public/private: Private (nonprofit). Total Faculty: 50. Student/faculty Ratio: 6:1. Students in Parent Institution: 4,800

PROGRAMS
Masters offered in: Conducting; music history, literature, and theory; music performance; music theory and composition; musicology and ethnomusicology; piano and organ; violin, viola, guitar, and other stringed instruments; voice and opera. Doctorate offered in: Music performance; music theory and composi-

tion; piano and organ; violin, viola, guitar, and other stringed instruments; voice and opera.

STUDENT INFORMATION
Total Students in Program: 166. % Full-time: 96.

RESEARCH FACILITIES
Research Facilities: Center for Research on Parallel Computation, Computer and Information Technology Institute, Energy and Environmental Systems Institute, Institute of Biosciences and Bioengineering, Rice Quantum Institute.

EXPENSES/FINANCIAL AID
Annual Tuition: $21,200. Room & Board: $8,380. Fees: $854. Books and Supplies: $800. Types of Aid Available: Institutional work-study, loans, scholarships.

ADMISSIONS INFORMATION
Application Fee: $35. Regular Application Deadline: 1/3. Regular Notification: Rolling. Transfer Students Accepted? Yes. Number of Applications Received: 458. % of Applicants Accepted: 20. % Accepted Who Enrolled: 64.

Required Admission Factors: Letters of recommendation, transcript.

Program-Specific Admission Factors: Portfolio required of composition program applicants. Audition required of performance program applicants. Interview required of musicology program applicants.

RICE UNIVERSITY
Wiess School of Natural Sciences

Address: 6100 Main Street MS13, Houston, TX 77005

INSTITUTIONAL INFORMATION
Students in Parent Institution: 4,400.

STUDENT INFORMATION
Total Students in Program: 1,724. % Full-time: 97. % Female: 37.

RESEARCH FACILITIES
Research Facilities: Center for Research on Parallel Computation, Computer and Information Technology Institute, Energy and Environmental Systems Institute, Institute of Biosciences and Bioengineering, Rice Quantum Institute.

EXPENSES/FINANCIAL AID
Annual Tuition: $17,800. Fees: $250.

ADMISSIONS INFORMATION
Transfer Students Accepted? No. Number of Applications Received: 613. % of Applicants Accepted: 20. % Accepted Who Enrolled: 46.

EMPLOYMENT INFORMATION
Placement Office Available? Yes.

RIDER UNIVERSITY
Westminster Choir College—The School of Music of Rider University

Address: 2083 Lawrenceville Road, Lawrenceville, NJ 08648-3099
Admissions Phone: 609-921-7144 or 800-96-CHOIR
Admissions Fax: 609-921-2538 · Admissions E-mail: mtrittlo@rider.edu
Website: www.rider.edu

INSTITUTIONAL INFORMATION
Public/private: Private (nonprofit). Student/faculty Ratio: 2:1. Students in Parent Institution: 5,274.

STUDENT INFORMATION

Total Students in Program: 1,096. **% Full-time:** 19. **% Female:** 66.

EXPENSES/FINANCIAL AID

Annual Tuition: $21,820. **Room & Board:** $10,210. **Fees:** $480. **Books and Supplies:** $600. **Grants Range From:** $35-$11,320. **Loans Range From:** $100-$21,088. **% Receiving Financial Aid:** 94. **% Receiving Scholarships/Grants:** 30. **% Receiving Loans:** 62. **% Receiving Assistantships:** 35. **Average student debt, upon graduation:** $20,000.

ADMISSIONS INFORMATION

Application Fee: $40. **Transfer Students Accepted?** Yes. **Number of Applications Received:** 100. **% of Applicants Accepted:** 53. **% Accepted Who Enrolled:** 62. **Average GPA:** 3.5.
Required Admission Factors: Essays/personal statement, letters of recommendation, transcript.

ROBERT MORRIS UNIVERSITY
(FORMERLY ROBERT MORRIS COLLEGE)
School of Communications & Information Systems

Address: 881 Narrows Run Road, Moon Township, PA 15108-1189
Admissions Phone: 412-262-8304 · **Admissions Fax:** 412-299-2425
Admissions E-mail: laurenzi@rmu.edu

INSTITUTIONAL INFORMATION

Public/private: Private (nonprofit). **Evening Classes Available?** Yes. **Student/faculty Ratio:** 12:1. **Students in Parent Institution:** 4,719.

STUDENT INFORMATION

Total Students in Program: 906 **% Female:** 45.

RESEARCH FACILITIES

Research Facilities: Learning Factory, manufacturing center.

EXPENSES/FINANCIAL AID

Annual Tuition: $7,380. **Room & Board:** $8,480. **Books and Supplies:** $400. **Grants Range From:** $250-$3,000. **Loans Range From:** $300-$18,500. **% Receiving Financial Aid:** 28. **% Receiving Loans:** 19. **% Receiving Assistantships:** 1.

ADMISSIONS INFORMATION

Application Fee: $35. **Regular Notification:** Rolling. **Transfer Students Accepted?** Yes. **Transfer Policy:** No credit hours may be transferred into doctoral program. **Number of Applications Received:** 210. **% of Applicants Accepted:** 73. **% Accepted Who Enrolled:** 79. **Average GPA:** 3.2.
Required Admission Factors: Interview, letters of recommendation, transcript.
Program-Specific Admission Factors: 3 letters of recommendation, employer endorsement, and interview required of doctoral program applicants.

EMPLOYMENT INFORMATION

Placement Office Available? Yes. **% of master's grads employed in their field upon graduation:** 89. **Rate of placement:** 95%.

ROBERTS WESLEYAN COLLEGE
Graduate Programs

Address: 2301 Westside Drive, Rochester, NY 14624-1997
Admissions Phone: 716-594-6600 · **Admissions Fax:** 716-594-6585

INSTITUTIONAL INFORMATION

Public/private: Private (nonprofit). **Evening Classes Available?** Yes. **Students in Parent Institution:** 1,596.

STUDENT INFORMATION

Total Students in Program: 388. **% Full-time:** 55. **% Female:** 67.

EXPENSES/FINANCIAL AID

Grants Range From: $500-$3,600. **Loans Range From:** $18,500. **% Receiving Financial Aid:** 75. **% Receiving Scholarships/Grants:** 24. **% Receiving Loans:** 92.

ADMISSIONS INFORMATION

Application Fee: $35. **Regular Notification:** Rolling. **Transfer Students Accepted?** Yes. **Number of Applications Received:** 36. **% of Applicants Accepted:** 83. **% Accepted Who Enrolled:** 73.
Required Admission Factors: Essays/personal statement, letters of recommendation, transcript.

EMPLOYMENT INFORMATION

Placement Office Available? Yes. **% of master's grads employed in their field upon graduation:** 70. **Rate of placement:** 96%. **Average starting salary:** $34,000.

ROCHESTER INSTITUTE OF TECHNOLOGY
College of Imaging Arts & Sciences

Address: 60 Lomb Memorial Drive, Rochester, NY 14623

INSTITUTIONAL INFORMATION

Public/private: Private (nonprofit). **Students in Parent Institution:** 13,230.

RESEARCH FACILITIES

Research Facilities: RIT Research Corporation, Center for Integrated Manufacturing Studies, Center for Imaging Science, Center for Microelectronic Engineering, National Technical Institute for the Deaf.

EXPENSES/FINANCIAL AID

Annual Tuition: $20,142.

ADMISSIONS INFORMATION

Application Fee: $40. **Regular Notification:** Rolling. **Transfer Students Accepted?** No. **Number of Applications Received:** 2,054. **% of Applicants Accepted:** 54.
Required Admission Factors: Essays/personal statement, letters of recommendation, transcript.
Other Admission Factors: Minimum 3.0 GPA and portfolio required.

EMPLOYMENT INFORMATION

Placement Office Available? Yes.

ROCHESTER INSTITUTE OF TECHNOLOGY
College of Liberal Arts

Address: 60 Lomb Memorial Drive, Rochester, NY 14623

INSTITUTIONAL INFORMATION

Public/private: Private (nonprofit). **Students in Parent Institution:** 13,230.

RESEARCH FACILITIES

Research Facilities: RIT Research Corporation, Center for Integrated Manufacturing Studies, Center for Imaging Science, Center for Microelectronic Engineering, National Technical Institute for the Deaf.

EXPENSES/FINANCIAL AID

Annual Tuition: In-state $20,142.

ADMISSIONS INFORMATION

Application Fee: $40. **Regular Notification:** Rolling. **Transfer Students Accepted?** Yes. **Number of Applications Received:** 2,054. **% of Applicants Accepted:** 54.

Required Admission Factors: Essays/personal statement, GRE, interview, letters of recommendation, transcript.
Other Admission Factors: Minimum GRE scores of 550 Verbal, 500 Quantitative, 500 Analytical, and minimum 3.0 GPA required.

EMPLOYMENT INFORMATION
Placement Office Available? Yes.

ROCHESTER INSTITUTE OF TECHNOLOGY
College of Science

Address: 60 Lomb Memorial Drive, Rochester, NY 14623

INSTITUTIONAL INFORMATION
Public/private: Private (nonprofit). **Evening Classes Available?** Yes. **Students in Parent Institution:** 13,230.

RESEARCH FACILITIES
Research Facilities: RIT Research Corporation, Center for Integrated Manufacturing Studies, Center for Imaging Science, Center for Microelectronic Engineering, National Technical Institute for the Deaf.

EXPENSES/FINANCIAL AID
Annual Tuition: $20,142.

ADMISSIONS INFORMATION
Application Fee: $40. **Regular Notification:** Rolling. **Transfer Students Accepted?** Yes. **Number of Applications Received:** 2,054. **% of Applicants Accepted:** 54.
Required Admission Factors: Essays/personal statement, GRE, letters of recommendation, transcript.
Other Admission Factors: Minimum 3.0 GPA required.

EMPLOYMENT INFORMATION
Placement Office Available? Yes.

ROCKHURST UNIVERSITY
Communication Sciences/Disorders Program

Address: 1100 Rockhurst Road, Kansas City, MO 64110-2561
Admissions Phone: 816-501-4097 · **Admissions Fax:** 816-501-4241
Admissions E-mail: graduate.admission@rockhurst.edu
Website: www.rockhurst.edu/admission/grad/csd/welcome.asp

INSTITUTIONAL INFORMATION
Public/private: Private (nonprofit). **Evening Classes Available?** Yes. **Total Faculty:** 8. **% Faculty Female:** 100. **% Faculty Part-time:** 12. **Student/faculty Ratio:** 7:1. **Students in Parent Institution:** 2,764.

STUDENT INFORMATION
Total Students in Program: 48. **% Full-time:** 77. **% Female:** 98. **% Minority:** 10.

RESEARCH FACILITIES
Research Facilities: Richardson Science Center.

EXPENSES/FINANCIAL AID
Annual Tuition: $7,380. **Room & Board:** $5,800. **Fees:** $30. **Books and Supplies:** $90. **Grants Range From:** $500-$12,000. **Loans Range From:** $100-$18,500. **Types of Aid Available:** Graduate assistantships, loans.

ADMISSIONS INFORMATION
Application Fee: $25. **Regular Application Deadline:** 8/22. **Regular Notification:** Rolling. **Transfer Students Accepted?** Yes. **Number of Applications Received:** 41. **% of Applicants Accepted:** 39. **% Accepted Who Enrolled:** 100.

Required Admission Factors: Essays/personal statement, GRE, interview, letters of recommendation, transcript.
Other Admission Factors: Minimum 3.0 GPA (3.0 in major) required.
Program-Specific Admission Factors: Prerequisite course work sheet.

EMPLOYMENT INFORMATION
Placement Office Available? Yes.

ROCKHURST UNIVERSITY
Master of Education

Address: 1100 Rockhurst Road, Kansas City, MO 64110-2561
Admissions Phone: 816-501-4097 · **Admissions Fax:** 816-501-4241
Admissions E-mail: graduate.admission@rockhurst.edu
Website: www.rockhurst.edu/admission/grad/med/welcome.asp

INSTITUTIONAL INFORMATION
Public/private: Private (nonprofit). **Evening Classes Available?** Yes. **Total Faculty:** 14. **% Faculty Female:** 71. **% Faculty Part-time:** 29. **Student/faculty Ratio:** 16:1. **Students in Parent Institution:** 2,764.

STUDENT INFORMATION
Total Students in Program: 176. **% Full-time:** 35. **% Female:** 70. **% Minority:** 22.

RESEARCH FACILITIES
Research Facilities: Richardson Science Center.

EXPENSES/FINANCIAL AID
Annual Tuition: $5,400. **Room & Board:** $5,800. **Fees:** $30. **Books and Supplies:** $90. **Grants Range From:** $500-$12,000. **Loans Range From:** $100-$18,500.

ADMISSIONS INFORMATION
Application Fee: $25. **Regular Application Deadline:** 8/22. **Regular Notification:** Rolling. **Transfer Students Accepted?** Yes. **Transfer Policy:** Minimum 3.0 GPA required. **Number of Applications Received:** 137. **% of Applicants Accepted:** 77. **% Accepted Who Enrolled:** 74.
Required Admission Factors: Essays/personal statement, letters of recommendation, transcript.
Other Admission Factors: Minimum 2.5 GPA required.

EMPLOYMENT INFORMATION
Placement Office Available? Yes.

ROCKHURST UNIVERSITY
Occupational Therapy Program

Address: 1100 Rockhurst Road, Kansas City, MO 64110-2561
Admissions Phone: 816-501-4097 · **Admissions Fax:** 816-501-4241
Admissions E-mail: graduate.admission@rockhurst.edu
Website: www.rockhurst.edu/admission/grad/ot/welcome.asp

INSTITUTIONAL INFORMATION
Public/private: Private (nonprofit). **Total Faculty:** 6. **% Faculty Female:** 100. **% Faculty Part-time:** 33. **Student/faculty Ratio:** 9:1. **Students in Parent Institution:** 2,764.

STUDENT INFORMATION
Total Students in Program: 42. **% Full-time:** 100. **% Female:** 93. **% Minority:** 14.

RESEARCH FACILITIES
Research Facilities: Richardson Science Center.

EXPENSES/FINANCIAL AID
Annual Tuition: $7,380. **Room & Board:** $5,800. **Fees:** $30. **Books and Supplies:** $90. **Grants Range From:** $500-$12,000. **Loans Range From:** $100-$18,500. **Types of Aid Available:** Graduate assistantships, loans.

ADMISSIONS INFORMATION

Application Fee: $25. **Regular Application Deadline:** 8/22. **Regular Notification:** Rolling. **Transfer Students Accepted?** Yes. **Number of Applications Received:** 34. **% of Applicants Accepted:** 74. **% Accepted Who Enrolled:** 68.
Required Admission Factors: Essays/personal statement, letters of recommendation, transcript.
Recommended Admission Factors: Interview.
Other Admission Factors: Minimum 3.0 GPA required.
Program-Specific Admission Factors: Prerequisite course work sheet, observation hours completed.

EMPLOYMENT INFORMATION

Placement Office Available? Yes.

ROCKHURST UNIVERSITY
Physical Therapy Program

Address: 1100 Rockhurst Road, Kansas City, MO 64110-2561
Admissions Phone: 816-501-4097 · **Admissions Fax:** 816-501-4241
Admissions E-mail: graduate.admission@rockhurst.edu
Website: www.rockhurst.edu/admission/grad/pt/welcome.asp

INSTITUTIONAL INFORMATION

Public/private: Private (nonprofit). **Total Faculty:** 8. **% Faculty Female:** 62. **% Faculty Part-time:** 12. **Student/faculty Ratio:** 8:1. **Students in Parent Institution:** 2,764.

STUDENT INFORMATION

Total Students in Program: 68. **% Full-time:** 71. **% Female:** 71. **% Minority:** 15. **% International:** 1.

RESEARCH FACILITIES

Research Facilities: Richardson Science Center.

EXPENSES/FINANCIAL AID

Annual Tuition: $7,380. **Room & Board:** $5,800. **Fees:** $30. **Books and Supplies:** $90. **Grants Range From:** $500-$12,000. **Loans Range From:** $100-$18,500. **Types of Aid Available:** Graduate assistantships, loans.

ADMISSIONS INFORMATION

Application Fee: $25. **Regular Application Deadline:** 8/22. **Regular Notification:** Rolling. **Transfer Students Accepted?** Yes. **Number of Applications Received:** 72. **% of Applicants Accepted:** 56. **% Accepted Who Enrolled:** 72.
Required Admission Factors: Essays/personal statement, letters of recommendation, transcript.
Recommended Admission Factors: Interview.
Other Admission Factors: Minimum 3.0 GPA required.
Program-Specific Admission Factors: Prerequisite course work sheet, physical therapy experience.

EMPLOYMENT INFORMATION

Placement Office Available? Yes.

ROSE-HULMAN INSTITUTE OF TECHNOLOGY
Graduate Programs

Address: 5500 Wabash Avenue, Terre Haute, IN 47803
Admissions Phone: 812-877-8403 · **Admissions Fax:** 812-877-8061
Admissions E-mail: teresa.l.gosnell@rose-hulman.edu

INSTITUTIONAL INFORMATION

Public/private: Private (nonprofit). **Evening Classes Available?** Yes. **Total Faculty:** 132. **% Faculty Female:** 14. **% Faculty Part-time:** 11. **Student/faculty Ratio:** 1:1. **Students in Parent Institution:** 1,725.

STUDENT INFORMATION

Total Students in Program: 144. **% Full-time:** 40. **% Female:** 17.

RESEARCH FACILITIES

Research Facilities: Center for Applied Optics Studies, Eli Lilly & Co. Applied Life Sciences Research Center, Imaging Systems Lab, Center for Industrial Statistics, John T. Meyers Center for Technological Research with Industry.

EXPENSES/FINANCIAL AID

Annual Tuition: $21,792. **Fees:** $324. **Grants Range From:** $20,559-$28,059. **Loans Range From:** $1,000-$8,500. **% Receiving Financial Aid:** 52. **% Receiving Scholarships/Grants:** 47. **% Receiving Assistantships:** 21. **Number of Fellowships Granted Each Year:** 9. **Average amount of individual fellowships per year:** $25,000. **Number of Teaching/Research Assistantships Granted Each Year:** 4. **Average Salary Stipend:** $2,500.

ADMISSIONS INFORMATION

Regular Notification: Rolling. **Transfer Students Accepted?** Yes. **Number of Applications Received:** 88. **% of Applicants Accepted:** 75. **% Accepted Who Enrolled:** 74. **Average GPA:** 3.3. **Average GRE Verbal:** 376. **Average GRE Quantitative:** 650. **Average GRE Analytical:** 521.
Required Admission Factors: Letters of recommendation, transcript.
Other Admission Factors: Minimum 3.0 GPA required.

EMPLOYMENT INFORMATION

Placement Office Available? Yes. **% Employed Within 6 Months:** 98. **Rate of placement:** 98%. **Average starting salary:** $68,000.

RUTGERS UNIVERSITY—CAMDEN
Graduate School—Camden

Address: 311 North 5ᵗʰ Street, Camden, NJ 08102
Admissions Phone: 856-225-6056 · **Admissions Fax:** 856-225-6498

INSTITUTIONAL INFORMATION

Public/private: Public. **Evening Classes Available?** Yes. **Students in Parent Institution:** 5,135.

STUDENT INFORMATION

Total Students in Program: 658. **% Full-time:** 20. **% Female:** 51.

RESEARCH FACILITIES

Research Facilities: Walter Rand Institute of Public Affairs.

EXPENSES/FINANCIAL AID

Annual Tuition: In-state $6,776. / Out-of-state $9,936. **Room & Board:** $7,374. **Number of Fellowships Granted Each Year:** 20. **Average amount of individual fellowships per year:** 1,000. **Number of Teaching/Research Assistantships Granted Each Year:** 17. **Average Salary Stipend:** $6,500.

ADMISSIONS INFORMATION

Application Fee: $50. **Regular Notification:** Rolling. **Transfer Students Accepted?** Yes. **Number of Applications Received:** 562. **% of Applicants Accepted:** 33. **Average GPA:** 3.2. **Average GRE Verbal:** 506. **Average GRE Quantitative:** 544. **Average GRE Analytical:** 563.
Required Admission Factors: Essays/personal statement, GRE, letters of recommendation, transcript.
Program-Specific Admission Factors: GRE required for all programs except master in library studies. GRE subject exam (English Literature) required of English program applicants.

EMPLOYMENT INFORMATION

Placement Office Available? Yes.

RUTGERS UNIVERSITY—NEW BRUNSWICK
Edward J. Bloustein School of Planning & Public Policy

Address: College Avenue, New Brunswick, NJ 08901
Admissions Phone: 732-932-7711 · **Admissions Fax:** 732-932-8731
Admissions E-mail: macvee@rci.rutgers.edu

INSTITUTIONAL INFORMATION
Public/private: Public. **Students in Parent Institution:** 35,237.

STUDENT INFORMATION
Total Students in Program: 7,098. **% Full-time:** 37. **% Female:** 62.

RESEARCH FACILITIES
Research Facilities: More than 50 research centers and bureaus.

EXPENSES/FINANCIAL AID
Annual Tuition: In-state $6,776. / Out-of-state $9,936. **Room & Board:** $7,374. **Types of Aid Available:** 1. **Number of Fellowships Granted Each Year:** 12. **Average amount of individual fellowships per year:** $22,000. **Number of Teaching/Research Assistantships Granted Each Year:** 28. **Average Salary Stipend:** $14,000.

ADMISSIONS INFORMATION
Application Fee: $50. **Transfer Students Accepted?** No. **Number of Applications Received:** 230. **% of Applicants Accepted:** 73. **% Accepted Who Enrolled:** 39. **Average GPA:** 3.26. **Average GRE Verbal:** 550. **Average GRE Quantitative:** 610. **Average GRE Analytical:** 630.
Required Admission Factors: Essays/personal statement, GRE, letters of recommendation, transcript.
Other Admission Factors: Minimum grade average of B required.

RUTGERS UNIVERSITY—NEW BRUNSWICK
Graduate School of Applied & Professional Psychology

Address: College Avenue, New Brunswick, NJ 08901
Admissions Phone: 732-932-7711 · **Admissions Fax:** 732-932-8231
Admissions E-mail: macvee@rci.rutgers.edu

INSTITUTIONAL INFORMATION
Public/private: Public. **Total Faculty:** 16. **Students in Parent Institution:** 35,237.

STUDENT INFORMATION
Total Students in Program: 7,098. **% Full-time:** 37. **% Female:** 62.

RESEARCH FACILITIES
Research Facilities: More than 50 research centers and bureaus.

EXPENSES/FINANCIAL AID
Annual Tuition: In-state $6,776. / Out-of-state $9,936. **Room & Board:** $7,374.

ADMISSIONS INFORMATION
Application Fee: $40. **Transfer Students Accepted?** Yes. **Number of Applications Received:** 469. **% of Applicants Accepted:** 10. **% Accepted Who Enrolled:** 67. **Average GPA:** 3.51. **Average GRE Verbal:** 579. **Average GRE Quantitative:** 607. **Average GRE Analytical:** 620.
Required Admission Factors: Essays/personal statement, GRE, letters of recommendation, transcript.

RUTGERS UNIVERSITY—NEW BRUNSWICK
Mason Gross School of the Arts

Address: College Avenue, New Brunswick, NJ 08901
Admissions Phone: 732-932-7711 · **Admissions Fax:** 732-932-8231
Admissions E-mail: macvee@rci.rutgers.edu

INSTITUTIONAL INFORMATION
Public/private: Public. **Students in Parent Institution:** 35,237.

STUDENT INFORMATION
Total Students in Program: 7,098. **% Full-time:** 37. **% Female:** 62.

RESEARCH FACILITIES
Research Facilities: More than 50 research centers and bureaus.

EXPENSES/FINANCIAL AID
Annual Tuition: In-state $6,776. / Out-of-state $9,936. **Room & Board:** $7,374.

ADMISSIONS INFORMATION
Application Fee: $50. **Regular Notification:** Rolling. **Transfer Students Accepted?** Yes. **Number of Applications Received:** 485. **% of Applicants Accepted:** 30. **% Accepted Who Enrolled:** 62. **Average GPA:** 3.45.
Required Admission Factors: Essays/personal statement, letters of recommendation, transcript.
Program-Specific Admission Factors: Audition and diagnostic exams in music history and theory required of music program applicants. Writing sample required of doctorate in music arts program applicants. Audition required of acting program applicants. Portfolio required of playwriting, design/stage management program applicants.

RUTGERS UNIVERSITY—NEW BRUNSWICK
School of Communication, Information & Library Studies

Address: College Avenue, New Brunswick, NJ 08901
Admissions Phone: 732-932-7711 · **Admissions Fax:** 732-932-8231

INSTITUTIONAL INFORMATION
Public/private: Public. **Students in Parent Institution:** 35,237.

STUDENT INFORMATION
Total Students in Program: 7,098. **% Full-time:** 37. **% Female:** 62.

RESEARCH FACILITIES
Research Facilities: More than 50 research centers and bureaus.

EXPENSES/FINANCIAL AID
Annual Tuition: In-state $6,776. / Out-of-state $9,936. **Room & Board:** $7,374. **Average Salary Stipend:** $14,000.

ADMISSIONS INFORMATION
Application Fee: $40. **Transfer Students Accepted?** Yes. **Number of Applications Received:** 497. **% of Applicants Accepted:** 76. **% Accepted Who Enrolled:** 73. **Average GPA:** 3.22. **Average GRE Verbal:** 552. **Average GRE Quantitative:** 566. **Average GRE Analytical:** 575.
Required Admission Factors: Essays/personal statement, GRE, letters of recommendation, transcript.
Program-Specific Admission Factors: Minimum grade average of B required of master of library science program applicants. Minimum GRE score of 1000 and minimum 3.0 GPA required of master of communication/information studies program applicants.

RUTGERS UNIVERSITY—NEW BRUNSWICK
School of Social Work

Address: College Avenue, New Brunswick, NJ 08901
Admissions Phone: 732-932-7711 · **Admissions Fax:** 732-932-8231
Admissions E-mail: macvee@rci.rutgers.edu

INSTITUTIONAL INFORMATION
Public/private: Public. **Students in Parent Institution:** 35,237.

STUDENT INFORMATION
Total Students in Program: 7,098. **% Full-time:** 37. **% Female:** 62.

RESEARCH FACILITIES
Research Facilities: More than 50 research centers and bureaus.

EXPENSES/FINANCIAL AID
Annual Tuition: In-state $6,776. / Out-of-state $9,936. **Room & Board:** $7,374.

ADMISSIONS INFORMATION
Application Fee: $50. **Regular Notification:** Rolling. **Transfer Students Accepted?** No. **Number of Applications Received:** 600. **% of Applicants Accepted:** 74. **% Accepted Who Enrolled:** 57. **Average GPA:** 3.27.
Required Admission Factors: Essays/personal statement, letters of recommendation, transcript.
Other Admission Factors: Minimum grade average of B required.

RUTGERS UNIVERSITY—NEW BRUNSWICK
The Graduate School—New Brunswick

Address: Graduate and Professional Admissions, 18 Bishop Place,
New Brunswick, NJ 08901
Admissions Phone: 732-932-7711 · **Admissions Fax:** 732-932-8231
Admissions E-mail: gradadm@rci.rutgers.edu · **Website:** http://gradstudy.rutgers.edu

INSTITUTIONAL INFORMATION
Public/private: Public. **Total Faculty:** 2,285. **% Faculty Female:** 35. **% Faculty Part-time:** 34. **Student/faculty Ratio:** 3:1. **Students in Parent Institution:** 35,318.

PROGRAMS
Masters offered in: Aerospace, aeronautical, and astronautical engineering; agricultural/biological engineering and bioengineering; anthropology; astronomy; biochemistry/biophysics and molecular biology; biochemistry; biological and biomedical sciences; biomathematics and bioinformatics; biomedical/medical engineering; biophysics; botany/plant biology; cell/cellular biology and histology; ceramic sciences and engineering; chemical engineering; chemistry; civil engineering; classics and classical languages, literatures, and linguistics; comparative literature; computer engineering; economics; electrical, electronics, and communications engineering; engineering; foreign languages/modern languages; French language and literature; geography; geological and earth sciences/geosciences; German language and literature; humanities/humanistic studies; industrial engineering; Italian language and literature; liberal arts and sciences studies and humanities; linguistic, comparative, and related language studies and servies; linguistics; materials engineering; mathematics; mechanical engineering; meteorology; microbiology; molecular genetics; molecular pharmacology; multi/interdisciplinary studies; neurobiology and neurophysiology; operations research; pharmacology; philosophy; physics; physiology; sociology; Spanish language and literature; urban studies/affairs. **Doctorate offered in:** Aerospace, aeronautical, and astronautical engineering; agricultural/biological engineering and bioengineering; American history (United States); anthropology; astronomy; biochemistry/biophysics and molecular biology; biochemistry; biological and biomedical engineering.

STUDENT INFORMATION
Total Students in Program: 7,953. **% Full-time:** 50. **% Female:** 63. **% Minority:** 18. **% International:** 22.

RESEARCH FACILITIES
Research Facilities: More than 50 research centers and bureaus.

EXPENSES/FINANCIAL AID
Annual Tuition: In-state $8,952. / Out-of-state $13,124. **Room & Board (On/off Campus):** $8,426/$11,399. **Fees:** $1,077. **Books and Supplies:** $1,150. **% Receiving Financial Aid:** 65. **Number of Fellowships Granted Each Year:** 627. **Average amount of individual fellowships per year:** $13,800. **Number of Teaching/Research Assistantships Granted Each Year:** 1,377. **Average Salary Stipend:** $13,800.

ADMISSIONS INFORMATION
Application Fee: $50. **Regular Application Deadline:** 10/3. **Regular Notification:** Rolling. **Transfer Students Accepted?** No. **Number of Applications Received:** 10,731. **% of Applicants Accepted:** 21. **% Accepted Who Enrolled:** 56. **Average GPA:** 3.4. **Average GRE Verbal:** 554. **Average GRE Quantitative:** 707. **Average GRE Analytical:** 678. **Average GRE Analytical Writing:** 4.5.
Required Admission Factors: Essays/personal statement, GRE, letters of recommendation, transcript.
Other Admission Factors: GPA, test results, and other requirements varie by program. Admission is competitive.
Program-Specific Admission Factors: Writing sample required of anthropology, doctoral art history, English literature, history, philosphy, and doctoral sociology program applicants. Text analysis required of Spanish program applicants. Writing sample or portfolio required of music program applicants.

RUTGERS UNIVERSITY—NEWARK
Graduate School

Address: 249 University Avenue, Blumenthal Hall, Newark, NJ 07102-1872
Admissions Phone: 973-353-5205 · **Admissions Fax:** 973-353-1440

INSTITUTIONAL INFORMATION
Public/private: Public. **Evening Classes Available?** Yes. **Students in Parent Institution:** 9,352.

STUDENT INFORMATION
Total Students in Program: 2,766. **% Full-time:** 25. **% Female:** 46.

RESEARCH FACILITIES
Research Facilities: Center for Molecular and Behavioral Neural Sciences, Center for Global Studies and Governance, Cornwall Center for Metropolitan Studies.

EXPENSES/FINANCIAL AID
Annual Tuition: In-state $6,776. / Out-of-state $9,936. **Room & Board:** $7,374. **% Receiving Financial Aid:** 27. **Number of Fellowships Granted Each Year:** 44. **Average amount of individual fellowships per year:** 12,000. **Number of Teaching/Research Assistantships Granted Each Year:** 159. **Average Salary Stipend:** $13,350.

ADMISSIONS INFORMATION
Application Fee: $50. **Regular Notification:** Rolling. **Transfer Students Accepted?** Yes. **Number of Applications Received:** 1,307. **% of Applicants Accepted:** 53. **% Accepted Who Enrolled:** 67. **Average GPA:** 3.28. **Average GRE Verbal:** 486. **Average GRE Quantitative:** 553. **Average GRE Analytical:** 560.
Required Admission Factors: Essays/personal statement, GRE, letters of recommendation, transcript.
Other Admission Factors: Minimum 3.0 GPA required.
Program-Specific Admission Factors: Writing sample required of creative writing program applicants.

EMPLOYMENT INFORMATION
Placement Office Available? Yes.

RUTGERS UNIVERSITY—NEWARK
School of Criminal Justice

Address: 249 University Avenue, Blumenthal Hall, Newark, NJ 07102-1872
Admissions Phone: 973-353-5205 · **Admissions Fax:** 973-353-1440

INSTITUTIONAL INFORMATION
Public/private: Public. **Students in Parent Institution:** 9,352.

STUDENT INFORMATION
Total Students in Program: 2,766. **% Full-time:** 25. **% Female:** 46.

RESEARCH FACILITIES
Research Facilities: Center for Molecular and Behavioral Neural Sciences, Center for Global Studies and Governance, Cornwall Center for Metropolitan Studies.

EXPENSES/FINANCIAL AID
Annual Tuition: In-state $6,776. / Out-of-state $9,936. **Room & Board:** $7,374. **% Receiving Financial Aid:** 27.

ADMISSIONS INFORMATION
Application Fee: $50. **Regular Notification:** Rolling. **Transfer Students Accepted?** No. **Number of Applications Received:** 67. **% of Applicants Accepted:** 63. **% Accepted Who Enrolled:** 55. **Average GPA:** 3.27. **Average GRE Verbal:** 494. **Average GRE Quantitative:** 568. **Average GRE Analytical:** 610.
Required Admission Factors: Essays/personal statement, GRE, letters of recommendation, transcript.
Other Admission Factors: Minimum 3.0 GPA required.

EMPLOYMENT INFORMATION
Placement Office Available? Yes. **% Employed Within 6 Months:** 90. **% of master's/doctoral grads employed in their field upon graduation:** 90/100.

SACRED HEART SCHOOL OF THEOLOGY
Professional Program

Address: 7335 South Highway 100, PO Box 429, Hales Corners, WI 53130-0429
Admissions Phone: 414-529-6984 · **Admissions Fax:** 414-529-6999

INSTITUTIONAL INFORMATION
Public/private: Private (nonprofit). **Evening Classes Available?** Yes. **Students in Parent Institution:** 146.

STUDENT INFORMATION
Total Students in Program: 38. **% Female:** 47.

EXPENSES/FINANCIAL AID
Annual Tuition: $5,850. **Fees:** $100. **Books and Supplies:** $400. **% Receiving Financial Aid:** 3.

ADMISSIONS INFORMATION
Application Fee: $25. **Regular Notification:** Rolling. **Transfer Students Accepted?** Yes. **Transfer Policy:** Transfer applicants should contact the dean. **Number of Applications Received:** 32. **% of Applicants Accepted:** 100. **% Accepted Who Enrolled:** 97. **Average GPA:** 2.5.
Required Admission Factors: Essays/personal statement, transcript.
Other Admission Factors: Minimum 2.0 GPA required.

EMPLOYMENT INFORMATION
Placement Office Available? Yes. **% Employed Within 6 Months:** 100. **Rate of placement:** 100%.

SACRED HEART UNIVERSITY
Graduate Admissions

Address: 5151 Park Avenue, Fairfield, CT 06825
Admissions Phone: 203-365-7619 · **Admissions Fax:** 203-365-4732
Admissions E-mail: gradstudies@sacredheart.edu
Website: www.sacredheart.edu/graduate

INSTITUTIONAL INFORMATION
Public/private: Private (nonprofit). **Evening Classes Available?** Yes. **Total Faculty:** 143. **% Faculty Female:** 52. **% Faculty Part-time:** 57. **Student/faculty Ratio:** 13:1. **Students in Parent Institution:** 5,730.

PROGRAMS
Masters offered in: Business administration/management, chemistry, computer and information sciences, education, elementary education and teaching, family practice nurse/nurse practitioner, health/health care administration/management, liberal arts and sciences studies and humanities, nursing/registered nurse training (RN, ASN, BSN, MSN), nursing administration (MSN, MS, PhD), occupational therapy/therapist, physical therapy/therapist, reading teacher education, rehabilitation and therapeutic professions, religion/religious studies, secondary education and teaching. **First Professional degree offered in:** Physical therapy/therapist.

STUDENT INFORMATION
Total Students in Program: 1,681. **% Full-time:** 31. **% Female:** 68. **% Minority:** 11. **% International:** 2.

RESEARCH FACILITIES
Research Facilities: Center for Christian-Jewish Understanding, Sacred Heart University Polling Institute.

EXPENSES/FINANCIAL AID
Annual Tuition: $5,850. **Room & Board:** $8,000. **Fees:** $230. **Books and Supplies:** $800. **Loans Range From:** $1,000-$18,500. **% Receiving Financial Aid:** 13. **% Receiving Loans:** 90. **% Receiving Assistantships:** 10. **Types of Aid Available:** Graduate assistantships, loans. **Assistantship Compensation Includes:** Partial tuition remission, salary/stipend. **Average Salary Stipend:** $7,500.

ADMISSIONS INFORMATION
Application Fee: $50. **Regular Notification:** Rolling. **Transfer Students Accepted?** Yes. **Transfer Policy:** Transfer credits must be approved by the program director. **Number of Applications Received:** 552. **% of Applicants Accepted:** 76. **% Accepted Who Enrolled:** 80. **Average GPA:** 3.0.
Required Admission Factors: GMAT, letters of recommendation, transcript. Praxis I.

EMPLOYMENT INFORMATION
Placement Office Available? Yes. **Rate of placement:** 95%.

THE SAGE COLLEGES
Sage Graduate School

Address: 45 Ferry Street, Troy, NY 12180
Admissions Phone: 518-244-6878 · **Admissions Fax:** 518-244-6880
Admissions E-mail: lawrez@sage.edu · **Website:** www.sage.edu/SGS

INSTITUTIONAL INFORMATION
Public/private: Private (nonprofit). **Evening Classes Available?** Yes. **Total Faculty:** 78. **% Faculty Female:** 85. **Student/faculty Ratio:** 9:1. **Students in Parent Institution:** 994.

STUDENT INFORMATION
Total Students in Program: 994. **% Full-time:** 34. **% Female:** 83. **% Minority:** 9. **% International:** 1.

RESEARCH FACILITIES

Research Facilities: Affiliation with Albany Law School, Albany Medical Center, Albany College of Pharmacy.

EXPENSES/FINANCIAL AID

Annual Tuition: $7,200. **Fees:** $100. **Books and Supplies:** $800. **Grants Range From:** $500-$3,000. **Loans Range From:** $500-$18,500. **% Receiving Financial Aid:** 65. **% Receiving Scholarships/Grants:** 2. **% Receiving Loans:** 85. **% Receiving Assistantships:** 6. **Number of Teaching/Research Assistantships Granted Each Year:** 3.

ADMISSIONS INFORMATION

Application Fee: $40. **Priority Application Deadline:** 4/1. **Regular Application Deadline:** 9/1. **Regular Notification:** Rolling. **Transfer Students Accepted?** Yes. **Number of Applications Received:** 118. **% of Applicants Accepted:** 51. **% Accepted Who Enrolled:** 52. **Average GPA:** 3.0. **Required Admission Factors:** Essays/personal statement, letters of recommendation, transcript. **Recommended Admission Factors:** GRE, interview. **Other Admission Factors:** Minimum 2.75 GPA required; provisional admission possible for applicants with GPA below minimum.

EMPLOYMENT INFORMATION

Placement Office Available? Yes. **% Employed Within 6 Months:** 65. **% of master's grads employed in their field upon graduation:** 65. **Rate of placement:** 91%. **Average starting salary:** $45,000.

SAGINAW VALLEY STATE UNIVERSITY
College of Arts & Behavioral Sciences

Address: 7400 Bay Road, University Center, MI 48710
Admissions Phone: 517-790-4259 · **Admissions Fax:** 517-790-0180
Admissions E-mail: klopez@tardis.svsu.edu

INSTITUTIONAL INFORMATION

Public/private: Public. **Evening Classes Available?** Yes. **Student/faculty Ratio:** 9:1. **Students in Parent Institution:** 8,054.

STUDENT INFORMATION

Total Students in Program: 1,352. **% Full-time:** 5. **% Female:** 72.

EXPENSES/FINANCIAL AID

Annual Tuition: In-state $4,541. / Out-of-state $8,975. **Room & Board:** $7,450. **Loans Range From:** $3,002-$4,070. **% Receiving Financial Aid:** 5. **% Receiving Loans:** 9. **Average student debt, upon graduation:** $8,986.

ADMISSIONS INFORMATION

Application Fee: $25. **Regular Notification:** Rolling. **Transfer Students Accepted?** Yes. **Number of Applications Received:** 31. **% of Applicants Accepted:** 100. **% Accepted Who Enrolled:** 71. **Average GPA:** 3.08. **Required Admission Factors:** Letters of recommendation, transcript. **Other Admission Factors:** Minimum 2.75 overall GPA (minimum 3.0 in political science and criminal justice) required.

EMPLOYMENT INFORMATION

Placement Office Available? Yes.

SAINT FRANCIS SEMINARY
Graduate Programs

Address: 3257 South Lake Drive, St. Francis, WI 53235
Admissions Phone: 414-747-6411 · **Admissions Fax:** 414-747-6442
Admissions E-mail: mwitczak@sfs.edu

INSTITUTIONAL INFORMATION

Public/private: Private (nonprofit). **Students in Parent Institution:** 66.

STUDENT INFORMATION

Total Students in Program: 37 **% Female:** 76.

RESEARCH FACILITIES

Research Facilities: Salzman Library.

EXPENSES/FINANCIAL AID

Annual Tuition: In-state $8,400. **Fees:** $40. **Books and Supplies:** $1,000. **% Receiving Financial Aid:** 70. **Average student debt, upon graduation:** $3,000.

ADMISSIONS INFORMATION

Application Fee: $25. **Regular Notification:** Rolling. **Transfer Students Accepted?** Yes. **Number of Applications Received:** 24. **Required Admission Factors:** Essays/personal statement, interview, letters of recommendation, transcript.

SAINT JOSEPH'S COLLEGE (MAINE)
Graduate & Professional Studies

Address: 278 White's Bridge Road, Standish, ME 04084-5263
Admissions Phone: 800-752-4723 · **Admissions Fax:** 207-892-7480
Admissions E-mail: info@sjcme.edu · **Website:** www.sjcme.edu/gps

INSTITUTIONAL INFORMATION

Public/private: Private (nonprofit). **Total Faculty:** 39. **% Faculty Female:** 54. **% Faculty Part-time:** 85. **Students in Parent Institution:** 5,140.

PROGRAMS

Masters offered in: Adult and continuing education and teaching; business administration/management; education leadership and administration; educational, instructional, and curriculum supervision; health teacher education; health/health care administration/management; nursing administration (MSN, MS, PhD); pastoral studies/counseling; resort management; secondary education and teaching; teacher education and professional development, specific levels and methods; theology/theological studies.

STUDENT INFORMATION

Total Students in Program: 1,800 **% Female:** 72.

EXPENSES/FINANCIAL AID

Annual Tuition: $4,140. **Fees:** $100. **Books and Supplies:** $350. **Grants Range From:** $500-$10,000. **Loans Range From:** $500-$18,500. **% Receiving Financial Aid:** 67. **% Receiving Loans:** 100.

ADMISSIONS INFORMATION

Application Fee: $50. **Regular Application Deadline:** 9/1. **Regular Notification:** Rolling. **Transfer Students Accepted?** Yes. **Transfer Policy:** Transfer applicants should complete application. **Number of Applications Received:** 400. **% of Applicants Accepted:** 96. **% Accepted Who Enrolled:** 100. **Required Admission Factors:** Essays/personal statement, letters of recommendation, transcript.

EMPLOYMENT INFORMATION

Placement Office Available? Yes. **% Employed Within 6 Months:** 100. **% of master's grads employed in their field upon graduation:** 100. **Rate of placement:** 100%. **Average starting salary:** $75,000.

SAINT LOUIS UNIVERSITY
The Graduate School

Address: 3634 Lindell Boulevard, Verhaegen Hall, St. Louis, MO 63108
Admissions Phone: 314-977-2240 · **Admissions Fax:** 314-977-3943
Admissions E-mail: grequest@slu.edu · **Website:** www.slu.edu/colleges/gr

INSTITUTIONAL INFORMATION

Public/private: Private (nonprofit). **Student/faculty Ratio:** 12:1. **Students in Parent Institution:** 11,422.

PROGRAMS

Masters offered in: Administration of special education; aerospace, aeronautical, and astronautical engineering; agricultural/biological engineering and bioengineering; American history (United States); American literature (United States); anatomy; applied mathematics; atmospheric sciences and meteorology; audiology/audiologist and hearing sciences; audiology/audiologist and speech-language pathology/pathologist; Bible/Biblical studies; biochemistry/biophysics and molecular biology; biochemistry; biological and physical sciences; biology/ biological sciences; biomedical/medical engineering; biotechnology; botany/ plant biology; business administration and management; cell biology and anatomy; cell/cellular and molecular biology; cell/cellular biology and histology; chemistry; clinical psychology; clinical/medical social work; cognitive psychology and psycholinguistics; college student counseling and personnel services; communication disorders; communications and media studies; communications studies/speech communication and rhetoric; community health and preventive medicine; corrections and criminal justice; counselor education/school counseling and guidance services; creative writing; criminal justice/law enforcement administration; curriculum and instruction; developmental and child psychology; education leadership and administration; education; education/teaching of individuals in early childhood special education programs; education/teaching of individuals who are developmentally delayed; education/teaching of individuals with autism; education/teaching of individuals with specific learning disabilities; education/teaching of individuals with speech or language impairments; educational evaluation and research; educational, instructional, and curriculum supervision; endodontics/endodontology (certification, MS, PhD); English composition; English language and literature; English language and literature/letters; European history; experimental psychology; finance; foods, nutrition, and related services; foreign languages/modern languages; French language and literature; genetics; geological/geophysical engineering; geology/ earth science; geophysics and seismology; health information/medical records administration/administrator; health services administration; health services/allied health; health/health care administration/management; higher education/ higher education administration; history; human nutrition; immunology; industrial and organizational psychology; international public health/international health; law (LLB, JD); management information systems; mathematics and computer science; mathematics and statistics; mathematics; medical microbiology and bacteriology; medicine (MD); medieval and renaissance studies; meteorology; microbiology; molecular biochemistry; molecular biology; neuroanatomy; nursing/registered nurse training (RN, ASN, BSN, MSN); nursing; nutrition sciences; occupational health and industrial hygiene; orthodontics/ orthodontology (certification, MS, PhD); periodontics/periodontology (certification, MS, PhD); pharmacology; philosophy and religion; philosophy; physician assistant; physiology; plant molecular biology; plant pathology/phytopathology; plant physiology; psychology; public administration; public health (MPh, DPh); public policy analysis; real estate; religion/religious studies; religious education; romance languages, literatures, and linguistics; social work; Spanish language and literature; special education and teaching; special education; speech-language pathology/pathologist; statistics; theology/theological studies; urban education and leadership; urban studies/affairs; zoology/animal biology. **Doctorate offered in:** Administration of special education; aerospace, aeronautical, and astronautical engineering; agricultural/biological engineering and bioengineering; American history (United States); American literature (United States); anatomy; applied mathematics. **First Professional degree offered in:** Early childhood education and teaching; elementary education and teaching; junior high/intermediate/middle school education and teaching; kindergarten/preschool education and teaching; secondary education and teaching; teacher education, multiple levels.

STUDENT INFORMATION

Total Students in Program: 2,077. **% Full-time:** 43. **% International:** 10.

EXPENSES/FINANCIAL AID

Annual Tuition: $11,340. **Room & Board (On/off Campus):** $10,160/

$7,000. **Fees:** $40. **Books and Supplies:** $1,000. **Grants Range From:** $15-$24,000. **Loans Range From:** $800-$81,134. **% Receiving Financial Aid:** 80. **% Receiving Scholarships/Grants:** 10. **% Receiving Loans:** 60. **% Receiving Assistantships:** 25. **Types of Aid Available:** Fellowships, graduate assistantships, grants, institutional work-study, loans, scholarships. work study. **Average student debt, upon graduation:** $24,501. **Number of Fellowships Granted Each Year:** 20. **Average amount of individual fellowships per year:** $17,000. **Number of Teaching/Research Assistantships Granted Each Year:** 450. **Assistantship Compensation Includes:** Full tuition remission, salary/stipend. **Average Salary Stipend:** $13,000.

ADMISSIONS INFORMATION

Application Fee: $40. **Priority Application Deadline:** 7/1. **Regular Application Deadline:** 7/1. **Regular Notification:** Rolling. **Transfer Students Accepted?** Yes. **Number of Applications Received:** 1,500. **% of Applicants Accepted:** 47. **% Accepted Who Enrolled:** 79.
Required Admission Factors: Essays/personal statement, letters of recommendation, transcript.

EMPLOYMENT INFORMATION

Placement Office Available? Yes. **% Employed Within 6 Months:** 92. **Rate of placement:** 3%.

SAINT LOUIS UNIVERSITY
School of Social Service

Address: 221 North Grand Boulevard, St. Louis, MO 63103-2097
Admissions Phone: 314-977-2240 · **Admissions Fax:** 314-977-3943
Admissions E-mail: bureschm@slu.edu

INSTITUTIONAL INFORMATION

Public/private: Private (nonprofit). **Student/faculty Ratio:** 7:1. **Students in Parent Institution:** 13,873.

STUDENT INFORMATION

Total Students in Program: 2,657. **% Full-time:** 35. **% Female:** 63.

EXPENSES/FINANCIAL AID

Annual Tuition: $11,340. **Room & Board:** $10,160. **Books and Supplies:** $1,000. **Grants Range From:** $15-$22,898. **Loans Range From:** $800-$81,134. **% Receiving Financial Aid:** 51. **% Receiving Scholarships/Grants:** 63. **% Receiving Loans:** 69. **Average student debt, upon graduation:** $24,108. **Number of Fellowships Granted Each Year:** 80. **Average amount of individual fellowships per year:** $10,000.

ADMISSIONS INFORMATION

Application Fee: $40. **Transfer Students Accepted?** Yes. **Number of Applications Received:** 358. **% of Applicants Accepted:** 32. **% Accepted Who Enrolled:** 65.
Required Admission Factors: GRE, letters of recommendation, transcript.

EMPLOYMENT INFORMATION

Placement Office Available? Yes. **Rate of placement:** 3%.

SAINT MARTIN'S COLLEGE
Master's in Teaching Program

Address: 5300 Pacific Avenue SE, Lacey, WA 98503
Admissions Phone: 360-438-4333

INSTITUTIONAL INFORMATION

Public/private: Private (nonprofit). **Evening Classes Available?** Yes. **Total Faculty:** 12. **Student/faculty Ratio:** 4:1. **Students in Parent Institution:** 1,399.

STUDENT INFORMATION

Total Students in Program: 301. % Full-time: 28. % Female: 55.

EXPENSES/FINANCIAL AID

Annual Tuition: $15,560. Fees: $130. Books and Supplies: $700. Grants Range From: $500-$4,148. Loans Range From: $500-$18,500. % Receiving Financial Aid: 100. % Receiving Scholarships/Grants: 1. % Receiving Loans: 98. Average student debt, upon graduation: $40,000.

ADMISSIONS INFORMATION

Application Fee: $35. Regular Notification: Rolling. Transfer Students Accepted? Yes. Number of Applications Received: 10. % of Applicants Accepted: 100. % Accepted Who Enrolled: 100. Average GPA: 3.0 Average GRE Verbal: 397. Average GRE Quantitative: 453. Average GRE Analytical: 463.

Required Admission Factors: Essays/personal statement, interview, letters of recommendation, transcript.

Other Admission Factors: Minimum 3.0 GPA required.

EMPLOYMENT INFORMATION

% Employed Within 6 Months: 100. % of master's grads employed in their field upon graduation: 100. Rate of placement: 96%.

SAINT MARTIN'S COLLEGE
Counseling Psychology Program

Address: 5300 Pacific Avenue SE, Lacey, WA 98503
Admissions Phone: 360-438-4560

INSTITUTIONAL INFORMATION

Public/private: Private (nonprofit). Evening Classes Available? Yes. Student/faculty Ratio: 30:1. Students in Parent Institution: 1,399.

STUDENT INFORMATION

Total Students in Program: 301. % Full-time: 28. % Female: 55.

EXPENSES/FINANCIAL AID

Annual Tuition: $15,560. Fees: $130. Books and Supplies: $700. Grants Range From: $500-$4,148. Loans Range From: $500-$18,500. % Receiving Scholarships/Grants: 1. % Receiving Loans: 98. Average student debt, upon graduation: $10,000 Number of Fellowships Granted Each Year: 1. Average amount of individual fellowships per year: $1,500. Number of Teaching/Research Assistantships Granted Each Year: 1.

ADMISSIONS INFORMATION

Application Fee: $35. Regular Notification: Rolling. Transfer Students Accepted? Yes. Number of Applications Received: 60. % of Applicants Accepted: 58. % Accepted Who Enrolled: 86. Average GPA: 3.2.

Required Admission Factors: Essays/personal statement, interview, letters of recommendation, transcript.

EMPLOYMENT INFORMATION

% Employed Within 6 Months: 50. % of master's grads employed in their field upon graduation: 85. Rate of placement: 96%.

SAINT MARTIN'S COLLEGE
Master's in Engineering Management Program

Address: 5300 Pacific Avenue SE, Lacey, WA 98503
Admissions Phone: 360-438-4587 · Admissions Fax: 360-438-4522
Admissions E-mail: dstout@stmartin.edu

INSTITUTIONAL INFORMATION

Public/private: Private (nonprofit). Evening Classes Available? Yes. Student/faculty Ratio: 5:1. Students in Parent Institution: 1,399.

STUDENT INFORMATION

Total Students in Program: 301. % Full-time: 28. % Female: 55.

EXPENSES/FINANCIAL AID

Annual Tuition: $15,560. Fees: $130. Books and Supplies: $700. Grants Range From: $500-$4,148. Loans Range From: $500-$18,500. % Receiving Scholarships/Grants: 1. % Receiving Loans: 98.

ADMISSIONS INFORMATION

Application Fee: $35. Regular Notification: Rolling. Transfer Students Accepted? Yes. Number of Applications Received: 24. % of Applicants Accepted: 33. % Accepted Who Enrolled: 100. Average GPA: 3.35.

Required Admission Factors: Essays/personal statement, interview, letters of recommendation, transcript.

Other Admission Factors: Minimum 2.8 GPA, professional engineer's license, or approval of admissions comittee required.

EMPLOYMENT INFORMATION

% Employed Within 6 Months: 100. % of master's grads employed in their field upon graduation: 100. Rate of placement: 96%.

SAINT MARY COLLEGE
Graduate Programs—Psychology

Address: 4100 South Fourth Street, Leavenworth, KS 66048-5082
Admissions Phone: 913-345-8288 · Admissions Fax: 913-345-2802

INSTITUTIONAL INFORMATION

Public/private: Private (nonprofit). Evening Classes Available? Yes. Student/faculty Ratio: 11:1. Students in Parent Institution: 786.

STUDENT INFORMATION

Total Students in Program: 280. % Full-time: 3. % Female: 77.

EXPENSES/FINANCIAL AID

Annual Tuition: $4,860. Books and Supplies: $600. Loans Range From: $210-$46,998. % Receiving Loans: 100.

ADMISSIONS INFORMATION

Application Fee: $25. Regular Notification: Rolling. Transfer Students Accepted? Yes. Number of Applications Received: 10. % of Applicants Accepted: 90. % Accepted Who Enrolled: 100. Average GPA: 3.3.

Required Admission Factors: Essays/personal statement, interview, letters of recommendation, transcript.

Other Admission Factors: Minimum 2.75 GPA required.

SAINT PAUL SCHOOL OF THEOLOGY
Graduate Program

Address: 5123 Truman Road, Kansas City, MO 64127
Admissions Phone: 800-825-0378 · Admissions Fax: 816-483-9605
Admissions E-mail: admis@spst.edu

INSTITUTIONAL INFORMATION

Public/private: Private (nonprofit). Student/faculty Ratio: 18:1. Students in Parent Institution: 257.

STUDENT INFORMATION

Total Students in Program: 257. % Full-time: 49. % Female: 55.

EXPENSES/FINANCIAL AID

Annual Tuition: $5,580. Grants Range From: $50-$242. Loans Range From: $1,000-$8,500. % Receiving Financial Aid: 80. % Receiving Scholarships/Grants: 97. % Receiving Loans: 3. Average student debt, upon graduation: $17,000.

ADMISSIONS INFORMATION

Application Fee: $25. **Regular Notification:** Rolling. **Transfer Students Accepted?** Yes. **Number of Applications Received:** 102. **Average GPA:** 3.2.

Required Admission Factors: Essays/personal statement, letters of recommendation, transcript.

Other Admission Factors: Minimum 2.75 GPA required.

SAINT PETER'S COLLEGE
Graduate Programs

Address: 2641 Kennedy Boulevard, Jersey City, NJ 07306-5997
Admissions Phone: 201-915-9216 · **Admissions Fax:** 201-432-5860

INSTITUTIONAL INFORMATION

Public/private: Private (nonprofit). **Evening Classes Available?** Yes. **Total Faculty:** 26. **% Faculty Female:** 12. **% Faculty Part-time:** 38. **Students in Parent Institution:** 3,863.

STUDENT INFORMATION

Total Students in Program: 426. **% Full-time:** 23. **% Female:** 46.

EXPENSES/FINANCIAL AID

Annual Tuition: $13,392.

ADMISSIONS INFORMATION

Application Fee: $20. **Regular Notification:** Rolling. **Transfer Students Accepted?** Yes. **Number of Applications Received:** 62. **% of Applicants Accepted:** 85. **% Accepted Who Enrolled:** 42. **Average GPA:** 2.7. **Required Admission Factors:** Essays/personal statement, transcript. **Other Admission Factors:** Minimum GMAT score of 400 or minimum MAT score of 40, and 3 letters of recommendation required.

EMPLOYMENT INFORMATION

Placement Office Available? Yes. **Rate of placement:** 92%.

SAINT VINCENT DE PAUL REGIONAL SEMINARY
Graduate Programs

Address: 10701 South Military Trail, Boynton Beach, FL 33436-4899
Admissions Phone: 561-732-4424 · **Admissions Fax:** 561-737-2205

INSTITUTIONAL INFORMATION

Public/private: Private (nonprofit). **Students in Parent Institution:** 105.

STUDENT INFORMATION

Total Students in Program: 15. **% Full-time:** 13. **% Female:** 40.

EXPENSES/FINANCIAL AID

Annual Tuition: In-state $9,500. / Out-of-state $10,500. **Books and Supplies:** $800. **Grants Range From:** $14,500-$15,500. **Loans Range From:** $1,900-$3,800. **% Receiving Financial Aid:** 100. **% Receiving Scholarships/Grants:** 100. **% Receiving Loans:** 17. **Average student debt, upon graduation:** $4,962.

ADMISSIONS INFORMATION

Transfer Students Accepted? Yes. **Transfer Policy:** Minimum grade C required for MDiv transfer applicants; minimum grade of B required. **Number of Applications Received:** 33. **% of Applicants Accepted:** 97. **% Accepted Who Enrolled:** 94.

Required Admission Factors: Essays/personal statement, interview, letters of recommendation, transcript.

Other Admission Factors: Minimum 2.0 GPA required of MDiv program applicants. Minimum 3.0 GPA required of MA program applicants.

SAINT XAVIER UNIVERSITY
Graduate Programs

Address: 3700 West 103rd Street, Chicago, IL 60655
Admissions Phone: 773-298-3053 · **Admissions Fax:** 773-298-3951
Admissions E-mail: graduateadmisison@sxu.edu
Website: www.sxu.edu/academics/grprograms.asp

INSTITUTIONAL INFORMATION

Public/private: Private (nonprofit). **Evening Classes Available?** Yes. **Student/faculty Ratio:** 16:1. **Students in Parent Institution:** 5,709

PROGRAMS

Masters offered in: Adult health nurse/nursing; business administration and management; computer science; counselor education/school counseling and guidance services; curriculum and instruction; E-commerce/electronic commerce; early childhood education and teaching; education; educational administration and supervision; elementary education and teaching; family practice nurse/nurse practitioner; finance and financial management services; finance; financial planning and services; health services administration; marketing/marketing management; music teacher education; nonprofit/public/organizational management; nursing clinical specialist; nursing; psychiatric/mental health nurse/nursing; public health (MPh, DPh); public health, community nurse, nursing; secondary education and teaching; special education; speech-language pathology/pathologist. **First Professional degree offered in:** Pastoral studies/counseling.

STUDENT INFORMATION

Total Students in Program: 2,639. **% Full-time:** 4. **% Female:** 81. **% Minority:** 27. **% International:** 1.

RESEARCH FACILITIES

Research Facilities: Athletic Center, Campus Ministry, Counseling and Career Services, Learning Center and Disabilities Services.

EXPENSES/FINANCIAL AID

Annual Tuition: $10,350. **Fees:** $100. **Books and Supplies:** $500. **Grants Range From:** $452-$2,868. **Loans Range From:** $105-$18,500. **% Receiving Financial Aid:** 25. **% Receiving Scholarships/Grants:** 17. **% Receiving Loans:** 86. **% Receiving Assistantships:** 8. **Types of Aid Available:** Graduate assistantships, loans, scholarships.

ADMISSIONS INFORMATION

Application Fee: $35. **Priority Application Deadline:** 7/1. **Regular Application Deadline:** 8/1. **Regular Notification:** Rolling. **Transfer Students Accepted?** Yes. **Transfer Policy:** Request for review of transfer credit is required of transfer applicants. **Number of Applications Received:** 1,487. **% of Applicants Accepted:** 70. **% Accepted Who Enrolled:** 78. **Average GPA:** 3. **Average GRE Verbal:** 500. **Average GRE Quantitative:** 500. **Average GRE Analytical Writing:** 4.

Required Admission Factors: Essays/personal statement, letters of recommendation, transcript.

Other Admission Factors: Minimum 3.0 GPA and minimum combined GRE score of 1000.

EMPLOYMENT INFORMATION

% Employed Within 6 Months: 100. **Rate of placement:** 98%.

SALEM INTERNATIONAL UNIVERSITY
Graduate Programs

Address: 223 West Main Street, Salem, WV 26426
Admissions Phone: 800-283-4562 · **Admissions Fax:** 304-782-5592
Admissions E-mail: admissions@salemiu.edu

INSTITUTIONAL INFORMATION

Public/private: Private (nonprofit). **Student/faculty Ratio:** 16:1. **Students in Parent Institution:** 537.

STUDENT INFORMATION

Total Students in Program: 82. **% Full-time:** 33. **% Female:** 73.

RESEARCH FACILITIES

Research Facilities: Barker Equestrian Center, Fort New Salem Appalachian Museum, bioscience facilities.

EXPENSES/FINANCIAL AID

Loans Range From: $2,500-$10,000. **% Receiving Financial Aid:** 14. **% Receiving Loans:** 75. **% Receiving Assistantships:** 25. **Average student debt, upon graduation:** $21,182. **Number of Teaching/Research Assistantships Granted Each Year:** 3. **Average Salary Stipend:** $7,200.

ADMISSIONS INFORMATION

Application Fee: $25. **Regular Notification:** Rolling. **Transfer Students Accepted?** Yes. **Transfer Policy:** Credits to be transferred must be from comparable accredited university. **Number of Applications Received:** 87. **% of Applicants Accepted:** 95. **% Accepted Who Enrolled:** 95. **Average GPA:** 3.5.
Required Admission Factors: Letters of recommendation, transcript.
Other Admission Factors: Minimum 2.5 GPA required; minimum 3.0 GPA recommended.
Program-Specific Admission Factors: Equine experience required for equine education specialization.

SALISBURY UNIVERSITY
(FORMERLY SALISBURY STATE UNIVERSITY)
Fulton School of Liberal Arts

Address: 1101 Camden Avenue, Salisbury, MD 21801
Admissions Phone: 410-543-6161 · **Admissions Fax:** 410-546-6016
Admissions E-mail: gegrodzicki@ssu.edu

INSTITUTIONAL INFORMATION

Public/private: Public. **Evening Classes Available?** Yes. **Student/faculty Ratio:** 8:1. **Students in Parent Institution:** 6,421.

STUDENT INFORMATION

Total Students in Program: 538. **% Full-time:** 20. **% Female:** 69.

RESEARCH FACILITIES

Research Facilities: The Graduate House, Center for Economic Education, Center for Technology in Education, European American Business Institute, Mid Atlantic Sales and Marketing Institute, Perdue Center for Professional Development, Lower Shore Manufacturing Network.

EXPENSES/FINANCIAL AID

Annual Tuition: In-state $3,024. / Out-of-state $6,048. **Fees:** $72. **Books and Supplies:** $500. **Grants Range From:** $200-$1,500. **Loans Range From:** $1,000-$15,000. **% Receiving Scholarships/Grants:** 17. **% Receiving Loans:** 34. **% Receiving Assistantships:** 20. **Average Salary Stipend:** $625.

ADMISSIONS INFORMATION

Application Fee: $30. **Regular Notification:** Rolling. **Transfer Students Accepted?** No. **Number of Applications Received:** 28.
Required Admission Factors: GRE, letters of recommendation, transcript.
Other Admission Factors: Minimum 3.0 GPA required.

SAMFORD UNIVERSITY
Howard College of Arts & Sciences

Address: 800 Lakeshore Drive, Birmingham, AL 35229
Admissions Phone: 205-726-2944 · **Admissions Fax:** 205-726-2479
Admissions E-mail: rnhunsin@samford.edu
Website: www.samford.edu/schools/artsci/biology/envm.html

INSTITUTIONAL INFORMATION

Public/private: Private (nonprofit). **Total Faculty:** 8. **% Faculty Female:** 12. **% Faculty Part-time:** 12. **Student/faculty Ratio:** 1:1. **Students in Parent Institution:** 4,416.

PROGRAMS

Masters offered in: Environmental control technologies/technicians.

STUDENT INFORMATION

Total Students in Program: 21. **% Full-time:** 24. **% Female:** 48. **% Minority:** 5.

RESEARCH FACILITIES

Research Facilities: Vulcan Materials Center.

EXPENSES/FINANCIAL AID

Annual Tuition: $12,292. **Grants Range From:** $1,688-$2,000. **Loans Range From:** $1,679-$18,150. **% Receiving Financial Aid:** 59. **% Receiving Scholarships/Grants:** 9. **% Receiving Loans:** 59. **Types of Aid Available:** Grants, institutional work-study, loans, scholarships. **Average student debt, upon graduation:** $15,617.

ADMISSIONS INFORMATION

Application Fee: $25. **Regular Notification:** Rolling. **Transfer Students Accepted?** Yes. **Transfer Policy:** Maximum 9 credit hours with a minimum grade of B may be transferred. **Number of Applications Received:** 12. **% of Applicants Accepted:** 92. **% Accepted Who Enrolled:** 55. **Average GRE Verbal:** 460. **Average GRE Quantitative:** 600.
Required Admission Factors: GRE, letters of recommendation, MAT, transcript.
Other Admission Factors: Minimum 3.0 GPA required.

SAMFORD UNIVERSITY
School of Performing Arts,
Division of Music

Address: 800 Lakeshore Drive, Birmingham, AL 35229
Admissions Phone: 205-726-2496 · **Admissions Fax:** 205-726-2165
Admissions E-mail: parichar@samford.edu · **Website:** www.samford.edu

INSTITUTIONAL INFORMATION

Public/private: Private (nonprofit). **Total Faculty:** 18. **% Faculty Female:** 28. **% Faculty Part-time:** 22. **Student/faculty Ratio:** 1:1. **Students in Parent Institution:** 4,379.

PROGRAMS

Masters offered in: Music pedagogy, music.

STUDENT INFORMATION

Total Students in Program: 12. **% Full-time:** 83. **% Female:** 58.

EXPENSES/FINANCIAL AID

Annual Tuition: $6,894. **Grants Range From:** $65-$25,050. **Loans Range From:** $221-$26,700. **% Receiving Financial Aid:** 100. **% Receiving Scholarships/Grants:** 61. **% Receiving Loans:** 73. **Average student debt, upon graduation:** $15,495.

ADMISSIONS INFORMATION

Application Fee: $25. **Regular Application Deadline:** 7/15. **Regular Notification:** Rolling. **Transfer Students Accepted?** Yes. **Number of Applica-

tions Received: 7. % of Applicants Accepted: 86. % Accepted Who Enrolled: 50. Average GPA: 3.6.
Required Admission Factors: Interview, transcript.
Program-Specific Admission Factors: Audition required for admission to programs in church music. Alabama teaching certificate required for admission to traditional program in music education.

EMPLOYMENT INFORMATION
% Employed Within 6 Months: 75.

SAMUEL MERRITT COLLEGE
Graduate Programs

Address: 370 Hawthorne Avenue, Oakland, CA 94609
Admissions Phone: 510-869-6976 · **Admissions Fax:** 510-869-6525
Admissions E-mail: jgartens@samuelmerritt.edu · **Website:** www.samuelmerritt.edu

INSTITUTIONAL INFORMATION
Public/private: Private (nonprofit). **Evening Classes Available?** Yes. **Student/faculty Ratio:** 12:1. **Students in Parent Institution:** 714.

PROGRAMS
Masters offered in: Family practice nurse/nurse practitioner, nurse anesthetist, nursing/registered nurse training (RN, ASN, BSN, MSN), occupational therapy/therapist, physician assistant. **Doctorate offered in:** Physical therapy/therapist, podiatric medicine/podiatry (DPM).

STUDENT INFORMATION
Total Students in Program: 436. **% Full-time:** 90. **% Female:** 79.

ADMISSIONS INFORMATION
Application Fee: $50. **Regular Application Deadline:** 1/15. **Regular Notification:** Rolling. **Transfer Students Accepted?** No. **Number of Applications Received:** 154. **% of Applicants Accepted:** 73. **% Accepted Who Enrolled:** 64. **Average GPA:** 3.25. **Average GRE Verbal:** 488. **Average GRE Quantitative:** 492. **Average GRE Analytical:** 557.
Required Admission Factors: Essays/personal statement, interview, letters of recommendation, transcript.
Other Admission Factors: Please go to our website or call the Office of Admission at 510-869-6976 for specific program requirements.
Program-Specific Admission Factors: GRE required of CRNA, DPT, MOT program applicants. MCAT or GRE required for DPM program applicants.

EMPLOYMENT INFORMATION
Average starting salary: $95,701.

SAN DIEGO STATE UNIVERSITY
College of Arts & Letters

Address: 5300 Campanile Drive, San Diego, CA 92182-8020
Admissions Phone: 619-594-0884 · **Admissions Fax:** 619-594-3908
Admissions E-mail: gra@mail.sdsu.edu · **Website:** www-rohan.sdsu.edu/dept/calweb/

INSTITUTIONAL INFORMATION
Public/private: Public. **Evening Classes Available?** Yes. **Total Faculty:** 206. **% Faculty Female:** 42. **Students in Parent Institution:** 32,803.

PROGRAMS
Masters offered in: American/United States studies/civilization; anthropology; Asian studies/civilization; Central/Middle and Eastern European studies; comparative literature; creative writing; economics; English language and literature; English language and literature/letters; ethnic, cultural minority, and gender studies; European studies/civilization; French language and literature; geography; German language and literature; Hispanic American, Puerto Rican, and Mexican American/Chicano studies; history; humanities/humanistic stud-

ies; international business; international economics; Japanese language and literature; Latin American studies; liberal arts and sciences studies and humanities; liberal arts and sciences/liberal studies; linguistics; multi/interdisciplinary studies; philosophy; political science and government; public/applied history and archival administration; religion/religious studies; Russian language and literature; Russian studies; social sciences; sociology; Spanish language and literature; speech and rhetorical studies; urban studies/affairs; women's studies.

STUDENT INFORMATION
Total Students in Program: 747. **% Full-time:** 45. **% Female:** 58. **% Minority:** 25. **% International:** 9.

RESEARCH FACILITIES
Research Facilities: More than 40 institutional research centers.

EXPENSES/FINANCIAL AID
Annual Tuition: $2,698. **Room & Board:** $11,000. **Fees:** $6,768. **Books and Supplies:** $1,200. **Grants Range From:** $100-$5,000. **Loans Range From:** $100-$18,500. **Types of Aid Available:** Fellowships, graduate assistantships, grants, institutional work-study, loans, scholarships. **Assistantship Compensation Includes:** Salary/stipend.

ADMISSIONS INFORMATION
Application Fee: $55. **Priority Application Deadline:** 5/1. **Regular Application Deadline:** 9/1. **Regular Notification:** Rolling. **Transfer Students Accepted?** Yes. **Transfer Policy:** Maximum number of credit hours that may be transferred varies by program. **Number of Applications Received:** 710. **% of Applicants Accepted:** 53. **% Accepted Who Enrolled:** 69. **Average GPA:** 3.3.
Required Admission Factors: GRE, letters of recommendation, transcript.
Other Admission Factors: Minimum 2.85 GPA required for most programs; other requirements vary by program.

EMPLOYMENT INFORMATION
Placement Office Available? Yes. **Rate of placement:** 83%.

SAN DIEGO STATE UNIVERSITY
College of Professional Studies
& Fine Arts

Address: 5300 Campanile Drive, San Diego, CA 92182-8020
Admissions Phone: 619-594-0884 · **Admissions Fax:** 619-594-3908
Admissions E-mail: gra@mail.sdsu.edu · **Website:** http://psfa.sdsu.edu

INSTITUTIONAL INFORMATION
Public/private: Public. **Evening Classes Available?** Yes. **Total Faculty:** 125. **% Faculty Female:** 37. **Students in Parent Institution:** 32,803.

PROGRAMS
Masters offered in: Advertising; art/art studies; communications studies/speech communication and rhetoric; communications technologies and support services; communications, journalism, and related fields; criminal justice/law enforcement administration; criminal justice/safety studies; dance; drama and dramatics/theater arts; dramatic/theater arts and stagecraft; family and consumer economics and related services; film/video and photographic arts; foods, nutrition, and related services; foods, nutrition, and wellness studies; graphic design; health and physical education; hospitality administration/management; industrial design; journalism; kinesiology and exercise science; mass communications/media studies; music performance; music; music/music and performing arts studies; parks, recreation, and leisure studies; public administration and services; public administration; public relations/image management.

STUDENT INFORMATION
Total Students in Program: 516. **% Full-time:** 49. **% Female:** 61. **% Minority:** 19. **% International:** 9.

RESEARCH FACILITIES
Research Facilities: More than 40 institutional research centers.

Complete Book of Graduate Programs in the Arts and Sciences

EXPENSES/FINANCIAL AID

Annual Tuition: $2,698. **Room & Board:** $11,000. **Fees:** $6,768. **Books and Supplies:** $810. **Grants Range From:** $100-$5,000. **Loans Range From:** $100-$18,500. **Types of Aid Available:** Fellowships, graduate assistantships, grants, institutional work-study, loans, scholarships. **Number of Teaching/Research Assistantships Granted Each Year:** 174.

ADMISSIONS INFORMATION

Application Fee: $55. **Priority Application Deadline:** 5/1. **Regular Application Deadline:** 9/1. **Regular Notification:** Rolling. **Transfer Students Accepted?** Yes. **Transfer Policy:** Maximum number of credit hours that may be transferred varies by program. **Number of Applications Received:** 694. **% of Applicants Accepted:** 35. **% Accepted Who Enrolled:** 44. **Average GPA:** 3.3.
Required Admission Factors: Essays/personal statement, GRE, letters of recommendation, transcript.
Other Admission Factors: Minimum 2.85 GPA in final 60 semester hours required.

EMPLOYMENT INFORMATION

Placement Office Available? Yes.

SAN DIEGO STATE UNIVERSITY
College of Sciences

Address: 5300 Campanile Drive, San Diego, CA 92182-8020
Admissions Phone: 619-594-0884 · **Admissions Fax:** 619-594-3908
Admissions E-mail: gra@mail.sddsu.edu · **Website:** www.sci.sdsu.edu/cos/

INSTITUTIONAL INFORMATION

Public/private: Public. **Total Faculty:** 170. **% Faculty Female:** 24. **Students in Parent Institution:** 32,803.

PROGRAMS

Masters offered in: Applied mathematics, astronomy, biological and biomedical sciences, botany/plant biology, chemical physics, chemistry, computer and information sciences, environmental science, environmental studies, genetics, geology/earth science, mathematics and statistics, mathematics, microbiology, molecular biology, natural resources conservation and research, physical sciences, physics, physiology, psychology, statistics. **Doctorate offered in:** Chemistry, clinical psychology, computer science, mathematics and statistics.

STUDENT INFORMATION

Total Students in Program: 906. **% Full-time:** 40. **% Female:** 46. **% Minority:** 22. **% International:** 28.

RESEARCH FACILITIES

Research Facilities: More than 40 institutional research centers.

EXPENSES/FINANCIAL AID

Annual Tuition: $2,698. **Room & Board:** $11,000. **Fees:** $6,768. **Books and Supplies:** $1,200. **Grants Range From:** $100-$5,000. **Loans Range From:** $100-$18,500. **Types of Aid Available:** Fellowships, graduate assistantships, grants, institutional work-study, loans, scholarships. **Number of Teaching/Research Assistantships Granted Each Year:** 323.

ADMISSIONS INFORMATION

Application Fee: $55. **Priority Application Deadline:** 5/1. **Regular Application Deadline:** 9/1. **Regular Notification:** Rolling. **Transfer Students Accepted?** Yes. **Number of Applications Received:** 1,220. **% of Applicants Accepted:** 41. **% Accepted Who Enrolled:** 30. **Average GPA:** 3.3.
Required Admission Factors: Essays/personal statement, GRE, letters of recommendation, transcript.
Other Admission Factors: Minimum 2.85 GPA in final 60 semester hours required. Minimum GRE scores of 540 Verbal, 610 Quantitative, and 600 Analytical, minimum GRE subject score in the 60th percentile, and minimum 3.0 GPA in biology or science major recommended.

Program-Specific Admission Factors: GRE subject exam in biology required of ecology and systematics program applicants.

EMPLOYMENT INFORMATION

Placement Office Available? Yes. **Rate of placement:** 83%.

SAN FRANCISCO THEOLOGICAL SEMINARY
Graduate Programs

Address: 2 Kensington Road, San Anselmo, CA 94960
Admissions Phone: 415-258-6531 · **Admissions Fax:** 415-258-1608
Admissions E-mail: gpulido@sfts.edu

INSTITUTIONAL INFORMATION

Public/private: Private (nonprofit). **Total Faculty:** 24. **Students in Parent Institution:** 700.

STUDENT INFORMATION

Total Students in Program: 700.

EXPENSES/FINANCIAL AID

Annual Tuition: In-state $7,600. **Fees:** $50. **Books and Supplies:** $1,000.

ADMISSIONS INFORMATION

Application Fee: $35. **Regular Notification:** Rolling. **Transfer Students Accepted?** Yes.
Required Admission Factors: Essays/personal statement, letters of recommendation, transcript.
Other Admission Factors: Minimum 3.0 GPA recommended.

EMPLOYMENT INFORMATION

Placement Office Available? Yes.

SAN JOSE STATE UNIVERSITY
College of Applied Science & Arts

Address: One Washington Square, San Jose, CA 95192-0009

INSTITUTIONAL INFORMATION

Public/private: Public. **Students in Parent Institution:** 26,698.

STUDENT INFORMATION

Total Students in Program: 5,406. **% Full-time:** 40. **% Female:** 65.

RESEARCH FACILITIES

Research Facilities: Institute for Radiation Sciences, Institute for Research and Development in Education, Institute for Research in Child Development, Institute for Research in Environmental Engineering and Science, Institute for Social Responsibility.

EXPENSES/FINANCIAL AID

Annual Tuition: $4,428. **Room & Board (On/off Campus):** $6,786/$25,000. **Fees:** $1,987.

ADMISSIONS INFORMATION

Transfer Students Accepted? No. **Transfer Policy:** Maximum 6 credit hours may be transferred into most programs.
Required Admission Factors: Transcript.
Other Admission Factors: Minimum 3.0 GPA required for most programs.
Program-Specific Admission Factors: 3 letters of recommendation required of some programs.

SAN JOSE STATE UNIVERSITY
College of Humanities & the Arts

Address: One Washington Square, San Jose, CA 95192-0009

INSTITUTIONAL INFORMATION
Public/private: Public. **Students in Parent Institution:** 26,698.

STUDENT INFORMATION
Total Students in Program: 5,406. **% Full-time:** 40. **% Female:** 65.

RESEARCH FACILITIES
Research Facilities: Institute for Radiation Sciences, Institute for Research and Development in Education, Institute for Research in Child Development, Institute for Research in Environmental Engineering and Science, Institute for Social Responsibility.

EXPENSES/FINANCIAL AID
Annual Tuition: $4,428. **Room & Board (On/off Campus):** $6,786/$25,000. **Fees:** $1,987.

ADMISSIONS INFORMATION
Transfer Students Accepted? No. **Transfer Policy:** Maximum 6 credit hours may be transferred into most programs.
Required Admission Factors: Transcript.
Other Admission Factors: Minimum 3.0 GPA required for most programs.
Program-Specific Admission Factors: Portfolio required of theater program applicants.

SAN JOSE STATE UNIVERSITY
College of Science

Address: One Washington Square, San Jose, CA 95192-0009

INSTITUTIONAL INFORMATION
Public/private: Public. **Students in Parent Institution:** 26,698.

STUDENT INFORMATION
Total Students in Program: 5,406. **% Full-time:** 40. **% Female:** 65.

RESEARCH FACILITIES
Research Facilities: Institute for Radiation Sciences, Institute for Research and Development in Education, Institute for Research in Child Development, Institute for Research in Environmental Engineering and Science, Institute for Social Responsibility.

EXPENSES/FINANCIAL AID
Annual Tuition: $4,428. **Room & Board (On/off Campus):** $6,786/$25,000. **Fees:** $1,987.

ADMISSIONS INFORMATION
Transfer Students Accepted? No.

SAN JOSE STATE UNIVERSITY
College of Social Work

Address: One Washington Square, San Jose, CA 95192-0009
Admissions Phone: 408-924-5849 · **Admissions Fax:** 408-924-5892

INSTITUTIONAL INFORMATION
Public/private: Public. **Evening Classes Available?** Yes. **Students in Parent Institution:** 26,698.

STUDENT INFORMATION
Total Students in Program: 5,406. **% Full-time:** 40. **% Female:** 65.

RESEARCH FACILITIES
Research Facilities: Institute for Radiation Sciences, Institute for Research and Development in Education, Institute for Research in Child Development, Institute for Research in Environmental Engineering and Science, Institute for Social Responsibility.

EXPENSES/FINANCIAL AID
Annual Tuition: $4,428. **Room & Board (On/off Campus):** $6,786/$25,000. **Fees:** $1,987.

ADMISSIONS INFORMATION
Transfer Students Accepted? No. **Number of Applications Received:** 257. **% of Applicants Accepted:** 67. **% Accepted Who Enrolled:** 85.
Required Admission Factors: Essays/personal statement, letters of recommendation, transcript.
Other Admission Factors: Minimum 2.5 GPA required.
Program-Specific Admission Factors: Volunteer or paid work in human services recommended of social work program applicants.

SAVANNAH COLLEGE OF ART AND DESIGN
Graduate Program

Address: 342 Bull Street, PO Box 3146, Savannah, GA 31402-3146
Admissions Phone: 800-869-7223 · **Admissions Fax:** 912-525-5983
Admissions E-mail: tmorrow@scad.edu

INSTITUTIONAL INFORMATION
Public/private: Private (nonprofit). **Evening Classes Available?** Yes. **Student/faculty Ratio:** 6:1. **Students in Parent Institution:** 4,923.

STUDENT INFORMATION
Total Students in Program: 674. **% Full-time:** 85. **% Female:** 50.

EXPENSES/FINANCIAL AID
Annual Tuition: $17,775. **Room & Board:** $7,300. **Books and Supplies:** $800. **% Receiving Financial Aid:** 60. **Average student debt, upon graduation:** $17,000.

ADMISSIONS INFORMATION
Application Fee: $50. **Regular Notification:** Rolling. **Transfer Students Accepted?** Yes. **Number of Applications Received:** 651. **% of Applicants Accepted:** 77. **% Accepted Who Enrolled:** 43.
Required Admission Factors: Letters of recommendation, transcript.
Program-Specific Admission Factors: Academic paper required of art history, architectural history, and historic preservation program applicants. GRE or portfolio required of architecture track III program applicants.

EMPLOYMENT INFORMATION
Placement Office Available? Yes. **Rate of placement:** 86%.

SAVANNAH STATE UNIVERSITY
Graduate Programs

Address: State College Branch, Savannah, GA 31404
Admissions Phone: 912-356-2181 · **Admissions Fax:** 912-356-2256
Admissions E-mail: jacksonr@savstate.edu

INSTITUTIONAL INFORMATION
Public/private: Public. **Evening Classes Available?** Yes. **Students in Parent Institution:** 2,286.

STUDENT INFORMATION
Total Students in Program: 116. **% Full-time:** 31. **% Female:** 75.

RESEARCH FACILITIES
Research Facilities: Survey Research Center.

EXPENSES/FINANCIAL AID

Annual Tuition: In-state $3,640. / Out-of-state $14,520. **Fees:** $548. **Books and Supplies:** $800. **Number of Fellowships Granted Each Year:** 14,000. **Average amount of individual fellowships per year:** $4,666. **Number of Teaching/Research Assistantships Granted Each Year:** 15,500. **Average Salary Stipend:** $1,200.

ADMISSIONS INFORMATION

Application Fee: $20. **Regular Notification:** Rolling. **Transfer Students Accepted?** Yes. **Number of Applications Received:** 61. **% of Applicants Accepted:** 57. **% Accepted Who Enrolled:** 89.
Required Admission Factors: Essays/personal statement, GRE, letters of recommendation, transcript.
Other Admission Factors: Minimum GRE score in the 50th percentile and minimum 2.6 GPA required.
Program-Specific Admission Factors: 4 letters of recommendation required for some programs.

SAYBROOK GRADUATE SCHOOL AND RESEARCH CENTER
Graduate Programs

Address: 747 Front Street, Third Floor, San Francisco, CA 94111-1920
Admissions Phone: 415-394-6166 · **Admissions Fax:** 415-433-9271
Admissions E-mail: admissions@saybrook.edu · **Website:** www.saybrook.edu

INSTITUTIONAL INFORMATION

Public/private: Private (nonprofit). **Students in Parent Institution:** 517.

STUDENT INFORMATION

Total Students in Program: 517. **% Full-time:** 100. **% Female:** 69. **% Minority:** 15. **% International:** 3.

RESEARCH FACILITIES

Research Facilities: Rollo May Center for Humanistic Studies.

EXPENSES/FINANCIAL AID

Annual Tuition: $15,800. **Fees:** $1,275. **Books and Supplies:** $1,500. **Grants Range From:** $100-$3,000. **Loans Range From:** $100-$18,500. **% Receiving Financial Aid:** 60. **% Receiving Scholarships/Grants:** 10. **% Receiving Loans:** 95. **Types of Aid Available:** Fellowships, loans, scholarships. **Average student debt, upon graduation:** $50,000.

ADMISSIONS INFORMATION

Application Fee: $50. **Priority Application Deadline:** 6/1. **Regular Application Deadline:** 8/15. **Regular Notification:** Rolling. **Transfer Students Accepted?** Yes. **Transfer Policy:** Transcript from an accredited school required of applicants who wish to receive transfer credits. **Number of Applications Received:** 225. **% of Applicants Accepted:** 51. **% Accepted Who Enrolled:** 67. **Average GPA:** 3.0.
Required Admission Factors: Essays/personal statement, letters of recommendation, transcript.
Other Admission Factors: Minimum 3.0 GPA.

EMPLOYMENT INFORMATION

% Employed Within 6 Months: 100.

SCHOOL FOR INTERNATIONAL TRAINING
Graduate Programs

Address: PO Box 676 Kipling Road, Brattleboro, VT 05302-0676
Admissions Phone: 800-336-1616 · **Admissions Fax:** 802-258-3500
Admissions E-mail: admissions@sit.edu · **Website:** www.sit.edu

INSTITUTIONAL INFORMATION

Public/private: Private (nonprofit). **Students in Parent Institution:** 202.

PROGRAMS

Masters offered in: Area, ethnic, cultural, and gender studies; education; English/language arts teacher education; foreign language teacher education; foreign languages, literatures, and linguistics; French language and literature; intercultural/multicultural and diversity studies; international and comparative education; international relations and affairs; international/global studies; linguistics; organizational behavior studies; peace studies and conflict resolution; Spanish language and literature; teaching English as a second or foreign language/ESL language instructor; teaching English or French as a second or foreign language; teaching French as a second or foreign language.

STUDENT INFORMATION

Total Students in Program: 658. **% Full-time:** 31. **% Female:** 75. **% Minority:** 10. **% International:** 19.

RESEARCH FACILITIES

Research Facilities: Center for Teacher Education, Training, and Research (CTETR) and Center for Professional Development.

EXPENSES/FINANCIAL AID

Annual Tuition: $24,120. **Room & Board:** $7,545. **Fees:** $2,316. **Books and Supplies:** $1,100. **Grants Range From:** $500-$33,000. **Loans Range From:** $8,500-$24,500. **% Receiving Financial Aid:** 75. **% Receiving Scholarships/Grants:** 87. **% Receiving Loans:** 75. **Types of Aid Available:** Fellowships, grants, institutional work-study, loans, scholarships. **Average student debt, upon graduation:** $28,500.

ADMISSIONS INFORMATION

Application Fee: $45. **Priority Application Deadline:** 3/1. **Regular Application Deadline:** 9/1. **Regular Notification:** Rolling. **Transfer Students Accepted?** No. **Number of Applications Received:** 813. **% of Applicants Accepted:** 61. **% Accepted Who Enrolled:** 41. **Average GPA:** 3.3.
Required Admission Factors: Essays/personal statement, letters of recommendation, transcript.
Other Admission Factors: TOEFL score minimum requirements for nonnative speakers of English are 213 on the computer-based test or 550 on the paper test.

EMPLOYMENT INFORMATION

Placement Office Available? Yes. **% Employed Within 6 Months:** 90. **Rate of placement:** 90%. **Average starting salary:** $45,000.

SCHOOL OF THE MUSEUM OF FINE ARTS, BOSTON/TUFTS UNIVERSITY
Graduate Program

Address: 230 The Fenway, Boston, MA 02115
Admissions Phone: 617-369-3626 · **Admissions Fax:** 617-369-3679
Admissions E-mail: admissions@smfa.edu · **Website:** www.smfa.edu

INSTITUTIONAL INFORMATION

Public/private: Private (nonprofit). **Student/faculty Ratio:** 10:1. **Students in Parent Institution:** 780.

PROGRAMS

Masters offered in: Art teacher education, ceramic arts and ceramics, drawing, fine arts and art studies, fine/studio arts, metal and jewelry arts, painting, printmaking, sculpture.

STUDENT INFORMATION

Total Students in Program: 116. **% Full-time:** 100. **% Female:** 71. **% Minority:** 9. **% International:** 7.

RESEARCH FACILITIES

Research Facilities: Reciprocity with all schools in the Pro-Arts Consortium.

EXPENSES/FINANCIAL AID

Books and Supplies: $1,250. **Grants Range From:** $1,000-$11,000. **Loans Range From:** $8,500-$18,500. **% Receiving Financial Aid:** 78. **% Receiving Scholarships/Grants:** 100. **% Receiving Assistantships:** 50. **Average student debt, upon graduation:** $37,000. **Number of Teaching/Research Assistantships Granted Each Year:** 45. **Average Salary Stipend:** $1,000.

ADMISSIONS INFORMATION

Application Fee: $60. **Priority Application Deadline:** 1/15. **Regular Application Deadline:** 1/15. **Regular Notification:** Rolling. **Transfer Students Accepted?** No. **Number of Applications Received:** 256. **% of Applicants Accepted:** 32. **% Accepted Who Enrolled:** 62.

Required Admission Factors: Essays/personal statement, letters of recommendation, portfolio, transcript.

Other Admission Factors: TOEFL for non-English speaking applicants is also required.

THE SCHOOL OF PUBLIC AFFAIRS
Baruch College—CUNY

Address: One Bernard Baruch Way, Box C-0406, New York, NY 10010-5585
Admissions Phone: 212-802-5921 · **Admissions Fax:** 212-802-5928
Admissions E-mail: spa_admissions@baruch.cuny.edu
Website: www.baruch.cuny.edu/spa

INSTITUTIONAL INFORMATION

Public/private: Public. **Evening Classes Available?** Yes. **Total Faculty:** 55. **% Faculty Female:** 44. **% Faculty Part-time:** 36. **Student/faculty Ratio:** 20:1. **Students in Parent Institution:** 15,608.

PROGRAMS

Masters offered in: Education leadership and administration; education; educational administration and supervision; educational, instructional, and curriculum supervision; elementary and middle school administration/principalship; higher education/higher education administration; public administration and services; public administration; public policy analysis; secondary school administration/principalship; urban education and leadership.

STUDENT INFORMATION

Total Students in Program: 637. **% Full-time:** 25. **% Female:** 70. **% Minority:** 31.

RESEARCH FACILITIES

Research Facilities: Baruch Survey Research Unit; Center for Innovation and Leadership in Government; Center on Equality, Pluralism, and Policy; The Center for Educational Leadership; The Nonprofit Group.

EXPENSES/FINANCIAL AID

Annual Tuition: In-state $230. / Out-of-state $425. **Fees:** $38. **Books and Supplies:** $550. **Grants Range From:** $200-$11,000. **% Receiving Financial Aid:** 20. **Types of Aid Available:** Graduate assistantships, loans. **Number of Fellowships Granted Each Year:** 1. **Average amount of individual fellowships per year:** $20,000. **Number of Teaching/Research Assistantships Granted Each Year:** 11. **Assistantship Compensation Includes:** Salary/stipend. **Average Salary Stipend:** $9,000.

ADMISSIONS INFORMATION

Application Fee: $125. **Priority Application Deadline:** 5/1. **Regular Application Deadline:** 6/15. **Regular Notification:** Rolling. **Transfer Students Accepted?** Yes. **Transfer Policy:** Prior to orientation, please provide the admissions office with syllabi, course descriptions, reading lists, and an official transcript for each course they would like to transfer. **Number of Applications Received:** 456. **% of Applicants Accepted:** 68. **% Accepted Who Enrolled:** 76. **Average GPA:** 3.4. **Average GRE Verbal:** 570. **Average GRE Quantitative:** 600. **Average GRE Analytical Writing:** 5.

Required Admission Factors: Essays/personal statement, GRE, letters of recommendation, transcript.

Other Admission Factors: Minimum 3.0 GPA recommended.
Program-Specific Admission Factors: The GRE requirment may be waived for students with cumulative GPA above 3.0 or those who already hold a graduate degree. A minimum of 3.5 years of management experience is required of applicants to the executive MPA program.

EMPLOYMENT INFORMATION

Placement Office Available? Yes. **% Employed Within 6 Months:** 85. **% of master's grads employed in their field upon graduation:** 80. **Rate of placement:** 85%. **Average starting salary:** $57,000.

SCHOOL OF VISUAL ARTS
Graduate Programs

Address: 209 East 23rd Street, New York, NY 10010-3994
Admissions Phone: 212-592-2106 · **Admissions Fax:** 212-592-2288
Admissions E-mail: gradadmissions@adm.schoolofvisualarts.edu

INSTITUTIONAL INFORMATION

Public/private: Private (proprietary). **Student/faculty Ratio:** 3:1. **Students in Parent Institution:** 5,312.

STUDENT INFORMATION

Total Students in Program: 326. **% Full-time:** 92. **% Female:** 57.

EXPENSES/FINANCIAL AID

Room & Board: $9,700. **Fees:** $1,730. **Grants Range From:** $75-$8,550. **Loans Range From:** $8,500-$20,500. **% Receiving Scholarships/Grants:** 43. **% Receiving Loans:** 74. **% Receiving Assistantships:** 17.

ADMISSIONS INFORMATION

Application Fee: $60. **Transfer Students Accepted?** Yes. **Number of Applications Received:** 993. **% of Applicants Accepted:** 26. **% Accepted Who Enrolled:** 58. **Average GPA:** 2.96.

Required Admission Factors: Letters of recommendation, transcript.

EMPLOYMENT INFORMATION

Placement Office Available? Yes. **% of master's grads employed in their field upon graduation:** 93. **Rate of placement:** 93%.

THE SCRIPPS RESEARCH INSTITUTE
Graduate Programs

Address: 10550 North Torrey Pines Road, TPC 19, La Jolla, CA 92037
Admissions Phone: 858-784-8469 · **Admissions Fax:** 858-784-2802
Admissions E-mail: gradprgm@scripps.edu

INSTITUTIONAL INFORMATION

Public/private: Private (nonprofit). **Students in Parent Institution:** 144.

STUDENT INFORMATION

Total Students in Program: 144. **% Full-time:** 100. **% Female:** 29.

ADMISSIONS INFORMATION

Transfer Students Accepted? No. **Number of Applications Received:** 328. **% of Applicants Accepted:** 25. **% Accepted Who Enrolled:** 28.
Required Admission Factors: Essays/personal statement, GRE, interview, letters of recommendation, transcript.

EMPLOYMENT INFORMATION

% Employed Within 6 Months: 100. **% of doctoral grads employed in their field upon graduation:** 100.

SEATTLE PACIFIC UNIVERSITY
College of Arts & Sciences

Address: 3307 Third Avenue West, Suite 111, Seattle, WA 98119

INSTITUTIONAL INFORMATION
Public/private: Private (nonprofit). **Evening Classes Available?** Yes. **Student/faculty Ratio:** 17:1. **Students in Parent Institution:** 3,491.

STUDENT INFORMATION
Total Students in Program: 799. **% Full-time:** 27. **% Female:** 65.

RESEARCH FACILITIES
Research Facilities: On-campus family therapy clinic.

EXPENSES/FINANCIAL AID
Books and Supplies: $657. **Grants Range From:** $250-$2,500. **Loans Range From:** $1,500-$32,000. **% Receiving Financial Aid:** 70. **% Receiving Scholarships/Grants:** 3. **% Receiving Loans:** 99. **Number of Teaching/Research Assistantships Granted Each Year:** 5 **Average Salary Stipend:** $3,500.

ADMISSIONS INFORMATION
Application Fee: $50. **Transfer Students Accepted?** Yes. **Transfer Policy:** Maximum 9 credit hours with a minimum grade of B taken within the last 5 years may be transferred. **Number of Applications Received:** 118. **% of Applicants Accepted:** 75. **% Accepted Who Enrolled:** 67. **Average GPA:** 3.3.
Required Admission Factors: Essays/personal statement, letters of recommendation, transcript.
Other Admission Factors: Minimum GRE score of 950 or minimum MAT score of 35, and minimum 3.0 GPA in last 45 quarter credits (30 semester credits) or overall (whichever is higher) required of marriage/family therapy program applicants.

SEATTLE UNIVERSITY
College of Arts & Sciences

Address: 900 Broadway, Seattle, WA 98122-4340
Admissions Phone: 206-296-2000 · **Admissions Fax:** 206-296-5656
Admissions E-mail: grad-admissions@seattleu.edu

INSTITUTIONAL INFORMATION
Public/private: Private (nonprofit). **Student/faculty Ratio:** 6:1. **Students in Parent Institution:** 5,981.

STUDENT INFORMATION
Total Students in Program: 1,542. **% Full-time:** 23. **% Female:** 58.

EXPENSES/FINANCIAL AID
Room & Board: $7,683. **Grants Range From:** $298-$17,288. **Loans Range From:** $480-$46,930. **% Receiving Scholarships/Grants:** 41. **% Receiving Loans:** 74.

ADMISSIONS INFORMATION
Application Fee: $55. **Transfer Students Accepted?** No. **Transfer Policy:** Maximum 10 credit hours may be transferred into the public administration program. **Number of Applications Received:** 77. **% of Applicants Accepted:** 66. **% Accepted Who Enrolled:** 76. **Average GPA:** 3.04. **Average GRE Verbal:** 504. **Average GRE Quantitative:** 606. **Average GRE Analytical:** 572.
Required Admission Factors: Essays/personal statement, interview, letters of recommendation, transcript.
Other Admission Factors: Minimum 3.0 GPA required.
Program-Specific Admission Factors: 3 letters of recommendation, autobiography, and experience in the field required of psychology program applicants; 1 letter of recommendation from employer, resume, and letter of intent required of public administration program applicants.

EMPLOYMENT INFORMATION
Placement Office Available? Yes.

SETON HALL UNIVERSITY
College of Arts & Sciences

Address: 400 South Orange Avenue, South Orange, NJ 07079-2689
Admissions Phone: 973-761-9430 · **Admissions Fax:** 973-761-9453
Admissions E-mail: gradserv@shu.edu · **Website:** http://artsci.shu.edu

INSTITUTIONAL INFORMATION
Public/private: Private (nonprofit). **Evening Classes Available?** Yes. **Students in Parent Institution:** 8,337.

PROGRAMS
Masters offered in: American literature (United States); arts management; Asian studies/civilization; biochemistry; chemistry; Christian studies; communications studies/speech communication and rhetoric; English literature (British and commonwealth); experimental psychology; health/health care administration/management; human services; Jewish/Judaic studies; microbiology; nonprofit/public/organizational management; organizational communications, public relations, and advertising; public administration and services; public administration; religion/religious studies. **Doctorate offered in:** Biochemistry, biological and biomedical sciences, chemistry.

STUDENT INFORMATION
Total Students in Program: 3,392. **% Full-time:** 23. **% Female:** 55.

EXPENSES/FINANCIAL AID
Annual Tuition: $15,576. **Fees:** $655. **Books and Supplies:** $700. **% Receiving Loans:** 96. **% Receiving Assistantships:** 4. **Types of Aid Available:** Graduate assistantships, institutional work-study, partial scholarships. **Number of Teaching/Research Assistantships Granted Each Year:** 41. **Assistantship Compensation Includes:** Salary/stipend. **Average Salary Stipend:** $7,000.

ADMISSIONS INFORMATION
Application Fee: $50. **Regular Application Deadline:** 7/1. **Regular Notification:** Rolling. **Transfer Students Accepted?** Yes. **Transfer Policy:** Must be approved by department chair person or director. **Number of Applications Received:** 288. **% of Applicants Accepted:** 97. **% Accepted Who Enrolled:** 74. **Average GPA:** 3.0.
Required Admission Factors: Essays/personal statement, letters of recommendation, transcript.
Other Admission Factors: Minimum GPA of 3.0.

EMPLOYMENT INFORMATION
Placement Office Available? Yes.

SETON HALL UNIVERSITY
John C. Whitehead School of Diplomacy and International Relations

Address: 400 South Orange Avenue, South Orange, NJ 07079
Admissions Phone: 973-275-2515 · **Admissions Fax:** 973-275-2519
Admissions E-mail: diplomat@shu.edu · **Website:** http://diplomacy.shu.edu

INSTITUTIONAL INFORMATION
Public/private: Private (nonprofit). **Evening Classes Available?** Yes. **Total Faculty:** 33. **% Faculty Female:** 36. **% Faculty Part-time:** 70. **Student/faculty Ratio:** 12:1. **Students in Parent Institution:** 8,409.

PROGRAMS
Masters offered in: African studies; Asian studies/civilization; development economics and international development; European studies/civilization; inter-

national business, trade, and tax law (LLM, JSD, S/JD); international business; international economics; international law and legal studies (LLM, JSD, S/JD); international relations and affairs; Latin American studies; Near and Middle Eastern studies.

STUDENT INFORMATION

Total Students in Program: 194. **% Full-time:** 83. **% Female:** 49.

RESEARCH FACILITIES

Research Facilities: Alberto Italian Studies Institute, Asia Center, Center for Public Service, Institute for Service Learning, Nonprofit Sector Resource Institute, Puerto Rican Institute, International Institute for Clergy Formation.

EXPENSES/FINANCIAL AID

Annual Tuition: $15,188. **Fees:** $405. **Books and Supplies:** $500. **Loans Range From:** $200-$10,000. **Types of Aid Available:** Graduate assistantships, institutional work-study, loans, scholarships. **Assistantship Compensation Includes:** Full tuition remission, salary/stipend. **Average Salary Stipend:** $5,000.

ADMISSIONS INFORMATION

Application Fee: $50. **Priority Application Deadline:** 4/1. **Regular Application Deadline:** 8/1. **Regular Notification:** Rolling. **Transfer Students Accepted?** Yes. **Number of Applications Received:** 306. **% of Applicants Accepted:** 52. **% Accepted Who Enrolled:** 61. **Average GPA:** 3.4. **Average GRE Verbal:** 540. **Average GRE Quantitative:** 630. **Average GRE Analytical Writing:** 5.
Required Admission Factors: Essays/personal statement, letters of recommendation, transcript.

EMPLOYMENT INFORMATION

Placement Office Available? Yes. **Rate of placement:** 88%. **Average starting salary:** $41,000.

SETON HILL UNIVERSITY
Graduate Programs

Address: 1 Seton Hill Drive, Greensburg, PA 15601-1599
Admissions Phone: 724-838-4283 · **Admissions Fax:** 724-830-1891
Admissions E-mail: gadmit@setonhill.edu · **Website:** www.setonhill.edu

INSTITUTIONAL INFORMATION

Public/private: Private (nonprofit). **Evening Classes Available?** Yes. **Total Faculty:** 42. **% Faculty Female:** 52. **% Faculty Part-time:** 60. **Student/faculty Ratio:** 14:1. **Students in Parent Institution:** 1,730.

PROGRAMS

Masters offered in: Art therapy/therapist, business administration/management, creative writing, educational/instructional media design, elementary and middle school administration/principalship, marriage and family therapy/counseling, physician assistant, special education.

STUDENT INFORMATION

Total Students in Program: 361. **% Full-time:** 28. **% Female:** 78.

RESEARCH FACILITIES

Research Facilities: National Education Center for Women in Business.

EXPENSES/FINANCIAL AID

Annual Tuition: $9,900. **Room & Board:** $7,000. **Fees:** $90. **Books and Supplies:** $200. **Grants Range From:** $225-$4,725. **Loans Range From:** $2,000-$15,000. **% Receiving Scholarships/Grants:** 80. **Average student debt, upon graduation:** $27,321.

ADMISSIONS INFORMATION

Application Fee: $30. **Regular Application Deadline:** 8/15. **Regular Notification:** Rolling. **Transfer Students Accepted?** Yes. **Transfer Policy:** Individual program directors will determine the transfer of credit. **Number of Applications Received:** 151. **% of Applicants Accepted:** 89. **% Accepted Who Enrolled:** 73. **Average GPA:** 3.0.

Required Admission Factors: Essays/personal statement, letters of recommendation, transcript.
Other Admission Factors: Minimum 3.0 GPA required.
Program-Specific Admission Factors: Art portfolio for art therapy masters.

EMPLOYMENT INFORMATION

Placement Office Available? Yes. **% Employed Within 6 Months:** 90. **Rate of placement:** 98%. **Average starting salary:** $30,000.

SHENANDOAH UNIVERSITY
School of Arts & Sciences

Address: 1460 University Drive, Winchester, VA 22601
Admissions Phone: 540-665-4581 · **Admissions Fax:** 540-665-4627
Admissions E-mail: admit@su.edu

INSTITUTIONAL INFORMATION

Public/private: Private (nonprofit). **Evening Classes Available?** Yes. **Student/faculty Ratio:** 15:1. **Students in Parent Institution:** 2,451.

STUDENT INFORMATION

Total Students in Program: 724. **% Full-time:** 39. **% Female:** 68.

EXPENSES/FINANCIAL AID

Annual Tuition: $9,360. **Room & Board:** $6,400. **Books and Supplies:** $2,000. **Grants Range From:** $300-$12,350. **Loans Range From:** $500-$18,500. **% Receiving Financial Aid:** 89. **% Receiving Scholarships/Grants:** 66. **% Receiving Loans:** 83. **% Receiving Assistantships:** 2. **Number of Fellowships Granted Each Year:** 415. **Average amount of individual fellowships per year:** $2,204.

ADMISSIONS INFORMATION

Application Fee: $30. **Transfer Students Accepted?** Yes. **Number of Applications Received:** 150. **% of Applicants Accepted:** 81. **% Accepted Who Enrolled:** 79.
Required Admission Factors: GRE, letters of recommendation, transcript.
Other Admission Factors: Minimum 2.8 GPA required.
Program-Specific Admission Factors: Teaching license required for some concentrations of MSEd program.

EMPLOYMENT INFORMATION

Placement Office Available? Yes. **% Employed Within 6 Months:** 100. **% of master's grads employed in their field upon graduation:** 100. **Rate of placement:** 70%.

SHENANDOAH UNIVERSITY
Shenandoah University Graduate School

Address: 1460 University Drive, Winchester, VA 22601
Admissions Phone: 540-665-4581 · **Admissions Fax:** 540-665-4627
Admissions E-mail: admit@su.edu · **Website:** www.su.edu

INSTITUTIONAL INFORMATION

Public/private: Private (nonprofit). **Evening Classes Available?** Yes. **Student/faculty Ratio:** 2:1. **Students in Parent Institution:** 2,451.

STUDENT INFORMATION

Total Students in Program: 1,200. **% Full-time:** 100. **% Female:** 41.

EXPENSES/FINANCIAL AID

Annual Tuition: $9,360. **Room & Board:** $6,400. **Books and Supplies:** $2,000. **Grants Range From:** $300-$12,350. **Loans Range From:** $500-$18,500. **% Receiving Financial Aid:** 89. **% Receiving Scholarships/Grants:** 66. **% Receiving Loans:** 83. **% Receiving Assistantships:** 2. **Number of Fellowships Granted Each Year:** 119. **Average amount of individual fellowships per year:** 1,573. **Number of Teaching/Research Assistantships Granted Each Year:** 10.

ADMISSIONS INFORMATION

Application Fee: $30. Regular Application Deadline: 5/30. Regular Notification: 7/1. Transfer Students Accepted? Yes. Transfer Policy: Transfer applicants must submit evidence of good standing at the previously college attended and an official transcript of degree(s) and/or credit(s) earned at all institutions previously attended. Conservatory applicants in selected programs of study must successfully complete an audition prior to the admission decision. Number of Applications Received: 1,200. % of Applicants Accepted: 33. % Accepted Who Enrolled: 45. Average GPA: 3.4. Average GRE Verbal: 520. Average GRE Quantitative: 520. Average GRE Analytical: 500. Average GRE Analytical Writing: 4.
Required Admission Factors: Transcript, GRE subject exam(s) in doctor of education in administrative leadership.
Other Admission Factors: Minimum 2.8 required for all programs.

EMPLOYMENT INFORMATION

Placement Office Available? Yes. % of master's/doctoral grads employed in their field upon graduation: 80/100. Rate of placement: 70%.

SHIPPENSBURG UNIVERSITY OF PENNSYLVANIA
College of Arts & Sciences

Address: 1871 Old Main Drive, Shippensburg, PA 17257-2299
Admissions Phone: 717-477-1213 · Admissions Fax: 717-477-4016
Admissions E-mail: jgcret@wharf.ship.edu
Website: www.ship.edu/academic/art.html

INSTITUTIONAL INFORMATION

Public/private: Public. Students in Parent Institution: 7,011.

STUDENT INFORMATION

Total Students in Program: 1,021. % Full-time: 18. % Female: 66.

EXPENSES/FINANCIAL AID

Annual Tuition: In-state $4,600. / Out-of-state $7,554. Fees: $374. Books and Supplies: $850. Grants Range From: $100-$2,000. Loans Range From: $100-$12,000. % Receiving Financial Aid: 70. % Receiving Scholarships/Grants: 5. % Receiving Loans: 65. % Receiving Assistantships: 15. Types of Aid Available: 1. Average student debt, upon graduation: $17,500. Number of Teaching/Research Assistantships Granted Each Year: 62.

ADMISSIONS INFORMATION

Application Fee: $30. Regular Notification: Rolling. Transfer Students Accepted? Yes. Number of Applications Received: 170. % of Applicants Accepted: 72. % Accepted Who Enrolled: 84.
Required Admission Factors: Transcript.
Other Admission Factors: Minimum 2.75 GPA required.
Program-Specific Admission Factors: Minimum 2.75 GPA, GRE or MAT if GPA is below minimum, 6 credit hours in psychology, statistics course, and personal goals statement required of psychology program applicants.

EMPLOYMENT INFORMATION

Placement Office Available? Yes.

SHIPPENSBURG UNIVERSITY OF PENNSYLVANIA
School of Graduate Studies

Address: 1871 Old Main Drive, Shippensburg, PA 17257-2299
Admissions Phone: 717-477-1213 · Admissions Fax: 717-477-4016
Admissions E-mail: admiss@ship.edu · Website: www.ship.edu

INSTITUTIONAL INFORMATION

Public/private: Public. Total Faculty: 155. % Faculty Female: 41. % Faculty Part-time: 14. Student/faculty Ratio: 7:1. Students in Parent Institution: 7,653.

PROGRAMS

Masters offered in: Biology/biological sciences; business administration and management; college student counseling and personnel services; communications studies, speech communication, and rhetoric; computer and information sciences; counselor education/school counseling and guidance services; criminal justice/safety studies; curriculum and instruction; elementary and middle school administration/principalship; environmental studies; gerontology; history; information science/studies; organizational behavior studies; psychology; public administration; reading teacher education; special education.

STUDENT INFORMATION

Total Students in Program: 1,074. % Full-time: 22. % Female: 69. % Minority: 4. % International: 1.

EXPENSES/FINANCIAL AID

Annual Tuition: In-state $5,518. / Out-of-state $8,830. Room & Board: $6,135. Fees: $908. Books and Supplies: $900. Grants Range From: $1,000-$3,200. Loans Range From: $150-$18,500. % Receiving Financial Aid: 30. % Receiving Scholarships/Grants: 2. % Receiving Loans: 66. % Receiving Assistantships: 58. % Receiving Other Aid: 63. Types of Aid Available: Graduate assistantships, grants, institutional work-study, loans, scholarships, residence hall directors. Average student debt, upon graduation: $15,000. Assistantship Compensation Includes: Full tuition remission, salary/stipend.

ADMISSIONS INFORMATION

Application Fee: $30. Priority Application Deadline: 6/1. Regular Notification: Rolling. Transfer Students Accepted? Yes. Transfer Policy: College transcript. statement of good standing, and must satisfy all other admissions requirements. Credit earned more than 5 years prior to start of graduate program does not qualify for transfer credit. Number of Applications Received: 648. % of Applicants Accepted: 64. % Accepted Who Enrolled: 77. Average GRE Verbal: 486. Average GRE Quantitative: 555. Average GRE Analytical: 610.
Required Admission Factors: Transcript.
Other Admission Factors: Minimum 2.75 GPA required. If less than 2.75 other evidence of ability to successfully complete the program applied to will be required.
Program-Specific Admission Factors: Please refer to specific program information online at www.ship.edu/catalog.

EMPLOYMENT INFORMATION

Placement Office Available? Yes.

SILVER LAKE COLLEGE
Graduate Studies

Address: 2406 South Alverno Road, Manitowoc, WI 54220-9319
Admissions Phone: 920-686-6371 · Admissions Fax: 920-684-7082

INSTITUTIONAL INFORMATION

Public/private: Private (nonprofit). Evening Classes Available? Yes. Student/faculty Ratio: 10:1. Students in Parent Institution: 1,259.

STUDENT INFORMATION

Total Students in Program: 541. % Full-time: 28. % Female: 76.

EXPENSES/FINANCIAL AID

Annual Tuition: $5,310. Books and Supplies: $60. Grants Range From: $1,700-$13,000. Loans Range From: $1,900-$18,000. % Receiving Financial Aid: 9. % Receiving Scholarships/Grants: 17. % Receiving Loans: 83. Average student debt, upon graduation: $10,337.

ADMISSIONS INFORMATION

Application Fee: $30. **Regular Notification:** Rolling. **Transfer Students Accepted?** Yes. **Transfer Policy:** Minimum grade average of B required of transfer applicants.
Required Admission Factors: Essays/personal statement, letters of recommendation, transcript.
Other Admission Factors: Minimum 3.0 GPA recommended.

EMPLOYMENT INFORMATION

Placement Office Available? Yes. **Rate of placement:** 78%.

SIMMONS COLLEGE
College of Arts & Sciences

Address: 300 The Fenway, Boston, MA 02115
Admissions Phone: 617-521-2915 · **Admissions Fax:** 617-521-3058
Admissions E-mail: GSA@simmons.edu · **Website:** www.simmons.edu/gradstudies

INSTITUTIONAL INFORMATION

Public/private: Private (nonprofit). **Evening Classes Available?** Yes. **Student/faculty Ratio:** 10:1. **Students in Parent Institution:** 3,340.

PROGRAMS

Masters offered in: Area, ethnic, cultural, and gender studies; bilingual and multilingual education; classics and classical languages, literatures, and linguistics; communications technologies and support services; communications, journalism, and related fields; creative writing; curriculum and instruction; education leadership and administration; education; educational administration and supervision; educational, instructional, and curriculum supervision; elementary and middle school administration/principalship; elementary education and teaching; English language and literature; ethnic, cultural minority, and gender studies; foreign languages/modern languages; gay/lesbian studies; general studies; history; history; humanities/humanistic studies; junior high/intermediate/middle school education and teaching; liberal arts and sciences studies and humanities; liberal arts and sciences/liberal studies; multicultural education; organizational communications, public relations, and advertising; secondary education and teaching; secondary school administration/principalship; Spanish language and literature; special education and teaching; special education; superintendency and educational system administration; teacher education and professional development, specific levels and methods; teacher education and professional development, specific subject areas; teacher education, multiple levels; teaching English as a second or foreign language/ESL language instructor; urban education and leadership; women's studies.

STUDENT INFORMATION

Total Students in Program: 2,116. **% Full-time:** 31. **% Female:** 88.

EXPENSES/FINANCIAL AID

Annual Tuition: $15,288. **Fees:** $20. **Books and Supplies:** $600. **Grants Range From:** $500-$14,640. **Loans Range From:** $1,000-$18,500. **% Receiving Financial Aid:** 80. **% Receiving Scholarships/Grants:** 47. **% Receiving Loans:** 100. **% Receiving Assistantships:** 3. **Average student debt, upon graduation:** $23,592. **Number of Fellowships Granted Each Year:** 17. **Average amount of individual fellowships per year:** $2,284. **Number of Teaching/Research Assistantships Granted Each Year:** 5.

ADMISSIONS INFORMATION

Application Fee: $35. **Priority Application Deadline:** 8/1. **Regular Application Deadline:** 8/1. **Regular Notification:** Rolling. **Transfer Students Accepted?** Yes. **Number of Applications Received:** 421. **% of Applicants Accepted:** 95. **% Accepted Who Enrolled:** 71. **Average GPA:** 3.0.
Required Admission Factors: Essays/personal statement, letters of recommendation, transcript.
Program-Specific Admission Factors: 3 letters of recommendation required for some programs.

EMPLOYMENT INFORMATION

Placement Office Available? Yes.

SIMMONS COLLEGE
Graduate School of Library & Information Science

Address: 300 The Fenway, Boston, MA 02115
Admissions Phone: 617-521-2800 · **Admissions Fax:** 617-521-3192
Admissions E-mail: gslis@simmons.edu · **Website:** www.simmons.edu/gslis

INSTITUTIONAL INFORMATION

Public/private: Private (nonprofit). **Total Faculty:** 42. **% Faculty Female:** 60. **% Faculty Part-time:** 60. **Student/faculty Ratio:** 16:1. **Students in Parent Institution:** 4,121

PROGRAMS

Masters offered in: Library science/librarianship. **Doctorate offered in:** Library science/librarianship.

STUDENT INFORMATION

Total Students in Program: 678. **% Full-time:** 20. **% Female:** 82.

EXPENSES/FINANCIAL AID

Annual Tuition: $25,920. **Room & Board (On/off Campus):** $11,000/$12,000. **Fees:** $60. **Books and Supplies:** $600. **Types of Aid Available:** Grants, loans.

ADMISSIONS INFORMATION

Application Fee: $35. **Regular Application Deadline:** 7/1. **Regular Notification:** Rolling. **Transfer Students Accepted?** Yes. **Transfer Policy:** Students must petition the faculty for approval of transfer credit hours, all of which must come from an ALA accredited program. **Number of Applications Received:** 342. **% of Applicants Accepted:** 86. **% Accepted Who Enrolled:** 54. **Average GPA:** 3.4.
Required Admission Factors: Essays/personal statement, letters of recommendation, transcript.
Other Admission Factors: Minimum 3.0 GPA required; GRE (Verbal and Quantitative) required if GPA is below minimum and applicant holds no advanced degree.
Program-Specific Admission Factors: Dual degree archives/history students must submit a writing sample of 5 to 7 pages in length.

EMPLOYMENT INFORMATION

Placement Office Available? Yes. **% Employed Within 6 Months:** 22. **Rate of placement:** 79%. **Average starting salary:** $36,768.

SIMMONS COLLEGE
Graduate School of Social Work

Address: 300 The Fenway, Boston, MA 02115
Admissions Phone: 617-521-3920 · **Admissions Fax:** 617-521-3980
Admissions E-mail: mable.millner@simmons.edu

INSTITUTIONAL INFORMATION

Public/private: Private (nonprofit). **Student/faculty Ratio:** 8:1. **Students in Parent Institution:** 3,340.

STUDENT INFORMATION

Total Students in Program: 2,116. **% Full-time:** 31. **% Female:** 88.

EXPENSES/FINANCIAL AID

Annual Tuition: $15,288. **Fees:** $20. **Books and Supplies:** $600. **Grants Range From:** $500-$14,640. **Loans Range From:** $1,000-$18,500. **% Receiving Financial Aid:** 100. **% Receiving Scholarships/Grants:** 47. **%**

Receiving Loans: 100. % Receiving Assistantships: 3. Average student debt, upon graduation: $34,569.

ADMISSIONS INFORMATION

Application Fee: $45. Regular Notification: Rolling. Transfer Students Accepted? Yes. Transfer Policy: Personal statement and letter from current dean or faculty advisor required of transfer applicants. Number of Applications Received: 373. % of Applicants Accepted: 84. % Accepted Who Enrolled: 49. Average GPA: 3.2.
Required Admission Factors: Essays/personal statement, letters of recommendation, transcript.
Other Admission Factors: Minimum 3.0 GPA in last 2 years required.
Program-Specific Admission Factors: MAT required of PhD program applicants.

EMPLOYMENT INFORMATION

Placement Office Available? Yes. % Employed Within 6 Months: 77. % of master's/doctoral grads employed in their field upon graduation: 77/100. Average starting salary: $45,500.

SLIPPERY ROCK UNIVERSITY OF PENNSYLVANIA
College of Arts & Sciences

Address: 14 Maltby Drive, Slippery Rock, PA 16057
Admissions Phone: 724-738-2051 · Admissions Fax: 724-738-2908
Admissions E-mail: carla.hradisky@sru.edu

INSTITUTIONAL INFORMATION

Public/private: Public. Evening Classes Available? Yes. Students in Parent Institution: 7,197.

STUDENT INFORMATION

Total Students in Program: 697. % Full-time: 47. % Female: 70.

RESEARCH FACILITIES

Research Facilities: Marine Science Consortium with research facilities at Wallops Island, VA.

EXPENSES/FINANCIAL AID

Annual Tuition: In-state $4,600. / Out-of-state $7,554. Room & Board: $5,558. Fees: $1,246. Books and Supplies: $640. Grants Range From: $500-$4,600. Loans Range From: $200-$11,500. % Receiving Financial Aid: 80. % Receiving Scholarships/Grants: 4. % Receiving Loans: 75. % Receiving Assistantships: 42. Number of Teaching/Research Assistantships Granted Each Year: 100. Average Salary Stipend: $4,000.

ADMISSIONS INFORMATION

Application Fee: $25. Regular Notification: Rolling. Transfer Students Accepted? Yes. Number of Applications Received: 20. % of Applicants Accepted: 65. % Accepted Who Enrolled: 100. Average GPA: 3.25.
Required Admission Factors: GRE, letters of recommendation, transcript.
Other Admission Factors: Minimum 2.75 GPA and minimum GRE score of 1350 required.

EMPLOYMENT INFORMATION

Placement Office Available? Yes. Rate of placement: 96%.

SLIPPERY ROCK UNIVERSITY OF PENNSYLVANIA
School of Physical Therapy

Address: 14 Maltby Drive, Slippery Rock, PA 16057
Admissions Phone: 724-738-2051 · Admissions Fax: 724-738-2908
Admissions E-mail: carla.hradisky@sru.edu

INSTITUTIONAL INFORMATION

Public/private: Public. Students in Parent Institution: 7,197.

STUDENT INFORMATION

Total Students in Program: 697. % Full-time: 47. % Female: 70.

RESEARCH FACILITIES

Research Facilities: Marine Science Consortium with research facilities at Wallops Island, VA.

EXPENSES/FINANCIAL AID

Annual Tuition: In-state $4,600. / Out-of-state $7,554. Room & Board: $5,558. Fees: $1,246. Books and Supplies: $640. Grants Range From: $500-$4,600. Loans Range From: $200-$11,500. % Receiving Financial Aid: 29. % Receiving Scholarships/Grants: 4. % Receiving Loans: 75. % Receiving Assistantships: 42.

ADMISSIONS INFORMATION

Application Fee: $35. Regular Notification: Rolling. Transfer Students Accepted? No. Number of Applications Received: 269. % of Applicants Accepted: 22. % Accepted Who Enrolled: 100.
Required Admission Factors: Essays/personal statement, GRE, interview, letters of recommendation, transcript.
Other Admission Factors: Minimum 3.0 GPA and minimum GRE score of 1350 required.

EMPLOYMENT INFORMATION

Placement Office Available? Yes. Rate of placement: 96%.

SMITH COLLEGE
School for Social Work

Address: Lilly Hall, Office of Admission, Northampton, MA 01063
Admissions Phone: 413-585-7960 · Admissions Fax: 413-585-7990
Admissions E-mail: sswadmis@smith.edu · Website: www.smith.edu/ssw

INSTITUTIONAL INFORMATION

Public/private: Private (nonprofit). Student/faculty Ratio: 4:1. Students in Parent Institution: 3,040.

PROGRAMS

Masters offered in: Clinical/medical social work. Doctorate offered in: Clinical/medical social work.

STUDENT INFORMATION

Total Students in Program: 95. % Full-time: 316. % Female: 85.

EXPENSES/FINANCIAL AID

Annual Tuition: $14,062. Room & Board: $2,343. Fees: $45. Books and Supplies: $600. Grants Range From: $1,500-$15,000. Loans Range From: $1,000-$18,500. % Receiving Financial Aid: 74. % Receiving Scholarships/Grants: 100. % Receiving Loans: 100. Average student debt, upon graduation: $43,000.

ADMISSIONS INFORMATION

Application Fee: $60. Priority Application Deadline: 1/5. Regular Application Deadline: 2/21. Regular Notification: Rolling. Transfer Students Accepted? Yes. Transfer Policy: 1 full academic year of master's in social work education in an accredited program required of transfer applicants. Number of Applications Received: 244. % of Applicants Accepted: 89. % Accepted Who Enrolled: 59.
Required Admission Factors: Essays/personal statement, letters of recommendation, transcript.
Other Admission Factors: Minimum 3.0 GPA, at least 20 semester hours completed in social psychology and/or biological science, and at least 1 year of paid or volunteer experience in human services required.

EMPLOYMENT INFORMATION

Placement Office Available? Yes.

SMITH COLLEGE
Smith College Office of Graduate Study

Address: Northampton, MA 01063
Admissions Phone: 413-585-3050 · **Admissions Fax:** 413-585-3054
Admissions E-mail: dsiegel@smith.edu

INSTITUTIONAL INFORMATION
Public/private: Private (nonprofit). **Student/faculty Ratio:** 10:1. **Students in Parent Institution:** 3,040.

STUDENT INFORMATION
Total Students in Program: 95. **% Full-time:** 64. **% Female:** 85.

EXPENSES/FINANCIAL AID
Annual Tuition: $24,550. **Books and Supplies:** $600. **Grants Range From:** $2,455-$24,550. **Loans Range From:** $2,200-$18,500. **% Receiving Scholarships/Grants:** 52. **% Receiving Loans:** 37. **% Receiving Other Aid:** 5. **Number of Fellowships Granted Each Year:** 29. **Average amount of individual fellowships per year:** $9,840.

ADMISSIONS INFORMATION
Application Fee: $50. **Transfer Students Accepted?** Yes. **Number of Applications Received:** 163. **% of Applicants Accepted:** 62. **% Accepted Who Enrolled:** 60.
Required Admission Factors: Essays/personal statement, letters of recommendation, transcript.
Other Admission Factors: Paper from an advanced undergraduate course required.

EMPLOYMENT INFORMATION
Placement Office Available? Yes.

SOAS (UNIVERSITY OF LONDON)
School of Oriental and African Studies

Address: Thornhaugh Street, Russell Square, London, WC1H OXG United Kingdom
Admissions Phone: +4420-7074-5100 · **Admissions Fax:** +4420-7075-5089
Admissions E-mail: registrar@soas.ac.uk · **Website:** www.soas.ac.uk

INSTITUTIONAL INFORMATION
Public/private: Public. **Students in Parent Institution:** 3,485

STUDENT INFORMATION
Total Students in Program: 1,661. **% Full-time:** 74. **% Female:** 60. **% Minority:** 48. **% International:** 40.

ADMISSIONS INFORMATION
Application Fee: $50. **Regular Application Deadline:** 6/30. **Regular Notification:** Rolling. **Transfer Students Accepted?** No. **Number of Applications Received:** 4,612. **% of Applicants Accepted:** 70. **% Accepted Who Enrolled:** 37.
Required Admission Factors: Letters of recommendation, transcript.
Other Admission Factors: UK first degree (2.1) or equivalent (3.5) required for taught master's programs. Good master's degree required for consideration for research degree programs.

SONOMA STATE UNIVERSITY
Institute of Interdisciplinary Studies

Address: 1801 East Cotati Avenue, Rohnert Park, CA 94928

INSTITUTIONAL INFORMATION
Public/private: Public. **Students in Parent Institution:** 7,402.

STUDENT INFORMATION
Total Students in Program: 1,191. **% Full-time:** 54. **% Female:** 72.

RESEARCH FACILITIES
Research Facilities: Anthropological Studies Center, Center for Management and Business Research, Center for Teaching and Professional Development, Wine Marketing Institute, Pan-Pacific Exchange.

EXPENSES/FINANCIAL AID
Annual Tuition: $7,380. **Fees:** $2,006. **Books and Supplies:** $846. **Grants Range From:** $100. **Loans Range From:** $100-$18,500. **% Receiving Scholarships/Grants:** 39. **% Receiving Loans:** 42.

ADMISSIONS INFORMATION
Transfer Students Accepted? No.

EMPLOYMENT INFORMATION
Placement Office Available? Yes.

SONOMA STATE UNIVERSITY
School of Arts & Humanities

Address: 1801 East Cotati Avenue, Rohnert Park, CA 94928

INSTITUTIONAL INFORMATION
Public/private: Public. **Students in Parent Institution:** 7,402.

STUDENT INFORMATION
Total Students in Program: 1,191. **% Full-time:** 54. **% Female:** 72.

RESEARCH FACILITIES
Research Facilities: Anthropological Studies Center, Center for Management and Business Research, Center for Teaching and Professional Development, Wine Marketing Institute, Pan-Pacific Exchange.

EXPENSES/FINANCIAL AID
Annual Tuition: $7,380. **Fees:** $2,006. **Books and Supplies:** $846. **Grants Range From:** $100. **Loans Range From:** $100-$18,500. **% Receiving Scholarships/Grants:** 39. **% Receiving Loans:** 42.

ADMISSIONS INFORMATION
Transfer Students Accepted? No.

EMPLOYMENT INFORMATION
Placement Office Available? Yes.

SONOMA STATE UNIVERSITY
School of Natural Sciences

Address: 1801 East Cotati Avenue, Rohnert Park, CA 94928

INSTITUTIONAL INFORMATION
Public/private: Public. **Students in Parent Institution:** 7,402.

STUDENT INFORMATION
Total Students in Program: 1,191. **% Full-time:** 54. **% Female:** 72.

RESEARCH FACILITIES
Research Facilities: Anthropological Studies Center, Center for Management and Business Research, Center for Teaching and Professional Development, Wine Marketing Institute, Pan-Pacific Exchange.

EXPENSES/FINANCIAL AID
Annual Tuition: $7,380. **Fees:** $2,006. **Books and Supplies:** $846. **Grants Range From:** $100. **Loans Range From:** $100-$18,500. **% Receiving Scholarships/Grants:** 39. **% Receiving Loans:** 42.

ADMISSIONS INFORMATION
Transfer Students Accepted? No.

EMPLOYMENT INFORMATION
Placement Office Available? Yes.

SONOMA STATE UNIVERSITY
School of Social Sciences

Address: 1801 East Cotati Avenue, Rohnert Park, CA 94928

INSTITUTIONAL INFORMATION
Public/private: Public. **Students in Parent Institution:** 7,402.

STUDENT INFORMATION
Total Students in Program: 1,191. **% Full-time:** 54. **% Female:** 72.

RESEARCH FACILITIES
Research Facilities: Anthropological Studies Center, Center for Management and Business Research, Center for Teaching and Professional Development, Wine Marketing Institute, Pan-Pacific Exchange.

EXPENSES/FINANCIAL AID
Annual Tuition: $7,380. **Fees:** $2,006. **Books and Supplies:** $846. **Grants Range From:** $100. **Loans Range From:** $100-$18,500. **% Receiving Scholarships/Grants:** 39. **% Receiving Loans:** 42.

ADMISSIONS INFORMATION
Transfer Students Accepted? No.

EMPLOYMENT INFORMATION
Placement Office Available? Yes.

SOUTH CAROLINA STATE UNIVERSITY
Graduate Studies

Address: 300 College Street, NE, PO Box 7127, Orangeburg, SC 29117-7127

INSTITUTIONAL INFORMATION
Public/private: Public. **Students in Parent Institution:** 4,899.

STUDENT INFORMATION
Total Students in Program: 790. **% Full-time:** 40. **% Female:** 79.

EXPENSES/FINANCIAL AID
Annual Tuition: In-state $3,654. / Out-of-state $7,200. **Room & Board:** $3,806. **Fees:** $1,827. **Books and Supplies:** $1,000.

ADMISSIONS INFORMATION
Transfer Students Accepted? No.

SOUTH DAKOTA STATE UNIVERSITY
College of Arts & Science

Address: Administration 130, Box 2201, Brookings, SD 57007
Admissions Phone: 605-688-4181 · **Admissions Fax:** 605-688-6167
Admissions E-mail: ruth.manson@sdstate.edu
Website: www.sdstate.edu/Academics/CollegeOfArtsAndScience/Index.cfm

INSTITUTIONAL INFORMATION
Public/private: Public. **Evening Classes Available?** Yes. **Total Faculty:** 58. **% Faculty Female:** 21. **Students in Parent Institution:** 10,561.

PROGRAMS
Masters offered in: Animal sciences; chemistry; communications studies, speech communication, and rhetoric; engineering; English language and literature; health and physical education/fitness; journalism; mathematics; nursing administration (MSN, MS, PhD); sociology; wildlife and wildlands sciences and management. **Doctorate offered in:** Sociology.

STUDENT INFORMATION
Total Students in Program: 136. **% Full-time:** 29. **% Female:** 55. **% Minority:** 12.

RESEARCH FACILITIES
Research Facilities: Agricultural Experiment Station, Animal Disease Research & Diagonistic Lab, E.A. Martin Program in Human Nutrition, Oak Lake Field Station.

EXPENSES/FINANCIAL AID
Annual Tuition: In-state $1,969. / Out-of-state $5,804. **Fees:** $1,254. **Books and Supplies:** $800. **Grants Range From:** $500-$7,500. **Loans Range From:** $500-$18,500. **% Receiving Financial Aid:** 57. **% Receiving Scholarships/Grants:** 4. **% Receiving Loans:** 53. **% Receiving Assistantships:** 45. **Types of Aid Available:** Graduate assistantships, institutional work-study, loans, scholarships. **Average student debt, upon graduation:** $16,660. **Assistantship Compensation Includes:** Partial tuition remission, salary/stipend. **Average Salary Stipend:** $10,707.

ADMISSIONS INFORMATION
Application Fee: $35. **Transfer Students Accepted?** Yes. **Number of Applications Received:** 91. **% of Applicants Accepted:** 85. **% Accepted Who Enrolled:** 73. **Average GPA:** 3.3.
Required Admission Factors: GRE, transcript.
Other Admission Factors: An applicant may be admitted with a GPA of 3.0 or higher (on 4.0 scale), which is also required for assistantship consideration. An applicant may be admitted conditionally with a 2.75 or higher GPA.

EMPLOYMENT INFORMATION
Placement Office Available? Yes.

SOUTH DAKOTA STATE UNIVERSITY
College of Family & Consumer Sciences

Address: Administration 130, Box 2201, Brookings, SD 57007
Admissions Phone: 605-688-5758 · **Admissions Fax:** 605-688-6167
Admissions E-mail: ruth_manson@sdstate.edu
Website: www3.sdstate.edu/Academics/CollegeOfFamilyAndConsumerSciences/Index.cfm

INSTITUTIONAL INFORMATION
Public/private: Public. **Evening Classes Available?** Yes. **Total Faculty:** 18. **% Faculty Female:** 78. **Students in Parent Institution:** 10,561.

STUDENT INFORMATION
Total Students in Program: 1,222. **% Female:** 2.

RESEARCH FACILITIES
Research Facilities: Agricultural Experiment Station, Animal Disease Research & Diagonistic Lab, E.A. Martin Program in Human Nutrition, Oak Lake Field Station.

EXPENSES/FINANCIAL AID
Annual Tuition: In-state $1,969. / Out-of-state $5,804. **Fees:** $1,254. **Books and Supplies:** $800. **Grants Range From:** $500-$7,500. **Loans Range From:** $500-$18,500. **% Receiving Financial Aid:** 57. **% Receiving Scholarships/Grants:** 4. **% Receiving Loans:** 53. **% Receiving Assistantships:** 45. **Types of Aid Available:** Graduate assistantships, institutional work-study, loans, scholarships. **Average student debt, upon graduation:** $16,660. **Assistantship Compensation Includes:** Partial tuition remission, salary/stipend. **Average Salary Stipend:** $10,707.

ADMISSIONS INFORMATION
Application Fee: $35. **Transfer Students Accepted?** Yes. **Number of Applications Received:** 11. **% of Applicants Accepted:** 55. **% Accepted Who Enrolled:** 67. **Average GPA:** 3.5.
Required Admission Factors: GRE, transcript.
Other Admission Factors: Minimum 2.8 GPA required. An applicant may be admitted with a GPA of 3.0 or higher (on 4.0 scale), which is also required for

---

assistantship consideration. An applicant may be admitted conditionally with a 2.75 to 2.99 GPA.

EMPLOYMENT INFORMATION

Placement Office Available? Yes. % Employed Within 6 Months: 100. % of master's grads employed in their field upon graduation: 100. Average starting salary: $35,000.

SOUTHEASTERN LOUISIANA UNIVERSITY
College of Arts & Sciences

Address: SLU 10752, Hammond, LA 70402
Admissions Phone: 800-222-7358 · Admissions Fax: 504-549-5632
Admissions E-mail: jmercante@selu.edu

INSTITUTIONAL INFORMATION

Public/private: Public. Total Faculty: 80. Students in Parent Institution: 14,535.

STUDENT INFORMATION

Total Students in Program: 1,615. % Full-time: 27.

RESEARCH FACILITIES

Research Facilities: Turtle Cove Environmental Research Station, SLU Business Research Center, Florida Parishes Social Science Research Center.

EXPENSES/FINANCIAL AID

Annual Tuition: In-state $2,412. / Out-of-state $6,408. Grants Range From: $75-$5,000. Loans Range From: $100-$18,000. % Receiving Scholarships/Grants: 5. % Receiving Loans: 58. % Receiving Assistantships: 37. Number of Teaching/Research Assistantships Granted Each Year: 54. Average Salary Stipend: $2,200.

ADMISSIONS INFORMATION

Application Fee: $20. Regular Notification: Rolling. Transfer Students Accepted? Yes. Transfer Policy: Maximum 1/3 of credit hours required may be transferred with a minimum grade of B. Number of Applications Received: 55. % of Applicants Accepted: 95.
Required Admission Factors: GRE, transcript.
Other Admission Factors: Minimum GRE score of 850, minimum 2.5 GPA, and minimum 24 credit hours of course work in major area required.

EMPLOYMENT INFORMATION

Placement Office Available? Yes.

SOUTHERN CALIFORNIA COLLEGE OF OPTOMETRY
Professional Program

Address: 2575 Yorba Linda Boulevard, Fullerton, CA 92831-1699
Admissions Phone: 714-449-7444 · Admissions Fax: 714-992-7878
Admissions E-mail: pberryman@scco.edu

INSTITUTIONAL INFORMATION

Public/private: Private (nonprofit). Student/faculty Ratio: 8:1. Students in Parent Institution: 379.

EXPENSES/FINANCIAL AID

Annual Tuition: $20,150. Fees: $90. Books and Supplies: $1,000. % Receiving Financial Aid: 95. Average student debt, upon graduation: $80,000.

ADMISSIONS INFORMATION

Application Fee: $50. Regular Notification: Rolling. Transfer Students Accepted? No. Number of Applications Received: 381. % of Applicants Accepted: 40. % Accepted Who Enrolled: 63. Average GPA: 3.39.

Required Admission Factors: Essays/personal statement, interview, letters of recommendation, transcript.
Other Admission Factors: Minimum OAT academic average of 300 and minimum 2.0 GPA required.

EMPLOYMENT INFORMATION

Placement Office Available? Yes. % Employed Within 6 Months: 100.

SOUTHERN ILLINOIS UNIVERSITY EDWARDSVILLE
College of Arts & Sciences

Address: Box 1047, Edwardsville, IL 62026-1080
Admissions Phone: 618-650-3160 · Admissions Fax: 618-650-2081

INSTITUTIONAL INFORMATION

Public/private: Public. Evening Classes Available? Yes. Students in Parent Institution: 12,193.

STUDENT INFORMATION

Total Students in Program: 2,422. % Full-time: 31. % Female: 60.

RESEARCH FACILITIES

Research Facilities: Dental implant clinic, nursing psychomotor skills lab, engineering labs.

EXPENSES/FINANCIAL AID

Annual Tuition: In-state $2,712. / Out-of-state $5,424. Fees: $573. Books and Supplies: $1,109. Grants Range From: $508-$12,000. Loans Range From: $1,061-$18,500. % Receiving Scholarships/Grants: 80. % Receiving Loans: 30. % Receiving Assistantships: 1.

ADMISSIONS INFORMATION

Application Fee: $25. Regular Notification: Rolling. Transfer Students Accepted? Yes. Transfer Policy: Maximum 1/3 of total credit hours required may be transferred. Number of Applications Received: 330. % of Applicants Accepted: 55.
Required Admission Factors: Essays/personal statement, transcript.
Other Admission Factors: Minimum 2.5 GPA required.

EMPLOYMENT INFORMATION

Placement Office Available? Yes. Rate of placement: 75%.

SOUTHERN METHODIST UNIVERSITY
Dedman College

Address: 3225 University Boulevard, Dallas Hall, Room 332, PO Box 750240, Dallas, TX 75275
Admissions Phone: 214-768-4345 · Admissions Fax: 214-768-4235
Admissions E-mail: bphillip@smu.edu · Website: www.smu.edu/graduate

INSTITUTIONAL INFORMATION

Public/private: Private (nonprofit). Evening Classes Available? Yes. Total Faculty: 236. Students in Parent Institution: 10,064.

STUDENT INFORMATION

Total Students in Program: 3,363. % Full-time: 26. % Female: 38.

RESEARCH FACILITIES

Research Facilities: Center for Southwest Studies, Cary M. Maguire Center for Ethics and Responsibility, Department of Marketing, TAGER TV Network System, Institute for the Study of Earth and Man.

EXPENSES/FINANCIAL AID

Annual Tuition: In-state $13,878. Room & Board: $7,855. Fees: $2,346. % Receiving Financial Aid: 68. Average student debt, upon graduation:

$21,192. **Number of Teaching/Research Assistantships Granted Each Year:** 4.

ADMISSIONS INFORMATION

Application Fee: $60. **Priority Application Deadline:** 2/1. **Regular Application Deadline:** 6/1. **Regular Notification:** Rolling. **Transfer Students Accepted?** Yes. **Transfer Policy:** Transfer applicants course descriptions must fit required courses. **Number of Applications Received:** 458. **% of Applicants Accepted:** 68. **% Accepted Who Enrolled:** 35. **Average GRE Verbal:** 546. **Average GRE Quantitative:** 682.
Required Admission Factors: GRE, letters of recommendation, transcript. **Other Admission Factors:** Minimum 3.0 GPA and statement of purpose required, writing samples for history and English.

EMPLOYMENT INFORMATION

Placement Office Available? Yes. **Rate of placement:** 98%.

SOUTHERN METHODIST UNIVERSITY
Meadows School of the Arts

Address: Room 1150 Owen Arts Center, 6101 Bishop Boulevard, Dallas, TX 75205
Admissions Phone: 214-768-3765 · **Admissions Fax:** 214-768-3272
Admissions E-mail: jcherry@smu.edu · **Website:** www.smu.edu/meadows

INSTITUTIONAL INFORMATION

Public/private: Private (nonprofit). **Total Faculty:** 129. **% Faculty Female:** 37. **Students in Parent Institution:** 10,064.

PROGRAMS

Masters offered in: Acting; art history, criticism, and conservation; art/art studies; arts management; ceramic arts and ceramics; conducting; dance; drawing; fine/studio arts; intermedia/multimedia; music history, literature, and theory; music pedagogy; music performance; music theory and composition; music; music/music and performing arts studies; painting; photography; piano and organ; printmaking; radio and television broadcasting technology/technician; radio and television; sculpture; technical theater/theater design and technology; violin, viola, guitar, and other stringed instruments; voice and opera.

STUDENT INFORMATION

Total Students in Program: 200. **% Full-time:** 99. **% Female:** 635.

RESEARCH FACILITIES

Research Facilities: Hamon Arts Library.

EXPENSES/FINANCIAL AID

Annual Tuition: $14,634. **Room & Board:** $7,995. **Fees:** $1,872. **Books and Supplies:** $200. **Grants Range From:** $8,000-$26,866. **Loans Range From:** $500-$18,500.

ADMISSIONS INFORMATION

Application Fee: $50. **Priority Application Deadline:** 2/1. **Regular Application Deadline:** 6/1. **Regular Notification:** Rolling. **Transfer Students Accepted?** No. **Number of Applications Received:** 263. **% of Applicants Accepted:** 47. **% Accepted Who Enrolled:** 70.
Required Admission Factors: Essays/personal statement, letters of recommendation, transcript.
Other Admission Factors: Some, but not all, programs require a minimum GPA of 3.0. The television/radio program requires a minimum 450 on the Verbal portion of the GRE.
Program-Specific Admission Factors: Audition required of theater acting and most music applicants. Portfolio required of studio art and theater design applicants. Sample research paper required of art history, music history, music theory, music education, and music therapy applicants.

SOUTHERN NAZARENE UNIVERSITY
Graduate College

Address: 6729 Northwest 39th Expressway, Bethany, OK 73008
Admissions Phone: 405-491-6316 · **Admissions Fax:** 405-491-6686

INSTITUTIONAL INFORMATION

Public/private: Private (nonprofit). **Evening Classes Available?** Yes. **Students in Parent Institution:** 2,013.

STUDENT INFORMATION

Total Students in Program: 308. **% Full-time:** 86. **% Female:** 56.

EXPENSES/FINANCIAL AID

Annual Tuition: $6,372.

ADMISSIONS INFORMATION

Application Fee: $25. **Regular Notification:** Rolling. **Transfer Students Accepted?** Yes.
Required Admission Factors: Essays/personal statement, interview, transcript.
Other Admission Factors: Minimum 2.7 GPA (3.0 in the last 60 credit hours) required.

SOUTHERN OREGON UNIVERSITY
School of Arts & Letters

Address: 1250 Siskiyou Boulevard, Ashland, OR 97520

INSTITUTIONAL INFORMATION

Public/private: Public. **Students in Parent Institution:** 5,493.

STUDENT INFORMATION

Total Students in Program: 614. **% Full-time:** 31. **% Female:** 67.

EXPENSES/FINANCIAL AID

Annual Tuition: In-state $6,111. / Out-of-state $10,755. **Grants Range From:** $199-$13,542. **Loans Range From:** $211-$18,500. **% Receiving Scholarships/Grants:** 28. **% Receiving Loans:** 100. **% Receiving Assistantships:** 3.

ADMISSIONS INFORMATION

Transfer Students Accepted? No.
Required Admission Factors: GRE, letters of recommendation, transcript.
Other Admission Factors: Minimum GRE score of 1500 and minimum 3.0 GPA required.

EMPLOYMENT INFORMATION

Placement Office Available? Yes. **Rate of placement:** 68%.

SOUTHERN OREGON UNIVERSITY
School of Sciences

Address: 1250 Siskiyou Boulevard, Ashland, OR 97520
Admissions Phone: 541-552-6411

INSTITUTIONAL INFORMATION

Public/private: Public. **Students in Parent Institution:** 5,493.

STUDENT INFORMATION

Total Students in Program: 614. **% Full-time:** 31. **% Female:** 67.

EXPENSES/FINANCIAL AID

Annual Tuition: In-state $6,111. / Out-of-state $10,755. **Grants Range From:** $199-$13,542. **Loans Range From:** $211-$18,500. **% Receiving Scholarships/Grants:** 28. **% Receiving Loans:** 100. **% Receiving Assistantships:** 3. **Average Salary Stipend:** $1,179.

ADMISSIONS INFORMATION

Application Fee: $50. Regular Notification: Rolling. Transfer Students Accepted? Yes. % Accepted Who Enrolled: 72. Average GPA: 3.65. Required Admission Factors: GRE, letters of recommendation, transcript. Program-Specific Admission Factors: Minimum GRE score of 1400 and minimum 3.0 GPA required of computer science program applicants.

EMPLOYMENT INFORMATION

Placement Office Available? Yes. % Employed Within 6 Months: 95. Rate of placement: 68%.

SOUTHERN POLYTECHNIC STATE UNIVERSITY
College of Arts & Sciences

Address: 1100 South Marietta Parkway, Marietta, GA 30060-2896
Admissions Phone: 770-528-7281 · Admissions Fax: 770-528-7292
Admissions E-mail: vhead@spsu.edu

INSTITUTIONAL INFORMATION

Public/private: Public. Evening Classes Available? Yes. Student/faculty Ratio: 23:1. Students in Parent Institution: 3,525.

STUDENT INFORMATION

Total Students in Program: 556. % Full-time: 29. % Female: 43.

EXPENSES/FINANCIAL AID

Annual Tuition: In-state $1,686. / Out-of-state $6,762. Fees: $408. Books and Supplies: $1,000. Grants Range From: $1,100. Loans Range From: $1,800-$18,500. % Receiving Scholarships/Grants: 2. % Receiving Loans: 100. % Receiving Assistantships: 15. % Receiving Other Aid: 4. Number of Teaching/Research Assistantships Granted Each Year: 27 Average Salary Stipend: $1,500.

ADMISSIONS INFORMATION

Regular Notification: Rolling. Transfer Students Accepted? Yes. Transfer Policy: Good standing at previous institution required of transfer applicants. % Accepted Who Enrolled: 79.
Required Admission Factors: Essays/personal statement, letters of recommendation, transcript.

EMPLOYMENT INFORMATION

Placement Office Available? Yes. % Employed Within 6 Months: 79. Rate of placement: 85%. Average starting salary: $70,000.

SOUTHERN UNIVERSITY AND AGRICULTURAL AND MECHANICAL COLLEGE
Graduate Studies

Address: Southern Branch Post Office, Baton Rouge, LA 70813
Admissions Phone: 888-223-1460 or 225-771-5390
Admissions Fax: 225-771-5723

INSTITUTIONAL INFORMATION

Public/private: Public. Evening Classes Available? Yes. Total Faculty: 150. % Faculty Female: 32. % Faculty Part-time: 4. Student/faculty Ratio: 5:1. Students in Parent Institution: 9,095.

STUDENT INFORMATION

Total Students in Program: 1,247. % Full-time: 37. % Female: 74.

RESEARCH FACILITIES

Research Facilities: Center for Energy & Environmental Studies, Health Research Center.

EXPENSES/FINANCIAL AID

Annual Tuition: In-state $2,682. / Out-of-state $8,474. Books and Supplies: $900. Loans Range From: $8,500-$12,857. % Receiving Financial Aid: 76.

% Receiving Scholarships/Grants: 46. % Receiving Loans: 60. Number of Fellowships Granted Each Year: 2. Average amount of individual fellowships per year: 28,000. Number of Teaching/Research Assistantships Granted Each Year: 28.

ADMISSIONS INFORMATION

Application Fee: $5. Regular Notification: Rolling. Transfer Students Accepted? Yes. Transfer Policy: Proof of eligibility to re-enter previous school required of transfer applicants. Number of Applications Received: 435. % of Applicants Accepted: 100. % Accepted Who Enrolled: 91. Average GPA: 2.75. Average GRE Verbal: 344. Average GRE Quantitative: 376. Average GRE Analytical: 365.
Required Admission Factors: GRE, letters of recommendation, transcript. Program-Specific Admission Factors: Minimum 2.5 GPA required of master's degree program applicants. Minimum 3.0 GPA required of doctoral degree program applicants.

EMPLOYMENT INFORMATION

Placement Office Available? Yes. Rate of placement: 48%.

SOUTHERN UNIVERSITY AT NEW ORLEANS
Graduate Programs

Address: 6400 Press Drive, New Orleans, LA 70126
Admissions Phone: 504-284-5484 · Admissions Fax: 504-284-5506
Admissions E-mail: lhaynes@ml1.suno.edu

INSTITUTIONAL INFORMATION

Public/private: Public. Evening Classes Available? Yes. Student/faculty Ratio: 15:1. Students in Parent Institution: 4,121.

STUDENT INFORMATION

Total Students in Program: 357. % Full-time: 64. % Female: 76.

RESEARCH FACILITIES

Research Facilities: Student/faculty research lab.

EXPENSES/FINANCIAL AID

Annual Tuition: In-state $2,448. / Out-of-state $4,660. Fees: $50. Books and Supplies: $200. Average Salary Stipend: $5,500.

ADMISSIONS INFORMATION

Application Fee: $25. Transfer Students Accepted? Yes. Transfer Policy: Maximum 9 semester hours may be transferred with a minimum grade of B. Number of Applications Received: 22. Average GPA: 2.9.
Required Admission Factors: Essays/personal statement, GRE, letters of recommendation, transcript.
Other Admission Factors: Minimum 2.7 GPA required.

EMPLOYMENT INFORMATION

Placement Office Available? Yes. % Employed Within 6 Months: 75. % of master's/doctoral grads employed in their field upon graduation: 75/ 11. Rate of placement: 90%.

SOUTHERN UNIVERSITY AT NEW ORLEANS
School of Social Work

Address: 6400 Press Drive, New Orleans, LA 70126
Admissions Phone: 504-286-5484 · Admissions Fax: 504-284-5506
Admissions E-mail: lhaynes@ml1.suno.edu

INSTITUTIONAL INFORMATION

Public/private: Public. Evening Classes Available? Yes. Students in Parent Institution: 4,121.

STUDENT INFORMATION

Total Students in Program: 357. % Full-time: 64. % Female: 76.

RESEARCH FACILITIES

Research Facilities: Student/faculty research lab.

EXPENSES/FINANCIAL AID

Annual Tuition: In-state $2,448. / Out-of-state $4,660. Fees: $50. Books and Supplies: $200. Average amount of individual fellowships per year: 500.

ADMISSIONS INFORMATION

Application Fee: $25. Regular Notification: Rolling. Transfer Students Accepted? Yes. Transfer Policy: Maximum 9 credit hours may be transferred with minimum grade of B. Number of Applications Received: 200. % of Applicants Accepted: 68. % Accepted Who Enrolled: 85.
Required Admission Factors: Essays/personal statement, GRE, letters of recommendation, transcript.
Other Admission Factors: Minimum 2.5 GPA required.

EMPLOYMENT INFORMATION

Placement Office Available? Yes. % Employed Within 6 Months: 80. % of master's grads employed in their field upon graduation: 70. Rate of placement: 90%.

SOUTHERN UTAH UNIVERSITY
College of Performing & Visual Arts

Address: 351 West Center, Cedar City, UT 84720
Admissions Phone: 435-586-7743 · Admissions Fax: 435-865-8223
Admissions E-mail: abbott@suu.edu · Website: www.suu.edu/pua/mfa

INSTITUTIONAL INFORMATION

Public/private: Public. Student/faculty Ratio: 8:1. Students in Parent Institution: 6,095.

STUDENT INFORMATION

Total Students in Program: 211. % Full-time: 32. % Female: 46.

EXPENSES/FINANCIAL AID

Annual Tuition: In-state $1,612. / Out-of-state $5,984. Books and Supplies: $1,036. Grants Range From: $50-$10,035. Loans Range From: $500-$8,500. % Receiving Financial Aid: 100. % Receiving Scholarships/Grants: 80. % Receiving Loans: 66. Number of Teaching/Research Assistantships Granted Each Year: 8 Average Salary Stipend: $11,250.

ADMISSIONS INFORMATION

Application Fee: $40. Transfer Students Accepted? No. Number of Applications Received: 10. % of Applicants Accepted: 80. % Accepted Who Enrolled: 100. Average GPA: 3.29. Average GRE Verbal: 445. Average GRE Quantitative: 457. Average GRE Analytical: 572.
Required Admission Factors: Essays/personal statement, GRE, interview, letters of recommendation, transcript.
Other Admission Factors: Minimum 3.0 GPA required.
Program-Specific Admission Factors: Resume of professional and academic experience required of some applicants.

EMPLOYMENT INFORMATION

Placement Office Available? Yes. Rate of placement: 96%.

SOUTHERN WESLEYAN UNIVERSITY
Graduate Programs

Address: Wesleyan Drive, Central, SC 29630
Admissions Phone: 864-639-2112 or 800-264-5327
Admissions Fax: 864-639-4050 · Admissions E-mail: tgriffin@swu.edu

INSTITUTIONAL INFORMATION

Public/private: Private (nonprofit). Evening Classes Available? Yes. Students in Parent Institution: 1,803.

STUDENT INFORMATION

Total Students in Program: 79. % Full-time: 100. % Female: 43.

EXPENSES/FINANCIAL AID

Annual Tuition: $6,480. Fees: $920. Loans Range From: $5,000-$18,500. Average student debt, upon graduation: $20,000.

ADMISSIONS INFORMATION

Application Fee: $25. Regular Notification: Rolling. Transfer Students Accepted? Yes.
Required Admission Factors: Essays/personal statement, letters of recommendation, transcript.
Other Admission Factors: Minimum 2.7 GPA required.

SOUTHWEST BAPTIST UNIVERSITY
College of Science & Mathematics

Address: 1600 University Avenue, Bolivar, MO 65613-2597
Admissions Phone: 417-328-1672 · Admissions Fax: 417-328-1658
Admissions E-mail: pt@sbuniv.edu · Website: www.sbuniv.edu/PT/index.htm

INSTITUTIONAL INFORMATION

Public/private: Private (proprietary). Total Faculty: 5. % Faculty Female: 40. Student/faculty Ratio: 9:1. Students in Parent Institution: 3,445.

STUDENT INFORMATION

Total Students in Program: 44. % Full-time: 100. % Female: 52. % Minority: 7.

EXPENSES/FINANCIAL AID

Annual Tuition: $17,000. Fees: $422. Books and Supplies: $1,000. Loans Range From: $10,000-$18,000. % Receiving Financial Aid: 70. % Receiving Loans: 100.

ADMISSIONS INFORMATION

Application Fee: $25. Regular Application Deadline: 12/31. Regular Notification: Rolling. Transfer Students Accepted? Yes. Number of Applications Received: 26. % of Applicants Accepted: 88. % Accepted Who Enrolled: 70. Average GPA: 3.3. Average GRE Verbal: 423. Average GRE Quantitative: 487. Average GRE Analytical: 420.
Required Admission Factors: Essays/personal statement, GRE, interview, letters of recommendation, transcript.
Other Admission Factors: Minimum 2.75 GPA (minimum 3.0 in prerequisite courses) and minimum 40 hours of physical therapy experience required.

EMPLOYMENT INFORMATION

% Employed Within 6 Months: 90. Rate of placement: 100%. Average starting salary: $45,000.

SOUTHWEST MISSOURI STATE UNIVERSITY
College of Arts & Letters

Address: 901 South National, Springfield, MO 65804
Admissions Phone: 417-836-5335 · Admissions Fax: 417-836-6888
Admissions E-mail: derekmallett@smsu.edu

INSTITUTIONAL INFORMATION

Public/private: Public. Evening Classes Available? Yes. Students in Parent Institution: 17,703.

STUDENT INFORMATION

Total Students in Program: 3,004. % Full-time: 28. % Female: 65.

RESEARCH FACILITIES

Research Facilities: Plant Science Research Center.

EXPENSES/FINANCIAL AID

Annual Tuition: In-state $2,286. / Out-of-state $4,572. **Room & Board (On/off Campus):** $6,512/$6,783. **Fees:** $418. **Books and Supplies:** $500. **Grants Range From:** $150-$4,364. **Loans Range From:** $1,000-$19,500. **% Receiving Scholarships/Grants:** 13. **% Receiving Loans:** 47. **% Receiving Assistantships:** 38. **Average Salary Stipend:** $6,150.

ADMISSIONS INFORMATION

Application Fee: $25. **Regular Notification:** Rolling. **Transfer Students Accepted?** Yes. **Number of Applications Received:** 49. **% of Applicants Accepted:** 94. **% Accepted Who Enrolled:** 100. **Average GPA:** 3.17. **Required Admission Factors:** Transcript. **Other Admission Factors:** Minimum 3.0 GPA required.

EMPLOYMENT INFORMATION

Placement Office Available? Yes. **Rate of placement:** 75%.

SOUTHWEST MISSOURI STATE UNIVERSITY
College of Natural & Applied Sciences

Address: 901 South National, Springfield, MO 65804
Admissions Phone: 417-836-5335 · **Admissions Fax:** 417-836-6888
Admissions E-mail: derekmallett@smsu.edu

INSTITUTIONAL INFORMATION

Public/private: Public. **Students in Parent Institution:** 17,703.

STUDENT INFORMATION

Total Students in Program: 3,004. **% Full-time:** 28. **% Female:** 65.

RESEARCH FACILITIES

Research Facilities: Plant Science Research Center.

EXPENSES/FINANCIAL AID

Annual Tuition: In-state $2,286. / Out-of-state $4,572. **Room & Board (On/off Campus):** $6,512/$6,783. **Fees:** $418. **Books and Supplies:** $500. **Grants Range From:** $150-$4,364. **Loans Range From:** $1,000-$19,500. **% Receiving Scholarships/Grants:** 13. **% Receiving Loans:** 47. **% Receiving Assistantships:** 38. **Average Salary Stipend:** $6,150.

ADMISSIONS INFORMATION

Application Fee: $25. **Regular Notification:** Rolling. **Transfer Students Accepted?** Yes. **Number of Applications Received:** 38. **% of Applicants Accepted:** 87. **% Accepted Who Enrolled:** 100. **Required Admission Factors:** GRE, transcript. **Other Admission Factors:** Minimum 2.75 GPA (3.0 in biology) on last 60 credit hours required.

EMPLOYMENT INFORMATION

Placement Office Available? Yes. **Rate of placement:** 75%.

SOUTHWEST MISSOURI STATE UNIVERSITY
College of Humanities & Public Affairs

Address: 901 South National, Springfield, MO 65804
Admissions Phone: 417-836-5335 · **Admissions Fax:** 417-836-6888
Admissions E-mail: derekmallett@smsu.edu

INSTITUTIONAL INFORMATION

Public/private: Public. **Evening Classes Available?** Yes. **Students in Parent Institution:** 17,703.

STUDENT INFORMATION

Total Students in Program: 3,004. **% Full-time:** 28. **% Female:** 65.

RESEARCH FACILITIES

Research Facilities: Plant Science Research Center.

EXPENSES/FINANCIAL AID

Annual Tuition: In-state $2,286. / Out-of-state $4,572. **Room & Board (On/off Campus):** $6,512/$6,783. **Fees:** $418. **Books and Supplies:** $500. **Grants Range From:** $150-$4,364. **Loans Range From:** $1,000-$19,500. **% Receiving Scholarships/Grants:** 13. **% Receiving Loans:** 47. **% Receiving Assistantships:** 38. **Average Salary Stipend:** $6,150.

ADMISSIONS INFORMATION

Application Fee: $25. **Regular Notification:** Rolling. **Transfer Students Accepted?** Yes. **Number of Applications Received:** 38. **% of Applicants Accepted:** 89. **% Accepted Who Enrolled:** 100. **Average GPA:** 3.03. **Required Admission Factors:** GRE, transcript. **Program-Specific Admission Factors:** Minimum 2.75 GPA required of history program applicants. Minimum 3.0 GPA required of public administration program applicants. Minimum 3.2 GPA required of religious studies applicants.

EMPLOYMENT INFORMATION

Placement Office Available? Yes. **Rate of placement:** 75%.

SOUTHWESTERN COLLEGE (KANSAS)
Graduate Program

Address: 100 College Street, Winfield, KS 67156-2499
Admissions Phone: 316-221-8236 · **Admissions Fax:** 316-221-8344
Admissions E-mail: scadmit@jinx.sckans.edu

INSTITUTIONAL INFORMATION

Public/private: Private (nonprofit). **Evening Classes Available?** Yes. **Student/faculty Ratio:** 13:1. **Students in Parent Institution:** 1,143.

STUDENT INFORMATION

Total Students in Program: 29 **% Female:** 48.

RESEARCH FACILITIES

Research Facilities: Winfield Professional Studies, Witchita East Professional Studies, Witchita West Professional Studies.

EXPENSES/FINANCIAL AID

Books and Supplies: $600. **Loans Range From:** $2,600-$8,705. **% Receiving Loans:** 78.

ADMISSIONS INFORMATION

Regular Notification: Rolling. **Transfer Students Accepted?** Yes. **Transfer Policy:** Maximum 6 credit hours with a minimum grade of 3.0 may be transferred. **Number of Applications Received:** 8. **Required Admission Factors:** Transcript. **Other Admission Factors:** Minimum 3.0 GPA required.

EMPLOYMENT INFORMATION

Placement Office Available? Yes. **% of master's grads employed in their field upon graduation:** 100.

SOUTHWESTERN OKLAHOMA STATE UNIVERSITY
School of Arts & Sciences

Address: 100 Campus Drive, Weatherford, OK 73096-3098
Admissions Phone: 580-774-3216
Admissions E-mail: spurgea@swosu.edu

INSTITUTIONAL INFORMATION

Public/private: Public. **Evening Classes Available?** Yes. **Students in Parent Institution:** 4,453.

STUDENT INFORMATION

Total Students in Program: 258. **% Full-time:** 29. **% Female:** 59.

RESEARCH FACILITIES

Research Facilities: Gulf Coast Research Lab.

EXPENSES/FINANCIAL AID

Annual Tuition: $1,458. Room & Board: $3,000. Fees: $40.

ADMISSIONS INFORMATION

Application Fee: $15. Regular Notification: Rolling. Transfer Students Accepted? Yes. Number of Applications Received: 2. % of Applicants Accepted: 100.
Required Admission Factors: Letters of recommendation, transcript.
Other Admission Factors: Minimum 2.5 GPA required.

EMPLOYMENT INFORMATION

Placement Office Available? Yes.

SPALDING UNIVERSITY
School of Professional Psychology

Address: 851 South Fourth Street, School of Professional Psychology, Louisville, KY 40203
Admissions Phone: 502-585-7127 · Admissions Fax: 502-585-7159
Admissions E-mail: esimpson@spalding.edu · Website: www.spalding.edu

INSTITUTIONAL INFORMATION

Public/private: Private (nonprofit). Evening Classes Available? Yes. Total Faculty: 29. % Faculty Female: 55. % Faculty Part-time: 66. Student/faculty Ratio: 5:1. Students in Parent Institution: 1,800.

STUDENT INFORMATION

Total Students in Program: 150. % Full-time: 100. % Female: 263.

EXPENSES/FINANCIAL AID

Annual Tuition: $12,320. Fees: $330. Books and Supplies: $1,000. Grants Range From: $560-$10,080. % Receiving Financial Aid: 49. % Receiving Scholarships/Grants: 24. % Receiving Loans: 62. % Receiving Assistantships: 15. Types of Aid Available: Graduate assistantships, loans, scholarships.

ADMISSIONS INFORMATION

Application Fee: $30. Regular Application Deadline: 1/15. Regular Notification: 4/1. Transfer Students Accepted? Yes. Transfer Policy: Maximum 9 credit hours may be transferred into master's programs. Number of Applications Received: 101. % of Applicants Accepted: 62. % Accepted Who Enrolled: 44. Average GPA: 3.6. Average GRE Verbal: 480. Average GRE Quantitative: 560. Average GRE Analytical: 500.
Required Admission Factors: Essays/personal statement, GRE, interview, letters of recommendation, transcript.
Other Admission Factors: Minimum GRE score of 1000 and minimum 3.0 GPA recommended. School of professional psychology application, 3-page autobiography, writting sample, 3 letters of recommendation, and CV required.

SPRING ARBOR UNIVERSITY
School of Adult Studies

Address: 106 East Main Street, Spring Arbor, MI 49283
Admissions Phone: 517-750-6654 · Admissions Fax: 517-750-6602
Admissions E-mail: cpavey@arbor.edu

INSTITUTIONAL INFORMATION

Public/private: Private (nonprofit). Evening Classes Available? Yes. Student/faculty Ratio: 18:1. Students in Parent Institution: 1,582.

STUDENT INFORMATION

Total Students in Program: 443. % Full-time: 60. % Female: 66.

EXPENSES/FINANCIAL AID

Annual Tuition: In-state $5,202. Fees: $75. Books and Supplies: $396. % Receiving Financial Aid: 27. Average student debt, upon graduation: $7,500.

ADMISSIONS INFORMATION

Application Fee: $30. Regular Notification: Rolling. Transfer Students Accepted? Yes. Transfer Policy: Maximum 8 credit hours taken within the last 6 years may be transferred. Number of Applications Received: 90. % of Applicants Accepted: 66. % Accepted Who Enrolled: 100. Average GPA: 3.0.
Required Admission Factors: Letters of recommendation, transcript.
Other Admission Factors: Minimum 3.0 GPA required. Writing and computer skills recommended.

SPRING HILL COLLEGE
Liberal Arts Program

Address: 4000 Dauphin Street, Mobile, AL 36608
Admissions Phone: 251-380-3094 · Admissions Fax: 251-460-2190
Admissions E-mail: grad@shc.edu

INSTITUTIONAL INFORMATION

Public/private: Private (nonprofit). Evening Classes Available? Yes. Student/faculty Ratio: 2:1. Students in Parent Institution: 1,484.

STUDENT INFORMATION

Total Students in Program: 257. % Full-time: 8. % Female: 70.

EXPENSES/FINANCIAL AID

Annual Tuition: $3,510. Fees: $20. Books and Supplies: $600. Grants Range From: $184-$4,435. Loans Range From: $500-$18,500. % Receiving Loans: 69. % Receiving Assistantships: 1.

ADMISSIONS INFORMATION

Application Fee: $25. Regular Notification: Rolling. Transfer Students Accepted? Yes. Transfer Policy: Maximum 9 credit hours with a minimum grade of B may be transferred.
Required Admission Factors: Transcript.
Other Admission Factors: Minimum 3.0 GPA required for unconditional admission; MAT may be required if GPA is below minimum.

EMPLOYMENT INFORMATION

Placement Office Available? Yes.

SPRINGFIELD COLLEGE
School of Graduate Studies

Address: 263 Alden Street, Springfield, MA 01109-3797
Admissions Phone: 413-748-3479 · Admissions Fax: 413-748-3694
Admissions E-mail: donald_shaw_jr@spfldcol.edu

INSTITUTIONAL INFORMATION

Public/private: Private (nonprofit). Evening Classes Available? Yes. Student/faculty Ratio: 7:1. Students in Parent Institution: 4,716.

PROGRAMS

Masters offered in: Art therapy/therapist, education, health teacher education, health/health care administration/management, kinesiology and exercise science, medical/clinical assistant, occupational therapy/therapist, physical education teaching and coaching, physical therapy/therapist, psychology, rehabilitation counseling/counselor, sports and fitness administration/management.

STUDENT INFORMATION

Total Students in Program: 1,408. % Full-time: 69. % Female: 68.

EXPENSES/FINANCIAL AID

Annual Tuition: $12,912. Room & Board: $5,640. Fees: $25. Books and Supplies: $800. Grants Range From: $2,000-$9,324. Loans Range From: $500-$22,500. % Receiving Financial Aid: 68. % Receiving Scholarships/Grants: 3. % Receiving Loans: 91. % Receiving Assistantships: 10. Number of Fellowships Granted Each Year: 4. Average amount of individual fellowships per year: $9,324. Number of Teaching/Research Assistantships Granted Each Year: 125. Average Salary Stipend: $4,000.

ADMISSIONS INFORMATION

Application Fee: $40. Regular Notification: Rolling. Transfer Students Accepted? Yes. Transfer Policy: Maximum 6 credit hours may be transferred into programs that require 48 semester hours. Number of Applications Received: 980. % of Applicants Accepted: 83. % Accepted Who Enrolled: 51. Average GPA: 3.15.
Required Admission Factors: Essays/personal statement, letters of recommendation, transcript.
Other Admission Factors: Minimum 2.5 GPA required.
Program-Specific Admission Factors: Minimum 3.0 GPA required of social work, physical therapy, and physician assistant program applicants and recommended for art therapy and psychology program applicants.

EMPLOYMENT INFORMATION

Placement Office Available? Yes. % of master's/doctoral grads employed in their field upon graduation: 80/100. Rate of placement: 99%. Average starting salary: $40,000.

ST. AMBROSE UNIVERSITY
College of Arts & Sciences

Address: 518 West Locust Street, Davenport, IA 52803
Admissions Phone: 563-333-6308 · Admissions Fax: 563-333-6243
Admissions E-mail: shumphry@sau.edu

INSTITUTIONAL INFORMATION

Student/faculty Ratio: 7:1. Students in Parent Institution: 3,011.

STUDENT INFORMATION

Total Students in Program: 895. % Full-time: 32. % Female: 59.

EXPENSES/FINANCIAL AID

Annual Tuition: $8,208. Books and Supplies: $85. Grants Range From: $648-$13,890. Loans Range From: $1,500-$25,500. % Receiving Financial Aid: 33. % Receiving Scholarships/Grants: 7. % Receiving Loans: 96. % Receiving Assistantships: 8. Average student debt, upon graduation: $13,000 Average Salary Stipend: $400.

ADMISSIONS INFORMATION

Application Fee: $25. Regular Notification: Rolling. Transfer Students Accepted? Yes. Transfer Policy: Maximum 12 credit hours may be transferred into pastoral studies program. Number of Applications Received: 50. % of Applicants Accepted: 94. % Accepted Who Enrolled: 81.
Required Admission Factors: Letters of recommendation, transcript.
Other Admission Factors: Minimum 3.0 GPA required.
Program-Specific Admission Factors: At least 9 credit horus of theology and 2 years of ministry experience required of pastoral studies program applicants. Minimum 3 letters of recommendation required of social work program applicants.

EMPLOYMENT INFORMATION

Placement Office Available? Yes. % of master's grads employed in their field upon graduation: 96. Rate of placement: 98%.

ST. AMBROSE UNIVERSITY
College of Human Services

Address: 518 West Locust Street, Davenport, IA 52803
Admissions Phone: 563-333-6308 · Admissions Fax: 563-333-6243
Admissions E-mail: shumphry@sau.edu

INSTITUTIONAL INFORMATION

Evening Classes Available? Yes. Student/faculty Ratio: 10:1. Students in Parent Institution: 3,011.

STUDENT INFORMATION

Total Students in Program: 895. % Full-time: 32. % Female: 59.

EXPENSES/FINANCIAL AID

Annual Tuition: $8,208. Books and Supplies: $85. Grants Range From: $648-$13,890. Loans Range From: $1,500-$25,500. % Receiving Financial Aid: 30. % Receiving Scholarships/Grants: 7. % Receiving Loans: 96. % Receiving Assistantships: 8. Average student debt, upon graduation: $13,000. Number of Teaching/Research Assistantships Granted Each Year: 24. Average Salary Stipend: $200.

ADMISSIONS INFORMATION

Application Fee: $25. Transfer Students Accepted? Yes. Number of Applications Received: 200. % of Applicants Accepted: 88. % Accepted Who Enrolled: 76.
Required Admission Factors: Letters of recommendation, transcript.
Other Admission Factors: Minimum 2.8 GPA required of some programs.
Program-Specific Admission Factors: Minimum 2.75 GPA required of MEd program applicants. Minimum 3.0 GPA required of criminal justice program applicants. Minimum 3.3 GPA required of physical therpay track I program applicants; minimum GRE score of 1500.

EMPLOYMENT INFORMATION

Placement Office Available? Yes. % of master's grads employed in their field upon graduation: 96. Rate of placement: 98%.

ST. BONAVENTURE UNIVERSITY
School of Arts & Sciences

Address: PO Box D, St. Bonaventure, NY 14778-2284
Admissions Phone: 716-375-2021 · Admissions Fax: 716-375-4015
Admissions E-mail: gradsch@sbu.edu

INSTITUTIONAL INFORMATION

Public/private: Private (nonprofit). Total Faculty: 45. % Faculty Female: 36. Students in Parent Institution: 2,755.

STUDENT INFORMATION

Total Students in Program: 598. % Full-time: 46. % Female: 66.

RESEARCH FACILITIES

Research Facilities: Franciscan Institute.

EXPENSES/FINANCIAL AID

Annual Tuition: In-state $12,720. % Receiving Financial Aid: 48. Average student debt, upon graduation: $16,000.

ADMISSIONS INFORMATION

Application Fee: $35. Regular Notification: Rolling. Transfer Students Accepted? Yes. Number of Applications Received: 12. % of Applicants Accepted: 83. % Accepted Who Enrolled: 50. Average GPA: 2.7. Average GRE Verbal: 404. Average GRE Quantitative: 500. Average GRE Analytical: 516.
Required Admission Factors: GRE, letters of recommendation, transcript.
Other Admission Factors: Minimum 2.75 GPA and health certificate required.

Program-Specific Admission Factors: Minimum GRE score of 1000 required of psychology program applicants.

EMPLOYMENT INFORMATION
Placement Office Available? Yes.

ST. BONAVENTURE UNIVERSITY
School of Graduate Studies

Address: PO Box D, St. Bonaventure, NY 14778
Admissions Phone: 716-375-2021 · Admissions Fax: 716-375-4015
Admissions E-mail: gradsch@sbu.edu · Website: http://grad.sbu.edu

INSTITUTIONAL INFORMATION
Public/private: Private (nonprofit). Evening Classes Available? Yes.

PROGRAMS
Masters offered in: Business administration/management; communications, journalism, and related fields; counselor education/school counseling and guidance services; education leadership and administration; education; English language and literature; health teacher education; organizational behavior studies; reading teacher education; secondary education and teaching; theology/theological studies.

EXPENSES/FINANCIAL AID
Annual Tuition: $590. Room & Board: $6,530. Books and Supplies: $1,000. Types of Aid Available: graduate assistantships, institutional work-study, loans, scholarships.

ADMISSIONS INFORMATION
Priority Application Deadline: 3/15. Regular Application Deadline: 6/1. Regular Notification: Rolling. Transfer Students Accepted? Yes. Transfer Policy: Transfer applicants must speak directly to the appropriate program director to inquire about receiving transfer credit. Number of Applications Received: 316. % of Applicants Accepted: 79. % Accepted Who Enrolled: 86.
Required Admission Factors: Letters of recommendation, transcript.
Other Admission Factors: A 3.0 cumulative GPA is the working standard for most of our programs.
Program-Specific Admission Factors: MSEd adolescence education initial certification applicants must submit a passing score for the content specialty test and the liberal arts & science test.

ST. CHARLES BORROMEO SEMINARY
Graduate Programs

Address: 100 East Wynnewood Road, Wynnewood, PA 19096
Admissions Phone: 610-667-3394 · Admissions Fax: 610-667-9267
Admissions E-mail: vreascs@aol.com

INSTITUTIONAL INFORMATION
Public/private: Private (nonprofit). Total Faculty: 34. % Faculty Female: 21. Student/faculty Ratio: 7:1. Students in Parent Institution: 485.

STUDENT INFORMATION
Total Students in Program: 105. % Full-time: 19. % Female: 43.

EXPENSES/FINANCIAL AID
Annual Tuition: $9,580. Books and Supplies: $600.

ADMISSIONS INFORMATION
Regular Notification: Rolling. Transfer Students Accepted? Yes. Transfer Policy: Recommendation of the diocese or religious community required of transfer applicants to the seminary. Number of Applications Received: 83. % of Applicants Accepted: 96. % Accepted Who Enrolled: 100.
Required Admission Factors: Letters of recommendation, transcript.

ST. CLOUD STATE UNIVERSITY
College of Fine Arts & Humanities

Address: 720 Fourth Avenue South, St. Cloud, MN 56301
Admissions Phone: 320-255-2113 · Admissions Fax: 320-654-5371

INSTITUTIONAL INFORMATION
Public/private: Public. Evening Classes Available? Yes. Students in Parent Institution: 14,758.

STUDENT INFORMATION
Total Students in Program: 1,246. % Full-time: 34. % Female: 65.

EXPENSES/FINANCIAL AID
Annual Tuition: In-state $3,564. / Out-of-state $5,005. Books and Supplies: $1,315. Loans Range From: $272-$11,554. % Receiving Financial Aid: 18. Average student debt, upon graduation: $15,625.

ADMISSIONS INFORMATION
Application Fee: $20. Regular Notification: Rolling. Transfer Students Accepted? Yes. Number of Applications Received: 34. % of Applicants Accepted: 88. % Accepted Who Enrolled: 90. Average GPA: 3.32. Average GRE Verbal: 480. Average GRE Quantitative: 509.
Required Admission Factors: Essays/personal statement, GRE, letters of recommendation, transcript.
Other Admission Factors: Minimum GRE score of 1000 (or minimum section score of 480 Verbal) and minimum 2.75 GPA required.

EMPLOYMENT INFORMATION
Placement Office Available? Yes.

ST. CLOUD STATE UNIVERSITY
College of Social Sciences

Address: 720 Fourth Avenue South, St. Cloud, MN 56301
Admissions Phone: 320-255-2113 · Admissions Fax: 320-654-5371

INSTITUTIONAL INFORMATION
Public/private: Public. Evening Classes Available? Yes. Students in Parent Institution: 14,758.

STUDENT INFORMATION
Total Students in Program: 1,246. % Full-time: 34. % Female: 65.

EXPENSES/FINANCIAL AID
Annual Tuition: In-state $3,564. / Out-of-state $5,005. Books and Supplies: $1,315. Loans Range From: $272-$11,554. % Receiving Financial Aid: 18. Average student debt, upon graduation: $15,475. Average Salary Stipend: $6,500.

ADMISSIONS INFORMATION
Application Fee: $20. Regular Notification: Rolling. Transfer Students Accepted? Yes. Number of Applications Received: 71. % of Applicants Accepted: 90. Average GPA: 3.22. Average GRE Verbal: 458. Average GRE Quantitative: 485.
Required Admission Factors: GRE, letters of recommendation, transcript.
Other Admission Factors: Minimum GRE score of 1000 (or minimum section score of 480 Verbal) and minimum 2.75 GPA required.

EMPLOYMENT INFORMATION
Placement Office Available? Yes.

ST. EDWARD'S UNIVERSITY
Master of Arts in Counseling

Address: 3001 South Congress Avenue, Austin, TX 78704
Admissions Phone: 512-448-8600 · **Admissions Fax:** 512-428-1032
Admissions E-mail: seu.grad@admin.stedwards.edu
Website: www.stedwards.edu/mac

INSTITUTIONAL INFORMATION
Public/private: Private (nonprofit). **Evening Classes Available?** Yes.

PROGRAMS
Masters offered in: Counseling psychology.

STUDENT INFORMATION
Total Students in Program: 171. **% Full-time:** 30.

EXPENSES/FINANCIAL AID
Annual Tuition: $8,460. **Fees:** $45. **Books and Supplies:** $300. **Types of Aid Available:** Institutional work-study, loans, scholarships.

ADMISSIONS INFORMATION
Application Fee: $45. **Priority Application Deadline:** 7/1. **Regular Application Deadline:** 8/1. **Regular Notification:** Rolling. **Transfer Students Accepted?** Yes. **Transfer Policy:** Graduate transfer credit must be completed with a 3.0 or higher, subject to approval of dean or program director. **Number of Applications Received:** 72. **% of Applicants Accepted:** 78. **% Accepted Who Enrolled:** 82.
Required Admission Factors: Essays/personal statement, transcript.
Other Admission Factors: Minimum GPA of 3.0 in last 60 hours or 2.75 overall

ST. EDWARD'S UNIVERSITY
Master of Arts in Human Services

Address: 3001 South Congress Avenue, Austin, TX 78704
Admissions Phone: 512-448-8600 · **Admissions Fax:** 512-428-1032
Admissions E-mail: seu.grad@admin.stedwards.edu · **Website:** www.stedwards.edu

INSTITUTIONAL INFORMATION
Public/private: Private (nonprofit). **Evening Classes Available?** Yes. **Student/faculty Ratio:** 17:1.

PROGRAMS
Masters offered in: Health/health care administration/management, human resources management/personnel administration, human services, peace studies and conflict resolution, public administration and services, sports and fitness administration/management.

STUDENT INFORMATION
Total Students in Program: 67. **% Full-time:** 16.

EXPENSES/FINANCIAL AID
Annual Tuition: $8,460. **Fees:** $45. **Books and Supplies:** $300. **Types of Aid Available:** Institutional work-study, loans, scholarships.

ADMISSIONS INFORMATION
Application Fee: $45. **Priority Application Deadline:** 7/1. **Regular Application Deadline:** 8/1. **Regular Notification:** Rolling. **Transfer Students Accepted?** Yes. **Number of Applications Received:** 30. **% of Applicants Accepted:** 80. **% Accepted Who Enrolled:** 75.
Required Admission Factors: Essays/personal statement, transcript.
Other Admission Factors: Minimum GRE score of 1000 on Verbal and Quantitative sections or minimum GMAT of 500, and minimum 2.75 GPA in last 60 credit hours required.

ST. EDWARD'S UNIVERSITY
Master of Liberal Arts Program

Address: 3001 South Congress Avenue, Austin, TX 78704
Admissions Phone: 512-448-8600 · **Admissions Fax:** 512-428-1032
Admissions E-mail: seu.grad@admin.stedwards.edu
Website: www.stedwards.edu/mla

INSTITUTIONAL INFORMATION
Public/private: Private (nonprofit). **Evening Classes Available?** Yes. **Students in Parent Institution:** 4,443.

PROGRAMS
Masters offered in: Humanities/humanistic studies, liberal arts and sciences studies and humanities, liberal arts and sciences/liberal studies, multi/interdisciplinary studies.

STUDENT INFORMATION
Total Students in Program: 80. **% Full-time:** 14. **% Female:** 485.

EXPENSES/FINANCIAL AID
Annual Tuition: $8,460. **Fees:** $45. **Books and Supplies:** $300. **Types of Aid Available:** Institutional work-study, loans, scholarships.

ADMISSIONS INFORMATION
Application Fee: $45. **Priority Application Deadline:** 7/1. **Regular Application Deadline:** 8/1. **Regular Notification:** Rolling. **Transfer Students Accepted?** Yes. **Transfer Policy:** Graduate transfer credit must have a grade of at least 3.0 and is subject to the discretion of the dean or program director. **Number of Applications Received:** 30. **% of Applicants Accepted:** 87. **% Accepted Who Enrolled:** 88.
Required Admission Factors: Essays/personal statement, interview, transcript.
Other Admission Factors: Minimum 2.75 GPA in last 60 credit hours of undergraduate study required.

ST. EDWARD'S UNIVERSITY
Master of Science in Organizational Leadership and Ethics

Address: 3001 South Congress Avenue, Austin, TX 78704
Admissions Phone: 512-448-8600 · **Admissions Fax:** 512-428-1032
Admissions E-mail: seu.grad@admin.stedwards.edu
Website: www.stedwards.edu/gsm/msole

INSTITUTIONAL INFORMATION
Public/private: Private (nonprofit). **Evening Classes Available?** Yes.

PROGRAMS
Masters offered in: Ethics, multi/interdisciplinary studies.

STUDENT INFORMATION
Total Students in Program: 56. **% Full-time:** 4.

ADMISSIONS INFORMATION
Application Fee: $45. **Priority Application Deadline:** 7/1. **Regular Application Deadline:** 8/1. **Regular Notification:** Rolling. **Transfer Students Accepted?** Yes. **Transfer Policy:** Graduate transfer credit must be completed with a 3.0 or higher, subject to the approval of the dean or program director. **Number of Applications Received:** 22. **% of Applicants Accepted:** 77. **% Accepted Who Enrolled:** 71.
Required Admission Factors: Essays/personal statement, transcript.
Other Admission Factors: Minimum 2.75 GPA in last 60 hours

ST. FRANCIS XAVIER UNIVERSITY
Graduate Studies

Address: PO Box 5000, Antigonish, Nova Scotia, B2G 2W5, Canada
Admissions Phone: 902-867-2219 · **Admissions Fax:** 902-867-2329
Admissions E-mail: jtaylor@stfx.edu

INSTITUTIONAL INFORMATION
Public/private: Private (nonprofit). **Evening Classes Available?** Yes. **Student/faculty Ratio:** 2:1. **Students in Parent Institution:** 4,080.

STUDENT INFORMATION
Total Students in Program: 75. **% Full-time:** 19. **% Female:** 55.

EXPENSES/FINANCIAL AID
Room & Board: $6,500. **Fees:** $341.

ADMISSIONS INFORMATION
Application Fee: $30. **Regular Notification:** Rolling. **Transfer Students Accepted?** Yes. **Number of Applications Received:** 85. **% of Applicants Accepted:** 44.
Required Admission Factors: Letters of recommendation, transcript.
Other Admission Factors: Minimum grade average of 70 required.

EMPLOYMENT INFORMATION
Placement Office Available? Yes.

ST. GEORGE'S UNIVERSITY
Graduate Studies

Address: North American Correspondent, 1 East Main Street, Bay Shore, NY 11706
Admissions Phone: 631-665-8500 · **Admissions Fax:** 631-665-5590
Admissions E-mail: sguinfo@sgu.edu · **Website:** www.sgu.edu

INSTITUTIONAL INFORMATION
Public/private: Private (proprietary). **Student/faculty Ratio:** 1:1. **Students in Parent Institution:** 2,945.

PROGRAMS
Masters offered in: Anatomy, microbiology. **Doctorate offered in:** Anatomy, microbiology.

RESEARCH FACILITIES
Research Facilities: Windward Island Research and Education Foundation, an independent charitable research institute located on the Grenada Campus.

EXPENSES/FINANCIAL AID
Annual Tuition: $15,000. **Room & Board:** $9,900. **Books and Supplies:** $1,000. **Grants Range From:** $1,200-$12,000. **Loans Range From:** $500-$3,500. **% Receiving Financial Aid:** 79. **% Receiving Scholarships/Grants:** 79. **% Receiving Loans:** 51. **Types of Aid Available:** Grants, loans, scholarships. **Average student debt, upon graduation:** $10,000.

ADMISSIONS INFORMATION
Application Fee: $75. **Regular Application Deadline:** 6/15. **Transfer Students Accepted?** Yes.
Required Admission Factors: Essays/personal statement, interview, letters of recommendation, transcript.
Recommended Admission Factors: GRE.

ST. JOHN'S UNIVERSITY
College of Liberal Arts & Sciences

Address: 8000 Utopia Parkway, Jamaica, NY 11439
Admissions Phone: 718-990-2000 · **Admissions Fax:** 718-990-2096
Admissions E-mail: armstrop@stjohns.edu

INSTITUTIONAL INFORMATION
Public/private: Private (nonprofit). **Evening Classes Available?** Yes. **Total Faculty:** 461. **% Faculty Female:** 38. **% Faculty Part-time:** 54. **Students in Parent Institution:** 18,621.

STUDENT INFORMATION
Total Students in Program: 3,450. **% Full-time:** 20. **% Female:** 66.

RESEARCH FACILITIES
Research Facilities: Center for Asian Studies, Speech and Hearing Clinic, Center for Psychological Services, Writing Center.

EXPENSES/FINANCIAL AID
Annual Tuition: $14,520. **Room & Board:** $6,800. **Fees:** $150. **Books and Supplies:** $1,000. **Grants Range From:** $100. **Loans Range From:** $200. **% Receiving Financial Aid:** 63. **% Receiving Scholarships/Grants:** 13. **% Receiving Loans:** 33. **% Receiving Assistantships:** 7. **Average student debt, upon graduation:** $26,123. **Number of Fellowships Granted Each Year:** 91. **Average amount of individual fellowships per year:** $14,666. **Number of Teaching/Research Assistantships Granted Each Year:** 72. **Average Salary Stipend:** $12,240.

ADMISSIONS INFORMATION
Application Fee: $40. **Regular Notification:** Rolling. **Transfer Students Accepted?** Yes. **Transfer Policy:** Maximum 12 credit hours with a minimum 3.0 GPA and catalog description of course may be transferred. **Number of Applications Received:** 1,036. **% of Applicants Accepted:** 42. **% Accepted Who Enrolled:** 48. **Average GPA:** 3.4. **Average GRE Verbal:** 480. **Average GRE Quantitative:** 538. **Average GRE Analytical:** 548.
Required Admission Factors: Essays/personal statement, letters of recommendation, transcript.
Other Admission Factors: Minimum 3.0 GPA required.
Program-Specific Admission Factors: Interview required of library science, clinical psychology, school psychology (PsyD), English, and modern world history program applicants. GRE required of school psychology, clinical psychology, and English program applicants.

EMPLOYMENT INFORMATION
Placement Office Available? Yes. **% Employed Within 6 Months:** 69.

ST. JOHN'S UNIVERSITY
College of Professional Studies

Address: 8000 Utopia Parkway, Jamaica, NY 11439
Admissions Phone: 718-990-2000 · **Admissions Fax:** 718-990-2046
Admissions E-mail: admissions@stjohns.edu

INSTITUTIONAL INFORMATION
Public/private: Private (nonprofit). **Total Faculty:** 286. **% Faculty Female:** 37. **% Faculty Part-time:** 67. **Students in Parent Institution:** 18,621.

STUDENT INFORMATION
Total Students in Program: 3,450. **% Full-time:** 20. **% Female:** 66.

RESEARCH FACILITIES
Research Facilities: Center for Asian Studies, Speech and Hearing Clinic, Center for Psychological Services, Writing Center.

EXPENSES/FINANCIAL AID
Annual Tuition: $14,520. **Room & Board:** $6,800. **Fees:** $150. **Books and Supplies:** $1,000. **Grants Range From:** $100. **Loans Range From:** $200. **% Receiving Financial Aid:** 60. **% Receiving Scholarships/Grants:** 13. **% Receiving Loans:** 33. **% Receiving Assistantships:** 7.

ADMISSIONS INFORMATION
Application Fee: $40. **Regular Notification:** Rolling. **Transfer Students Accepted?** No. **Transfer Policy:** Letter of good standing frorm current institution required of transfer applicants. **Number of Applications Received:** 21. **% of Applicants Accepted:** 95. **% Accepted Who Enrolled:** 80. **Average GPA:** 3.0.

Required Admission Factors: Essays/personal statement, letters of recommendation, transcript.
Other Admission Factors: Minimum 3.0 GPA required.

EMPLOYMENT INFORMATION
Placement Office Available? Yes.

ST. JOSEPH'S COLLEGE (PATCHOGUE, NY)
School of Arts & Sciences

Address: 155 West Roe Boulevard, Patchogue, NY 11772
Admissions Phone: 631-447-3219 · **Admissions Fax:** 631-447-1734

INSTITUTIONAL INFORMATION
Public/private: Private (proprietary). **Student/faculty Ratio:** 15:1. **Students in Parent Institution:** 3,236.

STUDENT INFORMATION
Total Students in Program: 121. **% Full-time:** 34. **% Female:** 88.

EXPENSES/FINANCIAL AID
Annual Tuition: $7,182. **Loans Range From:** $5,000-$10,500. **% Receiving Financial Aid:** 50. **% Receiving Loans:** 100. **Average student debt, upon graduation:** $9,000.

ADMISSIONS INFORMATION
Application Fee: $25. **Regular Notification:** Rolling. **Transfer Students Accepted?** Yes. **Number of Applications Received:** 52. **% of Applicants Accepted:** 63. **% Accepted Who Enrolled:** 79. **Average GPA:** 3.43.
Required Admission Factors: Essays/personal statement, interview, letters of recommendation, transcript.
Other Admission Factors: Minimum 3.0 GPA required.

EMPLOYMENT INFORMATION
% Employed Within 6 Months: 100. **% of master's grads employed in their field upon graduation:** 97.

ST. JOSEPH'S UNIVERSITY
Graduate School of Arts & Sciences

Address: 5600 City Avenue, Philadelphia, PA 19131
Admissions Phone: 610-660-1289 · **Admissions Fax:** 610-660-1264

INSTITUTIONAL INFORMATION
Public/private: Private (nonprofit). **Evening Classes Available?** Yes. **Students in Parent Institution:** 6,484.

STUDENT INFORMATION
Total Students in Program: 2,331. **% Full-time:** 13. **% Female:** 55.

EXPENSES/FINANCIAL AID
Annual Tuition: $9,180. **Books and Supplies:** $350.

ADMISSIONS INFORMATION
Application Fee: $30. **Regular Notification:** Rolling. **Transfer Students Accepted?** Yes. **Average GPA:** 3.0.
Required Admission Factors: GRE, letters of recommendation, transcript.
Other Admission Factors: Resume required.

EMPLOYMENT INFORMATION
Placement Office Available? Yes.

ST. LOUIS COLLEGE OF PHARMACY
St. Louis College of Pharmacy

Address: 4588 Parkview Place, St. Louis, MO 63110
Admissions Phone: 314-367-8700 · **Admissions Fax:** 314-446-8310
Admissions E-mail: pkulage@stlcop.edu · **Website:** www.stlcop.edu

INSTITUTIONAL INFORMATION
Public/private: Private (nonprofit). **Total Faculty:** 107. **% Faculty Female:** 57. **% Faculty Part-time:** 40. **Student/faculty Ratio:** 13:1. **Students in Parent Institution:** 991.

PROGRAMS
Masters offered in: Pharmacy administration and pharmacy policy and regulatory affairs (MS, PhD). **First Professional degree offered in:** Pharmacy (PharMD, BS/BPharm).

STUDENT INFORMATION
Total Students in Program: 991. **% Full-time:** 100.

EXPENSES/FINANCIAL AID
Room & Board (On/off Campus): $7,133/$7,200. **Books and Supplies:** $1,000. **Types of Aid Available:** Grants, institutional work-study, loans, scholarships.

ADMISSIONS INFORMATION
Application Fee: $50. **Priority Application Deadline:** 10/31. **Regular Application Deadline:** 10/31. **Regular Notification:** Rolling. **Transfer Students Accepted?** Yes. **Transfer Policy:** PCAT minimum of 60. All applicants must go through PharmCAS system. **Number of Applications Received:** 714. **% of Applicants Accepted:** 45. **% Accepted Who Enrolled:** 78. **Average GPA:** 3.7.
Required Admission Factors: Essays/personal statement, letters of recommendation, transcript.

EMPLOYMENT INFORMATION
% Employed Within 6 Months: 100. **% of master's/first professional grads employed in their field upon graduation:** 100/100. **Rate of placement:** 99%. **Average starting salary:** $80,000.

ST. MARY-OF-THE-WOODS COLLEGE
Art Therapy Program

Address: St. Mary-of-the-Woods, IN 47876
Admissions Phone: 812-535-5162 · **Admissions Fax:** 812-535-4613
Admissions E-mail: gradadms@smwc.edu

INSTITUTIONAL INFORMATION
Public/private: Private (nonprofit). **Student/faculty Ratio:** 3:1. **Students in Parent Institution:** 1,439.

STUDENT INFORMATION
Total Students in Program: 85.

EXPENSES/FINANCIAL AID
Annual Tuition: $6,030. **Grants Range From:** $300-$600. **% Receiving Scholarships/Grants:** 100. **Average student debt, upon graduation:** $12,600.

ADMISSIONS INFORMATION
Application Fee: $35. **Regular Notification:** Rolling. **Transfer Students Accepted?** Yes. **Number of Applications Received:** 3. **% of Applicants Accepted:** 100. **% Accepted Who Enrolled:** 67. **Average GPA:** 3.0.
Required Admission Factors: Essays/personal statement, interview, letters of recommendation, transcript.
Other Admission Factors: Minimum 2.5 GPA and at least 12 semester hours in psychology and 15 semester hours in studio art required.

ST. MARY-OF-THE-WOODS COLLEGE
Earth Literacy Program

Address: St. Mary-of-the-Woods College, St. Mary of the Woods, IN 47876
Admissions Phone: 812-535-5160 · **Admissions Fax:** 812-535-5127
Admissions E-mail: mldolan@smwc.edu · **Website:** www.smwc.edu

INSTITUTIONAL INFORMATION
Public/private: Private (nonprofit). **Total Faculty:** 12. **% Faculty Female:** 75. **% Faculty Part-time:** 100. **Student/faculty Ratio:** 4:1. **Students in Parent Institution:** 1,300.

PROGRAMS
Masters offered in: Art therapy/therapist, music therapy/therapist, natural resources/conservation, pastoral studies/counseling.

STUDENT INFORMATION
Total Students in Program: 50. **% Full-time:** 4. **% Female:** 90. **% Minority:** 2. **% International:** 2.

EXPENSES/FINANCIAL AID
Annual Tuition: $1,456. **Room & Board:** $530. **Books and Supplies:** $150. **% Receiving Financial Aid:** 36. **% Receiving Loans:** 100.

ADMISSIONS INFORMATION
Application Fee: $35. **Regular Application Deadline:** 9/1. **Regular Notification:** Rolling. **Transfer Students Accepted?** Yes. **Number of Applications Received:** 13. **% of Applicants Accepted:** 100. **% Accepted Who Enrolled:** 62. **Average GPA:** 3.39.
Required Admission Factors: Essays/personal statement, letters of recommendation, transcript.
Other Admission Factors: Minimum 2.5 GPA required.

EMPLOYMENT INFORMATION
% Employed Within 6 Months: 100. **% of master's grads employed in their field upon graduation:** 100.

ST. MARY-OF-THE-WOODS COLLEGE
Music Therapy

Address: St. Mary-of-the-Woods, IN 47876
Admissions Phone: 812-535-5107 · **Admissions Fax:** 812-535-4900
Admissions E-mail: gradadms@smwc.edu

INSTITUTIONAL INFORMATION
Public/private: Private (nonprofit). **Student/faculty Ratio:** 2:1. **Students in Parent Institution:** 1,439.

STUDENT INFORMATION
Total Students in Program: 85.

EXPENSES/FINANCIAL AID
Annual Tuition: $6,030. **Grants Range From:** $300-$600. **% Receiving Scholarships/Grants:** 100.

ADMISSIONS INFORMATION
Application Fee: $35. **Regular Notification:** Rolling. **Transfer Students Accepted?** Yes. **Number of Applications Received:** 2. **% of Applicants Accepted:** 100. **% Accepted Who Enrolled:** 100. **Average GPA:** 3.62.
Required Admission Factors: Essays/personal statement, interview, letters of recommendation, transcript.
Other Admission Factors: Minimum 2.5 GPA, music therapy credential, diagnostic music exam, and at least 9 credit hours of psychology required.

ST. MARY'S COLLEGE OF CALIFORNIA
School of Liberal Arts

Address: 1928 Saint Mary's Road, Moraga, CA 94556
Admissions Phone: 925-631-4377 · **Admissions Fax:** 925-631-4965

INSTITUTIONAL INFORMATION
Public/private: Private (nonprofit). **Student/faculty Ratio:** 15:1. **Students in Parent Institution:** 4,136.

STUDENT INFORMATION
Total Students in Program: 462. **% Full-time:** 30. **% Female:** 87.

EXPENSES/FINANCIAL AID
Grants Range From: $480-$12,000. **Loans Range From:** $1,000-$18,500. **% Receiving Scholarships/Grants:** 32. **% Receiving Loans:** 71. **% Receiving Assistantships:** 1.

ADMISSIONS INFORMATION
Application Fee: $25. **Regular Notification:** Rolling. **Transfer Students Accepted?** Yes. **Average GPA:** 3.0.
Required Admission Factors: Essays/personal statement, letters of recommendation, transcript.
Other Admission Factors: Minimum 2.75 GPA required.

EMPLOYMENT INFORMATION
Placement Office Available? Yes. **Rate of placement:** 60%.

ST. MARY'S UNIVERSITY OF MINNESOTA
Graduate Programs

Address: 2510 Park Avenue South, Minneapolis, MN 55404
Admissions Phone: 612-874-9877 · **Admissions Fax:** 612-874-7108

INSTITUTIONAL INFORMATION
Evening Classes Available? Yes. **Total Faculty:** 239. **% Faculty Female:** 45. **Students in Parent Institution:** 6,688.

STUDENT INFORMATION
Total Students in Program: 6,542. **% Full-time:** 4. **% Female:** 63.

EXPENSES/FINANCIAL AID
Annual Tuition: $3,960. **Books and Supplies:** $300.

ADMISSIONS INFORMATION
Application Fee: $20. **Regular Notification:** Rolling. **Transfer Students Accepted?** Yes.
Required Admission Factors: Essays/personal statement, interview, transcript.
Other Admission Factors: Minimum 2.75 GPA required.

STATE UNIVERSITY OF NEW YORK AT ALBANY
College of Arts & Sciences

Address: 1400 Washington Avenue, Albany, NY 12222
Admissions Phone: 518-442-3980 · **Admissions Fax:** 518-442-3922
Admissions E-mail: graduate@uamail.albany.edu
Website: www.albany.edu/graduate/index.html

INSTITUTIONAL INFORMATION
Public/private: Public. **Evening Classes Available?** Yes. **Total Faculty:** 1,133. **% Faculty Female:** 40. **% Faculty Part-time:** 47. **Student/faculty Ratio:** 10:1. **Students in Parent Institution:** 16,293.

PROGRAMS

Masters offered in: Accounting; African American/Black studies; anthropology; art/art studies; atmospheric sciences and meteorology; biology teacher education; biometry/biometrics; business administration/management; chemistry teacher education; chemistry; city/urban, community, and regional planning; classics and classical languages, literatures, and linguistics; computer and information sciences; counseling psychology; criminology; curriculum and instruction; demography/population studies; directing and theatrical production; economics; education leadership and administration; education; educational statistics and research methods; English language and literature; English/language arts teacher education; environmental health; fine/studio arts; French language and literature; French language teacher education; geography; geology/earth science; German language teacher education; information science/studies; Latin American studies; Latin teacher education; liberal arts and sciences/liberal studies; library science/librarianship; linguistics; mathematics teacher education; mathematics; nonprofit/public/organizational management; philosophy; physics teacher education; physics; political science and government; psychology; public administration and services; public administration; public health (MPh, DPh); public policy analysis; reading teacher education; Russian language and literature; school psychology; social studies teacher education; social work; sociology; Spanish language and literature; Spanish language teacher education; special education; speech and rhetorical studies; taxation; teaching English as a second or foreign language/ESL language instructor; urban education and leadership; urban studies/affairs; women's studies. **Doctorate offered in:** Anthropology, atmospheric sciences and meteorology, biometry/biometrics, chemistry, clinical psychology, cognitive psychology and psycholinguistics, computer and information sciences, counseling psychology, criminology.

STUDENT INFORMATION

Total Students in Program: 4,905. **% Full-time:** 44. **% Female:** 62.

RESEARCH FACILITIES

Research Facilities: Over 50 research centers and institutes.

EXPENSES/FINANCIAL AID

Annual Tuition: In-state $6,900. / Out-of-state $10,500. **Room & Board:** $6,923. **Fees:** $990. **Books and Supplies:** $800. **Types of Aid Available:** Fellowships, graduate assistantships, grants, institutional work-study, loans, scholarships.

ADMISSIONS INFORMATION

Application Fee: $60. **Regular Notification:** Rolling. **Transfer Students Accepted?** Yes. **Transfer Policy:** Varies by program. **Number of Applications Received:** 4,522. **% of Applicants Accepted:** 48. **% Accepted Who Enrolled:** 54.

Required Admission Factors: Essays/personal statement, letters of recommendation, transcript.

Other Admission Factors: Varies by program.

STATE UNIVERSITY OF NEW YORK AT BUFFALO
College of Arts and Sciences

Address: Joseph Syracuse, c/o Dean's Office, 810 Clemens Hall, UB
North Campus, Buffalo, NY 14260
Admissions Phone: 716-645-2711 · **Admissions Fax:** 716-645-3888
Admissions E-mail: jcs32@buffalo.edu · **Web Address:** www.cas.buffalo.edu

INSTITUTIONAL INFORMATION

Public/private: Public. **Evening Classes Available?** Yes. **Students in Parent Institution:** 24,830.

PROGRAMS

Masters offered in: African studies; African American/black studies; American Indian/Native American studies; American/United States studies/civilization; anthropology; anthropology; applied economics; art/art studies; Asian American studies; biochemistry, biophysics and molecular biology; biochemistry/biophysics and molecular biology; biochemistry; bioinformatics; biological and physical sciences; biophysics; Caribbean studies; cartography; cell biology and anatomy; cell/cellular and molecular biology; chemistry; chemistry; classics and classical languages, literatures, and linguistics; classics and classical languages, literatures, and linguistics; comparative literature; design and applied arts; economics; economics; English composition; English language and literature; English language and literature/letters; film/video and photographic arts; fine arts and art studies; foreign languages/modern languages; French language and literature; geography; geography; geology/earth science; German language and literature; Germanic languages, literatures, and linguistics; Germanic languages, literatures, and linguistics; history; history; humanities/humanistic studies; intermedia/multimedia; international economics; liberal arts and sciences studies and humanities; linguistics; mathematics and computer science; mathematics; mathematics; molecular biochemistry; molecular biology; molecular biophysics; multi/interdisciplinary studies; music history, literature, and theory; music performance; music theory and composition; music; music/music and performing arts studies; musicology and ethnomusicology; natural sciences; philosophy; philosophy; physical sciences; physical sciences; physics; physics; political science and government; political science and government; psychology; psychology; romance languages, literatures, and linguistics; romance languages, literatures, and linguistics; social sciences; social sciences; sociology; Spanish language and literature; women's studies. **Doctorate offered in:** American Indian/Native American studies; American/United States studies/civilization; anthropology; anthropology; applied economics; biological and physical sciences; cartography; chemistry; chemistry; classics and classical languages. **First Professional degree offered in:** Molecular biochemistry; molecular biology; molecular biophysics.

STUDENT INFORMATION

Total Students in Program: 6,310. **% Full-time:** 52. **% Female:** 52.

RESEARCH FACILITIES

Research Facilities: More than 40 interdisciplinary research centers and institutes.

EXPENSES/FINANCIAL AID

Annual Tuition: In-state $6,900. / Out-of-state $10,500. **Fees:** $1,097. **Books and Supplies:** $1,000. **Grants Range From:** $100-$16,663. **Loans Range From:** $100-$16,663. **% Receiving Financial Aid:** 51. **% Receiving Scholarships/Grants:** 32. **% Receiving Loans:** 29. **% Receiving Assistantships:** 31. **Types of Aid Available:** Fellowships, graduate assistantships, grants, institutional work-study, loans, scholarships. **Number of Fellowships Granted Each Year:** 32. **Average amount of individual fellowships per year:** $16,000. **Number of Teaching/Research Assistantships Granted Each Year:** 389. **Average Salary Stipend:** $5,500.

ADMISSIONS INFORMATION

Application Fee: $35. **Regular Application Deadline:** 4/1. **Regular Notification:** Rolling. **Transfer Students Accepted?** Yes. **Transfer Policy:** Each graduate program determines its own admission requirements. **Number of Applications Received:** 2,655. **% of Applicants Accepted:** 42. **% Accepted Who Enrolled:** 19. **Average GPA:** 3.31. **Average GRE Verbal:** 521. **Average GRE Quantitative:** 757. **Average GRE Analytical:** 675.

Required Admission Factors: GRE, letters of recommendation, transcript.
Other Admission Factors: Minimum 3.0 GPA required. GRE required for applicants and fellowship candidates. TOEFL scores required for international students (minimum 550 paper; 213 computer).

EMPLOYMENT INFORMATION

Placement Office Available? Yes. **Rate of placement:** 97%.

STATE UNIVERSITY OF NEW YORK— BINGHAMTON UNIVERSITY
Harpur College of Arts & Sciences

Address: PO Box 6000, Binghamton, NY 13902-6000
Admissions Phone: 607-777-2151 · **Admissions Fax:** 607-777-2501
Admissions E-mail: gradad@binghamton.edu ·
Web Address: gradschool.binghamton.edu/

INSTITUTIONAL INFORMATION
Public/Private: Public. **Student/Faculty Ratio:** 20:1. **Students in Parent Institution:** 12,564.

RESEARCH FACILITIES
Research Facilities: Center for Learning & Teaching, Center for Intelligent Systems, Center for Cognitive & Psycholinguistic Sciences, Center for Computing Technologies, Center for Developmental Psychobiology, Center for Leadership Studies, Center for Medieval & Early Reniassance.

EXPENSES/FINANCIAL AID
Annual Tuition: In-state $5,100. / Out-of-state $8,416. **Books and Supplies:** $750. **Grants Range From:** $4,000-$15,000. **Loans Range From:** $1,000-$19,213. **% Receiving Financial Aid:** 71. **% Receiving Scholarships/Grants:** 10. **% Receiving Assistantships:** 64. **Number of fellowships granted each year:** 99. **Average amount of individual fellowships per year:** $8,000. **Number of teaching/research assistantships granted each year:** 441. **Average Salary Stipend:** $8,100.

ADMISSIONS INFORMATION
Application Fee: $55. **Priority Application Deadline:** 1/1. **Regular Application Deadline:** 6/30. **Regular Notification:** Rolling. **Transfer Students Accepted?** No. **Number of Applications Received:** 1,053. **% of Applicants Accepted:** 54. **% Accepted Who Enrolled:** 39. **Average GRE Verbal:** 544. **Average GRE Quantitative:** 603. **Average GRE Analytical:** 606.
Required Admission Factors: Essays/personal statement, letters of recommendation, transcript.
Other Admission Factors: Minimum GPA 3.0, minimum TOEFL required for English-Second-Language international students 550 paper, 213 computer.

EMPLOYMENT INFORMATION
Placement Office Available? Yes.

STATE UNIVERSITY OF NEW YORK AT BUFFALO
School of Social Work

Address: 685 Baldy Hall, Buffalo, NY 14260
Admissions Phone: 716-645-3381 · **Admissions Fax:** 716-645-3456
Admissions E-mail: sw-info@buffalo.edu · **Website:** www.socialwork.buffalo.edu

INSTITUTIONAL INFORMATION
Public/private: Public. **Evening Classes Available?** Yes. **Students in Parent Institution:** 24,830.

PROGRAMS
Masters offered in: Clinical/medical social work, community organization and advocacy, mental health counseling/counselor, social work, substance abuse/addiction counseling, youth services/administration.

STUDENT INFORMATION
Total Students in Program: 9,438. **% Full-time:** 100.

EXPENSES/FINANCIAL AID
Annual Tuition: In-state $6,900. / Out-of-state $10,920.

ADMISSIONS INFORMATION
Application Fee: $65. **Regular Application Deadline:** 3/1. **Transfer Students Accepted?** Yes. **Transfer Policy:** Transfer applicants must be from CSWE-accredited social work programs. **Number of Applications Received:** 324. **% of Applicants Accepted:** 89. **% Accepted Who Enrolled:** 76. **Average GPA:** 3.3. **Average GRE Verbal:** 427. **Average GRE Quantitative:** 481. **Average GRE Analytical:** 501.
Required Admission Factors: Essays/personal statement, letters of recommendation, transcript.
Other Admission Factors: Minimum 24 undergraduate credit hours in liberal arts required, including 6 credits in the humanities and 6 credits in the social sciences.
Program-Specific Admission Factors: BSW (no more than 6 years old) and 3.0 QPA required for admission to advanced standing.

EMPLOYMENT INFORMATION
Placement Office Available? Yes. **Rate of placement:** 97%.

STATE UNIVERSITY OF NEW YORK AT BUFFALO
School of Informatics

Address: Buffalo, NY 14260

INSTITUTIONAL INFORMATION
Public/private: Public. **Evening Classes Available?** Yes. **Student/faculty Ratio:** 17:1. **Students in Parent Institution:** 24,830.

STUDENT INFORMATION
Total Students in Program: 6,310. **% Full-time:** 52. **% Female:** 52.

RESEARCH FACILITIES
Research Facilities: More than 40 interdisciplinary research centers and institutes.

EXPENSES/FINANCIAL AID
Annual Tuition: In-state $5,100. / Out-of-state $8,416. **Room & Board:** $2,554. **Fees:** $935. **Books and Supplies:** $939. **Grants Range From:** $100-$16,663. **Loans Range From:** $100-$16,663. **% Receiving Financial Aid:** 25. **% Receiving Scholarships/Grants:** 32. **% Receiving Loans:** 29. **% Receiving Assistantships:** 31. **Average Salary Stipend:** $8,400.

ADMISSIONS INFORMATION
Application Fee: $35. **Regular Notification:** Rolling. **Transfer Students Accepted?** Yes. **Transfer Policy:** Maximum 6 credit hours with a minimum grade of B and no more than 2 years old may be transferred. **Number of Applications Received:** 176. **% of Applicants Accepted:** 75. **% Accepted Who Enrolled:** 62. **Average GPA:** 3.2.
Required Admission Factors: Essays/personal statement, letters of recommendation, transcript.
Other Admission Factors: Minimum 3.0 GPA required.

EMPLOYMENT INFORMATION
Placement Office Available? Yes. **% Employed Within 6 Months:** 70. **% of master's grads employed in their field upon graduation:** 90. **Rate of placement:** 97%. **Average starting salary:** $33,000.

STATE UNIVERSITY OF NEW YORK AT BUFFALO
Roswell Park Cancer Institute

Address: Elm and Carlton Streets, Buffalo, NY 14263
Admissions Phone: 716-845-2339 · **Admissions Fax:** 716-845-8178
Admissions E-mail: craig.johnson@roswellpark.org
Website: www.roswellpark.org/document_40.html

INSTITUTIONAL INFORMATION
Public/private: Public. **Total Faculty:** 120. **% Faculty Female:** 34. **Student/faculty Ratio:** 2:1. **Students in Parent Institution:** 26,830.

STUDENT INFORMATION
Total Students in Program: 6,310. **% Full-time:** 63. **% Female:** 52.

RESEARCH FACILITIES
Research Facilities: More than 40 interdisciplinary research centers and institutes.

EXPENSES/FINANCIAL AID
Annual Tuition: In-state $7,000. / Out-of-state $10,500. **Room & Board (On/off Campus):** $2,554/$7,600. **Fees:** $935. **Books and Supplies:** $939. **Grants Range From:** $100-$16,663. **Loans Range From:** $100-$16,663. **% Receiving Scholarships/Grants:** 32. **% Receiving Loans:** 29. **% Receiving Assistantships:** 31. **Types of Aid Available:** Fellowships, graduate assistantships, loans, scholarships. research assistantships. **Number of Fellowships Granted Each Year:** 25. **Average amount of individual fellowships per year:** $21,000. **Number of Teaching/Research Assistantships Granted Each Year:** 120. **Average Salary Stipend:** $21,000.

ADMISSIONS INFORMATION
Application Fee: $35. **Priority Application Deadline:** 1/1. **Regular Application Deadline:** 6/1. **Regular Notification:** Rolling. **Transfer Students Accepted?** Yes. **Number of Applications Received:** 300. **% of Applicants Accepted:** 33. **% Accepted Who Enrolled:** 50. **Average GPA:** 3.3. **Average GRE Verbal:** 550. **Average GRE Quantitative:** 600. **Average GRE Analytical:** 600.
Required Admission Factors: Essays/personal statement, GRE, interview, letters of recommendation, transcript.
Other Admission Factors: Minimum GRE score in the 50th percentile and minimum 3.0 GPA required.
Program-Specific Admission Factors: GRE Subject Test Required for International Applicants

EMPLOYMENT INFORMATION
Placement Office Available? Yes. **% Employed Within 6 Months:** 95. **% of doctoral grads employed in their field upon graduation:** 100. **Rate of placement:** 97%. **Average starting salary:** $35,000.

STATE UNIVERSITY OF NEW YORK AT STONY BROOK
College of Arts & Sciences

Address: Stony Brook, NY 11794
Website: www.grad. suny.sb.edu

INSTITUTIONAL INFORMATION
Public/private: Public. **Students in Parent Institution:** 19,924.

STUDENT INFORMATION
Total Students in Program: 6,098. **% Full-time:** 41. **% Female:** 58.

RESEARCH FACILITIES
Research Facilities: Marine Sciences Research Center, Brookhaven National Lab, Cold Spring Harbor Lab.

EXPENSES/FINANCIAL AID
Annual Tuition: In-state $5,100. / Out-of-state $8,416. **Fees:** $480. **Books and Supplies:** $750.

ADMISSIONS INFORMATION
Application Fee: $50. **Regular Notification:** Rolling. **Transfer Students Accepted?** No.
Required Admission Factors: GRE, letters of recommendation, transcript.
Other Admission Factors: Minimum 2.75 GPA required.

EMPLOYMENT INFORMATION
Placement Office Available? Yes.

STATE UNIVERSITY OF NEW YORK AT STONY BROOK
School of Professional Development

Address: Stony Brook, NY 11794
Website: www.grad. suny.sb.edu

INSTITUTIONAL INFORMATION
Public/private: Public. **Students in Parent Institution:** 19,924.

STUDENT INFORMATION
Total Students in Program: 6,098. **% Full-time:** 41. **% Female:** 58.

RESEARCH FACILITIES
Research Facilities: Marine Sciences Research Center, Brookhaven National Lab, Cold Spring Harbor Lab.

EXPENSES/FINANCIAL AID
Annual Tuition: In-state $5,100. / Out-of-state $8,416. **Fees:** $480. **Books and Supplies:** $750.

ADMISSIONS INFORMATION
Transfer Students Accepted? No.

EMPLOYMENT INFORMATION
Placement Office Available? Yes.

STATE UNIVERSITY OF NEW YORK AT STONY BROOK
Marine Sciences Research Center

Address: Stony Brook, NY 11794
Website: www.grad. suny.sb.edu

INSTITUTIONAL INFORMATION
Public/private: Public. **Students in Parent Institution:** 19,924.

STUDENT INFORMATION
Total Students in Program: 6,098. **% Full-time:** 41. **% Female:** 58.

RESEARCH FACILITIES
Research Facilities: Marine Sciences Research Center, Brookhaven National Lab, Cold Spring Harbor Lab.

EXPENSES/FINANCIAL AID
Annual Tuition: In-state $5,100. / Out-of-state $8,416. **Fees:** $480. **Books and Supplies:** $750.

ADMISSIONS INFORMATION
Transfer Students Accepted? No.

EMPLOYMENT INFORMATION
Placement Office Available? Yes.

STATE UNIVERSITY OF NEW YORK AT STONY BROOK
The Graduate School

Address: 2401 Computer Science Building, Stony Brook, NY 11794-4433
Admissions Phone: 631-632-GRAD · **Admissions Fax:** 631-632-7243
Admissions E-mail: Graduate.School@sunysb.edu · **Website:** www.grad.sunysb.edu

INSTITUTIONAL INFORMATION
Public/private: Public. **Students in Parent Institution:** 21,685.

STUDENT INFORMATION
Total Students in Program: 5,749. **% Full-time:** 50. **% Female:** 61.

RESEARCH FACILITIES
Research Facilities: Brookhaven National Lab, Cold Spring Harbor Lab, Marine Sciences Research Center.

EXPENSES/FINANCIAL AID
Annual Tuition: In-state $6,900. / Out-of-state $10,500. **Room & Board:** $8,600. **Fees:** $526. **Books and Supplies:** $900. **Grants Range From:** $18,555-$26,900. **% Receiving Scholarships/Grants:** 70. **% Receiving Assistantships:** 75. **Types of Aid Available:** Fellowships, graduate assistantships, grants, institutional work-study, loans, scholarships. **Assistantship Compensation Includes:** Full tuition remission, partial tuition remission, salary/stipend. **Average Salary Stipend:** $13,000.

ADMISSIONS INFORMATION
Application Fee: $60. **Regular Application Deadline:** 1/15. **Regular Notification:** Rolling. **Transfer Students Accepted?** Yes. **Transfer Policy:** Requirement for master's programs only. No maximum requirement for doctoral programs. **Number of Applications Received:** 5,473. **% of Applicants Accepted:** 31. **% Accepted Who Enrolled:** 43. **Average GPA:** 3.6. **Required Admission Factors:** Essays/personal statement, GRE, letters of recommendation, transcript.
Other Admission Factors: 3.0 undergraduate GPA.

EMPLOYMENT INFORMATION
Placement Office Available? Yes.

STATE UNIVERSITY OF NEW YORK AT STONY BROOK
School of Social Welfare

Address: Stony Brook, NY 11794
Admissions Phone: 516-444-3149

INSTITUTIONAL INFORMATION
Public/private: Public. **Students in Parent Institution:** 19,924.

STUDENT INFORMATION
Total Students in Program: 6,098. **% Full-time:** 41. **% Female:** 58.

RESEARCH FACILITIES
Research Facilities: Marine Sciences Research Center, Brookhaven National Lab, Cold Spring Harbor Lab.

EXPENSES/FINANCIAL AID
Annual Tuition: In-state $5,100. / Out-of-state $8,416. **Fees:** $480. **Books and Supplies:** $750.

ADMISSIONS INFORMATION
Application Fee: $50. **Transfer Students Accepted?** No.
Required Admission Factors: Letters of recommendation, transcript.

EMPLOYMENT INFORMATION
Placement Office Available? Yes.

STATE UNIVERSITY OF NEW YORK COLLEGE AT BROCKPORT
School of Arts & Performance

Address: 350 New Campus Drive, Brockport, NY 14420-2915
Admissions Phone: 716-395-5465

INSTITUTIONAL INFORMATION
Public/private: Public. **Students in Parent Institution:** 8,524

STUDENT INFORMATION
Total Students in Program: 1,773. **% Full-time:** 17. **% Female:** 64.

EXPENSES/FINANCIAL AID
Annual Tuition: In-state $5,100. / Out-of-state $8,416. **Fees:** $513. **Books and Supplies:** $800.

ADMISSIONS INFORMATION
Application Fee: $50. **Transfer Students Accepted?** No. **Transfer Policy:** Maximum number of credit hours that may be transferred varies by program. **Required Admission Factors:** Transcript.
Program-Specific Admission Factors: Audition requied of dance program applicants.

EMPLOYMENT INFORMATION
Placement Office Available? Yes. **Rate of placement:** 95%.

STATE UNIVERSITY OF NEW YORK COLLEGE AT CORTLAND
School of Professional Studies

Address: PO Box 2000, Cortland, NY 13045
Admissions Phone: 607-753-4712 · **Admissions Fax:** 607-753-5998
Admissions E-mail: marky@em.cortland.edu

INSTITUTIONAL INFORMATION
Public/private: Public. **Evening Classes Available?** Yes. **Total Faculty:** 14. **Student/faculty Ratio:** 13:1. **Students in Parent Institution:** 7,178

STUDENT INFORMATION
Total Students in Program: 1,530. **% Full-time:** 17. **% Female:** 68.

RESEARCH FACILITIES
Research Facilities: Distance Learning Centers, smart classrooms.

EXPENSES/FINANCIAL AID
Annual Tuition: In-state $3,400. / Out-of-state $8,300. **Fees:** $774. **Books and Supplies:** $700. **Grants Range From:** $200-$3,000. **Loans Range**

From: $100-$3,900. **% Receiving Scholarships/Grants:** 22. **% Receiving Loans:** 71. **% Receiving Assistantships:** 6.

ADMISSIONS INFORMATION

Application Fee: $50. **Regular Notification:** Rolling. **Transfer Students Accepted?** Yes. **Number of Applications Received:** 352. **% of Applicants Accepted:** 89. **% Accepted Who Enrolled:** 71.
Required Admission Factors: Transcript.
Other Admission Factors: Minimum 2.5 GPA required for most programs.
Program-Specific Admission Factors: State provisional certification required for some programs.

EMPLOYMENT INFORMATION

Placement Office Available? Yes. **Rate of placement:** 81%.

STATE UNIVERSITY OF NEW YORK COLLEGE AT CORTLAND
Graduate Studies

Address: PO Box 2000, Brockway Hall 122, Cortland, NY 13045
Admissions Phone: 607-753-4711 · **Admissions Fax:** 607-753-5998
Admissions E-mail: gradstudies@cortland.edu
Website: www.cortland.edu/gradstudies

INSTITUTIONAL INFORMATION

Public/private: Public. **Student/faculty Ratio:** 13:1. **Students in Parent Institution:** 7,319.

PROGRAMS

Masters offered in: Bilingual and multilingual education; biology teacher education; chemistry teacher education; chemistry; education leadership and administration; education; educational administration and supervision; elementary and middle school administration/principalship; elementary education and teaching; English language and literature; French language and literature; French language teacher education; geography teacher education; geology/earth science; health and physical education; health and physical education/fitness; health teacher education; history teacher education; history; junior high/intermediate/middle school education and teaching; mathematics teacher education; mathematics; parks, recreation, and leisure facilities management; parks, recreation, and leisure studies; physical education teaching and coaching; physics teacher education; physics; reading teacher education; science teacher education/general science teacher education; secondary education and teaching; secondary school administration/principalship; social science teacher education; social studies teacher education; Spanish language and literature; Spanish language teacher education; special education; teacher education and professional development, specific subject areas; teacher education, multiple levels; teaching English as a second or foreign language/ESL language instructor; teaching English or French as a second or foreign language.

STUDENT INFORMATION

Total Students in Program: 1,536. **% Full-time:** 19. **% Female:** 68.

RESEARCH FACILITIES

Research Facilities: Distance Learning Centers, smart classrooms; Centers for the Aging, Multicultural, and Gender Studies.

EXPENSES/FINANCIAL AID

Annual Tuition: In-state $3,450. / Out-of-state $5,250. **Fees:** $430. **Books and Supplies:** $800. **Grants Range From:** $200-$3,000. **Loans Range From:** $100-$3,900. **% Receiving Financial Aid:** 50. **% Receiving Scholarships/Grants:** 22. **% Receiving Loans:** 71. **% Receiving Assistantships:** 6.
Types of Aid Available: Fellowships, graduate assistantships, grants, loans, scholarships. **Number of Teaching/Research Assistantships Granted Each Year:** 17. **Assistantship Compensation Includes:** Partial tuition remission, salary/stipend.

ADMISSIONS INFORMATION

Application Fee: $65. **Regular Application Deadline:** 12/1. **Transfer Students Accepted?** Yes. **Number of Applications Received:** 389. **% of Applicants Accepted:** 89. **% Accepted Who Enrolled:** 90. **Average GPA:** 2.7.
Required Admission Factors: Letters of recommendation, transcript.
Program-Specific Admission Factors: Exercise science requires GPA of 3.0 and 1000 combined score on GRE.

EMPLOYMENT INFORMATION

Placement Office Available? Yes. **% Employed Within 6 Months:** 94. **% of master's grads employed in their field upon graduation:** 90. **Rate of placement:** 90%. **Average starting salary:** $32,000.

STATE UNIVERSITY OF NEW YORK COLLEGE AT ONEONTA
Graduate Studies

Address: Ravine Parkway, Oneonta, NY 13820
Admissions Phone: 607-436-2523,-800-SUNY-123 · **Admissions Fax:** 607-436-3084
Admissions E-mail: gradoffice@oneonta.edu · **Website:** www.oneonta.edu

INSTITUTIONAL INFORMATION

Public/private: Public. **Evening Classes Available?** Yes. **Students in Parent Institution:** 5,745.

PROGRAMS

Masters offered in: Biology/biological sciences, counselor education/school counseling and guidance services, education, geology/earth science, public/applied history and archival administration.

STUDENT INFORMATION

Total Students in Program: 283. **% Full-time:** 20. **% Female:** 76.

RESEARCH FACILITIES

Research Facilities: Biological field station on Otsego Lake

EXPENSES/FINANCIAL AID

Annual Tuition: In-state $5,010. / Out-of-state $8,416. **Fees:** $641. **Books and Supplies:** $500. **Types of Aid Available:** Fellowships, graduate assistantships, grants, institutional work-study, loans, scholarships.

ADMISSIONS INFORMATION

Application Fee: $50. **Regular Notification:** Rolling. **Transfer Students Accepted?** Yes. **Number of Applications Received:** 115. **% of Applicants Accepted:** 48. **% Accepted Who Enrolled:** 75.
Required Admission Factors: GRE, transcript.
Other Admission Factors: Minimum 2.8 GPA (3.0 in major) required.
Program-Specific Admission Factors: Initial teacher certification is required for education programs.

EMPLOYMENT INFORMATION

Placement Office Available? Yes.

STATE UNIVERSITY OF NEW YORK COLLEGE AT OSWEGO
College of Arts & Sciences

Address: 602 Culkin Hall, Oswego, NY 13126
Admissions Phone: 315-312-3152 · **Admissions Fax:** 315-312-3577
Admissions E-mail: narayan@oswegeo.edu

INSTITUTIONAL INFORMATION

Public/private: Public. **Evening Classes Available?** Yes. **Students in Parent Institution:** 8,407.

STUDENT INFORMATION

Total Students in Program: 1,345. **% Full-time:** 25. **% Female:** 65.

EXPENSES/FINANCIAL AID

Annual Tuition: In-state $5,100. / Out-of-state $8,416. **Room & Board:** $8,096. **Fees:** $485. **Books and Supplies:** $700. **Average amount of individual fellowships per year:** $10,000. **Number of Teaching/Research Assistantships Granted Each Year:** 10. **Average Salary Stipend:** $3,800.

ADMISSIONS INFORMATION

Application Fee: $50. **Regular Notification:** Rolling. **Transfer Students Accepted?** No. **Number of Applications Received:** 46. **% of Applicants Accepted:** 85.

Required Admission Factors: Essays/personal statement, GRE, letters of recommendation, transcript.

EMPLOYMENT INFORMATION

Placement Office Available? Yes.

STATE UNIVERSITY OF NEW YORK COLLEGE AT PLATTSBURGH
Center for Lifelong Learning

Address: 101 Broad Street, Plattsburgh, NY 12901
Admissions Phone: 518-564-2050 or 800-388-6473
Admissions Fax: 518-564-2052 · **Admissions E-mail:** graduate@plattsburgh.edu

INSTITUTIONAL INFORMATION

Public/private: Public. **Evening Classes Available?** Yes. **Students in Parent Institution:** 6,153.

STUDENT INFORMATION

Total Students in Program: 776. **% Full-time:** 38. **% Female:** 73.

RESEARCH FACILITIES

Research Facilities: Center for Ethics in Public Life, Teacher Resource Center, Alzheimer's Disease Assistance Center.

EXPENSES/FINANCIAL AID

Annual Tuition: In-state $5,100. / Out-of-state $8,416. **Fees:** $559. **% Receiving Financial Aid:** 12.

ADMISSIONS INFORMATION

Application Fee: $50. **Transfer Students Accepted?** Yes. **Number of Applications Received:** 26. **% of Applicants Accepted:** 81.

Required Admission Factors: Letters of recommendation, transcript.
Other Admission Factors: Minimum 2.5 GPA required.

EMPLOYMENT INFORMATION

Placement Office Available? Yes. **% Employed Within 6 Months:** 25. **% of master's grads employed in their field upon graduation:** 20. **Rate of placement:** 85%.

STATE UNIVERSITY OF NEW YORK COLLEGE AT POTSDAM
School of Arts & Sciences

Address: 44 Pierrepont Avenue, Potsdam, NY 13676-2294
Admissions Phone: 315-267-2165 · **Admissions Fax:** 315-267-4802
Admissions E-mail: murphysl@potsdam.edu

INSTITUTIONAL INFORMATION

Public/private: Public. **Students in Parent Institution:** 4,238.

STUDENT INFORMATION

Total Students in Program: 651. **% Full-time:** 45. **% Female:** 59.

EXPENSES/FINANCIAL AID

Annual Tuition: In-state $5,100. / Out-of-state $8,416. **Fees:** $315. **Books and Supplies:** $500. **Number of Teaching/Research Assistantships Granted Each Year:** 1. **Average Salary Stipend:** $3,000.

ADMISSIONS INFORMATION

Application Fee: $50. **Regular Notification:** Rolling. **Transfer Students Accepted?** Yes. **Number of Applications Received:** 4. **% of Applicants Accepted:** 100. **% Accepted Who Enrolled:** 100. **Average GPA:** 2.96.
Required Admission Factors: Essays/personal statement, letters of recommendation, transcript.
Other Admission Factors: Minimum 2.75 GPA in last 60 semester hours required.

EMPLOYMENT INFORMATION

Placement Office Available? Yes.

STATE UNIVERSITY OF NEW YORK COLLEGE AT POTSDAM
Crane School of Music

Address: 44 Pierrepont Avenue, Potsdam, NY 13676-2294
Admissions Phone: 315-267-2165 · **Admissions Fax:** 315-267-4802
Admissions E-mail: murphsyl@potsdam.edu

INSTITUTIONAL INFORMATION

Public/private: Public. **Students in Parent Institution:** 4,238.

STUDENT INFORMATION

Total Students in Program: 651. **% Full-time:** 45. **% Female:** 59.

EXPENSES/FINANCIAL AID

Annual Tuition: In-state $5,100. / Out-of-state $8,416. **Fees:** $315. **Books and Supplies:** $500. **Number of Teaching/Research Assistantships Granted Each Year:** 2. **Average Salary Stipend:** $3,000.

ADMISSIONS INFORMATION

Application Fee: $50. **Regular Notification:** Rolling. **Transfer Students Accepted?** Yes. **Number of Applications Received:** 29. **% of Applicants Accepted:** 97. **% Accepted Who Enrolled:** 86. **Average GPA:** 3.26.
Required Admission Factors: Essays/personal statement, letters of recommendation, transcript.
Other Admission Factors: Minimum 3.0 GPA required; provisional admission possible for applicants with minimum 2.75 GPA.

EMPLOYMENT INFORMATION

Placement Office Available? Yes.

STATE UNIVERSITY OF NEW YORK— COLLEGE OF ENVIRONMENTAL SCIENCE AND FORESTRY
Graduate Studies Programs

Address: Syracuse, NY 13210
Admissions Phone: 315-470-6599 · **Admissions Fax:** 315-470-6978
Admissions E-mail: rhfrey@esf.edu

INSTITUTIONAL INFORMATION

Public/private: Public. **Total Faculty:** 26. **% Faculty Female:** 12. **% Faculty Part-time:** 12. **Students in Parent Institution:** 1,845.

STUDENT INFORMATION

Total Students in Program: 584. **% Full-time:** 49.

RESEARCH FACILITIES

Research Facilities: Adirondack Ecological Center, Institute for Environmental Policy and Planning, Cellulose Research Institute.

EXPENSES/FINANCIAL AID

Annual Tuition: In-state $5,100. / Out-of-state $8,416. **Fees:** $268. **Books and Supplies:** $600. **Grants Range From:** $100-$1,000. **Loans Range From:** $500-$18,500. **% Receiving Financial Aid:** 52. **% Receiving Scholarships/Grants:** 30. **% Receiving Loans:** 70. **% Receiving Assistantships:** 18. **Average student debt, upon graduation:** $25,800. **Number of Teaching/Research Assistantships Granted Each Year:** 11. **Average Salary Stipend:** $8,309.

ADMISSIONS INFORMATION

Application Fee: $50. **Regular Notification:** Rolling. **Transfer Students Accepted?** Yes. **Number of Applications Received:** 341. **% of Applicants Accepted:** 74. **% Accepted Who Enrolled:** 50.
Required Admission Factors: Essays/personal statement, GRE, letters of recommendation, transcript.
Program-Specific Admission Factors: Portfolio recommended of master's in landscape architecture program applicants.

EMPLOYMENT INFORMATION

Placement Office Available? Yes.

STATE UNIVERSITY OF NEW YORK—
EMPIRE STATE COLLEGE
Graduate Programs

Address: One Union Avenue, Saratoga Springs, NY 12866
Admissions Phone: 518-587-2100, ext. 429

INSTITUTIONAL INFORMATION

Public/private: Public. **Students in Parent Institution:** 8,009.

STUDENT INFORMATION

Total Students in Program: 337. **% Full-time:** 9. **% Female:** 64.

EXPENSES/FINANCIAL AID

Annual Tuition: In-state $3,888. / Out-of-state $6,372. **Fees:** $307. **Grants Range From:** $100-$3,500. **Loans Range From:** $500-$18,500. **% Receiving Loans:** 98.

ADMISSIONS INFORMATION

Application Fee: $50. **Regular Notification:** Rolling. **Transfer Students Accepted?** Yes.
Required Admission Factors: Essays/personal statement, letters of recommendation, transcript.

STATE UNIVERSITY OF NEW YORK—
FASHION INSTITUTE OF TECHNOLOGY
School of Graduate Studies

Address: Seventh Avenue at 27th Street, Office of the Dean, E 315, New York, NY 10001-5992
Admissions Phone: 212-217-5714 · **Admissions Fax:** 212-217-5156
Admissions E-mail: fitinfo@fitnyc.edu · **Web Address:** www.fitnyc.edu/graduatestudies

INSTITUTIONAL INFORMATION

Public/private: Public. **Evening Classes Available?** Yes. **Students in Parent Institution:** 12,579.

PROGRAMS

Masters offered in: Art history, criticism and conservation; museology/museum studies. **First Professional degree offered in:** Marketing

STUDENT INFORMATION

Total Students in Program: 112. **% Full-time:** 100.

RESEARCH FACILITIES

Research Facilities: Because of FIT's location, students can take advantage of the cultural richness of New York-museums, galleries, libraries, conservation laboratories, and other professional resources.

EXPENSES/FINANCIAL AID

Annual Tuition: In-state $7,110. / Out-of-state $10,920. **Fees:** $370. **Grants Range From:** $250-$10,223. **Loans Range From:** $250-$10,223. **Types of Aid Available:** Fellowships, grants, institutional work-study, loans, scholarships.

ADMISSIONS INFORMATION

Application Fee: $25. **Priority Application Deadline:** 2/15. **Regular Application Deadline:** 4/15. **Regular Notification:** Rolling. **Transfer Students Accepted?** Yes. **Number of Applications Received:** 115. **% of Applicants Accepted:** 58. **% Accepted Who Enrolled:** 78. **Average GPA:** 3.0.
Required Admission Factors: Letters of recommendation, transcript.
Other Admission Factors: Minimum 3.0 GPA required.
Program-Specific Admission Factors: Applicants to the master of arts programs, fashion and textile studies and art market are required to have completed two years of undergraduate coursework in art history and foreign language.

EMPLOYMENT INFORMATION

Placement Office Available? Yes. **% Employed Within 6 Months:** 80. **Rate of placement:** 60%. **Average starting salary:** $30,000.

STATE UNIVERSITY OF NEW YORK—NEW PALTZ
College of Liberal Arts & Sciences

Address: 75 South Manheim Boulevard, New Paltz, NY 12561-2499
Admissions Phone: 914-257-3285

INSTITUTIONAL INFORMATION

Public/private: Public. **Students in Parent Institution:** 7,344.

STUDENT INFORMATION

Total Students in Program: 1,696.

RESEARCH FACILITIES

Research Facilities: Clean room (engineering), electron microscope.

EXPENSES/FINANCIAL AID

Annual Tuition: In-state $2,550. / Out-of-state $4,208. **Room & Board:** $600. **Fees:** $558.

ADMISSIONS INFORMATION

Application Fee: $50. **Transfer Students Accepted?** No.
Required Admission Factors: GRE, transcript.
Other Admission Factors: Minimum 3.0 GPA required.
Program-Specific Admission Factors: 3 letters of recommendation required of psychology and sociology program applicants. GRE subject exam (psychology) required of psychology program applicants.

EMPLOYMENT INFORMATION

Placement Office Available? Yes.

STATE UNIVERSITY OF NEW YORK—NEW PALTZ
School of Fine & Performing Arts

Address: 75 South Manheim Boulevard, New Paltz, NY 12561-2499
Admissions Phone: 914-257-3285

INSTITUTIONAL INFORMATION
Public/private: Public. **Students in Parent Institution:** 7,344.

STUDENT INFORMATION
Total Students in Program: 1,696.

RESEARCH FACILITIES
Research Facilities: Clean room (engineering), electron microscope.

EXPENSES/FINANCIAL AID
Annual Tuition: In-state $2,550. / Out-of-state $4,208. **Room & Board:** $600. **Fees:** $558.

ADMISSIONS INFORMATION
Application Fee: $50. **Regular Notification:** Rolling. **Transfer Students Accepted?** No. **Transfer Policy:** Maximum 6 credit hours may be transferred into MA and MS programs.
Required Admission Factors: Essays/personal statement, letters of recommendation, transcript.
Other Admission Factors: Minimum 3.0 GPA, 3 letters of recommendation from former art teachers, and portfolio required.

EMPLOYMENT INFORMATION
Placement Office Available? Yes.

STATE UNIVERSITY OF NEW YORK—UPSTATE MEDICAL UNIVERSITY (FOMERLY SUNY HEALTH SCIENCE CENTER AT SYRACUSE)
College of Graduate Studies

Address: 155 Elizabeth Blackwell Street, Syracuse, NY 13210
Admissions Phone: 315-464-4538 · **Admissions Fax:** 315-464-4544

INSTITUTIONAL INFORMATION
Public/private: Public. **Students in Parent Institution:** 1,130.

STUDENT INFORMATION
Total Students in Program: 659. **% Female:** 47.

EXPENSES/FINANCIAL AID
Fees: $130. **Average Salary Stipend:** $15,300.

ADMISSIONS INFORMATION
Application Fee: $40. **Regular Notification:** Rolling. **Transfer Students Accepted?** No. **Number of Applications Received:** 114. **% of Applicants Accepted:** 40. **% Accepted Who Enrolled:** 46. **Average GPA:** 3.4. **Average GRE Verbal:** 510. **Average GRE Quantitative:** 634. **Average GRE Analytical:** 615.
Required Admission Factors: Letters of recommendation, transcript.
Other Admission Factors: Minimum GRE score of 600 and minimum 3.0 GPA required.

EMPLOYMENT INFORMATION
% Employed Within 6 Months: 10. **% of master's/doctoral grads employed in their field upon graduation:** 100/100.

STATE UNIVERSITY OF NEW YORK— PURCHASE COLLEGE
Conservatory of Dance

Address: 735 Anderson Hill Road, Purchase, NY 10577
Admissions Phone: 914-251-6700 · **Admissions Fax:** 914-251-6314
Admissions E-mail: admissn@purchase.edu · **Website:** www.purchase.edu

INSTITUTIONAL INFORMATION
Public/private: Public. **Student/faculty Ratio:** 3:1. **Students in Parent Institution:** 4,080.

STUDENT INFORMATION
Total Students in Program: 138. **% Full-time:** 93. **% Female:** 56.

EXPENSES/FINANCIAL AID
Annual Tuition: In-state $3,400. / Out-of-state $8,300. **Room & Board:** $8,900. **Fees:** $597. **Books and Supplies:** $1,400. **Grants Range From:** $550-$8,100. **Loans Range From:** $5,000-$18,500. **% Receiving Financial Aid:** 100. **% Receiving Scholarships/Grants:** 35. **% Receiving Loans:** 40. **% Receiving Assistantships:** 5. **Average student debt, upon graduation:** $9,672. **Average Salary Stipend:** $2,000.

ADMISSIONS INFORMATION
Application Fee: $50. **Regular Application Deadline:** 4/2. **Regular Notification:** Rolling. **Transfer Students Accepted?** Yes. **Number of Applications Received:** 19. **% of Applicants Accepted:** 21. **% Accepted Who Enrolled:** 100.
Required Admission Factors: Essays/personal statement, interview, transcript.

EMPLOYMENT INFORMATION
Placement Office Available? Yes.

STATE UNIVERSITY OF NEW YORK— PURCHASE COLLEGE
Conservatory of Music

Address: 735 Anderson Hill Road, Purchase, NY 10577
Admissions Phone: 914-251-6700 · **Admissions Fax:** 914-251-6314
Admissions E-mail: admissn@purchase.edu

INSTITUTIONAL INFORMATION
Public/private: Public. **Student/faculty Ratio:** 5:1. **Students in Parent Institution:** 4,080.

STUDENT INFORMATION
Total Students in Program: 138. **% Full-time:** 93. **% Female:** 56.

EXPENSES/FINANCIAL AID
Annual Tuition: In-state $3,400. / Out-of-state $8,300. **Room & Board:** $8,900. **Fees:** $597. **Books and Supplies:** $1,400. **Grants Range From:** $550-$8,100. **Loans Range From:** $5,000-$18,500. **% Receiving Financial Aid:** 67. **% Receiving Scholarships/Grants:** 35. **% Receiving Loans:** 40. **% Receiving Assistantships:** 5. **Average student debt, upon graduation:** $9,672. **Number of Teaching/Research Assistantships Granted Each Year:** 1.

ADMISSIONS INFORMATION
Application Fee: $50. **Regular Application Deadline:** 3/2. **Regular Notification:** Rolling. **Transfer Students Accepted?** Yes. **Number of Applications Received:** 112. **% of Applicants Accepted:** 62. **% Accepted Who Enrolled:** 75. **Average GPA:** 3.16.
Required Admission Factors: Essays/personal statement, transcript.

EMPLOYMENT INFORMATION
Placement Office Available? Yes.

STATE UNIVERSITY OF NEW YORK—
PURCHASE COLLEGE
Conservatory of Theater Arts & Film

Address: 735 Anderson Hill Road, Purchase, NY 10577
Admissions Phone: 914-251-6700 · **Admissions Fax:** 914-251-6314
Admissions E-mail: admissn@purchase.edu · **Website:** www.purchase.edu

INSTITUTIONAL INFORMATION
Public/private: Public. **Total Faculty:** 10. **Student/faculty Ratio:** 2:1. **Students in Parent Institution:** 4,080.

STUDENT INFORMATION
Total Students in Program: 138. **% Full-time:** 93. **% Female:** 56.

EXPENSES/FINANCIAL AID
Annual Tuition: In-state $3,400. / Out-of-state $8,300. **Room & Board:** $8,900. **Fees:** $597. **Books and Supplies:** $1,400. **Grants Range From:** $550-$8,100. **Loans Range From:** $5,000-$18,500. **% Receiving Financial Aid:** 100. **% Receiving Scholarships/Grants:** 35. **% Receiving Loans:** 40. **% Receiving Assistantships:** 5. **Average student debt, upon graduation:** $9,672.

ADMISSIONS INFORMATION
Application Fee: $50. **Regular Application Deadline:** 4/1. **Regular Notification:** Rolling. **Transfer Students Accepted?** Yes. **Number of Applications Received:** 17. **% of Applicants Accepted:** 47. **% Accepted Who Enrolled:** 50.
Required Admission Factors: Interview, letters of recommendation, transcript.
Other Admission Factors: Portfolio required.

EMPLOYMENT INFORMATION
Placement Office Available? Yes.

STATE UNIVERSITY OF NEW YORK—
PURCHASE COLLEGE
School of Art & Design

Address: 735 Anderson Hill Road, Purchase, NY 10577
Admissions Phone: 914-251-6700 · **Admissions Fax:** 914-251-6314
Admissions E-mail: admissn@purchase.edu · **Website:** www.purchase.edu

INSTITUTIONAL INFORMATION
Public/private: Public. **Student/faculty Ratio:** 3:1. **Students in Parent Institution:** 4,080.

STUDENT INFORMATION
Total Students in Program: 138. **% Full-time:** 93. **% Female:** 56.

EXPENSES/FINANCIAL AID
Annual Tuition: In-state $3,400. / Out-of-state $8,300. **Room & Board:** $8,900. **Fees:** $597. **Books and Supplies:** $1,400. **Grants Range From:** $550-$8,100. **Loans Range From:** $5,000-$18,500. **% Receiving Financial Aid:** 44. **% Receiving Scholarships/Grants:** 35. **% Receiving Loans:** 40. **% Receiving Assistantships:** 5. **Average student debt, upon graduation:** $9,672. **Number of Teaching/Research Assistantships Granted Each Year:** 5. **Average Salary Stipend:** $2,000.

ADMISSIONS INFORMATION
Application Fee: $50. **Regular Application Deadline:** 2/2. **Regular Notification:** Rolling. **Transfer Students Accepted?** No. **Number of Applications Received:** 64. **% of Applicants Accepted:** 22. **% Accepted Who Enrolled:** 64.
Required Admission Factors: Essays/personal statement, interview, transcript.

EMPLOYMENT INFORMATION
Placement Office Available? Yes.

STATE UNIVERSITY OF WEST GEORGIA
College of Arts & Sciences

Address: 1600 Maple Street, Carrollton, GA 30118-0001
Admissions Phone: 770-836-6419 · **Admissions Fax:** 770-830-2301
Admissions E-mail: gradsch@westga.edu · **Website:** www.westga.edu/~gradsch/

INSTITUTIONAL INFORMATION
Public/private: Public. **Evening Classes Available?** Yes. **Students in Parent Institution:** 8,415.

PROGRAMS
Masters offered in: Art teacher education; biology teacher education; computer science; English language and literature; English/language arts teacher education; foreign language teacher education; history teacher education; history; mathematics teacher education; music teacher education; nursing administration (MSN, MS, PhD); psychology; public administration; public, applied history, and archival administration; science teacher education/general science teacher education; social sciences; social studies teacher education; sociology.

STUDENT INFORMATION
Total Students in Program: 1,643. **% Full-time:** 6. **% Female:** 75.

RESEARCH FACILITIES
Research Facilities: Teacher Education Lab & Software Library.

EXPENSES/FINANCIAL AID
Annual Tuition: In-state $1,160. / Out-of-state $4,640. **Room & Board:** $2,583. **Fees:** $536. **Books and Supplies:** $600. **Grants Range From:** $150-$4,959. **Loans Range From:** $500-$8,500. **% Receiving Scholarships/Grants:** 20. **% Receiving Loans:** 66.

ADMISSIONS INFORMATION
Application Fee: $20. **Priority Application Deadline:** 3/4. **Regular Application Deadline:** 7/4. **Regular Notification:** Rolling. **Transfer Students Accepted?** Yes. **Average GPA:** 3.08. **Average GRE Verbal:** 499. **Average GRE Quantitative:** 522.
Required Admission Factors: GRE, letters of recommendation, transcript.
Other Admission Factors: Minimum GRE section scores of 400 (Verbal and Quantitative), minimum 2.5 GPA, and proof of immunization required.
Program-Specific Admission Factors: Narrative statement required of some applicants.

EMPLOYMENT INFORMATION
Placement Office Available? Yes. **Rate of placement:** 78%.

STEPHEN F. AUSTIN STATE UNIVERSITY
Arthur Temple College of Forestry

Address: Box 6109, Nacogdoches, TX 75962-6109
Admissions Phone: 936-468-3301 · **Admissions Fax:** 936.468-2489
Admissions E-mail: mfountain@sfasu.edu · **Website:** www.sfasu.edu/forestry

INSTITUTIONAL INFORMATION
Public/private: Public. **Student/faculty Ratio:** 4:1. **Students in Parent Institution:** 11,484.

STUDENT INFORMATION
Total Students in Program: 1,238. **% Full-time:** 35. **% Female:** 63.

RESEARCH FACILITIES
Research Facilities: SFA Science Research Center.

EXPENSES/FINANCIAL AID

Annual Tuition: In-state $3,155. / Out-of-state $5,567. Room & Board: $4,448. Fees: $48. Books and Supplies: $200. Number of Teaching/Research Assistantships Granted Each Year: 27. Average Salary Stipend: $6,400.

ADMISSIONS INFORMATION

Application Fee: $25. Priority Application Deadline: 8/1. Regular Application Deadline: 8/1. Regular Notification: Rolling. Transfer Students Accepted? Yes. Transfer Policy: Maximum 6 credit hours may be transferred into masters thesis programs; maximum 12 credit hours may be transferred into PhD program. Number of Applications Received: 21. % of Applicants Accepted: 86. % Accepted Who Enrolled: 61.
Required Admission Factors: GRE, transcript.
Other Admission Factors: Minimum 2.8 GPA overall and 3.0 GPA for last 60 credit hours required. Minimum GRE of 900 for combined Quantitative and Verbal portions. Apriori identification of major professor.

EMPLOYMENT INFORMATION

Placement Office Available? Yes.

STEVENS INSTITUTE OF TECHNOLOGY
Graduate School

Address: Castle Point on Hudson, Hoboken, NJ 07030
Admissions Phone: 201-216-5234 · Admissions Fax: 201-216-8044
Admissions E-mail: edowns@stevens-tech.edu · Website: www.stevens.edu

INSTITUTIONAL INFORMATION

Public/private: Private (nonprofit). Evening Classes Available? Yes. Total Faculty: 320. % Faculty Part-time: 50. Students in Parent Institution: 2,841.

PROGRAMS

Masters offered in: Applied mathematics; architectural engineering; biochemistry; biological and biomedical sciences; business administration/management; business/managerial operations; chemical engineering; chemistry; civil engineering; computer and information sciences and support services; computer and information sciences; computer engineering; computer systems networking and telecommunications; electrical, electronics, and communications engineering; engineering physics; engineering; environmental/environmental health engineering; human resources management/personnel administration; industrial management; management information systems and services; management information systems; materials engineering; materials science; mathematics and statistics; mathematics; mechanical engineering; ocean engineering; organizational behavior studies; physical sciences; physics; polymer/plastics engineering; statistics; structural engineering. Doctorate offered in: Applied mathematics, architectural engineering, biochemistry, biological and biomedical sciences, business/managerial operations, chemical engineering, chemistry, civil engineering, computer and information sciences and support services.

STUDENT INFORMATION

Total Students in Program: 2,841. % Full-time: 25. % Female: 27.

EXPENSES/FINANCIAL AID

Annual Tuition: $15,660. Fees: $90. Books and Supplies: $1,100. Grants Range From: $2,000-$31,000. Loans Range From: $100-$18,500.

ADMISSIONS INFORMATION

Application Fee: $40. Regular Application Deadline: 8/1. Regular Notification: Rolling. Transfer Students Accepted? Yes. Number of Applications Received: 2,498. % of Applicants Accepted: 61. % Accepted Who Enrolled: 54. Average GPA: 3.5.
Required Admission Factors: GMAT, GRE, transcript.
Other Admission Factors: Minimum 3.0 GPA and 2 letters of recommendation required.

EMPLOYMENT INFORMATION

Placement Office Available? Yes. % Employed Within 6 Months: 70. Rate of placement: 60%. Average starting salary: $50,000.

SUFFOLK UNIVERSITY
College of Arts & Sciences

Address: 8 Ashburton Place, Boston, MA 02108
Admissions Phone: 617-573-8302 · Admissions Fax: 617-523-0116
Admissions E-mail: gradadmission@admin.suffolk.edu · Website: www.suffolk.edu

INSTITUTIONAL INFORMATION

Public/private: Private (nonprofit). Evening Classes Available? Yes. Total Faculty: 66. Student/faculty Ratio: 6:1. Students in Parent Institution: 6,690.

PROGRAMS

Masters offered in: Advertising, education leadership and administration, education, elementary and middle school administration/principalship, higher education/higher education administration, mass communications/media studies, public relations/image management. Doctorate offered in: Clinical psychology.

STUDENT INFORMATION

Total Students in Program: 1,527. % Full-time: 17. % Female: 52.

RESEARCH FACILITIES

Research Facilities: Beacon Hill Institute for Public Policy Research.

EXPENSES/FINANCIAL AID

Fees: $80. Books and Supplies: $500. Grants Range From: $400-$16,920. Loans Range From: $2,000-$32,370. % Receiving Financial Aid: 36. % Receiving Scholarships/Grants: 5. % Receiving Loans: 98. Average student debt, upon graduation: $24,342. Number of Fellowships Granted Each Year: 114. Average amount of individual fellowships per year: $6,000.

ADMISSIONS INFORMATION

Application Fee: $35. Regular Notification: Rolling. Transfer Students Accepted? Yes. Number of Applications Received: 360. % of Applicants Accepted: 78. % Accepted Who Enrolled: 52. Average GPA: 3.0.
Required Admission Factors: Essays/personal statement, GRE, letters of recommendation, transcript.
Other Admission Factors: Minimum 2.75 GPA required.

EMPLOYMENT INFORMATION

Placement Office Available? Yes. % of master's grads employed in their field upon graduation: 50. Rate of placement: 95%. Average starting salary: $10,000.

SUL ROSS STATE UNIVERSITY
Graduate Programs

Address: Alpine, TX 79832
Admissions Phone: 915-837-8052 · Admissions Fax: 915-837-8431

INSTITUTIONAL INFORMATION

Public/private: Public. Evening Classes Available? Yes. Students in Parent Institution: 2,418.

STUDENT INFORMATION

Total Students in Program: 600 % Female: 65.

RESEARCH FACILITIES

Research Facilities: Chihuahua Desert Research Institute, physical science materials characterization lab, Center for Big Bend Studies.

EXPENSES/FINANCIAL AID

Annual Tuition: In-state $1,224. / Out-of-state $5,076. **Room & Board:** $8,500. **Fees:** $60. **Books and Supplies:** $350. **% Receiving Financial Aid:** 50. **Average student debt, upon graduation:** $17,500.

ADMISSIONS INFORMATION

Regular Notification: Rolling. **Transfer Students Accepted?** Yes. **Number of Applications Received:** 14. **% of Applicants Accepted:** 21. **Average GPA:** 3.0.
Required Admission Factors: Transcript.

EMPLOYMENT INFORMATION

Placement Office Available? Yes.

SUL ROSS STATE UNIVERSITY
School of Arts & Sciences

Address: Highway 90 East, Alpine, TX 79832
Admissions Phone: 415-837-8052 · **Admissions Fax:** 415-837-8431
Admissions E-mail: colman@sul-ross-1.sulross.edu · **Website:** www.sulross.edu

INSTITUTIONAL INFORMATION

Public/private: Public. **Evening Classes Available?** Yes. **Students in Parent Institution:** 2,418.

STUDENT INFORMATION

Total Students in Program: 600. **% Female:** 65.

RESEARCH FACILITIES

Research Facilities: Chihuahua Desert Research Institute, physical science materials characterization lab, Center for Big Bend Studies.

EXPENSES/FINANCIAL AID

Annual Tuition: In-state $1,224. / Out-of-state $5,076. **Room & Board:** $8,500. **Fees:** $60. **Books and Supplies:** $350.

ADMISSIONS INFORMATION

Application Fee: $25. **Regular Application Deadline:** 8/20. **Regular Notification:** Rolling. **Transfer Students Accepted?** Yes. **Average GRE Verbal:** 510. **Average GRE Quantitative:** 400. **Average GRE Analytical:** 470. **Required Admission Factors:** Transcript.
Other Admission Factors: Minimum 2.5 GPA in last 60 credit hours required.

EMPLOYMENT INFORMATION

Placement Office Available? Yes.

SYRACUSE UNIVERSITY
College of Arts & Sciences

Address: 303 Bowne Hall, Syracuse, NY 13244
Admissions Phone: 315-443-4492

INSTITUTIONAL INFORMATION

Public/private: Private (nonprofit). **Evening Classes Available?** Yes. **Students in Parent Institution:** 17,371.

STUDENT INFORMATION

Total Students in Program: 5,337. **% Full-time:** 53. **% Female:** 53.

RESEARCH FACILITIES

Research Facilities: Northeast Parallel Architecture Center.

EXPENSES/FINANCIAL AID

Annual Tuition: In-state $9,522. **Fees:** $354.

ADMISSIONS INFORMATION

Application Fee: $40. **Transfer Students Accepted?** No. **Number of Applications Received:** 1,062. **% of Applicants Accepted:** 31. **% Accepted Who Enrolled:** 46.
Required Admission Factors: GRE.

SYRACUSE UNIVERSITY
Maxwell School of Citizenship & Public Affairs

Address: 303 Bowne Hall, Syracuse University, Syracuse, NY 13244
Admissions Phone: 315-443-4492 · **Admissions Fax:** 315-443-3423
Admissions E-mail: grad@syr.edu · **Website:** http://gradsch.syr.edu

INSTITUTIONAL INFORMATION

Public/private: Private (nonprofit). **Total Faculty:** 146. **% Faculty Female:** 32. **% Faculty Part-time:** 3. **Student/faculty Ratio:** 18:1. **Students in Parent Institution:** 18,247.

PROGRAMS

Masters offered in: Anthropology, economics, geography, history, international relations and affairs, political science and government, public administration, sociology. **Doctorate offered in:** Anthropology, economics, geography, history, international relations and affairs, political science and government, public administration, sociology.

STUDENT INFORMATION

Total Students in Program: 855. **% Full-time:** 70. **% Female:** 50. **% Minority:** 11. **% International:** 30.

RESEARCH FACILITIES

Research Facilities: Program on Analysis & Resolution of Conflict, Center for Environmental Policy & Administration, Center for Policy Research, Center for Technology & Information Policy, Project Legal, Campbell Institute, Global Affairs Institute, South Asia Center.

EXPENSES/FINANCIAL AID

Annual Tuition: $19,344. **Room & Board:** $10,980. **Fees:** $1,366. **Books and Supplies:** $1,160. **% Receiving Financial Aid:** 40. **% Receiving Scholarships/Grants:** 33. **% Receiving Loans:** 82. **% Receiving Other Aid (federal work-study):** 20. **Types of Aid Available:** Fellowships, graduate assistantships, grants, institutional work-study, loans, scholarships. **Number of Fellowships Granted Each Year:** 21. **Average amount of individual fellowships per year:** 14,500. **Number of Teaching/Research Assistantships Granted Each Year:** 162. **Assistantship Compensation Includes:** Full tuition remission, partial tuition remission, salary/stipend. **Average Salary Stipend:** $9,400.

ADMISSIONS INFORMATION

Application Fee: $65. **Priority Application Deadline:** 1/10. **Regular Application Deadline:** 2/1. **Regular Notification:** Rolling. **Transfer Students Accepted?** Yes. **Number of Applications Received:** 987. **% of Applicants Accepted:** 34. **% Accepted Who Enrolled:** 46. **Average GPA:** 3.5. **Average GRE Verbal:** 569. **Average GRE Quantitative:** 656. **Average GRE Analytical:** 638. **Average GRE Analytical Writing:** 4.9.
Required Admission Factors: Essays/personal statement, GRE, letters of recommendation, transcript.
Recommended Admission Factors: Interview.
Program-Specific Admission Factors: Written statement for anthropology; statement of academic plans for international relations and public administration; written statement for political science, social science, and sociology.

EMPLOYMENT INFORMATION

Placement Office Available? Yes. **% Employed Within 6 Months:** 90. **% of master's/doctoral/first professional grads employed in their field upon graduation:** 78/75/62. **Rate of placement:** 95%. **Average starting salary:** $48,000.

SYRACUSE UNIVERSITY
S.I. Newhouse School of Public Communications

Address: 215 University Place, Syracuse, NY 13244
Admissions Phone: 315-443-4039 · **Admissions Fax:** 315-443-3946
Admissions E-mail: pcgrad@syr.edu · **Website:** http://newhouse.syr.edu

INSTITUTIONAL INFORMATION
Public/private: Private (nonprofit). **Students in Parent Institution:** 18,605.

PROGRAMS
Masters offered in: Advertising; broadcast journalism; business, management, marketing, and related support services; communications, journalism, and related fields; digital communications and media/multimedia; journalism; mass communications/media studies; photojournalism; public relations/image management; radio and television. **Doctorate offered in:** Mass communications/media studies.

STUDENT INFORMATION
Total Students in Program: 260. **% Full-time:** 100.

RESEARCH FACILITIES
Research Facilities: Transactional Records Access Clearinghouse, Center for the Study of Popular Television, Gene Media Forum.

EXPENSES/FINANCIAL AID
Annual Tuition: $29,016. **Room & Board:** $7,500. **Fees:** $400. **Books and Supplies:** $500. **Grants Range From:** $5,000-$26,000. **Loans Range From:** $2,500-$30,000. **% Receiving Financial Aid:** 30. **Assistantship Compensation Includes:** Partial tuition remission, salary/stipend.

ADMISSIONS INFORMATION
Application Fee: $65. **Regular Application Deadline:** 2/1. **Regular Notification:** 3/15. **Transfer Students Accepted?** No. **Number of Applications Received:** 650. **% of Applicants Accepted:** 62. **% Accepted Who Enrolled:** 50. **Average GPA:** 3.4. **Average GRE Verbal:** 550. **Average GRE Quantitative:** 600. **Average GRE Analytical:** 660. **Average GRE Analytical Writing:** 5.
Required Admission Factors: Essays/personal statement, GRE, letters of recommendation, transcript.
Other Admission Factors: TOEFL is required of all international applicants. A minimum of 600 paper/250 computer is required.
Program-Specific Admission Factors: Writing samples required for arts journalism applicants. Portfolio required of photography program applicants. GMAT may be taken in place of GRE for media management applicants.

EMPLOYMENT INFORMATION
% Employed Within 6 Months: 90. **Average starting salary:** $28,000.

SYRACUSE UNIVERSITY
School of Information Studies

Address: 303 Bowne Hall, Syracuse, NY 13244
Admissions Phone: 315-443-4492 · **Admissions Fax:** 315-443-5673
Admissions E-mail: ist@syr.edu · **Website:** www.ist.syr.edu

INSTITUTIONAL INFORMATION
Public/private: Private (nonprofit). **Total Faculty:** 42. **% Faculty Female:** 36. **Students in Parent Institution:** 17,371.

PROGRAMS
Masters offered in: Communications technologies and support services, computer and information systems security, computer systems networking and telecommunications, information resources management/CIO training, information science/studies, library science/librarianship, management information sys-

tems and services. **Doctorate offered in:** Computer systems networking and telecommunications, information science/studies, library science/librarianship.

STUDENT INFORMATION
Total Students in Program: 592. **% Full-time:** 43. **% Female:** 57. **% Minority:** 25. **% International:** 30.

RESEARCH FACILITIES
Research Facilities: Center for Digital Commerce, Center for Emerging Network Technologies, Center for Natural Language Processing, Convergence Center: Security Assurance Institute, Center for Digital Literacy, Information Institute of Syracuse.

EXPENSES/FINANCIAL AID
Annual Tuition: $14,508. **Room & Board:** $10,980. **Fees:** $325. **Books and Supplies:** $1,160. **Grants Range From:** $1,500-$39,022. **Loans Range From:** $100-$29,334. **% Receiving Financial Aid:** 9. **% Receiving Scholarships/Grants:** 2. **% Receiving Loans:** 90. **% Receiving Assistantships:** 6. **% Receiving Other Aid (university fellowships):** 25. **Types of Aid Available:** Fellowships, graduate assistantships, grants, institutional work-study, loans, scholarships. **Number of Fellowships Granted Each Year:** 2. **Average amount of individual fellowships per year:** $47,334. **Number of Teaching/Research Assistantships Granted Each Year:** 32. **Assistantship Compensation Includes:** Full tuition remission, salary/stipend. **Average Salary Stipend:** $11,000.

ADMISSIONS INFORMATION
Application Fee: $65. **Regular Application Deadline:** 2/15. **Regular Notification:** Rolling. **Transfer Students Accepted?** No. **Number of Applications Received:** 371. **% of Applicants Accepted:** 64. **% Accepted Who Enrolled:** 44. **Average GPA:** 3.3.
Required Admission Factors: Essays/personal statement, GRE, letters of recommendation, transcript.
Other Admission Factors: GPA of 3.0 or better, GRE scores (combined) of 1000.
Program-Specific Admission Factors: Certificate of advanced studies in school media requires a master's of library and information science.

EMPLOYMENT INFORMATION
Placement Office Available? Yes. **% Employed Within 6 Months:** 75. **% of master's/doctoral grads employed in their field upon graduation:** 75/75. **Rate of placement:** 75%. **Average starting salary:** $40,000.

TARLETON STATE UNIVERSITY
College of Liberal & Fine Arts

Address: Box T-0350, Stephenville, TX 76402
Admissions Phone: 254-968-9104 · **Admissions Fax:** 254-968-9670
Admissions E-mail: gradoffice@tarleton.edu

INSTITUTIONAL INFORMATION
Public/private: Public. **Evening Classes Available?** Yes. **Students in Parent Institution:** 7,545.

STUDENT INFORMATION
Total Students in Program: 1,322. **% Full-time:** 21. **% Female:** 63.

EXPENSES/FINANCIAL AID
Annual Tuition: In-state $1,386. / Out-of-state $5,076. **Fees:** $462. **Books and Supplies:** $250. **Loans Range From:** $2,625-$8,500.

ADMISSIONS INFORMATION
Application Fee: $25. **Regular Notification:** Rolling. **Transfer Students Accepted?** Yes. **Number of Applications Received:** 124. **% of Applicants Accepted:** 90. **% Accepted Who Enrolled:** 72.
Required Admission Factors: GRE, transcript.
Other Admission Factors: Minimum 3.0 GPA required.

TEMPLE UNIVERSITY
College of Liberal Arts

Address: 1803 North Broad Street, Philadelphia, PA 19122-6095
Admissions Phone: 215-204-8583 · **Admissions Fax:** 215-204-3731
Admissions E-mail: GraduateSchool@temple.edu · **Website:** www.temple.edu/cla

INSTITUTIONAL INFORMATION
Public/private: Public. **Total Faculty:** 119. **% Faculty Female:** 30. **% Faculty Part-time:** 8. **Student/faculty Ratio:** 4:1. **Students in Parent Institution:** 33,286.

PROGRAMS
Masters offered in: African American/Black studies; anthropology; clinical psychology; computer and information sciences; counseling psychology; creative writing; criminal justice, safety studies; developmental and child psychology; economics; educational psychology; English language and literature; experimental psychology; geography; history; liberal arts and sciences/liberal studies; linguistics; mathematics; philosophy; political science and government; psychology; religion/religious studies; school psychology; social psychology; social work; sociology; Spanish language and literature; speech and rhetorical studies; urban studies/affairs. **Doctorate offered in:** African American/Black studies; anthropology; clinical psychology; cognitive psychology and psycholinguistics; computer and information sciences; counseling psychology; criminal justice, safety studies; developmental and child psychology.

STUDENT INFORMATION
Total Students in Program: 789. **% Full-time:** 53. **% Female:** 52. **% Minority:** 24. **% International:** 8.

RESEARCH FACILITIES
Research Facilities: Attention to Teaching and Teaching Improvement Center, Center for African American History and Culture, Center for Frontier Sciences, Center for Intergenerational Learning, Center for Public Policy.

EXPENSES/FINANCIAL AID
Annual Tuition: In-state $7,236. / Out-of-state $10,476. **Room & Board:** $8,250. **Fees:** $460. **Books and Supplies:** $1,200. **Loans Range From:** $1,000-$18,500. **% Receiving Financial Aid:** 30. **% Receiving Scholarships/Grants:** 10. **% Receiving Loans:** 75. **% Receiving Assistantships:** 7. **Types of Aid Available:** Fellowships, graduate assistantships, grants, institutional work-study, loans, scholarships. **Number of Teaching/Research Assistantships Granted Each Year:** 225. **Assistantship Compensation Includes:** Full tuition remission, salary/stipend.

ADMISSIONS INFORMATION
Application Fee: $40. **Regular Application Deadline:** 3/1. **Regular Notification:** Rolling. **Transfer Students Accepted?** Yes. **Transfer Policy:** Maximum 20% of total required credit hours may be transferred into master's programs. **Number of Applications Received:** 939. **% of Applicants Accepted:** 42. **% Accepted Who Enrolled:** 47. **Average GPA:** 3.3. **Average GRE Verbal:** 585. **Average GRE Quantitative:** 594.
Required Admission Factors: Essays/personal statement, letters of recommendation, transcript.

EMPLOYMENT INFORMATION
Placement Office Available? Yes. **% Employed Within 6 Months:** 1. **Rate of placement:** 65%.

TEMPLE UNIVERSITY
Esther Boyer College of Music

Address: 1803 North Broad Street, Philadelphia, PA 19122-6095
Admissions Phone: 215-204-8301 · **Admissions Fax:** 215-204-4957

INSTITUTIONAL INFORMATION
Public/private: Public. **Student/faculty Ratio:** 10:1. **Students in Parent Institution:** 28,355.

STUDENT INFORMATION
Total Students in Program: 6,844. **% Full-time:** 28. **% Female:** 59.

RESEARCH FACILITIES
Research Facilities: Attention to Teaching and Teaching Improvement Center, Center for African American History and Culture, Center for Frontier Sciences, Center for Intergenerational Learning, Center for Public Policy.

EXPENSES/FINANCIAL AID
Annual Tuition: In-state $6,642. / Out-of-state $9,612. **Room & Board:** $8,250. **Fees:** $350. **Books and Supplies:** $1,200. **Loans Range From:** $1,000-$18,500. **% Receiving Scholarships/Grants:** 10. **% Receiving Loans:** 75. **% Receiving Assistantships:** 7.

ADMISSIONS INFORMATION
Application Fee: $40. **Regular Notification:** Rolling. **Transfer Students Accepted?** Yes. **Transfer Policy:** Maximum 6 semester hours may be transferred into master's programs; maximum 12 semester hours may be transferred. **Number of Applications Received:** 262. **% of Applicants Accepted:** 36. **% Accepted Who Enrolled:** 60.
Required Admission Factors: Essays/personal statement, letters of recommendation, transcript.
Other Admission Factors: Minimum 2.8 GPA required.

EMPLOYMENT INFORMATION
Placement Office Available? Yes. **Rate of placement:** 65%.

TEMPLE UNIVERSITY
School of Communications & Theater

Address: 1803 North Broad Street, Philadelphia, PA 19122-6095
Admissions Phone: 215-204-8422 · **Admissions Fax:** 215-204-6641
Admissions E-mail: murphyp@temple.edu

INSTITUTIONAL INFORMATION
Public/private: Public. **Students in Parent Institution:** 28,355.

STUDENT INFORMATION
Total Students in Program: 6,844. **% Full-time:** 28. **% Female:** 59.

RESEARCH FACILITIES
Research Facilities: Attention to Teaching and Teaching Improvement Center, Center for African American History and Culture, Center for Frontier Sciences, Center for Intergenerational Learning, Center for Public Policy.

EXPENSES/FINANCIAL AID
Annual Tuition: In-state $6,642. / Out-of-state $9,612. **Room & Board:** $8,250. **Fees:** $350. **Books and Supplies:** $1,200. **Loans Range From:** $1,000-$18,500. **% Receiving Scholarships/Grants:** 10. **% Receiving Loans:** 75. **% Receiving Assistantships:** 7. **Number of Fellowships Granted Each Year:** 6. **Number of Teaching/Research Assistantships Granted Each Year:** 58. **Average Salary Stipend:** $11,000.

ADMISSIONS INFORMATION
Application Fee: $40. **Transfer Students Accepted?** Yes. **Transfer Policy:** Maximum 20% of total required credit hours may be transferred into master's programs. **Number of Applications Received:** 328. **% of Applicants Accepted:** 41. **% Accepted Who Enrolled:** 44. **Average GPA:** 3.37. **Average**

GRE Verbal: 550. **Average GRE Quantitative:** 570.
Required Admission Factors: Essays/personal statement, letters of recommendation, transcript.
Other Admission Factors: Minimum 3.0 GPA in major or in last 2 years required.
Program-Specific Admission Factors: Portfolio required of some theater program applicants.

EMPLOYMENT INFORMATION
Placement Office Available? Yes. **Rate of placement:** 65%.

TEMPLE UNIVERSITY
Tyler School of Art

Address: 1803 North Broad Street, Philadelphia, PA 19122-6095
Admissions Phone: 215-782-2875
Admissions E-mail: tylerart@vm.temple.edu · **Website:** www.temple.edu/tyler

INSTITUTIONAL INFORMATION
Public/private: Public. **Student/faculty Ratio:** 2:1. **Students in Parent Institution:** 28,355.

STUDENT INFORMATION
Total Students in Program: 6,844. **% Full-time:** 28. **% Female:** 59.

RESEARCH FACILITIES
Research Facilities: Attention to Teaching and Teaching Improvement Center, Center for African American History and Culture, Center for Frontier Sciences, Center for Intergenerational Learning, Center for Public Policy.

EXPENSES/FINANCIAL AID
Annual Tuition: In-state $6,642. / Out-of-state $9,612. **Room & Board:** $8,250. **Fees:** $350. **Books and Supplies:** $1,200. **Loans Range From:** $1,000-$18,500. **% Receiving Scholarships/Grants:** 10. **% Receiving Loans:** 75. **% Receiving Assistantships:** 7.

ADMISSIONS INFORMATION
Application Fee: $40. **Transfer Students Accepted?** Yes. **Transfer Policy:** Maximum 20% of total required credit hours may be transferred into master's programs. **Number of Applications Received:** 790. **% of Applicants Accepted:** 58. **% Accepted Who Enrolled:** 55. **Average GPA:** 3.2.
Required Admission Factors: Essays/personal statement, letters of recommendation, transcript.

EMPLOYMENT INFORMATION
Placement Office Available? Yes. **Rate of placement:** 65%.

TENNESSEE STATE UNIVERSITY
College of Arts & Sciences

Address: 3500 John A. Merritt Boulevard, Nashville, TN 37209-1561

INSTITUTIONAL INFORMATION
Public/private: Public. **Evening Classes Available?** Yes. **Students in Parent Institution:** 8,715.

STUDENT INFORMATION
Total Students in Program: 1,654. **% Full-time:** 30. **% Female:** 66.

RESEARCH FACILITIES
Research Facilities: Cooperative Agricultural Research Program, Research Infrastructure in Minority Institutions, NASA Research Center, Centers of Excellence.

EXPENSES/FINANCIAL AID
Annual Tuition: In-state $3,884. / Out-of-state $10,356. **Room & Board:** $4,690. **% Receiving Financial Aid:** 70. **Number of Fellowships Granted**

Each Year: 15. **Average amount of individual fellowships per year:** $15,000. **Average Salary Stipend:** $15,000.

ADMISSIONS INFORMATION
Application Fee: $25. **Regular Notification:** Rolling. **Transfer Students Accepted?** Yes. **Transfer Policy:** Maximum 12 semester hours may be transferred into master's program; maximum 6 semester hours may be transferred. **Number of Applications Received:** 60. **% of Applicants Accepted:** 60. **% Accepted Who Enrolled:** 58.
Required Admission Factors: Letters of recommendation, transcript.
Program-Specific Admission Factors: 3 letters of recommendation required of biology program applicants; 2 letters of recommendation required of mathematics program applicants. Minimum 2.5 GPA, minimum MAT score of 25, and minimum 18 semester hours of undergraduate work in major required.

EMPLOYMENT INFORMATION
Placement Office Available? Yes. **% of master's grads employed in their field upon graduation:** 20.

TENNESSEE STATE UNIVERSITY
Institute of Government

Address: 3500 John A. Merritt Boulevard, Nashville, TN 37209-1561
Admissions Phone: 615-963-5901 · **Admissions Fax:** 615-963-5963
Admissions E-mail: eallen@tnstate.edu

INSTITUTIONAL INFORMATION
Public/private: Public. **Evening Classes Available?** Yes. **Student/faculty Ratio:** 8:1. **Students in Parent Institution:** 8,715.

STUDENT INFORMATION
Total Students in Program: 1,654. **% Full-time:** 30. **% Female:** 66.

RESEARCH FACILITIES
Research Facilities: Cooperative Agricultural Research Program, Research Infrastructure in Minority Institutions, NASA Research Center, Centers of Excellence.

EXPENSES/FINANCIAL AID
Annual Tuition: In-state $3,884. / Out-of-state $10,356. **Room & Board:** $4,690. **Average Salary Stipend:** $7,500.

ADMISSIONS INFORMATION
Application Fee: $25. **Regular Notification:** Rolling. **Transfer Students Accepted?** Yes. **Transfer Policy:** Maximum 12 credit hours may be transferred into master's program; maximum 6 credit hours may be transferred. **Number of Applications Received:** 54. **% of Applicants Accepted:** 65. **% Accepted Who Enrolled:** 71.
Required Admission Factors: Essays/personal statement, letters of recommendation, transcript.

EMPLOYMENT INFORMATION
Placement Office Available? Yes.

TENNESSEE STATE UNIVERSITY
School of Graduate Studies

Address: 3500 John A. Merritt Boulevard, Nashville, TN 37209-1561
Admissions Phone: 615-963-5901 · **Admissions Fax:** 615-963-5963
Admissions E-mail: mbennett@picard.tnstate.edu

INSTITUTIONAL INFORMATION
Public/private: Public. **Evening Classes Available?** Yes. **Students in Parent Institution:** 8,715.

STUDENT INFORMATION
Total Students in Program: 1,654. **% Full-time:** 30. **% Female:** 66.

RESEARCH FACILITIES

Research Facilities: Cooperative Agricultural Research Program, Research Infrastructure in Minority Institutions, NASA Research Center, Centers of Excellence.

EXPENSES/FINANCIAL AID

Annual Tuition: In-state $3,884. / Out-of-state $10,356. Room & Board: $4,690. Average Salary Stipend: $7,500.

ADMISSIONS INFORMATION

Application Fee: $25. Regular Notification: Rolling. Transfer Students Accepted? Yes. Transfer Policy: Maximum 6 credit hours may be transferred into master's programs; maximum 12 credit hours may be transferred. Number of Applications Received: 772. % of Applicants Accepted: 63. % Accepted Who Enrolled: 73.

Required Admission Factors: Essays/personal statement, letters of recommendation, transcript.

EMPLOYMENT INFORMATION

Placement Office Available? Yes.

TENNESSEE TECHNOLOGICAL UNIVERSITY
College of Arts & Sciences

Address: Box 5006 TTU, Cookeville, TN 38505
Admissions Phone: 931-372-3233 · Admissions Fax: 931-372-3497

INSTITUTIONAL INFORMATION

Public/private: Public. Student/faculty Ratio: 2:1. Students in Parent Institution: 8,653.

STUDENT INFORMATION

Total Students in Program: 1,554. % Full-time: 25. % Female: 49.

EXPENSES/FINANCIAL AID

Annual Tuition: In-state $3,942. / Out-of-state $10,414. Fees: $100. Books and Supplies: $700. % Receiving Financial Aid: 100. Number of Teaching/Research Assistantships Granted Each Year: 30. Average Salary Stipend: $532.

ADMISSIONS INFORMATION

Application Fee: $25. Regular Notification: Rolling. Transfer Students Accepted? Yes. Transfer Policy: Maximum 9 credit hours may be transferred into master's program. Number of Applications Received: 32. % of Applicants Accepted: 50. % Accepted Who Enrolled: 12. Average GPA: 3.35. Average GRE Verbal: 493. Average GRE Quantitative: 583. Average GRE Analytical: 597.

Required Admission Factors: GRE, letters of recommendation, transcript. Other Admission Factors: Minimum combined GRE score of 1500 required. Minimum 3.0 GPA required of master's program applicants. Minimum 3.5 GPA required of doctoral program applicants. Acceptance by advisor required before admission to college is offered.

EMPLOYMENT INFORMATION

Placement Office Available? Yes. % Employed Within 6 Months: 90. % of master's grads employed in their field upon graduation: 50. Average starting salary: $28,000.

TEXAS A&M INTERNATIONAL UNIVERSITY
College of Arts & Humanities

Address: 5201 University Boulevard, Laredo, TX 78041
Admissions Phone: 956-326-2200 · Admissions Fax: 956-326-2199
Admissions E-mail: mrrosillo@tamiu.edu

INSTITUTIONAL INFORMATION

Public/private: Public. Evening Classes Available? Yes. Student/faculty Ratio: 14:1. Students in Parent Institution: 3,016.

STUDENT INFORMATION

Total Students in Program: 777. % Full-time: 18. % Female: 59.

RESEARCH FACILITIES

Research Facilities: Texas Center for Border Economics and Enterprise Development, Center for the Study of Western Hempisheric Trade.

EXPENSES/FINANCIAL AID

Annual Tuition: In-state $1,536. / Out-of-state $6,600. Fees: $574. Books and Supplies: $642.

ADMISSIONS INFORMATION

Regular Notification: Rolling. Transfer Students Accepted? Yes. Required Admission Factors: GRE, transcript. Other Admission Factors: Minimum 3.0 GPA in upper-level courses required.

EMPLOYMENT INFORMATION

Placement Office Available? Yes.

TEXAS A&M UNIVERSITY—COLLEGE STATION
College of Geosciences

Address: College Station, TX 77843
Admissions Phone: 979-845-1044 · Admissions Fax: 979-845-0727

INSTITUTIONAL INFORMATION

Public/private: Public. Student/faculty Ratio: 3:1. Students in Parent Institution: 44,026.

STUDENT INFORMATION

Total Students in Program: 7,291. % Full-time: 73. % Female: 38.

RESEARCH FACILITIES

Research Facilities: Research Cyclotron, research reactor, visualization laboratory, biotechnology research center.

EXPENSES/FINANCIAL AID

Annual Tuition: In-state $3,024. / Out-of-state $8,088. Fees: $1,095. Books and Supplies: $800. % Receiving Financial Aid: 81. Number of Fellowships Granted Each Year: 14. Average amount of individual fellowships per year: 12,000. Number of Teaching/Research Assistantships Granted Each Year: 180. Average Salary Stipend: $1,200.

ADMISSIONS INFORMATION

Application Fee: $50. Regular Notification: Rolling. Transfer Students Accepted? Yes. Transfer Policy: Maximum 12 credit hours may be transferred into master's programs. Number of Applications Received: 120. % of Applicants Accepted: 72. % Accepted Who Enrolled: 57. Average GPA: 3.51. Average GRE Verbal: 513. Average GRE Quantitative: 665. Average GRE Analytical: 589.

Required Admission Factors: Essays/personal statement, GRE, letters of recommendation, transcript. Other Admission Factors: Minimum GRE score in the 50th percentile and minimum 3.0 GPA required.

EMPLOYMENT INFORMATION

Placement Office Available? Yes.

TEXAS A&M UNIVERSITY—COLLEGE STATION
College of Liberal Arts

Address: Admissions Processing, Texas A&M University, PO Box 40001, College Station, TX 77842-4001
Admissions Phone: 979-845-1044 · **Admissions Fax:** 409-845-1596
Admissions E-mail: admissions@tamu.edu · **Website:** http://clla.tamu.edu/

INSTITUTIONAL INFORMATION
Public/private: Public. **Students in Parent Institution:** 44,026.

STUDENT INFORMATION
Total Students in Program: 7,291. **% Full-time:** 73. **% Female:** 38.

RESEARCH FACILITIES
Research Facilities: Research Cyclotron, research reactor, visualization laboratory, biotechnology research center.

EXPENSES/FINANCIAL AID
Annual Tuition: In-state $3,024. / Out-of-state $8,088. **Fees:** $1,095. **Books and Supplies:** $800. **Types of Aid Available:** 1. **Number of Fellowships Granted Each Year:** 36. **Average amount of individual fellowships per year:** $3,000. **Number of Teaching/Research Assistantships Granted Each Year:** 350. **Average Salary Stipend:** $10,500.

ADMISSIONS INFORMATION
Application Fee: $50. **Regular Application Deadline:** 9/1. **Regular Notification:** Rolling. **Transfer Students Accepted?** Yes. **Number of Applications Received:** 1,000. **% of Applicants Accepted:** 15. **% Accepted Who Enrolled:** 67.
Required Admission Factors: Essays/personal statement, GRE, letters of recommendation, transcript.
Other Admission Factors: Minimum combined GRE score of 1000 (Verbal and Quantitative) and minimum 3.0 GPA required.

EMPLOYMENT INFORMATION
Placement Office Available? Yes.

TEXAS A&M UNIVERSITY—COLLEGE STATION
College of Science

Address: College Station, TX 77843

INSTITUTIONAL INFORMATION
Public/private: Public. **Students in Parent Institution:** 44,026.

STUDENT INFORMATION
Total Students in Program: 7,291. **% Full-time:** 73. **% Female:** 38.

RESEARCH FACILITIES
Research Facilities: Research Cyclotron, research reactor, visualization laboratory, biotechnology research center.

EXPENSES/FINANCIAL AID
Annual Tuition: In-state $3,024. / Out-of-state $8,088. **Fees:** $1,095. **Books and Supplies:** $800.

ADMISSIONS INFORMATION
Transfer Students Accepted? No.
Required Admission Factors: GRE, letters of recommendation, transcript.

EMPLOYMENT INFORMATION
Placement Office Available? Yes.

TEXAS A&M UNIVERSITY—COMMERCE
College of Arts & Sciences

Address: PO Box 3011, Commerce, TX 75429
Admissions Phone: 903-886-5163 · **Admissions Fax:** 903-886-5165
Admissions E-mail: Tammi_Thompson@tamu-commerce.edu
Website: www7.tamu-commerce.edu/

INSTITUTIONAL INFORMATION
Public/private: Public. **Evening Classes Available?** Yes. **Total Faculty:** 154. **% Faculty Female:** 26. **% Faculty Part-time:** 12. **Student/faculty Ratio:** 17:1. **Students in Parent Institution:** 8,359.

PROGRAMS
Masters offered in: Agriculture, computer and information sciences, drama and dramatics/theater arts, E-commerce/electronic commerce, economics, educational psychology, fine/studio arts, history, marketing/marketing management, music pedagogy, psychology, school psychology, social work, sociology. **Doctorate offered in:** Educational psychology.

STUDENT INFORMATION
Total Students in Program: 3,329. **% Full-time:** 25. **% Female:** 65.

RESEARCH FACILITIES
Research Facilities: Jerry D. Morris Recreation Center for health improvement, Children's Learning Center, Math Skills Center, Writing Center, Synergy Lab, Graduate Counsel.

EXPENSES/FINANCIAL AID
Annual Tuition: In-state $3,254. / Out-of-state $8,486. **Room & Board:** $5,004. **Fees:** $1,100. **Books and Supplies:** $900. **Grants Range From:** $200-$5,000. **Loans Range From:** $200-$15,000. **% Receiving Scholarships/Grants:** 30. **% Receiving Loans:** 82. **Types of Aid Available:** Graduate assistantships, grants, institutional work-study, loans, scholarships. **Number of Teaching/Research Assistantships Granted Each Year:** 27. **Average Salary Stipend:** $7,875.

ADMISSIONS INFORMATION
Application Fee: $35. **Priority Application Deadline:** 6/1. **Regular Application Deadline:** 8/1. **Regular Notification:** Rolling. **Transfer Students Accepted?** Yes. **Transfer Policy:** Minimum grade average of B required of transfer applicants. Graduate level courses from an accredited university. **Number of Applications Received:** 1,508. **% of Applicants Accepted:** 63. **% Accepted Who Enrolled:** 70. **Average GPA:** 3.0.
Required Admission Factors: Transcript.
Other Admission Factors: Minimum 3.0 GPA.

EMPLOYMENT INFORMATION
Placement Office Available? Yes. **% Employed Within 6 Months:** 75. **% of master's/doctoral grads employed in their field upon graduation:** 70/80. **Rate of placement:** 50%. **Average starting salary:** $45,000.

TEXAS A&M UNIVERSITY—CORPUS CHRISTI
College of Arts & Humanities

Address: 6300 Ocean Drive, Corpus Christi, TX 78412
Admissions Phone: 512-994-2651 · **Admissions Fax:** 512-994-5844
Admissions E-mail: dmead@tamucc.edu

INSTITUTIONAL INFORMATION
Public/private: Public. **Evening Classes Available?** Yes. **Students in Parent Institution:** 5,545.

STUDENT INFORMATION
Total Students in Program: 1,207. **% Female:** 63.

EXPENSES/FINANCIAL AID

Annual Tuition: In-state $1,954. / Out-of-state $7,090.

ADMISSIONS INFORMATION

Application Fee: $10. **Regular Notification:** Rolling. **Transfer Students Accepted?** Yes. **Number of Applications Received:** 86. **% of Applicants Accepted:** 100. **% Accepted Who Enrolled:** 100.
Required Admission Factors: GRE, transcript.
Program-Specific Admission Factors: Recommendation required of some programs. Essay required of interdisciplinary study program applicants.

TEXAS A&M UNIVERSITY—KINGSVILLE
College of Arts & Sciences

Address: MSC 105, Kingsville, TX 78363
Admissions Phone: 361-593-2808 · **Admissions Fax:** 361-593-3412

INSTITUTIONAL INFORMATION

Public/private: Public. **Students in Parent Institution:** 6,150.

STUDENT INFORMATION

Total Students in Program: 1,142. **% Full-time:** 37. **% Female:** 56.

RESEARCH FACILITIES

Research Facilities: Caesar Kleberg Wildlife Research Institute, Citrus Center.

EXPENSES/FINANCIAL AID

Annual Tuition: In-state $2,607. / Out-of-state $9,057. **Books and Supplies:** $562.

ADMISSIONS INFORMATION

Application Fee: $15. **Regular Notification:** Rolling. **Transfer Students Accepted?** No. **Average GRE Verbal:** 424. **Average GRE Quantitative:** 477. **Average GRE Analytical:** 490.
Required Admission Factors: GRE, transcript.

EMPLOYMENT INFORMATION

Placement Office Available? Yes.

TEXAS A&M UNIVERSITY—TEXARKANA
Graduate Studies

Address: 2600 North Robison Road
PO Box 5518, Texarkana, TX 75505-5518
Admissions Phone: 903-223-3047 · **Admissions Fax:** 903-832-8890
Admissions E-mail: carol.moore@tamut.edu

INSTITUTIONAL INFORMATION

Public/private: Public. **Evening Classes Available?** Yes. **Student/faculty Ratio:** 15:1. **Students in Parent Institution:** 1,197.

STUDENT INFORMATION

Total Students in Program: 405. **% Full-time:** 17. **% Female:** 71.

EXPENSES/FINANCIAL AID

Annual Tuition: In-state $1,785. / Out-of-state $5,583. **Books and Supplies:** $860. **Grants Range From:** $100-$2,500. **Loans Range From:** $100-$8,500. **% Receiving Scholarships/Grants:** 79. **% Receiving Loans:** 51.

ADMISSIONS INFORMATION

Regular Notification: Rolling. **Transfer Students Accepted?** Yes. **Number of Applications Received:** 132. **% of Applicants Accepted:** 100. **% Accepted Who Enrolled:** 77.
Required Admission Factors: Letters of recommendation, transcript.
Other Admission Factors: Minimum GMAT score of 400 and minimum 2.75 GPA on last 60 credit hours (or minimum GRE score of 850 and minimum 3.0 GPA on last 60 credit hours) required.

EMPLOYMENT INFORMATION

Placement Office Available? Yes. **Rate of placement:** 92%.

TEXAS CHRISTIAN UNIVERSITY
AddRan College of Humanities & Social Sciences

Address: TCU Box 297023, Graduate Studies & Research, Fort Worth, TX 76129
Admissions Phone: 817-257-7160 · **Admissions Fax:** 817-257-7709
Admissions E-mail: bmelhart@tcu.edu

INSTITUTIONAL INFORMATION

Public/private: Private (nonprofit). **Total Faculty:** 114. **Students in Parent Institution:** 7,775.

STUDENT INFORMATION

Total Students in Program: 857. **% Full-time:** 39. **% Female:** 54.

RESEARCH FACILITIES

Research Facilities: Center for Remote Sensing, Experimental Mesocosm Facility, Lake Worth Fish Hatchery, NMR Facility, X-ray Defraction Facility.

EXPENSES/FINANCIAL AID

Annual Tuition: In-state $7,560. **Fees:** $1,540. **Grants Range From:** $1,000-$10,350. **% Receiving Financial Aid:** 51. **% Receiving Scholarships/Grants:** 16. **% Receiving Loans:** 61. **% Receiving Assistantships:** 58. **Average student debt, upon graduation:** $9,988. **Number of Fellowships Granted Each Year:** 8. **Average amount of individual fellowships per year:** $11,744. **Number of Teaching/Research Assistantships Granted Each Year:** 161.

ADMISSIONS INFORMATION

Regular Notification: Rolling. **Transfer Students Accepted?** Yes.
Required Admission Factors: Essays/personal statement, GRE, letters of recommendation, transcript.
Other Admission Factors: Minimum 3.0 GPA required.

EMPLOYMENT INFORMATION

Placement Office Available? Yes.

TEXAS CHRISTIAN UNIVERSITY
College of Communication

Address: TCU Box 297023, Graduate Studies & Research, Fort Worth, TX 76129
Admissions Phone: 817-257-5917 · **Admissions Fax:** 817-257-5921
Admissions E-mail: D.Whillock@TCU.EDU

INSTITUTIONAL INFORMATION

Public/private: Private (nonprofit). **Students in Parent Institution:** 7,775.

STUDENT INFORMATION

Total Students in Program: 857. **% Full-time:** 39. **% Female:** 54.

RESEARCH FACILITIES

Research Facilities: Center for Remote Sensing, Experimental Mesocosm Facility, Lake Worth Fish Hatchery, NMR Facility, X-ray Defraction Facility.

EXPENSES/FINANCIAL AID

Annual Tuition: In-state $7,560. **Fees:** $1,540. **Grants Range From:** $1,000-$10,350. **% Receiving Scholarships/Grants:** 16. **% Receiving Loans:** 61. **% Receiving Assistantships:** 58.

ADMISSIONS INFORMATION

Application Fee: $50. **Regular Application Deadline:** 4/15. **Regular Notification:** Rolling. **Transfer Students Accepted?** Yes.
Required Admission Factors: Essays/personal statement, GRE, letters of recommendation, transcript.

Other Admission Factors: Must have 3 letters of recommendation. Must have a statement of no more than 250 words describing academic/professional objectives.

EMPLOYMENT INFORMATION
Placement Office Available? Yes.

TEXAS CHRISTIAN UNIVERSITY
College of Fine Arts

Address: TCU Box 297550, Graduate Studies & Research, Fort Worth, TX 76129
Admissions Phone: 817-257-7603 · **Admissions Fax:** 817-257-5672
Admissions E-mail: h.j.butler@tcu.edu · **Website:** www.cfagraduate.tcu.edu

INSTITUTIONAL INFORMATION
Public/private: Private (nonprofit). **Total Faculty:** 78. **Students in Parent Institution:** 7,775.

STUDENT INFORMATION
Total Students in Program: 857. **% Full-time:** 39. **% Female:** 54.

RESEARCH FACILITIES
Research Facilities: Center for Remote Sensing, Experimental Mesocosm Facility, Lake Worth Fish Hatchery, NMR Facility, X-ray Defraction Facility.

EXPENSES/FINANCIAL AID
Annual Tuition: In-state $7,560. **Fees:** $1,540. **Grants Range From:** $1,000-$10,350. **% Receiving Financial Aid:** 51. **% Receiving Scholarships/Grants:** 16. **% Receiving Loans:** 61. **% Receiving Assistantships:** 58. **Average student debt, upon graduation:** $9,988. **Number of Teaching/Research Assistantships Granted Each Year:** 62.

ADMISSIONS INFORMATION
Application Fee: $50. **Regular Application Deadline:** 8/5. **Regular Notification:** Rolling. **Transfer Students Accepted?** Yes. **Number of Applications Received:** 88. **% of Applicants Accepted:** 62. **% Accepted Who Enrolled:** 51. **Average GPA:** 3.6. **Average GRE Verbal:** 560. **Average GRE Quantitative:** 580.
Required Admission Factors: Essays/personal statement, letters of recommendation, transcript.
Other Admission Factors: Minimum 3.0 GPA required.
Program-Specific Admission Factors: Audition required of music program applicants. (International students may send in a tape or CD.)

EMPLOYMENT INFORMATION
Placement Office Available? Yes.

TEXAS STATE UNIVERSITY—SAN MARCOS
College of Applied Arts

Address: 601 University Drive, San Marcos, TX 78666-5709
Admissions Phone: 512-245-2581 · **Admissions Fax:** 512-245-8365
Admissions E-mail: gradcollege@txstate.edu · **Website:** www.txstate.edu/appliedarts

INSTITUTIONAL INFORMATION
Public/private: Public. **Evening Classes Available?** Yes. **Total Faculty:** 16. **% Faculty Female:** 44. **% Faculty Part-time:** 25. **Student/faculty Ratio:** 13:1. **Students in Parent Institution:** 26,783.

PROGRAMS
Masters offered in: Agricultural teacher education, criminal justice/law enforcement administration, human development and family studies, industrial technology/technician, multi/interdisciplinary studies, trade and industrial teacher education.

STUDENT INFORMATION
Total Students in Program: 217. **% Full-time:** 25. **% Female:** 59. **% Minority:** 35. **% International:** 1.

RESEARCH FACILITIES
Research Facilities: Edwards Aquifer Research and Data Center, Polymer Research Group.

EXPENSES/FINANCIAL AID
Annual Tuition: In-state $3,168. / Out-of-state $8,136. **Room & Board (On/off Campus):** $5,310/$6,800. **Fees:** $1,112. **Books and Supplies:** $770. **Grants Range From:** $50-$10,000. **Loans Range From:** $162-$12,102. **% Receiving Scholarships/Grants:** 77. **% Receiving Loans:** 23. **Types of Aid Available:** Graduate assistantships, grants, loans, scholarships. **Number of Teaching/Research Assistantships Granted Each Year:** 19. **Average Salary Stipend:** $8,892.

ADMISSIONS INFORMATION
Application Fee: $40. **Regular Application Deadline:** 6/15. **Regular Notification:** Rolling. **Transfer Students Accepted?** Yes. **Number of Applications Received:** 83. **% of Applicants Accepted:** 77. **% Accepted Who Enrolled:** 94. **Average GPA:** 3.2. **Average GRE Verbal:** 439. **Average GRE Quantitative:** 508.
Required Admission Factors: GRE, transcript.
Other Admission Factors: Minimum GRE score of 900 and minimum 2.75 GPA in last 60 credit hours required for most programs.

EMPLOYMENT INFORMATION
Placement Office Available? Yes.

TEXAS STATE UNIVERSITY—SAN MARCOS
College of Fine Arts & Communication

Address: 601 University Drive, JCK 280, San Marcos, TX 78666-5709
Admissions Phone: 512-245-2581 · **Admissions Fax:** 512-245-8365
Admissions E-mail: gradcollege@txstate.edu
Website: www.finearts.txstate.edu/finearts.html

INSTITUTIONAL INFORMATION
Public/private: Public. **Evening Classes Available?** Yes. **Total Faculty:** 29. **% Faculty Female:** 45. **% Faculty Part-time:** 7. **Student/faculty Ratio:** 8:1. **Students in Parent Institution:** 26,783.

PROGRAMS
Masters offered in: Drama and dramatics/theater arts, mass communications/media studies, music teacher education, music, speech, and rhetorical studies.

STUDENT INFORMATION
Total Students in Program: 142. **% Full-time:** 58. **% Female:** 65. **% Minority:** 19. **% International:** 7.

RESEARCH FACILITIES
Research Facilities: Edwards Aquifer Research and Data Center, Polymer Research Group.

EXPENSES/FINANCIAL AID
Annual Tuition: In-state $3,168. / Out-of-state $8,136. **Room & Board (On/off Campus):** $6,049/$6,800. **Fees:** $1,112. **Books and Supplies:** $770. **Grants Range From:** $50-$10,000. **Loans Range From:** $162-$12,102. **% Receiving Scholarships/Grants:** 77. **% Receiving Loans:** 23. **Types of Aid Available:** Graduate assistantships, grants, loans, scholarships. **Number of Teaching/Research Assistantships Granted Each Year:** 3. **Average Salary Stipend:** $2,209.

ADMISSIONS INFORMATION
Application Fee: $40. **Regular Application Deadline:** 6/15. **Regular Notification:** Rolling. **Transfer Students Accepted?** Yes. **Transfer Policy:** Some programs have earlier deadlines than the general ones listed (mass communication: 4/15). Please visit the graduate college division of the Texas State website for more information. **Number of Applications Received:** 72. **% of Appli-**

cants Accepted: 62. **% Accepted Who Enrolled:** 100. **Average GPA:** 3.4. **Average GRE Verbal:** 479. **Average GRE Quantitative:** 548. **Average GRE Analytical:** 535.

Required Admission Factors: Essays/personal statement, GRE, transcript. **Other Admission Factors:** Minimum GRE score of 900 and minimum 2.75 GPA in final 60 credit hours prior to receiving bachelor's degree or minimum 2.75 GPA in final 60 credit hours required.

Program-Specific Admission Factors: 200-400 word statement of academic and professional goals required of speech communication program applicants. Minimum GRE score of 1000 with minimum section scores of 500 and minimum 3.0 GPA in last 60 credit hours required of mass communication program.

EMPLOYMENT INFORMATION

Placement Office Available? Yes.

TEXAS STATE UNIVERSITY—SAN MARCOS
College of Science

Address: 601 University Drive, San Marcos, TX 78666-5709
Admissions Phone: 512-245-2581 · **Admissions Fax:** 512-245-8365
Admissions E-mail: gradcollege@txstate.edu · **Website:** www.science.txstate.edu

INSTITUTIONAL INFORMATION

Public/private: Public. **Evening Classes Available?** Yes. **Total Faculty:** 63. **% Faculty Female:** 22. **% Faculty Part-time:** 5. **Student/faculty Ratio:** 8:1. **Students in Parent Institution:** 26,783.

PROGRAMS

Masters offered in: Applied mathematics; aquatic biology/limnology; biochemistry; biology teacher education; biology/biological sciences; chemistry; computer and information sciences; computer programming, programmer; ecology; industrial technology/technician; mathematics teacher education; mathematics; physics. **Doctorate offered in:** Natural resources/conservation.

STUDENT INFORMATION

Total Students in Program: 522. **% Full-time:** 46. **% Female:** 46. **% Minority:** 23. **% International:** 19.

RESEARCH FACILITIES

Research Facilities: Edwards Aquifer Research and Data Center, Polymer Research Group, anthropology forensics laboratory, observatory with 17-inch telescope.

EXPENSES/FINANCIAL AID

Annual Tuition: In-state $3,168. / Out-of-state $8,136. **Room & Board (On/off Campus):** $5,310/$6,800. **Fees:** $1,112. **Books and Supplies:** $770. **Grants Range From:** $50-$10,000. **Loans Range From:** $162-$12,102. **% Receiving Scholarships/Grants:** 77. **% Receiving Loans:** 23. **Types of Aid Available:** Graduate assistantships, grants, loans, scholarships. **Number of Teaching/Research Assistantships Granted Each Year:** 172. **Assistantship Compensation Includes:** Salary/stipend. **Average Salary Stipend:** $9,783.

ADMISSIONS INFORMATION

Application Fee: $40. **Regular Application Deadline:** 6/15. **Regular Notification:** Rolling. **Transfer Students Accepted?** Yes. **Number of Applications Received:** 218. **% of Applicants Accepted:** 77. **% Accepted Who Enrolled:** 89. **Average GPA:** 3.3. **Average GRE Verbal:** 475. **Average GRE Quantitative:** 641.
Required Admission Factors: GRE, transcript.
Other Admission Factors: Department of biology and computer science: Minimum GRE score of 1000 and minimum 2.75 GPA in final 60 credit hours required. Department of chemistry and biochemistry: Minimum GRE score of 950 and minimum 2.75 GPA in final 60 hours.

EMPLOYMENT INFORMATION

Placement Office Available? Yes.

TEXAS STATE UNIVERSITY—SAN MARCOS
College of Liberal Arts

Address: 601 University Drive, San Marcos, TX 78666-5709
Admissions Phone: 512-245-2581 · **Admissions Fax:** 512-245-8365
Admissions E-mail: gradcollege@txstate.edu
Website: www.txstate.edu/liberalarts

INSTITUTIONAL INFORMATION

Public/private: Public. **Evening Classes Available?** Yes. **Total Faculty:** 114. **% Faculty Female:** 32. **% Faculty Part-time:** 9. **Student/faculty Ratio:** 8:1. **Students in Parent Institution:** 26,783.

PROGRAMS

Masters offered in: Anthropology; cartography; counseling psychology; creative writing; English language and literature; environmental science; geography; health/medical psychology; history teacher education; history; international/global studies; land use planning, management, and development; legal assistant/paralegal; multi/interdisciplinary studies; political science and government; public administration; school psychology; sociology; technical and business writing. **Doctorate offered in:** Cartography, geography.

STUDENT INFORMATION

Total Students in Program: 895. **% Full-time:** 40. **% Female:** 56. **% Minority:** 26. **% International:** 2.

RESEARCH FACILITIES

Research Facilities: Edwards Aquifer Research and Data Center, Polymer Research Group, Center for the Study of the Southwest, Center for the Study of Ethnic and Gender Issues, Music History Center.

EXPENSES/FINANCIAL AID

Annual Tuition: In-state $3,168. / Out-of-state $8,136. **Room & Board (On/off Campus):** $5,310/$6,800. **Fees:** $1,112. **Books and Supplies:** $770. **Grants Range From:** $50-$10,000. **Loans Range From:** $162-$12,102. **% Receiving Scholarships/Grants:** 77. **% Receiving Loans:** 23. **Types of Aid Available:** Graduate assistantships, grants, loans, scholarships. **Number of Teaching/Research Assistantships Granted Each Year:** 165. **Average Salary Stipend:** $9,900.

ADMISSIONS INFORMATION

Application Fee: $40. **Regular Application Deadline:** 6/15. **Regular Notification:** Rolling. **Transfer Students Accepted?** Yes. **Number of Applications Received:** 487. **% of Applicants Accepted:** 66. **% Accepted Who Enrolled:** 91. **Average GPA:** 3.3. **Average GRE Verbal:** 489. **Average GRE Quantitative:** 522.
Required Admission Factors: GRE, transcript.
Other Admission Factors: Minimum GRE score of 900 and minimum 2.5 GPA in final 60 credit hours prior to receiving bachelor's degree or minimum 2.75 GPA in final 60 credit hours required.
Program-Specific Admission Factors: Minimum 3.0 GPA in 24 credit hours of history required of history program applicants. Minimum GRE score of 900 and minimum 2.75 GPA, or minimum GRE score of 1000 and minimum 2.5 GPA required of public administration program applicants.

EMPLOYMENT INFORMATION

Placement Office Available? Yes.

TEXAS TECH UNIVERSITY
College of Arts & Sciences

Address: Box 41030, Lubbock, TX 79409-1030
Admissions Phone: 806-742-2787 · **Admissions Fax:** 806-742-4038
Admissions E-mail: gradschool@ttu.edu · **Website:** www.gradschool.ttu.edu

INSTITUTIONAL INFORMATION

Public/private: Public. **Evening Classes Available?** Yes. **Student/faculty Ratio:** 15:1. **Students in Parent Institution:** 28,325.

PROGRAMS

Masters offered in: Analytical chemistry; anthropology; art/art studies; atmospheric sciences and meteorology; chemical physics; chemistry; classical, Mediterranean, and Near Eastern/Oriental studies and archaeology; counseling psychology; drama and dramatics/theater arts; economics; educational psychology; experimental psychology; geology/earth science; geophysics and seismology; health and physical education; inorganic chemistry; intercultural/multicultural and diversity studies; international relations and affairs; international/global studies; kinesiology and exercise science; mathematics and statistics; mathematics; multi/interdisciplinary studies; museology/museum studies; music history, literature, and theory; music performance; organic chemistry; philosophy; physical and theoretical chemistry; physics; political science and government; psychology; public administration and services; public administration; public policy analysis; sociology; statistics; urban studies/affairs; visual and performing arts. **Doctorate offered in:** Analytical chemistry; ballet; chemical physics; chemistry; clinical psychology; conducting; counseling psychology; crafts/craft design, folk art and artisanry; dance; dance, drama, and dramatics; theater arts.

STUDENT INFORMATION

Total Students in Program: 4,311. **% Full-time:** 100. **% Female:** 37.

RESEARCH FACILITIES

Research Facilities: International Textile Research Center, Water Resource Center, Wind Engineering Research Center, Institute for Disaster Research, Center for Research in Industrial Automation and Robotics, Texas Wine Marketing Research Center, Center for the Study of Addiction.

EXPENSES/FINANCIAL AID

Annual Tuition: In-state $4,132. / Out-of-state $11,380. **Fees:** $5,100. **Books and Supplies:** $800. **Grants Range From:** $1-$5,000. **Loans Range From:** $1-$5,000. **% Receiving Financial Aid:** 57. **Types of Aid Available:** Fellowships, graduate assistantships, grants, institutional work-study, loans, scholarships. **Number of Teaching/Research Assistantships Granted Each Year:** 10. **Average Salary Stipend:** $10,000.

ADMISSIONS INFORMATION

Application Fee: $50. **Regular Application Deadline:** 9/1. **Regular Notification:** Rolling. **Transfer Students Accepted?** Yes. **Transfer Policy:** Admission requirements and maximum number of credit hours that may be transferred varies by program. **Number of Applications Received:** 5,000. **% of Applicants Accepted:** 22. **% Accepted Who Enrolled:** 100. **Average GPA:** 3.45.
Required Admission Factors: GRE, letters of recommendation, transcript. **Other Admission Factors:** GRE requirements vary by department. Minimum 3.0 GPA in last 60 credit hours recommended.

EMPLOYMENT INFORMATION

Placement Office Available? Yes. **% Employed Within 6 Months:** 50. **Rate of placement:** 68%. **Average starting salary:** $62,300.

TEXAS TECH UNIVERSITY
College of Human Sciences

Address: Box 41030, Lubbock, TX 79409-1030
Admissions Phone: 806-742-2787 · **Admissions Fax:** 806-742-4038
Admissions E-mail: gradschool@ttu.edu · **Website:** www.gradschool.ttu.edu

INSTITUTIONAL INFORMATION

Public/private: Public. **Student/faculty Ratio:** 19:1. **Students in Parent Institution:** 24,558.

PROGRAMS

Masters offered in: Child development; consumer economics; family and consumer economics and related services; family and consumer sciences/human sciences; family and consumer sciences/human sciences; family systems; food service, waiter/waitress, and dining room management/manager; foods, nutrition, and wellness studies; human development and family studies; human development, family studies, and related services; restaurant, culinary, and catering management. **Doctorate offered in:** Child development; consumer economics; family and consumer economics and related services; family, and consumer sciences, human sciences; family and consumer sciences/human sciences; family systems; foods, nutrition, and wellness studies.

STUDENT INFORMATION

Total Students in Program: 3,389. **% Full-time:** 127. **% Female:** 48.

RESEARCH FACILITIES

Research Facilities: International Textile Research Center, Water Resource Center, Wind Engineering Research Center, Institute for Disaster Research, Center for Research in Industrial Automation and Robotics, Texas Wine Marketing Research.

EXPENSES/FINANCIAL AID

Annual Tuition: In-state $4,132. / Out-of-state $11,380. **Fees:** $2,100. **Books and Supplies:** $900. **% Receiving Financial Aid:** 75. **Types of Aid Available:** Fellowships, graduate assistantships, grants, institutional work-study, loans, scholarships. **Average Salary Stipend:** $10,000.

ADMISSIONS INFORMATION

Application Fee: $50. **Regular Application Deadline:** 3/1. **Regular Notification:** Rolling. **Transfer Students Accepted?** Yes. **Transfer Policy:** Admission requirements and maximum number of credit hours that may be transferred varies by program. **Number of Applications Received:** 300. **% of Applicants Accepted:** 19. **Average GPA:** 3.47.
Required Admission Factors: GRE, transcript.
Recommended Admission Factors: Letters of recommendation.
Other Admission Factors: GRE requirements vary by department. Minimum 3.0 GPA in last 60 credit hours recommended.

EMPLOYMENT INFORMATION

Placement Office Available? Yes. **% Employed Within 6 Months:** 65. **Rate of placement:** 68%. **Average starting salary:** $62,500.

TEXAS TECH UNIVERSITY
College of Mass Communications

Address: Box 41030, Lubbock, TX 79409
Admissions Phone: 806-742-2787 · **Admissions Fax:** 806-742-4038
Admissions E-mail: gradschool@ttu.edu · **Website:** www.gradschool.ttu.edu

INSTITUTIONAL INFORMATION

Public/private: Public.

STUDENT INFORMATION

Total Students in Program: 29. **% Full-time:** 14,866.

EXPENSES/FINANCIAL AID

Annual Tuition: In-state $4,132. / Out-of-state $11,380. **Fees:** $2,100. **Books and Supplies:** $800. **Types of Aid Available:** Fellowships, graduate assistantships, grants, institutional work-study, loans, scholarships. **Assistantship Compensation Includes:** Partial tuition remission, salary/stipend. **Average Salary Stipend:** $10,000.

ADMISSIONS INFORMATION

Application Fee: $50. **Regular Application Deadline:** 4/1. **Regular Notification:** Rolling. **Transfer Students Accepted?** Yes. **Number of Applications Received:** 38. **% of Applicants Accepted:** 39. **% Accepted Who Enrolled:** 47. **Average GPA:** 3.4.
Required Admission Factors: Essays/personal statement, GRE, letters of recommendation, transcript.

TEXAS WOMAN'S UNIVERSITY
College of Arts & Sciences

Address: PO Box 425589, Denton, TX 76204-5589
Admissions Phone: 866-809-6130 · **Admissions Fax:** 940-898-3079
Admissions E-mail: Holly.Kiser@exchange.twu.edu · **Website:** www.twu.edu

INSTITUTIONAL INFORMATION

Public/private: Public. **Evening Classes Available?** Yes. **Student/faculty Ratio:** 12:1. **Students in Parent Institution:** 8,624.

STUDENT INFORMATION

Total Students in Program: 3,894. **% Full-time:** 27. **% Female:** 86.

RESEARCH FACILITIES

Research Facilities: Center for Research on Women's Health.

EXPENSES/FINANCIAL AID

Annual Tuition: In-state $2,044. / Out-of-state $5,932. **Fees:** $955. **Books and Supplies:** $576.

ADMISSIONS INFORMATION

Application Fee: $30. **Priority Application Deadline:** 7/1. **Regular Application Deadline:** 7/1. **Regular Notification:** Rolling. **Transfer Students Accepted?** Yes. **Transfer Policy:** Transfer credits are applied by department approval. Usually 3 to 6 hours are acceptable.
Required Admission Factors: Transcript.
Other Admission Factors: Minumum GPA 3.0.

EMPLOYMENT INFORMATION

Placement Office Available? Yes.

TEXAS WOMAN'S UNIVERSITY
School of Library & Information Studies

Address: PO Box 425589, Denton, TX 76204-5589
Admissions Phone: 940-898-3073 · **Admissions Fax:** 940-898-3019
Admissions E-mail: Holly.Kiser@exchange.twu.edu

INSTITUTIONAL INFORMATION

Public/private: Public. **Students in Parent Institution:** 8,624.

STUDENT INFORMATION

Total Students in Program: 3,894. **% Full-time:** 27. **% Female:** 86.

RESEARCH FACILITIES

Research Facilities: Center for Research on Women's Health.

EXPENSES/FINANCIAL AID

Annual Tuition: In-state $2,044. / Out-of-state $5,932. **Fees:** $955. **Books and Supplies:** $576.

ADMISSIONS INFORMATION

Application Fee: $30. **Regular Notification:** Rolling. **Transfer Students Accepted?** No.
Required Admission Factors: GRE, transcript.
Other Admission Factors: Minimum 3.0 GPA in last 60 credit hours required.

EMPLOYMENT INFORMATION

Placement Office Available? Yes.

TEXAS WOMAN'S UNIVERSITY
School of Occupational Therapy

Address: PO Box 425589, Denton, TX 76204-5589
Admissions Phone: 940-898-3073 · **Admissions Fax:** 940-898-3079
Admissions E-mail: Holly.Kiser@exchange.twu.edu

INSTITUTIONAL INFORMATION

Public/private: Public. **Students in Parent Institution:** 8,624.

STUDENT INFORMATION

Total Students in Program: 3,894. **% Full-time:** 27. **% Female:** 86.

RESEARCH FACILITIES

Research Facilities: Center for Research on Women's Health.

EXPENSES/FINANCIAL AID

Annual Tuition: In-state $2,044. / Out-of-state $5,932. **Fees:** $955. **Books and Supplies:** $576.

ADMISSIONS INFORMATION

Application Fee: $100. **Regular Notification:** Rolling. **Transfer Students Accepted?** Yes.
Required Admission Factors: GRE, transcript.
Program-Specific Admission Factors: Minimum 3.0 GPA required of MA and master of occupational therapy program applicants. Minimum 3.2 GPA required of PhD program applicants. At least 20 clock hours of observation in occupational therapy treatment settings required of master of occupational therapy program applicants.

EMPLOYMENT INFORMATION

Placement Office Available? Yes.

TEXAS WOMAN'S UNIVERSITY
School of Physical Therapy

Address: PO Box 425589, Denton, TX 76204-5589
Admissions Phone: 940-898-3073 · **Admissions Fax:** 940-898-3079
Admissions E-mail: Holly.Kiser@exchange.twu.edu

INSTITUTIONAL INFORMATION

Public/private: Public. **Student/faculty Ratio:** 12:1. **Students in Parent Institution:** 8,624.

STUDENT INFORMATION

Total Students in Program: 3,894. **% Full-time:** 27. **% Female:** 86.

RESEARCH FACILITIES

Research Facilities: Center for Research on Women's Health.

EXPENSES/FINANCIAL AID

Annual Tuition: In-state $2,044. / Out-of-state $5,932. **Fees:** $955. **Books and Supplies:** $576.

ADMISSIONS INFORMATION

Application Fee: $100. **Regular Notification:** Rolling. **Transfer Students Accepted?** No.
Required Admission Factors: Essays/personal statement, GRE, letters of recommendation, transcript.
Other Admission Factors: Minimum 3.0 GPA in last 60 credit hours required.

EMPLOYMENT INFORMATION

Placement Office Available? Yes.

THOMAS JEFFERSON UNIVERSITY
Jefferson College of Graduate Studies

Address: 1020 Locust Street, Room M-46, Philadelphia, PA 19107-6799
Admissions Phone: 215-503-4400 · **Admissions Fax:** 215-503-3433
Admissions E-mail: jessie.pervall@jefferson.edu · **Website:** www.jefferson.edu/jcgs

INSTITUTIONAL INFORMATION
Public/private: Private (nonprofit). **Total Faculty:** 183. **% Faculty Female:** 31. **Students in Parent Institution:** 2,332.

PROGRAMS
Masters offered in: Adult health nurse/nursing; biochemistry, biophysics, and molecular biology; biotechnology; clinical/medical laboratory technician/assistant (certificate); developmental biology and embryology; family practice nurse/nurse practitioner; health services/allied health; microbiology; nursing/registered nurse training (RN, ASN, BSN, MSN); nursing administration (MSN, MS, PhD); nursing; occupational therapy assistant; occupational therapy/therapist; pediatric nurse/nursing; pharmacology; physical therapy assistant; physical therapy/therapist; public health (MPh, DPh). **Doctorate offered in:** Biochemistry/biophysics and molecular biology, biochemistry, cell biology and anatomy, cell/cellular and molecular biology, cell/cellular biology and anatomical sciences, genetics, microbiological sciences and immunology.

STUDENT INFORMATION
Total Students in Program: 601. **% Full-time:** 44. **% Female:** 68. **% Minority:** 14. **% International:** 5.

RESEARCH FACILITIES
Research Facilities: Computer access to Medline, Health, CCIS.

EXPENSES/FINANCIAL AID
Annual Tuition: $14,460. **Books and Supplies:** $800. **Grants Range From:** $23,460-$23,460. **Loans Range From:** $500-$30,000. **% Receiving Financial Aid:** 54. **% Receiving Scholarships/Grants:** 7. **% Receiving Loans:** 54. **Types of Aid Available:** Fellowships, graduate assistantships, loans, scholarships. **Average student debt, upon graduation:** $50,000. **Number of Fellowships Granted Each Year:** 25. **Average amount of individual fellowships per year:** $40,235. **Assistantship Compensation Includes:** Salary/stipend. **Average Salary Stipend:** $5,000.

ADMISSIONS INFORMATION
Application Fee: $40. **Priority Application Deadline:** 3/1. **Regular Application Deadline:** 8/1. **Regular Notification:** Rolling. **Transfer Students Accepted?** Yes. **Transfer Policy:** Maximum 18 credit hours may be transferred into PhD programs; maximum 9 credit hours may be transferred into MS programs. **Number of Applications Received:** 838. **% of Applicants Accepted:** 37. **% Accepted Who Enrolled:** 59. **Average GPA:** 3.2. **Average GRE Verbal:** 500. **Average GRE Quantitative:** 570. **Average GRE Analytical:** 550. **Average GRE Analytical Writing:** 4.2.
Required Admission Factors: Essays/personal statement, GRE, letters of recommendation, transcript.
Other Admission Factors: Minimum GRE score of 1100 (Verbal and Quantitative) and minimum 3.0 GPA required.
Program-Specific Admission Factors: MAT acceptable in lieu of GRE for MS health professions programs. MCAT is required for combined MD/PhD Program.

THOMAS JEFFERSON UNIVERSITY
Kimmel Cancer Center

Address: 1025 Walnut Street, Philadelphia, PA 19107
Admissions Phone: 215-503-6687 · **Admissions Fax:** 215-503-0622
Admissions E-mail: jim.keen@mail.tju.edu

INSTITUTIONAL INFORMATION
Public/private: Private (nonprofit). **Total Faculty:** 73. **Students in Parent Institution:** 2,764.

STUDENT INFORMATION
Total Students in Program: 595. **% Full-time:** 45.

RESEARCH FACILITIES
Research Facilities: Computer access to Medline, Health, CCIS.

EXPENSES/FINANCIAL AID
Annual Tuition: $14,500. **Books and Supplies:** $800. **Grants Range From:** $18,000-$21,000. **% Receiving Financial Aid:** 100. **% Receiving Scholarships/Grants:** 7. **% Receiving Loans:** 54. **Number of Fellowships Granted Each Year:** 15. **Average amount of individual fellowships per year:** $31,500.

ADMISSIONS INFORMATION
Application Fee: $40. **Regular Notification:** Rolling. **Transfer Students Accepted?** Yes. **Number of Applications Received:** 146. **% of Applicants Accepted:** 18. **% Accepted Who Enrolled:** 44. **Average GPA:** 3.26. **Average GRE Verbal:** 538. **Average GRE Quantitative:** 640. **Average GRE Analytical:** 650.
Required Admission Factors: Essays/personal statement, GRE, letters of recommendation, transcript.

EMPLOYMENT INFORMATION
% Employed Within 6 Months: 100.

TOWSON UNIVERSITY
College of Graduate Studies & Research

Address: 8000 York Road, Towson, MD 21252
Admissions Phone: 410-704-2501 · **Admissions Fax:** 410-704-4675
Admissions E-mail: grads@towson.edu · **Website:** http://grad.towson.edu

INSTITUTIONAL INFORMATION
Public/private: Public. **Evening Classes Available?** Yes. **Students in Parent Institution:** 16,980.

STUDENT INFORMATION
Total Students in Program: 3,021. **% Full-time:** 23. **% Female:** 75.

RESEARCH FACILITIES
Research Facilities: Regional Economic Studies Institute, Institute for Teaching and Research on Women, Center for Applied Information Technology, Center for Geographic Information Sciences.

EXPENSES/FINANCIAL AID
Annual Tuition: In-state $3,798. / Out-of-state $7,830. **Fees:** $976.

ADMISSIONS INFORMATION
Application Fee: $40. **Regular Application Deadline:** 8/1. **Regular Notification:** Rolling. **Transfer Students Accepted?** Yes.
Required Admission Factors: Transcript.
Other Admission Factors: Minimum 3.0 GPA required (2.5 or 2.75 GPA required for conditional admission based on the program of study).

EMPLOYMENT INFORMATION
Placement Office Available? Yes.

TRENT UNIVERSITY
Graduate Programs

Address: Nassau Mills Road, Peterborough, Ontario, K9J 7B8, Canada
Admissions Phone: 705-748-1245 · **Admissions Fax:** 705-748-1587
Admissions E-mail: scarr@trentu.ca

INSTITUTIONAL INFORMATION

Public/private: Public. **Students in Parent Institution:** 162.

STUDENT INFORMATION

Total Students in Program: 162. **% Full-time:** 77. **% Female:** 52.

EXPENSES/FINANCIAL AID

Fees: $450. **Grants Range From:** $1,000-$17,000.

ADMISSIONS INFORMATION

Application Fee: $50. **Regular Notification:** Rolling. **Transfer Students Accepted?** Yes. **Number of Applications Received:** 185. **% of Applicants Accepted:** 47. **% Accepted Who Enrolled:** 69.
Required Admission Factors: Letters of recommendation, transcript.
Other Admission Factors: Minimum grade average of B+ in last 10 credit hours required.

TREVECCA NAZARENE UNIVERSITY
Graduate Psychology Program

Address: 333 Murfreesboro Road, Nashville, TN 37210
Admissions Phone: 615-248-1417 · **Admissions Fax:** 615-248-1366
Admissions E-mail: admissions_psy@trevecca.edu · **Website:** www.trevecca.edu

INSTITUTIONAL INFORMATION

Public/private: Private (nonprofit). **Evening Classes Available?** Yes. **Total Faculty:** 19. **% Faculty Female:** 32. **% Faculty Part-time:** 84. **Students in Parent Institution:** 1,911.

PROGRAMS

Masters offered in: Marriage and family therapy/counseling, psychology.

STUDENT INFORMATION

Total Students in Program: 173. **% Full-time:** 80. **% Female:** 81.

EXPENSES/FINANCIAL AID

Annual Tuition: $5,760. **Room & Board:** $6,046. **% Receiving Loans:** 100. **Types of Aid Available:** Loans.

ADMISSIONS INFORMATION

Application Fee: $25. **Transfer Students Accepted?** Yes. **Transfer Policy:** Maximum 9 credit hours with a minimum grade of B may be transferred from a regionally accredited institution. **Number of Applications Received:** 44. **% of Applicants Accepted:** 64.
Required Admission Factors: Letters of recommendation, transcript.
Other Admission Factors: Minimum GRE score of 800 or minimum MAT score of 30 and minimum 2.7 GPA required.
Program-Specific Admission Factors: Minimum 15 semester hours of psychology course work required of counseling psychology program applicants.

EMPLOYMENT INFORMATION

Placement Office Available? Yes.

TRINITY COLLEGE
Graduate Program

Address: 300 Summit Street, Hartford, CT 06106-3100
Admissions Phone: 860-297-2527 · **Admissions Fax:** 860-297-2529
Admissions E-mail: grad-studies@trincoll.edu
Website: www.trincoll.edu/depts/gradstud/

INSTITUTIONAL INFORMATION

Public/private: Private (nonprofit). **Evening Classes Available?** Yes. **Student/faculty Ratio:** 7:1. **Students in Parent Institution:** 2,249.

STUDENT INFORMATION

Total Students in Program: 185. **% Full-time:** 5. **% Female:** 49.

RESEARCH FACILITIES

Research Facilities: Watkinson Library, CTW Library, and member of the Hartford Consortium.

EXPENSES/FINANCIAL AID

Fees: $100. **Grants Range From:** $450-$900. **% Receiving Financial Aid:** 20. **% Receiving Scholarships/Grants:** 50. **% Receiving Loans:** 10. **Average student debt, upon graduation:** $6,000.

ADMISSIONS INFORMATION

Application Fee: $50. **Regular Notification:** Rolling. **Transfer Students Accepted?** Yes. **Transfer Policy:** Maximum 2 courses or 6 semester hours may be transferred. **Number of Applications Received:** 80. **% of Applicants Accepted:** 98. **% Accepted Who Enrolled:** 96. **Average GPA:** 3.3.
Required Admission Factors: Essays/personal statement, letters of recommendation, transcript.
Other Admission Factors: Minimum 3.0 GPA and writing sample required.
Program-Specific Admission Factors: Portfolio required of creative writing program applicants.

EMPLOYMENT INFORMATION

% Employed Within 6 Months: 95. **% of master's grads employed in their field upon graduation:** 95.

TRINITY EPISCOPAL SCHOOL FOR MINISTRY
Graduate Program

Address: 311 Eleventh Street, Ambridge, PA 15003
Admissions Phone: 724-266-3838 · **Admissions Fax:** 724-266-4617
Admissions E-mail: tesm@tesm.edu

INSTITUTIONAL INFORMATION

Public/private: Private (nonprofit). **Evening Classes Available?** Yes. **Students in Parent Institution:** 189.

STUDENT INFORMATION

Total Students in Program: 112. **% Full-time:** 75. **% Female:** 25.

EXPENSES/FINANCIAL AID

Annual Tuition: $6,840. **Books and Supplies:** $900. **Loans Range From:** $3,000-$18,500. **% Receiving Financial Aid:** 25. **% Receiving Scholarships/Grants:** 45. **% Receiving Loans:** 55. **Average student debt, upon graduation:** $10,000.

ADMISSIONS INFORMATION

Application Fee: $25. **Regular Notification:** Rolling. **Transfer Students Accepted?** Yes.
Required Admission Factors: Essays/personal statement, interview, letters of recommendation, transcript.

EMPLOYMENT INFORMATION

Placement Office Available? Yes. **% Employed Within 6 Months:** 100. **% of master's grads employed in their field upon graduation:** 100. **Rate of placement:** 100%. **Average starting salary:** $50,000.

TRINITY INTERNATIONAL UNIVERSITY
Graduate School

Address: 2065 Half Day Road, Deerfield, IL 60015
Admissions Phone: 847-317-6900 or 800-533-0975
Admissions Fax: 847-317-8097 · **Admissions E-mail:** kbotton@tiu.edu

INSTITUTIONAL INFORMATION

Public/private: Private (nonprofit). **Evening Classes Available?** Yes. **Students in Parent Institution:** 2,152.

STUDENT INFORMATION

Total Students in Program: 627. % Full-time: 42. % Female: 27.

RESEARCH FACILITIES

Research Facilities: Bannockburn Institute for Christianity and Contemporary Culture.

EXPENSES/FINANCIAL AID

Annual Tuition: $10,440. Room & Board: $13,000. Books and Supplies: $800. Grants Range From: $1,000-$3,000. Loans Range From: $500-$13,500.

ADMISSIONS INFORMATION

Application Fee: $25. Regular Notification: Rolling. Transfer Students Accepted? Yes. Transfer Policy: Review of transfer credits required of transfer applicants. Number of Applications Received: 27. % of Applicants Accepted: 41. % Accepted Who Enrolled: 82. Average GPA: 3.18. Required Admission Factors: Essays/personal statement, GRE, letters of recommendation, transcript.
Other Admission Factors: Minimum 3.0 GPA required.

EMPLOYMENT INFORMATION

Placement Office Available? Yes.

TRINITY UNIVERSITY
Accounting Program

Address: 715 Stadium Drive, San Antonio, TX 78212-7200
Admissions Phone: 210-999-7296 · Admissions Fax: 210-999-8134

INSTITUTIONAL INFORMATION

Public/private: Private (nonprofit). Student/faculty Ratio: 15:1. Students in Parent Institution: 2,662.

STUDENT INFORMATION

Total Students in Program: 215. % Full-time: 50. % Female: 59.

EXPENSES/FINANCIAL AID

Annual Tuition: $16,140. % Receiving Financial Aid: 80. Number of Teaching/Research Assistantships Granted Each Year: 12. Average Salary Stipend: $5,900.

ADMISSIONS INFORMATION

Application Fee: $30. Transfer Students Accepted? Yes. Number of Applications Received: 23. % of Applicants Accepted: 96. % Accepted Who Enrolled: 68. Average GPA: 3.55.
Required Admission Factors: Letters of recommendation, transcript.
Other Admission Factors: Minimum 3.0 GPA overall and in accounting courses and at least 6 accounting courses required.

EMPLOYMENT INFORMATION

% Employed Within 6 Months: 100. % of master's grads employed in their field upon graduation: 95. Average starting salary: $50,000.

TRINITY UNIVERSITY
Master of Arts in Teaching

Address: One Trinity Place, San Antonio, TX 78212-7200
Admissions Phone: 210-999-7501 · Admissions Fax: 210-999-7592
Admissions E-mail: krussell@trinity.edu
Website: http://trinity.edu/education/graduate

INSTITUTIONAL INFORMATION

Public/private: Private (nonprofit). Total Faculty: 228. % Faculty Female: 30. Student/faculty Ratio: 10:1. Students in Parent Institution: 2,707.

STUDENT INFORMATION

Total Students in Program: 226. % Full-time: 59. % Female: 64.

EXPENSES/FINANCIAL AID

Annual Tuition: $18,402. Room & Board: $7,290. % Receiving Financial Aid: 98.

ADMISSIONS INFORMATION

Application Fee: $30. Regular Application Deadline: 11/1. Regular Notification: Rolling. Transfer Students Accepted? No. Number of Applications Received: 56. % of Applicants Accepted: 82. % Accepted Who Enrolled: 87. Average GPA: 3.3. Average GRE Verbal: 503. Average GRE Quantitative: 587.
Required Admission Factors: Interview, letters of recommendation, transcript.
Other Admission Factors: Minimum 3.0 GPA required, Praxis II (in certification area), THEA (exemptions available).
Program-Specific Admission Factors: Please contact the department of education for more specific program requirements.

EMPLOYMENT INFORMATION

Placement Office Available? Yes. % Employed Within 6 Months: 100. % of master's grads employed in their field upon graduation: 100. Rate of placement: 100%. Average starting salary: $33,000.

TRINITY UNIVERSITY
School Psychology Program

Address: One Trinity Place, San Antonio, TX 78212-7200
Admissions Phone: 210-999-7501 · Admissions Fax: 210-999-7592
Admissions E-mail: smireles@trinity.edu
Website: www.trinity.edu/education/graduate

INSTITUTIONAL INFORMATION

Public/private: Private (nonprofit). Evening Classes Available? Yes. Student/faculty Ratio: 10:1. Students in Parent Institution: 2,707.

STUDENT INFORMATION

Total Students in Program: 226. % Full-time: 59. % Female: 64.

EXPENSES/FINANCIAL AID

Annual Tuition: $18,402. Room & Board: $7,290. Fees: $100. Books and Supplies: $400. % Receiving Financial Aid: 100. Average Salary Stipend: $400.

ADMISSIONS INFORMATION

Application Fee: $30. Priority Application Deadline: 2/1. Regular Application Deadline: 2/1. Regular Notification: 2/15. Transfer Students Accepted? Yes. Number of Applications Received: 34. % of Applicants Accepted: 41. % Accepted Who Enrolled: 93. Average GPA: 3.5.
Required Admission Factors: GRE, interview, letters of recommendation, transcript.
Other Admission Factors: Minimum 3.0 GPA required. Undergraduate degree in psychology or education preferred.

EMPLOYMENT INFORMATION

% Employed Within 6 Months: 100.

TRINITY WESTERN UNIVERSITY
School of Graduate Studies

Address: 7600 Glover Road, Langley, British Columbia, V2Y 1Y1, Canada
Admissions Phone: 604-888-7511 · Admissions Fax: 604-513-2010
Admissions E-mail: kamiem@twu.ca

INSTITUTIONAL INFORMATION

Public/private: Private (nonprofit). **Student/faculty Ratio:** 20:1. **Students in Parent Institution:** 183.

STUDENT INFORMATION

Total Students in Program: 183.

RESEARCH FACILITIES

Research Facilities: Dead Sea Scrolls Institute, International Network on Personal Meaning. .

EXPENSES/FINANCIAL AID

Annual Tuition: $8,280. **Fees:** $200. **Books and Supplies:** $500. **Grants Range From:** $350-$960. **Loans Range From:** $8,840. **% Receiving Financial Aid:** 93. **% Receiving Scholarships/Grants:** 90. **% Receiving Loans:** 70.

ADMISSIONS INFORMATION

Application Fee: $35. **Transfer Students Accepted?** Yes. **Number of Applications Received:** 110. **% of Applicants Accepted:** 57. **% Accepted Who Enrolled:** 100. **Average GPA:** 3.3. **Average GRE Verbal:** 500. **Average GRE Quantitative:** 500. **Average GRE Analytical:** 500.
Required Admission Factors: Essays/personal statement, letters of recommendation, transcript.
Other Admission Factors: Minimum 3.3 GPA required.

EMPLOYMENT INFORMATION

% Employed Within 6 Months: 60.

TROY STATE UNIVERSITY
College of Arts & Sciences

Address: University Avenue, Troy, AL 36082
Admissions Phone: 334-670-3178 · **Admissions Fax:** 334-670-3733
Admissions E-mail: bcamp@trojan.troyst.edu

INSTITUTIONAL INFORMATION

Public/private: Public. **Evening Classes Available?** Yes. **Students in Parent Institution:** 6,299.

STUDENT INFORMATION

Total Students in Program: 1,697. **% Full-time:** 36. **% Female:** 65.

EXPENSES/FINANCIAL AID

Annual Tuition: In-state $3,020. / Out-of-state $6,040. **Fees:** $276. **Books and Supplies:** $360. **Grants Range From:** $850-$2,250. **Loans Range From:** $8,500-$18,500. **% Receiving Scholarships/Grants:** 11. **% Receiving Loans:** 81. **% Receiving Assistantships:** 4.

ADMISSIONS INFORMATION

Application Fee: $20. **Regular Notification:** Rolling. **Transfer Students Accepted?** Yes. **Transfer Policy:** Maximum 12 credit hours with a minimum grade of B taken for graduate credit from a regionally.
Required Admission Factors: Transcript.
Other Admission Factors: Minimum GRE score of 850 or minimum MAT score of 33 and minimum 2.5 GPA required.

EMPLOYMENT INFORMATION

Placement Office Available? Yes.

TROY STATE UNIVERSITY
University College

Address: University Avenue, Troy, AL 36082
Admissions Phone: 334-670-3170 · **Admissions Fax:** 334-670-3770
Admissions E-mail: tjones@trojan.troyst.edu

INSTITUTIONAL INFORMATION

Public/private: Public. **Evening Classes Available?** Yes. **Students in Parent Institution:** 6,299.

STUDENT INFORMATION

Total Students in Program: 1,697. **% Full-time:** 36. **% Female:** 65.

EXPENSES/FINANCIAL AID

Annual Tuition: In-state $3,020. / Out-of-state $6,040. **Fees:** $276. **Books and Supplies:** $360. **Grants Range From:** $850-$2,250. **Loans Range From:** $8,500-$18,500. **% Receiving Financial Aid:** 18. **% Receiving Scholarships/Grants:** 11. **% Receiving Loans:** 81. **% Receiving Assistantships:** 4.

ADMISSIONS INFORMATION

Application Fee: $20. **Regular Notification:** Rolling. **Transfer Students Accepted?** Yes. **Transfer Policy:** Maximum 12 credit hours with a minimum grade of B taken for graduate credit from a regionally. **Number of Applications Received:** 210. **% of Applicants Accepted:** 93. **% Accepted Who Enrolled:** 97. **Average GPA:** 2.8.
Required Admission Factors: GRE, interview, transcript.
Other Admission Factors: Minimum GRE score of 850, minimum MAT score of 33, and minimum 2.5 GPA required.

EMPLOYMENT INFORMATION

Placement Office Available? Yes.

TRUMAN STATE UNIVERSITY
Communications Disorders Program

Address: 100 East Normal Street, MC 203, Kirksville, MO 63501
Admissions Phone: 660-785-4109 · **Admissions Fax:** 660-785-7460
Admissions E-mail: gradinfo@truman.edu · **Website:** http://gradschool.truman.edu

INSTITUTIONAL INFORMATION

Public/private: Public. **Total Faculty:** 6. **% Faculty Female:** 83. **% Faculty Part-time:** 33. **Students in Parent Institution:** 6,136.

PROGRAMS

Masters offered in: Communication disorders.

STUDENT INFORMATION

Total Students in Program: 211. **% Full-time:** 88. **% Female:** 56.

EXPENSES/FINANCIAL AID

Annual Tuition: In-state $4,320. / Out-of-state $7,542. **Fees:** $50. **Books and Supplies:** $500. **Grants Range From:** $100-$6,344. **Loans Range From:** $200-$15,120. **% Receiving Financial Aid:** 80. **Types of Aid Available:** Fellowships. **Number of Fellowships Granted Each Year:** 20.

ADMISSIONS INFORMATION

Regular Application Deadline: 6/1. **Regular Notification:** Rolling. **Transfer Students Accepted?** Yes. **Number of Applications Received:** 20. **% of Applicants Accepted:** 65. **% Accepted Who Enrolled:** 23. **Average GPA:** 3.5. **Average GRE Verbal:** 441. **Average GRE Quantitative:** 566. **Average GRE Analytical Writing:** 4.5.
Required Admission Factors: Essays/personal statement, GRE, letters of recommendation, transcript.
Other Admission Factors: Minimum 3.0 GPA required.

EMPLOYMENT INFORMATION

Placement Office Available? Yes. **% Employed Within 6 Months:** 100. **% of master's grads employed in their field upon graduation:** 100. **Rate of placement:** 100%. **Average starting salary:** $30,000.

TULANE UNIVERSITY
Graduate School of Arts & Sciences

Address: 6823 St. Charles Avenue, New Orleans, LA 70118
Admissions Phone: 504-865-5100 · Admissions Fax: 504-865-5274
Admissions E-mail: deboraht@mailhost.tcs.tulane.edu

INSTITUTIONAL INFORMATION
Public/private: Private (nonprofit). Students in Parent Institution: 11,945.

STUDENT INFORMATION
Total Students in Program: 2,630. % Full-time: 77. % Female: 51.

RESEARCH FACILITIES
Research Facilities: Regional Primate Center, Mid-American Research Center, Center for Urban Initiatives, Murphy Institute of Political Economy, Center for Research on Women, Center for Bioenvironment Research, Language Labs.

EXPENSES/FINANCIAL AID
Annual Tuition: $24,675. Fees: $2,160. Books and Supplies: $1,000. % Receiving Financial Aid: 90. Number of Fellowships Granted Each Year: 75. Average amount of individual fellowships per year: $10,000. Number of Teaching/Research Assistantships Granted Each Year: 425. Average Salary Stipend: $10,000.

ADMISSIONS INFORMATION
Application Fee: $45. Transfer Students Accepted? No. Transfer Policy: Maximum 12 credit hours may be transferred into master's programs, 24 into doctoral programs. Number of Applications Received: 1,124. % of Applicants Accepted: 36. % Accepted Who Enrolled: 53. Average GPA: 3.3. Average GRE Verbal: 567. Average GRE Quantitative: 641. Average GRE Analytical: 634.
Required Admission Factors: Essays/personal statement, GRE, letters of recommendation, transcript.
Other Admission Factors: Minimum GRE score of 1100 and minimum 3.0 GPA required.

EMPLOYMENT INFORMATION
Placement Office Available? Yes.

TULANE UNIVERSITY
School of Social Work

Address: 6823 St. Charles Avenue, New Orleans, LA 70118
Admissions Phone: 504-865-5314 · Admissions Fax: 504-862-8727

INSTITUTIONAL INFORMATION
Public/private: Private (nonprofit). Evening Classes Available? Yes. Students in Parent Institution: 11,945.

STUDENT INFORMATION
Total Students in Program: 2,630. % Full-time: 77. % Female: 51.

RESEARCH FACILITIES
Research Facilities: Regional Primate Center, Mid-American Research Center, Center for Urban Initiatives, Murphy Institute of Political Economy, Center for Research on Women, Center for Bioenvironment Research, language labs.

EXPENSES/FINANCIAL AID
Annual Tuition: $24,675. Fees: $2,160. Books and Supplies: $1,000. % Receiving Financial Aid: 90. Average student debt, upon graduation: $37,000.

ADMISSIONS INFORMATION
Application Fee: $25. Regular Notification: Rolling. Transfer Students Accepted? Yes. Transfer Policy: Maximum 29 credit hours with a minimum 3.5 GPA may be transferred. Number of Applications Received: 197. % of Applicants Accepted: 85. % Accepted Who Enrolled: 40. Average GPA: 3.2.
Required Admission Factors: Essays/personal statement, letters of recommendation, transcript.
Other Admission Factors: Minimum 3.0 GPA required. Minimum GRE score of 1000 if GPA is below minimum.

EMPLOYMENT INFORMATION
Placement Office Available? Yes. % Employed Within 6 Months: 80. % of master's grads employed in their field upon graduation: 10. Average starting salary: $30,000.

TUSCULUM COLLEGE
Graduate School

Address: PO Box 5093, Greeneville, TN 37743-9997
Admissions Phone: 423-636-7300, ext. 330 · Admissions Fax: 423-638-5181
Admissions E-mail: dwood@tusculum.edu

INSTITUTIONAL INFORMATION
Public/private: Private (nonprofit). Evening Classes Available? Yes. Students in Parent Institution: 1,681.

STUDENT INFORMATION
Total Students in Program: 304. % Full-time: 99. % Female: 72.

EXPENSES/FINANCIAL AID
Annual Tuition: $5,635. Fees: $75. Books and Supplies: $600. Loans Range From: $8,500-$13,160. % Receiving Scholarships/Grants: 8. % Receiving Loans: 99. % Receiving Other Aid: 6.

ADMISSIONS INFORMATION
Regular Notification: Rolling. Transfer Students Accepted? Yes. Number of Applications Received: 163. % of Applicants Accepted: 97. % Accepted Who Enrolled: 91.
Required Admission Factors: Essays/personal statement, letters of recommendation, transcript.
Other Admission Factors: Minimum 2.75 GPA from last 60 credit hours and 3 years of professional experience required.

EMPLOYMENT INFORMATION
Placement Office Available? Yes.

UNION INSTITUTE & UNIVERSITY (FORMERLY THE UNION INSTITUTE)
The Graduate College

Address: 440 East McMillan Street, Cincinnati, OH 45206-1925
Admissions Phone: 800-486-3116 · Admissions Fax: 513-861-0779

INSTITUTIONAL INFORMATION
Public/private: Private (nonprofit). Student/faculty Ratio: 13:1. Students in Parent Institution: 1,812.

STUDENT INFORMATION
Total Students in Program: 1,122. % Full-time: 100. % Female: 61.

RESEARCH FACILITIES
Research Facilities: Center for Public Policy, Center for Women, Office of Social Responsibility.

EXPENSES/FINANCIAL AID
Annual Tuition: $9,392. Books and Supplies: $700. Grants Range From: $1,000-$12,750. Loans Range From: $1,000-$18,500. % Receiving Financial Aid: 56. % Receiving Scholarships/Grants: 2. % Receiving Loans: 98. Average student debt upon graduation: $53,000.

ADMISSIONS INFORMATION

Application Fee: $50. **Regular Notification:** Rolling. **Transfer Students Accepted?** No. **Number of Applications Received:** 397. **% of Applicants Accepted:** 71. **% Accepted Who Enrolled:** 94.

Required Admission Factors: Essays/personal statement, letters of recommendation, transcript.

Other Admission Factors: Evidence of ability to do doctoral-level research required.

UNION THEOLOGICAL SEMINARY (NY)
Graduate Program

Address: 3041 Broadway, New York, NY 10027-0003
Admissions Phone: 212-662-7100 · **Admissions Fax:** 212-280-1416
Admissions E-mail: dmcdonagh@uts.columbia.edu
Web Address: www.uts.columbia.edu

INSTITUTIONAL INFORMATION

Public/private: Private (nonprofit). **Student/faculty Ratio:** 15:1. **Students in Parent Institution:** 283.

STUDENT INFORMATION

Total Students in Program: 221. **% Full-time:** 62. **% Female:** 60.

EXPENSES/FINANCIAL AID

Annual Tuition: $14,000. **Room & Board:** $10,080. **Fees:** $1,300. **Books and Supplies:** $1,300. **Grants Range From:** $5,000-$24,640. **Loans Range From:** $1,000-$18,500. **% Receiving Financial Aid:** 90. **% Receiving Scholarships/Grants:** 80. **% Receiving Loans:** 80. **% Receiving Assistantships:** 15. **Average student debt upon graduation:** $31,500. **Number of Fellowships Granted Each Year:** 28. **Average amount of individual fellowships per year:** $19,600. **Number of Teaching/Research Assistantships Granted Each Year:** 23. **Average Salary Stipend:** $2,100.

ADMISSIONS INFORMATION

Application Fee: $50. **Priority Application Deadline:** 2/15. **Regular Application Deadline:** 7/15. **Regular Notification:** Rolling. **Transfer Students Accepted?** Yes. **Transfer Policy:** Minimum grade of B in courses to be transferred required of transfer applicants. **Number of Applications Received:** 124. **% of Applicants Accepted:** 81. **% Accepted Who Enrolled:** 55.

Required Admission Factors: Essays/personal statement, letters of recommendation, transcript.

Recommended Admission Factors: Interview.

Program-Specific Admission Factors: GRE required of doctoral program applicants.

UNION THEOLOGICAL SEMINARY AND PRESBYTERIAN SCHOOL OF CHRISTIAN EDUCATION
Graduate Program

Address: 3401 Brook Road, Richmond, VA 23227
Admissions Phone: 804-355-0671 · **Admissions Fax:** 804-355-3919

INSTITUTIONAL INFORMATION

Public/private: Private (nonprofit). **Student/faculty Ratio:** 11:1. **Students in Parent Institution:** 610.

STUDENT INFORMATION

Total Students in Program: 344.

RESEARCH FACILITIES

Research Facilities: Carl Howie Center for Science, Religion, and the Arts; Center on Aging; Institute for Reformed Theology.

EXPENSES/FINANCIAL AID

Room & Board: $14,380. **Fees:** $170. **Books and Supplies:** $1,100. **% Receiving Financial Aid:** 85. **% Receiving Scholarships/Grants:** 100. **% Receiving Loans:** 40. **Average student debt upon graduation:** $5,000.

ADMISSIONS INFORMATION

Application Fee: $45. **Transfer Students Accepted?** Yes. **Transfer Policy:** Maximum 16 courses may be transferred into the MDiv program. **Number of Applications Received:** 245. **% of Applicants Accepted:** 59. **% Accepted Who Enrolled:** 67. **Average GPA:** 3.13.

Required Admission Factors: Essays/personal statement, GRE, letters of recommendation, transcript.

Program-Specific Admission Factors: GRE required of PhD program applicants.

EMPLOYMENT INFORMATION

Placement Office Available? Yes. **Rate of placement:** 98%.

UNITED STATES INTERNATIONAL UNIVERSITY
College of Arts & Sciences

Address: 10455 Pomerado Road, San Diego, CA 92131
Admissions Phone: 858-635-4772 · **Admissions Fax:** 858-635-4739
Admissions E-mail: admissions@usiu.edu

INSTITUTIONAL INFORMATION

Public/private: Private (nonprofit). **Evening Classes Available?** Yes. **Student/faculty Ratio:** 20:1. **Students in Parent Institution:** 1,335.

STUDENT INFORMATION

Total Students in Program: 813. **% Full-time:** 41. **% Female:** 57.

EXPENSES/FINANCIAL AID

Annual Tuition: $9,720. **Fees:** $390. **Books and Supplies:** $846. **Grants Range From:** $800-$6,600. **Loans Range From:** $500-$20,000. **% Receiving Financial Aid:** 64. **% Receiving Scholarships/Grants:** 29. **% Receiving Loans:** 70. **% Receiving Assistantships:** 5. **Average student debt upon graduation:** $32,692. **Number of Fellowships Granted Each Year:** 2. **Average amount of individual fellowships per year:** $2,696. **Number of Teaching/Research Assistantships Granted Each Year:** 2.

ADMISSIONS INFORMATION

Application Fee: $40. **Regular Notification:** Rolling. **Transfer Students Accepted?** Yes. **Number of Applications Received:** 148. **% of Applicants Accepted:** 59. **% Accepted Who Enrolled:** 60. **Average GPA:** 3.26. **Average GRE Verbal:** 415. **Average GRE Quantitative:** 479.

Required Admission Factors: Essays/personal statement, GRE, letters of recommendation, transcript.

Other Admission Factors: Minimum 2.5 GPA required.

Program-Specific Admission Factors: GRE or MAT and 3 letters of recommendation required of doctoral program applicants.

EMPLOYMENT INFORMATION

Placement Office Available? Yes.

UNITED THEOLOGICAL SEMINARY
Graduate Program

Address: 1810 Harvard Boulevard, Dayton, OH 45406
Admissions Phone: 937-278-5817 · **Admissions Fax:** 937-278-1218
Admissions E-mail: utsadmis@united.edu

INSTITUTIONAL INFORMATION

Public/private: Private (nonprofit). **Evening Classes Available?** Yes. **Student/faculty Ratio:** 10:1. **Students in Parent Institution:** 322.

STUDENT INFORMATION
Total Students in Program: 180. % Full-time: 92. % Female: 38.

RESEARCH FACILITIES
Research Facilities: Center for Supervisory Studies, Center for Evangelical United Brethren Heritage.

EXPENSES/FINANCIAL AID
Annual Tuition: $10,680. Room & Board: $306. Fees: $500. Books and Supplies: $600. Grants Range From: $500-$10,760. Loans Range From: $2,000-$16,000. % Receiving Financial Aid: 43. % Receiving Scholarships/Grants: 35. % Receiving Loans: 33. Average student debt upon graduation: $23,348.

ADMISSIONS INFORMATION
Application Fee: $40. Regular Notification: Rolling. Transfer Students Accepted? Yes. Transfer Policy: Transcript, application, $20 fee, and 3 recommendations required of international applicants. Number of Applications Received: 91. % of Applicants Accepted: 95. % Accepted Who Enrolled: 66. Average GPA: 3.2.
Required Admission Factors: Essays/personal statement, interview, letters of recommendation, transcript.
Other Admission Factors: Minimum 2.5 GPA required.

UNIVERSITÉ LAVAL
Graduate Studies

Address: Cite Universitaire, Quebec City, G1K 7P4 Canada
Admissions Phone: 418-656-3080 or 877-785-2825 · Admissions Fax: 418-656-5216
Admissions E-mail: reg@reg.ulaval.ca · Web Address: www.ulaval.ca

INSTITUTIONAL INFORMATION
Public/private: Private (nonprofit). Students in Parent Institution: 12,644.

STUDENT INFORMATION
Total Students in Program: 1,894. % Full-time: 66. % Female: 55.

RESEARCH FACILITIES
Research Facilities: Numerous research centers.

EXPENSES/FINANCIAL AID
Fees: $50. Books and Supplies: $1,000. Grants Range From: $500-$39,000. % Receiving Scholarships/Grants: 39. % Receiving Loans: 91.

ADMISSIONS INFORMATION
Application Fee: $30. Regular Notification: Rolling. Transfer Students Accepted? Yes. Number of Applications Received: 5,521. % of Applicants Accepted: 61. % Accepted Who Enrolled: 56.
Required Admission Factors: Letters of recommendation, transcript.

EMPLOYMENT INFORMATION
Placement Office Available? Yes. Rate of placement: 92%.

THE UNIVERSITY OF AKRON
Buchtel College of Arts & Sciences

Address: 302 Buchtel Common, Akron, OH 44325-1901
Admissions Phone: 330-972-7880 · Admissions Fax: 330-972-7222
Admissions E-mail: rcreel@uakron.edu · Website: www.uakron.edu/colleges/artsci/

INSTITUTIONAL INFORMATION
Public/private: Public. Evening Classes Available? Yes. Total Faculty: 264. % Faculty Female: 26. % Faculty Part-time: 21. Students in Parent Institution: 24,335.

PROGRAMS
Masters offered in: Applied mathematics; chemistry; city/urban, community, and regional planning; computer and information sciences; counseling psychology; economics; English composition; English language and literature; geography; geology/earth science; history; mathematics; physics; political science and government; psychology; public administration; sociology; Spanish language and literature; statistics. Doctorate offered in: Applied mathematics, chemistry, counseling psychology, history, industrial and organizational psychology, psychology, sociology, urban studies/affairs.

STUDENT INFORMATION
Total Students in Program: 3,597. % Full-time: 47. % Female: 58. % International: 17.

RESEARCH FACILITIES
Research Facilities: Ray C. Bliss Institute of Political Science, Center for Collaboration and Inquiry, Center for Conflict Management, Center for Environmental Studies, Center for Organizational Research, Center for Policy Studies.

EXPENSES/FINANCIAL AID
Annual Tuition: In-state $4,992. / Out-of-state $8,564. Room & Board: $6,268. Fees: $654. Loans Range From: $4,000-$15,000. % Receiving Financial Aid: 100. % Receiving Assistantships: 32. Types of Aid Available: Graduate assistantships, grants, institutional work-study, scholarships. Number of Teaching/Research Assistantships Granted Each Year: 771.

ADMISSIONS INFORMATION
Application Fee: $40. Regular Notification: Rolling. Transfer Students Accepted? Yes. Transfer Policy: Credits cannot be transferred until full admission has been granted and 12 graduate credits have been taken with a 3.0 GPA. Number of Applications Received: 580. % of Applicants Accepted: 56. % Accepted Who Enrolled: 54.
Required Admission Factors: Transcript.
Other Admission Factors: 2.75 GPA required for full admission; GRE score requirements set by departments.
Program-Specific Admission Factors: Some programs may require letters of recommendation; personal interview; personal essay; writing sample; higher minimum GPA requirements for program entry may be determined by departments.

EMPLOYMENT INFORMATION
Placement Office Available? Yes.

THE UNIVERSITY OF AKRON
College of Fine & Applied Arts

Address: Guzzetta Hall 260, Akron, OH 44325-1001
Admissions Phone: 330-972-7543 · Admissions Fax: 330-972-5844
Admissions E-mail: auburn@uakron.edu · Website: www.uakron.edu/colleges/faa/

INSTITUTIONAL INFORMATION
Public/private: Public. Total Faculty: 173. % Faculty Female: 56. % Faculty Part-time: 49. Students in Parent Institution: 24,335.

PROGRAMS
Masters offered in: Apparel and textiles; audiology/audiologist and hearing sciences; audiology/audiologist and speech-language pathology/pathologist; child development; communications studies/speech communication and rhetoric; conducting; directing and theatrical production; family and consumer sciences/human sciences; fashion/apparel design; foods, nutrition, and wellness studies; interior design; music history, literature, and theory; music performance; music theory and composition; music; music/music and performing arts studies; piano and organ; social work; speech-language pathology/pathologist; violin, viola, guitar, and other stringed instruments; voice and opera. Doctorate offered in: Audiology/audiologist and hearing sciences.

STUDENT INFORMATION
Total Students in Program: 3,597. % Full-time: 47. % Female: 58. % International: 17.

RESEARCH FACILITIES

Research Facilities: WZIP (FM radio station); Ballet Center, Sandefur Theater, Daum Theater, Center for Child Development, Audiology and Speech Center, Center for Family Studies.

EXPENSES/FINANCIAL AID

Annual Tuition: In-state $4,992. / Out-of-state $8,564. **Room & Board:** $6,268. **Fees:** $654. **Loans Range From:** $4,000-$15,000. **% Receiving Financial Aid:** 100. **% Receiving Assistantships:** 32. **Types of Aid Available:** Graduate assistantships, grants, institutional work-study, scholarships. **Number of Fellowships Granted Each Year:** 325. **Assistantship Compensation Includes:** Full tuition remission, partial tuition remission, salary/stipend.

ADMISSIONS INFORMATION

Application Fee: $40. **Regular Notification:** Rolling. **Transfer Students Accepted?** Yes. **Transfer Policy:** Credits cannot be transferred until 12 graduate credits are taken with 3.0 GPA. Maximum one-third of credit hours required for program may be transferred. **Number of Applications Received:** 267. **% of Applicants Accepted:** 66. **% Accepted Who Enrolled:** 65.

Required Admission Factors: Transcript.
Other Admission Factors: Minimum 2.75 GPA required for full admission; GRE score requirements are set by the departments.
Program-Specific Admission Factors: Family and consumer sciences: GRE (1220 on all three parts); letter of career goals; 2 letters of recommendation; personal interview (if necessary). Doctor of audiology: 3.0 or higher GPA; 3 letters of recommendation; GRE scores; personal statement.

EMPLOYMENT INFORMATION

Placement Office Available? Yes.

THE UNIVERSITY OF ALABAMA
College of Arts & Sciences

Address: Box 870100, Tuscaloosa, AL 35487-0100
Admissions Phone: 205-348-5921 · **Admissions Fax:** 205-348-0400

INSTITUTIONAL INFORMATION
Public/private: Public.

STUDENT INFORMATION
Total Students in Program: 5,335. **% Full-time:** 73. **% Female:** 52.

EXPENSES/FINANCIAL AID
Annual Tuition: In-state $3,000. / Out-of-state $8,000. **% Receiving Loans:** 30. **% Receiving Assistantships:** 40.

ADMISSIONS INFORMATION
Application Fee: $25. **Regular Notification:** Rolling. **Transfer Students Accepted?** No. **Number of Applications Received:** 578. **% of Applicants Accepted:** 68. **% Accepted Who Enrolled:** 62.
Required Admission Factors: Letters of recommendation, transcript.
Other Admission Factors: Minimum 3.0 GPA required.

EMPLOYMENT INFORMATION
Placement Office Available? Yes.

THE UNIVERSITY OF ALABAMA
College of Communication and Information Sciences

Address: Box 870100, Tuscaloosa, AL 35487-0100
Admissions Phone: 205-348-8593 · **Admissions Fax:** 205-348-6774

INSTITUTIONAL INFORMATION
Public/private: Public.

STUDENT INFORMATION
Total Students in Program: 5,335. **% Full-time:** 73. **% Female:** 52.

EXPENSES/FINANCIAL AID
Annual Tuition: In-state $3,000. / Out-of-state $8,000. **% Receiving Loans:** 30. **% Receiving Assistantships:** 40.

ADMISSIONS INFORMATION
Application Fee: $25. **Regular Notification:** Rolling. **Transfer Students Accepted?** No. **Number of Applications Received:** 259. **% of Applicants Accepted:** 53. **% Accepted Who Enrolled:** 73.
Required Admission Factors: Letters of recommendation, transcript.
Other Admission Factors: Minimum 3.0 GPA required.

EMPLOYMENT INFORMATION
Placement Office Available? Yes.

THE UNIVERSITY OF ALABAMA
College of Human Environmental Sciences

Address: Box 870100, Tuscaloosa, AL 35487-0100
Admissions Phone: 205-348-5921 · **Admissions Fax:** 205-348-0400
Website: http://ches.ua.edu

INSTITUTIONAL INFORMATION
Public/private: Public.

STUDENT INFORMATION
Total Students in Program: 5,335. **% Full-time:** 73. **% Female:** 52.

EXPENSES/FINANCIAL AID
Annual Tuition: In-state $3,000. / Out-of-state $8,000. **% Receiving Loans:** 30. **% Receiving Assistantships:** 40.

ADMISSIONS INFORMATION
Transfer Students Accepted? No. **Number of Applications Received:** 85. **% of Applicants Accepted:** 72. **% Accepted Who Enrolled:** 51.

EMPLOYMENT INFORMATION
Placement Office Available? Yes.

THE UNIVERSITY OF ALABAMA
School of Social Work

Address: Box 870100, Tuscaloosa, AL 35487-0100
Admissions Phone: 205-348-5921 · **Admissions Fax:** 205-348-0400

INSTITUTIONAL INFORMATION
Public/private: Public.

STUDENT INFORMATION
Total Students in Program: 5,335. **% Full-time:** 73. **% Female:** 52.

EXPENSES/FINANCIAL AID
Annual Tuition: In-state $3,000. / Out-of-state $8,000. **% Receiving Loans:** 30. **% Receiving Assistantships:** 40.

ADMISSIONS INFORMATION
Application Fee: $25. **Transfer Students Accepted?** No. **Number of Applications Received:** 115. **% of Applicants Accepted:** 61. **% Accepted Who Enrolled:** 63.
Required Admission Factors: Letters of recommendation, transcript.
Other Admission Factors: Minimum 3.0 GPA required.

EMPLOYMENT INFORMATION
Placement Office Available? Yes.

UNIVERSITY OF ALABAMA AT BIRMINGHAM
School of Arts & Humanities

Address: 1530 Third Avenue South, Birmingham, AL 35294
Admissions Phone: 205-934-8227 · **Admissions Fax:** 205-934-8413

INSTITUTIONAL INFORMATION
Public/private: Public. **Students in Parent Institution:** 14,951.

STUDENT INFORMATION
Total Students in Program: 3,641. **% Full-time:** 65. **% Female:** 61.

RESEARCH FACILITIES
Research Facilities: Learning Center, Educational Technology Services, Civitan International Research Center, Laser and Photonics Research Center.

EXPENSES/FINANCIAL AID
Annual Tuition: In-state $2,688. / Out-of-state $5,376. **Room & Board:** $2,998. **Fees:** $562. **Books and Supplies:** $900.

ADMISSIONS INFORMATION
Application Fee: $35. **Regular Notification:** Rolling. **Transfer Students Accepted?** No. **Number of Applications Received:** 20. **% of Applicants Accepted:** 75. **% Accepted Who Enrolled:** 20.
Required Admission Factors: GRE, transcript.
Other Admission Factors: Minimum GRE section scores of 500, minimum grade average of B (overall or last 60 semester hours), and previous academic work appropriate to selected academic area required.
Program-Specific Admission Factors: Minimum 4th semester-level foreign language required of English program applicants. Minimum grade average of B in art history and related areas required of art history program applicants.

EMPLOYMENT INFORMATION
Placement Office Available? Yes.

UNIVERSITY OF ALABAMA AT BIRMINGHAM
School of Natural Sciences & Mathematics

Address: 1530 Third Avenue South, Birmingham, AL 35294
Admissions Phone: 205-934-8227 · **Admissions Fax:** 205-934-8413

INSTITUTIONAL INFORMATION
Public/private: Public. **Students in Parent Institution:** 14,951.

STUDENT INFORMATION
Total Students in Program: 3,641. **% Full-time:** 65. **% Female:** 61.

RESEARCH FACILITIES
Research Facilities: Learning Center, Educational Technology Services, Civitan International Research Center, Laser and Photonics Research Center.

EXPENSES/FINANCIAL AID
Annual Tuition: In-state $2,688. / Out-of-state $5,376. **Room & Board:** $2,998. **Fees:** $562. **Books and Supplies:** $900.

ADMISSIONS INFORMATION
Application Fee: $35. **Regular Notification:** Rolling. **Transfer Students Accepted?** No. **Number of Applications Received:** 398. **% of Applicants Accepted:** 55. **% Accepted Who Enrolled:** 17.
Required Admission Factors: GRE, letters of recommendation, transcript.
Other Admission Factors: Minimum GRE section scores of 500, minimum grade average of B (overall or in last 60 semester hours), and previous academic work appropriate to selected academic area required.
Program-Specific Admission Factors: Substantial background in computer science and mathematics required.

EMPLOYMENT INFORMATION
Placement Office Available? Yes.

UNIVERSITY OF ALABAMA AT BIRMINGHAM
School of Social & Behavioral Sciences

Address: 1530 Third Avenue South, Birmingham, AL 35294
Admissions Phone: 205-934-8277 · **Admissions Fax:** 205-934-8413

INSTITUTIONAL INFORMATION
Public/private: Public. **Students in Parent Institution:** 14,951.

STUDENT INFORMATION
Total Students in Program: 3,641. **% Full-time:** 65. **% Female:** 61.

RESEARCH FACILITIES
Research Facilities: Learning Center, Educational Technology Services, Civitan International Research Center, Laser and Photonics Research Center.

EXPENSES/FINANCIAL AID
Annual Tuition: In-state $2,688. / Out-of-state $5,376. **Room & Board:** $2,998. **Fees:** $562. **Books and Supplies:** $900.

ADMISSIONS INFORMATION
Application Fee: $35. **Regular Notification:** Rolling. **Transfer Students Accepted?** No. **Number of Applications Received:** 382. **% of Applicants Accepted:** 33. **% Accepted Who Enrolled:** 28.
Required Admission Factors: GRE, transcript.
Other Admission Factors: Minimum GRE section scores of 500, minimum grade average of B (overall or in last 60 semester hours), and previous academic work appropriate to selected academic area required.
Program-Specific Admission Factors: Minimum GRE section scores of 600 and minimum 3.2 GPA (overall and in psychology courses) required of doctoral psychology program applicants. Minimum GRE score of 1150 and minimum 3.0 GPA overall, 3.2 GPA in last 60 semester hours, or 3.5 GPA in previous undergraduate major.

EMPLOYMENT INFORMATION
Placement Office Available? Yes.

UNIVERSITY OF ALABAMA IN HUNTSVILLE
College of Liberal Arts

Address: 301 Sparkman Drive, Huntsville, AL 35899
Admissions Phone: 256-824-6002 · **Admissions Fax:** 256-824-6349
Admissions E-mail: emslieg@email.uah.edu

INSTITUTIONAL INFORMATION
Public/private: Public. **Evening Classes Available?** Yes. **Student/faculty Ratio:** 2:1. **Students in Parent Institution:** 6,563.

STUDENT INFORMATION
Total Students in Program: 1,343. **% Full-time:** 36. **% Female:** 42.

RESEARCH FACILITIES
Research Facilities: Center for Space Plasma and Aeronomic Research, Center for Robotics, Research Institute, Center for Applied Optics, Center for Economic Research, Center for the Management of Technology, Johnson Research Center, Information Technology Systems Lab.

EXPENSES/FINANCIAL AID
Annual Tuition: In-state $4,408. / Out-of-state $9,054. **Room & Board:** $6,520. **Books and Supplies:** $720. **Grants Range From:** $59-$10,500. **Loans Range From:** $400-$16,970. **% Receiving Financial Aid:** 49. **% Receiving Scholarships/Grants:** 17. **% Receiving Loans:** 27. **% Receiving Assistantships:** 56. **Average student debt upon graduation:** $19,644. **Number of Teaching/Research Assistantships Granted Each Year:** 21. **Average Salary Stipend:** $877.

ADMISSIONS INFORMATION

Application Fee: $35. **Regular Notification:** Rolling. **Transfer Students Accepted?** Yes. **Number of Applications Received:** 50. **% of Applicants Accepted:** 82. **% Accepted Who Enrolled:** 61. **Average GPA:** 3.39. **Average GRE Verbal:** 521. **Average GRE Quantitative:** 509. **Average GRE Analytical:** 546.
Required Admission Factors: Transcript.
Other Admission Factors: Minimum 3.0 GPA required.
Program-Specific Admission Factors: Minimum GRE combined score of 1000 (Verbal and Quantitative), minimum 3.25 GPA, 3 letters of recommendation, and paper required of psychology program applicants. Minimum GRE score of 1140 required of English program applicants. Minimum MAT score of 50.

EMPLOYMENT INFORMATION

Placement Office Available? Yes. **Rate of placement:** 83%.

UNIVERSITY OF ALABAMA IN HUNTSVILLE
College of Science

Address: 301 Sparkman Drive, Huntsville, AL 35899
Admissions Phone: 256-890-6002 · **Admissions Fax:** 256-890-6349
Admissions E-mail: emslieg@email.uah.edu

INSTITUTIONAL INFORMATION

Public/private: Public. **Evening Classes Available?** Yes. **Student/faculty Ratio:** 4:1. **Students in Parent Institution:** 6,563.

STUDENT INFORMATION

Total Students in Program: 1,343. **% Full-time:** 36. **% Female:** 42.

RESEARCH FACILITIES

Research Facilities: Center for Space Plasma and Aeronomic Research, Center for Robotics. Research Institute, Center for Applied Optics, Center for Economic Research, Center for the Management of Technology, Johnson Research Center, Information Technology Systems Lab.

EXPENSES/FINANCIAL AID

Annual Tuition: In-state $4,408. / Out-of-state $9,054. **Room & Board:** $6,520. **Books and Supplies:** $720. **Grants Range From:** $59-$10,500. **Loans Range From:** $400-$16,970. **% Receiving Financial Aid:** 46. **% Receiving Scholarships/Grants:** 17. **% Receiving Loans:** 27. **% Receiving Assistantships:** 56. **Average student debt upon graduation:** $32,201. **Number of Teaching/Research Assistantships Granted Each Year:** 133. **Average Salary Stipend:** $869.

ADMISSIONS INFORMATION

Application Fee: $35. **Regular Notification:** Rolling. **Transfer Students Accepted?** Yes. **Number of Applications Received:** 221. **% of Applicants Accepted:** 74. **% Accepted Who Enrolled:** 56. **Average GPA:** 3.44. **Average GRE Verbal:** 478. **Average GRE Quantitative:** 675. **Average GRE Analytical:** 585.
Required Admission Factors: GRE, transcript.
Other Admission Factors: Minimum GRE score of 1500, minimum 3.0 GPA, and at least 1 year of chemistry (1 semester each of chemistry and biochemistry), and 1 statistics course required.

EMPLOYMENT INFORMATION

Placement Office Available? Yes. **Rate of placement:** 83%.

UNIVERSITY OF ALASKA—FAIRBANKS
Graduate School

Address: PO Box 757480, Fairbanks, AK 99775-7480
Admissions Phone: 907-474-7464 · **Admissions Fax:** 907-474-1984
Admissions E-mail: fyapply@uaf.edu

INSTITUTIONAL INFORMATION

Public/private: Public. **Evening Classes Available?** Yes. **Student/faculty Ratio:** 11:1. **Students in Parent Institution:** 7,142.

STUDENT INFORMATION

Total Students in Program: 831. **% Full-time:** 63. **% Female:** 53.

RESEARCH FACILITIES

Research Facilities: Geophysical Institute, Institute of Arctic Biology, Institute of Marine Sciences, Institute of Northern Engineering, Cooperative Institute for Arctic Engineering.

EXPENSES/FINANCIAL AID

Annual Tuition: In-state $4,272. / Out-of-state $8,328. **Room & Board:** $5,840. **Fees:** $960. **Books and Supplies:** $650.

ADMISSIONS INFORMATION

Application Fee: $35. **Regular Notification:** Rolling. **Transfer Students Accepted?** Yes. **Transfer Policy:** Maximum 1/3 of total required credit hours may be transferred. **Number of Applications Received:** 302. **% of Applicants Accepted:** 88. **% Accepted Who Enrolled:** 94. **Average GRE Verbal:** 517. **Average GRE Quantitative:** 632. **Average GRE Analytical:** 617.
Required Admission Factors: Letters of recommendation, transcript.
Other Admission Factors: Minimum 3.0 GPA, resume, and statement of academic goals required.

EMPLOYMENT INFORMATION

Placement Office Available? Yes.

UNIVERSITY OF ARKANSAS
Fulbright College of Arts & Sciences

Address: 119 Ozark Hall, Fayetteville, AR 72701

INSTITUTIONAL INFORMATION

Public/private: Public. **Students in Parent Institution:** 2,278.

STUDENT INFORMATION

Total Students in Program: 2,278. **% Full-time:** 65. **% Female:** 48.

RESEARCH FACILITIES

Research Facilities: Arkansas Biotechnology Center, Arkansas Center for Technology Transfer, Arkansas Household Research Panel, Arkansas Leadership Academy, Arkansas Research and Training Center in Vocational Rehabilitation, Arkansas Water Resources Center.

EXPENSES/FINANCIAL AID

Annual Tuition: In-state $4,502. / Out-of-state $10,670. **Fees:** $473. **Books and Supplies:** $800.

ADMISSIONS INFORMATION

Transfer Students Accepted? No.

EMPLOYMENT INFORMATION

Placement Office Available? Yes.

UNIVERSITY OF ARKANSAS—LITTLE ROCK
College of Arts, Humanities, & Social Science

Address: 2801 South University Avenue, Little Rock, AR 72204
Admissions Phone: 501-569-3206

INSTITUTIONAL INFORMATION
Public/private: Public. **Students in Parent Institution:** 10,959.

STUDENT INFORMATION
Total Students in Program: 1,847. **% Full-time:** 27. **% Female:** 71.

RESEARCH FACILITIES
Research Facilities: Arkansas Institute for Economic Advancement, Arkansas Institute of Government, Graduate Institute of Technology.

EXPENSES/FINANCIAL AID
Annual Tuition: In-state $2,808. / Out-of-state $6,012. **Room & Board:** $3,900. **Fees:** $297. **Books and Supplies:** $100.

ADMISSIONS INFORMATION
Transfer Students Accepted? Yes. **Number of Applications Received:** 76. **% of Applicants Accepted:** 32. **% Accepted Who Enrolled:** 29.
Required Admission Factors: GRE, transcript.
Other Admission Factors: Minimum 2.7 GPA and letters of recommendation required for most programs.
Program-Specific Admission Factors: Portfolio and statement of objectives required of art program applicants. Statistics course required of applied psychology program applicants. Portfolio required of writing program applicants. Minimum GRE score of 800 recommended of applied psychology program.

EMPLOYMENT INFORMATION
Placement Office Available? Yes.

UNIVERSITY OF ARKANSAS—LITTLE ROCK
College of Professional Studies

Address: 2801 South University Avenue, Little Rock, AR 72204
Admissions Phone: 501-569-3209

INSTITUTIONAL INFORMATION
Public/private: Public. **Students in Parent Institution:** 10,959.

STUDENT INFORMATION
Total Students in Program: 1,847. **% Full-time:** 27. **% Female:** 71.

RESEARCH FACILITIES
Research Facilities: Arkansas Institute for Economic Advancement, Arkansas Institute of Government, Graduate Institute of Technology.

EXPENSES/FINANCIAL AID
Annual Tuition: In-state $2,808. / Out-of-state $6,012. **Room & Board:** $3,900. **Fees:** $297. **Books and Supplies:** $100.

ADMISSIONS INFORMATION
Transfer Students Accepted? No. **Number of Applications Received:** 327. **% of Applicants Accepted:** 31. **% Accepted Who Enrolled:** 37.
Required Admission Factors: GRE, letters of recommendation, transcript.
Other Admission Factors: Minimum MAT score of 40 (or GRE score of 1000), and minimum 2.7 GPA required of applicants to most programs.
Program-Specific Admission Factors: Summer preparatory course required of interpersonal/organizational communication program applicants.

EMPLOYMENT INFORMATION
Placement Office Available? Yes.

UNIVERSITY OF ARKANSAS—MONTICELLO
School of Forest Resources

Address: PO Box 3478, Monticello, AR 71656-3478
Admissions Phone: 870-460-1026 · **Admissions Fax:** 870-460-1933
Admissions E-mail: admissions@uamont.edu

INSTITUTIONAL INFORMATION
Public/private: Public. **Evening Classes Available?** Yes. **Total Faculty:** 16. **% Faculty Female:** 6. **Student/faculty Ratio:** 2:1. **Students in Parent Institution:** 2,254.

STUDENT INFORMATION
Total Students in Program: 131. **% Full-time:** 22. **% Female:** 68.

EXPENSES/FINANCIAL AID
Annual Tuition: In-state $1,764. / Out-of-state $4,104. **Fees:** $14. **Books and Supplies:** $800. **Grants Range From:** $1,960-$2,940. **Loans Range From:** $1,600-$8,500. **% Receiving Financial Aid:** 95. **% Receiving Scholarships/ Grants:** 2. **% Receiving Loans:** 81. **% Receiving Assistantships:** 14. **Number of Teaching/Research Assistantships Granted Each Year:** 8. **Average Salary Stipend:** $11,000.

ADMISSIONS INFORMATION
Regular Notification: Rolling. **Transfer Students Accepted?** Yes. **Number of Applications Received:** 25. **% of Applicants Accepted:** 40. **% Accepted Who Enrolled:** 80. **Average GPA:** 3.0.
Required Admission Factors: Essays/personal statement, GRE, letters of recommendation, transcript.
Other Admission Factors: Minimum 2.7 GPA required.

UNIVERSITY OF BALTIMORE
Yale Gordon College of Liberal Arts

Address: 1420 North Charles Street, Baltimore, MD 21201
Admissions Phone: 877-APPLY-UB · **Admissions Fax:** 410-837-4793
Admissions E-mail: rcthomas@ubmail.ubalt.edu

INSTITUTIONAL INFORMATION
Public/private: Public. **Evening Classes Available?** Yes. **Students in Parent Institution:** 4,611.

STUDENT INFORMATION
Total Students in Program: 1,724. **% Full-time:** 26. **% Female:** 54.

RESEARCH FACILITIES
Research Facilities: Institute for Publications Design, the Hoffberger Center for Professional Ethics, the Information Systems Research Center, and the William Donald Schaefer Center for Public Policy Studies.

EXPENSES/FINANCIAL AID
Annual Tuition: In-state $5,832. / Out-of-state $8,424. **Books and Supplies:** $730.

ADMISSIONS INFORMATION
Application Fee: $30. **Regular Notification:** Rolling. **Transfer Students Accepted?** Yes. **Transfer Policy:** Transfer applicants are required to meet with faculty chairperson. **Number of Applications Received:** 453. **% of Applicants Accepted:** 79. **% Accepted Who Enrolled:** 78.
Required Admission Factors: GRE, transcript.
Other Admission Factors: Minimum 3.0 GPA, letter of intent, and resume required.
Program-Specific Admission Factors: Portfolio required of publications design program applicants.

EMPLOYMENT INFORMATION
Placement Office Available? Yes.

UNIVERSITY OF BRIDGEPORT
Nutrition Institute

Address: 126 Park Avenue, Bridgeport, CT 06601
Admissions Phone: 203-576-4370 · **Admissions Fax:** 203-576-4941
Admissions E-mail: admit@bridgeport.edu
Web Address: www.bridgeport.edu/ub/nu/

INSTITUTIONAL INFORMATION

Public/private: Private (nonprofit). **Students in Parent Institution:** 2,686.

STUDENT INFORMATION

Total Students in Program: 1,232. **% Full-time:** 42. **% Female:** 57.

RESEARCH FACILITIES

Research Facilities: Connecticut Technologies Institute (CTI), Center for Venture Management, New England Center for Regional & International Studies.

EXPENSES/FINANCIAL AID

Room & Board: $8,120. **Fees:** $100. **Books and Supplies:** $1,050. **Grants Range From:** $500-$5,000. **Loans Range From:** $500-$18,500. **% Receiving Scholarships/Grants:** 11. **% Receiving Loans:** 79.

ADMISSIONS INFORMATION

Application Fee: $40. **Regular Application Deadline:** 7/1. **Regular Notification:** Rolling. **Transfer Students Accepted?** Yes. **Transfer Policy:** Transfer students should have the prerequisites and a minimum of a 2.75 GPA. **Required Admission Factors:** Essays/personal statement, letters of recommendation, transcript.
Other Admission Factors: 2.75 GPA.
Program-Specific Admission Factors: Prerequisites include anatomy and physiology, biochemistry, and basic nutrition.

EMPLOYMENT INFORMATION

Placement Office Available? Yes.

UNIVERSITY OF BRITISH COLUMBIA
Faculty of Graduate Studies

Address: 180-6371 Crescent Road, Vancouver, British Columbia, BC V6T 1Z2 Canada
Admissions Phone: 604-822-0954 · **Admissions Fax:** 614-822-8742
Admissions E-mail: onlineap@interchange.ubc.ca · **Web Address:** www.grad.ubc.ca

INSTITUTIONAL INFORMATION

Public/private: Public. **Students in Parent Institution:** 31,500.

PROGRAMS

Masters offered in: Administration of special education; advanced general dentistry (certificate, MS, PhD); advanced legal research/studies (LLM, MCL, MLI, MSL, JSD/SJD); agricultural and food products processing; agricultural and horticultural plant breeding; agricultural animal breeding; agricultural economics; agricultural production operations; agricultural production operations; agricultural operations and related sciences; agriculture; agronomy and crop science; American Indian/Native American languages, literatures, and linguistics; American/United States studies/civilization; anatomy; ancient studies/civilization; ancient/classical greek language and literature; animal health; animal nutrition; animal sciences; animal sciences; animal/livestock husbandry and production; anthropology; applied mathematics; aquaculture; architecture (BArch, BA/BS, MArch, MA/MS, PhD); architecture and related programs; area studies; art history, criticism, and conservation; art/art studies; art/art studies; artificial intelligence and robotics; Asian studies/civilization; astronomy; astrophysics; atmospheric sciences and meteorology; audiology/audiologist and hearing sciences; balkans studies; baltic studies; biochemistry; bioinformatics; biological and physical sciences; botany/plant biology; business administration/management; cell biology and anatomy; cell/cellular and molecular biology; cell/cellular biology and histology; Central/Middle and Eastern European studies; chemical engineering; chemistry; Chinese studies; city/urban, community, and regional planning; civil engineering; classical, mediterranean, and Near Eastern/Oriental studies and archaeology; classics and classical languages, literatures, and linguistics; clinical psychology; college student counseling and personnel services; comparative literature; computer and information sciences and support services; computer and information sciences; computer and information sciences; computer engineering; computer graphics; computer science; computer systems analysis/analyst; counseling psychology; counselor education/school counseling and guidance services; creative writing; crop production; curriculum and instruction; dairy science; drama and dramatics/theater arts; East Asian languages, literatures, and linguistics; East Asian studies; economics; education leadership and administration; education; education; education/teaching of individuals in early childhood special education programs; educational assessment, evaluation, and research; educational assessment, testing, and measurement; educational evaluation and research; educational psychology; educational statistics and research methods; educational, instructional, and curriculum supervision; electrical, electronics and communications engineering; engineering physics; engineering; English language and literature; English language and literature/letters; environmental design/architecture; environmental science; environmental studies; ethnic, cultural minority, and gender studies; European studies/civilization; family and consumer sciences/home economics teacher education; film/cinema studies; fine/studio arts; fishing and fisheries sciences and management; food science and technology; food science; food technology and processing; foreign languages and literatures; foreign languages/modern languages; forest management/forest resources management; forest resources production and management; forest sciences; forest technology/technician; forestry; French language and literature; French studies; gay/lesbian studies; genetic counseling/counselor; genetics; geography; geological/geophysical engineering; geology/earth science; geophysics and seismology; German language and literature; German studies; Germanic languages, literatures, and linguistics; health and physical education; health communications; health services/allied health; health/health care administration/management; higher education/higher education administration; history; horticultural science; hospital and health care facilities administration/management; human nutrition; human/medical genetics; information science/studies; information technology; interior architecture; Japanese studies; journalism; Korean studies; land use planning and management/development; landscape architecture (BS, BSLA, BLA, MSLA, MLA, PhD); law, legal services, and legal studies; legal research and advanced professional studies; linguistics; livestock management; marine biology and biological oceanography; materials engineering; mathematics teacher education; mathematics; mechanical engineering; medical microbiology and bacteriology; microbiological sciences and immunology; microbiology; mining and mineral engineering; molecular biochemistry; molecular biology; multi/interdisciplinary studies; music teacher education; music; music/music and performing arts studies; natural resource economics; natural resources and conservation; natural resources conservation and research; natural resources management and policy; natural resources management and policy; natural resources/conservation; Near and Middle Eastern studies; neuroscience; nursing; occupational health and industrial hygiene; occupational therapy/therapist; oceanography, chemical and physical; oncology and cancer biology; pacific area/pacific rim studies; pathology/experimental pathology; periodontics/periodontology (certificate, MS, PhD); pharmacology; pharmacy (PharmD, BS/BPharm); philosophy; physical anthropology; physical education teaching and coaching; physical therapy/therapist; physics; physiology; physiology, pathology and related sciences; plant protection and integrated pest management; plant sciences; playwriting and screenwriting; political science and government; poultry science; psychology teacher education; psychology; range science and management; regional studies (U.S., Canadian, foreign); religion/religious studies; school librarian/school library media specialist; school psychology; science teacher education/general science teacher education; social studies teacher education; social work; sociology; soil chemistry and physics; soil microbiology; soil science and agronomy; soil sciences; South Asian languages, literatures, and linguistics; South Asian studies; Southeast Asian languages, literatures, and linguistics; Southeast Asian studies; Spanish and Iberian studies; Spanish language and literature; special education and teaching; special education; statistics; student counseling and personnel services; teacher education and professional development, specific levels and methods; teacher education and professional development, specific subject areas; teaching English as a second or foreign language/ESL language instructor; Ural-altaic and Central Asian studies; urban forestry; visual and performing arts; water, wetlands, and marine resources management. **Doctorate offered in:** Administration of special education; advanced general dentistry (Certificate, MS, PhD); advanced legal research/studies (LLM, MCL, MLI, MSL, JSD/SJD); agricultural and food products processing.

STUDENT INFORMATION
Total Students in Program: 6,500. **% Full-time:** 108.

EXPENSES/FINANCIAL AID
Annual Tuition: In-state $15,000. / Out-of-state $20,000. **Types of Aid Available:** Fellowships, graduate assistantships, grants, institutional work-study, loans, scholarships, tuition fee awards, international partial scholarships.

ADMISSIONS INFORMATION
Application Fee: $150. **Priority Application Deadline:** 1/1. **Regular Application Deadline:** 3/1. **Regular Notification:** Rolling. **Transfer Students Accepted?** Yes. **Transfer Policy:** Admission requirements for transfers vary in the different graduate programs. Contact program in which you are interested for information.
Required Admission Factors: Letters of recommendation, transcript.
Other Admission Factors: Minimum 3.3 GPA required.
Program-Specific Admission Factors: Requirements for graduate programs vary. Please review the programs on our website at www.grad.ubc.ca and contact specific ones to find out their specific admission requirements.

EMPLOYMENT INFORMATION
Placement Office Available? Yes.

UNIVERSITY OF BRITISH COLUMBIA— DEPARTMENT OF MECHANICAL ENGINEERING
Faculty of Applied Science

Address: Graduate Secretary (Mechanical Engineering), 2324 Main Mall, Vancouver, British Columbia, BC V6T 1Z4 Canada
Admissions Phone: 604-822-2781 · **Admissions Fax:** 604-822-2403
Admissions E-mail: secgrad@mech.ubc.ca · **Web Address:** www.mech.ubc.ca

INSTITUTIONAL INFORMATION
Public/private: Public. **Student/faculty Ratio:** 3:1. **Students in Parent Institution:** 31,500.

PROGRAMS
Masters offered in: Mechanical engineering. **Doctorate offered in:** Mechanical engineering. **First Professional degree offered in:** Mechanical engineering.

STUDENT INFORMATION
Total Students in Program: 6,500. **% Full-time:** 2.

RESEARCH FACILITIES
Research Facilities: TRIUME.

EXPENSES/FINANCIAL AID
Annual Tuition: In-state $15,000. / Out-of-state $20,000. **% Receiving Financial Aid:** 75. **Number of Teaching/Research Assistantships Granted Each Year:** 95. **Average Salary Stipend:** $1,500.

ADMISSIONS INFORMATION
Application Fee: $65. **Regular Notification:** Rolling. **Transfer Students Accepted?** Yes. **Transfer Policy:** Maximum 12 credits may be transferred into masters program upon approval, after enrollment; maximum 6 credits may be transferred into doctoral program upon approval, after enrollment. **Number of Applications Received:** 600. **% of Applicants Accepted:** 12. **% Accepted**

Who Enrolled: 86. **Average GPA:** 3.5. **Average GRE Verbal:** 491. **Average GRE Quantitative:** 733. **Average GRE Analytical:** 680.
Required Admission Factors: Letters of recommendation, transcript.
Other Admission Factors: Minimum 3.34 GPA or minimum grade of B required of Canadian and U.S. applicants.

EMPLOYMENT INFORMATION
Placement Office Available? Yes.

UNIVERSITY OF CALIFORNIA—BERKELEY
Graduate School of Journalism

Address: 121 North Gate Hall, #5860, Berkeley, CA 94720
Admissions Phone: 510-642-3383 · **Admissions Fax:** 510-643-9136
Admissions E-mail: applysoj@berkeley.edu
Web Address: www.journalism.berkeley.edu

INSTITUTIONAL INFORMATION
Public/private: Public. **Students in Parent Institution:** 31,011.

PROGRAMS
Masters offered in: Journalism.

STUDENT INFORMATION
Total Students in Program: 114. **% Full-time:** 100. **% Female:** 56. **% Minority:** 30. **% International:** 9.

EXPENSES/FINANCIAL AID
Annual Tuition: $14,939. **Room & Board:** $13,330. **Fees:** $7,456. **Books and Supplies:** $1,240. **Grants Range From:** $500-$4,000. **Loans Range From:** $500-$18,500. **% Receiving Financial Aid:** 75. **Types of Aid Available:** Fellowships, graduate assistantships, grants, institutional work-study, loans, scholarships. researcher positions only in dept.

ADMISSIONS INFORMATION
Application Fee: $60. **Priority Application Deadline:** 12/12. **Regular Application Deadline:** 12/12. **Transfer Students Accepted?** No. **Number of Applications Received:** 461. **% of Applicants Accepted:** 16. **% Accepted Who Enrolled:** 72. **Average GPA:** 3.5. **Average GRE Verbal:** 630. **Average GRE Quantitative:** 610.
Required Admission Factors: Essays/personal statement, GRE, letters of recommendation, transcript. TOEFL required of international applicants, in lieu of GRE.
Other Admission Factors: The minimum graduate admission requirements are a bachelor's degree or recognized equivalent from an accredited institution and a satisfactory scholastic average, usually a minimum GPA of 3.0 (B) for all coursework completed after initial 60 credits.

EMPLOYMENT INFORMATION
Placement Office Available? Yes.

UNIVERSITY OF CALIFORNIA—BERKELEY
Richard & Rhoda Goldman School of Public Policy

Address: 2607 Hearst Avenue, #7320, Berkeley, CA 94720-7320
Admissions Phone: 510-642-1940 · **Admissions Fax:** 510-643-9657
Admissions E-mail: gsppadm@socrates.berkeley.edu
Web Address: www.gspp.berkeley.edu

INSTITUTIONAL INFORMATION
Public/private: Public. **Students in Parent Institution:** 31,011.

STUDENT INFORMATION
Total Students in Program: 8,625 **% Female:** 45.

RESEARCH FACILITIES

Research Facilities: Lawrence Berkeley Lab.

EXPENSES/FINANCIAL AID

Annual Tuition: $4,492. Fees: $2,197.

ADMISSIONS INFORMATION

TRANSFER STUDENTS ACCEPTED? NO.

EMPLOYMENT INFORMATION

Placement Office Available? Yes.

UNIVERSITY OF CALIFORNIA—DAVIS
Graduate Programs

Address: 250 Mark Hall, Davis, CA 95616-8678
Admissions Phone: 530-752-9297 · Admissions Fax: 530-752-6363
Admissions E-mail: cjjurado@ucdavis.edu

INSTITUTIONAL INFORMATION

Public/private: Public. Students in Parent Institution: 25,260.

STUDENT INFORMATION

Total Students in Program: 3,179. % Full-time: 100. % Female: 48.

RESEARCH FACILITIES

Research Facilities: Center for Geotechnical Modeling, Center for Image Processing and Integrated Computing, Institute for Transportation Studies, Advanced Design and Manufacturing Systems Program, the Advanced Highway and Maintenance and Construction Technology Center.

EXPENSES/FINANCIAL AID

Annual Tuition: $10,244. Fees: $4,591. Grants Range From: $41-$35,746. Loans Range From: $175-$36,912. % Receiving Scholarships/Grants: 15. % Receiving Loans: 13. % Receiving Assistantships: 45.

ADMISSIONS INFORMATION

Application Fee: $40. Regular Notification: Rolling. Transfer Students Accepted? Yes. Number of Applications Received: 1,263. % of Applicants Accepted: 34. % Accepted Who Enrolled: 43. Average GRE Verbal: 599. Average GRE Quantitative: 624. Average GRE Analytical: 617. Required Admission Factors: Essays/personal statement, GRE, transcript.

EMPLOYMENT INFORMATION

Placement Office Available? Yes.

UNIVERSITY OF CALIFORNIA—IRVINE
Claire Trevor School of the Arts

Address: 120 Administration Building, Irvine, CA 92697-3180
Admissions Phone: 949-824-6646 · Admissions Fax: 949-824-2450
Admissions E-mail: afujitan@uci.edu · Web Address: www.arts.uci.edu

INSTITUTIONAL INFORMATION

Public/private: Public. Students in Parent Institution: 17,221.

STUDENT INFORMATION

Total Students in Program: 2,868 % Female: 39.

RESEARCH FACILITIES

Research Facilities: Cancer Research Institute, Center for the Neurobiology of Learning and Memory, Developmental Biology Center, Institute for Transportation Studies, Critical Theory Institute.

EXPENSES/FINANCIAL AID

Annual Tuition: $10,322.

ADMISSIONS INFORMATION

Application Fee: $60. Regular Application Deadline: 1/15. Transfer Students Accepted? Yes. Number of Applications Received: 299. % of Applicants Accepted: 20. % Accepted Who Enrolled: 85. Average GPA: 3.48. Required Admission Factors: GRE, letters of recommendation, transcript. Other Admission Factors: Minimum 3.0 GPA and 3 letters of recommendation required.
Program-Specific Admission Factors: Auditions are required of the following programs: MFA in dance; MFA in drama, emphasis in acting; MFA in music, emphasis in performance.

EMPLOYMENT INFORMATION

Placement Office Available? Yes.

UNIVERSITY OF CALIFORNIA—IRVINE
School of Biological Sciences

Address: 120 Administration Building, Irvine, CA 92697-3180
Admissions Phone: 714-824-8145 · Admissions Fax: 714-824-7407
Admissions E-mail: damurphy@uci.edu

INSTITUTIONAL INFORMATION

Public/private: Public. Total Faculty: 86. Students in Parent Institution: 17,221.

STUDENT INFORMATION

Total Students in Program: 2,868 % Female: 39.

RESEARCH FACILITIES

Research Facilities: Cancer Research Institute, Center for the Neurobiology of Learning and Memory, Developmental Biology Center, Institute for Transportation Studies, Critical Theory Institute.

EXPENSES/FINANCIAL AID

Annual Tuition: $10,322.

ADMISSIONS INFORMATION

Application Fee: $40. Transfer Students Accepted? No. Number of Applications Received: 398. % of Applicants Accepted: 30. % Accepted Who Enrolled: 38. Average GPA: 3.5. Average GRE Verbal: 601. Average GRE Quantitative: 695. Average GRE Analytical: 683. Required Admission Factors: GRE, transcript. Other Admission Factors: Minimum 3.0 GPA and 3 letters of recommendation required.

EMPLOYMENT INFORMATION

Placement Office Available? Yes.

UNIVERSITY OF CALIFORNIA—IRVINE
School of Humanities

Address: 120 Administration Building, Irvine, CA 92697-3180
Admissions Phone: 714-824-4303 · Admissions Fax: 714-824-1360
Admissions E-mail: rjhumphr@uci.edu · Web Address: www.humanities.uci.edu/SOH/

INSTITUTIONAL INFORMATION

Public/private: Public. Students in Parent Institution: 17,221.

STUDENT INFORMATION

Total Students in Program: 2,868. % Full-time: 15. % Female: 39.

RESEARCH FACILITIES

Research Facilities: Cancer Research Institute, Center for the Neurobiology of Learning and Memory, Developmental Biology Center, Institute for Transportation Studies, Critical Theory Institute.

EXPENSES/FINANCIAL AID
Annual Tuition: In-state $8,567. / Out-of-state $23,507.**Types of Aid Available:** Fellowships, graduate assistantships, grants, loans.

ADMISSIONS INFORMATION
Application Fee: $60. **Regular Application Deadline:** 1/15. **Transfer Students Accepted?** No. **Number of Applications Received:** 768. **% of Applicants Accepted:** 21. **% Accepted Who Enrolled:** 54. **Average GPA:** 3.64. **Average GRE Verbal:** 621. **Average GRE Quantitative:** 604. **Average GRE Analytical:** 623.
Required Admission Factors: Essays/personal statement, GRE, transcript.
Other Admission Factors: Minimum 3.0 GPA and 3 letters of recommendation required.

EMPLOYMENT INFORMATION
Placement Office Available? Yes.

UNIVERSITY OF CALIFORNIA—IRVINE
School of Physical Sciences

Address: 120 Administration Building, Irvine, CA 92697-3180

INSTITUTIONAL INFORMATION
Public/private: Public. **Students in Parent Institution:** 17,221.

STUDENT INFORMATION
Total Students in Program: 2,868 **% Female:** 39.

RESEARCH FACILITIES
Research Facilities: Cancer Research Institute, Center for the Neurobiology of Learning and Memory, Developmental Biology Center, Institute for Transportation Studies, Critical Theory Institute.

EXPENSES/FINANCIAL AID
Annual Tuition: $10,322.

ADMISSIONS INFORMATION
TRANSFER STUDENTS ACCEPTED? NO.

EMPLOYMENT INFORMATION
Placement Office Available? Yes.

UNIVERSITY OF CALIFORNIA—IRVINE
School of Social Ecology

Address: 120 Administration Building, Irvine, CA 92697-3180
Admissions Phone: 714-824-5918

INSTITUTIONAL INFORMATION
Public/private: Public. **Students in Parent Institution:** 17,221.

STUDENT INFORMATION
Total Students in Program: 2,868 **% Female:** 39.

RESEARCH FACILITIES
Research Facilities: Cancer Research Institute, Center for the Neurobiology of Learning and Memory, Developmental Biology Center, Institute for Transportation Studies, Critical Theory Institute.

EXPENSES/FINANCIAL AID
Annual Tuition: $10,322.

ADMISSIONS INFORMATION
Application Fee: $40. **Transfer Students Accepted?** No. **Number of Applications Received:** 233. **% of Applicants Accepted:** 27. **% Accepted Who Enrolled:** 50. **Average GPA:** 3.45. **Average GRE Verbal:** 568. **Average GRE Quantitative:** 616. **Average GRE Analytical:** 641.
Required Admission Factors: GRE, transcript.

Other Admission Factors: Minimum 3.0 GPA and 3 letters of recommendation required.

EMPLOYMENT INFORMATION
Placement Office Available? Yes.

UNIVERSITY OF CALIFORNIA—IRVINE
School of Social Sciences

Address: 120 Administration Building, Irvine, CA 92697-3180
Admissions Phone: 714-824-4074

INSTITUTIONAL INFORMATION
Public/private: Public. **Students in Parent Institution:** 17,221.

STUDENT INFORMATION
Total Students in Program: 2,868 **% Female:** 39.

RESEARCH FACILITIES
Research Facilities: Cancer Research Institute, Center for the Neurobiology of Learning and Memory, Developmental Biology Center, Institute for Transportation Studies, Critical Theory Institute.

EXPENSES/FINANCIAL AID
Annual Tuition: $10,322.

ADMISSIONS INFORMATION
Application Fee: $40. **Transfer Students Accepted?** No. **Number of Applications Received:** 335. **% of Applicants Accepted:** 30. **% Accepted Who Enrolled:** 51. **Average GPA:** 3.56. **Average GRE Verbal:** 602. **Average GRE Quantitative:** 673. **Average GRE Analytical:** 657.
Required Admission Factors: GRE, transcript.
Other Admission Factors: Minimum 3.0 GPA and 3 letters of recommendation required.

EMPLOYMENT INFORMATION
Placement Office Available? Yes.

UNIVERSITY OF CALIFORNIA—RIVERSIDE
College of Humanities, Arts, & Social Sciences

Address: 900 University Avenue, Riverside, CA 92521
Admissions Phone: 909-787-3313 · **Admissions Fax:** 909-787-2238
Admissions E-mail: grdadmis@ucr.edu

INSTITUTIONAL INFORMATION
Public/private: Public. **Students in Parent Institution:** 14,329.

STUDENT INFORMATION
Total Students in Program: 1,662. **% Full-time:** 97. **% Female:** 49.

RESEARCH FACILITIES
Research Facilities: Agricultural Experiment Station, Air Pollution Research Center, Center for Bibliographic Studies and Research, California Educational Research Cooperative, Center for Ideas and Society, Center for Environmental Research and Technology.

EXPENSES/FINANCIAL AID
Annual Tuition: $10,704. **Room & Board:** $8,100. **Fees:** $5,193. **Books and Supplies:** $1,300.

ADMISSIONS INFORMATION
Application Fee: $40. **Transfer Students Accepted?** No. **Number of Applications Received:** 664. **% of Applicants Accepted:** 37. **% Accepted Who Enrolled:** 41. **Average GPA:** 3.52. **Average GRE Verbal:** 594. **Average GRE Quantitative:** 612. **Average GRE Analytical:** 620.

Required Admission Factors: Essays/personal statement, GRE, transcript. **Other Admission Factors:** Minimum combined GRE (Verbal and Quantitative) score of 1100, minimum 3.2 GPA required.

EMPLOYMENT INFORMATION
Placement Office Available? Yes. **Rate of placement:** 97%.

UNIVERSITY OF CALIFORNIA—SAN DIEGO
Graduate School of International Relations & Pacific Studies

Address: 9500 Gilman Drive, 0520, La Jolla, CA 92093-0520
Admissions Phone: 858-534-5914 · **Admissions Fax:** 858-534-1135
Admissions E-mail: irps-apply@ucsd.edu · **Web Address:** www.irps.ucsd.edu

INSTITUTIONAL INFORMATION
Public/private: Public. **Total Faculty:** 66. **% Faculty Part-time:** 61. **Student/faculty Ratio:** 11:1. **Students in Parent Institution:** 290.

PROGRAMS
Masters offered in: International relations and affairs. **Doctorate offered in:** Economics, international relations and affairs, political science and government.

STUDENT INFORMATION
Total Students in Program: 290. **% Full-time:** 100. **% Female:** 50. **% International:** 40.

RESEARCH FACILITIES
Research Facilities: Asia Pacific Economic Cooperation (APEC), Study Center, Center for U.S.—Mexican Studies, Information Storage Industry Center (ISIC), Institute on Global Conflict and Cooperation (IGCC), Korea Pacific Program (KPP), Strategic Community Consulting (SCC).

EXPENSES/FINANCIAL AID
Annual Tuition: $12,245. **Fees:** $11,810. **Books and Supplies:** $600. **Grants Range From:** $1,500-$15,000. **Types of Aid Available:** Fellowships, graduate assistantships, grants. **Assistantship Compensation Includes:** Partial tuition remission, salary/stipend.

ADMISSIONS INFORMATION
Application Fee: $60. **Priority Application Deadline:** 12/1. **Regular Application Deadline:** 2/1. **Transfer Students Accepted?** No. **Number of Applications Received:** 511. **% of Applicants Accepted:** 67. **% Accepted Who Enrolled:** 40. **Average GPA:** 3.4. **Average GRE Verbal:** 550. **Average GRE Quantitative:** 680. **Average GRE Analytical Writing:** 4.5.
Required Admission Factors: Essays/personal statement, letters of recommendation, transcript.
Other Admission Factors: A minimum grade point average of 3.0 in undergraduate upper-division course work is required for admission to graduate study at IR/PS.
Program-Specific Admission Factors: Applicants to the MPIA program may take either the GRE or the GMAT exam. Applicants to the PhD program must take the GRE. All application materials for PhD applicants must arrive (not postmarked) by 1/15.

UNIVERSITY OF CALIFORNIA—SAN DIEGO
Graduate Studies

Address: 9500 Gilman Drive, La Jolla, CA 92093-0003
Admissions Phone: 858-534-3554 · **Admissions Fax:** 858-822-5690
Admissions E-mail: gradadmissions@ucsd.edu · **Web Address:** www.ogsr.ucsd.edu/

INSTITUTIONAL INFORMATION
Public/private: Public. **Students in Parent Institution:** 23,266.

PROGRAMS
Masters offered in: Aerospace, aeronautical, and astronautical engineering; agricultural/biological engineering and bioengineering; applied mathematics; biochemistry; biophysics; business administration/management; chemical engineering; computer engineering; curriculum and instruction; education/teaching of individuals with hearing impairments, including deafness; electrical, electronics, and communications engineering; elementary education and teaching; ethnic, cultural minority, and gender studies; French language and literature; Germanic languages, literatures, and linguistics; history; junior high/intermediate/middle school education and teaching; Latin American studies; materials science; mathematics; music/music and performing arts studies; Spanish language and literature; statistics; structural engineering; visual and performing arts. **Doctorate offered in:** Aerospace, aeronautical, and astronautical engineering; agricultural/biological engineering and bioengineering; audiology/audiologist and hearing sciences; biochemistry; bioinformatics; biophysics; chemical engineering; computer engineering; dance. **First Professional degree offered in:** Medicine (MD).

STUDENT INFORMATION
Total Students in Program: 3,697. **% Full-time:** 98. **% Minority:** 9. **% International:** 22.

EXPENSES/FINANCIAL AID
Annual Tuition: In-state $8,615. / Out-of-state $23,576. **Room & Board (On/off campus):** $7,250/$8,783. **Books and Supplies:** $1,275. **Types of Aid Available:** Fellowships, graduate assistantships, grants, loans, scholarships. **Assistantship Compensation Includes:** Full tuition remission, salary/stipend. **Average Salary Stipend:** $12,000.

ADMISSIONS INFORMATION
Application Fee: $60. **Regular Application Deadline:** 3/15. **Regular Notification:** Rolling. **Transfer Students Accepted?** No. **Number of Applications Received:** 11,154. **% of Applicants Accepted:** 23. **% Accepted Who Enrolled:** 39. **Average GPA:** 3.0. **Average GRE Verbal:** 620. **Average GRE Quantitative:** 760. **Average GRE Analytical:** 750. **Average GRE Analytical Writing:** 5.
Required Admission Factors: GRE, letters of recommendation, transcript.
Other Admission Factors: TOEFL required of all international applicants whose native language is not English or who were not enrolled, full-time, for a minimum of 1 year in an academic program at an English speaking institution. Statement of Purpose: 2,500 word limit.

EMPLOYMENT INFORMATION
Placement Office Available? Yes. **% Employed Within Six Months:** 72. **Average starting salary:** $65,000.

UNIVERSITY OF CALIFORNIA—SAN DIEGO
Scripps Institute of Oceanography

Address: 9500 Gilman Drive, La Jolla, CA 92093-0003
Admissions Phone: 858-534-3554 · **Admissions Fax:** 858-822-5690
Admissions E-mail: siodept@sio.ucsd.edu · **Web Address:** www.siograddept.ucsd.edu

INSTITUTIONAL INFORMATION
Public/private: Public. **Total Faculty:** 28. **Student/faculty Ratio:** 12:1. **Students in Parent Institution:** 23,266.

PROGRAMS
Masters offered in: Geological and earth sciences/geosciences; oceanography, chemical and physical. **Doctorate offered in:** Geological and earth sciences/geosciences; oceanography, chemical and physical.

STUDENT INFORMATION
Total Students in Program: 3,697. **% Full-time:** 92. **% Female:** 40. **% Minority:** 9. **% International:** 22.

EXPENSES/FINANCIAL AID

Annual Tuition: In-state $8,926. / Out-of-state $23,963. **Room & Board (On/off campus):** $7,250/$8,783. **Books and Supplies:** $1,275. **% Receiving Scholarships/Grants:** 15. **% Receiving Assistantships:** 72. **Types of Aid Available:** Fellowships, graduate assistantships, grants, loans, scholarships. **Assistantship Compensation Includes:** Full tuition remission, salary/stipend. **Average Salary Stipend:** $16,059.

ADMISSIONS INFORMATION

Application Fee: $60. **Regular Application Deadline:** 1/7. **Regular Notification:** Rolling. **Transfer Students Accepted?** Yes. **Number of Applications Received:** 389. **% of Applicants Accepted:** 19. **% Accepted Who Enrolled:** 57. **Average GPA:** 3.0. **Average GRE Verbal:** 610. **Average GRE Quantitative:** 750. **Average GRE Analytical:** 740. **Average GRE Analytical Writing:** 5.
Required Admission Factors: GRE, letters of recommendation, transcript. TOEFL—see below, GRE subject exam(s) in GRE biology for marine biology major only.
Other Admission Factors: Prefers the online statement of purpose—2,500 word limit. TOEFL required of all international applicants whose native language is not English or who were not enrolled, full-time, for a minimum of 1 year in an academic program at an English speaking postsecondary institution.
Program-Specific Admission Factors: Your application will not be considered unless a pre-application has been approved by earth sciences. This applies only to earth sciences BS/MS applications and not to other SIO majors.

EMPLOYMENT INFORMATION

Placement Office Available? Yes. **% Employed Within Six Months:** 84.

UNIVERSITY OF CALIFORNIA—SANTA CRUZ
Graduate Programs

Address: 1156 High Street, Santa Cruz, CA 95064
Admissions Phone: 831-459-2301

INSTITUTIONAL INFORMATION

Public/private: Public. **Students in Parent Institution:** 9,932.

STUDENT INFORMATION

Total Students in Program: 1,056. **% Full-time:** 100. **% Female:** 49.

RESEARCH FACILITIES

Research Facilities: Bilingual Research Center, Center for Nonlinear Science, Institute for Marine Sciences, Insitute of Tectonics, Santa Cruz Instute for Particle Physics, University of California Observatories/Lick Observatory, Arboretum.

EXPENSES/FINANCIAL AID

Annual Tuition: $8,984. **Fees:** $4,950. **Books and Supplies:** $801.

ADMISSIONS INFORMATION

Application Fee: $40. **Transfer Students Accepted?** No. **Number of Applications Received:** 2,140. **% of Applicants Accepted:** 30. **% Accepted Who Enrolled:** 47.
Required Admission Factors: Essays/personal statement, GRE, transcript. **Other Admission Factors:** GRE subject exam may be required for some programs.

EMPLOYMENT INFORMATION

Placement Office Available? Yes.

UNIVERSITY OF CENTRAL ARKANSAS
College of Fine Arts & Communications

Address: Graduate School Admissions—Third Floor Torreyson Library, Room 328, Conway, AR 72035-0001
Admissions Phone: 501-450-3124 · **Admissions Fax:** 501-450-5066
Admissions E-mail: janed@ecom.uca.edu

INSTITUTIONAL INFORMATION

Public/private: Public. **Evening Classes Available?** Yes. **Student/faculty Ratio:** 1:1. **Students in Parent Institution:** 8,461.

STUDENT INFORMATION

Total Students in Program: 990. **% Full-time:** 43. **% Female:** 76.

RESEARCH FACILITIES

Research Facilities: Axciom Corporation, National Center for Toxological Research.

EXPENSES/FINANCIAL AID

Annual Tuition: In-state $4,404. / Out-of-state $8,484. **Fees:** $106. **Books and Supplies:** $700. **Grants Range From:** $833-$1,391. **Loans Range From:** $2,155-$4,366. **Average Salary Stipend:** $633.

ADMISSIONS INFORMATION

Application Fee: $25. **Regular Notification:** Rolling. **Transfer Students Accepted?** Yes.
Required Admission Factors: GRE, transcript.
Other Admission Factors: Minimum 2.7 GPA required.

EMPLOYMENT INFORMATION

Placement Office Available? Yes. **Rate of placement:** 15%.

UNIVERSITY OF CENTRAL ARKANSAS
College of Liberal Arts

Address: Graduate School Admissions—Third Floor Torreyson Library, Room 328, Conway, AR 72035-0001
Admissions Phone: 501-450-3124 · **Admissions Fax:** 501-450-5066
Admissions E-mail: janed@ecom.uca.edu

INSTITUTIONAL INFORMATION

Public/private: Public. **Evening Classes Available?** Yes. **Student/faculty Ratio:** 1:1. **Students in Parent Institution:** 8,461.

STUDENT INFORMATION

Total Students in Program: 990. **% Full-time:** 43. **% Female:** 76.

RESEARCH FACILITIES

Research Facilities: Axciom Corporation, National Center for Toxological Research.

EXPENSES/FINANCIAL AID

Annual Tuition: In-state $4,404. / Out-of-state $8,484. **Fees:** $106. **Books and Supplies:** $700. **Grants Range From:** $833-$1,391. **Loans Range From:** $2,155-$4,366. **Average Salary Stipend:** $5,700.

ADMISSIONS INFORMATION

Application Fee: $25. **Regular Notification:** Rolling. **Transfer Students Accepted?** Yes.
Required Admission Factors: GRE, transcript.
Other Admission Factors: Minimum 2.7 GPA required.

EMPLOYMENT INFORMATION

Placement Office Available? Yes. **Rate of placement:** 15%.

UNIVERSITY OF CENTRAL ARKANSAS
College of Natural Sciences & Math

Address: Graduate School Admissions, Third Floor Torreyson Library, Room 328, Conway, AR 72035-0001
Admissions Phone: 501-450-3124 · **Admissions Fax:** 501-450-5066
Admissions E-mail: nancyg@ecom.uca.edu

INSTITUTIONAL INFORMATION
Public/private: Public. **Evening Classes Available?** Yes. **Student/faculty Ratio:** 1:1. **Students in Parent Institution:** 8,461.

STUDENT INFORMATION
Total Students in Program: 990. **% Full-time:** 43. **% Female:** 76.

RESEARCH FACILITIES
Research Facilities: Axciom Corporation, National Center for Toxological Research.

EXPENSES/FINANCIAL AID
Annual Tuition: In-state $4,404. / Out-of-state $8,484. **Fees:** $106. **Books and Supplies:** $700. **Grants Range From:** $833-$1,391. **Loans Range From:** $2,155-$4,366. **Average Salary Stipend:** $5,700.

ADMISSIONS INFORMATION
Application Fee: $25. **Regular Notification:** Rolling. **Transfer Students Accepted?** Yes. **Transfer Policy:** Maximum 12 credit hours may be transferred, depending on length of program, if taken within the last. **Average GPA:** 3.2. **Average GRE Verbal:** 310. **Average GRE Quantitative:** 558. **Average GRE Analytical:** 445.
Required Admission Factors: GRE, transcript.
Other Admission Factors: Minimum 2.7 GPA or minimum 3.0 GPA for last 60 credit hours of coursework required.

EMPLOYMENT INFORMATION
Placement Office Available? Yes. **Rate of placement:** 15%.

UNIVERSITY OF CENTRAL FLORIDA
College of Arts & Sciences

Address: 4000 Central Florida Boulevard, Orlando, FL 32816
Admissions Phone: 407-823-2766 · **Admissions Fax:** 407-823-6442
Admissions E-mail: graduate@mail.ucf.edu · **Web Address:** www.graduate.ucf.edu

INSTITUTIONAL INFORMATION
Public/private: Public. **Students in Parent Institution:** 41,102.

STUDENT INFORMATION
Total Students in Program: 930. **% Full-time:** 48. **% International:** 9.

RESEARCH FACILITIES
Research Facilities: Institute for Simulation and Training, Florida Solar Energy Center, Center for Research and Education in Optics and Lasers, Research Park.

EXPENSES/FINANCIAL AID
Annual Tuition: In-state $3,658. / Out-of-state $12,748. **Books and Supplies:** $800. **Grants Range From:** $500-$18,500. **Loans Range From:** $500-$18,500. **% Receiving Financial Aid:** 66. **% Receiving Loans:** 75. **% Receiving Assistantships:** 34. **Average student debt upon graduation:** $26,598. **Number of Fellowships Granted Each Year:** 217. **Average amount of individual fellowships per year:** $4,118. **Number of Teaching/Research Assistantships Granted Each Year:** 160.

ADMISSIONS INFORMATION
Application Fee: $30. **Priority Application Deadline:** 2/1. **Regular Notification:** Rolling. **Transfer Students Accepted?** Yes. **Transfer Policy:** Maximum 9 credit hours may be transferred from an accredited institution. **Number**

of Applications Received: 1,068. **% of Applicants Accepted:** 50. **% Accepted Who Enrolled:** 56. **Average GPA:** 3.0. **Average GRE Verbal:** 498. **Average GRE Quantitative:** 580. **Average GRE Analytical:** 560.
Required Admission Factors: GRE, transcript.
Other Admission Factors: Minimum GRE score of 1000 (Verbal and Quantitative) and minimum 3.0 GPA required.
Program-Specific Admission Factors: Application deadlines vary; please visit website for verification: www.graduate.ucf.edu.

EMPLOYMENT INFORMATION
Placement Office Available? Yes. **Rate of placement:** 96%.

UNIVERSITY OF CENTRAL FLORIDA
School of Optics

Address: 4000 Central Florida Boulevard, Orlando, FL 32816
Admissions Phone: 407-823-2766 · **Admissions Fax:** 407-823-6442
Admissions E-mail: graduate@mail.ucf.edu · **Web Address:** www.graduate.ucf.edu

INSTITUTIONAL INFORMATION
Public/private: Public. **Students in Parent Institution:** 41,102.

STUDENT INFORMATION
Total Students in Program: 115. **% Full-time:** 65. **% International:** 63.

RESEARCH FACILITIES
Research Facilities: Institute for Simulation and Training, Florida Solar Energy Center, Center for Research and Education in Optics and Lasers, Research Park.

EXPENSES/FINANCIAL AID
Annual Tuition: In-state $3,658. / Out-of-state $12,748. **Books and Supplies:** $800. **Grants Range From:** $500-$18,500. **Loans Range From:** $500-$18,500. **% Receiving Financial Aid:** 75. **% Receiving Loans:** 75. **% Receiving Assistantships:** 34. **Average student debt upon graduation:** $26,598. **Number of Fellowships Granted Each Year:** 41. **Average amount of individual fellowships per year:** $6,388. **Number of Teaching/Research Assistantships Granted Each Year:** 38.

ADMISSIONS INFORMATION
Application Fee: $30. **Priority Application Deadline:** 2/1. **Regular Application Deadline:** 7/15. **Regular Notification:** Rolling. **Transfer Students Accepted?** Yes. **Number of Applications Received:** 184. **% of Applicants Accepted:** 52. **% Accepted Who Enrolled:** 26. **Average GPA:** 3.0. **Average GRE Verbal:** 478. **Average GRE Quantitative:** 770. **Average GRE Analytical:** 664.
Required Admission Factors: GRE, letters of recommendation, transcript.
Other Admission Factors: Minimum 3.0 GPA and minimum GRE score of 1000 required.

EMPLOYMENT INFORMATION
Placement Office Available? Yes. **Rate of placement:** 96%.

UNIVERSITY OF CHARLESTON
School of Humanities & Social Sciences

Address: 66 George Street, Charleston, SC 29424
Admissions Phone: 843-953-5614 · **Admissions Fax:** 843-953-1434

INSTITUTIONAL INFORMATION
Public/private: Public. **Evening Classes Available?** Yes. **Students in Parent Institution:** 10,854.

STUDENT INFORMATION
Total Students in Program: 1,602. **% Full-time:** 14. **% Female:** 85.

RESEARCH FACILITIES

Research Facilities: Member of ORAU, research opportunites with NOAA, Grice Marine Lab

EXPENSES/FINANCIAL AID

Annual Tuition: In-state $3,630. / Out-of-state $7,910.

ADMISSIONS INFORMATION

Application Fee: $35. Regular Notification: Rolling. Transfer Students Accepted? Yes. Transfer Policy: Maximum 12 credit hours may be transferred into most programs. Number of Applications Received: 59. % of Applicants Accepted: 58. % Accepted Who Enrolled: 62.
Required Admission Factors: Essays/personal statement, GRE, interview, letters of recommendation, transcript.
Other Admission Factors: Minimum GRE score of 1000 (Verbal plus Quantitative) required.

EMPLOYMENT INFORMATION

Placement Office Available? Yes.

UNIVERSITY OF CHARLESTON
School of Science & Mathematics

Address: 66 George Street, Charleston, SC 29424
Admissions Phone: 843-406-4000 · Admissions Fax: 843-406-4001

INSTITUTIONAL INFORMATION

Public/private: Public. Students in Parent Institution: 10,854.

STUDENT INFORMATION

Total Students in Program: 1,602. % Full-time: 14. % Female: 85.

RESEARCH FACILITIES

Research Facilities: Member of ORAU, research opportunites with NOAA, Grice Marine Lab.

EXPENSES/FINANCIAL AID

Annual Tuition: In-state $3,630. / Out-of-state $7,910.

ADMISSIONS INFORMATION

Application Fee: $35. Transfer Students Accepted? No. Number of Applications Received: 78. % of Applicants Accepted: 42.
Required Admission Factors: GRE, letters of recommendation, transcript.
Other Admission Factors: Background in biology, chemistry, physics, and calculus required.

EMPLOYMENT INFORMATION

Placement Office Available? Yes.

UNIVERSITY OF CHICAGO
Irving B. Harris School of Public Policy Studies

Address: 5801 South Ellis Avenue, Room 228, Chicago, IL 60637
Admissions Phone: 773-702-8401 · Admissions Fax: 773-702-0926
Admissions E-mail: eb-cohen@uchicago.edu

INSTITUTIONAL INFORMATION

Total Faculty: 26. Student/faculty Ratio: 8:1. Students in Parent Institution: 12,226.

STUDENT INFORMATION

Total Students in Program: 8,660. % Full-time: 75. % Female: 39.

RESEARCH FACILITIES

Research Facilities: Centers for International Studies, East Asian Studies, East European and Russian Studies, Latin American Studies, Middle Eastern Studies, South Asia Language Studies, and Urban Studies, Fermi-Lab, Argonne National Lab, Field Museum of Natural History.

EXPENSES/FINANCIAL AID

Annual Tuition: $27,360. Fees: $429. Books and Supplies: $1,575. % Receiving Financial Aid: 80. Number of Fellowships Granted Each Year: 75. Average amount of individual fellowships per year: $10,000. Number of Teaching/Research Assistantships Granted Each Year: 10. Average Salary Stipend: $10.

ADMISSIONS INFORMATION

Application Fee: $50. Transfer Students Accepted? Yes. Transfer Policy: Maximum one year of credit hours may be transferred. Number of Applications Received: 371. % of Applicants Accepted: 81. % Accepted Who Enrolled: 33. Average GPA: 3.4. Average GRE Verbal: 550. Average GRE Quantitative: 630. Average GRE Analytical: 640.
Required Admission Factors: Essays/personal statement, GRE, letters of recommendation, transcript.

EMPLOYMENT INFORMATION

Placement Office Available? Yes. % Employed Within Six Months: 100. % of masters/doctoral grads employed in their field upon graduation: 100/100. Average starting salary: $100,000.

UNIVERSITY OF CINCINNATI
College—Conservatory of Music

Address: PO Box 210003, Cincinnati, OH 45221-0003
Admissions Phone: 513-556-5463 · Admissions Fax: 513-556-1028
Admissions E-mail: paul.hillner@uc.edu · Web Address: www.ccm.uc.edu

INSTITUTIONAL INFORMATION

Public/private: Public. Total Faculty: 143. % Faculty Female: 30. % Faculty Part-time: 38. Student/faculty Ratio: 15:1. Students in Parent Institution: 33,583.

PROGRAMS

Masters offered in: Acting; conducting; jazz/jazz studies; music history, literature, and theory; music management and merchandising; music performance; music theory and composition; music/music and performing arts studies; musicology and ethnomusicology; piano and organ; technical theater/theater design and technology; violin, viola, guitar, and other stringed instruments; visual and performing arts; voice and opera. Doctorate offered in: Conducting; music history, literature, and theory; music performance; music theory and composition; music/music and performing arts studies; musicology and ethnomusicology; piano and organ; violin, viola, guitar, and other stringed instruments. First Professional degree offered in: Conducting; music history, literature, and theory; music performance; music theory and composition; music/music and performing arts studies; musicology and ethnomusicology; piano and organ; violin, viola, guitar, and other stringed instruments.

STUDENT INFORMATION

Total Students in Program: 6,744. % Full-time: 51. % Female: 55.

RESEARCH FACILITIES

Research Facilities: Institute for Policy Research, Center for Urban and Regional Analysis, Biomedical Chemistry Research Center, Center for Hazardous Waste Research.

EXPENSES/FINANCIAL AID

Annual Tuition: In-state $8,601. / Out-of-state $17,031. Fees: $1,374. Books and Supplies: $300. Grants Range From: $4,300-$27,000. Loans Range From: $300-$18,500. % Receiving Financial Aid: 98. % Receiving Scholarships/Grants: 98. Types of Aid Available: Fellowships, graduate assistantships, grants, institutional work-study, loans, scholarships. Number of Teaching/Research Assistantships Granted Each Year: 160. Assistantship Compensation Includes: Full tuition remission, salary/stipend.

ADMISSIONS INFORMATION

Application Fee: $90. **Priority Application Deadline:** 12/1. **Regular Application Deadline:** 2/15. **Regular Notification:** Rolling. **Transfer Students Accepted?** Yes. **Transfer Policy:** Same as regular admissions found in our CCM application handbook: http://www.ccm.uc.edu/pdf/CCMhandbook0405.pdf. **Number of Applications Received:** 1,135. **% of Applicants Accepted:** 29. **% Accepted Who Enrolled:** 69. **Average GPA:** 3.6. **Average GRE Verbal:** 465. **Average GRE Quantitative:** 561. **Average GRE Analytical:** 560. **Average GRE Analytical Writing:** 4.06.
Required Admission Factors: Essays/personal statement, GRE, interview, letters of recommendation, transcript.
Other Admission Factors: Minimum GPA of 3.0 required to be eligible for scholarship awards.
Program-Specific Admission Factors: Individual requirements for all programs can be found in our CCM admissions hanbook: http://www.ccm.uc.edu/pdf/CCMhandbook0405.pdf.

EMPLOYMENT INFORMATION

Placement Office Available? Yes.

UNIVERSITY OF CINCINNATI
McMicken College of Arts & Sciences

Address: PO Box 210627, Cincinnati, OH 45221-0627
Admissions Phone: 513-556-1100 · **Admissions Fax:** 513-556-3477

INSTITUTIONAL INFORMATION

Public/private: Public. **Evening Classes Available?** Yes. **Students in Parent Institution:** 33,583.

STUDENT INFORMATION

Total Students in Program: 6,744. **% Full-time:** 51. **% Female:** 55.

RESEARCH FACILITIES

Research Facilities: Institute for Policy Research, Center for Urban and Regional Analysis, Biomedical Chemistry Research center, Center for Hazardous Waste Research.

EXPENSES/FINANCIAL AID

Annual Tuition: In-state $5,700. / Out-of-state $10,887. **Fees:** $187.

ADMISSIONS INFORMATION

Application Fee: $30. **Regular Notification:** Rolling. **Transfer Students Accepted?** Yes. **Number of Applications Received:** 1,009. **% of Applicants Accepted:** 39. **% Accepted Who Enrolled:** 61. **Average GPA:** 3.35. **Average GRE Verbal:** 519. **Average GRE Quantitative:** 598. **Average GRE Analytical:** 602.
Required Admission Factors: GRE, letters of recommendation, transcript.

UNIVERSITY OF CINCINNATI
School of Social Work

Address: PO Box 210627, Cincinnati, OH 45221-0627
Admissions Phone: 513-556-4614 · **Admissions Fax:** 513-556-2077
Admissions E-mail: gerald.bostwick@uc.edu

INSTITUTIONAL INFORMATION

Public/private: Public. **Evening Classes Available?** Yes. **% Faculty Female:** 100. **Students in Parent Institution:** 33,583.

STUDENT INFORMATION

Total Students in Program: 6,744. **% Full-time:** 51. **% Female:** 55.

RESEARCH FACILITIES

Research Facilities: Institute for Policy Research, Center for Urban and Regional Analysis, Biomedical Chemistry Research center, Center for Hazardous Waste Research.

EXPENSES/FINANCIAL AID

Annual Tuition: In-state $5,700. / Out-of-state $10,887. **Fees:** $187.

ADMISSIONS INFORMATION

Application Fee: $30. **Regular Notification:** Rolling. **Transfer Students Accepted?** Yes. **Number of Applications Received:** 309. **% of Applicants Accepted:** 57. **% Accepted Who Enrolled:** 52.
Required Admission Factors: Essays/personal statement, transcript.
Other Admission Factors: Minimum 3.0 GPA required.

UNIVERSITY OF COLORADO AT BOULDER
College of Arts & Sciences

Address: Campus Box 26, Boulder, CO 80309-0026
Admissions Phone: 303-492-7294 · **Admissions Fax:** 303-492-4944
Web Address: www.colorado.edu/ArtsSciences/

INSTITUTIONAL INFORMATION

Public/private: Public. **Students in Parent Institution:** 29,609.

STUDENT INFORMATION

Total Students in Program: 5,123. **% Full-time:** 31. **% Female:** 45.

RESEARCH FACILITIES

Research Facilities: Institute for Behavioral Genetics, Institute for Behavioral Science, Institute for Cognitive Science, Laboratory for Atmospheric and Space Physics, Institute for Arctic and Alpine Research, Cooperative Institute for Research in Environmental Studies.

EXPENSES/FINANCIAL AID

Annual Tuition: In-state $3,474. / Out-of-state $16,624. **Fees:** $744.

ADMISSIONS INFORMATION

Transfer Students Accepted? Yes.
Required Admission Factors: Transcript.
Other Admission Factors: Minimum 2.75 GPA required. Other requirements vary by program.

UNIVERSITY OF COLORADO AT BOULDER
College of Music

Address: Campus Box 26, Boulder, CO 80309-0026
Admissions Phone: 303-492-2207 · **Admissions Fax:** 303-492-6352
Web Address: www.colorado.edu/music

INSTITUTIONAL INFORMATION

Public/private: Public. **Students in Parent Institution:** 29,609.

STUDENT INFORMATION

Total Students in Program: 5,123. **% Full-time:** 31. **% Female:** 45.

RESEARCH FACILITIES

Research Facilities: Institute for Behavioral Genetics, Institute for Behavioral Science, Institute for Cognitive Science, Laboratory for Atmospheric and Space Physics, Institute for Arctic and Alpine Research, Cooperative Institute for Research in Environmental Studies.

EXPENSES/FINANCIAL AID

Annual Tuition: In-state $3,474. / Out-of-state $16,624. **Fees:** $744.

ADMISSIONS INFORMATION

Transfer Students Accepted? Yes.
Required Admission Factors: Transcript.
Other Admission Factors: Minimum 2.75 GPA required. Other requirements vary by program.

UNIVERSITY OF COLORADO AT BOULDER
School of Journalism &
Mass Communication

Address: Campus Box 26, Boulder, CO 80309-0026
Admissions Phone: 303-492-0507 · **Admissions Fax:** 303-492-0969
Web Address: www.colorado.edu/journalism

INSTITUTIONAL INFORMATION
Public/private: Public. **Students in Parent Institution:** 29,609.

STUDENT INFORMATION
Total Students in Program: 5,123. **% Full-time:** 31. **% Female:** 45.

RESEARCH FACILITIES
Research Facilities: Institute for Behavioral Genetics, Institute for Behavioral Science, Institute for Cognitive Science, Laboratory for Atmospheric and Space Physics, Institute for Arctic and Alpine Research, Cooperative Institute for Research in Environmental Studies.

EXPENSES/FINANCIAL AID
Annual Tuition: In-state $3,474. / Out-of-state $16,624. **Fees:** $744.

ADMISSIONS INFORMATION
Transfer Students Accepted? Yes.
Required Admission Factors: Transcript.
Other Admission Factors: Minimum 2.75 GPA required. Other requirements vary by program.

UNIVERSITY OF COLORADO
AT COLORADO SPRINGS
College of Letters, Arts, & Sciences

Address: Austin Bluffs Parkway
PO Box 7150, Colorado Springs, CO 80933-7150
Admissions Phone: 719-262-3383 · **Admissions Fax:** 719-262-3116

INSTITUTIONAL INFORMATION
Public/private: Public. **Evening Classes Available?** Yes. **Students in Parent Institution:** 6,933.

STUDENT INFORMATION
Total Students in Program: 1,812. **% Full-time:** 54. **% Female:** 51.

RESEARCH FACILITIES
Research Facilities: More than 20 institutional research centers.

EXPENSES/FINANCIAL AID
Annual Tuition: In-state $3,156. / Out-of-state $10,593. **Room & Board (On/off campus):** $6,473/$6,988. **Fees:** $531. **Books and Supplies:** $700. **Grants Range From:** $250-$9,898. **Loans Range From:** $477-$18,500. **% Receiving Scholarships/Grants:** 21. **% Receiving Loans:** 85.

ADMISSIONS INFORMATION
Application Fee: $60. **Regular Notification:** Rolling. **Transfer Students Accepted?** Yes.
Required Admission Factors: Essays/personal statement, letters of recommendation, transcript.
Other Admission Factors: Writing sample required.

UNIVERSITY OF COLORADO
AT COLORADO SPRINGS
Graduate School of Public Affairs

Address: Austin Bluffs Parkway
PO Box 7150, Colorado Springs, CO 80933-7150
Admissions Phone: 719-262-4182 · **Admissions Fax:** 719-262-4183
Admissions E-mail: fraingue@mail.uccs.edu

INSTITUTIONAL INFORMATION
Public/private: Public. **Evening Classes Available?** Yes. **Students in Parent Institution:** 6,933.

STUDENT INFORMATION
Total Students in Program: 1,812. **% Full-time:** 54. **% Female:** 51.

RESEARCH FACILITIES
Research Facilities: More than 20 institutional research centers.

EXPENSES/FINANCIAL AID
Annual Tuition: In-state $3,156. / Out-of-state $10,593. **Room & Board (On/off campus):** $6,473/$6,988. **Fees:** $531. **Books and Supplies:** $700. **Grants Range From:** $250-$9,898. **Loans Range From:** $477-$18,500. **% Receiving Scholarships/Grants:** 21. **% Receiving Loans:** 85.

ADMISSIONS INFORMATION
Application Fee: $60. **Regular Notification:** Rolling. **Transfer Students Accepted?** Yes. **Number of Applications Received:** 20. **% of Applicants Accepted:** 95. **% Accepted Who Enrolled:** 95. **Average GPA:** 3.2.
Required Admission Factors: Essays/personal statement, GRE, transcript.
Other Admission Factors: Minimum 2.75 GPA required, minimum GRE score of 1000 recommended.

UNIVERSITY OF COLORADO AT DENVER
Graduate School of Public Affairs

Address: Box 173364, Campus Box 167, Denver, CO 80217-3364
Admissions Phone: 303-556-5970 · **Admissions Fax:** 303-556-5971
Admissions E-mail: pwolfe@gspa.cudenver.edu

INSTITUTIONAL INFORMATION
Public/private: Public. **Evening Classes Available?** Yes. **Student/faculty Ratio:** 7:1. **Students in Parent Institution:** 10,863.

STUDENT INFORMATION
Total Students in Program: 4,500. **% Full-time:** 30. **% Female:** 55.

RESEARCH FACILITIES
Research Facilities: Center for Research in Applied Language, Bioengineering Lab, Soil Research Center, TeleMedia Center, Transportation Research Center, National Leadership Institute on Aging, Center for Applied Psychology.

EXPENSES/FINANCIAL AID
Annual Tuition: In-state $3,284. / Out-of-state $13,380. **Room & Board:** $8,000. **Fees:** $475. **Books and Supplies:** $720. **Grants Range From:** $33-$13,096. **Loans Range From:** $330-$23,850. **% Receiving Financial Aid:** 14. **% Receiving Scholarships/Grants:** 39. **% Receiving Loans:** 78. **Average student debt upon graduation:** $17,535. **Number of Fellowships Granted Each Year:** 1. **Average amount of individual fellowships per year:** $2,000. **Number of Teaching/Research Assistantships Granted Each Year:** 5. **Average Salary Stipend:** $500.

ADMISSIONS INFORMATION
Application Fee: $50. **Regular Notification:** Rolling. **Transfer Students Accepted?** Yes. **Number of Applications Received:** 178. **% of Applicants Accepted:** 76. **% Accepted Who Enrolled:** 65.

Required Admission Factors: Essays/personal statement, letters of recommendation, transcript.

Other Admission Factors: Minimum 3.0 GPA (2.75 for masters in criminal justice) and essay required, minimum GRE score of 1000 (Quantitative plus Verbal) recommended.

EMPLOYMENT INFORMATION

Placement Office Available? Yes.

UNIVERSITY OF COLORADO AT DENVER AND HEALTH SCIENCES CENTER
College of Liberal Arts & Sciences

Address: Campus Box 167, PO Box 173364, (physical location 1250 Fourteenth Street), Denver, CO 80217-3364
Admissions Phone: 303-556-2557 · **Admissions Fax:** 303-556-4861
Admissions E-mail: Tammy.Stone@cudenver.edu ·
Web Address: www.cudenver.edu/

INSTITUTIONAL INFORMATION

Public/private: Public. **Evening Classes Available?** Yes. **Student/faculty Ratio:** 16:1. **Students in Parent Institution:** 10,863.

PROGRAMS

Masters offered in: American literature (United States), anthropology, applied economics, applied mathematics, chemistry, communications and media studies, communications studies/speech communication and rhetoric, creative writing, economics, English composition, English language and literature, history, humanities/humanistic studies, mass communications/media studies, natural sciences, political science and government, social sciences, social sciences, sociology. **Doctorate offered in:** Applied mathematics, behavioral sciences.

STUDENT INFORMATION

Total Students in Program: 4,500. **% Full-time:** 30. **% Female:** 55.

RESEARCH FACILITIES

Research Facilities: Center for Research in Applied Language, Bioengineering Lab, Soil Research Center, TeleMedia Center, Transportation Research Center, National Leadership Institute on Aging, Center for Applied Psychology.

EXPENSES/FINANCIAL AID

Annual Tuition: In-state $3,284. / Out-of-state $13,380. **Room & Board:** $8,000. **Fees:** $475. **Books and Supplies:** $720. **Grants Range From:** $33-$13,096. **Loans Range From:** $330-$23,850. **% Receiving Scholarships/Grants:** 39. **% Receiving Loans:** 78. **Average student debt upon graduation:** $17,513

ADMISSIONS INFORMATION

Application Fee: $50. **Regular Application Deadline:** 2/15. **Transfer Students Accepted?** Yes. **Transfer Policy:** 5000 level classes, grade of B- or higher, approval of the program and dean. **Number of Applications Received:** 372. **% of Applicants Accepted:** 54. **% Accepted Who Enrolled:** 65.

Required Admission Factors: Essays/personal statement, letters of recommendation, transcript.

Other Admission Factors: Other requirements vary by program.

EMPLOYMENT INFORMATION

Placement Office Available? Yes.

UNIVERSITY OF DALLAS
Braniff Graduate School of Liberal Arts

Address: Braniff Graduate School, Liberal Arts
1845 East Northgate Drive, 1845 East Northgate Drive, Irving, TX 75062-4736
Admissions Phone: 972-721-5106 · **Admissions Fax:** 972-721-5280
Admissions E-mail: graduate@acad.udallas.edu
Web Address: www.udallas.edu/braniff

INSTITUTIONAL INFORMATION

Public/private: Private (nonprofit). **Student/faculty Ratio:** 12:1. **Students in Parent Institution:** 3,170.

PROGRAMS

Masters offered in: American government and politics (United States), ceramic arts and ceramics, education, English language and literature, fine/studio arts, humanities/humanistic studies, painting, pastoral counseling and specialized ministries, philosophy, political science and government, printmaking, psychology, religious education, sculpture, theology/theological studies. **Doctorate offered in:** English language and literature; philosophy; political science and government.

STUDENT INFORMATION

Total Students in Program: 2,027. **% Full-time:** 17. **% Female:** 44.

RESEARCH FACILITIES

Research Facilities: Comprehensive data on 12,000 publicly traded companies and 800 business journals. Center for the Study of Democratic Citizenship

EXPENSES/FINANCIAL AID

Annual Tuition: $8,640. **Room & Board:** $7,200. **Fees:** $270. **Books and Supplies:** $300. **Grants Range From:** $3,000-$16,000. **Loans Range From:** $9,976-$18,500. **% Receiving Financial Aid:** 95. **% Receiving Scholarships/Grants:** 95. **Types of Aid Available:** Fellowships, graduate assistantships, loans, scholarships. **Average student debt upon graduation:** $16,189. **Number of Fellowships Granted Each Year:** 35. **Average amount of individual fellowships per year:** $4,000. **Number of Teaching/Research Assistantships Granted Each Year:** 10. **Assistantship Compensation Includes:** Full tuition remission, salary/stipend. **Average Salary Stipend:** $3,000.

ADMISSIONS INFORMATION

Application Fee: $40. **Regular Application Deadline:** 2/15. **Regular Notification:** Rolling. **Transfer Students Accepted?** Yes. **Transfer Policy:** Credits are transferable only from accredited institutions and must have been taken within 6 years prior to acceptance in the program. Transfer of graduate credits earned at other institutions is not automatic. Only courses with a grade of B or better may be considered for transfer. No more than 12 credits can be transferred into the doctoral program. **Number of Applications Received:** 10. **% of Applicants Accepted:** 100. **Average GPA:** 3.5. **Average GRE Verbal:** 558. **Average GRE Quantitative:** 583. **Average GRE Analytical:** 612.

Required Admission Factors: Letters of recommendation, transcript. TOEFL or ELT required for non-English-speaking, international students.

Other Admission Factors: Statement of aims and intellectual autobiography required. In some cases, writing samples are required. See www.udallas.edu/braniff for specific information.

Program-Specific Admission Factors: Special students—those enrolled in graduate courses but not, seeking a degree—should be at least 21 years old and have completed an undergraduate degree.

EMPLOYMENT INFORMATION

Placement Office Available? Yes.

UNIVERSITY OF DAYTON
College of Arts & Sciences

Address: 300 College Park, Dayton, OH 45469-1620
Admissions Phone: 937-229-2390

INSTITUTIONAL INFORMATION
Public/private: Private (nonprofit). **Evening Classes Available?** Yes. Students in Parent Institution: 10,763.

STUDENT INFORMATION
Total Students in Program: 2,581. % Full-time: 26. % Female: 61.

RESEARCH FACILITIES
Research Facilities: Research Institute.

EXPENSES/FINANCIAL AID
Annual Tuition: $5,266. **Fees:** $150. **Number of Teaching/Research Assistantships Granted Each Year:** 60.

ADMISSIONS INFORMATION
Application Fee: $30. **Regular Notification:** Rolling. **Transfer Students Accepted?** Yes. **Transfer Policy:** Maximum 36 credits may be transferred into doctoral programs. **Number of Applications Received:** 253. **% of Applicants Accepted:** 75. **% Accepted Who Enrolled:** 49. **Average GRE Verbal:** 406. **Average GRE Quantitative:** 432. **Average GRE Analytical:** 532. **Required Admission Factors:** GRE, letters of recommendation, transcript. **Program-Specific Admission Factors:** Minimum 3.0 GPA required for masters programs; 3.5 GPA requied for doctoral programs.

EMPLOYMENT INFORMATION
Placement Office Available? Yes. Rate of placement: 97%.

UNIVERSITY OF DELAWARE
College of Arts & Sciences

Address: Newark, DE 19716
Admissions Phone: 302-831-2129 · **Admissions Fax:** 302-831-8745

INSTITUTIONAL INFORMATION
Public/private: Public. **Student/faculty Ratio:** 2:1. **Students in Parent Institution:** 21,206.

STUDENT INFORMATION
Total Students in Program: 3,108. % Full-time: 71. % Female: 49.

RESEARCH FACILITIES
Research Facilities: Center for Composite Materials, Center for Applied Coastal Research, Center for Molecular and Engineering Thermodynamics, Center for Catalytic Science and Technology, Orthopedic and Biomechanical Engineering Center.

EXPENSES/FINANCIAL AID
Annual Tuition: In-state $4,380. / Out-of-state $12,750. **Fees:** $382. **% Receiving Financial Aid:** 69. **Number of Fellowships Granted Each Year:** 126. **Average amount of individual fellowships per year:** $9,113. **Number of Teaching/Research Assistantships Granted Each Year:** 450.

ADMISSIONS INFORMATION
Application Fee: $50. **Regular Notification:** Rolling. **Transfer Students Accepted?** Yes. **Number of Applications Received:** 2,119. **% of Applicants Accepted:** 36. **% Accepted Who Enrolled:** 40. **Average GPA:** 3.46. **Average GRE Verbal:** 515. **Average GRE Quantitative:** 611. **Average GRE Analytical:** 608.
Required Admission Factors: Essays/personal statement, GRE, letters of recommendation, transcript.
Program-Specific Admission Factors: GRE subject exam required for some programs.

EMPLOYMENT INFORMATION
Placement Office Available? Yes.

UNIVERSITY OF DELAWARE
Graduate College of Marine Studies

Address: Newark, DE 19716
Admissions Phone: 302-831-2129 · **Admissions Fax:** 302-831-8745

INSTITUTIONAL INFORMATION
Public/private: Public. **Student/faculty Ratio:** 4:1. **Students in Parent Institution:** 21,206.

STUDENT INFORMATION
Total Students in Program: 3,108. % Full-time: 71. % Female: 49.

RESEARCH FACILITIES
Research Facilities: Center for Composite Materials, Center for Applied Coastal Research, Center for Molecular and Engineering Thermodynamics, Center for Catalytic Science and Technology, Orthopedic and Biomechanical Engineering Center.

EXPENSES/FINANCIAL AID
Annual Tuition: In-state $4,380. / Out-of-state $12,750. **Fees:** $382. **% Receiving Financial Aid:** 67. **Number of Fellowships Granted Each Year:** 7. **Average amount of individual fellowships per year:** $11,358. **Number of Teaching/Research Assistantships Granted Each Year:** 58.

ADMISSIONS INFORMATION
Application Fee: $50. **Regular Notification:** Rolling. **Transfer Students Accepted?** Yes. **Number of Applications Received:** 121. **% of Applicants Accepted:** 38. **% Accepted Who Enrolled:** 52. **Average GPA:** 3.37. **Average GRE Verbal:** 549. **Average GRE Quantitative:** 685. **Average GRE Analytical:** 613.
Required Admission Factors: Essays/personal statement, GRE, interview, letters of recommendation, transcript.

EMPLOYMENT INFORMATION
Placement Office Available? Yes.

UNIVERSITY OF DENVER
Extended Learning

Address: University Park, Denver, CO 80208
Admissions Phone: 303-871-3155 · **Admissions Fax:** 303-871-3033
Admissions E-mail: jjohnsen@du.edu

INSTITUTIONAL INFORMATION
Public/private: Private (nonprofit). **Evening Classes Available?** Yes. **Student/faculty Ratio:** 15:1. **Students in Parent Institution:** 9,444.

STUDENT INFORMATION
Total Students in Program: 5,452. % Full-time: 55. % Female: 55.

RESEARCH FACILITIES
Research Facilities: Center for Judaic Studies, Center for Latin American Studies, Child Study Center, High Altitude Research Lab, Law Enforcement Technology Center, Rocky Mountain Conservation Center, Ricks Center.

EXPENSES/FINANCIAL AID
Annual Tuition: $21,456. **Fees:** $159. **Grants Range From:** $75-$21,456. **Loans Range From:** $150-$18,500. **% Receiving Scholarships/Grants:** 24. **% Receiving Loans:** 49. **% Receiving Assistantships:** 35.

ADMISSIONS INFORMATION
Application Fee: $25. **Regular Notification:** Rolling. **Transfer Students Accepted?** Yes.

Required Admission Factors: Essays/personal statement, letters of recommendation, transcript.
Other Admission Factors: Minimum 3.0 GPA (minimum 2.5 GPA for conditional acceptance) required.

EMPLOYMENT INFORMATION
Placement Office Available? Yes. **Rate of placement:** 95%.

UNIVERSITY OF DENVER
Faculty of Arts, Humanities, & Social Sciences

Address: University Park, Denver, CO 80208
Admissions Phone: 303-871-2305

INSTITUTIONAL INFORMATION
Public/private: Private (nonprofit). **Students in Parent Institution:** 9,444.

STUDENT INFORMATION
Total Students in Program: 5,452. **% Full-time:** 55. **% Female:** 55.

RESEARCH FACILITIES
Research Facilities: Center for Judaic Studies, Center for Latin American Studies, Child Study Center, High Altitude Research Lab, Law Enforcement Technology Center, Rocky Mountain Conservation Center, Ricks Center.

EXPENSES/FINANCIAL AID
Annual Tuition: $21,456. **Fees:** $159. **Grants Range From:** $75-$21,456. **Loans Range From:** $150-$18,500. **% Receiving Scholarships/Grants:** 24. **% Receiving Loans:** 49. **% Receiving Assistantships:** 35.

ADMISSIONS INFORMATION
Application Fee: $40. **Transfer Students Accepted?** Yes. **Transfer Policy:** Minimum grade average of B required of transfer applicants. **Number of Applications Received:** 954. **% of Applicants Accepted:** 50. **% Accepted Who Enrolled:** 30.
Required Admission Factors: GRE, transcript.
Program-Specific Admission Factors: Audition required of music program applicants.

EMPLOYMENT INFORMATION
Placement Office Available? Yes. **Rate of placement:** 95%.

UNIVERSITY OF DENVER
Graduate School of International Studies

Address: University Park, Denver, CO 80208
Admissions Phone: 303-871-2544 · **Admissions Fax:** 303-871-3585
Admissions E-mail: gsisadm@du.edu

INSTITUTIONAL INFORMATION
Public/private: Private (nonprofit). **Evening Classes Available?** Yes. **Students in Parent Institution:** 9,444.

STUDENT INFORMATION
Total Students in Program: 5,452. **% Full-time:** 55. **% Female:** 55.

RESEARCH FACILITIES
Research Facilities: Center for Judaic Studies, Center for Latin American Studies, Child Study Center, High Altitude Research Lab, Law Enforcement Technology Center, Rocky Mountain Conservation Center, Ricks Center.

EXPENSES/FINANCIAL AID
Annual Tuition: $21,456. **Fees:** $159. **Grants Range From:** $75-$21,456. **Loans Range From:** $150-$18,500. **% Receiving Scholarships/Grants:** 24. **% Receiving Loans:** 49. **% Receiving Assistantships:** 35.

ADMISSIONS INFORMATION
Application Fee: $50. **Transfer Students Accepted?** Yes. **Number of Applications Received:** 504. **% of Applicants Accepted:** 75. **% Accepted Who Enrolled:** 22. **Average GPA:** 3.3. **Average GRE Verbal:** 520. **Average GRE Quantitative:** 580. **Average GRE Analytical:** 600.
Required Admission Factors: Essays/personal statement, GRE, letters of recommendation, transcript.

EMPLOYMENT INFORMATION
Placement Office Available? Yes. **Rate of placement:** 95%.

UNIVERSITY OF DENVER
Graduate School of Professional Psychology

Address: 2460 South Vine Street, Room 102, Denver, CO 80208
Admissions Phone: 303-871-3873 · **Admissions Fax:** 303-871-7656
Admissions E-mail: gsppinfo@du.edu · **Web Address:** www.du.edu/gspp

INSTITUTIONAL INFORMATION
Public/private: Private (nonprofit). **Student/faculty Ratio:** 15:1. **Students in Parent Institution:** 9,444.

PROGRAMS
Masters offered in: Forensic psychology; psychology. **Doctorate offered in:** Clinical psychology; forensic psychology; psychoanalysis and psychoptherapy.

STUDENT INFORMATION
Total Students in Program: 5,452. **% Full-time:** 55. **% Female:** 55.

RESEARCH FACILITIES
Research Facilities: Center for Judaic Studies, Center for Latin American Studies, Child Study Center, High Altitude Research Lab, Law Enforcement Technology Center, Rocky Mountain Conservation Center, Ricks Center.

EXPENSES/FINANCIAL AID
Annual Tuition: $32,880. **Fees:** $200. **Books and Supplies:** $2,000. **Grants Range From:** $75-$21,456. **Loans Range From:** $150-$18,500. **% Receiving Financial Aid:** 80. **% Receiving Scholarships/Grants:** 24. **% Receiving Loans:** 49. **% Receiving Assistantships:** 35. **Types of Aid Available:** Fellowships, grants, institutional work-study, loans, scholarships.

ADMISSIONS INFORMATION
Application Fee: $50. **Priority Application Deadline:** 12/15. **Regular Application Deadline:** 1/6. **Regular Notification:** Rolling. **Transfer Students Accepted?** Yes. **Transfer Policy:** Maximum 45 quarter hours or 30 semester hours may be transferred into the PsyD program. **Number of Applications Received:** 300. **% of Applicants Accepted:** 13. **% Accepted Who Enrolled:** 100. **Average GPA:** 3.5. **Average GRE Verbal:** 550. **Average GRE Quantitative:** 550. **Average GRE Analytical:** 550. **Average GRE Analytical Writing:** 4.5.
Required Admission Factors: Essays/personal statement, GRE, interview, letters of recommendation, transcript.
Recommended Admission Factors: GRE subject exam(s) in psychology.
Other Admission Factors: Minimum 6 months of supervised relevant work experience required. Four references from academic and supervisory sources required. Abnormal, child, experimental, learning, personality, and statistics psychology courses required.
Program-Specific Admission Factors: Applicants must complete the GSPP application and the supplemental materials by the application deadline for consideration.

EMPLOYMENT INFORMATION
Placement Office Available? Yes. **% Employed Within Six Months:** 75. **Rate of placement:** 95%. **Average starting salary:** $35,000.

UNIVERSITY OF DENVER
Graduate School of Social Work

Address: University Park, 2148 South High Street, Denver, CO 80208
Admissions Phone: 303-871-2841 · **Admissions Fax:** 303-871-2845
Admissions E-mail: gssw-admission@du.edu · **Web Address:** www.du.edu/gssw

INSTITUTIONAL INFORMATION
Public/private: Private (nonprofit). **Total Faculty:** 68. **% Faculty Female:** 66. **% Faculty Part-time:** 66. **Student/faculty Ratio:** 15:1. **Students in Parent Institution:** 9,444.

PROGRAMS
Masters offered in: Clinical pastoral counseling/patient counseling, clinical/medical social work, community health services/liaison/counseling, corrections and criminal justice, juvenile corrections, marriage and family therapy/counseling, mental and social health services and allied professions, mental health counseling/counselor, psychoanalysis and psychoptherapy, psychology, social sciences, social work, substance abuse/addiction counseling. **First Professional degree offered in:** Social work.

STUDENT INFORMATION
Total Students in Program: 5,452. **% Full-time:** 55. **% Female:** 55.

RESEARCH FACILITIES
Research Facilities: Center for Judaic Studies, Center for Latin American Studies, Child Study Center, High Altitude Research Lab, Law Enforcement Technology Center, Rocky Mountain Conservation Center.

EXPENSES/FINANCIAL AID
Annual Tuition: $24,264. **Room & Board:** $10,043. **Fees:** $159. **Books and Supplies:** $1,500. **% Receiving Financial Aid:** 95. **Types of Aid Available:** Fellowships, graduate assistantships, grants, institutional work-study, loans, scholarships, child welfare stipends. **Number of Fellowships Granted Each Year:** 4. **Average amount of individual fellowships per year:** $6,250. **Number of Teaching/Research Assistantships Granted Each Year:** 8. **Assistantship Compensation Includes:** Full tuition remission, partial tuition remission, salary/stipend. **Average Salary Stipend:** $8,800.

ADMISSIONS INFORMATION
Application Fee: $50. **Priority Application Deadline:** 2/1. **Regular Application Deadline:** 8/1. **Regular Notification:** Rolling. **Transfer Students Accepted?** Yes. **Number of Applications Received:** 381. **Average GPA:** 3.2.
Required Admission Factors: Essays/personal statement, letters of recommendation, transcript. Liberal arts requirement—20 semester hours/30 quarter hours.
Other Admission Factors: Minimum 3.0 GPA required.
Program-Specific Admission Factors: Applicants to the two-year MSW Program must have a baccalaureate degree in an academic discipline other than social work. The degree must be earned at a college or university accredited by a regional accrediting body.

EMPLOYMENT INFORMATION
Placement Office Available? Yes. **% Employed Within Six Months:** 80. **Rate of placement:** 95%. **Average starting salary:** $34,000.

UNIVERSITY OF FINDLAY
Graduate and Special Programs

Address: 1000 North Main Street, Findlay, OH 45840-3695
Admissions Phone: 419-434-4538 · **Admissions Fax:** 419-434-4822
Admissions E-mail: gradinfo@findlay.edu · **Web Address:** www.findlay.edu

INSTITUTIONAL INFORMATION
Public/private: Private (nonprofit). **Evening Classes Available?** Yes. **Student/faculty Ratio:** 18:1. **Students in Parent Institution:** 4,585.

STUDENT INFORMATION
Total Students in Program: 1,458. **% Full-time:** 36. **% Female:** 62.

EXPENSES/FINANCIAL AID
Annual Tuition: $419. **Room & Board:** $3,637. **Fees:** $45. **Books and Supplies:** $300. **Grants Range From:** $1,000-$10,500. **Loans Range From:** $1,000-$10,500. **% Receiving Financial Aid:** 90. **% Receiving Loans:** 100. **% Receiving Assistantships:** 5. **Average student debt upon graduation:** $12,000. **Number of Fellowships Granted Each Year:** 30. **Average amount of individual fellowships per year:** $4,300. **Number of Teaching/Research Assistantships Granted Each Year:** 27. **Average Salary Stipend:** $6,000.

ADMISSIONS INFORMATION
Application Fee: $25. **Regular Application Deadline:** 8/30. **Regular Notification:** Rolling. **Transfer Students Accepted?** Yes. **Transfer Policy:** Need to submit official transcript. **Number of Applications Received:** 385. **% of Applicants Accepted:** 60. **% Accepted Who Enrolled:** 99. **Average GPA:** 3.2.
Required Admission Factors: Transcript.
Other Admission Factors: Minimum 3.0 GPA in last 60 hours of undergraduate course work required; GMAT required if GPA is below minimum.
Program-Specific Admission Factors: MALS, TESOL, 3 letters of recommendation and personal statement required.

EMPLOYMENT INFORMATION
Placement Office Available? Yes. **% Employed Within Six Months:** 99. **Rate of placement:** 94%. **Average starting salary:** $65,000.

UNIVERSITY OF FLORIDA
College of Design, Construction, & Planning

Address: Gainesville, FL 32611
Admissions Phone: 352-392-4836 · **Admissions Fax:** 352-392-7266
Admissions E-mail: ajdasta@ufl.edu

INSTITUTIONAL INFORMATION
Public/private: Public. **Total Faculty:** 87. **Students in Parent Institution:** 45,114.

STUDENT INFORMATION
Total Students in Program: 9,309. **% Full-time:** 75. **% Female:** 48.

RESEARCH FACILITIES
Research Facilities: More than 100 interdisciplinary research centers, bureaus, and institutes.

EXPENSES/FINANCIAL AID
Annual Tuition: In-state $3,460. / Out-of-state $12,120. **Books and Supplies:** $700. **Number of Fellowships Granted Each Year:** 6. **Number of Teaching/Research Assistantships Granted Each Year:** 59.

ADMISSIONS INFORMATION
Application Fee: $20. **Regular Notification:** Rolling. **Transfer Students Accepted?** Yes. **Number of Applications Received:** 236. **% of Applicants Accepted:** 58. **% Accepted Who Enrolled:** 39. **Average GPA:** 3.26.
Required Admission Factors: GRE, transcript.
Other Admission Factors: Minimum GRE score of 1000 (Verbal & Quantitative) and minimum 3.0 GPA required.

EMPLOYMENT INFORMATION
Placement Office Available? Yes.

UNIVERSITY OF FLORIDA
College of Fine Arts

Address: Gainesville, FL 32611
Admissions Phone: 352-392-0207 · **Admissions Fax:** 352-392-3802
Admissions E-mail: pad@ufl.edu

INSTITUTIONAL INFORMATION
Public/private: Public. **Total Faculty:** 81. **Students in Parent Institution:** 45,114.

STUDENT INFORMATION
Total Students in Program: 9,309. **% Full-time:** 75. **% Female:** 48.

RESEARCH FACILITIES
Research Facilities: More than 100 interdisciplinary research centers, bureaus, and institutes.

EXPENSES/FINANCIAL AID
Annual Tuition: In-state $3,460. / Out-of-state $12,120. **Books and Supplies:** $700.

ADMISSIONS INFORMATION
Application Fee: $20. **Regular Notification:** Rolling. **Transfer Students Accepted?** Yes. **Number of Applications Received:** 194. **% of Applicants Accepted:** 47. **% Accepted Who Enrolled:** 75. **Average GPA:** 3.49. **Required Admission Factors:** GRE, transcript.
Other Admission Factors: Minimum GRE score of 1000 (Verbal & Quantitative) and minimum 3.0 GPA required.
Program-Specific Admission Factors: Interview required of theater program applicants.

EMPLOYMENT INFORMATION
Placement Office Available? Yes.

UNIVERSITY OF FLORIDA
College of Journalism & Communications

Address: PO Box 118400, Gainesville, FL 32611
Admissions Phone: 352-392-6557 · **Admissions Fax:** 352-392-1794
Admissions E-mail: gradapps@jou.ufl.edu · **Web Address:** www.jou.ufl.edu/grad

INSTITUTIONAL INFORMATION
Public/private: Public. **Total Faculty:** 48. **Students in Parent Institution:** 45,114.

STUDENT INFORMATION
Total Students in Program: 9,309. **% Full-time:** 75. **% Female:** 48.

RESEARCH FACILITIES
Research Facilities: More than 100 interdisciplinary research centers, bureaus, and institutes.

EXPENSES/FINANCIAL AID
Annual Tuition: In-state $3,460. / Out-of-state $12,120. **Books and Supplies:** $700.

ADMISSIONS INFORMATION
Application Fee: $20. **Regular Notification:** Rolling. **Transfer Students Accepted?** Yes. **Number of Applications Received:** 382. **% of Applicants Accepted:** 46. **% Accepted Who Enrolled:** 41. **Average GPA:** 3.34. **Required Admission Factors:** GRE, transcript.
Other Admission Factors: Minimum GRE score of 1000 (Verbal and Quantitative) and minimum 3.0 GPA required.

EMPLOYMENT INFORMATION
Placement Office Available? Yes.

UNIVERSITY OF FLORIDA
College of Liberal Arts & Sciences

Address: Gainesville, FL 32611
Admissions Phone: 352-392-2230 · **Admissions Fax:** 352-392-3584
Admissions E-mail: arlene@clas.ufl.edu

INSTITUTIONAL INFORMATION
Public/private: Public. **Total Faculty:** 885. **Students in Parent Institution:** 45,114.

STUDENT INFORMATION
Total Students in Program: 9,309. **% Full-time:** 75. **% Female:** 48.

RESEARCH FACILITIES
Research Facilities: More than 100 interdisciplinary research centers, bureaus, and institutes.

EXPENSES/FINANCIAL AID
Annual Tuition: In-state $3,460. / Out-of-state $12,120. **Books and Supplies:** $700.

ADMISSIONS INFORMATION
Application Fee: $20. **Regular Notification:** Rolling. **Transfer Students Accepted?** Yes. **Number of Applications Received:** 1,921. **% of Applicants Accepted:** 36. **% Accepted Who Enrolled:** 50. **Average GPA:** 3.61. **Required Admission Factors:** GRE, transcript.
Other Admission Factors: Minimum GRE score of 1000 (Verbal & Quantitative) and minimum 3.0 GPA required for most programs.
Program-Specific Admission Factors: Writing sample required of philosophy program applicants. 1,000-word statement required of religion program applicants. Minimum GRE score of 1100 and minimum 3.2 GPA required of anthropology program applicants.

EMPLOYMENT INFORMATION
Placement Office Available? Yes.

UNIVERSITY OF FLORIDA
School of Forest Resources & Conservation

Address: Gainesville, FL 32611
Admissions Phone: 352-846-0853
Admissions E-mail: cla@gnv.ifas.ufl.edu

INSTITUTIONAL INFORMATION
Public/private: Public. **Students in Parent Institution:** 45,114.

STUDENT INFORMATION
Total Students in Program: 9,309. **% Full-time:** 75. **% Female:** 48.

RESEARCH FACILITIES
Research Facilities: More than 100 interdisciplinary research centers, bureaus, and institutes.

EXPENSES/FINANCIAL AID
Annual Tuition: In-state $3,460. / Out-of-state $12,120. **Books and Supplies:** $700.

ADMISSIONS INFORMATION
Transfer Students Accepted? No. **Number of Applications Received:** 36. **% of Applicants Accepted:** 50. **% Accepted Who Enrolled:** 83. **Average GPA:** 3.37. **Average GRE Verbal:** 541. **Average GRE Quantitative:** 644.

EMPLOYMENT INFORMATION
Placement Office Available? Yes.

UNIVERSITY OF GEORGIA
College of Family & Consumer Sciences

Address: Athens, GA 30602
Admissions Phone: 706-542-1787 · **Admissions Fax:** 706-542-9480
Admissions E-mail: jsander@arches.uga.edu

INSTITUTIONAL INFORMATION
Public/private: Public. **Students in Parent Institution:** 32,505.

STUDENT INFORMATION
Total Students in Program: 5,573. % Full-time: 67. % Female: 59.

RESEARCH FACILITIES
Research Facilities: Numerous research centers.

EXPENSES/FINANCIAL AID
Annual Tuition: In-state $3,156. / Out-of-state $12,624. Fees: $786. **Books and Supplies:** $610. **Loans Range From:** $200-$18,500. **Number of Teaching/Research Assistantships Granted Each Year:** 63.

ADMISSIONS INFORMATION
Application Fee: $30. Regular Notification: Rolling. **Transfer Students Accepted?** Yes. **Number of Applications Received:** 180. **% of Applicants Accepted:** 39. **% Accepted Who Enrolled:** 56. **Average GPA:** 3.4. **Average GRE Verbal:** 510. **Average GRE Quantitative:** 580. **Average GRE Analytical:** 600.
Required Admission Factors: GRE, letters of recommendation, transcript. **Other Admission Factors:** Minimum GRE score of 1000, minimum 3.0 GPA, and statement of goals required.
Program-Specific Admission Factors: Biographical sketch and report of the number of supervised clinical hours required of doctoral marriage/family therapy specialization program applicants.

EMPLOYMENT INFORMATION
Placement Office Available? Yes. **% Employed Within Six Months:** 92. **% of masters/doctoral grads employed in their field upon graduation:** 90/100.

UNIVERSITY OF GEORGIA
Franklin College of Arts & Sciences

Address: Athens, GA 30602
Admissions Phone: 706-542-1787 · **Admissions Fax:** 706-542-9480
Admissions E-mail: jsandor@arches.uga.edu

INSTITUTIONAL INFORMATION
Public/private: Public. **Students in Parent Institution:** 32,505.

STUDENT INFORMATION
Total Students in Program: 5,573. % Full-time: 67. % Female: 59.

RESEARCH FACILITIES
Research Facilities: Numerous research centers.

EXPENSES/FINANCIAL AID
Annual Tuition: In-state $3,156. / Out-of-state $12,624. Fees: $786. **Books and Supplies:** $610. **Loans Range From:** $200-$18,500.

ADMISSIONS INFORMATION
Application Fee: $30. **Transfer Students Accepted?** No.
Required Admission Factors: GRE, letters of recommendation, transcript. **Other Admission Factors:** Rank in top half of undergraduate class required.

EMPLOYMENT INFORMATION
Placement Office Available? Yes.

UNIVERSITY OF GEORGIA
Grady College of Journalism & Mass Comunication

Address: Athens, GA 30602
Admissions Phone: 706-542-7833 · **Admissions Fax:** 706-542-2183

INSTITUTIONAL INFORMATION
Public/private: Public. **Student/faculty Ratio:** 4:1. **Students in Parent Institution:** 32,505.

STUDENT INFORMATION
Total Students in Program: 5,573. % Full-time: 67. % Female: 59.

RESEARCH FACILITIES
Research Facilities: Numerous research centers.

EXPENSES/FINANCIAL AID
Annual Tuition: In-state $3,156. / Out-of-state $12,624. **Fees:** $786. **Books and Supplies:** $610. **Loans Range From:** $200-$18,500. **% Receiving Financial Aid:** 39. **Number of Teaching/Research Assistantships Granted Each Year:** 25 **Average Salary Stipend:** $7,200.

ADMISSIONS INFORMATION
Application Fee: $30. **Transfer Students Accepted?** Yes. **Number of Applications Received:** 247. **% of Applicants Accepted:** 31. **% Accepted Who Enrolled:** 57. **Average GPA:** 3.0.
Required Admission Factors: Essays/personal statement, GRE, letters of recommendation, transcript.
Other Admission Factors: Minimum GRE score of 1000 and minimum 3.0 GPA required.

EMPLOYMENT INFORMATION
Placement Office Available? Yes. **% of mastersgrads employed in their field upon graduation:** 100.

UNIVERSITY OF GEORGIA
School of Environmental Design

Address: Athens, GA 30602
Admissions Phone: 706-542-1787 · **Admissions Fax:** 706-542-9480
Admissions E-mail: makeller@arches.uga.edu

INSTITUTIONAL INFORMATION
Public/private: Public. **Students in Parent Institution:** 32,505.

STUDENT INFORMATION
Total Students in Program: 5,573. % Full-time: 67. % Female: 59.

RESEARCH FACILITIES
Research Facilities: Numerous research centers.

EXPENSES/FINANCIAL AID
Annual Tuition: In-state $3,156. / Out-of-state $12,624. **Fees:** $786. **Books and Supplies:** $610. **Loans Range From:** $200-$18,500.

ADMISSIONS INFORMATION
Application Fee: $30. **Transfer Students Accepted?** No.
Required Admission Factors: GRE, letters of recommendation, transcript. **Other Admission Factors:** Rank in top half of undergraduate class required.

EMPLOYMENT INFORMATION
Placement Office Available? Yes.

UNIVERSITY OF GEORGIA
School of Social Work

Address: Athens, GA 30602
Admissions Phone: 706-542-1787 or 706-542-5421 · **Admissions Fax:** 706-542-9480
Admissions E-mail: makeller@arches.uga.edu

INSTITUTIONAL INFORMATION
Public/private: Public. **Evening Classes Available?** Yes. **Student/faculty Ratio:** 15:1. **Students in Parent Institution:** 32,505.

STUDENT INFORMATION
Total Students in Program: 5,573. **% Full-time:** 67. **% Female:** 59.

RESEARCH FACILITIES
Research Facilities: Numerous research centers.

EXPENSES/FINANCIAL AID
Annual Tuition: In-state $3,156. / Out-of-state $12,624. **Fees:** $786. **Books and Supplies:** $610. **Loans Range From:** $200-$18,500. **% Receiving Financial Aid:** 35. **Number of Teaching/Research Assistantships Granted Each Year:** 9. **Average Salary Stipend:** $5,965.

ADMISSIONS INFORMATION
Application Fee: $30. **Regular Notification:** Rolling. **Transfer Students Accepted?** Yes. **Number of Applications Received:** 422. **% of Applicants Accepted:** 39. **Average GPA:** 3.23.
Required Admission Factors: GRE, letters of recommendation, transcript.
Other Admission Factors: Personal narrative and rank in top half of undergraduate class required.
Program-Specific Admission Factors: Minimum GRE score of 1000, minimum 3.0 GPA on undergraduate work with a 3.4 GPA on graduate work, resume, at least 18 semester hours in behavioral and social sciences, and professional writing samples required of doctoral program applicants.

EMPLOYMENT INFORMATION
Placement Office Available? Yes.

UNIVERSITY OF GEORGIA
Warnell School of Forest Resources

Address: Athens, GA 30602
Admissions Phone: 706-542-1787 · **Admissions Fax:** 706-542-9480
Admissions E-mail: jsandor@archers.uga.edu

INSTITUTIONAL INFORMATION
Public/private: Public. **Students in Parent Institution:** 32,505.

STUDENT INFORMATION
Total Students in Program: 5,573. **% Full-time:** 67. **% Female:** 59.

RESEARCH FACILITIES
Research Facilities: Numerous research centers.

EXPENSES/FINANCIAL AID
Annual Tuition: In-state $3,156. / Out-of-state $12,624. **Fees:** $786. **Books and Supplies:** $610. **Loans Range From:** $200-$18,500. **% Receiving Financial Aid:** 89. **Average Salary Stipend:** $38,875.

ADMISSIONS INFORMATION
Application Fee: $30. **Regular Notification:** Rolling. **Transfer Students Accepted?** Yes. **Number of Applications Received:** 57. **% of Applicants Accepted:** 79. **% Accepted Who Enrolled:** 82. **Average GPA:** 3.19. **Average GRE Verbal:** 515. **Average GRE Quantitative:** 645.
Required Admission Factors: Essays/personal statement, GRE, letters of recommendation, transcript.
Other Admission Factors: Minimum 3.0 undergraduate GPA required.

EMPLOYMENT INFORMATION
Placement Office Available? Yes.

UNIVERSITY OF GREAT FALLS
College of Graduate Studies

Address: 1301 20th Street South, Great Falls, MT 59405
Admissions Phone: 406-791-5200 · **Admissions Fax:** 406-791-5209
Admissions E-mail: enroll@ugf.edu · **Web Address:** www.ugf.edu

INSTITUTIONAL INFORMATION
Public/private: Private (nonprofit). **Evening Classes Available?** Yes. **Total Faculty:** 26. **% Faculty Female:** 54. **% Faculty Part-time:** 42. **Student/faculty Ratio:** 6:1. **Students in Parent Institution:** 764.

STUDENT INFORMATION
Total Students in Program: 93. **% Full-time:** 37. **% Female:** 129. **% Minority:** 14. **% International:** 2.

RESEARCH FACILITIES
Research Facilities: Neuropsychology center.

EXPENSES/FINANCIAL AID
Annual Tuition: $7,600. **Room & Board:** $5,670. **Fees:** $460. **Books and Supplies:** $750. **Grants Range From:** $1,000-$3,000. **Loans Range From:** $4,990-$1,850. **% Receiving Financial Aid:** 65. **% Receiving Scholarships/Grants:** 2. **% Receiving Loans:** 65. **Types of Aid Available:** Institutional work-study, loans, scholarships. **Average student debt upon graduation:** $30,000

ADMISSIONS INFORMATION
Application Fee: $50. **Priority Application Deadline:** 6/1. **Regular Application Deadline:** 8/15. **Regular Notification:** Rolling. **Transfer Students Accepted?** Yes. **Transfer Policy:** Transfer credits cannot be older than 5 years upon transfer to UGF. **Number of Applications Received:** 50. **% of Applicants Accepted:** 82. **% Accepted Who Enrolled:** 63. **Average GPA:** 3.4. **Average GRE Verbal:** 450. **Average GRE Quantitative:** 450. **Average GRE Analytical:** 400.
Required Admission Factors: Essays/personal statement, interview, letters of recommendation, transcript.
Other Admission Factors: Minimum 3.0 GPA required.
Program-Specific Admission Factors: Master of arts in teaching requires a BA/BS with a teacheable major.

EMPLOYMENT INFORMATION
Placement Office Available? Yes. **% Employed Within Six Months:** 80. **% of masters grads employed in their field upon graduation:** 100. **Rate of placement:** 80%. **Average starting salary:** $40,000.

UNIVERSITY OF GUELPH
College of Arts

Address: Guelph, Ontario, N1G 2W1 Canada

INSTITUTIONAL INFORMATION
Public/private: Public. **Students in Parent Institution:** 13,890.

STUDENT INFORMATION
Total Students in Program: 1,734. **% Full-time:** 94. **% Female:** 54.

RESEARCH FACILITIES
Research Facilities: Center for Land and Water Stewardship, Center for Genetic Improvement of Livestock, Center for Toxicology, Center for Study of Animal Welfare, Guelph Turfgrass Institute, Institute of Technology, Institute for Environmental Policy and Stewardship.

EXPENSES/FINANCIAL AID

Annual Tuition: In-state $4,989. / Out-of-state $7,392. **Room & Board:** $10,305. **Fees:** $405. **Books and Supplies:** $1,170. **Grants Range From:** $2,000-$25,000. **Loans Range From:** $500-$5,000.

ADMISSIONS INFORMATION

Application Fee: $60. **Transfer Students Accepted?** Yes.
Required Admission Factors: Essays/personal statement, letters of recommendation, transcript.
Program-Specific Admission Factors: Writing samples required of English literature and drama program applicants.

EMPLOYMENT INFORMATION

Placement Office Available? Yes. **Rate of placement:** 96%.

UNIVERSITY OF GUELPH
College of Biological Science

Address: Guelph, Ontario, N1G 2W1 Canada

INSTITUTIONAL INFORMATION

Public/private: Public. **Student/faculty Ratio:** 3:1. **Students in Parent Institution:** 13,890.

STUDENT INFORMATION

Total Students in Program: 1,734. **% Full-time:** 94. **% Female:** 54.

RESEARCH FACILITIES

Research Facilities: Center for Land and Water Stewardship, Center for Genetic Improvement of Livestock, Center for Toxicology, Center for Study of Animal Welfare, Guelph Turfgrass Institute, Institute of Technology, Institute for Environmental Policy and Stewardship.

EXPENSES/FINANCIAL AID

Annual Tuition: In-state $4,989. / Out-of-state $7,392. **Room & Board:** $10,305. **Fees:** $405. **Books and Supplies:** $1,170. **Grants Range From:** $2,000-$25,000. **Loans Range From:** $500-$5,000.

ADMISSIONS INFORMATION

Application Fee: $60. **Regular Notification:** Rolling. **Transfer Students Accepted?** No.
Required Admission Factors: Letters of recommendation, transcript.
Program-Specific Admission Factors: Minimum grade average of B required of masters in zoology program applicants. Minimum grade average of A-minusrequired of doctoral in zoology program applicants.

EMPLOYMENT INFORMATION

Placement Office Available? Yes. **Rate of placement:** 96%.

UNIVERSITY OF GUELPH
College of Social & Applied Human Sciences

Address: Guelph, Ontario, N1G 2W1 Canada
Web Address: www.csahs.uoguelph.ca

INSTITUTIONAL INFORMATION

Public/private: Public. **Students in Parent Institution:** 13,890.

STUDENT INFORMATION

Total Students in Program: 1,734. **% Full-time:** 94. **% Female:** 54.

RESEARCH FACILITIES

Research Facilities: Center for Land and Water Stewardship, Center for Genetic Improvement of Livestock, Center for Toxicology, Center for Study of Animal Welfare, Guelph Turfgrass Institute, Institute of Technology, Institute for Environmental Policy and Stewardship.

EXPENSES/FINANCIAL AID

Annual Tuition: In-state $4,989. / Out-of-state $7,392. **Room & Board:** $10,305. **Fees:** $405. **Books and Supplies:** $1,170. **Grants Range From:** $2,000-$25,000. **Loans Range From:** $500-$5,000.

ADMISSIONS INFORMATION

Application Fee: $60. **Transfer Students Accepted?** No.
Required Admission Factors: Letters of recommendation, transcript.
Program-Specific Admission Factors: Minimum 3.5 GPA and GRE score of 600 (500 for general experimental psychology program) required of psychology program applicants. Minimum grade average of B-minus required of consumer studies program applicants.

EMPLOYMENT INFORMATION

Placement Office Available? Yes. **Rate of placement:** 96%.

UNIVERSITY OF GUELPH
Interdepartmental Programs

Address: Guelph, Ontario, N1G 2W1 Canada

INSTITUTIONAL INFORMATION

Public/private: Public. **Students in Parent Institution:** 13,890.

STUDENT INFORMATION

Total Students in Program: 1,734. **% Full-time:** 94. **% Female:** 54.

RESEARCH FACILITIES

Research Facilities: Center for Land and Water Stewardship, Center for Genetic Improvement of Livestock, Center for Toxicology, Center for Study of Animal Welfare, Guelph Turfgrass Institute, Institute of Technology, Institute for Environmental Policy and Stewardship.

EXPENSES/FINANCIAL AID

Annual Tuition: In-state $4,989. / Out-of-state $7,392. **Room & Board:** $10,305. **Fees:** $405. **Books and Supplies:** $1,170. **Grants Range From:** $2,000-$25,000. **Loans Range From:** $500-$5,000.

ADMISSIONS INFORMATION

Application Fee: $60. **Regular Notification:** Rolling. **Transfer Students Accepted?** No.
Required Admission Factors: Letters of recommendation, transcript.
Program-Specific Admission Factors: Minimum grade average of B in last two years of undergraduate study and relevant work experience or educational training recommended of aquaculture program applicants.

EMPLOYMENT INFORMATION

Placement Office Available? Yes. **Rate of placement:** 96%.

UNIVERSITY OF HARTFORD
College of Arts & Sciences

Address: 200 Bloomfield Avenue, West Hartford, CT 06117
Admissions Phone: 860-768-4371 · **Admissions Fax:** 860-768-5160
Admissions E-mail: westenfel@mail.hartford.edu

INSTITUTIONAL INFORMATION

Public/private: Private (nonprofit). **Evening Classes Available?** Yes. **Student/faculty Ratio:** 6:1. **Students in Parent Institution:** 6,895.

STUDENT INFORMATION

Total Students in Program: 1,528. **% Full-time:** 35. **% Female:** 63.

EXPENSES/FINANCIAL AID

Annual Tuition: $18,626. **Fees:** $220. **Books and Supplies:** $558. **% Receiving Scholarships/Grants:** 4. **% Receiving Loans:** 76. **% Receiving Assistantships:** 20.

ADMISSIONS INFORMATION

Application Fee: $40. **Regular Notification:** Rolling. **Transfer Students Accepted?** Yes. **Number of Applications Received:** 331. % of Applicants Accepted: 65. % Accepted Who Enrolled: 40.
Required Admission Factors: Essays/personal statement, GRE, letters of recommendation, transcript.
Other Admission Factors: Minimum B average recommended of psychology program applicants.

EMPLOYMENT INFORMATION

Placement Office Available? Yes.

UNIVERSITY OF HARTFORD
Hartford Art School

Address: 200 Bloomfield Avenue, West Hartford, CT 06117
Admissions Phone: 860-768-4371 · **Admissions Fax:** 860-768-5160
Admissions E-mail: westenfel@mail.hartford.edu

INSTITUTIONAL INFORMATION

Public/private: Private (nonprofit). **Evening Classes Available?** Yes. **Student/faculty Ratio:** 2:1. **Students in Parent Institution:** 6,895.

STUDENT INFORMATION

Total Students in Program: 1,528. **% Full-time:** 35. **% Female:** 63.

EXPENSES/FINANCIAL AID

Annual Tuition: $18,626. **Fees:** $220. **Books and Supplies:** $558. **% Receiving Financial Aid:** 90. **% Receiving Scholarships/Grants:** 4. **% Receiving Loans:** 76. **% Receiving Assistantships:** 20. **Number of Fellowships Granted Each Year:** 10. **Average amount of individual fellowships per year:** $6,000.

ADMISSIONS INFORMATION

Application Fee: $40. **Transfer Students Accepted?** Yes. **Transfer Policy:** Maximum 6 credit hours may be transferred with a minimum grade of B. **Number of Applications Received:** 36. **% of Applicants Accepted:** 33. **% Accepted Who Enrolled:** 67. **Average GPA:** 3.0.
Required Admission Factors: Letters of recommendation, transcript.
Other Admission Factors: Minimum 3.0 GPA required.

EMPLOYMENT INFORMATION

Placement Office Available? Yes. **% Employed Within Six Months:** 50. **% of masters employed in their field upon graduation:** 100.

UNIVERSITY OF HARTFORD
Hartt School

Address: 200 Bloomfield Avenue, West Hartford, CT 06117
Admissions Phone: 860-768-4371 · **Admissions Fax:** 860-768-5160
Admissions E-mail: westenfel@mail.hartford.edu

INSTITUTIONAL INFORMATION

Public/private: Private (nonprofit). **Evening Classes Available?** Yes. **Student/faculty Ratio:** 3:1. **Students in Parent Institution:** 6,895.

STUDENT INFORMATION

Total Students in Program: 1,528. **% Full-time:** 35. **% Female:** 63.

EXPENSES/FINANCIAL AID

Annual Tuition: $18,626. **Fees:** $220. **Books and Supplies:** $558. **% Receiving Financial Aid:** 95. **% Receiving Scholarships/Grants:** 4. **% Receiving Loans:** 76. **% Receiving Assistantships:** 20.

ADMISSIONS INFORMATION

Application Fee: $40. **Regular Notification:** Rolling. **Transfer Students Accepted?** Yes. **Transfer Policy:** Maximum 6 credit hours may be transferred

---

into masters program; maximum 12 credit hours may be transferred. **Number of Applications Received:** 196. **% of Applicants Accepted:** 65. **% Accepted Who Enrolled:** 44. **Average GPA:** 2.8.
Required Admission Factors: Essays/personal statement, interview, letters of recommendation, transcript.
Program-Specific Admission Factors: Research paper, music history, and music theory exams required of doctoral applicants.

EMPLOYMENT INFORMATION

Placement Office Available? Yes.

UNIVERSITY OF HOUSTON
College of Liberal Arts & Social Sciences

Address: 4800 Calhoun, Houston, TX 77204-2163
Admissions Phone: 713-743-3000 · **Admissions Fax:** 713-743-2990
Admissions E-mail: smintz@uh.edu · **Web Address:** www.class.uh.edu

INSTITUTIONAL INFORMATION

Public/private: Public. **Evening Classes Available?** Yes. **Total Faculty:** 211. **% Faculty Female:** 33. **% Faculty Part-time:** 9. **Student/faculty Ratio:** 8:1. **Students in Parent Institution:** 32,123.

PROGRAMS

Masters offered in: American history (United States); American literature (United States); anthropology; art/art studies; communications, journalism, and related fields; creative writing; design and visual communications; drama and dramatics/theater arts; economics; English language and literature; English literature (British and commonwealth); European history; foreign languages, literatures, and linguistics; history; interior design; mass communications/media studies; music history, literature, and theory; music pedagogy; music performance; music theory and composition; music/music and performing arts studies; painting; philosophy; photography; political science and government; public relations/image management; sculpture; sociology; Spanish language and literature. **Doctorate offered in:** See above.

STUDENT INFORMATION

Total Students in Program: 6,231. **% Full-time:** 47. **% Female:** 54.

RESEARCH FACILITIES

Research Facilities: The university includes more than 40 institutional research centers. Research funding at the University of Houston continues to grow and is now more than $72 million a year.

EXPENSES/FINANCIAL AID

Annual Tuition: In-state $1,512. / Out-of-state $5,310. **Room & Board:** $7,502. **Fees:** $1,308. **Books and Supplies:** $800. **Grants Range From:** $1,413-$4,000. **Loans Range From:** $2,800-$12,000. **% Receiving Financial Aid:** 65. **Types of Aid Available:** Fellowships, graduate assistantships, institutional work-study, scholarships. **Average student debt upon graduation:** $14,000. **Number of Fellowships Granted Each Year:** 8. **Average amount of individual fellowships per year:** $5,000. **Number of Teaching/Research Assistantships Granted Each Year:** 1,250. **Assistantship Compensation Includes:** Full tuition remission, salary/stipend. **Average Salary Stipend:** $928.

ADMISSIONS INFORMATION

Application Fee: $35. **Regular Application Deadline:** 7/1. **Regular Notification:** Rolling. **Transfer Students Accepted?** Yes. **Transfer Policy:** Requirements are the same as those used for new graduate students. Credits may be given to transfer students for advanced courses where 1) a grade of A or B was earned, 2) these courses were taken at another regionally accredited organization, and 3) if the individual UH department approves the transfer. Also please note that the following programs only admit students in the fall: Clinical psychology; industrial/organizational psychology; creative writing; counseling psychology, PhD; educational psychology, PhD; English; art; social psychology; political science; and counseling, MEd. **Number of Applications Received:**

690. **% of Applicants Accepted:** 44. **% Accepted Who Enrolled:** 67. **Average GRE Verbal:** 466. **Average GRE Quantitative:** 511. **Average GRE Analytical:** 517.
Required Admission Factors: Essays/personal statement, GRE, transcript. **Other Admission Factors:** Minimum 3.0 GPA (3.0 in major), statement of intent, and writing sample required.
Program-Specific Admission Factors: Writing sample required of creative writing program applicants. Minimum GRE Verbal score of 620 and subject score of 600 required of English doctoral program applicants. Minimum GRE subject score of 550 required of masters English program applicants.

EMPLOYMENT INFORMATION
Placement Office Available? Yes. **% of masters/doctoral grads employed in their field upon graduation:** 35/40. **Rate of placement:** 86%.

UNIVERSITY OF HOUSTON
College of Natural Sciences & Mathematics

Address: 4800 Calhoun, Houston, TX 77204-2163
Admissions Phone: 713-743-2611

INSTITUTIONAL INFORMATION
Public/private: Public. **Student/faculty Ratio:** 6:1. **Students in Parent Institution:** 32,123.

STUDENT INFORMATION
Total Students in Program: 6,231. **% Full-time:** 47. **% Female:** 54.

RESEARCH FACILITIES
Research Facilities: More than 40 institutional research centers.

EXPENSES/FINANCIAL AID
Annual Tuition: In-state $1,512. / Out-of-state $5,310. **Room & Board:** $7,502. **Fees:** $1,308. **% Receiving Financial Aid:** 91. **Number of Teaching/Research Assistantships Granted Each Year:** 84. **Average Salary Stipend:** $13,440.

ADMISSIONS INFORMATION
Application Fee: $75. **Regular Notification:** Rolling. **Transfer Students Accepted?** Yes. **Number of Applications Received:** 614. **Average GRE Verbal:** 437. **Average GRE Quantitative:** 703. **Average GRE Analytical:** 595.
Required Admission Factors: Essays/personal statement, GRE, letters of recommendation, transcript.
Other Admission Factors: Minimum GRE score of 1100 Verbal and Quantitative and minimum 3.0 GPA required.

EMPLOYMENT INFORMATION
Placement Office Available? Yes. **% of doctoral grads employed in their field upon graduation:** 90. **Rate of placement:** 86%.

UNIVERSITY OF HOUSTON
Graduate School of Social Work

Address: 4800 Calhoun, Houston, TX 77204-2163
Admissions Phone: 713-743-8078 · **Admissions Fax:** 713-743-8149
Admissions E-mail: msampson@uh.edu

INSTITUTIONAL INFORMATION
Public/private: Public. **Evening Classes Available?** Yes. **Student/faculty Ratio:** 9:1. **Students in Parent Institution:** 32,123.

STUDENT INFORMATION
Total Students in Program: 6,231. **% Full-time:** 47. **% Female:** 54.

RESEARCH FACILITIES
Research Facilities: More than 40 institutional research centers.

EXPENSES/FINANCIAL AID
Annual Tuition: In-state $1,512. / Out-of-state $5,310. **Room & Board:** $7,502. **Fees:** $1,308. **Average student debt upon graduation:** $12,000. **Number of Fellowships Granted Each Year:** 3. **Average amount of individual fellowships per year:** $7,000.

ADMISSIONS INFORMATION
Application Fee: $45. **Regular Notification:** Rolling. **Transfer Students Accepted?** Yes. **Transfer Policy:** Maximum 9 credit hours with syllabi may be transferred. **Number of Applications Received:** 150. **% of Applicants Accepted:** 77. **% Accepted Who Enrolled:** 90.
Required Admission Factors: Essays/personal statement, GRE, letters of recommendation, transcript.
Other Admission Factors: Minimum 3.0 GPA (2.6 GPA for conditional admission) required.

EMPLOYMENT INFORMATION
Placement Office Available? Yes. **% Employed Within Six Months:** 78. **% of masters grads employed in their field upon graduation:** 48. **Rate of placement:** 86%. **Average starting salary:** $32,000.

UNIVERSITY OF HOUSTON
Moores School of Music

Address: 4800 Calhoun, Houston, TX 77204-2163
Admissions Phone: 713-743-3314 · **Admissions Fax:** 713-743-3166
Admissions E-mail: hpollack@uh.edu

INSTITUTIONAL INFORMATION
Public/private: Public. **Student/faculty Ratio:** 3:1. **Students in Parent Institution:** 32,123.

STUDENT INFORMATION
Total Students in Program: 6,231. **% Full-time:** 47. **% Female:** 54.

RESEARCH FACILITIES
Research Facilities: More than 40 institutional research centers.

EXPENSES/FINANCIAL AID
Annual Tuition: In-state $1,512. / Out-of-state $5,310. **Room & Board:** $7,502. **Fees:** $1,308. **% Receiving Financial Aid:** 80. **Number of Fellowships Granted Each Year:** 12. **Average amount of individual fellowships per year:** $12,000. **Number of Teaching/Research Assistantships Granted Each Year:** 30. **Average Salary Stipend:** $5,000.

ADMISSIONS INFORMATION
Regular Notification: Rolling. **Transfer Students Accepted?** Yes. **Transfer Policy:** Maximum 9 credit hours with syllabi and a minimum grade of B may be transferred. **Number of Applications Received:** 111. **% of Applicants Accepted:** 49. **% Accepted Who Enrolled:** 91. **Average GRE Verbal:** 392. **Average GRE Quantitative:** 481. **Average GRE Analytical:** 451.
Required Admission Factors: GRE, letters of recommendation, transcript.
Other Admission Factors: Minimum 3.2 GPA recommended.
Program-Specific Admission Factors: Minimum GRE score of 500 Verbal and 500 analytical recommend of doctoral program applicants. Writing sample required of doctoral program applicants.

EMPLOYMENT INFORMATION
Placement Office Available? Yes. **% Employed Within Six Months:** 100. **% of masters/doctoral grads employed in their field upon graduation:** 100/100. **Rate of placement:** 86%.

UNIVERSITY OF HOUSTON
School of Communication

Address: 4800 Calhoun, Houston, TX 77204-2163
Admissions Phone: 713-743-2873 · **Admissions Fax:** 713-743-2876
Admissions E-mail: wdouglas@uh.edu

INSTITUTIONAL INFORMATION
Public/private: Public. **Evening Classes Available?** Yes. **Student/faculty Ratio:** 3:1. **Students in Parent Institution:** 32,123.

STUDENT INFORMATION
Total Students in Program: 6,231. **% Full-time:** 47. **% Female:** 54.

RESEARCH FACILITIES
Research Facilities: More than 40 institutional research centers.

EXPENSES/FINANCIAL AID
Annual Tuition: In-state $1,512. / Out-of-state $5,310. **Room & Board:** $7,502. **Fees:** $1,308. **% Receiving Financial Aid:** 8. **Number of Teaching/Research Assistantships Granted Each Year:** 5. **Average Salary Stipend:** $8,651.

ADMISSIONS INFORMATION
Application Fee: $25. **Regular Notification:** Rolling. **Transfer Students Accepted?** Yes. **Number of Applications Received:** 64. **% of Applicants Accepted:** 38. **% Accepted Who Enrolled:** 54. **Average GPA:** 3.0. **Average GRE Verbal:** 485. **Average GRE Quantitative:** 527. **Average GRE Analytical:** 507.
Required Admission Factors: GRE, transcript.
Other Admission Factors: Minimum GRE score of 500 Verbal, 500 Quantitative, and minimum overall 3.0 GPA (3.0 in communication) required for full admission; minimum GRE score of 450 Verbal and 450 Quantitative required for conditional admission.

EMPLOYMENT INFORMATION
Placement Office Available? Yes. **Rate of placement:** 86%.

UNIVERSITY OF HOUSTON
School of Theater

Address: 4800 Calhoun, Houston, TX 77204-2163
Admissions Phone: 713-743-3000 · **Admissions Fax:** 713-743-2990

INSTITUTIONAL INFORMATION
Public/private: Public. **Student/faculty Ratio:** 4:1. **Students in Parent Institution:** 32,123.

STUDENT INFORMATION
Total Students in Program: 6,231. **% Full-time:** 47. **% Female:** 54.

RESEARCH FACILITIES
Research Facilities: More than 40 institutional research centers.

EXPENSES/FINANCIAL AID
Annual Tuition: In-state $1,512. / Out-of-state $5,310. **Room & Board:** $7,502. **Fees:** $1,308. **% Receiving Financial Aid:** 85. **Number of Teaching/Research Assistantships Granted Each Year:** 3.

ADMISSIONS INFORMATION
Regular Notification: Rolling. **Transfer Students Accepted?** Yes. **Transfer Policy:** Maximum 12 credit hours may be transferred from an accredited institution. **Number of Applications Received:** 15. **% of Applicants Accepted:** 87. **% Accepted Who Enrolled:** 62. **Average GPA:** 3.0. **Average GRE Verbal:** 540. **Average GRE Quantitative:** 503. **Average GRE Analytical:** 538.
Required Admission Factors: GRE, letters of recommendation, transcript.
Other Admission Factors: Minimum GRE score of 500 Verbal and minimum 3.0 GPA required.

EMPLOYMENT INFORMATION
Placement Office Available? Yes. **% Employed Within Six Months:** 60. **% of masters grads employed in their field upon graduation:** 85. **Rate of placement:** 86%.

UNIVERSITY OF HOUSTON—CLEAR LAKE
School of Human Sciences & Humanities

Address: 2700 Bay Area Boulevard, Houston, TX 77058-1098
Admissions Phone: 281-283-3333 · **Admissions Fax:** 281-283-3405
Admissions E-mail: smithjohnf@cl.uh.edu

INSTITUTIONAL INFORMATION
Public/private: Public. **Evening Classes Available?** Yes. **Total Faculty:** 46. **% Faculty Female:** 43. **Students in Parent Institution:** 7,580.

STUDENT INFORMATION
Total Students in Program: 3,634. **% Full-time:** 30. **% Female:** 59.

EXPENSES/FINANCIAL AID
Annual Tuition: In-state $1,512. / Out-of-state $4,554. **Fees:** $1,204. **Books and Supplies:** $1,126. **Loans Range From:** $2,750-$5,500. **% Receiving Financial Aid:** 19. **Average student debt upon graduation:** $13,813

ADMISSIONS INFORMATION
Application Fee: $30. **Transfer Students Accepted?** Yes. **Number of Applications Received:** 261. **% of Applicants Accepted:** 100. **% Accepted Who Enrolled:** 59. **Average GPA:** 3.0.
Required Admission Factors: GRE, transcript.
Program-Specific Admission Factors: Minimum GRE score of 900, minimum 3.25 GPA, transcript. interview and essay required of professional psychology program applicants.

EMPLOYMENT INFORMATION
Placement Office Available? Yes.

UNIVERSITY OF HOUSTON—CLEAR LAKE
School of Natural & Applied Sciences

Address: 2700 Bay Area Boulevard, Houston, TX 77058-1098
Admissions Phone: 281-283-3711
Admissions E-mail: smithjohnf@cl.uh.edu

INSTITUTIONAL INFORMATION
Public/private: Public. **Evening Classes Available?** Yes. **Students in Parent Institution:** 7,580.

STUDENT INFORMATION
Total Students in Program: 3,634. **% Full-time:** 30. **% Female:** 59.

EXPENSES/FINANCIAL AID
Annual Tuition: In-state $1,512. / Out-of-state $4,554. **Fees:** $1,204. **Books and Supplies:** $1,126. **Loans Range From:** $2,750-$5,500. **% Receiving Financial Aid:** 19. **Average student debt upon graduation:** $12,165

ADMISSIONS INFORMATION
Application Fee: $30. **Regular Notification:** Rolling. **Transfer Students Accepted?** Yes. **Number of Applications Received:** 177. **% of Applicants Accepted:** 100. **% Accepted Who Enrolled:** 87.
Required Admission Factors: GRE, transcript.
Other Admission Factors: Minimum GRE score of 1500, minimum 3.0 GPA on last 60 credit hours, and appropriate foundation courses required.

EMPLOYMENT INFORMATION
Placement Office Available? Yes.

UNIVERSITY OF HOUSTON—VICTORIA
Graduate Studies

Address: 2506 East Red River, Victoria, TX 77901-4450
Admissions Phone: 512-576-3151

INSTITUTIONAL INFORMATION
Public/private: Public. **Evening Classes Available?** Yes. **Students in Parent Institution:** 1,491.

STUDENT INFORMATION
Total Students in Program: 403. **% Full-time:** 20. **% Female:** 70.

RESEARCH FACILITIES
Research Facilities: Center for Children.

EXPENSES/FINANCIAL AID
Annual Tuition: In-state $972. / Out-of-state $4,464. **Fees:** $40. **Books and Supplies:** $400. **Grants Range From:** $114-$5,400. **Loans Range From:** $750-$14,000. **% Receiving Scholarships/Grants:** 85. **% Receiving Loans:** 66.

ADMISSIONS INFORMATION
Regular Notification: Rolling. **Transfer Students Accepted?** Yes. **Average GPA:** 3.0.
Required Admission Factors: GRE, transcript.
Other Admission Factors: Minimum 3.0 GPA required.

EMPLOYMENT INFORMATION
Placement Office Available? Yes.

UNIVERSITY OF IDAHO
College of Letters, Arts, & Social Sciences

Address: Moscow, ID 83844-3017
Admissions Phone: 208-885-4001 · **Admissions Fax:** 208-885-6198
Admissions E-mail: gadms@uidaho.edu · **Web Address:** www.uidaho.edu/cogs

INSTITUTIONAL INFORMATION
Public/private: Public. **Students in Parent Institution:** 12,067.

RESEARCH FACILITIES
Research Facilities: Aquaculture Research Institute, Center for Applied Thermodynamic Studies, Center for Hazardous Waste Remediation Research, Institute for Materials and Advanced Processes, Idaho Water Resources Research Institute, Microelectronics Research Institute.

EXPENSES/FINANCIAL AID
Annual Tuition: In-state $1,630. / Out-of-state $4,630. **Books and Supplies:** $1,130. **Number of Teaching/Research Assistantships Granted Each Year:** 563.

ADMISSIONS INFORMATION
Application Fee: $35. **Regular Notification:** Rolling. **Transfer Students Accepted?** Yes. **Transfer Policy:** Maximum 12 credit hours may be transferred into masters programs. **Number of Applications Received:** 1,519. **% of Applicants Accepted:** 54. **% Accepted Who Enrolled:** 53.
Required Admission Factors: Transcript.
Other Admission Factors: Minimum 2.8 GPA required; test requirements vary by program.

EMPLOYMENT INFORMATION
Placement Office Available? Yes.

UNIVERSITY OF IDAHO
College of Natural Resources

Address: Moscow, ID 83844-3017
Admissions Phone: 208-885-4001 · **Admissions Fax:** 208-885-6198
Admissions E-mail: rwallins@uidaho.edu · **Web Address:** www.uidaho.edu/cogs

INSTITUTIONAL INFORMATION
Public/private: Public. **Students in Parent Institution:** 12,067.

RESEARCH FACILITIES
Research Facilities: Aquaculture Research Institute, Center for Applied Thermodynamic Studies, Center for Hazardous Waste Remediation Research, Institute for Materials and Advanced Processes, Idaho Water Resources Research Institute, Microelectronics Research Institute.

EXPENSES/FINANCIAL AID
Annual Tuition: In-state $1,630. / Out-of-state $4,630. **Books and Supplies:** $1,130. **Number of Teaching/Research Assistantships Granted Each Year:** 563.

ADMISSIONS INFORMATION
Application Fee: $35. **Regular Notification:** Rolling. **Transfer Students Accepted?** Yes. **Transfer Policy:** Maximum 12 credit hours may be transferred into masters programs. **Number of Applications Received:** 1,519. **% of Applicants Accepted:** 54. **% Accepted Who Enrolled:** 53.
Required Admission Factors: GRE, transcript.
Other Admission Factors: Minimum 2.8 GPA required; test requirements vary by program.

EMPLOYMENT INFORMATION
Placement Office Available? Yes.

UNIVERSITY OF ILLINOIS AT URBANA-CHAMPAIGN
College of Communications

Address: 901 West Illinois, Urbana, IL 61801
Admissions Phone: 217-333-2350

INSTITUTIONAL INFORMATION
Public/private: Public. **Students in Parent Institution:** 38,415.

STUDENT INFORMATION
Total Students in Program: 9,052. **% Full-time:** 74. **% Female:** 44.

RESEARCH FACILITIES
Research Facilities: Numerous institutional research facilities.

EXPENSES/FINANCIAL AID
Annual Tuition: In-state $5,226. / Out-of-state $13,046. **Fees:** $1,240. **Books and Supplies:** $740. **Grants Range From:** $500-$15,000. **Loans Range From:** $5-$18,500. **% Receiving Loans:** 75. **% Receiving Assistantships:** 65. **Average Salary Stipend:** $5,300.

ADMISSIONS INFORMATION
Application Fee: $40. **Transfer Students Accepted?** Yes. **Number of Applications Received:** 123. **% of Applicants Accepted:** 27. **% Accepted Who Enrolled:** 61. **Average GPA:** 3.65. **Average GRE Verbal:** 580. **Average GRE Quantitative:** 600. **Average GRE Analytical:** 625.
Required Admission Factors: Essays/personal statement, GRE, letters of recommendation, transcript.
Other Admission Factors: Minimum 3.0 GPA required.
Program-Specific Admission Factors: Minimum GRE section scores of 500 required of advertising program applicants. Minimum 3.0 graduate-level GPA and 3 letters of recommendation required of communications (PhD) program applicants. Writing sample and broadcast tape sample required of journalism program applicants.

EMPLOYMENT INFORMATION
Placement Office Available? Yes.

UNIVERSITY OF ILLINOIS AT URBANA-CHAMPAIGN
College of Fine & Applied Arts

Address: 901 West Illinois, Urbana, IL 61801 **Web Address:** www.faa.uiuc.edu

INSTITUTIONAL INFORMATION
Public/private: Public. Students in Parent Institution: 38,415.

STUDENT INFORMATION
Total Students in Program: 9,052. % Full-time: 74. % Female: 44.

RESEARCH FACILITIES
Research Facilities: Numerous institutional research facilities.

EXPENSES/FINANCIAL AID
Annual Tuition: In-state $5,226. / Out-of-state $13,046. Fees: $1,240. Books and Supplies: $740. Grants Range From: $500-$15,000. Loans Range From: $5-$18,500. % Receiving Financial Aid: 100. % Receiving Loans: 75. % Receiving Assistantships: 65. Number of Fellowships Granted Each Year: 4. Average amount of individual fellowships per year: $4,000. Number of Teaching/Research Assistantships Granted Each Year: 28. Average Salary Stipend: $4,250.

ADMISSIONS INFORMATION
Application Fee: $40. Transfer Students Accepted? No. Number of Applications Received: 65. % of Applicants Accepted: 66. % Accepted Who Enrolled: 47. Average GPA: 3.3. Average GRE Verbal: 510. Average GRE Quantitative: 660. Average GRE Analytical: 600.
Required Admission Factors: Letters of recommendation, transcript.
Other Admission Factors: Minimum 3.0 GPA required.
Program-Specific Admission Factors: Portfolio required of MFA design, acting, and landscape architecture program applicants.

EMPLOYMENT INFORMATION
Placement Office Available? Yes.

UNIVERSITY OF ILLINOIS AT URBANA-CHAMPAIGN
College of Liberal Arts & Sciences

Address: 901 West Illinois, Urbana, IL 61801
Admissions Phone: 217-333-1350

INSTITUTIONAL INFORMATION
Public/private: Public. Students in Parent Institution: 38,415.

STUDENT INFORMATION
Total Students in Program: 9,052. % Full-time: 74. % Female: 44.

RESEARCH FACILITIES
Research Facilities: Numerous institutional research facilities.

EXPENSES/FINANCIAL AID
Annual Tuition: In-state $5,226. / Out-of-state $13,046. Fees: $1,240. Books and Supplies: $740. Grants Range From: $500-$15,000. Loans Range From: $5-$18,500. % Receiving Loans: 75. % Receiving Assistantships: 65.

ADMISSIONS INFORMATION
Application Fee: $50. Transfer Students Accepted? No.
Required Admission Factors: Transcript.

EMPLOYMENT INFORMATION
Placement Office Available? Yes.

UNIVERSITY OF ILLINOIS AT URBANA-CHAMPAIGN
Graduate School of Library & Information Science

Address: 501 East Daniel Street, Champaign, IL 61820-6211
Admissions Phone: 217-333-3280 · **Admissions Fax:** 217-244-3302
Admissions E-mail: apply@alexia.lis.uiuc.edu · **Web Address:** www.lis.uiuc.edu

INSTITUTIONAL INFORMATION
Public/private: Public. Total Faculty: 32. % Faculty Female: 38. % Faculty Part-time: 44. Student/faculty Ratio: 17:1. Students in Parent Institution: 40,360.

STUDENT INFORMATION
Total Students in Program: 10,338. % Full-time: 92. % Minority: 7. % International: 35.

RESEARCH FACILITIES
Research Facilities: Numerous institutional research facilities. Center for Children's Books, Information Systems Research Lab (ISRL), Library Research Center (LRC), Mortenson Center for International Library Programs, National Center for Supercomputing Applications.

EXPENSES/FINANCIAL AID
Annual Tuition: In-state $7,260. / Out-of-state $19,260. Room & Board: $4,207. Fees: $1,664. Books and Supplies: $740. Grants Range From: $500-$15,000. Loans Range From: $1,000-$18,500. % Receiving Loans: 75. % Receiving Assistantships: 65. Types of Aid Available: Fellowships, graduate assistantships, loans, scholarships. Number of Fellowships Granted Each Year: 35. Average amount of individual fellowships per year: $16,834. Number of Teaching/Research Assistantships Granted Each Year: 166. Average Salary Stipend: $12,000.

ADMISSIONS INFORMATION
Application Fee: $40. Regular Application Deadline: 3/1. Regular Notification: 3/30. Transfer Students Accepted? Yes. Transfer Policy: Petition to transfer required of transfer applicants if coming from another UIUC graduate department. Regular application if transferring from another ALA-accredited LIS program. Number of Applications Received: 765. % of Applicants Accepted: 45. % Accepted Who Enrolled: 63. Average GPA: 3.5.
Required Admission Factors: Essays/personal statement, letters of recommendation, transcript.
Other Admission Factors: Minimum 3.0 GPA required.

EMPLOYMENT INFORMATION
Placement Office Available? Yes. % Employed Within Six Months: 93. % of doctoral grads employed in their field upon graduation: 100. Rate of placement: 80%. Average starting salary: $40,000.

UNIVERSITY OF ILLINOIS AT URBANA-CHAMPAIGN
School of Art & Design

Address: 901 West Illinois, Urbana, IL 61801
Admissions Phone: 217-333-0642 · **Admissions Fax:** 217-244-7688
Admissions E-mail: m-biddle@staff.uiuc.edu · **Web Address:** www.art.uiuc.edu

INSTITUTIONAL INFORMATION

Public/private: Public. **Student/faculty Ratio:** 2:1. **Students in Parent Institution:** 38,415.

STUDENT INFORMATION

Total Students in Program: 9,052. **% Full-time:** 74. **% Female:** 44.

RESEARCH FACILITIES

Research Facilities: Numerous institutional research facilities.

EXPENSES/FINANCIAL AID

Annual Tuition: In-state $5,226. / Out-of-state $13,046. **Fees:** $1,240. **Books and Supplies:** $740. **Grants Range From:** $500-$15,000. **Loans Range From:** $5-$18,500. **% Receiving Financial Aid:** 25. **% Receiving Loans:** 75. **% Receiving Assistantships:** 65. **Number of Fellowships Granted Each Year:** 10. **Average amount of individual fellowships per year:** $5,000. **Number of Teaching/Research Assistantships Granted Each Year:** 75. **Average Salary Stipend:** $5,300.

ADMISSIONS INFORMATION

Application Fee: $40. **Transfer Students Accepted?** No. **Number of Applications Received:** 385. **% of Applicants Accepted:** 15. **% Accepted Who Enrolled:** 46. **Average GPA:** 3.52.
Required Admission Factors: Essays/personal statement, interview, letters of recommendation, transcript.
Other Admission Factors: Minimum 3.0 GPA required.
Program-Specific Admission Factors: Portfolio required of art education program applicants. Writing sample required of art education and art history program applicants.

EMPLOYMENT INFORMATION

Placement Office Available? Yes. **% of masters/doctoral grads employed in their field upon graduation:** 50/100. **Average starting salary:** $40,000.

UNIVERSITY OF ILLINOIS AT URBANA-CHAMPAIGN
School of Music

Address: 1114 West Nevada Street, Urbana, IL 61801
Admissions Phone: 217-244-7899 · **Admissions Fax:** 217-244-4585
Admissions E-mail: musadm@music.uiuc.edu · **Web Address:** www.music.uiuc.edu

INSTITUTIONAL INFORMATION

Public/private: Public. **Student/faculty Ratio:** 5:1. **Students in Parent Institution:** 38,415.

PROGRAMS

Masters offered in: Conducting; jazz/jazz studies; music history, literature, and theory; music pedagogy; music performance; music teacher education; music theory and composition; music; music/music and performing arts studies; musicology and ethnomusicology; piano and organ; violin, viola, guitar, and other stringed instruments; voice and opera. **Doctorate offered in:** Conducting; jazz/jazz studies; music history, literature, and theory; music pedagogy; music performance; music teacher education; music theory and composition; music; music/music and performing arts studies; musicology and ethnomusicology.

STUDENT INFORMATION

Total Students in Program: 9,052. **% Full-time:** 74. **% Female:** 44.

RESEARCH FACILITIES

Research Facilities: Numerous institutional research facilities.

EXPENSES/FINANCIAL AID

Annual Tuition: In-state $7,146. / Out-of-state $19,146. **Room & Board:** $8,550. **Fees:** $1,624. **Books and Supplies:** $1,150. **Grants Range From:** $500-$15,000. **Loans Range From:** $5-$18,500. **% Receiving Loans:** 75. **% Receiving Assistantships:** 65. **Types of Aid Available:** Fellowships, gradu-

ate assistantships. **Number of Fellowships Granted Each Year:** 7. **Average amount of individual fellowships per year:** $6,000. **Number of Teaching/Research Assistantships Granted Each Year:** 120. **Average Salary Stipend:** $5,300.

ADMISSIONS INFORMATION

Application Fee: $40. **Priority Application Deadline:** 1/1. **Regular Application Deadline:** 1/1. **Regular Notification:** Rolling. **Transfer Students Accepted?** Yes. **Number of Applications Received:** 594. **% of Applicants Accepted:** 61. **% Accepted Who Enrolled:** 55. **Average GPA:** 3.6.
Required Admission Factors: Essays/personal statement, interview, letters of recommendation, transcript.
Other Admission Factors: Minimum 3.0 GPA required.
Program-Specific Admission Factors: Audition required of graduate performance, conducting, and vocal accompanying and coaching candidates.

EMPLOYMENT INFORMATION

Placement Office Available? Yes.

UNIVERSITY OF ILLINOIS AT URBANA-CHAMPAIGN
School of Social Work

Address: 1207 West Oregon, Urbana, IL 61801
Admissions Phone: 217-333-2261 · **Admissions Fax:** 217-244-5220
Admissions E-mail: social@uiuc.edu · **Web Address:** www.social.uiuc.edu

INSTITUTIONAL INFORMATION

Public/private: Public. **Evening Classes Available?** Yes. **Student/faculty Ratio:** 15:1. **Students in Parent Institution:** 38,415.

PROGRAMS

Masters offered in: Social sciences. **Doctorate offered in:** Social sciences.

STUDENT INFORMATION

Total Students in Program: 9,052. **% Full-time:** 74. **% Female:** 44.

RESEARCH FACILITIES

Research Facilities: Numerous institutional research facilities.

EXPENSES/FINANCIAL AID

Annual Tuition: In-state $5,226. / Out-of-state $13,046. **Fees:** $1,240. **Books and Supplies:** $740. **Grants Range From:** $500-$15,000. **Loans Range From:** $5-$18,500. **% Receiving Financial Aid:** 75. **% Receiving Loans:** 75. **% Receiving Assistantships:** 65. **Number of Fellowships Granted Each Year:** 11. **Average amount of individual fellowships per year:** $17,000. **Number of Teaching/Research Assistantships Granted Each Year:** 30. **Average Salary Stipend:** $560.

ADMISSIONS INFORMATION

Application Fee: $40. **Priority Application Deadline:** 12/15. **Regular Application Deadline:** 1/15. **Transfer Students Accepted?** Yes. **Number of Applications Received:** 289. **% of Applicants Accepted:** 48. **% Accepted Who Enrolled:** 75. **Average GPA:** 3.56. **Average GRE Verbal:** 430. **Average GRE Quantitative:** 613. **Average GRE Analytical:** 467.
Required Admission Factors: Essays/personal statement, letters of recommendation, transcript.
Other Admission Factors: Minimum 3.0 GPA on final 60 credit hours (90 quarter hours) and at least 20 credit hours of social sciences required.
Program-Specific Admission Factors: GRE required of PhD and dual degree program applicants.

EMPLOYMENT INFORMATION

Placement Office Available? Yes. **% Employed Within Six Months:** 94.

UNIVERSITY OF KANSAS
College of Liberal Arts & Sciences

Address: 200 Strong Hall, 1450 Jayhawk Boulevard, Lawrence, KS 66045
Admissions Phone: 785-864-4898 · **Admissions Fax:** 785-864-5331
Admissions E-mail: clasdean@ku.edu · **Web Address:** www.clas.ku.edu

INSTITUTIONAL INFORMATION
Public/private: Public. **Total Faculty:** 572. **Students in Parent Institution:** 28,329.

STUDENT INFORMATION
Total Students in Program: 6,979. **% Full-time:** 53. **% Female:** 55.

RESEARCH FACILITIES
Research Facilities: Bioscience Center, Cancer Center, Institute for Life Span Studies, Center for Aging, Center for the Humanities, Kansas Biological and Geological Survey, Mental Retardation and Human Development Research Center.

EXPENSES/FINANCIAL AID
Annual Tuition: In-state $2,640. / Out-of-state $8,400. **Fees:** $458.

ADMISSIONS INFORMATION
Application Fee: $25. **Regular Notification:** Rolling. **Transfer Students Accepted?** Yes. **Number of Applications Received:** 1,843. **% of Applicants Accepted:** 34. **% Accepted Who Enrolled:** 67.
Other Admission Factors: Minimum 3.0 GPA required.

EMPLOYMENT INFORMATION
Placement Office Available? Yes.

UNIVERSITY OF KANSAS
School of Fine Arts

Address: Lawrence, KS 66045
Admissions Phone: 913-864-3421 · **Admissions Fax:** 913-864-5387
Admissions E-mail: majordan@ku.edu

INSTITUTIONAL INFORMATION
Public/private: Public. **Total Faculty:** 97. **% Faculty Female:** 9. **Student/faculty Ratio:** 6:1. **Students in Parent Institution:** 28,329.

STUDENT INFORMATION
Total Students in Program: 6,979. **% Full-time:** 53. **% Female:** 55.

RESEARCH FACILITIES
Research Facilities: Bioscience Center, Cancer Center, Institute for Life Span Studies, Center for Aging, Center for the Humanities, Kansas Biological and Geological Survey, Mental Retardation and Human Development Research Center.

EXPENSES/FINANCIAL AID
Annual Tuition: In-state $2,640. / Out-of-state $8,400. **Fees:** $458. **Number of Teaching/Research Assistantships Granted Each Year:** 62.

ADMISSIONS INFORMATION
Application Fee: $25. **Regular Notification:** Rolling. **Transfer Students Accepted?** Yes. **Number of Applications Received:** 181. **% of Applicants Accepted:** 46. **% Accepted Who Enrolled:** 70. **Average GPA:** 3.0.
Required Admission Factors: Letters of recommendation, transcript.
Other Admission Factors: Minimum 3.0 GPA required.
Program-Specific Admission Factors: Supporting materials required of musicology, music theory, and composition program applicants.

EMPLOYMENT INFORMATION
Placement Office Available? Yes.

UNIVERSITY OF KANSAS
School of Social Welfare

Address: MSW Program, 1545 Lilac Lane, Lawrence, KS 66045
Admissions Phone: 785-864-8956 · **Admissions Fax:** 785-864-5277
Admissions E-mail: admissionsMSW@ku.edu · **Web Address:** www.socwel.ku.edu

INSTITUTIONAL INFORMATION
Public/private: Public. **Total Faculty:** 24. **% Faculty Female:** 62. **Student/faculty Ratio:** 18:1. **Students in Parent Institution:** 28,329.

PROGRAMS
Masters offered in: Social work. **Doctorate offered in:** Social work. **First Professional degree offered in:** Social work.

STUDENT INFORMATION
Total Students in Program: 6,979. **% Full-time:** 53. **% Female:** 55.

RESEARCH FACILITIES
Research Facilities: Bioscience Center, Cancer Center, Institute for Life Span Studies, Center for Aging, Center for the Humanities, Kansas Biological and Geological Survey, Mental Retardation and Human Development Research Center.

EXPENSES/FINANCIAL AID
Annual Tuition: In-state $5,721. / Out-of-state $14,691. **Fees:** $574. **Books and Supplies:** $600. **Grants Range From:** $600-$2,200. **% Receiving Financial Aid:** 22. **% Receiving Scholarships/Grants:** 100. **Types of Aid Available:** Graduate assistantships, scholarships.

ADMISSIONS INFORMATION
Application Fee: $30. **Regular Application Deadline:** 2/15. **Regular Notification:** 4/15. **Transfer Students Accepted?** Yes. **Transfer Policy:** Transfer students accepted from accredited masters in social work programs only. **Number of Applications Received:** 328. **% of Applicants Accepted:** 72. **% Accepted Who Enrolled:** 73. **Average GPA:** 3.3.
Required Admission Factors: Essays/personal statement, letters of recommendation, transcript.
Other Admission Factors: Minimum cumulative GPA of 3.0 or higher. Work and volunteer history required.
Program-Specific Admission Factors: Minimum 3.0 GPA required of masters program applicants. Minimum 3.5 GPA required of doctoral program applicants. Bachelors in social work required of advanced standing program applicants.

EMPLOYMENT INFORMATION
% Employed Within Six Months: 80. **Average starting salary:** $35,000.

UNIVERSITY OF KANSAS
William Allen White School of Journalism & Mass Communications

Address: Lawrence, KS 66045
Admissions Phone: 785-864-7649 · **Admissions Fax:** 785-864-5318
Admissions E-mail: jbroholm@ukans.edu

INSTITUTIONAL INFORMATION
Public/private: Public. **Total Faculty:** 24. **Students in Parent Institution:** 28,329.

STUDENT INFORMATION
Total Students in Program: 6,979. **% Full-time:** 53. **% Female:** 55.

RESEARCH FACILITIES
Research Facilities: Bioscience Center, Cancer Center, Institute for Life Span Studies, Center for Aging, Center for the Humanities, Kansas Biological and Geological Survey, Mental Retardation and Human Development Research Center.

EXPENSES/FINANCIAL AID

Annual Tuition: In-state $2,640. / Out-of-state $8,400. Fees: $458.

ADMISSIONS INFORMATION

Application Fee: $25. Transfer Students Accepted? No. Number of Applications Received: 66. % of Applicants Accepted: 33. % Accepted Who Enrolled: 95. Average GPA: 3.0. Average GRE Verbal: 566. Average GRE Quantitative: 585. Average GRE Analytical: 619.
Required Admission Factors: GRE, letters of recommendation, transcript.
Other Admission Factors: Minimum GRE score of 500 Verbal and minimum 3.0 GPA required.

EMPLOYMENT INFORMATION

Placement Office Available? Yes. % Employed Within Six Months: 70. % of masters grads employed in their field upon graduation: 60.

UNIVERSITY OF MARY
Graduate Program

Address: 7500 University Drive, Bismarck, ND 58501-9652
Admissions Phone: 701-255-7500 · Admissions Fax: 701-255-7687
Admissions E-mail: rkrieg@umary.edu

INSTITUTIONAL INFORMATION

Public/private: Private (nonprofit). Evening Classes Available? Yes. Student/faculty Ratio: 12:1. Students in Parent Institution: 2,343.

STUDENT INFORMATION

Total Students in Program: 337

EXPENSES/FINANCIAL AID

Annual Tuition: $5,220. Room & Board (On/off campus): $1,950/$1,930. Grants Range From: $300-$2,750. Loans Range From: $2,000-$18,500. % Receiving Scholarships/Grants: 10. % Receiving Loans: 90. % Receiving Assistantships: 5.

ADMISSIONS INFORMATION

Application Fee: $15. Regular Notification: Rolling. Transfer Students Accepted? Yes. Transfer Policy: Minimum 3.0 GPA required of transfer applicants. Number of Applications Received: 180. % of Applicants Accepted: 96. % Accepted Who Enrolled: 96. Average GPA: 3.0.
Required Admission Factors: Essays/personal statement, letters of recommendation, transcript.
Other Admission Factors: Minimum 2.75 GPA required.

EMPLOYMENT INFORMATION

Placement Office Available? Yes. Rate of placement: 94%.

UNIVERSITY OF MARY HARDIN-BAYLOR
School of Sciences & Humanities

Address: 900 College Street, Belton, TX 76513-2599
Admissions Phone: 254-295-4520 · Admissions Fax: 254-295-5049
Admissions E-mail: stheodore@umbb.edu

INSTITUTIONAL INFORMATION

Public/private: Private (nonprofit). Evening Classes Available? Yes. Student/faculty Ratio: 8:1. Students in Parent Institution: 2,590.

STUDENT INFORMATION

Total Students in Program: 189. % Full-time: 16. % Female: 71.

EXPENSES/FINANCIAL AID

Annual Tuition: $5,940. Fees: $400. Books and Supplies: $750. Grants Range From: $200-$3,600. Loans Range From: $500-$8,500. % Receiving Financial Aid: 100. % Receiving Scholarships/Grants: 20. % Receiving Loans: 80.

ADMISSIONS INFORMATION

Application Fee: $35. Regular Notification: Rolling. Transfer Students Accepted? Yes. Transfer Policy: Maximum 6 credit hours may be transferred with a minimum grade average of B. Average GPA: 2.9. Average GRE Verbal: 430. Average GRE Quantitative: 440. Average GRE Analytical: 460.
Required Admission Factors: GRE, interview, letters of recommendation, transcript.
Other Admission Factors: Minimum GRE scores of 900 Verbal and Quantitative and 400 analytical and minimum 2.75 GPA required for most programs.
Program-Specific Admission Factors: In-state teacher certificate required of public school counselor program applicants.

UNIVERSITY OF MARY WASHINGTON
James Monroe Center for Graduate & Professional Studies

Address: 1301 College Avenue, Fredericksburg, VA 22401-5358
Admissions Phone: 540-654-1038 · Admissions Fax: 540-654-1070
Admissions E-mail: cferrell@mwc.edu

INSTITUTIONAL INFORMATION

Public/private: Public. Evening Classes Available? Yes. Student/faculty Ratio: 10:1. Students in Parent Institution: 3,840.

STUDENT INFORMATION

Total Students in Program: 39 % Female: 74.

EXPENSES/FINANCIAL AID

Annual Tuition: In-state $2,646. / Out-of-state $6,084. Books and Supplies: $200. % Receiving Financial Aid: 5. Average student debt upon graduation: $2,000.

ADMISSIONS INFORMATION

Application Fee: $35. Regular Notification: Rolling. Transfer Students Accepted? Yes. Number of Applications Received: 13. % of Applicants Accepted: 92. % Accepted Who Enrolled: 100. Average GPA: 3.5.
Required Admission Factors: Essays/personal statement, interview, transcript.
Other Admission Factors: Minimum 3.0 GPA required.

UNIVERSITY OF MARYLAND—BALTIMORE
Graduate School

Address: 515 West Lombard Street, Suite 208, Baltimore, MD 21201
Admissions Phone: 410-706-7131 · Admissions Fax: 410-706-3473
Admissions E-mail: gradinfo@umaryland.edu
Web Address: http://graduate.umaryland.edu/

INSTITUTIONAL INFORMATION

Public/private: Public. Students in Parent Institution: 5,602.

PROGRAMS

Masters offered in: Biostatistics, clinical laboratory science/medical technology/technologist, dental hygiene/hygienist, dental public health and education (Certificate, MS/MPH, PhD/DPH), environmental toxicology, family practice nurse practitioner, human/medical genetics, maternal/child health nurse/nursing, nursing—registered nurse training (RN, ASN, BSN, MSN), nursing administration (MSN, MS, PhD), nursing science (MS, PhD), oral biology and pathology (MS, PhD), pathology/experimental pathology, pathology/pathologist assistant, pediatric nurse/nursing, pharmacology, physiology, public health/community nurse/nursing, toxicology. Doctorate offered in: See above.

STUDENT INFORMATION

Total Students in Program: 1,146. % Full-time: 46.

RESEARCH FACILITIES

Research Facilities: Center for Vaccine Development, Center for Child Welfare, Center for Aging, Center for Health Services, Center for Persistent Pain, Center for Disease Prevention, Center for Health Policy.

EXPENSES/FINANCIAL AID

Annual Tuition: In-state $6,576. / Out-of-state $11,790. **Room & Board:** $6,700. **Fees:** $460. **Books and Supplies:** $1,000. **Grants Range From:** $500-$5,000. **Loans Range From:** $500-$18,500. **Types of Aid Available:** Fellowships, graduate assistantships, institutional work-study, loans, scholarships. **Assistantship Compensation Includes:** Full tuition remission, salary/stipend. **Average Salary Stipend:** $19,500.

ADMISSIONS INFORMATION

Application Fee: $50. **Priority Application Deadline:** 1/15. **Regular Application Deadline:** 1/7. **Regular Notification:** Rolling. **Transfer Students Accepted?** Yes. **Number of Applications Received:** 1,002. **% of Applicants Accepted:** 48. **% Accepted Who Enrolled:** 68. **Average GPA:** 3.4. **Required Admission Factors:** Essays/personal statement, GRE, letters of recommendation, transcript. TOEFL or IELTS. **Other Admission Factors:** Minimum 3.0 GPA required.

EMPLOYMENT INFORMATION

Placement Office Available? Yes.

UNIVERSITY OF MARYLAND—BALTIMORE
School of Social Work

Address: 621 West Lombard Street, Baltimore, MD 21201
Admissions Phone: 410-706-3602 · **Admissions Fax:** 410-706-6046

INSTITUTIONAL INFORMATION

Public/private: Public. **Students in Parent Institution:** 5,337.

RESEARCH FACILITIES

Research Facilities: Center for Vaccine Development, Center for Child Welfare, Center for Aging, Center for Health Services, Center for Persistent Pain, Center for Disease Prevention, Center for Health Policy.

EXPENSES/FINANCIAL AID

Annual Tuition: In-state $6,576. / Out-of-state $11,730. **Room & Board:** $6,000.

ADMISSIONS INFORMATION

Application Fee: $50. **Regular Notification:** Rolling. **Transfer Students Accepted?** Yes.
Required Admission Factors: Essays/personal statement, GRE, interview, transcript.
Other Admission Factors: Minimum 3.0 GPA and MSW degree required.

EMPLOYMENT INFORMATION

Placement Office Available? Yes.

UNIVERSITY OF MARYLAND—BALTIMORE COUNTY
Graduate School

Address: 1000 Hilltop Circle, Baltimore, MD 21250
Admissions Phone: 410-455-2537 · **Admissions Fax:** 410-455-1130
Admissions E-mail: umbcgrad@umbc.edu · **Web Address:** www.umbc.edu/gradschool

INSTITUTIONAL INFORMATION

Public/private: Public. **Evening Classes Available?** Yes. **Total Faculty:** 949. **% Faculty Part-time:** 31. **Student/faculty Ratio:** 3:1. **Students in Parent Institution:** 11,852.

STUDENT INFORMATION

Total Students in Program: 2,184. **% Full-time:** 39. **% Female:** 53. **% Minority:** 15. **% International:** 21.

RESEARCH FACILITIES

Research Facilities: Imaging Research Center, Howard Hughes Medical Institute Lab, Molecular Biology Lab, Joint Center for Earth Systems Technology, MD Institute for Policy Analysis, Research Center for Health Program Development & Management, Shriver Center.

EXPENSES/FINANCIAL AID

Annual Tuition: In-state $5,256. / Out-of-state $8,640. **Room & Board:** $7,150. **Fees:** $1,044. **Books and Supplies:** $700. **Grants Range From:** $500-$8,000. **Loans Range From:** $100-$18,500. **% Receiving Financial Aid:** 47. **% Receiving Scholarships/Grants:** 4. **% Receiving Loans:** 22. **% Receiving Assistantships:** 53. **% Receiving Other Aid (work-study, tuition waiver):** 21. **Average student debt upon graduation:** $25,000

ADMISSIONS INFORMATION

Application Fee: $50. **Priority Application Deadline:** 1/1. **Regular Application Deadline:** 6/1. **Regular Notification:** Rolling. **Transfer Students Accepted?** Yes. **Transfer Policy:** Maximum 6 credit hours may be transferred into graduate programs from a regionally accredited institution. **Number of Applications Received:** 2,140. **% of Applicants Accepted:** 51. **% Accepted Who Enrolled:** 55. **Average GRE Verbal:** 521. **Average GRE Quantitative:** 615. **Average GRE Analytical:** 607.
Required Admission Factors: Essays/personal statement, letters of recommendation, transcript.
Other Admission Factors: Minimum 3.0 GPA required.

EMPLOYMENT INFORMATION

Placement Office Available? Yes. **Rate of placement:** 92%.

UNIVERSITY OF MARYLAND—COLLEGE PARK
College of Arts & Humanities

Address: University of Maryland, College Park, Box G, Mitchell Building, College Park, MD 20742
Admissions Phone: 301-405-0376 · **Admissions Fax:** 301-314-9305
Admissions E-mail: grshool@deans.umd.edu
Web Address: www.vprgs.umd.edu/gss/admission.htm

INSTITUTIONAL INFORMATION

Public/private: Public. **Total Faculty:** 285. **% Faculty Female:** 41. **% Faculty Part-time:** 4. **Student/faculty Ratio:** 4:1. **Students in Parent Institution:** 34,933.

STUDENT INFORMATION

Total Students in Program: 876. **% Full-time:** 78. **% Female:** 59. **% Minority:** 14. **% International:** 29.

EXPENSES/FINANCIAL AID

Annual Tuition: In-state $6,678. / Out-of-state $12,618. **Fees:** $877. **Books and Supplies:** $1,159. **Loans Range From:** $400-$18,500. **% Receiving Financial Aid:** 76. **% Receiving Scholarships/Grants:** 91. **% Receiving Loans:** 34. **% Receiving Assistantships:** 64. **Types of Aid Available:** Fellowships, graduate assistantships, grants, loans, scholarships. **Number of Teaching/Research Assistantships Granted Each Year:** 527. **Average Salary Stipend:** $12,986.

ADMISSIONS INFORMATION

Application Fee: $50. **Transfer Students Accepted?** Yes. **Number of Applications Received:** 1,803. **% Accepted Who Enrolled:** 6. **Average GPA:** 3.5. **Average GRE Verbal:** 531. **Average GRE Quantitative:** 664. **Average GRE Analytical:** 674. **Average GRE Analytical Writing:** 4.8.
Required Admission Factors: Essays/personal statement, letters of recommendation, transcript.
Other Admission Factors: Minimum 3.0 GPA required.

Program-Specific Admission Factors: GRE required of art history/archaeology, comparative literature, geography, history, music, and philosophy program applicants; recommended of French language/literature program applicants. Minimum 3.5 GPA in English classes required of English program applicants.

UNIVERSITY OF MARYLAND—COLLEGE PARK
College of Behavioral & Social Sciences

Address: University of Maryland, College Park, Box G, Mitchell Building, College Park, MD 20742
Admissions Phone: 301-405-0376 · Admissions Fax: 301-314-9305
Admissions E-mail: grschool@deans.umd.edu
Web Address: www.vprgs.umd.edu/gss/admission.htm

INSTITUTIONAL INFORMATION

Public/private: Public. Total Faculty: 179. % Faculty Female: 29. % Faculty Part-time: 2. Student/faculty Ratio: 5:1. Students in Parent Institution: 34,933.

STUDENT INFORMATION

Total Students in Program: 876. % Full-time: 78. % Female: 59. % Minority: 14. % International: 29.

EXPENSES/FINANCIAL AID

Annual Tuition: In-state $6,678. / Out-of-state $12,618. Fees: $877. Books and Supplies: $1,159. Loans Range From: $400-$18,500. % Receiving Financial Aid: 74. % Receiving Scholarships/Grants: 94. % Receiving Loans: 31. % Receiving Assistantships: 70. Types of Aid Available: Fellowships, graduate assistantships, grants, loans, scholarships. Number of Teaching/Research Assistantships Granted Each Year: 445. Average Salary Stipend: $12,938.

ADMISSIONS INFORMATION

Application Fee: $50. Transfer Students Accepted? Yes. Number of Applications Received: 1,908. % of Applicants Accepted: 15. % Accepted Who Enrolled: 50. Average GPA: 3.5. Average GRE Verbal: 531. Average GRE Quantitative: 664. Average GRE Analytical: 674. Average GRE Analytical Writing: 4.8.
Required Admission Factors: Essays/personal statement, letters of recommendation, transcript.
Other Admission Factors: Minimum 3.0 GPA required.
Program-Specific Admission Factors: GRE required for most programs; recommended for psychology program applicants. GRE or MAT required for human development program applicants. GRE subject exam required of economics program applicants. Minimum GRE score of 1000 required of family studies program.

UNIVERSITY OF MARYLAND—COLLEGE PARK
College of Chemical & Life Sciences

Address: University of Maryland, College Park, Box G, Mitchell Building, College Park, MD 20742
Admissions Phone: 301-405-0376 · Admissions Fax: 301-314-9305
Admissions E-mail: grschool@deans.umd.edu
Web Address: www.vprgs.umd.edu/gss/admission.htm

INSTITUTIONAL INFORMATION

Public/private: Public. Total Faculty: 107. % Faculty Female: 25. Student/faculty Ratio: 6:1. Students in Parent Institution: 34,933.

STUDENT INFORMATION

Total Students in Program: 667. % Full-time: 72. % Female: 56. % Minority: 9. % International: 24.

EXPENSES/FINANCIAL AID

Annual Tuition: In-state $6,678. / Out-of-state $12,618. Fees: $877. Books and Supplies: $1,159. Loans Range From: $400-$18,500. % Receiving Scholarships/Grants: 56. % Receiving Loans: 11. % Receiving Assistantships: 27. Types of Aid Available: Fellowships, graduate assistantships, grants, loans, scholarships. Number of Teaching/Research Assistantships Granted Each Year: 362. Average Salary Stipend: $15,474.

ADMISSIONS INFORMATION

Application Fee: $50. Transfer Students Accepted? No. Number of Applications Received: 698. % of Applicants Accepted: 13. % Accepted Who Enrolled: 67. Average GPA: 3.3. Average GRE Verbal: 528. Average GRE Quantitative: 690. Average GRE Analytical: 686. Average GRE Analytical Writing: 4.6.
Required Admission Factors: GRE, letters of recommendation, transcript.
Other Admission Factors: Minimum 3.0 GPA required.

UNIVERSITY OF MARYLAND—COLLEGE PARK
College of Information Studies

Address: University of Maryland, College Park, Box G, Mitchell Building, College Park, MD 20742
Admissions Phone: 301-405-0376 · Admissions Fax: 301-314-9305
Admissions E-mail: grschool@deans.umd.edu
Web Address: www.vprgs.umd.edu/gss/admission.htm

INSTITUTIONAL INFORMATION

Public/private: Public. Total Faculty: 10. % Faculty Female: 60. Student/faculty Ratio: 36:1. Students in Parent Institution: 34,933.

STUDENT INFORMATION

Total Students in Program: 357. % Full-time: 46. % Female: 78. % Minority: 17. % International: 7.

EXPENSES/FINANCIAL AID

Annual Tuition: In-state $6,678. / Out-of-state $12,618. Fees: $877. Books and Supplies: $1,159. Loans Range From: $400-$18,500. % Receiving Financial Aid: 56. % Receiving Scholarships/Grants: 59. % Receiving Loans: 65. % Receiving Assistantships: 33. Types of Aid Available: Fellowships, graduate assistantships, grants, loans, scholarships. Number of Teaching/Research Assistantships Granted Each Year: 24. Average Salary Stipend: $12,526.

ADMISSIONS INFORMATION

Application Fee: $50. Transfer Students Accepted? Yes. Number of Applications Received: 317. % of Applicants Accepted: 52. % Accepted Who Enrolled: 55. Average GPA: 3.4. Average GRE Verbal: 558. Average GRE Quantitative: 642. Average GRE Analytical: 636. Average GRE Analytical Writing: 4.8.
Required Admission Factors: Essays/personal statement, GRE, letters of recommendation, transcript.
Other Admission Factors: Minimum 3.0 GPA required.

UNIVERSITY OF MARYLAND—COLLEGE PARK
Philip Merrill College of Journalism

Address: University of Maryland, Collge Park, Box G, Mitchell Building, College Park, MD 20742
Admissions Phone: 301-405-0376 · Admissions Fax: 301-314-9305
Admissions E-mail: grschool@deans.umd.edu
Web Address: www.vprgs.umd.edu/gss/admission.htm

INSTITUTIONAL INFORMATION

Public/private: Public. Total Faculty: 17. % Faculty Female: 35. % Faculty Part-time: 6. Student/faculty Ratio: 4:1. Students in Parent Institution: 34,933.

STUDENT INFORMATION

Total Students in Program: 74. % Full-time: 77. % Female: 64. % Minority: 39. % International: 9.

EXPENSES/FINANCIAL AID

Annual Tuition: In-state $6,678. / Out-of-state $12,618. Fees: $877. Books and Supplies: $1,159. Loans Range From: $400-$18,500. % Receiving Financial Aid: 100. % Receiving Scholarships/Grants: 66. % Receiving Loans: 58. % Receiving Assistantships: 28. Types of Aid Available: Fellowships, graduate assistantships, grants, loans, scholarships. Number of Teaching/Research Assistantships Granted Each Year: 16. Average Salary Stipend: $13,643.

ADMISSIONS INFORMATION

Application Fee: $50. Transfer Students Accepted? Yes. Number of Applications Received: 213. % of Applicants Accepted: 22. % Accepted Who Enrolled: 26. Average GPA: 3.3. Average GRE Verbal: 508. Average GRE Quantitative: 588. Average GRE Analytical: 634. Average GRE Analytical Writing: 4.9.

Required Admission Factors: Essays/personal statement, GRE, letters of recommendation, transcript.

Other Admission Factors: Minimum 3.0 GPA required.

UNIVERSITY OF MARYLAND—COLLEGE PARK
School of Public Affairs

Address: University of Maryland, College Park, Box G, Mitchell Building, College Park, MD 20742
Admissions Phone: 301-405-0376 · **Admissions Fax:** 301-314-9305
Admissions E-mail: grschool@deans.umd.edu
Web Address: www.vprgs.umd.edu/gss/admission.htm

INSTITUTIONAL INFORMATION

Public/private: Public. Evening Classes Available? Yes. Total Faculty: 13. % Faculty Female: 8. % Faculty Part-time: 8. Student/faculty Ratio: 13:1. Students in Parent Institution: 34,933.

PROGRAMS

Masters offered in: Environmental studies, international relations and affairs, international/global studies, public administration, public policy analysis. Doctorate offered in: Environmental studies, international relations and affairs, international/global studies, public administration, public policy analysis. First Professional degree offered in: Environmental studies, international relations and affairs, international/global studies, public administration, public policy analysis.

STUDENT INFORMATION

Total Students in Program: 170. % Full-time: 63. % Female: 52. % Minority: 12. % International: 15.

EXPENSES/FINANCIAL AID

Annual Tuition: In-state $8,352. / Out-of-state $15,768. Fees: $877. Books and Supplies: $1,159. Loans Range From: $400-$18,500. % Receiving Financial Aid: 99. % Receiving Scholarships/Grants: 69. % Receiving Loans: 50. % Receiving Assistantships: 32. Types of Aid Available: Fellowships, graduate assistantships, grants, loans, scholarships. Number of Teaching/Research Assistantships Granted Each Year: 52. Average Salary Stipend: $12,249.

ADMISSIONS INFORMATION

Application Fee: $50. Priority Application Deadline: 1/1. Regular Application Deadline: 4/15. Regular Notification: Rolling. Transfer Students Accepted? Yes. Transfer Policy: Transfer of eligible courses taken prior to entering MSPA program are subject to the approval of advisor and assistant dean/director of student affairs. Number of Applications Received: 405. % of Applicants Accepted: 32. % Accepted Who Enrolled: 26. Average GPA: 3.4. Average GRE Verbal: 549. Average GRE Quantitative: 659.

Average GRE Analytical: 689. Average GRE Analytical Writing: 4.9.
Required Admission Factors: Essays/personal statement, GRE, letters of recommendation, transcript.
Other Admission Factors: Minimum 3.0 GPA and completion of college level math required.

UNIVERSITY OF MARYLAND—EASTERN SHORE
School of Graduate Studies

Address: Backbone Road, Child Development Center, Room 1137, Princess Anne, MD 21853
Admissions Phone: 410-651-6507/7966 · **Admissions Fax:** 410-651-7571
Admissions E-mail: cdignasias@mail.umes.edu · **Web Address:** www.umes.edu

INSTITUTIONAL INFORMATION

Public/private: Public. Evening Classes Available? Yes. Students in Parent Institution: 3,771.

PROGRAMS

Masters offered in: Agricultural teacher education; agricultural, agricultural operations, and related sciences; art teacher education; biology teacher education; business teacher education; chemistry teacher education; computer science; counselor education/school counseling and guidance services; criminology; English/language arts teacher education; environmental science; family and consumer sciences/home economics teacher education; mathematics teacher education; music teacher education; rehabilitation counseling/counselor; social studies teacher education; special education and teaching; technology teacher education/industrial arts teacher education. Doctorate offered in: Education leadership and administration; environmental science; food science and technology; multi/interdisciplinary studies; physical therapy/therapist.

STUDENT INFORMATION

Total Students in Program: 392. % Full-time: 62. % Female: 63. % International: 11.

RESEARCH FACILITIES

Research Facilities: Food Science and Technology building.

EXPENSES/FINANCIAL AID

Annual Tuition: In-state $2,718. / Out-of-state $4,896.Loans Range From: $8,500-$12,000. % Receiving Scholarships/Grants: 3. % Receiving Loans: 90. % Receiving Assistantships: 2. Number of Teaching/Research Assistantships Granted Each Year: 8. Average Salary Stipend: $9,000.

ADMISSIONS INFORMATION

Application Fee: $30. Regular Application Deadline: 3/1. Regular Notification: Rolling. Transfer Students Accepted? Yes. Transfer Policy: Masters programs—6 credits and doctoral programs—up to 12. Number of Applications Received: 155. % of Applicants Accepted: 99. % Accepted Who Enrolled: 60. Average GPA: 3.4.

Required Admission Factors: Essays/personal statement, letters of recommendation, transcript.
Other Admission Factors: Minimum 3.0 GPA required.
Program-Specific Admission Factors: See individual programs.

EMPLOYMENT INFORMATION

Placement Office Available? Yes. % Employed Within Six Months: 100. % of masters grads employed in their field upon graduation: 95. Rate of placement: 75%. Average starting salary: $36,000.

UNIVERSITY OF MASSACHUSETTS—AMHERST
College of Humanities & Fine Arts

Address: 140 Hicks Way, Amherst, MA 01003
Admissions Phone: 413-545-0721 · Admissions Fax: 413-577-0010
Admissions E-mail: gradinfo@resgs.umass.edu
Web Address: www.umass.edu/gradschool

INSTITUTIONAL INFORMATION
Public/private: Public. Students in Parent Institution: 22,509.

STUDENT INFORMATION
Total Students in Program: 4,721. % Full-time: 47. % Female: 52.

RESEARCH FACILITIES
Research Facilities: Population research institute, polymer research institute, environmental institute.

EXPENSES/FINANCIAL AID
Annual Tuition: In-state $5,193. / Out-of-state $11,032. Loans Range From: $1,000-$18,500. % Receiving Loans: 35.

ADMISSIONS INFORMATION
Application Fee: $40. Regular Application Deadline: 2/1. Regular Notification: Rolling. Transfer Students Accepted? No.
Admission Factors: 2.8 minimum GPA for admission
Program-Specific Admission Factors: Some programs require portfolios and/or writing samples.

EMPLOYMENT INFORMATION
Placement Office Available? Yes.

UNIVERSITY OF MASSACHUSETTS—AMHERST
College of Natural Resources & the Environment

Address: 140 Hicks Way, Amherst, MA 01003
Admissions Phone: 413-545-0721 · Admissions Fax: 413-577-0010
Admissions E-mail: gradinfo@resgs.umass.edu
Web Address: www.umass.edu/gradschool

INSTITUTIONAL INFORMATION
Public/private: Public. Students in Parent Institution: 22,509.

STUDENT INFORMATION
Total Students in Program: 4,721. % Full-time: 47. % Female: 52.

RESEARCH FACILITIES
Research Facilities: Population research institute, polymer research institute, environmental institute.

EXPENSES/FINANCIAL AID
Annual Tuition: In-state $5,193. / Out-of-state $11,032. Loans Range From: $1,000-$18,500. % Receiving Loans: 35.

ADMISSIONS INFORMATION
Application Fee: $40. Regular Application Deadline: 2/1. Regular Notification: Rolling. Transfer Students Accepted? No.
Required Admission Factors: GRE, letters of recommendation, transcript.
Other Admission Factors: 2.8 required for admission

EMPLOYMENT INFORMATION
Placement Office Available? Yes.

UNIVERSITY OF MASSACHUSETTS—AMHERST
College of Natural Sciences & Mathematics

Address: 140 Hicks Way, Amherst, MA 01003
Admissions Phone: 413-545-0721 · Admissions Fax: 413-577-0010
Admissions E-mail: gradinfo@resgs.umass.edu
Web Address: www.umass.edu/gradschool

INSTITUTIONAL INFORMATION
Public/private: Public. Students in Parent Institution: 22,509.

STUDENT INFORMATION
Total Students in Program: 4,721. % Full-time: 47. % Female: 52.

RESEARCH FACILITIES
Research Facilities: Population research institute, polymer research institute, environmental institute.

EXPENSES/FINANCIAL AID
Annual Tuition: In-state $5,193. / Out-of-state $11,032. Loans Range From: $1,000-$18,500. % Receiving Loans: 35.

ADMISSIONS INFORMATION
Application Fee: $40. Regular Application Deadline: 2/1. Regular Notification: Rolling. Transfer Students Accepted? No.
Required Admission Factors: Letters of recommendation, transcript.
Other Admission Factors: 2.8 minimum GPA required for admission

EMPLOYMENT INFORMATION
Placement Office Available? Yes.

UNIVERSITY OF MASSACHUSETTS—AMHERST
College of Social & Behavioral Sciences

Address: 140 Hicks Way, Amherst, MA 01003
Admissions Phone: 413-545-0721 · Admissions Fax: 413-577-0010
Admissions E-mail: gradinfo@resgs.umass.edu
Web Address: www.umass.edu/gradschool

INSTITUTIONAL INFORMATION
Public/private: Public. Students in Parent Institution: 22,509.

STUDENT INFORMATION
Total Students in Program: 4,721. % Full-time: 47. % Female: 52.

RESEARCH FACILITIES
Research Facilities: Population research institute, polymer research institute, environmental institute.

EXPENSES/FINANCIAL AID
Annual Tuition: In-state $5,193. / Out-of-state $11,032. Loans Range From: $1,000-$18,500. % Receiving Loans: 35.

ADMISSIONS INFORMATION
Application Fee: $40. Regular Application Deadline: 2/1. Transfer Students Accepted? No.
Required Admission Factors: Letters of recommendation, transcript.
Other Admission Factors: 2.8 required for admission

EMPLOYMENT INFORMATION
Placement Office Available? Yes.

UNIVERSITY OF MASSACHUSETTS—AMHERST
Isenberg School of Management

Address: 140 Hicks Way, Amherst, MA 01003
Admissions Phone: 413-545-0721 · **Admissions Fax:** 413-577-0010
Admissions E-mail: gradinfo@resgs.umass.edu
Web Address: www.umass.edu/gradschool

INSTITUTIONAL INFORMATION
Public/private: Public.

PROGRAMS
Masters offered in: Public administration.

EXPENSES/FINANCIAL AID
Annual Tuition: In-state $2,640. / Out-of-state $9,937. **Room & Board (On/off campus):** $6,189/$8,376. **Fees:** $4,113. **Books and Supplies:** $600. **% Receiving Financial Aid:** 60. **% Receiving Assistantships:** 95. **Types of Aid Available:** Fellowships, graduate assistantships. **Number of Fellowships Granted Each Year:** 1. **Average amount of individual fellowships per year:** $16,750. **Number of Teaching/Research Assistantships Granted Each Year:** 18. **Assistantship Compensation Includes:** Full tuition remission, salary/stipend. **Average Salary Stipend:** $5,600.

ADMISSIONS INFORMATION
Application Fee: $40. **Regular Application Deadline:** 2/1. **Regular Notification:** Rolling. **Transfer Students Accepted?** Yes. **Transfer Policy:** Not more than 6 credits of grade B or better may be transferred from other institutions with the consent of the department and approval of the graduate dean. These transfer credits must have been awarded within 3 years of a student's entrance into the masters degree program.
Required Admission Factors: Essays/personal statement, GRE, letters of recommendation, transcript. TOEFL test is required of international students.
Recommended Admission Factors: Interview.

EMPLOYMENT INFORMATION
% Employed Within Six Months: 90. **Rate of placement:** 100%. **Average starting salary:** $45,000.

UNIVERSITY OF MASSACHUSETTS—BOSTON
College of Arts & Sciences

Address: 100 Morrissey Boulevard, Boston, MA 02125-3393
Admissions Phone: 617-287-6000 · **Admissions Fax:** 617-287-6236

INSTITUTIONAL INFORMATION
Public/private: Public. **Evening Classes Available?** Yes. **Students in Parent Institution:** 12,923.

STUDENT INFORMATION
Total Students in Program: 3,112

RESEARCH FACILITIES
Research Facilities: 20 institutes and college-based centers.

EXPENSES/FINANCIAL AID
Annual Tuition: In-state $2,590. / Out-of-state $9,760. **Room & Board:** $1,000. **Fees:** $3,530. **Books and Supplies:** $750. **Grants Range From:** $200-$2,040. **Loans Range From:** $100-$18,500. **% Receiving Financial Aid:** 17. **% Receiving Scholarships/Grants:** 22. **% Receiving Loans:** 65. **% Receiving Assistantships:** 11. **Average student debt upon graduation:** $18,949. **Number of Teaching/Research Assistantships Granted Each Year:** 135.

ADMISSIONS INFORMATION
Application Fee: $25. **Transfer Students Accepted?** No. **Number of Applications Received:** 962. **% of Applicants Accepted:** 49. **% Accepted Who Enrolled:** 57.

Required Admission Factors: Essays/personal statement, letters of recommendation, transcript.
Other Admission Factors: Minimum 2.75 GPA required.
Program-Specific Admission Factors: Writing sample required of American studies and English program applicants. Resume required of clinical psychology program applicants.

EMPLOYMENT INFORMATION
Placement Office Available? Yes.

UNIVERSITY OF MASSACHUSETTS—BOSTON
College of Public & Community Service

Address: 100 Morrissey Boulevard, Boston, MA 02125-3393
Admissions Phone: 617-287-6000 · **Admissions Fax:** 617-287-6236
Admissions E-mail: bos.gadm@umb.edu

INSTITUTIONAL INFORMATION
Public/private: Public. **Evening Classes Available?** Yes. **Students in Parent Institution:** 12,923.

STUDENT INFORMATION
Total Students in Program: 3,112

RESEARCH FACILITIES
Research Facilities: 20 institutes and college-based centers.

EXPENSES/FINANCIAL AID
Annual Tuition: In-state $2,590. / Out-of-state $9,760. **Room & Board:** $1,000. **Fees:** $3,530. **Books and Supplies:** $750. **Grants Range From:** $200-$2,040. **Loans Range From:** $100-$18,500. **% Receiving Financial Aid:** 17. **% Receiving Scholarships/Grants:** 22. **% Receiving Loans:** 65. **% Receiving Assistantships:** 11. **Average student debt upon graduation:** $18,949. **Number of Teaching/Research Assistantships Granted Each Year:** 35.

ADMISSIONS INFORMATION
Application Fee: $25. **Transfer Students Accepted?** No. **Number of Applications Received:** 169. **% of Applicants Accepted:** 66. **% Accepted Who Enrolled:** 68.
Required Admission Factors: Essays/personal statement, letters of recommendation, transcript.
Other Admission Factors: Minimum 2.75 GPA required.
Program-Specific Admission Factors: GRE required of doctoral program in gerontology applicants. GRE or MAT required of dispute resolution program applicants. MAT required of human services program applicants.

EMPLOYMENT INFORMATION
Placement Office Available? Yes.

UNIVERSITY OF MASSACHUSETTS— DARTMOUTH
College of Arts & Sciences

Address: 285 Old Westport Road, North Dartmouth, MA 02747-2300
Admissions Phone: 508-999-8604 · **Admissions Fax:** 508-999-8183

INSTITUTIONAL INFORMATION
Public/private: Public. **Students in Parent Institution:** 7,122.

PROGRAMS
Masters offered in: Clinical psychology; Portuguese language and literature; psychology.

STUDENT INFORMATION
Total Students in Program: 699. **% Full-time:** 37. **% Female:** 53.

RESEARCH FACILITIES

Research Facilities: Robert F. Kennedy Assassination Archive, Center for Marine Science and Technology.

EXPENSES/FINANCIAL AID

Annual Tuition: In-state $2,071. / Out-of-state $8,099. **Room & Board (On/off campus):** $6,224/$5,071. **Books and Supplies:** $600. **% Receiving Financial Aid:** 15. **Average student debt upon graduation:** $9,425. **Number of Teaching/Research Assistantships Granted Each Year:** 110.

ADMISSIONS INFORMATION

Application Fee: $25. **Regular Notification:** Rolling. **Transfer Students Accepted?** Yes. **Number of Applications Received:** 119. **% of Applicants Accepted:** 67. **% Accepted Who Enrolled:** 52. **Average GRE Verbal:** 531. **Average GRE Quantitative:** 632. **Average GRE Analytical:** 643. **Required Admission Factors:** Essays/personal statement, letters of recommendation, transcript. **Recommended Admission Factors:** GRE, interview, GRE subject exam(s) in psychology.

EMPLOYMENT INFORMATION

Placement Office Available? Yes.

UNIVERSITY OF MASSACHUSETTS— DARTMOUTH
College of Visual & Performing Arts

Address: 285 Old Westport Road, North Dartmouth, MA 02747-2300
Admissions Phone: 508-999-8604 · **Admissions Fax:** 508-999-8183

INSTITUTIONAL INFORMATION

Public/private: Public. **Evening Classes Available?** Yes. **Students in Parent Institution:** 7,122.

STUDENT INFORMATION

Total Students in Program: 699. **% Full-time:** 37. **% Female:** 53.

RESEARCH FACILITIES

Research Facilities: Robert F. Kennedy Assassination Archive, Center for Marine Science and Technology.

EXPENSES/FINANCIAL AID

Annual Tuition: In-state $2,071. / Out-of-state $8,099. **Room & Board (On/off campus):** $6,224/$5,071. **Books and Supplies:** $600. **Number of Teaching/Research Assistantships Granted Each Year:** 37.

ADMISSIONS INFORMATION

Application Fee: $25. **Regular Notification:** Rolling. **Transfer Students Accepted?** No. **Number of Applications Received:** 83. **% of Applicants Accepted:** 61. **% Accepted Who Enrolled:** 53. **Required Admission Factors:** Essays/personal statement, letters of recommendation, transcript. **Other Admission Factors:** Minimum 3.0 GPA required.

EMPLOYMENT INFORMATION

Placement Office Available? Yes.

UNIVERSITY OF MASSACHUSETTS—LOWELL
College of Arts & Sciences

Address: One University Avenue, Lowell, MA 01854
Admissions Phone: 978-934-2380 or 800-656-GRAD · **Admissions Fax:** 978-934-3010

INSTITUTIONAL INFORMATION

Public/private: Public. **Evening Classes Available?** Yes. **Students in Parent Institution:** 9,562.

STUDENT INFORMATION

Total Students in Program: 2,503. **% Full-time:** 24. **% Female:** 46.

RESEARCH FACILITIES

Research Facilities: 30 research centers.

EXPENSES/FINANCIAL AID

Annual Tuition: In-state $1,610. / Out-of-state $6,000. **Books and Supplies:** $500.

ADMISSIONS INFORMATION

Application Fee: $20. **Regular Notification:** Rolling. **Transfer Students Accepted?** Yes. **Transfer Policy:** Maximum 12 credit hours may be transferred into masters programs; maximum 24 credit hours may be transferred. **Number of Applications Received:** 655. **% of Applicants Accepted:** 55. **Average GPA:** 3.0. **Required Admission Factors:** GRE, letters of recommendation, transcript. **Other Admission Factors:** Minimum 2.8 GPA required.

EMPLOYMENT INFORMATION

Placement Office Available? Yes.

THE UNIVERSITY OF MEMPHIS
College of Arts & Sciences

Address: Administration Building #317, Memphis, TN 38152
Admissions Phone: 901-678-2911 · **Admissions Fax:** 901-678-3003
Admissions E-mail: wcrump@adlan.memphis.edu

INSTITUTIONAL INFORMATION

Public/private: Public. **Evening Classes Available?** Yes. **Students in Parent Institution:** 19,986.

STUDENT INFORMATION

Total Students in Program: 4,265. **% Full-time:** 41. **% Female:** 58.

RESEARCH FACILITIES

Research Facilities: Center for Earthquake Research & Information, Center for Research on Women, Center for the Study of Higher Education, Institute of Egyptian Art & Archaeology, Speech & Hearing Center, Bureau of Business & Economic Research.

EXPENSES/FINANCIAL AID

Annual Tuition: In-state $3,410. / Out-of-state $8,670. **Room & Board:** $3,520. **Fees:** $68. **Books and Supplies:** $900. **Loans Range From:** $200-$18,500.

ADMISSIONS INFORMATION

Application Fee: $5. **Regular Notification:** Rolling. **Transfer Students Accepted?** Yes. **Required Admission Factors:** GRE, transcript. **Other Admission Factors:** Minimum 2.0 GPA required.

EMPLOYMENT INFORMATION

Placement Office Available? Yes.

THE UNIVERSITY OF MEMPHIS
School of Audiology & Speech-Language Pathology

Address: Administration Building #317, Memphis, TN 38152

INSTITUTIONAL INFORMATION

Public/private: Public. **Students in Parent Institution:** 19,986.

STUDENT INFORMATION

Total Students in Program: 4,265. **% Full-time:** 41. **% Female:** 58.

RESEARCH FACILITIES

Research Facilities: Center for Earthquake Research & Information, Center for Research on Women, Center for the Study of Higher Education, Institute of Egyptian Art & Archaeology, Speech & Hearing Center, Bureau of Business & Economic Research.

EXPENSES/FINANCIAL AID

Annual Tuition: In-state $3,410. / Out-of-state $8,670. **Room & Board:** $3,520. **Fees:** $68. **Books and Supplies:** $900. **Loans Range From:** $200-$18,500.

ADMISSIONS INFORMATION

Transfer Students Accepted? No.

EMPLOYMENT INFORMATION

Placement Office Available? Yes.

THE UNIVERSITY OF MEMPHIS
College of Communication & Fine Arts

Address: Administration Building #317, Memphis, TN 38152
Admissions Phone: 901-678-2911 · **Admissions Fax:** 901-678-3003
Admissions E-mail: wcrump@adlan.memphis.edu

INSTITUTIONAL INFORMATION

Public/private: Public. **Evening Classes Available?** Yes. **Students in Parent Institution:** 19,986.

STUDENT INFORMATION

Total Students in Program: 4,265. **% Full-time:** 41. **% Female:** 58.

RESEARCH FACILITIES

Research Facilities: Center for Earthquake Research & Information, Center for Research on Women, Center for the Study of Higher Education, Institute of Egyptian Art & Archaeology, Speech & Hearing Center, Bureau of Business & Economic Research.

EXPENSES/FINANCIAL AID

Annual Tuition: In-state $3,410. / Out-of-state $8,670. **Room & Board:** $3,520. **Fees:** $68. **Books and Supplies:** $900. **Loans Range From:** $200-$18,500.

ADMISSIONS INFORMATION

Application Fee: $5. **Regular Notification:** Rolling. **Transfer Students Accepted?** Yes.
Required Admission Factors: GRE, interview, transcript.

EMPLOYMENT INFORMATION

Placement Office Available? Yes.

UNIVERSITY OF MIAMI
College of Arts & Sciences

Address: PO Box 248004, Coral Gables, FL 33124-8004
Admissions Phone: 305-284-3188 · **Admissions Fax:** 305-284-4686
Admissions E-mail: gradadmin@mail.as.miami.edu · **Web Address:** www.as.miami.edu

INSTITUTIONAL INFORMATION

Public/private: Private (nonprofit). **Total Faculty:** 250. **% Faculty Female:** 32. **Students in Parent Institution:** 15,250.

PROGRAMS

Masters offered in: American history (United States), American literature (United States), biology/biological sciences, chemistry, clinical psychology, computer and information sciences, creative writing, English language and literature, English language and literature/letters, English literature (British and commonwealth), European history, fine/studio arts, geography, history,

international relations and affairs, Latin American studies, liberal arts and sciences/liberal studies, mathematics and statistics, mathematics, multi/interdisciplinary studies, natural resources/conservation, philosophy, physics, psychology, sociology. **Doctorate offered in:** See above.

STUDENT INFORMATION

Total Students in Program: 596. **% Full-time:** 83. **% Female:** 56. **% Minority:** 32. **% International:** 21.

EXPENSES/FINANCIAL AID

Annual Tuition: $20,714. **Room & Board:** $8,602. **Fees:** $100. **Books and Supplies:** $1,044. **Grants Range From:** $7,000-$17,000. **Types of Aid Available:** Graduate assistantships. **Number of Teaching/Research Assistantships Granted Each Year:** 358. **Assistantship Compensation Includes:** Full tuition remission, partial tuition remission, salary/stipend. **Average Salary Stipend:** $13,013.

ADMISSIONS INFORMATION

Application Fee: $50. **Regular Application Deadline:** 2/1. **Regular Notification:** Rolling. **Transfer Students Accepted?** Yes. **Number of Applications Received:** 1,001. **% of Applicants Accepted:** 27. **% Accepted Who Enrolled:** 54. **Average GPA:** 3.5. **Average GRE Verbal:** 548. **Average GRE Quantitative:** 645. **Average GRE Analytical:** 674. **Average GRE Analytical Writing:** 4.6.
Required Admission Factors: GRE, letters of recommendation, transcript. **Other Admission Factors:** Minimum 3.0 GPA and minimum combined GRE score of 1000 required.

EMPLOYMENT INFORMATION

Placement Office Available? Yes.

UNIVERSITY OF MIAMI
Rosenstiel School of Marine
& Atmospheric Science

Address: Graduate Studies Office, 4600 Rickenbacker Causeway, Miami, FL 33149
Admissions Phone: 305-361-4155 · **Admissions Fax:** 305-361-4771
Admissions E-mail: gso@rsmas.miami.edu · **Web Address:** www.rsmas.miami.edu

INSTITUTIONAL INFORMATION

Public/private: Private (nonprofit). **Total Faculty:** 112. **% Faculty Female:** 21. **% Faculty Part-time:** 1. **Student/faculty Ratio:** 2:1. **Students in Parent Institution:** 186.

PROGRAMS

Masters offered in: Acoustics; atmospheric chemistry and climatology; atmospheric physics and dynamics; atmospheric sciences and meteorology; atmospheric sciences and meteorology; environmental studies; geological and earth sciences/geosciences; geology/earth science; geophysics and seismology; hydrology and water resources science; meteorology; natural resource economics; natural resources management and policy; oceanography, chemical and physical; physics; water, wetlands, and marine resources management. **Doctorate offered in:** See above.

STUDENT INFORMATION

Total Students in Program: 186. **% Full-time:** 96. **% Female:** 48. **% Minority:** 8. **% International:** 27.

RESEARCH FACILITIES

Research Facilities: School-owned 96' research catamaran vessel (R/V F.G. Walton Smith), Center for Sustainable Fisheries, Pew Institute, Marine & Freshwater Biomedical Science Center, National Center for Caribbean Coral Reef Research, Center for Southeastern Tropical Advancement.

EXPENSES/FINANCIAL AID

Annual Tuition: $18,180. **Room & Board:** $17,000. **Fees:** $760. **Books and Supplies:** $200. **Grants Range From:** $7,000-$40,000. **Loans Range From:** $1,200-$18,500. **% Receiving Financial Aid:** 87. **Types of Aid Available:**

Fellowships, graduate assistantships, grants, institutional work-study, loans, scholarships. **Number of Fellowships Granted Each Year:** 1. **Average amount of individual fellowships per year:** $40,000. **Number of Teaching/Research Assistantships Granted Each Year:** 20. **Assistantship Compensation Includes:** Full tuition remission, salary/stipend. **Average Salary Stipend:** $20,000.

ADMISSIONS INFORMATION

Application Fee: $50. **Priority Application Deadline:** 1/1. **Regular Application Deadline:** 1/1. **Regular Notification:** Rolling. **Transfer Students Accepted?** Yes. **Transfer Policy:** Same as new applicants. **Number of Applications Received:** 270. **% of Applicants Accepted:** 30. **% Accepted Who Enrolled:** 58. **Average GPA:** 3.3. **Average GRE Verbal:** 526. **Average GRE Quantitative:** 677. **Average GRE Analytical:** 655.

Required Admission Factors: Essays/personal statement, GRE, letters of recommendation, transcript.

Other Admission Factors: Minimum 3.0 GPA and minimum 75th percentile GRE required.

EMPLOYMENT INFORMATION

% Employed Within Six Months: 95. **Average starting salary:** $40,000.

UNIVERSITY OF MIAMI
School of Communication

Address: PO Box 248127, Coral Gables, FL 33124
Admissions Phone: 305-284-5236 · **Admissions Fax:** 305-284-5205
Admissions E-mail: sumiller@miami.edu · **Web Address:** www.miami.edu/com

INSTITUTIONAL INFORMATION

Public/private: Private (nonprofit). **Evening Classes Available?** Yes. **Student/faculty Ratio:** 10:1. **Students in Parent Institution:** 13,963.

STUDENT INFORMATION

Total Students in Program: 3,246. **% Full-time:** 79. **% Female:** 51.

EXPENSES/FINANCIAL AID

Annual Tuition: $16,182. **Room & Board:** $7,400. **Fees:** $194. **Books and Supplies:** $934. **Grants Range From:** $7,000-$17,000. **% Receiving Financial Aid:** 35. **Number of Teaching/Research Assistantships Granted Each Year:** 34.

ADMISSIONS INFORMATION

Application Fee: $50. **Priority Application Deadline:** 3/1. **Regular Notification:** Rolling. **Transfer Students Accepted?** Yes. **Transfer Policy:** Maximum 6 credit hours may be transferred into masters programs that require less than 36 credits. **Number of Applications Received:** 231. **% of Applicants Accepted:** 65. **% Accepted Who Enrolled:** 37. **Average GPA:** 3.23. **Average GRE Verbal:** 510. **Average GRE Quantitative:** 580. **Average GRE Analytical:** 569.

Required Admission Factors: GRE, letters of recommendation, transcript. **Program-Specific Admission Factors:** Minimum GRE score of 1000 (Verbal and Quantitative) and minimum 3.0 GPA required of masters program applicants. Minimum GRE score of 1100 (Verbal and Quantitative), minimum 3.3 undergraduate GPA, and minimum 3.5 graduate GPA required of doctoral program applicants.

EMPLOYMENT INFORMATION

Placement Office Available? Yes.

UNIVERSITY OF MIAMI
School of International Studies

Address: 210 Ferre Building
PO Box 248125, Coral Gables, FL 33124-2220
Admissions Phone: 305-284-4173 · **Admissions Fax:** 305-284-4406

INSTITUTIONAL INFORMATION

Public/private: Private (nonprofit). **Evening Classes Available?** Yes. **Students in Parent Institution:** 13,963.

STUDENT INFORMATION

Total Students in Program: 3,246. **% Full-time:** 79. **% Female:** 51.

EXPENSES/FINANCIAL AID

Annual Tuition: $16,182. **Room & Board:** $7,400. **Fees:** $194. **Books and Supplies:** $934. **Grants Range From:** $7,000-$17,000.

ADMISSIONS INFORMATION

Application Fee: $50. **Regular Notification:** Rolling. **Transfer Students Accepted?** Yes. **Transfer Policy:** Maximum of 6 credit hours may be transferred into masters programs. **Number of Applications Received:** 115. **% of Applicants Accepted:** 79. **% Accepted Who Enrolled:** 32. **Average GRE Verbal:** 523. **Average GRE Quantitative:** 579. **Average GRE Analytical:** 590.

Required Admission Factors: Essays/personal statement, GRE, letters of recommendation, transcript.

Other Admission Factors: Minimum 3.0 GPA required.

EMPLOYMENT INFORMATION

Placement Office Available? Yes.

UNIVERSITY OF MIAMI
School of Music

Address: 210 Ferre Building, PO Box 248125, Coral Gables, FL 33124-2220
Admissions Phone: 305-284-2446 · **Admissions Fax:** 305-284-6475
Admissions E-mail: ed.asmus@miami.edu
Web Address: http://www.music.miami.edu/gradstudies

INSTITUTIONAL INFORMATION

Public/private: Private (nonprofit). **Evening Classes Available?** Yes. **Student/faculty Ratio:** 5:1. **Students in Parent Institution:** 13,963.

STUDENT INFORMATION

Total Students in Program: 3,246. **% Full-time:** 79. **% Female:** 51.

EXPENSES/FINANCIAL AID

Annual Tuition: $16,182. **Room & Board:** $7,400. **Fees:** $194. **Books and Supplies:** $934. **Grants Range From:** $7,000-$17,000. **% Receiving Financial Aid:** 65. **Number of Fellowships Granted Each Year:** 2. **Average amount of individual fellowships per year:** $27,600. **Number of Teaching/Research Assistantships Granted Each Year:** 58. **Average Salary Stipend:** $7,400.

ADMISSIONS INFORMATION

Application Fee: $65. **Regular Notification:** Rolling. **Transfer Students Accepted?** Yes. **Number of Applications Received:** 179. **% of Applicants Accepted:** 68. **% Accepted Who Enrolled:** 63. **Average GPA:** 3.57. **Average GRE Verbal:** 480. **Average GRE Quantitative:** 573. **Average GRE Analytical:** 575.

Required Admission Factors: Letters of recommendation, transcript. **Other Admission Factors:** Minimum 3.0 GPA required.

Program-Specific Admission Factors: GRE required for all doctoral and MMus programs except performance. Writing portfolio required of composition program applicants.

EMPLOYMENT INFORMATION
Placement Office Available? Yes.

UNIVERSITY OF MICHIGAN—ANN ARBOR
College of Literature, Science, & the Arts

Address: Ann Arbor, MI 48109

INSTITUTIONAL INFORMATION
Public/private: Public. Students in Parent Institution: 40,393.

STUDENT INFORMATION
Total Students in Program: 13,691. % Full-time: 82. % Female: 42.

RESEARCH FACILITIES
Research Facilities: The Insititute for Social Research.

EXPENSES/FINANCIAL AID
Annual Tuition: In-state $11,654. / Out-of-state $23,132. Books and Supplies: $860.

ADMISSIONS INFORMATION
Regular Application Deadline: 12/15. Transfer Students Accepted? No.

EMPLOYMENT INFORMATION
Placement Office Available? Yes.

UNIVERSITY OF MICHIGAN—ANN ARBOR
Rackham School of Graduate Studies

Address: 915 East Washington Street, Ann Arbor, MI 48109-1070
Admissions Phone: 734-764-8129 · **Admissions Fax:** 734-647-7740
Admissions E-mail: rackadmis@umich.edu · **Web Address:** www.rackham.umich.edu/

INSTITUTIONAL INFORMATION
Public/private: Public. Students in Parent Institution: 40,393.

STUDENT INFORMATION
Total Students in Program: 13,691. % Full-time: 82. % Female: 42.

RESEARCH FACILITIES
Research Facilities: The Insititute for Social Research.

EXPENSES/FINANCIAL AID
Annual Tuition: In-state $11,654. / Out-of-state $23,132. Books and Supplies: $860.

ADMISSIONS INFORMATION
Application Fee: $60. Regular Application Deadline: 12/15. Transfer Students Accepted? Yes. Transfer Policy: No transfer of credit hours is accepted for doctoral programs.
Required Admission Factors: Essays/personal statement, GRE, letters of recommendation, transcript.

EMPLOYMENT INFORMATION
Placement Office Available? Yes.

UNIVERSITY OF MICHIGAN—ANN ARBOR
School of Art & Design

Address: Ann Arbor, MI 48109
Admissions Phone: 734-763-5247 · **Admissions Fax:** 734-936-0469

INSTITUTIONAL INFORMATION
Public/private: Public. Students in Parent Institution: 40,393.

STUDENT INFORMATION
Total Students in Program: 13,691. % Full-time: 82. % Female: 42.

RESEARCH FACILITIES
Research Facilities: The Insititute for Social Research.

EXPENSES/FINANCIAL AID
Annual Tuition: In-state $11,654. / Out-of-state $23,132. Books and Supplies: $860. Number of Teaching/Research Assistantships Granted Each Year: 30. Average Salary Stipend: $2,484.

ADMISSIONS INFORMATION
Application Fee: $55. Transfer Students Accepted? Yes. Number of Applications Received: 94. % of Applicants Accepted: 30. % Accepted Who Enrolled: 68.
Required Admission Factors: Essays/personal statement, letters of recommendation, transcript.
Other Admission Factors: Minimum 3.0 GPA required.

EMPLOYMENT INFORMATION
Placement Office Available? Yes.

UNIVERSITY OF MICHIGAN—ANN ARBOR
School of Information

Address: 403B West Hall, 550 East University Avenue, Ann Arbor, MI 48109-1092
Admissions Phone: 734-763-2285 · **Admissions Fax:** 734-615-3587
Admissions E-mail: si.admissions@umich.edu

INSTITUTIONAL INFORMATION
Public/private: Public. Evening Classes Available? Yes. Students in Parent Institution: 40,393.

PROGRAMS
Masters offered in: Animation, interactive technology, video graphics and special effects; audiovisual communications technologies/technicians; business, management, marketing, and related support services; business/corporate communications; business/managerial economics; communications technologies and support services; communications technology/technician; communications, journalism, and related fields; computer and information sciences and support services; computer and information sciences; computer and information systems security; computer graphics; computer software and media applications; computer systems analysis/analyst; computer systems networking and telecommunications; computer/information technology services administration and management; cultural resources management and policy analysis; data warehousing/mining and database administration; development economics and international development; digital communications and media/multimedia; E-commerce/electronic commerce; entrepreneurship/entrepreneurial studies; graphic communications; graphic communications; historic preservation and conservation; historic preservation and conservation; information resources management/CIO training; information science/studies; information technology; international marketing; knowledge management; library science; library science/librarianship; management information systems and services; management information systems; management science; management sciences and quantitative methods; marketing research; marketing; marketing/marketing management; multi/interdisciplinary studies; museology/museum studies; nonprofit/public/organizational management; organizational communication; organizational communications, public relations, and advertising; prepress/desktop publishing and digital imaging design; public relations/image management; publishing; radio, television, and digital communications; sales, distribution, and marketing operations; science, technology and society; social sciences; social sciences; systems administration/administrator; systems science and theory; web page, digital/multimedia and information resources design; web/multimedia management and webmaster. Doctorate offered in: See above.

STUDENT INFORMATION
Total Students in Program: 13,691. % Full-time: 82. % Female: 42.

RESEARCH FACILITIES
Research Facilities: The Insititute for Social Research.

EXPENSES/FINANCIAL AID
Annual Tuition: In-state $11,654. / Out-of-state $23,132. Books and Supplies: $860.

ADMISSIONS INFORMATION
Application Fee: $60. Priority Application Deadline: 2/1. Regular Application Deadline: 5/1. Regular Notification: Rolling. Transfer Students Accepted? Yes. Number of Applications Received: 247. % of Applicants Accepted: 84. % Accepted Who Enrolled: 41. Average GPA: 3.2.
Required Admission Factors: Essays/personal statement, GRE, letters of recommendation, transcript.
Other Admission Factors: Minimum 3.0 GPA and resume required.

EMPLOYMENT INFORMATION
Placement Office Available? Yes.

UNIVERSITY OF MICHIGAN—ANN ARBOR
School of Music

Address: 1100 Baits Drive, 2290 Moore Building, Ann Arbor, MI 48109
Admissions Phone: 734-764-0593 · Admissions Fax: 734-763-5097
Admissions E-mail: music.admissions@umich.edu
Web Address: www.music.umich.edu

INSTITUTIONAL INFORMATION
Public/private: Public. Students in Parent Institution: 40,393.

PROGRAMS
Masters offered in: Conducting; jazz/jazz studies; music pedagogy; music performance; music theory and composition; music; piano and organ; violin, viola, guitar, and other stringed instruments; voice and opera. Doctorate offered in: Conducting; music pedagogy; music performance; music theory and composition; music; musicology and ethnomusicology; piano and organ; violin, viola, guitar, and other stringed instruments; voice and opera.

EXPENSES/FINANCIAL AID
Annual Tuition: In-state $13,098. / Out-of-state $26,342. Room & Board: $8,938. Books and Supplies: $1,066. Types of Aid Available: Fellowships, graduate assistantships, institutional work-study, scholarships.

ADMISSIONS INFORMATION
Application Fee: $75. Priority Application Deadline: 12/1. Regular Application Deadline: 12/1. Regular Notification: Rolling. Transfer Students Accepted? Yes.
Required Admission Factors: Essays/personal statement, letters of recommendation, transcript.
Other Admission Factors: Minimum 3.0 GPA required. TOEFL—588 paper/237 computer.
Program-Specific Admission Factors: Audition and/or interview required of music program applicants.

UNIVERSITY OF MICHIGAN—ANN ARBOR
School of Public Policy

Address: Ann Arbor, MI 48109

INSTITUTIONAL INFORMATION
Public/private: Public. Students in Parent Institution: 40,393.

STUDENT INFORMATION

Total Students in Program: 13,691. % Full-time: 82. % Female: 42.

RESEARCH FACILITIES
Research Facilities: The Insititute for Social Research.

EXPENSES/FINANCIAL AID
Annual Tuition: In-state $11,654. / Out-of-state $23,132. Books and Supplies: $860.

ADMISSIONS INFORMATION
Transfer Students Accepted? No.

EMPLOYMENT INFORMATION
Placement Office Available? Yes.

UNIVERSITY OF MICHIGAN—ANN ARBOR
School of Social Work

Address: 1080 South University, Room 1748, Ann Arbor, MI 48109-1106
Admissions Phone: 734-764-3309 · Admissions Fax: 734-936-1961
Admissions E-mail: ssw.msw.info@umich.edu · Web Address: www.ssw.umich.edu

INSTITUTIONAL INFORMATION
Public/private: Public. Students in Parent Institution: 40,393.

PROGRAMS
Masters offered in: Clinical/medical social work.

STUDENT INFORMATION
Total Students in Program: 13,691. % Full-time: 82. % Female: 42.

RESEARCH FACILITIES
Research Facilities: The Insititute for Social Research.

EXPENSES/FINANCIAL AID
Annual Tuition: In-state $11,654. / Out-of-state $23,132. Books and Supplies: $860.

ADMISSIONS INFORMATION
Application Fee: $50. Priority Application Deadline: 3/1. Regular Application Deadline: 6/1. Regular Notification: Rolling. Transfer Students Accepted? Yes. Transfer Policy: Must submit the following additional materials: 1) transfer statement indicating the reasons for why they are requesting transfer from one MSW program to another, 2) recommendation from faculty advisor of the prior MSW program, and 3) copy of field work evaluations, if enrolled in field work in previous MSW program.
Required Admission Factors: Essays/personal statement, letters of recommendation, transcript.
Other Admission Factors: Prior academic record must reflect a liberal arts perspective including 20 academic semester credits in psychology, sociology, anthropology, economincs, history, political science, government, and/or languages.
Program-Specific Admission Factors: Admission to the MSW degree program is possible for a limited number of persons who do not hold a baccalaureate degree.

EMPLOYMENT INFORMATION
Placement Office Available? Yes.

UNIVERSITY OF MICHIGAN—DEARBORN
College of Arts, Sciences, & Letters

Address: 4901 Evergreen Road, 1080 AB, Dearborn, MI 48128-1491
Admissions Phone: 313-593-1183 · Admissions Fax: 313-593-5552
Admissions E-mail: ehiggs@umd.umich.edu

INSTITUTIONAL INFORMATION
Public/private: Public. Evening Classes Available? Yes. Students in Parent Institution: 8,484.

STUDENT INFORMATION
Total Students in Program: 1,790. % Full-time: 4. % Female: 40.

RESEARCH FACILITIES
Research Facilities: Environmental Center, numerous engineering labs.

EXPENSES/FINANCIAL AID
Annual Tuition: In-state $5,511./Out-of-state $14,320. Books and Supplies: $600. Grants Range From: $1,000-$3,000. Loans: $18,500. % Receiving Financial Aid: 2.

ADMISSIONS INFORMATION
Application Fee: $55. Regular Notification: Rolling. Transfer Students Accepted? Yes. Number of Applications Received: 19. % of Applicants Accepted: 100. % Accepted Who Enrolled: 79. Average GPA: 3.3. Required Admission Factors: Essays/personal statement, interview, transcript.
Other Admission Factors: Minimum 3.0 GPA required in last 60 credit hours.

EMPLOYMENT INFORMATION
Placement Office Available? Yes. % of masters grads employed in their field upon graduation: 95. Rate of placement: 95%.

UNIVERSITY OF MICHIGAN—FLINT
Rackham School of Graduate Studies

Address: 303 East Kearsley, Flint, MI 48502-2186
Admissions Phone: 810-762-3171 · Admissions Fax: 810-766-6789

INSTITUTIONAL INFORMATION
Public/private: Public. Evening Classes Available? Yes. Students in Parent Institution: 6,316.

STUDENT INFORMATION
Total Students in Program: 530. % Full-time: 18. % Female: 48.

EXPENSES/FINANCIAL AID
Annual Tuition: In-state $4,330./Out-of-State $4,763. Number of Fellowships Granted Each Year: 4.

ADMISSIONS INFORMATION
Application Fee: $55. Transfer Students Accepted? No. Number of Applications Received: 23. % of Applicants Accepted: 91. % Accepted Who Enrolled: 86. Average GPA: 3.1.
Required Admission Factors: Essays/personal statement, transcript.
Other Admission Factors: Minimum 3.0 GPA required.
Program-Specific Admission Factors: Knowledge of the operation of public institutions, microeconomic principles, and analytical tools required masters in public administration program applicants. Minimum 24 hours of undergraduate course work in the humanities and social sciences required of masters in liberal studies program.

EMPLOYMENT INFORMATION
Placement Office Available? Yes.

UNIVERSITY OF MINNESOTA—DULUTH
College of Liberal Arts

Address: 431 Darland Administration, Duluth, MN 55812

INSTITUTIONAL INFORMATION
Public/private: Public. Students in Parent Institution: 9,850.

STUDENT INFORMATION
Total Students in Program: 667. % Full-time: 85. % Female: 56.

RESEARCH FACILITIES
Research Facilities: Large Lakes Observatory, sea grant.

EXPENSES/FINANCIAL AID
Annual Tuition: In-state $5,745. / Out-of-state $11,480. Room & Board: $6,000. Fees: $1,650. Books and Supplies: $1,800. % Receiving Scholarships/Grants: 30. % Receiving Loans: 25. % Receiving Assistantships: 43.

ADMISSIONS INFORMATION
Transfer Students Accepted? No.

EMPLOYMENT INFORMATION
Placement Office Available? Yes.

UNIVERSITY OF MINNESOTA—DULUTH
Graduate School

Address: 431 Darland Administration, Duluth, MN 55812

INSTITUTIONAL INFORMATION
Public/private: Public. Students in Parent Institution: 9,850.

STUDENT INFORMATION
Total Students in Program: 667. % Full-time: 85. % Female: 56.

RESEARCH FACILITIES
Research Facilities: Large Lakes Observatory, sea grant.

EXPENSES/FINANCIAL AID
Annual Tuition: In-state $5,745. / Out-of-state $11,480. Room & Board: $6,000. Fees: $1,650. Books and Supplies: $1,800. % Receiving Scholarships/Grants: 30. % Receiving Loans: 25. % Receiving Assistantships: 43.

ADMISSIONS INFORMATION
Transfer Students Accepted? No.

EMPLOYMENT INFORMATION
Placement Office Available? Yes.

UNIVERSITY OF MINNESOTA—DULUTH
School of Fine Arts

Address: 431 Darland Administration, Duluth, MN 55812

INSTITUTIONAL INFORMATION
Public/private: Public. Students in Parent Institution: 9,850.

STUDENT INFORMATION
Total Students in Program: 667. % Full-time: 85. % Female: 56.

RESEARCH FACILITIES
Research Facilities: Large Lakes Observatory, sea grant.

EXPENSES/FINANCIAL AID
Annual Tuition: In-state $5,745. / Out-of-state $11,480. Room & Board: $6,000. Fees: $1,650. Books and Supplies: $1,800. % Receiving Scholarships/Grants: 30. % Receiving Loans: 25. % Receiving Assistantships: 43.

ADMISSIONS INFORMATION
Transfer Students Accepted? No.

EMPLOYMENT INFORMATION
Placement Office Available? Yes.

UNIVERSITY OF MISSOURI—COLUMBIA
College of Arts & Science

Address: 210 Jesse Hall, University of Missouri—Columbia, Columbia, MO 65211
Admissions Phone: 573-882-6311 · **Admissions Fax:** 573-884-5454
Admissions E-mail: gradadmin@missouri.edu
Web Address: http://coas.missouri.edu/

INSTITUTIONAL INFORMATION
Public/private: Public. **Students in Parent Institution:** 25,398.

PROGRAMS
Masters offered in: Anthropology, applied mathematics, chemistry, economics, English language and literature, French studies, geography, geology/earth science, German studies, history, mass communications/media studies, mathematics, music/music and performing arts studies, philosophy, physics, political science and government, psychology, religion/religious studies, Russian studies, sociology, Spanish and Iberian studies, statistics, visual and performing arts. **Doctorate offered in:** See above.

STUDENT INFORMATION
Total Students in Program: 1,022. **% Full-time:** 60. **% Female:** 44.

RESEARCH FACILITIES
Research Facilities: Capsule Pipeline Research Center, Center for Surface Science and Plasma Technology, Power Electronics Research Center, University of Missouri Research Reactor Center, John M. Dalton Cardiovascular Research Center.

EXPENSES/FINANCIAL AID
Annual Tuition: In-state $5,306. / Out-of-state $8,048. **Fees:** $553. **Books and Supplies:** $746. **Types of Aid Available:** Fellowships, graduate assistantships, grants, loans, scholarships.

ADMISSIONS INFORMATION
Application Fee: $45. **Regular Application Deadline:** 1/1. **Regular Notification:** Rolling. **Transfer Students Accepted?** Yes. **Transfer Policy:** Admission requirements vary by department.
Required Admission Factors: Essays/personal statement, letters of recommendation, transcript.
Other Admission Factors: Minimum requirements vary by department.

UNIVERSITY OF MISSOURI—COLUMBIA
College of Human Environmental Sciences

Address: 210 Jesse Hall, University of Missouri—Columbia, Columbia, MO 65211
Admissions Phone: 573-882-6311 · **Admissions Fax:** 573-884-5454
Admissions E-mail: gradadmin@missouri.edu
Web Address: http://web.missouri.edu/~hes/

INSTITUTIONAL INFORMATION
Public/private: Public. **Students in Parent Institution:** 25,398.

PROGRAMS
Masters offered in: Apparel and textiles, architecture (BArch, BA/BS, MArch, MA/MS, PhD), family and consumer sciences/human sciences, human nutrition, work and family studies. **Doctorate offered in:** Apparel and textiles, architecture (BArch, BA/BS, MArch, MA/MS, PhD), family and consumer sciences/human sciences, human nutrition, work and family studies.

STUDENT INFORMATION
Total Students in Program: 120. **% Full-time:** 70. **% Female:** 66.

RESEARCH FACILITIES
Research Facilities: Capsule Pipeline Research Center, Center for Surface

Science and Plasma Technology, Power Electronics Research Center, University of Missouri Research Reactor Center, John M. Dalton Cardiovascular Research Center, Industrial and Technological Development.

EXPENSES/FINANCIAL AID
Annual Tuition: In-state $5,306. / Out-of-state $8,048. **Fees:** $553. **Books and Supplies:** $746. **% Receiving Financial Aid:** 20. **Types of Aid Available:** Fellowships, graduate assistantships, grants, loans, scholarships. **Average amount of individual fellowships per year:** $5,000. **Number of Teaching/Research Assistantships Granted Each Year:** 20. **Average Salary Stipend:** $5,000.

ADMISSIONS INFORMATION
Application Fee: $45. **Regular Notification:** Rolling. **Transfer Students Accepted?** Yes.
Required Admission Factors: GRE, letters of recommendation, transcript.
Other Admission Factors: Minimum GRE score of 1500 and minimum 3.0 GPA required.
Program-Specific Admission Factors: Portfolio required of design program applicants.

UNIVERSITY OF MISSOURI—COLUMBIA
School of Accountancy

Address: 210 Jesse Hall, University of Missouri—Columbia, Columbia, MO 65211
Admissions Phone: 573-882-6311 · **Admissions Fax:** 573-884-5454
Admissions E-mail: gradadmin@missouri.edu
Web Address: http://business.missouri.edu/43/default.aspx

INSTITUTIONAL INFORMATION
Public/private: Public. **Students in Parent Institution:** 25,398.

PROGRAMS
Masters offered in: Accounting. **Doctorate offered in:** Accounting.

STUDENT INFORMATION
Total Students in Program: 309. **% Full-time:** 86. **% Female:** 35.

RESEARCH FACILITIES
Research Facilities: Capsule Pipeline Research Center, Center for Surface Science and Plasma Technology, Power Electronics Research Center, University of Missouri Research Reactor Center, John M. Dalton Cardiovascular Research Center, Industrial and Technological Development.

EXPENSES/FINANCIAL AID
Annual Tuition: In-state $5,306. / Out-of-state $8,048. **Fees:** $553. **Books and Supplies:** $746. **% Receiving Financial Aid:** 100. **Types of Aid Available:** Graduate assistantships, grants, loans, scholarships. **Number of Teaching/Research Assistantships Granted Each Year:** 25.

ADMISSIONS INFORMATION
Application Fee: $45. **Transfer Students Accepted?** Yes. **Transfer Policy:** Maximum 6 credit hours may be transferred into masters program.
Required Admission Factors: Essays/personal statement, GMAT, letters of recommendation, transcript.
Program-Specific Admission Factors: Minimum 3.0 GPA and minimum GMAT score of 600 required of masters program applicants. Minimum 3.5 GPA, minimum GMAT score of 650 and 3 letters of recommendation required of doctoral program applicants.

EMPLOYMENT INFORMATION
Placement Office Available? Yes.

UNIVERSITY OF MISSOURI—COLUMBIA
School of Journalism

Address: 210 Jesse Hall, University of Missouri-Columbia, Columbia, MO 65211
Admissions Phone: 573-882-6311 · **Admissions Fax:** 573-884-5454
Admissions E-mail: gradadmin@missouri.edu
Web Address: http://journalism.missouri.edu/

INSTITUTIONAL INFORMATION
Public/private: Public. **Students in Parent Institution:** 25,398.

PROGRAMS
Masters offered in: Broadcast journalism; journalism; journalism, mass communications/media studies; photojournalism. **Doctorate offered in:** Broadcast journalism; journalism; journalism, mass communications/media studies; photojournalism.

STUDENT INFORMATION
Total Students in Program: 246. **% Full-time:** 70. **% Female:** 62.

RESEARCH FACILITIES
Research Facilities: Capsule Pipeline Research Center, Center for Surface Science and Plasma Technology, Power Electronics Research Center, University of Missouri Research Reactor Center, John M. Dalton Cardiovascular Research Center, Industrial and Technological Development.

EXPENSES/FINANCIAL AID
Annual Tuition: In-state $5,306. / Out-of-state $8,048. **Fees:** $553. **Books and Supplies:** $746. **Types of Aid Available:** Fellowships, graduate assistantships, grants, loans, scholarships.

ADMISSIONS INFORMATION
Application Fee: $45. **Transfer Students Accepted?** Yes. **Transfer Policy:** Maximum 6 credit hours may be transferred with approval.
Required Admission Factors: Essays/personal statement, GRE, letters of recommendation, transcript.
Other Admission Factors: Minimum GRE Verbal and Quantitative score of 1000 and minimum 3.0 GPA on last 60 credit hours required.

EMPLOYMENT INFORMATION
Placement Office Available? Yes. **% of masters/doctoralgrads employed in their field upon graduation:** 45/95.

UNIVERSITY OF MISSOURI—KANSAS CITY
College of Arts & Sciences

Address: 5100 Rock Hill Road, Kansas City, MO 64110
Admissions Phone: 816-235-1136 · **Admissions Fax:** 816-235-5191
Admissions E-mail: college@umkc.edu
Web Address: http://iml.umkc.edu/a&s/

INSTITUTIONAL INFORMATION
Public/private: Public. **Evening Classes Available?** Yes.

PROGRAMS
Masters offered in: Analytical chemistry; art history, criticism, and conservation; chemistry; criminal justice/law enforcement administration; drama and dramatics/theater arts; economics; English language and literature; history; inorganic chemistry; liberal arts and sciences/liberal studies; mathematics; organic chemistry; physical and theoretical chemistry; physics; playwriting and screenwriting; political science and government; polymer chemistry; psychology; romance languages, literatures, and linguistics; social work; sociology; statistics; technical theater/theater design and technology. **Doctorate offered in:** See above.

EXPENSES/FINANCIAL AID
Annual Tuition: In-state $4,258. / Out-of-state $7,242. **Room & Board (On/off campus):** $7,270/$7,130. **Fees:** $429. **Books and Supplies:** $880. **Grants Range From:** $100-$31,476. **Loans Range From:** $1,000-$44,187. **% Receiving Financial Aid:** 40. **% Receiving Scholarships/Grants:** 31. **% Receiving Loans:** 91. **Types of Aid Available:** Graduate assistantships, grants, institutional work-study, loans, scholarships.

ADMISSIONS INFORMATION
Application Fee: $35. **Regular Application Deadline:** 8/22. **Transfer Students Accepted?** Yes. **Transfer Policy:** Maximum 6 credit hours may be transferred into most programs.
Required Admission Factors: Transcript.
Other Admission Factors: Scores, requirements, and application deadlines are different from department to department. Please contact the Office of Admissions at 816-235-1111 or e-mail us at admit@umkc.edu for information.

EMPLOYMENT INFORMATION
Placement Office Available? Yes.

UNIVERSITY OF MISSOURI—KANSAS CITY
Conservatory of Music

Address: 5100 Rock Hill Road, Kansas City, MO 64110
Admissions Phone: 816-235-2900 · **Admissions Fax:** 816-235-5269
Admissions E-mail: elswickj@umkc.edu · **Web Address:** www.umkc.edu/conservatory

INSTITUTIONAL INFORMATION
Public/private: Public. **Students in Parent Institution:** 14,244.

PROGRAMS
Masters offered in: Conducting; music history, literature, and theory; music pedagogy; music performance; music theory and composition; music; music and performing arts studies; piano and organ; violin, viola, guitar, and other stringed instruments; voice and opera. **Doctorate offered in:** Conducting; music pedagogy; music performance; music; music and performing arts studies; piano and organ; violin, viola, guitar, and other stringed instruments; voice and opera.

STUDENT INFORMATION
Total Students in Program: 3,263. **% Full-time:** 31. **% Female:** 61.

EXPENSES/FINANCIAL AID
Annual Tuition: In-state $4,258. / Out-of-state $7,242. **Room & Board:** $7,270. **Fees:** $429. **Books and Supplies:** $880. **Grants Range From:** $100-$31,476. **Loans Range From:** $1,000-$44,187. **% Receiving Financial Aid:** 40. **% Receiving Scholarships/Grants:** 31. **% Receiving Loans:** 91. **Types of Aid Available:** Graduate assistantships, grants, institutional work-study, loans, scholarships. **Number of Fellowships Granted Each Year:** 12. **Average amount of individual fellowships per year:** $7,000. **Number of Teaching/Research Assistantships Granted Each Year:** 40. **Average Salary Stipend:** $4,500.

ADMISSIONS INFORMATION
Application Fee: $35. **Priority Application Deadline:** 2/1. **Regular Application Deadline:** 8/22. **Regular Notification:** Rolling. **Transfer Students Accepted?** Yes. **Transfer Policy:** Letters of recommendation required of transfer applicants. **Number of Applications Received:** 210. **% of Applicants Accepted:** 68. **Average GPA:** 3.0.
Required Admission Factors: Interview, transcript.
Program-Specific Admission Factors: Portfolio, performance and/or papers required for MA program applicants.

EMPLOYMENT INFORMATION
Placement Office Available? Yes.

UNIVERSITY OF MISSOURI—KANSAS CITY
School of Biological Sciences

Address: 5100 Rock Hill Road, Kansas City, MO 64110
Admissions Phone: 816-235-5246 · **Admissions Fax:** 816-235-5158
Admissions E-mail: SBS-grad@umkc.edu · **Web Address:** www.umkc.edu/sbs

INSTITUTIONAL INFORMATION
Public/private: Public. **Students in Parent Institution:** 14,244.

PROGRAMS
Masters offered in: Biochemistry; molecular biology.

STUDENT INFORMATION
Total Students in Program: 3,263. **% Full-time:** 31. **% Female:** 61.

EXPENSES/FINANCIAL AID
Annual Tuition: In-state $4,258. / Out-of-state $7,242. **Room & Board (On/ off campus):** $7,270/$7,130. **Fees:** $429. **Books and Supplies:** $880. **Grants Range From:** $100-$31,476. **Loans Range From:** $1,000-$44,187. **% Receiving Financial Aid:** 30. **% Receiving Scholarships/Grants:** 31. **% Receiving Loans:** 91. **Types of Aid Available:** Graduate assistantships, grants, institutional work-study, loans, scholarships. **Number of Teaching/Research Assistantships Granted Each Year:** 20.

ADMISSIONS INFORMATION
Application Fee: $35. **Regular Application Deadline:** 8/22. **Regular Notification:** Rolling. **Transfer Students Accepted?** Yes. **Number of Applications Received:** 48. **% of Applicants Accepted:** 33. **Average GPA:** 3.0. **Average GRE Verbal:** 475. **Average GRE Quantitative:** 670. **Average GRE Analytical:** 640.
Required Admission Factors: Essays/personal statement, GRE, letters of recommendation, transcript.
Other Admission Factors: Minimum GRE score of 1500 and minimum 3.0 GPA required.
Program-Specific Admission Factors: Interview required of biology program applicants.

EMPLOYMENT INFORMATION
Placement Office Available? Yes.

UNIVERSITY OF MISSOURI—KANSAS CITY
School of Graduate Studies

Address: 5100 Rock Hill Road, Kansas City, MO 64110
Admissions Phone: 816-235-1161 · **Admissions Fax:** 816-235-1057
Admissions E-mail: graduate@umkc.edu · **Web Address:** www.umkc.edu/sgs

INSTITUTIONAL INFORMATION
Public/private: Public. **Students in Parent Institution:** 14,244.

PROGRAMS
Masters offered in: Pharmacy (PharmD, BS/BPharm). **Doctorate offered in:** Cell/cellular biology and histology, chemistry, clinical psychology, community psychology, computer programming/programmer, economics, education, engineering, English composition, English language and literature.

STUDENT INFORMATION
Total Students in Program: 3,263. **% Full-time:** 31. **% Female:** 61.

EXPENSES/FINANCIAL AID
Annual Tuition: In-state $4,258. / Out-of-state $7,242. **Room & Board:** $7,270. **Fees:** $429. **Books and Supplies:** $880. **Grants Range From:** $100-$31,476. **Loans Range From:** $1,000-$44,187. **% Receiving Financial Aid:** 40. **% Receiving Scholarships/Grants:** 31. **% Receiving Loans:** 91. **Types of Aid Available:** Graduate assistantships, grants, institutional work-study, loans, scholarships.

ADMISSIONS INFORMATION
Application Fee: $35. **Priority Application Deadline:** 2/1. **Regular Application Deadline:** 8/23. **Transfer Students Accepted?** Yes. **Number of Applications Received:** 330. **% of Applicants Accepted:** 29.
Required Admission Factors: Essays/personal statement, GRE, transcript.
Program-Specific Admission Factors: Writing sample and plan of study may be required for some programs.

EMPLOYMENT INFORMATION
Placement Office Available? Yes.

UNIVERSITY OF MISSOURI—ROLLA
College of Arts & Sciences

Address: 1870 Miner Circle106 Parker Hall, Rolla, MO 65409-0910
Admissions Phone: 573-341-4315 · **Admissions Fax:** 573-341-4082
Admissions E-mail: admissions@umr.edu · **Web Address:** www.umr.edu

INSTITUTIONAL INFORMATION
Public/private: Public. **Students in Parent Institution:** 5,459.

STUDENT INFORMATION
Total Students in Program: 227. **% Full-time:** 87. **% Female:** 27. **% Minority:** 6. **% International:** 59.

RESEARCH FACILITIES
Research Facilities: Center for Infrastructure Engineering Systems, Environmental Research Center, Intelligent Systems Center, Electronic Materials Applied Research Center, Nuclear Reactor Facility, Rock Mechanics and Explosive Research Center.

EXPENSES/FINANCIAL AID
Annual Tuition: In-state $4,259. / Out-of-state $11,502. **Room & Board:** $5,453. **Fees:** $820. **Books and Supplies:** $850. **Grants Range From:** $400-$12,299. **Loans Range From:** $400-$19,471. **% Receiving Financial Aid:** 85. **% Receiving Scholarships/Grants:** 54. **% Receiving Loans:** 21. **% Receiving Assistantships:** 63. **Types of Aid Available:** Fellowships, graduate assistantships, grants, institutional work-study, loans, scholarships. **Average student debt upon graduation:** $17,991. **Number of Fellowships Granted Each Year:** 20 **Average amount of individual fellowships per year:** $3,300. **Number of Teaching/Research Assistantships Granted Each Year:** 113. **Assistantship Compensation Includes:** Full tuition remission, partial tuition remission, salary/stipend.

ADMISSIONS INFORMATION
Application Fee: $50. **Regular Application Deadline:** 7/15. **Regular Notification:** Rolling. **Transfer Students Accepted?** Yes. **Number of Applications Received:** 260. **% of Applicants Accepted:** 63. **% Accepted Who Enrolled:** 24. **Average GRE Verbal:** 507. **Average GRE Quantitative:** 741. **Average GRE Analytical:** 659.
Required Admission Factors: GRE, letters of recommendation, transcript.
Other Admission Factors: Varies by department.
Program-Specific Admission Factors: Varies by department.

EMPLOYMENT INFORMATION
Placement Office Available? Yes. **Rate of placement:** 96%.

UNIVERSITY OF MISSOURI—ST. LOUIS
College of Arts & Sciences

Address: Graduate School Admissions
8001 Natural Bridge Road, St. Louis, MO 63121-4499
Admissions Phone: 314-516-5458 · **Admissions Fax:** 314-516-6759
Admissions E-mail: pbarton@umsl.edu

INSTITUTIONAL INFORMATION

Public/private: Public. **Evening Classes Available?** Yes. **Students in Parent Institution:** 12,134.

STUDENT INFORMATION

Total Students in Program: 2,353. **% Full-time:** 19. **% Female:** 68.

RESEARCH FACILITIES

Research Facilities: Center for Molecular Electronics, International Center for Tropical Ecology, Center for Science and Technology, Center for Neurodynamics, Center for Trauma Recovery.

EXPENSES/FINANCIAL AID

Annual Tuition: In-state $4,932. / Out-of-state $12,504. **Room & Board (On/off campus):** $5,235/$6,480. **Fees:** $500. **Number of Teaching/Research Assistantships Granted Each Year:** 164. **Average Salary Stipend:** $9,900.

ADMISSIONS INFORMATION

Application Fee: $25. **Regular Notification:** Rolling. **Transfer Students Accepted?** Yes. **Transfer Policy:** Maximum 1/3 of total credit hours required may be transferred with a minimum grade of B. **Number of Applications Received:** 2,219. **% of Applicants Accepted:** 64. **% Accepted Who Enrolled:** 47.
Required Admission Factors: Transcript.
Other Admission Factors: Minimum 2.75 GPA required.

EMPLOYMENT INFORMATION

Placement Office Available? Yes.

UNIVERSITY OF NEBRASKA—LINCOLN
College of Arts & Sciences

Address: 14th and R Streets, Lincoln, NE 68588
Admissions Phone: 402-472-2878 · **Admissions Fax:** 402-472-3834
Admissions E-mail: ggross2@unl.edu

INSTITUTIONAL INFORMATION

Public/private: Public. **Evening Classes Available?** Yes. **Students in Parent Institution:** 22,764.

STUDENT INFORMATION

Total Students in Program: 4,309. **% Full-time:** 48. **% Female:** 52.

RESEARCH FACILITIES

Research Facilities: Center for Genetics and Biomaterials Research.

EXPENSES/FINANCIAL AID

Annual Tuition: In-state $2,412. / Out-of-state $6,223. **Fees:** $725. **Books and Supplies:** $790. **Grants Range From:** $200-$12,000. **Loans Range From:** $200-$20,100. **% Receiving Financial Aid:** 36. **% Receiving Scholarships/Grants:** 5. **% Receiving Loans:** 56. **% Receiving Assistantships:** 61. **Average student debt upon graduation:** $21,397. **Number of Fellowships Granted Each Year:** 103. **Average amount of individual fellowships per year:** $4,146. **Number of Teaching/Research Assistantships Granted Each Year:** 559. **Average Salary Stipend:** $10,202.

ADMISSIONS INFORMATION

Application Fee: $35. **Regular Notification:** Rolling. **Transfer Students Accepted?** Yes. **Number of Applications Received:** 1,063. **% of Applicants Accepted:** 36. **% Accepted Who Enrolled:** 51.
Required Admission Factors: GRE, transcript.
Program-Specific Admission Factors: GRE required for most programs. Statement of purpose or writing sample required of applicants to many programs.

EMPLOYMENT INFORMATION

Placement Office Available? Yes. **Rate of placement:** 76%.

UNIVERSITY OF NEBRASKA—LINCOLN
College of Fine & Performing Arts

Address: 14th and R Streets, Lincoln, NE 68588
Admissions Phone: 402-472-2878 · **Admissions Fax:** 402-472-3834
Admissions E-mail: ggross2@unl.edu

INSTITUTIONAL INFORMATION

Public/private: Public. **Evening Classes Available?** Yes. **Students in Parent Institution:** 22,764.

STUDENT INFORMATION

Total Students in Program: 4,309. **% Full-time:** 48. **% Female:** 52.

RESEARCH FACILITIES

Research Facilities: Center for Genetics and Biomaterials Research.

EXPENSES/FINANCIAL AID

Annual Tuition: In-state $2,412. / Out-of-state $6,223. **Fees:** $725. **Books and Supplies:** $790. **Grants Range From:** $200-$12,000. **Loans Range From:** $200-$20,100. **% Receiving Financial Aid:** 61. **% Receiving Scholarships/Grants:** 5. **% Receiving Loans:** 56. **% Receiving Assistantships:** 61. **Average student debt upon graduation:** $19,014. **Number of Fellowships Granted Each Year:** 18. **Average amount of individual fellowships per year:** $2,577. **Number of Teaching/Research Assistantships Granted Each Year:** 88. **Average Salary Stipend:** $7,455.

ADMISSIONS INFORMATION

Application Fee: $35. **Regular Notification:** Rolling. **Transfer Students Accepted?** Yes. **Transfer Policy:** Maximum 1/2 of total credit hours required may be transferred. **Number of Applications Received:** 177. **% of Applicants Accepted:** 51. **% Accepted Who Enrolled:** 57.
Required Admission Factors: Letters of recommendation, transcript.

EMPLOYMENT INFORMATION

Placement Office Available? Yes. **Rate of placement:** 76%.

UNIVERSITY OF NEBRASKA—LINCOLN
School of Biological Sciences

Address: 14th and R Streets, Lincoln, NE 68588
Admissions Phone: 402-472-2878 · **Admissions Fax:** 402-472-3834
Admissions E-mail: ggross2@unl.edu

INSTITUTIONAL INFORMATION

Public/private: Public. **Evening Classes Available?** Yes. **Students in Parent Institution:** 22,764.

STUDENT INFORMATION

Total Students in Program: 4,309. **% Full-time:** 48. **% Female:** 52.

RESEARCH FACILITIES

Research Facilities: Center for Genetics and Biomaterials Research.

EXPENSES/FINANCIAL AID

Annual Tuition: In-state $2,412. / Out-of-state $6,223. **Fees:** $725. **Books and Supplies:** $790. **Grants Range From:** $200-$12,000. **Loans Range From:** $200-$20,100. **% Receiving Financial Aid:** 39. **% Receiving Scholarships/Grants:** 5. **% Receiving Loans:** 56. **% Receiving Assistantships:** 61. **Number of Fellowships Granted Each Year:** 2. **Average amount of individual fellowships per year:** $3,250. **Number of Teaching/Research Assistantships Granted Each Year:** 65. **Average Salary Stipend:** $9,273.

ADMISSIONS INFORMATION

Application Fee: $35. **Regular Notification:** Rolling. **Transfer Students Accepted?** Yes. **Number of Applications Received:** 182. **% of Applicants Accepted:** 16. **% Accepted Who Enrolled:** 57.

Required Admission Factors: Essays/personal statement, letters of recommendation, transcript.
Other Admission Factors: Requirements vary by program.

EMPLOYMENT INFORMATION
Placement Office Available? Yes. **Rate of placement:** 76%.

UNIVERSITY OF NEBRASKA—OMAHA
College of Arts & Sciences

Address: 60th and Dodge Streets, Omaha, NE 68182-0005
Admissions Phone: 402-554-2341 · **Admissions Fax:** 402-554-3143

INSTITUTIONAL INFORMATION
Public/private: Public. **Students in Parent Institution:** 13,479.

STUDENT INFORMATION
Total Students in Program: 2,785. **% Full-time:** 22. **% Female:** 61.

EXPENSES/FINANCIAL AID
Annual Tuition: In-state $1,890. / Out-of-state $4,545.

ADMISSIONS INFORMATION
Application Fee: $35. **Transfer Students Accepted?** Yes. **Transfer Policy:** Maximum 1/3 of total credits required may be transferred. **Number of Applications Received:** 181. **% of Applicants Accepted:** 81. **% Accepted Who Enrolled:** 59. **Average GPA:** 3.0.
Required Admission Factors: Transcript.
Other Admission Factors: Minimum 3.0 GPA required.

EMPLOYMENT INFORMATION
Placement Office Available? Yes.

UNIVERSITY OF NEBRASKA—OMAHA
College of Fine Arts

Address: 60th and Dodge Streets, Omaha, NE 68182-0005
Admissions Phone: 402-554-2341 · **Admissions Fax:** 402-554-3143

INSTITUTIONAL INFORMATION
Public/private: Public. **Students in Parent Institution:** 13,479.

STUDENT INFORMATION
Total Students in Program: 2,785. **% Full-time:** 22. **% Female:** 61.

EXPENSES/FINANCIAL AID
Annual Tuition: In-state $1,890. / Out-of-state $4,545.

ADMISSIONS INFORMATION
Application Fee: $35. **Transfer Students Accepted?** Yes. **Transfer Policy:** Maximum 1/3 of total credits may be transferred. **Number of Applications Received:** 18. **% of Applicants Accepted:** 83. **% Accepted Who Enrolled:** 53.
Required Admission Factors: Essays/personal statement, transcript.
Other Admission Factors: Minimum 3.0 GPA required.

EMPLOYMENT INFORMATION
Placement Office Available? Yes.

UNIVERSITY OF NEBRASKA—OMAHA
College of Public Affairs & Community Service

Address: 60th and Dodge Streets, Omaha, NE 68182-0005
Admissions Phone: 402-554-2341 · **Admissions Fax:** 402-554-3143

INSTITUTIONAL INFORMATION
Public/private: Public. **Students in Parent Institution:** 13,479.

STUDENT INFORMATION
Total Students in Program: 2,785. **% Full-time:** 22. **% Female:** 61.

EXPENSES/FINANCIAL AID
Annual Tuition: In-state $1,890. / Out-of-state $4,545.

ADMISSIONS INFORMATION
Application Fee: $35. **Transfer Students Accepted?** Yes. **Transfer Policy:** Maximum 1/3 of total credits required may be transferred. **Number of Applications Received:** 300. **% of Applicants Accepted:** 70. **% Accepted Who Enrolled:** 65. **Average GPA:** 3.0.
Required Admission Factors: Essays/personal statement, transcript.
Other Admission Factors: Minimum 3.0 GPA required.

EMPLOYMENT INFORMATION
Placement Office Available? Yes.

UNIVERSITY OF NEVADA—LAS VEGAS
College of Fine Arts

Address: 4505 South Maryland Parkway
Box 451017, Las Vegas, NV 89154-1017
Admissions Phone: 702-895-4210 · **Admissions Fax:** 702-895-4194

INSTITUTIONAL INFORMATION
Public/private: Public. **Students in Parent Institution:** 22,040.

STUDENT INFORMATION
Total Students in Program: 4,303. **% Full-time:** 28. **% Female:** 62.

RESEARCH FACILITIES
Research Facilities: Desert Bridge Research Center, Work and Leisure Research Center, Center for Economic Education, International Gaming Institute, Center for Survey Research, National Supercomputer Center for Energy Research, Lake Mead Limnological Research Center.

EXPENSES/FINANCIAL AID
Annual Tuition: In-state $1,863. / Out-of-state $7,215. **Number of Teaching/Research Assistantships Granted Each Year:** 50. **Average Salary Stipend:** $8,707.

ADMISSIONS INFORMATION
Application Fee: $40. **Regular Notification:** Rolling. **Transfer Students Accepted?** No. **Number of Applications Received:** 117. **% of Applicants Accepted:** 56. **% Accepted Who Enrolled:** 69.
Required Admission Factors: Letters of recommendation, transcript.
Other Admission Factors: Minimum 2.75 GPA required.

EMPLOYMENT INFORMATION
Placement Office Available? Yes.

UNIVERSITY OF NEVADA—LAS VEGAS
College of Liberal Arts

Address: 4505 South Maryland Parkway
Box 451017, Las Vegas, NV 89154-1017
Admissions Phone: 702-895-3401 · **Admissions Fax:** 702-895-4097

INSTITUTIONAL INFORMATION
Public/private: Public. **Students in Parent Institution:** 22,040.

STUDENT INFORMATION
Total Students in Program: 4,303. **% Full-time:** 28. **% Female:** 62.

RESEARCH FACILITIES

Research Facilities: Desert Bridge Research Center, Work and Leisure Research Center, Center for Economic Education, International Gaming Institute, Center for Survey Research, National Supercomputer Center for Energy Research, Lake Mead Limnological Research Center.

EXPENSES/FINANCIAL AID

Annual Tuition: In-state $1,863. / Out-of-state $7,215. **Number of Teaching/Research Assistantships Granted Each Year:** 91. **Average Salary Stipend:** $8,797.

ADMISSIONS INFORMATION

Application Fee: $40. **Regular Notification:** Rolling. **Transfer Students Accepted?** No. **Number of Applications Received:** 191. **% of Applicants Accepted:** 48. **% Accepted Who Enrolled:** 74.
Required Admission Factors: Letters of recommendation, transcript.
Other Admission Factors: Minimum 2.75 GPA required.

EMPLOYMENT INFORMATION

Placement Office Available? Yes.

UNIVERSITY OF NEVADA—LAS VEGAS
College of Sciences

Address: 4505 South Maryland Parkway
Box 451017, Las Vegas, NV 89154-1017
Admissions Phone: 702-895-3487 · **Admissions Fax:** 702-895-4159

INSTITUTIONAL INFORMATION

Public/private: Public. **Students in Parent Institution:** 22,040.

STUDENT INFORMATION

Total Students in Program: 4,303. **% Full-time:** 28. **% Female:** 62.

RESEARCH FACILITIES

Research Facilities: Desert Bridge Research Center, Work and Leisure Research Center, Center for Economic Education, International Gaming Institute, Center for Survey Research, National Supercomputer Center for Energy Research, Lake Mead Limnological Research Center.

EXPENSES/FINANCIAL AID

Annual Tuition: In-state $1,863. / Out-of-state $7,215.

ADMISSIONS INFORMATION

Application Fee: $40. **Transfer Students Accepted?** No. **Number of Applications Received:** 92. **% of Applicants Accepted:** 60. **% Accepted Who Enrolled:** 62.

EMPLOYMENT INFORMATION

Placement Office Available? Yes.

UNIVERSITY OF NEVADA—LAS VEGAS
Greenspun College of Urban Affairs

Address: 4505 South Maryland Parkway
Box 451017, Las Vegas, NV 89154-1017
Admissions Phone: 702-895-3291 · **Admissions Fax:** 702-895-4231

INSTITUTIONAL INFORMATION

Public/private: Public. **Students in Parent Institution:** 22,040.

STUDENT INFORMATION

Total Students in Program: 4,303. **% Full-time:** 28. **% Female:** 62.

RESEARCH FACILITIES

Research Facilities: Desert Bridge Research Center, Work and Leisure Research Center, Center for Economic Education, International Gaming Insti-

---

tute, Center for Survey Research, National Supercomputer Center for Energy Research, Lake Mead Limnological Research Center.

EXPENSES/FINANCIAL AID

Annual Tuition: In-state $1,863. / Out-of-state $7,215. **Number of Teaching/Research Assistantships Granted Each Year:** 23. **Average Salary Stipend:** $8,500.

ADMISSIONS INFORMATION

Application Fee: $40. **Regular Notification:** Rolling. **Transfer Students Accepted?** No. **Number of Applications Received:** 182. **% of Applicants Accepted:** 70. **% Accepted Who Enrolled:** 64.
Required Admission Factors: GRE, letters of recommendation, transcript.
Other Admission Factors: Minimum 2.75 GPA required.

EMPLOYMENT INFORMATION

Placement Office Available? Yes.

UNIVERSITY OF NEVADA—RENO
College of Human & Community Sciences

Address: Mail Stop 326, Reno, NV 89557-0035
Admissions Phone: 775-784-6869 · **Admissions Fax:** 775-784-6064
Admissions E-mail: gradschool@unr.edu

INSTITUTIONAL INFORMATION

Public/private: Public. **Students in Parent Institution:** 12,659.

STUDENT INFORMATION

Total Students in Program: 2,807. **% Full-time:** 36. **% Female:** 58.

RESEARCH FACILITIES

Research Facilities: Biological Resources Research Center, Bridge Rsearch and Information Center, Candida Adherence Mycology Research Unit, Center for Basque Studies, Center for Economic Development, Center for Environmental Arts and Humanities.

EXPENSES/FINANCIAL AID

Annual Tuition: In-state $1,872. / Out-of-state $7,444. **Fees:** $57.

ADMISSIONS INFORMATION

Application Fee: $40. **Transfer Students Accepted?** Yes. **Number of Applications Received:** 92. **% of Applicants Accepted:** 68. **% Accepted Who Enrolled:** 90.
Required Admission Factors: Letters of recommendation, transcript.

EMPLOYMENT INFORMATION

Placement Office Available? Yes.

UNIVERSITY OF NEVADA—RENO
College of Liberal Arts

Address: Mail Stop 326, Reno, NV 89557-0035
Admissions Phone: 775-784-6869 · **Admissions Fax:** 775-784-6064
Admissions E-mail: gradadmissions@unr.edu · **Web Address:** www.unr.edu/grad/

INSTITUTIONAL INFORMATION

Public/private: Public. **Evening Classes Available?** Yes. **Students in Parent Institution:** 12,659.

PROGRAMS

Masters offered in: Anthropology; clinical psychology; communications studies/speech, communication, and rhetoric; English language and literature; experimental psychology; foreign languages/modern languages; history; music; philosophy; psychology; sociology. **Doctorate offered in:** Anthropology; clinical psychology; English language and literature; experimental psychology; history; psychology; social psychology; social sciences.

STUDENT INFORMATION

Total Students in Program: 2,807. **% Full-time:** 36. **% Female:** 58.

RESEARCH FACILITIES

Research Facilities: Biological Resources Research Center, Bridge Rsearch and Information Center, Candida Adherence Mycology Research Unit, Center for Basque Studies, Center for Economic Development, Center for Environmental Arts and Humanities.

EXPENSES/FINANCIAL AID

Annual Tuition: In-state $1,872. / Out-of-state $7,444. **Fees:** $57. **Average Salary Stipend:** $9,500.

ADMISSIONS INFORMATION

Application Fee: $60. **Regular Application Deadline:** 3/1. **Regular Notification:** Rolling. **Transfer Students Accepted?** Yes. **Transfer Policy:** You may transfer nine credit hours for master students and 24 credit hours for PhD students. (See website.) Each program has its own individual application deadline. **Number of Applications Received:** 373. **% of Applicants Accepted:** 48. **% Accepted Who Enrolled:** 91.
Required Admission Factors: Transcript.
Other Admission Factors: 2.75 GPA for most programs. (See website for individual program differences.) Minimum of 500 TOEFL score for international students. (See websites for differences in programs.)
Program-Specific Admission Factors: Each program has its own application deadline.

EMPLOYMENT INFORMATION

Placement Office Available? Yes.

UNIVERSITY OF NEVADA—RENO
Donald W. Reynolds School of Journalism

Address: Mail Stop 326, Reno, NV 89557-0035
Admissions Phone: 775-784-6869 · **Admissions Fax:** 775-784-6064
Admissions E-mail: gradschool@unr.edu

INSTITUTIONAL INFORMATION

Public/private: Public. **Students in Parent Institution:** 12,659.

STUDENT INFORMATION

Total Students in Program: 2,807. **% Full-time:** 36. **% Female:** 58.

RESEARCH FACILITIES

Research Facilities: Biological Resources Research Center, Bridge Rsearch and Information Center, Candida Adherence Mycology Research Unit, Center for Basque Studies, Center for Economic Development, Center for Environmental Arts and Humanities, Center for Environmental

EXPENSES/FINANCIAL AID

Annual Tuition: In-state $1,872. / Out-of-state $7,444. **Fees:** $57.

ADMISSIONS INFORMATION

Transfer Students Accepted? No. **Number of Applications Received:** 16. **% of Applicants Accepted:** 44. **% Accepted Who Enrolled:** 57.
Required Admission Factors: GRE, transcript.
Other Admission Factors: Statement of intent and 3 letters of recommendation required. Minimum GRE score of 1500 and minimum 3.0 GPA recommended.

EMPLOYMENT INFORMATION

Placement Office Available? Yes.

UNIVERSITY OF NEW ENGLAND
College of Arts & Sciences

Address: Hills Beach Road, Biddeford, ME 04005
Admissions Phone: 207-283-0171, ext. 4225 · **Admissions Fax:** 207-286-3678
Admissions E-mail: sgaffney@mailbox.une.edu

INSTITUTIONAL INFORMATION

Public/private: Private (nonprofit). **Students in Parent Institution:** 2,834.

STUDENT INFORMATION

Total Students in Program: 989. **% Full-time:** 56. **% Female:** 77.

EXPENSES/FINANCIAL AID

Annual Tuition: $7,560. **Fees:** $240. **Books and Supplies:** $1,350. **Grants Range From:** $500-$1,000. **Loans Range From:** $1,000-$25,000. **% Receiving Scholarships/Grants:** 20. **% Receiving Loans:** 90. **% Receiving Assistantships:** 2.

ADMISSIONS INFORMATION

Application Fee: $40. **Regular Notification:** Rolling. **Transfer Students Accepted?** No. **Number of Applications Received:** 264. **% of Applicants Accepted:** 92. **% Accepted Who Enrolled:** 60.
Required Admission Factors: Essays/personal statement, letters of recommendation, transcript.
Program-Specific Admission Factors: Teaching certificate and proficiency required of education program applicants.

UNIVERSITY OF NEW HAMPSHIRE
Graduate School

Address: 105 Main Street—Thompson Hall, Graduate School, Durham, NH 03824
Admissions Phone: 603-862-3000 · **Admissions Fax:** 603-862-0275
Admissions E-mail: grad.school@unh.edu · **Web Address:** www.gradschool.unh.edu

INSTITUTIONAL INFORMATION

Public/private: Public. **Evening Classes Available?** Yes. **Total Faculty:** 605.

STUDENT INFORMATION

Total Students in Program: 2,324. **% Full-time:** 48. **% Female:** 58. **% Minority:** 4. **% International:** 11.

RESEARCH FACILITIES

Research Facilities: Agricultural experiment station, earth, ocean, and space study.

EXPENSES/FINANCIAL AID

Annual Tuition: In-state $6,300. / Out-of-state $15,720. **Fees:** $1,059. **% Receiving Financial Aid:** 26. **% Receiving Scholarships/Grants:** 13. **% Receiving Assistantships:** 55. **Number of Fellowships Granted Each Year:** 15. **Number of Teaching/Research Assistantships Granted Each Year:** 132. **Average Salary Stipend:** $10,800.

ADMISSIONS INFORMATION

Application Fee: $60. **Priority Application Deadline:** 2/15. **Regular Application Deadline:** 7/1. **Regular Notification:** Rolling. **Transfer Students Accepted?** No. **Transfer Policy:** An applicant can transfer up to 8 credits toward a degree from an outside institution. **Number of Applications Received:** 1,785. **% of Applicants Accepted:** 71. **% Accepted Who Enrolled:** 50. **Average GPA:** 3.31. **Average GRE Verbal:** 520. **Average GRE Quantitative:** 615. **Average GRE Analytical:** 517. **Average GRE Analytical Writing:** 5.0.
Required Admission Factors: Essays/personal statement, letters of recommendation, transcript.

Other Admission Factors: Recommended GRE section scores of 500 and recommended 3.0 GPA required or higher.

Program-Specific Admission Factors: Varies a great deal for each department. Please contact the department at UNH for details or visit the grad school website at www.gradschool.unh.edu.

EMPLOYMENT INFORMATION
Placement Office Available? Yes.

UNIVERSITY OF NEW HAVEN
College of Arts & Sciences

Address: 300 Orange Avenue, West Haven, CT 06516
Admissions Phone: 203-932-7133 · **Admissions Fax:** 203-932-7137
Admissions E-mail: psommers@charger.newhaven.edu

INSTITUTIONAL INFORMATION
Public/private: Private (nonprofit). **Evening Classes Available?** Yes. Students in Parent Institution: 4,349.

STUDENT INFORMATION
Total Students in Program: 1,812. **% Full-time:** 37. **% Female:** 48.

RESEARCH FACILITIES
Research Facilities: Bureau of Business Research, Center for Family Business, Institute of Analytical and Environmental Chemistry, Center for Study of Crime Victims Rights.

EXPENSES/FINANCIAL AID
Annual Tuition: $11,340. **Fees:** $39. **Books and Supplies:** $600. **Loans Range From:** $100-$18,500.

ADMISSIONS INFORMATION
Application Fee: $50. **Regular Notification:** Rolling. **Transfer Students Accepted?** Yes.
Required Admission Factors: Letters of recommendation, transcript.

EMPLOYMENT INFORMATION
Placement Office Available? Yes. **Rate of placement:** 95%.

UNIVERSITY OF NEW HAVEN
School of Public Safety & Professional Studies

Address: 300 Orange Avenue, West Haven, CT 06516
Admissions Phone: 203-932-7133 · **Admissions Fax:** 203-932-7137
Admissions E-mail: psommers@charger.newhaven.edu

INSTITUTIONAL INFORMATION
Public/private: Private (nonprofit). **Evening Classes Available?** Yes. Students in Parent Institution: 4,349.

STUDENT INFORMATION
Total Students in Program: 1,812. **% Full-time:** 37. **% Female:** 48.

RESEARCH FACILITIES
Research Facilities: Bureau of Business Research, Center for Family Business, Institute of Analytical and Environmental Chemistry, Center for Study of Crime Victims Rights.

EXPENSES/FINANCIAL AID
Annual Tuition: $11,340. **Fees:** $39. **Books and Supplies:** $600. **Loans Range From:** $100-$18,500.

ADMISSIONS INFORMATION
Application Fee: $50. **Regular Notification:** Rolling. **Transfer Students Accepted?** Yes.

Required Admission Factors: Letters of recommendation, transcript.

EMPLOYMENT INFORMATION
Placement Office Available? Yes. **Rate of placement:** 95%.

UNIVERSITY OF NEW MEXICO
College of Arts & Sciences

Address: 107 Humanities Building, Albuquerque, NM 87131-1041
Admissions Phone: 505-277-4621 · **Admissions Fax:** 505-277-0351

INSTITUTIONAL INFORMATION
Public/private: Public. **Students in Parent Institution:** 24,900.

STUDENT INFORMATION
Total Students in Program: 4,284. **% Full-time:** 46. **% Female:** 56.

EXPENSES/FINANCIAL AID
Annual Tuition: In-state $2,175. / Out-of-state $4,712. **Fees:** $32. **Grants Range From:** $1,200-$8,000. **% Receiving Loans:** 34. **% Receiving Assistantships:** 32.

ADMISSIONS INFORMATION
Application Fee: $40. **Transfer Students Accepted?** Yes. **Transfer Policy:** Maximum one-half of total credit hours required may be transferred. **Number of Applications Received:** 1,324. **% of Applicants Accepted:** 38. **% Accepted Who Enrolled:** 62. **Average GPA:** 3.0.
Required Admission Factors: Essays/personal statement, letters of recommendation, transcript.
Other Admission Factors: Minimum 3.0 GPA required for most programs.

EMPLOYMENT INFORMATION
Placement Office Available? Yes.

UNIVERSITY OF NEW MEXICO
College of Fine Arts

Address: 107 Humanities Building, Albuquerque, NM 87131-1041
Admissions Phone: 505-277-2711

INSTITUTIONAL INFORMATION
Public/private: Public. **Evening Classes Available?** Yes. **Students in Parent Institution:** 24,900.

STUDENT INFORMATION
Total Students in Program: 4,284. **% Full-time:** 46. **% Female:** 56.

EXPENSES/FINANCIAL AID
Annual Tuition: In-state $2,175. / Out-of-state $4,712. **Fees:** $32. **Grants Range From:** $1,200-$8,000. **Loans Range From:** $1-$18,500. **% Receiving Financial Aid:** 80. **% Receiving Loans:** 34. **% Receiving Assistantships:** 32.

ADMISSIONS INFORMATION
Application Fee: $40. **Transfer Students Accepted?** Yes. **Number of Applications Received:** 292. **% of Applicants Accepted:** 28. **% Accepted Who Enrolled:** 56. **Average GPA:** 3.0.
Required Admission Factors: Essays/personal statement, letters of recommendation, transcript.
Program-Specific Admission Factors: Essay required of music program applicants; writing sample required of art history program applicants. Video required of choreography program applicants. Script required of playwriting program applicants.

EMPLOYMENT INFORMATION
Placement Office Available? Yes.

UNIVERSITY OF NEW ORLEANS
College of Liberal Arts

Address: New Orleans, LA 70148
Admissions Phone: 504-280-6595 · **Admissions Fax:** 504-280-5522
Admissions E-mail: rssad@uno.edu

INSTITUTIONAL INFORMATION

Public/private: Public. **Evening Classes Available?** Yes. **Student/faculty Ratio:** 4:1. **Students in Parent Institution:** 17,014.

STUDENT INFORMATION

Total Students in Program: 4,047. **% Full-time:** 36. **% Female:** 61.

EXPENSES/FINANCIAL AID

Annual Tuition: In-state $3,402. / Out-of-state $10,801. **Fees:** $150. **Books and Supplies:** $1,150. **Grants Range From:** $1,356-$9,756. **Loans Range From:** $500-$10,500. **% Receiving Scholarships/Grants:** 43. **% Receiving Loans:** 42. **% Receiving Assistantships:** 27. **Average Salary Stipend:** $3,950.

ADMISSIONS INFORMATION

Application Fee: $20. **Regular Notification:** Rolling. **Transfer Students Accepted?** Yes. **Transfer Policy:** Minimum grade average of B and statement of good standing required of transfer applicants. **Number of Applications Received:** 318. **% of Applicants Accepted:** 52. **% Accepted Who Enrolled:** 82.
Required Admission Factors: GRE, transcript.
Other Admission Factors: Minimum 2.5 GPA required.

EMPLOYMENT INFORMATION

Placement Office Available? Yes. **Rate of placement:** 82%.

UNIVERSITY OF NEW ORLEANS
College of Sciences

Address: New Orleans, LA 70148
Admissions Phone: 504-280-6595 · **Admissions Fax:** 504-280-5522
Admissions E-mail: rssad@uno.edu

INSTITUTIONAL INFORMATION

Public/private: Public. **Evening Classes Available?** Yes. **Student/faculty Ratio:** 4:1. **Students in Parent Institution:** 17,014.

STUDENT INFORMATION

Total Students in Program: 4,047. **% Full-time:** 36. **% Female:** 61.

EXPENSES/FINANCIAL AID

Annual Tuition: In-state $3,402. / Out-of-state $10,801. **Fees:** $150. **Books and Supplies:** $1,150. **Grants Range From:** $1,356-$9,756. **Loans Range From:** $500-$10,500. **% Receiving Scholarships/Grants:** 43. **% Receiving Loans:** 42. **% Receiving Assistantships:** 27.

ADMISSIONS INFORMATION

Application Fee: $20. **Regular Notification:** Rolling. **Transfer Students Accepted?** Yes. **Number of Applications Received:** 362. **% of Applicants Accepted:** 49. **% Accepted Who Enrolled:** 46. **Average GRE Verbal:** 510. **Average GRE Quantitative:** 680.
Required Admission Factors: GRE, letters of recommendation, transcript. **Other Admission Factors:** Minimum GRE scores of 500 Verbal and 500 Quantitative required.

EMPLOYMENT INFORMATION

Placement Office Available? Yes. **Rate of placement:** 82%.

UNIVERSITY OF NEW ORLEANS
College of Urban & Public Affairs

Address: New Orleans, LA 70148
Admissions Phone: 504-280-5473 · **Admissions Fax:** 504-280-6272
Admissions E-mail: rssad@uno.edu

INSTITUTIONAL INFORMATION

Public/private: Public. **Evening Classes Available?** Yes. **Student/faculty Ratio:** 8:1. **Students in Parent Institution:** 17,014.

STUDENT INFORMATION

Total Students in Program: 4,047. **% Full-time:** 36. **% Female:** 61.

EXPENSES/FINANCIAL AID

Annual Tuition: In-state $3,402. / Out-of-state $10,801. **Fees:** $150. **Books and Supplies:** $1,150. **Grants Range From:** $1,356-$9,756. **Loans Range From:** $500-$10,500. **% Receiving Financial Aid:** 15. **% Receiving Scholarships/Grants:** 43. **% Receiving Loans:** 42. **% Receiving Assistantships:** 27. **Average Salary Stipend:** $850.

ADMISSIONS INFORMATION

Transfer Students Accepted? Yes. **Transfer Policy:** Maximum 12 credit hours may be transferred into masters programs; maximum 24 credit hours into PhD programs. **Number of Applications Received:** 83. **% of Applicants Accepted:** 46. **% Accepted Who Enrolled:** 29.
Required Admission Factors: Essays/personal statement, GRE, letters of recommendation, transcript.
Other Admission Factors: Minimum 2.5 GPA required of masters program applicants; minimum 3.0 GPA required of PhD program applicants.
Program-Specific Admission Factors: GRE or GMAT required of public administration program applicants.

EMPLOYMENT INFORMATION

Placement Office Available? Yes. **Rate of placement:** 82%.

UNIVERSITY OF NORTH ALABAMA
College of Arts & Sciences

Address: Morrison Avenue, Florence, AL 35632-0001
Admissions Phone: 256-765-4608 · **Admissions Fax:** 256-765-4329
Admissions E-mail: swilson@unanov.una.edu

INSTITUTIONAL INFORMATION

Public/private: Public. **Evening Classes Available?** Yes. **Students in Parent Institution:** 5,601.

STUDENT INFORMATION

Total Students in Program: 657. **% Full-time:** 16. **% Female:** 67.

EXPENSES/FINANCIAL AID

Annual Tuition: In-state $2,214. / Out-of-state $4,428. **Room & Board:** $4,734. **Fees:** $302.

ADMISSIONS INFORMATION

Application Fee: $25. **Regular Notification:** Rolling. **Transfer Students Accepted?** Yes.
Required Admission Factors: GRE, transcript.
Other Admission Factors: Minimum 2.75 GPA required.

EMPLOYMENT INFORMATION

Placement Office Available? Yes.

UNIVERSITY OF NORTH CAROLINA—ASHEVILLE
Graduate Programs

Address: One University Heights, Asheville, NC 28804-3299
Admissions Phone: 704-251-6227 · **Admissions Fax:** 704-251-6614
Admissions E-mail: uldricks@unca.edu

INSTITUTIONAL INFORMATION
Public/private: Public. **Evening Classes Available?** Yes. **Students in Parent Institution:** 3,092.

STUDENT INFORMATION
Total Students in Program: 56. **% Full-time:** 5. **% Female:** 55.

EXPENSES/FINANCIAL AID
Annual Tuition: In-state: $1,725. / Out-of-state: $6,382. **% Receiving Financial Aid:** 10.

ADMISSIONS INFORMATION
Application Fee: $25. **Regular Notification:** Rolling. **Transfer Students Accepted?** Yes. **Transfer Policy:** Maximum 6 credit hours may be transferred. **Number of Applications Received:** 12. **% of Applicants Accepted:** 83. **% Accepted Who Enrolled:** 100. **Average GPA:** 3.2.
Required Admission Factors: Essays/personal statement, interview, transcript.
Other Admission Factors: Minimum 3.25 GPA required.

EMPLOYMENT INFORMATION
Placement Office Available? Yes.

UNIVERSITY OF NORTH CAROLINA—
CHAPEL HILL
College of Arts & Sciences

Address: Chapel Hill, NC 27599-9100

INSTITUTIONAL INFORMATION
Public/private: Public. **Students in Parent Institution:** 22,845.

STUDENT INFORMATION
Total Students in Program: 6,499

RESEARCH FACILITIES
Research Facilities: Institute for Research in Social Sciences, Carolina Population Center, Center for Health Promotion & Disease Prevention, Institute on Aging, Center for Health Services Research.

EXPENSES/FINANCIAL AID
Annual Tuition: In-state $3,448. / Out-of-state $13,759.

ADMISSIONS INFORMATION
Application Fee: $55. **Transfer Students Accepted?** No. **Number of Applications Received:** 5,867. **% of Applicants Accepted:** 23. **% Accepted Who Enrolled:** 44. **Average GPA:** 3.56.
Other Admission Factors: Minimum GRE score of 1000 and minimum 3.0 GPA required.

EMPLOYMENT INFORMATION
Placement Office Available? Yes.

UNIVERSITY OF NORTH CAROLINA—
CHAPEL HILL
School of Information & Library Science

Address: 100 Manning Hall, Chapel Hill, NC 27599-3360
Admissions Phone: 919-962-8366 · **Admissions Fax:** 919-962-8071
Admissions E-mail: info@ils.unc.edu · **Web Address:** www.ils.unc.edu

INSTITUTIONAL INFORMATION
Public/private: Public. **Evening Classes Available?** Yes. **Student/faculty Ratio:** 15:1. **Students in Parent Institution:** 26,000.

PROGRAMS
Masters offered in: Information science/studies, library science, library science/librarianship. **Doctorate offered in:** Information science/studies, library science, library science/librarianship.

STUDENT INFORMATION
Total Students in Program: 10,039.

RESEARCH FACILITIES
Research Facilities: Institute for Research in Social Sciences, Carolina Population Center, Center for Health Promotion & Disease Prevention, Institute on Aging, Center for Health Services Research.

EXPENSES/FINANCIAL AID
Annual Tuition: In-state $3,012. / Out-of-state $14,461. **Fees:** $1,031. **Books and Supplies:** $900. **% Receiving Financial Aid:** 50. **Types of Aid Available:** Graduate assistantships, scholarships. **Number of Fellowships Granted Each Year:** 52. **Average amount of individual fellowships per year:** $4,000. **Number of Teaching/Research Assistantships Granted Each Year:** 81.

ADMISSIONS INFORMATION
Application Fee: $60. **Regular Application Deadline:** 6/15. **Regular Notification:** Rolling. **Transfer Students Accepted?** Yes. **Transfer Policy:** Maximum 6 semester hours may be transferred into doctoral programs. **Number of Applications Received:** 316. **% of Applicants Accepted:** 53. **% Accepted Who Enrolled:** 51. **Average GPA:** 3.4. **Average GRE Verbal:** 601. **Average GRE Quantitative:** 637. **Average GRE Analytical:** 641.
Required Admission Factors: Essays/personal statement, GRE, letters of recommendation, transcript.

EMPLOYMENT INFORMATION
Placement Office Available? Yes. **% of doctoral grads employed in their field upon graduation:** 100.

UNIVERSITY OF NORTH CAROLINA—
CHAPEL HILL
School of Journalism & Mass Communication

Address: Campus Box 3365, Carroll Hall, Chapel Hill, NC 27599-3365
Admissions Phone: 919-962-3372 · **Admissions Fax:** 919-962-0620
Admissions E-mail: jomcgrad@email.unc.edu · **Web Address:** www.jomc.unc.edu

INSTITUTIONAL INFORMATION
Public/private: Public. **Student/faculty Ratio:** 3:1. **Students in Parent Institution:** 26,359.

PROGRAMS
Masters offered in: Advertising; broadcast journalism; journalism; journalism; mass communications/media studies; photojournalism; public relations/image management; radio, television, and digital communications. **Doctorate offered in:** Mass communications/media studies.

STUDENT INFORMATION
Total Students in Program: 7,857. % Full-time: 55.

RESEARCH FACILITIES
Research Facilities: Institute for Research in Social Sciences, Carolina Population Center, Center for Health Promotion & Disease Prevention, Institute on Aging, Center for Health Services Research, Odum Institute.

EXPENSES/FINANCIAL AID
Annual Tuition: In-state $6,046. / Out-of-state $17,935. Fees: $1,105. Books and Supplies: $600. Grants Range From: $10,000-$18,500. Loans Range From: $1,000-$20,000. % Receiving Financial Aid: 77. % Receiving Assistantships: 100. Types of Aid Available: Graduate assistantships. Number of Teaching/Research Assistantships Granted Each Year: 64. Assistantship Compensation Includes: Full tuition remission, salary/stipend. Average Salary Stipend: $8,800.

ADMISSIONS INFORMATION
Application Fee: $60. Regular Application Deadline: 1/1. Regular Notification: Rolling. Transfer Students Accepted? No. Number of Applications Received: 282. % of Applicants Accepted: 19. % Accepted Who Enrolled: 69. Average GRE Verbal: 610. Average GRE Quantitative: 630. Average GRE Analytical: 660. Average GRE Analytical Writing: 5. Required Admission Factors: Essays/personal statement, GRE, letters of recommendation, transcript. Other Admission Factors: Minimum GRE score in the 55th percentile for Verbal, 50th percentile for Quantitative and Analytical, minimum 3.0 GPA, and letter of intent required.

EMPLOYMENT INFORMATION
Placement Office Available? Yes. % Employed Within Six Months: 75. Rate of placement: 90%. Average starting salary: $35,000.

UNIVERSITY OF NORTH CAROLINA— CHAPEL HILL
School of Social Work

Address: 301 Pittsboro Street, CB# 3550, Chapel Hill, NC 27599-3550
Admissions Phone: 919-962-6442 · Admissions Fax: 919-843-8562
Admissions E-mail: ltw2517@email.unc.edu · Web Address: www.ssw.unc.edu

INSTITUTIONAL INFORMATION
Public/private: Public. Total Faculty: 88. % Faculty Female: 68. % Faculty Part-time: 35. Student/faculty Ratio: 5:1. Students in Parent Institution: 26,359.

PROGRAMS
Masters offered in: Social sciences. Doctorate offered in: Social sciences.

STUDENT INFORMATION
Total Students in Program: 332. % Full-time: 53. % Female: 84. % Minority: 21. % International: 1.

RESEARCH FACILITIES
Research Facilities: Institute for Research in Social Sciences, Carolina Population Center, Center for Health Promotion & Disease Prevention, Institute on Aging, Center for Health Services Research.

EXPENSES/FINANCIAL AID
Annual Tuition: In-state $3,163. / Out-of-state $15,394. Room & Board (On/off campus): $4,540/$6,200. Fees: $1,706. Books and Supplies: $500. Grants Range From: $100-$15,000. Loans Range From: $250-$16,000. % Receiving Financial Aid: 60. % Receiving Scholarships/Grants: 18. % Receiving Loans: 59. % Receiving Assistantships: 2. Average student debt upon graduation: $13,750. Number of Fellowships Granted Each Year: 5. Average amount of individual fellowships per year: $12,000. Number of Teaching/Research Assistantships Granted Each Year: 15.

Assistantship Compensation Includes: Full tuition remission, partial tuition remission, salary/stipend.

ADMISSIONS INFORMATION
Application Fee: $60. Priority Application Deadline: 1/1. Regular Application Deadline: 2/15. Regular Notification: Rolling. Transfer Students Accepted? No. Number of Applications Received: 424. % of Applicants Accepted: 59. % Accepted Who Enrolled: 69. Average GPA: 3.5. Average GRE Verbal: 521. Average GRE Quantitative: 549. Average GRE Analytical: 598. Required Admission Factors: Essays/personal statement, GRE, letters of recommendation, transcript. Other Admission Factors: Minimum 3.0 GPA and minimum rank of 50th percentile on Verbal and Quantitative sections of GRE recommended. Program-Specific Admission Factors: Advanced Standing applicants must submit a field instruction form, course information form, and field evaluation.

EMPLOYMENT INFORMATION
Placement Office Available? Yes. % Employed Within Six Months: 95. Rate of placement: 95%. Average starting salary: $25,000.

UNIVERSITY OF NORTH CAROLINA—CHARLOTTE
College of Arts & Sciences

Address: 9201 University City Boulevard, Charlotte, NC 28223-0001
Admissions Phone: 704-687-3366 · Admissions Fax: 704-687-3279
Admissions E-mail: jwwatson@email.uncc.edu

INSTITUTIONAL INFORMATION
Public/private: Public. Students in Parent Institution: 16,844.

STUDENT INFORMATION
Total Students in Program: 2,688. % Full-time: 26. % Female: 57.

RESEARCH FACILITIES
Research Facilities: Cameron Applied Research Center.

EXPENSES/FINANCIAL AID
Annual Tuition: In-state $2,178. / Out-of-state $9,448. Room & Board: $5,618. Grants Range From: $400-$9,000. Loans Range From: $3,000-$18,500. % Receiving Scholarships/Grants: 25. % Receiving Loans: 57. % Receiving Assistantships: 62.

ADMISSIONS INFORMATION
Application Fee: $35. Regular Notification: Rolling. Transfer Students Accepted? Yes. Number of Applications Received: 395. % of Applicants Accepted: 60. % Accepted Who Enrolled: 68. Required Admission Factors: Transcript.

EMPLOYMENT INFORMATION
Placement Office Available? Yes.

UNIVERSITY OF NORTH CAROLINA— GREENSBORO
College of Arts & Sciences

Address: 1000 Spring Garden Street, Greensboro, NC 27412
Admissions Phone: 336-334-5596 · Admissions Fax: 336-334-4424
Admissions E-mail: inquiries@uncg.edu · Web Address: www.uncg.edu/grs

INSTITUTIONAL INFORMATION
Public/private: Public. Evening Classes Available? Yes. Students in Parent Institution: 14,328.

STUDENT INFORMATION
Total Students in Program: 641. % Full-time: 39. % Female: 58.

RESEARCH FACILITIES

Research Facilities: Center for Study of Social Issues, Center for Educational Research & Evaluation, Center for Global Business Education & Research, Center for Childcare Workforce, Statistical Counsuling Center.

EXPENSES/FINANCIAL AID

Annual Tuition: In-state $1,798. / Out-of-state $12,362. **Fees:** $1,038. **Books and Supplies:** $1,136. **Grants Range From:** $1,000-$15,000. **Loans Range From:** $200-$18,500. % **Receiving Scholarships/Grants:** 5. % **Receiving Loans:** 90. **Number of Fellowships Granted Each Year:** 14. **Average amount of individual fellowships per year:** $5,000. **Number of Teaching/Research Assistantships Granted Each Year:** 279.

ADMISSIONS INFORMATION

Application Fee: $35. **Regular Application Deadline:** 7/1. **Transfer Students Accepted?** Yes. **Number of Applications Received:** 888. % **of Applicants Accepted:** 35. % **Accepted Who Enrolled:** 60. **Average GPA:** 3.3. **Average GRE Verbal:** 517. **Average GRE Quantitative:** 568. **Average GRE Analytical:** 561.

Required Admission Factors: Essays/personal statement, GRE, interview, letters of recommendation, transcript.

Other Admission Factors: Minimum 3.0 GPA required of applicants to most programs.

Program-Specific Admission Factors: Portfolio required of applicants to design, film/video production, and technical writing certificate programs.

EMPLOYMENT INFORMATION

Placement Office Available? Yes.

UNIVERSITY OF NORTH CAROLINA—GREENSBORO
School of Human Environmental Sciences

Address: 1000 Spring Garden Street, Greensboro, NC 27412
Admissions Phone: 336-334-5596 · **Admissions Fax:** 336-334-4424
Admissions E-mail: m_grasso@uncg.edu

INSTITUTIONAL INFORMATION

Public/private: Public. **Evening Classes Available?** Yes. **Student/faculty Ratio:** 2:1. **Students in Parent Institution:** 13,372.

STUDENT INFORMATION

Total Students in Program: 3,086. % **Full-time:** 35. % **Female:** 71.

RESEARCH FACILITIES

Research Facilities: Center for Study of Social Issues, Center for Educational Research & Evaluation, Center for Global Business Education & Research, Center for Childcare Workforce, Statistical Counsuling Center.

EXPENSES/FINANCIAL AID

Annual Tuition: In-state $2,208. / Out-of-state $10,662. **Fees:** $946. **Books and Supplies:** $700. **Grants Range From:** $1,000-$15,000. **Loans Range From:** $200-$18,500. % **Receiving Scholarships/Grants:** 5. % **Receiving Loans:** 90. **Number of Fellowships Granted Each Year:** 7. **Average amount of individual fellowships per year:** $2,500. **Number of Teaching/Research Assistantships Granted Each Year:** 94. **Average Salary Stipend:** $5,000.

ADMISSIONS INFORMATION

Application Fee: $35. **Transfer Students Accepted?** Yes. **Number of Applications Received:** 226. % **of Applicants Accepted:** 49. % **Accepted Who Enrolled:** 82. **Average GRE Verbal:** 460. **Average GRE Quantitative:** 527. **Average GRE Analytical:** 542.

Required Admission Factors: Essays/personal statement, GRE, letters of recommendation, transcript.

Other Admission Factors: Minimum 3.0 GPA and minimum combined GRE score of 1000 required.

EMPLOYMENT INFORMATION

Placement Office Available? Yes.

UNIVERSITY OF NORTH CAROLINA—GREENSBORO
School of Music

Address: 1000 Spring Garden Street, Greensboro, NC 27412
Admissions Phone: 336-334-5596 · **Admissions Fax:** 336-334-4424
Admissions E-mail: b_bartel@office.uncg.edu

INSTITUTIONAL INFORMATION

Public/private: Public. **Evening Classes Available?** Yes. **Student/faculty Ratio:** 3:1. **Students in Parent Institution:** 13,372.

STUDENT INFORMATION

Total Students in Program: 3,086. % **Full-time:** 35. % **Female:** 71.

RESEARCH FACILITIES

Research Facilities: Center for Study of Social Issues, Center for Educational Research & Evaluation, Center for Global Business Education & Research, Center for Childcare Workforce, Statistical Counsuling Center.

EXPENSES/FINANCIAL AID

Annual Tuition: In-state $2,208. / Out-of-state $10,662. **Fees:** $946. **Books and Supplies:** $700. **Grants Range From:** $1,000-$15,000. **Loans Range From:** $200-$18,500. % **Receiving Financial Aid:** 50. % **Receiving Scholarships/Grants:** 5. % **Receiving Loans:** 90. **Number of Fellowships Granted Each Year:** 5. **Average amount of individual fellowships per year:** $7,400. **Number of Teaching/Research Assistantships Granted Each Year:** 61. **Average Salary Stipend:** $4,000.

ADMISSIONS INFORMATION

Application Fee: $35. **Regular Notification:** Rolling. **Transfer Students Accepted?** Yes. **Number of Applications Received:** 87. % **of Applicants Accepted:** 69. % **Accepted Who Enrolled:** 82. **Average GRE Verbal:** 480. **Average GRE Quantitative:** 527. **Average GRE Analytical:** 542.

Required Admission Factors: GRE, interview, letters of recommendation, transcript.

Other Admission Factors: Minimum 3.0 GPA in major required.

EMPLOYMENT INFORMATION

Placement Office Available? Yes.

UNIVERSITY OF NORTH CAROLINA—PEMBROKE
Graduate Studies

Address: PO Box 1510, Pembroke, NC 28372
Admissions Phone: 910-521-6271 · **Admissions Fax:** 910-521-6497

INSTITUTIONAL INFORMATION

Public/private: Public. **Evening Classes Available?** Yes. **Students in Parent Institution:** 3,648.

STUDENT INFORMATION

Total Students in Program: 369. % **Full-time:** 7. % **Female:** 67.

EXPENSES/FINANCIAL AID

Annual Tuition: In-state $1,788. / Out-of-state $9,058. **Room & Board:** $2,165. **Books and Supplies:** $1,500. % **Receiving Financial Aid:** 30. % **Receiving Loans:** 20. % **Receiving Assistantships:** 10. **Average student debt upon graduation:** $6,000. **Number of Teaching/Research Assistantships Granted Each Year:** 25. **Average Salary Stipend:** $3,000.

ADMISSIONS INFORMATION

Application Fee: $25. **Regular Notification:** Rolling. **Transfer Students Accepted?** Yes. **Average GPA:** 3.0. **Average GRE Verbal:** 350. **Average GRE Quantitative:** 400. **Average GRE Analytical:** 350. **Required Admission Factors:** GRE, letters of recommendation, transcript. **Other Admission Factors:** Minimum 2.5 GPA required.

EMPLOYMENT INFORMATION

Placement Office Available? Yes.

UNIVERSITY OF NORTH DAKOTA
College of Arts & Sciences

Address: Graduate School
PO Box 8178, Grand Forks, ND 58202-8178
Admissions Phone: 701-777-2947 · **Admissions Fax:** 701-777-3619
Admissions E-mail: gradschool@mail.und.nodak.edu

INSTITUTIONAL INFORMATION

Public/private: Public. **Student/faculty Ratio:** 3:1. **Students in Parent Institution:** 11,031.

STUDENT INFORMATION

Total Students in Program: 1,492. **% Full-time:** 20. **% Female:** 56.

RESEARCH FACILITIES

Research Facilities: Energy & Environmental Research Center, Center for Rural Health, Institute for Remote Sensing, Bureau of Governmental Affairs, Bureau of Educational Services & Applied Research, Human Nutrition Research Center, Center for Innovation & Business Development.

EXPENSES/FINANCIAL AID

Annual Tuition: In-state $2,814. / Out-of-state $7,514. **Fees:** $484. **Books and Supplies:** $500. **Average Salary Stipend:** $9,000.

ADMISSIONS INFORMATION

Application Fee: $30. **Regular Notification:** Rolling. **Transfer Students Accepted?** Yes. **Number of Applications Received:** 166. **% of Applicants Accepted:** 70. **% Accepted Who Enrolled:** 70. **Average GPA:** 3.36. **Average GRE Verbal:** 479. **Average GRE Quantitative:** 583. **Average GRE Analytical:** 568. **Required Admission Factors:** Essays/personal statement, letters of recommendation, transcript. **Other Admission Factors:** Minimum 3.0 GPA required for masters programs. Minimum 3.5 GPA required for doctoral programs. **Program-Specific Admission Factors:** Writing samples required for psychology, history, and English programs.

EMPLOYMENT INFORMATION

Placement Office Available? Yes.

UNIVERSITY OF NORTH FLORIDA
College of Arts & Sciences

Address: 4567 St. Johns Bluff Road South, Jacksonville, FL 32224-2645
Admissions Phone: 904-620-1360 · **Admissions Fax:** 904-620-1362
Admissions E-mail: jmowen@unf.edu · **Web Address:** www.unf.edu/coas

INSTITUTIONAL INFORMATION

Public/private: Public. **Evening Classes Available?** Yes. **Students in Parent Institution:** 12,992.

STUDENT INFORMATION

Total Students in Program: 1,858. **% Full-time:** 26. **% Female:** 66.

RESEARCH FACILITIES

Research Facilities: Florida Institute of Education, Center for Public Leadership, Center for Entrepreneurial Studies.

EXPENSES/FINANCIAL AID

Annual Tuition: In-state $3,081. / Out-of-state $10,410. **Room & Board:** $6,750. **Books and Supplies:** $600. **Grants Range From:** $125-$8,000. **Loans Range From:** $317-$16,405. **% Receiving Scholarships/Grants:** 22. **% Receiving Loans:** 64. **% Receiving Assistantships:** 14.

ADMISSIONS INFORMATION

Application Fee: $20. **Regular Notification:** Rolling. **Transfer Students Accepted?** Yes. **Number of Applications Received:** 225. **% of Applicants Accepted:** 39. **% Accepted Who Enrolled:** 62. **Average GPA:** 3.34. **Average GRE Verbal:** 486. **Average GRE Quantitative:** 532. **Required Admission Factors:** GRE, transcript. **Other Admission Factors:** Minimum GRE score of 1000 and minimum 3.0 GPA required.

EMPLOYMENT INFORMATION

Placement Office Available? Yes.

UNIVERSITY OF NORTH TEXAS
College of Arts & Sciences

Address: Toulouse School of Graduate Studies
Box 305459, Denton, TX 76203-3797
Admissions Phone: 940-465-2497 · **Admissions Fax:** 940-565-4517

INSTITUTIONAL INFORMATION

Public/private: Public. **Evening Classes Available?** Yes. **Student/faculty Ratio:** 17:1. **Students in Parent Institution:** 32,432.

STUDENT INFORMATION

Total Students in Program: 6,983. **% Full-time:** 31. **% Female:** 52.

EXPENSES/FINANCIAL AID

Annual Tuition: In-state $2,064. / Out-of-state $4,002. **Fees:** $610. **Books and Supplies:** $900. **Grants Range From:** $250-$2,500. **Loans Range From:** $100-$12,000. **% Receiving Financial Aid:** 31. **% Receiving Scholarships/Grants:** 85. **% Receiving Loans:** 84.

ADMISSIONS INFORMATION

Application Fee: $25. **Regular Notification:** Rolling. **Transfer Students Accepted?** Yes. **Required Admission Factors:** GRE, transcript. **Other Admission Factors:** Minimum GRE score of 800 (400 Verbal) and minimum 3.0 GPA required. **Program-Specific Admission Factors:** Minimum 3.4 GPA required for doctoral degree applicants.

EMPLOYMENT INFORMATION

Placement Office Available? Yes.

UNIVERSITY OF NORTH TEXAS
College of Music

Address: Toulouse School of Graduate Studies
Box 305459, Denton, TX 76203-3797
Admissions Phone: 940-565-3733 · **Admissions Fax:** 940-565-2002
Admissions E-mail: ebaird@music.unt.edu

INSTITUTIONAL INFORMATION

Public/private: Public. **Evening Classes Available?** Yes. **Student/faculty Ratio:** 17:1. **Students in Parent Institution:** 32,432.

STUDENT INFORMATION

Total Students in Program: 6,983. % Full-time: 31. % Female: 52.

EXPENSES/FINANCIAL AID

Annual Tuition: In-state $2,064. / Out-of-state $4,002. Fees: $610. Books and Supplies: $900. Grants Range From: $250-$2,500. Loans Range From: $100-$12,000. % Receiving Financial Aid: 31. % Receiving Scholarships/Grants: 85. % Receiving Loans: 84.

ADMISSIONS INFORMATION

Application Fee: $25. Regular Notification: Rolling. Transfer Students Accepted? Yes.
Required Admission Factors: GRE, transcript.
Other Admission Factors: Minimum GRE score of 800 and minimum 3.0 GPA required.

EMPLOYMENT INFORMATION

Placement Office Available? Yes.

UNIVERSITY OF NORTH TEXAS
School of Community Service

Address: Toulouse School of Graduate Studies
Box 305459, Denton, TX 76203-3797
Admissions Phone: 940-565-2239 · Admissions Fax: 940-565-4663

INSTITUTIONAL INFORMATION

Public/private: Public. Evening Classes Available? Yes. Student/faculty Ratio: 17:1. Students in Parent Institution: 32,432.

STUDENT INFORMATION

Total Students in Program: 6,983. % Full-time: 31. % Female: 52.

EXPENSES/FINANCIAL AID

Annual Tuition: In-state $2,064. / Out-of-state $4,002. Fees: $610. Books and Supplies: $900. Grants Range From: $250-$2,500. Loans Range From: $100-$12,000. % Receiving Financial Aid: 31. % Receiving Scholarships/Grants: 85. % Receiving Loans: 84.

ADMISSIONS INFORMATION

Application Fee: $25. Regular Notification: Rolling. Transfer Students Accepted? Yes.
Required Admission Factors: GRE, transcript.
Other Admission Factors: Minimum GRE score of 800 (400 Verbal) and minimum 3.0 GPA required.
Program-Specific Admission Factors: Minimum 3.4 GPA required of doctoral program applicants.

EMPLOYMENT INFORMATION

Placement Office Available? Yes.

UNIVERSITY OF NORTH TEXAS
School of Library & Information Sciences

Address: Toulouse School of Graduate Studies
Box 305459, Denton, TX 76203-3797
Admissions Phone: 940-565-2445 · Admissions Fax: 940-565-3101
Admissions E-mail: tohen@lis.admin.unt.edu

INSTITUTIONAL INFORMATION

Public/private: Public. Evening Classes Available? Yes. Student/faculty Ratio: 17:1. Students in Parent Institution: 32,432.

STUDENT INFORMATION

Total Students in Program: 6,983. % Full-time: 31. % Female: 52.

EXPENSES/FINANCIAL AID

Annual Tuition: In-state $2,064. / Out-of-state $4,002. Fees: $610. Books and Supplies: $900. Grants Range From: $250-$2,500. Loans Range From: $100-$12,000. % Receiving Financial Aid: 31. % Receiving Scholarships/Grants: 85. % Receiving Loans: 84.

ADMISSIONS INFORMATION

Application Fee: $25. Regular Notification: Rolling. Transfer Students Accepted? Yes.
Required Admission Factors: GRE, transcript.
Other Admission Factors: Minimum GRE score of 1000 (400 Verbal) and minimum 2.8 GPA required.
Program-Specific Admission Factors: Minimum 3.0 GPA required of doctoral program applicants.

EMPLOYMENT INFORMATION

Placement Office Available? Yes.

UNIVERSITY OF NORTH TEXAS
School of Visual Arts

Address: Toulouse School of Graduate Studies
Box 305459, Denton, TX 76203-3797
Admissions Phone: 940-565-4004 · Admissions Fax: 940-565-4717
Admissions E-mail: dtaylor@art.unt.edu

INSTITUTIONAL INFORMATION

Public/private: Public. Evening Classes Available? Yes. Student/faculty Ratio: 17:1. Students in Parent Institution: 32,432.

STUDENT INFORMATION

Total Students in Program: 6,983. % Full-time: 31. % Female: 52.

EXPENSES/FINANCIAL AID

Annual Tuition: In-state $2,064. / Out-of-state $4,002. Fees: $610. Books and Supplies: $900. Grants Range From: $250-$2,500. Loans Range From: $100-$12,000. % Receiving Financial Aid: 31. % Receiving Scholarships/Grants: 85. % Receiving Loans: 84.

ADMISSIONS INFORMATION

Application Fee: $25. Regular Notification: Rolling. Transfer Students Accepted? Yes.
Required Admission Factors: GRE, transcript.
Other Admission Factors: Minimum GRE score of 800 (400 Verbal) and minimum 3.0 GPA required.
Program-Specific Admission Factors: Minimum 3.4 GPA required of doctoral program applicants.

EMPLOYMENT INFORMATION

Placement Office Available? Yes.

UNIVERSITY OF NORTHERN COLORADO
College of Arts & Sciences

Address: Greeley, CO 80639
Admissions Phone: 970-351-2831 · Admissions Fax: 970-351-2731
Admissions E-mail: gradsch@unco.edu

INSTITUTIONAL INFORMATION

Public/private: Public. Students in Parent Institution: 12,233.

STUDENT INFORMATION

Total Students in Program: 2,020. % Full-time: 50. % Female: 73.

RESEARCH FACILITIES

Research Facilities: Math & Science Teaching Center, Center for Applied Research.

EXPENSES/FINANCIAL AID

Annual Tuition: In-state $2,549. / Out-of-state $10,459. Fees: $631. Books and Supplies: $800. Grants Range From: $50-$16,744. Loans Range From: $126-$12,077. % Receiving Financial Aid: 84. % Receiving Scholarships/Grants: 68. % Receiving Loans: 57. Number of Teaching/Research Assistantships Granted Each Year: 70. Average Salary Stipend: $8,178.

ADMISSIONS INFORMATION

Application Fee: $35. Transfer Students Accepted? No. Number of Applications Received: 118. % of Applicants Accepted: 73. % Accepted Who Enrolled: 65. Average GPA: 3.54. Average GRE Verbal: 497. Average GRE Quantitative: 591. Average GRE Analytical: 595. Required Admission Factors: Letters of recommendation, transcript. Other Admission Factors: Minimum 3.0 GPA required.

EMPLOYMENT INFORMATION

Placement Office Available? Yes. Rate of placement: 98%.

UNIVERSITY OF NORTHERN COLORADO
College of Performing & Visual Arts

Address: Greeley, CO 80639
Admissions Phone: 970-351-2831 · Admissions Fax: 970-351-2731
Admissions E-mail: gradsch@unico.edu

INSTITUTIONAL INFORMATION

Public/private: Public. Evening Classes Available? Yes. Students in Parent Institution: 12,233.

STUDENT INFORMATION

Total Students in Program: 2,020. % Full-time: 50. % Female: 73.

RESEARCH FACILITIES

Research Facilities: Math & Science Teaching Center, Center for Applied Research.

EXPENSES/FINANCIAL AID

Annual Tuition: In-state $2,549. / Out-of-state $10,459. Fees: $631. Books and Supplies: $800. Grants Range From: $50-$16,744. Loans Range From: $126-$12,077. % Receiving Financial Aid: 74. % Receiving Scholarships/Grants: 68. % Receiving Loans: 57. Number of Teaching/Research Assistantships Granted Each Year: 25. Average Salary Stipend: $5,835.

ADMISSIONS INFORMATION

Application Fee: $30. Transfer Students Accepted? Yes. Number of Applications Received: 72. % of Applicants Accepted: 61. % Accepted Who Enrolled: 66. Average GPA: 3.57. Average GRE Verbal: 513. Average GRE Quantitative: 519. Average GRE Analytical: 570. Required Admission Factors: Letters of recommendation, transcript. Other Admission Factors: Minimum 3.0 GPA required.

EMPLOYMENT INFORMATION

Placement Office Available? Yes. Rate of placement: 98%.

UNIVERSITY OF NORTHERN IOWA
College of Humanities & Fine Arts

Address: 1222 West 27th Street, Cedar Falls, IA 50614-0006
Admissions Phone: 319-273-2725

INSTITUTIONAL INFORMATION

Public/private: Public. Evening Classes Available? Yes. Students in Parent Institution: 14,070.

STUDENT INFORMATION

Total Students in Program: 1,596. % Full-time: 36. % Female: 66.

EXPENSES/FINANCIAL AID

Annual Tuition: In-state $3,704. / Out-of-state $9,122. Fees: $232. Books and Supplies: $776.

ADMISSIONS INFORMATION

Application Fee: $20. Regular Notification: Rolling. Transfer Students Accepted? Yes. Number of Applications Received: 217. % of Applicants Accepted: 70. % Accepted Who Enrolled: 54. Average GPA: 3.0. Required Admission Factors: Transcript.

EMPLOYMENT INFORMATION

Placement Office Available? Yes.

UNIVERSITY OF NORTHERN IOWA
College of Natural Sciences

Address: 1222 West 27th Street, Cedar Falls, IA 50614-0006
Admissions Phone: 319-273-2585 · Admissions Fax: 319-273-2893

INSTITUTIONAL INFORMATION

Public/private: Public. Evening Classes Available? Yes. Students in Parent Institution: 14,070.

STUDENT INFORMATION

Total Students in Program: 1,596. % Full-time: 36. % Female: 66.

EXPENSES/FINANCIAL AID

Annual Tuition: In-state $3,704. / Out-of-state $9,122. Fees: $232. Books and Supplies: $776.

ADMISSIONS INFORMATION

Application Fee: $20. Regular Notification: Rolling. Transfer Students Accepted? Yes. Number of Applications Received: 87. % of Applicants Accepted: 66. % Accepted Who Enrolled: 60. Average GPA: 3.0. Required Admission Factors: Essays/personal statement, interview, letters of recommendation, transcript.

EMPLOYMENT INFORMATION

Placement Office Available? Yes.

UNIVERSITY OF NORTHERN IOWA
College of Social & Behavioral Sciences

Address: 1222 West 27th Street, Cedar Falls, IA 50614-0006
Admissions Phone: 319-273-2221 · Admissions Fax: 319-273-2222

INSTITUTIONAL INFORMATION

Public/private: Public. Evening Classes Available? Yes. Students in Parent Institution: 14,070.

STUDENT INFORMATION

Total Students in Program: 1,596. % Full-time: 36. % Female: 66.

EXPENSES/FINANCIAL AID

Annual Tuition: In-state $3,704. / Out-of-state $9,122. Fees: $232. Books and Supplies: $776.

ADMISSIONS INFORMATION

Application Fee: $20. Regular Notification: Rolling. Transfer Students Accepted? Yes. Number of Applications Received: 107. % of Applicants Accepted: 75. % Accepted Who Enrolled: 58. Average GPA: 3.0. Required Admission Factors: Transcript. Program-Specific Admission Factors: Interview and essay required for some programs.

EMPLOYMENT INFORMATION

Placement Office Available? Yes.

UNIVERSITY OF NORTHERN IOWA
School of Music

Address: 1222 West 27th Street, Cedar Falls, IA 50614-0006
Admissions Phone: 319-273-2173 · Admissions Fax: 319-273-7320

INSTITUTIONAL INFORMATION

Public/private: Public. Evening Classes Available? Yes. Students in Parent Institution: 14,070.

STUDENT INFORMATION

Total Students in Program: 1,596. % Full-time: 36. % Female: 66.

EXPENSES/FINANCIAL AID

Annual Tuition: In-state $3,704. / Out-of-state $9,122. Fees: $232. Books and Supplies: $776.

ADMISSIONS INFORMATION

Application Fee: $20. Regular Notification: Rolling. Transfer Students Accepted? Yes. Number of Applications Received: 23. % of Applicants Accepted: 61. % Accepted Who Enrolled: 71. Average GPA: 3.0. Required Admission Factors: Essays/personal statement, letters of recommendation, transcript.
Program-Specific Admission Factors: 3 letters of recommendation required of MA program applicants. Interview required of some programs.

EMPLOYMENT INFORMATION

Placement Office Available? Yes.

UNIVERSITY OF NOTRE DAME
College of Arts & Letters

Address: Notre Dame, IN 46556
Admissions Phone: 219-631-7706 · Admissions Fax: 219-631-4183
Admissions E-mail: grad.ad.1@nd.edu

INSTITUTIONAL INFORMATION

Public/private: Private (nonprofit). Student/faculty Ratio: 2:1. Students in Parent Institution: 10,301.

STUDENT INFORMATION

Total Students in Program: 1,746. % Full-time: 94. % Female: 35.

RESEARCH FACILITIES

Research Facilities: Center for Philosophy of Religion, Medieval Institute, Kellogg Institute for International Studies, Kroc Institute for International Peace Studies, Cushwa Center for Study of American Catholicism, and Center for Bioengineering and Pollution Control.

EXPENSES/FINANCIAL AID

Annual Tuition: $21,500. Fees: $25. Books and Supplies: $800. Grants Range From: $300-$20,800. Loans Range From: $200-$32,270. % Receiving Financial Aid: 100. % Receiving Scholarships/Grants: 97. % Receiving Loans: 34. % Receiving Assistantships: 65. Number of Fellowships Granted Each Year: 186. Average amount of individual fellowships per year: $11,000. Number of Teaching/Research Assistantships Granted Each Year: 214. Average Salary Stipend: $10,300.

ADMISSIONS INFORMATION

Application Fee: $25. Regular Notification: Rolling. Transfer Students Accepted? Yes. Transfer Policy: Maximum 6 credit hours may be transferred from an incomplete masters; 24 from a complete masters. Number of Applications Received: 1,791. % of Applicants Accepted: 18. % Accepted Who Enrolled: 6. Average GPA: 3.58. Average GRE Verbal: 585. Average GRE

Quantitative: 628. Average GRE Analytical: 629.
Required Admission Factors: Essays/personal statement, GRE, letters of recommendation, transcript.
Other Admission Factors: Minimum 3.0 GPA required.

EMPLOYMENT INFORMATION

Placement Office Available? Yes.

UNIVERSITY OF NOTRE DAME
College of Science

Address: Notre Dame, IN 46556
Admissions Phone: 219-631-7706 · Admissions Fax: 219-631-6630

INSTITUTIONAL INFORMATION

Public/private: Private (nonprofit). Student/faculty Ratio: 2:1. Students in Parent Institution: 10,301.

STUDENT INFORMATION

Total Students in Program: 1,746. % Full-time: 94. % Female: 35.

RESEARCH FACILITIES

Research Facilities: Center for Philosophy of Religion, Medieval Institute, Kellogg Institute for International Studies, Kroc Institute for International Peace Studies, Cushwa Center for Study of American Catholicism, and Center for Bioengineering and Pollution Control.

EXPENSES/FINANCIAL AID

Annual Tuition: $21,500. Fees: $25. Books and Supplies: $800. Grants Range From: $300-$20,800. Loans Range From: $200-$32,270. % Receiving Financial Aid: 100. % Receiving Scholarships/Grants: 97. % Receiving Loans: 34. % Receiving Assistantships: 65. Number of Fellowships Granted Each Year: 10. Average amount of individual fellowships per year: $14,000. Number of Teaching/Research Assistantships Granted Each Year: 133. Average Salary Stipend: $12,500.

ADMISSIONS INFORMATION

Application Fee: $25. Regular Notification: Rolling. Transfer Students Accepted? Yes. Transfer Policy: Maximum 6 credit hours may be transferred from an incomplete masters; 24 from a complete masters. Number of Applications Received: 213. % of Applicants Accepted: 20. % Accepted Who Enrolled: 50. Average GPA: 3.47. Average GRE Verbal: 550. Average GRE Quantitative: 703. Average GRE Analytical: 670.
Required Admission Factors: Essays/personal statement, GRE, letters of recommendation, transcript.
Other Admission Factors: Minimum 3.0 GPA required.

EMPLOYMENT INFORMATION

Placement Office Available? Yes.

UNIVERSITY OF OKLAHOMA
College of Arts & Sciences

Address: 1000 ASP, Room 313, Norman, OK 73019
Admissions Phone: 405-325-3811 · Admissions Fax: 405-325-5346
Admissions E-mail: ap@ou.edu

INSTITUTIONAL INFORMATION

Public/private: Public. Evening Classes Available? Yes. Students in Parent Institution: 21,622.

STUDENT INFORMATION

Total Students in Program: 3,379. % Full-time: 56. % Female: 48.

RESEARCH FACILITIES

Research Facilities: Fred Jones Museum of Art, Oklahoma Museum of Natural History, Sarkeys Energy Center, Western history collection, history of science collection.

EXPENSES/FINANCIAL AID

Annual Tuition: In-state $2,208. / Out-of-state $7,140. **Fees:** $560. **Books and Supplies:** $899. **Grants Range From:** $100-$3,000. **Loans Range From:** $200-$18,500. **% Receiving Financial Aid:** 79. **% Receiving Scholarships/Grants:** 80. **% Receiving Loans:** 55. **% Receiving Assistantships:** 30. **Number of Teaching/Research Assistantships Granted Each Year:** 506. **Average Salary Stipend:** $10,775.

ADMISSIONS INFORMATION

Application Fee: $25. **Regular Notification:** Rolling. **Transfer Students Accepted?** Yes. **Number of Applications Received:** 1,420. **% of Applicants Accepted:** 65. **% Accepted Who Enrolled:** 55.
Required Admission Factors: Transcript.
Other Admission Factors: Minimum 3.0 GPA required; other requirements vary by program.

EMPLOYMENT INFORMATION

Placement Office Available? Yes.

UNIVERSITY OF OKLAHOMA
College of Fine Arts

Address: 1000 ASP, Room 313, Norman, OK 73019
Admissions Phone: 405-325-3811 · **Admissions Fax:** 405-325-5346
Admissions E-mail: ap@ou.edu

INSTITUTIONAL INFORMATION

Public/private: Public. **Evening Classes Available?** Yes. **Students in Parent Institution:** 21,622.

STUDENT INFORMATION

Total Students in Program: 3,379. **% Full-time:** 56. **% Female:** 48.

RESEARCH FACILITIES

Research Facilities: Fred Jones Museum of Art, Oklahoma Museum of Natural History, Sarkeys Energy Center, Western history collection, history of science collection.

EXPENSES/FINANCIAL AID

Annual Tuition: In-state $2,208. / Out-of-state $7,140. **Fees:** $560. **Books and Supplies:** $899. **Grants Range From:** $100-$3,000. **Loans Range From:** $200-$18,500. **% Receiving Financial Aid:** 71. **% Receiving Scholarships/Grants:** 80. **% Receiving Loans:** 55. **% Receiving Assistantships:** 30. **Number of Teaching/Research Assistantships Granted Each Year:** 94. **Average Salary Stipend:** $8,305.

ADMISSIONS INFORMATION

Application Fee: $25. **Regular Notification:** Rolling. **Transfer Students Accepted?** Yes. **Number of Applications Received:** 139. **% of Applicants Accepted:** 50. **% Accepted Who Enrolled:** 70.
Required Admission Factors: Interview, transcript.
Other Admission Factors: Minimum 3.0 GPA required.

EMPLOYMENT INFORMATION

Placement Office Available? Yes.

UNIVERSITY OF OKLAHOMA
College of Geosciences

Address: 1000 ASP, Room 313, Norman, OK 73019
Admissions Phone: 405-325-3811 · **Admissions Fax:** 405-325-5346
Admissions E-mail: ap@ou.edu

INSTITUTIONAL INFORMATION

Public/private: Public. **Evening Classes Available?** Yes. **Students in Parent Institution:** 21,622.

STUDENT INFORMATION

Total Students in Program: 3,379. **% Full-time:** 56. **% Female:** 48.

RESEARCH FACILITIES

Research Facilities: Fred Jones Museum of Art, Oklahoma Museum of Natural History, Sarkeys Energy Center, Western history collection, history of science collection.

EXPENSES/FINANCIAL AID

Annual Tuition: In-state $2,208. / Out-of-state $7,140. **Fees:** $560. **Books and Supplies:** $899. **Grants Range From:** $100-$3,000. **Loans Range From:** $200-$18,500. **% Receiving Financial Aid:** 90. **% Receiving Scholarships/Grants:** 80. **% Receiving Loans:** 55. **% Receiving Assistantships:** 30. **Number of Teaching/Research Assistantships Granted Each Year:** 42. **Average Salary Stipend:** $11,244.

ADMISSIONS INFORMATION

Regular Notification: Rolling. **Transfer Students Accepted?** Yes. **Transfer Policy:** Maximum 25% of total credit hours required may be transferred into a program requiring up to 36 credits. **Number of Applications Received:** 44. **% of Applicants Accepted:** 43. **% Accepted Who Enrolled:** 58.
Required Admission Factors: Essays/personal statement, GRE, letters of recommendation, transcript.
Other Admission Factors: Departmental application required.
Program-Specific Admission Factors: Minimum 3.0 GPA required of masters degree program applicants. Minimum 3.25 required of doctoral degree program applicants.

EMPLOYMENT INFORMATION

Placement Office Available? Yes. **% Employed Within Six Months:** 95.

UNIVERSITY OF OKLAHOMA
College of Journalism & Mass Communications

Address: 1000 ASP, Room 313, Norman, OK 73019
Admissions Phone: 405-325-3811 · **Admissions Fax:** 405-325-5346
Admissions E-mail: ap@ou.edu

INSTITUTIONAL INFORMATION

Public/private: Public. **Evening Classes Available?** Yes. **Students in Parent Institution:** 21,622.

STUDENT INFORMATION

Total Students in Program: 3,379. **% Full-time:** 56. **% Female:** 48.

RESEARCH FACILITIES

Research Facilities: Fred Jones Museum of Art, Oklahoma Museum of Natural History, Sarkeys Energy Center, Western history collection, history of science collection.

EXPENSES/FINANCIAL AID

Annual Tuition: In-state $2,208. / Out-of-state $7,140. **Fees:** $560. **Books and Supplies:** $899. **Grants Range From:** $100-$3,000. **Loans Range From:** $200-$18,500. **% Receiving Financial Aid:** 76. **% Receiving Scholarships/Grants:** 80. **% Receiving Loans:** 55. **% Receiving Assistantships:** 30. **Number of Teaching/Research Assistantships Granted Each Year:** 13. **Average Salary Stipend:** $8,632.

ADMISSIONS INFORMATION

Application Fee: $25. **Transfer Students Accepted?** Yes. **Number of Applications Received:** 23. **% of Applicants Accepted:** 52. **% Accepted Who Enrolled:** 67.
Required Admission Factors: Essays/personal statement, GRE, letters of recommendation, transcript.
Other Admission Factors: Minimum 3.0 GPA required; other requirements vary by program.

EMPLOYMENT INFORMATION

Placement Office Available? Yes.

UNIVERSITY OF OKLAHOMA
College of Liberal Studies

Address: 1700 ASP, Suite 226, Norman, OK 73072-6400
Admissions Phone: 405-325-1061-or-800-522-4389
Admissions Fax: 405-325-7132 · **Admissions E-mail:** nancee@ou.edu
Web Address: www.ou.edu/cls/Prospective/Masters/mlsadmission.htm

INSTITUTIONAL INFORMATION

Public/private: Public. **Students in Parent Institution:** 21,622.

STUDENT INFORMATION

Total Students in Program: 3,379. **% Full-time:** 56. **% Female:** 48.

RESEARCH FACILITIES

Research Facilities: Fred Jones Museum of Art, Oklahoma Museum of Natural History, Sarkeys Energy Center, Western history collection, history of science collection.

EXPENSES/FINANCIAL AID

Annual Tuition: In-state $2,208. / Out-of-state $7,140. **Fees:** $560. **Books and Supplies:** $899. **Grants Range From:** $100-$3,000. **Loans Range From:** $200-$18,500. **% Receiving Scholarships/Grants:** 80. **% Receiving Loans:** 55. **% Receiving Assistantships:** 30. **Number of Teaching/Research Assistantships Granted Each Year:** 1 **Average Salary Stipend:** $9,363.

ADMISSIONS INFORMATION

Application Fee: $25. **Regular Application Deadline:** 6/1. **Regular Notification:** Rolling. **Transfer Students Accepted?** Yes. **Number of Applications Received:** 7. **% of Applicants Accepted:** 86.
Required Admission Factors: Essays/personal statement, transcript.
Other Admission Factors: Minimum 3.0 GPA required; alternate admissions possible for applicants whose GPA does not meet minimum.

EMPLOYMENT INFORMATION

Placement Office Available? Yes.

UNIVERSITY OF OREGON
College of Arts & Sciences

Address: Eugene, OR 97403-1217

INSTITUTIONAL INFORMATION

Public/private: Public. **Students in Parent Institution:** 17,801.

STUDENT INFORMATION

Total Students in Program: 3,227. **% Full-time:** 67. **% Female:** 54.

RESEARCH FACILITIES

Research Facilities: Institute for a Sustainable Environment, Institute for Community Arts, Institute for the Development of Educational Achievement, Institute for Industrial Relations, Institute of Molecular Biology, Institute of Neuroscience.

EXPENSES/FINANCIAL AID

Annual Tuition: In-state $6,228. / Out-of-state $11,375. **Fees:** $1,125. **Books and Supplies:** $800. **Number of Teaching/Research Assistantships Granted Each Year:** 1,200.

ADMISSIONS INFORMATION

Application Fee: $50. **Transfer Students Accepted?** Yes. **Number of Applications Received:** 1,281. **% of Applicants Accepted:** 19.
Required Admission Factors: Essays/personal statement, letters of recommendation, transcript.

Other Admission Factors: Minimum 3.0 GPA (3.3 for some programs) required.

EMPLOYMENT INFORMATION

Placement Office Available? Yes.

UNIVERSITY OF OREGON
School of Journalism & Communication

Address: 1275 University of Oregon, Eugene, OR 97403-1217
Admissions Phone: 541-346-2136 · **Admissions Fax:** 541-346-2211
Admissions E-mail: gradinfo@jcomm.uoregon.edu
Web Address: http://jcomm.uoregon.edu/

INSTITUTIONAL INFORMATION

Public/private: Public. **Total Faculty:** 25. **% Faculty Female:** 32. **% Faculty Part-time:** 92. **Student/faculty Ratio:** 4:1. **Students in Parent Institution:** 20,000.

PROGRAMS

Masters offered in: Advertising; communications and media studies; communications, journalism, and related fields; health communications; journalism; journalism; mass communications/media studies; public relations/image management; publishing. **Doctorate offered in:** Communications and media studies; communications, journalism, and related fields; health communications; mass communications/media studies. **First Professional degree offered in:** Advertising; journalism; journalism; public relations/image management.

STUDENT INFORMATION

Total Students in Program: 3,227. **% Full-time:** 67. **% Female:** 54.

RESEARCH FACILITIES

Research Facilities: Institute for a Sustainable Environment, Institute for Community Arts, Institute for the Development of Educational Achievement, Institute for Industrial Relations, Institute of Molecular Biology, Institute of Neuroscience.

EXPENSES/FINANCIAL AID

Annual Tuition: In-state $9,900. / Out-of-state $17,000. **Room & Board:** $7,000. **Fees:** $1,125. **Books and Supplies:** $900. **Grants Range From:** $500-$2,000. **Loans Range From:** $5,000-$20,000. **% Receiving Financial Aid:** 75. **% Receiving Scholarships/Grants:** 40. **Types of Aid Available:** Fellowships, graduate assistantships, scholarships. **Number of Fellowships Granted Each Year:** 30. **Average amount of individual fellowships per year:** $13,000. **Number of Teaching/Research Assistantships Granted Each Year:** 30. **Average Salary Stipend:** $4,900.

ADMISSIONS INFORMATION

Application Fee: $50. **Regular Application Deadline:** 1/1. **Transfer Students Accepted?** Yes. **Transfer Policy:** Same as for regular admission. **Number of Applications Received:** 150. **% of Applicants Accepted:** 30. **% Accepted Who Enrolled:** 69. **Average GPA:** 3.8. **Average GRE Verbal:** 600. **Average GRE Quantitative:** 600.
Required Admission Factors: Essays/personal statement, GRE, letters of recommendation, transcript.
Other Admission Factors: Minimum GRE score of 1100 (Verbal and Quantitative), minimum 3.0 GPA, resume, and portfolio required. TOEFL of 600 required for international students.

EMPLOYMENT INFORMATION

Placement Office Available? Yes. **% Employed Within Six Months:** 78. **% of masters/doctoral grads employed in their field upon graduation:** 75/100. **Rate of placement:** 90%. **Average starting salary:** $35,000.

UNIVERSITY OF OREGON
School of Music

Address: Eugene, OR 97403-1217
Admissions Phone: 541-346-5664 · **Admissions Fax:** 541-346-0723

INSTITUTIONAL INFORMATION
Public/private: Public. **Students in Parent Institution:** 17,801.

STUDENT INFORMATION
Total Students in Program: 3,227. **% Full-time:** 67. **% Female:** 54.

RESEARCH FACILITIES
Research Facilities: Institute for a Sustainable Environment, Institute for Community Arts, Institute for the Development of Educational Achievement, Institute for Industrial Relations, Institute of Molecular Biology, Institute of Neuroscience.

EXPENSES/FINANCIAL AID
Annual Tuition: In-state $6,228. / Out-of-state $11,375. **Fees:** $1,125. **Books and Supplies:** $800. **% Receiving Financial Aid:** 80. **Number of Fellowships Granted Each Year:** 65 **Average amount of individual fellowships per year:** $10,800 **Number of Teaching/Research Assistantships Granted Each Year:** 65 **Average Salary Stipend:** $3,700.

ADMISSIONS INFORMATION
Application Fee: $50. **Regular Notification:** Rolling. **Transfer Students Accepted?** Yes. **Number of Applications Received:** 93. **% of Applicants Accepted:** 58. **% Accepted Who Enrolled:** 76. **Average GPA:** 3.5.
Required Admission Factors: Essays/personal statement, GRE, letters of recommendation, transcript.
Other Admission Factors: Minimum 3.0 GPA required.
Program-Specific Admission Factors: Interview required of conducting and composition program applicants.

EMPLOYMENT INFORMATION
Placement Office Available? Yes.

UNIVERSITY OF PENNSYLVANIA
Annenberg School for Communication

Address: Philadelphia, PA 19104

INSTITUTIONAL INFORMATION
Public/private: Private (nonprofit). **Total Faculty:** 15. **% Faculty Female:** 20. **Students in Parent Institution:** 21,200.

STUDENT INFORMATION
Total Students in Program: 7,392. **% Full-time:** 74. **% Female:** 49.

RESEARCH FACILITIES
Research Facilities: Over 70 research centers.

EXPENSES/FINANCIAL AID
Annual Tuition: $25,750. **Room & Board (On/off campus):** $12,904/$8,244. **Fees:** $1,612. **Books and Supplies:** $760.

ADMISSIONS INFORMATION
Application Fee: $65. **Transfer Students Accepted?** No. **Number of Applications Received:** 576. **% of Applicants Accepted:** 5. **% Accepted Who Enrolled:** 83.
Required Admission Factors: Essays/personal statement, GRE, interview, letters of recommendation, transcript.

EMPLOYMENT INFORMATION
Placement Office Available? Yes.

UNIVERSITY OF PENNSYLVANIA
School of Arts & Sciences

Address: 3401 Walnut Street, Suite 322A, Philadelphia, PA 19104-6228
Admissions Phone: 215-573-5816 · **Admissions Fax:** 215-573-8068
Admissions E-mail: gdasadmis@sas.upenn.edu · **Web Address:** www.upenn.edu/GAS

INSTITUTIONAL INFORMATION
Public/private: Private (nonprofit). **Total Faculty:** 441. **% Faculty Female:** 24. **Students in Parent Institution:** 21,200.

STUDENT INFORMATION
Total Students in Program: 7,392. **% Full-time:** 74. **% Female:** 49.

RESEARCH FACILITIES
Research Facilities: Over 70 research centers.

EXPENSES/FINANCIAL AID
Annual Tuition: $25,750. **Room & Board (On/off campus):** $12,904/$8,244. **Fees:** $1,612. **Books and Supplies:** $760.

ADMISSIONS INFORMATION
Application Fee: $70. **Priority Application Deadline:** 12/15. **Regular Application Deadline:** 12/15. **Regular Notification:** Rolling. **Transfer Students Accepted?** Yes. **Transfer Policy:** Maximum 8 credit units may be transferred into some programs. New students must complete application process. **Number of Applications Received:** 3,527. **% of Applicants Accepted:** 26. **% Accepted Who Enrolled:** 36. **Average GRE Verbal:** 612. **Average GRE Quantitative:** 669. **Average GRE Analytical:** 682.
Required Admission Factors: Essays/personal statement, letters of recommendation, transcript.
Other Admission Factors: Minimum 3.0 GPA required for most programs.

EMPLOYMENT INFORMATION
Placement Office Available? Yes.

UNIVERSITY OF PENNSYLVANIA
School of Design

Address: 110 Meyerson Hall, Philadelphia, PA 19104-6311
Admissions Phone: 215-898-6520 · **Admissions Fax:** 215-573-3927
Admissions E-mail: admissions@design.upenn.edu
Web Address: www.design.upenn.edu/

INSTITUTIONAL INFORMATION
Public/private: Private (nonprofit). **Students in Parent Institution:** 22,768.

PROGRAMS
Masters offered in: Architecture (BArch, BA/BS, MArch, MA/MS, PhD); architecture and related programs; art/art studies; city/urban, community, and regional planning; design and visual communications; fine arts and art studies; fine/studio arts; intermedia/multimedia; landscape architecture (BS, BSLA, BLA, MSLA, MLA, PhD); painting; photography; printmaking; sculpture; visual and performing arts. **Doctorate offered in:** Architectural history and criticism; architecture (BArch, BA/BS, MArch, MA/MS, PhD); city/urban, community, and regional planning; landscape architecture (BS, BSLA, BLA, MSLA, MLA, PhD). **First Professional degree offered in:** Architecture (BArch, BA/BS, MArch, MA/MS, PhD), landscape architecture (BS, BSLA, BLA, MSLA, MLA, PhD).

STUDENT INFORMATION
Total Students in Program: 606. **% Full-time:** 100. **% Female:** 592.

RESEARCH FACILITIES
Research Facilities: Over 70 research centers.

EXPENSES/FINANCIAL AID
Annual Tuition: $28,040. **Room & Board (On/off campus):** $8,500/$8,230.

Fees: $4,030. **Books and Supplies:** $1,500. **Grants Range From:** $2,000-$20,000. **Loans Range From:** $1,000-$45,000. **% Receiving Financial Aid:** 60. **Types of Aid Available:** Fellowships, graduate assistantships, grants, institutional work-study, loans, scholarships. **Average student debt upon graduation:** $70,000. **Number of Fellowships Granted Each Year:** 4. **Average amount of individual fellowships per year:** $45,670. **Number of Teaching/Research Assistantships Granted Each Year:** 79. **Average Salary Stipend:** $2,000.

ADMISSIONS INFORMATION

Application Fee: $70. **Regular Application Deadline:** 1/15. **Regular Notification:** 3/22. **Transfer Students Accepted?** Yes. **Number of Applications Received:** 1,377. **% of Applicants Accepted:** 47. **% Accepted Who Enrolled:** 40. **Average GPA:** 3.3. **Average GRE Verbal:** 534. **Average GRE Quantitative:** 664. **Average GRE Analytical:** 646.
Required Admission Factors: Essays/personal statement, GRE, letters of recommendation, transcript.
Program-Specific Admission Factors: Portfolio required of art, architecture, and landscape architecture program applicants.

EMPLOYMENT INFORMATION

Placement Office Available? Yes.

UNIVERSITY OF PENNSYLVANIA
School of Social Work

Address: Philadelphia, PA 19104
Admissions Phone: 215-898-5521

INSTITUTIONAL INFORMATION

Public/private: Private (nonprofit). **Students in Parent Institution:** 21,200.

STUDENT INFORMATION

Total Students in Program: 7,392. **% Full-time:** 74. **% Female:** 49.

RESEARCH FACILITIES

Research Facilities: Over 70 research centers.

EXPENSES/FINANCIAL AID

Annual Tuition: $25,750. **Room & Board (On/off campus):** $12,904/$8,244. **Fees:** $1,612. **Books and Supplies:** $760.

ADMISSIONS INFORMATION

Application Fee: $65. **Regular Notification:** Rolling. **Transfer Students Accepted?** Yes. **Transfer Policy:** Maximum 18 credit hours may be transferred into masters programs. **Number of Applications Received:** 346. **% of Applicants Accepted:** 77. **% Accepted Who Enrolled:** 46.
Required Admission Factors: Essays/personal statement, letters of recommendation, transcript.
Program-Specific Admission Factors: Minimum 3.0 GPA required of doctoral program applicants.

EMPLOYMENT INFORMATION

Placement Office Available? Yes.

UNIVERSITY OF PITTSBURGH
Faculty of Arts & Sciences

Address: 5141 Sennott Square, Pittsburgh, PA 15260
Admissions Phone: 412-624-6094 · **Admissions Fax:** 412-624-5299
Admissions E-mail: walters@fcas.pitt.edu · **Web Address:** www.fas.pitt.edu

INSTITUTIONAL INFORMATION

Public/private: Public. **Students in Parent Institution:** 23,901.

STUDENT INFORMATION

Total Students in Program: 1,489. **% Full-time:** 88. **% Female:** 47. **% Minority:** 8. **% International:** 35.

RESEARCH FACILITIES

Research Facilities: University Center for International Studies.

EXPENSES/FINANCIAL AID

Annual Tuition: In-state $11,744. / Out-of-state $22,938. **Room & Board:** $6,500. **Fees:** $540. **Books and Supplies:** $900. **% Receiving Financial Aid:** 75. **Types of Aid Available:** Fellowships, graduate assistantships, institutional work-study, loans.

ADMISSIONS INFORMATION

Application Fee: $40. **Priority Application Deadline:** 1/15. **Regular Application Deadline:** 1/30. **Regular Notification:** Rolling. **Transfer Students Accepted?** Yes. **Transfer Policy:** Maximum of 6 credit hours may be transferred into masters programs. Maximum 24 credit hours may be transferred into doctoral programs. **Number of Applications Received:** 3,222. **% of Applicants Accepted:** 31. **% Accepted Who Enrolled:** 32. **Average GPA:** 3.5. **Average GRE Verbal:** 562. **Average GRE Quantitative:** 675. **Average GRE Analytical:** 669.
Required Admission Factors: Essays/personal statement, letters of recommendation, transcript.
Other Admission Factors: Minimum 3.0 GPA required.
Program-Specific Admission Factors: 3 letters of recommendation may be required of some programs.

EMPLOYMENT INFORMATION

Placement Office Available? Yes.

UNIVERSITY OF PITTSBURGH
Graduate School of Public & International Affairs

Address: Office of Student Services, 3L03 Posvar Hall, Pittsburgh, PA 15260
Admissions Phone: 412-648-7640 · **Admissions Fax:** 412-648-7641
Admissions E-mail: gspia@pitt.edu · **Web Address:** www.gspia.pitt.edu

INSTITUTIONAL INFORMATION

Public/private: Public. **Evening Classes Available?** Yes. **Student/faculty Ratio:** 10:1. **Students in Parent Institution:** 26,329.

STUDENT INFORMATION

Total Students in Program: 440. **% Full-time:** 91. **% Female:** 878.

RESEARCH FACILITIES

Research Facilities: University Center for International Studies.

EXPENSES/FINANCIAL AID

Annual Tuition: In-state $9,410. / Out-of-state $19,376. **Fees:** $480. **Books and Supplies:** $500. **% Receiving Financial Aid:** 33. **Average student debt upon graduation:** $20,000 **Number of Fellowships Granted Each Year:** 86 **Average amount of individual fellowships per year:** $6,000. **Number of Teaching/Research Assistantships Granted Each Year:** 5. **Average Salary Stipend:** $11,520.

ADMISSIONS INFORMATION

Application Fee: $40. **Regular Application Deadline:** 2/1. **Regular Notification:** Rolling. **Transfer Students Accepted?** Yes. **Transfer Policy:** Maximum 12 credit hours may be transferred into masters programs; 30 may be transferred into the doctoral program. **Number of Applications Received:** 640. **% of Applicants Accepted:** 73. **% Accepted Who Enrolled:** 40. **Average GPA:** 3.4. **Average GRE Verbal:** 632. **Average GRE Quantitative:** 720. **Average GRE Analytical:** 684. **Average GRE Analytical Writing:** 5.5.
Required Admission Factors: Essays/personal statement, letters of recommendation, transcript.
Recommended Admission Factors: Interview.

Other Admission Factors: Minimum 3.0 GPA required.
Program-Specific Admission Factors: Minimum combined GRE score of 1050 (Verbal and Quantitative) and 4.5 on Analytical Writing and Writing Sample required of doctoral program applicants. GRE recommended of masters program applicants.

EMPLOYMENT INFORMATION
Placement Office Available? Yes. **% Employed Within Six Months:** 90. **% of masters/doctoral grads employed in their field upon graduation:** 90/90. **Average starting salary:** $47,000.

UNIVERSITY OF PITTSBURGH
School of Information Science

Address: 4200 Fifth Avenue, Pittsburgh, PA 15260
Admissions Phone: 412-624-5146 · **Admissions Fax:** 412-624-5231
Admissions E-mail: mbiagini@mail.sis.pitt.edu

INSTITUTIONAL INFORMATION
Public/private: Public. **Evening Classes Available?** Yes. **Student/faculty Ratio:** 26:1. **Students in Parent Institution:** 26,329.

STUDENT INFORMATION
Total Students in Program: 7,058. **% Full-time:** 58. **% Female:** 55.

RESEARCH FACILITIES
Research Facilities: University Center for International Studies.

EXPENSES/FINANCIAL AID
Annual Tuition: In-state $9,410. / Out-of-state $19,376. **Fees:** $480. **Books and Supplies:** $500. **% Receiving Financial Aid:** 27. **Number of Fellowships Granted Each Year:** 3. **Average amount of individual fellowships per year:** $13,809. **Number of Teaching/Research Assistantships Granted Each Year:** 24. **Average Salary Stipend:** $4,495.

ADMISSIONS INFORMATION
Application Fee: $40. **Regular Notification:** Rolling. **Transfer Students Accepted?** No. **Transfer Policy:** Maximum 6 credit hours with department approval may be transferred. **Number of Applications Received:** 194. **% of Applicants Accepted:** 92. **% Accepted Who Enrolled:** 63. **Average GPA:** 3.0.
Required Admission Factors: Essays/personal statement, letters of recommendation, transcript.
Other Admission Factors: Minimum 3.0 GPA required.

EMPLOYMENT INFORMATION
Placement Office Available? Yes. **% Employed Within Six Months:** 63. **% of doctoral grads employed in their field upon graduation:** 100. **Average starting salary:** $40,000.

UNIVERSITY OF PITTSBURGH
School of Social Work

Address: 4200 Fifth Avenue, Pittsburgh, PA 15260
Admissions Phone: 412-624-6346 · **Admissions Fax:** 412-624-6323

INSTITUTIONAL INFORMATION
Public/private: Public. **Student/faculty Ratio:** 25:1. **Students in Parent Institution:** 26,329.

STUDENT INFORMATION
Total Students in Program: 7,058. **% Full-time:** 58. **% Female:** 55.

RESEARCH FACILITIES
Research Facilities: University Center for International Studies.

EXPENSES/FINANCIAL AID
Annual Tuition: In-state $9,410. / Out-of-state $19,376. **Fees:** $480. **Books and Supplies:** $500. **% Receiving Financial Aid:** 30. **Average student debt upon graduation:** $10,000. **Number of Teaching/Research Assistantships Granted Each Year:** 19. **Average Salary Stipend:** $5,300.

ADMISSIONS INFORMATION
Application Fee: $40. **Transfer Students Accepted?** Yes. **Transfer Policy:** Field placement evaluation required of transfer applicants. **Number of Applications Received:** 531. **% of Applicants Accepted:** 72. **% Accepted Who Enrolled:** 62. **Average GPA:** 3.0.
Required Admission Factors: Essays/personal statement, letters of recommendation, transcript.
Other Admission Factors: Minimum 3.0 GPA required.

EMPLOYMENT INFORMATION
Placement Office Available? Yes. **% Employed Within Six Months:** 96. **% of masters/doctoral grads employed in their field upon graduation:** 81/90. **Average starting salary:** $65,000.

UNIVERSITY OF PORTLAND
College of Arts & Sciences

Address: 5000 North Willamette Boulevard, Portland, OR 97203-5798
Admissions Phone: 503-943-7107 · **Admissions Fax:** 503-943-7178
Admissions E-mail: gradschl@up.edu

INSTITUTIONAL INFORMATION
Public/private: Private (nonprofit). **Students in Parent Institution:** 2,956.

STUDENT INFORMATION
Total Students in Program: 437. **% Full-time:** 31. **% Female:** 59.

RESEARCH FACILITIES
Research Facilities: Orrico Hall, Swindells Hall, science building.

EXPENSES/FINANCIAL AID
Annual Tuition: In-state $11,838. **Books and Supplies:** $700.

ADMISSIONS INFORMATION
Application Fee: $45. **Regular Notification:** Rolling. **Transfer Students Accepted?** Yes. **Number of Applications Received:** 35. **% of Applicants Accepted:** 46.
Required Admission Factors: Essays/personal statement, GRE, letters of recommendation, transcript.
Other Admission Factors: Minimum 3.0 GPA required for most programs.

EMPLOYMENT INFORMATION
Placement Office Available? Yes.

UNIVERSITY OF PUERTO RICO—MAYAGUEZ
College of Arts & Sciences

Address: PO Box 5000, Mayaguez, Puerto Rico 00681-5000

INSTITUTIONAL INFORMATION
Public/private: Public. **Students in Parent Institution:** 12,603.

STUDENT INFORMATION
Total Students in Program: 799. **% Full-time:** 82. **% Female:** 46.

RESEARCH FACILITIES
Research Facilities: Agricultural Resource Station, Agricultural Extension Center, Research and Development Center.

EXPENSES/FINANCIAL AID
Annual Tuition: In-state $1,950. / Out-of-state $3,388. **Room & Board:** $8,000. **Fees:** $885. **Books and Supplies:** $1,500.

ADMISSIONS INFORMATION

Transfer Students Accepted? No.

EMPLOYMENT INFORMATION

Placement Office Available? Yes.

UNIVERSITY OF PUERTO RICO—
RIO PIEDRAS CAMPUS
College of Humanities

Address: PO Box 21790, UPR Station, Rio Piedras, Puerto Rico 00931-1790
Admissions Phone: 787-764-0000, ext. 3541 · **Admissions Fax:** 787-763-5899
Admissions E-mail: humagrad@rrpac.upr.clu.edu

INSTITUTIONAL INFORMATION

Public/private: Public. Evening Classes Available? Yes. Student/faculty Ratio: 5:1. Students in Parent Institution: 21,539.

STUDENT INFORMATION

Total Students in Program: 3,056. % Full-time: 60. % Female: 67.

RESEARCH FACILITIES

Research Facilities: 14 research centers.

EXPENSES/FINANCIAL AID

Annual Tuition: In-state $1,200. / Out-of-state $3,500. Fees: $70. Books and Supplies: $1,500. Grants Range From: $1,000-$3,000. Loans Range From: $3,000-$8,500. % Receiving Financial Aid: 36. % Receiving Scholarships/Grants: 60. % Receiving Loans: 90. Number of Teaching/Research Assistantships Granted Each Year: 9. Average Salary Stipend: $7,000.

ADMISSIONS INFORMATION

Application Fee: $15. Transfer Students Accepted? Yes. Transfer Policy: Maximum 1/3 of total credit hours required may be transferred. Number of Applications Received: 139. % of Applicants Accepted: 81. % Accepted Who Enrolled: 91. Average GPA: 3.0.
Required Admission Factors: Essays/personal statement, letters of recommendation, transcript.
Other Admission Factors: Minimum 3.0 GPA required.

EMPLOYMENT INFORMATION

Placement Office Available? Yes. % Employed Within Six Months: 98. % of masters/doctoral grads employed in their field upon graduation: 98/100. Rate of placement: 45%. Average starting salary: $30,000.

UNIVERSITY OF PUERTO RICO—
RIO PIEDRAS CAMPUS
College of Social Sciences

Address: PO Box 21790, UPR Station, Rio Piedras, Puerto Rico 00931-1790
Admissions Phone: 787-764-0000, ext. 4152 · **Admissions Fax:** 787-763-5599

INSTITUTIONAL INFORMATION

Public/private: Public. Evening Classes Available? Yes. Student/faculty Ratio: 17:1. Students in Parent Institution: 21,539.

STUDENT INFORMATION

Total Students in Program: 3,056. % Full-time: 60. % Female: 67.

RESEARCH FACILITIES

Research Facilities: 14 research centers.

EXPENSES/FINANCIAL AID

Annual Tuition: In-state $1,200. / Out-of-state $3,500. Fees: $70. Books and Supplies: $1,500. Grants Range From: $1,000-$3,000. Loans Range From: $3,000-$8,500. % Receiving Financial Aid: 36. % Receiving Scholarships/

Grants: 60. % Receiving Loans: 90. Average Salary Stipend: $7,000.

ADMISSIONS INFORMATION

Application Fee: $26. Transfer Students Accepted? Yes. Transfer Policy: Maximum 1/3 of total credit hours required may be transferred. Number of Applications Received: 879. % of Applicants Accepted: 48. % Accepted Who Enrolled: 100. Average GPA: 3.3.
Required Admission Factors: Essays/personal statement, interview, letters of recommendation, transcript.
Other Admission Factors: Minimum 3.0 GPA required.

EMPLOYMENT INFORMATION

Placement Office Available? Yes. % Employed Within Six Months: 98. % of masters/doctoral grads employed in their field upon graduation: 98/100. Rate of placement: 45%. Average starting salary: $30,000.

UNIVERSITY OF PUERTO RICO—RIO PIEDRAS
Faculty of Natural Sciences

Address: PO Box 21790, UPR Station, Rio Piedras, Puerto Rico 00931-1790
Admissions Phone: 787-764-0000

INSTITUTIONAL INFORMATION

Public/private: Public. Student/faculty Ratio: 5:1. Students in Parent Institution: 21,539.

STUDENT INFORMATION

Total Students in Program: 3,056. % Full-time: 60. % Female: 67.

RESEARCH FACILITIES

Research Facilities: 14 research centers.

EXPENSES/FINANCIAL AID

Annual Tuition: In-state $1,200. / Out-of-state $3,500. Fees: $70. Books and Supplies: $1,500. Grants Range From: $1,000-$3,000. Loans Range From: $3,000-$8,500. % Receiving Financial Aid: 36. % Receiving Scholarships/Grants: 60. % Receiving Loans: 90. Number of Teaching/Research Assistantships Granted Each Year: 126 Average Salary Stipend: $7,000.

ADMISSIONS INFORMATION

Application Fee: $15. Transfer Students Accepted? Yes. Transfer Policy: Maximum 1/3 of total credit hours required may be transferred. Number of Applications Received: 137. % of Applicants Accepted: 62. % Accepted Who Enrolled: 73. Average GPA: 3.0. Average GRE Verbal: 374. Average GRE Quantitative: 492. Average GRE Analytical: 443.
Required Admission Factors: Letters of recommendation, transcript.
Other Admission Factors: Minimum 3.0 GPA, full command of Spanish language, and good command of English required.
Program-Specific Admission Factors: 3 letters of recommendation required of some programs.

EMPLOYMENT INFORMATION

Placement Office Available? Yes. % Employed Within Six Months: 98. % of masters/doctoral grads employed in their field upon graduation: 98/100. Rate of placement: 45%. Average starting salary: $40,000.

UNIVERSITY OF PUERTO RICO—
RIO PIEDRAS CAMPUS
Graduate School of Planning

Address: PO Box 21790, UPR Station, Rio Piedras, Puerto Rico 00931-1790
Admissions Phone: 787-764-0000, ext. 3182
Admissions Fax: 787-763-5375 · **Admissions E-mail:** aest_egp@hotmail.com

INSTITUTIONAL INFORMATION

Public/private: Public. Evening Classes Available? Yes. Student/faculty Ratio: 11:1. Students in Parent Institution: 21,539.

STUDENT INFORMATION

Total Students in Program: 3,056. % Full-time: 60. % Female: 67.

RESEARCH FACILITIES

Research Facilities: 14 research centers.

EXPENSES/FINANCIAL AID

Annual Tuition: In-state $1,200. / Out-of-state $3,500. Fees: $70. Books and Supplies: $1,500. Grants Range From: $1,000-$3,000. Loans Range From: $3,000-$8,500. % Receiving Financial Aid: 36. % Receiving Scholarships/ Grants: 60. % Receiving Loans: 90. Number of Teaching/Research Assistantships Granted Each Year: 6 Average Salary Stipend: $7,000.

ADMISSIONS INFORMATION

Application Fee: $15. Transfer Students Accepted? Yes. Number of Applications Received: 58. % of Applicants Accepted: 83. % Accepted Who Enrolled: 58. Average GPA: 3.0.
Required Admission Factors: Interview, letters of recommendation.
Other Admission Factors: Minimum 3.0 GPA and coursework in mathematics, statistics, sociology, and economics required.

EMPLOYMENT INFORMATION

Placement Office Available? Yes. % Employed Within Six Months: 99. % of masters grads employed in their field upon graduation: 99. Rate of placement: 45%. Average starting salary: $30,000.

UNIVERSITY OF PUERTO RICO— RIO PIEDRAS CAMPUS
School of Public Communication

Address: PO Box 21790, UPR Station, Rio Piedras, Puerto Rico 00931-1790
Admissions Phone: 787-764-0000, ext. 5037 · Admissions Fax: 787-763-5390

INSTITUTIONAL INFORMATION

Public/private: Public. Evening Classes Available? Yes. Student/faculty Ratio: 5:1. Students in Parent Institution: 21,539.

STUDENT INFORMATION

Total Students in Program: 3,056. % Full-time: 60. % Female: 67.

RESEARCH FACILITIES

Research Facilities: 14 research centers.

EXPENSES/FINANCIAL AID

Annual Tuition: In-state $1,200. / Out-of-state $3,500. Fees: $70. Books and Supplies: $1,500. Grants Range From: $1,000-$3,000. Loans Range From: $3,000-$8,500. % Receiving Financial Aid: 36. % Receiving Scholarships/ Grants: 60. % Receiving Loans: 90. Number of Teaching/Research Assistantships Granted Each Year: 5 Average Salary Stipend: $7,000.

ADMISSIONS INFORMATION

Application Fee: $15. Transfer Students Accepted? Yes. Transfer Policy: Maximum 1/3 of total credit hours required may be transferred. Number of Applications Received: 41. % of Applicants Accepted: 61. % Accepted Who Enrolled: 84. Average GPA: 3.0.
Required Admission Factors: Essays/personal statement, interview, letters of recommendation, transcript.
Other Admission Factors: Minimum 3.0 GPA, reading knowledge of another romance language, and bachelor's degree in communication required.

EMPLOYMENT INFORMATION

Placement Office Available? Yes. % Employed Within Six Months: 98. Rate of placement: 45%. Average starting salary: $25,000.

UNIVERSITY OF PUGET SOUND
School of Occupational Therapy

Address: 1500 North Warner Street, Tacoma, WA 98416-1062
Admissions Phone: 253-879-3211 · Admissions Fax: 253-897-3993
Admissions E-mail: admission@ups.edu · Web Address: www.ups.edu/ot/

INSTITUTIONAL INFORMATION

Public/private: Private (nonprofit). Total Faculty: 12. % Faculty Female: 67. % Faculty Part-time: 58. Student/faculty Ratio: 5:1. Students in Parent Institution: 2,760.

PROGRAMS

Masters offered in: Occupational therapy/therapist.

STUDENT INFORMATION

Total Students in Program: 32. % Full-time: 62. % Female: 97. % Minority: 22.

RESEARCH FACILITIES

Research Facilities: The program operates a student on-campus clinic, providing pre-fieldwork experience under the guidance of expert clinicians, that is required of all students.

EXPENSES/FINANCIAL AID

Annual Tuition: $23,850. Room & Board: $6,400. Books and Supplies: $1,000. Grants Range From: $500-$14,100. Loans Range From: $2,000-$35,904. % Receiving Financial Aid: 90.57. % Receiving Scholarships/ Grants: 62.5. % Receiving Loans: 93.75. % Receiving Other Aid (Work-study): 37.5. Types of Aid Available: Fellowships, grants, loans, scholarships. Average student debt upon graduation: $40,623. Number of Fellowships Granted Each Year: 13. Average amount of individual fellowships per year: $4,800.

ADMISSIONS INFORMATION

Application Fee: $65. Priority Application Deadline: 1/15. Regular Application Deadline: 1/15. Regular Notification: 3/15. Transfer Students Accepted? Yes. Transfer Policy: 26 semester hours (6.5 courses) for professional entry-level; 8 semester hours (2 courses) for post-professional. Requirements: College transcripts, letter of transfer request, and letter from current program affirming good academic standing. Number of Applications Received: 37. % of Applicants Accepted: 95. % Accepted Who Enrolled: 29. Average GRE Verbal: 467.4. Average GRE Quantitative: 569.4.
Required Admission Factors: Essays/personal statement, GRE, letters of recommendation, transcript.
Other Admission Factors: GPA minimum of 3.0 for undergraduate work or 3.25 in last 2 years.
Program-Specific Admission Factors: For post-professional MSOT program a bachelor's degree in occupational therapy, an introductory statistics course, and a letter of reference from a work supervisor or mentor are required. No GRE is required of post-professional applicants.

EMPLOYMENT INFORMATION

Placement Office Available? Yes. % Employed Within Six Months: 70. % of masters grads employed in their field upon graduation: 40. Average starting salary: $45,000.

UNIVERSITY OF PUGET SOUND
School of Physical Therapy

Address: 1500 North Warner Street, Tacoma, WA 98416-1062
Admissions Phone: 253-879-3211 · Admissions Fax: 253-879-3993
Admissions E-mail: admission@ups.edu · Web Address: www.ups.edu/pt/

INSTITUTIONAL INFORMATION

Public/private: Private (nonprofit). **Total Faculty:** 13. **% Faculty Female:** 85. **% Faculty Part-time:** 62. **Student/faculty Ratio:** 10:1. **Students in Parent Institution:** 2,760.

PROGRAMS

First Professional degree offered in: Physical therapy/therapist.

STUDENT INFORMATION

Total Students in Program: 93. **% Full-time:** 95. **% Female:** 75. **% Minority:** 19. **% International:** 1.

RESEARCH FACILITIES

Research Facilities: All faculty members actively integrate students into their research. Motion analysis equipment available.

EXPENSES/FINANCIAL AID

Annual Tuition: $19,080. **Room & Board:** $6,400. **Books and Supplies:** $1,000. **Grants Range From:** $1,000-$21,522. **Loans Range From:** $2,643-$29,279. **% Receiving Financial Aid:** 81.73. **% Receiving Scholarships/Grants:** 34.12. **% Receiving Loans:** 94.12. **% Receiving Other Aid (Work-study):** 41.18. **Types of Aid Available:** Fellowships, grants, loans, scholarships. **Average student debt upon graduation:** $47,831. **Number of Fellowships Granted Each Year:** 12. **Average amount of individual fellowships per year:** $6,250.

ADMISSIONS INFORMATION

Application Fee: $65. **Regular Application Deadline:** 1/15. **Regular Notification:** Rolling. **Transfer Students Accepted?** No. **Number of Applications Received:** 91. **% of Applicants Accepted:** 79. **% Accepted Who Enrolled:** 47. **Average GPA:** 3.5. **Average GRE Verbal:** 470. **Average GRE Quantitative:** 610.
Required Admission Factors: Essays/personal statement, GRE, letters of recommendation, transcript.
Other Admission Factors: Overall undergraduate GPA 3.0; GPA of anatomy, physiology, and physics courses (including labs) combined=3.0
Program-Specific Admission Factors: Exposure to the practice of physical therapy, either volunteer or paid, sufficient to articulate an understanding of the scope of the profession in admission essays. (No minimum number of hours.)

EMPLOYMENT INFORMATION

% Employed Within Six Months: 99.

UNIVERSITY OF REDLANDS
Alfred North Whitehead College for Lifelong Learning

Address: 1200 East Colton Avenue, PO Box 3080, Redlands, CA 92373-0999
Admissions Phone: 909-793-2121, ext. 4931
Admissions Fax: 909-335-5325

INSTITUTIONAL INFORMATION

Public/private: Private (nonprofit). **Evening Classes Available?** Yes. **Student/faculty Ratio:** 12:1. **Students in Parent Institution:** 4,143.

STUDENT INFORMATION

Total Students in Program: 1,127. **% Full-time:** 97. **% Female:** 55.

EXPENSES/FINANCIAL AID

Books and Supplies: $693. **Grants Range From:** $1,000-$10,000. **Loans Range From:** $8,500-$18,500. **% Receiving Financial Aid:** 80. **% Receiving Scholarships/Grants:** 3. **% Receiving Loans:** 79. **% Receiving Assistantships:** 14.

ADMISSIONS INFORMATION

Regular Notification: Rolling. **Transfer Students Accepted?** No. **Number of Applications Received:** 280. **% of Applicants Accepted:** 67. **% Accepted Who Enrolled:** 18. **Average GPA:** 3.13.

Required Admission Factors: Essays/personal statement, interview, letters of recommendation, transcript.
Other Admission Factors: Minimum 3.0 GPA required.

EMPLOYMENT INFORMATION

Placement Office Available? Yes. **% Employed Within Six Months:** 99. **% of masters grads employed in their field upon graduation:** 99. **Rate of placement:** 65%. **Average starting salary:** $69,000.

UNIVERSITY OF REDLANDS
Communicative Disorders Program

Address: 1200 East Colton Avenue, PO Box 3080, Redlands, CA 92373-0999
Admissions Phone: 909-335-4061 · **Admissions Fax:** 909-335-5192
Admissions E-mail: walker@uor.edu

INSTITUTIONAL INFORMATION

Public/private: Private (nonprofit). **Student/faculty Ratio:** 8:1. **Students in Parent Institution:** 4,143.

STUDENT INFORMATION

Total Students in Program: 1,127. **% Full-time:** 97. **% Female:** 55.

EXPENSES/FINANCIAL AID

Books and Supplies: $693. **Grants Range From:** $1,000-$10,000. **Loans Range From:** $8,500-$18,500. **% Receiving Financial Aid:** 100. **% Receiving Scholarships/Grants:** 3. **% Receiving Loans:** 79. **% Receiving Assistantships:** 14. **Number of Teaching/Research Assistantships Granted Each Year:** 6 **Average Salary Stipend:** $1,500.

ADMISSIONS INFORMATION

Application Fee: $40. **Regular Notification:** Rolling. **Transfer Students Accepted?** Yes. **Number of Applications Received:** 63. **% of Applicants Accepted:** 86. **% Accepted Who Enrolled:** 48. **Average GPA:** 3.5. **Average GRE Verbal:** 470. **Average GRE Quantitative:** 500. **Average GRE Analytical:** 500.
Required Admission Factors: Essays/personal statement, GRE, letters of recommendation.
Other Admission Factors: Minimum 3.0 GPA required.

EMPLOYMENT INFORMATION

Placement Office Available? Yes. **% Employed Within Six Months:** 99. **% of masters grads employed in their field upon graduation:** 95. **Rate of placement:** 65%. **Average starting salary:** $48,000.

UNIVERSITY OF REDLANDS
School of Music

Address: 1200 East Colton Avenue, PO Box 3080, Redlands, CA 92373-0999
Admissions Phone: 909-335-4014 · **Admissions Fax:** 909-748-6343
Admissions E-mail: music@redlands.edu · **Web Address:** www.redlands.edu

INSTITUTIONAL INFORMATION

Public/private: Private (nonprofit). **Evening Classes Available?** Yes. **Student/faculty Ratio:** 8:1. **Students in Parent Institution:** 4,143.

STUDENT INFORMATION

Total Students in Program: 1,127. **% Full-time:** 97. **% Female:** 55.

EXPENSES/FINANCIAL AID

Books and Supplies: $693. **Grants Range From:** $1,000-$10,000. **Loans Range From:** $8,500-$18,500. **% Receiving Financial Aid:** 80. **% Receiving Scholarships/Grants:** 3. **% Receiving Loans:** 79. **% Receiving Assistantships:** 14. **Number of Teaching/Research Assistantships Granted Each Year:** 5.

ADMISSIONS INFORMATION

Application Fee: $40. Priority Application Deadline: 4/1. Regular Application Deadline: 5/1. Regular Notification: Rolling. Transfer Students Accepted? Yes. Number of Applications Received: 9. % of Applicants Accepted: 78. % Accepted Who Enrolled: 100. Average GPA: 3.44. Required Admission Factors: Letters of recommendation, transcript. Other Admission Factors: Minimum 3.0 GPA required. Bachelor's degree needs to be in music. Program-Specific Admission Factors: Audition required in person or by tape if over 200 miles away.

EMPLOYMENT INFORMATION

Placement Office Available? Yes. % Employed Within Six Months: 90. % of masters grads employed in their field upon graduation: 90. Rate of placement: 65%.

UNIVERSITY OF REGINA
Faculty of Graduate Studies & Research

Address: Regina, Saskatchewan, S4S 0A2 Canada
Admissions Phone: 306-585-4161 · Admissions Fax: 306-585-4893

INSTITUTIONAL INFORMATION

Public/private: Public. Evening Classes Available? Yes. Student/faculty Ratio: 3:1. Students in Parent Institution: 11,581.

STUDENT INFORMATION

Total Students in Program: 946. % Full-time: 25. % Female: 54.

EXPENSES/FINANCIAL AID

Annual Tuition: $2,375. Room & Board (On/off campus): $6,200/$9,000. Books and Supplies: $865. Number of Fellowships Granted Each Year: 2. Average amount of individual fellowships per year: $9,418. Number of Teaching/Research Assistantships Granted Each Year: 100. Average Salary Stipend: $800.

ADMISSIONS INFORMATION

Application Fee: $55. Regular Notification: Rolling. Transfer Students Accepted? No. Number of Applications Received: 537. % of Applicants Accepted: 43. Required Admission Factors: Letters of recommendation, transcript. Program-Specific Admission Factors: Audition required of music program applicants.

UNIVERSITY OF SAINT FRANCIS
Graduate School

Address: 2701 Spring Street, Fort Wayne, IN 46808
Admissions Phone: 219-434-3279 · Admissions Fax: 219-434-7590
Admissions E-mail: dmcmahon@sf.edu

INSTITUTIONAL INFORMATION

Public/Private: Private (nonprofit). Evening Classes Available? Yes. Student/Faculty Ratio: 19:1. Students in Parent Institution: 1,688.

STUDENT INFORMATION

Total Students in Program: 200. % Full Time: 22. % Female: 72.

EXPENSES/FINANCIAL AID

Annual Tuition: In-state $7,740. Fees: $500. Books and Supplies: $850. Grants Range From: $1,000-$5,070. Loans Range From: $428-$14,897. % Receiving Financial Aid: 62. % Receiving Scholarships/Grants: 50. % Receiving Loans: 71. % Receiving Assistantships: 8.

ADMISSIONS INFORMATION

Application Fee: $20. Regular Notification: Rolling. Transfer Students

Accepted? Yes. Transfer Policy: Maximum 15 credit hours with a minimum grade of "B" taken within the past five years may be transferred. Number of Applications Received: 129. % of Applicants Accepted: 84. % Accepted Who Enrolled: 48. Required Admission Factors: transcript. Recommended Admission Factors: Other Admission Factors: Minimum 2.5 GPA required. Program-Specific Admission Factors: Minimum GMAT score of 400 and minimum 2.0 GPA required of business program applicants.

EMPLOYMENT INFORMATION

Placement Office Available? Yes. % Employed Within 6 Months: 95. % of master's grads employed in their field upon graduation: 95. Rate of placement: 95%.

UNIVERSITY OF SAN DIEGO
College of Arts & Sciences

Address: 5998 Alcala Park, San Diego, CA 92110-2492
Admissions Phone: 619-260-4524 · Admissions Fax: 619-260-4158
Admissions E-mail: grads@sandiego.edu
Web Address: www.sandiego.edu/gradmiss

INSTITUTIONAL INFORMATION

Public/Private: Private (nonprofit). Evening Classes Available? Yes. Total Faculty: 31. % Faculty Female: 45. % Faculty Part Time: 29. Students in Parent Institution: 7,262

PROGRAMS

Masters offered in: Drama and dramatics/theater arts, general; English language and literature, general; history, general; international relations and affairs; pastoral studies/counseling; peace studies and conflict resolution; theology/theological studies

STUDENT INFORMATION

Total Students in Program: 198 % Full Time: 30. % Female: 53. % Minority: 11. % International: 5.

EXPENSES/FINANCIAL AID

Annual Tuition: $14,850 Fees: $126. Books and Supplies: $1,220. Grants Range From: $100-$5,400. Loans Range From: $200-$27,588. Types of Aid Available: Fellowships, grants, loans, scholarships.

ADMISSIONS INFORMATION

Application Fee: $45. Priority Application Deadline: 5/1. Regular Application Deadline: 8/1. Regular Notification: Rolling. Transfer Students Accepted? Yes. Transfer Policy: Transferred units must be from accredited institutions; maximum number of transferable units varies. Number of Applications Received: 450. % of Applicants Accepted: 33. % Accepted Who Enrolled: 36. Required Admission Factors: Essays/personal statement, GRE, letters of recommendation, transcript. Other Admission Factors: Minimum 3.0 GPA required of most applicants. Three letters of recommendation required. Program-Specific Admission Factors: Minimum 3.0 GPA in last 50% of undergraduate work required of history program applicants. Minimum GRE score of 500 on each section and minimum 3.0 GPA required of international relations program applicants. Scholastic Level Exam and minimum 3.0 GPA required.

EMPLOYMENT INFORMATION

Placement Office Available? Yes. % Employed Within 6 Months: 90. Rate of placement: 96%. Average starting salary: $45,000.

UNIVERSITY OF SAN FRANCISCO
College of Professional Studies

Address: 2130 Fulton Street, San Francisco, CA 94117-1080
Admissions Phone: 415-422-4723

INSTITUTIONAL INFORMATION
Public/Private: Private (nonprofit). **Evening Classes Available?** Yes. Students in Parent Institution: 7,803

STUDENT INFORMATION
Total Students in Program: 2,355 % Full Time: 50. % Female: 62.

EXPENSES/FINANCIAL AID
Room & Board: $9,610. **Books and Supplies:** $750. **Grants Range From:** $5,400-$13,000. **Loans Range From:** $14,200-$32,000. **% Receiving Financial Aid:** 34. **% Receiving Scholarships/Grants:** 9. **% Receiving Loans:** 60. **% Receiving Assistantships:** 7. **Average student debt, upon graduation:** $21,473.

ADMISSIONS INFORMATION
Application Fee: $35. **Regular Notification:** Rolling. **Transfer Students Accepted?** Yes. **Number of Applications Received:** 244. **% of Applicants Accepted:** 89. **% Accepted Who Enrolled:** 65.
Required Admission Factors: Essays/personal statement, letters of recommendation, transcript.
Other Admission Factors: Minimum 2.7 GPA (3.0 in last 60 credit hours) and resume required.

EMPLOYMENT INFORMATION
Placement Office Available? Yes.

UNIVERSITY OF SAN FRANCISCO
College of Arts & Sciences

Address: 2130 Fulton Street, San Francisco, CA 94117-1080
Admissions Phone: 415-422-GRAD · **Admissions Fax:** 415-422-2217
Admissions E-mail: fascis@usfca.edu ·

INSTITUTIONAL INFORMATION
Public/Private: Private (nonprofit). **Students in Parent Institution:** 7,803.

STUDENT INFORMATION
Total Students in Program: 2,355 % Full Time: 50. % Female: 62.

EXPENSES/FINANCIAL AID
Room & Board: $9,610. **Books and Supplies:** $750. **Grants Range From:** $5,400-$13,000. **Loans Range From:** $14,200-$32,000. **% Receiving Scholarships/Grants:** 9. **% Receiving Loans:** 60. **% Receiving Assistantships:** 7. **Transfer Students Accepted?** No.

EMPLOYMENT INFORMATION
Placement Office Available? Yes.

UNIVERSITY OF SASKATCHEWAN
College of Graduate Studies & Research

Address: Saskatoon, Saskatchewan, S7N 0W0 Canada
Admissions Phone: 306-966-5751 · **Admissions Fax:** 306-966-5756
Web Address: www.usask.ca/cgsr/

INSTITUTIONAL INFORMATION
Public/Private: Public. **Students in Parent Institution:** 1,767

STUDENT INFORMATION
Total Students in Program: 1,767 % Full Time: 75.

EXPENSES/FINANCIAL AID
Annual Tuition: In-state $2,520.

ADMISSIONS INFORMATION
Application Fee: $50. **Regular Notification:** Rolling. **Transfer Students Accepted?** No.
Required Admission Factors: Letters of recommendation, transcript.

UNIVERSITY OF SCRANTON
Graduate School

Address: 800 Linden Street, O'Hara Hall, Room 219, Scranton, PA 18510-4631
Admissions Phone: 570-941-7600 · **Admissions Fax:** 570-941-5995
Admissions E-mail: goonanj1@scranton.edu
Web Address: www.scranton.edu/graduateschool

INSTITUTIONAL INFORMATION
Public/Private: Private (nonprofit). **Evening Classes Available?** Yes. Students in Parent Institution: 4,795.

STUDENT INFORMATION
Total Students in Program: 750 % Full Time: 31. % Female: 64. % International: 13.

EXPENSES/FINANCIAL AID
Annual Tuition: $12,936. **Fees:** $50. **Books and Supplies:** $900. **% Receiving Assistantships:** 10. **Number of teaching/research assistantships granted each year:** 70 **Average Salary Stipend:** $7,000.

ADMISSIONS INFORMATION
Application Fee: $50. **Priority Application Deadline:** 11/1. **Regular Application Deadline:** 3/1. **Regular Notification:** Rolling. **Transfer Students Accepted?** Yes. **Transfer Policy:** Grade of B or better. Courses must be parallel to those in our curriculum. **Number of Applications Received:** 663. **% of Applicants Accepted:** 90. **% Accepted Who Enrolled:** 44. **Average GPA:** 3.3.
Required Admission Factors: Essays/personal statement, letters of recommendation, transcript, TOEFL, IELTS, or STEP for International Students.
Other Admission Factors: Minimum 2.75 GPA required. Some programs require a higher minimum GPA.
Program-Specific Admission Factors: Minimum nine credit hours of philosophy and 15 credit hours of theology required of theology program applicants. Minimum 18 credit hours in upper division history courses required of history program applicants. At least one year of chemistry, physical, an

EMPLOYMENT INFORMATION
Placement Office Available? Yes.

UNIVERSITY OF SOUTH ALABAMA
College of Arts & Sciences

Address: 245 Administration Building, Mobile, AL 36688-0002
Admissions Phone: 251-460-6280 · **Admissions Fax:** 251-460-7928

INSTITUTIONAL INFORMATION
Public/Private: Public. **Evening Classes Available?** Yes. **Student/Faculty Ratio:** 1:1. **Students in Parent Institution:** 12,122.

STUDENT INFORMATION
Total Students in Program: 2,299 % Full Time: 60. % Female: 69.
Annual Tuition: In-state $3,048. / Out-of-state $6,096. **Room & Board:**

$2,792. **Fees:** $320. **Books and Supplies:** $800. **Loans Range From:** $500-$27,500. **% Receiving Scholarships/Grants:** 16. **% Receiving Loans:** 100. **% Receiving Assistantships:** 9. **Number of teaching/research assistantships granted each year:** 55 **Average Salary Stipend:** $4,000.

ADMISSIONS INFORMATION

Application Fee: $25. **Regular Notification:** Rolling. **Transfer Students Accepted?** Yes. **Transfer Policy:** Maximum nine credit hours with minimum grade of B may be transferred into master's degree program. **Number of Applications Received:** 122. **% of Applicants Accepted:** 71. **% Accepted Who Enrolled:** 68.
Required Admission Factors: GRE, letters of recommendation, transcript. **Other Admission Factors:** Minimum 3.0 GPA and sufficient course study in major required.
Program-Specific Admission Factors:

EMPLOYMENT INFORMATION

Placement Office Available? Yes.

UNIVERSITY OF SOUTH CAROLINA
College of Journalism &
Mass Communications

Address: 901 Sumter Street, Suite 304, Columbia, SC 29208
Admissions Phone: 803-777-4102 · **Admissions Fax:** 803-777-4103

INSTITUTIONAL INFORMATION

Public/Private: Public. **Evening Classes Available?** Yes. **Students in Parent Institution:** 23,699.

RESEARCH FACILITIES

Research Facilities: Center for Mechanics of Materials & Nondestructive Evaluation, Center for Retailing, Earth Sciences & Resources Institute, Electron Microscopy Center, Institute of International Studies, Institute for Southern Studies, Human Resource Research Center.

EXPENSES/FINANCIAL AID

Annual Tuition: In-state $2,007. / Out-of-state $4,264. **Fees:** $100. **Books and Supplies:** $600. **Number of teaching/research assistantships granted each year:** 6 **Average Salary Stipend:** $5,000.

ADMISSIONS INFORMATION

Application Fee: $35. **Transfer Students Accepted?** Yes. **Transfer Policy:** Maximum nine credit hours may be transferred into most programs; 12 may be transferred into some programs. **Number of Applications Received:** 96. **% of Applicants Accepted:** 55. **% Accepted Who Enrolled:** 51.
Required Admission Factors: GRE, letters of recommendation, transcript. **Recommended Admission Factors:**
Other Admission Factors: Minimum 3.0 GPA required.
Program-Specific Admission Factors: Minimum GRE score of 1500 (500 on Verbal section) required of master's program applicants. Minimum GRE score of 1800 (600 on Verbal section) required of doctoral program applicants.

EMPLOYMENT INFORMATION

Placement Office Available? Yes. **% Employed Within 6 Months:** 100. **% of master's/doctoral grads employed in their field upon graduation:** 69/100.

UNIVERSITY OF SOUTH CAROLINA
College of Science & Mathematics

Address: 901 Sumter Street, Suite 304, Columbia, SC 29208
Admissions Phone: 803-777-4243 · **Admissions Fax:** 803-777-2972

INSTITUTIONAL INFORMATION

Public/Private: Public. **Evening Classes Available?** Yes. **Total Faculty:** 160. **Student/Faculty Ratio:** 4:1. **Students in Parent Institution:** 23,699

RESEARCH FACILITIES

Research Facilities: Center for Mechanics of Materials & Nondestructive Evaluation, Center for Retailing, Earth Sciences & Resources Institute, Electron Microscopy Center, Institute of International Studies, Institute for Southern Studies, Human Resource Research Center.

EXPENSES/FINANCIAL AID

Annual Tuition: In-state $2,007. / Out-of-state $4,264. **Fees:** $100. **Books and Supplies:** $600. **% Receiving Financial Aid:** 100. **Number of fellowships granted each year:** 20 **Average amount of individual fellowships per year:** $8000. **Number of teaching/research assistantships granted each year:** 50. **Average Salary Stipend:** $12,000.

ADMISSIONS INFORMATION

Application Fee: $35. **Regular Notification:** Rolling. **Transfer Students Accepted?** Yes. **Number of Applications Received:** 300. **% of Applicants Accepted:** 67. **% Accepted Who Enrolled:** 68. **Average GRE Verbal:** 513. **Average GRE Quantitative:** 687. **Average GRE Analytical:** 630.
Required Admission Factors: GRE, transcript.
Recommended Admission Factors:
Other Admission Factors: Minimum 3.0 GPA required.

EMPLOYMENT INFORMATION

Placement Office Available? Yes. **Average starting salary:** $60,000.

UNIVERSITY OF SOUTH CAROLINA
College of Social Work

Address: 901 Sumter Street, Suite 304, Columbia, SC 29208
Admissions Phone: 803-777-5291 · **Admissions Fax:** 803-777-3498
Admissions E-mail: crolley@gwm.sc.edu

INSTITUTIONAL INFORMATION

Public/Private: Public. **Student/Faculty Ratio:** 17:1. **Students in Parent Institution:** 23,699.

RESEARCH FACILITIES

Research Facilities: Center for Mechanics of Materials & Nondestructive Evaluation, Center for Retailing, Earth Sciences & Resources Institute, Electron Microscopy Center, Institute of International Studies, Institute for Southern Studies, Human Resource Research Center.

EXPENSES/FINANCIAL AID

Annual Tuition: In-state $2,007. / Out-of-state $4,264. **Fees:** $100. **Books and Supplies:** $600. **% Receiving Financial Aid:** 75. **Number of fellowships granted each year:** 2. **Average amount of individual fellowships per year:** $4000. **Number of teaching/research assistantships granted each year:** 125. **Average Salary Stipend:** $3,000.

ADMISSIONS INFORMATION

Application Fee: $35. **Transfer Students Accepted?** Yes. **Number of Applications Received:** 650. **% of Applicants Accepted:** 55. **% Accepted Who Enrolled:** 66. **Average GPA:** 3.4.
Required Admission Factors: Essays/personal statement, GRE, letters of recommendation, transcript.
Recommended Admission Factors:
Other Admission Factors: Minimum 3.0 GPA and autobiography required; GRE required of applicants with GPA below minimum. Work and volunteer experience recommended.

EMPLOYMENT INFORMATION

Placement Office Available? Yes.

UNIVERSITY OF SOUTH CAROLINA
College of Library & Information Science

Address: 901 Sumter Street, Suite 304, Columbia, SC 29208
Admissions Phone: 803-777-3887 · **Admissions Fax:** 803-777-0457
Admissions E-mail: nbeitz@sc.edu

INSTITUTIONAL INFORMATION
Public/Private: Public. **Students in Parent Institution:** 23,699.

RESEARCH FACILITIES
Research Facilities: Center for Mechanics of Materials & Nondestructive Evaluation, Center for Retailing, Earth Sciences & Resources Institute, Electron Microscopy Center, Institute of International Studies, Institute for Southern Studies, Human Resource Research Center.

EXPENSES/FINANCIAL AID
Annual Tuition: In-state $2,007. / Out-of-state $4,264. **Fees:** $100. **Books and Supplies:** $600. **Number of fellowships granted each year:** 11 Average amount of individual fellowships per year: $1000. **Average Salary Stipend:** $1,250.

ADMISSIONS INFORMATION
Application Fee: $35. **Regular Notification:** Rolling. **Transfer Students Accepted?** Yes. **Number of Applications Received:** 154. **% of Applicants Accepted:** 94. **% Accepted Who Enrolled:** 93. **Average GPA:** 3.3. **Average GRE Verbal:** 553. **Average GRE Quantitative:** 555. **Average GRE Analytical:** 587.
Required Admission Factors: Essays/personal statement, interview, letters of recommendation, transcript.
Recommended Admission Factors:
Other Admission Factors: Minimum GRE score of 950 Verbal and Quantitative or Verbal and Analytical or minimum MAT score of 50, minimum 3.0 GPA, and two letters of recommendation required.

EMPLOYMENT INFORMATION
Placement Office Available? Yes. **% Employed Within 6 Months:** 82.

UNIVERSITY OF SOUTH CAROLINA
School of Music

Address: 901 Sumter Street, Suite 304, Columbia, SC 29208
Admissions Phone: 803-777-4106 · **Admissions Fax:** 803-777-6508
Admissions E-mail: wbates@mozart.sc.edu

INSTITUTIONAL INFORMATION
Public/Private: Public. **Student/Faculty Ratio:** 7:1. **Students in Parent Institution:** 23,699.

RESEARCH FACILITIES
Research Facilities: Center for Mechanics of Materials & Nondestructive Evaluation, Center for Retailing, Earth Sciences & Resources Institute, Electron Microscopy Center, Institute of International Studies, Institute for Southern Studies, Human Resource Research Center.

EXPENSES/FINANCIAL AID
Annual Tuition: In-state $2,007. / Out-of-state $4,264. **Fees:** $100. **Books and Supplies:** $600. **% Receiving Financial Aid:** 66. **Number of fellowships granted each year:** 2. **Average amount of individual fellowships per year:** $500. **Number of teaching/research assistantships granted each year:** 10. **Average Salary Stipend:** $6,000.

ADMISSIONS INFORMATION
Application Fee: $35. **Regular Notification:** Rolling. **Transfer Students Accepted?** Yes. **Number of Applications Received:** 72. **% of Applicants Accepted:** 75. **Average GPA:** 3.65. **Average GRE Verbal:** 480. **Average GRE Quantitative:** 570. **Average GRE Analytical:** 570.

Required Admission Factors: Essays/personal statement, interview, letters of recommendation, transcript.
Recommended Admission Factors:
Other Admission Factors:
Program-Specific Admission Factors: Minimum 3.0 GPA (3.2 in music) required of master's program applicants. Minimum 3.5 GPA in graduate work required of doctoral program applicants.

EMPLOYMENT INFORMATION
Placement Office Available? Yes. **% Employed Within 6 Months:** 89. **% of master's/doctoral grads employed in their field upon graduation:** 85/92.

UNIVERSITY OF SOUTH CAROLINA
School of the Environment

Address: 901 Sumter Street, Suite 304, Columbia, SC 29208
Admissions Phone: 803-777-4243 · **Admissions Fax:** 803-777-2972

INSTITUTIONAL INFORMATION
Public/Private: Public. **Students in Parent Institution:** 23,699.

RESEARCH FACILITIES
Research Facilities: Center for Mechanics of Materials & Nondestructive Evaluation, Center for Retailing, Earth Sciences & Resources Institute, Electron Microscopy Center, Institute of International Studies, Institute for Southern Studies, Human Resource Research Center.

EXPENSES/FINANCIAL AID
Annual Tuition: In-state $2,007. / Out-of-state $4,264. **Fees:** $100. **Books and Supplies:** $600.

ADMISSIONS INFORMATION
Application Fee: $35. **Regular Notification:** Rolling. **Transfer Students Accepted?** Yes. **Number of Applications Received:** 33. **% of Applicants Accepted:** 58. **% Accepted Who Enrolled:** 79. **Average GPA:** 3.37. **Average GRE Verbal:** 449. **Average GRE Quantitative:** 558. **Average GRE Analytical:** 530.
Required Admission Factors: Essays/personal statement, GRE, letters of recommendation, transcript.
Other Admission Factors: Minimum 3.0 GPA and minimum GRE score of 1050 (Verbal plus Quantitative) required.

EMPLOYMENT INFORMATION
Placement Office Available? Yes. **% Employed Within 6 Months:** 100.

UNIVERSITY OF SOUTH CAROLINA
College of Criminal Justice

Address: 901 Sumter Street, Suite 304, Columbia, SC 29208
Admissions Phone: 803-777-7088 · **Admissions Fax:** 803-777-9600

INSTITUTIONAL INFORMATION
Public/Private: Public. **Evening Classes Available?** Yes. **Students in Parent Institution:** 23,699.

RESEARCH FACILITIES
Research Facilities: Center for Mechanics of Materials & Nondestructive Evaluation, Center for Retailing, Earth Sciences & Resources Institute, Electron Microscopy Center, Institute of International Studies, Institute for Southern Studies, Human Resource Research Center.

EXPENSES/FINANCIAL AID
Annual Tuition: In-state $2,007. / Out-of-state $4,264. **Fees:** $100. **Books and Supplies:** $600.

ADMISSIONS INFORMATION

Application Fee: $35. **Regular Notification:** Rolling. **Transfer Students Accepted?** Yes. **Transfer Policy:** Maximum 12 credit hours with a minimum grade of B and petition of transfer required of transfers. **Number of Applications Received:** 44. **% of Applicants Accepted:** 57. **% Accepted Who Enrolled:** 60. **Average GPA:** 3.16. **Average GRE Verbal:** 520. **Average GRE Quantitative:** 550.
Required Admission Factors: Essays/personal statement, letters of recommendation, transcript.
Recommended Admission Factors:
Other Admission Factors: Minimum GRE score of 1000 and minimum 3.0 GPA required.

EMPLOYMENT INFORMATION

Placement Office Available? Yes.

UNIVERSITY OF SOUTH CAROLINA
College of Liberal Arts

Address: 901 Sumter Street, Suite 304, Columbia, SC 29208
Admissions Phone: 803-777-4243 · **Admissions Fax:** 803-777-2972
Admissions E-mail: aw@ss1.csd.sc.edu

INSTITUTIONAL INFORMATION

Public/Private: Public. **Evening Classes Available?** Yes. **Students in Parent Institution:** 23,699.

RESEARCH FACILITIES

Research Facilities: Center for Mechanics of Materials & Nondestructive Evaluation, Center for Retailing, Earth Sciences & Resources Institute, Electron Microscopy Center, Institute of International Studies, Institute for Southern Studies, Human Resource Research Center.

EXPENSES/FINANCIAL AID

Annual Tuition: In-state $2,007. / Out-of-state $4,264. **Fees:** $100. **Books and Supplies:** $600.

ADMISSIONS INFORMATION

Application Fee: $35. **Transfer Students Accepted?** Yes. **Transfer Policy:** Maximum 12 semester hours may be transferred with minimum grade of B.
Required Admission Factors: GRE, letters of recommendation, transcript.
Program-Specific Admission Factors: Writing sample required of philosophy, art history, and comparative literature program applicants. Three letters of recommendation required of some programs.

EMPLOYMENT INFORMATION

Placement Office Available? Yes.

UNIVERSITY OF SOUTH DAKOTA AT VERMILLION
College of Fine Arts

Address: 414 East Clark Street, Vermillion, SD 57069

INSTITUTIONAL INFORMATION

Public/Private: Public. **Evening Classes Available?** Yes. **Students in Parent Institution:** 7,544.

STUDENT INFORMATION

Total Students in Program: 1,530

EXPENSES/FINANCIAL AID

Annual Tuition: In-state $1,706. / Out-of-state $5,027. **Room & Board:** $3,670. **Fees:** $1,062. **Books and Supplies:** $500. **Average Salary Stipend:** $1,970.

ADMISSIONS INFORMATION

Application Fee: $15. **Regular Notification:** Rolling. **Transfer Students Accepted?** Yes.
Required Admission Factors: letters of recommendation, transcript.
Recommended Admission Factors:
Other Admission Factors:
Program-Specific Admission Factors:

EMPLOYMENT INFORMATION

Placement Office Available? Yes.

UNIVERSITY OF SOUTH DAKOTA AT VERMILLION
College of Arts & Sciences

Address: 414 East Clark Street, Vermillion, SD 57069

INSTITUTIONAL INFORMATION

Public/Private: Public. **Evening Classes Available?** Yes. **Students in Parent Institution:** 7,544.

STUDENT INFORMATION

Total Students in Program: 1,530.

EXPENSES/FINANCIAL AID

Annual Tuition: In-state $1,706. / Out-of-state $5,027. **Room & Board:** $3,670. **Fees:** $1,062. **Books and Supplies:** $500. **Number of teaching/research assistantships granted each year:** 120 **Average Salary Stipend:** $8,900.

ADMISSIONS INFORMATION

Application Fee: $15. **Regular Notification:** Rolling. **Transfer Students Accepted?** Yes. **Number of Applications Received:** 17. **% of Applicants Accepted:** 76. **% Accepted Who Enrolled:** 31. **Average GPA:** 3.08. **Average GRE Verbal:** 538. **Average GRE Quantitative:** 728. **Average GRE Analytical:** 620.
Required Admission Factors: Letters of recommendation, transcript.
Other Admission Factors: Minimum 2.7 GPA required.

EMPLOYMENT INFORMATION

Placement Office Available? Yes.

UNIVERSITY OF SOUTH FLORIDA
College of Fine Arts

Address: 4202 East Fowler Avenue, Tampa, FL 33620
Admissions Phone: 813-974-3660 · **Admissions Fax:** 813-974-2091
Admissions E-mail: jmoore@arts.usf.edu

INSTITUTIONAL INFORMATION

Public/Private: Public. **Student/Faculty Ratio:** 16:1. **Students in Parent Institution:** 35,561.

STUDENT INFORMATION

Total Students in Program: 7,795 **% Full Time:** 36. **% Female:** 62.

EXPENSES/FINANCIAL AID

Annual Tuition: In-state $2,789. / Out-of-state $9,606. **% Receiving Financial Aid:** 48. **Types of Aid Available:** 1. **Average student debt, upon graduation:** $17,321 **Number of fellowships granted each year:** 2 **Average amount of individual fellowships per year:** $7,500. **Number of teaching/research assistantships granted each year:** 47. **Average Salary Stipend:** $3,510.

ADMISSIONS INFORMATION

Application Fee: $20. **Regular Notification:** Rolling. **Transfer Students Accepted?** Yes. **Number of Applications Received:** 78. **% of Applicants**

Accepted: 53. **% Accepted Who Enrolled:** 78. **Average GPA:** 3.2. **Average GRE Verbal:** 514. **Average GRE Quantitative:** 534.
Required Admission Factors: Transcript.
Recommended Admission Factors:
Other Admission Factors: Minimum GRE score of 1000 and minimum 2.5 GPA or minimum GRE score of 800 and minimum 3.0 GPA required.
Program-Specific Admission Factors: Graduate Theory Assessment Test required of music program applicants.

UNIVERSITY OF SOUTH FLORIDA
Psychology Department—Industrial/ Organizational Psychology Program

Address: 4202 East Fowler Avenue, Tampa, FL 33620
Admissions Phone: 813-974-0379 · **Admissions Fax:** 813-974-4617
Admissions E-mail: wallyb@pdi-corp.com

INSTITUTIONAL INFORMATION
Public/Private: Public. **Student/Faculty Ratio:** 6:1. **Students in Parent Institution:** 35,561.

STUDENT INFORMATION
Total Students in Program: 7,795. **% Full Time:** 36. **% Female:** 62.

EXPENSES/FINANCIAL AID
Annual Tuition: In-state $2,789. / Out-of-state $9,606. **% Receiving Financial Aid:** 100. **Number of fellowships granted each year:** 1. **Average amount of individual fellowships per year:** $9,400. **Number of teaching/ research assistantships granted each year:** 15 **Average Salary Stipend:** $10,000.

ADMISSIONS INFORMATION
Application Fee: $20. **Transfer Students Accepted?** No. **Number of Applications Received:** 130. **% of Applicants Accepted:** 18. **% Accepted Who Enrolled:** 39. **Average GPA:** 3.9. **Average GRE Verbal:** 600. **Average GRE Quantitative:** 690.
Required Admission Factors: Essays/personal statement, GRE, letters of recommendation, transcript.
Recommended Admission Factors:
Other Admission Factors: Minimum GRE Verbal and Quantitative score of 1100 and minimum 3.5 GPA required.

EMPLOYMENT INFORMATION
% Employed Within 6 Months: 95. **% of doctoral grads employed in their field upon graduation:** 80.

UNIVERSITY OF SOUTH FLORIDA
College of Arts & Sciences

Address: 4202 East Fowler Avenue, Tampa, FL 33620
Admissions Phone: 813-974-6922 · **Admissions Fax:** 813-974-4075
Admissions E-mail: coch@cas.usf.edu · **Web Address:** www.cas.usf.edu

INSTITUTIONAL INFORMATION
Public/Private: Public. **Students in Parent Institution:** 35,561

PROGRAMS
Masters offered in: African-American/Black studies; audiology/audiologist and speech-language pathology/pathologist; English language and literature, general; environmental studies; French language and literature; liberal arts and sciences/liberal studies; library science/librarianship; mass communications/ media studies; Spanish language and literature; speech and rhetorical studies.
Doctorate offered in: Audiology/audiologist and hearing sciences; audiology/ audiologist and speech-language pathology/pathologist; English language and literature, general; speech and rhetorical studies

STUDENT INFORMATION
Total Students in Program: 7,795 **% Full Time:** 36. **% Female:** 62.

EXPENSES/FINANCIAL AID
Annual Tuition: In-state $2,789. / Out-of-state $9,606. **Fees:** $3,600. **Books and Supplies:** $800. **Grants Range From:** $250-$25,000. **Loans Range From:** $8,500-$18,500. **Types of Aid Available:** Fellowships, graduate assistantships, grants, institutional work-study, loans, scholarships. **Number of fellowships granted each year:** 14. **Average amount of individual fellowships per year:** $11,000. **Number of teaching/research assistantships granted each year:** 1,200. **Assistantship compensation includes:** Partial tuition remission, salary/stipend. **Average Salary Stipend:** $8,000.

ADMISSIONS INFORMATION
Application Fee: $30. **Priority Application Deadline:** 6/1. **Regular Application Deadline:** 6/1. **Regular Notification:** Rolling. **Transfer Students Accepted?** Yes. **Number of Applications Received:** 2,040. **% of Applicants Accepted:** 37. **% Accepted Who Enrolled:** 69. **Average GPA:** 0. **Average GRE Verbal:** 494. **Average GRE Quantitative:** 553. **Average GRE Analytical:** 544.
Required Admission Factors: GRE, transcript.

UNIVERSITY OF SOUTHERN CALIFORNIA
School of Social Work

Address: 655 W. 34th Street, Social Work Center, Room 114, Los Angeles, CA 90089-0411
Admissions Phone: 213-740-2013 · **Admissions Fax:** 213-740-0789
Admissions E-mail: carriel@usc.edu · **Web Address:** www.usc.edu/socialwork

INSTITUTIONAL INFORMATION
Public/Private: Private (nonprofit). **Evening Classes Available?** Yes. **Student/Faculty Ratio:** 9:1. **Students in Parent Institution:** 28,766

EXPENSES/FINANCIAL AID
Annual Tuition: In-state $11,099. **Fees:** $334. **Books and Supplies:** $1,000. **Grants Range From:** $10,000-$14,000. **% Receiving Financial Aid:** 90. **Average student debt, upon graduation:** $35,000

ADMISSIONS INFORMATION
Application Fee: $65. **Priority Application Deadline:** 2/1. **Regular Application Deadline:** 4/1. **Transfer Students Accepted?** Yes. **Transfer Policy:** Syllabi, transcripts, and evaluations of prior graduate social work curriculum required of transfer. **Number of Applications Received:** 600. **% of Applicants Accepted:** 50. **% Accepted Who Enrolled:** 73. **Average GPA:** 3.13.
Required Admission Factors: Essays/personal statement, letters of recommendation, transcript.
Recommended Admission Factors:
Other Admission Factors: Minimum 3.0 GPA required.
Program-Specific Admission Factors: Nurse Social Work Practitioner option applicants need to be a registered nurse.

EMPLOYMENT INFORMATION
Placement Office Available? Yes.

UNIVERSITY OF SOUTHERN CALIFORNIA
School of Policy, Planning, & Development

Address: USC School of Policy, Planning, and Development, Ralph and Goldy Lewis Hall, Room 111, Los Angeles, CA 90089-0626
Admissions Phone: 213-740-6842 · **Admissions Fax:** 213-740-7573
Admissions E-mail: colaner@usc.edu · **Web Address:** www.usc.edu/schools/sppd

INSTITUTIONAL INFORMATION

Public/Private: Private (nonprofit). **Evening Classes Available?** Yes. **Students in Parent Institution:** 31,000.

STUDENT INFORMATION

Total Students in Program: 15,000. **% International:** 32.

EXPENSES/FINANCIAL AID

Annual Tuition: $11,099. **Fees:** $334. **Books and Supplies:** $1,000. **Grants Range From:** $10,000-$14,000. **% Receiving Financial Aid:** 65. **Average student debt, upon graduation:** $30,000. **Number of fellowships granted each year:** 125. **Average amount of individual fellowships per year:** $7,000 **Number of teaching/research assistantships granted each year:** 3. **Average Salary Stipend:** $12,000.

ADMISSIONS INFORMATION

Application Fee: $65. **Priority Application Deadline:** 2/1. **Regular Application Deadline:** 7/1. **Regular Notification:** Rolling. **Transfer Students Accepted?** Yes. **Number of Applications Received:** 1,050. **% of Applicants Accepted:** 60. **% Accepted Who Enrolled:** 42. **Average GPA:** 3.23. **Average GRE Verbal:** 525. **Average GRE Quantitative:** 645.
Required Admission Factors: Essays/personal statement, GRE, letters of recommendation, transcript.
Other Admission Factors: Minimum GRE score of 500 Verbal and 500 Quantitative and minimum 3.0 GPA required.
Program-Specific Admission Factors: MRED program requires at least two years of professional experience in the real estate development field.

EMPLOYMENT INFORMATION

Placement Office Available? Yes.

UNIVERSITY OF SOUTHERN CALIFORNIA
School of Theater

Address: University Park, Los Angeles, CA 90089-0913
Admissions Phone: 213-740-1286 · **Admissions Fax:** 213-821-1193
Admissions E-mail: tabithat@usc.edu

INSTITUTIONAL INFORMATION

Public/Private: Private (nonprofit). **Students in Parent Institution:** 28,766.

EXPENSES/FINANCIAL AID

Annual Tuition: $11,099. **Fees:** $334. **Books and Supplies:** $1,000. **Grants Range From:** $10,000-$14,000. **Number of teaching/research assistantships granted each year:** 11. **Average Salary Stipend:** $5,600.

ADMISSIONS INFORMATION

Application Fee: $55. **Regular Notification:** Rolling. **Transfer Students Accepted?** Yes. **Number of Applications Received:** 27. **% of Applicants Accepted:** 44. **% Accepted Who Enrolled:** 92. **Average GPA:** 3.0
Required Admission Factors: Essays/personal statement, GRE, letters of recommendation, transcript.
Other Admission Factors: Minimum 3.0 GPA required.

EMPLOYMENT INFORMATION

Placement Office Available? Yes.

UNIVERSITY OF SOUTHERN CALIFORNIA
School of Fine Arts

Address: University Park, Los Angeles, CA 90089-0913
Admissions Phone: 213-740-9153 · **Admissions Fax:** 213-740-8938
Admissions E-mail: finearts@mizar.usc.edu

INSTITUTIONAL INFORMATION

Public/Private: Private (nonprofit). **Evening Classes Available?** Yes. **Student/Faculty Ratio:** 15:1. **Students in Parent Institution:** 28,766.

EXPENSES/FINANCIAL AID

Annual Tuition: $11,099. **Fees:** $334. **Books and Supplies:** $1,000. **Grants Range From:** $10,000-$14,000. **% Receiving Financial Aid:** 85. **Average student debt, upon graduation:** $15,000 **Number of teaching/research assistantships granted each year:** 8. **Average Salary Stipend:** $5,670.

ADMISSIONS INFORMATION

Transfer Students Accepted? No. **Number of Applications Received:** 63. **% of Applicants Accepted:** 54. **% Accepted Who Enrolled:** 53. **Average GPA:** 3.13. **Average GRE Verbal:** 503.
Required Admission Factors: Essays/personal statement, letters of recommendation, transcript.
Recommended Admission Factors:
Other Admission Factors: Minimum 3.0 GPA required.
Program-Specific Admission Factors:

EMPLOYMENT INFORMATION

Placement Office Available? Yes. **% Employed Within 6 Months:** 40. **% of master's/doctoral/first professional grads employed in their field upon graduation:** 30/NR/NR. **Average starting salary:** $32,000.

UNIVERSITY OF SOUTHERN CALIFORNIA
School of Urban Planning & Development

Address: University Park, Los Angeles, CA 90089-0913
Admissions Phone: 213-740-2052 · **Admissions Fax:** 213-740-1160
Admissions E-mail: jbgraff@rcf.usc.edu

INSTITUTIONAL INFORMATION

Public/Private: Private (nonprofit). **Students in Parent Institution:** 28,766

EXPENSES/FINANCIAL AID

Annual Tuition: $11,099. **Fees:** $334. **Books and Supplies:** $1,000. **Grants Range From:** $10,000-$14,000. **Average Salary Stipend:** $665.

ADMISSIONS INFORMATION

Application Fee: $55. **Regular Notification:** Rolling. **Transfer Students Accepted?** No. **Number of Applications Received:** 275. **% of Applicants Accepted:** 50. **% Accepted Who Enrolled:** 62. **Average GPA:** 3.2.
Required Admission Factors: Essays/personal statement, letters of recommendation, transcript.
Recommended Admission Factors:
Other Admission Factors: Minimum GMAT score of 550 (GRE score of 1000, LSAT score of 150) and minimum 3.0 GPA required.
Program-Specific Admission Factors: Writing sample required of PhD program applicants.

EMPLOYMENT INFORMATION

Placement Office Available? Yes.

UNIVERSITY OF SOUTHERN CALIFORNIA
Thornton School of Music

Address: 817 West 34th Street, UUC 218, Los Angeles, CA 90089-2991
Admissions Phone: 213-740-8986 · **Admissions Fax:** 213-740-8995
Admissions E-mail: uscmusic@usc.edu · **Web Address:** www.usc.edu/music

INSTITUTIONAL INFORMATION

Public/Private: Private (nonprofit). **Total Faculty:** 175. **Student/Faculty Ratio:** 3:1. **Students in Parent Institution:** 30,000.

PROGRAMS

Masters offered in: Conducting; jazz/jazz studies; music history, literature, and theory; music pedagogy; music performance, general; music theory and composition; music, other; piano and organ; violin, viola, guitar, and other stringed instruments; voice and opera. **Doctorate offered in:** Jazz/jazz studies;

music history, literature, and theory; music pedagogy; music performance, general; music theory and composition; music, other; musicology and ethnomusicology; piano and organ; violin, viola, guitar, and other stringed instruments; voice.

STUDENT INFORMATION

Total Students in Program: 486 **% Full Time:** 100. **% Female:** 53. **% Minority:** 45. **% International:** 31.

RESEARCH FACILITIES

Research Facilities: Polish Music Reference Center.

EXPENSES/FINANCIAL AID

Annual Tuition: $16,156. **Room & Board:** $10,000. **Fees:** $2,300. **Books and Supplies:** $700. **Grants Range From:** $1,000-$20,000. **Loans Range From:** $1,000-$30,000. **% Receiving Financial Aid:** 90. **Types of Aid Available:** Graduate assistantships, institutional work-study, loans, scholarships. **Number of teaching/research assistantships granted each year:** 66 **Assistantship compensation includes:** Full tuition remission, salary/stipend. **Average Salary Stipend:** $8,000.

ADMISSIONS INFORMATION

Application Fee: $65. **Priority Application Deadline:** 12/1. **Regular Application Deadline:** 2/1. **Transfer Students Accepted?** Yes. **Transfer Policy:** Maximum of 4 units may be transferred into master's programs; maximum of 30 units may be transferred into doctoral programs. **Number of Applications Received:** 695. **% of Applicants Accepted:** 34. **% Accepted Who Enrolled:** 63. **Average GPA:** 3.6.
Required Admission Factors: Essays/personal statement, interview, letters of recommendation, transcript.
Recommended Admission Factors:
Other Admission Factors: Minimum GRE score of 1000 and minimum 3.0 GPA required.
Program-Specific Admission Factors: Composition program applicants must submit 3 compositions and transcripts to Music Admissions. Thesis or writing sample required of applicants to music education and musicology programs. Please see our website for further admission requirements.

EMPLOYMENT INFORMATION

% Employed Within 6 Months: 75. **Rate of placement:** 80%. **Average starting salary:** $45,000.

UNIVERSITY OF SOUTHERN CALIFORNIA
Annenberg School for Communication

Address: University Park, 3502 Watt Way ASC 140, Los Angeles, CA 90089-0281
Admissions Phone: 213-821-0770 · **Admissions Fax:** 213-821-5574
Admissions E-mail: ascadm@usc.edu · **Web Address:** www.annenberg.usc.edu

INSTITUTIONAL INFORMATION

Public/Private: Private (nonprofit). **Evening Classes Available?** Yes. **Student/Faculty Ratio:** 9:1. **Students in Parent Institution:** 28,766.

PROGRAMS

Masters offered in: Broadcast journalism; communications studies/speech communication and rhetoric; journalism, other; journalism; organizational communications, public relations, and advertising, other; public relations/image management. **Doctorate offered in:** Communications and media studies, other; communications studies/speech communication and rhetoric; mass communications/media studies; organizational communication, general. **First Professional degree offered in:** Mass communications/media studies.

STUDENT INFORMATION

RESEARCH FACILITIES

Research Facilities: Norman Lear Center, Institute for Justice in Journalism, USC Annenberg Getty Arts Program, Online Journalism Review, Sexual Orien-

tation Issues in the News, Local Broadcast News Initative, Center for the Study of Journalism and Democracy.

EXPENSES/FINANCIAL AID

Annual Tuition: $11,099. **Fees:** $334. **Books and Supplies:** $1,000. **Grants Range From:** $10,000-$14,000. **% Receiving Financial Aid:** 40. **Number of fellowships granted each year:** 1. **Average amount of individual fellowships per year:** $14,000. **Number of teaching/research assistantships granted each year:** 30 **Average Salary Stipend:** $12,501.

ADMISSIONS INFORMATION

Application Fee: $55. **Regular Application Deadline:** 6/1. **Regular Notification:** Rolling. **Transfer Students Accepted?** No. **Transfer Policy:** Maximum four credit hours may be transferred into master's programs, 12 into doctoral programs. **Number of Applications Received:** 420. **% of Applicants Accepted:** 40. **% Accepted Who Enrolled:** 47. **Average GPA:** 3.34. **Average GRE Verbal:** 532. **Average GRE Quantitative:** 593. **Average GRE Analytical:** 580.
Required Admission Factors: Essays/personal statement, GRE, letters of recommendation, transcript.
Other Admission Factors: 3.0 and or 1000 GRE

EMPLOYMENT INFORMATION

Placement Office Available? Yes. **% of master's/doctoral grads employed in their field upon graduation:** 85/90. **Average starting salary:** $38,000.

UNIVERSITY OF SOUTHERN CALIFORNIA
College of Letters, Arts, & Sciences

Address: University Park, Los Angeles, CA 90089-0911
Admissions Phone: 213-740-1111 · **Admissions Fax:** 213-740-1556
Admissions E-mail: gradadm@usc.edu · **Web Address:** www.usc.edu/admission

INSTITUTIONAL INFORMATION

Public/Private: Private (nonprofit). **Students in Parent Institution:** 28,766

PROGRAMS

Masters offered in: Mathematics, general. **Doctorate offered in:** American/United States studies/civilization; applied mathematics; art history, criticism, and conservation; chemistry, general; economics, general; geography; geology/earth science, general; history, general; international relations and affairs; mathematic

STUDENT INFORMATION

Total Students in Program: 1,493 **% Full Time:** 100.

EXPENSES/FINANCIAL AID

Annual Tuition: $11,099. **Fees:** $45. **Books and Supplies:** $1,000. **Grants Range From:** $10,000-$14,000. **Types of Aid Available:** Fellowships, graduate assistantships, grants, institutional work-study, loans, scholarships. **Number of fellowships granted each year:** 120. **Number of teaching/research assistantships granted each year:** 450. **Average Salary Stipend:** $16,000.

ADMISSIONS INFORMATION

Application Fee: $55. **Transfer Students Accepted?** Yes. **Number of Applications Received:** 2,324. **% of Applicants Accepted:** 15. **% Accepted Who Enrolled:** 64. **Average GPA:** 3.4. **Average GRE Verbal:** 570. **Average GRE Quantitative:** 692.
Required Admission Factors: GRE, letters of recommendation, transcript.

EMPLOYMENT INFORMATION

Placement Office Available? Yes.

UNIVERSITY OF SOUTHERN CALIFORNIA
Leonard Davis School of Gerontology

Address: University Park, Los Angeles, CA 90089-0913
Admissions Phone: 213-740-5156 · **Admissions Fax:** 213-740-0792
Admissions E-mail: bknight@usc.edu ·

INSTITUTIONAL INFORMATION
Public/Private: Private (nonprofit). **Students in Parent Institution:** 28,766

EXPENSES/FINANCIAL AID
Annual Tuition: $11,099. **Fees:** $334. **Books and Supplies:** $1,000. **Grants Range From:** $10,000-$14,000. **% Receiving Financial Aid:** 75.

ADMISSIONS INFORMATION
Application Fee: $55. **Regular Notification:** Rolling. **Transfer Students Accepted?** Yes. **Number of Applications Received:** 80. **% of Applicants Accepted:** 50. **% Accepted Who Enrolled:** 95. **Average GRE Verbal:** 510. **Average GRE Quantitative:** 490.
Required Admission Factors: Essays/personal statement, GRE, letters of recommendation, transcript.
Other Admission Factors: Minimum GRE score of 1000 (Verbal plus Quantitative) and minimum 3.0 GPA required.
Program-Specific Admission Factors:

EMPLOYMENT INFORMATION
Placement Office Available? Yes.

UNIVERSITY OF SOUTHERN COLORADO
College of Humanities & Social Sciences

Address: 2200 Bonforte Boulevard, Pueblo, CO 81001
Admissions Phone: 719-549-2461 · **Admissions Fax:** 719-549-2419
Admissions E-mail: kangas@uscolo.edu

INSTITUTIONAL INFORMATION
Public/Private: Public. **Students in Parent Institution:** 5,811

STUDENT INFORMATION
Total Students in Program: 689 **% Full Time:** 11. **% Female:** 68.

RESEARCH FACILITIES
Research Facilities: Minority Biomedical Research Support Program, Nature Center, Center for Teaching, Learning, and Research.

EXPENSES/FINANCIAL AID
Annual Tuition: In-state $1,808. / Out-of-state $8,448. **Fees:** $462. **Books and Supplies:** $500. **Grants Range From:** $500-$2,500. **Loans Range From:** $500-$18,500. **% Receiving Financial Aid:** 80. **% Receiving Scholarships/Grants:** 58. **% Receiving Loans:** 79. **% Receiving Assistantships:** 7. **Average student debt, upon graduation:** $18,000

ADMISSIONS INFORMATION
Application Fee: $25. **Regular Notification:** Rolling. **Transfer Students Accepted?** Yes. **Transfer Policy:** Maximum nine credit hours with a minimum grade average of B may be transferred.
Required Admission Factors: GRE, transcript.

EMPLOYMENT INFORMATION
Placement Office Available? Yes.

UNIVERSITY OF SOUTHERN INDIANA
Social Work Department

Address: 8600 University Boulevard, Evansville, IN 47712
Admissions Phone: 812-464-1843 · **Admissions Fax:** 812-465-1116
Admissions E-mail: socwork@usi.edu
Web Address: www.usi.edu/gradstud/social.asp

INSTITUTIONAL INFORMATION
Public/Private: Public. **Evening Classes Available?** Yes. **Total Faculty:** 11. **% Faculty Female:** 64. **% Faculty Part Time:** 9. **Student/Faculty Ratio:** 19:1. **Students in Parent Institution:** 10,050.

PROGRAMS
Masters offered in: Social work.

STUDENT INFORMATION
Total Students in Program: 81. **% Full Time:** 62. **% Female:** 89. **% Minority:** 6.

EXPENSES/FINANCIAL AID
Annual Tuition: In-state $3,335. / Out-of-state $6,588. **Room & Board (On/Off Campus):** $5,140/$7,162. **Fees:** $60. **Books and Supplies:** $850. **Grants Range From:** $500-$1,500. **Loans Range From:** $1,300-$23,183. **% Receiving Financial Aid:** 66. **% Receiving Scholarships/Grants:** 3.7. **% Receiving Loans:** 90.1. **% Receiving Assistantships:** 2.5. **% Receiving Other Aid (Tuition reimbursement):** 3.7. **Types of Aid Available:** Graduate assistantships, grants, institutional work-study, loans, scholarships, **Average student debt, upon graduation:** $23,147

ADMISSIONS INFORMATION
Application Fee: $25. **Regular Application Deadline:** 1/12. **Regular Notification:** Rolling. **Transfer Students Accepted?** Yes. **Number of Applications Received:** 73. **% of Applicants Accepted:** 63. **% Accepted Who Enrolled:** 85. **Average GPA:** 3.2.
Required Admission Factors: Essays/personal statement, letters of recommendation, transcript.
Recommended Admission Factors:
Other Admission Factors: Minimum 2.8 GPA with a minimum 3.0 GPA on prerequisites or minimum 3.0 GPA on last 60 semester hours required.
Program-Specific Admission Factors: BSW required of advanced standing program applicants.

EMPLOYMENT INFORMATION
Placement Office Available? Yes.

UNIVERSITY OF SOUTHERN INDIANA
Graduate Studies and Sponsored Research

Address: 8600 University Boulevard, Evansville, IN 47712
Admissions Phone: 812-465-7015 · **Admissions Fax:** 812-465-7152
Admissions E-mail: gssr@usi.edu · **Web Address:** www.usi.edu/gradstud/

INSTITUTIONAL INFORMATION
Public/Private: Public. **Evening Classes Available?** Yes. **Total Faculty:** 76. **% Faculty Female:** 42. **% Faculty Part Time:** 30. **Student/Faculty Ratio:** 21:1. **Students in Parent Institution:** 10,050.

PROGRAMS
Masters offered in: Accounting; business administration/management; elementary education and teaching; health and medical administrative services, other; liberal arts and sciences/liberal studies; nursing—registered nurse training (RN, ASN, BSN, MSN); occupational therapy assistant; operations management and supervision; public administration; secondary education and teaching; social work.

STUDENT INFORMATION

Total Students in Program: 833 % Full Time: 14. % Female: 73. % Minority: 2. % International: 2.

EXPENSES/FINANCIAL AID

Annual Tuition: In-state $3,335. / Out-of-state $6,588. Room & Board (On/Off Campus): $5,140/$7,162. Fees: $60. Books and Supplies: $850. Grants Range From: $500-$3,705. Loans Range From: $1,100-$23,183. % Receiving Financial Aid: 14. % Receiving Scholarships/Grants: 19. % Receiving Loans: 71. % Receiving Assistantships: 2. % Receiving Other Aid (Tuition reimbursement and federal work study): 19. Types of Aid Available: Graduate assistantships, grants, institutional work-study, loans, scholarships, Average student debt, upon graduation: $13,487

ADMISSIONS INFORMATION

Application Fee: $25. Regular Application Deadline: 8/15. Regular Notification: Rolling. Transfer Students Accepted? Yes. Number of Applications Received: 502. % of Applicants Accepted: 81. % Accepted Who Enrolled: 69. Average GPA: 3.3. Average GRE Verbal: 433. Average GRE Quantitative: 503. Average GRE Analytical Writing: 4.1.
Required Admission Factors: Transcript.
Other Admission Factors: Written statement of interest required.

EMPLOYMENT INFORMATION

Placement Office Available? Yes.

UNIVERSITY OF SOUTHERN MISSISSIPPI
College of Marine Science

Address: Southern Station, Hattiesburg, MS 39406

INSTITUTIONAL INFORMATION

Public/Private: Public. Student/Faculty Ratio: 6:1. Students in Parent Institution: 14,510.

STUDENT INFORMATION

Total Students in Program: 2,366. % Full Time: 52. % Female: 63.

RESEARCH FACILITIES

Research Facilities: Gulf Coast Research Lab.

EXPENSES/FINANCIAL AID

Annual Tuition: In-state $2,870. / Out-of-state $5,972. Books and Supplies: $500. Grants Range From: $2,986-$5,376. Loans Range From: $8,500-$18,500. % Receiving Scholarships/Grants: 42. % Receiving Loans: 54.

ADMISSIONS INFORMATION

Regular Notification: Rolling. Transfer Students Accepted? Yes.
Required Admission Factors: Essays/personal statement, GRE, letters of recommendation, transcript.
Program-Specific Admission Factors: Three letters of recommendation required of some programs.

EMPLOYMENT INFORMATION

Placement Office Available? Yes. % Employed Within 6 Months: 90. Rate of placement: 76%.

UNIVERSITY OF SOUTHERN MISSISSIPPI
College of Arts and Letters

Address: 118 College Drive #10066, Hattiesburg, MS 39406-0001
Admissions Phone: 601-266-5137 · Admissions Fax: 601-266-5138
Admissions E-mail: Susan.Siltanen@usm.edu
Web Address: www.usm.edu/graduatestudies/

INSTITUTIONAL INFORMATION

Public/Private: Public. Total Faculty: 228. % Faculty Female: 42. % Faculty Part Time: 22. Student/Faculty Ratio: 3:1. Students in Parent Institution: 15,253.

STUDENT INFORMATION

Total Students in Program: 483 % Full Time: 57. % Female: 54. % Minority: 17. % International: 7.

RESEARCH FACILITIES

Research Facilities: Gulf Coast Research Lab.

EXPENSES/FINANCIAL AID

Annual Tuition: In-state $4,106. / Out-of-state $9,276. Room & Board: $5,119. Books and Supplies: $700. Grants Range From: $2,986-$5,376. Loans Range From: $8,500-$18,500. % Receiving Financial Aid: 84. % Receiving Scholarships/Grants: 42. % Receiving Loans: 48. Number of fellowships granted each year: 326 Average amount of individual fellowships per year: $15,000. Number of teaching/research assistantships granted each year: 478 Assistantship compensation includes: full tuition remission, salary/stipend. Average Salary Stipend: $10,000.

ADMISSIONS INFORMATION

Application Fee: $25. Regular Notification: Rolling. Transfer Students Accepted? Yes. Number of Applications Received: 301. % of Applicants Accepted: 77. % Accepted Who Enrolled: 62. Average GRE Verbal: 470. Average GRE Quantitative: 482. Average GRE Analytical: 501. Average GRE Analytical Writing: 4.
Required Admission Factors: GRE, letters of recommendation, transcript.
Other Admission Factors: Minimum 3.0 GPA required for most programs.
Program-Specific Admission Factors:

EMPLOYMENT INFORMATION

Placement Office Available? Yes. Rate of placement: 76%.

UNIVERSITY OF ST. AUGUSTINE
FOR HEALTH SCIENCES
Institute of Physical Therapy

Address: One University Boulevard, St. Augustine, FL 32086
Admissions Phone: 904-826-0084 · Admissions Fax: 904-826-0083
Admissions E-mail: jcook@usa.edu

INSTITUTIONAL INFORMATION

Public/Private: Private (proprietary). Students in Parent Institution: 320.

STUDENT INFORMATION

Total Students in Program: 320 % Full Time: 86. % Female: 56.

EXPENSES/FINANCIAL AID

Annual Tuition: $16,000. Fees: $200. Books and Supplies: $300.

ADMISSIONS INFORMATION

Application Fee: $50.Transfer Students Accepted? Yes. Number of Applications Received: 154. % of Applicants Accepted: 58. % Accepted Who Enrolled: 43. Average GPA: 3.25. Average GRE Verbal: 500. Average GRE Quantitative: 500. Average GRE Analytical: 600.
Required Admission Factors: Essays/personal statement, GRE, letters of recommendation, transcript.

Other Admission Factors: Minimum 3.0 GPA and minimum GRE Verbal and Quantitative score of 1000 recommended.

EMPLOYMENT INFORMATION
% Employed Within 6 Months: 100. **% of master's/doctoral grads employed in their field upon graduation:** 100/100/NR. **Rate of placement:** 100%.

UNIVERSITY OF ST. AUGUSTINE FOR HEALTH SCIENCES
Institute of Occupational Therapy

Address: One University Boulevard, St. Augustine, FL 32086
Admissions Phone: 904-826-0084 · **Admissions Fax:** 904-826-0085
Admissions E-mail: jcook@usa.edu

INSTITUTIONAL INFORMATION
Public/Private: Private (proprietary). **Students in Parent Institution:** 320.

STUDENT INFORMATION
Total Students in Program: 320 **% Full Time:** 86. **% Female:** 56.

EXPENSES/FINANCIAL AID
Annual Tuition: $16,000. **Fees:** $200. **Books and Supplies:** $300.

ADMISSIONS INFORMATION
Application Fee: $50. **Transfer Students Accepted?** Yes. **Number of Applications Received:** 39. **% of Applicants Accepted:** 74. **% Accepted Who Enrolled:** 41. **Average GPA:** 3. **Average GRE Verbal:** 450. **Average GRE Quantitative:** 450. **Average GRE Analytical:** 450.
Required Admission Factors: Essays/personal statement, GRE, letters of recommendation, transcript.
Recommended Admission Factors:
Other Admission Factors: Minimum 3.0 GPA and minimum GRE Verbal and Quantitative score of 1000 recommended.

EMPLOYMENT INFORMATION
% Employed Within 6 Months: 100. **% of master's grads employed in their field upon graduation:** 100. **Rate of placement:** 100%.

UNIVERSITY OF ST. FRANCIS
College of Graduate Studies

Address: 500 Wilcox Street, Joliet, IL 60435
Admissions Phone: 800-735-4723 · **Admissions Fax:** 815-740-3537
Admissions E-mail: gradinfo@stfrancis.edu

INSTITUTIONAL INFORMATION
Public/Private: Private (nonprofit). **Evening Classes Available?** Yes.

STUDENT INFORMATION
Total Students in Program: 1,212.

EXPENSES/FINANCIAL AID
Annual Tuition: $3,600. **Books and Supplies:** $400.

ADMISSIONS INFORMATION
Application Fee: $25. **Regular Notification:** Rolling. **Transfer Students Accepted?** Yes. **Number of Applications Received:** 305. **% of Applicants Accepted:** 100. **% Accepted Who Enrolled:** 86. **Average GPA:** 3.0
Required Admission Factors: Essays/personal statement, transcript.
Other Admission Factors: Minimum 2.75 GPA, computer competency, and two years of managerial experience or GMAT required.
Program-Specific Admission Factors: Prerequisites required for MBA program.

EMPLOYMENT INFORMATION
Placement Office Available? Yes. **Rate of placement:** 93%.

UNIVERSITY OF ST. THOMAS
Master of Liberal Arts Program

Address: 3800 Montrose Boulevard, Houston, TX 77006-4696
Admissions Phone: 713-525-6951 · **Admissions Fax:** 713-525-6924
Admissions E-mail: jgk@stthom.edu

INSTITUTIONAL INFORMATION
Public/Private: Private (nonprofit). **Evening Classes Available?** Yes. **Students in Parent Institution:** 2,897.

STUDENT INFORMATION
Total Students in Program: 863. **% Full Time:** 23. **% Female:** 60.

EXPENSES/FINANCIAL AID
Annual Tuition: $8,550. **Room & Board:** $7,330. **Fees:** $33. **Books and Supplies:** $684. **Grants Range From:** $200-$12,300. **Loans Range From:** $2,248-$18,500. **% Receiving Financial Aid:** 12. **% Receiving Scholarships/Grants:** 42. **% Receiving Loans:** 96. **Number of fellowships granted each year:** 1. **Average amount of individual fellowships per year:** $1,290.

ADMISSIONS INFORMATION
Application Fee: $35. **Regular Notification:** Rolling. **Transfer Students Accepted?** No. **Transfer Policy:** Maximum six credit horus with a minimum 3.0 GPA may be transferred. **Number of Applications Received:** 49. **% of Applicants Accepted:** 100. **% Accepted Who Enrolled:** 73.
Required Admission Factors: Essays/personal statement, interview, letters of recommendation, transcript.
Other Admission Factors: Minimum 2.5 GPA required.

UNIVERSITY OF ST. THOMAS
Center for Thomistic Studies

Address: 3800 Montrose Boulevard, Houston, TX 77006-4696
Admissions Phone: 713-525-3591 · **Admissions Fax:** 713-942-3464
Admissions E-mail: mac@stthom.edu

INSTITUTIONAL INFORMATION
Public/Private: Private (nonprofit). **Student/Faculty Ratio:** 3:1. **Students in Parent Institution:** 2,897.

STUDENT INFORMATION
Total Students in Program: 863. **% Full Time:** 23. **% Female:** 60.

EXPENSES/FINANCIAL AID
Annual Tuition: In-state $8,550. **Room & Board:** $7,330. **Fees:** $33. **Books and Supplies:** $684. **Grants Range From:** $200-$12,300. **Loans Range From:** $2,248-$18,500. **% Receiving Financial Aid:** 30. **% Receiving Scholarships/Grants:** 42. **% Receiving Loans:** 96. **Number of fellowships granted each year:** 8. **Average amount of individual fellowships per year:** $5,015

ADMISSIONS INFORMATION
Regular Notification: Rolling. **Transfer Students Accepted?** No. **Number of Applications Received:** 4. **% of Applicants Accepted:** 100. **% Accepted Who Enrolled:** 100. **Average GRE Verbal:** 600. **Average GRE Quantitative:** 548. **Average GRE Analytical:** 643.
Required Admission Factors: GRE, letters of recommendation, transcript.
Program-Specific Admission Factors: Language exam required of doctoral program applicants. At least 18 hours of philosophy required of master's program applicants.

UNIVERSITY OF ST. THOMAS (MINNESOTA)
Graduate School of Professional Psychology

Address: 1000 La Salle Avenue, TMH451, Minneapolis, MN 55403
Admissions Phone: 651-962-4650 · **Admissions Fax:** 651-962-4651
Admissions E-mail: gradpsych@stthomas.edu
Web Address: www.stthomas.edu/gradpsych

INSTITUTIONAL INFORMATION
Public/Private: Private (nonprofit). **Evening Classes Available?** Yes. **Total Faculty:** 18. **% Faculty Female:** 44. **% Faculty Part Time:** 50. **Student/Faculty Ratio:** 17:1. **Students in Parent Institution:** 11,079.

PROGRAMS
Masters offered in: Counseling psychology. **Doctorate offered in:** Counseling psychology.

STUDENT INFORMATION
Total Students in Program: 5,843 **% Full Time:** 18. **% Female:** 51. **% Minority:** 20.

RESEARCH FACILITIES
Research Facilities: Aspen Institute, Center for Entreprenurship, Center for Health and Medical Affairs, Management Center, Minnesota Center for Corporate Responsiblity, Center for Nonprofit Management, Center for Real Estate Education, Institute for Creative Studies.

EXPENSES/FINANCIAL AID
Annual Tuition: $431. **Room & Board (On/Off Campus):** $9,572/$5,580. **Fees:** $50. **Books and Supplies:** $800. **Grants Range From:** $100-$15,000. **Loans Range From:** $750-$27,500. **% Receiving Financial Aid:** 45. **% Receiving Scholarships/Grants:** 25. **% Receiving Loans:** 68. **% Receiving Assistantships:** 2. **Types of Aid Available:** Graduate assistantships, grants, loans, **Average student debt, upon graduation:** $28,821. **Average Salary Stipend:** $3,000.

ADMISSIONS INFORMATION
Application Fee: $50. **Regular Application Deadline:** 4/1. **Transfer Students Accepted?** Yes. **Transfer Policy:** Maximum nine credit hours may be transferred into master's programs only. **Number of Applications Received:** 80. **% of Applicants Accepted:** 44. **% Accepted Who Enrolled:** 89. **Average GPA:** 3.4. **Average GRE Verbal:** 490. **Average GRE Quantitative:** 560. **Average GRE Analytical:** 630.
Required Admission Factors: Essays/personal statement, interview, letters of recommendation, transcript.
Program-Specific Admission Factors: GRE is required for PsyD applicants. MAT or GRE is required for MA applicants.

UNIVERSITY OF ST. THOMAS (MINNESOTA)
College of Arts & Science

Address: 2115 Summit Avenue, St. Paul, MN 55105-1096

INSTITUTIONAL INFORMATION
Public/Private: Private (nonprofit). **Evening Classes Available?** Yes. **Students in Parent Institution:** 11,359.

STUDENT INFORMATION
Total Students in Program: 5,816. **% Full Time:** 12. **% Female:** 51.

RESEARCH FACILITIES
Research Facilities: Aspen Institute, Center for Entreprenurship, Center for Health and Medical Affairs, Management Center, Minnesota Center for Corporate Responsiblity, Center for Nonprofit Management, Center for Real Estate Education, Institute for Creative Studies.

EXPENSES/FINANCIAL AID
Annual Tuition: In-state. **Room & Board (On/Off Campus):** $9,572/$5,580. **Fees:** $50. **Books and Supplies:** $750. **Grants Range From:** $100-$15,000. **Loans Range From:** $750-$27,500. **% Receiving Financial Aid:** 42. **% Receiving Scholarships/Grants:** 25. **% Receiving Loans:** 68. **% Receiving Assistantships:** 2. **Average student debt, upon graduation:** $9,930. **Number of fellowships granted each year:** 6. **Average amount of individual fellowships per year:** $4,000. **Number of teaching/research assistantships granted each year:** 1. **Average Salary Stipend:** $1,212.

ADMISSIONS INFORMATION
Application Fee: $50. **Transfer Students Accepted?** No. **Transfer Policy:** Maximum six credit hours with a minimum grade of B may be transferred. **Number of Applications Received:** 48. **% of Applicants Accepted:** 100. **% Accepted Who Enrolled:** 56. **Average GPA:** 3.0
Required Admission Factors: Interview, letters of recommendation, transcript.
Other Admission Factors: Minimum 3.0 GPA required.
Program-Specific Admission Factors: Minimum 3.0 GPA, five courses in literature, and writing sample required of English program applicants. Writing sample and personal statement required of art history program applicants. Minimum 3.0 GPA and bachelor's degree in music or music education required.

UNIVERSITY OF ST. THOMAS (MINNESOTA)
School of Social Work

Address: 2115 Summit Avenue, St. Paul, MN 55105-1096
Admissions Phone: 651-962-5810 or 651-690-6933
Admissions Fax: 651-690-6024 or 651-962-5819
Admissions E-mail: mjgeuntzel@stthomas.edu

INSTITUTIONAL INFORMATION
Public/Private: Private (nonprofit). **Evening Classes Available?** Yes. **Students in Parent Institution:** 11,359.

STUDENT INFORMATION
Total Students in Program: 5,816. **% Full Time:** 12. **% Female:** 51.

RESEARCH FACILITIES
Research Facilities: Aspen Institute, Center for Entreprenurship, Center for Health and Medical Affairs, Management Center, Minnesota Center for Corporate Responsiblity, Center for Nonprofit Management, Center for Real Estate Education, Institute for Creative Studies.

EXPENSES/FINANCIAL AID
Room & Board (On/Off Campus): $9,572/$5,580. **Fees:** $50. **Books and Supplies:** $750. **Grants Range From:** $100-$15,000. **Loans Range From:** $750-$27,500. **% Receiving Financial Aid:** 75. **% Receiving Scholarships/Grants:** 25. **% Receiving Loans:** 68. **% Receiving Assistantships:** 2. **Average student debt, upon graduation:** $31,785. **Number of teaching/research assistantships granted each year:** 20. **Average Salary Stipend:** $962.

ADMISSIONS INFORMATION
Application Fee: $25. **Transfer Students Accepted?** Yes. **Number of Applications Received:** 161. **% of Applicants Accepted:** 79. **% Accepted Who Enrolled:** 68.
Required Admission Factors: Essays/personal statement, letters of recommendation, transcript.
Other Admission Factors: Minimum 3.0 GPA required.

UNIVERSITY OF ST. THOMAS (MINNESOTA)
School of Applied Science

Address: 2115 Summit Avenue, St. Paul, MN 55105-1096
Admissions Phone: 651-962-5501 or 651-962-5750
Admissions Fax: 651-962-5543 or 651-962-6419
Admissions E-mail: bmfloz1@stthomas.edu

INSTITUTIONAL INFORMATION
Public/Private: Private (nonprofit). **Evening Classes Available?** Yes. **Students in Parent Institution:** 11,359.

STUDENT INFORMATION
Total Students in Program: 5,816. **% Full Time:** 12. **% Female:** 51.

RESEARCH FACILITIES
Research Facilities: Aspen Institute, Center for Entreprenurship, Center for Health and Medical Affairs, Management Center, Minnesota Center for Corporate Responsiblity, Center for Nonprofit Management, Center for Real Estate Education, Institute for Creative Studies.

EXPENSES/FINANCIAL AID
Room & Board (On/Off Campus): $9,572/$5,580. **Fees:** $50. **Books and Supplies:** $750. **Grants Range From:** $100-$15,000. **Loans Range From:** $750-$27,500. **% Receiving Financial Aid:** 17. **% Receiving Scholarships/Grants:** 25. **% Receiving Loans:** 68. **% Receiving Assistantships:** 2. **Average student debt, upon graduation:** $19,873 **Average Salary Stipend:** $1,284.

ADMISSIONS INFORMATION
Application Fee: $30. **Regular Notification:** Rolling. **Transfer Students Accepted?** Yes.
Required Admission Factors: Essays/personal statement, transcript.
Other Admission Factors: Minimum 2.7 GPA required.

UNIVERSITY OF TENNESSEE
College of Human Ecology

Address: 218 Student Services Building, Knoxville, TN 37996-0220
Admissions Phone: 423-974-3251 · **Admissions Fax:** 423-974-6541

INSTITUTIONAL INFORMATION
Public/Private: Public. **Evening Classes Available?** Yes. **Students in Parent Institution:** 26,494.

STUDENT INFORMATION
Total Students in Program: 6,599. **% Full Time:** 62. **% Female:** 53.

RESEARCH FACILITIES
Research Facilities: More than 20 institutional research centers.

EXPENSES/FINANCIAL AID
Annual Tuition: In-state $3,078. / Out-of-state $7,722.

ADMISSIONS INFORMATION
Application Fee: $15. **Transfer Students Accepted?** Yes. **Number of Applications Received:** 152. **% of Applicants Accepted:** 47. **% Accepted Who Enrolled:** 53.
Required Admission Factors: GRE, transcript.
Other Admission Factors: Minimum 2.7 GPA required.

EMPLOYMENT INFORMATION
Placement Office Available? Yes.

UNIVERSITY OF TENNESSEE
College of Arts & Sciences

Address: 218 Student Services Building, Knoxville, TN 37996-0220
Admissions Phone: 423-974-3251 · **Admissions Fax:** 423-974-6541

INSTITUTIONAL INFORMATION
Public/Private: Public. **Evening Classes Available?** Yes. **Students in Parent Institution:** 26,494.

STUDENT INFORMATION
Total Students in Program: 6,599. **% Full Time:** 62. **% Female:** 53.

RESEARCH FACILITIES
Research Facilities: More than 20 institutional research centers.

EXPENSES/FINANCIAL AID
Annual Tuition: In-state $3,078. / Out-of-state $7,722.

ADMISSIONS INFORMATION
Application Fee: $15. **Transfer Students Accepted?** Yes. **Number of Applications Received:** 999. **% of Applicants Accepted:** 25. **% Accepted Who Enrolled:** 56.
Required Admission Factors: transcript.
Other Admission Factors: Minimum 2.7 GPA required.

EMPLOYMENT INFORMATION
Placement Office Available? Yes.

UNIVERSITY OF TENNESSEE SPACE INSTITUTE
Graduate Programs

Address: B.H. Goethert Parkway, Tullahoma, TN 37388
Admissions Phone: 931-393-7432 · **Admissions Fax:** 931-393-7346

INSTITUTIONAL INFORMATION
Public/Private: Public. **Students in Parent Institution:** 268

EXPENSES/FINANCIAL AID
Annual Tuition: In-state $4,730. / Out-of-state $15,028. **Fees:** $90. **Books and Supplies:** $300. **% Receiving Assistantships:** 21.

ADMISSIONS INFORMATION
Application Fee: $35. **Regular Notification:** Rolling. **Transfer Students Accepted?** Yes. **Number of Applications Received:** 283. **% of Applicants Accepted:** 55. **% Accepted Who Enrolled:** 21.
Required Admission Factors: GRE, transcript.
Other Admission Factors: Minimum 2.7 GPA required.

EMPLOYMENT INFORMATION
Placement Office Available? Yes.

UNIVERSITY OF TEXAS—PAN AMERICAN
College of Arts & Humanities

Address: 1201 West University Drive, Edinburg, TX 78539

INSTITUTIONAL INFORMATION
Public/Private: Public. **Evening Classes Available?** Yes. **Students in Parent Institution:** 12,760.

STUDENT INFORMATION
Total Students in Program: 1,574. **% Full Time:** 22. **% Female:** 64.

EXPENSES/FINANCIAL AID
Annual Tuition: In-state $1,876. / Out-of-state $5,746. **Books and Supplies:** $1,200.

ADMISSIONS INFORMATION

Transfer Students Accepted? No. Transfer Policy: Maximum 12 credit hours with dean's approval may be transferred. Number of Applications Received: 66. % of Applicants Accepted: 100. % Accepted Who Enrolled: 61.

Required Admission Factors: Essays/personal statement, GRE, letters of recommendation, transcript.

EMPLOYMENT INFORMATION

Placement Office Available? Yes.

UNIVERSITY OF TEXAS—PAN AMERICAN
College of Social & Behavioral Sciences

Address: 1201 West University Drive, Edinburg, TX 78539

INSTITUTIONAL INFORMATION

Public/Private: Public. Evening Classes Available? Yes. Student/Faculty Ratio: 12:1. Students in Parent Institution: 12,760.

STUDENT INFORMATION

Total Students in Program: 1,574 % Full Time: 22. % Female: 64.

EXPENSES/FINANCIAL AID

Annual Tuition: In-state $1,876. / Out-of-state $5,746. Books and Supplies: $1,200. % Receiving Financial Aid: 40. Number of teaching/research assistantships granted each year: 4

ADMISSIONS INFORMATION

Transfer Students Accepted? No. Transfer Policy: Letter of approval from the dean required of transfer applicants. Number of Applications Received: 22. % of Applicants Accepted: 86. % Accepted Who Enrolled: 79. Average GPA: 3.0

Required Admission Factors: Essays/personal statement, GRE, transcript.

EMPLOYMENT INFORMATION

Placement Office Available? Yes. % of master's grads employed in their field upon graduation: 50.

UNIVERSITY OF TEXAS AT ARLINGTON
School of Urban & Public Affairs

Address: P.O. Box 19088, Arlington, TX 76019

INSTITUTIONAL INFORMATION

Public/Private: Public. Students in Parent Institution: 20,424.

STUDENT INFORMATION

Total Students in Program: 4,975. % Full Time: 41. % Female: 55.

RESEARCH FACILITIES

Research Facilities: More than 30 school-supported/affiliated research centers.

EXPENSES/FINANCIAL AID

Annual Tuition: In-state $2,913. / Out-of-state $6,981. Books and Supplies: $600. Grants Range From: $400-$6,000. Loans Range From: $500-$18,000. % Receiving Scholarships/Grants: 80. % Receiving Loans: 35.

ADMISSIONS INFORMATION

Transfer Students Accepted? No.

EMPLOYMENT INFORMATION

Placement Office Available? Yes.

UNIVERSITY OF TEXAS AT ARLINGTON
College of Science

Address: P.O. Box 19088, Arlington, TX 76019

INSTITUTIONAL INFORMATION

Public/Private: Public. Students in Parent Institution: 20,424.

STUDENT INFORMATION

Total Students in Program: 4,975. % Full Time: 41. % Female: 55.

RESEARCH FACILITIES

Research Facilities: More than 30 school-supported/affiliated research centers.

EXPENSES/FINANCIAL AID

Annual Tuition: In-state $2,913. / Out-of-state $6,981. Books and Supplies: $600. Grants Range From: $400-$6,000. Loans Range From: $500-$18,000. % Receiving Scholarships/Grants: 80. % Receiving Loans: 35.

ADMISSIONS INFORMATION

Transfer Students Accepted? No.
Required Admission Factors: GRE, transcript.

EMPLOYMENT INFORMATION

Placement Office Available? Yes.

UNIVERSITY OF TEXAS AT ARLINGTON
Graduate School

Address: PO Box 19088, Arlington, TX 76019

INSTITUTIONAL INFORMATION

Public/Private: Public. Students in Parent Institution: 20,424.

STUDENT INFORMATION

Total Students in Program: 4,975. % Full Time: 41. % Female: 55.

RESEARCH FACILITIES

Research Facilities: More than 30 school-supported/affiliated research centers.

EXPENSES/FINANCIAL AID

Annual Tuition: In-state $2,913. / Out-of-state $6,981. Books and Supplies: $600. Grants Range From: $400-$6,000. Loans Range From: $500-$18,000. % Receiving Scholarships/Grants: 80. % Receiving Loans: 35.

ADMISSIONS INFORMATION

Transfer Students Accepted? No.

EMPLOYMENT INFORMATION

Placement Office Available? Yes.

UNIVERSITY OF TEXAS AT ARLINGTON
School of Social Work

Address: PO Box 19088, Arlington, TX 76019

INSTITUTIONAL INFORMATION

Public/Private: Public. Students in Parent Institution: 20,424.

STUDENT INFORMATION

Total Students in Program: 4,975. % Full Time: 41. % Female: 55.

RESEARCH FACILITIES

Research Facilities: More than 30 school-supported/affiliated research centers.

EXPENSES/FINANCIAL AID
Annual Tuition: In-state $2,913. / Out-of-state $6,981. **Books and Supplies:** $600. **Grants Range From:** $400-$6,000. **Loans Range From:** $500-$18,000. **% Receiving Scholarships/Grants:** 80. **% Receiving Loans:** 35.

ADMISSIONS INFORMATION
Transfer Students Accepted? No.

EMPLOYMENT INFORMATION
Placement Office Available? Yes.

UNIVERSITY OF TEXAS AT ARLINGTON
College of Liberal Arts

Address: PO Box 19088, Arlington, TX 76019

INSTITUTIONAL INFORMATION
Public/Private: Public. **Students in Parent Institution:** 20,424.

STUDENT INFORMATION
Total Students in Program: 4,975. **% Full Time:** 41. **% Female:** 55.

RESEARCH FACILITIES
Research Facilities: More than 30 school-supported/affiliated research centers.

EXPENSES/FINANCIAL AID
Annual Tuition: In-state $2,913. / Out-of-state $6,981. **Books and Supplies:** $600. **Grants Range From:** $400-$6,000. **Loans Range From:** $500-$18,000. **% Receiving Scholarships/Grants:** 80. **% Receiving Loans:** 35.

ADMISSIONS INFORMATION
Transfer Students Accepted? No.

EMPLOYMENT INFORMATION
Placement Office Available? Yes.

UNIVERSITY OF TEXAS AT AUSTIN
College of Fine Arts

Address: Austin, TX 78712-1157
Admissions Phone: 512-475-7390 · **Admissions Fax:** 512-475-7395
Admissions E-mail: adwjp@utxdp.dp.utexas.edu

INSTITUTIONAL INFORMATION
Public/Private: Public. **Total Faculty:** 165. **Students in Parent Institution:** 48,318.

STUDENT INFORMATION
Total Students in Program: 9,779. **% Female:** 51.

RESEARCH FACILITIES
Research Facilities: More than 50 institutional research centers.

EXPENSES/FINANCIAL AID
Annual Tuition: In-state $3,780. / Out-of-state $10,110. **Grants Range From:** $200-$17,000. **Loans Range From:** $1,000-$20,000.

ADMISSIONS INFORMATION
Regular Notification: Rolling. **Transfer Students Accepted?** Yes. **Transfer Policy:** Maximum six credit hours may be transferred into master's programs. **Required Admission Factors:** Essays/personal statement, interview, letters of recommendation, transcript. **Other Admission Factors:** Minimum GRE score of 1000 and minimum 3.0 GPA recommended.

EMPLOYMENT INFORMATION
Placement Office Available? Yes.

UNIVERSITY OF TEXAS AT AUSTIN
Lyndon B. Johnson
School of Public Affairs

Address: PO Box Y, Austin, TX 78713-8925
Admissions Phone: 512-471-4292 · **Admissions Fax:** 512-471-8455
Admissions E-mail: lbjadmit@mail.utexas.edu · **Web Address:** www.utexas.edu/lbj/

INSTITUTIONAL INFORMATION
Public/Private: Public. **Total Faculty:** 24. **Students in Parent Institution:** 48,318.

STUDENT INFORMATION
Total Students in Program: 9,779 **% Female:** 51.

RESEARCH FACILITIES
Research Facilities: More than 50 institutional research centers.

EXPENSES/FINANCIAL AID
Annual Tuition: In-state $3,780. / Out-of-state $10,110. **Grants Range From:** $200-$17,000. **Loans Range From:** $1,000-$20,000.

ADMISSIONS INFORMATION
Regular Application Deadline: 1/15. **Regular Notification:** Rolling. **Transfer Students Accepted?** Yes. **Transfer Policy:** Maximum six credit hours may be transferred into master's programs. **Number of Applications Received:** 313. **% of Applicants Accepted:** 61. **% Accepted Who Enrolled:** 53. **Average GPA:** 3.5. **Average GRE Verbal:** 570. **Average GRE Quantitative:** 627. **Average GRE Analytical:** 627.
Required Admission Factors: Essays/personal statement, GRE, letters of recommendation, transcript.
Other Admission Factors: Minimum GRE score of 1000 and minimum 3.0 GPA recommended.

EMPLOYMENT INFORMATION
Placement Office Available? Yes.

UNIVERSITY OF TEXAS AT AUSTIN
Graduate School of Library &
Information Science

Address: Austin, TX 78712-1157
Admissions Phone: 512-475-7390 · **Admissions Fax:** 512-475-7395
Admissions E-mail: adwjp@utxdp.dp.utexas.edu

INSTITUTIONAL INFORMATION
Public/Private: Public. **Total Faculty:** 16. **Students in Parent Institution:** 48,318.

STUDENT INFORMATION
Total Students in Program: 9,779. **% Female:** 51.

RESEARCH FACILITIES
Research Facilities: More than 50 institutional research centers.

EXPENSES/FINANCIAL AID
Annual Tuition: In-state $3,780. / Out-of-state $10,110. **Grants Range From:** $200-$17,000. **Loans Range From:** $1,000-$20,000.

ADMISSIONS INFORMATION

Regular Notification: Rolling. **Transfer Students Accepted?** Yes. **Transfer Policy:** Maximum six credit hours may be transferred into master's programs. **Number of Applications Received:** 255. **% of Applicants Accepted:** 73. **% Accepted Who Enrolled:** 48. **Average GPA:** 3.5. **Average GRE Verbal:** 586. **Average GRE Quantitative:** 594. **Average GRE Analytical:** 600.
Required Admission Factors: GRE, letters of recommendation, transcript.
Recommended Admission Factors:
Other Admission Factors: Minimum GRE score of 1000 and minimum 3.0 GPA recommended.

EMPLOYMENT INFORMATION

Placement Office Available? Yes.

UNIVERSITY OF TEXAS AT AUSTIN
College of Communication

Address: Austin, TX 78712-1157
Admissions Phone: 512-475-7390 · **Admissions Fax:** 512-475-7395
Admissions E-mail: adwjp@utxdp.dp.utexas.edu

INSTITUTIONAL INFORMATION

Public/Private: Public. **Total Faculty:** 102. **Students in Parent Institution:** 48,318.

STUDENT INFORMATION

Total Students in Program: 9,779. **% Female:** 51.

RESEARCH FACILITIES

Research Facilities: More than 50 institutional research centers.

EXPENSES/FINANCIAL AID

Annual Tuition: In-state $3,780. / Out-of-state $10,110. **Grants Range From:** $200-$17,000. **Loans Range From:** $1,000-$20,000.

ADMISSIONS INFORMATION

Regular Notification: Rolling. **Transfer Students Accepted?** Yes. **Transfer Policy:** Maximum six credit hours may be transferred into master's programs.
Required Admission Factors: GRE, letters of recommendation, transcript.
Other Admission Factors: Minimum GRE score of 1000 and minimum 3.0 GPA recommended.

EMPLOYMENT INFORMATION

Placement Office Available? Yes.

UNIVERSITY OF TEXAS AT AUSTIN
College of Liberal Arts

Address: Austin, TX 78712-1157
Admissions Phone: 512-475-7390 · **Admissions Fax:** 512-475-7395
Admissions E-mail: adwjp@utxdp.dp.utexas.edu

INSTITUTIONAL INFORMATION

Public/Private: Public. **Total Faculty:** 549. **Students in Parent Institution:** 48,318.

STUDENT INFORMATION

Total Students in Program: 9,779. **% Female:** 51.

RESEARCH FACILITIES

Research Facilities: More than 50 institutional research centers.

EXPENSES/FINANCIAL AID

Annual Tuition: In-state $3,780. / Out-of-state $10,110. **Grants Range From:** $200-$17,000. **Loans Range From:** $1,000-$20,000.

ADMISSIONS INFORMATION

Regular Notificaion: Rolling. **Transfer Students Accepted?** Yes. **Transfer Policy:** Maximum six credit hours may be transferred into master's programs.
Required Admission Factors: Essays/personal statement, GRE, letters of recommendation, transcript.

EMPLOYMENT INFORMATION

Placement Office Available? Yes.

UNIVERSITY OF TEXAS AT AUSTIN
School of Social Work

Address: Austin, TX 78712-1157
Admissions Phone: 512-475-7390 · **Admissions Fax:** 512-475-7395
Admissions E-mail: adwjp@utxdp.dp.utexas.edu

INSTITUTIONAL INFORMATION

Public/Private: Public. **Total Faculty:** 33. **Students in Parent Institution:** 48,318.

STUDENT INFORMATION

Total Students in Program: 9,779. **% Female:** 51.

RESEARCH FACILITIES

Research Facilities: More than 50 institutional research centers.

EXPENSES/FINANCIAL AID

Annual Tuition: In-state $3,780. / Out-of-state $10,110. **Grants Range From:** $200-$17,000. **Loans Range From:** $1,000-$20,000.

ADMISSIONS INFORMATION

Regular Notification: Rolling. **Transfer Students Accepted?** Yes. **Transfer Policy:** Maximum six credit hours may be transferred into master's programs. **Number of Applications Received:** 279. **% of Applicants Accepted:** 82. **% Accepted Who Enrolled:** 59. **Average GPA:** 3.4. **Average GRE Verbal:** 501. **Average GRE Quantitative:** 543. **Average GRE Analytical:** 543.
Required Admission Factors: GRE, letters of recommendation, transcript.
Recommended Admission Factors:
Other Admission Factors: Minimum GRE score of 1000 and minimum 3.0 GPA recommended.

EMPLOYMENT INFORMATION

Placement Office Available? Yes.

UNIVERSITY OF TEXAS AT AUSTIN
College of Natural Sciences

Address: Austin, TX 78712-1157
Admissions Phone: 512-475-7390 · **Admissions Fax:** 512-475-7395
Admissions E-mail: paver@mail.utexas.edu

INSTITUTIONAL INFORMATION

Public/Private: Public. **Total Faculty:** 387. **Students in Parent Institution:** 48,318.

STUDENT INFORMATION

Total Students in Program: 9,779. **% Female:** 51.

RESEARCH FACILITIES

Research Facilities: More than 50 institutional research centers.

EXPENSES/FINANCIAL AID

Annual Tuition: In-state $3,780. / Out-of-state $10,110. **Grants Range From:** $200-$17,000. **Loans Range From:** $1,000-$20,000.

ADMISSIONS INFORMATION

Regular Notification: Rolling. **Transfer Students Accepted?** Yes.
Required Admission Factors: Essays/personal statement, GRE, letters of recommendation, transcript.

EMPLOYMENT INFORMATION

Placement Office Available? Yes.

UNIVERSITY OF TEXAS AT BROWNSVILLE
College of Liberal Arts

Address: 80 Fort Brown, Brownsville, TX 78520
Admissions Phone: 956-544-8254 · **Admissions Fax:** 956-983-7279
Admissions E-mail: abel@utb1.utb.edu

INSTITUTIONAL INFORMATION

Public/Private: Public. **Evening Classes Available?** Yes. **Total Faculty:** 46.
% Faculty Female: 33. **Students in Parent Institution:** 9,076.

STUDENT INFORMATION

Total Students in Program: 689.

RESEARCH FACILITIES

Research Facilities: Center for Business and Education.

EXPENSES/FINANCIAL AID

Annual Tuition: In-state $4,320. / Out-of-state $9,369. **Grants Range From:**
$432-$864. **% Receiving Financial Aid:** 100.

ADMISSIONS INFORMATION

Application Fee: $15. **Regular Notification:** Rolling. **Transfer Students
Accepted?** Yes. **Number of Applications Received:** 14. **% of Applicants
Accepted:** 100. **% Accepted Who Enrolled:** 79.
Required Admission Factors: GRE, letters of recommendation, transcript.
Other Admission Factors: Minimum GRE score of 800 (Verbal and Quantitative or analytical) and minimum 3.0 GPA required.

EMPLOYMENT INFORMATION

Placement Office Available? Yes. **Rate of placement:** 90%.

UNIVERSITY OF TEXAS AT DALLAS
School of Natural Science & Mathematics

Address: P.O. Box 830688, AD 29, Richardson, TX 75083-0688

INSTITUTIONAL INFORMATION

Public/Private: Public. **Evening Classes Available?** Yes. **Total Faculty:** 77.
% Faculty Female: 10. **Student/Faculty Ratio:** 3:1. **Students in Parent
Institution:** 10,945.

STUDENT INFORMATION

Total Students in Program: 4,385. **% Full Time:** 36. **% Female:** 46.

RESEARCH FACILITIES

Research Facilities: Carolyn Lipshy Galersein Women's Center, Cecil & Ida
Green Center for the Study of Science & Society, Callier Center for Communication Disorders, Communication and Learning Center, Center for International Accounting Development.

EXPENSES/FINANCIAL AID

Annual Tuition: In-state $2,016. / Out-of-state $7,080. **Fees:** $1,177. **Books
and Supplies:** $1,000. **Grants Range From:** $500-$3,000. **Loans Range
From:** $200-$18,000. **% Receiving Financial Aid:** 40. **% Receiving Scholarships/Grants:** 15. **% Receiving Loans:** 75. **% Receiving Assistantships:**
5.

ADMISSIONS INFORMATION

Application Fee: $25. **Regular Notification:** Rolling. **Transfer Students
Accepted?** Yes. **Number of Applications Received:** 378. **% of Applicants
Accepted:** 62. **% Accepted Who Enrolled:** 27.
Required Admission Factors: Essays/personal statement, GRE, letters of recommendation, transcript.
Program-Specific Admission Factors: Minimum GRE score of 1000 (Verbal
and Quantitative), calculus, general physics, organic chemistry, biochemistry,
and general biology (including genetics) required of biology program applicants. Degree equivalent to B.S. in chemistry required of chemistry applicants.

EMPLOYMENT INFORMATION

Placement Office Available? Yes.

UNIVERSITY OF TEXAS AT DALLAS
School of Human Development

Address: P.O. Box 830688, AD 29, Richardson, TX 75083-0688
Admissions Phone: 972-883-2342 · **Admissions Fax:** 972-883-2599
Admissions E-mail: chendl@utdallas.edu

INSTITUTIONAL INFORMATION

Public/Private: Public. **Total Faculty:** 37. **% Faculty Female:** 54. **Student/
Faculty Ratio:** 6:1. **Students in Parent Institution:** 10,945.

STUDENT INFORMATION

Total Students in Program: 4,385. **% Full Time:** 36. **% Female:** 46.

RESEARCH FACILITIES

Research Facilities: Carolyn Lipshy Galersein Women's Center, Cecil & Ida
Green Center for the Study of Science & Society, Callier Center for Communication Disorders, Communication and Learning Center, Center for International Accounting Development.

EXPENSES/FINANCIAL AID

Annual Tuition: In-state $2,016. / Out-of-state $7,080. **Fees:** $1,177. **Books
and Supplies:** $1,000. **Grants Range From:** $500-$3,000. **Loans Range
From:** $200-$18,000. **% Receiving Financial Aid:** 65. **% Receiving Scholarships/Grants:** 15. **% Receiving Loans:** 75. **% Receiving Assistantships:**
5. **Number of teaching/research assistantships granted each year:** 60

ADMISSIONS INFORMATION

Application Fee: $25. **Regular Notification:** Rolling. **Transfer Students
Accepted?** Yes. **Number of Applications Received:** 298. **% of Applicants
Accepted:** 43. **% Accepted Who Enrolled:** 53.
Required Admission Factors: Essays/personal statement, GRE, interview,
letters of recommendation, transcript.
Recommended Admission Factors:
Other Admission Factors: Minimum GRE Verbal and Quantitative score of
1000 required.

EMPLOYMENT INFORMATION

Placement Office Available? Yes.

UNIVERSITY OF TEXAS AT DALLAS
School of General Studies

Address: P.O. Box 830688, AD 29, Richardson, TX 75083-0688
Admissions Phone: 972-883-2342 · **Admissions Fax:** 972-883-2599
Admissions E-mail: chendl@utdallas.edu

INSTITUTIONAL INFORMATION

Public/Private: Public. **Evening Classes Available?** Yes. **Total Faculty:** 6.
% Faculty Female: 33. **Student/Faculty Ratio:** 5:1. **Students in Parent
Institution:** 10,945.

STUDENT INFORMATION

Total Students in Program: 4,385. % Full Time: 36. % Female: 46.

RESEARCH FACILITIES

Research Facilities: Carolyn Lipshy Galersein Women's Center, Cecil & Ida Green Center for the Study of Science & Society, Callier Center for Communication Disorders, Communication and Learning Center, Center for International Accounting Development.

EXPENSES/FINANCIAL AID

Annual Tuition: In-state $2,016. / Out-of-state $7,080. Fees: $1,177. Books and Supplies: $1,000. Grants Range From: $500-$3,000. Loans Range From: $200-$18,000. % Receiving Financial Aid: 1. % Receiving Scholarships/Grants: 15. % Receiving Loans: 75. % Receiving Assistantships: 5.

ADMISSIONS INFORMATION

Application Fee: $25. Regular Notification: Rolling. Transfer Students Accepted? Yes. Number of Applications Received: 14. % of Applicants Accepted: 93. % Accepted Who Enrolled: 92. Average GPA: 3.

Required Admission Factors: Essays/personal statement, GRE, letters of recommendation, transcript.

Recommended Admission Factors:

Other Admission Factors: Minimum GRE score of 1000 and minimum 3.0 GPA required; conditional admission possible for applicants not meeting minimums.

EMPLOYMENT INFORMATION

Placement Office Available? Yes.

UNIVERSITY OF TEXAS AT DALLAS
School of Social Sciences

Address: P.O. Box 830688, AD 29, Richardson, TX 75083-0688
Admissions Phone: 972-883-2342 · Admissions Fax: 972-883-2599
Admissions E-mail: ss-grad-unfo@utdallas.edu

INSTITUTIONAL INFORMATION

Public/Private: Public. Evening Classes Available? Yes. Total Faculty: 32. % Faculty Female: 16. Student/Faculty Ratio: 5:1. Students in Parent Institution: 10,945.

STUDENT INFORMATION

Total Students in Program: 4,385. % Full Time: 36. % Female: 46.

RESEARCH FACILITIES

Research Facilities: Carolyn Lipshy Galersein Women's Center, Cecil & Ida Green Center for the Study of Science & Society, Callier Center for Communication Disorders, Communication and Learning Center, Center for International Accounting Development.

EXPENSES/FINANCIAL AID

Annual Tuition: In-state $2,016. / Out-of-state $7,080. Fees: $1,177. Books and Supplies: $1,000. Grants Range From: $500-$3,000. Loans Range From: $200-$18,000. % Receiving Financial Aid: 18. % Receiving Scholarships/Grants: 15. % Receiving Loans: 75. % Receiving Assistantships: 5. Number of teaching/research assistantships granted each year: 30

ADMISSIONS INFORMATION

Application Fee: $25. Regular Notification: Rolling. Transfer Students Accepted? Yes. Number of Applications Received: 100. % of Applicants Accepted: 72. % Accepted Who Enrolled: 65. Average GPA: 3.

Required Admission Factors: Essays/personal statement, GRE, letters of recommendation, transcript.

Other Admission Factors: Minimum GRE score of 1000 and minimum 3.0 GPA required.

EMPLOYMENT INFORMATION

Placement Office Available? Yes.

UNIVERSITY OF TEXAS AT DALLAS
School of Arts & Humanities

Address: P.O. Box 830688, AD 29, Richardson, TX 75083-0688
Admissions Phone: 972-883-2342 · Admissions Fax: 972-883-2310
Admissions E-mail: soliday@utdallas.edu

INSTITUTIONAL INFORMATION

Public/Private: Public. Evening Classes Available? Yes. Total Faculty: 40. % Faculty Female: 35. Student/Faculty Ratio: 5:1. Students in Parent Institution: 10,945.

STUDENT INFORMATION

Total Students in Program: 4,385. % Full Time: 36. % Female: 46.

RESEARCH FACILITIES

Research Facilities: Carolyn Lipshy Galersein Women's Center, Cecil & Ida Green Center for the Study of Science & Society, Callier Center for Communication Disorders, Communication and Learning Center, Center for International Accounting Development.

EXPENSES/FINANCIAL AID

Annual Tuition: In-state $2,016. / Out-of-state $7,080. Fees: $1,177. Books and Supplies: $1,000. Grants Range From: $500-$3,000. Loans Range From: $200-$18,000. % Receiving Financial Aid: 7. % Receiving Scholarships/Grants: 15. % Receiving Loans: 75. % Receiving Assistantships: 5.

ADMISSIONS INFORMATION

Application Fee: $25. Regular Notification: Rolling. Transfer Students Accepted? Yes. Transfer Policy: Maximum 15 credit hours may be transferred into master's programs; maximum 36 credit hours may be transferred. Number of Applications Received: 72. % of Applicants Accepted: 75. % Accepted Who Enrolled: 70. Average GPA: 3.3.

Required Admission Factors: Essays/personal statement, GRE, letters of recommendation, transcript.

Recommended Admission Factors:

Other Admission Factors: Minimum GRE score of 1050 and minimum 3.0 GPA required. Applicants taking the revised GRE must complete General Test Package One.

Program-Specific Admission Factors: Some training across arts and humanities fields required.

EMPLOYMENT INFORMATION

Placement Office Available? Yes.

UNIVERSITY OF TEXAS AT EL PASO
College of Science

Address: 500 West University Avenue, El Paso, TX 79968
Admissions Phone: 915-747-5491 · Admissions Fax: 915-747-5788
Admissions E-mail: sjordan@utep.edu

INSTITUTIONAL INFORMATION

Public/Private: Public. Evening Classes Available? Yes. Students in Parent Institution: 16,220.

STUDENT INFORMATION

Total Students in Program: 2,578. % Full Time: 36. % Female: 57.

EXPENSES/FINANCIAL AID

Annual Tuition: In-state $816. / Out-of-state $6,384. Fees: $992. Books and Supplies: $492.

ADMISSIONS INFORMATION

Application Fee: $15. Transfer Students Accepted? Yes. Number of Applications Received: 29. % of Applicants Accepted: 41. Average GRE Verbal: 440. Average GRE Quantitative: 580. Average GRE Analytical: 509.

Required Admission Factors: GRE, transcript.
Other Admission Factors: Minimum GRE score of 450 and minimum 3.0 GPA recommended for unconditional admission.

EMPLOYMENT INFORMATION
Placement Office Available? Yes.

UNIVERSITY OF TEXAS AT EL PASO
College of Liberal Arts

Address: 500 West University Avenue, El Paso, TX 79968
Admissions Phone: 915-747-5491 · Admissions Fax: 915-474-5788
Admissions E-mail: sjordan@utep.edu

INSTITUTIONAL INFORMATION
Public/Private: Public. Evening Classes Available? Yes. Students in Parent Institution: 16,220.

STUDENT INFORMATION
Total Students in Program: 2,578. % Full Time: 36. % Female: 57.

EXPENSES/FINANCIAL AID
Annual Tuition: In-state $816. / Out-of-state $6,384. Fees: $992. Books and Supplies: $492.

ADMISSIONS INFORMATION
Application Fee: $15. Regular Notification: Rolling. Transfer Students Accepted? Yes. Number of Applications Received: 199. % of Applicants Accepted: 47. % Accepted Who Enrolled: 78. Average GRE Verbal: 520. Average GRE Quantitative: 490. Average GRE Analytical: 525.
Required Admission Factors: GRE, transcript.
Recommended Admission Factors:
Other Admission Factors: Minimum GRE score of 450 and minimum 3.0 GPA recommended for unconditional admission.
Program-Specific Admission Factors: Writing sample required of MFA program applicants.

EMPLOYMENT INFORMATION
Placement Office Available? Yes.

UNIVERSITY OF TEXAS AT SAN ANTONIO
The Graduate School

Address: 6900 North Loop 1604 West, San Antonio, TX 78249
Admissions Phone: 210-458-4330 · Admissions Fax: 210-458-4332
Admissions E-mail: graduatestudies@utsa.edu · Web Address: www.utsa.edu/graduate

INSTITUTIONAL INFORMATION
Public/Private: Public. Evening Classes Available? Yes. Students in Parent Institution: 26,175.

STUDENT INFORMATION
Total Students in Program: 3,638. % Female: 60. % Minority: 46. % International: 9.

EXPENSES/FINANCIAL AID
Annual Tuition: In-state $172. / Out-of-state $688.

ADMISSIONS INFORMATION
Application Fee: $40. Priority Application Deadline: 10/1. Regular Application Deadline: 11/1. Regular Notification: Rolling. Transfer Students Accepted? Yes. Number of Applications Received: 1,251. % of Applicants Accepted: 62. % Accepted Who Enrolled: 71. Average GPA: 3.
Required Admission Factors: Transcript.
Recommended Admission Factors:
Other Admission Factors: Minimum GPA 3.0

UNIVERSITY OF TEXAS AT SAN ANTONIO
College of Science

Address: 6900 North Loop 1604 West, San Antonio, TX 78249-0603
Admissions Phone: 210-458-4330 · Admissions Fax: 210-458-4332
Admissions E-mail: graduatestudies@utsa.edu
Web Address: http://www.utsa.edu/cds/index.htm

INSTITUTIONAL INFORMATION
Public/Private: Public. Evening Classes Available? Yes. Total Faculty: 130. Students in Parent Institution: 18,450.

EXPENSES/FINANCIAL AID
Annual Tuition: In-state $1,980. / Out-of-state $5,868. Fees: $660.

ADMISSIONS INFORMATION
Application Fee: $25. Regular Notification: Rolling. Transfer Students Accepted? Yes. Transfer Policy: Maximum of six semester hours may be transferred. Number of Applications Received: 393. % of Applicants Accepted: 56. % Accepted Who Enrolled: 52.
Required Admission Factors: GRE, transcript.
Other Admission Factors: Minimum 3.0 GPA required.

EMPLOYMENT INFORMATION
Placement Office Available? Yes.

UNIVERSITY OF TEXAS AT SAN ANTONIO
College of Public Policy

Address: 501 West Durango Boulevard, San Antonio, TX 78207
Admissions Phone: 210-458-2530 · Admissions Fax: 210-458-2531
Admissions E-mail: graduatestudies@utsa.edu · Web Address: utsa.edu/copp/

INSTITUTIONAL INFORMATION
Public/Private: Public. Evening Classes Available? Yes. Total Faculty: 24. % Faculty Female: 38. % Faculty Part Time: 4.

PROGRAMS
Masters offered in: Criminal justice/law enforcement administration; public administration; social work.

RESEARCH FACILITIES
Research Facilities: Center for Policy Studies, Culture and Policy Institute.

EXPENSES/FINANCIAL AID
Annual Tuition: In-state $1,980. / Out-of-state $5,868. Fees: $660. Types of Aid Available: Graduate assistantships, scholarships,

ADMISSIONS INFORMATION
Application Fee: $25. Regular Application Deadline: 7/1. Regular Notification: Rolling. Transfer Students Accepted? Yes. Number of Applications Received: 85.
Required Admission Factors: Essays/personal statement, letters of recommendation, transcript.
Other Admission Factors: Minimum 3.0 GPA required for unconditional admission.

EMPLOYMENT INFORMATION
Placement Office Available? Yes.

UNIVERSITY OF TEXAS AT SAN ANTONIO
College of Liberal & Fine Arts

Address: 6900 North Loop 1604 West, San Antonio, TX 78249-0603
Admissions Phone: 210-458-4330 · **Admissions Fax:** 210-458-4332
Admissions E-mail: graduatestudies@utsa.edu
Web Address: colfa2.utsa.edu/home2/index.htm

INSTITUTIONAL INFORMATION
Public/Private: Public. **Evening Classes Available?** Yes. **Total Faculty:** 357. **% Faculty Female:** 32. **% Faculty Part Time:** 20. **Student/Faculty Ratio:** 10:1. **Students in Parent Institution:** 18,450.

PROGRAMS
Masters offered in: American government and politics (United States); American history (United States); American literature (United States); anthropology, other; anthropology; archeology; art history, criticism and conservation; art/art studies, general; creative writing; English composition; English language and literature, general; English language and literature/letters, other; English literature (British and Commonwealth); experimental psychology; history, general; music performance, general; music/music and performing arts studies, general; physical anthropology; piano and organ; political science and government, general; political science and government, other; psychology, general; sociology; spanish and iberian studies; speech and rhetorical studies; technical and business writing; violin, viola, guitar, and other stringed instruments; voice and opera. **Doctorate offered in:** American literature (United States); English composition; English language and literature, general; English language and literature/letters, other; English literature (British and Commonwealth). **First Professional degree offered in:** fine/studio arts, general.

RESEARCH FACILITIES
Research Facilities: Canter for Archeological Research, Culture & Policy Institute, Women's Studies Institute, Institute of Music Research, Institute of Texan Cultures, Institute of Law and Public Affairs, Hispanic Research Center, Metropolitan Research Center.

EXPENSES/FINANCIAL AID
Annual Tuition: In-state $2,376. / Out-of-state $6,300. **Room & Board (On/Off Campus):** $7,656/$6,300. **Fees:** $774. **Books and Supplies:** $900. **Loans Range From:** $5,000-$18,500. **Types of Aid Available:** Fellowships, graduate assistantships, grants, institutional work-study, loans, scholarships.

ADMISSIONS INFORMATION
Application Fee: $40. **Priority Application Deadline:** n/a. **Regular Application Deadline:** 7/1. **Regular Notification:** Rolling. **Transfer Students Accepted?** Yes. **Transfer Policy:** Must meet college and program requirements. **Number of Applications Received:** 96. **% of Applicants Accepted:** 49. **% Accepted Who Enrolled:** 60.
Required Admission Factors: Transcript.
Other Admission Factors: College minimum is 3.0. Some programs require higher GPA. A lower GPA is allowed on a discretionary case-by-case basis.
Program-Specific Admission Factors: GRE required of some programs. Portfolio required for art program applicants. Anthropology, psychology, and the MFA programs require separate application. Music requires an audition.

EMPLOYMENT INFORMATION
Placement Office Available? Yes.

THE UNIVERSITY OF TEXAS AT TYLER
College of Arts and Sciences

Address: 3900 University Boulevard, Tyler, TX 75799
Admissions Phone: 903-566-7368 · **Admissions Fax:** 903-566-7377
Admissions E-mail: mgrissom@mail.uttyl.edu
Website: www.uttyler.edu/cas/index.htm

INSTITUTIONAL INFORMATION
Public/private: Public. **Evening Classes Available?** Yes. **Students in Parent Institution:** 4,760.

PROGRAMS
Masters offered in: Criminal justice/safety studies, English language and literature, history, mathematics, political science and government, public administration, sociology.

EXPENSES/FINANCIAL AID
Annual Tuition: In-state $1,450/Out-of-state $5,302. **Grants Range From:** $200-$2,700. **Loans Range From:** $500-$18,500. **% Receiving Scholarships/Grants:** 33. **% Receiving Loans:** 64.

ADMISSIONS INFORMATION
Regular Notification: Rolling. **Transfer Students Accepted?** Yes.
Required Admission Factors: GRE, transcript.
Other Admission Factors: Minimum GRE score of 1000 required.
Program-Specific Admission Factors: Minimum 2.5 GPA required of public administration and political science program applicants. Minimum 3.0 GPA required of history and English program applicants.

EMPLOYMENT INFORMATION
Placement Office Available? Yes.

UNIVERSITY OF TEXAS OF THE PERMIAN BASIN
College of Arts & Sciences

Address: 4901 East University, Odessa, TX 79762
Admissions Phone: 915-552-2220

INSTITUTIONAL INFORMATION
Public/Private: Public. **Students in Parent Institution:** 2,193.

STUDENT INFORMATION
Total Students in Program: 583. **% Full Time:** 16. **% Female:** 63.

RESEARCH FACILITIES
Research Facilities: J.B. Shepperd Public Leadership Institute.

EXPENSES/FINANCIAL AID
Annual Tuition: In-state $1,314. / Out-of-state $4,896. **Fees:** $458.

ADMISSIONS INFORMATION
Transfer Students Accepted? No. **Number of Applications Received:** 8. **% of Applicants Accepted:** 100. **% Accepted Who Enrolled:** 88.
Required Admission Factors: GRE, transcript.

THE UNIVERSITY OF THE ARTS
Philadelphia College of Art & Design

Address: 320 South Broad Street, Philadelphia, PA 19102
Admissions Phone: 800-616-ARTS · **Admissions Fax:** 215-717-6045
Admissions E-mail: belliott@uarts.edu · **Website:** www.uarts.edu

INSTITUTIONAL INFORMATION
Public/private: Private (nonprofit). **Students in Parent Institution:** 2,150.

PROGRAMS
Masters offered in: Art teacher education, ceramic arts and ceramics, education, industrial design, museology/museum studies, music teacher education, painting, printmaking; sculpture.

STUDENT INFORMATION
Total Students in Program: 157. **% Full-time:** 66. **% Female:** 76. **% International:** 8.

RESEARCH FACILITIES

Research Facilities: Borowsky Center for Publication Arts, Design for Thinking Research Institute.

EXPENSES/FINANCIAL AID

Annual Tuition: $20,860. Room & Board (On/off Campus): $7,800/$9,100. Fees: $850. Books and Supplies: $2,000. Grants Range From: $2,000-$6,800. Loans Range From: $7,800-$18,500. % Receiving Financial Aid: 75. % Receiving Scholarships/Grants: 70. % Receiving Loans: 90. Average student debt, upon graduation: $27,000. Number of Fellowships Granted Each Year: 68. Average amount of individual fellowships per year: 6,250.

ADMISSIONS INFORMATION

Application Fee: $50. Priority Application Deadline: 2/1. Regular Application Deadline: 2/1. Regular Notification: Rolling. Transfer Students Accepted? Yes. Number of Applications Received: 169. % of Applicants Accepted: 63. % Accepted Who Enrolled: 58. Average GPA: 3.34. Required Admission Factors: Essays/personal statement, letters of recommendation, transcript.
Recommended Admission Factors: GRE, interview.
Other Admission Factors: Minimum 3.0 GPA in major required.
Program-Specific Admission Factors: MAT visual arts: Candidate must hold BFA or BA in art or equivalent with 45 credits in studio art and 12 crdits in art history with a B or better.

THE UNIVERSITY OF THE ARTS
Philadelphia College of Performing Arts

Address: 320 South Broad Street, Philadelphia, PA 19102
Admissions Phone: 800-616-ARTS · Admissions Fax: 215-717-6045
Admissions E-mail: admissions@uarts.edu · Website: www.uarts.edu

INSTITUTIONAL INFORMATION

Public/private: Private (nonprofit). Students in Parent Institution: 2,150.

PROGRAMS

Masters offered in: Jazz/jazz studies, music teacher education.

STUDENT INFORMATION

Total Students in Program: 17. % Full-time: 94. % Female: 18.

RESEARCH FACILITIES

Research Facilities: Borowsky Center for Publication Arts, Design for Thinking Research Institute.

EXPENSES/FINANCIAL AID

Annual Tuition: $20,860. Room & Board (On/off Campus): $7,800/$9,300. Fees: $850. Books and Supplies: $2,000. Grants Range From: $2,000-$6,800. Loans Range From: $7,800-$18,500. % Receiving Financial Aid: 75. % Receiving Scholarships/Grants: 70. % Receiving Loans: 90. Average student debt, upon graduation: $27,000. Number of Fellowships Granted Each Year: 14. Average amount of individual fellowships per year: 6,250.

ADMISSIONS INFORMATION

Application Fee: $50. Priority Application Deadline: 2/1. Regular Application Deadline: 2/1. Transfer Students Accepted? Yes. Number of Applications Received: 28. % of Applicants Accepted: 82. % Accepted Who Enrolled: 65. Average GPA: 3.3.
Required Admission Factors: Essays/personal statement, letters of recommendation, transcript.
Recommended Admission Factors: Interview.
Other Admission Factors: Minimum 3.0 GPA in major required.

UNIVERSITY OF THE DISTRICT OF COLUMBIA
College of Arts & Sciences

Address: 4200 Connecticut Avenue, NW, Washington, DC 20008
Admissions Phone: 202-274-5011 · Admissions Fax: 202-274-6180

INSTITUTIONAL INFORMATION

Public/Private: Public. Evening Classes Available? Yes. Students in Parent Institution: 5,358.

STUDENT INFORMATION

Total Students in Program: 350. % Full Time: 28. % Female: 70.

EXPENSES/FINANCIAL AID

Annual Tuition: In-state $2,070. / Out-of-state $4,710. Books and Supplies: $400. Grants Range From: $400-$1,200. Loans Range From: $1,113-$4,780. % Receiving Scholarships/Grants: 45. % Receiving Loans: 50.

ADMISSIONS INFORMATION

Application Fee: $20. Transfer Students Accepted? No.
Required Admission Factors: Essays/personal statement, GRE, letters of recommendation, transcript.
Other Admission Factors: Minimum 3.0 GPA required.

EMPLOYMENT INFORMATION

Placement Office Available? Yes.

UNIVERSITY OF THE INCARNATE WORD
School of Graduate Studies & Research

Address: 4301 Broadway, San Antonio, TX 78209-6397
Admissions Phone: 210-829-3157 · Admissions Fax: 210-805-3559
Admissions E-mail: hinojosa@universe.uiwtx.edu

INSTITUTIONAL INFORMATION

Public/Private: Private (nonprofit). Evening Classes Available? Yes. Student/Faculty Ratio: 15:1. Students in Parent Institution: 3,702.

STUDENT INFORMATION

Total Students in Program: 699. % Full Time: 19. % Female: 66.

EXPENSES/FINANCIAL AID

Annual Tuition: In-state $8,010. Fees: $150. Books and Supplies: $800. Loans Range From: $5,000-$10,000.

ADMISSIONS INFORMATION

Application Fee: $20. Regular Notification: Rolling. Transfer Students Accepted? Yes. Number of Applications Received: 374. % of Applicants Accepted: 79. % Accepted Who Enrolled: 67.
Required Admission Factors: Transcript.
Recommended Admission Factors:
Other Admission Factors: Minimum GRE score of 1200 or MAT score of 40 and minimum 2.5 GPA required.

EMPLOYMENT INFORMATION

Placement Office Available? Yes.

UNIVERSITY OF THE PACIFIC
Conservatory of Music

Address: 3601 Pacific Avenue, Stockton, CA 95211
Admissions Phone: 209-946-2261 · Admissions Fax: 209-946-2858
Admissions E-mail: dwolfe@uop.edu

INSTITUTIONAL INFORMATION

Public/Private: Private (nonprofit). Students in Parent Institution: 5,634.

STUDENT INFORMATION

Total Students in Program: 582. % Full Time: 57. % Female: 62.

RESEARCH FACILITIES

Research Facilities: Masonic Speech-Language Clinic.

EXPENSES/FINANCIAL AID

Annual Tuition: $21,152. Number of teaching/research assistantships granted each year: 2.

ADMISSIONS INFORMATION

Application Fee: $50. Regular Notification: Rolling. Transfer Students Accepted? No. Number of Applications Received: 9. % of Applicants Accepted: 89. % Accepted Who Enrolled: 25.

Required Admission Factors: Essays/personal statement, GRE, letters of recommendation, transcript.

Other Admission Factors: Minimum 3.0 GPA required.

EMPLOYMENT INFORMATION

Placement Office Available? Yes.

UNIVERSITY OF THE PACIFIC
Arts & Sciences

Address: 3601 Pacific Avenue, Stockton, CA 95211
Admissions Phone: 209-946-2261 · Admissions Fax: 209-946-2858
Admissions E-mail: salton@uop.edu

INSTITUTIONAL INFORMATION

Public/Private: Private (nonprofit). Students in Parent Institution: 5,634.

STUDENT INFORMATION

Total Students in Program: 582. % Full Time: 57. % Female: 62.

RESEARCH FACILITIES

Research Facilities: Masonic Speech-Language Clinic.

EXPENSES/FINANCIAL AID

Annual Tuition: $21,152. Number of teaching/research assistantships granted each year: 30. Average Salary Stipend: $8,600.

ADMISSIONS INFORMATION

Application Fee: $50.Transfer Students Accepted? Yes. Number of Applications Received: 64. % of Applicants Accepted: 61. % Accepted Who Enrolled: 62.

Required Admission Factors: Essays/personal statement, GRE, letters of recommendation, transcript.

Other Admission Factors: Minimum 3.0 GPA required.

EMPLOYMENT INFORMATION

Placement Office Available? Yes.

UNIVERSITY OF THE SACRED HEART
Graduate Programs

Address: P.O. Box 12383, San Juan, Puerto Rico 00914-0383
Admissions Phone: 787-728-1515,-extension-3237 · Admissions Fax: 787-727-7880
Admissions E-mail: a_nieves@uscsi.usc.clu.edu

INSTITUTIONAL INFORMATION

Evening Classes Available? Yes. Total Faculty: 12. % Faculty Female: 75. % Faculty Part Time: 50. Students in Parent Institution: 5,154.

STUDENT INFORMATION

Total Students in Program: 388. % Full Time: 12. % Female: 62.

EXPENSES/FINANCIAL AID

Annual Tuition: $2,430. Fees: $240.

ADMISSIONS INFORMATION

Application Fee: $25. Regular Notification: Rolling. Transfer Students Accepted? Yes.

Required Admission Factors: Essays/personal statement, interview, transcript.

Other Admission Factors: Minimum test score of 500 and minimum 2.75 GPA required.

Program-Specific Admission Factors: Courses in statistical analysis and elementary accounting required of management of information systems program applicants. Courses in Quantitative methos, elementary accounting, and adminstrative theory required of tax program applicants.

UNIVERSITY OF THE SCIENCES IN PHILADELPHIA
College of Graduate Studies

Address: 600 South 43rd Street, Philadelphia, PA 19104-4495
Admissions Phone: 215-596-8937 · Admissions Fax: 215-895-1185
Admissions E-mail: graduate@usip.edu

INSTITUTIONAL INFORMATION

Public/Private: Private (nonprofit). Evening Classes Available? Yes. Students in Parent Institution: 127.

STUDENT INFORMATION

Total Students in Program: 127. % Full Time: 40. % Female: 59.

RESEARCH FACILITIES

Research Facilities: McNeil Research Center, Institute for Pharmaceutical Economics, Pharmacology-Toxicology Research Center.

EXPENSES/FINANCIAL AID

Annual Tuition: $25,683. Room & Board: $8,148. Fees: $26. Grants Range From: $4,436-$26,619. % Receiving Financial Aid: 50. % Receiving Assistantships: 50. Average student debt, upon graduation: $45,000 Number of fellowships granted each year: 4 Average amount of individual fellowships per year: $13,500. Number of teaching/research assistantships granted each year: 27.

ADMISSIONS INFORMATION

Application Fee: $45. Regular Notification: Rolling. Transfer Students Accepted? Yes. Number of Applications Received: 116. % of Applicants Accepted: 62. % Accepted Who Enrolled: 62. Average GPA: 3.2.

Required Admission Factors: Essays/personal statement, letters of recommendation, transcript.

Other Admission Factors: Minimum combined GRE score of 1500 with no single score lower than 400 required.

UNIVERSITY OF TOLEDO
College of Arts & Sciences

Address: 2801 West Bancroft Street, Toledo, OH 43606-3390
Admissions Phone: 419-530-4723 · Admissions Fax: 419-530-4724
Admissions E-mail: grdsch@utnet.utoledo.edu
Web Address: http://www.utoledo.edu/colleges/as

INSTITUTIONAL INFORMATION

Public/Private: Public. Evening Classes Available? Yes. Students in Parent Institution: 20,313.

RESEARCH FACILITIES

Research Facilities: Instrumentation Center, Lake Erie Center, Center for Visual Arts, Scott Park Learning Resource Center, Carlson Library, LaValley Law Library.

EXPENSES/FINANCIAL AID

Annual Tuition: In-state $3,167. / Out-of-state $6,847. **Fees:** $464. **Books and Supplies:** $700. **Grants Range From:** $7,200-$17,000. **Loans Range From:** $100-$18,000. **% Receiving Assistantships:** 33.

ADMISSIONS INFORMATION

Application Fee: $30. **Regular Notification:** Rolling. **Transfer Students Accepted?** Yes. **Number of Applications Received:** 407. **% of Applicants Accepted:** 53. **% Accepted Who Enrolled:** 67. **Average GPA:** 3.2. **Average GRE Verbal:** 470. **Average GRE Quantitative:** 592. **Average GRE Analytical:** 562.
Required Admission Factors: Essays/personal statement, letters of recommendation, transcript.
Other Admission Factors: Minimum 2.7 GPA required.

EMPLOYMENT INFORMATION

Placement Office Available? Yes.

UNIVERSITY OF TORONTO
Graduate Programs

Address: 63 St. George Street, Toronto, Ontario, M5S 2Z9 Canada
Admissions Phone: 416-978-6614 · **Admissions Fax:** 416-978-4367

INSTITUTIONAL INFORMATION

Public/Private: Public. **Total Faculty:** 641. **Students in Parent Institution:** 9,546.

STUDENT INFORMATION

Total Students in Program: 9,546. **% Full Time:** 77. **% Female:** 55.

RESEARCH FACILITIES

Research Facilities: Addiction Research Foundation, Clark Institute of Psychiatry, Pontifical Institute of Medieval Studies, Institute for Theoretical Astrophysics, Ontario Center for Materials Research, Banting and Best Department of Medical Research.

EXPENSES/FINANCIAL AID

Room & Board (On/Off Campus): $600/$800. **Grants Range From:** $1,000-$20,000. **Loans Range From:** $9,600-$9,600.

ADMISSIONS INFORMATION

Application Fee: $85. **Regular Notification:** Rolling. **Transfer Students Accepted?** No. **Number of Applications Received:** 1,651. **% of Applicants Accepted:** 59. **% Accepted Who Enrolled:** 46.
Required Admission Factors: Letters of recommendation, transcript.
Program-Specific Admission Factors: Minimum grade average of B required of master's program applicants. Minimum grade average of B+ required of doctoral program applicants.

UNIVERSITY OF TULSA
Henry Kendall College of Arts & Sciences

Address: University of Tulsa Graduate School, 600 South College Avenue, Tulsa, OK 74104
Admissions Phone: 918-631-2336 or 800-882-4723 · **Admissions Fax:** 918-631-2156
Admissions E-mail: grad@utulsa.edu · **Web Address:** www.utulsa.edu/graduate

INSTITUTIONAL INFORMATION

Public/Private: Private (nonprofit). **Student/Faculty Ratio:** 3:1. **Students in Parent Institution:** 4,174.

STUDENT INFORMATION

Total Students in Program: 219. **% Full Time:** 81. **% Female:** 66. **% Minority:** 10. **% International:** 5.

RESEARCH FACILITIES

Research Facilities: Mary K. Chapman Center for Communication Disorders, Lithic Technology Journal, Center for Community Research and Development, James Joyce Quarterly, Tulsa Studies in Women's Literature, Online Modernist Journals Project.

EXPENSES/FINANCIAL AID

Annual Tuition: $11,340. **Room & Board (On/Off Campus):** $7,238/$5,850. **Fees:** $60. **Books and Supplies:** $1,000. **Grants Range From:** $5,175-$15,200. **Loans Range From:** $1,000-$12,000. **% Receiving Financial Aid:** 86. **Types of Aid Available:** Fellowships, graduate assistantships, institutional work-study, loans, scholarships. **Average student debt, upon graduation:** $6,984 **Number of fellowships granted each year:** 6 **Average amount of individual fellowships per year:** $11,000. **Number of teaching/research assistantships granted each year:** 98. **Average Salary Stipend:** $10,000.

ADMISSIONS INFORMATION

Application Fee: $30. **Regular Application Deadline:** 8/5. **Regular Notification:** Rolling. **Transfer Students Accepted?** Yes. **Transfer Policy:** Maximum six credit hours may be transferred into master's programs; maximum 12 credit hours may be transferred into PhD programs. **Number of Applications Received:** 248. **% of Applicants Accepted:** 66. **% Accepted Who Enrolled:** 52. **Average GPA:** 3.4. **Average GRE Verbal:** 514. **Average GRE Quantitative:** 575. **Average GRE Analytical:** 598. **Average GRE Analytical Writing:** 4.8.
Required Admission Factors: Essays/personal statement, letters of recommendation, transcript.
Other Admission Factors: Minimum 3.0 GPA and acceptable GRE scores required.
Program-Specific Admission Factors: Portfolio required for admission to MFA program in art.

EMPLOYMENT INFORMATION

Placement Office Available? Yes. **% Employed Within 6 Months:** 84. **% of master's/doctoral grads employed in their field upon graduation:** 89/92. **Rate of placement:** 91%. **Average starting salary:** $38,000.

UNIVERSITY OF UTAH
College of Humanities

Address: 310 Park Building, Salt Lake City, UT 84112
Admissions Phone: 801-581-7283 · **Admissions Fax:** 801-581-7864
Admissions E-mail: lprigmo@ssbi.saff.utah.edu

INSTITUTIONAL INFORMATION

Public/Private: Public. **Student/Faculty Ratio:** 2:1. **Students in Parent Institution:** 25,981.

STUDENT INFORMATION

Total Students in Program: 4,859. **% Full Time:** 66. **% Female:** 42.

EXPENSES/FINANCIAL AID

Annual Tuition: In-state $7,891. / Out-of-state $21,631. **% Receiving Financial Aid:** 33.

ADMISSIONS INFORMATION

Application Fee: $40. **Regular Notification:** Rolling. **Transfer Students Accepted?** Yes.
Required Admission Factors: Essays/personal statement, GRE, letters of recommendation, transcript.
Other Admission Factors: Minimum 3.0 GPA required for most programs.
Program-Specific Admission Factors: GRE required of history, English, and communication program applicants; recommended of philosophy program applicants. Minimum GRE score in the 65th percentile required of history program applicants. Minimum GRE section scores of 500 required of communications program applicants.

EMPLOYMENT INFORMATION

Placement Office Available? Yes.

UNIVERSITY OF UTAH
College of Social & Behavioral Science

Address: 310 Park Building, Salt Lake City, UT 84112
Admissions Phone: 801-581-7283 · Admissions Fax: 801-585-7864

INSTITUTIONAL INFORMATION

Public/Private: Public. **Evening Classes Available?** Yes. **Student/Faculty Ratio:** 3:1. **Students in Parent Institution:** 25,981.

STUDENT INFORMATION

Total Students in Program: 4,859. **% Full Time:** 66. **% Female:** 42.

EXPENSES/FINANCIAL AID

Annual Tuition: In-state $7,891. / Out-of-state $21,631. **% Receiving Financial Aid:** 33.

ADMISSIONS INFORMATION

Application Fee: $50. **Transfer Students Accepted?** No.
Required Admission Factors: Essays/personal statement, GRE, letters of recommendation, transcript.
Other Admission Factors: Minimum 3.0 GPA required.

EMPLOYMENT INFORMATION

Placement Office Available? Yes.

UNIVERSITY OF UTAH
Graduate School of Social Work

Address: 310 Park Building, Salt Lake City, UT 84112
Admissions Phone: 801-581-5103 · Admissions Fax: 801-585-3219
Admissions E-mail: lsmith@socwk.utah.edu

INSTITUTIONAL INFORMATION

Public/Private: Public. **Evening Classes Available?** Yes. **Student/Faculty Ratio:** 14:1. **Students in Parent Institution:** 25,981.

STUDENT INFORMATION

Total Students in Program: 4,859. **% Full Time:** 66. **% Female:** 42.

EXPENSES/FINANCIAL AID

Annual Tuition: In-state $7,891. / Out-of-state $21,631. **% Receiving Financial Aid:** 32. **Number of fellowships granted each year:** 86. **Average amount of individual fellowships per year:** $1,750. **Number of teaching/research assistantships granted each year:** 2. **Average Salary Stipend:** $4,000.

ADMISSIONS INFORMATION

Application Fee: $40. **Regular Notification:** Rolling. **Transfer Students Accepted?** Yes. **Transfer Policy:** Letter of good standing required of transfer applicants. **Number of Applications Received:** 365. **% of Applicants Accepted:** 35. **% Accepted Who Enrolled:** 81. **Average GPA:** 3.6. **Average GRE Verbal:** 550. **Average GRE Quantitative:** 500. **Average GRE Analytical:** 525.
Required Admission Factors: Essays/personal statement, letters of recommendation, ranscript.
Other Admission Factors: Minimum 3.0 GPA (cumulative or upper-division) required.

EMPLOYMENT INFORMATION

Placement Office Available? Yes.

UNIVERSITY OF UTAH
College of Fine Arts

Address: 310 Park Building, Salt Lake City, UT 84112
Admissions Phone: 801-581-7283 · Admissions Fax: 801-585-7864

INSTITUTIONAL INFORMATION

Public/Private: Public. **Student/Faculty Ratio:** 2:1. **Students in Parent Institution:** 25,981.

STUDENT INFORMATION

Total Students in Program: 4,859 **% Full Time:** 66. **% Female:** 42.

EXPENSES/FINANCIAL AID

Annual Tuition: In-state $7,891. / Out-of-state $21,631. **% Receiving Financial Aid:** 33.

ADMISSIONS INFORMATION

Application Fee: $40. **Transfer Students Accepted?** No.
Required Admission Factors: Essays/personal statement, letters of recommendation, transcript.
Other Admission Factors: Minimum 3.0 GPA required for most programs.
Program-Specific Admission Factors: Film portfolio and interview required of film production program applicants. Interview required of stage directing program applicants. Interview recommended of modern dance and music program applicants.

EMPLOYMENT INFORMATION

Placement Office Available? Yes.

UNIVERSITY OF VERMONT
Graduate College

Address: 85 South Prospect Street, Burlington, VT 05405-0160
Admissions Phone: 802-656-2699 · Admissions Fax: 802-656-0519
Admissions E-mail: graduate.admissions@uvm.edu
Web Address: www.uvm.edu/~gradcoll/

INSTITUTIONAL INFORMATION

Public/Private: Public. **Evening Classes Available?** Yes. **Students in Parent Institution:** 10,970.

PROGRAMS

Masters offered in: Adult health nurse/nursing; agricultural economics; agricultural/biological engineering and bioengineering; anatomy; ancient studies/civilization; animal nutrition; animal sciences, general; biochemistry/biophysics and molecular biology; biochemistry; biology/biological sciences, general; biomedical/medical engineering; biostatistics; botany/plant biology; business administration and management, general ; business administration/management; cell/cellular and molecular biology; chemistry teacher education; chemistry, general; civil engineering, general; classics and classical languages, literatures, and linguistics, general; clinical psychology; communication disorders, general; community organization and advocacy; computer and information sciences, general; computer and information sciences, general; computer engineering, general; counselor education/school counseling and guidance services; curriculum and instruction; dairy science; education leadership and administration, general; education, general; educational, instructional, and curriculum supervision; electrical, electronics and communications engineering; elementary and middle school administration/principalship; elementary education and teaching; English language and literature, general; environmental/environmental health engineering; experimental psychology; family practice nurse nurse practitioner; fishing and fisheries sciences and management; food science; forestry, general; french language and literature; geology/earth science, general; German language and literature; higher education/higher education administration; historic preservation and conservation; history, general; junior high/intermediate/middle school education and teaching; materials science; mathematics teacher education; mathematics, general; mechanical engineering; microbiology, general; molecular biology; molecular biophysics; molecular genetics; molecular physiology; natural resources management and policy, general; natural resources/conservation, general; neuroanatomy; neurobiology and neurophysiology; neuroscience; nursing—registered nurse training (rn, asn, bsn, msn); nutrition sciences; pathology/experimental pathology; pharmacology; physics teacher education; physics, general; plant sciences, general; psychology, general; public administration; public health/community nurse/nursing; secondary education and teaching; secondary school administration/principalship; social work; soil science and agronomy, general; special education, general; speech-language pathology/pathologist; statistics, general; structural biology; teacher education, multiple levels; water resources engineering; wildlife and wildlands sciences and management. **Doctorate offered in:** Anatomy; animal nutrition; animal sciences, general; biochemistry/biophysics and molecular biology; biochemistry; biology/biological sciences, general; botany/plant biology; cell/cellular and molecular biology; chemistry, general; civil engineering, gener **First Professional degree offered in:** Mdicine (MD)

STUDENT INFORMATION
Total Students in Program: 1,300 % Full Time: 100. % Female: 58. % Minority: 5. % International: 12.

RESEARCH FACILITIES
Research Facilities: Center for Research on Vermont, Center for Rural Studies, Center for Groundwater Remediation Design, Center for Food Entrepreneurship, Clinical Research Center, Gund Institute for Ecological Economics, Proctor Maple Research Center, Rubenstein Ecosystems

EXPENSES/FINANCIAL AID
Annual Tuition: In-state $6,516. / Out-of-state $1,728. Fees: $428. **Number of fellowships granted each year:** 50 **Number of teaching/research assistantships granted each year:** 475 **Assistantship compensation includes:** full tuition remission, partial tuition remission, salary/stipend. **Average Salary Stipend:** $13,200.

ADMISSIONS INFORMATION
Application Fee: $35. Regular Notification: Rolling. **Transfer Students Accepted?** Yes. **Transfer Policy:** Application deadlines are the same for all applicants. Transfer credit limits are 9 for master's programs and the EdD; 24 for the Ph.D. **Number of Applications Received:** 1,934. **% of Applicants Accepted:** 46. **% Accepted Who Enrolled:** 51.
Required Admission Factors: Essays/personal statement, letters of recommendation, transcript.
Recommended Admission Factors:
Other Admission Factors: There are no firm GPA or test score cutoffs. Decisions are based upon consideration of all materials. Consult individual program web sites for required/recommended preparation.
Program-Specific Admission Factors: See www.uvm.edu/~gradcoll/overviewgradmajors1.html for application requirements, including tests, where applicable, and specific program deadlines.

EMPLOYMENT INFORMATION
Placement Office Available? Yes.

UNIVERSITY OF VICTORIA
Faculty of Graduate Studies

Address: P.O. Box 3025, STN CSC, Victoria, British Columbia, V8W 2Y2 Canada
Admissions Phone: 250-472-4657 · Admissions Fax: 250-721-6225
Admissions E-mail: garo@uvic.ca · Web Address: http://web.uvic.ca/grar

INSTITUTIONAL INFORMATION
Public/Private: Public. Students in Parent Institution: 18,219.

STUDENT INFORMATION
Total Students in Program: 2,146. % Full Time: 84.

RESEARCH FACILITIES
Research Facilities: Center for Earth and Ocean Research, Center for Forest Biology, Center for Studies in Religion and Society, Center on Aging, Institute

for Dispute Resolution, Center for Asia-Pacific Initiatives, Canada Center for Climate Modelling and Prediction.

EXPENSES/FINANCIAL AID
Room & Board: $2,640. Fees: $392. Grants Range From: $50-$13,400. **Number of fellowships granted each year:** 50 **Average amount of individual fellowships per year:** $13,000.

ADMISSIONS INFORMATION
Application Fee: $50. Regular Notification: Rolling. **Transfer Students Accepted?** Yes. **Transfer Policy:** Maximum number of credit hours which may be transferred varies by program. **Number of Applications Received:** 2,098. **% of Applicants Accepted:** 33. **% Accepted Who Enrolled:** 54. Required Admission Factors: Letters of recommendation, transcript. Other Admission Factors: Minimum grade average of <#7f>B" required.

UNIVERSITY OF VIRGINIA
Graduate School of Arts & Sciences

Address: Cabell Hall 437, Charlottesville, VA 22903
Admissions Phone: 434-924-7184 · Admissions Fax: 434-924-6737
Admissions E-mail: grad-a-s@virginia.edu
Web Address: artsandsciences.virginia.edu/grad/

INSTITUTIONAL INFORMATION
Public/Private: Public. Students in Parent Institution: 19,643.

STUDENT INFORMATION
Total Students in Program: 1,812. % Full Time: 100. % Female: 234.

RESEARCH FACILITIES
Research Facilities: More than a dozen institutional research centers.

EXPENSES/FINANCIAL AID
Annual Tuition: In-state $3,988. / Out-of-state $17,078. Fees: $1,190. **Books and Supplies:** $800.

ADMISSIONS INFORMATION
Application Fee: $40. Priority Application Deadline: 12/1. Regular Application Deadline: 4/15. Regular Notification: Rolling. **Transfer Students Accepted?** Yes. **Transfer Policy:** Transfer students are not accepted into master's programs; some may be approved for doctoral program. **Number of Applications Received:** 4,024. **% of Applicants Accepted:** 30. **% Accepted Who Enrolled:** 34. **Average GPA:** 3.5. **Average GRE Verbal:** 602. **Average GRE Quantitative:** 684. **Average GRE Analytical:** 671.
Required Admission Factors: Essays/personal statement, GRE, interview, letters of recommendation, transcript.

EMPLOYMENT INFORMATION
Placement Office Available? Yes.

UNIVERSITY OF WASHINGTON
College of Arts & Sciences

Address: G-1 Communications Building, Box 353770 – University of Washington, Seattle, WA 98195
Admissions Phone: 206-543-5929 · Admissions Fax: 206-685-3234
Admissions E-mail: uwgrad@u.washington.edu
Web Address: www.grad.washington.edu/admissions/adminfo.html

INSTITUTIONAL INFORMATION
Public/Private: Public. Students in Parent Institution: 45,587.

STUDENT INFORMATION
Total Students in Program: 9,308. % Full Time: 81. % Female: 50.

RESEARCH FACILITIES
Research Facilities: Center for the Humanities, Center for Law and Justice, Center on Human Development and Disability, Center for Urban Horticulture,

Applied Physics Laboratory, Friday Harbor Laboratories, Medical Center/ Harborview Medical Center, Quaternary Research Center.

EXPENSES/FINANCIAL AID
Annual Tuition: In-state $5,539. / Out-of-state $14,376. **Fees:** $384. **Books and Supplies:** $924.

ADMISSIONS INFORMATION
Transfer Students Accepted? No.

EMPLOYMENT INFORMATION
Placement Office Available? Yes.

UNIVERSITY OF WASHINGTON
College of Forest Resources

Address: Seattle, WA 98195

INSTITUTIONAL INFORMATION
Public/Private: Public. **Students in Parent Institution:** 45,587.

STUDENT INFORMATION
Total Students in Program: 9,308. **% Full Time:** 81. **% Female:** 50.

RESEARCH FACILITIES
Research Facilities: Center for the Humanities, Center for Law and Justice, Center on Human Development and Disability, Center for Urban Horticulture, Applied Physics Laboratory, Friday Harbor Laboratories, Medical Center/ Harborview Medical Center, Quaternary Research Center.

EXPENSES/FINANCIAL AID
Annual Tuition: In-state $5,539. / Out-of-state $14,376. **Fees:** $384. **Books and Supplies:** $924.

ADMISSIONS INFORMATION
Transfer Students Accepted? No.

EMPLOYMENT INFORMATION
Placement Office Available? Yes.

UNIVERSITY OF WASHINGTON
Graduate School

Address: Seattle, WA 98195

INSTITUTIONAL INFORMATION
Public/Private: Public. **Students in Parent Institution:** 45,587.

STUDENT INFORMATION
Total Students in Program: 9,308. **% Full Time:** 81. **% Female:** 50.

RESEARCH FACILITIES
Research Facilities: Center for the Humanities, Center for Law and Justice, Center on Human Development and Disability, Center for Urban Horticulture, Applied Physics Laboratory, Friday Harbor Laboratories, Medical Center/ Harborview Medical Center, Quaternary Research Center.

EXPENSES/FINANCIAL AID
Annual Tuition: In-state $5,539. / Out-of-state $14,376. **Fees:** $384. **Books and Supplies:** $924.

ADMISSIONS INFORMATION
Transfer Students Accepted? No.

EMPLOYMENT INFORMATION
Placement Office Available? Yes.

UNIVERSITY OF WASHINGTON
College of Ocean & Fishery Sciences

Address: Seattle, WA 98195

INSTITUTIONAL INFORMATION
Public/Private: Public. **Students in Parent Institution:** 45,587.

STUDENT INFORMATION
Total Students in Program: 9,308. **% Full Time:** 81. **% Female:** 50.

RESEARCH FACILITIES
Research Facilities: Center for the Humanities, Center for Law and Justice, Center on Human Development and Disability, Center for Urban Horticulture, Applied Physics Laboratory, Friday Harbor Laboratories, Medical Center/ Harborview Medical Center, Quaternary Research Center.

EXPENSES/FINANCIAL AID
Annual Tuition: In-state $5,539. / Out-of-state $14,376. **Fees:** $384. **Books and Supplies:** $924.

ADMISSIONS INFORMATION
Transfer Students Accepted? No.

EMPLOYMENT INFORMATION
Placement Office Available? Yes.

UNIVERSITY OF WASHINGTON
Graduate School of Public Affairs

Address: 109B Parrington Hall, Box 353055, Seattle, WA 98195
Admissions Phone: 206-616-1613 · **Admissions Fax:** 206-543-1096
Admissions E-mail: smithjpn@u.washington.edu
Web Address: www.evans.washington.edu

INSTITUTIONAL INFORMATION
Public/Private: Public. **Evening Classes Available?** Yes. **Students in Parent Institution:** 45,587.

STUDENT INFORMATION
Total Students in Program: 9,308. **% Full Time:** 81. **% Female:** 50.

RESEARCH FACILITIES
Research Facilities: Center for the Humanities, Center for Law and Justice, Center on Human Development and Disability, Center for Urban Horticulture, Applied Physics Laboratory, Friday Harbor Laboratories, Medical Center/ Harborview Medical Center, Quaternary Research Center.

EXPENSES/FINANCIAL AID
Annual Tuition: In-state $5,539. / Out-of-state $14,376. **Fees:** $384. **Books and Supplies:** $924.

ADMISSIONS INFORMATION
Application Fee: $45. **Priority Application Deadline:** 2/1. **Regular Application Deadline:** 2/1. **Regular Notification:** Rolling. **Transfer Students Accepted?** No. **Transfer Policy:** Up to 12 credits can be transferred once the applicant is accepted, and assuming that the credits meet all the conditions set by the school.
Required Admission Factors: Essays/personal statement, GRE, letters of recommendation, transcript.
Recommended Admission Factors:
Other Admission Factors: Minimum GPA: 3.0
No minimum GRE, but average is around 600 for Quantitative and Verbal. Taking a stats and micro economics class before starting program is recommended.
Program-Specific Admission Factors: GRE is not required for the Executive MPA program only.

EMPLOYMENT INFORMATION
Placement Office Available? Yes.

UNIVERSITY OF WASHINGTON
School of Social Work

Address: Seattle, WA 98195

INSTITUTIONAL INFORMATION
Public/Private: Public. **Students in Parent Institution:** 45,587

STUDENT INFORMATION
Total Students in Program: 9,308 **% Full Time:** 81. **% Female:** 50.

RESEARCH FACILITIES
Research Facilities: Center for the Humanities, Center for Law and Justice, Center on Human Development and Disability, Center for Urban Horticulture, Applied Physics Laboratory, Friday Harbor Laboratories, Medical Center/Harborview Medical Center, Quaternary Research Ce

EXPENSES/FINANCIAL AID
Annual Tuition: In-state $5,539. / Out-of-state $14,376. **Fees:** $384. **Books and Supplies:** $924.

ADMISSIONS INFORMATION
Transfer Students Accepted? No.

EMPLOYMENT INFORMATION
Placement Office Available? Yes.

UNIVERSITY OF WATERLOO
Faculty of Arts

Address: 200 University Avenue West, Waterloo, Ontario, ON N2L 3G1 Canada
Admissions Phone: 519-888-4567, ext. 5411 · **Admissions Fax:** 519-746-3051
Admissions E-mail: gsoffice@uwaterloo.ca · **Web Address:** www.grad.uwaterloo.ca

INSTITUTIONAL INFORMATION
Public/Private: Public. **Students in Parent Institution:** 22,181.

PROGRAMS
Masters offered in: Accounting and finance; Canadian government and politics; cognitive psychology and psycholinguistics; developmental and child psychology; economics, general; English language and literature, general; fine/studio arts, general; French language and literature; French studies; German language and literature; German studies; history, general; industrial and organizational psychology; philosophy; political science and government, general; public/applied history and archival administration; Russian language and literature; russian studies; social psychology; sociology; technical and business writing. **Doctorate offered in:** Applied economics; clinical psychology; cognitive psychology and psycholinguistics; developmental and child psychology; English language and literature, general; German language and literature; German studies; history, general; industrial and organization. **First Professional degree offered in:** accounting; entrepreneurship/entrepreneurial studies; taxation.

STUDENT INFORMATION
Total Students in Program: 2,778. **% Full Time:** 82.

EXPENSES/FINANCIAL AID
Annual Tuition: In-state $5,391. / Out-of-state $13,701. **Books and Supplies:** $900.

ADMISSIONS INFORMATION
Application Fee: $75. **Regular Application Deadline:** 2/1. **Regular Notification:** Rolling. **Transfer Students Accepted?** Yes. **Transfer Policy:** Maximum one-half of total credit hours required may be transferred into MA programs. **Number of Applications Received:** 1,159. **% of Applicants Accepted:** 23. **% Accepted Who Enrolled:** 73. **Average GPA:** 3.2.

Required Admission Factors: letters of recommendation, transcript.
Other Admission Factors: Minimum 3.0 average
Program-Specific Admission Factors: See http://www.grad.uwaterloo.ca/students/applicrequirements.asp.

UNIVERSITY OF WATERLOO
Faculty of Science

Address: 200 University Avenue West, Waterloo, Ontario, ON N2L 3G1 Canada
Admissions Phone: 519-888-4567, ext. 5411 · **Admissions Fax:** 519-746-3051
Admissions E-mail: gsoffice@uwaterloo.ca · **Web Address:** www.grad.uwaterloo.ca

INSTITUTIONAL INFORMATION
Public/Private: Public. **Students in Parent Institution:** 22,122.

PROGRAMS
Masters offered in: Actuarial science; applied economics; biochemistry; biology/biological sciences, general; chemistry, general; clinical psychology; cognitive psychology and psycholinguistics; developmental and child psychology; economics, general; English language and literature, general; English language and literature/letters, other; finance, general; fine/studio arts, general; French language and literature; geography; geology/earth science, general; German language and literature; history, general; industrial and organizational psychology; management science, general; philosophy; physics, general; political science and government, general; psychology, general; public/applied history and archival administration; Russian language and literature; social psychology; sociology; taxation. **Doctorate offered in:** Accounting; actuarial science; applied economics; biochemistry; biology/biological sciences, general; chemistry, general; cognitive psychology and psycholinguistics; developmental and child psychology; English language and literature, general; English lan **First Professional degree offered in:** Optometry (OD)

STUDENT INFORMATION
Total Students in Program: 2,042 **% Full Time:** 80.

EXPENSES/FINANCIAL AID
Annual Tuition: In-state $5,391. / Out-of-state $13,701. **Books and Supplies:** $900. **Average Salary Stipend:** $16,500.

ADMISSIONS INFORMATION
Application Fee: $75. **Regular Application Deadline:** 7/1. **Regular Notification:** Rolling. **Transfer Students Accepted?** Yes.
Required Admission Factors: Letters of recommendation, transcript.
Other Admission Factors: Minimum 3.0 average in a four-year bachelor's degree.
Program-Specific Admission Factors: See http://www.grad.uwaterloo.ca/students/applicrequirements.asp for details.

UNIVERSITY OF WATERLOO
Faculty of Mathematics

Address: University Avenue West, Waterloo, Ontario, ON N2L 3G1 Canada
Admissions Phone: 519-888-4567 ext.-5411 · **Admissions Fax:** 519-746-3051
Admissions E-mail: gsoffice@uwaterloo.ca · **Web Address:** www.grad.uwaterloo.ca

INSTITUTIONAL INFORMATION
Public/Private: Public. **Total Faculty:** 137. **Students in Parent Institution:** 22,122.

PROGRAMS
Masters offered in: Applied mathematics; computer science; mathematics and statistics, other; mathematics, other; statistics, general. **Doctorate offered in:** Applied mathematics; computer science; mathematics and statistics, other; mathematics, other; statistics, general.

STUDENT INFORMATION

Total Students in Program: 2,042. % Full Time: 80.

EXPENSES/FINANCIAL AID

Annual Tuition: In-state $5,391. / Out-of-state $13,701. Books and Supplies: $900.

ADMISSIONS INFORMATION

Application Fee: $75. Regular Application Deadline: 2/1. Regular Notification: Rolling. Transfer Students Accepted? Yes. Number of Applications Received: 351. % of Applicants Accepted: 49. % Accepted Who Enrolled: 55.
Required Admission Factors: Letters of recommendation, transcript.
Other Admission Factors: 3.0/4.0 see www.grad.uwaterloo.ca for details

---

UNIVERSITY OF WATERLOO
Faculty of Environmental Studies

Address: 200 University Avenue West, Waterloo, Ontario, ON N2L 3G1 Canada
Admissions Phone: 519-888-4567, extension-5411 · Admissions Fax: 519-746-3051
Admissions E-mail: gsoffice@uwaterloo.ca · Web Address: www.grad.uwaterloo.ca

INSTITUTIONAL INFORMATION

Public/Private: Public. Students in Parent Institution: 22,122.

PROGRAMS

Masters offered in: architecture (BArch, BA/BS, MArch, MA/MS, PhD); city/urban, community and regional planning; environmental studies; geography.
Doctorate offered in: City/urban, community and regional planning; geography.

STUDENT INFORMATION

Total Students in Program: 2,042. % Full Time: 80.

EXPENSES/FINANCIAL AID

Annual Tuition: In-state $5,391. / Out-of-state $13,701. Books and Supplies: $900.

ADMISSIONS INFORMATION

Application Fee: $75. Regular Application Deadline: 2/1. Regular Notification: Rolling. Transfer Students Accepted? Yes.
Required Admission Factors: Letters of recommendation, transcript.
Other Admission Factors: 3.0 on a 4.0 scale is the minimum university academic admission requirement.
Program-Specific Admission Factors: See http://www.grad.uwaterloo.ca/students/applicrequirements.asp.

UNIVERSITY OF WEST ALABAMA
School of Graduate Studies

Address: Highway 11, Livingston, AL 35470
Admissions Phone: 205-652-3647 · Admissions Fax: 205-652-3670
Admissions E-mail: jbe@uwa.edu

INSTITUTIONAL INFORMATION

Public/Private: Public. Evening Classes Available? Yes. Student/Faculty Ratio: 19:1. Students in Parent Institution: 1,974.

STUDENT INFORMATION

Total Students in Program: 349. % Full Time: 50. % Female: 76.

EXPENSES/FINANCIAL AID

Annual Tuition: In-state $3,192. / Out-of-state $6,384. Room & Board: $4,274. Fees: $110. Books and Supplies: $700. % Receiving Financial Aid: 41. % Receiving Loans: 100.

ADMISSIONS INFORMATION

Application Fee: $20. Regular Notification: Rolling. Transfer Students Accepted? Yes. Number of Applications Received: 73. % of Applicants Accepted: 86. % Accepted Who Enrolled: 81.
Required Admission Factors: Transcript.
Other Admission Factors: Minimum 2.75 GPA required.

UNIVERSITY OF WEST FLORIDA
College of Arts & Sciences

Address: 11000 University Parkway, Pensacola, FL 32514-5750
Admissions Phone: 850-474-2235 · Admissions Fax: 850-474-3360
Admissions E-mail: admissions@uwf.edu · Web Address: uwf.edu

INSTITUTIONAL INFORMATION

Public/Private: Public. Students in Parent Institution: 9,518.

PROGRAMS

Masters offered in: Anthropology; communications studies/speech communication and rhetoric; computer and information sciences, general; English language and literature, general; history, general; humanities/humanistic studies; information technology; mathematics teacher education; mathematics, general; political science and government, general; psychology, general.

STUDENT INFORMATION

Total Students in Program: 361. % Full Time: 45. % Female: 61. % International: 3.

RESEARCH FACILITIES

Research Facilities: Institute for Archeology, Institute for Interdisciplinary Study of Human and Machine Cognition, Small Business Development Center, HAAS Center for Business Research & Economic Development.

EXPENSES/FINANCIAL AID

Annual Tuition: In-state $4,986. / Out-of-state $18,649. Room & Board (On/Off Campus): $6,000/$6,000. Fees: $28. Books and Supplies: $800. Loans Range From: $1,000-$8,500. Types of Aid Available: Fellowships, graduate assistantships, grants, institutional work-study, loans, scholarships. Number of fellowships granted each year: 40. Average amount of individual fellowships per year: $500. Number of teaching/research assistantships granted each year: 110. Average Salary Stipend: $1,000.

ADMISSIONS INFORMATION

Application Fee: $30. Regular Application Deadline: 6/1. Regular Notification: Rolling. Transfer Students Accepted? Yes. Number of Applications Received: 256. % of Applicants Accepted: 69. % Accepted Who Enrolled: 61. Average GPA: 3.4.
Required Admission Factors: GRE, transcript.
Other Admission Factors: Minimum 3.0 GPA required.

EMPLOYMENT INFORMATION

Placement Office Available? Yes.

UNIVERSITY OF WEST FLORIDA
College of Professional Studies

Address: 11000 University Parkway, Pensacola, FL 32514-5750
Admissions Phone: 850-474-2230 · Admissions Fax: 850-474-3360
Admissions E-mail: admissions@uwf.edu · Web Address: http://uwf.edu

INSTITUTIONAL INFORMATION

Public/Private: Public. Evening Classes Available? Yes. Students in Parent Institution: 9,518.

PROGRAMS

Masters offered in: Community health services/liaison/counseling; curriculum and instruction; education leadership and administration, general; educational/instructional media design; health and physical education, general; public administration; special education, general. **Doctorate offered in:** Curriculum and instruction.

STUDENT INFORMATION

Total Students in Program: 697 % **Full Time:** 21. % **Female:** 75. %

RESEARCH FACILITIES

Research Facilities: Institute for Archeology, Institute for Interdisciplinary Study of Human and Machine Cognition, Small Business Development Center, HAAS Center for Business Research & Economic Development.

EXPENSES/FINANCIAL AID

Annual Tuition: In-state $4,986. / Out-of-state $18,649. **Room & Board:** $6,000. **Fees:** $28. **Books and Supplies:** $800. **Loans Range From:** $200-$8,500. **Types of Aid Available:** Fellowships, graduate assistantships, grants, institutional work-study, loans, scholarships, **Number of fellowships granted each year:** 62 **Average amount of individual fellowships per year:** $353.15

ADMISSIONS INFORMATION

Application Fee: $30. **Regular Application Deadline:** 6/1. **Regular Notification:** Rolling. **Transfer Students Accepted?** Yes. **Number of Applications Received:** 315. % **of Applicants Accepted:** 79. % **Accepted Who Enrolled:** 69. **Average GPA:** 3.3.
Required Admission Factors: GRE, transcript.

EMPLOYMENT INFORMATION

Placement Office Available? Yes.

UNIVERSITY OF WEST GEORGIA (UWG)
The Graduate School

Address: 1601 Maple Street, Cobb Hall, Carrollton, GA 30118-4180
Admissions Phone: 678-839-6419 · **Admissions Fax:** 678-839-5949
Admissions E-mail: gradsch@westga.edu · **Web Address:** www.westga.edu/~gradsch/

INSTITUTIONAL INFORMATION

Public/Private: Public. **Evening Classes Available?** Yes. **Total Faculty:** 185. % **Faculty Female:** 43. % **Faculty Part Time:** 12. **Student/Faculty Ratio:** 5:1. **Students in Parent Institution:** 10,216.

PROGRAMS

Masters offered in: Accounting; art teacher education; biology teacher education; biology/biological sciences, general; business administration and management, general ; business teacher education; computer science; counselor education/school counseling and guidance services; education leadership and administration, general; education/teaching of individuals with emotional disturbances; education/teaching of individuals with mental retardation; education/teaching of individuals with specific learning disabilities; educational/instructional media design; elementary education and teaching; English language and literature, general; English/language arts teacher education; French language teacher education; geography; gerontology; history, general; junior high/intermediate/middle school education and teaching; mathematics teacher education; music performance, general; music teacher education; nursing—registered nurse training (EN, ASN, BSN, MSN); physical education teaching and coaching; psychology, general; public administration; reading teacher education; science teacher education/general science teacher education; social studies teacher education; sociology; Spanish language teacher education; speech-language pathology/pathologist. **Doctorate offered in:** Education, other. **First Professional degree offered in:** Business teacher education; counselor education/school counseling and guidance services; education leadership and administration, general; education/teaching of individuals with emotional disturbances; education/teaching of individuals with mental retardation.

STUDENT INFORMATION

Total Students in Program: 1,937. % **Full Time:** 20. % **Female:** 77. % **Minority:** 25. % **International:** 2.

RESEARCH FACILITIES

Research Facilities: Teacher Education Lab & Software Library.

EXPENSES/FINANCIAL AID

Annual Tuition: In-state $1,998. / Out-of-state $7,974. **Room & Board:** $4,406. **Fees:** $536. **Books and Supplies:** $600. **Grants Range From:** $150-$4,959. **Loans Range From:** $500-$8,500. % **Receiving Scholarships/Grants:** 20. % **Receiving Loans:** 66. **Assistantship compensation includes:** full tuition remission, salary/stipend. **Average Salary Stipend:** $1,500.

ADMISSIONS INFORMATION

Application Fee: $20. **Regular Application Deadline:** 8/2. **Regular Notification:** Rolling. **Transfer Students Accepted?** No. **Transfer Policy:** The Graduate School at the State University of West Georgia does not have "transfer" students. There is also no specific deadline for the application. These individuals would need to apply like any other applicant seeking admission. Students who have completed graduate work at another institution and are seeking enrollment to our graduate programs would need only to apply and with approval from the dean of the graduate school and the department, a student can transfer a maximum of six graduate semester hours towards a degree offered by West Georgia. **Number of Applications Received:** 777. % **of Applicants Accepted:** 78. % **Accepted Who Enrolled:** 48.
Required Admission Factors: GMAT, GRE, letters of recommendation, transcript, PRAXIS Series (Education Majors only); TOEFL,
Other Admission Factors: GRE—Min. test score varies by program. The minimum for most programs in the College of Arts & Sciences and the College of Education require 400 Verbal/400 Quantitative or Analytical Scores (test scores taken prior to October 2002).
Program-Specific Admission Factors: Please see www.westga.edu/~gradsch/ and click on "Graduate Admissions" for more detailed information.

EMPLOYMENT INFORMATION

Placement Office Available? Yes. % **Employed Within 6 Months:** 80. **Rate of placement:** 80%.

UNIVERSITY OF WISCONSIN—EAU CLAIRE
School of Human Sciences & Services

Address: 105 Garfield Avenue, Eau Claire, WI 54701
Admissions Phone: 715-836-4733 · **Admissions E-mail:** kluncl@uwec.edu

INSTITUTIONAL INFORMATION

Public/Private: Public. **Students in Parent Institution:** 10,549.

STUDENT INFORMATION

Total Students in Program: 448. % **Full Time:** 24. % **Female:** 77.

EXPENSES/FINANCIAL AID

Annual Tuition: In-state $4,437. / Out-of-state $13,918. **Grants Range From:** $100-$9,673. **Loans Range From:** $169-$11,569. % **Receiving Financial Aid:** 72. % **Receiving Scholarships/Grants:** 42. % **Receiving Loans:** 66. % **Receiving Assistantships:** 3. **Number of fellowships granted each year:** 8 **Average amount of individual fellowships per year:** $500 **Number of teaching/research assistantships granted each year:** 8 **Average Salary Stipend:** $4,300.

ADMISSIONS INFORMATION

Application Fee: $45. **Regular Notification:** Rolling. **Transfer Students Accepted?** Yes. **Number of Applications Received:** 82. % **of Applicants Accepted:** 83. % **Accepted Who Enrolled:** 25.
Required Admission Factors: GRE, letters of recommendation, transcript.

EMPLOYMENT INFORMATION

Placement Office Available? Yes. **Rate of placement:** 99%.

UNIVERSITY OF WISCONSIN—EAU CLAIRE
Graduate Studies

Address: 105 Garfield Avenue, Eau Claire, WI 54701
Admissions Phone: 715-836-4733 · **Admissions Fax:** 715-836-4892
Admissions E-mail: graduate@uwec.edu
Web Address: www.uwec.edu/graduate/index/htm

INSTITUTIONAL INFORMATION

Public/Private: Public. **Total Faculty:** 312. **% Faculty Female:** 34. **% Faculty Part Time:** 4. **Student/Faculty Ratio:** 2:1. **Students in Parent Institution:** 10,540.

STUDENT INFORMATION

Total Students in Program: 506 **% Full Time:** 21. **% Female:** 70. **% Minority:** 5. **% International:** 2.

EXPENSES/FINANCIAL AID

Annual Tuition: In-state $5,922. / Out-of-state $16,531. **Room & Board:** $4,580. **Books and Supplies:** $500. **Grants Range From:** $100-$6,100. **Loans Range From:** $1,000-$23,339. **% Receiving Financial Aid:** 32. **% Receiving Scholarships/Grants:** 11. **% Receiving Loans:** 23. **% Receiving Assistantships:** 3. **Types of Aid Available:** Fellowships, graduate assistantships, grants, institutional work-study, loans, scholarships. **Average student debt, upon graduation:** $8,100. **Number of fellowships granted each year:** 3. **Average amount of individual fellowships per year:** $500. **Number of teaching/research assistantships granted each year:** 15. **Average Salary Stipend:** $5,000.

ADMISSIONS INFORMATION

Application Fee: $45. **Priority Application Deadline:** 3/1. **Regular Application Deadline:** 9/1. **Regular Notification:** Rolling. **Transfer Students Accepted?** Yes. **Number of Applications Received:** 275. **% of Applicants Accepted:** 7.
Required Admission Factors: Transcript.
Other Admission Factors: Minimum 2.75 GPA (or minimum 2.9 GPA in last 10 credit hours) required.

EMPLOYMENT INFORMATION

Placement Office Available? Yes. **Rate of placement:** 99%.

UNIVERSITY OF WISCONSIN—GREEN BAY
Graduate Studies

Address: 2420 Nicolet Drive, Green Bay, WI 54311-7001
Admissions Phone: 920-465-2111 · **Admissions Fax:** 920-465-5754
Admissions E-mail: gradstu@uwgb.edu · **Web Address:** www.uwgb.edu/gradstu

INSTITUTIONAL INFORMATION

Public/Private: Public. **Evening Classes Available?** Yes. **Total Faculty:** 44. **% Faculty Female:** 34. **Students in Parent Institution:** 5,400.

PROGRAMS

Masters offered in: Business administration/management; business/managerial operations, other; education, other; environmental science; management science, general; natural resource economics; natural resources management and policy, general; public administration; public policy analysis; social work; teacher education and professional development, specific levels and methods, other; water, wetlands, and marine resources management; youth services/administration.

STUDENT INFORMATION

Total Students in Program: 163 **% Full Time:** 28. **% Female:** 58.

EXPENSES/FINANCIAL AID

Annual Tuition: In-state $5,996. / Out-of-state $16,606. **Room & Board (On/Off Campus):** $3,561/$6,050. **Fees:** $10. **Books and Supplies:** $600. **% Receiving Financial Aid:** 14. **% Receiving Assistantships:** 12. **% Receiving Other Aid (Research grants and contracts.):** 2. **Types of Aid Available:** Graduate assistantships, institutional work-study, loans, research grants and contracts.

ADMISSIONS INFORMATION

Application Fee: $45. **Priority Application Deadline:** 4/1. **Regular Application Deadline:** 8/1. **Regular Notification:** Rolling. **Transfer Students Accepted?** Yes. **Number of Applications Received:** 1. **% of Applicants Accepted:** 100. **% Accepted Who Enrolled:** 100.
Required Admission Factors: Essays/personal statement, letters of recommendation, transcript.
Other Admission Factors: Minimum 3.0 GPA required.
Program-Specific Admission Factors: A pre-application is required for the master of social work program.

EMPLOYMENT INFORMATION

Placement Office Available? Yes. **% Employed Within 6 Months:** 90. **% of master's grads employed in their field upon graduation:** 90. **Rate of placement:** 99%. **Average starting salary:** $32,000.

UNIVERSITY OF WISCONSIN—LA CROSSE
College of Liberal Studies/School Psychology

Address: 2517 State Street, 115 Graff Main Hall, UW-La Crosse, La Crosse, WI 54601
Admissions Phone: 608-785-8939 · **Admissions Fax:** 608-785-8443
Admissions E-mail: dixon.robe@uwlax.edu
Web Address: www.uwlax.edu/graduate/psychology

INSTITUTIONAL INFORMATION

Public/Private: Public. **Total Faculty:** 3. **% Faculty Female:** 67. **Student/Faculty Ratio:** 12:1. **Students in Parent Institution:** 7,846.

PROGRAMS

Masters offered in: School psychology.

STUDENT INFORMATION

Total Students in Program: 35 **% Full Time:** 100. **% Female:** 89.

EXPENSES/FINANCIAL AID

Annual Tuition: In-state $6,088. / Out-of-state $16,698. **Room & Board (On/Off Campus):** $4,570/$3,000. **Fees:** $75. **Books and Supplies:** $500. **Grants Range From:** $250-$1,000. **Loans Range From:** $500-$5,098. **% Receiving Financial Aid:** 100. **% Receiving Loans:** 100. **% Receiving Assistantships:** 8. **% Receiving Other Aid:** 92. **Types of Aid Available:** Graduate assistantships, grants, institutional work-study, loans, scholarships. **Average student debt, upon graduation:** $10,000. **Number of teaching/research assistantships granted each year:** 3. **Assistantship compensation includes:** Partial tuition remission, salary/stipend.

ADMISSIONS INFORMATION

Application Fee: $45. **Priority Application Deadline:** 1/15. **Regular Application Deadline:** 1/15. **Regular Notification:** Rolling. **Transfer Students Accepted?** Yes. **Transfer Policy:** Graduate program directors have discretion in evaluating transfer credits and determinng if graduate courses taken at other institutions may apply to a student's program of study at UW—La Crosse. In addition to reviewing official transcripts, graduate program directors may request to review a course syllabus, written assignments, and examinations in order to assist them in their evaluation of transferring credits. **Number of Applications Received:** 30. **% of Applicants Accepted:** 57. **% Accepted Who Enrolled:** 71. **Average GPA:** 3.6. **Average GRE Verbal:** 483. **Average GRE Quantitative:** 612. **Average GRE Analytical Writing:** 5.

Required Admission Factors: Essays/personal statement, GRE, letters of recommendation, transcript.
Recommended Admission Factors: GRE subject exam(s) in psychology.
Other Admission Factors: Minimum of 2.85 GPA required to be admitted to UW—La Crosse. GPA averages for those admitted into the School Psychology Program range from 3.0-3.5.
Program-Specific Admission Factors: Admissions essay is in the form of a personal statement and an independent writing sample. We also require a resume.

EMPLOYMENT INFORMATION

Placement Office Available? Yes. **% Employed Within 6 Months:** 100. **Rate of placement:** 100%. **Average starting salary:** $36,918.

UNIVERSITY OF WISCONSIN—LA CROSSE
Physical Therapy Program

Address: 1725 State St., La Crosse, WI 54601
Admissions Phone: 608-785-8470 · **Admissions Fax:** 608-785-6647
Admissions E-mail: pt@uwlax.edu · **Web Address:** www.uwlax.edu/pt/

INSTITUTIONAL INFORMATION

Public/Private: Public.

RESEARCH FACILITIES

Research Facilities: La Crosse Medical Health Science Consortium

ADMISSIONS INFORMATION

Application Fee: $30. **Regular Application Deadline:** 2/1. **Regular Notification:** Rolling. **Transfer Students Accepted?** Yes. **Transfer Policy:** Interested students should contact Dr. Dennis Fater via e-mail fater.denn@uwlax.edu or by phone 608-785-8471.
Required Admission Factors: Essays/personal statement, letters of recommendation, transcript.
Recommended Admission Factors:
Other Admission Factors: 3.0 minimum GPA

UNIVERSITY OF WISCONSIN—MADISON
School of Human Ecology

Address: 1300 Linden Drive, Madison, WI 53706
Admissions Phone: 608-263-2381-or-608-265-8698
Admissions Fax: 608-265-3616 · **Admissions E-mail:** canderson1@wisc.edu
Web Address: www.sohe.wisc.edu

INSTITUTIONAL INFORMATION

Public/Private: Public. **Total Faculty:** 47. **% Faculty Female:** 68. **Students in Parent Institution:** 41,588.

STUDENT INFORMATION

Total Students in Program: 8,924. **% Full Time:** 100.

RESEARCH FACILITIES

Research Facilities: Helen Louise Allen Textile Collection, Retail Center, Gallery of Design.

EXPENSES/FINANCIAL AID

Annual Tuition: In-state $6,361. / Out-of-state $20,499. **Room & Board (On/Off Campus):** $4,923/$16,716. **Books** and **Supplies:** $680.

ADMISSIONS INFORMATION

Application Fee: $45. **Priority Application Deadline:** 2/6. **Regular Application Deadline:** 2/6. **Regular Notification:** Rolling. **Transfer Students Accepted?** Yes. **Average GPA:** 3.0
Required Admission Factors: Essays/personal statement, letters of recommendation, transcript.
Other Admission Factors: Minimum 3.0 GPA required.

UNIVERSITY OF WISCONSIN—MADISON
School of Journalism & Mass Communication

Address: 5115 Vilas Hall, 821 University Ave, Madison, WI 53706
Admissions Phone: 608-262-3691 · **Admissions Fax:** 608-262-1361
Admissions E-mail: info@journalism.wisc.edu · **Web Address:** www.journalism.wisc.edu

INSTITUTIONAL INFORMATION

Public/Private: Public. **Students in Parent Institution:** 40,072.

STUDENT INFORMATION

Total Students in Program: 8,744. **% Full Time:** 80. **% Female:** 47.

RESEARCH FACILITIES

Research Facilities: Numerous research centers.

EXPENSES/FINANCIAL AID

Annual Tuition: In-state $6,361. / Out-of-state $20,499. **Room & Board (On/Off Campus):** $4,923/$16,716. **Books** and **Supplies:** $680.

ADMISSIONS INFORMATION

Application Fee: $45. **Regular Application Deadline:** 12/1. **Regular Notification:** 2/25. **Transfer Students Accepted?** Yes. **Number of Applications Received:** 121. **% of Applicants Accepted:** 60. **% Accepted Who Enrolled:** 32. **Average GPA:** 3.6. **Average GRE Verbal:** 589. **Average GRE Quantitative:** 655. **Average GRE Analytical:** 630. **Average GRE Analytical Writing:** 5.
Required Admission Factors: Essays/personal statement, GRE, letters of recommendation, transcript.
Other Admission Factors: 3.0 for MA degree/3.5 for PhD degree.
1000 GRE (combined Verbal and Quantitative) and 5.0 on Analytical Writing.

UNIVERSITY OF WISCONSIN—MADISON
School of Social Work

Address: 217 Bascom Hall, 500 Lincoln Drive, Madison, WI 53706

INSTITUTIONAL INFORMATION

Public/Private: Public. **Students in Parent Institution:** 40,072.

STUDENT INFORMATION

Total Students in Program: 8,744. **% Full Time:** 80. **% Female:** 47.

RESEARCH FACILITIES

Research Facilities: Numerous research centers.

EXPENSES/FINANCIAL AID

Annual Tuition: In-state $6,361. / Out-of-state $20,499. **Room & Board (On/Off Campus):** $4,923/$16,716. **Books** and **Supplies:** $680.

ADMISSIONS INFORMATION

Transfer Students Accepted? No.

UNIVERSITY OF WISCONSIN—MADISON
The Graduate School

Address: 228 Bascom Hall 500 Lincoln Drive, Madison, WI 53706
Admissions Phone: 608-262-2433 · **Admissions Fax:** 608-265-6742

INSTITUTIONAL INFORMATION
Public/Private: Public. **Total Faculty:** 4057. **% Faculty Female:** 34. **% Faculty Part Time:** 20. **Students in Parent Institution:** 41,588.

STUDENT INFORMATION
Total Students in Program: 8,924. **% Full Time:** 81. **% Female:** 48. **% Minority:** 8. **% International:** 26.

RESEARCH FACILITIES
Research Facilities: Numerous research centers.

EXPENSES/FINANCIAL AID
Annual Tuition: In-state $7,600. / Out-of-state $22,863. **Room & Board (On/ Off Campus):** $7,200/$16,716. **Fees:** $585. **Books and Supplies:** $680. **Types of Aid Available:** Fellowships, graduate assistantships, grants, institutional work-study, loans, scholarships.

ADMISSIONS INFORMATION
Application Fee: $45. **Regular Notification:** Rolling. **Transfer Students Accepted?** No. **Number of Applications Received:** 16,284. **% of Applicants Accepted:** 28. **% Accepted Who Enrolled:** 46. **Average GRE Verbal:** 558. **Average GRE Quantitative:** 660. **Average GRE Analytical:** 648. **Required Admission Factors:** transcript.
Other Admission Factors: GPA-3.0, departmental GPA requirement may be higher.

UNIVERSITY OF WISCONSIN—PARKSIDE
College of Arts & Sciences

Address: PO Box 2000
900 Wood Road, Kenosha, WI 53141-2000
Admissions Phone: 262-595-2547 · **Admissions Fax:** 262-595-2056
Admissions E-mail: melvin.thomson@uwp.edu

INSTITUTIONAL INFORMATION
Public/Private: Public. **Student/Faculty Ratio:** 1:1. **Students in Parent Institution:** 5,016.

STUDENT INFORMATION
Total Students in Program: 117. **% Full Time:** 11. **% Female:** 49.

EXPENSES/FINANCIAL AID
Annual Tuition: In-state $4,542. / Out-of-state $14,366. **Fees:** $150. **Books and Supplies:** $800. **Grants Range From:** $1,200-$2,400. **Loans Range From:** $200-$7,468. **% Receiving Financial Aid:** 57. **Number of teaching/ research assistantships granted each year:** 8

ADMISSIONS INFORMATION
Application Fee: $45. **Regular Notification:** Rolling. **Transfer Students Accepted?** Yes. **Number of Applications Received:** 4. **% of Applicants Accepted:** 100. **% Accepted Who Enrolled:** 50. **Average GRE Verbal:** 417. **Average GRE Quantitative:** 613. **Average GRE Analytical:** 593.
Required Admission Factors: Essays/personal statement, GRE, letters of recommendation, transcript.
Other Admission Factors: Minimum 3.0 GPA and background in biology, chemistry, math, and physics required.

EMPLOYMENT INFORMATION
Placement Office Available? Yes. **% Employed Within 6 Months:** 100. **% of master's employed in their field upon graduation:** 100. **Rate of placement:** 100%.

UNIVERSITY OF WISCONSIN—PLATTEVILLE
Graduate Programs

Address: One University Plaza, Platteville, WI 53818
Admissions Phone: 608-342-1125 · **Admissions Fax:** 608-342-1122
Admissions E-mail: Admit@uwplatt.edu
Web Address: www.uwplatt.edu/registrar/gradschool.html

INSTITUTIONAL INFORMATION
Public/Private: Public. **Evening Classes Available?** Yes. **Students in Parent Institution:** 5,540.

STUDENT INFORMATION
Total Students in Program: 386. **% Full Time:** 46. **% Female:** 69.

EXPENSES/FINANCIAL AID
Annual Tuition: In-state $4,838. / Out-of-state $15,252. **% Receiving Scholarships/Grants:** 10. **% Receiving Loans:** 40. **% Receiving Assistantships:** 25.

ADMISSIONS INFORMATION
Application Fee: $45. **Regular Application Deadline:** 8/1. **Transfer Students Accepted?** Yes.
Required Admission Factors: Transcript.
Other Admission Factors: Minimum 2.75 GPA or minimum 2.9 GPA in the last 60 credit hours required.

UNIVERSITY OF WISCONSIN—STEVENS POINT
College of Professional Studies

Address: 2100 Main Street, Stevens Point, WI 54481
Admissions Phone: 715-346-2441 · **Admissions Fax:** 715-346-3296
Admissions E-mail: cglennon@uwsp.edu · **Web Address:** www.uwsp.edu/cps

INSTITUTIONAL INFORMATION
Public/Private: Public. **Total Faculty:** 33. **% Faculty Part Time:** 0. **Students in Parent Institution:** 9,023.

PROGRAMS
Masters offered in: Communication disorders, general; education, general; family and community services; human nutrition; teacher education and professional development, specific subject areas, other.

STUDENT INFORMATION
Total Students in Program: 185. **% Full Time:** 37. **% Female:** 85.

EXPENSES/FINANCIAL AID
Annual Tuition: In-state $5,342. / Out-of-state $15,952. **Room & Board:** $4,094. **Fees:** $568. **Books and Supplies:** $450. **Grants Range From:** $500-$1,000. **Loans Range From:** $200-$11,000. **Types of Aid Available:** Graduate assistantships.

ADMISSIONS INFORMATION
Application Fee: $45. **Regular Application Deadline:** 5/1. **Regular Notification:** Rolling. **Transfer Students Accepted?** Yes. **Number of Applications Received:** 82. **% of Applicants Accepted:** 72. **% Accepted Who Enrolled:** 61. **Average GPA:** 3.5.
Required Admission Factors: Transcript.

UNIVERSITY OF WISCONSIN—STEVENS POINT
College of Fine Arts & Communication

Address: 2100 Main Street, Stevens Point, WI 54481
Admissions Phone: 715-346-2441 · **Admissions Fax:** 715-346-3296
Admissions E-mail: cglennon@uwsp.edu · **Web Address:** www.uwsp.edu/cnr/

INSTITUTIONAL INFORMATION

Public/Private: Public. **Total Faculty:** 37. **% Faculty Part Time:** 5. **Students in Parent Institution:** 9,023.

PROGRAMS

Masters offered in: Communications studies/speech communication and rhetoric; music teacher education.

STUDENT INFORMATION

Total Students in Program: 32. **% Full Time:** 22. **% Female:** 62.

EXPENSES/FINANCIAL AID

Annual Tuition: In-state $5,342. / Out-of-state $15,952. **Room & Board:** $4,094. **Fees:** $568. **Books and Supplies:** $450. **Grants Range From:** $500-$1,000. **Loans Range From:** $200-$11,000. **Types of Aid Available:** Graduate assistantships.

ADMISSIONS INFORMATION

Application Fee: $45. **Priority Application Deadline:** 3/1. **Regular Application Deadline:** 5/1. **Regular Notification:** Rolling. **Transfer Students Accepted?** Yes. **Number of Applications Received:** 24. **% of Applicants Accepted:** 54. **% Accepted Who Enrolled:** 54. **Average GPA:** 3.6. **Required Admission Factors:** Transcript.

UNIVERSITY OF WISCONSIN—STEVENS POINT
College of Natural Resources

Address: 2100 Main Street, Stevens Point, WI 54481
Admissions Phone: 715-346-2441 · **Admissions Fax:** 715-346-3296
Admissions E-mail: cglennon@uwsp.edu · **Web Address:** www.uwsp.edu/cnr/

INSTITUTIONAL INFORMATION

Public/Private: Public. **Total Faculty:** 35. **% Faculty Part Time:** 11. **Students in Parent Institution:** 9,023.

PROGRAMS

Masters offered in: Natural resources/conservation, general.

STUDENT INFORMATION

Total Students in Program: 54 **% Full Time:** 44. **% Female:** 56.

RESEARCH FACILITIES

Research Facilities: Central Wisconsin Environmental Station, Treehaven Field Station, Schmeeckle Reserve, Global Environmental Managment Education Center, Center for Land Use Education, Center for Watershed Science Education, Central Wisconsin Groundwater Center.

EXPENSES/FINANCIAL AID

Annual Tuition: In-state $5,342. / Out-of-state $15,952. **Room & Board:** $4,094. **Fees:** $568. **Books and Supplies:** $450. **Grants Range From:** $500-$1,000. **Loans Range From:** $200-$11,000. **Types of Aid Available:** Graduate assistantships.

ADMISSIONS INFORMATION

Application Fee: $45. **Regular Application Deadline:** 3/15. **Regular Notification:** Rolling. **Transfer Students Accepted?** Yes. **Number of Applications Received:** 42. **% of Applicants Accepted:** 40. **% Accepted Who Enrolled:** 65. **Average GPA:** 3.5. **Required Admission Factors:** GRE, transcript.

UNIVERSITY OF WISCONSIN—STOUT
College of Human Development

Address: 130 Bowman Hall, Menomonie, WI 54751
Admissions Phone: 715-232-2211 · **Admissions Fax:** 715-232-2413
Admissions E-mail: johnsona@uwstout.edu · **Web Address:** www.uwstout.edu/grad/

INSTITUTIONAL INFORMATION

Public/Private: Public. **Evening Classes Available?** Yes. **Students in Parent Institution:** 7,738.

STUDENT INFORMATION

Total Students in Program: 488. **% Full Time:** 57. **% Female:** 58.

EXPENSES/FINANCIAL AID

Annual Tuition: In-state $5,084. / Out-of-state $15,694. **Room & Board (On/Off Campus):** $3,942/$3,945. **Fees:** $600. **Books and Supplies:** $300. **Grants Range From:** $100-$9,093. **Loans Range From:** $106-$15,296. **% Receiving Financial Aid:** 40. **% Receiving Scholarships/Grants:** 17. **% Receiving Loans:** 85. **% Receiving Other Aid (tuition waivers):** 15. **Types of Aid Available:** Graduate assistantships, institutional work-study, loans, scholarships, federal work study, tuition waivers. **Average student debt, upon graduation:** $24,889 **Assistantship compensation includes:** Partial tuition remission, salary/stipend.

ADMISSIONS INFORMATION

Application Fee: $45. **Regular Application Deadline:** 2/1. **Regular Notification:** Rolling. **Transfer Students Accepted?** Yes. **Number of Applications Received:** 170. **% of Applicants Accepted:** 91. **% Accepted Who Enrolled:** 77.
Required Admission Factors: Transcript.
Program-Specific Admission Factors: Minimum 2.75 GPA required for most programs. GRE required of applicants to applied psychology program.

EMPLOYMENT INFORMATION

Placement Office Available? Yes. **Rate of placement:** 98%.

UNIVERSITY OF WISCONSIN—SUPERIOR
Graduate Studies

Address: Belknap & Catlin, P.O. Box 2000, Superior, WI 54880-4500
Admissions Phone: 715-394-8295 · **Admissions Fax:** 715-394-8040
Admissions E-mail: gradstudy@uwsuper.edu
Web Address: www.uwsuper.edu/graduate

INSTITUTIONAL INFORMATION

Public/Private: Public. **Evening Classes Available?** Yes. **Student/Faculty Ratio:** 5:1. **Students in Parent Institution:** 2,883.

STUDENT INFORMATION

Total Students in Program: 378. **% Full Time:** 26. **% Female:** 65.

RESEARCH FACILITIES

Research Facilities: Lake Superior Research Center.

EXPENSES/FINANCIAL AID

Annual Tuition: In-state $6,000. / Out-of-state $16,610. **Room & Board:** $5,454. **Books and Supplies:** $700. **Grants Range From:** $354-$11,478. **Loans Range From:** $1,700-$9,700. **% Receiving Financial Aid:** 53. **% Receiving Assistantships:** 1. **Types of Aid Available:** Loans. **Average student debt, upon graduation:** $5,796 **Number of fellowships granted each year:** 12 **Average amount of individual fellowships per year:** $1,000 **Number of teaching/research assistantships granted each year:** 12 **Average Salary Stipend:** $10,000.

ADMISSIONS INFORMATION

Application Fee: $45. **Priority Application Deadline:** 4/1. **Regular Application Deadline:** 9/1. **Regular Notification:** Rolling. **Transfer Students Accepted?** Yes. **Transfer Policy:** Maximum 14 credit hours with a minimum grade of "B." EdAd allows 12 credits. **Number of Applications Received:** 57. **% of Applicants Accepted:** 95. **% Accepted Who Enrolled:** 41. **Average GPA:** 3. **Average GRE Verbal:** 480. **Average GRE Quantitative:** 550. **Average GRE Analytical:** 550.
Required Admission Factors: Transcript.
Recommended Admission Factors:
Other Admission Factors: Minimum 2.75 GPA required for unconditional admission; 2.25 required for probational admission.
Program-Specific Admission Factors: Art (Art/Th): Portfolio, two letters
Art (His/Ed): Two letters
Comm Arts: Essay
Counseling: Statement, three letters, GRE/MAT, CPI, and interview.
Educ Admin (MSE): two letters, two-page professional leadership statement, resume, teaching license.

EMPLOYMENT INFORMATION

Placement Office Available? Yes. **% of master's grads employed in their field upon graduation:** 90. **Rate of placement:** 92%. **Average starting salary:** $50,000.

UNIVERSITY OF WISCONSIN—WHITEWATER
College of Arts & Communication

Address: 800 West Main Street, Roseman 2015, Whitewater, WI 53190
Admissions Phone: 262-472-1006 · **Admissions Fax:** 262-472-5027
Admissions E-mail: gradschl@uww.edu · **Web Address:** www.uww.edu

INSTITUTIONAL INFORMATION

Public/Private: Public. **Evening Classes Available?** Yes. **Students in Parent Institution:** 10,441.

STUDENT INFORMATION

Total Students in Program: 1,207. **% Female:** 66.

EXPENSES/FINANCIAL AID

Annual Tuition: In-state $3,259. / Out-of-state $9,906. **Room & Board:** $3,502.

ADMISSIONS INFORMATION

Application Fee: $45. **Priority Application Deadline:** 7/1. **Regular Application Deadline:** 8/15. **Regular Notification:** Rolling. **Transfer Students Accepted?** Yes. **Transfer Policy:** Transfer credit forms are needed for each course wishing to transfer.
Required Admission Factors: Letters of recommendation, transcript.

UNIVERSITY OF WYOMING
College of Arts & Sciences

Address: P.O. Box 3108, Laramie, WY 82071
Admissions Phone: 307-766-2287 · **Admissions Fax:** 307-766-4042
Admissions E-mail: juliea@uwyo.edu

INSTITUTIONAL INFORMATION

Public/Private: Public. **Students in Parent Institution:** 10,941.

STUDENT INFORMATION

Total Students in Program: 2,073. **% Full Time:** 38. **% Female:** 57.

RESEARCH FACILITIES

Research Facilities: Wyoming National Park Research Center, Survey Research Center.

EXPENSES/FINANCIAL AID

Annual Tuition: In-state $3,116. / Out-of-state $8,198. **Fees:** $20. **Books and Supplies:** $680. **Grants Range From:** $100-$8,100. **Loans Range From:** $179-$8,500. **% Receiving Financial Aid:** 63. **% Receiving Scholarships/Grants:** 41. **% Receiving Loans:** 32. **% Receiving Assistantships:** 48. **Average student debt, upon graduation:** $16,168. **Number of teaching/research assistantships granted each year:** 563. **Average Salary Stipend:** $8,667.

ADMISSIONS INFORMATION

Application Fee: $40. **Regular Notification:** Rolling. **Transfer Students Accepted?** Yes. **Transfer Policy:** Maximum nine credit hours with a minimum grade of B may be transferred into master's programs.
Required Admission Factors: GRE, letters of recommendation, transcript.
Other Admission Factors: Minimum 3.0 GPA required.
Program-Specific Admission Factors: Minimum GRE score of 900 (Verbal plus Quantitative) required of MS and MA program applicants, minimum GRE score of 1000 (Verbal plus Quantitative) required of PhD program applicants.

EMPLOYMENT INFORMATION

Placement Office Available? Yes.

URSULINE COLLEGE
Graduate Studies

Address: 2550 Lander Road, Pepper Pike, OH 44124
Admissions Phone: 440-646-8119 · **Admissions Fax:** 440-684-6088
Admissions E-mail: chackney@ursuline.edu

INSTITUTIONAL INFORMATION

Public/Private: Private (nonprofit). **Evening Classes Available?** Yes. **Student/Faculty Ratio:** 10:1. **Students in Parent Institution:** 1,281.

STUDENT INFORMATION

Total Students in Program: 262. **% Full Time:** 19. **% Female:** 82.

EXPENSES/FINANCIAL AID

Annual Tuition: $9,612. **Room & Board:** $6,400. **Books** and **Supplies:** $600. **Grants Range From:** $400-$5,000. **Loans Range From:** $200-$18,500. **% Receiving Financial Aid:** 73. **% Receiving Scholarships/Grants:** 5. **% Receiving Loans:** 90.

ADMISSIONS INFORMATION

Application Fee: $25. **Regular Notification:** Rolling. **Transfer Students Accepted?** Yes. **Transfer Policy:** Maximum six credit hours with a minimum grade average of B may be transferred. **Number of Applications Received:** 235. **% of Applicants Accepted:** 50. **% Accepted Who Enrolled:** 100. **Average GPA:** 3.0
Required Admission Factors: Interview, transcript.
Other Admission Factors: Minimum 3.0 GPA required.

UTAH STATE UNIVERSITY
College of Humanities, Arts, & Social Sciences

Address: 900 Old Main Hill, Logan, UT 84322-0900
Admissions Phone: 435-797-1189 · **Admissions Fax:** 435-797-1192
Admissions E-mail: gradsch@cc.usu.edu

INSTITUTIONAL INFORMATION

Public/Private: Public. **Evening Classes Available?** Yes. **Student/Faculty Ratio:** 1:1. **Students in Parent Institution:** 20,158.

STUDENT INFORMATION

Total Students in Program: 2,293. **% Female:** 40.

RESEARCH FACILITIES

Research Facilities: Agricultural Experiment Station, Engineering Experiment Station, Center for Water Resources Research, Ecology Center, Center for Atmospheric and Space Sciences, Center for Persons with Disabilities, Institute of Political Economy, Economics Research Center.

EXPENSES/FINANCIAL AID

Annual Tuition: In-state $2,000. / Out-of-state $5,883. **Fees:** $447. **Books and Supplies:** $700. **Loans Range From:** $8,500-$18,500. **% Receiving Financial Aid:** 80. **Types of Aid Available:** 1. **Number of fellowships granted each year:** 5. **Number of teaching/research assistantships granted each year:** 50. **Average Salary Stipend:** $8,000.

ADMISSIONS INFORMATION

Application Fee: $40. **Regular Notification:** Rolling. **Transfer Students Accepted?** Yes. **Transfer Policy:** Transfer request, current department sign-off on progress, and request to new department for conside. **Number of Applications Received:** 157. **% of Applicants Accepted:** 70. **% Accepted Who Enrolled:** 62. **Average GPA:** 3.58. **Average GRE Verbal:** 584. **Average GRE Quantitative:** 618. **Average GRE Analytical:** 646.

Required Admission Factors: Essays/personal statement, GRE, letters of recommendation, transcript.

Other Admission Factors: Minimum GRE score in the 40th percentile (Verbal and Quantitative) and minimum 3.0 GPA required.

EMPLOYMENT INFORMATION

Placement Office Available? Yes. **Rate of placement:** 98%.

UTAH STATE UNIVERSITY
College of Science

Address: 900 Old Main Hill, Logan, UT 84322-0900
Admissions Phone: 435-797-1189 · **Admissions Fax:** 435-797-1192

INSTITUTIONAL INFORMATION

Public/Private: Public. **Evening Classes Available?** Yes. **Student/Faculty Ratio:** 2:1. **Students in Parent Institution:** 20,158.

STUDENT INFORMATION

Total Students in Program: 2,293. **% Female:** 40.

RESEARCH FACILITIES

Research Facilities: Agricultural Experiment Station, Engineering Experiment Station, Center for Water Resources Research, Ecology Center, Center for Atmospheric and Space Sciences, Center for Persons with Disabilities, Institute of Political Economy, Economics Research Center.

EXPENSES/FINANCIAL AID

Annual Tuition: In-state $2,000. / Out-of-state $5,883. **Fees:** $447. **Books and Supplies:** $700. **Loans Range From:** $8,500-$18,500. **% Receiving Financial Aid:** 76. **Types of Aid Available:** 1. **Number of fellowships**

granted each year: 10. **Number of teaching/research assistantships granted each year:** 141. **Average Salary Stipend:** $14,000.

ADMISSIONS INFORMATION

Application Fee: $40. **Regular Notification:** Rolling. **Transfer Students Accepted?** No. **Number of Applications Received:** 391. **% of Applicants Accepted:** 48. **% Accepted Who Enrolled:** 42. **Average GPA:** 3.53. **Average GRE Verbal:** 598. **Average GRE Quantitative:** 666. **Average GRE Analytical:** 640.

Required Admission Factors: GRE, letters of recommendation, transcript.

Other Admission Factors: Minimum GRE Verbal and Quantitative score in the 40th percentile and minimum 3.0 GPA required.

EMPLOYMENT INFORMATION

Placement Office Available? Yes. **Rate of placement:** 98%.

UTAH STATE UNIVERSITY
School of Accountancy

Address: 900 Old Main Hill, Logan, UT 84322-0900
Admissions Phone: 435-797-1189 · **Admissions Fax:** 435-797-1192
Admissions E-mail: gradsch@cc.usu.edu

INSTITUTIONAL INFORMATION

Public/Private: Public. **Student/Faculty Ratio:** 5:1. **Students in Parent Institution:** 20,158.

STUDENT INFORMATION

Total Students in Program: 2,293. **% Female:** 40.

RESEARCH FACILITIES

Research Facilities: Agricultural Experiment Station, Engineering Experiment Station, Center for Water Resources Research, Ecology Center, Center for Atmospheric and Space Sciences, Center for Persons with Disabilities, Institute of Political Economy, Economics Research Center.

EXPENSES/FINANCIAL AID

Annual Tuition: In-state $2,000. / Out-of-state $5,883. **Fees:** $447. **Books and Supplies:** $700. **Loans Range From:** $8,500-$18,500. **Types of Aid Available:** 1. **Number of teaching/research assistantships granted each year:** 2.

ADMISSIONS INFORMATION

Application Fee: $40. **Regular Notification:** Rolling. **Transfer Students Accepted?** Yes. **Number of Applications Received:** 33. **% of Applicants Accepted:** 82. **% Accepted Who Enrolled:** 52. **Average GPA:** 3.48. **Average GRE Verbal:** 590. **Average GRE Quantitative:** 745. **Average GRE Analytical:** 680.

Required Admission Factors: Essays/personal statement, letters of recommendation, transcript.

Other Admission Factors: Minimum GMAT score in the 40th percentile, minimum 3.0 GPA, and minimum entrance formula of 1150 (200 times GPA plus GMAT) required.

EMPLOYMENT INFORMATION

Placement Office Available? Yes. **% Employed Within 6 Months:** 96. **% of master's grads employed in their field upon graduation:** 100. **Rate of placement:** 98%. **Average starting salary:** $40,000.

UTAH STATE UNIVERSITY
College of Natural Resources

Address: 900 Old Main Hill, Logan, UT 84322-0900
Admissions Phone: 435-797-1189 · **Admissions Fax:** 434-797-1192

INSTITUTIONAL INFORMATION

Public/Private: Public. **Student/Faculty Ratio:** 2:1. **Students in Parent Institution:** 20,158.

STUDENT INFORMATION

Total Students in Program: 2,293. **% Female:** 40.

RESEARCH FACILITIES

Research Facilities: Agricultural Experiment Station, Engineering Experiment Station, Center for Water Resources Research, Ecology Center, Center for Atmospheric and Space Sciences, Center for Persons with Disabilities, Institute of Political Economy, Economics Research Center.

EXPENSES/FINANCIAL AID

Annual Tuition: In-state $2,000. / Out-of-state $5,883. **Fees:** $447. **Books and Supplies:** $700. **Loans Range From:** $8,500-$18,500. **Types of Aid Available:** 1. **Number of fellowships granted each year:** 7. **Number of teaching/research assistantships granted each year:** 85. **Average Salary Stipend:** $11,000.

ADMISSIONS INFORMATION

Application Fee: $40. **Regular Notification:** Rolling. **Transfer Students Accepted?** No. **Number of Applications Received:** 118. **% of Applicants Accepted:** 42. **% Accepted Who Enrolled:** 64. **Average GPA:** 3.07. **Average GRE Verbal:** 480. **Average GRE Quantitative:** 670. **Average GRE Analytical:** 490.
Required Admission Factors: Essays/personal statement, GRE, transcript.
Other Admission Factors: Minimum GRE Verbal and Quantitative score in the 40th percentile and minimum 3.0 GPA required.

EMPLOYMENT INFORMATION

Placement Office Available? Yes. **% Employed Within 6 Months:** 100. **% of master's/doctoral grads employed in their field upon graduation:** 100/100. **Rate of placement:** 98%. **Average starting salary:** $60,000.

UTAH STATE UNIVERSITY
College of Family Life

Address: 900 Old Main Hill, Logan, UT 84322-0900
Admissions Phone: 435-797-1189 · **Admissions Fax:** 435-797-1192
Admissions E-mail: gradsch@cc.usu.edu

INSTITUTIONAL INFORMATION

Public/Private: Public. **Student/Faculty Ratio:** 3:1. **Students in Parent Institution:** 20,158.

STUDENT INFORMATION

Total Students in Program: 2,293 **% Female:** 40.

RESEARCH FACILITIES

Research Facilities: Agricultural Experiment Station, Engineering Experiment Station, Center for Water Resources Research, Ecology Center, Center for Atmospheric and Space Sciences, Center for Persons with Disabilities, Institute of Political Economy, Economics Research Center.

EXPENSES/FINANCIAL AID

Annual Tuition: In-state $2,000. / Out-of-state $5,883. **Fees:** $447. **Books and Supplies:** $700. **Loans Range From:** $8,500-$18,500. **% Receiving Financial Aid:** 37. **Number of fellowships granted each year:** 6. **Number of teaching/research assistantships granted each year:** 45. **Average Salary Stipend:** $12,000.

ADMISSIONS INFORMATION

Application Fee: $40. **Transfer Students Accepted?** Yes. **Transfer Policy:** Transfer request, current department sign-off on progress, and request to new department for conside. **Number of Applications Received:** 143. **% of Applicants Accepted:** 33. **% Accepted Who Enrolled:** 40. **Average GPA:** 3.47. **Average GRE Verbal:** 580. **Average GRE Quantitative:** 625. **Average GRE Analytical:** 658.

Required Admission Factors: Essays/personal statement, letters of recommendation, transcript.
Other Admission Factors: Minimum GRE score in the 40th percentile (Verbal and quantitative), minimum MAT score in the 40th percentile, and minimum 3.0 GPA required.
Program-Specific Admission Factors: Essay and interview required of marriage/family therapy program applicants.

EMPLOYMENT INFORMATION

Placement Office Available? Yes. **% of master's/doctoral employed in their field upon graduation:** 90/100. **Rate of placement:** 98%. **Average starting salary:** $45,000.

VALDOSTA STATE UNIVERSITY
College of Arts

Address: 1500 North Patterson Street, Valdosta, GA 31698
Admissions Phone: 229-333-5694 · **Admissions Fax:** 229-245-3853
Admissions E-mail: jtomberl@valdosta.edu

INSTITUTIONAL INFORMATION

Public/Private: Public. **Evening Classes Available?** Yes. **Students in Parent Institution:** 8,232.

STUDENT INFORMATION

Total Students in Program: 1,309. **% Full Time:** 33. **% Female:** 78.

EXPENSES/FINANCIAL AID

Annual Tuition: In-state $1,746. / Out-of-state $6,966. **Fees:** $694. **Books and Supplies:** $750. **Grants Range From:** $200-$250. **Loans Range From:** $200-$12,000. **% Receiving Scholarships/Grants:** 2. **% Receiving Loans:** 90. **% Receiving Assistantships:** 8. **Number of teaching/research assistantships granted each year:** 6 **Average Salary Stipend:** $1,226.

ADMISSIONS INFORMATION

Application Fee: $20. **Regular Notification:** Rolling. **Transfer Students Accepted?** Yes. **Number of Applications Received:** 13. **% of Applicants Accepted:** 85. **% Accepted Who Enrolled:** 36. **Average GPA:** 3.0
Required Admission Factors: GRE, transcript.

EMPLOYMENT INFORMATION

Placement Office Available? Yes. **Rate of placement:** 75%.

VALDOSTA STATE UNIVERSITY
College of Social Work

Address: 1500 North Patterson Street, Valdosta, GA 31698
Admissions Phone: 229-333-5694 · **Admissions Fax:** 229-245-3853
Admissions E-mail: jtomberl@valdosta.edu

INSTITUTIONAL INFORMATION

Public/Private: Public. **Evening Classes Available?** Yes. **Students in Parent Institution:** 8,232.

STUDENT INFORMATION

Total Students in Program: 1,309. **% Full Time:** 33. **% Female:** 78.

EXPENSES/FINANCIAL AID

Annual Tuition: In-state $1,746. / Out-of-state $6,966. **Fees:** $694. **Books and Supplies:** $750. **Grants Range From:** $200-$250. **Loans Range From:** $200-$12,000. **% Receiving Scholarships/Grants:** 2. **% Receiving Loans:** 90. **% Receiving Assistantships:** 8. **Number of teaching/research assistantships granted each year:** 2. **Average Salary Stipend:** $1,226.

ADMISSIONS INFORMATION

Application Fee: $20. **Transfer Students Accepted?** Yes. **Number of Applications Received:** 72. **% of Applicants Accepted:** 42. **% Accepted Who Enrolled:** 53. **Average GPA:** 3.0

Required Admission Factors: Essays/personal statement, GRE, letters of recommendation, transcript.
Other Admission Factors: Minimum GRE score of 800 and minimum 3.0 GPA required.

EMPLOYMENT INFORMATION
Placement Office Available? Yes. Rate of placement: 75%.

VALDOSTA STATE UNIVERSITY
College of Arts & Sciences

Address: 1500 North Patterson Street, Valdosta, GA 31698
Admissions Phone: 229-333-5694 · Admissions Fax: 229-345-3853
Admissions E-mail: eclark@valdosta.edu

INSTITUTIONAL INFORMATION
Public/Private: Public. Evening Classes Available? Yes. Students in Parent Institution: 8,232.

STUDENT INFORMATION
Total Students in Program: 1,309. % Full Time: 33. % Female: 78.

EXPENSES/FINANCIAL AID
Annual Tuition: In-state $1,746. / Out-of-state $6,966. Fees: $694. Books and Supplies: $750. Grants Range From: $200-$250. Loans Range From: $200-$12,000. % Receiving Scholarships/Grants: 2. % Receiving Loans: 90. % Receiving Assistantships: 8. Average Salary Stipend: $1,226.

ADMISSIONS INFORMATION
Application Fee: $20. Regular Notification: Rolling. Transfer Students Accepted? Yes. Number of Applications Received: 114. % of Applicants Accepted: 82. % Accepted Who Enrolled: 44. Average GRE Verbal: 480. Average GRE Quantitative: 510. Average GRE Analytical: 560.
Required Admission Factors: Essays/personal statement, GRE, letters of recommendation, transcript.
Other Admission Factors: Minimum 2.5 GPA required.

EMPLOYMENT INFORMATION
Placement Office Available? Yes. Rate of placement: 75%.

VANGUARD UNIVERSITY OF SOUTHERN CALIFORNIA
Graduate Program in Clinical Psychology

Address: 55 Fair Drive, Costa Mesa, CA 92626
Admissions Phone: 714-966-5499 · Admissions Fax: 714-966-5471
Admissions E-mail: gradadmissions@vanguard.edu
Web Address: www.vanguard.edu/gradpsych/

INSTITUTIONAL INFORMATION
Public/Private: Private (nonprofit). Evening Classes Available? Yes. Student/Faculty Ratio: 10:1. Students in Parent Institution: 2,155.

STUDENT INFORMATION
Total Students in Program: 313. % Full Time: 38. % Female: 56.

RESEARCH FACILITIES
Research Facilities: Center for Urban Studies and Ethnic Leadership, Wilson Center for Pentecostal Studies, Costa Rica Study Center, Jerusalem University College.

EXPENSES/FINANCIAL AID
Annual Tuition: $15,402. Fees: $50. Books and Supplies: $630. Grants Range From: $500-$10,500. Loans Range From: $2,000-$18,500. % Receiving Financial Aid: 92. % Receiving Scholarships/Grants: 83. % Receiving Loans: 65. % Receiving Assistantships: 5. Types of Aid Available:

scholarships, assistantships for 2nd year students. Average student debt, upon graduation: $38,398. Number of teaching/research assistantships granted each year: 4 Average Salary Stipend: $2,000.

ADMISSIONS INFORMATION
Application Fee: $45. Priority Application Deadline: 4/1. Regular Application Deadline: 7/1. Regular Notification: Rolling. Transfer Students Accepted? Yes. Transfer Policy: Maximum six semester units may be transferred with letter and syllabus of courses to be transferred. Number of Applications Received: 89. % of Applicants Accepted: 44. % Accepted Who Enrolled: 67. Average GPA: 3.5.
Required Admission Factors: Essays/personal statement, letters of recommendation, transcript.
Other Admission Factors: Minimum 3.0 GPA from an accredited school required. Developmental psychology, abnormal psychology, and new or old testament survey are all required prerequisites for the program.

EMPLOYMENT INFORMATION
% Employed Within 6 Months: 89.

VASSAR COLLEGE
Graduate Programs

Address: 124 Raymond Avenue, Poughkeepsie, NY 12604

INSTITUTIONAL INFORMATION
Public/Private: Private (nonprofit). Students in Parent Institution: 2,439.

RESEARCH FACILITIES
Research Facilities: Class of 1951 Observatory, special collections library, electron microscope.

EXPENSES/FINANCIAL AID
Annual Tuition: $25,890. Fees: $400. Books and Supplies: $820.

ADMISSIONS INFORMATION
Transfer Students Accepted? No.
Required Admission Factors: Interview, transcript.

EMPLOYMENT INFORMATION
Placement Office Available? Yes.

VIRGINIA COMMONWEALTH UNIVERSITY
Graduate School

Address: 1001 Grove Avenue, Richmond, VA 23284
Admissions Phone: 804-828-6916 · Admissions Fax: 804-828-6949
Admissions E-mail: vcu-grad@vcu.edu · Web Address: www.vcu.edu/graduate

INSTITUTIONAL INFORMATION
Public/Private: Public. Evening Classes Available? Yes. Total Faculty: 983. % Faculty Part Time: 0. Students in Parent Institution: 28,462.

STUDENT INFORMATION
Total Students in Program: 4,694. % Full Time: 54. % Female: 67. % Minority: 19. % International: 8.

EXPENSES/FINANCIAL AID
Annual Tuition: In-state $8,088. / Out-of-state $21,208. Fees: $662. Books and Supplies: $600. Grants Range From: $2,000-$20,000. Loans Range From: $1,500-$30,000. Types of Aid Available: Fellowships, graduate assistantships, institutional work-study, loans, scholarships. Assistantship compensation includes: Full tuition remission, partial tuition remission, salary/stipend. Average Salary Stipend: $7,500.

ADMISSIONS INFORMATION
Application Fee: $50. Priority Application Deadline: 2/1. Regular Application Deadline: 8/15. Regular Notification: Rolling. Transfer Students

Accepted? Yes. **Number of Applications Received:** 4,445. **% of Applicants Accepted:** 52. **% Accepted Who Enrolled:** 66. **Average GPA:** 3.3.
Required Admission Factors: Essays/personal statement, letters of recommendation, transcript.

VIRGINIA COMMONWEALTH UNIVERSITY
Sport Leadership Graduate Program

Address: 1300 W. Broad St., Richmond, VA 23284
Admissions Phone: 804-828-7821 · **Admissions Fax:** 804-828-4938
Admissions E-mail: sportscenter@vcu.edu · **Web Address:** www.vcu.edu/sportscenter

INSTITUTIONAL INFORMATION
Public/Private: Public. **Evening Classes Available?** Yes.

ADMISSIONS INFORMATION
Application Fee: $50. **Regular Application Deadline:** 5/15. **Regular Notification:** Rolling. **Transfer Students Accepted?** Yes. **Transfer Policy:** must meet same requirements. **Average GPA:** 2.9.
Required Admission Factors: Essays/personal statement, GRE, letters of recommendation, mat, transcript.
Recommended Admission Factors: Interview.

VIRGINIA COMMONWEALTH UNIVERSITY
Center for Public Policy

Address: 1001 Grove Avenue, Moseley House, PO Box 843051, Richmond, VA 23284-3051
Admissions Phone: 804-828-6916 · **Admissions Fax:** 804-828-6949
Admissions E-mail: vcu-grad@vcu.edu · **Web Address:** www.vcu.edu/graduate

INSTITUTIONAL INFORMATION
Public/Private: Public. **Students in Parent Institution:** 26,685.

PROGRAMS
Masters offered in: Accounting and business/management; accounting; acting; adult and continuing education administration; adult and continuing education and teaching; adult health nurse/nursing; advertising; analytical chemistry; applied mathematics; art history, criticism and conservation; art teacher education; art/art studies, general; biochemistry; biomedical/medical engineering; biostatistics; business administration/management; business/commerce, general; ceramic arts and ceramics; chemistry teacher education; chemistry, general; city/urban, community and regional planning; clinical laboratory science/medical technology/technologist; clinical pastoral counseling/patient counseling; computer and information sciences, general; conducting; counselor education/school counseling and guidance services; crafts/craft design, folk art and artisanry; creative writing; criminal justice/law enforcement administration; curriculum and instruction; dental clinical sciences, general (MS, PhD); design and visual communications, general; drama and dance teacher education; drama and dramatics/theater arts, general; economics, general; education leadership and administration, general; education/teaching of individuals with emotional disturbances; education/teaching of individuals with hearing impairments, including deafness; education/teaching of individuals with mental retardation; education/teaching of individuals with multiple disabilities; education/teaching of individuals with specific learning disabilities; education/teaching of the gifted and talented; educational administration and supervision, other; educational, instructional, and curriculum supervision; elementary and middle school administration/principalship; elementary education and teaching; engineering, general; English composition; English language and literature, general; English/language arts teacher education; environmental studies; family practice nurse nurse practitioner; fiber, textile and weaving arts; finance, gen-

eral; fine arts and art studies, other; fine/studio arts, general; foreign language teacher education; forensic science and technology; French language teacher education; German language teacher education; gerontology; health and physical education, general; health and physical education/fitness, other; health services/allied health, general; health teacher education; health/health care administration/management; history teacher education; history, general; human resources management and services, other; human resources management/personnel administration, general; inorganic chemistry; junior high/intermediate/middle school education and teaching; kinesiology and exercise science; management information systems, general; marketing/marketing management, general; mass communications/media studies; maternal/child health nurse/nursing; mathematics teacher education; mathematics, general; medicinal and pharmaceutical chemistry (MS, PhD); metal and jewelry arts; molecular biology; multi/interdisciplinary studies, other; museology/museum studies; music performance, general; music teacher education; music theory and composition; music/music and performing arts studies, general; nurse anesthetist; nursing—registered nurse training (RN, ASN, BSN, MSN); occupational therapy/therapist; organic chemistry; organizational behavior studies; painting; parks, recreation and leisure studies; pastoral studies/counseling; pathology/experimental pathology; pediatric nurse/nursing; pharmacology and toxicology; pharmacy administration and pharmacy policy and regulatory affairs (MS, PhD); photography; physical and theoretical chemistry; physical education teaching and coaching; physics, general; physiology, general; printmaking; psychiatric/mental health nurse/nursing; public administration; public health, general (MPH, DPH); public health/community nurse/nursing; reading teacher education; real estate; rehabilitation counseling/counselor; sculpture; secondary education and teaching; secondary school administration/principalship; social work; sociology; spanish language teacher education; special education and teaching, other; special education, general; sports and fitness administration/management; statistics, general; substance abuse/addiction counseling; superintendency and educational system administration; surgical nurse/nursing; taxation; urban studies/affairs; visual and performing arts, general. **Doctorate offered in:** Accounting and business/management; analytical chemistry; art history, criticism and conservation; biochemistry; biomedical/medical engineering; business/commerce, general; chemical physics; chemistry, general; clinical psychology; counseling psychology. **First Professional degree offered in:** Dentistry (DDS, DMD); medicine (MD); pharmacy (PharmD, BS/BPharm); physical therapy/therapist.

STUDENT INFORMATION
Total Students in Program: 4,680. **% Full Time:** 48. **% Female:** 67. **% Minority:** 20. **% International:** 8.

RESEARCH FACILITIES
Research Facilities: Anderson Art Gallery Conservation Laboratory, MCV Burn Trauma Clinic, Virginia Institute for Developmental Disabilities, Massey Cancer Center, School of Pharmacy's Pharmacokinetics Laboratory, Virginia Real Estate Research Center, Center for Economic Education.

EXPENSES/FINANCIAL AID
Annual Tuition: In-state $7,030. / Out-of-state $17,196. **Types of Aid Available:** Fellowships, graduate assistantships, grants, institutional work-study, scholarships.

ADMISSIONS INFORMATION
Application Fee: $50. **Regular Application Deadline:** N/A. **Regular Notification:** Rolling. **Transfer Students Accepted?** Yes. **Transfer Policy:** Contact program director or consult the online version of "VCU Graduate and Professional Programs Bulletin" at http://www.vcu.edu/graduate. **Number of Applications Received:** 30.
Required Admission Factors: Essays/personal statement, gmat, GRE, letters of recommendation, transcript.

EMPLOYMENT INFORMATION
Placement Office Available? Yes.

VIRGINIA COMMONWEALTH UNIVERSITY
Center for Environmental Studies

Address: 1001 Grove Avenue, Richmond, VA 23284-3051
Admissions Phone: 804-828-6916 · **Admissions Fax:** 804-828-6949
Admissions E-mail: gcgarman@vcu.edu · **Web Address:** www.vcu.edu/graduate

INSTITUTIONAL INFORMATION
Public/Private: Public. **Students in Parent Institution:** 26,685.

STUDENT INFORMATION
Total Students in Program: 4,308. **% Full Time:** 52. **% Female:** 66. **% International:** 8.

RESEARCH FACILITIES
Research Facilities: Anderson Art Gallery Conservation Laboratory, MCV Burn Trauma Clinic, Virginia Institute for Developmental Disabilities, Massey Cancer Center, School of Pharmacy's Pharmacokinetics Laboratory, Virginia Real Estate Research Center, Center for Economic Education.

EXPENSES/FINANCIAL AID
Annual Tuition: In-state $7,030. / Out-of-state $17,196. **Types of Aid Available:** Fellowships, graduate assistantships, grants, institutional work-study, scholarships.

ADMISSIONS INFORMATION
Application Fee: $50. **Regular Notification:** Rolling. **Transfer Students Accepted?** Yes. **Transfer Policy:** Contact program director or consult the online version of the Graduate and Professional Programs Bulletin at http://www.vcu.edu/graduate. **Number of Applications Received:** 24. **% of Applicants Accepted:** 83. **% Accepted Who Enrolled:** 85.
Required Admission Factors: Essays/personal statement, GRE, letters of recommendation, transcript.

EMPLOYMENT INFORMATION
Placement Office Available? Yes.

VIRGINIA COMMONWEALTH UNIVERSITY
School of the Arts

Address: 1001 Grove Avenue, Richmond, VA 23284-3051
Admissions Phone: 804-828-6916 · **Admissions Fax:** 804-828-6949
Admissions E-mail: jseipel@saturn.vcu.edu · **Web Address:** www.vcu.edu/graduate

INSTITUTIONAL INFORMATION
Public/Private: Public. **Students in Parent Institution:** 26,685.

STUDENT INFORMATION
Total Students in Program: 4,308. **% Full Time:** 52. **% Female:** 66. **% International:** 8.

RESEARCH FACILITIES
Research Facilities: Anderson Art Gallery Conservation Laboratory, MCV Burn Trauma Clinic, Virginia Institute for Developmental Disabilities, Massey Cancer Center, School of Pharmacy's Pharmacokinetics Laboratory, Virginia Real Estate Research Center, Center for Economic Education.

EXPENSES/FINANCIAL AID
Annual Tuition: In-state $7,030. / Out-of-state $17,196. **Types of Aid Available:** Fellowships, graduate assistantships, grants, institutional work-study, scholarships.

ADMISSIONS INFORMATION
Application Fee: $50. **Regular Notification:** Rolling. **Transfer Students Accepted?** Yes. **Transfer Policy:** Contact program director or consult the online version of the Graduate and Professional Programs Bulletin at http://www.vcu.edu/graduate. **Number of Applications Received:** 406. **% of Applicants Accepted:** 38. **% Accepted Who Enrolled:** 62.

Required Admission Factors: Essays/personal statement, letters of recommendation, transcript.

EMPLOYMENT INFORMATION
Placement Office Available? Yes.

VIRGINIA COMMONWEALTH UNIVERSITY
School of Social Work

Address: 901 West Franklin Street, Richmond, VA 23284-3051
Admissions Phone: 804-828-6916 · **Admissions Fax:** 804-828-6949
Admissions E-mail: acasebol@saturn.vcu.edu

INSTITUTIONAL INFORMATION
Public/Private: Public. **Evening Classes Available?** Yes. **Students in Parent Institution:** 25,001.

STUDENT INFORMATION
Total Students in Program: 6,345. **% Full Time:** 38. **% Female:** 63.

RESEARCH FACILITIES
Research Facilities: Anderson Art Gallery Conservation Laboratory, MCV Burn Trauma Clinic, Virginia Institute for Developmental Disabilities, Massey Cancer Center, School of Pharmacy's Pharmacokinetics Laboratory, Virginia Real Estate Research Center, Center for Economic Education.

EXPENSES/FINANCIAL AID
Annual Tuition: In-state $5,443. / Out-of-state $13,893. **Room & Board:** $5,912.

ADMISSIONS INFORMATION
Application Fee: $30. **Regular Notification:** Rolling. **Transfer Students Accepted?** No. **Number of Applications Received:** 478. **% of Applicants Accepted:** 78. **% Accepted Who Enrolled:** 55.
Required Admission Factors: Essays/personal statement, letters of recommendation, transcript.

EMPLOYMENT INFORMATION
Placement Office Available? Yes.

VIRGINIA COMMONWEALTH UNIVERSITY
College of Humanities & Sciences

Address: 901 West Franklin Street, Richmond, VA 23284-3051
Admissions Phone: 804-828-6916 · **Admissions Fax:** 804-828-6949
Admissions E-mail: asneden@saturn.vcu.edu

INSTITUTIONAL INFORMATION
Public/Private: Public. **Students in Parent Institution:** 25,001.

STUDENT INFORMATION
Total Students in Program: 6,345. **% Full Time:** 38. **% Female:** 63.

RESEARCH FACILITIES
Research Facilities: Anderson Art Gallery Conservation Laboratory, MCV Burn Trauma Clinic, Virginia Institute for Developmental Disabilities, Massey Cancer Center, School of Pharmacy's Pharmacokinetics Laboratory, Virginia Real Estate Research Center, Center for Economic Education.

EXPENSES/FINANCIAL AID
Annual Tuition: In-state $5,443. / Out-of-state $13,893. **Room & Board:** $5,912.

ADMISSIONS INFORMATION
Application Fee: $30. **Regular Notification:** Rolling. **Transfer Students Accepted?** No. **Number of Applications Received:** 1,025. **% of Applicants Accepted:** 39. **% Accepted Who Enrolled:** 70.
Required Admission Factors: Essays/personal statement, letters of recommendation, transcript.

EMPLOYMENT INFORMATION
Placement Office Available? Yes.

VIRGINIA POLYTECHNIC INSTITUTE AND STATE UNIVERSITY
College of Natural Resources

Address: Blacksburg, VA 24061-0202
Admissions Phone: 540-231-7051 · **Admissions Fax:** 540-231-7664
Admissions E-mail: rbush@vt.edu · **Web Address:** http://www.cnr.vt.edu

INSTITUTIONAL INFORMATION
Public/Private: Public. Students in Parent Institution: 25,783.

STUDENT INFORMATION
Total Students in Program: 3,618. % Full Time: 83. % Female: 38.

RESEARCH FACILITIES
Research Facilities: More than 60 research centers.

EXPENSES/FINANCIAL AID
Annual Tuition: In-state $4,347. / Out-of-state $7,317. Fees: $872.

ADMISSIONS INFORMATION
Transfer Students Accepted? No.

EMPLOYMENT INFORMATION
Placement Office Available? Yes.

VIRGINIA POLYTECHNIC INSTITUTE AND STATE UNIVERSITY
College of Arts & Sciences

Address: Blacksburg, VA 24061-0202

INSTITUTIONAL INFORMATION
Public/Private: Public. Total Faculty: 1,410. Students in Parent Institution: 25,783.

STUDENT INFORMATION
Total Students in Program: 3,618. % Full Time: 83. % Female: 38.

RESEARCH FACILITIES
Research Facilities: More than 60 research centers.

EXPENSES/FINANCIAL AID
Annual Tuition: In-state $4,347. / Out-of-state $7,317. Fees: $872.

ADMISSIONS INFORMATION
Transfer Students Accepted? No. Number of Applications Received: 1,518. % of Applicants Accepted: 39. % Accepted Who Enrolled: 49.

EMPLOYMENT INFORMATION
Placement Office Available? Yes.

VIRGINIA STATE UNIVERSITY
School of Graduate Studies, Research, & Outreach

Address: 1 Hayden Drive, PO Box 9080, Petersburg, VA 23806-2096
Admissions Phone: 804-524-5985 · **Admissions Fax:** 804-524-5105

INSTITUTIONAL INFORMATION
Public/Private: Public. Evening Classes Available? Yes. Students in Parent Institution: 4,674.

STUDENT INFORMATION
Total Students in Program: 785. % Full Time: 6. % Female: 74.

EXPENSES/FINANCIAL AID
Annual Tuition: In-state $4,170. / Out-of-state $10,538. Number of fellowships granted each year: 35. Number of teaching/research assistantships granted each year: 5. Average Salary Stipend: $8.

ADMISSIONS INFORMATION
Application Fee: $25. Regular Notification: Rolling. Transfer Students Accepted? No. Number of Applications Received: 230. % of Applicants Accepted: 84. % Accepted Who Enrolled: 89. Average GPA: 2.6. Required Admission Factors: GRE, transcript.
Other Admission Factors: Minimum 2.0 GPA required.

EMPLOYMENT INFORMATION
Placement Office Available? Yes.

WAKE FOREST UNIVERSITY
Graduate School of Arts and Sciences

Address: 1834 Wake Forest Road, PO Box 7487 Reynolda Station, Winston-Salem, NC 27109
Admissions Phone: 336-758-5301 · **Admissions Fax:** 336-758-4230
Admissions E-mail: gradschl@wfu.edu · **Web Address:** www.wfu.edu/graduate

INSTITUTIONAL INFORMATION
Public/Private: Private (nonprofit). Total Faculty: 509. Students in Parent Institution: 6,504.

PROGRAMS
Masters offered in: Accounting; biology/biological sciences; chemistry; communications studies/speech, communication, and rhetoric; computer and information sciences; counselor education/school counseling and guidance services; English language and literature; kinesiology and exercise science; liberal arts and sciences/liberal studies; mathematics; pastoral studies/counseling; physics; psychology; religion/religious studies; secondary education and teaching. Doctorate offered in: Biology/biological sciences; chemistry; physics.

STUDENT INFORMATION
Total Students in Program: 422. % Full-time: 79. % Female: 57. % Minority: 9. % International: 10.

EXPENSES/FINANCIAL AID
Annual Tuition: $23,310. Room & Board: $8,255. Fees: $710. Books and Supplies: $1,000. Grants Range From: $30-$23,310. Loans Range From: $2,000-$24,000. % Receiving Financial Aid: 76.5. % Receiving Scholarships/Grants: 44. % Receiving Loans: 46. % Receiving Assistantships: 42. Types of Aid Available: Fellowships, graduate assistantships, loans, scholarships. Number of Fellowships Granted Each Year: 37 Average amount of individual fellowships per year: 4000. Number of Teaching/Research Assistantships Granted Each Year: 110 Assistantship Compensation Includes: Full tuition remission, salary/stipend. Average Salary Stipend: $10,500.

ADMISSIONS INFORMATION
Application Fee: $25. Regular Application Deadline: 1/15. Regular Notification: Rolling. Transfer Students Accepted? Yes. Number of Applications Received: 642. % of Applicants Accepted: 36. % Accepted Who Enrolled: 82. Average GPA: 3.5. Average GRE Verbal: 546. Average GRE Quantitative: 645. Average GRE Analytical: 637. Average GRE Analytical Writing: 4.81.
Required Admission Factors: Essays/personal statement, GRE, letters of recommendation, transcript.
Recommended Admission Factors: GRE subject exam(s) in Chemistry, English, Physics, Psychology.
Other Admission Factors: Minimum 3.0 GPA and minimum GRE score of 1100 recommended.

WALLA WALLA COLLEGE
Department of Biological Sciences

Address: 204 South College Avenue, College Place, WA 99324
Admissions Phone: 509-527-2421 · **Admissions Fax:** 509-527-2253

INSTITUTIONAL INFORMATION
Public/Private: Private (nonprofit). **Student/Faculty Ratio:** 1:1. **Students in Parent Institution:** 1,823.

STUDENT INFORMATION
Total Students in Program: 246. **% Full-time:** 88. **% Female:** 78.

RESEARCH FACILITIES
Research Facilities: Rosario Beach marine station.

EXPENSES/FINANCIAL AID
Annual Tuition: $16,497. **Room & Board:** $10,100. **Books and Supplies:** $1,575. **Grants Range From:** $300-$7,700. **Loans Range From:** $500-$19,500. **% Receiving Financial Aid:** 100. **% Receiving Scholarships/Grants:** 95. **% Receiving Loans:** 82. **% Receiving Assistantships:** 3. **Average student debt, upon graduation:** $40,500. **Number of Teaching/Research Assistantships Granted Each Year:** 3. **Average Salary Stipend:** $4,040.

ADMISSIONS INFORMATION
Application Fee: $50. **Regular Notification:** Rolling. **Transfer Students Accepted?** Yes. **Transfer Policy:** Minimum grade of B required of transfer applicants. **Number of Applications Received:** 4. **% of Applicants Accepted:** 100. **% Accepted Who Enrolled:** 100. **Average GPA:** 3.28. **Average GRE Verbal:** 482. **Average GRE Quantitative:** 552. **Average GRE Analytical:** 587.
Required Admission Factors: Essays/personal statement, GRE, letters of recommendation, transcript.
Other Admission Factors: Minimum 2.75 GPA required.

EMPLOYMENT INFORMATION
Placement Office Available? Yes. **Rate of placement:** 78%.

WALLA WALLA COLLEGE
School of Social Work

Address: 204 South College Avenue, College Place, WA 99324
Admissions Phone: 509-527-2590 · **Admissions Fax:** 509-527-2434
Admissions E-mail: gruske@wwc.edu

INSTITUTIONAL INFORMATION
Public/Private: Private (nonprofit). **Evening Classes Available?** Yes. **Students in Parent Institution:** 1,823.

STUDENT INFORMATION
Total Students in Program: 246. **% Full-time:** 88. **% Female:** 78.

RESEARCH FACILITIES
Research Facilities: Rosario Beach marine station.

EXPENSES/FINANCIAL AID
Annual Tuition: $16,497. **Room & Board:** $10,100. **Books and Supplies:** $1,575. **Grants Range From:** $300-$7,700. **Loans Range From:** $500-$19,500. **% Receiving Financial Aid:** 90. **% Receiving Scholarships/Grants:** 95. **% Receiving Loans:** 82. **% Receiving Assistantships:** 3. **Average student debt, upon graduation:** $40,500.

ADMISSIONS INFORMATION
Application Fee: $50. **Regular Notification:** Rolling. **Transfer Students Accepted?** Yes. **Transfer Policy:** Maximum 12 credit hours with a minimum grade of B may be transferred. **Number of Applications Received:** 182. **% of**

Applicants Accepted: 98. **% Accepted Who Enrolled:** 77. **Average GPA:** 3.32.
Required Admission Factors: Essays/personal statement, letters of recommendation, transcript.
Other Admission Factors: Minimum 2.75 GPA required.

EMPLOYMENT INFORMATION
Placement Office Available? Yes. **Rate of placement:** 78%.

WALSH COLLEGE OF ACCOUNTANCY & BUSINESS ADMINISTRATION
Graduate Programs

Address: 3838 Livernois Road, PO Box 7006, Troy, MI 48007-7006
Admissions Phone: 248-689-8282 ext. 215 · **Admissions Fax:** 248-254-2520
Admissions E-mail: dzalapi@walshcollege.edu

INSTITUTIONAL INFORMATION
Public/Private: Private (nonprofit). **Evening Classes Available?** Yes. **Students in Parent Institution:** 2,978.

STUDENT INFORMATION
Total Students in Program: 1,808. **% Full-time:** 4. **% Female:** 50.

EXPENSES/FINANCIAL AID
Annual Tuition: $8,586. **Fees:** $330. **Books and Supplies:** $1,000. **Grants Range From:** $150-$6,275. **Loans Range From:** $500-$8,500. **% Receiving Scholarships/Grants:** 28. **% Receiving Loans:** 23.

ADMISSIONS INFORMATION
Application Fee: $25. **Regular Notification:** Rolling. **Transfer Students Accepted?** Yes. **Number of Applications Received:** 765. **% of Applicants Accepted:** 77. **% Accepted Who Enrolled:** 73. **Average GPA:** 3.
Required Admission Factors: Transcript.
Other Admission Factors: Minimum 2.75 GPA required.

EMPLOYMENT INFORMATION
Placement Office Available? Yes. **% Employed Within 6 Months:** 85. **% of master's grads employed in their field upon graduation:** 85. **Average starting salary:** $70,000.

WARREN WILSON COLLEGE
The MFA Program for Writers

Address: 701 Warren Wilson Road, Swannanoa, NC 28778
Admissions Phone: 828-771-3715 · **Admissions Fax:** 828-771-7005
Admissions E-mail: agrimmi@warren-wilson.edu
Web Address: www.warren-wilson.edu/~mfa/

INSTITUTIONAL INFORMATION
Public/Private: Private (nonprofit). **Total Faculty:** 41. **% Faculty Female:** 44. **Student/Faculty Ratio:** 3:1. **Students in Parent Institution:** 786.

PROGRAMS
Masters offered in: Creative writing.

STUDENT INFORMATION
Total Students in Program: 72. **% Full-time:** 100. **% Female:** 72. **% Minority:** 11.

EXPENSES/FINANCIAL AID
Annual Tuition: $8,800. **Fees:** $950.

ADMISSIONS INFORMATION
Application Fee: $70. **Priority Application Deadline:** 9/1. **Regular Application Deadline:** 9/1. **Regular Notification:** 10/15. **Transfer Students**

Accepted? No. **Number of Applications Received:** 206. **% of Applicants Accepted:** 8. **Average GPA:** 3.5.
Required Admission Factors: Essays/personal statement, letters of recommendation, transcript.
Other Admission Factors: Manuscript of 25 fiction pages or 10 poetry pages required.

WARTBURG THEOLOGICAL SEMINARY
Graduate Program

Address: 333 Wartburg Place, PO Box 5004, Dubuque, IA 52004-6004
Admissions Phone: 319-589-0204 · **Admissions Fax:** 319-589-0333
Admissions E-mail: dteig@wartburgseminary.edu

INSTITUTIONAL INFORMATION
Public/Private: Private (nonprofit). **Students in Parent Institution:** 185.

STUDENT INFORMATION
Total Students in Program: 48. **% Full-time:** 81. **% Female:** 60.

EXPENSES/FINANCIAL AID
Annual Tuition: $6,000. **Fees:** $225. **Books and Supplies:** $850. **Grants Range From:** $100-$6,000. **Loans Range From:** $2,000-$18,500. **% Receiving Financial Aid:** 65. **% Receiving Scholarships/Grants:** 85. **% Receiving Loans:** 75. **Average student debt, upon graduation:** $14,600.

ADMISSIONS INFORMATION
Application Fee: $25. **Regular Application Deadline:** 8/5. **Regular Notification:** Rolling. **Transfer Students Accepted?** Yes. **Transfer Policy:** Letter of good standing from school of origin required of transfer applicants. **Number of Applications Received:** 68. **% of Applicants Accepted:** 82. **% Accepted Who Enrolled:** 66. **Average GPA:** 3.1.
Required Admission Factors: Essays/personal statement, letters of recommendation, transcript.
Other Admission Factors: Minimum 2.5 GPA, autobiography, and demonstrated writing ability required.
Program-Specific Admission Factors: One year of college-level Greek required of MDiv program applicants.

WASHBURN UNIVERSITY
College of Arts & Sciences

Address: 1700 College Avenue, Topeka, KS 66621

INSTITUTIONAL INFORMATION
Public/Private: Public. **Students in Parent Institution:** 5,917.

STUDENT INFORMATION
Total Students in Program: 623. **% Full-time:** 25. **% Female:** 64.

EXPENSES/FINANCIAL AID
Annual Tuition: In-state $2,700. / Out-of-state $5,526. **Fees:** $28. **Grants Range From:** $400-$11,833. **Loans Range From:** $105-$18,500. **% Receiving Scholarships/Grants:** 40. **% Receiving Loans:** 93.

ADMISSIONS INFORMATION
Application Fee: $30. **Transfer Students Accepted?** Yes. **Transfer Policy:** Maximum 9 credit hours may be transferred into liberal studies and MEd programs.
Required Admission Factors: Letters of recommendation, transcript.
Program-Specific Admission Factors: Minimum 2.5 GPA required of psychology program applicants. Minimum MAT score of 42 and minimum 2.75 GPA required of MEd program applicants. Minimum 3.0 GPA required of liberal studies program applicants.

EMPLOYMENT INFORMATION
Placement Office Available? Yes.

WASHBURN UNIVERSITY
School of Applied Studies

Address: 1700 College Avenue, Topeka, KS 66621
Admissions Phone: 785-231-1010 · **Admissions Fax:** 785-231-1039
Admissions E-mail: ron.tannehill@washburn.edu · **Web Address:** www.washburn.edu

INSTITUTIONAL INFORMATION
Public/Private: Public. **Evening Classes Available?** Yes. **Total Faculty:** 10. **% Faculty Female:** 20. **% Faculty Part-time:** 30. **Students in Parent Institution:** 5,917.

PROGRAMS
Masters offered in: Corrections administration, criminal justice/law enforcement administration.

STUDENT INFORMATION
Total Students in Program: 623. **% Full-time:** 25. **% Female:** 64.

EXPENSES/FINANCIAL AID
Annual Tuition: In-state $2,700. / Out-of-state $5,526. **Fees:** $28. **Books and Supplies:** $1,000. **Grants Range From:** $400-$11,833. **Loans Range From:** $105-$18,500. **% Receiving Scholarships/Grants:** 40. **% Receiving Loans:** 93. **Types of Aid Available:** Loans.

ADMISSIONS INFORMATION
Application Fee: $35. **Regular Application Deadline:** 4/1. **Regular Notification:** Rolling. **Transfer Students Accepted?** Yes. **Transfer Policy:** Transfer course work must have at least a "B" grade except law school credits which must have at least a C grade. Transfer course work must be criminal justice related. **Number of Applications Received:** 35. **% of Applicants Accepted:** 91. **% Accepted Who Enrolled:** 94. **Average GPA:** 3.4.
Required Admission Factors: Essays/personal statement, letters of recommendation, transcript.
Recommended Admission Factors: Interview.
Other Admission Factors: Minimum 3.0 GPA required to avoid MAT, or other admissions tests, and be admitted as a full-standing student.
Program-Specific Admission Factors: Appropiate liberal arts classes required of social work program applicants.

EMPLOYMENT INFORMATION
Placement Office Available? Yes. **% Employed Within 6 Months:** 90. **Rate of placement:** 90%. **Average starting salary:** $36,000.

WASHINGTON THEOLOGICAL UNION
Graduate Programs

Address: 6896 Laurel Street, NW, Washington, DC 20012
Admissions Phone: 202-726-8800, ext. 5210 · **Admissions Fax:** 202-726-1716
Admissions E-mail: admissions@wtu.edu · **Web Address:** www.wtu.edu

INSTITUTIONAL INFORMATION
Public/Private: Private (nonprofit). **Evening Classes Available?** Yes. **Total Faculty:** 37. **% Faculty Female:** 43. **% Faculty Part-time:** 57. **Student/Faculty Ratio:** 13:1. **Students in Parent Institution:** 266.

PROGRAMS
Masters offered in: Divinity/ministry (BD, MDiv), pastoral studies/counseling, theology/theological studies.

STUDENT INFORMATION
Total Students in Program: 266. **% Full-time:** 34. **% Female:** 49.

RESEARCH FACILITIES

Research Facilities: Washington Theological Union co-publishes the New Theology Review. Our location in Washington DC, facilitates our emphasis on being at the center of the discussion between faith and political life.

EXPENSES/FINANCIAL AID

Annual Tuition: $10,500. **Room & Board (On/Off Campus):** $9,000/$13,700. **Fees:** $250. **Books and Supplies:** $900. **Grants Range From:** $300-$21,000. **Loans Range From:** $300-$18,500. **% Receiving Financial Aid:** 30. **% Receiving Scholarships/Grants:** 50. **% Receiving Loans:** 20. **% Receiving Other Aid (Partners in Ministry is a tuition discount of 33%):** 30. **Types of Aid Available:** Grants, loans, scholarships. partners in ministry for lay part-time students. **Average student debt, upon graduation:** $15,000

ADMISSIONS INFORMATION

Application Fee: $30. **Priority Application Deadline:** 5/31. **Regular Application Deadline:** 8/15. **Regular Notification:** Rolling. **Transfer Students Accepted?** Yes. **Transfer Policy:** Maximum number of credits that may be transferred is 1/3 of total required for degree. Courses accepted must closely resemble courses offered at WTU. **Number of Applications Received:** 100. **% of Applicants Accepted:** 80. **% Accepted Who Enrolled:** 81. **Average GPA:** 3.2.

Required Admission Factors: Essays/personal statement, interview, letters of recommendation, transcript.

Other Admission Factors: Minimum 3.0 GPA preferred, some leeway is given.

Program-Specific Admission Factors: Philosophy and religious studies required of MA and MDiv program applicants.

EMPLOYMENT INFORMATION

% Employed Within 6 Months: 80. **% of master's/first professional grads employed in their field upon graduation:** 75/100. **Rate of placement:** 90%. **Average starting salary:** $24,000.

WASHINGTON UNIVERSITY
Graduate School of Arts & Sciences

Address: One Brookings Drive, Campus Box 1187, St. Louis, MO 63130
Admissions Phone: 314-935-6880 · **Admissions Fax:** 314-935-4887
Admissions E-mail: GraduateSchool@artsci.wustl.edu
Web Address: www.artsci.wustl.edu/GSAS

INSTITUTIONAL INFORMATION

Public/Private: Private (nonprofit). **Evening Classes Available?** Yes. **Students in Parent Institution:** 12,187.

STUDENT INFORMATION

Total Students in Program: 4,335. **% Full-time:** 68. **% Female:** 47.

EXPENSES/FINANCIAL AID

Annual Tuition: $25,700. **% Receiving Financial Aid:** 95. **Number of Fellowships Granted Each Year:** 200. **Average amount of individual fellowships per year:** $11,250. **Number of Teaching/Research Assistantships Granted Each Year:** 750. **Average Salary Stipend:** $11,250.

ADMISSIONS INFORMATION

Application Fee: $35. **Regular Application Deadline:** 1/15. **Regular Notification:** Rolling. **Transfer Students Accepted?** Yes. **Transfer Policy:** Maximum 6 credit hours may be transferred into master's programs; maximum 24 credit hours may be transferred into doctoral programs. **Number of Applications Received:** 2,662. **% of Applicants Accepted:** 26. **% Accepted Who Enrolled:** 49.

Required Admission Factors: Essays/personal statement, GRE, letters of recommendation, transcript.

Program-Specific Admission Factors: Writing sample required of humanities and social sciences program applicants.

EMPLOYMENT INFORMATION

Placement Office Available? Yes. **% Employed Within 6 Months:** 98. **% of doctoral grads employed in their field upon graduation:** 97.

WASHINGTON UNIVERSITY
School of Art

Address: One Brookings Drive
Box 1187, St. Louis, MO 63130
Admissions Phone: 314-935-4761 · **Admissions Fax:** 314-935-6462
Admissions E-mail: sdott@art.wustl.edu

INSTITUTIONAL INFORMATION

Public/Private: Private (nonprofit). **Students in Parent Institution:** 12,187.

STUDENT INFORMATION

Total Students in Program: 4,335. **% Full-time:** 68. **% Female:** 47.

EXPENSES/FINANCIAL AID

Annual Tuition: $25,700. **% Receiving Financial Aid:** 100. **Average Salary Stipend:** $2,000.

ADMISSIONS INFORMATION

Application Fee: $30. **Transfer Students Accepted?** No. **Number of Applications Received:** 67. **% of Applicants Accepted:** 48. **% Accepted Who Enrolled:** 41. **Average GPA:** 3.45.

Required Admission Factors: Essays/personal statement, letters of recommendation, transcript.

EMPLOYMENT INFORMATION

Placement Office Available? Yes.

WASHINGTON UNIVERSITY IN ST. LOUIS
George Warren Brown
School of Social Work

Address: One Brookings Drive, Campus Box 1196, St. Louis, MO 63130
Admissions Phone: 314-935-6676 · **Admissions Fax:** 314-935-4859
Admissions E-mail: msw@wustl.edu · **Web Address:** gwbweb.wustl.edu

INSTITUTIONAL INFORMATION

Public/Private: Private (nonprofit). **Students in Parent Institution:** 12,187.

STUDENT INFORMATION

Total Students in Program: 4,335. **% Full-time:** 68. **% Female:** 47.

EXPENSES/FINANCIAL AID

Annual Tuition: $25,700.

ADMISSIONS INFORMATION

Application Fee: $40. **Regular Application Deadline:** 8/1. **Regular Notification:** Rolling. **Transfer Students Accepted?** Yes. **Number of Applications Received:** 600. **% of Applicants Accepted:** 67. **% Accepted Who Enrolled:** 44. **Average GPA:** 3.4.

Required Admission Factors: Essays/personal statement, letters of recommendation, transcript.

Other Admission Factors: Minimum cummulative undergraduate GPA is 3.0 on a 4.0 scale.

EMPLOYMENT INFORMATION

Placement Office Available? Yes.

WAYLAND BAPTIST UNIVERSITY
Graduate Programs

Address: 1900 West Seventh Street, Plainview, TX 79072
Admissions Phone: 806-291-3420 · **Admissions Fax:** 806-291-1950
Admissions E-mail: admityou@wbu.edu · **Web Address:** www.wbu.edu

INSTITUTIONAL INFORMATION

Public/Private: Private (nonprofit). **Total Faculty:** 16. **% Faculty Female:** 38. **% Faculty Part-time:** 19. **Student/Faculty Ratio:** 2:1. **Students in Parent Institution:** 1,067.

PROGRAMS

Masters offered in: Biological and physical sciences, business administration/management, Christian studies, curriculum and instruction.

STUDENT INFORMATION

Total Students in Program: 57. **% Full-time:** 18. **% Female:** 60. **% International:** 4.

EXPENSES/FINANCIAL AID

Annual Tuition: $5,310. **Room & Board:** $3,420. **Fees:** $400. **Books and Supplies:** $574. **Grants Range From:** $650-$6,689. **Loans Range From:** $4,018-$11,504. **% Receiving Financial Aid:** 96. **% Receiving Scholarships/Grants:** 79. **% Receiving Loans:** 57. **Types of Aid Available:** Grants, institutional work-study, loans, scholarships.

ADMISSIONS INFORMATION

Application Fee: $35. **Regular Notification:** Rolling. **Transfer Students Accepted?** Yes. **Number of Applications Received:** 9. **% of Applicants Accepted:** 100. **% Accepted Who Enrolled:** 89. **Average GPA:** 3.5. **Average GRE Verbal:** 421. **Average GRE Quantitative:** 450.
Required Admission Factors: GRE, GMAT, or MAT; transcript.
Other Admission Factors: Minimum entry point total of 16 ([GMAT score divided by 60] plus [GPA times 3] or [(GRE verbal plus GRE quantitative) divided by 100] plus [GPA times 3]) required for regular admission. A GMAT score of 45 or higher and a GPA of 3.0 or higher.

EMPLOYMENT INFORMATION

Placement Office Available? Yes.

WAYNE STATE COLLEGE
Graduate Studies

Address: 1111 Main Street, Wayne, NE 68787
Admissions Phone: 402-375-7234 · **Admissions Fax:** 402-375-7204
Admissions E-mail: admit1@wsc.edu · **Web Address:** www.wsc.edu

INSTITUTIONAL INFORMATION

Public/Private: Public. **Evening Classes Available?** Yes. **Total Faculty:** 52. **% Faculty Female:** 62. **% Faculty Part-time:** 100. **Students in Parent Institution:** 3,398.

PROGRAMS

Masters offered in: Business administration/management, college student counseling and personnel services, counselor education/school counseling and guidance services, curriculum and instruction, education leadership and administration, elementary and middle school administration/principalship, English/language arts teacher education, history teacher education, mathematics teacher education, physical education teaching and coaching, science teacher education/general science teacher education, secondary school administration/principalship, social science teacher education, special education, speech teacher education, student counseling and personnel services, superintendency and educational system administration.

STUDENT INFORMATION

Total Students in Program: 648. **% Full-time:** 6. **% Female:** 74. **% Minority:** 3. **% International:** 1.

RESEARCH FACILITIES

Research Facilities: Social Sciences Research Center

EXPENSES/FINANCIAL AID

Annual Tuition: In-state $110 / Out-of-state $220 (per credit). **Room & Board:** $3,920. **Fees:** $33. **Books and Supplies:** $720. **Types of Aid Available:** Graduate assistantships, loans. **Number of Teaching/Research Assistantships Granted Each Year:** 30 **Assistantship Compensation Includes:** Full tuition remission, salary/stipend. **Average Salary Stipend:** $4,000.

ADMISSIONS INFORMATION

Application Fee: $30. **Regular Notification:** Rolling. **Transfer Students Accepted?** Yes.
Required Admission Factors: GMAT, GRE, letters of recommendation, transcript.
Other Admission Factors: Minimum 2.75 undergraduate GPA required for MSE & EDS admissions. MBA admissions is determined by a combination of upper level undergraduate GPA and score on the GMAT.
Program-Specific Admission Factors: GRE required for MSE and EDS. GMAT required for MBA.

EMPLOYMENT INFORMATION

Placement Office Available? Yes.

WAYNE STATE UNIVERSITY
College of Fine, Performing, & Communication Arts

Address: 656 West Kirby Street, Detroit, MI 48202
Admissions Phone: 313-577-5342 · **Admissions Fax:** 313-577-5355

INSTITUTIONAL INFORMATION

Public/Private: Public. **Evening Classes Available?** Yes. **Total Faculty:** 100. **Students in Parent Institution:** 30,408.

STUDENT INFORMATION

Total Students in Program: 9,575. **% Full-time:** 29. **% Female:** 57.

RESEARCH FACILITIES

Research Facilities: Karmano's Cancer Institute.

EXPENSES/FINANCIAL AID

Annual Tuition: In-state $4,984 / Out-of-state $11,011. **Room & Board:** $8,940. **Fees:** $442. **Books and Supplies:** $654. **Number of Teaching/Research Assistantships Granted Each Year:** 13. **Average Salary Stipend:** $12,923.

ADMISSIONS INFORMATION

Application Fee: $20. **Transfer Students Accepted?** Yes. **Number of Applications Received:** 53. **% of Applicants Accepted:** 70. **% Accepted Who Enrolled:** 65. **Average GPA:** 3. **Average GRE Verbal:** 500. **Average GRE Quantitative:** 600. **Average GRE Analytical:** 600.
Required Admission Factors: Transcript.

EMPLOYMENT INFORMATION

Placement Office Available? Yes.

WAYNE STATE UNIVERSITY
College of Liberal Arts

Address: 656 West Kirby Street, Detroit, MI 48202
Admissions Phone: 313-577-2170 · **Admissions Fax:** 313-577-2903

INSTITUTIONAL INFORMATION
Public/Private: Public. **Evening Classes Available?** Yes. **Total Faculty:** 247. **Students in Parent Institution:** 30,408.

STUDENT INFORMATION
Total Students in Program: 9,575. **% Full-time:** 29. **% Female:** 57.

RESEARCH FACILITIES
Research Facilities: Karmano's Cancer Institute.

EXPENSES/FINANCIAL AID
Annual Tuition: In-state $4,984 / Out-of-state $11,011. **Room & Board:** $8,940. **Fees:** $442. **Books and Supplies:** $654.

ADMISSIONS INFORMATION
Application Fee: $20. **Regular Notification:** Rolling. **Transfer Students Accepted?** Yes.
Required Admission Factors: Transcript.

EMPLOYMENT INFORMATION
Placement Office Available? Yes.

WAYNE STATE UNIVERSITY
College of Science

Address: 42 West Warren, Detroit, MI 48202
Admissions Phone: 313-577-3577 · **Admissions Fax:** 313-577-7536
Admissions E-mail: admissions@wayne.edu
Web Address: www.admissions.wayne.edu

INSTITUTIONAL INFORMATION
Public/Private: Public. **Evening Classes Available?** Yes. **Total Faculty:** 266. **Students in Parent Institution:** 30,408.

PROGRAMS
Masters offered in: Analytical chemistry, applied mathematics, artificial intelligence and robotics, biology technician/biotechnology laboratory technician, biotechnology, chemistry, clinical psychology, cognitive psychology and psycholinguistics, computer and information sciences, computer science, computer software and media applications, computer systems networking and telecommunications, developmental and child psychology, human nutrition, industrial and organizational psychology, inorganic chemistry, liberal arts and sciences studies and humanities, liberal arts and sciences/liberal studies, mathematics, organic chemistry, physical and theoretical chemistry, physical sciences, physics, social psychology. **Doctorate offered in:** Analytical chemistry, artificial intelligence and robotics, chemistry, clinical psychology, cognitive psychology and psycholinguistics, computer and information sciences, computer science, computer software and media applications.

STUDENT INFORMATION
Total Students in Program: 9,575. **% Full-time:** 29. **% Female:** 57.

RESEARCH FACILITIES
Research Facilities: Karmano's Cancer Institute.

EXPENSES/FINANCIAL AID
Annual Tuition: In-state $4,984. / Out-of-state $11,011. **Room & Board:** $8,940. **Fees:** $442. **Books and Supplies:** $654.

ADMISSIONS INFORMATION
Application Fee: $50. **Priority Application Deadline:** 7/1. **Regular Application Deadline:** 7/15. **Regular Notification:** Rolling. **Transfer Students Accepted?** Yes. **Transfer Policy:** Varies by department.
Required Admission Factors: Transcript.
Other Admission Factors: 2.6
Program-Specific Admission Factors: Varies by department

EMPLOYMENT INFORMATION
Placement Office Available? Yes.

WAYNE STATE UNIVERSITY
College of Urban, Labor, & Metropolitan Affairs

Address: 656 West Kirby Street, Detroit, MI 48202

INSTITUTIONAL INFORMATION
Public/Private: Public. **Total Faculty:** 31. **Students in Parent Institution:** 30,408.

STUDENT INFORMATION
Total Students in Program: 9,575. **% Full-time:** 29. **% Female:** 57.

RESEARCH FACILITIES
Research Facilities: Karmano's Cancer Institute.

EXPENSES/FINANCIAL AID
Annual Tuition: In-state $4,984. / Out-of-state $11,011. **Room & Board:** $8,940. **Fees:** $442. **Books and Supplies:** $654.

ADMISSIONS INFORMATION
Application Fee: $20. **Transfer Students Accepted?** No.
Required Admission Factors: Transcript.

EMPLOYMENT INFORMATION
Placement Office Available? Yes.

WAYNE STATE UNIVERSITY
School of Social Work

Address: 4756 Cass, Thompson Home, Detroit, MI 48202
Admissions Phone: 313-577-4409 · **Admissions Fax:** 313-577-4266
Admissions E-mail: ac2027@wayne.edu · **Web Address:** www.socialwork.wayne.edu

INSTITUTIONAL INFORMATION
Public/Private: Public. **Evening Classes Available?** Yes. **Total Faculty:** 102. **Students in Parent Institution:** 33,091.

STUDENT INFORMATION
Total Students in Program: 509. **% Full-time:** 66. **% Female:** 1065.

RESEARCH FACILITIES
Research Facilities: Karmano's Cancer Institute.

EXPENSES/FINANCIAL AID
Annual Tuition: In-state $10,475. / Out-of-state $20,799. **Room & Board:** $8,940. **Fees:** $432. **Books and Supplies:** $700. **Grants Range From:** $500-$2,000. **Loans Range From:** $500-$500. **Types of Aid Available:** loans, scholarships.

ADMISSIONS INFORMATION
Priority Application Deadline: 1/31. **Regular Application Deadline:** 2/28. **Regular Notification:** Rolling. **Transfer Students Accepted?** Yes. **Transfer Policy:** Good standing at previous institution required of transfer applicants. **Number of Applications Received:** 500. **% of Applicants Accepted:** 54. **% Accepted Who Enrolled:** 94. **Average GPA:** 3.1.

Required Admission Factors: Essays/personal statement, letters of recommendation, transcript.
Other Admission Factors: Minimum 2.6 GPA required; minimum 3.0 GPA preferred.

EMPLOYMENT INFORMATION

Placement Office Available? Yes. **% Employed Within 6 Months:** 100. **% of master's grads employed in their field upon graduation:** 100. **Rate of placement:** 100%. **Average starting salary:** $34,000.

WEBER STATE UNIVERSITY
College of Social & Behavioral Sciences

Address: 1137 University Circle, Ogden, UT 84408-1137
Admissions Phone: 801-626-6743 · **Admissions Fax:** 801-626-6747
Admissions E-mail: kgillespie@weber.edu

INSTITUTIONAL INFORMATION

Public/Private: Public. **Total Faculty:** 11. **% Faculty Female:** 9. **% Faculty Part-time:** 36. **Students in Parent Institution:** 16,051.

STUDENT INFORMATION

Total Students in Program: 197. **% Full-time:** 31. **% Female:** 58.

EXPENSES/FINANCIAL AID

Fees: $448. **Books and Supplies:** $900.

ADMISSIONS INFORMATION

Application Fee: $15. **Priority Application Deadline:** 2/15. **Regular Notification:** Rolling. **Transfer Students Accepted?** No.
Required Admission Factors: Essays/personal statement, GRE, transcript.
Other Admission Factors: Minimum GRE score in the 60th percentile, minimum 3.0 GPA, experience, and progression in the criminal justice field required.

EMPLOYMENT INFORMATION

Placement Office Available? Yes. **Rate of placement:** 80%.

WEBSTER UNIVERSITY
School of Communication

Address: 470 East Lockwood, St. Louis, MO 63119-3194
Admissions Phone: 314-968-7100 · **Admissions Fax:** 314-968-7116

INSTITUTIONAL INFORMATION

Public/Private: Private (nonprofit). **Evening Classes Available?** Yes. **Student/Faculty Ratio:** 27:1. **Students in Parent Institution:** 17,279.

STUDENT INFORMATION

Total Students in Program: 12,632. **% Full-time:** 29. **% Female:** 53.

EXPENSES/FINANCIAL AID

Annual Tuition: $6,894. **Grants Range From:** $200-$5,000. **Loans Range From:** $200-$18,500. **% Receiving Financial Aid:** 42. **% Receiving Scholarships/Grants:** 2. **% Receiving Loans:** 98. **Average student debt, upon graduation:** $15,945.

ADMISSIONS INFORMATION

Application Fee: $25. **Regular Notification:** Rolling. **Transfer Students Accepted?** Yes. **Number of Applications Received:** 128. **% of Applicants Accepted:** 82. **% Accepted Who Enrolled:** 92.
Required Admission Factors: Interview, transcript.
Other Admission Factors: Background in media and undergraduate media courses required. Students must meet with an advisor prior to enrollment.

EMPLOYMENT INFORMATION

Placement Office Available? Yes. **% Employed Within 6 Months:** 78. **% of master's grads employed in their field upon graduation:** 83. **Rate of placement:** 94%. **Average starting salary:** $40,000.

WEBSTER UNIVERSITY
College of Arts & Sciences

Address: 470 East Lockwood, St. Louis, MO 63119-3194
Admissions Phone: 314-968-7100 · **Admissions Fax:** 314-968-7116

INSTITUTIONAL INFORMATION

Public/Private: Private (nonprofit). **Student/Faculty Ratio:** 16:1. **Students in Parent Institution:** 17,279.

STUDENT INFORMATION

Total Students in Program: 12,632. **% Full-time:** 29. **% Female:** 53.

EXPENSES/FINANCIAL AID

Annual Tuition: $6,894. **Grants Range From:** $200-$5,000. **Loans Range From:** $200-$18,500. **% Receiving Financial Aid:** 42. **% Receiving Scholarships/Grants:** 2. **% Receiving Loans:** 98. **Average student debt, upon graduation:** $15,945

ADMISSIONS INFORMATION

Application Fee: $25. **Transfer Students Accepted?** No. **Number of Applications Received:** 434. **% of Applicants Accepted:** 93. **% Accepted Who Enrolled:** 99.
Required Admission Factors: Interview, transcript.

EMPLOYMENT INFORMATION

Placement Office Available? Yes. **% Employed Within 6 Months:** 87. **% of master's grads employed in their field upon graduation:** 91. **Rate of placement:** 94%. **Average starting salary:** $30,000.

WEBSTER UNIVERSITY
College of Fine Arts

Address: 470 East Lockwood, St. Louis, MO 63119-3194
Admissions Phone: 314-968-7100 · **Admissions Fax:** 314-968-7116

INSTITUTIONAL INFORMATION

Public/Private: Private (nonprofit). **Evening Classes Available?** Yes. **Student/Faculty Ratio:** 15:1. **Students in Parent Institution:** 17,279.

STUDENT INFORMATION

Total Students in Program: 12,632. **% Full-time:** 29. **% Female:** 53.

EXPENSES/FINANCIAL AID

Annual Tuition: $6,894. **Grants Range From:** $200-$5,000. **Loans Range From:** $200-$18,500. **% Receiving Financial Aid:** 42. **% Receiving Scholarships/Grants:** 2. **% Receiving Loans:** 98. **Average student debt, upon graduation:** $15,945

ADMISSIONS INFORMATION

Application Fee: $25. **Regular Notification:** Rolling. **Transfer Students Accepted?** Yes. **Number of Applications Received:** 19. **% of Applicants Accepted:** 89. **% Accepted Who Enrolled:** 82.
Required Admission Factors: Essays/personal statement, interview, letters of recommendation, transcript.

EMPLOYMENT INFORMATION

Placement Office Available? Yes. **% Employed Within 6 Months:** 95. **Rate of placement:** 94%.

WEST CHESTER UNIVERSITY OF PENNSYLVANIA
College of Arts & Sciences

Address: High Street and University Avenue, West Chester, PA 19383
Admissions Phone: 610-436-2943 · **Admissions Fax:** 610-436-2763
Admissions E-mail: gradstudy@wcupa.edu · **Web Address:** www.wcupa.edu

INSTITUTIONAL INFORMATION
Public/Private: Public. **Evening Classes Available?** Yes. **Students in Parent Institution:** 12,152.

STUDENT INFORMATION
Total Students in Program: 1,950. **% Full-time:** 20. **% Female:** 68.

RESEARCH FACILITIES
Research Facilities: Center for the Study of Connectivity and Databases, Center for Procurement Assistance.

EXPENSES/FINANCIAL AID
Annual Tuition: In-state $5,518 / Out-of-state $8,830. **Room & Board:** $5,360. **Fees:** $1,002. **Books and Supplies:** $800. **Types of Aid Available:** Graduate assistantships, loans. **Number of Teaching/Research Assistantships Granted Each Year:** 65. **Assistantship Compensation Includes:** Full tuition remission, partial tuition remission, salary/stipend. **Average Salary Stipend:** $5,000.

ADMISSIONS INFORMATION
Application Fee: $35. **Regular Application Deadline:** 10/15. **Regular Notification:** Rolling. **Transfer Students Accepted?** Yes. **Transfer Policy:** Transfer applicants must apply for transfer of credit.
Required Admission Factors: Letters of recommendation, transcript.
Other Admission Factors: Minimum 2.5 GPA required.
Program-Specific Admission Factors: Writing sample required of English program applicants. 2 letters of recommendation and statement of professional goals required of history program applicants. 3 letters of recommendation and GRE subject exam required of psychology program applicants.

EMPLOYMENT INFORMATION
Placement Office Available? Yes.

WEST CHESTER UNIVERSITY OF PENNSYLVANIA
School of Music

Address: High Street and University Avenue, West Chester, PA 19383
Admissions Phone: 610-436-2943 · **Admissions Fax:** 610-436-2763
Admissions E-mail: gradstudy@wcupa.edu

INSTITUTIONAL INFORMATION
Public/Private: Public. **Evening Classes Available?** Yes. **Students in Parent Institution:** 12,152.

STUDENT INFORMATION
Total Students in Program: 1,950. **% Full-time:** 20. **% Female:** 68.

RESEARCH FACILITIES
Research Facilities: Center for the Study of Connectivity and Databases, Center for Procurement Assistance.

EXPENSES/FINANCIAL AID
Annual Tuition: In-state $3,780 / Out-of-state $6,610. **Fees:** $660. **Books and Supplies:** $650.

ADMISSIONS INFORMATION
Application Fee: $25. **Regular Notification:** Rolling. **Transfer Students Accepted?** No. **Transfer Policy:** Transfer applicants must apply for transfer of credit.
Required Admission Factors: Essays/personal statement, transcript.
Recommended Admission Factors:

Other Admission Factors: Minimum 2.5 GPA required.
Program-Specific Admission Factors: Interview and audition required of music theory program applicants.

EMPLOYMENT INFORMATION
Placement Office Available? Yes.

WEST TEXAS A&M UNIVERSITY
College of Fine Arts & Humanities

Address: 2501 Fourth Avenue, Canyon, TX 79016
Admissions Phone: 806-651-2730 · **Admissions Fax:** 806-651-2733
Admissions E-mail: vnelson@mail.wtamu.edu ·

INSTITUTIONAL INFORMATION
Public/Private: Public. **Evening Classes Available?** Yes. **Students in Parent Institution:** 6,348.

STUDENT INFORMATION
Total Students in Program: 808. **% Full-time:** 24. **% Female:** 56.

RESEARCH FACILITIES
Research Facilities: Kilgore Research Center, Alternative Energy Institute, Dryland Agriculture Institute, Texas Engingeering Experiment Station.

EXPENSES/FINANCIAL AID
Annual Tuition: In-state $2,214 / Out-of-state $7,398. **Fees:** $1,062. **Books and Supplies:** $300. **Grants Range From:** $200-$1,000. **Loans Range From:** $8,500-$18,500. **% Receiving Scholarships/Grants:** 62. **% Receiving Loans:** 58. **Average Salary Stipend:** $6,500.

ADMISSIONS INFORMATION
Regular Notification: Rolling. **Transfer Students Accepted?** Yes. **Transfer Policy:** Maximum 1/3 of total credit hours may be transferred. **Number of Applications Received:** 14.
Required Admission Factors: GRE, transcript.
Other Admission Factors: Minimum combined GRE score of 650 (verbal plus quantitative or analytical) required.

EMPLOYMENT INFORMATION
Placement Office Available? Yes. **Rate of placement:** 80%.

WEST VIRGINIA UNIVERSITY
College of Creative Arts

Address: PO Box 6009
Admissions & Records, Morgantown, WV 26506-6009
Admissions Phone: 304-293-4841 · **Admissions Fax:** 304-293-3550
Admissions E-mail: wwinsor@wvu.edu · **Web Address:** http://www.wvu.edu/~ccarts

INSTITUTIONAL INFORMATION
Public/Private: Public. **Students in Parent Institution:** 21,987.

STUDENT INFORMATION
Total Students in Program: 5,307. **% Full-time:** 46. **% Female:** 61.

RESEARCH FACILITIES
Research Facilities: More than 30 institutional research centers.

EXPENSES/FINANCIAL AID
Annual Tuition: In-state $3,242. / Out-of-state $9,106. **Books and Supplies:** $720.

ADMISSIONS INFORMATION
Application Fee: $45. **Regular Notification:** Rolling. **Transfer Students Accepted?** Yes. **Number of Applications Received:** 111. **% of Applicants Accepted:** 22.
Required Admission Factors: Transcript.

Program-Specific Admission Factors: Minimum 3.0 GPA required of doctoral program applicants. Minimum 2.75 GPA required of art program applicants. Minimum 2.5 GPA and portfolio required of theater program applicants. 3 letters of recommendation required of art and theater program applications.

EMPLOYMENT INFORMATION

Placement Office Available? Yes. **Rate of placement:** 96%.

WEST VIRGINIA UNIVERSITY
Eberly College of Arts & Sciences

Address: PO Box 6286, Graduation Records, Morgantown, WV 26506-6286
Admissions Phone: 304-293-2505 · **Admissions Fax:** 304-293-6858
Admissions E-mail: fred.king@mail.wvu.edu · **Web Address:** www.as.wvu.edu/graduate

INSTITUTIONAL INFORMATION

Public/Private: Public. **Students in Parent Institution:** 21,987.

STUDENT INFORMATION

Total Students in Program: 5,307. **% Full-time:** 46. **% Female:** 61.

RESEARCH FACILITIES

Research Facilities: More than 30 institutional research centers.

EXPENSES/FINANCIAL AID

Annual Tuition: In-state $3,242 / Out-of-state $9,106. **Books and Supplies:** $720.

ADMISSIONS INFORMATION

Application Fee: $55. **Regular Application Deadline:** 8/4. **Regular Notification:** Rolling. **Transfer Students Accepted?** Yes. **Average GRE Verbal:** 469. **Average GRE Quantitative:** 602. **Average GRE Analytical:** 560. **Required Admission Factors:** Transcript.

EMPLOYMENT INFORMATION

Placement Office Available? Yes. **% Employed Within 6 Months:** 40. **% of masters/doctoral grads employed in their field upon graduation:** 30/60. **Rate of placement:** 96%. **Average starting salary:** $80,000.

WEST VIRGINIA UNIVERSITY
Perley Isaac Reed School of Journalism

Address: PO Box 6009, Admissions & Records, Morgantown, WV 26506-6009
Admissions Phone: 304-293-3505 · **Admissions Fax:** 304-293-3072
Admissions E-mail: kurt.schimmel@mail.wvu.edu
Web Address: http://www.wvu.edu/~journals/

INSTITUTIONAL INFORMATION

Public/Private: Public. **Students in Parent Institution:** 21,987.

STUDENT INFORMATION

Total Students in Program: 5,307. **% Full-time:** 46. **% Female:** 61.

RESEARCH FACILITIES

Research Facilities: More than 30 institutional research centers.

EXPENSES/FINANCIAL AID

Annual Tuition: In-state $3,242. / Out-of-state $9,106. **Books and Supplies:** $720.

ADMISSIONS INFORMATION

Application Fee: $45. **Regular Notification:** Rolling. **Transfer Students Accepted?** Yes. **Number of Applications Received:** 32. **% of Applicants Accepted:** 53.
Required Admission Factors: GRE, transcript.
Other Admission Factors: Minimum 3.0 GPA and writing samples required.

EMPLOYMENT INFORMATION

Placement Office Available? Yes. **Rate of placement:** 96%.

WESTERN CAROLINA UNIVERSITY
College of Arts & Sciences

Address: Cullowhee, NC 28723
Admissions Phone: 828-227-7398 · **Admissions Fax:** 828-227-7480
Admissions E-mail: kowen@wcu.edu

INSTITUTIONAL INFORMATION

Public/Private: Public. **Evening Classes Available?** Yes. **Total Faculty:** 132. **% Faculty Female:** 22. **Student/Faculty Ratio:** 2:1. **Students in Parent Institution:** 6,699.

STUDENT INFORMATION

Total Students in Program: 1,088. **% Full-time:** 37. **% Female:** 66.

RESEARCH FACILITIES

Research Facilities: Highlands Biological Station, Mountain Aquaculture Center, Mountain Research Center, Developmental Evaluation Center.

EXPENSES/FINANCIAL AID

Annual Tuition: In-state $1,084. / Out-of-state $8,354. **Room & Board:** $6,174. **Fees:** $1,171. **Books and Supplies:** $800. **Grants Range From:** $500-$20,000. **Loans Range From:** $500-$17,920. **% Receiving Scholarships/Grants:** 34. **% Receiving Loans:** 56. **% Receiving Assistantships:** 54.

ADMISSIONS INFORMATION

Application Fee: $35. **Regular Notification:** Rolling. **Transfer Students Accepted?** Yes. **Transfer Policy:** Maximum 6 credit hours with a minimum grade of B may be transferred. **Number of Applications Received:** 115. **% of Applicants Accepted:** 76. **% Accepted Who Enrolled:** 51. **Average GPA:** 3.0. **Average GRE Verbal:** 484. **Average GRE Quantitative:** 501. **Average GRE Analytical:** 537.
Required Admission Factors: Essays/personal statement, GRE, letters of recommendation, transcript.
Other Admission Factors: Minimum grade average of B required.

EMPLOYMENT INFORMATION

Placement Office Available? Yes.

WESTERN CAROLINA UNIVERSITY
College of Applied Sciences

Address: Cullowhee, NC 28723
Admissions Phone: 828-227-7398 · **Admissions Fax:** 828-227-7480
Admissions E-mail: kowen@wcu.edu

INSTITUTIONAL INFORMATION

Public/Private: Public. **Evening Classes Available?** Yes. **Total Faculty:** 38. **% Faculty Female:** 66. **Student/Faculty Ratio:** 3:1. **Students in Parent Institution:** 6,699.

STUDENT INFORMATION

Total Students in Program: 1,088. **% Full-time:** 37. **% Female:** 66.

RESEARCH FACILITIES

Research Facilities: Highlands Biological Station, Mountain Aquaculture Center, Mountain Research Center, Developmental Evaluation Center.

EXPENSES/FINANCIAL AID

Annual Tuition: In-state $1,084. / Out-of-state $8,354. **Room & Board:** $6,174. **Fees:** $1,171. **Books and Supplies:** $800. **Grants Range From:** $500-$20,000. **Loans Range From:** $500-$17,920. **% Receiving Scholarships/Grants:** 34. **% Receiving Loans:** 56. **% Receiving Assistantships:** 54.

ADMISSIONS INFORMATION

Application Fee: $35. **Regular Notification:** Rolling. **Transfer Students Accepted?** Yes. **Transfer Policy:** Maximum 6 semester hours with a minimum grade of B may be transferred. **Number of Applications Received:** 109. **% of Applicants Accepted:** 66. **% Accepted Who Enrolled:** 33. **Average GPA:** 3.0. **Average GRE Verbal:** 484. **Average GRE Quantitative:** 501. **Average GRE Analytical:** 537.

Required Admission Factors: Essays/personal statement, GRE, letters of recommendation, transcript.

Program-Specific Admission Factors: Minimum 8 semester hours each of human anatomy, physiology chemistry, and general physics, 6 semester hours of social sciences, and 3 semester hours of statistics required of physical therapy program applicants.

EMPLOYMENT INFORMATION

Placement Office Available? Yes.

WESTERN ILLINOIS UNIVERSITY
College of Arts & Sciences

Address: 1 University Circle, Macomb, IL 61455
Admissions Phone: 309-298-1806 · **Admissions Fax:** 309-298-2345
Admissions E-mail: Grad-Office@wiu.edu · **Web Address:** www.wiu.edu/grad

INSTITUTIONAL INFORMATION

Public/Private: Public. **Evening Classes Available?** Yes. **Total Faculty:** 408. **% Faculty Female:** 30. **% Faculty Part-time:** 4. **Student/Faculty Ratio:** 17:1. **Students in Parent Institution:** 13,469.

PROGRAMS

Masters offered in: College student counseling and personnel services; communication disorders; computer and information sciences; counselor education/school counseling and guidance services; drama and dramatics/theater arts; education leadership and administration; educational/instructional media design; elementary education and teaching; gerontology; health teacher education; manufacturing technology/technician; mathematics; music history, literature, and theory; music performance; music theory and composition; physical education teaching and coaching; radio and television; reading teacher education; secondary education and teaching; social and philosophical foundations of education; special education.

STUDENT INFORMATION

Total Students in Program: 2,442. **% Full-time:** 35. **% Female:** 62.

RESEARCH FACILITIES

Research Facilities: Alice Kibbe Life Science Station, Frank J. Horn Field Campus, aquatic studies link with the John G. Shield Aquarium in Chicago (where research and teaching are conducted).

EXPENSES/FINANCIAL AID

Annual Tuition: In-state $3,450. / Out-of-state $6,900. **Room & Board:** $5,366. **Fees:** $1,270. **Books and Supplies:** $510. **Grants Range From:** $50-$8,000. **Loans Range From:** $500-$15,000. **% Receiving Financial Aid:** 44. **% Receiving Scholarships/Grants:** 51. **% Receiving Loans:** 34. **% Receiving Assistantships:** 33. **% Receiving Other Aid (employment):** 11. **Types of Aid Available:** Graduate assistantships, institutional work-study, loans, scholarships. **Average student debt, upon graduation:** $13,800. **Number of Teaching/Research Assistantships Granted Each Year:** 590. **Assistantship Compensation Includes:** Full tuition remission, salary/stipend. **Average Salary Stipend:** $5,600.

ADMISSIONS INFORMATION

Application Fee: $30. **Regular Application Deadline:** 8/1. **Regular Notification:** Rolling. **Transfer Students Accepted?** Yes. **Number of Applications Received:** 1,681. **% of Applicants Accepted:** 83. **% Accepted Who Enrolled:** 47.

Required Admission Factors: Transcript.

Other Admission Factors: Cumulative GPA for undergraduate work of at least 2.5 or have a 2.75 or higher average for last 2 years of undergraduate work **Program-Specific Admission Factors:** For biology: GPA of 2.70 for undergrad work or 3.0 or higher for last 2 years of undergrad work. For English: GPA of 2.75 overall and 3.0 in English courses. For history: cumulative GPA of 2.75 or 3.0 for last 2 years of undergrad work.

EMPLOYMENT INFORMATION

Placement Office Available? Yes.

WESTERN ILLINOIS UNIVERSITY
College of Fine Arts & Communication

Address: 1 University Circle, Macomb, IL 61455
Admissions Phone: 309-298-1806 · **Admissions Fax:** 309-298-2345
Admissions E-mail: Grad-Office@wiu.edu · **Web Address:** www.wiu.edu/grad

INSTITUTIONAL INFORMATION

Public/Private: Public. **Students in Parent Institution:** 13,089.

PROGRAMS

Masters offered in: Communication disorders; drama and dramatics/theater arts; music history, literature, and theory; music performance; music theory and composition; radio and television.

STUDENT INFORMATION

Total Students in Program: 2,437. **% Full-time:** 31. **% Female:** 65.

RESEARCH FACILITIES

Research Facilities: Alice Kibbe Life Science Station, Frank J. Horn Field Campus, aquatic studies link with the John G. Shield Aquarium in Chicago (where research and teaching are conducted).

EXPENSES/FINANCIAL AID

Annual Tuition: In-state $2,588. / Out-of-state $5,175. **Room & Board:** $5,366. **Fees:** $649. **Books and Supplies:** $500. **Types of Aid Available:** Graduate assistantships, institutional work-study, loans. **Assistantship Compensation Includes:** Full tuition remission, salary/stipend. **Average Salary Stipend:** $5,864.

ADMISSIONS INFORMATION

Transfer Students Accepted? No.

EMPLOYMENT INFORMATION

Placement Office Available? Yes.

WESTERN KENTUCKY UNIVERSITY
Potter College of Arts, Humanities, & Social Sciences

Address: One Big Red Way, Bowling Green, KY 42101-3576
Admissions Phone: 270-745-2446 · **Admissions Fax:** 270-745-6950
Admissions E-mail: elmer.gray@wku.edu

INSTITUTIONAL INFORMATION

Public/Private: Public. **Students in Parent Institution:** 15,479.

STUDENT INFORMATION

Total Students in Program: 2,244. **% Full-time:** 22. **% Female:** 72.

RESEARCH FACILITIES

Research Facilities: Applied Research and Technology Program of Distinction, Karst Geology—Mammoth Cave.

EXPENSES/FINANCIAL AID

Annual Tuition: $2,734. **Room & Board:** $3,940. **Books and Supplies:** $400. **Grants Range From:** $110-$10,500. **Loans Range From:** $100-

$12,500. **% Receiving Financial Aid:** 32. **% Receiving Scholarships/Grants:** 39. **% Receiving Loans:** 56. **Average student debt, upon graduation:** $12,268. **Number of Teaching/Research Assistantships Granted Each Year:** 30. **Average Salary Stipend:** $6,000.

ADMISSIONS INFORMATION

Application Fee: $30. **Regular Notification:** Rolling. **Transfer Students Accepted?** Yes. **Transfer Policy:** Good standing at previous school required of transfer applicants. **Number of Applications Received:** 105. **% of Applicants Accepted:** 62. **% Accepted Who Enrolled:** 65. **Average GPA:** 3.24. **Average GRE Verbal:** 482. **Average GRE Quantitative:** 510. **Average GRE Analytical:** 556.
Required Admission Factors: GRE, transcript.
Other Admission Factors: Minimum score of 3300 (GRE times GPA) required.

EMPLOYMENT INFORMATION

Placement Office Available? Yes. **Rate of placement:** 85%.

WESTERN MICHIGAN UNIVERSITY
College of Arts & Sciences

Address: 1903 West Michigan Ave, Kalamazoo, MI 49008
Admissions Phone: 269-387-2000 · **Admissions Fax:** 269-387-2096
Admissions E-mail: paula.boodt@wmich.edu · **Web Address:** www.wmich.edu

INSTITUTIONAL INFORMATION

Public/Private: Public. **Evening Classes Available?** Yes. **Total Faculty:** 626. **% Faculty Female:** 39. **% Faculty Part-time:** 30. **Students in Parent Institution:** 29,178.

PROGRAMS

Masters offered in: Anthropology, applied economics, applied mathematics, biological and biomedical sciences, chemistry, clinical psychology, communications studies/speech communication and rhetoric, counseling psychology, creative writing, English language and literature, geography, geology/earth science, history, mathematics, medieval and renaissance studies, physical sciences, physics, political science and government, public administration and services, public administration, religion/religious studies, social work, sociology, Spanish language and literature, statistics. **Doctorate offered in:** Anthropology, applied economics, biological and biomedical sciences, clinical psychology, counseling psychology, English language and literature, experimental psychology, geology/earth science, history, mathematics.

STUDENT INFORMATION

Total Students in Program: 1,308. **% Full-time:** 100. **% Female:** 54. **% Minority:** 11. **% International:** 19.

RESEARCH FACILITIES

Research Facilities: Medieval Institute, Center for the Study of Ethics in Society, Geographic Information Systems, Human Performance Institute, Paper and Printing Pilot Plants, Non-wood Fibers Center, Environmental Research Center, Biological Imaging Center.

EXPENSES/FINANCIAL AID

Annual Tuition: In-state $4,920. / Out-of-state $12,083. **Room & Board (On/Off Campus):** $6,128/$6,472. **Fees:** $602. **Books and Supplies:** $1,340. **Grants Range From:** $200-$6,000. **Loans Range From:** $200-$8,000. **% Receiving Scholarships/Grants:** 10. **% Receiving Loans:** 35. **% Receiving Assistantships:** 18. **% Receiving Other Aid (12% work):** 12. **Types of Aid Available:** Fellowships, graduate assistantships, grants, institutional work-study, loans, scholarships.

ADMISSIONS INFORMATION

Application Fee: $25. **Regular Application Deadline:** 7/1. **Regular Notification:** Rolling. **Transfer Students Accepted?** Yes. **Number of Applications Received:** 2,214. **% of Applicants Accepted:** 47. **% Accepted Who Enrolled:** 25. **Average GPA:** 3.0.
Required Admission Factors: Transcript.

WESTERN MICHIGAN UNIVERSITY
College of Fine Arts

Address: 1903 West Michigan Ave, Kalamazoo, MI 49008
Admissions Phone: 269-387-2000 · **Admissions Fax:** 269-387-2096
Admissions E-mail: paula.boodt@wmich.edu · **Web Address:** www.wmich.edu

INSTITUTIONAL INFORMATION

Public/Private: Public. **Evening Classes Available?** Yes. **Total Faculty:** 135. **% Faculty Female:** 44. **% Faculty Part-time:** 35. **Students in Parent Institution:** 29,178.

PROGRAMS

Masters offered in: Fine/studio arts; music.

STUDENT INFORMATION

Total Students in Program: 88. **% Full-time:** 70. **% Female:** 53. **% Minority:** 5. **% International:** 17.

RESEARCH FACILITIES

Research Facilities: Medieval Institute, Center for the Study of Ethics in Society, Geographic Information Systems, Human Performance Institute, Paper and Printing Pilot Plants, Non-wood Fibers Center, Environmental Research Center, Biological Imaging Center.

EXPENSES/FINANCIAL AID

Annual Tuition: In-state $4,920. / Out-of-state $12,083. **Room & Board (On/Off Campus):** $6,128/$6,472. **Fees:** $602. **Books and Supplies:** $1,340. **Grants Range From:** $500-$6,000. **Loans Range From:** $200-$8,000. **% Receiving Scholarships/Grants:** 10. **% Receiving Loans:** 35. **% Receiving Assistantships:** 18. **% Receiving Other Aid (12% work):** 12. **Types of Aid Available:** Fellowships, graduate assistantships, grants, institutional work-study, loans, scholarships.

ADMISSIONS INFORMATION

Application Fee: $25. **Regular Application Deadline:** 7/1. **Transfer Students Accepted?** Yes. **Transfer Policy:** All official transcripts must be presented. **Number of Applications Received:** 182. **% of Applicants Accepted:** 55. **% Accepted Who Enrolled:** 31. **Average GPA:** 3.0.
Required Admission Factors: Transcript.
Other Admission Factors: Minimum 3.0 GPA required.

WESTERN OREGON UNIVERSITY
School of Liberal Arts & Sciences

Address: 345 North Monmouth Avenue, Monmouth, OR 97361
Admissions Phone: 503-838-8211 · **Admissions Fax:** 503-838-8067
Admissions E-mail: marshaa@wou.edu

INSTITUTIONAL INFORMATION

Public/Private: Public. **Evening Classes Available?** Yes. **Student/Faculty Ratio:** 6:1. **Students in Parent Institution:** 4,225.

STUDENT INFORMATION

Total Students in Program: 316. **% Full-time:** 35. **% Female:** 69.

RESEARCH FACILITIES

Research Facilities: Educational Evaluation Center, Regional Resource Center on Deafness, Teaching Research Center.

EXPENSES/FINANCIAL AID

Annual Tuition: In-state $6,147. / Out-of-state $10,848. **Books and Supplies:** $900. **Grants Range From:** $500-$5,300. **Loans Range From:** $3,000-$18,500. **% Receiving Scholarships/Grants:** 1. **% Receiving Loans:** 75. **% Receiving Assistantships:** 7. **Number of Teaching/Research Assistantships Granted Each Year:** 2. **Average Salary Stipend:** $676.

ADMISSIONS INFORMATION

Application Fee: $50. **Regular Notification:** Rolling. **Transfer Students Accepted?** Yes. **Transfer Policy:** Maximum 15 quarter hours may be transferred. **Average GPA:** 3.06. **Average GRE Verbal:** 290. **Average GRE Quantitative:** 290. **Average GRE Analytical:** 300.
Required Admission Factors: Transcript.
Other Admission Factors: Minimum MAT score of 30 or minimum average GRE score of 450 in Analytical, Quantitative, and Verbal sections or minimum 3.0 GPA in last 90 quarter hours (60 semester hours) required.

EMPLOYMENT INFORMATION

Placement Office Available? Yes. **% of master's grads employed in their field upon graduation:** 100. **Rate of placement:** 98%. **Average starting salary:** $32,000.

WESTERN SEMINARY
Graduate Programs

Address: 5511 Southeast Hawthorne Boulevard, Portland, OR 97215-3399
Admissions Phone: 503-517-1800 or 877-517-1800 · **Admissions Fax:** 503-517-1801
Admissions E-mail: admiss@westernseminary.edu
Web Address: www.westernseminary.edu

INSTITUTIONAL INFORMATION

Public/Private: Private (nonprofit). **Evening Classes Available?** Yes. **Total Faculty:** 77. **% Faculty Part-time:** 69. **Students in Parent Institution:** 626.

PROGRAMS

Masters offered in: Counseling psychology, divinity/ministry (BD, MDiv), missions/missionary studies and missiology, pastoral counseling and specialized ministries, pastoral studies/counseling, psychology, theological and ministerial studies, theology/theological studies, youth ministry. **Doctorate offered in:** Divinity/ministry (BD, MDiv), missions/missionary studies and missiology. **First Professional degree offered in:** Divinity/ministry (BD, MDiv).

STUDENT INFORMATION

Total Students in Program: 626. **% Full-time:** 13. **% Female:** 32. **% Minority:** 27. **% International:** 4.

RESEARCH FACILITIES

Research Facilities: World View Center.

EXPENSES/FINANCIAL AID

Annual Tuition: $7,680. **Books and Supplies:** $350. **Grants Range From:** $100-$2,500. **Loans Range From:** $500-$10,000. **% Receiving Financial Aid:** 25. **Types of Aid Available:** Graduate assistantships, grants, loans, scholarships. church partnerships.

ADMISSIONS INFORMATION

Application Fee: $50. **Regular Application Deadline:** 9/1. **Regular Notification:** Rolling. **Transfer Students Accepted?** Yes. **Number of Applications Received:** 237. **% of Applicants Accepted:** 91. **% Accepted Who Enrolled:** 86. **Average GPA:** 3.0.
Required Admission Factors: Essays/personal statement, letters of recommendation, transcript.
Other Admission Factors: Minimum 2.5 GPA required.
Program-Specific Admission Factors: Minimum 3.0 GPA required of MA program applicants.

EMPLOYMENT INFORMATION

Placement Office Available? Yes. **% Employed Within 6 Months:** 25. **% of masters/doctoral grads employed in their field upon graduation:** 60/100. **Rate of placement:** 90%. **Average starting salary:** $40,000.

WESTERN THEOLOGICAL SEMINARY
Graduate Program

Address: 101 East 13th Street, Holland, MI 49423
Admissions Phone: 616-392-8555 · **Admissions Fax:** 616-392-7717
Admissions E-mail: tim@westernsem.org

INSTITUTIONAL INFORMATION

Public/Private: Private (nonprofit). **Evening Classes Available?** Yes. **Student/Faculty Ratio:** 12:1. **Students in Parent Institution:** 169

STUDENT INFORMATION

Total Students in Program: 70. **% Full-time:** 60. **% Female:** 43.

EXPENSES/FINANCIAL AID

Annual Tuition: $6,448. **Fees:** $60. **Books and Supplies:** $600. **Grants Range From:** $500-$5,500. **Loans Range From:** $2,500-$17,000. **% Receiving Scholarships/Grants:** 90. **% Receiving Loans:** 25.

ADMISSIONS INFORMATION

Application Fee: $30. **Regular Notification:** Rolling. **Transfer Students Accepted?** Yes. **Transfer Policy:** Maximum 66 semester hours may be transferred. **Number of Applications Received:** 108. **% of Applicants Accepted:** 75. **% Accepted Who Enrolled:** 91. **Average GPA:** 3.
Required Admission Factors: Essays/personal statement, interview, letters of recommendation, transcript.

EMPLOYMENT INFORMATION

Placement Office Available? Yes. **% Employed Within 6 Months:** 80. **% of master's/doctoral employed in their field upon graduation:** 80/100. **Rate of placement:** 95%.

WESTERN WASHINGTON UNIVERSITY
College of Fine & Performing Arts

Address: 516 High Street, Bellingham, WA 98225-9037
Admissions Phone: 360-650-3170 · **Admissions Fax:** 360-650-6811
Admissions E-mail: gradschl@wwu.edu · **Web Address:** www.wwu.edu

INSTITUTIONAL INFORMATION

Public/Private: Public. **Students in Parent Institution:** 12,940.

PROGRAMS

Masters offered in: Art/art studies; drama and dramatics/theater arts; music/music and performing arts studies.

STUDENT INFORMATION

Total Students in Program: 13. **% Full-time:** 92. **% Female:** 85.

RESEARCH FACILITIES

Research Facilities: Shannon Point Marine Center.

EXPENSES/FINANCIAL AID

Annual Tuition: In-state $5,310. / Out-of-state $16,070. **Room & Board (On/Off Campus):** $5,945/$7,200. **Fees:** $567. **Books and Supplies:** $1,500. **Grants Range From:** $100-$5,000. **Loans Range From:** $100-$18,500. **% Receiving Scholarships/Grants:** 35. **% Receiving Loans:** 87. **% Receiving Assistantships:** 29. **Types of Aid Available:** Graduate assistantships, institutional work-study, loans, scholarships. **Number of Teaching/Research Assistantships Granted Each Year:** 6. **Assistantship Compensation Includes:** Partial tuition remission, salary/stipend. **Average Salary Stipend:** $8,937.

ADMISSIONS INFORMATION

Application Fee: $35. **Regular Application Deadline:** 6/1. **Regular Notification:** Rolling. **Transfer Students Accepted?** Yes. **Transfer Policy:** Transfer credits must be from an accredited institution with a grade of B, 3.0, or better, taken no more than 3 years prior to the applicant's WWU admission date. **Number of Applications Received:** 12. **% of Applicants Accepted:** 83. **% Accepted Who Enrolled:** 90. **Average GPA:** 3.0.

Required Admission Factors: GMAT, letters of recommendation, transcript. TOEFL for non-native English speaking applicants.
Recommended Admission Factors: GRE subject exam(s) in psychology.
Other Admission Factors: Minimum 3.0 GPA in last 60 semester/90 quarter credit hours required.
Program-Specific Admission Factors: Interview or audition required of theater program applicants. Audition required for music performance applicants.

EMPLOYMENT INFORMATION

Placement Office Available? Yes. **% Employed Within 6 Months:** 75. **% of master's grads employed in their field upon graduation:** 70. **Rate of placement:** 87%. **Average starting salary:** $40,000.

WESTERN WASHINGTON UNIVERSITY
College of Humanities and Social Sciences

Address: 516 High Street, Bellingham, WA 98225
Admissions Phone: 360-650-3170 · **Admissions Fax:** 360-650-6811
Admissions E-mail: gradschool@wwu.edu · **Web Address:** www.wwu.edu/gradschool

INSTITUTIONAL INFORMATION

Public/Private: Public. **Students in Parent Institution:** 12,940.

STUDENT INFORMATION

Total Students in Program: 24. **% Full-time:** 817. **% Female:** 604. **% Minority:** 33. **% International:** 29.

RESEARCH FACILITIES

Research Facilities: Shannon Point Marine Research Center.

EXPENSES/FINANCIAL AID

Annual Tuition: In-state $5,310. / Out-of-state $16,170. **Fees:** $567. **Books and Supplies:** $1,200. **Grants Range From:** $100-$5,000. **Loans Range From:** $100-$18,500. **Types of Aid Available:** Graduate assistantships, institutional work-study, loans, scholarships. **Number of Teaching/Research Assistantships Granted Each Year:** 62. **Average Salary Stipend:** $8,973.

ADMISSIONS INFORMATION

Application Fee: $35. **Priority Application Deadline:** 1/31. **Regular Application Deadline:** 6/1. **Regular Notification:** Rolling. **Transfer Students Accepted?** Yes. **Transfer Policy:** Same admission requirements as for initial admissions. **Number of Applications Received:** 371. **% of Applicants Accepted:** 54. **% Accepted Who Enrolled:** 63. **Average GPA:** 3.0.
Required Admission Factors: Essays/personal statement, GRE, letters of recommendation, transcript.
Other Admission Factors: Minimum 3.0 GPA.

EMPLOYMENT INFORMATION

Placement Office Available? Yes. **% Employed Within 6 Months:** 75. **Rate of placement:** 75%. **Average starting salary:** $36,000.

WESTERN WASHINGTON UNIVERSITY
Huxley College of the Environment

Address: 516 High Street, Bellingham, WA 98225-9037
Admissions Phone: 360-650-3170 · **Admissions Fax:** 360-650-6811
Admissions E-mail: gradschool@wwu.edu · **Web Address:** www.wwu.edu/gradschl

INSTITUTIONAL INFORMATION

Public/Private: Public. **Students in Parent Institution:** 12,307.

PROGRAMS

Masters offered in: Biological and physical sciences; education; geography.

STUDENT INFORMATION

Total Students in Program: 76. **% Full-time:** 62. **% Female:** 50. **% Minority:** 3. **% International:** 7.

RESEARCH FACILITIES

Research Facilities: Shannon Point Marine Center.

EXPENSES/FINANCIAL AID

Annual Tuition: In-state $5,133. / Out-of-state $16,070. **Room & Board (On/Off Campus):** $6,000/$7,200. **Fees:** $537. **Books and Supplies:** $1,200. **Grants Range From:** $100-$5,000. **Loans Range From:** $100-$18,500. **Types of Aid Available:** Fellowships, graduate assistantships, grants, institutional work-study, loans, scholarships. **Number of Teaching/Research Assistantships Granted Each Year:** 30 **Assistantship Compensation Includes:** Partial tuition remission, salary/stipend. **Average Salary Stipend:** $8,937.

ADMISSIONS INFORMATION

Application Fee: $35. **Priority Application Deadline:** 1/31. **Regular Application Deadline:** 6/1. **Transfer Students Accepted?** No. **Transfer Policy:** Credit must be from an accredited institution; cannot have been used for other degrees; must be graded with B or better; must be graduate level; cannot be older than 3 years from year of admission. **Number of Applications Received:** 97. **% of Applicants Accepted:** 56. **% Accepted Who Enrolled:** 61. **Average GPA:** 3.0.
Required Admission Factors: Essays/personal statement, GRE, letters of recommendation, transcript.
Other Admission Factors: Minimum 3.0 GPA in last 60 credit hours required.

EMPLOYMENT INFORMATION

Placement Office Available? Yes. **% Employed Within 6 Months:** 50. **% of master's grads employed in their field upon graduation:** 85. **Rate of placement:** 87%. **Average starting salary:** $32,000.

WESTMINSTER SEMINARY CALIFORNIA
Graduate Programs

Address: 1725 Bear Valley Parkway, Escondido, CA 92027
Admissions Phone: 760-480-8474 · **Admissions Fax:** 760-480-0252
Admissions E-mail: info@wscal.edu · **Web Address:** www.wscal.edu

INSTITUTIONAL INFORMATION

Public/Private: Private (nonprofit). **Evening Classes Available?** Yes. **Student/Faculty Ratio:** 10:1. **Students in Parent Institution:** 186

STUDENT INFORMATION

Total Students in Program: 50. **% Full-time:** 64.

EXPENSES/FINANCIAL AID

Annual Tuition: In-state $8,225. / Out-of-state. **Fees:** $20. **Books and Supplies:** $800. **Grants Range From:** $400-$9,000. **Loans Range From:** $2,000-$18,500. **% Receiving Financial Aid:** 66. **% Receiving Scholarships/Grants:** 65. **% Receiving Loans:** 35. **Average student debt, upon graduation:** $19,500.

ADMISSIONS INFORMATION

Application Fee: $30. **Priority Application Deadline:** 5/30. **Regular Application Deadline:** 9/1. **Regular Notification:** Rolling. **Transfer Students Accepted?** Yes. **Transfer Policy:** No transfer credit of languages/placement testing. Only courses in which a grade of C or above was received. Application must include transcript and catalogue of courses. At least 36 hours must be completed at WSC. No transfer credit given for work previously used as basis for awarding of other masters or doctoral degree by another institution. **Number of Applications Received:** 55. **% of Applicants Accepted:** 98. **% Accepted Who Enrolled:** 67. **Average GPA:** 3.14.
Required Admission Factors: Essays/personal statement, letters of recommendation, transcript.

Other Admission Factors: Minimum 2.7 GPA required. May accept lower with probationary status.

WESTMINSTER COLLEGE OF SALT LAKE CITY
School of Arts & Sciences

Address: 1840 South 1300 East, Salt Lake City, UT 84105-3697
Admissions Phone: 801-832-2200 · **Admissions Fax:** 801-832-3101
Admissions E-mail: admispub@westminstercollege.edu
Web Address: www.westminstercollege.edu

INSTITUTIONAL INFORMATION
Public/Private: Private (nonprofit). **Evening Classes Available?** Yes. **Total Faculty:** 11. **% Faculty Female:** 55. **% Faculty Part-time:** 55. **Student/Faculty Ratio:** 14:1. **Students in Parent Institution:** 2,403.

PROGRAMS
Masters offered in: Communications, journalism, and related fields.

STUDENT INFORMATION
Total Students in Program: 88. **% Full-time:** 23. **% Female:** 69.

EXPENSES/FINANCIAL AID
Annual Tuition: $696. **Fees:** $200. **Books and Supplies:** $900. **Grants Range From:** $500-$13,000. **Loans Range From:** $1,000-$18,500. **% Receiving Financial Aid:** 58. **% Receiving Scholarships/Grants:** 12. **% Receiving Loans:** 55. **Types of Aid Available:** Loans.

ADMISSIONS INFORMATION
Application Fee: $30. **Regular Application Deadline:** 8/26. **Regular Notification:** Rolling. **Transfer Students Accepted?** Yes. **Transfer Policy:** Same admission requirements for new applicants. **Number of Applications Received:** 29. **% of Applicants Accepted:** 76. **% Accepted Who Enrolled:** 91. **Average GPA:** 3.3.
Required Admission Factors: Essays/personal statement, transcript.
Other Admission Factors: Minimum 3.0 GPA, resume, and writing sample required.

WESTMINSTER THEOLOGICAL SEMINARY
Graduate Programs

Address: Church Road and Willow Grove Avenue, Glenside, PA 19118
Admissions Phone: 215-887-5511 · **Admissions Fax:** 215-887-5404
Admissions E-mail: admissions@wts.edu · **Web Address:** www.wts.edu

INSTITUTIONAL INFORMATION
Public/Private: Private (nonprofit). **Evening Classes Available?** Yes. **Students in Parent Institution:** 910.

STUDENT INFORMATION
Total Students in Program: 691. **% Full-time:** 44. **% Female:** 13.

EXPENSES/FINANCIAL AID
Annual Tuition: $8,235. **Fees:** $60. **Books and Supplies:** $200. **Grants Range From:** $500-$10,200. **Loans Range From:** $500-$18,500. **% Receiving Scholarships/Grants:** 25. **% Receiving Loans:** 20.

ADMISSIONS INFORMATION
Application Fee: $40. **Priority Application Deadline:** 3/1. **Regular Application Deadline:** 8/30. **Transfer Students Accepted?** Yes. **Number of Applications Received:** 355. **% of Applicants Accepted:** 79. **% Accepted Who Enrolled:** 69. **Average GPA:** 3.0
Required Admission Factors: Essays/personal statement, letters of recommendation, transcript.

Other Admission Factors: Minimum 3.0 GPA required.
Program-Specific Admission Factors: GRE required for PhD.

WESTON JESUIT SCHOOL OF THEOLOGY
Graduate Programs

Address: 3 Phillips Place, Cambridge, MA 02138-3495
Admissions Phone: 617-492-1960 · **Admissions Fax:** 617-492-5833
Admissions E-mail: admissionsinfo@wjst.edu · **Web Address:** www.wjst.edu

INSTITUTIONAL INFORMATION
Public/Private: Private (nonprofit). **Student/Faculty Ratio:** 10:1. **Students in Parent Institution:** 240.

PROGRAMS
Masters offered in: Divinity/ministry (BD, MDiv), theological and ministerial studies, theological studies and religious vocations, theology/theological studies. **Doctorate offered in:** Divinity/ministry (BD, MDiv, theological studies and religious vocations. **First Professional degree offered in:** Divinity/ministry (BD, MDiv), theological studies and religious vocations.

STUDENT INFORMATION
Total Students in Program: 157. **% Full-time:** 92.

RESEARCH FACILITIES
Research Facilities: Member of the Boston Theological Institute.

EXPENSES/FINANCIAL AID
Annual Tuition: $14,444. **Room & Board:** $8,000. **Fees:** $530. **Books and Supplies:** $900. **Grants Range From:** $1,000-$14,444. **Loans Range From:** $1,000-$18,500. **% Receiving Financial Aid:** 60. **% Receiving Scholarships/Grants:** 100. **% Receiving Loans:** 42. **Types of Aid Available:** Graduate assistantships, grants, loans, scholarships. **Average student debt, upon graduation:** $27,000.

ADMISSIONS INFORMATION
Application Fee: $50. **Priority Application Deadline:** 3/15. **Regular Application Deadline:** 8/15. **Regular Notification:** Rolling. **Transfer Students Accepted?** Yes. **Number of Applications Received:** 151. **% of Applicants Accepted:** 58. **Average GPA:** 3.3. **Average GRE Verbal:** 600. **Average GRE Quantitative:** 550. **Average GRE Analytical:** 600. **Average GRE Analytical Writing:** 5.
Required Admission Factors: Essays/personal statement, letters of recommendation, transcript.
Recommended Admission Factors: GRE, interview.
Other Admission Factors: GRE or MAT required if applicant has not completed any graduate course work.

EMPLOYMENT INFORMATION
Placement Office Available? Yes. **% Employed Within 6 Months:** 95. **Rate of placement:** 97%. **Average starting salary:** $28,000.

WHEATON COLLEGE
Graduate School

Address: Graduate Admissions Office, 501 College Avenue, Wheaton, IL 60187
Admissions Phone: 630-752-5195 · **Admissions Fax:** 630-752-5935
Admissions E-mail: gradadm@wheaton.edu · **Web Address:** www.wheatongrad.com

INSTITUTIONAL INFORMATION
Public/Private: Private (nonprofit). **Evening Classes Available?** Yes. **Total Faculty:** 53. **% Faculty Female:** 21. **Student/Faculty Ratio:** 14:1. **Students in Parent Institution:** 2,944.

PROGRAMS

Masters offered in: Archeology, Bible/biblical studies, clinical psychology, history, missions/missionary studies and missiology, multi/interdisciplinary studies, religious education, secondary education and teaching, teaching English as a second or foreign language/ESL language instructor, theological studies and religious vocations, theology/theological studies, youth ministry. **Doctorate offered in:** Bible/Biblical studies, clinical psychology, theology/theological studies.

STUDENT INFORMATION

Total Students in Program: 514. **% Full-time:** 57. **% Female:** 51.

RESEARCH FACILITIES

Research Facilities: Billy Graham Center Archives, Wade Center.

EXPENSES/FINANCIAL AID

Annual Tuition: $464. **Room & Board:** $6,434. **Fees:** $1,250. **Books and Supplies:** $662. **Grants Range From:** $875-$14,154. **Loans Range From:** $1,000-$31,000. **% Receiving Financial Aid:** 31. **% Receiving Scholarships/Grants:** 94. **% Receiving Loans:** 62. **Average student debt, upon graduation:** $27,326. **Number of Teaching/Research Assistantships Granted Each Year:** 10. **Assistantship Compensation Includes:** Salary/stipend.

ADMISSIONS INFORMATION

Application Fee: $30. **Priority Application Deadline:** 3/1. **Regular Application Deadline:** 5/1. **Transfer Students Accepted?** Yes. **Transfer Policy:** Same as all applicants; maximum 25% of degree credit hours may be transferred for master's programs; 30 semester hours may be transferred for PsyD. **Number of Applications Received:** 539. **% of Applicants Accepted:** 63. **Average GPA:** 3.4. **Average GRE Verbal:** 565. **Average GRE Quantitative:** 565. **Average GRE Analytical:** 565.
Required Admission Factors: Essays/personal statement, GRE, letters of recommendation, transcript.
Other Admission Factors: MA minimum 2.75 GPA required.
Program-Specific Admission Factors: PhD minimum 3.5 GPA, PsyD minimum 3.0 GPA

EMPLOYMENT INFORMATION

Placement Office Available? Yes. **% Employed Within 6 Months:** 80. **% of master's grads employed in their field upon graduation:** 80. **Rate of placement:** 80%. **Average starting salary:** $33,000.

WHEELING JESUIT UNIVERSITY
Department of Physical Therapy Program

Address: 316 Washington Avenue, Wheeling, WV 26003
Admissions Phone: 304-243-2068 or 866-243-2068 · **Admissions Fax:** 304-243-2042
Admissions E-mail: wjupt@wju.edu
Web Address: www.wju.edu/academics/department/PT.asp

INSTITUTIONAL INFORMATION

Public/Private: Private (nonprofit). **Student/Faculty Ratio:** 10:1. **Students in Parent Institution:** 1,466.

STUDENT INFORMATION

Total Students in Program: 217. **% Full-time:** 38. **% Female:** 62.

RESEARCH FACILITIES

Research Facilities: NASA's National Technology Transfer Center, NASA's Classroom of the Future, Center for Educational Technologies.

EXPENSES/FINANCIAL AID

Annual Tuition: $7,740. **Room & Board:** $5,880. **Fees:** $145. **Grants Range From:** $300-$9,620. **Loans Range From:** $1,805-$28,500. **% Receiving Scholarships/Grants:** 21. **% Receiving Loans:** 65. **% Receiving Assistantships:** 26.

ADMISSIONS INFORMATION

Application Fee: $25. **Priority Application Deadline:** 1/15. **Regular Application Deadline:** 7/31. **Regular Notification:** Rolling. **Transfer Students Accepted?** No. **Number of Applications Received:** 29. **% of Applicants Accepted:** 79. **% Accepted Who Enrolled:** 70.
Required Admission Factors: Essays/personal statement, GRE, interview, letters of recommendation, transcript.
Other Admission Factors: Minimum 3.0 GPA overall and in math/sciene prerequisites and at 80 hours of observation or volunteer work recommended.

EMPLOYMENT INFORMATION

Placement Office Available? Yes.

WHEELING JESUIT UNIVERSITY
Master of Applied Theology Program

Address: 316 Washington Avenue, Wheeling, WV 26003
Admissions Phone: 304-243-2344 · **Admissions Fax:** 304-243-4441
Admissions E-mail: ccarroll@wju.edu
Web Address: www.wju.edu/academics/departments/theology/main.asp

INSTITUTIONAL INFORMATION

Public/Private: Private (nonprofit). **Evening Classes Available?** Yes. **Total Faculty:** 1. **% Faculty Female:** 100. **% Faculty Part-time:** 100. **Student/Faculty Ratio:** 12:1. **Students in Parent Institution:** 1,699.

PROGRAMS

Masters offered in: Theological and ministerial studies.

STUDENT INFORMATION

Total Students in Program: 12. **% Female:** 67.

RESEARCH FACILITIES

Research Facilities: NASA's National Technology Transfer Center, NASA's Classroom of the Future, Center for Educational Technologies.

EXPENSES/FINANCIAL AID

Annual Tuition: $1,410.

ADMISSIONS INFORMATION

Application Fee: $25. **Regular Application Deadline:** 8/15. **Regular Notification:** Rolling. **Transfer Students Accepted?** Yes. **Transfer Policy:** Same as for other students.
Required Admission Factors: Essays/personal statement, letters of recommendation, transcript.
Other Admission Factors: Minimum 2.75 GPA and satisfactory grades in Introuction to Bible, Introduction to Theology, Introduction to Morality, and general psychology courses required.

EMPLOYMENT INFORMATION

Placement Office Available? Yes.

WHEELING JESUIT UNIVERSITY
Master of Mathmatics/Science Education Program

Address: 316 Washington Avenue, Wheeling, WV 26003
Admissions Phone: 800-873-7665 · **Admissions Fax:** 304-243-4441
Admissions E-mail: hljones@wju.edu · **Web Address:** www.wju.edu

INSTITUTIONAL INFORMATION

Public/Private: Private (nonprofit). **Total Faculty:** 1. **% Student/Faculty Ratio:** 10:1. **Students in Parent Institution:** 1,699.

PROGRAMS

Masters offered in: Mathematics teacher education, science teacher education/general science teacher education.

STUDENT INFORMATION

Total Students in Program: 10. **% Female:** 80.

RESEARCH FACILITIES

Research Facilities: NASA's National Technology Transfer Center, NASA's Classroom of the Future, Center for Educational Technologies.

EXPENSES/FINANCIAL AID

Annual Tuition: $495. **Room & Board:** $6,520. **Fees:** $210. **Books and Supplies:** $250. **% Receiving Financial Aid:** 100. **% Receiving Scholarships/Grants:** 100. **Types of Aid Available:** Loans, scholarships.

ADMISSIONS INFORMATION

Application Fee: $25. **Regular Application Deadline:** 5/1. **Regular Notification:** Rolling. **Transfer Students Accepted?** No.
Required Admission Factors: Essays/personal statement, transcript.
Other Admission Factors: 2.75 minimum GPA; must be currently teaching math or science, grades 6-12. Must have Internet access.

EMPLOYMENT INFORMATION

Placement Office Available? Yes.

WHEELING JESUIT UNIVERSITY
MS in Accounting Program

Address: 316 Washington Avenue, Wheeling, WV 26003
Admissions Phone: 304-243-2250 · **Admissions Fax:** 304-243-4441
Admissions E-mail: adulted@wju.edu
Web Address: www.wju.edu/academics/business/msa.asp

INSTITUTIONAL INFORMATION

Public/Private: Private (nonprofit). **Evening Classes Available?** Yes. **Total Faculty:** 2. **% Faculty Part-time:** 50. **Student/Faculty Ratio:** 10:1. **Students in Parent Institution:** 1,699.

PROGRAMS

Masters offered in: Accounting, business administration/management.

STUDENT INFORMATION

Total Students in Program: 10. **% Full-time:** 50. **% Female:** 60.

RESEARCH FACILITIES

Research Facilities: NASA's National Technology Transfer Center, NASA's Classroom of the Future, Center for Educational Technologies.

EXPENSES/FINANCIAL AID

Annual Tuition: $8,910. **Room & Board:** $3,300. **Fees:** $185. **Books and Supplies:** $500. **Types of Aid Available:** graduate assistantships, loans. **Assistantship Compensation Includes:** Full tuition remission, salary/stipend. **Average Salary Stipend:** $5,500.

ADMISSIONS INFORMATION

Application Fee: $25. **Regular Application Deadline:** 8/15. **Regular Notification:** Rolling. **Transfer Students Accepted?** Yes. **Transfer Policy:** Same as for other students; minimum of 24 credits must be completed at WJU. **Average GPA:** 2.7.
Required Admission Factors: Letters of recommendation, transcript.
Recommended Admission Factors: Interview.
Other Admission Factors: 2.8 GPA; prerequisite undergraduate accounting and business courses.

EMPLOYMENT INFORMATION

Placement Office Available? Yes.

WHEELOCK COLLEGE
Graduate School

Address: 200 The Riverway, Boston, MA 02215-4176
Admissions Phone: 617-879-2178 or 800-734-5215 · **Admissions Fax:** 617-232-7127
Admissions E-mail: msheehan@wheelock.edu

INSTITUTIONAL INFORMATION

Public/Private: Private (nonprofit). **Evening Classes Available?** Yes. **Students in Parent Institution:** 1,081.

STUDENT INFORMATION

Total Students in Program: 439. **% Full-time:** 40. **% Female:** 96.

RESEARCH FACILITIES

Research Facilities: Center for Child Care Policy & Training, Center for Parenting Studies, Center for International Education & Leadership.

EXPENSES/FINANCIAL AID

Annual Tuition: In-state $10,350. **Grants Range From:** $3,000-$8,000. **Loans Range From:** $122-$18,500. **% Receiving Financial Aid:** 88. **% Receiving Scholarships/Grants:** 31. **% Receiving Loans:** 92. **% Receiving Assistantships:** 5.

ADMISSIONS INFORMATION

Application Fee: $35. **Regular Notification:** Rolling. **Transfer Students Accepted?** Yes. **Number of Applications Received:** 169. **% of Applicants Accepted:** 88. **% Accepted Who Enrolled:** 61. **Average GPA:** 2.9.
Required Admission Factors: Essays/personal statement, letters of recommendation, transcript.
Other Admission Factors: Minimum 2.7 GPA required.
Program-Specific Admission Factors: Interview required of TSSN, birth-3, and leadership program applicants.

EMPLOYMENT INFORMATION

Placement Office Available? Yes. **% Employed Within 6 Months:** 96. **Rate of placement:** 92%.

WICHITA STATE UNIVERSITY
College of Fine Arts

Address: 1845 Fairmount, Wichita, KS 67260
Admissions Phone: 316-978-3389 or 316-978-3522 or 316-978-3555
Admissions Fax: 316-978-3951 · **Admissions E-mail:** smith2@twsuvm.uc.twsu.edu

INSTITUTIONAL INFORMATION

Public/Private: Public. **Evening Classes Available?** Yes. **Student/Faculty Ratio:** 2:1. **Students in Parent Institution:** 14,810.

STUDENT INFORMATION

Total Students in Program: 3,433. **% Full-time:** 30. **% Female:** 57.

RESEARCH FACILITIES

Research Facilities: Center for Economic Development & Business Research, Hugo Wall Center for Urban Studies, National Institute for Aviation Research, Center for Energy Studies, Kansas Public Finance Center, Midwest Criminal Justice Institute.

EXPENSES/FINANCIAL AID

Annual Tuition: In-state $1,888. / Out-of-state $6,129. **Fees:** $379. **Books and Supplies:** $760. **Number of Teaching/Research Assistantships Granted Each Year:** 49. **Average Salary Stipend:** $3,845.

ADMISSIONS INFORMATION

Application Fee: $40. **Regular Notification:** Rolling. **Transfer Students Accepted?** Yes. **Number of Applications Received:** 45. **% of Applicants Accepted:** 58.

Required Admission Factors: Essays/personal statement, transcript.
Other Admission Factors: Minimum 2.75 GPA required.

EMPLOYMENT INFORMATION
Placement Office Available? Yes.

WICHITA STATE UNIVERSITY
Fairmount College of Liberal Arts & Sciences

Address: 1845 Fairmount, Wichita, KS 67260

INSTITUTIONAL INFORMATION
Public/Private: Public. **Students in Parent Institution:** 14,810.

STUDENT INFORMATION
Total Students in Program: 3,433. **% Full-time:** 30. **% Female:** 57.

RESEARCH FACILITIES
Research Facilities: Center for Economic Development & Business Research, Hugo Wall Center for Urban Studies, National Institute for Aviation Research, Center for Energy Studies, Kansas Public Finance Center, Midwest Criminal Justice Institute.

EXPENSES/FINANCIAL AID
Annual Tuition: In-state $1,888 / Out-of-state $6,129. **Fees:** $379. **Books and Supplies:** $760.

ADMISSIONS INFORMATION
Transfer Students Accepted? No. **Number of Applications Received:** 746. **% of Applicants Accepted:** 45.

EMPLOYMENT INFORMATION
Placement Office Available? Yes.

WICHITA STATE UNIVERSITY
Hugo Wall School of Urban and Public Affairs

Address: 1845 Fairmount, Wichita, KS 67260

INSTITUTIONAL INFORMATION
Public/Private: Public. **Student/Faculty Ratio:** 8:1. **Students in Parent Institution:** 14,810.

STUDENT INFORMATION
Total Students in Program: 3,433. **% Full-time:** 30. **% Female:** 57.

RESEARCH FACILITIES
Research Facilities: Center for Economic Development & Business Research, Hugo Wall Center for Urban Studies, National Institute for Aviation Research, Center for Energy Studies, Kansas Public Finance Center, Midwest Criminal Justice Institute.

EXPENSES/FINANCIAL AID
Annual Tuition: In-state $1,888. / Out-of-state $6,129. **Fees:** $379. **Books and Supplies:** $760. **Number of Teaching/Research Assistantships Granted Each Year:** 16. **Average Salary Stipend:** $3,675.

ADMISSIONS INFORMATION
Transfer Students Accepted? No. **Number of Applications Received:** 29. **% of Applicants Accepted:** 72.
Required Admission Factors: Interview, transcript.

EMPLOYMENT INFORMATION
Placement Office Available? Yes.

WICHITA STATE UNIVERSITY
School of Community Affairs

Address: 1845 Fairmount, Wichita, KS 67260

INSTITUTIONAL INFORMATION
Public/Private: Public. **Student/Faculty Ratio:** 4:1. **Students in Parent Institution:** 14,810.

STUDENT INFORMATION
Total Students in Program: 3,433. **% Full-time:** 30. **% Female:** 57.

RESEARCH FACILITIES
Research Facilities: Center for Economic Development & Business Research, Hugo Wall Center for Urban Studies, National Institute for Aviation Research, Center for Energy Studies, Kansas Public Finance Center, Midwest Criminal Justice Institute.

EXPENSES/FINANCIAL AID
Annual Tuition: In-state $1,888 / Out-of-state $6,129. **Fees:** $379. **Books and Supplies:** $760. **Number of Teaching/Research Assistantships Granted Each Year:** 17. **Average Salary Stipend:** $3,743.

ADMISSIONS INFORMATION
Transfer Students Accepted? No. **Number of Applications Received:** 34. **% of Applicants Accepted:** 59.
Required Admission Factors: Interview, transcript.

EMPLOYMENT INFORMATION
Placement Office Available? Yes.

WICHITA STATE UNIVERSITY
School of Social Work

Address: 1845 Fairmount, Wichita, KS 67260

INSTITUTIONAL INFORMATION
Public/Private: Public. **Student/Faculty Ratio:** 7:1. **Students in Parent Institution:** 14,810.

STUDENT INFORMATION
Total Students in Program: 3,433. **% Full-time:** 30. **% Female:** 57.

RESEARCH FACILITIES
Research Facilities: Center for Economic Development & Business Research, Hugo Wall Center for Urban Studies, National Institute for Aviation Research, Center for Energy Studies, Kansas Public Finance Center, Midwest Criminal Justice Institute.

EXPENSES/FINANCIAL AID
Annual Tuition: In-state $1,888 / Out-of-state $6,129. **Fees:** $379. **Books and Supplies:** $760. **Number of Teaching/Research Assistantships Granted Each Year:** 2. **Average Salary Stipend:** $6,862.

ADMISSIONS INFORMATION
Transfer Students Accepted? No. **Number of Applications Received:** 60. **% of Applicants Accepted:** 47.
Required Admission Factors: Interview, transcript.

EMPLOYMENT INFORMATION
Placement Office Available? Yes.

WIDENER UNIVERSITY
Institute for Graduate Clinical Psychology

Address: One University Place, Chester, PA 19013
Admissions Phone: 610-499-1209 · **Admissions Fax:** 610-499-4625
Admissions E-mail: Graduate.Psychology@widener.edu
Web Address: www.widener.edu

INSTITUTIONAL INFORMATION
Public/Private: Private (nonprofit). **Total Faculty:** 58. **% Faculty Female:** 53. **% Faculty Part-time:** 78. **Student/Faculty Ratio:** 3:1.

STUDENT INFORMATION
Total Students in Program: 163. **% Full-time:** 100.

EXPENSES/FINANCIAL AID
Annual Tuition: $18,600. **Fees:** $150. **Books and Supplies:** $800. **Grants Range From:** $375-$8,000. **Loans Range From:** $2,834-$30,210. **% Receiving Scholarships/Grants:** 20. **% Receiving Loans:** 93. **% Receiving Assistantships:** 8. **Types of Aid Available:** Graduate assistantships, institutional work-study, loans, scholarships. **Average student debt, upon graduation:** $90,000

ADMISSIONS INFORMATION
Application Fee: $75. **Regular Application Deadline:** 12/31. **Regular Notification:** 4/1. **Transfer Students Accepted?** No. **Number of Applications Received:** 280. **% of Applicants Accepted:** 25. **% Accepted Who Enrolled:** 58. **Average GPA:** 3.4. **Average GRE Verbal:** 574. **Average GRE Quantitative:** 656. **Average GRE Analytical:** 651. **Average GRE Analytical Writing:** 5.5.
Required Admission Factors: Essays/personal statement, GRE, interview, letters of recommendation, transcript.
Other Admission Factors: Minium GRE verbal score of 600 and minimum quantitative score of 600 required.

EMPLOYMENT INFORMATION
Placement Office Available? Yes. **% Employed Within 6 Months:** 95. **% of doctoral grads employed in their field upon graduation:** 98. **Rate of placement:** 81%. **Average starting salary:** $35,000.

WIDENER UNIVERSITY
College of Arts & Sciences

Address: One University Place, Chester, PA 19013

INSTITUTIONAL INFORMATION
Public/Private: Private (nonprofit). **Evening Classes Available?** Yes. **Students in Parent Institution:** 6,917.

STUDENT INFORMATION
Total Students in Program: 1,914. **% Full-time:** 30.

EXPENSES/FINANCIAL AID
Fees: $15. **Grants Range From:** $375-$8,000. **Loans Range From:** $2,834-$30,210. **% Receiving Scholarships/Grants:** 20. **% Receiving Loans:** 93. **% Receiving Assistantships:** 17. **% Receiving Other Aid:** 43.

ADMISSIONS INFORMATION
Application Fee: $25. **Regular Notification:** Rolling. **Transfer Students Accepted?** Yes. **Transfer Policy:** Maximum 6 credit hours may be transferred into most programs; 12 may be transferred into liberal studies. **Number of Applications Received:** 20. **% of Applicants Accepted:** 90. **% Accepted Who Enrolled:** 39. **Average GPA:** 3.2.

Required Admission Factors: Essays/personal statement, letters of recommendation, transcript.
Program-Specific Admission Factors: Interview required of liberal studies program applicants. Minimum 3.0 GPA required of criminal justice program applicants; recommended of prublic administration program applicants.

EMPLOYMENT INFORMATION
Placement Office Available? Yes. **Rate of placement:** 81%.

WILKES UNIVERSITY
Graduate Programs

Address: PO Box 111, Wilkes-Barre, PA 18766
Admissions Phone: 570-408-4160 · **Admissions Fax:** 570-408-7860
Admissions E-mail: admissions@wilkes.edu · **Web Address:** www.wilkes.edu

INSTITUTIONAL INFORMATION
Public/Private: Private (nonprofit). **Evening Classes Available?** Yes. **Students in Parent Institution:** 4,390.

PROGRAMS
Masters offered in: Biology teacher education; business administration/management; chemistry teacher education; education; electrical, electronics, and communications engineering; elementary and middle school administration/principalship; elementary education and teaching; English/language arts teacher education; history teacher education; mathematics teacher education; mathematics; nursing—registered nurse training (RN, ASN, BSN, MSN); teacher education and professional development, specific subject areas. **First Professional degree offered in:** Pharmacy (PharMD/BPharm).

STUDENT INFORMATION
Total Students in Program: 2,335. **% Full-time:** 16. **% Female:** 67. **% Minority:** 2. **% International:** 1.

EXPENSES/FINANCIAL AID
Annual Tuition: $15,600. **Fees:** $312. **Books and Supplies:** $900. **Types of Aid Available:** Graduate assistantships.

ADMISSIONS INFORMATION
Application Fee: $35. **Regular Application Deadline:** 9/1. **Regular Notification:** Rolling. **Transfer Students Accepted?** Yes.
Required Admission Factors: Letters of recommendation, transcript.
Recommended Admission Factors: GRE.

EMPLOYMENT INFORMATION
Placement Office Available? Yes.

WILLIAM PATERSON UNIVERSITY OF NEW JERSEY
College of the Arts & Communication

Address: 300 Pompton Road, Wayne, NJ 07470
Admissions Phone: 973-720-2237 · **Admissions Fax:** 973-720-2035

INSTITUTIONAL INFORMATION
Public/Private: Public. **Evening Classes Available?** Yes. **Students in Parent Institution:** 9,945.

RESEARCH FACILITIES
Research Facilities: Graduate Research Center, Department of Instruction and Research Technology, Center for Research.

EXPENSES/FINANCIAL AID
Annual Tuition: In-state $5,787. / Out-of-state $8,415. **Room & Board:** $5,270. **Books and Supplies:** $300. **Average Salary Stipend:** $6,000.

ADMISSIONS INFORMATION

Application Fee: $35. **Regular Notification:** Rolling. **Transfer Students Accepted?** Yes. **Transfer Policy:** Maximum 6 credit hours with a minimum grade of B may be transferred.
Required Admission Factors: Letters of recommendation, transcript.
Recommended Admission Factors:
Other Admission Factors: Minimum 2.75 GPA required.

WILLIAM PATERSON UNIVERSITY OF NEW JERSEY
College of the Humanities & Social Sciences

Address: 300 Pompton Road, Wayne, NJ 07470
Admissions Phone: 973-720-2237 · **Admissions Fax:** 973-720-2035
Admissions E-mail: graduate@wpunj.edu
Web Address: www.wpunj.edu/cohss/graduate.htm

INSTITUTIONAL INFORMATION

Public/Private: Public. **Evening Classes Available?** Yes. **Students in Parent Institution:** 9,945.

PROGRAMS

Masters offered in: Bilingual and multilingual education, clinical psychology, English language and literature, history, international relations and affairs, public policy analysis, sociology, teaching English as a second or foreign language/ESL language instructor.

RESEARCH FACILITIES

Research Facilities: Graduate Research Center, Department of Instruction and Research Technology, Center for Research, History Computer Laboratory, Public Policy Resource Center, Writing Center, Language Multimedia Center.

EXPENSES/FINANCIAL AID

Annual Tuition: In-state $5,787. / Out-of-state $8,415. **Room & Board:** $5,270. **Books and Supplies:** $300. **Average Salary Stipend:** $6,000.

ADMISSIONS INFORMATION

Application Fee: $35. **Regular Notification:** Rolling. **Transfer Students Accepted?** Yes. **Transfer Policy:** Maximum 6 credit hours with a minimum grade of B may be transferred.
Required Admission Factors: Essays/personal statement, GMAT, GRE, letters of recommendation, transcript.
Other Admission Factors: Minimum 3.0 GPA required. Clinical psychology requires interviews in some cases.
Program-Specific Admission Factors: 3 letters of recommendation required of applied.

WILLIAM WOODS UNIVERSITY
Graduate & Adult Studies

Address: One University Avenue, Fulton, MO 65251-1098
Admissions Phone: 800-995-3199 · **Admissions Fax:** 573-592-1164
Admissions E-mail: btutt@williamwoods.edu

INSTITUTIONAL INFORMATION

Public/Private: Private (nonprofit). **Evening Classes Available?** Yes. **Student/Faculty Ratio:** 14:1. **Students in Parent Institution:** 1,659.

STUDENT INFORMATION

Total Students in Program: 670. **% Full-time:** 99. **% Female:** 63.

EXPENSES/FINANCIAL AID

Fees: $45. **Loans Range From:** $200-$8,960. **% Receiving Financial Aid:** 41. **% Receiving Loans:** 41. **% Receiving Assistantships:** 8.

ADMISSIONS INFORMATION

Application Fee: $25. **Regular Notification:** Rolling. **Transfer Students Accepted?** Yes. **Number of Applications Received:** 250. **% of Applicants Accepted:** 98. **% Accepted Who Enrolled:** 98.
Required Admission Factors: Essays/personal statement, letters of recommendation, transcript.
Other Admission Factors: Minimum 2.5 GPA and two years of work experience required. ·

WILLIAMS COLLEGE
Graduate Program

Address: Williamstown, MA 01267
Admissions Phone: 413-597-2476 or 413-458-9545

INSTITUTIONAL INFORMATION

Public/Private: Private (nonprofit). **Students in Parent Institution:** 2,031.

STUDENT INFORMATION

Total Students in Program: 49. **% Full-time:** 100. **% Female:** 63.

EXPENSES/FINANCIAL AID

Annual Tuition: $23,500. **Fees:** $2,100. **Books and Supplies:** $500. **Grants Range From:** $10,000-$35,000.

ADMISSIONS INFORMATION

Application Fee: $50. **Transfer Students Accepted?** No. **Number of Applications Received:** 210. **% of Applicants Accepted:** 43. **% Accepted Who Enrolled:** 36.
Required Admission Factors: Letters of recommendation, transcript.
Program-Specific Admission Factors: Minimum GRE score of 500, essay, and 4 letters of recommendation required of history of art program applicants; interview recommended. One letter of recommendation required of developmental economics program applicants.

EMPLOYMENT INFORMATION

Placement Office Available? Yes.

WILMINGTON COLLEGE
Graduate Programs

Address: 320 DuPont Highway, New Castle, DE 19720
Admissions Phone: 302-328-9407 · **Admissions Fax:** 302-328-5902
Admissions E-mail: inquire@wilmcoll.edu
Web Address: www.wilmcoll.edu/admission/

INSTITUTIONAL INFORMATION

Public/Private: Private (nonprofit). **Evening Classes Available?** Yes. **Students in Parent Institution:** 5,298.

STUDENT INFORMATION

Total Students in Program: 1,371. **% Full-time:** 18. **% Female:** 68.

EXPENSES/FINANCIAL AID

Annual Tuition: $4,410. **Fees:** $50. **Books and Supplies:** $300. **Grants Range From:** $500-$1,000. **Loans Range From:** $3,000-$18,500. **% Receiving Scholarships/Grants:** 5. **% Receiving Loans:** 95.

ADMISSIONS INFORMATION

Application Fee: $25. **Regular Application Deadline:** 9/14. **Regular Notification:** Rolling. **Transfer Students Accepted?** Yes. **Transfer Policy:** Official transcripts forwarded directly to Office of Admissions required of transfer applicants. **Number of Applications Received:** 1,468. **% of Applicants Accepted:** 98. **% Accepted Who Enrolled:** 79. **Average GPA:** 2.5. **Required Admission Factors:** Letters of recommendation, transcript. **Other Admission Factors:** Minimum 2.0 GPA and undergraduate prerequisites required.

EMPLOYMENT INFORMATION

Placement Office Available? Yes. **Rate of placement:** 85%.

WINEBRENNER THEOLOGICAL SEMINARY
Graduate Program

Address: 950 North Main Street, Findlay, OH 45840
Admissions Phone: 800-992-4987 · **Admissions Fax:** 419-434-4267
Admissions E-mail: admissions@winebrenner.edu
Web Address: www.winebrenner.edu

INSTITUTIONAL INFORMATION

Public/Private: Private (nonprofit). **Student/Faculty Ratio:** 6:1. **Students in Parent Institution:** 94.

STUDENT INFORMATION

Total Students in Program: 28. **% Full-time:** 46. **% Female:** 46.

EXPENSES/FINANCIAL AID

Annual Tuition: $7,484. **Fees:** $36. **Books and Supplies:** $600.

ADMISSIONS INFORMATION

Application Fee: $25. **Priority Application Deadline:** 8/1. **Regular Application Deadline:** 8/1. **Transfer Students Accepted?** Yes.
Required Admission Factors: Essays/personal statement, interview, letters of recommendation, transcript.

WINONA STATE UNIVERSITY
College of Liberal Arts

Address: Winona, MN 55987
Admissions Phone: 507-457-5038 ·
Admissions E-mail: pchristensen@winona.msus.edu

INSTITUTIONAL INFORMATION

Public/Private: Public. **Evening Classes Available?** Yes. **Students in Parent Institution:** 7,386.

STUDENT INFORMATION

Total Students in Program: 614. **% Full-time:** 25. **% Female:** 65.

EXPENSES/FINANCIAL AID

Annual Tuition: In-state $2,850. / Out-of-state $6,350. **Fees:** $550. **Books and Supplies:** $600. **Grants Range From:** $1,700-$250. **Loans Range From:** $500-$8,500. **% Receiving Scholarships/Grants:** 12. **% Receiving Loans:** 98. **% Receiving Assistantships:** 5. **Number of Teaching/Research Assistantships Granted Each Year:** 6. **Average Salary Stipend:** $5,500.

ADMISSIONS INFORMATION

Application Fee: $20. **Regular Notification:** Rolling. **Transfer Students Accepted?** Yes. **Number of Applications Received:** 4. **% of Applicants Accepted:** 100. **% Accepted Who Enrolled:** 100.
Required Admission Factors: Transcript.
Other Admission Factors: Minimum 3.0 GPA required.

EMPLOYMENT INFORMATION

Placement Office Available? Yes. **Rate of placement:** 90%.

WINTHROP UNIVERSITY
College of Arts & Sciences

Address: 701 Oakland Avenue, Rock Hill, SC 29733
Admissions Phone: 803-323-2204 · **Admissions Fax:** 803-323-2292
Admissions E-mail: johnsons@winthrop.edu
Web Address: www.winthrop.edu/graduate-studies

INSTITUTIONAL INFORMATION

Public/Private: Public. **Evening Classes Available?** Yes. **Students in Parent Institution:** 6,447.

PROGRAMS

Masters offered in: Biology/biological sciences, developmental and child psychology, English language and literature, human nutrition, liberal arts and sciences/liberal studies, Spanish language and literature.

STUDENT INFORMATION

Total Students in Program: 125. **% Full-time:** 58. **% Female:** 72. **% Minority:** 18. **% International:** 5.

EXPENSES/FINANCIAL AID

Annual Tuition: In-state $7,508. / Out-of-state $13,824. **Room & Board:** $4,992. **Fees:** $20. **Books and Supplies:** $900. **Grants Range From:** $100-$4,000. **Loans Range From:** $200-$16,000. **% Receiving Scholarships/Grants:** 8. **% Receiving Loans:** 79. **% Receiving Assistantships:** 13.

ADMISSIONS INFORMATION

Application Fee: $35. **Transfer Students Accepted?** Yes. **Required Admission Factors:** GRE.

EMPLOYMENT INFORMATION

Placement Office Available? Yes. **Rate of placement:** 24%.

WINTHROP UNIVERSITY
College of Visual & Performing Arts

Address: 701 Oakland Avenue, Rock Hill, SC 29733
Admissions Phone: 803-323-2204 · **Admissions Fax:** 803-323-2292
Admissions E-mail: carpenterl@winthrop.edu
Web Address: www.winthrop.edu/graduate-studies

INSTITUTIONAL INFORMATION

Public/Private: Public. **Evening Classes Available?** Yes. **Students in Parent Institution:** 6,447.

PROGRAMS

Masters offered in: Conducting, fine/studio arts, music.

STUDENT INFORMATION

Total Students in Program: 328. **% Full-time:** 33.

EXPENSES/FINANCIAL AID

Annual Tuition: In-state $7,508. / Out-of-state $13,824. **Room & Board:** $4,992. **Fees:** $20. **Books and Supplies:** $900. **Grants Range From:** $100-$4,000. **Loans Range From:** $200-$16,000. **% Receiving Scholarships/Grants:** 8. **% Receiving Loans:** 79. **% Receiving Assistantships:** 13.

ADMISSIONS INFORMATION

Application Fee: $35. **Priority Application Deadline:** 3/1. **Regular Application Deadline:** 3/1. **Regular Notification:** Rolling. **Transfer Students Accepted?** Yes.
Required Admission Factors: Transcript.
Other Admission Factors: Minimum GRE score of 800 and minimum 3.0 GPA required.
Program-Specific Admission Factors: MAT (minimum score of 40) required of art/design program applicants.

EMPLOYMENT INFORMATION

Placement Office Available? Yes. Rate of placement: 24%.

WISCONSIN SCHOOL OF PROFESSIONAL PSYCHOLOGY
Graduate Program

Address: 9120 West Hampton Avenue, Suite 212, Milwaukee, WI 53225
Admissions Phone: 414-464-9777 · **Admissions Fax:** 414-358-5590
Admissions E-mail: admissions@wspp.edu · **Web Address:** www.wspp.edu

INSTITUTIONAL INFORMATION

Public/Private: Private (nonprofit). **Evening Classes Available?** Yes. **Student/Faculty Ratio:** 7:1. **Students in Parent Institution:** 67.

PROGRAMS

Masters offered in: Clinical psychology. **Doctorate offered in:** Clinical psychology.

STUDENT INFORMATION

Total Students in Program: 65. **% Full-time:** 48. **% Female:** 75.

RESEARCH FACILITIES

Research Facilities: Psychology Center (Outpatient Mental Health Clinic).

EXPENSES/FINANCIAL AID

Annual Tuition: $11,700. **Fees:** $100. **Books and Supplies:** $800. **Grants Range From:** $1,000-$18,500. **Loans Range From:** $9,000-$17,800. **% Receiving Financial Aid:** 20. **% Receiving Loans:** 100. **Types of Aid Available:** Graduate assistantships, scholarships.

ADMISSIONS INFORMATION

Application Fee: $75. **Priority Application Deadline:** 4/15. **Regular Application Deadline:** 7/31. **Regular Notification:** Rolling. **Transfer Students Accepted?** Yes. **Transfer Policy:** Same as applying for regular status. **Number of Applications Received:** 45. **% of Applicants Accepted:** 27. **% Accepted Who Enrolled:** 92. **Average GPA:** 3.2. **Average GRE Verbal:** 500. **Average GRE Quantitative:** 500. **Average GRE Analytical:** 500. **Average GRE Analytical Writing:** 5.

Required Admission Factors: Essays/personal statement, GRE, letters of recommendation, transcript. GRE subject exam(s) in clinical psychology. **Other Admission Factors:** Minimum 3.2 GPA and references required.

EMPLOYMENT INFORMATION

% Employed Within 6 Months: 90. **% of doctoral grads employed in their field upon graduation:** 100. **Rate of placement:** 100%. **Average starting salary:** $40,000.

WORCESTER POLYTECHNIC INSTITUTE
Graduate Studies

Address: 100 Institute Road, Worcester, MA 01609
Admissions Phone: 508-831-5301 · **Admissions Fax:** 508-831-5717
Admissions E-mail: grad_studies@wpi.edu · **Web Address:** www.grad.wpi.edu

INSTITUTIONAL INFORMATION

Public/Private: Private (nonprofit). **Evening Classes Available?** Yes. **Total Faculty:** 323. **% Faculty Female:** 19. **% Faculty Part-time:** 27. **Student/Faculty Ratio:** 12:1. **Students in Parent Institution:** 3,545.

PROGRAMS

Masters offered in: Aerospace, aeronautical, and astronautical engineering; agricultural/biological engineering and bioengineering; biochemistry; biological and biomedical sciences; biomedical/medical engineering; biotechnology; business administration/management; business, management, marketing, and re-

lated support services; business/commerce; ceramic sciences and engineering; chemical engineering; chemistry; chemistry; civil engineering; computer and information sciences; computer and information systems security; computer engineering; computer graphics; computer programming; computer programming, specific applications; computer programming/programmer; computer science; computer software and media applications; computer systems analysis/analyst; computer systems networking and telecommunications; data warehousing/mining and database administration; E-commerce/electronic commerce; electrical, electronics, and communications engineering; engineering; engineering; environmental/environmental health engineering; information technology; manufacturing engineering; marketing; materials engineering; materials science; mathematics; mechanical engineering; operations management and supervision; physics; system, networking, and LAN/WAN management/manager. **Doctorate offered in:** Aerospace, aeronautical, and astronautical engineering; agricultural/biological engineering and bioengineering; biological and biomedical sciences; biomedical/medical engineering; biotechnology; ceramic sciences and engineering; chemical engineering.

STUDENT INFORMATION

Total Students in Program: 786. **% Full-time:** 55. **% Female:** 25.

RESEARCH FACILITIES

Research Facilities: Research affiliations with Tufts University, University of Massachusetts Medical Center, Alden Research Lab, Massachusetts Biotechnology Research Institute, Central Massachusetts Manufacturing Partnership, Manufacturing Assistance Center.

EXPENSES/FINANCIAL AID

Annual Tuition: $15,444. **Fees:** $50. **Books and Supplies:** $750. **Grants Range From:** $15,444-$36,384. **Loans Range From:** $4,000-$18,500. **% Receiving Financial Aid:** 41. **% Receiving Scholarships/Grants:** 28. **% Receiving Loans:** 17. **% Receiving Assistantships:** 41. **Average student debt, upon graduation:** $15,000. **Number of Fellowships Granted Each Year:** 35. **Average amount of individual fellowships per year:** $28,972. **Number of Teaching/Research Assistantships Granted Each Year:** 217. **Average Salary Stipend:** $1,397.

ADMISSIONS INFORMATION

Application Fee: $70. **Priority Application Deadline:** 2/1. **Regular Application Deadline:** 8/1. **Regular Notification:** Rolling. **Transfer Students Accepted?** Yes. **Number of Applications Received:** 1,171. **% of Applicants Accepted:** 67. **% Accepted Who Enrolled:** 35. **Average GRE Verbal:** 498. **Average GRE Quantitative:** 745.

Required Admission Factors: Letters of recommendation, transcript. **Recommended Admission Factors:** GRE subject exam(s) in mathematics test recommended for mathematics department.

EMPLOYMENT INFORMATION

Placement Office Available? Yes. **Rate of placement:** 90%.

WRIGHT STATE UNIVERSITY
College of Liberal Arts

Address: 3640 Colonel Glenn Highway, Dayton, OH 45435
Admissions Phone: 937-775-2976 · **Admissions Fax:** 937-775-3781
Admissions E-mail: jerry.malicki@wright.edu

INSTITUTIONAL INFORMATION

Public/Private: Public. **Evening Classes Available?** Yes. **Students in Parent Institution:** 15,702.

STUDENT INFORMATION

Total Students in Program: 3,123. **% Full-time:** 34. **% Female:** 60.

EXPENSES/FINANCIAL AID

Annual Tuition: In-state $6,198. / Out-of-state $10,794. **Room & Board (On/Off Campus):** $5,193/$5,600. **Books and Supplies:** $750. **Average Salary Stipend:** $5,000.

456

ADMISSIONS INFORMATION

Application Fee: $25. **Regular Notification:** Rolling. **Transfer Students Accepted?** Yes. **Number of Applications Received:** 112. **% of Applicants Accepted:** 76.
Required Admission Factors: Essays/personal statement, transcript.
Other Admission Factors: Minimum 2.7 GPA or minimum 2.5 GPA overall with minimum 3.0 GPA in last 90 quarter hours required.
Program-Specific Admission Factors: Additional requirements vary by program.

EMPLOYMENT INFORMATION

Placement Office Available? Yes. **Rate of placement:** 93%.

WRIGHT STATE UNIVERSITY
College of Science & Mathematics

Address: 3640 Colonel Glenn Highway, Dayton, OH 45435

INSTITUTIONAL INFORMATION

Public/Private: Public. **Students in Parent Institution:** 15,702.

STUDENT INFORMATION

Total Students in Program: 3,123. **% Full-time:** 34. **% Female:** 60.

EXPENSES/FINANCIAL AID

Annual Tuition: In-state $6,198. / Out-of-state $10,794. **Room & Board (On/ Off Campus):** $5,193/$5,600. **Books and Supplies:** $750.

ADMISSIONS INFORMATION

Transfer Students Accepted? No.

EMPLOYMENT INFORMATION

Placement Office Available? Yes. **Rate of placement:** 93%.

WRIGHT STATE UNIVERSITY
School of Professional Psychology

Address: 3640 Colonel Glenn Highway, Dayton, OH 45435
Admissions Phone: 937-775-3492 · **Admissions E-mail:** opetrie@sirius.wright.edu

INSTITUTIONAL INFORMATION

Public/Private: Public. **Students in Parent Institution:** 15,702.

STUDENT INFORMATION

Total Students in Program: 3,123. **% Full-time:** 34. **% Female:** 60.

EXPENSES/FINANCIAL AID

Annual Tuition: In-state $6,198. / Out-of-state $10,794. **Room & Board (On/ Off Campus):** $5,193/$5,600. **Books and Supplies:** $750.

ADMISSIONS INFORMATION

Application Fee: $30. **Transfer Students Accepted?** Yes. **Number of Applications Received:** 315. **% of Applicants Accepted:** 11. **% Accepted Who Enrolled:** 79. **Average GPA:** 3.06. **Average GRE Verbal:** 560. **Average GRE Quantitative:** 590. **Average GRE Analytical:** 610.
Required Admission Factors: Essays/personal statement, GRE, interview, transcript.

EMPLOYMENT INFORMATION

Placement Office Available? Yes. **Rate of placement:** 93%.

XAVIER UNIVERSITY
College of Arts & Sciences

Address: 3800 Victory Parkway, Cincinnati, OH 45207-6541
Admissions Phone: 513-745-3360 · **Admissions Fax:** 513-745-1048
Admissions E-mail: cooperj@xu.edu · **Web Address:** www.xavier.edu/cas/

INSTITUTIONAL INFORMATION

Public/Private: Private (nonprofit). **Evening Classes Available?** Yes. **Student/Faculty Ratio:** 13:1. **Students in Parent Institution:** 6,668.

PROGRAMS

Masters offered in: English language and literature, humanities/humanistic studies, theology/theological studies.

STUDENT INFORMATION

Total Students in Program: 74. **% Full-time:** 11. **% Female:** 54. **% Minority:** 8.

ADMISSIONS INFORMATION

Application Fee: $35. **Regular Application Deadline:** 8/25. **Regular Notification:** Rolling. **Transfer Students Accepted?** Yes. **Transfer Policy:** Courses in which a grade of A or B is earned are transferable. **Number of Applications Received:** 41. **% of Applicants Accepted:** 56. **% Accepted Who Enrolled:** 48.
Required Admission Factors: Transcript.
Other Admission Factors: Minimum MAT score of 400 and minimum GPA of 2.7 for Theology. Minimum 3.2 GPA required of English.
Program-Specific Admission Factors:

EMPLOYMENT INFORMATION

Placement Office Available? Yes.

XAVIER UNIVERSITY
College of Social Sciences

Address: 3800 Victory Parkway, Cincinnati, OH 45207-6541
Admissions Phone: 513-745-3360 · **Admissions Fax:** 513-745-1048
Admissions E-mail: cooperj@xu.edu · **Web Address:** www.xavier.edu/css

INSTITUTIONAL INFORMATION

Public/Private: Private (nonprofit). **Evening Classes Available?** Yes. **Student/Faculty Ratio:** 16:1. **Students in Parent Institution:** 6,668.

PROGRAMS

Masters offered in: Art teacher education, biology teacher education, chemistry teacher education, clinical psychology, community health services/liaison/ counseling, counselor education/school counseling and guidance services, criminal justice/law enforcement administration, criminology, education leadership and administration, education, English/language arts teacher education, experimental psychology, French language teacher education, German language teacher education, health services administration, health services/allied health, health/health care administration/management, history teacher education, industrial and organizational psychology, junior high/intermediate/middle school education and teaching, mathematics teacher education, Montessori teacher education, music teacher education, nursing administration (MSN, MS, PhD), occupational therapy/therapist, physical education teaching and coaching, reading teacher education, secondary education and teaching, social science teacher education, Spanish language teacher education, special education.
Doctorate offered in: Clinical psychology.

STUDENT INFORMATION

Total Students in Program: 1,778. **% Full-time:** 30. **% Female:** 74. **% Minority:** 7.

ADMISSIONS INFORMATION

Application Fee: $35. **Regular Application Deadline:** 8/25. **Regular Notification:** Rolling. **Transfer Students Accepted?** Yes. **Transfer Policy:** Maximum 6 credit hours may be transferred into masters programs; for the doctorate in psychology the allowable number of transfer credit hours may vary. **Number of Applications Received:** 1,053. **% of Applicants Accepted:** 56. **% Accepted Who Enrolled:** 69.
Required Admission Factors: Transcript.
Program-Specific Admission Factors: Minimum 2.8 GPA (3.0 in psychology classes) required of masters psychology program applicants. Minimum 3.0 GPA (3.25 in psychology classes) required of doctoral psychology program applicants. Minimum 2.8 GPA required of nursing program applicants.

EMPLOYMENT INFORMATION

Placement Office Available? Yes.

XAVIER UNIVERSITY OF LOUISIANA
Graduate School

Address: One Drexel Drive, New Orleans, LA 70125
Admissions Phone: 504-483-7487 · **Admissions Fax:** 504-485-7921
Admissions E-mail: mrobinson@xula.edu

INSTITUTIONAL INFORMATION

Public/Private: Private (nonprofit). **Evening Classes Available?** Yes. **Student/Faculty Ratio:** 15:1. **Students in Parent Institution:** 3,761.

STUDENT INFORMATION

Total Students in Program: 244. **% Full-time:** 76. **% Female:** 64.

EXPENSES/FINANCIAL AID

Annual Tuition: $3,600. **Fees:** $10. **Books and Supplies:** $450.

ADMISSIONS INFORMATION

Application Fee: $30. **Regular Notification:** Rolling. **Transfer Students Accepted?** Yes. **Number of Applications Received:** 41. **% of Applicants Accepted:** 93. **% Accepted Who Enrolled:** 39. **Average GPA:** 3.0. **Average GRE Verbal:** 400. **Average GRE Quantitative:** 475.
Required Admission Factors: GRE, letters of recommendation, transcript. **Other Admission Factors:** Minimum GRE score of 800, minimum MAT score of 30, minimum 2.5 GPA, and 2 professional references required.

YALE UNIVERSITY
School of Art

Address: POBox 208339, 1156 Chapel Street, New Haven, CT 06520-8339
Admissions Phone: 203-432-2600
Admissions E-mail: artschool.info@yale.edu · **Web Address:** www.yale.edu/art

INSTITUTIONAL INFORMATION

Public/Private: Private (nonprofit). **Total Faculty:** 102. **% Faculty Female:** 37. **% Faculty Part-time:** 91. **Students in Parent Institution:** 11,017.

PROGRAMS

Masters offered in: Graphic design, painting, photography, printmaking, sculpture.

STUDENT INFORMATION

Total Students in Program: 119. **% Full-time:** 100.

EXPENSES/FINANCIAL AID

Annual Tuition: $21,760 **Fees:** $660. **Books and Supplies:** $1,030. **% Receiving Financial Aid:** 80. **Number of Teaching/Research Assistantships Granted Each Year:** 56.

ADMISSIONS INFORMATION

Application Fee: $75. **Regular Application Deadline:** 1/15. **Regular Notification:** 2/15. **Transfer Students Accepted?** No. **Number of Applications Received:** 1,100. **% of Applicants Accepted:** 5. **% Accepted Who Enrolled:** 95.
Required Admission Factors: Essays/personal statement, interview, letters of recommendation, transcript.

YALE UNIVERSITY
School of Drama

Address: PO Box 208325, 149 York Street, New Haven, CT 06520-8235
Admissions Phone: 203-432-1507 · **Admissions Fax:** 203-432-9668
Admissions E-mail: maria.leveton@yale.edu · **Web Address:** www.yale.edu/drama

INSTITUTIONAL INFORMATION

Public/Private: Private (nonprofit). **Total Faculty:** 83. **% Faculty Female:** 36. **Students in Parent Institution:** 11,017.

PROGRAMS

Masters offered in: Acting; design and visual communications; directing and theatrical production; playwriting and screenwriting; technical theater/theater design and technology; theater literature, history, and criticism. **Doctorate offered in:** Theater, literature, history, and criticism.

STUDENT INFORMATION

Total Students in Program: 200. **% Full-time:** 100.

EXPENSES/FINANCIAL AID

Annual Tuition: $19,795. **Fees:** $660. **Books and Supplies:** $1,030. **Grants Range From:** $1,500-$23,500. **Loans Range From:** $5,500-$14,000. **Types of Aid Available:** Institutional work-study, loans, scholarships.

ADMISSIONS INFORMATION

Application Fee: $80. **Priority Application Deadline:** 1/3. **Regular Application Deadline:** 2/1. **Regular Notification:** 4/1. **Transfer Students Accepted?** No. **Number of Applications Received:** 1,227. **% of Applicants Accepted:** 7. **% Accepted Who Enrolled:** 86. **Average GRE Verbal:** 600. **Average GRE Quantitative:** 600.
Required Admission Factors: Essays/personal statement, GRE, interview, letters of recommendation, transcript.

YESHIVA UNIVERSITY
Ferkauf Graduate School of Psychology

Address: 1300 Morris Park Avenue, Bronx, NY 10461
Admissions Phone: 718-430-3820 · **Admissions Fax:** 718-430-3960
Admissions E-mail: eschwart@yu.edu · **Web Address:** www.yu.edu/ferkauf/

INSTITUTIONAL INFORMATION

Public/Private: Private (nonprofit). **Students in Parent Institution:** 5,715.

STUDENT INFORMATION

Total Students in Program: 1,306. **% Full-time:** 64. **% Female:** 69.

EXPENSES/FINANCIAL AID

% Receiving Financial Aid: 50. **Average student debt, upon graduation:** $30,000. **Average Salary Stipend:** $2,000.

ADMISSIONS INFORMATION

Application Fee: $35. **Transfer Students Accepted?** Yes. **Number of Applications Received:** 415. **% of Applicants Accepted:** 42. **% Accepted Who Enrolled:** 56. **Average GPA:** 3.3. **Average GRE Verbal:** 550. **Average GRE Quantitative:** 550.

Required Admission Factors: Essays/personal statement, GRE, interview, letters of recommendation, transcript.
Other Admission Factors: Minimum GRE score of 1100, minimum 3.0 GPA, and personal statement required.

EMPLOYMENT INFORMATION
% Employed Within 6 Months: 90. **% of masters/doctoral grads employed in their field upon graduation:** 85/95.

YESHIVA UNIVERSITY
Wurzweiler School of Social Work

Address: Main Campus, 500 West 185th Street, New York, NY 10033-3201
Admissions Phone: 212-960-0810 · **Admissions Fax:** 212-960-0822
Admissions E-mail: wsswadmissions@ymail.yu.edu

INSTITUTIONAL INFORMATION
Public/Private: Private (nonprofit). **Evening Classes Available?** Yes. **Student/Faculty Ratio:** 9:1. **Students in Parent Institution:** 5,715.

STUDENT INFORMATION
Total Students in Program: 1,306. **% Full-time:** 64. **% Female:** 69.

EXPENSES/FINANCIAL AID
% Receiving Financial Aid: 70. **Average student debt, upon graduation:** $24,000.

ADMISSIONS INFORMATION
Application Fee: $35. **Regular Notification:** Rolling. **Transfer Students Accepted?** Yes. **Number of Applications Received:** 582. **% of Applicants Accepted:** 70. **% Accepted Who Enrolled:** 47. **Average GPA:** 3.1.
Required Admission Factors: Essays/personal statement, interview, transcript.
Other Admission Factors: Minimum 3.0 GPA required.

EMPLOYMENT INFORMATION
% Employed Within 6 Months: 90. **% of masters/doctoral grads employed in their field upon graduation:** 92/100. **Average starting salary:** $37,000.

YORK UNIVERSITY
Faculty of Graduate Studies

Address: 4700 Keele Street, North York, Ontario, M3J 1P3 Canada
Admissions Phone: 416-736-2100 · **Admissions Fax:** 416-736-5536

INSTITUTIONAL INFORMATION
Public/Private: Public. **Students in Parent Institution:** 37,900.

STUDENT INFORMATION
Total Students in Program: 3,910. **% Female:** 50.

EXPENSES/FINANCIAL AID
Annual Tuition: In-state $4,421. / Out-of-state $10,186. **Room & Board:** $630. **Books and Supplies:** $1,200.

ADMISSIONS INFORMATION
Application Fee: $60. **Regular Notification:** Rolling. **Transfer Students Accepted?** Yes.
Required Admission Factors: Transcript.

YOUNGSTOWN STATE UNIVERSITY
School of Graduate Studies

Address: One University Plaza, Youngstown, OH 44555-0001
Admissions Phone: 330-742-3091 · **Admissions Fax:** 330-742-1580
Admissions E-mail: jkweintz@cc.ysu.edu

INSTITUTIONAL INFORMATION
Public/Private: Public. **Evening Classes Available?** Yes. **Students in Parent Institution:** 11,787.

STUDENT INFORMATION
Total Students in Program: 1,168. **% Full-time:** 18. **% Female:** 63.

RESEARCH FACILITIES
Research Facilities: Center for Historic Preservation, Dale Ethics Center, Center for Photon-Induced Processes, Center for Engineering Research and Technology Transfer, Center for the Study of Young Adult and Children's Literature, Center for Biotechnology.

EXPENSES/FINANCIAL AID
Annual Tuition: In-state $2,826. / Out-of-state $6,336. **Fees:** $700. **Books and Supplies:** $900. **Loans Range From:** $100-$14,085. **Number of Teaching/Research Assistantships Granted Each Year:** 35. **Average Salary Stipend:** $6,000.

ADMISSIONS INFORMATION
Application Fee: $30. **Regular Notification:** Rolling. **Transfer Students Accepted?** Yes. **Number of Applications Received:** 358. **% of Applicants Accepted:** 94. **% Accepted Who Enrolled:** 82.
Required Admission Factors: Letters of recommendation, transcript.
Program-Specific Admission Factors: Minimum 2.7 GPA and essay required of English program applicants. Minimum 2.75 GPA and minimum 24 credit hours (undergraduate) of history coursework required of history program applicants.

EMPLOYMENT INFORMATION
Placement Office Available? Yes.

SCHOOL SAYS

In this section you'll find schools with extended listings describing admissions, curriculum, internships, and much more. This is your chance to get in-depth information on programs that interest you. The Princeton Review charges each school a small fee to be listed, and the editorial responsibility is solely that of the university.

ANTIOCH UNIVERSITY MCGREGOR

AT A GLANCE

Founded by Horace Mann, educational and social pioneer, Antioch University has been an innovator in higher education for 150 years. Today, Antioch is a five-campus university located in four states. Antioch University McGregor is one of those campuses. Antioch seeks to pass on to its graduates a legacy of passion for lifelong learning and commitment to the application of knowledge toward the betterment of our workplaces, communities and the wider society. We believe that education is most effective when students, faculty, staff, and administration unite as a community of learners.

Antioch University McGregor, established in 1988, offers academic programs for adults that are responsive to emerging societal needs. AUM is imbued with an entrepreneurial spirit and provides high quality, socially responsive, flexible, and innovative educational programs. Each program encourages critical thinking, provides opportunities for collaborative learning, emphasizes cultural diversity and an international perspective, and promotes the integration of life and work experience with academic knowledge. AUM's motto is "Be the difference."

PROGRAMS OF STUDY

Antioch University McGregor offers a master of arts (MA) in a field of choice through the Individualized Liberal and Professional Studies (ILPS) Program. In addition, master's-level distance programs in management for community college professionals and in conflict resolution are also offered. The programs combine a limited residency with online course work. Locally, the MA in management meets on Saturdays in Yellow Springs for six quarters, excluding summer. The School of Education offers MEd in various areas—early childhood education, middle childhood education, adolescent/young adult education and mild to moderate intervention (special education). All of these master's degrees fulfill the requirements for a teacher license in the State of Ohio. Additionally, the MEd in leadership provides the content that can also lead to the requirements for School Principal Licensure in the state.

A master of arts through the ILPS Program allows students to collaborate with an Antioch faculty adviser and experts in their field of study to design courses and—ultimately—their master of arts degree. This MA allows students to meet their own personal, educational, and professional needs while maintaining high academic standards. This is a limited-residency program with flexibility of design as a distance-learning program or as a program local to the student, depending on the student's preferences and academic resources.

The master of arts in management for community college professionals provides a unique educational experience for current and aspiring community college managers, faculty and administrators. The curriculum includes the traditional management disciplines while focusing on issues relevant to higher education. This is a limited-residency 2-year program. Courses are offered through a combination of face-to-face meetings and online study.

The master of arts in conflict resolution is an internationally recognized program with a reputation for graduating students who are highly skilled and knowledgeable theorist-practitioners. This is an 8-quarter, half-time program. Students attend two 14-day residencies, participate in online courses, and complete a practicum. The Intercultural Conflict Management Certificate Program parlays AUM's expertise in the field of conflict resolution to answer the growing societal call for leadership in this specific area in a year long series of courses awarding 22 graduate credits.

The Graduate Management Program incorporates a team-based approach across its entire curriculum. This local 2-year Saturday program provides the necessary expertise across the curriculum that is required to operate as a manager in the real world. Students in the graduate management program very often are able to apply classroom content to analyze and modify business practices immediately, dramatically illustrating Antioch's focus on taking theory to practice.

Antioch University McGregor's graduate level teacher licensure and post-graduate principal licensure programs are unique in delivery and content. Offered on weeknights, these students are pursuing credentials that identify them as highly qualified teachers as defined by the State of Ohio. In the summer, our Educational Leadership Summer Series provides numerous continued learning opportunities for local and regional educators.

FINANCIAL AID

Antioch participates in the Federal Stafford Loan, the Federal Perkins Loan, and Federal Work-Study Programs. Other payment options are available. Approximately 85 percent of students receive financial aid.

COST OF STUDY

Each program of study differs in cost depending on the number of credits needed to graduate. Antioch is a moderately priced private higher education institution. Average tuition costs to complete a graduate degree program range from $14,000 to $22,000.

LIVING AND HOUSING COSTS

Antioch University McGregor does not offer on-campus housing. Students commute or are enrolled in limited residency programs.

LOCATION

Antioch University McGregor is located in Yellow Springs, Ohio.

APPLYING

Applications are accepted throughout the year. Financial aid applications should be submitted 6 weeks before the quarter begins to ensure timely receipt of aid, loans, and grants. Applicants must take part in a personal interview with the admissions committee. GRE or GMAT scores are not required for admission. Applications may be submitted on-line at www.mcgregor.edu.

Correspondence and Information

Antioch University McGregor

Office of Student and Alumni Services

800 Livermore Street

Yellow Springs, OH 45387

Telephone: 937-769-1818

Fax: 937-769-1804

E-mail: sas@mcgregor.edu

Website: http://www.mcgregor.edu

BAYLOR UNIVERSITY

AT A GLANCE

Baylor University's MBA program provides you with the kind of personal, in-depth, hands-on learning that will best equip you to succeed in today's business world. Unlike traditional curricula that simply moves you through one business course after another, Baylor's MBA program integrates its core MBA courses across functional areas, giving you the opportunity to study business the way you do business.

Small classes, hosted at the university's state-of-the-art Hankamer School of Business in Waco, Texas, set the stage for an integrated learning experience that balances leading-edge business theory with practical, hands-on, real-world challenges.

DEGREES OFFERED

The Hankamer School of Business offers 12 graduate programs, including two joint programs with Baylor Law School. The largest program in Baylor Business is the full-time MBA. For students new to business education, Baylor offers the Integrated Management Seminar (IMS), designed specifically for students wanting to enter Baylor's MBA or MSIS program but needing business prerequisites. Once students pass the intensive one-semester IMS, they enter the first semester of the MBA or MSIS program. Programs include the master of business administration (MBA), executive MBA program in Dallas (EMBA), executive MBA program in Austin-Waco (EMBA), MBA-International Management (MBA-IM), MBA-Information Systems Management, (MBA-ISM), MBA/Master of Science in Information Systems (MBA/MSIS), Master of Science in Information Systems (MSIS), Master of Accountancy (MACC), Master of Taxation (MTAX), Master of Science in Economics (MS-ECO), Juris Doctorate/MBA (JD/MBA), and the Juris Doctorate/MTAX (JD/MTAX).

ACADEMIC PROGRAMS

MBA Program: The design of the MBA Core Courses centers around the business cycle of planning, implementation, and evaluation. Choose from a wide range of elective courses that allow you the opportunity to specialize or generalize, including Healthcare Administration, Information Systems, and Entrepreneurship. In as little as 16 months, you build the solid, overall business foundation you'll need to expand your career. During the summer semester, you can work in an internship, study abroad through an international exchange program, or take elective courses on campus.

FACILITIES

One of the strategic objectives of the Hankamer School of Business is to provide students with the tools to succeed in today's technology-fueled business environment. All Baylor business students take advantage of the wireless networking environment throughout the Baylor campus. One of the most visible aspects of Baylor's 10-year vision is the university's most ambitious construction and facilities improvement campaign ever, with $150 million in projects under construction and $50 million in other facilities in various stages of planning. You can follow our progress by accessing the "Building the Vision" page on the Baylor 2012 website. The Baylor library system was reorganized in 2002 as the 21st Century Library, which includes the university libraries and the electronic library divisions.

EXPENSES AND FINANCIAL AID

Dollar for dollar, you will get more from a Baylor graduate business education than almost anywhere in the country. Money magazine consistently ranks Baylor among the best values in the country. Our tuition is among the lowest of any major private university in the Southwest and one of the least expensive in the nation. Graduate scholarships, assistantships, and financial aid can make your graduate education a reality. Scholarships and graduate assistantships are awarded to qualified students each semester. Please see the website for additional information.

FACULTY

We believe a strong student-professor relationship can have dynamic, lifelong benefits and as a result, close mentoring relationships with faculty are a reality at Baylor. While it is possible at many large MBA programs for students to get lost in the shuffle, at Baylor you'll work with faculty members on academic and non-academic projects, such as personal goal setting, coursework plans, internship and career opportunities, or interviewing and placement. Your relationship with faculty members will help you sharpen your ambitions and form a solid basis upon which to develop the business acumen to succeed. While Baylor is known for its teaching excellence, the Hankamer School of Business recognized strength as an AACSB accredited school draws upon the expertise of the faculty as consultants and noted scholars. All professors teaching in the MBA programs hold doctorate degrees, are active in their professional fields, are business consultants, and are well published.

STUDENTS

Baylor offers an environment that will not only challenge you academically, but will nourish you personally. We are Texas's oldest university, and the world's largest Baptist university, committed to the unique mission of balancing mind and spirit.

Baylor offers a diverse community of people from around the world, including MBA students from a wide variety of states and many countries. International students comprise 25 percent of Baylor's MBA enrollment. This culturally diverse learning environment gives students the global perspective necessary to succeed in today's world market. The University International Programs Office and the International Graduate Student Association provide the support and guidance needed in adapting to American culture.

ADMISSIONS

Admission to Baylor Business is competitive. For the MBA program, we're looking for individuals with professional work experience, outstanding scholarship, a commitment to community service, and a motivation to pursue an intense graduate business program. MBA candidates should have strong analytical capabilities and communication skills. For programs other than the MBA, Baylor Business looks for the same qualities except professional work experience. Please see the website for additional information.

CAREER SERVICES AND PLACEMENT

Hundreds of employers consult Baylor's Career Services Center annually for potential Baylor graduate employees. One of the country's most sophisticated automation systems affords firms easy access to students' credentials. As a graduate business student, you will benefit from the individual attention of the associate director of MBA Career Services, who helps match candidates with potential employers for both full-time positions and internships.

For more information contact:

Laurie Wilson

Baylor University

One Bear Place #98013

1311 South 5th Street

Waco, Texas 76798

Telephone: 254-710-4163

E-mail: Laurie_Wilson@baylor.edu

Website: www.baylor.edu

BOSTON UNIVERSITY SCHOOL OF EDUCATION

AT A GLANCE

The Boston University School of Education has prepared classroom teachers and other education professionals since 1918. Our alumni are leaders in schools, community and government agencies, and corporations across the United States and around the globe. Through the Boston University/Boston Public Schools Collaborative, Boston University faculty and students have worked closely with the Boston Public Schools for more than 30 years. In 1989, Boston University entered into an unprecedented agreement to manage the public school system of Chelsea, Massachusetts, a system facing problems typical of many urban districts. With 20 percent of our full-time students from overseas, and the academic and cultural hub of Boston as our home, the School of Education offers a rich graduate experience.

CAMPUS AND LOCATION

Boston University is perfectly situated to enjoy the charm and beauty of the city of Boston and its many museums, theaters, and historic sites. The campus stretches along the banks of the Charles River, bringing boating, canoeing, and jogging to our doorstep. The streetcar that runs through campus connects students to the shopping, sporting, and cultural attractions of the city and to the more than 60 other colleges and universities in greater Boston. The School of Education is one of 17 schools and colleges that comprise Boston University. Students in the School of Education may choose from related classes taught at other schools when planning their graduate programs.

EXPENSES AND FINANCIAL AID
Tuition

2005-2006 rate	$985 per credit for full time or day classes
	$493 per credit for late afternoon or evening classes
Registration Fee	$40 per semester

FINANCIAL AID

Each year, Boston University School of Education offers $3 million in scholarship aid to full-time graduate students. Typical scholarships for the 2005-2006 academic year are set at $20,000 or $15,000. U.S. citizens and permanent residents may also apply for government loans and work-study. Scholarship applicants should submit the one page Graduate Application for Financial Assistance. U.S. citizens and permanent residents should also file the FAFSA form.

While most graduate aid is in the form of scholarships, graduate students may apply for research and teaching assistantships as well. The assistantship application is mailed with the acceptance letter.

For more information, visit our website: http://www.bu.edu/education/students/prospective/graduate/financial

STUDENTS

Boston University attracts students from 50 states and 140 countries. Our teaching programs are approved for licensure by the Commonwealth of Massachusetts, which has a reciprocal agreement with 44 other states.

ADMISSIONS

Most graduate programs review applications on a rolling basis, but the preferred deadline is February 15 for summer or fall enrollment or November 1 for January.

Master's applicants must hold a baccalaureate degree or equivalent from an accredited college or university and doctoral applicants must hold a master's degree.

A complete application includes

- Graduate Application, available online at www.bu.edu/education
- Official transcripts from each college or university attended
- Two or more letters of reference
- Statement of Objectives and Qualifications (a one to two page essay).

Doctoral applicants must also submit an analytical essay described at www.bu.edu/education/students/prospective/graduate/admissions/requirements

- Standardized Test score. Either the general GRE or the Miller Analogies Test score should be submitted. International doctoral applicants who have not earned a previous degree in English should also submit the TOEFL score. International master's applicants need only submit the TOEFL
- Application fee of $65.

Please contact us for additional information:

Graduate Admissions Office

Boston University School of Education

Two Sherborn Street

Boston, MA 02215

Telephone: 617-353-4237

E-mail: sedgrad@bu.edu

Website: www.bu.edu/education

EXPERIENCE BEYOND THE CLASSROOM

Graduate students at Boston University School of Education have tremendous opportunities to develop their skills and their resumes while earning a degree.

Among the affiliated programs that employ and train graduate students are:

- The Intergenerational Literacy Project, which teaches literacy skills to immigrant parents and their children
- Upward Bound at Boston University, which prepares urban high school students for college
- Boston University Initiative in Literacy Development, which employs Boston University School of Education graduate students as literacy tutors and supervisors in elementary literacy programs in schools, housing projects, and a public hospital
- The Early Childhood Learning Laboratory, a preschool located at the School of Education, is widely recognized for its innovative curriculum in developing cognitive and social skills for preschool children
- The Center for the Study of Communication and the Deaf provides community service the hearing parents of deaf children and workshops and presentations to area agencies. The center has recently received funding to investigate the role of ASL in the thinking of deaf children.

BROOKLYN COLLEGE OF THE CITY UNIVERSITY OF NY

AT A GLANCE

Brooklyn College of the City University of New York, founded in 1930, is a premier public liberal arts college respected nationally for its rigorous academic standards. Founded in 1935, the Division of Graduate Studies offers more than 60 master's degree and advanced certificate programs in the arts, education, humanities, social sciences, sciences, and professional studies.

CAMPUS AND LOCATION

Situated on a 26-acre campus of Georgian-styled buildings, broad lawns, and tree-lined walkways in the heart of the most dynamic borough of New York City, Brooklyn College was ranked "Most Beautiful Campus" in the United States in the 2003 edition of the Princeton Review's *The Best 345 Colleges*. Adding to the beauty of the campus is the dazzling new library, the most technologically advanced facility in the CUNY system, and a state-of-the-art student services and physical education building, currently under construction, which will open in 2007. The college's easy accessibility by subway or bus allows students to further enrich their educational experience through New York City's many cultural events and institutions.

DEGREES OFFERED

MA, MS, MFA, MPH, MS in education, MMus advanced certificate.

PROGRAMS & CURRICULUM

Communications, journalism, and related programs; computer and information sciences and support services; education; foreign languages, literatures, and linguistics; family and consumer sciences/human sciences; English language and literature/letters; liberal arts and sciences, general studies, and humanities; biological and biomedical sciences; mathematics and statistics; multi/interdisciplinary studies; parks, recreation, leisure and fitness studies; philosophy and religion; physical sciences; psychology; social sciences; visual and performing arts; health professions and related clinical sciences; business, management, marketing, and related support services; history.

FACILITIES

Information Technology Services provides Help Desk and on-site support to the college's students, faculty and staff. Brooklyn College maintains several large-scale public-access computing facilities, supplemented by departmental discipline-specific labs and electronic classrooms. Over 1,000 computers are available to students. The Atrium and Wolfe computer labs are open 24 hours a day, seven days a week, as well as the Morton and Angela Topfer Library Café, which contains 50 computers. The college maintains a sophisticated video-conferencing and multimedia facility. Brooklyn College students also have access to computing facilities provided by the CUNY/CIS central computing center. Dial-up and network access to mainframe resources and software applications may be arranged.

EXPENSES & FINANCIAL AID

The Division of Graduate Studies at Brooklyn College provides advanced education of superior quality at a comparatively modest tuition. Loans, college work-study, scholarships, graduate assistantships, fellowships, and internships may be available to qualified students.

Tuition for New York State residents is $2,720 per semester, or $230 per credit. For courses in which the number of hours a class meets each week exceeds the number of credits, students pay $230 per credit plus $65 for each additional class hour. Maximum tuition each term: $2,720. Tuition for out-of-state residents and international students is $5,100 for 12 credits, or $425 per credit. For courses in which the number of hours a class meets each week exceeds the number of credits, students pay $425 per credit plus $85 for each additional class hour. There is no maximum tuition each term.

Other anticipated costs include books/supplies, housing, transportation, food, and personal.

Graduate students are encouraged to apply for scholarship funding. Applications are available beginning in September for the following fall semester. They are available in paper form or may be completed online at http://depthome.brooklyn.cuny.edu/scholar.

STUDENTS

Today students from almost every state and more than 30 countries are working toward their master's degrees at Brooklyn College. The college's 15,300 undergraduate and graduate students represent the ethnic and cultural diversity of the borough.

ADMISSIONS

Admission to the Division of Research and Graduate Studies is determined by graduate faculty, departmental and/or program committees. All applicants are advised to review special admissions and matriculation requirements for each program as stated in the Brooklyn College bulletin. You may also apply online at https://websql.brooklyn.cuny.edu/admissions/graduate/. Brooklyn College utilizes a self managed application for admission to graduate study. It is the applicant's responsibility to gather all required materials and send them to Brooklyn College. Official standardized test score reports (TOEFL, GRE, MAT) should be sent under separate cover to Brooklyn College by the respective testing service centers. The following materials should be submitted to the Office of Admissions:

- Graduate application form
- Two letters of recommendation
- Official transcripts from all colleges and universities attended
- Application processing fee of $125.

Academic departments have different deadline dates for fall admissions. Programs that admit in the spring may have different filing dates as well. Students interested in finding out about the filing dates for specific programs should visit us on line at www.brooklyn.cuny.edu. For additional information, please contact admissions at 718-951-5001 or visit us on line at www.brooklyn.cuny.edu.

CAREER SERVICES & PLACEMENT

The Magner Center for Career Development and Internships offers a wide range of career programs to Brooklyn College undergraduates, graduate students, and alumni. The center assists students with finding internships and stipends, career counseling, resume writing, finding part- and full-time jobs, and sponsors on-campus recruiting.

CLAREMONT UNIVERSITY

AT A GLANCE

The Drucker School of Management, located in beautiful Claremont, California, is a unique management school dedicated to training people to become effective and ethical leaders and managers in whatever industries they serve. This focus stems from our belief that management is a liberal art, a human enterprise encompassing perspectives from the social and behavioral sciences. Named after one of the most prominent management thinkers of the 20th century, Peter F. Drucker, the Drucker MBA program offers a high quality interactive educational experience: small classes averaging 25 students per class and instruction from world renowned professors. Approximately 70 percent of our classroom instruction is either in discussion or case analysis format, and we incorporate team building in classroom projects and presentations.

CAMPUS AND LOCATION

Location: approximately 25 miles east of the city of Los Angeles and 6 miles west of Ontario International Airport in a small suburban college-town community.

Population: 34,000

Area and elevation: 14 square miles at an elevation of between 1,100 and 1,800 feet above sea level.

Climate: Average yearly temperature of 63 degrees with average annual rainfall of 17 inches.

Nestled in the foothills of the San Gabriel Mountains, this charming community is famous for its tree-lined streets, world-renowned colleges, and charming "old town" restaurants and shops. Claremont provides the atmosphere of a New England college town within comfortable driving distance of major Southern California attractions and sports stadiums.

DEGREES OFFERED

- MBA
- Master of Science in Financial Engineering
- Dual Degrees
- Executive MBA
- Certificate Series
- PhD in Management

MBA Program

Consistent with our vision, we attract students who already exhibit strong leadership and achievement skills or who clearly show the potential to develop such skills. These students typically wish to develop themselves both as individuals and as professional executives fully competent in the complex, globally connected economy, and recognize our focus on strategy, leadership, and risk management and our philosophy of management as a liberal art. The effectiveness of this positioning strategy is confirmed by the fact the Drucker School's MBA program was ranked 20th nationally in the General Management category in the *U.S. News & World Report*'s 2003 rankings.

EXPENSES AND FINANCIAL AID

Tuition: $17,021 full time (16 credits); $1,099/credit part time

Fees: $80

Books & Supplies: $400

Health Insurance: $225

Average Rent: $600–$700/month (not including meals). We have on-campus graduate apartments (first come first serve) and numerous off-campus housing resources/assistance.

Expenses: Expected expenses are approximately $12,000 per year, including housing, meals and entertainment.

Financial Aid: Merit- and need-based scholarships are available for U.S. and international students alike. Institutional financial aid is based on the applicant's professional work experience, academic qualifications, and GMAT score. To be considered, applicants must complete the Application for Institutional Financial Aid and have their entire application materials submitted by the financial aid deadline. Government loans (FAFSA—for U.S. citizens and permanent residents) and International Student loans are available.

THE SCHOOL AT A GLANCE

The Peter F. Drucker Graduate School of Management at Claremont Graduate University, located in beautiful Claremont, California, is a unique management school dedicated to training people to become effective and ethical leaders, strategists, and visionaries in whatever organization they serve. Our focus stems from the belief that management is a liberal art, a human enterprise encompassing perspectives from the social and behavioral sciences. This positions Drucker as a "Different School of Thought" and not just another business school.

In his book, *The New Realities*, Peter Drucker explains why management is a liberal art:

"Management is thus what tradition used to call a liberal art—'liberal' because it deals with the fundamentals of knowledge, self-knowledge, wisdom, and leadership; 'art' because it is practice and application. Managers draw on all the knowledge and insights of the humanities and the social sciences."

ADMISSIONS

The Peter F. Drucker Graduate School of Management at Claremont Graduate University prides itself in being "A Different School of Thought." Our student body is academically, professional, racially, and geographically diverse, and we do not require an undergraduate background in business or economics. Our aim is to create an environment that more realistically reflects the world around us.

We do not have minimum cut-offs for the GMAT and GPA as we attempt to individualize each student's application by evaluating the "whole person."

In order for an application to be complete, applicants must submit:
1) Application
2) Student profile sheet and application for institutional financial aid (if applicable)
3) 3 letters of reference (recommendation letters)
4) Official transcripts from every college/university attended
5) Personal statement (3–5 pages double-spaced)
6) Current resume
7) GMAT score
8) TOEFL score (for international students)

COLUMBIA U.—ENVIRONMENTAL SCIENCE & POLICY

AT A GLANCE

The master of public administration (MPA) program in environmental science and policy trains sophisticated public managers and policy makers, who apply innovative, systems-based thinking to environmental issues. The program challenges students to think systemically and act pragmatically. To meet this challenge, Columbia offers a top-quality graduate program in management and policy analysis that emphasizes practical skills and is enriched by ecological and planetary science. The program's approach reflects the system-level thinking that is needed to understand ecological interactions and maintain the health of the earth's interconnected ecological, institutional, economic, and social systems. Public policy and administration represents the core of the program, with the goal to provide students with the analytic, communication, and work skills required to be problem-solving earth systems professionals.

CAMPUS AND LOCATION

This 12-month program takes place at Columbia University's Morningside Heights Campus in New York City and at its Lamont-Doherty Earth Observatory in Palisades, New York, a 25-minute drive (or campus shuttle ride) from the main campus. During the summer six class sessions and special seminars will be held at Columbia University's beautiful Lamont campus, overlooking the Hudson River. All other courses are held on the Morningside Heights Campus on New York City's dynamic, diverse upper west side. Columbia's campus in Morningside Heights is one of the richest concentrations of educational resources and academic activity in the United States. Its 15 schools draw on a renowned faculty, making it among the country's most productive research centers. Students in the MPA program in environmental science and policy work closely with Columbia's Earth Institute, the world's leading academic center for the integrated study of Earth, its environment, and society

EXPENSES AND FINANCIAL AID

Participation in Columbia's MPA program in environmental science and policy requires a significant investment of time and money. Fellowships are available each year for a select number of incoming students and are awarded based on both need and merit.

Tuition

The program's tuition and fees for 2005–2006 will total $49,137. We estimate that living expenses are around $11,000, personal expenses are about $4,000. However, please keep in mind that these costs vary according to your personal choices.

Financial Aid

There are fellowships available based upon need and merit. The application deadline for students seeking fellowships is January 15. Long-term loans at low interest rates are available, including Federal Stafford Student Loans and Federal Perkins Loans. The Federal Work-Study Program is also available.

STUDENTS

Drawn from more than 75 countries, School of International and Public Affairs students are diverse, mature (the average age is 27), and intelligent individuals. The environmental science and policy program enrolls approximately 50 to 55 students each year.

ADMISSIONS

November 1 is the early admission deadline. Applicants who submit a completed application by that date are promised a decision by December 1. January 15 is the final application deadline for students seeking fellowships. February 15 is the final deadline for June admission. International applicants are encouraged to apply a month in advance of these deadlines.

- A bachelor's degree or its equivalent is required for admission.
- Advanced high school course work in chemistry and biology is strongly recommended.
- Qualification for admission is based upon the admissions committee's review of the applicant's file.
- Familiarity with environmental issues and microeconomics is strongly preferred.
- Any candidate who earned a bachelor's degree (or the international equivalent) from a country in which English is not the native language of instruction must submit the Test of English as a Foreign Language (TOEFL) scores or submit the test results of the Columbia University American Language Program (ALP) English Placement Test.
- Recent GRE scores are highly recommended.

Application material must include:

- A completed application form
- Official transcripts from all colleges, professional schools, and universities
- Three letters of evaluation. If possible, at least one of these should be from a member of the academic profession. Other letters may be from an employer, supervisor, or work associate
- A personal statement describing how one's professional and academic background has influenced the decision to pursue a career in the field of environmental science, policy, and management
- A curriculum vitae

For information concerning admission, financial aid, curriculum, and staff members, students should write to the address below.

Louise A. Rosen

Assistant Director, Master of Public Administration Program in Environmental Science and Policy

School of International and Public Affairs

1407 International Affairs

420 West 118th Street

New York, New York 10027

United States

Telephone: 212-854-3142

Fax: 212-864-4847

E-mail: lar46@columbia.edu

Website: www.columbia.edu/cu/mpaenvironment/

CAREER SERVICES AND PLACEMENT

The Office of Career Services, located in the School of International and Public Affairs, helps students in all stages of their search for employment, from career interviews to the writing of resumes and their submission to appropriate organizations. The office has a long-standing working relationship with scores of agencies and private organizations. The MPA program in environmental science and policy prepares highly marketable students for management and leadership roles in countless arenas of the global public and private sectors. Recent graduates have gone on to careers with NASA, the Center for Corporate Responsibility, EarthTech Environmental Consulting and Engineering, Forest Guardians, CH2M Hill, and the Agency for Toxic Substances and Disease Registry.

MONMOUTH UNIVERSITY

LOCATION & ENVIRONMENT

Monmouth University is located in a residential area of an attractive community near the Atlantic Ocean, approximately one hour away from the metropolitan attractions of New York City and Philadelphia. Monmouth enjoys the advantage of proximity (within its home county) to many high technology firms, financial institutions, and a thriving business/industrial sector. These places provide employment possibilities for Monmouth University graduates.

The university's 153-acre campus, considered one of the most beautiful in New Jersey, includes in its more than 50 different facilities a harmonious blend of historic and contemporary architectural styles.

PROGRAMS & CURRICULUM

The Graduate School administers the graduate programs through five academic schools: School of Business Administration; School of Education; The Wayne D. McMurray School of Humanities and Social Sciences; The Marjorie K. Unterberg School of Nursing & Health Studies; and the School of Science, Technology, and Engineering. The graduate school degree programs are designed to meet the educational needs of post-baccalaureate students who wish to acquire advanced knowledge and skills in their chosen fields of study and to engage in research and other scholarly activities. Classes are offered year-round, scheduled predominantly in the evening. The exception is the MSW program, which offers a full-time program during the day and part-time program during the evening.

Monmouth University's graduate school offers many opportunities for students interested in the arts and sciences.

The Wayne D. McMurray School of Humanities and Social Sciences offers seven master's degree programs including: corporate and public communication, criminal justice, history, English, liberal arts, social work, and psychological counseling. Graduate certificates are offered in criminal justice, three specific areas of communication, and professional counseling (a post-master's certificate program). All programs of study are directed toward preparing students for working and living in a global environment.

Monmouth University's School of Science, Technology, and Engineering awards master's degrees in computer science and software engineering. The computer science discipline offers tracks in telecommunications, computer networks, and intelligent information systems. For students interested in software engineering, the following tracks are available: telecommunications, embedded systems, information management, and software technology. Three graduate software engineering certificate programs are also available.

EXPENSES & FINANCIAL AID

For information on expenses for 2005–2006, please visit the university's website at www.monmouth.edu/admission/financialaid/pay/tuitionfees.asp.

Monmouth University believes that qualified students should not be denied an educational opportunity due to lack of financial resources and that financing a student's education should be a cooperative effort between the student and the institution. To that end, the staff of the Financial Aid Office is available to assist students in developing a comprehensive educational financial plan. Students and families are strongly encouraged to call or visit the Financial Aid Office at 732-571-3463 to engage in this planning process.

FACULTY

The graduate faculty provides the core of instruction in the graduate school at Monmouth University. Recognized for their scholarly achievements by peers in their fields, the members of the faculty provide a challenging classroom environment. The faculty brings insight from research and professional experience into the classroom. Graduate students are drawn into the ongoing, creative work of the faculty through classroom demonstration, as research assistants, and through attendance at professional meetings. Faculty members also serve as advisors and mentors to students, in many cases not only during the course of their studies but also after they graduate from the university.

Working directly with senior faculty who are engaged in research is a key element in graduate-level study. In recent interviews, a group of student leaders on campus unanimously agreed that the opportunity to work closely with faculty is the greatest single benefit of Monmouth's small class size and engaged faculty.

STUDENTS

Monmouth University, as described in its mission statement, is an independent, comprehensive institution of higher learning that emphasizes teaching and scholarship at the undergraduate and graduate levels. The university is dedicated to service in the public interest and, in particular, to the enhancement of the quality of life. Monmouth University is committed to providing a learning environment that enables men and women to pursue their educational goals, to reach their full potential, to determine the direction of their lives, and to contribute actively to their community and society.

Monmouth University, founded in 1933, was a two-year institution holding classes only in the evenings. For a time it appeared uncertain whether the college would have adequate funds to continue. With support from students and the community, however, the fledgling college survived the economic crisis and quickly assumed its present private status. In 1956 it was renamed Monmouth College and accredited by the state to offer four-year programs leading to the baccalaureate degree. Less than a decade later, it was authorized to offer master's degree programs. In 1995, the New Jersey Commission on Higher Education designated Monmouth a teaching university.

Today, Monmouth's student body enrollment is more than 6,000 and represents 22 states and 35 foreign countries.

ADMISSION

Graduates of colleges of recognized standing, whose records show evidence of ability to do graduate work, may apply for admission. Selection for all programs is based on the student's ability to do graduate work of high quality as shown by the distinction of the undergraduate record, particularly in the major, scores on appropriate admission tests, and/or other supporting documentation where required. Each program has its own set of admission requirements and all admissions decisions are approved by the program director of the department in which the student plans to earn a graduate degree.

The deadline for application for the fall semester is August 1; for the spring semester the date is December 1; and for summer sessions, the deadline is May 15. Qualified applicants are given consideration after the deadline on a space-available basis. Please note that applications for the fall term are only accepted for the MSW program until March 15 and for the corporate and public communication program until June 15.

For more information contact:

Kevin Roane, Director of Graduate Admission

Monmouth University

400 Cedar Avenue

West Long Branch, NJ 07764-1898

Telephone: 800-320-7754 or 732-571-3452

E-mail: kroane@monmouth.edu

Website: www.monmouth.edu

PARSONS SCHOOL OF DESIGN

AT A GLANCE

Parsons School of Design, a division of New School University, is one of the largest degree-granting colleges of art and design in the nation. Currently enrolled are about 2,400 undergraduate students, 500 graduate students, and 2,500 nondegree students from all 50 United States and from 60 countries. Parsons' main campuses are located in New York City's Greenwich Village and the Upper East Side at the Cooper-Hewitt National Design Museum. Graduate degrees are granted in architecture, design and technology, lighting design, painting and sculpture, photography, and the history of decorative arts. For further information on Parsons, call 212-229-8911 or visit the website at www.parsons.edu.

CAMPUS AND LOCATION

Urban Campus

    Greenwich Village (Main) Campus

    66 Fifth Avenue

    New York, NY 10011

    212-229-8911

Cooper Hewitt National Design Musuem (Decorative Arts NY Program)

    2 East 91st Street

    New York, NY 10128

The Smithsonian Associates (Decorative Arts DC Program)

    1100 Jefferson Drive, SW

    Washington, DC 20560

DEGREES OFFERED

MA: history of decorative arts (European & American)

MArch: architecture

MFA: design & technology, photography, fine arts, lighting design

PROGRAMS & CURRICULUM

Architecture (MArch)

Design and technology (MFA)

Fine arts (MFA)

History of decorative arts (MA)

Lighting design (MFA)

Photography (MFA)

EXPENSES & FINANCIAL AID

Tuition cost for 2004–2005: $29,290

More than 70 percent of students receive financial aid and/or loans.

ADMISSIONS

For all departments:

- Application deadline: 2/1
- $40 application fee
- Resume or CV
- Statement of intent/purpose
- Official copies of all college transcripts
- 2 letters of recommendation from faculty or people with whom you have worked professionally

ADDITIONAL DEPARTMENTAL REQUIREMENTS:

Architecture

- GRE scores (Verbal, Quantitative, Analytical)
- TOEFL score of 580 or higher (237 computerized)
- Portfolio (not to exceed 9"x12")
- Third letter of recommendation

Design and Technology

- TOEFL score of 580 or higher (237 computerized)
- Portfolio must be submitted as website URL, CD-Rom, DVD, videotape, or slides.

History of Decorative Arts

- Interview if residing within 200 miles of NY or DC campus
- Third letter of recommendation
- Minimum of 6 credits of art history (or equivalent experience)
- Sample of scholarly work (recommended)
- GRE scores (strongly recommended)
- TOEFL score of 650 (280 computerized)

Fine Arts

- TOEFL score of 580 (237 computerized)
- Portfolio of work (20 pieces) in slide or CD-ROM format with inventory list.

Lighting Design

- TOEFL score of 580 or higher (237 computerized)
- Portfolio (not to exceed 9"x12")

Photography

- TOEFL score of 550 or higher (213 computerized)
- Portfolio of work (20 pieces) in slide, CD-ROM, DVD, or video format.

PERU STATE COLLEGE

AT A GLANCE
In 1867 Nebraska achieved statehood and shortly thereafter the new state's legislature established a training school for teachers in the town of Peru. Peru State College's School of Education and Graduate Studies was first authorized to confer its bachelor of arts degree in 1949 and its bachelor of science degree in 1965. In 1986 the Board of Trustees approved a master of science in education program. Emerging from its role as a single-purpose teachers' college, Peru State College is now a regional state college offering a wide variety of programs to meet the challenging needs of today's students. Peru State College is also a recognized pioneer in accredited online higher education.

CAMPUS AND LOCATION
Peru State College, one of the oldest colleges west of the Mississippi, is located in Southeast Nebraska. We are approximately an hour's drive from Omaha or Lincoln and about two hours from Kansas City, MO. A proud member of the Nebraska Statewide Arboretum, Peru State College's "Campus of a Thousand Oaks" is bursting with greenery, trees, and a lush landscape, and the campus is accented by historical structures, sculptures, and landmarks. Our programs can also be pursued at our Southwest Omaha campus, as well as online. Peru State College offers a master of science in education in curriculum and instruction with two options: teaching and learning (formerly pedagogy) and instructional technology. Our graduate programs are designed to build upon the strengths and expertise of experienced teachers. Our reflective leadership framework is intended to extend the teachers' competencies in order to improve the performance of the students they teach.

EXPENSES AND FINANCIAL AID
Pursuing a graduate degree can require a significant investment of time and resources. Peru State College prides itself on offering one of the nation's most affordable graduate degrees in education. Our online programs are available wherever an Internet connection is available, and cost the same no matter where you live. We offer several payment options and financial aid which includes student loans. Peru State College has the lowest tuition and fees of any four-year institution in the State of Nebraska.

Main Peru Campus Classes:

Undergraduate, Nebraska resident: $95.00 per credit hour

Undergraduate, Non-resident: $190.00 per credit hour

Graduate, Nebraska resident: $120.25 per credit hour

Graduate, Non-resident: $240.50 per credit hour

Off-Campus Classes (Southwest Omaha Location):

Undergraduate, Nebraska resident: $112.00 per credit hour

Undergraduate, Non-resident: $207.00 per credit hour

Graduate, Nebraska resident: $137.25 per credit hour

Graduate, Non-resident: $257.50 per credit hour

Online Classes:

All *Undergraduate*: $110.00 per credit hour

All *Graduate*: $138.00 per credit hour

Other Anticipated Costs:

Books/supplies, housing, transportation.

FINANCIAL AID
For more information on Financial Aid, visit our website at www.peru.edu. Click on Current and Prospective Students, then Financial Aid.

STUDENTS
Peru State College School of Education and Graduate Studies students are certified teachers, non-certified education professionals and others who find themselves working with adults in teaching and learning situations. We offer convenient locations for face-to-face cohort-based classes and a complete online master's degree in education, Peru State serves students from southeast Nebraska, the American Midwest and the world.

ADMISSIONS
Faculty and staff are here to assist you in making your graduate educational experience the most fulfilling and rewarding time in your scholarly development. We invite you to call the main campus Monday–Friday, 8 A.M. to 5 P.M. (7:30 A.M. to 4:30 P.M. in summer) at 800-742-4412, choice #4, or stop by TJ Majors 207 on our main campus in Peru. If you are interest in the Instructional Technology program offered at the graduate center in southwest Omaha, please call (402) 595-1866.

Basic requirements:

• For admission, applicants must hold a baccalaureate degree or equivalent from an accredited college or university.

• Standardized test scores, GRE or MAT, are required from all applicants.

• Applicants must complete the graduate admission form and furnish official transcripts reflecting a minimum 3.0 GPA. Two letters of recommendation from persons acquainted with the applicant and capable of judging his or her ability to do graduate work. One letter should be from a college faculty person and one from a professional employment supervisor. Applicants must also be certified or eligible for certification as a classroom teacher K-12 and submit a copy of teaching certificate. (Those seeking the graduate degree who are not educators need not submit a teaching certificate.)

For more information on admissions, visit the website at www.peru.edu and click on Academics, then choose School of Education and Graduate Studies.

CAREER SERVICES AND PLACEMENT
Peru State College graduates enjoy a high rate of placement in secondary education career positions. Call us today for details at 800-742-4412, option #4.

ROOSEVELT UNIVERSITY

PROGRAMS OF STUDY

The Graduate Division of Roosevelt University offers master's degrees in accounting, biotechnology and chemical science, business administration (including real estate concentration), computer science, creative writing (MFA), economics, education (educational leadership, counseling and human services, early childhood, early-childhood professions, elementary education, reading, secondary education, special education, and teacher leadership), English, history, hospitality and tourism management, human resource management, information systems, integrated marketing communications, international business, journalism, mathematical sciences (including actuarial science), music (performance, theory, composition, jazz studies, musicology, orchestral studies, and vocal pedagogy), political science, psychology (clinical, professional, and industrial organization), public administration, sociology, Spanish, telecommunications, theater (performance and general theater studies), training and development, and women's and gender studies.

Doctor of education degrees in educational leadership and organizational change are available, as well as a PsyD degree in clinical psychology (APA accredited).

Certificate programs are available in biotechnology, chemical science, clinical child and family studies, computer science/telecommunications, e-learning, early childhood education, fraud examination, geographic information systems, hospitality and tourism, information systems, instructional design, online teaching, paralegal studies, public administration, real estate development, Stress Institute programs, and training and development.

RESEARCH FACILITIES

The Murray-Green Library holds more than 225,000 volumes and a variety of research materials including periodicals and microforms. A full staff is on duty to assist student researchers at the downtown campus, and research services are also available at the Schaumburg Campus. Roosevelt University is a member of the Illinois Library Computer Services Organization (ILCSO), which operates a statewide online circulation system embracing 45 of the largest libraries in Illinois. It is also backed up by the OCLC international bibliographic network and subscribes to numerous online electronic database services.

FINANCIAL AID

Grants, scholarships, and loans are available for qualified students in all programs of the graduate division. Assistantships that pay stipends and carry tuition waivers are offered in many programs. Graduate students may also apply for college work-study. Partial tuition grants are available to qualified full and part-time students. Many graduate students finance their education through loans or are reimbursed by their employers. Those interested in financial aid should see the Applying section below for deadlines.

COST OF STUDY

The 2005–2006 tuition is $688 per graduate semester hour. Fees included a general student fee of $150 per term and, in some programs, laboratory and other nominal fees.

LIVING AND HOUSING COSTS

University Center (UC) 525 S. State Street:

This newly constructed 18-story, state-of-the-art, multi-university residence hall is located just one block away from the Roosevelt University Auditorium Building. University Center houses students attending Roosevelt University, DePaul University and Columbia College Chicago. Enjoy a diverse community of fellow learners and live in an exciting neighborhood teeming with cultural and artistic entertainments. Best of all, you can choose a housing plan that fits your needs.

Herman Crown Center, 425 S. Wabash:

Located right next to the Roosevelt University Auditorium Building, Herman Crown Center means you can attend classes in January and leave behind your coat and gloves. This 17-story residence hall has only 13 rooms on each floor, making residence life exclusive and hospitable. Each room is fully furnished, and HCC has both double- and single-occupancy rooms, and full dining services.

The Marvin Moss Student Center of HCC is a free recreational facility complete with fitness center, game room, basketball courts, and locker rooms.

The Herman Crown Center also houses key administrative offices to benefit students and meet their individual needs: the Office of Residence Life, the Office of Student Activities, and the Office of International Programs.

STUDENT GROUP

Approximately 800 full-time and 2,400 part-time graduate students attend classes at Roosevelt. Students of varied backgrounds and ages from many states and more than 50 other countries pursue graduate studies at the university. Most work part-time or full-time and find Roosevelt's scheduling flexibility well suited to their schedules. In addition, courses and some programs are offered online. In 2004, Roosevelt University was ranked the most diverse master's university in the Midwest, according to the *U.S. News and World Report*.

LOCATION

Roosevelt University's main campus is in two Michigan Avenue locations—the Auditorium Building and the Center for Professional Advancement—in the heart of Chicago's cultural center. Both are within easy commuting distance by car or public transportation. Students can take advantage of the many events and activities in the city. The Albert A. Robin Campus is located in northwest suburban Schaumburg, approximately 30 miles from downtown Chicago. The university van schedules daily transport to and from each of the three campuses. In addition to the two main campus locations, Roosevelt is expanding its efforts to offer courses through partnerships with community colleges and corporations and through its Internet-based RU online program. Currently, one entire degree program, the master of arts in training and development, is available in a fully online format as well as on campus.

THE UNIVERSITY AT A GLANCE

From its founding as a private university in 1945, Roosevelt pioneered the education of adults and nontraditional students, creating a diverse learning environment for all students. Today, its educational programs are recognized nationwide, and students throughout Metropolitan Chicago and from around the world pursue degrees at its two campuses. Roosevelt's characteristics provide a number of graduate educational benefits: small classes that encourage an open exchange of ideas, outstanding faculty, excellent academic programs, scheduling flexibility to accommodate working students, and counseling and career planning services.

The Career Counseling and Placement Office assists students in finding part-time, full-time, and second-career positions. Its services remain available to Roosevelt graduates, who may take advantage of a full range of career counseling, planning, and placement opportunities.

APPLYING

Applicants can apply online or request applications at www.roosevelt.edu or by calling 1-877-APPLY RU. Priority deadlines for applications for admission are August 1 for the fall semester, December 1 for the spring semester, and April 15 for the summer terms. The priority application deadline for assistantships is February 15 for the following year and for partial scholarships the priority deadline is May 1 for fall and October 15 for spring. There is a $25 fee for domestic applications and $35 for international applications. International students must apply at least three months prior to the intended semester.

SAINT XAVIER UNIVERSITY

SAINT·XAVIER
UNIVERSITY

AT A GLANCE

The graduate programs at Saint Xavier University prepare students to assume positions of leadership in professional areas such as health care, business, technology, and education. Leadership in the profession implies the application of science and the exercise of art in addressing human and social problems of considerable complexity. Each program is designed to guide students toward advanced levels of analysis and argument, written discourse, reflective practice, and inquiry.

CAMPUS AND LOCATION

Saint Xavier University's Chicago Campus is located on 73 acres in a residential neighborhood in southwest Chicago. It is close enough to downtown Chicago for students to enjoy the cultural offerings of one of the nation's largest cities and distant enough to experience a sense of quiet and community. Saint Xavier University's Chicago Campus is home to the School of Education, the School of Nursing, the Graham School of Management, and the School of Arts and Sciences. The university's nearby Orland Park Campus also offers a variety of graduate programs, including several from the School of Education, The Graham School of Management, and the School of Arts and Sciences.

DEGREES OFFERED

Graduate students are awarded the degrees of master of applied computer science, master of arts, master of business administration, master of public health, master of science, master of science in nursing, or the joint master of science in nursing/master of business administration.

EXPENSES & FINANCIAL AID

Saint Xavier University is committed to making college education affordable. Tuition and fees are updated annually in the summer and are listed each semester in the graduate academic catalog.

Tuition 2005-2006: Education $550 per credit hour/$450 per credit hour for cohorts; MBA $600 per credit hour; nursing $575 per credit hour; speech $600 per credit hour; computer science $575 per credit hour. Mandatory fees: Application $35 (no fee for applying online); registration $25; student activity fee $30. Optional fees: Parking $70 (per academic year). Other anticipated costs: Books/supplies, housing, transportation More than 35 percent of Saint Xavier University graduate students receive some form of financial aid. Students interested in applying for financial assistance must complete a Free Application for Federal Student Aid (FAFSA). Some of the aid programs available include federal, state, and institutional programs. For more information, visit: http://www.sxu.edu/financial_aid/.

STUDENTS

Saint Xavier University admits qualified students without regard to race, religion, age, sex, color, or national or ethnic origin; the university does not discriminate against persons with disabilities who are otherwise qualified to participate in the intellectual and social life of the university.

ADMISSIONS

Application materials may be obtained from the Office of Graduate Admission or online at www.sxu.edu/admission. See individual program applications for further procedures, requirements and deadlines. All application materials should be sent directly to the Office of Graduate Admission. The director of admission will make the initial evaluation for admission. The file will then be sent to the appropriate program director for further review and an admission decision. The program director will promptly inform applicants of admission decisions. For further information, contact the Office of Graduate Admission at (773) 298-3053 or e-mail *graduateadmission@sxu.edu*.

ADDITIONAL INFORMATION

Saint Xavier University

Office of Graduate Admission

3700 W. 103rd Street

Chicago, IL 60655

Telephone: 773-298-3053

Fax: 773-298-3951

E-mail: graduateadmission@sxu.edu

Website: www.sxu.edu/admission/grad.asp

CAREER SERVICES & PLACEMENT

Counseling and Career Services offers a broad range of life/career services delivered by a knowledgeable and highly trained counseling and placement team. The services now include five functionally different but overlapping areas: personal counseling, career counseling and planning, experiential learning, alumni mentoring, and job placement. With respect for the needs of each individual student, the staff teaches/counsels a diverse student body about the skills they need to make responsible and satisfying life decisions and the choices they will make to achieve their personal and professional goals.

SUFFOLK UNIVERSITY

AT A GLANCE

With over 40 academic programs at the undergraduate and graduate levels, and a dedicated faculty made up of leading academics—both inside and outside the classroom—Suffolk has a program that's right for you. Our classroom discussion is lively and differing viewpoints are encouraged. Please take a moment to view our various programs and learn how to get connected to our community.

MISSION STATEMENT

The College of Arts and Sciences has as its credo that liberal learning prepares students of all ages and backgrounds to live more fulfilling lives, to appreciate and contribute to the communities of which they are members and to reach their ethical, personal, intellectual and financial goals. To help its students maximize their potential, the college emphasizes critical and analytical thinking through a rigorous "success skills" undergraduate core program in written and oral communication, computing, analyzing and integrating. Faculty scholarship supports diversified liberal arts concentrations available in the humanities, the natural sciences and the social sciences, along with graduate programs in several fields, most offering career-related professional program tracks and practical experience on or off campus.

CAMPUS AND LOCATION

Set on historic Beacon Hill, Suffolk is a private, urban university which offers students access to global resources. The Boston campus offers a wide range of undergraduate and graduate degrees in over 70 areas of study. The intellectual contributions of its faculty provide a diverse, challenging and uniquely supportive environment in which motivated and capable students flourish.

TUITION AND EXPENCES

Tuition depends on program and range between $440 and $1,060 per credit for part time students. Rates for full time students range between $7,215 and $13,425. There is also a $10 student activity fee

HOUSING

- Single Room: $5,730
- Double/Triple Room: $5,010
- Quad: $4,770

FINANCIAL AID

The Office of Financial Aid offers a variety of services and is staffed by financial aid professionals who are committed to helping students and their families finance a Suffolk University education. The cost of higher education represents a significant financial burden for many families. In an attempt to help alleviate this burden, there are four sources of financial aid available at Suffolk University: the federal government, the state government, the university, and private sources. Any undergraduate or graduate student enrolled in a degree or certificate program for at least six credit hours may apply for financial aid consideration.

Contact the Financial Aid Department with any questions:

Telephone: 617-573-8470

E-mail: finaid@admin.suffolk.edu

ADMISSIONS

Admission Requirements

- U.S. bachelor's degree from a regionally accredited college or university or an equivalent degree from another country (as determined by the Office of Graduate Admission)

Application material must include:

- Completed application
- Application fee of $35 (USD)
- Statement of professional goals (usually one or two pages)
- Transcripts of all prior academic work
- Current resume
- Two letters of recommendation
- Appropriate testing (GRE, MAT, GMAT, LSAT, MTEL). Please refer to your program of interest for testing requirements.

ADDITIONAL INFORMATION

To request additional information and application materials for graduate programs at Suffolk University to be mailed to you, please complete and submit the form found at http://www.suffolk.edu/gradadm/infoform_g.cfm; or complete and fax the form to the Graduate Admission office at 617-523-0116; or mail it to:

Graduate Admission Office

8 Ashburton Place

Boston, MA 02108

UNION UNIVERSITY GRADUATE COLLEGE

AT A GLANCE

The first rate faculty at The Graduate College deliver a relevant, accredited curriculum within a "small college" environment. It is our high-quality academic program, small size, and careful attention to the individual needs of each student that makes graduate study at our college such a rewarding experience. Almost all classes meet in the evening, enabling us to bring full- and part-time students together in an educationally valuable and exciting way.

CAMPUS AND LOCATION

The Graduate College is located on the Union College campus in Schenectady, New York which is centrally located between Montreal, Boston and New York City. The Capital District (Albany, Schenectady, and Troy) is a major education center with 55,000 students at a dozen colleges and universities, and the area's large array of businesses and government agencies offer extensive internship and career possibilities.

DEGREES OFFERED

The Graduate College offers two MBA degree programs:

• MBA (general—students choose an area of focus)

• MBA in healthcare management

Our MBA programs are accredited by AACSB (the Association to Advance Collegiate Schools of Business). Our innovative MBA in healthcare management is one of a select few that is dually accredited by AACSB and accredited by CAHME (the Commission on Accreditation of Healthcare Management Education).

The Graduate College offers three joint degree programs. In cooperation with Albany Law School, students can obtain a JD and MBA, while in cooperation with Albany College of Pharmacy they offer a joint pharmacy degree.

ACADEMIC PROGRAMS

MBA (general):

• The MBA core courses provides a solid foundation in business administration including probability, statistics, financial accounting, managerial accounting and finance, economics, marketing, operations management, managing people and business law.

• The MBA courses beyond the core allow the student to tailor the program to one's individual interests with a specific focus on finance, economics, marketing, operations, general management or global business.

• The capstone course is the last course one takes and integrates all the courses studied in the MBA program. The principle activity in the course is the development of a comprehensive business plan for a real company. This is done in small student teams. The teams present their final plans to a simulated investment panel of the businesses CEO's and venture capitalists.

• MBA program course requirements include 20 total courses: 10 required core courses, 2 required advanced courses, 8 elective advanced courses. 12 of the 20 courses must be completed at the Graduate College. A maximum of 8 waivers and transfers combined are allowed. An internship of 400 hours or relevant business experience is required. This is not considered one of the 20 courses.

The MBA (healthcare management):

• The MBA healthcare management core courses include introduction to health systems, managing ethically in a global environment, statistical modeling in management, financial and managerial accounting, economics, marketing management & strategy, and operations management.

• The MBA healthcare management required courses beyond the core include such courses as health care finance, health economics, health systems marketing and information systems, legal aspects of health care, health policy and managerial epidemiology, strategic issues for health care organizations.

• The MBA healthcare management offers an array of elective courses (students must take any three).

• The capstone course is typically the last course you take and is intended to integrate all the courses studied in the MBA healthcare management program.

• Program course requirements include 20 total courses: 10 required core courses, 7 required advanced courses, 3 elective advanced courses. 12 of the 20 courses must be completed at the Graduate College. A maximum of 8 waivers and transfers combined are allowed.

The internship is a valuable component of both MBA programs. Students have interned at many fine organizations in the Capital District and beyond including; GE, The AYCO Co., PricewaterhouseCoopers, Mobile Oil, Map Info, Physician groups practices, MVP Health Plan and more.

FACILITIES

Numerous facilities, resources, and services are at the disposal of The Graduate College's students.

EXPENSES AND FINANCIAL AID

Tuition for the MBA program for the academic year 2005–2006 is $20,750. Resource fees are $150. There is no on-campus housing for graduate students. Off-campus housing costs for room and board are approximately $8,800 per year.

Merit-based assistance is available to both U.S. and non-U.S. citizens. Competitive scholarships are awarded. Graduate student loans, part-time employment, internships and affordable graduate housing are available.

FACULTY

The Graduate College's distinguished faculty are readily accessible to students outside the classroom. With an average class size of 15, classes include open discussion and intensive feedback.

STUDENT BODY

There is almost an even number of full- and part-time students, ranging from accelerated undergraduates to CEOs, doctors, lawyers and entrepreneurs. Nineteen percent are international students. The program is designed for students ranging from those with no management background to those with years of experience.

ADMISSIONS

Applicants may seek admission throughout the year on a rolling basis. Notification of an admissions decision is made within four weeks of receipt of a completed application. Students may begin their study in any term. International students whose native language is not English must take the TOFEL exam.

Criteria for admissions in to the MBA programs include a student's postsecondary academic record, career objectives, personal recommendations, and standardized test scores. Course waivers and transfer credit may be approved up to a maximum of eight courses. In general, a minimum GPA of 3.0 is expected in previous academic work. Applicants must submit a $60 application fee, essays, three letters of recommendation, official GMAT test scores, and official transcripts of all previous academic work.

CAREER SERVICES & PLACEMENT

MBA faculty, the associate dean for career placement and the Career Development Center offer a variety of opportunities for MBA students and alumni to explore career paths and learn the job search and career development skills needed to advance in their longer-term careers. Career advising and placement services are available to all matriculated full- and part-time graduate students.

UNIVERSITY OF MASSACHUSETTS—DARTMOUTH

AT A GLANCE

The programs of the College of Arts and Sciences offer students the theoretical and practical foundations for careers in the sciences, humanities, and social sciences, and develop the understanding that enables an informed and independent life. Graduate programs offer small classes; close contact with faculty and undergraduates; excellent facilities for advanced study, research, and creative work, and individualized academic experiences.

MISSION STATEMENT

The University of Massachusetts-Dartmouth distinguishes itself as a vibrant public university actively engaged in personalized teaching and innovative research, and acting as an intellectual catalyst for regional economic, social, and cultural development.

CAMPUS AND LOCATION

UMass-Dartmouth is a part of the five-campus UMass system, UMD's main campus is on 710 wooded acres in Dartmouth, MA, with four satellite campuses in New Bedford and Fall River, and three cooperative sites in Barnstable (Cape Cod), and New Bedford. The university's coastal location grants easy access to Providence, Boston, Newport, Cape Cod and the islands of Martha's Vineyard and Nantucket.

FINACIAL AID

Financing your education is one of the most important issues you and your family face. The financial aid services office is committed to providing you with excellent customer service, timely delivery of information, and sensitivity to your individual financial concerns. UMass-Dartmouth participates in a wide variety of federal, state, institutional, and private financial aid programs. These programs include grants, scholarships and waivers, loans, and work opportunities.

TUITION AND EXPENCES

Such charges as tuition and fees, the policies associated with such charges, and academic or general university policies are subject to change without notice.

Tuition fees: 9 credits per semester

- Massachusetts resident: $1,553

- Non-Massachusetts resident: $6,074

Curriculum support fee: 9 credits per semester

- Massachusetts resident: $4,750

- Non-Massachusetts resident: $6,501

Tuition fees: 12 credits per semester

- Massachusetts resident: $2,071

- Non-Massachusetts resident: $8,099

Curriculum Support Fee: 12 credits per semester

- Massachusetts resident: $6,333

- Non-Massachusetts resident: $8,668

Attendance at UMass-Dartmouth also requires a number of fees to support student needs that include a curriculum support fee, an athletics fee, a student fee, a campus center fee, a health fee, and a MassPIRG fee.

STUDENT

There are a total of 8,299 students, including 6,535 undergraduates, 726 graduate students, and 1,407 continuing education students. By fall 2005, there will be 3,900 students living on campus. The student-faculty ratio is 16:1.

ADDMISSIONS

Applicants must hold a baccalaureate degree baccalaureate degree in an appropriate field from an accredited (if U.S.) institution. Applicants who lack a bachelor's degree may be considered for admission, in some programs, if they can demonstrate convincingly that they have the equivalent of a baccalaureate degree in the discipline of their choice.

Applicants from countries where English is not the national language and/or whose schooling has not been predominantly in English must take the Test of English as a Foreign Language (TOEFL) and pass with a score of at least 500 or 173 on the computer based test.

Application material must include:

- a completed application form

- the required fee of $35 for Massachusetts residents and $55 for out-of-state applicants

- at least 3 letters of recommendation

- official transcripts of all undergraduate and graduate records

- a personal statement, and reports of all required examinations

Suggested deadlines for application completion are:

- April 20 for September entrance

- November 15 for January entrance

The Office of Graduate Studies handles the graduate admissions process. For general inquiries, call 508-999-8604.

XAVIER UNIVERSITY

AT A GLANCE

The Xavier University Graduate Program in Health Services Administration (XUGPHSA) prepares individuals to assume leadership roles in a variety of health services organizations including hospitals, insurance companies, long-term care organizations, integrated delivery networks, HMOs and physician group practices.

The program has a long and successful history. Founded in 1958, it is one of the oldest in the United States. It has been continuously accredited by the Commission on Accreditation on Healthcare Management Education (CAHME) formerly known as the Accrediting Commission on Education in Health Services Administration (ACEHSA) since the commission's initiation in 1968. The program consists of four consecutive semesters of coursework, an eight-to 12-month residency and a master's project, for a total of 60 semester hours. The residency and master's project are required for graduation.

CAMPUS AND LOCATION

Founded in 1831, Xavier University is a private coeducational university located in Cincinnati, Ohio. Xavier provides a liberal arts education in the Catholic, Jesuit tradition. The university is the third-largest independent institution in Ohio, the sixth-oldest Catholic university in the nation, and one of 28 Jesuit colleges and universities nationwide.

Cincinnati has been rated as one of the nations' most livable cities. Xavier Univesity, a 10-minute drive from downtown, is ideally situated with easy access to Cincinnati's many attractions. The city offers unlimited dining, recreation, entertainment and cultural activities.

EXPENSES & FINANCIAL AID

The Xavier University Graduate Program in Health Services Administration realized that graduate school is an expensive investment. We are able to offer our students a variety of scholarship opportunities.

Tuition (updated annually):

2005-2006 rate $498 per credit hour

Parking (optional fee):

Full-time commuter $100/year

Part-time commuter $60/year

Other anticipated costs:

Books/supplies, housing and transportation

FINANCIAL AID

Students applying to the Graduate Program in Health Services Administration may be eligible for various scholarships including the MHSA Academic Scholarship and the MHSA Minority Scholarship.

Students may also be eligible to apply for Federal Financial aid. For more information on Federal Financial aid look to http://www.xavier.edu/financial_aid/.

STUDENTS

The Xavier University Graduate Program in Health Services Administration accepts students from all undergraduate backgrounds. Students actively participate in community service and leadership activities both on campus and in the community.

ADMISSIONS

Applications are considered for the admission into the Graduate Program in Health Services Administration until July 15 for fall admission. The program is a lock-step program and requires all students to begin in the fall semester. The following pieces of material are necessary to be considered for admission:

• Completed application form and $35 application fee

• Sealed official transcripts from all institutions where you have done undergraduate and graduate-level coursework

• Official copies of your GMAT or GRE score sent directly from the testing service

• Two completed recommendation forms

• Resume indicating all past educational and experiential activities

• Statement of Intent: A 1,000-1,200 word essay that addresses the following three questions: (1) Why do you wish to obtain a master's degree in health administration at Xavier University; (2) What are your career objectives and how will your prior education and experience assist you in achieving those objectives; and, (3) What are the three issues that have the greatest influence on the future of the health care system?

Prerequisites

A basic undergraduate or graduate level introductory accounting course and a basic undergraduate statistics course with a grade of "C" or better are required prerequisites. A passing grade is also acceptable.

Computer literacy is necessary, with a working knowledge of word processing and spreadsheet software.

Additionally, a course in microeconomics is highly recommended.

For additional information, contact the recruitment coordinator at:

Xavier University

Graduate Program in Health Services Administration

3800 Victory Parkway

Cincinnati, OH 45207-7331

Phone: 513-745-3687

Fax: 513-745-4301

E-mail: houyka@xavier.edu

Website: www.xavier.edu/mhsa

CAREER SERVICES & PLACEMENT

All full-time students in the Xavier University Graduate Program in Health Services Administration are required to complete an 8-12 month residency under the preceptorship of an executive level administrator in a health care organization. Residencies are available throughout the United States in hospitals, integrated delivery networks, insurance firms, group practices, long-term care organizations and consulting firms. Students on residency do receive a stipend. The average stipend in 2005 was $36,400. Graduate Program in Health Services Administration has consistently had 100 percent job placement for graduates within in three months of graduation.

INDEX BY LOCATION

FLORIDA

GEORGIA

HAWAII

IDAHO

ILLINOIS

MASSACHUSETTS

MICHIGAN

EGYPT

FRANCE

UNITED KINGDOM

ABOUT THE AUTHOR

Christopher Maier is a graduate of Dickinson College, a former staff writer for the Office of College Relations at Dickinson College, and a soon-to-be graduate of the MFA program at the University of Illinois at Urbana-Champaign, where he teaches courses in rhetoric and creative writing and serves as assistant editor for the literature/arts magazine Ninth Letter.

Manage Student Loan Debt Like A Pro

Upon arriving at your future alma mater as a freshman you will be asked one of the most important, yet most difficult questions of your life, "What do you want to do when you graduate?" For some, the answer to this question was as clear as day from the beginning. However for most, it was a question with an impossible answer. It is a question that all post high school graduates know is peering its ugly head around the corner, and inevitably, has to be answered.

After several days of thinking and mulling over the seemingly endless possibilities, speaking with advisors and conversing amongst friends, the decision is made and the course has been set. With the whisper of one single, simple little phrase, you begin the journey of the rest of your life.

Many of the professions that young people choose these days require a post secondary education of some sort. These specialized positions demand the highest level of skill, concentration, and more importantly, time and money.

Now that you have completed the first step along the path to accomplishing your ultimate goal and received your undergraduate degree, there are many decisions that need to be made, and many things that need to be considered. Taking into account the cost associated with receiving a specialized degree in a field such as medicine, money is on the top of most students' minds. "How will I pay for this? How will I repay my undergraduate loans while still attending school? What will happen when I graduate?"

In 1965, the Federal Government passed *The Higher Education Act*. This legislation was passed to strengthen the educational resources of our colleges and universities. It provides assistance for students wanting to enroll in postsecondary and higher education programs such as medical, law, or business school, and encourages more students to pursue their college and graduate school dreams.

Tuition increases have far outpaced the growth in personal and family income over the past two decades. For this reason, the need for private and federal aid has increased dramatically. As schools have become more expensive to attend, students and parents have been required to increase the amount of borrowing that they need under Federal Programs. As a result, the amount that students and parents have to pay on a monthly basis has also increased.

In order to address this problem and try to ease the financial burden on student borrowers, Congress passed the *Consolidation Loan Program* under the *Higher Education Act in 1986*. With this program, student loan borrowers are able to consolidate their multiple Federal Student Loans into one new Loan, while at the same time, extending their repayment term and locking in a fixed interest rate. By doing this, borrowers are able to lower their monthly payments enabling them to avoid delinquency and default.

THE FEDERAL CONSOLIDATION LOAN PROGRAM

The Federal Consolidation Loan Program is a unique program offered by the Federal Government that provides student loan borrowers with the following benefits:

- Lower monthly loan payments.

- Lock in a fixed interest rate for the life of the loan.

- Ability to merge all of the existing eligible federal loans into one new loan thereby making only one payment per month.

- Maintain their existing in-school deferment option if attending a graduate school and have no prepayment penalties. In-school deferment allows borrowers to postpone their payments while they are enrolled at least half time. While in deferment, all subsidized Stafford loans included in the consolidation will accrue zero interest.

- Availability of several repayment plans, including standard level payments, graduated payments, and income-based payments, allowing borrower to select the plan that best meets his or her needs.

- Potential interest rate reductions or other benefits, depending on the lender.

The Federal Consolidation Loan Program could be in the best interest of many students depending on the interest rates at the current time. There are no additional service fees for setting up a Consolidation Loan.

The eligibility guidelines for the program are very simple. In order to be eligible for a consolidation loan, a borrower must:

- Have outstanding loans made under the Federal Family Education Loan Program (FFELP), Direct, Perkins or Health Professions Student Loan (HPSL) program.

- Be in repayment period (including deferment and forbearance) or grace period.

- If a borrower is in default on their loans, certain rules/requirements apply in order to include these loans in the consolidation. Not all lenders will consolidate defaulted loans.

- Although Federal rules do not require a minimum balance many lenders may set minimum balance requirements. Typical minimums range from $5,000 to $10,000.

Qualifying Loans Under the Program:

Several types of student loans are eligible for Consolidation, including:

- Federal Family Education Loan Program (FFELP)

    Federal Subsidized and Unsubsidized Stafford Loans

    Federal PLUS Loans

    Federal Consolidation Loans

- Direct Loan Program

    Direct Subsidized and Unsubsidized Stafford Loans

    Direct PLUS loans

    Direct Consolidation Loans

- Perkins Loan Program

    Federal Perkins Loans

- Health Profession Student Loans (HPSL)

- Other

    Federal Education Assistance Loans (HEAL)

    Federal Nursing Student Loans (NSL)

CONSOLIDATION, WHEN IS THE RIGHT TIME?

A borrower can consolidate their student loans upon the completion of an undergraduate or graduate degree. As for those planning to attend postsecondary school, there are a few things to consider.

One of the great benefits of a higher education is the entitlement to in-school deferment on all federal loans. A borrower is legally entitled to this deferment even if they consolidate their student loans after they receive their undergraduate degree! The Department of Education states that students considered at least half-time (typically a minimum of six credit hours per semester) are not only eligible, but are legally guaranteed in-school deferment.

If this is the case, what is the benefit to consolidating only a portion of your student loans? All Stafford loans have variable interest rates prior to using the FFEL Consolidation Program. Once your loans have been consolidated the interest rate is locked in for the life of the loan and cannot go any higher. This is the primary and obvious reason to consolidate all eligible Stafford loans while still accumulating student loan debt.

The loans that will be taken out for postsecondary school may maintain their variable interest rates until the program is complete or the course load drops below half time. If the current interest rates are low in comparison to past years, you should secure whatever eligible debt you have incurred at these rates and consolidate the postsecondary school loans later. In fact, the option to roll all loans together or consolidate the remaining loans in a completely separate consolidation is something to be decided later.

The Six Month Grace Period = Opportunity for Big Savings

Most know that they do not necessarily have to begin paying off their student loans until six months after graduation. This six months is called a Grace Period or a period in which recently graduated students are awarded time to decide where they are going to live, find a job, etc. before they are required to make payments on their student loan debt.

Despite popular belief, the grace period typically may be the best time to consolidate student loans. When in a grace period, student loan interest rates are actually over a half of a percent lower than when the required payments begin six months after graduation.

STUDENT LOAN INTEREST RATES

Not all student loan borrowers have the same interest rate when they take advantage of the Consolidation Loan Program. This is not due to personal credit or the lender selected, but rather to government rules. A borrower's interest rate is determined by several factors.

FFELP Consolidation is a federal program and the actual interest rate is determined by a set of rules defined by the U.S. Department of Education. The fixed interest rates are determined by taking the weighted average of all of the loans being consolidated and rounding to the nearest 1/8th of a point.

Rates for Stafford and PLUS loans first disbursed on or after July 1, 1998, are adjusted on July 1 of each year based on the results of the last auction of the three-month Treasury bills before June 1st.

Many mailings and advertisements from Consolidation lenders offer the lowest possible rate and interest rate reductions. It is standard practice for companies to offer 0.25 percent reduction for making automatic EFT payments from a checking account. Many also offer a 1 percent interest rate reduction once a certain number of on-time payments have been received. The actual interest rate that is determined by the U.S. Department of Education is the maximum that a lender can charge and is the same from company to company.

Repayment Options

The Federal Consolidation Loan Program allows borrowers to get the best payoff terms without imposing penalties for early repayment. All Stafford loans are initially on a ten-year payoff plan, leaving many to opt for a nonpayment status such as deferment or forbearance when experiencing a cash flow problem in the short-term. Many borrowers want lower monthly payments, which will lengthen the payoff term. Switching to a longer-term payoff plan provides an immediate increase in short-term cash flow. Since there is no pre-payment penalty with the program, a borrower can make aggressive payments towards the principal at any time.

Most lenders do not require a borrower to accept the longer term associated with the repayment plans, so if they are opposed to it, other options exist. At the borrower's request, the servicer of his/her consolidation can adjust the payment plan to a ten-year payoff schedule. Borrowers are initially set up on the following terms based upon the balance of their Consolidation Loan:

- **10 years** for less than $7,500

- **12 years** for $7,500 to $10,000

- **15 years** for $10,000 to $20,000 ($20,000 balance monthly payment drop from $192 to $110)

- **20 years** for $20,000 to $40,000 ($35,000 balance monthly payment drop from $335 to $191)

- **25 years** for $40,000 to $60,000 ($50,000 balance monthly payment drop from $480 to $234)

- **30 years** for $60,000 and above ($100,000 balance monthly payment drop from $960 to $415)

A borrower may choose from the most suitable of four repayment plans:

- **Standard Repayment**

The monthly payment amount is fixed over the life of the Loan. The most popular plan is the level repayment method. Many borrowers choose this plan because they like the security and simplicity of a fixed monthly payment. However, more importantly, the level repayment plan usually is the least expensive in terms of total interest charges. The latter plans cost more because they slow down the repayment of the principal.

- **Graduated Repayment**

The Graduated Repayment Plan can vary from lender to lender, however many lenders offer more affordable interest only payments with the initial installments. After a certain number of the interest only payments the borrower will begin to pay down on the principle, resulting in higher payments. Other lenders offer pay increases every two years on the loans. The loan is repaid in the same time-frame as the Standard Repayment, but the total interest costs are slightly higher. The purpose of this payment plan is to provide the borrower more disposable income immediately upon beginning repayment.

- **Extended Repayment**

This plan allows the borrower to repay his/her Federal Consolidation Loans over a 25-year period under a level or graduated repayment schedule. To be eligible, the oldest Federal Stafford (subsidized and unsubsidized), Federal PLUS and/or Federal Consolidation Loan must have been disbursed on or after October 7, 1998 (borrowers who have pre-1998 loans can qualify for extended repayment if they consolidate all of the pre-1998 loans). In addition, the combined outstanding balance on all eligible Loans must be at least $30,000.01.

- **Income-sensitive repayment**

Initial monthly payments are based on monthly earnings and are adjusted annually, according to changes in income.

A new federal loan allows a borrower to consolidate again and restart a brand new term. While extending the repayment term may increase the overall amount of interest paid over the life of the loan, those who have higher debt often find the longer payoff schedule to be acceptable.

In addition to the choice of plans, the borrower can switch from one repayment plan to another at least once a year. There's no extra cost or penalty. All it takes is a phone call to his/her servicer or lender.

MAKING THE RIGHT DECISION

Now that all of the benefits of the Federal Consolidation Loan Program have been explained in their entirety, it is up to you, the borrower, to make the final decision. Find the company that offers the best explanation of terms, or find the one with the best incentives. Remember, the official interest rate formula is the same everywhere. The decision simply becomes a matter of personal choice. So what are you waiting for? Consolidate your student loans today and save money today!

The Graduate Loan Center, based in Chicago, Illinois, helps borrowers manage paying for the high cost of education by offering the Federal Consolidation Loan Program and Private Loan Programs. The Graduate Loan Center works with some of the nation's leading financial institutions, which combined have consolidated well over $1 billion in student loans. Call today to speak with one of our specially trained Financial Aid Advisors.

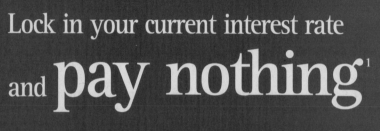

Law school students:

Lock in your current interest rate

and **pay nothing**[1]

until you complete law school

Call The Graduate Loan Center at 1-866-581-4GLC to find out how

Federal Student Loan Consolidation is a low-cost, government-backed program created to help you manage your student loan payments. Borrowers can take advantage of consolidation even while attending law school. Call now and you may be able to:

- **Lock in a fixed interest rate on your loan**
- **Make NO payments[1] until after you have completed law school**
- **Reconsolidate after graduation**

Call now and get started with one 15-minute phone call.

Call 1-866-581-4GLC
(581-4452)

For more information visit www.gradloancenter.com.   © 2005 The Graduate Loan Center

1 Repayment will begin immediately after borrower drops below half-time enrollment and there is no 6 month grace period. Terms and Conditions apply.

JAN 04 2006

Our Books *Help You Navigate the* College Admissions Process

Find the Right School

**Complete Book of Graduate Programs
in the Arts and Sciences**, 2006 Edition
0-375-76501-8 • $22.95/C$32.95

Best 237 Business Schools, 2006 Edition
0-375-76500-X • $22.95/C$32.95

Best 159 Law Schools, 2006 Edition
0-375-76498-4 • $22.95/C$32.95

Best 162 Medical Schools, 2006 Edition
0-375-76499-2 • $22.95/C$32.95

Get In

Cracking the GMAT, 2006 Edition
0-375-76476-3 • $20.00/C$27.00

Cracking the GMAT with CD-ROM,
2006 Edition
0-375-76477-1 • $35.95/C$49.95

Cracking the GRE, 2006 Edition
0-375-76474-7 • $20.00/C$27.00

Cracking the GRE with CD-ROM,
2006 Edition
0-375-76475-5 • $31.95/C$44.95

Cracking the LSAT, 2006 Edition
0-375-76478-X • $20.00/C$27.00

Cracking the LSAT with CD-ROM,
2006 Edition
0-375-76479-8 • $34.95/C$49.95

**Cracking the MCAT with
Practice Questions on CD-ROM**
0-375-76352-X • $59.95/C$79.95

Practice MCATs
0-375-76456-9 • $22.95/C$32.95

Available at Bookstores Everywhere.
PrincetonReview.com